*Empire of Liberty*

# The Oxford History of the United States

David M. Kennedy, *General Editor*

ROBERT MIDDLEKAUFF
## THE GLORIOUS CAUSE
*The American Revolution, 1763–1789*

GORDON S. WOOD
## EMPIRE OF LIBERTY
*A History of the Early Republic, 1789–1815*

DANIEL WALKER HOWE
## WHAT HATH GOD WROUGHT
*The Transformation of America, 1815–1848*

JAMES M. MCPHERSON
## BATTLE CRY OF FREEDOM
*The Civil War Era*

DAVID M. KENNEDY
## FREEDOM FROM FEAR
*The American People in Depression and War, 1929–1945*

JAMES T. PATTERSON
## GRAND EXPECTATIONS
*The United States, 1945–1974*

JAMES T. PATTERSON
## RESTLESS GIANT
*The United States from Watergate to Bush v. Gore*

GEORGE C. HERRING
## FROM COLONY TO SUPERPOWER
*U.S. Foreign Relations since 1776*

# EMPIRE OF LIBERTY

## A History of the Early Republic, 1789–1815

GORDON S. WOOD

OXFORD
UNIVERSITY PRESS

# OXFORD
UNIVERSITY PRESS

Oxford University Press, Inc., publishes works that further
Oxford University's objective of excellence
in research, scholarship, and education.

Oxford    New York
Auckland    Cape Town    Dar es Salaam    Hong Kong    Karachi
Kuala Lumpur    Madrid    Melbourne    Mexico City    Nairobi
New Delhi    Shanghai    Taipei    Toronto

With offices in
Argentina    Austria    Brazil    Chile    Czech Republic    France    Greece
Guatemala    Hungary    Italy    Japan    Poland    Portugal    Singapore
South Korea    Switzerland    Thailand    Turkey    Ukraine    Vietnam

Published by Oxford University Press, Inc.
198 Madison Avenue, New York, NY 10016
www.oup.com

First issued as an Oxford University Press paperback, 2011

Oxford is a registered trademark of Oxford University Press

Library of Congress Cataloging-in-Publication Data
Wood, Gordon S.
Empire of liberty : a history of the early Republic,
1789–1815 / Gordon S. Wood.
p. cm. — (Oxford history of the United States)
Includes bibliographical references and index.
ISBN 978-0-19-503914-6 (hardcover); 978-0-19-983246-0 (paperback)
1. United States—Civilization—1783–1865.
2. United States—Politics and government—1789–1815.   I. Title.
E310.W87 2009    973.4—dc22    2009010762

3    4    5    6    7    8    9
Printed in the United States of America
on acid-free paper

*To My Family*

# Acknowledgments

A project that has gone on as long as this one acquires a large number of debts, so many that it is dangerous to list any for fear of leaving someone out. For institutional support I am indebted to the Woodrow Wilson Center and the Huntington Library, both of which offered time off from teaching to work on the book. In addition, my home institution, Brown University, gave me several leaves that allowed me opportunities to do research and writing.

My students, both graduate and undergraduate, have been a continual source of stimulation, mainly by compelling me to clarify my ideas and arguments.

A number of colleagues have read portions of the manuscript—Michael Les Benedict, Steven Calabresi, Robert Gross, Bruce Mann, R. Kent Newmyer, and Steve Presser—and I am deeply indebted for their aid and corrections. Several friends suffered through the entire long manuscript—Richard Buel Jr., Patrick T. Conley, and Joanne Freeman—and I am eternally grateful for their taking on the task and for their helpful comments. Pat Conley in particular brought to bear on the manuscript not only his rich historical knowledge but as well a keen editorial eye for typos and other such errors. The editor of the Oxford History of the United States series, David Kennedy, offered very sensible advice, and I thank him for overseeing the whole project. The Oxford editor, Susan Ferber, has a good eye and ear for writing and made many valuable suggestions. My thanks also to the incomparable copy editor, India Cooper. Of course, in the end I am responsible for any errors that remain.

Since this book sums up a great deal of what I have learned about the early Republic over my entire career, I am deeply indebted to the many people who have helped me in one way or another over the past half century. But I owe the greatest debt to my wife, Louise, who has been editor and soulmate through the whole period.

# Contents

# Maps

# Editor's Introduction

Gordon S. Wood's *Empire of Liberty* takes its place in the Oxford History of the United States between two other notable volumes: Robert Middlekauff's *The Glorious Cause*, which masterfully covers the Revolutionary War era that immediately preceded the period covered here, and Daniel Walker Howe's *What Hath God Wrought*, which vividly evokes the cultural ferment and technological transformations that marked the years between the conclusion of the War of 1812 and the end of the Mexican War in 1848. The present volume addresses the astonishingly volatile, protean moment that lay between the achievement of national independence and the emergence of a swiftly maturing mass democracy and modern economy in the Jacksonian Era.

The two and a half decades bracketed by the signing of the Constitution in 1788 and the signing of the Treaty of Ghent in 1815, which ended the War of 1812, constituted one of the most precarious and consequential passages in American history. As the period opened, some four million Americans, one-fifth of them black slaves, dwelled between the Atlantic seaboard and the Appalachians, many of them itching to spill over the mountain crest into the untamed interior. They inhabited a new nation struggling to establish itself on a continent still coveted by hostile imperial powers, and still seething with Indians ever more determined to resist white encroachment. Their governments were founded on inspiring but untested political principles. They aspired to shape a society modeled on its European, especially English, antecedents, and yet unlike any seen before. Few seasons in American history have been pregnant with more momentous uncertainties.

Usually referred to as the "early national period," the era was clamorously contentious, urgently creative, and teeming with possibilities for failure. To the men and women who lived though that time, the fate of their fledgling republic was by no means secure, and the character of their communities was disconcertingly labile. History offered little guidance as to what the future might hold for a polyglot, restless, self-governing, and assertive people. They were rebellious by nature, rootless by circumstance, and ravenous to possess the vast territories that beckoned to their westward.

History's shores are littered with the wreckage of nascent nations that foundered before they could grow to stable maturity. Why should the fragile American ship of state, launched in 1776 and relaunched in 1788, be expected to enjoy a happier fate? In little more than a decade, the American people had thrown off the British yoke and jettisoned the Articles of Confederation—a record of bellicose lawbreaking and political inconstancy that gave scant promise of their ability to sustain viable governments or even a coherent and orderly society.

Yet somehow those mercurial and sometimes irascible Americans managed to lay the foundations of a resilient democratic political system that has endured for more than two centuries. The story of that remarkable and in many ways improbable accomplishment lies at the heart of this book.

In a series of admirably lucid chapters, Gordon Wood explains the formative origins of the nation's major governmental institutions and political practices. His account of the ways in which Congress evolved the protocols and procedures that would allow it to make law for a diverse and footloose people is particularly instructive. His analyses of the peculiar characteristics of American law, the role of the federal and state judiciaries, and the development of the signal doctrine of judicial review are exemplary, as is his deft discussion of the role of political parties—or "factions," as contemporaries called them—in determining the young republic's political destiny. So too is his analysis of the novel institution of the presidency, a tale in which George Washington figures prominently. Washington, along with Alexander Hamilton, John Adams, Thomas Jefferson, and James Madison, is also a central character in Wood's trenchant portrayal of the principles that guided America's earliest foreign policies, leaving precedents that would inform American diplomacy ever after.

But *Empire of Liberty*'s deepest subject is not simply the formal political system that Americans crafted in their first years of nationhood. Perhaps Gordon Wood's most original contribution in this book is his deeply engaging account of the development of a distinctively American democratic culture, a culture that shaped civil society in its manners and mores and values and behaviors every bit as deeply as it shaped the official organs of American government.

The men who made the Revolution and wrote the Constitution were for the most part cultured gentlemen, patrician squires who believed in the foundational republican principle of self-government, to be sure, but who also expected the common folk to defer to their "betters" when it came to running the country. The Federalists like Washington, Adams, and Hamilton who presided over the first decade of nationhood were often appalled by the egalitarian excesses unleashed by the Revolution. Ordinary men and women demanded to be addressed as "Mr." and "Mrs."—titles once reserved for the wealthy and highborn. Employers began to be called "boss," rather than "master." Indentured servitude, once common throughout the colonies, came to be regarded as an affront to democratic ideals and soon all but disappeared—though chattel slavery, the poisonous serpent in the American garden, stubbornly persisted, indeed, in these years began its fateful expansion westward.

The "middling sorts," a new social class composed of unprivileged but energetically striving merchants, artisans, and entrepreneurs, arose to dominate politics and define the very essence of the national character. They ferociously opposed all "monarchical" pretensions and insisted on nothing less than a society completely open to talent and industry. Their influence was felt in every sector of the nation's life, not only in politics but in commerce, religion, architecture, and the arts. Their great champion was Thomas Jefferson, the quirky and brilliant Virginia aristocrat who articulated the dearest aspirations of the common people, and whose enigmatic figure animates many of the pages that follow.

Matters of such moment and complexity pose unique challenges to the historian. Few if any scholars are more able than Gordon Wood to do these subjects justice. A lifetime of research and writing about the early American republic has given him an unmatched mastery of the source documents that are the historian's raw materials. Drawing on rich archives of letters, diaries, pamphlets, newspapers, and memoirs, *Empire of Liberty* gives voice to countless individuals who speak on almost every page with all the urgency of their own lives and all the color and flavor of their time—including of course the fabled Founders but also the brawling congressman Matthew Lyon, the dignified jurist John Marshall, the Shawnee prophet Tenskwatawa and his brother Tecumseh, and their nemesis, General William Henry Harrison, among many others.

The Oxford History of the United States aims to bring the best scholarship to the broadest possible audience. The series is dedicated to making history live for later generations. *Empire of Liberty* handsomely, artfully fulfills that purpose.

David M. Kennedy

# Abbreviations Used in Citations

| | |
|---|---|
| Adams, ed., *Works* | Charles Francis Adams, ed., *The Works of John Adams*, 10 vols. (Boston, 1850–1856) |
| JA, *Diary and Autobiography* | Lyman H. Butterfield et al., eds., *Diary and Autobiography of John Adams* (Cambridge, MA, 1961) |
| *Papers of Adams* | Robert J. Taylor et al., eds., *The Papers of John Adams* (Cambridge, MA, 1977–) |
| *Annals of Congress* | *Annals of the Congress of the United States*, comp. Joseph Gales (Washington, DC, 1834) |
| *Papers of Franklin* | Leonard W. Labaree et al., eds., *The Papers of Benjamin Franklin* (New Haven, 1959–) |
| *Franklin: Writings* | J. A. Leo Lemay, ed., *Benjamin Franklin: Writings* (New York, 1987) |
| *Papers of Hamilton* | Harold C. Syrett et al., eds., *The Papers of Alexander Hamilton*, 27 vols. (New York, 1962–1987) |
| *Hamilton: Writings* | Joanne B. Freeman, ed., *Alexander Hamilton: Writings* (New York, 2001) |

*Papers of Jefferson*                          Julian P. Boyd et al., eds., *The
                                               Papers of Thomas Jefferson*
                                               (Princeton, 1950–)

*Papers of Jefferson: Retirement Ser.*         J. Jefferson Looney et al., eds., *The
                                               Papers of Thomas Jefferson:
                                               Retirement Series* (Princeton,
                                               2004–)

Ford, ed., *Writings of Jefferson*             Paul L. Ford, ed., *The Writings
                                               of Thomas Jefferson*, 10 vols.
                                               (New York, 1892–1899)

L and B, eds., *Writings of                    A. A. Lipscomb and Albert Ellery
Jefferson*                                     Bergh, eds., *The Writings of
                                               Thomas Jefferson*, 20 vols.
                                               (Washington, DC, 1903)

*Jefferson: Writings*                          Merrill D. Peterson, ed., *Thomas
                                               Jefferson: Writings* (New York,
                                               1984)

*Papers of Madison*                            William T. Hutchinson et al., eds.,
                                               *The Papers of James Madison*,
                                               vols. 1–10 (Chicago, 1962–1977);
                                               Robert A. Rutland et al., eds.,
                                               vols. 11– (Charlottesville, 1977–)

*Papers of Madison: Secretary                  Robert J. Brugger et al., eds., *The
of State Ser.*                                 Papers of James Madison:
                                               Secretary of State Series*
                                               (Charlottesville, 1986)

*Papers of Madison:                            Robert A. Rutland et al., *The Papers
Presidential Ser.*                             of James Madison: Presidential
                                               Series* (Charlottesville, 1984–)

*Madison: Writings*                            Jack N. Rakove, ed., *James Madison:
                                               Writings* (New York, 1999)

*Papers of Marshall*                           Herbert A. Johnson et al., eds., *The
                                               Papers of John Marshall* (Chapel
                                               Hill, 1974–)

*Letters of Rush*                              Lyman H. Butterfield, ed., *Letters of
                                               Benjamin Rush*, 2 vols.
                                               (Princeton, 1951)

*Republic of Letters*                          James Morton Smith, ed., *The
                                               Republic of Letters: The
                                               Correspondence Between Thomas
                                               Jefferson and James Madison,
                                               1776–1826*, 3 vols. (New York, 1995)

| | |
|---|---|
| *Spur of Fame* | John A. Schutz and Douglass Adair, eds., *The Spur of Fame: Dialogues of John Adams and Benjamin Rush, 1805–1813* (San Marino, CA, 1966) |
| *Papers of Washington: Presidential Ser.* | W. W. Abbot et al., eds., *The Papers of George Washington: Presidential Series* (Charlottesville, 1987–) |
| *Papers of Washington: Retirement Ser.* | W. W. Abbot et al., eds., *The Papers of George Washington: Retirement Series* (Charlottesville, 1998–1999) |
| Fitzpatrick, ed., *Writings of Washington* | John C. Fitzpatrick, *The Writings of George Washington*, 39 vols. (Washington, DC, 1931–1944) |
| *Washington: Writings* | John H. Rhodehamel, ed., *George Washington: Writings* (New York, 1997) |
| AHR | *American Historical Review* |
| JAH | *Journal of American History* |
| JER | *Journal of the Early Republic* |
| WMQ | *William and Mary Quarterly*, 3d Ser. |
| JA | John Adams |
| BF | Benjamin Franklin |
| AH | Alexander Hamilton |
| TJ | Thomas Jefferson |
| JM | James Madison |
| BR | Benjamin Rush |
| GW | George Washington |

*Empire of Liberty*

# Introduction:
# Rip Van Winkle's America

During the second decade of the nineteenth century, writer Washington Irving developed an acute sense that his native land was no longer the same place it had been just a generation earlier. Irving had conservative and nostalgic sensibilities, and he sought to express some of his amazement at the transformation that had taken place in America by writing his story "Rip Van Winkle." Irving had his character Rip awaken from a sleep that had begun before the Revolution and had lasted twenty years. When Rip entered his old village, he immediately felt lost. The buildings, the faces, the names were all strange and incomprehensible. "The very village was altered—it was larger and more populous," and idleness, except among the aged, was no longer tolerated. "The very character of the people seemed changed. There was a busy, bustling disputatious tone about it, instead of the accustomed phlegm and drowsy tranquility"—a terrifying situation for Rip, who had had "an insuperable aversion to all kinds of profitable labour." Even the language was strange—"rights of citizens—elections—members of Congress—liberty...and other words which were a perfect babylonish jargon to the bewildered Van Winkle." When people asked him "on which side he voted" and "whether he was Federal or a Democrat," Rip could only stare "in vacant stupidity."[1]

"Rip Van Winkle" became the most popular of Irving's many stories, for early nineteenth-century Americans could appreciate Rip's bewilderment. Although superficially the political leadership seemed much the same—on the sign at the village inn the face of George Washington had simply replaced that of George III—beneath the surface Rip, like most Americans, knew that "every thing's changed." In a few short decades Americans had experienced a remarkable transformation in their society and culture, and, like Rip and his creator, many wondered what had happened and who they really were.[2]

1. Washington Irving, *The Sketch Book*, in *Washington Irving: History, Tales and Sketches*, ed. James W. Tuttleton (New York, 1983), 770–81.
2. Jeffrey Rubin-Dorsky, *Adrift in the Old World: The Psychological Pilgrimage of Washington Irving* (Chicago, 1988), 74–75.

Before the Revolution of 1776 America had been merely a collection of disparate British colonies composed of some two million subjects huddled along a narrow strip of the Atlantic coast—European outposts whose cultural focus was still London, the metropolitan center of the empire. Following the War of 1812 with Great Britain—often called the Second American Revolution—these insignificant provinces had become a single giant continental republic with nearly ten million citizens, many of whom had already spilled into the lands beyond the Appalachian Mountains. The cultural focus of this huge expansive nation was no longer abroad but was instead directed inward at its own boundless possibilities.

By 1815 Americans had experienced a transformation in the way they related to one another and in the way they perceived themselves and the world around them. And this transformation took place before industrialization, before urbanization, before railroads, and before any of the technological breakthroughs usually associated with modern social change. In the decades following the Revolution America changed so much and so rapidly that Americans not only became used to change but came to expect it and prize it.

The population grew dramatically, doubling every twenty years or so, as it had for several generations, more than twice the rate of growth of any European country. And people were on the move as never before. Americans spread themselves over half a continent at astonishing speeds. Between 1790 and 1820 New York's population quadrupled; Kentucky's multiplied nearly eight times. In a single decade Ohio grew from a virtual wilderness (except, of course, for the presence of the native Indians, whom white Americans scarcely acknowledged) to become more populous than most of the century-old colonies had been at the time of the Revolution. In a single generation Americans occupied more territory than they had occupied during the entire 150 years of the colonial period, and in the process killed or displaced tens of thousands of Indians.

Although most Americans in 1815 remained farmers living in rural areas, they had become, especially in the North, one of the most highly commercialized people in the world. They were busy buying and selling not only with the rest of the world but increasingly with one another, everyone, it seemed, trying to realize what *Niles' Weekly Register* declared was "the almost universal ambition to get forward."[3] Nowhere in the Western world was business and working for profit more praised and honored.

This celebration of work made a leisured slaveholding aristocracy in the South more and more anomalous. Slavery was widely condemned,

3. *Niles' Weekly Register*, 9 (1815), 238.

but it did not die in the new United States; indeed, it flourished—but only in the South. It spread across the Southern half of the country, and as it disappeared in the North, it became more deeply entrenched in the Southern economy. In a variety of ways—socially, culturally, and politically—the South began to see itself as a beleaguered minority in the bustling nation.

All these demographic and commercial changes could not help but affect every aspect of American life. Politics became democratized as more Americans gained the right to vote. The essentially aristocratic world of the Founding Fathers in which gentry leaders stood for election was largely replaced by a very different democratic world, a recognizably modern world of competing professional politicians who ran for office under the banners of modern political parties. Indeed, Americans became so thoroughly democratic that much of the period's political activity, beginning with the Constitution, was devoted to finding means and devices to tame that democracy. Most important perhaps, ordinary Americans developed a keen sense of their own worth—a sense that, living in the freest nation in the world, they were anybody's equal. Religion too was democratized and transformed. Not only were most of the traditional European-based religious establishments finally destroyed, but the modern world of many competing Christian denominations was created. By 1815 America had become the most evangelically Christian nation in the world.

Even Washington Irving, despite his deep affection for all things English and his anxiety over America's national identity, had to concede that the United States was "a country in a singular state of moral and physical development; a country," he said, "in which one of the greatest Political experiments in the history of the world is now performing." Obvious to all was "our rapidly growing importance and our matchless prosperity"— due, he said, "not merely to physical and local but also to moral causes...the political liberty, the general diffusion of knowledge, the prevalence of sound moral and religious principles, which give force and sustained energy to the character of a people."[4] Americans knew they were an experiment, but they were confident they could by their own efforts remake their culture, re-create what they thought and believed. Their Revolution told them that people's birth did not limit what they might become.

Suddenly, everything seemed possible. The Revolutionary leaders were faced with the awesome task of creating out of their British heritage their own separate national identity. They had an opportunity to realize an

4. Irving, *The Sketch Book*, in Tuttleton, ed., *Washington Irving*, 789.

ideal world, to put the broadminded and tolerant principles of the Enlightenment into practice, to become a homogeneous, compassionate, and cosmopolitan people, and to create the kind of free and ordered society and illustrious culture that people since the Greeks and Romans had yearned for.

But little worked out quite as the Founders expected. Not only did their belief in the Revolution's enlightened and liberty-loving principles, including their dedication to equality and popular government, contain within itself the source of its own disillusionment, but their high-minded promise to end slavery and respect the rights of the native peoples were no match for the surging demographic forces accelerated by the Revolution.

By 1815 the classical Enlightenment in America was over or popularized, and many of the ideals of the Revolution, including the hope of America's becoming the repository of Western art and culture, had been modified or perverted. Yet the changes were so complicated, so indeliberate, so much a medley of responses to fast-moving events that Americans scarcely knew how they had progressed from one point to another.

The transformation Americans had experienced was unintended, for the character they celebrated in Andrew Jackson and the Hunters of Kentucky—the romantic, undisciplined, and untutored heroes of the battle of New Orleans of 1815—was scarcely the character they had sought in 1789. The bumptious nationalism and the defiant abandonment of Europe expressed at the end of the War of 1812 were both repudiations of the enlightened and cosmopolitan ideals of the Revolution and attempts to come to terms with the largely unanticipated popular commercial society that had emerged from the Revolution.

By the end of that second war against Britain in 1815, the central impulses of the Revolution had run their course. Americans believed that their Republic was at last secure and independent, free from hostile mercantile empires and the ravages of the European wars that had tormented them for over two decades. Democracy and equality were no longer problematic issues to be debated; they had become articles of faith to be fulfilled. Americans thought they had finally become a nation—the only one that was free and democratic in a world of monarchies. With nearly an entire continent at their disposal, they believed that they were at last ready to exploit the great possibilities that lay before them. At the same time, however, many of them had come to realize that their future as a united and freedom-loving people was being thwarted by the continuing presence of slavery in their midst. Their grand experiment in republicanism was not over after all and would have to be further tested.

# 1

# Experiment in Republicanism

In 1788 the American minister to France, Thomas Jefferson, presented Thomas Lee Shippen, the son of a prominent Philadelphia family, to the French Court of Versailles. Young Shippen, who was studying law at the Inns of Court in London, was very excited; the young man, the nephew of Richard Henry and Arthur Lee of Virginia, was very socially conscious and, since he had "a little Vanity," was apt to "run wild after the tinsel of life." He had looked forward to his "Continental tour" with all its opportunities for cultivating "the acquaintance of titled men and Ladies of birth," whose names," a friend of the Shippen family regretfully observed, "he soon gets and…will never forget."[1]

Of course, nowhere in the world was there more tinsel and titles than at the Court of Versailles, more indeed than Shippen had ever imagined. The protocol was incredibly elaborate: arriving at half past ten, "we were not done bowing until near 2"; in fact, "the business of bowing" went on so long, Shippen told his father, that "any but a Scotchman would have been tired of [it]." So ceremonious and so luxurious was the French court that this pretentious Philadelphian could only gawk and feel himself a "stranger" in its midst. He could not help expressing amazement at the "Oriental splendor and magnificence" of it all. The riches, the sophistication, the pomp dazzled him. The pictures of the royal family were "larger than life." The members of the court had "all separate households and distinct portions of the Palace allotted to them," and "between them they expend 36,000,000 of livres a year." And the royal gardens—"What walks! What groves! What water works!" The situation of the "superb building" of the palace was "worthy of its grandeur, and both well suited to the Court of a great Nation." Versailles was an "enchanting paradise," all "very splendid," and filled with such ceremony and civility, said Shippen, as "I had never seen." Overawed, he could only puff with pride at having "received very uncommon marks of politeness and attention" from the nobles of the court.

1. William Stephen Smith to TJ, 9 Jan. 1788, *Papers of Jefferson*, 12: 501.

Although Shippen "upon the whole...was well pleased with the day," all the time he knew he was being snubbed. He sensed that the "oppressive...civilities" of the courtiers were condescending, that their polite questions only "served to shew rather a desire to be attentive to me, than to be informed of what they did not know already." The American, something of an aristocrat in Philadelphia but hardly one at Versailles, could not help feeling his difference; and that difference became a shield for his self-esteem. He was, after all, he told his father, a republican: geographically and socially he was from another world. The magnificence and elegance of Versailles both impressed and repulsed him. How many thousands of subjects, Shippen wondered, had been doomed to want and wretchedness by King Louis XIV's wasteful efforts "to shroud his person and adorn his reign" by building Versailles. He "revolted" at the "insufferable arrogance" of the present king, Louis XVI, and was even "more mortified at the suppleness and base complaisance of his attendants." To witness "the file of ambassadors, Envoys Ministers &c. in full dress...prostrating themselves before him emulous of each other in demonstrating their obsequious adulation" was even more distasteful. He rejoiced that he was not the subject of such a monarchy but the citizen of a republic— "more great because more virtuous"—where there were no hereditary distinctions, no "empty ornament and unmeaning grandeur," and "where the people respect sincerity, and acknowledge no other tyranny than that of Honor." He was proud of Mr. Jefferson, who was "the plainest man in the room, and the most destitute of ribbands, crosses and other insignia of rank." That America's minister was the person "most courted and most attended to (even by the Courtiers themselves)" persuaded Shippen that good sense, merit, and integrity inevitably commanded respect "even among those who cannot boast of their possession." He observed in the midst of all the splendor of the courtiers "an uneasiness and ennui in their faces which did not bespeak content or happiness." The whole wonderful and eye-opening experience convinced him "that *a certain degree of equality* is essential to human bliss. Happy above all Countries is our Country," he concluded, "where *that equality* is found, without destroying the necessary subordination."[2]

IN A BASIC SENSE the importance of the American Revolution was summed up in Thomas Shippen's day at Versailles. For nearly all Americans, as it was for Shippen, becoming republican was the deeply felt

2. Thomas Lee Shippen to William Shippen, 14 Feb.–26 March 1788, *Papers of Jefferson*, 12: 502–4; Gordon S. Wood, *The Creation of the American Republic, 1776–1787* (Chapel Hill, 1969), 46–47.

meaning of their revolution. They knew that by overthrowing monarchy and adopting republican governments in 1776 they had done more than eliminate a king and institute an elective system of government. Republicanism gave a moral, even utopian, significance to their revolution that had made their separation from Great Britain much more than a simple colonial rebellion. They were keenly aware that by becoming members of thirteen republics they had undertaken a bold and perhaps world-shattering experiment in self-government.

At the moment of independence that was how they thought of themselves—as thirteen separate republics. No American revolutionary even imagined the possibility of creating a strong continental-sized national republic similar to the one that was established by the Constitution a decade later in 1787–1788. In 1776 the only central authority that most Americans could conceive of was "a firm league of friendship," or a confederation, among the thirteen individual states, similar in many respects to the present-day European Union, held together by a kind of treaty in which each state retained "its sovereignty, freedom, and independence." This treaty of thirteen states held out the possibility and hope of other British provinces—Canada and East and West Florida—joining the Union. The treaty—the Articles of Confederation, as it was called—gave the United States of America a literal plural meaning that has since been lost.

Maintaining this confederation of republics would not be easy. Americans knew only too well that republics were very delicate polities that required a special kind of society—a society of equal and virtuous citizens. By throwing off monarchy and becoming republics, declared South Carolina physician and historian David Ramsay, Americans had "changed from subjects to citizens," and "the difference is immense." "Subjects," he said, "look up to a master, but citizens are so far equal, that none have hereditary rights superior to others."[3] Republics demanded far more morally from their citizens than monarchies did of their subjects. In monarchies each man's desire to do what was right in his own eyes could be restrained by fear or force, by patronage or honor, and by professional standing armies. By contrast, republics had to hold themselves together from the bottom up, ultimately, from their citizens' willingness to take up arms to defend their country and to sacrifice their private desires for the sake of the public good—from their "disinterestedness,"

---

3. David Ramsay, *A Dissertation on the Manner of Acquiring the Character and Privileges of a Citizen of the United States* (Charleston, SC, 1789), 3. On the Revolution's creation of a new volitional allegiance of citizenship, see James H. Kettner, *The Development of American Citizenship, 1608–1870* (Chapel Hill, 1978), 173–209.

which was a popular synonym for virtue. This reliance on the moral virtue of their citizens, on their capacity for self-sacrifice and impartiality of judgment, was what made republican governments historically so fragile.

Theorists from Plutarch in antiquity to Machiavelli in the Renaissance to Montesquieu in the mid-eighteenth century had argued that republics dependent upon the virtue of their citizens had to be small in size and martial in character; otherwise their citizens would have too many diverse interests and would not be able to cohere, defend themselves, and develop the proper spirit of self-sacrifice. The only republics existing in the eighteenth century—the Netherlands, the Swiss cantons, and the Italian city-states—were small and compact and no models for the sprawling United States of America. Large and socially diverse states that had tried to become republics—as England had in the seventeenth century—inevitably had ended up in military dictatorships like that of Oliver Cromwell.

As Shippen had suggested, republics were also supposed to have citizens who were more or less equal to one anther. They could have no legal or artificial aristocracies, no privileges conferred by governments, no positions based on social connections, marriage, or parentage. The social hierarchies that republics would permit would be based solely on individual merit and talent. Distinctions that did emerge would presumably have no time to harden or be perpetuated across generations. Consequently, this equality of opportunity, with individuals of successive generations rising and falling, would sustain a rough equality of condition.

Such an equality of condition was essential for republicanism. Since antiquity, theorists had assumed that a republican state required a general equality of property-holding among its citizens. Although most Americans in 1776 believed that not everyone in a republic had to have the same amount of property, a few radicals in 1776 did call for agrarian laws with "the power of lessening property when it became excessive in individuals."[4] All took for granted that a society could not long remain republican if a tiny minority controlled most of the wealth and the bulk of the population remained dependent servants or poor landless laborers. Equality was related to independence; indeed, Jefferson's original draft for the Declaration of Independence had stated that "all men are created equal & independent."[5] Since owning property made this independence possible,

4. Philadelphia *Pennsylvania Packet*, 26 Nov. 1776.
5. Jefferson's "original Rough draught" of the Declaration of Independence, *Papers of Jefferson*, 1: 423.

all the states retained some kind of property qualification for voting or for officeholding.

Most of the Revolutionary leaders thought of property in pre-modern, almost classical terms—as rentier property, what some eighteenth-century historians have called "proprietary wealth."[6] They conceived of it as a source of authority and independence, not as a commodity or as the source of productivity and capitalistic investment. The most traditional kind of proprietary property was, of course, land; but it could take other rentier forms, such as government bonds or money out on loan.

Yet equality meant even more than having many independent land-holders. The stress on the circulation of talent and on the ability of common people to elect those who had integrity and merit presumed a certain moral capacity in the populace as a whole. In the 1780s James Madison had his doubts about this moral capacity of the people stretched to the limit, but even he admitted that ordinary people had to have sufficient "virtue and intelligence to select men of virtue and wisdom" or "no theoretical checks, no form of government, can render us secure."[7] Good republicans had to believe in the common sense of the common people.

Jefferson was undoubtedly correct when he later explained that when he wrote the Declaration of Independence in 1776 its affirmation that "all men are created equal" was a widely shared belief. Writing the Declaration, he said, did not involve setting out "new principles, or new arguments, never before thought of," but simply placing "before mankind the common sense of the subject."[8] By the latter part of the eighteenth century, to be enlightened was to believe in the natural equality of all men and to believe in the self-evident truth that all men had certain inalienable rights.

By modern standards, this declaration and these claims of equal rights smack of hypocrisy, or worse, given the severe unequal status of women, the treatment of the native peoples, and the fact that one-fifth of the American population was enslaved. To be sure, "we should not forget the restrictions placed on rights by eighteenth-century men, but to stop there," cautions historian Lynn Hunt, "patting ourselves on the back for our own comparative 'advancement,' is to miss the point. How did these men, living in societies built on slavery, subordination, and seemingly natural

6. George V. Taylor, "Noncapitalist Wealth and the Origins of the French Revolution," *AHR*, 62 (1967), 469–96; William Doyle, *Origins of the French Revolution* (Oxford, 1980), 17–18.
7. Wood, *Creation of the American Republic*, 544.
8. TJ to Henry Lee, 8 May 1825, *Jefferson: Writings*, 1501.

subservience, ever come to imagine men not at all like them and, in some cases, women too as equals?"[9]

That many people had come to think of others as their equals was a crucially important development of the enlightened eighteenth century. Even those as aristocratic as the wealthy slaveholding planter William Byrd and Francis Fauquier, a colonial governor of Virginia, conceded that all men, even men of different nations and races, were born equal and that, in Byrd's words, "the principal difference between one people and another proceeds only from the differing opportunities of improvement." "White, Red, or Black; polished or unpolished," declared Governor Fauquier in 1760, "Men are Men."[10] Most acknowledged that at some basic level all people were alike, that people, in the words of a Pennsylvania minister in 1790, were "all partakers of the same common nature" and that only education and cultivation separated one person from another. These were explosive assumptions—assumptions that came to dominate American thinking in the several decades following the Revolution.[11]

Possessing a common nature linked people together in natural affection and morality, or so the most radical reformers believed. People, however humble and uneducated, possessed a sympathetic social instinct and a moral intuition that told them right from wrong. Indeed, some liberals thought that plain unlettered people had a stronger moral sense than educated gentlemen. "State a moral case to a ploughman and a professor," said Jefferson; "the former will decide it as well, and often better than the latter, because he has not been led astray by artificial rules."[12]

These ideas lay behind Jefferson's radical belief in minimal government. The most liberal-minded of the eighteenth century—those in the Revolution who had used terms from English politics and called themselves Whigs in opposition to the conservative and royalist Tories—tended to see society as beneficent and government as malevolent. Social honors, social distinctions, perquisites of office, business contracts, privileges and monopolies, even excessive property and wealth of various sorts—indeed,

9.  Lynn Hunt, *Inventing Human Rights* (New York, 2007), 19.
10. William Byrd, "History of the Dividing Line...1728," in Louis B. Wright, ed., *The Prose Works of William Byrd of Westover* (Cambridge, MA, 1966), 221; Fauquier to Jeffrey Amherst, 5 Oct. 1760, in Julie Richter, "The Impact of the Death of Governor Francis Fauquier on His Slaves and Their Families," *Colonial Williamsburg Interpreter* 18, no. 3 (Fall 1997), 2.
11. John Andrews, *A Sermon on the Importance of Mutual Kindness* (Philadelphia, 1790), 14.
12. Mark A. Noll, "Common Sense Traditions and American Evangelical Thought," *American Quarterly*, 37 (1985), 218; TJ to Peter Carr, 10 Aug. 1787, *Papers of Jefferson*, 12: 15.

all social iniquities and deprivations—seemed to flow from connections to government. "Society," said Thomas Paine in a brilliant summary of this radical Whig liberal view in *Common Sense*, "is produced by our wants and government by our wickedness." Society "promotes our happiness *positively* by uniting our affections," government "*negatively*" by restraining our vices." Society "encourages intercourse," government "creates distinctions."[13] If only the natural tendencies of people to love and care for one another were allowed to flow freely, unclogged by the artificial interference of government, particularly monarchical government, the most devout republicans like Paine and Jefferson believed, society would prosper and hold itself together.

Jefferson had so much confidence in the natural harmony of society that he sometimes came close to denying any role for government at all. During the 1780s he had little interest in strengthening the national government created by the Articles of Confederation. In his opinion the Confederation was little more than a temporary combination of the states brought together for the sole purpose of waging war against the British; with the peace it should be allowed to lapse. By December 1783 he thought "the constant session of Congress can not be necessary in time of peace." After clearing up the most urgent business, the delegates, he said, should "separate and return to our respective states, leaving only a Committee of the states," and thus "destroy the strange idea of their being a permanent body, which has unaccountably taken possession of the heads of their constituents, and occasions jealousies injurious to the public good."[14] This was a conception of the national government that Jefferson and some other optimistic republicans never entirely abandoned.

THE LIBERAL IDEAS that society was naturally harmonious and that everyone possessed a common moral and social sense were no utopian fantasies but the conclusions of what many enlightened thinkers took to be the modern science of society. While most clergymen continued to urge Christian love and charity upon their ordinary parishioners, many other educated and enlightened people sought to secularize Christian love and find in human nature itself a scientific imperative for loving one's neighbor as oneself. "Just as the regular motions and harmony of the heavenly bodies depend upon their mutual gravitation towards each other," said liberal Massachusetts preacher Jonathan Mayhew, so too did love and benevolence among

13. Thomas Paine, *Common Sense* (1776), in Philip S. Foner, ed., *The Complete Writings of Thomas Paine* (New York, 1969), 1: 4.
14. TJ to Marbois, 5 Dec. 1783, *Papers of Jefferson*, 6: 374.

people preserve "order and harmony" in society. Love between humans was the gravity of the moral world, and it could be studied and perhaps even manipulated more easily than the gravity of the physical world.[15] Enlightened thinkers like Lord Shaftesbury, Francis Hutcheson, and Adam Smith thus sought to discover these hidden forces that moved and held people together in the moral world, forces, they believed, that could match the great eighteenth-century scientific discoveries about the hidden forces— gravity, magnetism, electricity, and energy—that operated in the physical world. Out of such dreams was born modern social science.

Because this natural social or moral sense, said Scottish immigrant and Philadelphia lawyer James Wilson, made "a man capable of managing his own affairs, and answerable for his conduct toward others," it not only held society together but made republican and ultimately democratic government possible.[16] Indeed, for many American thinkers this natural sociability of people became a modern substitute for the ascetic classical virtue of antiquity.

Many intellectuals in the eighteenth century still clung to the value of the ancient masculine and martial virtues. Witness the acclaim that greeted Jacques-Louis David's classical republican painting *The Oath of the Horatii*, exhibited in Paris in 1786. But many others like David Hume had concluded that such classical republican virtue was too demanding and too severe for the enlightened civilized societies of eighteenth-century Europe. It was true, wrote Hume, that ancient Sparta and Rome were free republican states whose citizens were virtuous and self-sacrificing. But they were also small states that were almost continually in arms. That kind of classical martial virtue no longer made sense in the enlightened eighteenth-century age of sprawling commercial societies.[17]

A new kind of virtue was needed, and many English-speakers, including many Americans, found it in people's instinct to be sociable and sympathetic to one another. Virtue became less the harsh and martial self-sacrifice of antiquity and more the modern willingness to get along with others for the sake of peace and prosperity.

---

15. Geoffroy Atkinson, *The Sentimental Revolution: French Writers of 1690–1740* (Seattle, 1966); Norman S. Fiering, "Irresistible Compassion: An Aspect of Eighteenth-Century Sympathy and Humanitarianism," *Journal of the History of Ideas*, 37 (1976), 199–212; John B. Radner, "The Art of Sympathy in Eighteenth-Century British Moral Thought," *Studies in Eighteenth-Century Culture*, 9 (Madison, WI, 1979), 189–210; Andrew Burstein, *Sentimental Democracy: The Evolution of America's Romantic Self-Image* (New York, 1999).

16. James Wilson, "Lectures on Law" (1790–1791), *The Works of James Wilson*, ed. Robert Green McCloskey (Cambridge, MA, 1967), 1: 213.

17. David Hume, "Of Commerce," *Essays, Moral, Political, and Literary*, ed. Eugene F. Miller (Indianapolis, 1985), 262–63.

Everywhere in eighteenth-century America there was evidence of this natural conviviality and sociability—in coffeehouses, clubs, assemblies, and salons. People seemed more benevolent, conversations were more polite, and manners were more gracious than they had been in the past. From physician Alexander Hamilton's Tuesday Club in Maryland to John Trumbull's Friendly Club in Connecticut, groups of gentlemen up and down the North American continent gathered together periodically to discuss issues, write poetry, and share in each other's company.

With this spread of politeness and civility, classical virtue had gradually become domesticated. Mingling in drawing rooms, clubs, and coffeehouses created friendship and sympathy and helped to hold society together. Some even thought that commercial exchanges and the trust and credit they bred contributed to this new conception of virtue. This modern virtue seemed softer, less masculine, and less political than the virtue of the classical past and could be expressed by women as well as men. Indeed, some said that women were even more capable than men of sociability and benevolence.[18] Since republican America appeared to possess more of this moral or social sense, it seemed to some to be a much more encouraging place for women than monarchical Europe.

THE RADICAL BELIEF in the capacity of affection and benevolence to hold republican societies together may have been as unrealistic and as contrary to human nature as the traditional belief in ascetic classical virtue. Certainly hard-nosed skeptics, like Alexander Hamilton, came to doubt its efficacy. But many Revolutionary Americans imagined a new and better world emerging, a world, according to some clergymen, of "greater perfection and happiness than mankind has yet seen." In this New World Americans would build a harmonious republican society of "comprehensive benevolence" and become "the eminent example of every divine and social virtue."[19]

For some American leaders, however, the ink on the Declaration of Independence was scarcely dry before they began expressing doubts about the possibility of realizing the high hopes and dreams of the Revolution. During the following decade the doubts grew rapidly into a prevailing sense of crisis. By the 1780s the public press and private correspondence were filled with warnings that "our situation is critical and dangerous" and that "our vices" were plunging us into "national ruin."[20]

18. Jan Lewis, "The Republican Wife: Virtue and Seduction in the Early Republic," WMQ, 44 (1987), 689–721.
19. Wood, *Creation of the American Republic*, 117.
20. "Amicus Republicae," *Address to the Public* (Exeter, NH, 1786), in Charles S. Hyneman and Donald S. Lutz, eds., *American Political Writing During the Founding Era, 1760–1805* (Indianapolis, 1983), 1: 644.

The events of the 1780s seemed to point toward "some crisis, some revolution" that could not be predicted. Many, like New Yorker John Jay, secretary for foreign affairs under the Confederation, found themselves uneasy, "more so than during the war." Then there had been a "fixed object," and though the means and timing were questionable, few had doubted the ultimate victory. With the coming of peace in 1783 "the case is now altered." Americans could see ahead of them only "evils and calamities, but without being able to guess at the instrument, nature, or measure of them."[21] Philadelphia physician Benjamin Rush even thought that the American people were on the verge of "degenerating into savages or devouring each other like beasts of prey." Rush may have had a hyperactive imagination, but even the more sober and restrained George Washington was in 1786 astonished at the changes that had taken place in a decade's time. "From the high ground we stood upon, the plain path which invited our footsteps, to be so fallen! So lost! It is really mortifying."[22]

These expressions seem greatly exaggerated. Despite a temporary recession following the end of the war, the decade of the 1780s was generally a time of great expansion and release of energy. The population grew as never before or since; indeed, the 1780s witnessed the greatest demographic growth of any decade in American history. "There is not upon the face of the earth a body of people more happy or rising into consequence with more rapid stride, than the Inhabitants of the United States of America," the secretary of the Congress, Charles Thomson, told Jefferson in 1786. "Population is encreasing, new houses building, new lands clearing, new settlements forming, and new manufacture establishing with a rapidity beyond conception." Amid all the expressions of crisis, the mood among the common people was high, expectant, and far from bleak. "If we are undone," declared a bewildered South Carolinian, "we are the most splendidly ruined of any nation in the universe."[23]

Yet there are all these hand-wringing and despairing statements in the 1780s, which were often made not in the frenzy of public debate but in the privacy of letters to friends. Why would Americans have lost their

21. Charleston *South Carolina Gazette and General Advertiser*, 9 Aug. 1783; John Jay to GW, 27 June 1786, in Henry P. Johnston, ed., *The Correspondence and Public Papers of John Jay* (New York, 1890–93), 3: 204–5.

22. BR to David Ramsay, [March or April 1788], *Letters of Rush*, 1: 454; GW to Jay, 1 Aug. 1786, 18 May 1786, in Fitzpatrick, ed., *Writings of Washington*, 28: 503, 431–32.

23. Charles Thomson to TJ, 6 April 1786, *Papers of Jefferson*, 9: 380; Charleston *South Carolina Gazette and Public Advertiser*, 18–21 May 1785.

nerve so quickly? Why did some men, members of the gentlemanly elite, think America was in a crisis?

There were, of course, many defects in the Articles of Confederation that had become obvious by the 1780s. Lacking the powers to tax and to regulate the nation's commerce, the Confederation Congress could neither pay off the debts the United States had incurred during the Revolution nor retaliate against the mercantilist trade policies of the European states, particularly Great Britain. At the same time, the new republican confederacy was hard-pressed to maintain its independence in a world of hostile monarchical empires. Britain refused to send a minister to the United States and ignored its treaty obligations to evacuate from American territory in the Northwest. In the Southwest Spain refused to recognize American claims to the territory between Florida and the Ohio River and was trying to use its ability to close the Mississippi to American trade to bring American settlers moving into Kentucky and Tennessee under its control. By 1786 all these problems, both domestic and international, had created mounting pressure to reform the Articles.

Yet it was not the defects of the Articles of Confederation by themselves that were causing the sense of crisis. These defects were correctable and were scarcely capable of eliciting the many expressions of horror and despair.

To be sure, these defects did make possible the calling of the Philadelphia Convention in 1787 to amend the Articles. Almost every political leader in the country, including most of the later opponents of the Constitution, wanted something done to strengthen the Articles of Confederation and make the United States a more respectable nation. Since most were willing to grant the Congress at least a limited authority to tax and the power to regulate commerce, nearly everyone supported the meeting of the Convention, which presumably was only going to revise the Articles. Hence many were as surprised by the results as John Tyler of Virginia was. Tyler had expected the Convention to vote a necessary power to regulate commerce. "But," he said, "it never entered into my head that we should quit liberty and throw ourselves into the hands of an energetic government." Tyler, like many others who came to oppose the Constitution, discovered that the Convention had presented them with much more than they had bargained for.[24]

Thus the deficiencies of the Confederation themselves cannot account for the unprecedented nature of the Constitution created in 1787. By establishing a strong national government that operated directly on individuals, the Constitution went far beyond what the weaknesses of the

24. Editorial Note, *Papers of Jefferson*, 9: 208.

Articles demanded. Granting Congress the authority to raise revenue, to regulate trade, to pay off its debts, and to deal effectively in international affairs did not require the total scrapping of the Articles and the creation of an extraordinarily powerful and distant national government, the likes of which were virtually inconceivable a decade earlier. To James Madison, the putative father of the Constitution, the document of 1787 became the solution for the "multiplicity," "mutability," and "injustice" of state legislation over the previous decade, what were often referred to as the "excesses of democracy." It was the popular behavior of the state legislatures in the decade following the Declaration of Independence that lay behind the elite's sense of crisis.

The abuses of the state legislatures, said Madison, were "so frequent and so flagrant as to alarm the most stedfast friends of Republicanism"; and these abuses, he told Jefferson in the fall of 1787, "contributed more to that uneasiness which produced the Convention, and prepared the public mind for a general reform than those which accrued to our national character and interest from the inadequacy of the Confederation to its immediate objects."[25]

The Revolution had greatly democratized the state legislatures, both by increasing the number of their members and by broadening their electorates. Many ordinary men of more humble and rural origins and less education than had sat in the colonial assemblies had been elected as representatives. In New Hampshire, for example, the colonial assembly in 1765 had contained only thirty-four members, almost all well-to-do gentlemen from the coastal region around Portsmouth. By 1786 the state's house of representatives numbered eighty-eight members, most of whom were ordinary farmers or men of moderate wealth from the western areas of the state. In other states the changes were less striking but no less important. Many of the state capitals were moved from their former colonial locations on the eastern coastline to new sites in the interior.[26]

In all the states electioneering and the open competition for office had expanded dramatically, along with demands for greater public access to governmental activities. The number of contested elections and the turnover of legislative seats multiplied. During the eighteenth century the colonial assemblies had attained a high degree of stability with very little change in membership from year to year. The Revolution had reversed all that. By the 1780s annual elections of the legislatures (a radical innovation in most states) were often replacing half or more of the

25. JM to TJ, 24 Oct. 1787, *Papers of Jefferson*, 12: 276.
26. Jackson Turner Main, "Government by the People: The American Revolution and Democratization of the Legislatures," *WMQ*, 23 (1966), 391–407; Rosemarie Zagarri, *The Politics of Size: Representation in the United States, 1776–1850* (Ithaca, 1987).

representatives every year. The colonial assemblies had remained closed to the public; even the record of the legislators' votes had often been considered privileged information. The new republican legislatures built galleries and opened their proceedings to the public, and a growing number of newspapers, including dailies, began to report legislative debates.

Everywhere self-appointed leaders, speaking for newly aroused groups and localities, had taken advantage of the expanded suffrage and the annual elections to seek membership in the assemblies. New petty entrepreneurs like Abraham Yates Jr., a part-time lawyer and shoemaker of Albany, and William Findley, a Scots-Irish ex-weaver of western Pennsylvania, had vaulted into political leadership in the states. In the eyes of the more established gentlemen who had gone to Harvard or the College of New Jersey in Princeton, these popular upstarts with interests to promote seemed incapable of the kind of disinterested character that republican political leaders were supposed to display. Alexander Hamilton, for example, thought that Yates was "a man whose ignorance and perverseness are only surpassed by his pertinacity and conceit." The state legislatures, concluded Robert R. Livingston of New York, had become full of men "unimproved by education and unreformed by honor."[27]

Under these turbulent circumstances the state legislatures could scarcely fulfill what many Revolutionary leaders in 1776 had assumed was their republican responsibility to promote a unitary public interest distinguishable from the private and parochial interests of individuals. By the 1780s it was obvious to many, including Madison, that "a spirit of locality" was destroying "the aggregate interests of the community." Everywhere the gentry leaders complained of popular legislative practices that today are taken for granted—logrolling, horse-trading, and pork-barreling that benefited special and local interest groups. Each representative, grumbled Ezra Stiles, president of Yale College, was concerned only with the particular interests of his electors. Whenever a bill was read in the legislature, "every one instantly thinks how it will affect his constituents." Instead of electing men to office "for their abilities, integrity and patriotism," the people, said Stiles, were much more likely to vote for someone "from some mean, interested, or capricious motive."[28]

Parochial politics of this kind was not new to America; after all, the colonial assemblies had spent much of their time fixing the height of

---

27. Alfred F. Young, *The Democratic Republicans of New York: The Origins, 1763–1797* (Chapel Hill, 1967), 40, 27.

28. "Madison's Observations on Jefferson's Draft of a Constitution for Virginia" (1788), *Papers of Jefferson*, 6: 308–9; Ezra Stiles, "The United States Elevated to Glory and Honor" (1783), in John W. Thornton, ed., *The Pulpit of the American Revolution* (Boston, 1860), 420.

fence posts and adjudicating all sorts of petty local grievances. But the nature and scale of this post-Revolutionary parochial politics were new. Constituents were pressuring their representatives to legislate on behalf of their interests, which were usually economic or commercial. Taxes in the states were two to three times higher than they had been before the Revolution, and many people were angry, especially since many of the taxes were laid directly on polls and property. Thus farmers in debt urged the lowering of taxes, or at least greater reliance on tariffs rather than direct taxes on persons and land; they also advocated the suspension of court actions to recover debts and the continued printing of paper money. And although they were willing to resort to violence if the tax burden became too heavy, as events in several states revealed, they were discovering that electing the right candidates was more effective.

Other groups also had their special interests to promote. Merchants and creditors called for high taxes on land in place of tariffs, less paper money, the protection of private contracts, and the encouragement of foreign trade. Artisans lobbied for the regulation of the prices of agricultural products, the abolition of mercantile monopolies, and tariff protection against imported manufactured goods. Entrepreneurs everywhere petitioned for legal privileges and corporate grants. And in the state legislatures representatives of these interests were passing laws on their behalf, in effect, becoming judges in their own causes.

All this political scrambling among contending interests made lawmaking in the states seem chaotic. Laws, as the Vermont Council of Censors said in 1786 in a common complaint, were "altered—realtered—made better—made worse; and kept in such a fluctuating position, that persons in civil commission scarce know what is law."[29] Indeed, Madison in 1787 said that the states had enacted more laws in the decade since independence than had been enacted in the entire colonial period. No wonder he concluded that the lack of "*wisdom* and *steadiness*" in legislation was "the grievance complained of in all of our republics."[30]

All these legislative efforts to respond to the excited pleas and pressures of the various interests alienated as many people as they pleased and brought lawmaking itself into contempt, at least in the eyes of elites. By excessively printing paper money and creating currency inflation and by enacting laws on behalf of debtors, the popularly elected representatives in the state legislatures were violating the individual rights of creditors and other property-holders.

29. "Address of the Council of Censors," 14 Feb. 1786, in William Slade, ed., *Vermont State Papers* (Middlebury, VT, 1823), 540.
30. Wood, *Creation of the American Republic*, 405.

Bondholders and those with money out on loan were especially vulnerable to inflation, which is why many leaders became so frightened by the paper money emissions and other debtor relief legislation passed by the state assemblies in the 1780s. Inflation threatened not simply the livelihood of creditors and elites with proprietary wealth but their authority and independence as well. Although leaders like Madison often regarded the advocates of paper money and debtor relief schemes in the 1780s as little better than levelers, unconcerned with the rights of property, those popular advocates of paper money and easy credit were neither propertyless masses nor destitute radicals opposed to the private ownership of property. They were themselves property owners, sometimes wealthy ones, who believed in the sacredness of property as much as Madison. Only it was usually a different kind of property they were promoting—modern, risk-taking property, property as a commodity; dynamic, entrepreneurial property; venture capital, even when it was land; not money out on loan, but money borrowed; in fact, all the paper money that enterprising farmers and proto-businessmen clamored for in these years.

By the 1780s it seemed as if the majorities of the popular legislatures had become just as dangerous to individual liberties as the detested royal governors had been. "173 despots would surely be as oppressive as one," wrote Jefferson in 1785 in his *Notes on the State of Virginia*. "An elective despotism was not the government we fought for."[31]

Most alarming to leaders like Madison was the fact that these abuses of individual rights by the state legislatures were backed by the bulk of the electorates in each state. In the 1770s the Revolutionaries had not conceived of the possibility of the people becoming tyrannical. When Tories had suggested in 1775 that the people might indeed abuse their power, good Whig patriots like John Adams had dismissed the notion as illogical: "a democratic despotism is a contradiction in terms."[32] The crown or executive authority was the only possible source of tyranny; the people could never tyrannize themselves.

But by the 1780s many leaders had come to realize that the Revolution had unleashed social and political forces that they had not anticipated and that the "excesses of democracy" threatened the very essence of their republican revolution. The behavior of the state legislatures, in the despairing words of Madison, had called "into question the fundamental principle of republican Government, that the majority who rule in such governments are the safest Guardians both of Public Good and private

---

31. TJ, *Notes on the State of Virginia*, ed. William Peden (Chapel Hill, 1955), 120.
32. JA, "Novanglus," in Adams, ed., *Works*, 4: 79.

rights."[33] This was the issue that made the 1780s so critical to large numbers of American leaders.

Liberals everywhere in the Western world were anxiously watching to see what would happen to the new American republics. If the expectations of 1776 should prove illusionary, if republican self-government could not survive, then, as the English radical Richard Price told Americans in 1785, "the consequence will be, that the fairest experiment ever tried in human affairs will miscarry; and that a REVOLUTION which had revived the hopes of good men and promised an opening to better times, will become a discouragement to all future efforts in favour of liberty, and prove only an opening to a new scene of human degeneracy and misery."[34]

BY 1787 MANY of the Revolutionary leaders had retreated from the republican idealism of 1775–1776. People were not going to be selfless and keep their private interests out of the public arena after all. Almost from the outset Washington had realized that to expect ordinary people, such "as compose the bulk of an Army," to be "influenced by any other principles than those of Interest, is to look for what never did, and I fear never will happen." Even most officers could not be expected to sacrifice their private interests and their families for the sake of their country. "The few, therefore, who act upon Principles of disinterestedness," Washington concluded, "are, comparatively speaking, no more than a drop in the Ocean."[35]

Looking around at aggressive debtor farmers, engrossing merchants, and factious legislators, many could only conclude that private interest ruled most social relationships. The American people, wrote Governor William Livingston of New Jersey in a common reckoning of 1787, "do not exhibit the virtue that is necessary to support a republican government."[36] The behavior of the popularly elected state legislatures revealed to the Revolutionary leaders an unanticipated dark underside to democracy and equality. Because the Revolution had made the people the sole source of authority in the thirteen republics, there seemed little that could be done about it. In an untitled play written by Yale students and performed for their classmates in 1784, one of the characters is warned against speaking out against the will of the people. "I must confess," the character responds, "this is something very singular, that a person must be cautioned against

---

33. JM, "Vices of the Political System of the United States" (1787), *Madison: Writings*, 75.
34. Richard Price, *Observations on the Importance of the American Revolution* (Dublin, 1785), 85.
35. GW to John Hancock, 24 Sept. 1776, in Fitzpatrick, ed., *Writings of Washington*, 6: 107–8.
36. Theodore Sedgwick, *A Memoir of the Life of William Livingston* (New York, 1833), 403.

speaking his sentiments upon any political point in a free state. — but sir, we have a new set of folk lately come upon the stage."[37]

Most Revolutionary leaders had not foreseen a "new set of folk" emerging in politics. They knew, of course, that the common people could occasionally get out of hand and riot. In 1774 the conservative New Yorker Gouverneur Morris had warned that "the mob begin to think and reason. Poor reptiles! It is with them a vernal morning; they are struggling to cast off their winter's slough, they bask in the sunshine, and ere noon they will bite, depend upon it." Although many of the leaders certainly did begin to fear the spread of disorder among the lower orders and the possibility of coming "under the domination of a riotous mob," they had taken such occurrences more or less in stride for years.

Mobbing was one thing; having common people actually holding high offices of government was quite another, and Morris had not seen it coming. He had focused his fears on the mobs themselves while dismissing their leaders, Isaac Sears and John Lamb, as "unimportant persons."[38] Yet the crisis of the 1780s did not come from men like Sears and Lamb leading mobs; elites could deal with popular mobs, as they had in the past. Instead, the crisis came from the election in the 1780s of such "unimportant persons" to the state legislatures, in Sears's and Lamb's case to the New York assembly; in a republican elective system, that was a situation not so easily dealt with.

When the Revolutionary leaders had asserted that all men were created equal, most had not imagined that ordinary people, farmers, artisans, and other workers would actually come to hold high governmental office. Men were equal at birth and in their rights, but not in ability and character. "The *rights* of mankind are simple," said Benjamin Rush in 1787, expressing views that even those liberals like Jefferson with a magnanimous view of human nature would have endorsed. "They require no learning to unfold them. They are better *felt*, than explained. Hence in matters that relate to liberty, the mechanic and the philosopher, the farmer and the scholar, are all upon a footing. But the case is widely different with respect to *government*. It is a complicated science, and requires abilities and knowledge of a variety of other subjects, to understand it."[39]

Average Americans who had occupations and had to work with their hands for a living lacked the proper qualifications for virtuous and

---

37. Christopher Grasso, A *Speaking Aristocracy: Transforming Public Discourse in Eighteenth-Century Connecticut* (Chapel Hill, 1999), 386.
38. Morris to John Penn, 20 May 1774, in Merrill Jensen, ed., *American Colonial Documents to 1776* (London, 1955), 861–63.
39. [BR], "To the Freeman of the United States," *Pennsylvania Gazette*, 30 May 1787, in John P. Kaminski et al., eds., *Documentary History of the Ratification of the Constitution* (Madison, WI, 1976–), 13: 116.

disinterested public leadership. In the ideal polity, Aristotle had written thousands of years earlier, "the citizen must not live a mechanical or commercial life. Such a life is not noble, and it militates against virtue." According to Aristotle artisans, agricultural workers, even businessmen, could not be citizens. For men "must have leisure to develop their virtue and for the activities of a citizen."[40]

In the late eighteenth century some of this ancient prejudice against artisans and other workers participating in government still remained. "Nature never intended that such men should be profound politicians or able statesmen," declared Oxford-trained William Henry Drayton of South Carolina on the eve of the Revolution. How could "men who never were in a way to study, or to advise upon any points, but knew only rules how to cut up a beast in a market to the best advantage, to cobble an old shoe in the neatest manner, or to build a necessary house"—how could such men claim a role in government? They were not gentlemen.

THE DISTINCTION BETWEEN gentlemen and commoners, this "most ancient and universal of all Divisions of People," as John Adams called it, was a crucially important horizontal cleavage in a largely vertically organized eighteenth-century society in which most people were more aware of those above and below them than of those alongside them. This division may even have been more conspicuous to some contemporaries than the horizontal line separating freemen from slaves.[41]

A gentleman, as that eighteenth-century connoisseur of English manners Lord Chesterfield defined him, was "a man of good behavior, well bred, amiable, high-minded, who knows how to act in any society, in the company of any man."[42] Gentlemen, who composed 5 to 10 percent of American society—fewer in the South than in the North—walked and talked in certain ways and dressed distinctively and fashionably. In contrast to the plain shirts, leather aprons, and buckskin breeches of ordinary men, gentlemen wore lace ruffles, silk stockings, and other finery. Unlike common people, they wore wigs or powdered their hair. They learned to dance and sometimes to fence and to play a musical instrument. They prided themselves on their classical learning and often took great pains to display it. They even had their own sense of honor, which they sometimes upheld by challenging other gentlemen to duels.

40. Aristotle, *Politics*, VII.ix.1328b33, trans. T. A. Sinclair, rev. Trevor J. Saunders (New York, 1981), 415.

41. JA, Notes for "A Dissertation on the Canon and Feudal Law" (1765), *Papers of Adams*, 1: 107.

42. Henry Dwight Sedgwick, *In Praise of Gentlemen* (Boston, 1933), 130n.

Although American gentlemen, such as the Southern landed planters George Washington and Thomas Jefferson or the Northern attorneys John Adams and Alexander Hamilton, in no way resembled the elaborately titled English nobility or the legally privileged French aristocracy, they nonetheless tended to consider themselves as aristocrats, "natural aristocrats," as both Jefferson and the New York farmer and self-made merchant Melancton Smith called them.[43]

They were different from ordinary folk because as gentlemen they did not have occupations, which meant, as the New Yorker Smith said, they were "not obliged to use the pains and labour to procure property."[44] Being a lawyer, a physician, a clergyman, a military officer, in other words, being members of what were beginning to be called "professions," was not yet considered having an occupation. Lawyers, for example, often tried to assure themselves and others that they were really gentlemen who only occasionally practiced some law. For such men, such as young Thomas Shippen, law was not as much a skilled profession as it was a desirable attribute of a man of learning, one, as James Kent told his Columbia law students in 1794, that ought to be "usefully known by every Gentleman of Polite Education." Such gentlemen-lawyers were expected to read Horace as well as Blackstone, Cicero as well as Coke, history and poetry as well as common law books. Early in his adult life Jefferson had been a lawyer, but he scarcely resembled a modern practitioner calculating billable hours. He believed that the law, like all of learning, was important for a variety of reasons. "It qualifies a man to be useful to himself, to his neighbors, and to the public. It is the most certain stepping stone to preferment in the political line."[45]

Early in his career John Adams, the ambitious son of a small-town Massachusetts farmer, had struggled to fashion himself into a polite and enlightened gentleman. In 1761, at age twenty-six, he may have still been unsure of his own gentility, but at least he knew who was not a gentleman. That person was someone who "neither by Birth, Education, Office, Reputation, or Employment," nor by "Thought, Word, or Deed," could

43. TJ to JA, 28 Oct. 1813, in Lester J. Cappon, ed., *The Adams-Jefferson Letters: The Complete Correspondence Between Thomas Jefferson and Abigail and John Adams* (Chapel Hill, 1959), 2: 388; Debate in the New York Ratifying Convention, 17 June–26 July 1788, in Bernard Bailyn, ed., *The Debate on the Constitution* (New York, 1993), 2: 760, 761.

44. Debate in the New York Ratifying Convention, 17 June–26 July 1788, in Bailyn, ed., *The Debate on the Constitution*, 2: 761.

45. James Kent, "An Introductory Lecture to a Course of Law Lectures," (1794), in Hyneman and Lutz, eds., *American Political Writing During the Founding Era*, 2: 947; TJ to Thomas Mann Randolph Jr., 30 May 1790, *Papers of Jefferson*, 16: 449.

pass himself off as a gentleman. A person who springs "from ordinary Parents," who "can scarcely write his Name," whose "Business is Boating," who "never had any Commissions"—to call such a person a gentleman was "an arrant Prostitution of the Title."[46]

Adams had attended Harvard College, and that for him had clinched his gentility. By the time the Constitution was being written, he had come to know who a proper gentleman was: he was someone who had received a liberal arts education in a college. (Perhaps this became Adams's exclusive criterion of gentility precisely because the rivals of whom he was most jealous, Benjamin Franklin and George Washington, had not attended college.) "By gentlemen," he wrote in 1787, "are not meant the rich or the poor, the high-born or the low-born, the industrious or the idle: but all those who have received a liberal education, an ordinary degree of erudition in liberal arts and sciences. Whether by birth they be descended from magistrates and officers of government, or from husbandmen, merchants, mechanics, or laborers; or whether they be rich or poor."[47]

By a liberal arts education Adams meant acquiring all those genteel qualities that were supposed to be the prerequisites to becoming a political leader. It meant being cosmopolitan, standing on elevated ground in order to have a large view of human affairs, being free of the prejudices, parochialism, and religious enthusiasm of the vulgar and barbaric, and having the ability to make disinterested judgments about the various contending interests in the society. Of course, as Noah Webster said, having a liberal arts education—and becoming a gentleman—"disqualifies a man for business."[48] Conventional wisdom, in other words, held that businessmen could not be gentlemen.

Adam Smith in *Wealth of Nations* (1776) claimed that businessmen could not be good political leaders. Smith thought that businessmen in a modern complicated commercial society were too engaged in their occupations and the making of money to be able to make impartial judgments about the varied interests of their society. Only "those few...attached to no particular occupation themselves"—by which Smith meant the English landed gentry—"have leisure and inclination to examine the occupations of other people."[49]

46. JA, Jan. 1776, *Diary and Autobiography*, 1: 198.
47. JA, A *Defence of the Constitutions of Government of the United States* (1787–88), in Adams, ed., *Works*, 6: 185.
48. Noah Webster, "On the Education of Youth in America" (1790), in Frederick Rudolph, ed., *Essays on Education in the Early Republic* (Cambridge, MA, 1965), 56.
49. Adam Smith, An *Inquiry into the Nature and Causes of the Wealth of Nations*, ed. R. H. Campbell and A. S. Skinner (Oxford, 1976) (V.i.f 50–51), 2: 781–83.

These independent gentlemen of leisure who were presumed to be free of money-grubbing were expected to supply the necessary leadership in government. This leisure was what gave the slaveholding Virginians such an advantage in holding public office. Since well-to-do gentry were "exempted from the lower and less honourable employments," wrote the British philosopher Francis Hutcheson, they were "rather more than others obliged to an active life in some service to mankind. The publick has this claim upon them."[50] All the American Founders felt the weight of this claim, and they often agonized and complained about it.

The Revolutionary leaders did not conceive of politics as a profession and officeholding as a career. Like Jefferson, they believed that "in a virtuous government...public offices are what they should be, burthens to those appointed to them, which it would be wrong to decline, though foreseen to bring with them intense labor, and great private loss." They did not like electioneering or political parties, and they regarded public office as an obligation required of certain gentlemen because of their talents, independence, social preeminence, and leisure. Benjamin Franklin never thought his accomplishments in science could begin to compare with the public's demand for his service. He even went so far as to say that "the finest" of Newton's "Discoveries" could not have excused the great scientist's neglect of serving the commonwealth, if the public had needed him.[51] Franklin had always stressed that he was an independent gentleman whose offices were obligations thrust upon him. In not one of fourteen elections, he insisted, "did I ever appear as a candidate. I never did, directly or indirectly, solicit any man's vote."[52] Showing oneself eager for office was a sign of being unworthy of it, for the office-seeker probably had selfish views rather than the public good in mind.

Since politics was not yet regarded as a profession, the political officeholder was supposed to want to return to private life after serving the public; and this classical ideal remained strong. Washington's fame as a modern Cincinnatus in the 1780s came from his eagerness to surrender his sword and return to Mount Vernon. In ancient Rome, declared James Wilson, magistrates and army officers were always gentlemen-farmers, always willing to step down "from the elevation of office" and reassume "with contentment

50. Francis Hutcheson, A System of Moral Philosophy in Three Books (London, 1755), 2: 113.

51. TJ to Richard Henry Lee, 17 June 1779, in Ford, ed., Writings of Jefferson, 2: 192; TJ to William Duane, 1 Oct. 1812, in L and B, eds., Writings of Jefferson, 6: 80; TJ to Francis Willis, 13 April 1790, in Ford, ed., Writings of Jefferson, 5: 157; BF to Cadwallader Colden, 11 Oct. 1750, Papers of Franklin, 4: 68.

52. Bernard Bailyn, The Origins of American Politics (New York, 1968), 143; Gordon S. Wood, The Americanization of Benjamin Franklin (New York, 2004), 183.

and with pleasure, the peaceful labours of a rural and independent life."
John Dickinson's pose in 1767 as a "Pennsylvania Farmer" is incomprehensible except within this classical tradition. Dickinson was in fact a wealthy
and busy Philadelphia lawyer, but he needed to assure his readers that he
was free of marketplace interests by informing them at the outset that he was
a farmer, "contented" and "undisturbed by worldly hopes or fears."[53]

Those who had worldly hopes and fears, especially men, in Melancton Smith's words, who were "obliged to employ their time in their
respective callings," were presumed to have so many overpowering private interests as to be incapable of promoting the public interest. Prominent merchants dealing in international trade brought wealth into the
society and were thus valuable members of the community; but their
status as independent gentlemen was always tainted by their concern, as
the distinguished Massachusetts minister Charles Chauncey once put it,
to "serve their own private separate interest."[54] Wealthy merchants like
John Hancock and Henry Laurens who wanted a role in politics had
known this, and during the imperial crisis both had shed their mercantile business and sought to ennoble themselves. Hancock spent lavishly,
bought every imaginable luxury, and patronized everyone. He went
through the fortune he had inherited from his uncle, but in the process
he became the single most popular and powerful figure in Massachusetts politics during the last quarter of the eighteenth century. Laurens
knew only too well the contempt in which trading was held in aristocratic South Carolina, and in the 1760s he had begun curtailing his
merchant activities. During the Revolution he became president of the
Continental Congress and was able to sneer at all those merchants who
were still busy making money. "How hard it is," he had the gall to say in
1779, "for a rich or covetous man to enter heartily into the kingdom of
patriotism."[55]

If successful tradesmen and mechanics, such as Roger Sherman of
Connecticut, wanted high political office, they had to abandon their
occupations. Only when wealthy Benjamin Franklin had retired from his

53. Debate in the New York Ratifying Convention, 17 June–26 July 1788, in Bailyn, ed.,
    *Debate on the Constitution,* 2: 761; Wilson, "On the History of Property," in
    McCloskey, ed., *Works of Wilson,* 2: 716; John Dickinson, "Letters of a Farmer in
    Pennsylvania," in Paul L. Ford, ed., *The Writings of John Dickinson,* vol. 1, *Political
    Writings, 1764–1774* (Penn. Historical Society, *Memoirs,* 14 [Philadelphia, 1895]),
    307.
54. Charles Chauncey to Richard Price, 1774, in D. C. Thomas and Bernard Peach, eds.,
    *The Correspondence of Richard Price* (Durham, 1983), 1: 170.
55. David Duncan Wallace, *The Life of Henry Laurens* (New York, 1915), 335.

printing business in 1748 did "the Publick," as he wrote in his *Autobiography*, "now considering me as a Man of Leisure," lay hold of him and bring him into an increasing number of important political offices.[56] Thus, leisure in a classical sense was highly valued. In fact, the Virginia Revolutionaries in 1776 had originally adopted as the motto for the state seal *Deus nobis haec otia fecit* (God bestowed upon us this leisure). Only in 1779, after Jefferson and others protested that this was not the best message to set forth in the midst of a war, was the motto replaced by *Perseverando* (By persevering).[57]

Having sufficient leisure remained important for gentry status even in the North, which had far fewer slaves than the South. Members of the learned professions were usually considered gentlemen, particularly if they had been liberally educated in college. But were they impartial and disinterested? Were they free of the marketplace? Did they have enough leisure to be able to serve the public virtuously? The Philadelphia lawyer James Wilson thought so. So did Alexander Hamilton. In *Federalist* No. 35, Hamilton argued passionately that, unlike merchants, mechanics, and farmers, "the learned professions," by which he meant mainly lawyers, "truly form no distinct interest in society." Thus they "will feel a neutrality to the rivalships between the different branches of industry" and will be most likely to be "an impartial arbiter" between the diverse interests of the society.[58]

BY THE 1780s all these classical ideals of political leadership were losing much of their meaning, particularly in the Northern states. The line between the gentry and the common people, never very strong to begin with in America, was becoming seriously blurred. The distance that traditionally had separated the social ranks from one another was collapsing, and subordinates no longer felt the same awe and respect in the presence of their superiors that they had in the past. Everywhere, but especially in the North, growing numbers of ordinary folk used the popular and egalitarian rhetoric of the Revolution to challenge their so-called gentlemanly superiors. If only acquired and learned attributes and not those of blood and birth separated one man from another, then these challenges were hard to resist. Although the aspiring commoners lacked many of the attributes of gentility, more and more of them were becoming quite wealthy, literate, and independent; and they were aping the gentry

---

56. *The Autobiography of Benjamin Franklin*, ed. Leonard Labaree et al. (New Haven, 1964), 196.
57. TJ to John Page, 30 July 1776, *Papers of Jefferson*, 1: 482; Susan Dunn, *Dominion of Memories: Jefferson, Madison, and the Decline of Virginia* (New York, 2007), 31.
58. AH, *Federalist* No. 35.

in a variety of ways, particularly by displaying consumer goods that had traditionally belonged exclusively to the gentry.[59]

So scrambled was the social hierarchy becoming that men struggled to identify the various degrees and ranks that were emerging. Most people did not yet think explicitly in terms of modern "classes"—those horizontal layers of income and occupation standing in an antagonistic relationship to one another that would become common forms of identity in the nineteenth century. Instead, most late eighteenth-century commentators talked about sorts—"the better sort," "the meaner sort," "the ruder sort," "the lower sort," and, increasingly, "the middling sort."

These "middling sorts" were middling because they could not be classified either as gentlemen or as out-and-out commoners. They could not be gentlemen, because they had occupations and worked for a living with their hands; even artisans who employed dozens of journeymen-employees were regarded as something less than gentlemen. At the same time, however, these middling sorts, such as the petty New York merchants Isaac Sears and John Lamb, were often too well-off or too refined and knowledgeable to be placed among "the lower sort" or "the meaner sort." Of the three thousand adult males in Boston in 1790, for example, eighteen hundred or 60 percent made up the middling sort; they were the artisans or mechanics, the laboring proprietors, who held 36 percent of the taxable wealth of the city and constituted the majority of its property-holders.[60]

From the beginning of the eighteenth-century thinkers like Daniel Defoe had tried to explain and justify these emerging middling people, including the "working trades, who labour hard but feel no want."[61] These well-to-do working people with property, like the young printer Benjamin Franklin, increasingly had prided themselves on their separation from the common idleness and dissipation of the gentry above them and the property-less poor beneath them. "It was, in fact, the unique combination of work and property," as one perceptive scholar of this social group has put it, "that distinguished the 'middling sort' from the elite who owned but did not engage in productive labor, and from the wage earners who labored but did not own." These were the beginnings of what would become the middle class of the nineteenth century.[62]

59. T. H. Breen, *The Marketplace of Revolution: How Consumer Politics Shaped American Independence* (New York, 2004).

60. Lisa B. Lubow, "From Carpenter to Capitalist: The Business of Building in Postrevolutionary Boston," in Conrad Edrick Wright and Katheryn P. Viens, eds., *Entrepreneurs: The Boston Business Community, 1700–1850* (Boston, 1997), 181.

61. George Rudé, *Hanoverian London, 1714–1808* (Berkeley, 1971), 37, 56–57.

62. Lubow, "From Carpenter to Capitalist," in Wright and Viens, eds., *Entrepreneurs*, 185; Howard B. Rock, *Artisans of the New Republic: Tradesmen of New York City in the Age of Jefferson* (New York, 1979), 295–322.

Although the gentry still tended to lump these middling sorts who had occupations and worked openly for money with the lower orders of wage-earners in the single category of commoners, many of these middling people saw themselves as the equals of the so-called aristocracy or gentry and were eager to use the republican emphasis on equality to contest those above them. Many of them had wealth enough, and they could not see why they should not be regarded as gentlemen too. Or if they themselves were not to be considered gentlemen, then they hoped, as one Pennsylvania radical put it in 1775, to bring "gentlemen...down to our level," and ensure that "all ranks and conditions would come in for their just share of the wealth."[63] Other middling sorts were becoming increasingly self-conscious of their separate but equal status and began, for example, to contest the right of the gentry to sit in separate boxes in the theaters. Some of them even took to writing plays and building theaters designed for their own middling kind.[64]

Of course, there were immense differences among these middling sorts. The artisans or mechanics, for example, ranged from the very wealthy to the marginally poor. Some, such as bakers and bricklayers, required large amounts of capital for entry into the trade and thus were richer than most. Others, such as goldsmiths and clockmakers, required specialized skills that restricted their numbers and raised their incomes. And still others, such as weavers and shoemakers, were more lowly and poorer. But all these tradesmen and other middling persons tended to be united in a common antagonism to the would-be aristocracy above them.

The social struggle that took place during the three or four decades following the Revolution, especially in the Northern states of America, was essentially between these middling people and the gentry-aristocracy who claimed to be "exalted above the rest."[65] Everywhere, but particularly in the North, tens of thousands of ambitious middling men — commercial farmers, master artisans, traders, shopkeepers, petty merchants, and all those who later came to be called businessmen — were acquiring not only considerable wealth but also some learning, some politeness, and some awareness of the larger world.

By the 1780s the would-be aristocrats were finding it difficult to resist such challenges. In his debate with some middling sorts in the New York ratifying convention in 1788, Alexander Hamilton conceded that in

63. Terry Bouton, *Taming Democracy: "The People," the Founders, and the Troubled Ending of the American Revolution* (New York, 2007), 33.
64. Heather Nathans, *Early American Theater from the Revolution to Thomas Jefferson: Into the Hands of the People* (Cambridge, UK, 2003), 85, 92–100, 106–14.
65. Debate in the New York Ratifying Convention, 17 June–26 July 1788, in Bailyn, ed., *Debate on the Constitution*, 2: 773.

America every governor, every member of Congress, every magistrate, and every militia officer, indeed, "every distinguished man was an aristocrat."[66] If this were the case, then anyone elected or appointed to these offices thereby became a gentleman-aristocrat. The problem had become evident during the Revolutionary War. Much to the chagrin of the more established gentry, such middling sorts—"the Sons of Farmers or Mechanicks, who had quit the Plow or Workshop" to join the army as officers—had tried to use their commissions as junior officers to claim the status of gentlemen. Middling men elected to political office in the 1780s were doing the same: they were asserting their gentry status by the fact of election alone, without having acquired all the cultural attributes of gentlemen.[67]

These middling sorts launched the momentous social struggle that eventually turned them into the dominant "middle class" of the nineteenth century. When men at the time talked about the contest between the few and the many, or the aristocracy and the democracy, taking place in the society of the early Republic, it is this social struggle they are referring to.[68]

Historians have interpreted this complicated social struggle in very different ways. Some have denied that there was a social contest at all, contending that the Revolution had no social causes or consequences whatsoever and was simply a war for independence. Others have agreed that there was a struggle but have seen it in exclusively economic rather than social terms, with a few moneyed men exploiting the common workers. And still others have differed over who the contestants were and who was oppressing whom.[69] Yet the struggle was very real, and it

66. AH, New York Ratifying Convention, 21 June 1788, *Papers of Hamilton*, 5: 41.
67. Charles Royster, *A Revolutionary People at War: The Continental Army and the American Character, 1775–1783* (Chapel Hill, 1979), 87, 91.
68. AStuart M. Blumin, *The Emergence of the Middle Class: Social Experience in the American City, 1760–1900* (Cambridge, UK, 1989); Howard B. Rock, *Artisans of the New Republic: Tradesmen of New York City in the Age of Jefferson* (New York, 1979), 295–322.
69. Bernard Bailyn, *The Ideological Origins of the American Revolution*, enlarged ed. (Cambridge, MA, 1992), 321–79, sees the Constitution as the fulfillment of the Revolution with little or no social conflict involved. Beginning with J. Allen Smith, *Spirit of American Government, a Study of the Constitution: Its Origin, Influence and Relation to Democracy* (1907), and continuing with probably the most famous history book in American history, Charles Beard, *An Economic Interpretation of the Constitution* (1913), Progressive and Neo-Progressive historians have viewed the Constitution as an undemocratic document foisted on an unwilling populace. For modern versions of this Progressive interpretation, see Terry Bouton, *Taming Democracy: "The People," the Founders, and the Troubled Ending of the American Revolution* (New York, 2007); and Woody Holton, *Unruly Americans and the Origins of the Constitution* (New York, 2007).

fundamentally changed American society in the decades following the Revolution, particularly in the North.

THE FEDERAL CONSTITUTION of 1787 was designed in part to solve the problems created by the presence in the state legislatures of these middling men. In addition to correcting the deficiencies of the Articles of Confederation, the Constitution was intended to restrain the excesses of democracy and protect minority rights from overbearing majorities in the state legislatures. But could that be done within a republican framework? Some thought not. "You may think it very Extraordinary," Joseph Savage of New Jersey told his son in July 1787, "but the better sort of people are very desirous of a Monarchical government and are in daily Expectation of having it recommended by those Gentlemen in Philadelphia."[70] Of course, the middling sorts in the states did not think there was too much democracy in the various legislatures; on the contrary, because of the heavy taxes they were paying, they thought there was not enough democracy.

Certainly no one described the crisis of American politics in 1787 more acutely than did the thirty-six-year-old Virginian James Madison. Madison had become a member of the Continental Congress at age twenty-eight and was thoroughly familiar with the Confederation's weaknesses. Indeed, throughout the middle 1780s he, along with other national leaders, had wrestled with various schemes for overhauling the Articles of Confederation. But it was his experience serving in the Virginia assembly in 1784–1787 that convinced him that the real problem of American politics lay in the state legislatures. During the 1780s he saw many of his and Jefferson's plans for reform mangled by factional fighting and majoritarian confusion in the Virginia assembly. More than any other Founder, Madison questioned the conventional wisdom of the age concerning majority rule, the proper size for a republic, and the role of factions in society. His thinking about the problems of creating republican governments and his writing of the Virginia Plan in 1787, which became the working model for the Constitution, constituted one of the most creative moments in the history of American politics.

Yet Madison's conception of a proper national government expressed in his Virginia Plan was very different from that of many of his fellow supporters of the Constitution. Although Madison very much desired to transcend the states and build a nation in 1787, his idea of the role of the proposed central government was very judicial-like.

70. Joseph Savage to Samuel Phillips Savage, 17 July 1787, Savage Family, MG 836, New Jersey Historical Society. (I owe this reference to Brendan McConville.)

No government, Madison wrote in *Federalist* No. 10, could be just if parties, that is, people with private interests to promote, became judges in their own causes; indeed, interested majorities in the legislatures were no better in this respect than interested minorities. Madison's solution to this problem was to create a national government that he hoped would be a kind of impartial super-judge over all the competing interests in the society. The new Constitution would create, he said, a "disinterested & dispassionate umpire in disputes between different passions & interests" in the various states.[71] In fact, he hoped the new government might play the same super-political neutral role that the British king ideally had been supposed to play in the empire.

Madison had little or no interest in creating the sort of modern European-like war-making state with an energetic and powerful executive that other nationalists such as Alexander Hamilton wanted. In fact, Madison seems to have never much valued executive authority as a means of countering legislative abuses, even in the states, and his conception of the executive in the new national government remained hazy at best. As late as April 1787 he told Washington that he had "scarcely ventured as yet to form my own opinion either of the manner in which [the executive] ought to be constituted or of the authorities with which it ought to be cloathed."[72]

Through much of the Convention he assumed that the powers over appointment to offices and the conduct of foreign affairs would be assigned to the Senate, not the president. Only in mid-August 1787, three months into the Convention, when Madison and other nationalists became alarmed by the states gaining equal representation in the Senate, were these powers taken away from the state-dominated Senate and granted to the president. Madison and others so feared the state legislatures, each of which would elect two senators under the "Connecticut Compromise," that they no longer wanted the Senate to have the degree of power earlier granted to it when it would have been proportionally elected and would not have represented the states.

Although the final version of the new Constitution eliminated what Madison regarded as essential parts of his Virginia Plan, including proportional representation in both houses of Congress, it did retain the tripartite structure of an executive, a bicameral legislature, and a judiciary. The Constitution corrected the deficiencies of the Confederation by

---

71. JM to GW, 16 April 1787, *Madison: Writings*, 81.
72. JM to GW, 16 April 1787, *Madison: Writings*, 81. For Madison's downplaying of the executive in the state governments, see JM to Caleb Wallace, 23 August 1785, ibid., 41–42.

granting the new national government some extraordinary powers, powers that ambitious state-builders could exploit. The Convention, however, rejected Madison's impractical plan for a national congressional veto over all state laws, a rejection that Madison feared would doom the Constitution to failure. Instead, the Convention in Article I, Section 10, prohibited the states from exercising a remarkable number of powers, including levying import or export duties, printing paper money, and enacting various debtor relief laws and laws impairing contracts. But if these prohibitions were not enough to prevent the excesses of localist and interest-ridden democracy in the states, then the expanded and elevated structure of the federal government itself was designed to help.

Madison and other supporters of the Constitution—the Federalists, as they called themselves—hoped that an expanded national sphere of operation would prevent the diverse and clashing interests of the society from combining to create tyrannical majorities in the new national government. Madison understood that it had worked that way in American religion: the multiplicity of religious sects prevented any one of them from dominating the state and permitted the enlightened reason of liberal gentlemen like Jefferson and himself to shape public policy and church-state relations and to protect the rights of minorities. "In a free government," wrote Madison in *Federalist* No. 51, "the security for civil rights must be the same as that for religious rights. It consists in the one case in the multiplicity of interests, and in the other in the multiplicity of sects."[73]

Madison, however, did not expect the new federal government to be neutralized into inactivity by competition among these numerous diverse interests. He did not envision public policy or the common good of the national government emerging naturally from the give-and-take of hosts of clashing private interests. Instead, he expected that these interests would neutralize themselves in the society and allow liberally educated, rational men—men, he said, "whose enlightened views and virtuous sentiments render them superior to local prejudices, and to schemes of injustice"—to decide questions of the public good in a disinterested adjudicatory manner.[74]

As "an auxiliary desideratum" to his scheme, Madison predicted that the elevated and expanded sphere of national politics would act as a filter, refining the kind of men who would become these national umpires.[75] In a larger arena of national politics with an expanded electorate and a

---

73. JM, *Federalist* Nos. 57, 51.
74. JM, *Federalist* No. 10.
75. JM, "Vices of the Political System," *Madison: Writings*, 79.

smaller number of representatives, the people were more apt to ignore the illiberal narrow-minded men with "factious tempers" and "local prejudices," the middling men who had dominated the state legislatures in the 1780s, and instead elect to the new federal government only disinterested gentlemen.[76] One has only to compare the sixty-five representatives who were designated for the first national Congress with the thousand or more representatives in the state legislatures to understand what this filtering and refining process of the Constitution might mean socially and politically.

Most of the Revolutionary leaders, in other words, continued to hold out the possibility of virtuous politics, practiced by at least a few in the society. Amid all the scrambling of private interests, perhaps only a few were capable of becoming founders and legislators, who, as Hamilton said, from their "commanding eminence...look down with contempt upon every mean or interested pursuit." "The rich," declared Robert R. Livingston in the New York ratifying convention, possessed "a more disinterested emotion" than ordinary people, who tended to be "most occupied by their cares and distresses."[77] Even Jefferson admitted that only those few "whom nature has endowed with genius and virtue" could "be rendered by liberal education worthy to receive, and able to guard the sacred rights and liberties of their fellow citizens."[78] Only a few were liberally educated and cosmopolitan enough to have the breadth of perspective to comprehend all the different interests of the society; and only a few were independent and unbiased enough to adjudicate among these different interests and advance the public rather than a private good.

Such an elitist conception of the Constitution was bound to arouse opposition in an America that was becoming increasingly egalitarian and filled with ambitious middling people who wanted a say in how they were governed. Indeed, as John Dickinson warned his colleagues in the Philadelphia Convention, "when this plan goes forth, it will be attacked by the popular leaders. Aristocracy will be the watchword: the Shibboleth among its adversaries."[79]

---

76. JM to GW, 16 April 1787, to Edmund Randolph, 8 April 1787, *Papers of Madison*, 9: 384, 370; JM, *Federalist* No. 10; John Zvesper, "The Madisonian Systems," *Western Political Quarterly*, 37 (1984), 244–47.

77. Gerald Stourzh, *Alexander Hamilton and the Idea of Republican Government* (Stanford, 1970), 175; Debate in the New York Ratifying Convention, 17 June–26 July 1788, in Bailyn, ed., *Debate on the Constitution*, 2: 778.

78. TJ, "A Bill for a More General Diffusion of Knowledge" (1778), *Papers of Jefferson*, 2: 527.

79. Max Farrand, ed., *The Records of the Federal Convention of 1787* (New Haven, 1911, 1937), 2: 278.

Dickinson was not wrong. Confronted with the new elevated federal government, the opponents of the Constitution, or the Anti-Federalists, as they were called, could only conclude that the proposed Constitution was a document designed to foist an aristocratic government of "Powdered heads" on republican America.[80] Although some of the prominent Anti-Federalists, such as George Mason, Richard Henry Lee, and Elbridge Gerry, were themselves aristocratic gentlemen, most of the opponents of the Constitution were ordinary middling men such as Melancton Smith, William Findley, and John Lamb—spokesmen for the market farmers, shopkeepers, traders, and paper money borrowers who represented the future dominant force of American society, at least in the Northern states of America. And they did not hesitate to lash out at the Federalists for promoting a government in which, as the New York Anti-Federalist Smith put it, "none but the great will be chosen."[81]

In the egalitarian atmosphere created by the Revolution, no accusation could be more effective. The declaration in the Constitution that "no Title of Nobility shall be granted by the United States" was now interpreted to mean that no one should be set apart from the body of the people.[82] As the poet Joel Barlow noted, the very word "people" had come to mean something different in America than in Europe. In Europe the people remained only a portion of the society—the poor, the canaille, the rabble, the *miserables*, the *menu peuple*, the *Pöbel*. But in America, as Fisher Ames pointed out, "the class called vulgar, canaille, rabble, so numerous there, does not exist."[83] The people had become the whole society and were taking on a quasi-sacred character. In America there were no orders, no hereditary aristocracy, no estates separate from the people.

Some American gentry may have expressed contempt for ordinary folk in the privacy of their dining rooms, but it was no longer possible for an American leader to refer to the people in public as the common "herd." During the Virginia ratifying convention in June 1788 Edmund Randolph used just this term in reference to the people, and the popular demagogue Patrick Henry immediately called him on it. By likening the people

---

80. David Waldstreicher, *In the Midst of Perpetual Fetes: The Making of American Nationalism, 1776–1820* (Chapel Hill, 1997), 95.

81. Debate in the New York Ratifying Convention, 17 June–26 July 1788, in Bailyn, ed., *Debate on the Constitution*, 2: 761.

82. The Constitution, Article I, Section 8.

83. Joel Barlow, *Advice to the Privileged Orders in the Several States of Europe* (1792, 1795) (Ithaca, 1956), 17; Harry C. Payne, *The Philosophes and the People* (New Haven, 1976), 7–17; Fisher Ames, Dec. 1796, *Annals of Congress*, 4th Congress, 2nd session, 1642.

to a "herd," Henry charged, Randolph had "levelled and degraded [them] to the lowest degree," reducing them "from respectable independent citizens, to abject, dependent subjects or slaves." Randolph was forced to defensively declare "that he did not use that word to excite any odium, but merely to convey an idea of a multitude."[84] But clearly he would not use it again in public.

The suggestion of elitism in the Constitution put the Federalist gentry on the defensive. In the New York ratifying convention Robert R. Livingston and Alexander Hamilton vainly tried to evade all the Anti-Federalist talk of aristocracy, or what Livingston referred to as "the phantom aristocracy . . . the bugbear" of the Anti-Federalists. Hamilton claimed he hardly knew the meaning of the word "aristocracy," and he denied that any traditional aristocracy existed. He and gentlemen like him, he said, were not "men elevated to a perpetual rank above their fellow citizens and possessing powers entirely independent of them." But his middling opponents would not be put off by such an Old World definition, and they continued to pound away at the aristocratic character of the Federalist leaders, the "high-fliers," as Abraham Yates called them. This was just the beginning of accusations of aristocracy that would be repeated throughout the subsequent decades.[85]

In 1787–1788 the middling Anti-Federalists may have lost the struggle over ratification of the Constitution, but they had won the rhetorical battle over the role of the people in public life.

AMERICANS WERE SO EXCITED over the successful ratification of the Constitution that they momentarily forgot the deep differences that existed among themselves and among the various states and sections. Social animosities were put aside, and gentlemen and mechanics and other middling sorts celebrated the establishment of the Constitution together, mingling their ranks in parades "in a truly republican style."[86] Even though two states—North Carolina and Rhode Island—were still outside the Union, Americans greeted the ratification of the Constitution with more unanimity than at any time since the Declaration of Independence. "'Tis done!" declared Benjamin Rush in July 1788 with his usual impulsive enthusiasm. "We have become a nation." (He said this despite the Convention's having eliminated all references to the word "national"

84. Virginia Ratifying Convention, in John P. Kaminski and Gaspare J. Saladino, eds., *The Documentary History of the Constitution* (Madison, WI, 1999), 9: 1044–45.

85. Debate in the New York Ratifying Convention, 17 June–26 July 1788, in Bailyn, ed., *Debate on the Constitution*, 778–79; AH, New York Ratifying Convention, 21 June 1788, *Papers of Hamilton*, 5: 41; Young, *Democratic Republicans of New York*, 45.

86. Waldstreicher, *In the Midst of Perpetual Fetes*, 105.

in the Constitution.) The creation of the Constitution, said Rush, had produced "such a tide of joy as has seldom been felt in any age or country." It represented the "triumph of knowledge over ignorance, of virtue over vice, and of liberty over slavery." With a fifth of America's population still enslaved, the irony in that last phrase was lost on Rush, at least for the moment.[87]

Rush was not the only enthusiast. Although Washington did not believe that the people of the United States had become a nation, and indeed believed that they were far from it, he abandoned his earlier pessimism and looked forward to better days, indulging a "fond, perhaps an enthusiastic idea, that as the world is much less barbarous than it has been, its melioration must still be progressive." Everywhere Americans saw their "rising empire" at long last fulfilling the promises of the Enlightenment.[88]

The rebellion of the North American colonies took place at a propitious moment in the history of the West, a moment in which hopes of liberal and benevolent reform and making the world anew filled the air on both sides of the Atlantic. That the American Revolution occurred at the height of what later came to be called the Enlightenment made all the difference: the coincidence transformed what otherwise might have been a mere colonial rebellion into a world-historical event that promised, as Richard Price and other foreign liberals pointed out, a new future not just for Americans but for all humanity.

The settlement of America, John Adams had declared in 1765, was "the opening of a grand scene and design in Providence for the illumination of the ignorant, and the emancipation of the slavish part of mankind all over the earth."[89] The Revolution had become the climax of this grand historic drama. Enlightenment was spreading everywhere in the Western world, but nowhere more than in America. With the break from Great Britain complete and the Constitution ratified, many Americans thought that the United States, as Congress told the president in 1796, had become the "freest and most enlightened" nation in the world.[90]

---

87. BR to Elias Boudinot? Observations on the Federal Procession in Philadelphia, 9 July 1788, *Letters of Rush*, 1: 470–75.
88. Russell Blaine Nye, *The Cultural Life of the New Nation, 1776–1830* (New York, 1960), 30. For a fuller version of this argument, see Gordon S. Wood, "The American Enlightenment," in Gary L. McDowell and Jonathan O'Neill, eds., *America and Enlightenment Constitutionalism* (New York, 2006), 159–75.
89. JA, "Dissertation on the Feudal and Canon Law" (1765), in Gordon S. Wood, ed., *The Rising Glory of America, 1760–1820* (New York, 1971), 29.
90. Address to the President, Dec. 1796, *Annals of Congress*, 4th Congress, 2nd session, 1612, 1638, 1641–42.

For the people of these obscure provinces, "so recently," as Samuel Bryan of Pennsylvania admitted, "a rugged wilderness and the abode of savages and wild beasts," to claim to be the most enlightened nation on earth and to have "attained to a degree of improvement and greatness...of which history furnishes no parallel" seemed scarcely credible.[91] Americans had no sophisticated court life, no magnificent cities, no great concert halls, no lavish drawing rooms, and not much to speak of in the way of the fine arts. Indeed, throughout the first half of the eighteenth century most of the American colonists had been overwhelmed by a pervasive sense of their cultural inferiority. When confronted with the contrast between the achievements of metropolitan England and their provincial societies, they had felt only awe and mortification. American travelers in England had been continually astonished by the size and grandeur of English social and cultural life, by London and its excitement and social complexity, its buildings, its art, its extravagance and sumptuousness.

By 1789, however, much of this earlier colonial sense of inadequacy had fallen away. The Revolution was such an exhilarating psychological event precisely because it allowed Americans to transform their feelings of cultural inferiority into ones of superiority. Americans had thrown off the "prejudices" of the Old World and had adopted new liberal, enlightened, and rational ideas, said Thomas Paine. "We see with other eyes; we hear with other ears; and think with other thoughts, than those we formerly used." Ignorance was being expelled and could not return. "The mind once enlightened cannot again become dark."[92]

Many of the ambiguities colonial Americans had felt about the rural and provincial character of their society were now clarified. What some had seen as the crudities and limitations of American life could now be viewed as advantages for republican government. Independent American farmers no longer had to be regarded as primitive folk living on the edges of Western civilization and mired in the backwaters of history. Far from remaining on the periphery of the historical process, they now saw themselves suddenly cast into its center, leading the world to a new era of republican liberty. They would show the way in ridding society of superstition and barbarism and would gently bind together all parts of the globe through benevolence and commerce. "There cannot, from the history of mankind," declared John Winthrop of Massachusetts in 1788, "be produced an instance of rapid growth in extent, in

---

91. Bailyn, ed., *Debate on the Constitution* 1: 686.
92. Thomas Paine, "Letter to the Abbé Raynal," in Foner, ed., *Writings of Paine*, 2: 243–44.

numbers, in arts, and in trade, that will bear any comparison with our country."[93]

Yet despite the ratification of the Constitution, most Americans knew that they were not yet a nation, at least not in the European sense of the term. At the end of the Declaration of Independence the members of the Continental Congress had been able only to "mutually pledge to each other our Lives, our Fortunes, and our sacred Honor." In 1776 there was nothing else but themselves that they could have dedicated themselves to — no patria, no fatherland, no nation as yet.

Because of extensive immigration, America already had a diverse society, certainly more diverse than most European nations. In addition to seven hundred thousand people of African descent and tens of thousands of native Indians, all the peoples of Europe were present in the country. In the census of 1790 only 60 percent of the white population of well over three million remained English in ancestry. The rest were composed of a variety of ethnicities. Nearly 9 percent were German, over 8 percent were Scots, 6 percent were Scots-Irish, nearly 4 percent were Irish, and over 3 percent were Dutch; the remainder were made up of French, Swedes, Spanish, and people of unknown ethnicity. The Mid-Atlantic region was especially diverse.[94]

Yet in their early attempts to invent their nationhood, Americans did not celebrate the ethnic diversity of America in any modern sense. The French immigrant and author Hector St. John Crèvecoeur, in one of his ecstatic celebrations of the distinctiveness of the New World in his *Letters from an American Farmer* (1782), was not exaggerating by much when he described the American as "this new man," a product of "that strange mixture of blood, which you will find in no other country."[95] What the Revolutionary leaders emphasized, as Crèvecoeur's comment suggests, was not the multicultural variety of the different immigrants, but rather their remarkable acculturation and assimilation into one people, which, as the Massachusetts political and literary figure Fisher Ames pointed out, meant, "to use the modern jargon, nationalized."[96]

America, declared the enthusiastic president of Yale, Timothy Dwight, in his millennial eclogue *Greenfield Hill* (1794), was destined to be God's commonwealth composed of one people.

93. Bailyn, ed., *Debate on the Constitution*, 1: 765.
94. Liam Riordan, *Many Identities, One Nation: The Revolution and Its Legacy in the Mid-Atlantic* (Philadelphia, 2007).
95. Hector St. John Crèvecoeur, *Letters from an American Farmer* (New York, 1981), Letter III, 69.
96. Fisher Ames, "Falkland III," 10 Feb. 1801, *Works of Fisher Ames* (1854), ed. W. B. Allen (Indianapolis, 1983), 1: 216.

> One blood, one kindred, reach from sea to sea;
> One language spread; one tide of manners run;
> One scheme of science, and of morals one;
> And, God's own Word the structure, and the base,
> One faith extend, one worship, and one praise.[97]

The Revolutionary leaders' idea of a modern nation, shared by enlightened British, French, and German eighteenth-century reformers as well, was one that was homogeneous, not one fractured by differences of language, ethnicity, religion, and local customs. That enlightened dream of wanting to be a single people tended to trump all reality. John Jay lived in New York City, the most ethnically and religiously diverse place in all America, and was himself three-eighths French and five-eighths Dutch, without any English ancestry whatsoever. Nevertheless, Jay could declare with a straight face in *Federalist* No. 2 that "Providence has been pleased to give this one connected country to one united people—a people descended from the same ancestors, speaking the same language, professing the same religion, attached to the same principles of government, very similar in their manners and customs and who, by their joint counsels, arms, and efforts…have nobly established general liberty and independence."

Yet the fact that most Americans were of British heritage and spoke the same language as the subjects of the former mother country created problems of national identity that troubled the new Republic over the next several decades. Indeed, almost to the moment of independence the colonists had continued to define themselves as British, and only reluctantly came to see themselves as a separate people called Americans.[98] The colonists were well aware of the warning John Dickinson, the most important pamphleteer in America before Thomas Paine, had given them on the eve of independence. "If *we* are separated from our mother country," he asked in 1768, "what new form of government shall we adopt, and where shall we find another *Britain* to supply our loss? Torn from the body, to which we are united by religion, liberty, laws, affection, relation, language and commerce we must bleed at every vein."[99]

Could these colonists who had been British and who had celebrated their Britishness for generations become a truly independent people? How could one united people descended from the same ancestors, speaking the same language, and professing the same Protestant religion differentiate themselves from the people of the former mother country? These questions,

97. Timothy Dwight, *Greenfield Hill: A Poem in Seven Parts* (New York, 1794), 168.
98. Paul A. Varg, "The Advent of Nationalism, 1758–1776," *American Quarterly*, 16 (1964), 169–81.
99. Dickinson, "Letters from a Farmer in Pennsylvania," Ford, ed., *Writings of Dickinson*, 326.

perhaps more than any others, bedeviled the politics of the early decades of the new Republic's history. In the end many Americans came to believe that they had to fight another war with Great Britain in order to reaffirm their national independence and establish their elusive identity.

If they were to be a single national people with a national character, Americans would have to invent themselves, and in some sense the whole of American history has been the story of that invention. At first, they struggled with a proper name for their new country. On the tercentenary celebration of Columbus's discovery of America in 1792 one patriot suggested "the United States of Columbia" as a name for the new Republic. Poets, ranging from the female black slave Phillis Wheatley to the young Princeton graduate Philip Freneau, saw the logic of the name and thus repeatedly referred to the nation as Columbia. With the same rhythm and number of syllables, Columbia could easily replace Britannia in new compositions set to the music of traditional English songs. In his song "Columbia," written in 1777 but not published until 1783, Timothy Dwight, as an army chaplain at West Point, sought to shed the new Republic's colonial English heritage and create a land that existed outside of history.

> COLUMBIA, Columbia, to glory arise
> The queen of the world, and the child of the skies!
> Thy genius commands thee; with rapture behold,
> While ages on ages thy splendors unfold.
> Thy reign is the last, and the noblest of time,
> Most fruitful thy soil, most inviting thy clime;
> Let the crimes of the East ne'er encrimson thy name,
> Be freedom, and science, and virtue, thy fame.[100]

But the name did not stick. Neither did Dr. Samuel Mitchill's suggestion that the new nation be called Fredon or Fredonia and its people Fredonians. Despite Mitchill's argument that "we cannot be national in feeling and in fact until we have a national name," the country's designation remained "the United States of America," with its people appropriating the name that belonged to all the peoples of the New World—even though the term "Americans" actually had begun as a pejorative label the metropolitan English had applied to their inferior and far-removed colonists.[101]

---

100. Claudia L. Bushman, *America Discovers Columbus: How an Italian Explorer Became an American Hero* (Hanover, NH, 1992), 41–51.

101. Alan David Aberbach, *In Search of an American Identity: Samuel Latham Mitchill, Jeffersonian Nationalist* (New York, 1988), 154–56; Joseph Jones, "Hail, Fredonia!" *American Speech* (1934), 12–17; Richard L. Merritt, *Symbols of American Community*, 1735–1775 (New Haven, 1966); T. H. Breen, "Ideology and Nationalism on the Eve of the American Revolution: Revisions Once More in Need of Revising," *JAH*, 84 (1997), 13–39.

Lacking a unique name and ethnicity, the best Americans could do was to locate their national identity and character in something other than the traditional sources of nationhood. In the absence of a common nationality, Union often became a synonym for nation. But even more important in making them a distinctive people, they told themselves, was the fact that they were both peculiarly enlightened and ideally located along the process of social development.[102]

Educated Americans were fascinated by the widely held belief in successive stages of historical evolution that ranged from rude simplicity to refined complexity. The various theories of social progress current in the late eighteenth century had many sources, but especially important to the Americans was the four-stage theory that had been worked out by that remarkable group of eighteenth-century Scottish social scientists—Adam Smith, John Millar, Adam Ferguson, and Lord Kames. These thinkers posited four stages of evolutionary development based on differing modes of subsistence: hunting and gathering, pasturage, agriculture, and commerce. As societies grew in population, so the theory went, people were forced to find new ways of subsisting, and this need accounted for societies advancing from one stage to another.

Nearly every thinker saw the aboriginal inhabitants of America as the perfect representatives of the first stage, which Adam Smith called the "lowest and rudest state of society."[103] Indeed, it would be hard to exaggerate the extent to which the European discovery of the Indians in the New World influenced the emergence of the theory of different stages of history. Eighteenth-century theorists assumed that thousands of years in the past Europeans had been as savage as the Indians of America were in the present. The Indians helped create the notion, as John Locke put it, that "in the beginning all the world was *America*."[104]

If the American Indians represented the initial stage of history, then contemporary England and France represented the fourth and final stage of development, modern commercial society. This final stage of history

102. Address to the President, Dec. 1796, *Annals of Congress*, 4th Congress, 2nd session, 1612, 1638, 1641–42.

103. Adam Smith, *An Inquiry into the Nature and Causes of the Wealth of Nations* (Oxford, 1976) (Bk. V, ch. 1) 2: 689. The fullest account of the four-stage theory is Ronald L. Meek, *Social Science and the Ignoble Savage* (Cambridge, UK, 1976). For the eighteenth-century Americans' application of the four-stage theory to their society, see Drew R. McCoy, *The Elusive Republic: Political Economy in Jeffersonian America* (Chapel Hill, 1980), 13–47.

104. Eric Slauter, "Neoclassical Culture in a Society with Slaves: Race and Rights in the Age of Wheatley," *Early American Studies*, 2 (2004), 99–100; John Locke, *Two Treatises of Government*, ed. Peter Laslett (Cambridge, UK, 1960) (II, sect. 49), 301.

was characterized by much of what Americans lacked—sprawling poverty-ridden cities, over-refined manners, gross inequalities of rank, complex divisions of labor, and widespread manufacturing of luxuries. Americans, such as Samuel Stanhope Smith of Princeton, knew only too well "that human society can advance only to a certain point before it becomes corrupted, and begins to decline."[105] Many concluded that Britain and France and other highly developed nations were steeped in corruption, dependency, luxury, and self-indulgence and therefore had to be on the verge of dissolution.

American patriots in 1776 had been sure that England was so deeply implicated in the final stage of commerce that as a nation it could not last much longer. Indeed, over the next half century many Americans continued to expect and hope that overly refined and overpopulated England would soon fall apart in selfishness, extravagance, and dissipation.

By contrast, most white Americans located themselves much earlier on the progressive spectrum of history. "In the present age, our Country is in a medium between Barbarity and Refinement," declared the Reverend Nathanael Emmons of Massachusetts in 1787. "In such an age, the minds of men are strong and vigorous, being neither enfeebled by luxury, nor shackled by authority."[106] Americans had advanced far beyond the earliest stage of development in which the native peoples of the New World appeared to be strangely frozen. In fact, because of the proximity of the native "savages," educated Americans were anxious to emphasize their progress. Their society may have been simple and egalitarian in many respects, without the polish and refined characteristics of Europe, but they repeatedly told themselves that they had put the bloody barbarism and savage violence of the previous century well behind them. They were confident that their society was becoming more polite and commercially sophisticated, but, of course, not to the point reached by the decadent Old World. The American people may have lacked the fine arts of Europe, wrote John Adams, but in all other matters, especially agriculture, commerce, and government, they were superior. "In this respect," he said, "America is infinitely further removed from Barbarity, than Europe."[107]

AMERICANS ASSURED THEMSELVES that they were a young and forming people. Their youth, in fact, justified their lack of all the refinements that Thomas Shippen found so repulsive. Americans may have

105. Steven J. Novak, *The Rights of Youth: American Colleges and Student Revolt, 1798–1815* (Cambridge, MA, 1977), 58.

106. Nathanael Emmons, *The Dignity of Man. A Discourse Addressed to the Congregation in Franklin...*(Providence, 1787), 33.

107. JA, Translation of Thomas Pownall's *Memorial* (1780), *Papers of Adams*, 9: 199.

been raw and callow compared to Europeans, but, they told themselves, at least they were not overwhelmed by a debilitating luxury. They knew from history that too much politeness was just as bad as too much vulgarity. Look what had happened to ancient Rome when its society had become too sophisticated, too luxury-loving, too divided by extremes of rich and poor. Too much refinement eroded valor, and the Romans lost their will to fight for their liberty. Look too, they said, to what was happening to eighteenth-century England.

The English radical Whig historian Catherine Macaulay warned George Washington in 1790 of what was in store for Americans if they tried to "copy all the excesses" of England. By wallowing in "all the deceitful pleasures of a vicious dissipation," Americans "will overturn all the virtue which at present exists in the Country." Then "an inattention to public interest will prevail, and nothing be pursued but private gratification and emolument." Despite Macaulay's apprehensions that the American people were showing "a greater inclination to the fripperies of Europe, than a Classic simplicity," most Americans believed that their society was young enough to avoid these evils of over-refinement.[108]

Just as Americans lacked the corrupting luxury of Europe, so too, they constantly told themselves, were they without Europe's great distinctions of the wealthy few and the poverty-stricken many. Compared to Great Britain, America had a truncated society; it lacked both the great noble families with their legal titles and sumptuous wealth and the great masses of poor whose lives were characterized by unremitting toil and deprivation. In America, wrote Benjamin Franklin in one of the many expressions of the idea of American exceptionalism in these years, "a general happy Mediocrity" prevailed.[109]

Commentators were eager to turn the general middling character of America into an asset. "Here," wrote Crèvecoeur, "are no aristocratical families, no courts, no kings, no bishops, no ecclesiastical dominion, no invisible power giving to a few a very visible one, no great manufactures employing thousands, no great refinements of luxury. The rich and the poor are not so far removed from each other as they are in Europe." There was nothing in America remotely resembling the wretched poverty and the gin-soaked slums of London. America, continued Crèvecoeur, who wrote his essays before the Revolution that he eventually repudiated, was largely made up of "cultivators scattered over an immense territory," each of them working for himself. Nowhere in America, he said, ignoring

---

108. Macaulay to GW, June 1790, *Papers of Washington: Presidential Ser.*, 5: 573–75.
109. BF, "Information to Those Who Would Remove to America" (1784), *Franklin: Writings*, 975.

for the moment, as most American social commentators did, the big houses of the Southern planters and the slave quarters of hundreds of thousands of black Africans, could one find "the hostile castle and the haughty mansion, contrasted with the clay-built hut and miserable cabin, where cattle and men help to keep each other warm and dwell in meanness, smoke and indigence."[110]

This American yeomanry, Americans told themselves, was not to be compared to the illiterate peasantry of the European states. The fact that the great bulk of Americans were landowners radically separated them from the rest of the world. Even England had very few freeholders left: most English farmers were tenants, cottagers, or landless laborers, not like "the yeomanry of this country," said Noah Webster, which "consist[ed] of substantial independent freeholders, masters of their own persons and lords of their own soil."[111] Americans were a society, in other words, ideally suited for republicanism.

Because of the prevalence of land, declared Jefferson, Americans had no need to develop the kinds of extensive urban workshops and intensive manufacturing establishments that confined tens of thousand of Europeans to daily dependent drudgery. Most Americans assumed that they were living in the age of agriculture with only the beginning signs of entering the age of commerce. They could remain farmers, and what a providential blessing that was. For "those who labour in the earth," said Jefferson, in the most famous of his paeans to agriculture, "are the chosen people of God, if ever he had a chosen people, whose breasts he had made his peculiar deposit for substantial and genuine virtue."

It was precisely the prevalence of all these independent farmers that made possible virtuous republican government in America. They seemed to Jefferson and other Americans freer of the sorts of vicious temptations that prevented Europeans from adopting republicanism. As long as America rested on their independent shoulders, it was secure. "Corruption of morals in the mass of cultivators," said Jefferson, "is a phenomenon of which no age nor nation has furnished an example."[112]

Not only did Americans describe themselves as a nation of independent farmers, they saw themselves as a mighty multiplying people, indeed, the fastest-growing people in the Western world. Consequently, "our population," declared Ezra Stiles in 1783, "will soon overspread the vast territory from the Atlantick to the Mississippi, which in two generations will become a property superiour to that of Britain." This could only mean

---

110. Crèvecoeur, *Letters from an American Farmer*, Letter III, 67.
111. Noah Webster, *Dissertations on the English Language* (Boston, 1789), 288.
112. TJ, *Notes on the State of Virginia* (1785), *Jefferson: Writings*, 290.

that "God has great things in design and ... purposes to make of us a great people."[113]

Precisely because Americans were separated from Europe and, as Jefferson said in 1787, "remote from all other aid, we are obliged to invent and execute; to find means within ourselves, and not to lean on others."[114] The result of this American pragmatism, this ability "to surmount every difficulty by resolution and contrivance," was a general prosperity. White Americans enjoyed the highest standard of living in the world, and goods of all sorts were widely diffused throughout the society.[115]

Most important of all, America was the premier land of liberty. The Americans had always been a vigilant people, jealous of their liberty and, as Edmund Burke had noted, snuffing tyranny in every tainted breeze. They knew—the English radical Richard Price told them—that "a Spirit," originating in America, was arising in the Western world. This spirit promised "a State of Society more favourable to peace, virtue, Science, and liberty (and consequently to human happiness and dignity) than has yet been known.... The minds of men are becoming more enlighten'd, and the silly despots of the world are likely to be forced to respect human rights and to take care not to govern too much lest they should not govern at all."[116]

By the early 1790s Americans were not surprised that their country was in fact attracting refugees from the tyrannies of the Old World. The enlightened everywhere had come to recognize the United States as the special asylum for liberty. In the spring of 1794 the United Irishmen of Dublin sent the renowned scientist Joseph Priestley their best wishes as he fled from persecution in England to the New World. "You are going to a happier world—the world of Washington and Franklin.... You are going to a country where science is turned to better uses." Priestley was only the most famous of the many European refugees who arrived in America during the 1790s. Thus most Americans had every reason to congratulate themselves, as they did at every opportunity, for being, in scientist David Rittenhouse's words, "an asylum to the good, to the persecuted, and to the oppressed of other climes."[117]

Americans were free and independent because, as they repeatedly told themselves, they were an intelligent people who could not be easily

113. Burstein, *Sentimental Democracy*, 155; Joseph J. Ellis, *After the Revolution: Profiles of Early American Culture* (New York, 1979), 14.

114. TJ to Martha Jefferson, 28 March 1787, *Papers of Jefferson*, 11: 251.

115. TJ to Lafayette, 11 April 1787, *Papers of Jefferson*, 11: 285.

116. Richard Price to BF, 17 Sept. 1787, *Papers of Franklin*, unpublished.

117. Larry E. Tise, *The American Counterrevolution: A Retreat from Liberty, 1783–1800* (Mechanicsburg, PA, 1998), 35, 37.

fooled by their leaders. The Revolution itself had stimulated them. It had given "a spring to the active powers of the inhabitants," said South Carolina historian David Ramsay in 1789, "and set them on thinking, speaking, and acting far beyond that to which they had been accustomed."[118] Levels of literacy may not have been high by modern standards, but by eighteenth-century standards, at least for white Americans in the North, they were higher than almost any other place on earth and were rapidly climbing, especially for white women. All their reading made them enlightened. Jefferson was convinced that an American farmer rather than an English farmer had conceived of making the rim of a wheel from a single piece of wood. He knew it had to be an American because the idea had been suggested by Homer, and "ours are the only farmers who can read Homer."[119]

With the formation of the many state constitutions and especially with the formation of the federal Constitution of 1787 Americans had demonstrated to the world how to apply reason to politics. They knew that all previous nations had had their governments imposed on them by conquerors or by some supreme lawgivers or had found themselves ensnared by governments born in accident, caprice, or violence. They repeatedly assured themselves that they were, in John Jay's words, "the first people whom heaven has favoured with an opportunity of deliberating upon and choosing the forms of government under which they should live." With the scrapping of the Articles of Confederation and the creation of their new federal Constitution, declared David Ramsay, they showed that governments could be changed to fit new circumstances. They had therefore placed "the science of politics on a footing with the other sciences, by opening it to improvements from experience, and the discoveries of future ages."[120]

In addition, Americans thought that they were less superstitious and more rational than the peoples of Europe. They had actually carried out religious reforms that European liberals could only dream about. Many Americans were convinced that their Revolution, in the words of the New York constitution of 1777, had been designed to end the "spiritual oppression and intolerance wherewith the bigotry and ambition of weak and wicked priests" had "scourged mankind."[121] Not only had Americans achieved true religious liberty, not just the toleration that

---

118. David Ramsay, *The History of the American Revolution* (1789), ed. Lester H. Cohen (Indianapolis, 1990), 2: 630.
119. Edward T. Martin, *Thomas Jefferson: Scientist* (New York, 1952), 54.
120. Wood, *The Creation of the American Republic*, 127, 613; Burstein, *Sentimental Democracy*, 166.
121. Evarts B. Greene, *The Revolutionary Generation, 1763–1790* (New York, 1943), 80.

the English made so much of, but their blending of the various European religions and nationalities had made their society much more homogeneous than those of the Old World. The European migrants had been unable to bring all of their various regional and local cultures with them, and re-creating and sustaining many of the peculiar customs, craft holidays, and primitive practices of the Old World proved difficult. Consequently, morris dances, charivaries, skimmingtons, and other folk practices were much less common in America than in Britain or Europe. The New England Puritans, moreover, had banned many of these popular festivals and customs, including Christmas, and elsewhere the mixing and settling of different peoples had worn most of them away. In New England all that remained of Old World holidays was Pope's Day, November 5—the colonists' version of Guy Fawkes Day. Since enlightened elites everywhere in the Western world regarded these plebeian customs and holidays as remnants of superstition and barbarism, their relative absence in America was seen as an additional sign of the New World's precocious enlightenment.[122]

America had a common language, unlike the European nations, none of which was linguistically homogeneous. In 1789 the majority of Frenchmen did not speak French but were divided by a variety of provincial patois. Englishmen from Yorkshire were incomprehensible to those from Cornwall and vice versa. By contrast, Americans could understand one another from Maine to Georgia. It was very obvious why this should be so, said John Witherspoon, president of Princeton. Since Americans were "much more unsettled, and move frequently from place to place, they are not as liable to local peculiarities, either in accent or phraseology."[123] With the Revolution some Americans wished to carry this uniformity further. They wanted their language "purged of its barbaric dross" and made "as pure, simple, and systematic as our politics." It was bound to happen in any case. Republics, said John Adams, had always attained a greater "purity, copiousness, and perfection of language than other forms of government."[124]

122. Richard L. Bushman, "American High Style and Vernacular Cultures," *Colonial British America: Essays in the New History of the Early Modern Era*, ed. Jack P. Greene and J. R. Pole (Baltimore, 1984), 371–72.

123. Witherspoon, "The Druid, No. V," *Works of John Witherspoon*, 2d ed. (Philadelphia, 1802), 4: 417.

124. JA, 1780, in Adams, ed., *Works*, 8: 249–51, quoted in Dennis E. Baron, *Grammar and Good Taste: Reforming the American Language* (New Haven, 1982), 17. See Paul K. Longmore, "'They...Speak Better English than the English Do': Colonialism and the Origins of Linguistic Standardization in America," *Early American Literature* 40 (2005), 279–314.

Americans expected the development of an American English that would be different from the English of the former mother country, a language that would reflect the peculiar character of the American people. Noah Webster, who would eventually become famous for his American dictionary, thought that language had divided the English people from one another. The court and the upper ranks of the aristocracy set the standards of usage and thus put themselves at odds with the language spoken by the rest of the country. By contrast, America's standard was fixed by the general practice of the nation, and therefore Americans had "the fairest opportunity of establishing a national language, and of giving it uniformity and perspicuity, in North America, that ever presented itself to mankind." Indeed, Webster was convinced that Americans already "speak the most *pure English* now known in the world." Within a century and a half, he predicted, North America would be peopled with a hundred millions of people, "all speaking the same language." Nowhere else in the world would such large numbers of people "be able to associate and converse together like children of the same family."[125]

Others had even more grandiose visions for the spread of America's language. John Adams was among those who suggested that American English would eventually become "the next universal language." In 1789 even a French official agreed; in a moment of giddiness he actually predicted that American English was destined to replace diplomatic French as the language of the world. Americans, he said, "tempered by misfortune," were "more human, more generous, more tolerant, all qualities that make one want to share the opinions, adopt the customs, and speak the language of such a people."[126]

Americans believed that their English might conquer the world because they were the only true citizens of the world. To be enlightened was to be, as Washington said, "a citizen of the great republic of humanity at large." The Revolutionary leaders were always eager to demonstrate their cosmopolitanism; they aimed not at becoming more American but at becoming more enlightened. As yet they had little sense that loyalty to their state or nation was incompatible with their cosmopolitanism.[127]

125. Webster, *Dissertations on the English Language*, 21, 36, 288. See Michael P. Kramer, *Imagining Language in America: From the Revolution to the Civil War* (Princeton, 1992).
126. Burstein, *Sentimental Democracy*, 152.
127. Greene, *The Revolutionary Generation*, 418; Colin Bonwick, *English Radicals and the American Revolution* (Chapel Hill, 1977), 13–14; Alan D. McKillop, "Local Attachment and Cosmopolitanism—The Eighteenth-Century Pattern," in Frederick W. Hilles and Harold Bloom, eds., *From Sensibility to Romanticism: Essays Presented to Frederick A. Pottle* (Oxford, UK, 1965), 197.

David Ramsay claimed he was "a citizen of the world and therefore despise[d] national reflections." Yet he did not believe he was being "inconsistent" in hoping that the professions would be "administered to my country by its own sons." Joel Barlow did not think he was any less American just because he ran for election to the French National Convention in 1792–1793. The many state histories written in the aftermath of the Revolution were anything but celebrations of localism. Indeed, declared Ramsay, who wrote a history of his adopted state of South Carolina, they were testimonies to American cosmopolitanism; the state histories were designed to "wear away prejudices—rub off asperities and mould us into a homogeneous people."[128]

Intense local attachments were common to peasants and backward peoples, but educated gentlemen were supposed to be at home anywhere in the world. Indeed, to be free of local prejudices and parochial ties was what defined a liberally educated person. One's humanity was measured by one's ability to relate to strangers, and Americans prided themselves on their hospitality and their treatment of strangers, thus further contributing to the developing myth of their exceptionalism. Indeed, as Crèvecoeur pointed out, in America the concept of "stranger" scarcely seemed to exist: "A traveller in Europe becomes a stranger as soon as he quits his own kingdom; but it is otherwise here. We know, properly speaking, no strangers; this is every person's country; the variety of our soils, situations, climates, governments, and produce hath something which must please everyone."[129] "In what part of the globe," asked Benjamin Rush, "was the 'great family of mankind' given as a toast before it was given in the republican states of America?"[130]

THE INSTITUTION that many Americans believed best embodied these cosmopolitan ideals of fraternity was Freemasonry. Not only did Masonry create enduring national icons (like the pyramid and the all-seeing eye of Providence on the Great Seal of the United States), but it brought people together in new ways and helped fulfill the republican dream of reorganizing social relationships. It was a major means by which thousands of Americans could think of themselves as especially enlightened.

128. David Ramsay to John Eliot, 11 Aug. 1792, in Robert L. Brunhouse, ed., *David Ramsay, 1749–1815: Selections from His Writings*, American Philosophical Society, *Trans.*, n.s. 55, pt. 4 (1965), 133.
129. Crèvecoeur, *Letters from an American Farmer*, Letter III, 80.
130. Donald J. D'Elia, "Dr. Benjamin Rush and the American Medical Revolution," American Philosophical Society, *Proc.*, 110 (1966), 100.

Freemasonry took its modern meaning in Great Britain at the beginning of the eighteenth century. The first Grand Lodge was formed in London in 1717. By mid-century English Masonry was strong enough to provide inspiration and example to a worldwide movement. Although Masonry first appeared in the North American colonies in the 1730s, it grew slowly until mid-century, when membership suddenly picked up. By the eve of the Revolution dozens of lodges existed up and down the continent. Many of the Revolutionary leaders, including Washington, Franklin, Samuel Adams, James Otis, Richard Henry Lee, and Hamilton, were members of the fraternity.[131]

Freemasonry was a surrogate religion for enlightened men suspicious of traditional Christianity. It offered ritual, mystery, and communality without the enthusiasm and sectarian bigotry of organized religion. But Masonry was not only an enlightened institution; with the Revolution, it became a republican one as well. As George Washington said, it was "a lodge for the virtues."[132] The Masonic lodges had always been places where men who differed in everyday affairs—politically, socially, even religiously—could "all meet amicably, and converse sociably together." There in the lodges, the Masons told themselves, "we discover no estrangement of behavior, nor alienation of affection." Masonry had always sought unity and harmony in a society increasingly diverse and fragmented. It traditionally had prided itself on being, as one Mason put it, "the Center of Union and the means of conciliating friendship among men that might otherwise have remained at perpetual distance."[133]

Earlier in the eighteenth century the organization had usually been confined to urban elites noted for their social status and gentility. But in the decades immediately preceding the Revolution Masonry began broadening its membership and reaching out to small village and country elites and ambitious urban artisans without abandoning its earlier concern with genteel refinement. The Revolution disrupted the organization but revitalized the movement. In the decades following the Revolution Masonry exploded in numbers, fed by hosts of new recruits from middling levels of

---

131. Catherine L. Albanese, *Sons of the Fathers: The Civil Religion of the American Revolution* (Philadelphia, 1976), 129–30; J. M. Roberts, *The Mythology of the Secret Societies* (St. Albans, UK, 1974), 37; Conrad E. Wright, *The Transformation of Charity in Postrevolutionary New England* (Boston, 1992); Steven C. Bullock, *Revolutionary Brotherhood: Freemasonry and the Transformation of the American Social Order, 1730–1840* (Chapel Hill, 1996).

132. Bullock, *Revolutionary Brotherhood*, 139.

133. Charles Brockwell, *Brotherly Love Recommended in a Sermon Preached Before the Ancient and Honourable Society of Free and Accepted Masons in Christ-Church, Boston* (Boston, 1750), 14.

the society. There were twenty-one lodges in Massachusetts by 1779; in the next twenty years fifty new ones were created, reaching out to embrace even small isolated communities on the frontiers of the state. Everywhere the same expansion took place. Masonry transformed the social landscape of the early Republic.

Masonry began emphasizing its role in spreading republican virtue and civilization. It was, declared some New York Masons in 1795, designed to wipe "away those narrow and contracted Prejudices which are born in Darkness, and fostered in the Lap of ignorance."[134] Freemasonry repudiated the monarchical hierarchy of family and favoritism and created a new republican order that rested on "real Worth and personal Merit" and "brotherly affection and sincerity." At the same time, Masonry offered some measure of familiarity and personal relationships to a society that was experiencing greater mobility and increasing numbers of immigrants. It created an "artificial consanguinity," declared DeWitt Clinton of New York in 1793, that operated "with as much force and effect, as the natural relationship of blood."[135]

Despite its later reputation for exclusivity, Freemasonry became a way for American males of diverse origins and ranks to be brought together in republican fraternity, including, at least in Boston, free blacks.[136] That strangers, removed from their families and neighbors, could come together in such brotherly love seemed a vindication of the enlightened hope that the force of love might indeed be made to flow outward from the self. A Mason found himself "belonging, not to one particular place only, but to places without number, and in almost every quarter of the globe; to whom, by a kind of universal language, he can make himself known—and from whom we can, if in distress, be sure to receive relief and protection." This was the enlightened dream of people throughout the world being gently bound together through benevolence and fellow-feeling. And it seemed to many Americans that the nation now responsible for fulfilling that dream was the new United States.[137]

---

134. Bullock, *Revolutionary Brotherhood*, 148.
135. Ann Lipson, *Freemasonry in Federalist Connecticut, 1789–1832* (Princeton, 1977), 40; Josiah Bartlett, *A Discourse on the Origin, Progress and Design of Free Masonry* (Boston, 1793), 15; DeWitt Clinton, quoted in Steven C. Bullock, "A Pure and Sublime System: The Appeal of Post-Revolutionary Freemasonry," *JER*, 9 (1989), 371.
136. Bullock, *Revolutionary Brotherhood*, 109–33.
137. John Andrews, *A Sermon on the Importance of Mutual Kindness* (Philadelphia, 1790), 20.

# 2

# A Monarchical Republic

In 1789 the Federalists, the leaders of the new Republic who clung to the name used by the supporters of the Constitution in 1787–1788, were optimistic about forming the new government. The results of the elections in 1788 showed that most of the members of the new Congress had been supporters of the Constitution—at least forty-eight of the fifty-nine congressmen and eighteen of the twenty-two senators. And George Washington had been unanimously elected as the first president of the United States. Indeed, expectations were so high that some Federalists worried that disappointment was inevitable.[1] By 1789 even the leading opponents of the Constitution, the Anti-Federalists, had come to accept it, though of course with an expectation of it soon being amended. No one wanted to oppose the new national government without giving it what Washington called "a fair chance."[2]

By 1789 the most nationally minded of the Federalists such as Hamilton and Washington were determined to turn the United States into an integrated nation, a republic in its own right with the governmental power to act energetically in the public sphere. Monarchies all over Europe were trying to consolidate their scattered collections of small duchies, principalities, provinces, and city-states—nearly 350 of them—and to build strong consolidated nation-states.[3] But could a continental-sized republic like the new United States do the same? The very idea of a single republic "on an average one thousand miles in length, and eight hundred in breadth, and containing six million of white inhabitants all reduced to the same standard of morals, of habits, and of laws, is," the Anti-Federalists had warned, "in itself an absurdity, and contrary to the whole experience of mankind."[4]

1. Charlene Bangs Bickford and Kenneth R. Bowling, *Birth of the Nation: The First Federal Congress, 1789–1791* (New York, 1989), 6.
2. GW to Benjamin Lincoln, 28 Aug. 1788, *George Washington: A Collection*, ed. W. B. Allen (Indianapolis, 1988), 415.
3. Jack P. Greene, *Negotiated Authorities: Essays in Colonial Political and Constitutional History* (Charlottesville, 1994), 5.
4. "Agrippa Letters," in Paul L. Ford., ed., *Essays on the Constitution of the United States* (Brooklyn, 1892), 64–65.

By 1789 many of the Federalists had lost faith in the Revolutionary dream of 1776—that America could exist with a minimum of government. Some New England Federalists, "seeing and dreading the evils of democracy," according to one traveler in the 1790s, were even willing to "admit monarchy, or something like it."[5] The wealthy New England merchant Benjamin Tappan, father of the future abolitionists, was not alone in thinking that a good dose of monarchism was needed to offset the popular excesses of the American people. Even though Henry Knox, Washington's close friend, had given Tappan "a gentle check" for openly voicing such an opinion, Tappan told Knox that he could not "give up the Idea that monarchy in our present situation is become absolutely necessary to save the states from sinking into the lowest abyss of misery." Since he had "delivered my sentiment in all companies" and found it well received, he believed that "if matters were properly arranged it would be easily and soon effected," perhaps with the aid of the Society of the Cincinnati, the fraternal organization of former Revolutionary War officers. Even if nothing were done, Tappan intended to continue to be "a strong advocate for what I have suggested."[6]

Prevalent as this kind of thinking was in some parts of America in the late 1780s and early 1790s, the Federalists, even the high-toned ones, were not traditional monarchists. As pessimistic about republicanism as some Federalists may have been, most of them had little desire to return to the monarchical and patriarchal politics of the colonial ancien régime in which government had been treated as a source of personal and family aggrandizement. Nor did most of them believe that the restoration of monarchy was possible in America, at least not at the present time. Thus most Federalists believed that whatever aspects of monarchy they hoped to bring back into America would have to be placed within a republican framework. Indeed, Benjamin Rush described the new government in 1790 as one "which unites with the vigor of monarchy and the stability of aristocracy all the freedom of a simple republic."[7] Even though the Federalists never openly declared it to be their aim, perhaps they really intended to create another Augustan age, an age of stability and cultural

5. William Strickland, *Journal of a Tour in the United States of America, 1794–1795*, ed. Rev. J. E. Strickland (New York, 1971), 53. (I owe this citation to Brendan McConville.)

6. Benjamin Tappan to Henry Knox, April 1787, in Henry Knox Papers, Mass. Historical Society. (I owe this reference to Brendan McConville.) For the colonists' strong attraction to monarchy, see Brendan McConville, *The King's Three Faces: The Rise and Fall of Royal America, 1688–1776* (Chapel Hill, 2006).

7. BR, "To——: Information to Europeans Who Are Disposed to Migrate to the United States," 16 April 1790, *Letters of Rush*, 2: 556.

achievement following a revolutionary upheaval.[8] Augustus had after all sought to incorporate elements of monarchy into the Roman Empire while all the time talking about republicanism.

ARTICLE I OF THE CONSTITUTION, with its ten sections, is by far the longest article in the document. It is devoted to the Congress, and naturally, as the most republican part of the new national government, the Congress was the first institution to be organized. Indeed, during its first session, beginning in April 1789, it was virtually the entire central government. Although the president was inaugurated at the end of April, the subordinate executive offices were not filled until late in the summer; and the judiciary was not created until just before adjournment in the early fall. The short Article III of the Constitution had prescribed only a Supreme Court for the nation and had left the possibility of establishing other federal courts to the Congress's discretion.

The First Congress faced a unique challenge, and those congressmen and senators who gathered in New York in the spring of 1789 were awed by what lay ahead of them. Not only would the members of the Congress have to pass some promised amendments to the new Constitution, but they would have to fill out the bare framework of a government that the Philadelphia Convention had created, including the organization of the executive and judicial departments. Some therefore saw the First Congress as something in the nature of a "second constitutional convention." The responsibilities were daunting, and many congressmen and senators of the First Congress felt overwhelmed. They were, said James Madison, "in a wilderness without a single footstep to guide us. Our successors will have an easier task."[9]

The First Congress had difficulty even getting itself together. It took weeks for some members of the Congress to journey from their home states to the first national capital of New York City. Even the stage from Boston, traveling eighteen hours a day, took six days to get to New York. Philadelphia was three days away.[10] Although on March 4, 1789, fifty-nine

8. Linda K. Kerber, *Federalists in Dissent: Imagery and Ideology in Jeffersonian America* (Ithaca, 1970), 1–22. Washington declared that "the Augustan age is proverbial for intellectual refinement and elegance," but he never suggested that it had any anti-republican political significance. GW to Lafayette, 28 May 1788, *Washington: Writings*, 681.

9. Samuel Osgood to Elbridge Gerry, 19 Feb. 1789, in Merrill Jensen and Robert A. Becker, eds., *The Documentary History of the First Federal Elections* (Madison, WI, 1976–), 1: 657; JM to TJ, 30 June 1789, *Republic of Letters*, 618.

10. Thomas E. V. Smith, *The City of New York in the Year of Washington's Inauguration, 1789* (New York, 1889; Riverside, CT, 1972), 194, 102.

representatives and twenty-two senators were supposed to convene in New York, only a handful actually showed up. Over the next few weeks the members dribbled in, several each day. Not until April 1, 1789, did the House of Representatives have a quorum and was it able to organize itself for business; the Senate got its quorum a week later.

New York City became the first capital of the new government mainly by default: the peripatetic Confederation Congress after wandering from town to town had ended up there. With a population of about thirty thousand, New York was not yet as large as Philadelphia, which with its contiguous suburbs totaled forty-five thousand people, but it was growing rapidly. "New York," observed a French traveler in 1794, "is less citified than Philadelphia, but the bustle of trade is far greater." Since it had twice as many foreign-born as Philadelphia, it had a more cosmopolitan feel. Some thought it still had an aristocratic English tone left over from the occupation. "If there is one city on the American continent which above all others displays English luxury," observed the French visitor Brissot de Warville, "it is New York, where you can find all the English fashions," including ladies in "dresses which exposed much of their bosoms"—an expression of "indecency in republican women" that "scandalized" Brissot.[11] Still, what impressed everyone was the commercial hurly-burly of the city. With its superb deepwater harbor and burgeoning economy, New York would soon outdistance all the other port cities in people and commerce.[12]

In 1789 the city's growing population was confined to the tip of Manhattan, extending about a mile and a half up the river on the east side and a mile on the west side. Broadway was the central boulevard, but it was paved only to Vesey Street. Greenwich Village was considered out-of-town. There were over four hundred taverns in the city, and these were increasing in number faster than the population. Despite its being caught up in English luxury, New York's mostly narrow and dirty streets and the fact that it had not yet fully recovered from devastating fires in 1776 and 1778 kept the city from becoming too pretentious. Its people, however, were beginning to build houses at a phenomenal rate.

Federal Hall, which was to house the new Congress, was the old City Hall located at the corner of Wall and Nassau streets; it had been recently remodeled by the French engineer Pierre-Charles L'Enfant,

11. Edwin G. Burrows and Mike Wallace, *Gotham: A History of New York City to 1898* (New York, 1999), 301.
12. Kenneth Roberts and Anna M. Roberts, eds., *Moreau de St. Méry's American Journey* (1793–1798) (Garden City, NY, 1947), 146; David T. Gilchrist et al., eds., *The Growth of the Seaport Cities, 1790–1825* (Charlottesville, 1967), 33.

who filled the tympanum of the building's pediment with the eagle drawn from the Great Seal, with thirteen stars in the entablature beneath it, even though two states, North Carolina and Rhode Island, were still not part of the Union.

The First Congress that gathered in New York had been elected in 1788 by the people of the states, or in the case of the Senate, by the state legislatures. The Constitution had left to each state the mode of electing the House of Representatives. Given the Federalist desire to enlarge the electorate for each congressman and thus help to ensure that only the most distinguished and enlightened were elected, the major issue in the states had been whether to elect all the congressional representatives at-large or to elect them by district. In 1788 most of the large states (Massachusetts, New York, North Carolina, South Carolina, and Virginia) had elected their congressmen by districts, while most of the small states, along with Pennsylvania, had elected them statewide.[13] Some warned that district elections were apt to keep out "the man of abilities." Instead of getting a liberally educated and cosmopolitan congressman, district elections would likely result in a narrow-minded demagogue. He would be, wrote one sarcastic Marylander, someone who would "have nothing to recommend him but his supposed humility, who will not be too proud to court what are generally called the *poor folks*, shake them by the hand, ask them for their vote and interest, and, when an opportunity serves, treat them to a can of grog, and whilst drinking of it, join heartily in abusing what are called the *great people*."[14]

Many of the members of the Congress were quite distinguished. Twenty of them had attended the Philadelphia Convention, including James Madison, Robert Morris, Oliver Ellsworth, Rufus King, Roger Sherman, and Elbridge Gerry (who had left without signing). Many others had held prominent political or military positions during the Revolution, such as Richard Henry Lee, Jeremiah Wadsworth, Philip Schuyler, and Elias Boudinot. Only twenty had entered politics since the treaty of peace of 1783, and most of these were very young men. In short, most members of the Congress were men of experience and consequence. Indeed, Washington declared that "the new Congress on account of the

13. By the early 1790s most of the original thirteen states had selected a method of election that they would continue to use until 1842, when Congress passed a law requiring district elections. In 1791 Pennsylvania joined the large district-electing states. See Rosemarie Zagarri, *The Politics of Size: Representation in the United States, 1776–1850* (Ithaca, 1987), 105–24.

14. Baltimore *Maryland Journal*, 14 Nov. 1788, in Jensen and Becker, eds., *Documentary History of the First Federal Elections*, 2: 125.

self-created respectability and various talents of its Members, will not be inferior to any Assembly in the world."[15]

Still, when Madison looked over the list of those elected with him to the House of Representatives, the future looked troublesome. He saw only "a very scanty proportion who will share in the drudgery of business," and for the tasks ahead he could only foresee "contentions first between federal & antifederal parties, and then between Northern and Southern parties, which give additional disagreeableness to the prospect." His high hopes that the Congress might be free of the "vicious arts" of democracy that had plagued the states now seemed more doubtful. He was worried that too many men of "factious tempers" and "local prejudices" had been elected.[16]

THE HOUSE OF REPRESENTATIVES took seriously the belief that it was the more democratic branch of the legislature, much closer to the people than the supposedly aristocratic Senate. It certainly tended to act in a more popular manner. The members of the House paid little attention to ceremony and dignities and sometimes shocked the Senate with their raucous and disorderly behavior. At times three or four representatives would be on their feet at once, shouting invectives, attacking individuals violently, telling private stories, and making irrelevant speeches. During the First Congress, it certainly was by far busier than the Senate. In its first three sessions it considered 146 different public bills, while the Senate considered only 24.

The House decided at the outset to open its debates to the public. Since the British Parliament and the colonial legislatures had deliberately kept their legislative proceedings hidden from the outside world, this decision marked a significant innovation. Young James Kent, a future chancellor of New York, was an early visitor to the gallery and was overcome with emotion. He thought it was "a proud & glorious day" to have "all ranks and degrees of men" present in the gallery "looking upon an organ of popular will, just beginning to breathe the Breath of Life, & which might in some future age, much more truly than the Roman Senate, be regarded as 'the refuge of nations.'"[17]

15. GW to Lafayette, 29 Jan. 1789, *Papers of Washington: Presidential Ser.*, 1: 262.
16. Jack N. Rakove, "The Structure of Politics at the Accession of George Washington," in Richard Beeman et al., eds., *Beyond Confederation: Origins of the Constitution and American National Identity* (Chapel Hill, 1987), 286–87.
17. Raymond W. Smock, "The Institutional Development of the House of Representatives, 1789–1801," in Kenneth R. Bowling and Donald R. Kennon, eds., *The House and Senate in the 1790s: Petitioning, Lobbying, and Institutional Development* (Athens, OH, 2002), 326.

The long-run implications of this decision to allow the public to listen to debates were not yet apparent. Despite the opening of the House to the public, knowledge of Congress's activities by modern standards remained limited. Politics in 1789 was still very traditional in character, small and intimate; and political leaders relied, as they had in the past, mostly on private conversations and personal correspondence among "particular gentlemen" for their connections and information.[18] The practice of congressmen writing circular letters to constituents summarizing congressional business had not yet become common, and most congressmen communicated with their constituents back home simply by sending letters to prominent friends who would show them to a few other influential persons.[19]

Some constituents did communicate with their congressmen, mostly by using the time-honored English tradition of petitioning guaranteed by the First Amendment. More than six hundred petitions were presented to the First Congress on a variety of issues, including the prohibition of rum, the standardization of printings of the Bible, and, most famously, the abolition of slavery. During its first twelve years the House of Representatives received nearly three thousand petitions—indeed, more petitions in this brief period than had been received by the colonial Pennsylvania assembly during the last sixty years of its existence. Of course, since most people lived at a distance from the federal capital, they had to rely on sending petitions; but if they could, they sought other ways of influencing the Congress as well. Individuals traveled to the capital to make personal claims for different sorts of congressional action; these usually involved individual rather than policy matters and included veterans requesting pensions and military contractors seeking payment of old debts.[20]

Still, it was difficult for most people to know what their congressmen were saying or doing. There was no *Congressional Record* as yet and no verbatim reporting. The newspaper reporters who had access to the debates of the House of Representatives took down only what they thought might be interesting to readers. It was not until 1834 that all the early

18. Gordon S. Wood, "The Democratization of Mind in the American Revolution," in *Leadership in the American Revolution: Library of Congress Symposia on the American Revolution* (Washington, DC, 1974), 78.
19. Winifred E. A. Bernhard, *Fisher Ames: Federalist and Statesmen, 1758–1808* (Chapel Hill, 1965), 75, 104.
20. William C. diGiacomantonio, "Petitioners and Their Grievances: A View from the First Congress"; Richard R. John and Christopher J. Young, "Rites of Passage: Postal Petitioning as a Tool of Governance in the Age of Federalism"; and Jeffrey L. Pasley, "Private Access and Public Power: Gentility and Lobbying in the Early Congress," all in Bowling and Kennon, eds., *House and Senate in the 1790s*, 31, 100–109, 62–63.

reports and fragments of congressional debates were compiled and published as the *Annals of Congress.*

Yet the political world was undoubtedly changing. Congressmen increasingly felt themselves more accountable to the public out-of-doors than they had expected, and they began catering to that public in their speeches and debates. Benjamin Goodhue of Massachusetts complained of the delay in the proceedings produced by "the needless and lengthy harangues" of fellow congressmen "who have been frequently actuated by the vain display of their Oritorical abilities." Members became anxious about how they appeared, and how they sounded in public, and they fretted over the accuracy of transcriptions of their speeches in the press. Peter Silvester of New York, eager to be seen to "say something clever" in the House, asked a friend to "draw up some suitable speech for me, not too long nor too short."[21]

With all this desire for speech-making, congressional debates became longer and more frequent. The House of Representatives encouraged more open and free deliberations by its common practice of going into the Committee of the Whole, where the restrictions on discussion were looser and the rules governing debate less formal.[22] The House thereby became, as Fisher Ames complained, "a kind of Robin Hood society, where everything is debated."[23] Many Northern congressmen thought that the House was following the pattern of the Virginia House of Delegates in conducting much of its business as a Committee of the Whole, and thus they blamed the Virginians for the endless talk and the slowness of business. "Our great committee is too unwieldly," complained Ames. Fifty members or more trying to amend or clean up the language of a bill was "a great, clumsy machine...applied to the slightest and most delicate operations—the hoof of an elephant to the strokes of mezzotinto."[24]

Madison denied that the Committee of the Whole accounted for the delays; rather, there were "difficulties arising from novelty." "Scarcely a day passes," he told Edmund Randolph, "without some striking evidence of the delays and perplexities springing merely from the want of precedents." But "time will be a full remedy for this evil," and the Congress and the country would be better for going slowly.[25]

The debates were not only frequent and lengthy but sometimes remarkably thoughtful. Members of Congress had ample time to prepare their

21. Rakove, "Structure of Politics," in Beeman et al., eds., *Beyond Confederation,* 291.
22. Ralph V. Harlow, *The History of Legislative Methods in the Period Before 1825* (New Haven, 1917), 127.
23. Ames to Thomas Dwight, June 11, 1789, *Works of Fisher Ames* (1854), ed. W. B. Allen (Indianapolis, 1983), 1: 642.
24. Ames to Minot, July 8, 1789, *Works of Ames,* ed. Allen, 1: 683.
25. JM to Edmund Randolph, 31 May 1789, *Papers of Madison,* 12: 190.

speeches. Because there were few select committee meetings and other distractions, nearly all congressmen attended the daily five-hour sessions punctually, at least at first, and were usually attentive to what their colleagues had to say on the floor of the House.[26] Ames "listened," as he said, "with the most unwearied attention to the arguments urged on both sides" in order that "his own mind might be fully enlightened."[27]

Ames himself was an elegant and compelling speaker. Almost overnight his oratory established his reputation as one of the most able members of the House; indeed, people congratulated themselves on having visited the gallery of the House to hear him speak. Ames frequently wrote his friend George Minot about the techniques and mistakes of his performances in the House and commented on those of others. He thought Madison, for example, an impressive reasoner but concluded that speaking was "not his *forte*.... He speaks low, his person is little and ordinary," and he was "a little too much of a book politician."[28]

Yet Ames had no doubt that Madison was the "first man" of the House. Although Madison was shy, short, and soft-spoken, he impressed everyone he met. He was widely read with a sharp and questioning mind; indeed, he was probably the most intellectually creative political figure America has ever produced.

Madison had been born in 1751 into that class of Virginia slaveholding planters who dominated their society as few aristocracies have. Although his father's plantation was the wealthiest in Orange County, Virginia, it was not far removed from the raw frontier, and young Madison, like most of the Founders, became the first of his family to attend college, in his case the College of New Jersey (later Princeton). In college Madison revealed his intellectual intensity and earnestness. His father's plantation wealth enabled Madison, who complained endlessly of his poor health, to return home to study and contemplate what he might do with his life. By 1776, at age twenty-five, he had become a member of Virginia's Revolutionary convention. In 1777 he became a member of the eight-man Virginia Council of State. In 1780 he served in the Confederation Congress, and when his three-year term was up he had returned to Virginia and in 1784 was elected to the Virginia assembly. But all through the 1780s his interest in strengthening the national government grew to the point where he became the principal organizer of the 1787 convention that wrote the Constitution. He was eager to put the new government that he had helped create on a sound

---

26. During a single two-year Congress today, the House may hold as many as 4,500 committee meetings.
27. *Annals of Congress*, 1st Congress, 1st session (13 May 1789), I, 352.
28. Ames to George Richards Minot, 3 May 1789, *Works of Ames*, ed. Allen, 1: 569.

footing. Although he regarded the Constitution as something less than what he had wanted, he became known as its principal author.

Madison had originally been slated for a seat in the Senate, but when the Anti-Federalist leader Patrick Henry squelched that plan, he actually had to campaign against James Monroe for a seat in the House of Representatives. He told friends that he hated having to ask for votes. He had, he said, "an extreme distaste to steps having an electioneering appearance, altho' they should lead to an appointment in which I am disposed to serve the public."[29] At the outset he was a fervent nationalist who was eager to secure an independent revenue for the new government, to create the executive departments, and to win over the minds of the Anti-Federalists to the new union. He journeyed to New York early and waited impatiently for the rest of the Congress to assemble. And on April 8, 1789, two days after both houses mustered a quorum, he began introducing legislation.

Although he was not a strong speaker, he made 150 speeches in the first session of the First Congress alone. But Madison's extraordinary dominance over the proceedings of the First Congress came not merely from his reputation and his speech-making. His broad knowledge and careful preparation for what had to be done were even more important. He got ready for the opening debate on revenue in the House of Representatives by comparing the state laws on the subject and by collecting whatever statistical information he could on the commerce of the various states.[30] His colleagues reported that he was "a thorough master of almost every public question that can arise, or he will spare no pains to become so, if he happens to be in want of information." His tireless attention to detail and his range of activities were astonishing. Not only did he lead the House, but he was also the principal link between the legislature and the executive in these early months. He helped Washington draft his inaugural address to the Congress, then drafted the response of the House of Representatives to that address, and finally helped the president in his reply to that response.

THE SENATE CONSIDERED ITSELF distinctly superior to the "lower" house, so-called perhaps because the House chamber was on the first floor of Federal Hall, while the Senate chamber was on the second floor. Although the Senate was not entirely clear about its relationship to the various state legislatures, which, of course, were its electors, it certainly did have a very high-flown sense of its dignity. While the House was busy passing legislation, establishing revenue for the new government, and

29. Richard Labunski, *James Madison and the Struggle for the Bill of Rights* (New York, 2006), 145.

30. Editorial Note, *Papers of Madison*, 12: 54.

erecting the several executive departments, the Senate spent its time discussing ceremonies and rituals, perhaps because it had little else to do. During the first session it initiated only one piece of legislation, that establishing the judiciary. Things got so bad that the senators began coming to the Hall for only an hour or two in the morning. "We Used to stay in the Senate Chamber till about 2 O'Clock," confessed Senator William Maclay of Pennsylvania, "whether we did anything or not, by way of keeping up the Appearance of Business. But even this," he said, "we seem to have got over."[31] Fortunately for the senators, the public did not know much about their business practices: unlike the lower house, the Senate decided not to open its debates to the public.

Establishing rules of etiquette for the Senate proved difficult. How was the Senate to receive the president of the United States? How was the president to be addressed? How should the senators address one another? Should they call each other "right honorable" or not? Should they have a sergeant at arms, and if so what should he be called? Should they address the speaker of the lower house as "honorable" or not? They ransacked ancient and modern history for examples and precedents, wondering whether "the framers of the Constitution had in View the Two Kings of Sparta or the Two Consuls of Rome" when they created a president and vice-president, or whether a fourteenth-century Italian reformer obsessed with titles was an object lesson for them.[32]

Vice-President John Adams was especially confused. He knew he was vice-president of the United States (in which "I am nothing, but I may be everything"), but he was also president of the Senate. He was two officers at once, which perhaps, he said, was the reason the huge chair in which he sat was made wide enough to hold two persons. But Washington was coming to the Congress to be sworn in as president, and questions of etiquette needed to be answered. "When the President comes into the Senate, what shall I be?" Adams asked his colleagues, in obvious distress. He could not continue to be president of the Senate then, could he? "I wish gentlemen to think what I shall be." Overwhelmed with the burden of this dilemma, Adams threw himself back into his velvet canopied chair, while the senators looked on in silence, some of them having difficulty stifling a laugh.

In the long ensuing pause, Senator Oliver Ellsworth, one of the members of the Constitutional Convention and a judicial expert, nervously thumbed through the Constitution. Finally Ellsworth rose and solemnly addressed the vice-president. It was clear, he told Adams, that wherever

31. *The Diary of William Maclay and Other Notes on Senate Debates*, ed. Kenneth R. Bowling and Helen E. Veit (Baltimore, 1988), 253.
32. *Diary of Maclay*, 5–6, 27, 28, 37.

the senators were, "then Sir you must be at the head of them." But further than this—here Ellsworth looked aghast, as if some tremendous gulf had opened before him—"I shall not pretend to say."[33]

On the day of the president's inauguration, April 30, 1789, the vice-president and the Senate were even more uncertain about what to do. Adams, who, according to Senator Maclay of Pennsylvania, was wrapped up more than usual "in the Contemplation of his own importance," asked once again for direction from the Senate. When the president addressed the Congress, what should he as vice-president do? "How shall I behave?" he asked. What should the Congress do? Should it listen to the president seated or standing? From these questions a long debate followed, and the senators tried to recall how the English handled such matters. Senator Richard Henry Lee of Virginia remembered from his stay in England as a young man that the king addressed Parliament with the Lords seated and the Commons standing. But then Senator Ralph Izard of South Carolina reminded his colleagues how often he too had visited the English Parliament and told them that "the Commons stood because they had no seats to sit on." The vice-president compounded the confusion by saying that every time he had visited the Parliament on such occasions "there was always such a Crowd, and ladies along, that for his part he could not say how it was."[34]

Because of a mix-up in communications the Congress waited an hour and ten minutes for the president. When Washington finally arrived at about two in the afternoon, an awkward silence followed. Adams, who had been so atwitter about the proper way to receive the president, was so overawed that he was uncharacteristically rendered speechless. Eventually Washington, dressed in a dark-brown homespun suit, with white silk stockings and silver shoe-buckles, was led out to a balcony of Federal Hall so that the huge throngs of people outside could witness his being sworn in as president. Robert Livingston, chancellor (the leading judicial official) of New York, administered the oath of office, at the conclusion of which Washington, according to a contemporary newspaper account, kissed the Bible on which he had sworn the oath.[35] After Livingston proclaimed "Long Live George Washington, President of the

33. *Diary of Maclay*, 5–6.

34. *Diary of Maclay*, 11.

35. There is no contemporary evidence that he also said "so help me God" at the end of the oath; the matter is very controversial today. See Forrest Church, *So Help Me God: The Founding Fathers and the First Great Battle over Church and State* (New York, 2007), 445–49. Since the Judiciary Act of 1789 declared that the oath to be sworn by the justices of the Supreme Court and the other federal judges included the phrase "So help me God," it is likely that Washington may have also used the phrase (1 Cong. Ch. 20, 1 Stat. 73, Sec. 8). I owe this information to Steven G. Calabresi.

United States," the crowd erupted in shouting and cheering, so loud as to drown out the pealing of the church bells. When the president came to deliver his inaugural address he was so overcome by the gravity and solemnity of the occasion that he had a hard time reading his notes. According to Maclay, Washington seemed "agitated and embarrassed more than ever he was by the levelled Cannon or pointed Musket."[36] It was an awful moment for Washington and for the country. Washington told his friend Henry Knox that his assumption of the office of president was "accompanied with feelings not unlike those of a culprit who is going to the place of his execution."[37]

THE PRESIDENT IN HIS INAUGURAL ADDRESS offered very little guidance about what the Congress should do. Although the Constitution provided that the president periodically recommend to the Congress such measures as he judged necessary and expedient, Washington in his address actually made only one recommendation for congressional action. Believing that the role of the president was only to execute the laws, not to make them, he was remarkably indirect and circumspect with even this one recommendation. He suggested that the Congress use the amendment procedures of the Constitution in order to promote "the public harmony" and make "the characteristic rights of freemen...more impregnably fortified," without, however, making any alteration in the Constitution that "might endanger the benefits of an United and effective Government." This recommendation, he said, was in response to "the objections which have been urged against the System" of government created by the Constitution and "the degree of inquietude which has given birth to them."[38]

Many of the states had ratified the Constitution on the understanding that some changes would be made in order to protect people's rights, and popular expectation was high that amendments would be added as soon as possible. Although many members of Congress were not at all eager to begin tampering with the Constitution before they had even tried it out, Congress could not easily evade this concern for the citizens' rights. It was after all in defense of their rights that Americans had fought the Revolution.

Americans had inherited an English concern for personal rights against the power of the crown that went back centuries. They had prefaced at

---

36. *Diary of Maclay*, 13; Editorial Note, *Papers of Washington: Presidential Ser.*, 2: 155; Smith, *City of New York in the Year of Washington's Inauguration*, 230.
37. GW to Knox, 1 April 1789, *Washington: Writings*, 726.
38. GW, First Inaugural Address, 30 April 1789, *Washington: Writings*, 733.

least five of their Revolutionary state constitutions in 1776 with bills of rights and had inserted certain common law liberties in four other constitutions. It thus came as something of a surprise to many Americans to discover that the new federal Constitution contained no bill of rights. It was not that members of the Philadelphia Convention were uninterested in rights; to the contrary, the Constitution had been drafted in part to protect the rights of Americans.

But the Constitution was designed to protect the Americans' rights from the abusive power of the state legislatures. The Constitution had done so by forbidding the states in Article I, Section 10, from certain actions. In fact, the members of the Philadelphia Convention had not seriously considered adding to the Constitution a bill of rights that would restrict the power of the national government. As delegate James Wilson said, a bill of rights had "never struck the mind of any member," until George Mason, author of the Virginia Declaration of Rights of 1776, brought the issue up almost as an afterthought in the last days of the Convention, when it was voted down by every state delegation.

But the idea of a bill of rights was too deeply embedded in the Americans' consciousness to be so easily passed over. George Mason and other opponents of the new Constitution immediately stressed the absence of a bill of rights as a serious deficiency, and they soon come to realize that this was the best argument they had against the Constitution.

Because the Federalists believed that the frenzied advocacy of a bill of rights by the Anti-Federalists masked a basic desire to dilute the power of the national government, they were determined to resist all efforts to add amendments. Over and over again they said that the old-fashioned idea of an English bill of rights had lost its meaning in America. A bill of rights, they said, had been relevant in England where the ruler had rights and powers distinct from those of the people; there it had been used, as in the case of the Magna Carta of 1215 and the Bill of Rights of 1689, "to limit the king's prerogative."[39] But in the United States rulers had no pre-existing independent governmental power; all rights and powers belonged to the sovereign people who parceled out bits and pieces sparingly and temporarily to their various delegated agents. Since the federal Constitution implied that every power not expressly delegated to the general government was reserved in the people's hands, a declaration reserving specific rights belonging to the people, said James Wilson, was "superfluous and absurd."[40]

39. Gordon S. Wood, *The Creation of the American Republic, 1776–1787* (Chapel Hill, 1969), 539.
40. John Bach McMaster and Frederick D. Stone, eds., *Pennsylvania and the Federal Constitution, 1787–1788* (Philadelphia, 1888), 143–44, 313–16.

The Anti-Federalists were puzzled by these arguments. No other country in the world, said Patrick Henry, looked at government as a delegation of express powers. "All nations have adopted this construction—that all rights not expressly and unequivocally reserved to the people are impliedly and incidentally relinquished to rulers.... It is so in Great Britain; for every possible right, which is not reserved to the people by some express provision or compact, is within the king's prerogative.... It is so in Spain, Germany, and other parts of the world."[41] The Anti-Federalists, in other words, continued to presume in traditional terms that governmental powers naturally adhered in rulers with whom the people had to bargain in order to get explicit recognition of their rights.

The Federalists might have eventually been able to carry their case against such conventional thinking about government, had it not been for the intervention of Thomas Jefferson from his distant post as minister to France. Jefferson was not unsympathetic to the new Constitution and to a somewhat stronger national government, but he had little or no comprehension of the emerging and quite original political theory of the Federalists that underlay the new federal political system. For Jefferson, sensitive to the politically correct thinking of "the most enlightened and disinterested characters" of his liberal French friends who still believed that government was something to be bargained with, "a bill of rights is what the people are entitled to against every government on earth, general or particular, and what no just government should refuse, or rest on inference."[42] No matter that his friend Madison patiently tried to explain to him that attempting to write out the people's rights might actually have the effect of limiting them.[43] Jefferson knew, and that was enough, that "the enlightened part of Europe have given us the greatest credit for inventing this instrument of security for the rights of the people, and have been not a little surprised to see us so soon give it up."[44]

Jefferson's belief that the Constitution was basically deficient because of the absence of a bill of rights was picked up by Anti-Federalists already suspicious of the Constitution and its lack of a bill of rights and used with great effectiveness, especially in Virginia, Maryland, and Rhode Island.[45] The Federalists were defensive over the issue, and in several state ratifying conventions they had to agree to add a list of recommended amendments, nearly all of which advocated changing the structure of the new government. The Federalists concluded that it was better to accept these

41. Wood, *Creation of the American Republic*, 540–41.
42. TJ to John Jay, 23 May 1788, to JM, 20 Dec. 1787, *Papers of Jefferson*, 13: 190; 12: 440.
43. JM to TJ, 17 Oct. 1788, *Papers of Jefferson*, 14: 18.
44. TJ to Francis Hopkinson, 13 March 1789, *Papers of Jefferson*, 14: 650.
45. JM to TJ, 24 July 1788, *Papers of Jefferson*, 13: 412, 414.

amendments as recommendations rather than as conditions for ratification. Otherwise they might have seen the Constitution defeated or at least have had to heed calls for a second convention.[46]

With nearly two hundred suggested amendments coming out of the state ratifying conventions, and with his good friend Jefferson remaining obstinate on the issue, Madison reluctantly began changing his opinion on the advisability of a bill of rights.[47] Although in October 1788 he had told Jefferson that he had never believed the omission of a bill of rights to be "a material defect" of the Constitution, he now declared somewhat disingenuously that he had "always been in favor of a bill of rights" and would support its addition, especially since "it is anxiously desired by others."[48] In his hard-fought electoral campaign for the House of Representatives in the winter of 1788–1789, Madison had been compelled to make a public pledge, if elected, to work in the Congress for the adoption of a bill of rights.[49]

This promise made all the difference. If the Federalists, who dominated both houses of Congress in 1789, had had their way, there would have been no bill of rights. But once Madison's personal honor was involved, he was stubbornly bent on seeing it enacted. Besides, as he told a friend, a bill of rights would "kill the opposition everywhere, and by putting an end to the disaffection to the Govt. itself, enable the administration to venture on measures not otherwise safe."[50] Yet Madison was determined that his bill of rights would be mainly limited to the protection of personal rights and would not harm "the structure & stamina of the Government."[51] He sifted through the nearly two hundred suggested amendments made by the states, most of which suggested altering the powers and structure of the national government, including such matters as taxation, the regulation of elections, judicial authority, and presidential terms. Madison deliberately ignored these structural proposals and extracted mainly those concerned with personal rights that he thought no one could argue with.

On June 8, 1789, Madison proposed his nine amendments, most of which he believed could be inserted into Article I, Section 9, as

46. Robert Allen Rutland, *The Birth of the Bill of Rights, 1776–1791*, rev. ed. (Boston, 1983), 159–89.

47. On the origins of the Bill of Rights, see Patrick T. Conley and John P. Kaminiski, eds., *The Bill of Rights and the States: The Colonial and Revolutionary Origins of American Liberties* (Madison, WI, 1991); and Gordon S. Wood, "The Origins of the Bill of Rights," American Antiquarian Society, *Proc*, 101 (1992), 255–74.

48. JM to TJ, 17 Oct. 1788, *Papers of Jefferson*, 14: 18.

49. JM, "To a Resident of Spotsylvania County," 27 Jan. 1789, *Papers of Madison*, 11: 428–29.

50. JM to Richard Peters, 19 Aug. 1789, *Papers of Madison*, 12: 347.

51. JM to Edmund Randolph, 15 June 1789, *Papers of Madison*, 12: 219.

prohibitions on the Congress. He also included one amendment to be inserted into Article I, Section 10, that actually prohibited the states, and not just the federal government, from violating rights of conscience, freedom of the press, and trial by jury in criminal cases.

At first his Federalist colleagues in the House claimed that it was too early to bring up amendments. Discussing amendments would take up too much time, especially since there were other more important issues like collecting revenue that the Congress ought to be considering. They told Madison he had done his duty and fulfilled his promise to his constituents by introducing the amendments, and now he ought just to forget about them. But "as an honest man I *feel* my self bound," Madison said, and he hounded his colleagues relentlessly.[52]

In several elegant and well-crafted speeches Madison laid out the reasons why a bill of rights should not be delayed. It would quiet the minds of the people uneasy about the new government, help to bring North Carolina and Rhode Island into the Union, further secure the people's rights in public opinion without harming the government, and perhaps allow judges to become the peculiar guardians of these declared rights. He answered all the doubts and all the arguments against a bill of rights, most of which were the doubts and arguments he himself had earlier voiced.[53]

There is no question that it was Madison's personal prestige and his dogged persistence that saw the amendments through the Congress. There might have been a federal Constitution without Madison but certainly no Bill of Rights. Madison did not get all he wanted and in the form he wanted. His colleagues in the House eliminated his preamble, revised some of his other amendments, and placed them at the end of the Constitution instead of incorporating them into the body as he had wished. The House then sent seventeen amendments to the Senate. The upper house not only significantly altered these amendments, but it also compressed them into twelve, eliminating Madison's proposal to protect certain rights from the states, which he had considered "the most valuable" of all his amendments.[54] Two of the twelve amendments—on apportionment of the House and on congressional salaries—were lost in the initial ratification process.[55] Still, when all is said and done the

52. JM to Richard Peters, 19 Aug. 1789, *Papers of Madison*, 12: 347.
53. JM, June 1789, in Helen E. Veit et al., eds., *Creating the Bill of Rights: The Documentary Record from the First Federal Congress* (Baltimore, 1991), 66–68, 77–86.
54. JM, June 1789, in Veit et al., eds., *Creating the Bill of Rights*, 188.
55. One of Madison's proposed amendments—the one requiring a House election to take place before the Congress can raise its salaries—was finally ratified by the requisite number of states in 1992 and became Article XXVII of the Constitution that same year.

remaining ten amendments—immortalized as the Bill of Rights—were Madison's.

The First Amendment states that "Congress shall make no law respecting an establishment of religion, or prohibiting the free exercise thereof; or abridging the freedom of speech, or of the press; or the right of the people to assemble, and to petition the Government for a redress of grievances." This has been the most important amendment invoked by the courts in modern times, applying not just to the federal government but also to the states.[56]

The Second Amendment states that "a well regulated Militia, being necessary to the security of a free State, the right of the people to keep and bear Arms, shall not be infringed." Because of its awkward wording, this amendment has become one of the most controversial at the present time. Its framers, of course, had little awareness of the distinction drawn today between a collective and an individual right to bear arms, and certainly they had no modern conception of gun control.[57] The Third Amendment, expressing the long-standing English fear of standing armies, limits the power of the government to quarter troops in the homes of citizens. The Fourth Amendment prevents the government from unreasonable searches and seizures of persons and property—an issue in 1761 with which, according to John Adams, the fiery Boston patriot James Otis had given birth to "the child Independence."[58]

The Fifth Amendment guarantees the rights of those suspected of crime and prohibits the government from taking private property for public use without just compensation. Amendment VI recognizes the rights of criminal defendants, and Amendment VII protects the right to jury trial in certain civil trials. The Eighth Amendment prohibits excessive bail and fines and "cruel and unusual punishments."

The Ninth Amendment, which was very important to Madison, states that "the enumeration in the Constitution, of certain rights, shall not be construed to deny or disparage others retained by the people." And the Tenth Amend-

---

56. Up until the twentieth century, the Bill of Rights applied only to the federal government, a position endorsed by the Supreme Court in *Barron* v. *City of Baltimore* (1833). Only during the first half of the twentieth century did the Supreme Court contend that the Fourteenth Amendment (1868) incorporates or absorbs the First Amendment and other amendments of the Bill of Rights. On the doctrine of incorporation, see Akhil Reed Amar, *The Bill of Rights: Creation and Reconstitution* (New Haven, 1998), 215–30.

57. "Symposium on the Second Amendment: Fresh Looks," ed. Carl T. Bogus, *Chicago-Kent Law Review*, 76 (2000), 60–715; Saul Cornell, *A Well-Regulated Militia: The Founding Fathers and the Origins of Gun Control in America* (New York, 2006); Mark V. Tushnet, *Out of Range: Why the Constitution Can't End the Battle over Guns* (New York, 2007).

58. Leonard W. Levy, *Origins of the Bill of Rights* (New Haven, 1999), 157.

ment reserves to the states or the people all powers not delegated to the federal government and not prohibited to the states. Placing such a clause in the Constitution had been a point of particular concern for the Anti-Federalists. In the Virginia ratifying convention George Mason had warned that "unless this was done, many valuable and important rights would be concluded to be given up by implication." Indeed, he had said, "unless there were a Bill of Rights, implication might swallow up all our rights."[59]

In the early fall of 1789 the Congress passed the amendments and sent them to the states for ratification. By then many Federalists had come to see that a bill of rights might be a good thing after all. Not only was it the best way of undercutting the strength of Anti-Federalism in the country, but the Bill of Rights that emerged, as Hamilton pointed out, left "the structure of the government and the mass and distribution of its powers where they were."[60] Anti-Federalists in the Congress began to realize that Madison's rights-based amendments weakened the desire for a second convention and thus actually worked against their cause of fundamentally altering the Constitution. Madison's amendments, as opponents of the Constitution angrily came to realize, were "good for nothing" and were "calculated merely to amuse, or rather to deceive."[61] They affected "personal liberty alone, leaving the great points of the Judiciary & direct taxation &c. to stand as they are."[62] Before long the Federalists were expressing surprise that the Anti-Federalists had become such vigorous opponents of amendments, since they were originally their idea.[63]

Unlike the French Declaration of Rights of Man and Citizen issued by the National Assembly in 1789, the American Bill of Rights of 1791 was less a creative document than a defensive one. It made no universal claims but was rooted solely in the Americans' particular history.[64] It did not invent human rights that had not existed before, but mainly reiterated long-standing English common law rights. Unlike the French Declaration, which transcended law and the institutions of government and in fact became the source of government and even society itself, the American

59. Mason, 16 June 1788, in John P. Kaminiski and Gaspare J. Saladino, eds., *The Documentary History of the Ratification of the Constitution* (Madison, WI, 1976–), 10: 1326, 1328.
60. John C. Miller, *The Federalist Era, 1789–1801* (New York, 1960), 24.
61. William Grayson to Patrick Henry, 29 Sept. 1789, and Thomas Tudor Tucker to St. George Tucker, 2 Oct. 1789, in Veit et al., eds., *Creating the Bill of Rights*, 300.
62. Grayson to Henry, 12 June 1789, in William Wirt Henry, *Patrick Henry: Life, Correspondence and Speeches* (New York, 1891), 3: 391.
63. Thomas Hartley to Jasper Yeates, 16 Aug. 1789, and John Brown to William Irvine, 17 Aug. 1789, in Veit et al., eds., *Creating the Bill of Rights*, 279.
64. This is the theme of Conley and Kaminiski, eds., *Bill of Rights and the States*.

Bill of Rights was simply part of the familiar English customary law that worked to limit pre-existing governmental power. To find an American version of the French Declaration of Rights of Man and Citizen that asserted the natural, equal, and universal nature of human rights requires reaching back to the Declaration of Independence of 1776.

Under the circumstances the states ratified the first ten amendments slowly and without much enthusiasm between 1789 and 1791; several of the original states—Massachusetts, Connecticut, and Georgia—did not even bother. After ratification, most Americans promptly forgot about the first ten amendments to the Constitution. The Bill of Rights remained judicially dormant until the twentieth century.

THE ANTI-FEDERALISTS may have been concerned with rights, but most Federalists had believed that power was what was most needed in the new government. And power to the eighteenth-century American Revolutionaries essentially meant monarchy. If there were to be a good dose of monarchical power injected into the body politic, as many Federalists expected in 1787, the energetic center of that power would be the presidency. For that reason it was the office of the president that made many Americans most suspicious of the new government.

The presidency was a new office for Americans. The Confederation had had a Congress, but it had never possessed a single strong national executive.[65] Article II of the Constitution is very vague about the president's powers. All it says is that the executive power shall be vested in the president and that the president shall be the commander-in-chief of the army and the navy and the militia, when called into service of the United States.

Such an office was bound to remind Americans of the king they had just cast off. When James Wilson in the Philadelphia Convention had moved that the executive "consist of a single person," a long uneasy silence had followed. The delegates knew only too well what such an office implied. John Rutledge complained that "the people will think we are leaning too much towards Monarchy."[66] But the Convention had

65. Indeed, none of the states in 1787 possessed an executive with a four-year term; ten executives were elected annually, most of them by the legislature, and only the Massachusetts governor had a veto power similar to that given to the new federal president.
66. Max Farrand, ed., *The Records of the Federal Convention of 1787* (New Haven, 1911, 1937), 1: 65, 119; 2: 513. Article II is so vague that some Federalists seem to have assumed that the president had inherited all the prerogative powers wielded by the English crown except for those, such as the coining of money, the establishment of post offices, the constituting of courts, and the declaring of war, that Article I, Section 8 of the Constitution specifically granted to the Congress.

resisted these warnings and had gone on to make the new chief executive so strong, so king-like, only because the delegates expected George Washington to be the first president. The authority of the presidency would never "have been so great," privately admitted Pierce Butler of South Carolina, "had not many members cast their eyes towards General Washington as President; and shaped their Ideas of the Powers to a President, by their opinion of his Virtue."[67]

Washington's unanimous election as president was preordained. He was the only person in the country who automatically commanded the allegiance of all the people. He was probably the only American who possessed the dignity, patience, restraint, and reputation for republican virtue that the untried but potentially powerful office of the presidency needed at the outset.

Washington, with his tall, imposing figure, Roman nose, and stern, thin-lipped face, was already at age fifty-eight an internationally famous hero—not so much for his military exploits during the Revolutionary War as for his character. At one point during the war he could probably have become a king or dictator, as some wanted, but he had resisted these blandishments.[68] Washington always respected civilian superiority over the army, and at the moment of military victory in 1783 he had unconditionally surrendered his sword to the Congress. He promised not to take "any share in public business hereafter" and, like the Roman conqueror Cincinnatus, had returned to his farm. This self-conscious retirement from public life had electrified the world. All previous victorious generals in modern times—Cromwell, William of Orange, Marlborough—had sought political rewards commensurate with their military achievements. But not Washington. He seemed to epitomize public virtue and the proper character of a republican leader.

Following his formal retirement from public life in 1783, Washington understandably had hesitated to get involved in the movement for a new federal government during the 1780s. Nevertheless, he had reluctantly agreed to attend the Philadelphia Convention and had been elected its president. After the Constitution was ratified, Washington still thought he could retire to the domestic tranquility of Mount Vernon. But the rest of the country assumed that he would become the first president of the new nation. People said he was denied children in his private life so he could be the father of his country.

67. Pierce Butler to Weedon Butler, 5 May 1788, in Farrand, ed., *Records of the Federal Convention*, 3: 302.
68. Thornton Anderson, *Creating the Constitution: The Convention of 1787 and the First Congress* (University Park, PA, 1993), 168.

ONCE WASHINGTON WAS ELECTED, many people, including Jefferson, expected that he might be president for life, that he would be a kind of elective monarch, something not out of the question in the eighteenth century. Poland, after all, was an elective monarchy; and James Wilson pointed out that in the distant past "crowns, in general, were originally elective."[69] Many Americans in the 1790s took seriously the prospect of some sort of monarchy developing in America. "There is a natural inclination in mankind to Kingly Government," Benjamin Franklin had warned the Philadelphia Convention. In fact, many like Hugh Williamson of North Carolina in 1787 thought that the new American government "should at some time or other have a King."[70]

Although America becoming a monarchy might seem absurd, in 1789 it did not seem so at all. After all, Americans had been raised as subjects of monarchy and, in the opinion of some, still seemed emotionally to value the hereditary attributes of monarchy.[71] In 1794 an English traveler was struck by the degree to which New Englanders were becoming "Aristocrats" and were willing to "admit monarchy, or something like it, seeing and dreading the evils of democracy." They were, he noted, a "haughty" people, "proud of their families, which from their emigration near two centuries since, they trace...from the best blood in England....Most of them display their arms engraven over their door, or emblazoned over the Chimney Piece." A small matter perhaps, but to this foreign observer, "this little trait of pride is strongly indicative of national character."[72] No doubt for many Federalist gentlemen ancestry continued to be important. In visiting Britain, even devout republicans like Jefferson tended to look up their ancestors.

William Short, viewing the new Constitution from abroad, was not immediately frightened by the power of the executive. But the Virginia diplomat, who was Jefferson's protégé and successor in France, thought that "the President of the eighteenth century" would "form a stock on which will be grafted a King in the nineteenth." Others, like George Mason of Virginia, believed that the new government was destined to become "an elective monarchy," and still others, like Rawlins Lowndes of

69. TJ to David Humphreys, 18 March 1789, *Papers of Jefferson*, 14: 679; James Wilson, "Lectures on Law" (1790–1791), in *The Works of James Wilson*, ed. Robert Green McCloskey (Cambridge, MA, 1967), 1: 288.

70. Anderson, *Creating the Constitution*, 130–31.

71. Louise Burnham Dunbar, *A Study of "Monarchical" Tendencies in the United States from 1776 to 1801* (1922; New York, 1970), 127.

72. William Strickland, *Journal of a Tour in the United States of America, 1794–1795*, ed. Rev. J. E. Strickland (New York, 1971), 53.

South Carolina, assumed that the government so closely resembled the British form that everyone naturally expected "our changing from a republic to monarchy."[73] To add to the confusion, the line between monarchical and republican governments in the eighteenth century was often hazy at best, and some were already talking about monarchical republics and republican monarchies.[74]

Once Washington accepted the presidency, he inevitably found himself caught up in some monarchical trappings. His journey from Mount Vernon to the capital in New York in the spring of 1789, for example, took on the air of a royal procession. He was saluted by cannons and celebrated in elaborate ceremonies along the way. Everywhere he was greeted by triumphal rejoicing and acclamations of "Long live George Washington!" With Yale students debating the advantages of an elective over a hereditary king, suggestions of monarchy were very much in the air. Following Washington's unanimous election as president in the late winter of 1789, James McHenry of Maryland told him, "You are now a King, under a different name." McHenry, who later became Washington's secretary of war, wished the new president to "reign long and happy over us." It was not surprising, therefore, that some people referred to Washington's inauguration as a "coronation."[75]

So prevalent was the thinking that Washington resembled an elected monarch that some even expressed relief that he had no heirs.[76] Washington was sensitive to these popular anxieties about monarchy, and for a while he had thought of holding the presidency for only a year or so and then resigning and turning the office over to Vice-President John Adams. In the initial draft of his inaugural address he pointed out that "the Divine Providence hath not seen fit, that my blood should be transmitted or name perpetuated by the endearing though sometimes seducing channel of immediate offspring." He had, he wrote, "no child for whom I could wish to make a provision—no family to build in greatness upon my country's ruins." Although Madison talked him out of this draft, Washington's desire to show the public that he harbored no monarchical aspirations revealed just how widespread was the talk of monarchy.[77]

73. Dunbar, *Study of "Monarchical" Tendencies in the United States*, 99–100.
74. Anderson, *Creating the Constitution*, 132.
75. James McHenry to GW, 29 March 1789, *Papers of Washington: Presidential Ser.*, 1: 461; Winifred E. A. Bernard, *Fisher Ames: Federalist and Statesman, 1758–1808* (Chapel Hill, 1965), 92.
76. David W. Robson, *Educating Republicans: The College in the Era of the American Revolution, 1758–1800* (Westport, CT, 1985), 149; Smith, *City of New York in the Year of Washington's Inauguration*, 217–19.
77. GW, Draft of First Inaugural Address, c. Jan. 1789, *Washington: Writings*, 702–16.

Washington's sensitivity to public opinion made him uncertain about the role he ought to play as president. He had understood what to do as commander-in-chief of the army, but the presidency was a wholly new office with a longer term than that of any of the state governors. He realized that the new government was fragile and needed dignity, but how far in a monarchical European direction ought he go to achieve it? As president, Washington tried to refuse accepting any salary, just as he had as commander-in-chief: such a renunciation, he thought, would be evidence of his disinterestedness in serving his country.[78]

But as president he knew he needed to do more to enhance the dignity of the office. Keenly aware that whatever he did would become a precedent for the future, he sought advice from those close to him, including the vice-president and the man he would soon make his secretary of the treasury, Alexander Hamilton. How often should he meet with the public? How accessible should he be? Should he dine with members of Congress? Should he host state dinners? Could he ever have private dinners with friends? Should he make a tour of the United States? The only state ceremonies that late eighteenth-century Americans were familiar with were those of the European monarchies. Were they applicable to the young republic?

Hamilton thought that most people were "prepared for a pretty high tone in the demeanour of the Executive," but they probably would not accept as high a tone as was desirable. "Notions of equality," he said, were "yet...too general and too strong" for the president to be properly distanced from the other branches of the government. Note his widely held presumption—"yet"—that American society, following the progressive stages of development, would eventually become more unequal and hierarchic like the societies of Europe. In the meantime, Hamilton suggested, the president ought to follow the practice of "European Courts" as closely as he could. Only department heads, high-ranking diplomats, and senators—and not mere congressmen—should have access to the president. "Your Excellency," as Hamilton and many others continued to call Washington, might hold a half-hour levee (the English term for the king's receptions) no more than once a week, and then only for invited guests. He could give up to four formal entertainments a year, but in order to maintain the president's dignity he must never accept any invitations or call on anyone.[79] Adams for his part urged Washington to make a show of "splendor and majesty" for his office. The president needed an entourage

---

78. Congress decided that whether or not Washington wanted a salary he had to accept one—$25,000, out of which he was to pay all his expenses. David P. Currie, *The Constitution in Congress: The Federalist Period, 1789–1801* (Chicago, 1997), 33.

79. AH to GW, 5 May 1789, *Papers of Hamilton*, 5: 335–37.

of chamberlains, aides-de-camp, and masters of ceremonies to conduct the formalities of his office.

As uncomfortable as he often was with ceremony, Washington knew that he had to make the presidency "respectable," and when he became president he spared few expenses in doing so. Although he was compelled to accept his $25,000 presidential salary—an enormous sum for the age—he spent nearly $2,000 of it on liquor and wine for entertaining. In his public appearances he dressed the part, in a dignified dark suit with a ceremonial sword and hat. Usually he rode in an elaborately ornamented cream-colored coach drawn by four and sometimes six white horses, attended by four servants in orange-and-white livery, followed by his official family in other coaches.[80] Although he tried to offset this show of regal elegance by taking a walk each afternoon at two o'clock just like any other citizen, he remained an awesome character. He was, as Senator Maclay described him, "a cold formal Man," who seldom laughed in public.[81]

When Washington appeared in public, bands sometimes played "God Save the King." In his public pronouncements the president referred to himself in the third person. His dozens of state portraits were all modeled on those of European monarchs. Indeed, much of the iconography of the new nation, including its civic processions, was copied from monarchical symbolism. The fact that the capital, New York, was more aristocratic than any other city in the new Republic added to the monarchical atmosphere. Mrs. John Jay, the wife of the acting secretary of state and the future chief justice, and someone familiar with foreign courts, turned her home into the center of fashionable society and welcomed Lady Kitty Duer, Lady Mary Watts, Lady Christiana Griffin, and other American women who refused to accept simple republican forms of address. When Jefferson arrived in the spring of 1790 to assume his duties as secretary of state, he thought he was the only real republican in the capital.[82]

Concerned as he was with "the style proper for the Chief Magistrate," Washington conceded that a certain monarchical tone had to be made part of the government; and since he had always thought of himself as being on stage, he was willing, up to a point, to play the part of a republican

---

80. Leonard D. White, *The Federalists: A Study in Administrative History* (New York, 1948), 108.
81. *Diary of Maclay*, 182, 212.
82. Joanne B. Freeman, *Affairs of Honor: National Politics in the New Republic* (New Haven, 2001), 45–46; David Waldstreicher, *In the Midst of Perpetual Fetes: The Making of American Nationalism, 1776–1820* (Chapel Hill, 1997), 120–22; Barry Schwartz, *George Washington: The Making of an American Symbol* (New York, 1987), 53–54; Burrows and Wallace, *Gotham*, 301.

king. He was, as John Adams later caustically remarked, "the best actor of the presidency we have ever had."[83]

Washington was nearly as much of an aristocrat as America ever produced—in his acceptance of social hierarchy and in his belief that some were born to command and some to obey. Although he trusted the good sense of the people in the long run, he believed that they could easily be misled by demagogues. His great strength was his realism. He always sought, as he put it at the outset of the struggle against Britain, to "make the best of Mankind as they are, since we cannot have them as we wish." Ultimately, his view of human nature was much closer to Hamilton's than to Jefferson's. "The motives which predominate most human affairs," he wrote, are "self-love and self-interest."[84]

With these assumptions, he realized only too acutely the fragility of the new nation. As president he spent much of his time devising schemes for creating a stronger sense of nationhood. He understood the power of symbols, and his willingness to sit for long hours to have his many portraits painted was not to honor himself but to inspire the country's national spirit. Indeed, popular celebrations of Washington became a means of cultivating patriotism. It is not too much to say that for many Americans he stood for the Union.

He promoted roads and canals, a national university, and the post office—anything and everything that would bind the different states and sections together. Washington never took the unity of the country for granted but remained preoccupied throughout his presidency with creating the sinews of nationhood. Even in the social life of the "republican court" at the capital in New York and then after 1790 in Philadelphia, he and his wife, Martha, acted as matchmakers in bringing together couples from different parts of the United States. With their own marriage and those of other Virginia families as examples, the Washingtons tended to think of marriage in dynastic terms, as a means of consolidating a ruling aristocracy for the sprawling extent of America. During his presidency he and Martha arranged sixteen marriages, including that of James Madison and Dolley Payne.[85]

He undertook his two long royal-like tours through the Northern and Southern states in 1789–1791 in order to bring a semblance of the

83. GW to JM, 30 March 1789, *Papers of Washington: Presidential Ser.*, 1: 464–65; JA to Rush, 21 June 1811, *Spur of Fame*, 181.

84. GW to Philip Schuyler, 24 Dec. 1775, W.W. Abbot et al., eds., *The Papers of George Washington: Revolutionary War Series*, 2: 599–600 (Charlottesville, 1985– ); GW to JM, 3 Dec. 1784, *Papers of Madison*, 12: 478; GW to John Hancock, 24 Sept. 1776, Fitzpatrick, ed., *Writings of Washington*, 6: 107–8.

85. Don Higginbotham, *George Washington: Uniting a Nation* (Latham, MD, 2001), 62, drawing on the work of David Shields and Fredrika Teute.

government to the farthest reaches of the land and reinforce the loyalty of people who had never seen him. Everywhere he was welcomed by triumphal arches, ceremonies, and acclaim befitting a king.[86] His entourage included eleven horses, one of which was his white parade steed, Prescott. He had Prescott's hooves painted and polished before mounting him at the edge of every town in order to make a more dramatic entrance. In each town he exchanged elaborate ceremonial addresses with the local officials, addresses that some critics thought "favored too much of Monarchy to be used by Republicans, or to be received with pleasure by a president of a Commonwealth."[87]

Because of his concern for the Union, Washington was especially interested in the size and character of the White House and of the capital city that was to be named after him. The huge scale and imperial grandeur of the Federal City, as Washington modestly called it, owe much to his vision and his backing of the French-born engineer Pierre Charles L'Enfant as architect.[88]

L'Enfant had migrated from France in 1777 as one of the many foreign recruits to the Continental Army. In 1779 he became a captain of engineers and attracted the attention of Washington for his ability to stage festivals and design medals, including that of the Society of the Cincinnati. In 1782 he organized the elaborate celebration in Philadelphia marking the birth of the French dauphin, and in 1788 he designed the conversion of New York's City Hall into Federal Hall. Thus it was natural for L'Enfant to write Washington in 1789 outlining his plans for "the Capital of this vast Empire." L'Enfant proposed a capital that would "give an idea of the greatness of the empire as well as…engrave in every mind that sense of respect that is due to a place which is the seat of a supreme sovereignty."[89] His plan for the Federal City, he said, "should be drawn on such a Scale as to leave room for that aggrandizement & embellishment which the increase of the wealth of the Nation will permit it to pursue at any period however remote."[90]

Washington knew the site of the national capital had to be larger than that of any state capital. "Philadelphia," the president pointed out, "stood

---

86. Lisle A. Rose, *Prologue to Democracy: The Federalists in the South, 1789–1800* (Lexington, KY, 1968), 27–28.

87. Joseph J. Ellis, *His Excellency, George Washington* (New York, 2004), 195–96; Editorial Note, *Papers of Washington: Presidential. Ser.*, 8: 73–74.

88. C. M. Harris, "Washington's Gamble, L'Enfant's Dream: Politics, Design, and the Founding of the National Capital," WMQ, 56 (1999), 527–64.

89. Kenneth R. Bowling, "A Capital Before a Capitol: Republican Visions," in Donald R. Kennon, ed., *A Republic for the Ages: The United States Capitol and the Political Culture of the Early Republic* (Charlottesville, 1999), 45, 46.

90. Pierre L'Enfant to GW, 11 Sept. 1789, *Papers of Washington: Presidential Ser.*, 4: 15–17.

upon an area of three by two miles.... If the metropolis of *one State* occupied so much ground, what ought that of the United States to occupy?"[91]
He wanted the Federal City to become a great commercial metropolis in
the life of the nation and a place that would eventually rival any city in
Europe. The new national capital, he hoped, would become the energiz-
ing and centralizing force that would dominate local and sectional interests and unify the disparate states.

L'Enfant designed the capital, as he said, in order to fulfill *"the President's intentions."* The Frenchman conceived of a system of grand radial
avenues imposed on a grid of streets with great public squares and circles
and with the public buildings—the "grand edifices" of the "Congress
House" and the "President's Palace"—placed so as to take best advantage
of the vistas across the Potomac. Some of the early plans for the rotunda
of the Capitol even included a monumental tomb that was designed
eventually to hold the first president's body—a proposal that made Secretary of State Thomas Jefferson very uneasy.[92]

Although the final plans for the capital were less impressive than what
Washington originally envisioned, they were still grander than those others had in mind. If Jefferson had had his way, L'Enfant would never have
kept his job as long as he did, and the capital would have been smaller
and less magnificent—perhaps something on the order of a college cam-
pus, like Jefferson's later University of Virginia. Opposed as he was to
anything that smacked of monarchical Europe, Jefferson thought that
fifteen hundred acres would be enough for the Federal City.[93]

Obsessed with the new government's weakness, other Federalists were
even more eager than Washington to bolster its dignity and respectability.
Most believed that this could be best done by adopting some of the ceremony and majesty of monarchy—by making, for example, the celebration
of Washington's birthday, even while he was alive, rival that of the Fourth of
July. Like the king of England speaking to Parliament from the throne, the
president delivered his inaugural address personally to the Congress, and
like the two houses of Parliament, both houses of Congress formally
responded and then waited upon the president at his residence. The English monarchy was the model for the new republican government in other

91. GW to the Commissioners for the Federal District, 7 May 1791, *Papers of Washington: Presidential Ser.*, 8: 159.
92. Harris, "Washington's Gamble, L'Enfant's Dream," 542–43, 557; Neil Harris, *The Artist in American Society: The Formative Years, 1790–1860* (New York, 1966), 16–17, 42.
93. Kenneth R. Bowling, *The Creation of Washington, D.C.: The Idea and Location of the American Capital* (Fairfax, VA, 1991); Bowling, "A Capital Before a Capitol," in Kennon, ed., *Republic for the Ages*, 54; Dumas Malone, *Jefferson and the Rights of Man* (Boston, 1951), 372.

respects as well. The Senate, the body in the American government that most closely resembled the House of Lords, voted that writs of the federal government ought to be issued in the name of the president—just as writs in England were issued in the name of the king—to reinforce the idea that he was the source of all judicial power in the nation and that prosecutions ought to be carried out in his name. Although the House refused to go along, the Supreme Court used the Senate's form for its writs.

The Federalists made many such attempts to surround the new government with some of the attributes and trappings of monarchy. They drew up elaborate rules of etiquette at what critics soon denounced as the "American Court."[94] They established ceremonial levees for the president where, as critics said, Washington was "seen in public on Stated times like an Eastern Lama."[95] Although Washington was often relieved when some of these efforts at royalizing the presidency failed, he did believe that the weekly receptions, which were excruciatingly formal affairs where no one actually conversed, were a necessary compromise between meeting the public and maintaining the majesty of the presidency. They were "meant," he said, "to preserve the dignity & respect which was due the first magistrate."[96]

Critics like Senator Maclay thought that the "empty Ceremony" of the levees smacked of European court life and had no place in republican America.[97] Others went so far as to criticize the awkwardness of Washington's bows, which were described as being "more distant and stiff" than those of a king. It was not long before the administration was being denounced for its "monarchical practices."[98] Even the fact that the servants attending the receptions had their hair powdered seemed to portend monarchy.[99] But many Federalist leaders believed that a strong measure of monarchy was just what republican America needed.

Indeed, John Adams was probably the person in the new government most concerned with matters of ceremony and ritual. "Neither Dignity nor Authority," he wrote, "can be Supported in human Minds, collected into nations or any great numbers without a Splendor and Majesty, in Some degree, proportioned to them."[100] He rode to the Senate each day

---

94. *Diary of Maclay*, 21; Schwartz, *Washington: The Making of an American Symbol*, 62.

95. *Diary of Maclay*, 21.

96. GW to David Stuart, 26 July 1789, *Papers of Washington: Presidential Ser.*, 3: 322.

97. *Diary of Maclay*, 70.

98. Schwartz, *Washington: The Making of an American Symbol*, 62–63.

99. Abraham Flexner, *George Washington and the New Nation*, 1783–1793 (Boston, 1970), 3: 201.

100. White, *Federalists*, 108n; JA to GW, 17 May 1789, *Papers of Washington: Presidential Ser.*, 2: 314.

in an elaborate carriage attended by a driver in livery. He presided over
the Senate in a powdered wig and small sword. More perhaps than anything else in his career, Adams's infatuation with titles has made him
appear more than a little ridiculous in the eyes of later generations. Of
course, he appeared ridiculous even to some of his contemporaries, who
mocked him as "the Duke of Braintree" and "His Rotundity."[101]

But Adams was not alone in his interest in royal rituals. Many Federalists believed that titles and a hierarchy of distinctions were essential to the
well-being of any mature stable society. If the American people were not as
well suited for republican government, not as virtuous as Adams and other
old Revolutionaries had once hoped, then the resort to titles, as one of the
least objectionable of monarchical forms, made a great deal of sense.
Americans could have a portion of monarchy without fundamentally subverting their republicanism. America was a young society, Adams said, and
it should prepare for its maturity "at no very distant period of time" when
hereditary institutions might be more applicable. Adams said that he did
"not consider hereditary monarchy or aristocracy as 'rebellion against
nature'; on the contrary I esteem them both institutions of admirable wisdom and exemplary virtue in a certain stage of society in a great nation."
When America did come to resemble the European nations, then hereditary institutions would become "the hope of our posterity." "Our country is
not ripe for it in many respects and it is not yet necessary," said Adams,
"but our ship must ultimately land on that shore or be cast away."[102]

In the 1770s Adams had been at the forefront of the resistance movement and had acquired his reputation as a great patriot from his role in
engineering the Continental Congress's movement into revolution. He
had been the principal draftsman of the Massachusetts constitution of
1780, and at the end of the Revolutionary War he was the first minister
sent to the former mother country. On his return from the Court of
St. James's in 1789, many thought he had borrowed some of its monarchical attitudes. The three volumes of his *Defence of the Constitutions of
Government of the United States* had recently appeared, and they raised
doubts about Adams's republicanism. England, for example, had become
for Adams as much of a republic as America was, "a monarchical republic, it is true; but still a republic." In the same way, he labeled the government of his home state of Massachusetts "a limited Monarchy." So too,
he said, was the new national government "a limited Monarchy" or "a
monarchical republic," like England.[103]

101. John Ferling, *John Adams: A Life* (New York, 1992), 304.
102. Page Smith, *John Adams* (Garden City, NY, 1962), 2: 755.
103. Wood, *Creation of the American Republic*, 586.

Although Adams protested that he was "as much a republican as I was in 1775," many of his ideas seemed out of place in the America of 1789.[104] Since most of his fellow Americans had recently abandoned Adams's traditional conception of a mixed republic with its balance of monarchy, aristocracy, and democracy, his talk of "monarchical republics" was bound to confuse people and raise suspicions. The Senate, over which he as vice-president presided, soon became aware of what a curious person their new leader was.[105]

On April 30, 1789, the day of the president's inauguration, Vice-President Adams described Washington's address as "his most gracious Speech"—the words customarily applied to speeches of the British king. Senator William Maclay of Pennsylvania, the son of Scotch-Irish Presbyterian immigrants, thought himself to be the voice of simple republicanism. He saw Adams's phrase as the first step in the ladder of ascent to royalty, and he objected strenuously. Adams replied that this was just a simple phrase borrowed from British governmental practices and that American colonials had after all enjoyed a great deal of happiness using those practices; all he wanted, he said, was a respectable government. He suggested that perhaps he had been abroad in the 1780s too long and the temper of the American people had changed. At any rate, he said, if he had known in 1775 that it would come to this, that the American people would not accept a dignified government, "he never would have drawn his Sword."[106]

Adams became even more agitated over what to call the president, an issue that occupied much of the Senate's time during the first month of its existence. Even before coming to New York, Adams had discussed with colleagues in Massachusetts the proper title for the president. After all, the governor of the state carried the title of "His Excellency." Should not the president have a superior title? "A royal or at least a princely title," he told a friend, "will be found indispensably necessary to maintain the reputation, authority, and dignity of the President." Only something like "His Highness, or, if you will, His Most Benign Highness" would do.[107]

Others shared Adams's concern for a proper title for the president. Washington himself was said to have initially favored "His High Mightiness,

104. Ralph Ketcham, *James Madison: A Biography* (New York, 1971), 285; Smith, *John Adams*, 2: 755.
105. We know what went on in the Senate only because of the remarkable journal that Adams's nemesis, the straitlaced agrarian republican from western Pennsylvania, Senator William Maclay, kept of the Senate's debates during the first two years of the Congress. For the modern edition, see *The Diary of William Maclay and Other Notes on Senate Debates*, ed. Kenneth R. Bowling and Helen E. Veit (Baltimore, 1988).
106. *Diary of Maclay*, 16–17.
107. Smith, *John Adams*, 2: 755.

the President of the United States and Protector of Their Liberties."[108] After all, the Dutch leaders of the States-General of the United Provinces called themselves "Their High Mightinesses," and they were supposedly citizens of a republic. Some of the senators actually expressed their attraction to monarchy—very aware that what they said remained within the Senate chamber. Senator Ellsworth of Connecticut pointed out that divine authority and the Bible sanctioned kingly government, and Senator Izard of South Carolina stressed the antiquity of monarchy. Finding value in kings was all too much for the zealous republican Senator Maclay. He was on his feet many times in opposition to what he saw as "the foolerries fopperies finerries and pomp of Royal etiquette."[109]

But under Vice-President Adams's prodding, the senators continued to search for the proper title for Washington. "Excellency," suggested Izard. "Highness," said Lee. "Elective Highness," said another. Anything but mere "President." It seemed too common, said Ellsworth, and Adams agreed: there were after all "Presidents of Fire Companies and of a Cricket Club." What will other governments think of a president whose titles are less than those of even our own diplomatic corps? asked Adams. "What will the Common People of Foreign Countries, what will the Sailors and Soldiers say [about] George Washington, President of the United States?" His answer: "They will despise him *to all eternity*." Eventually, a Senate committee reported the title "His Highness the President of the United States of America, and Protector of their Liberties." When Jefferson learned of Adams's obsession with titles and the Senate's action, he could only shake his head and recall Benjamin Franklin's now-famous characterization of Adams as someone who was "always an honest man, often a great one, but sometimes absolutely mad."[110]

Madison in the House was troubled by all this senatorial talk of monarchy and majesty. He thought that this senatorial project of titles, if successful, would "give a deep wound to our infant government."[111] Madison, in fact, was emerging as the principal conscience of popular republicanism in the new government. Although in 1787 he had certainly wanted a stronger national government and had very much feared democracy in the state legislatures, he had never wavered in his commitment to republican simplicity and to the people's ultimate sovereignty; and he certainly had not anticipated the monarch-like government that some Federalists were now promoting.

108. Max Farrand, *The Framing of the Constitution of the United States* (New Haven, 1913), 163.
109. *Diary of Maclay*, 29.
110. TJ to JM, 29 July 1789, *Papers of Jefferson*, 15: 316.
111. JM to TJ, 23 May 1789, *Republic of Letters*, 612.

With others in the House warning that a presidential title would be the first step down the road to "a crown and hereditary succession," Madison had little difficulty in getting his fellow congressmen to vote for the simple republican title "President of the United States."[112] The Senate was forced to go along. By defeating the Senate's royalist impulses, Madison hoped to "shew to the friends of Republicanism," he told his friend Jefferson, "that our new Government was not meant to substitute either Monarchy or Aristocracy, and that the genius of the People is as yet adverse to both."[113] As much as anyone in the First Congress, Madison was responsible for whatever plain and unpretentious tone the new government acquired.

Silly as this debate over titles may seem, there were important issues at stake. By creating a single strong president, the new federal Constitution had undoubtedly moved America back toward the abandoned English monarchy. But just how far back toward monarchy should Americans go? Just how royal and kingly should America become? How much of the English monarchical model should the new government adopt? Despite the defeat of the Senate's proposal for royal-sounding titles, these questions would not go away and the tendencies toward monarchism remained.

It was natural for some Americans to look to the British monarchy for guidance in putting together their new state, especially since many of them thought America, like any young state, was bound to mature socially, become more unequal and class-ridden, and thus become more like the former mother country. But the Revolution had been a republican rejection of the monarchism of Great Britain, and therefore it was just as natural for other Americans to resent having British customs and institutions, as one congressman said, "hung about our necks in all our public proceedings, and observations from their practice perpetually sounding in our ears."[114] It was as if the Revolution against Great Britain were still going on.

WASHINGTON WAS RELIEVED that the controversy over his title had ended with the simple "President of the United States." Yet he was still faced with making the institution of the presidency strong and energetic. In fact, the presidency is the powerful office it is in large part because of Washington's initial behavior. Even in the simple matter of issuing a thanksgiving proclamation in the fall of 1789, Washington underlined the national character of the presidency. Some congressmen

112. David P. Currie, *The Constitution in Congress: The Federalist Period, 1789–1801* (Chicago, 1997), 35.
113. JM to TJ, 9 May 1789, *Republic of Letters*, 607.
114. *Annals of Congress*, 1st Congress, 1st session, 1: 363.

thought that their request to commemorate a day of thanksgiving would be sent to the governors of the separate states and carried out by them, as had been done under the Confederation. But Washington saw that issuing the proclamation directly to the people would enhance the authority of the national government.[115] He always understood power and how to use it. He had led an army and was running a plantation; indeed, he had more people working for him at Mount Vernon than he initially did in the federal government.

From the outset, he knew what the new government had to do. As he said as early as January 1789, his goal as president would be "to extricate my country from the embarrassments in which it is entangled, through want of credit; and to establish a general system of policy, which if pursued will insure permanent felicity to the Commonwealth."[116] Although he surrounded himself with brilliant advisors, including Hamilton as secretary of the treasury and Jefferson as secretary of state, he was always his own man and was determined that the government would speak with a single voice. He gave a great deal of authority to his cabinet ministers but always remained in control. He passed on letters he received to the appropriate department heads, and they referred letters they received to him. "By this means," Jefferson recalled in an 1801 memo to his own new cabinet, Washington was "always in accurate possession of all facts and proceedings in every part of the Union, and to whatsoever department they related; he formed a central point for the different branches; preserved a unity of object and action among them," and assumed responsibility for everything that was done.[117] Lacking the genius and intellectual confidence of the advisors, he consulted them often and moved slowly and cautiously to judgment; but when ready to act, he acted decisively, and in the case of controversial decisions he did not second-guess himself. He created an independent role for the president and made it the dominant figure in the government.

During the spring and summer of 1789 Congress created three executive departments—for foreign affairs, war, and finance. It soon followed with legislation establishing the offices of attorney general, postmaster general, superintendent of the land office, and the governor of the Northwest Territory. Although Congress created the departments and their heads and the president appointed other officers with the advice and consent of the Senate, many understood that these officers were to be

115. Glenn A. Phelps, *George Washington and American Constitutionalism* (Lawrence, KS, 1993), 128.

116. GW to Lafayette, 29 Jan. 1789, *Papers of Washington: Presidential Ser.*, 1: 263.

117. Forrest McDonald, *The American Presidency: An Intellectual History* (Lawrence, KS, 1994), 226.

merely agents of the president, in whom complete executive authority was vested. In other words, the president resembled a king, and his ministers spoke in his name and with his authority.

Others had different opinions of how the executive should be organized. Although the president appointed federal officials with the consent of the Senate, the Constitution said nothing about how they were to be removed, other than by impeachment. Some thought that all officers served during good behavior and could be removed only by impeachment. Others presumed that the president could remove his appointees but only with the Senate's approval. Hamilton in *Federalist* No. 77 had stated that the consent of the Senate would be necessary to remove officials as well as appoint them and that this check would contribute to the stability of the government. Many in the First Congress agreed. "A new President," warned Theodorick Bland of Virginia in May 1789, "might, by turning out the great officers, bring about a change of the ministry, and throw the affairs of the Union into disorder: would not this, in fact, make the President a monarch, and give him absolute power over all the great departments of Government?"[118]

Madison saw at once that denying the president the sole power of removal would create "a two-headed monster" and would prevent the president from having effective control over his administration. Despite congressional talk about the president gaining kingly powers, Madison in the summer of 1789 was far less fearful of monarchy than of legislative encroachment on the executive. "In our government," he said, it was "less necessary to guard against the abuse in the Executive Department...because it is not the stronger branch of the system, but the weaker."[119] Trusting Washington as he did, Madison fought strenuously for the right of the president and the president alone to remove from office all those appointed to executive positions. More than anyone else, he brought the members of the House around to accepting the idea of a strong and independent president, one who had full responsibility for seeing that the laws were faithfully executed.

But the Senate was not so easily convinced of the president's independence. It had a role in the appointing process and jealously guarded its prerogatives. Many senators simply assumed that because they consented to the appointment of executive officers they likewise had to consent to their removal. Other senators, however, were fearful that the Constitution

118. Robert P. Williams, ed., *The First Congress, March 4, 1789–March 3, 1791: A Compilation of Significant Debates* (New York, 1970), 193.
119. James Hart, *The American Presidency in Action, 1789: A Study in Constitutional History* (New York, 1948), 178–84.

would fail for lack of executive authority and thus were willing to concede the president's sole responsibility for removing officers. They actually invoked the example of the king of England—arguing that the president should have at least the same powers as the English crown. The Senate was evenly divided on the issue; only after Vice-President Adams's tie-breaking vote did it concede the right of the president to remove executive officials without its advice and consent.[120]

The consequences of such a close vote were immense: on it turned the future nature of the presidency. Indeed, as Madison noted in the House, the Congress's decisions on this issue of removal "will become the permanent exposition of the Constitution; and on a permanent exposition of the Constitution will depend the genius and character of the whole government."[121] If the Senate had been able to claim the right of approving the removal of presidential appointees, executive officials would have become dependent on the will of the Senate, and the United States would have created something similar to the English system of cabinet responsibility to Parliament.[122]

No one was more keenly aware of the importance of precedents being set than Washington. "Many things which appear of little importance in themselves and at the beginning, may have great and durable consequences for their having been established at the commencement of a new general Government," he warned. Better to get things right at the start, he said, than to try to alter them later "after they shall have been confirmed by habit."[123]

He was especially concerned with the relations between the president and the Senate. He envisioned the Senate's role in advising and consenting to appointments and treaties as that of a council, similar to what he had been used to as commander-in-chief, and thus he assumed that much of the advice and consent would be oral. The Senate was more uncertain about dealing with the president in person, for fear of being overawed. President Washington was willing to concede that appointments might be handled in writing, but he believed that in matters of treaties oral communications between the Senate and the president were "indispensably necessary."[124]

120. White, *Federalists*, 20–25; *Diary of Maclay*, 111, 113–14.
121. Williams, ed., *First Congress*, 216–17.
122. On the history and significance of the president's removal power, see Steven G. Calabresi and Christopher S. Yoo, *The Unitary Executive: Presidential Power from Washington to Bush* (New Haven, 2008).
123. GW to JM, 5 May 1789, GW to JA, 10 May 1789, *Papers of Washington*, 2: 216–17, 246–47.
124. Phelps, *Washington and American Constitutionalism*, 122, 169.

In August 1789 the president went to the Senate to get its advice and consent to a treaty he was negotiating with Southern Indian tribes. Adams, who presided, hastily read each section of the treaty and then asked the senators for their opinion. Because of noise from the streets, some of the senators could not hear what was read, and they requested to have the treaty read again. Then the senators began debating each section of the treaty, with Washington impatiently glaring at them. Some of them felt intimidated. Finally one senator moved that the treaty and all the accompanying documents that the president had brought with him be submitted to a committee for study. Washington started up in what Senator Maclay called "a Violent fret." In exasperation, the president cried, "This defeats every purpose of my coming here." He calmed down, but when he finally left the Senate chamber, he was overheard to say he would "be damned if he ever went there again." He did try two days later, but neither the president nor the Senate enjoyed this personal confrontation. The advice part of the Senate's role in treaty making was dropped.[125] When the president issued his Proclamation of Neutrality in 1793, he did not bother to ask for the consent of the Senate, and he thus further established the executive as the dominant authority in the conduct of foreign affairs.

THE MOST IMPORTANT MINISTER in the new administration was the secretary of the treasury, Alexander Hamilton.

Hamilton, aged thirty-four in 1789, impressed everyone he met.[126] Although he was only about five feet seven in height and slight in build, he had a commanding air, and men and women alike were readily attracted to him. In many respects he was a natural republican: born in the West Indies as the illegitimate son of a Scottish merchant ("the bastard brat of a Scotch pedlar," sneered John Adams), he had no interest in the monarchical claims of blood and family. He was rather more of a natural aristocrat than even Thomas Jefferson: at the beginning he had no estate or family to support him; his genius was all he had. And what genius it was! The worldly French politician and diplomat Talleyrand who knew kings and emperors ranked Hamilton as one of the two or three great men of the age.

At age sixteen Hamilton was employed as a clerk in a merchant's firm in St. Croix. But he yearned to escape from his "grov'ling" position — ideally by a war in which he could risk his life and win honor. Merchants

---

125. *Diary of Maclay*, 130; Phelps, *Washington and American Constitutionalism*, 170; Editorial Note, *Papers of Washington: Presidential Ser.*, 3: 526–27.
126. Hamilton was born in 1755, but he apparently believed that he was born in 1757, which would have made him think he was even more precocious than he was.

and friends in St. Croix recognized the boy's remarkable abilities and in 1772 sponsored his education in a preparatory school in New Jersey and then at King's College (later Columbia). He wrote some brilliant Revolutionary pamphlets while still a college student and soon was in the midst of the war he had longed for. He took part in the retreat of Washington's army across New Jersey and so impressed Washington that the commander-in-chief invited the young captain to join his staff as an aide-de-camp with the rank of lieutenant colonel. He had what one of his West Indian sponsors called a "laudable Ambition to Excell," and more than most young men of the age he wanted the glory and fame that came from military heroism.[127] More than once he courted death on the battlefield and took risks that left other officers shaking their heads at his fool-hardy valor. In 1781 he told Washington he would resign his commission unless he was given a command. Under this pressure, Washington yielded and made him a battalion and eventually a brigade commander at Yorktown in October 1781. Hamilton talked his way into leading a major bayonet assault on the British redoubts, and he made the most of his opportunity for gallantry, being first over the redoubt. The attack was successful, and though seven French and American soldiers were killed and fifteen wounded, Hamilton emerged unscathed.[128]

Because he was raised in the West Indies and came to the North American continent as a teenager, Hamilton had little of the emotional attachment to a particular colony or state that most of the other Founders had. He naturally thought nationally, and from the outset of the Revolution he focused his attention on the government of the United States. In 1781–1782 he wrote an extraordinary series of papers on ways of strengthening the Confederation. In 1782 New York elected him, at age twenty-seven, one of its representatives in Congress. There he met James Madison, and a fruitful collaboration for the strengthening of the national government was begun. This partnership led from the stymied efforts to add to the powers of the Confederation in the early 1780s to the Annapolis Convention in 1786, then to the Philadelphia Convention in 1787, and finally to the production of the *Federalist* papers on behalf of the Constitution. When Hamilton became secretary of the treasury, he had every reason to believe that this cooperation between himself and Madison, the Federalist leader in the House of Representatives, would continue.

Ultimately, however, Hamilton's image of what the federal government should be differed from Madison's. Instead of Madison's disinterested

127. Hugh Knox to AH, 28 July 1784, *Papers of Hamilton*, 3: 573.
128. Robert Middlekauff, *The Glorious Cause: The American Revolution, 1763–1789* (New York, 1982; rev. ed., New York, 2005), 587.

adjudicatory state, Hamilton envisioned the United States becoming a great powerful nation like Great Britain and the other states of modern Europe, led by an energetic government and designed, as he said, "for the accomplishment of great purposes."[129] As secretary of the treasury Hamilton was in a perfect position to realize his idea of what the United States should become. As if in emulation of Britain's famous prime minster and First Lord of the Treasury Sir Robert Walpole, who had successfully built up the British state in the early decades of the eighteenth century, Hamilton saw himself as a kind of prime minister to Washington's monarchical presidency. He sometimes even talked about "my administration." Because he believed that "most of the important measures of every government are connected with the treasury," he felt justified in meddling in the affairs of the other departments and in taking the lead in organizing and administering the government.[130]

Unlike Jefferson as head of the State Department and Knox as head of the War Department, Hamilton as secretary of the treasury had an extraordinary degree of authority and independence. Washington treated Jefferson and Knox as advisors only and often directly involved himself in the conduct of foreign affairs and military matters. But he treated Hamilton differently—essentially because he believed the Treasury Department was constitutionally different from the other departments. When Congress created the Departments of State and War in 1789, it simply declared that the secretaries were to perform such duties as the president required. When it created the Treasury Department, however, it made no mention of the president and instead required the secretary to report directly to the Congress. Unwilling to encroach on the authority of Congress, Washington thus gave Hamilton a much freer hand in running the treasury than he gave the other secretaries.[131]

Emboldened in this way, Hamilton even began interfering in the legislative business of Congress. Indeed, one of the reasons the House of Representatives in the early congresses dispensed with standing committees was because it soon came to rely on the heads of the executive departments, in particular, the secretary of the treasury, to draft most of its bills. At the end of July 1789 the House of Representatives set up a Committee of Ways and Means to advise it on financial matters, but on September 2, 1789, the Treasury Department was created. On September 11 Alexander

129. AH, Speech in New York Ratifying Convention, 28 June 1788, *Papers of Hamilton*, 5: 118.
130. White, *Federalists*, 117; Jacob E. Cooke, *Alexander Hamilton* (New York, 1982), 73; AH to Edward Carrington, 26 May 1792, *Papers of Hamilton*, 11: 442.
131. Freeman W. Meyer, "A Note on the Origins of the 'Hamiltonian' System," *WMQ*, 21 (1964), 579–88.

Hamilton was appointed secretary of the treasury, and six days later the House discharged its Committee of Ways and Means, stating that it would rely on Hamilton instead for its financial knowledge. Congress might as well go home, complained the dyspeptic William Maclay in 1791; "Mr. Hamilton is all powerful and fails in nothing which he attempts."[132] Not until 1795, after Hamilton's resignation from the Treasury Department, did the House reestablish its Ways and Means Committee.

Since opposition groups in Britain had traditionally considered the treasury as an important source of political corruption, some members of the First Congress regarded the new secretary of the treasury with suspicion—and with good reason: his opportunities for the abuse of patronage and influence were immense. The treasury was by far the largest department, with several dozen staff members in the treasury office and well over two thousand customs officials, revenue agents, and postmasters scattered around the country.[133] The secretary of the treasury began in 1789 with thirty-nine members in the central office, including six chief officers, thirty-one clerks, and two messengers; by 1792 this number had grown to ninety. By comparison, the other departments were tiny: at the outset the secretary of state had four clerks and a messenger, the secretary of war had only three clerks, and the attorney general had none, there being as yet no Department of Justice.

Yet by contemporary European standards the treasury headquarters staff was minuscule and marked by republican simplicity. A French visitor to the treasury office in 1794 was startled to find the secretary attended by only a single crudely dressed servant, seated at a plain pine table covered with a green cloth, his records laid on makeshift plank shelves, in a "ministerial office" whose furnishings could not have cost more than ten dollars—"Spartan customs" everywhere.[134]

As secretary of the treasury, Hamilton set out to do for American finances what the early eighteenth-century English monarchical government had done in laying the basis for England's stability and commercial supremacy. Although Hamilton denied being a monarchist, Gouverneur Morris later recalled that Hamilton was "on Principle opposed to republican and attached to monarchical Government."[135] During his five-hour speech in the Constitutional Convention Hamilton had declared that the British government was "the best in the world" and that "he doubted much whether any thing short of it would do in America."[136] However

132. *Diary of Maclay*, 377.
133. Rose, *Prologue to Democracy*, 29; White, *Federalists*, 123.
134. Roberts and Roberts, eds., *Moreau de St. Méry's American Journey*, 135–36.
135. Notes from Gouverneur Morris's Diary, 11 July 1804, *Papers of Hamilton*, 26: 324 n.
136. Farrand, ed., *Records of the Federal Convention*, 1: 288.

much his sentiments shifted between monarchy and republicanism, the monarchical government of England was certainly the model for his financial program in the 1790s. More than any other American, he saw England's eighteenth-century experience as an object lesson for the United States, and he deliberately set out to duplicate England's great achievements in political economy and public policy.

By the eighteenth century England had emerged from the chaos and civil wars of the seventeenth century, which had killed one king and deposed another, to become the dominant political and commercial power in the world. That this small island on the northern edge of Europe with a third of the population of continental France was able to build the greatest and richest empire since the fall of Rome was the miracle of the age. The eighteenth-century English "fiscal-military" state, in historian John Brewer's apt term, could mobilize wealth and wage war as no other state in history ever had. Its centralized administration rested on its bureaucratic ability to acquire and use knowledge, and it had developed an extraordinary capacity to tax and to borrow from its subjects without impoverishing them.[137]

Hamilton saw that the secret of England's success was its system of funded debt together with its banking structure and its market in public securities. By attempting to duplicate the English experience, Hamilton was flying in the face of several generations of bitter intellectual opposition to the commercialization of British society and the corruption of British politics. Most English writers of the century—whether famous Tory satirists like Alexander Pope and Jonathan Swift or little-remembered radical Whig publicists like John Trenchard and Thomas Gordon—had expressed a deep hostility to the great social, economic, and political changes taking place in eighteenth-century England. These critics thought that the general commercialization of English life, including the rise of trading companies, banks, stock markets, speculators, and new moneyed men, had undermined traditional values and threatened England with ruin. The monarchy and its minions had used patronage, the national debt, and the Bank of England to corrupt the society, including the House of Commons, and to build up the executive bureaucracy at the expense of the people's liberties, usually for the purpose of waging war. In the face of these frightening developments, both radical Whigs and estranged Tories alike had championed a so-called "country" opposition to the deceit and luxury of the "court" that surrounded the monarch. Some of these reformers were so radical that they were accused of

137. John Brewer, *The Sinews of Power: War, Money and the English State, 1688–1783* (New York, 1989), xix.

harboring republican sentiments. The radical Whigs called for expansion of the suffrage, more liberty for the press, greater freedom of religion, more representation in Parliament, and a substantial reduction in the crown's inflated power, including its standing army. These country-Whigs, in other words, were opposed to the very fiscal-military institutions and programs that had made Great Britain the most powerful nation in the world.

Americans were thoroughly familiar with these radical Whig and "country opposition" ideas, and in fact had used them to explain their separation from a corrupt and despotic Britain in the 1770s.[138] Any attempt to follow England's example was therefore bound to make many Americans uneasy.

Hamilton was extremely confident of his knowledge of commerce and finance, and he set forth his financial program in defiance of this critical libertarian and anti-capitalist literature. He dismissed the idea that the stability of government required that the diverse interests and occupations of people be represented. In his mind "the confidence of the people will easily be gained by a good administration."[139] In light of the inexperience of eighteenth-century Americans with positive state power, his program was truly breathtaking. Hamilton worked his remarkable program out in a series of four reports to Congress in 1790–1791: on credit (including duties and taxes), on a national bank, on a mint, and on manufactures. These reports, powerfully written and argued, established Hamilton as one of the greatest statesmen of his era.[140]

Drafting these impressive reports was one thing, however; implementing them in the face of widespread and deeply rooted country-Whig opposition thinking would prove to be quite another.

138. The fullest description of these "country-opposition" ideas can be found in Bernard Bailyn, *The Ideological Origins of the American Revolution* (Cambridge, MA, 1967).
139. Debate in the New York Ratifying Convention, 17 June–26 July 1788, in Bernard Bailyn, ed., *The Debate on the Constitution* (New York, 1993), 2: 768.
140. On Hamilton's "financial revolution," see Richard Sylla, "The Transition to a Monetary Union in the United States, 1787–1795," *Financial History Review*, 13 (2006), 73–95.

# 3

# The Federalist Program

On September 21, 1789, ten days after Hamilton's appointment as secretary of the treasury, the House of Representatives, stating that "an adequate provision for the public credit" was a "matter of high importance to the national honor and prosperity," directed the treasury secretary to "prepare a plan for that purpose."[1] Hamilton was more than ready. Long before he became secretary of the treasury Hamilton had been thinking about the problem of the $79 million debt from the Revolutionary War. In 1790 the amount owed foreigners—the French and Spanish governments and Dutch bankers—was about $12 million, including the arrears of interest, and was easily calculated. The domestic debt, that is, the debt the states and the federal governments owed their own citizens, was another matter. It was made up of a bewildering array of bills, notes, and certificates issued by various agencies of both the Confederation and state governments. Of the domestic debt about $42 million was owed by the federal government; the various state governments owed an estimated $25 million.

Hamilton had to untangle this mass of debts and set forth a plan of payment. He did so in a forty-thousand-word Report on Public Credit submitted to Congress on January 14, 1790, five months after he had taken office.

Hamilton had no doubt that the foreign debt had to be paid off in full, and every American leader agreed with him. Yet paying off the domestic debt was not so easily dealt with. He faced a variety of options. Perhaps the domestic debt could be scaled down, or some proportion of it repudiated, or at least a distinction could be drawn between the original and the present holders of the public securities. After all, during the 1780s much of the debt had been bought up by speculators at a fraction of its face value; and many of these speculators had little expectation that the debt and interest would be paid in full and in specie. But Hamilton thought that any attempt to repudiate the debt or to discriminate between its

---

1. Jacob E. Cooke, *Alexander Hamilton* (New York, 1982), 75.

original and present holders would be not only unjust to those who had taken the risk of purchasing the securities but ruinous to the honor and creditability of the nation. Only by paying its debts in full would the new government assure future creditors of its ability to meet its obligations. Besides, Hamilton had no objection to having the public debt concentrated in the hands of a few moneyed men, for he hoped to use the debt as a source of economic productivity for the nation.

In the boldest and most controversial part of his plan Hamilton proposed that the United States government assume the obligation of paying not just the federal government's $42 million of war debts but all $25 million of the states' debts as well. This, of course, would relieve the states of raising taxes to pay off their debts and would eliminate one of the major problems behind the democratic turbulence of the 1780s. But then, instead of immediately retiring either these assumed state debts or the Confederation's debts, Hamilton urged that the United States government "fund" them, that is, transform them into a more or less permanent debt on which annual interest would be regularly paid. The new national government would collect into a single package all the various federal and state notes, bonds, and loan certificates left over from the Revolutionary War and would issue new federal securities in their place with more or less the same value as the old debts. Lacking the tax revenues to retire immediately the principal of the debt, Hamilton hoped that regular payments of interest alone would convince creditors that the government was committed to paying it off eventually.

To reassure people further of the government's intention to retire all the debts in time, and to stabilize the prices of the new national securities, Hamilton proposed the creation of a sinking fund, which presumably would be used gradually to redeem the debt over the coming years. In fact, a sinking fund, as Adam Smith pointed out, "though instituted for the payment of old, facilitates very much the contracting of new debts."[2] Hamilton used the sinking fund to maintain the confidence of creditors in the government's securities; he had no intention of paying off the outstanding principal of the debt. Retiring the debt would only destroy its usefulness as money and as a means of attaching investors to the federal government.

With these funding plans Hamilton hoped to create a consolidated and permanent national debt that would strengthen America in the same way that the British national debt had strengthened Great Britain. The Federalists hoped to wean the people's affections away from their state

2. Edwin J. Perkins, *American Public Finance and Financial Services, 1700–1815* (Columbus, OH, 1994), 221.

governments and to get them to feel the power of what they hoped would become a consolidated national government. The Constitution had attempted to reduce drastically the power of the states. Article I, Section 10, among other things, had forbidden the states from levying tariffs or duties on imports or exports and had barred them from issuing paper money or bills of credit. As these were the principal means by which pre-modern governments raised money, their prohibition cut deeply into the fiscal competency of the state governments. Consequently, as Samuel Chase pointed out in the Maryland ratifying convention, the states would end up "without power, or respect and despised—they will sink into nothing, and be absorbed in the general government." Some Federalists actually hoped for this to happen—for the states eventually to be reduced to mere administrative units of the national government.[3]

Under the new system creditors would be drawn away from the states and attached to the new federal government. With the federal government's assumption of the states' war debts, the states would have no war debts to pay and thus would lose much of the need to tax their citizens as heavily as they had in the 1780s.[4] Some like Washington hoped that the states might in time have "no occasion for Taxes and consequently may abandon all the subjects of taxation to the Union," which would then become the principal political force in people's lives, especially in the lives of the propertied and wealthy creditor class.[5] The national government would levy customs duties and excise taxes to supply the revenue to make regular interest payments on the refunded debt. Indeed, more than 40 percent of this federal revenue in the 1790s went to pay interest on the funded debt.

Hamilton expected that these regular interest payments would make the United States the best credit risk in the world, as well as create an attractive system of investment for American moneyed groups that lacked the stable alternatives for investment that Europeans had. Whereas land in Europe was generally a very safe form of investment, in America it was highly speculative and very risky, as many speculators in the 1790s only too poignantly came to realize.

Besides giving investors a secure stake in the new national government, these new bonds, Hamilton hoped, would become part of the nation's money supply as negotiable instruments in business transactions. But for

3. Herbert J. Storing, ed., *The Complete Anti-Federalist* (Chicago, 1981), 5: 84–85.
4. Max M. Edling and Mark D. Kaplanoff, "Alexander Hamilton's Fiscal Reform: Transforming the Structure of Taxation in the Early Republic," *WMQ*, 61 (2004), 712–44.
5. Leonard D. White, *The Federalists: A Study in Administrative History* (New York, 1948), 404 n; GW, Plan of American Finance, c. Oct 1789, in Fitzpatrick, ed., *Writings of Washington*, 30: 454.

Hamilton an even more important source of money was a national bank. Indeed, Hamilton defined a bank for President Washington in 1791 in just these terms of creating money. "For the simplest and most precise idea of a bank," he wrote, "is a deposit of coin or other property as a fund for *circulating a credit* upon it, which is to answer the purpose of money."[6] Hamilton laid out his plans for a bank in a report submitted to Congress on December 14, 1790.

Most Americans in 1790 were not at all familiar with banks. In 1781 the Confederation Congress had set up the Bank of North America in Philadelphia, and by 1790 there were three more banks established in New York, Boston, and Baltimore. Yet compared to England, banking in America was new and undeveloped. Nothing in America resembled the array of different monetary notes and the dozens upon dozens of private and county banks scattered over eighteenth-century Great Britain. When the Bank of North America was first opened, it was "a novelty," said Thomas Willing, its president. Banking in America, he said, was "a pathless wilderness ground but little known to this side the Atlantic." English rules, arrangements, and bank bills were then unknown. "All was to us a mystery."[7]

So Hamilton's proposal for a national bank was bold and novel. He recommended that Congress grant a twenty-year charter to a corporation to be called the Bank of the United States (BUS). This central bank would be capitalized at $10 million, which was far more than all the specie, that is, gold and silver, in the country. One-fifth of the capital was to be provided by the government itself; the rest of the Bank's stock was to be sold to private investors, who could pay for up to three-fourths of the shares with government securities and the remaining one-fourth in gold or silver. This Bank of the United States, like its model the Bank of England, would be the only bank chartered by the national government. For fear of diluting its strength Hamilton actually opposed establishing branches of the Bank in states outside of Pennsylvania, though by 1805 eight branches had been created. Some Federalists hoped that the Bank of the United States would sooner or later absorb the state banks and monopolize all banking in the country.[8] Even if this proved impossible, the BUS would facilitate the payment of federal taxes and import duties, loan money to the United States, serve as the government's sole depository and fiscal agent, and act as a central control on the state banks, of

6. Bray Hammond, *Banks and Politics in America from the Revolution to the Civil War* (Princeton, 1957), 69.
7. Hammond, *Banks and Politics*, 66.
8. Hammond, *Banks and Politics*, 126–27; Fisher Ames to AH, 31 July 1791, AH to William Seton, 25 Nov. 1791, *Papers of Hamilton*, 8: 590–91; 9: 538–39.

which there were only four in 1791.[9] But most important, the Bank of the United States would create paper money.

The BUS would issue its notes as loans to private citizens, and these notes would become the principal circulating medium of money for a society that lacked an adequate supply of gold and silver coin. Above all, Hamilton wanted a paper money that would hold its value in relation to this specie. By being assured that the federal government would accept the Bank's notes at face value in payment of all taxes, holders of the notes would be less likely to redeem them for gold or silver coin—the only real money that most people in the eighteenth century trusted. The notes would pass from hand to hand without depreciating, even though a fraction of their worth was available in specie at any one time. Although many American leaders continued to believe, as John Adams did, that "every dollar of a bank bill that is issued beyond the quantity of gold and silver in the vaults, represents nothing, and is therefore a cheat upon somebody," these multiplying bank notes quickly broadened the foundation of the nation's economy.[10]

Yet it is important to emphasize that Hamilton's Bank would make money available only to large merchants and others who wanted short-term loans, ninety days or less. Most banks, including the BUS, as yet did not want to get involved in making long-term mortgage loans to farmers; to do so would tie up money for too long a time, as the Bank waited for the land-based loans to be paid back. But that would soon change, for most farmers and entrepreneurs needed long-term credit. In spite of opposition from Hamilton and the BUS, these farmers and entrepreneurs soon pressured their states to create state banks, many of them, that eventually gave them the credit they wanted. Hamilton's insensitivity to the entrepreneurial needs of these ordinary farmers and small businessmen suggests how little he and other Federalists appreciated the real sources of the capitalist future of America.

On January 28, 1791, Hamilton submitted his recommendations for establishing a national mint to Congress, where they met little opposition. America had been long plagued by a bewildering variety of foreign coins— English shillings, Spanish pistareens, French sous, and even German carolins—and had none of its own. Hamilton and others were convinced that a national coinage would make for a greater sense of nationhood. His report therefore had little that was original; indeed, much of it, especially the proposal for a decimal system, was borrowed from Jefferson.

9. Hammond, *Banks and Politics*, 126.
10. Hammond, *Banks and Politics*, 188, 196, 189. On Hamilton's vision, see Robert E. Wright, *The First Wall Street: Chestnut Street, Philadelphia, and the Birth of American Finance* (Chicago, 2005), 66–85.

Hamilton's final report on manufactures, completed in December 1791, laid out what a century later looked like prescient plans for industrializing the United States. Some historians have described this as his most creative and powerful proposal. But others have been less excited; some have even gone so far as to suggest that, unlike his interest in the other parts of his financial program, his heart was never really in manufacturing. He certainly took his time in writing it. As early as January 1790 the House of Representatives had directed Hamilton to "prepare a proper plan . . . for the encouragement and promotion of such manufactories as will tend to render the United States independent of other nations for essential, particularly for military, supplies."[11] Nearly two years later he completed it, with considerable help from Tench Coxe of Pennsylvania, whom Hamilton had appointed assistant secretary of the treasury in May 1790.

The delay did not signify Hamilton's lack of concern for manufacturing. Quite the contrary. His report went well beyond the House's directive. In a long essay, twice as long as the other reports, he set forth the need for the new country to develop manufacturing, not just to meet military requirements but also to create a more diversified and prosperous economy that would be more self-reliant and less dependent on European supplies. The report further elaborated his grand vision of a powerful, integrated, and wealthy war-making nation that would be the equal of any in Europe, including Great Britain.

This vision of what the United States might become was inevitably related to the Federalists' ideas of political economy. Initially, they wanted America to move as quickly as possible into the final stage of commercial and industrial development. If the United States continued to rely exclusively on agriculture as it had in the past, it would remain a rude and stagnant society. As a New England Federalist put it in 1789, "an agricultural nation which exports its raw materials, and imports its manufactures" could be neither "opulent" nor "powerful."[12]

American farmers produced more farm goods than they could use themselves. If Americans were to have reliable markets for their agricultural surplus, the Federalists thought, the country needed to develop modern commercial and manufacturing sectors and create a more balanced economy with a domestic market for its farm produce. Since the

---

11. Cooke, *Hamilton*, 98.
12. "A Citizen of the United States," *Observations on the Agriculture, Manufactures and Commerce of the United States* (New York, 1789), 18–19. Although this pamphlet had long been attributed to Tench Coxe, his authoritative biographer, Jacob E. Cooke, says this is erroneous; he believes the author was a New Englander. Jacob E. Cooke, *Tench Coxe and the Early Republic* (Chapel Hill, 1978), 150 n.

nation existed in an uncertain world, dominated by mercantilist powers, it could not rely on stable markets abroad for its farm surpluses. With the mercantilist powers able to cut back on their demand for American agricultural goods at will or find other sources, American farmers would always be faced with inadequate and fluctuating buyers of their produce. Yet America's consumers still wanted European, especially British, conveniences and manufactured goods. If the United States did not make these goods, then Americans would continue to import them, which in turn would create an adverse balance of trade. Since this lopsided trade had been the problem with America's economy in the colonial period, the mercantile-minded Federalists wanted to move what they took to be the underdeveloped American nation into commercial modernity.

Thus many Federalists hoped to use government to encourage domestic industry and manufacturing, not just of a household sort but large-scale manufacturing as well. They thought that such home industries might draw farm workers into manufacturing. Then these workers would become a market for America's agricultural surpluses, and the farmers in turn would buy their manufactured goods from American industrialists. By creating extensive domestic markets in this way, America would eventually become independent of Europe.

In his first annual message to Congress, in January 1790, President Washington had urged the promoting of manufacturing, the importing of "new and useful inventions from abroad," and the encouraging of "the exertions of skill and genius in producing them at home." The safety and interest of a free people, he had warned, required the promoting of "such manufactories, as to tend to render them independent on others, for essential, particularly for military supplies."[13] If the United States could not supply its own wants and needs, especially those having to do with war-making, then it would never, the Federalists believed, become a powerful, integrated, and independent fiscal-military state capable of confronting the European nations as equals.

But in 1791 Hamilton knew that realizing this vision would take time, three or four decades at least. Meanwhile, there were more pressing needs. Consequently, to fulfill the long-term development of manufacturing Hamilton made only some modest recommendations: some moderate protective tariffs for infant industries, bounties for the establishment of new manufacturing, prizes to encourage inventions, and exemptions from duties of some raw materials imported from abroad.

The report imaginatively contested much conventional wisdom by suggesting that domestic commerce, that is, Americans trading with one

---

13. GW, First Annual Message to Congress, 8 Jan. 1790, *Washington: Writings*, 750, 749.

another, might be as valuable to the prosperity of the country as international commerce. Yet in the end Hamilton tempered his boldness. His promotion of manufacturing was limited to the development of new industries, not to the protection of established industries threatened by more efficient foreign competition. At the same time, he offered no help or capital for small artisans and for household manufacturing. His tariff proposals were not actually protective; they were for revenue, and because the price of foreign manufactures had declined, he believed that additional duties would not seriously affect consumer prices. He did not like protective tariffs, preferring bounties, or direct governmental payments to businesses, which he believed were "the best" and "most efficacious means of encouraging manufactures."[14] Such bounties tended in fact to benefit articles exported rather than those manufactured for home consumption.

So even in his encouragement of manufacturing he never lost sight of the importance of the large merchant community engaged in overseas trade. Whatever measures he suggested for aiding American manufacturing posed no danger to the businesses of merchants importing British manufactures or to the revenues those imports provided for his fiscal program. Since his entire fiscal program depended on the customs duties flowing from a large overseas commerce, Hamilton was reluctant to weaken that overseas commerce for the sake of developing domestic commerce.[15]

In fact, Hamilton in writing his report on manufactures seems to have been thinking mostly of drumming up support for his and Coxe's Society for Establishing Useful Manufactures (SEUM)—an incorporated stock-issuing community in Paterson, New Jersey, that would be a model factory town for future American industrialization. He and Coxe hoped to get some of the moneyed men and large merchants who were investing heavily in the new federal public securities to place some of their capital in SEUM and thus moderate the excessive speculation in the national debt that was taking place.[16]

Hamilton was so wedded to a hierarchical view of society that he could only imagine industrial investment and development coming from the top down. Thus he was incapable of foreseeing that the actual source of America's manufacturing would come from below, from the ambitions,

14. AH, Report on the Subject of Manufactures, 5 Dec. 1791, *Papers of Hamilton*, 10: 298.
15. Edling and Kaplanoff, "Alexander Hamilton's Fiscal Reform," 740.
16. John R. Nelson Jr., *Liberty and Property: Political Economy and Policymaking in the New Nation, 1789–1812* (Baltimore, 1987), 37–48; John E. Crowley, *The Privileges of Independence: Neomercantilism and the American Revolution* (Baltimore, 1993), 146–55.

productivity, and investments of thousands upon thousands of middling artisans and craftsmen who eventually became America's businessmen. Hamilton's historical reputation as the prophet of America's industrial greatness therefore seems somewhat exaggerated. He certainly wanted a powerful and glorious nation, but he was no more capable of accurately foretelling the future than the other American leaders.

At the same time, however, there is no doubt that Hamilton and his program laid the basis for the supremacy of the national government over the states. By the middle of the 1790s the total tax revenue raised by the federal government was a bit more than $6 million, which was more than ten times the total tax revenue ($500,000) that all the states combined raised from direct taxation, still the states' major source of tax revenue. Expenditures were equally lopsided: while all the states' expenditures in the early 1790s totaled only a little more than $1 million a year, the federal government's expenditures in 1795 were $7.5 million. Finally, in terms of money borrowed by the governments, the national government over-whelmed the states. While the combined public debt of the states in 1796 was less than $4 million, the federal government's debt amounted to more than $80 million. The new national government might not have yet won the trust or the loyalties of the American people, but it certainly had come to dominate their pocketbooks.[17]

As ENTHUSIASTICALLY AS HAMILTON celebrated the commercial prosperity of the United States, his goal was as much political as economic. Hamilton wanted people to feel the presence of the new national govern-ment. As he had said in *Federalist* No. 27, the more the government "enters into those objects which touch the most active springs of the human heart, the greater will be the probability that it will conciliate the respect and attachment of the community." A government that was "continually at a distance and out of mind" could never engage the feelings of its citizens. Like all the Revolutionaries, Hamilton was preoccupied with finding adhe-sives to bind people together; but unlike Jefferson, Paine, and other liber-als, he counted on the government as the main source of cohesion.

The dream of Hamilton, Washington, and the other Federalists of a strong, consolidated, and prosperous national polity was not the disinter-ested adjudicatory state that Madison had envisioned but an illustrious, European-type state that would rival the great powers of Europe. "Our national government," Hamilton admitted, was presently "in its infancy," but eventually the United States would become the equal of the European monarchies on their own terms—terms that, as Washington said, were

17. Edling and Kaplanoff, "Alexander Hamilton's Fiscal Reform," 743–44.

"characteristic of wise and powerful Nations."[18] This meant a strong central bureaucratic government directing the economy and reaching to all parts of a united and integrated nation and possessing a powerful army and navy that commanded the respect of the whole world.

Building this monarchical republic would not be easy. The Federalists knew that the people were emotionally attached to their states, whose histories went back a century or more. They would have to somehow redirect their loyalties to the Union. Consolidating a country that was still largely rural and thinly populated added to their difficulties. In 1790 only five American cities had populations over 10,000: Philadelphia, New York, Boston, Charleston, and Baltimore. The most populous state, Virginia, with nearly 700,000 people, had no large cities. Norfolk with about 7,000 was the biggest; the new state capital, Richmond, had 3,700. North Carolina had no town with a population of more than two thousand. Lexington, Kentucky, was the largest town in the West, and it had only 834 inhabitants in 1790.

Bringing all these scattered people together, making a unified nation out of disparate sections, states, and communities without relying on idealistic republican attachments—this was the preoccupation of Washington and the Federalists, and it explains much of what he as president and the other Federalists did during the 1790s.

Instead of virtue and the natural sociability of people, Hamilton, Washington, and other Federalists saw only the ordinary individual's selfish pursuit of his own private interests and happiness. Social stability therefore required the harnessing of this self-interest. And this could best be done by appealing principally to the self-interest of the gentry and would-be gentry at the top of the society, including all those rich moneyed interests who lived off of unearned income.

Although Hamilton's financial program was designed with these moneyed interests in mind, it was never intended for their exclusive benefit. They would no doubt prosper from it, but that would be incidental to his larger economic and political plans. In addition to bringing prosperity to the whole country, Hamilton hoped that his new economic and fiscal measures would tie moneyed men and other influential individuals to the new central government. Hamilton may have believed that he and Washington and a few others were capable of disinterested judgment, but

18. AH to GW, 15 Sept. 1790, *Papers of Hamilton*, 70: 50; GW to Henry Knox, 28 Feb. 1785, quoted in John Lauritz Larson, "'Wisdom Enough to Improve Them': Navigation Projects and the Rising American Empire," in Ronald Hoffman and Peter J. Albert, eds., *Launching the 'Extended Republic': The Federalist Era* (Charlottesville, 1996), 235.

he knew that most people were not, and he intended to build the Federalist program on this realistic assessment of human nature.

Hamilton and most other Federalists were strongly committed to the traditional view of society as a hierarchy of degrees and ranks with people held together by vertical ties, and they believed that America would naturally move in that direction as soon as the disorder generated by the Revolution had subsided. Distinctions of status, rights of precedence, patron-client relations, and the duties owed by all to those above them—from the child's duty to a parent to the citizen's duty to the government—very much dominated Federalist thinking. Hamilton, for example, believed that "mechanics and manufacturers will always be inclined, with few exceptions, to give their votes to merchants, in preference to persons of their own professions or trades.... They know that the merchant is their natural patron and friend."[19] The Federalists were good republicans, in that they believed in election as the source of political leadership, but they also believed that election ought to result in government by patrons and by the wise and virtuous, in other words, by men like themselves.

The Revolution may have been about liberty, but by 1790 most Federalists believed that Americans were free of British control and should not have to think about liberty so exclusively and passionately anymore. Besides, the Federalists said, true liberty was reason and order, not licentiousness. Popular passions unleashed by the Revolution, they believed, had to be restrained. In the enthusiasm of the 1770s and 1780s too many Americans, it was said, had allowed talk of freedom and equality to go to their heads; they had run wild and had violated the hierarchical order that made all civilized society possible.

Although many Federalists were reluctant to voice their ideas about society publicly, most of them believed that the "distinctions of rank and condition in life" were natural and inevitable. "There must be," declared Boston minister and noted geographer Jedidiah Morse, "rulers and subjects, masters and servants, rich and poor. The human body is not perfect without all its members, some of which are more honourable than others; so it is with the body politic."[20] Some were born to rule, others were born to serve. That some were born to be "Philosophers, Legislators, and Statesmen," while others were "intended for working with their hands" was a common theme of conservatives everywhere. Talent should be allowed to rise, but once risen it should be respected by those beneath it. The ideal harmonious

19. AH, *Federalist* No. 35.
20. James M. Banner Jr., *To the Hartford Convention: The Federalists and the Origins of Party Politics in Massachusetts, 1789–1815* (New York, 1970), 57.

society was one that recognized "the necessity of subordination," one in which everyone found his proper place and did not try to attain a rank for which he was unsuited. What the Federalists wanted for America, in the opinion of critics, was "the European condition of society."[21]

No one was more convinced of the inevitability of the hierarchical structure of American society than the new secretary of the treasury. While Hamilton waited for American society to mature, he and the other Federalists would have to create artificially whatever the society was lacking naturally. Hamilton believed in a social hierarchy dominated by gentlemen, men of leisure, patrons who lived off unearned income—income that came from rents from tenants, fees, or interest from bonds or money out on loan. These few were the influential men who, like William Cooper of Otsego County, New York, ruled their local communities through their wealth and power. Hamilton hoped that political leaders could be drawn from this class of gentlemen, who ideally should not have interests to support while they held public office.

Despite having to leave office periodically to practice law, Hamilton tried strenuously to live up to this ideal. Others, like John Jay, fit the ideal more easily. They presumably had sufficient wealth and leisure to assume the burdens of public office without expecting high salaries or great monetary rewards. Still others, Hamilton knew, were speculators and stockjobbers who were eager only to make money off the government. Even though these moneyed men may have been selfish schemers, nevertheless, the new government needed their support, indeed, needed the support of all the influential people at the top of the society, whatever their character or level of virtue and disinterestedness. In traditional eighteenth-century fashion, Hamilton saw these few at the top extending their influence and patronage down through the various levels and degrees of the society. Hamilton, like most Federalists, assumed that politics was largely a matter of securing the support of these influential patrons. Capture these few, he thought, and a statesman inevitably captures the whole society.

The way to do so was to appeal to the interests of these few influentials. Interest—there was no better or firmer bond between people: he had known that from his earliest years at King's College and had

21. Joyce Appleby, *Capitalism and a New Social Order: The Republican Vision of the 1790s* (New York, 1984), 73; Perez Forbes, "An Election Sermon" (1795), in Charles S. Hyneman and Donald S. Lutz, eds., *American Political Writing During the Founding Era* (Indianapolis, 1983), 2: 993; Andrew Shankman, *Crucible of American Democracy: The Struggle to Fuse Egalitarianism and Capitalism in Jeffersonian Pennsylvania* (Lawrence, KS, 2004), 76.

repeated it over and over ever since. "Men will pursue their interest," he said in 1788. "It is as easy to change human nature, as to oppose the strong current of the selfish passions. A wise legislator will gently divert the channel, and direct it, if possible, to the public good." Although he later and rather defensively denied that he had ever made interest "the weightiest motive" behind his various programs, there is no doubt that he meant to strengthen central authority and the Union "by increasing the number of ligaments between the Government and the interests of Individuals."[22]

In effect, in the opposition language of the eighteenth-century Anglo-American world, Hamilton and the Federalists set out to "corrupt" American society. In much the same way as English ministers in the eighteenth century, especially Sir Robert Walpole, had built up the power of the British crown, the Federalists sought to use monarchical-like governmental influence both to tie the leading commercial interests to the government and to create new hierarchies of interest and dependency that would substitute for the absence of virtue and the apparently weak republican adhesives existing in America. Hamilton's financial program was designed not to make money for any particular group but to use patronage, like all the great European state-builders before him, to create a powerful nation-state.[23]

Beginning in 1789 the Federalists sought to form rings of local interests throughout the country loyal to the government. In communities up and down the continent, Washington, Hamilton, and the Federalist leaders used patronage of various sorts to create hierarchies of support for the new government. Unlike the practice of the states, where thousands of state, town, and county public functionaries were elected, all executive and judicial offices in the federal government, except for the president and vice-president, were appointed. As early as 1782 Hamilton had foreseen the importance of the federal government's having this immense power to appoint all its own officers. The goal of such appointments, said Hamilton, was "to create in the interior of each State, a mass of influence in favor of the Federal Government." Force alone could not support the government, and besides its use was disagreeable and unpredictable. Creating influence could best be accomplished "by interesting such a number of individuals in each State, in support of the Federal Government, as will be counterpoised to the ambition of others, and

22. AH, New York Ratifying Convention, 25 June 1788, *Papers of Hamilton*, 5: 85; AH, "The Defence of the Funding System" (July 1795), *Papers of Hamilton*, 13: 349.
23. Roger V. Gould, "Patron-Client Ties, State Centralization, and the Whiskey Rebellion," *American Journal of Sociology*, 102 (1996), 401.

will make it difficult to unite the people in opposition to the first and necessary measures of the Union."[24]

When he became head of the treasury, Hamilton had hundreds of officials to appoint and was thus in a prime position to carry out his aim. Since these customs officials, revenue agents, and postmasters were located in every large town and section of the United States and touched every aspect of economic life in America, they were important for building support for the new government, even among former opponents of the Constitution.[25] In addition to the treasury officials, the Federalists had other executive and judicial offices to fill, including territorial officials, Indian commissioners, ministers at foreign posts, judges, marshals, and a wide variety of subordinate personnel. Very few former Anti-Federalists were appointed; of those whose political position can be identified, only thirty-one appointees had been opposed to the Constitution in 1787–1788. But of these Anti-Federalist officeholders, only nine later became members of the Jeffersonian Republican party that would eventually emerge to contest the Federalist government; fifteen of the former Anti-Federalists became members of the Federalist party. Holding a national office, in other words, helped to reconcile people to the Constitution.[26]

Both Hamilton and Washington thought that former military officers would make particularly trustworthy supporters of the administration. Of 487 Federalist appointees old enough to have fought in the War for Independence, 134 had been officers in the Continental Army, and of these, 74 were members of the Society of the Cincinnati.[27] "The idea, that my former gallant Associates in the field are now about to receive, in a good national government, some compensation for the toils and dangers which they experienced in the course of a long and perilous war," said Washington in September 1788, "is particularly consolatory to me."[28] These were men who had demonstrated their virtue in the war and, most important, would remain loyal to him and to the new fledgling government. Indeed, so much were the members of the Cincinnati favored for appointments that the testy Senator Maclay thought that "we were to go on making Offices until all the Cincinnati were provided for." The Cincinnati, Maclay believed, were just another one of Hamilton's "Machines" of

24. AH, "Continentalist," VI, 4 July 1782, *Papers of Hamilton*, 3: 105–6.
25. White, *Federalists*, 117; Cooke, *Hamilton*, 73.
26. Carl E. Prince, *The Federalists and the Origins of the U.S. Civil Service* (New York, 1977), 271.
27. Andrew R. L. Cayton, "'Separate Interests' and the Nation-State: The Washington Administration and the Origins of Regionalism in the Trans-Appalachian West," *JAH*, 79 (1992–1993), 50–51; Prince, *Origins of the Civil Service*, 269–70.
28. GW to John Sullivan, 1 Sept. 1788, in Fitzpatrick, ed. *Writings of Washington*, 30: 86.

corruption with which he was attempting to move "heaven and earth in favor of his System."[29]

Hamilton and the Federalists assumed that these appointments would work as they did in monarchical governments. Offices in the judiciary or other parts of the federal government would be offered to important and respectable local figures who could be counted on to use their influence to suppress popular passions and control the society in which they lived. Since the system worked best if the appointed official was already an important and respected local figure with an existing clientele, Washington was apprehensive. Because those excluded from office were often provoked into opposition, he realized that making appointments would be "one of the most difficult and delicate parts of my office." Ideally what he wanted was to have one candidate for each office "of such clear pretensions as to secure him against competition."[30]

Sometimes it worked out that way, but more often the appointments aroused the resentments of those left out. This was certainly the case with Chancellor Robert R. Livingston, the wealthy New York landlord who had administered the oath of office to Washington on April 30, 1789. Two weeks after the inauguration Livingston had written to Washington asking for a high office in the new government, presumably secretary of the treasury or chief justice of the United States. But the president had Hamilton and John Jay, two other New Yorkers, in mind for these offices, and not wanting to have too many top officials from the same state, he had tried tactfully to put Livingston off. Furious at being snubbed, Livingston soon emerged as a leading opponent of the Federalist government. American society was never hierarchical enough, the aristocratic leaders were never readily identifiable enough, and the national offices were never numerous enough for the Federalist patronage system to create the kind of order and stability that Washington and Hamilton expected.

Nevertheless, by 1793 or so the Federalists had formed groups of "friends of government" in most of the states. The lines of connection of these centers of economic and political patronage ran from the federal executive through Congress down to the various localities. These federal-based patronage networks cut through the existing state-based patronage networks and tended to isolate those local elites who had no national connections. Indeed, much of the conflict among elites during the 1790s flowed from rivalries between national and state structures of political connections.

There is no doubt that in the 1790s federal officeholders possessed considerable political resources, including the ability to offer favors and legal pro-

29. *The Diary of William Maclay and Other Notes on Senate Debates*, ed. Kenneth R. Bowling and Helen E. Veit (Baltimore, 1988), 316, 200.
30. GW to Edward Rutledge, 5 May 1789, in Washington: *Writings*, 735–36.

tection for clients and to influence additional appointments.[31] Washington certainly saw the wisdom of relying on existing federal officials for advice. By consulting the representatives and senators from the states in which he was making appointments, he helped to keep some influential political leaders—Congressman John Steele and Senator Samuel Johnson from North Carolina, for example—tied to the Federalist cause even in the face of local popular opposition.[32] Hamilton for his part tried to gain the support of commercial interests in Congress and the states that would benefit from his financial program. He was most successful with those from New England and New York, but even in the agriculture-dominated South he was able to cultivate financial interests in Charleston and Richmond and to gain the backing of South Carolinians for the federal assumption of state debts.

Despite all these efforts, however, the Federalist structure was already anachronistic and ill-adapted to the restless democratic and capitalistic society that was rapidly emerging in America, especially in the Northern states of America. Consequently, the Federalists' Walpolean system of influence never captured many of the most dynamic interests in American society. Hamilton and other Federalist leaders concentrated on tying to the government the holders of traditional aristocratic proprietary wealth— mostly the big moneyed men and the rich merchants in the port cities— "who," said Hamilton, "are in every society the only firm supporters of government." They paid almost no attention to the new multiplying interests of those ordinary men who worked for a living—commercial farmers, small manufacturers, master artisans, and proto-businessmen who were emerging, particularly in the burgeoning middle regions of the country.[33]

31. Gould, "Patron-Client Ties," *American Journal of Sociology*, 102 (1996), 400–429.
32. Lisle A. Rose, *Prologue to Democracy: The Federalists in the South, 1789–1800* (Lexington, KY, 1968), 27.
33. This Federalist use of patronage resembles but was very different from the later Jacksonian "spoils system" that came to dominate political officeholding in mid-nineteenth-century America. Most of the Jacksonian officeholders were not socially visible and respectable men; indeed, most were precisely those sorts of ordinary middling men whom the Federalists had ignored. For the Jacksonians the criterion of appointment was not family, not social standing, not ability, not character, and not reputation, but connection to the Jacksonian Democratic Party. Nothing else was required. "The duties of all public offices," said President Andrew Jackson in his first annual message, "are, or at least admit of being made, so plain and simple that men of intelligence may readily qualify themselves for their performance." Political office was no longer to be a "species of property" belonging to prominent gentlemen simply because of their social rank or character. Jackson, First Annual Message, 8 Dec. 1829, in James D. Richardson, ed., *A Compilation of the Messages and Papers of the Presidents, 1789–1897* (Washington, DC, 1900), 2: 449; Lynn Marshall, "The Strange Stillbirth of the Whig Party," *AHR*, 72 (1972), 452.

THE FEDERALISTS REALIZED that patronage and other political adhesives would be worthless if the new national government lacked ultimate coercive power. As Washington declared in response to Shays's Rebellion, an uprising of several thousand farmers in western Massachusetts in the winter of 1786–1787, "influence is no government."[34] Force may have been uncertain in its results and distasteful for good republicans to use, but for most Federalists the possession of military power was essential to the existence of the government. Indeed, Washington and the Federalists believed that no nation-state could exist without a powerful army. Delegates to the Constitutional Convention of 1787, one-third of whom were veterans of the Continental Army, knew that force was inherent in the very nature of government, both to enforce the law and to repel foreign enemies. When Elbridge Gerry proposed in the Convention that no standing army exceed three thousand men, Washington is supposed to have made a countermotion that "no foreign enemy should invade the United States at any time, with more than three thousand troops." In the end the Constitution granted the federal government the right to establish and to use a standing army against both foreign foes and domestic insurrections.[35]

Because the idea of a standing army flew in the face of long-existing popular prejudices, the Federalists publicly avoided using the term. Nevertheless, they were committed to the peacetime maintenance of at least a small regular army not only as a model for the state militias and a nucleus for a wartime army but also as a source of security for the government.[36] Certainly Hamilton believed, as he declared in 1794, that "government can never [be] said to be established until some signal display, has manifested its power of military coercion."[37] From the beginning many Federalists, including Secretary of War Henry Knox, regarded a regular army backed by a cohesive federalized militia as "a strong corrective arm" necessary for the national government to meet all crises "whether from internal or external causes."[38]

AT THE MOMENT OF THE INAUGURATION of the new government, crises from external causes seemed the most pressing. These were crises

---

34. GW to Henry Lee, 31 Oct. 1786, *Washington: Writings*, 609.
35. James Hudson, ed., *Supplement to the Records of the Federal Convention of 1787* (New Haven, 1987), 229; Max Farrand, ed., *Records of the Federal Convention of 1787* (New Haven, 1911, 1937), 1: 246.
36. Richard H. Kohn, *Eagle and Sword: The Federalists and the Creation of the Military Establishment in America, 1783–1802* (New York, 1975), 76, 88.
37. Kohn, *Eagle and Sword*, 171.
38. Marcus Cunliffe, *Soldiers and Civilians: The Martial Spirit in America, 1775–1865* (Boston, 1968), 183.

that the weak Confederation government had been unable to deal with. They flowed from the fact that the Treaty of Paris in 1783 had given to the United States territory far beyond its actual settlements. The people of the original thirteen states occupied only about half of the territory of the newly enlarged country. Not only was this new territory occupied by Indians, but the borderlands of the trans-Appalachian West were dominated by Great Britain and Spain. Indeed, these European powers actually threatened the territorial integrity of the new nation. Much of the Federalists' diplomacy in the 1790s was devoted to removing these threats.

Although the British had lost thirteen of their North American colonies in 1783, they had established a new colony, Canada, whose southern boundaries pointed like a dagger at the heartland of the United States. Moreover, the British refused to evacuate their forts in the Northwest Territory of the United States, even though they had promised to do so in the peace treaty in 1783. These forts—at Michilimackinac and Detroit in the west, at Niagara and Oswego on Lake Ontario, at Oswegatchie on the St. Lawrence, and at Dutchman's Point and Point-au-Fer on Lake Champlain—controlled both the Indian country in the Northwest and the waterways along the American-Canadian border. Although the British had many reasons for continuing to hold these posts, they justified their action by claiming that the United States had prevented British subjects from recovering debts owed them by American citizens and thus had not fulfilled the terms of the peace treaty.

From their positions in Canada and the Northwest forts, the British encouraged the Indians to resist American demands for land, supported the formation of an Indian confederacy under the remarkable leadership of the Mohawk Joseph Brant, who had been educated at Eleazar Wheelock's school in Lebanon, Connecticut, and intrigued with dissident elements in the territories of Kentucky and Vermont. Levi Allen, one of the Allen brothers who had helped establish Vermont, actually tried to negotiate a commercial treaty with the British and get Britain to recognize Vermont's independence and possibly unite it with Canada. The Northwest borderlands of the United States were extremely vulnerable to British meddling.

The Southern boundary was even hazier and more open to exploitation by a European power. In the peace treaty the British had ceded to the United States the territory north of the 31st parallel, more or less the present boundary of Florida. But in a separate treaty in which the British returned Florida to Spain, the northern boundary of Florida was set much farther north. The Spanish claimed that the boundary ran at least as far north as the Yazoo River, which meant that much of present-day Alabama and Mississippi remained Spanish. The Spanish actually occupied Natchez, the most important settlement in the disputed region.

More important, Spain also held New Orleans and the Louisiana Territory. In 1762 France had given these possessions to Spain as payment for Spain's allying itself with France in the Seven Years' War against Great Britain. Spain welcomed this territory not because it had any ambitions to populate it or to make it profitable, but simply because it wanted to use it as a barrier to protect the silver mines of Mexico from the aggressive Anglo-American colonists to the north. Spanish officials saw only too clearly that every American who crossed the Appalachian Mountains and settled along the Ohio River and its tributaries weakened this territorial buffer. Yet if these Western settlers could not move their produce down the Mississippi to the Gulf of Mexico, they would have no reason to keep crossing the Appalachians into Kentucky and Tennessee.

Since the Spanish in the Southwest controlled the outlet to the sea for Western settlers seeking to market their produce, they, like the British in the Northwest, were in a position to intrigue with Indians and with dissident settlers who might be persuaded to separate from the United States. In fact, in 1784 in an effort to influence or to stop Americans moving into Kentucky and Tennessee, Spain closed the Mississippi River to American trade.

In response to this crisis, the American secretary of foreign affairs, John Jay, in 1785–1786 negotiated an agreement with the experienced Spanish minister to the United States, Don Diego de Gardoqui. Although the Confederation Congress had instructed Jay not to surrender America's right to navigate the Mississippi in his negotiations with the Spanish minister, Jay thought that giving up that right for twenty-five or thirty years in return for having access to Spanish markets was very attractive; and he was willing to connive with some New Englanders (who were flirting with separation from the Union) to get that access to Spanish markets. But out of fear of the Western settlers being denied an outlet to the Gulf of Mexico, Southerners led by James Monroe and Charles Pinckney prevented the nine-state majority in the Confederation Congress needed for a treaty, and the scheme failed. But the willingness of a majority of seven states to sacrifice Western interests for the sake of Eastern merchants convinced some Western leaders that perhaps they ought to listen to what Spain had to offer the Americans in the West. Hence was born what came to be called the "Spanish Conspiracy." It continued to plague the Southwest into the early years of the nineteenth century.

After the failure of the treaty, Gardoqui contacted some Western leaders, including John Brown, the representative of the Kentucky district of Virginia, James White, a congressman from North Carolina, and, most important, James Wilkinson, an ex–Revolutionary War officer, and tried to convince them that the future of Americans in the West belonged to

Spain. Spain offered trading licenses to Kentucky settlers, negotiated with leaders in Tennessee, and sought to attract Americans to settle in Spanish territory. Spain even enlisted Wilkinson as a paid agent of its government. Wilkinson secretly swore allegiance to the Spanish crown and for fifteen years received $2,000 a year as Agent 13 of the Spanish government, an arrangement not authenticated until the twentieth century. Wilkinson remained a central figure in the Spanish Conspiracy even after he became a lieutenant colonel and later general and commander of the U.S. Army. Even without knowing that he was a paid agent of Spain, John Randolph of Virginia said that Wilkinson was the only man he ever knew "who from the bark to the very core was a villain."[39]

Fears of a Spanish conspiracy were very real. At the end of the eighteenth century many Western settlers appeared ready to deal with any government that could benefit them. In 1784 Washington warned that the Westerners were "on a pivot. The touch of a feather would turn them any way." Even Jefferson in 1787 worried that because of the temptations of foreign powers and "the temper of the people" in the West, a "separation was possible at every moment."[40]

FROM THE OUTSET the Federalists knew that they faced difficulties in the newly acquired lands west of the Appalachians. The settlers were moving westward in massive numbers, and their relentless search for land was bound to be resisted by the Indians who possessed it. Like most other American leaders, the Federalists hoped not only that the West would be "a mine of vast wealth to the United States," as Madison had predicted in *Federalist* No. 38, but that it would be settled in an orderly and progressive fashion. They also anticipated, as Hamilton put it, "that it should be in great measure settled from abroad rather than at the entire expence of the Atlantic population."[41] The government anticipated drawing boundaries between the settlers and the Indians, care being taken, said Washington, "neither to yield nor to grasp at too much." But purchasing the Indians' rights to the land and protecting or assimilating them in a civilized manner depended on an organized and steady pace of white settlement. As Washington foresaw the process, "the gradual extension of our Settlements will as certainly cause the Savage as the Wolf to retire."[42]

39. Jon Latimer, *1812: War with America* (Cambridge, MA, 2007), 195.
40. Andrew R. L. Cayton, *The Frontier Republic: Ideology and Politics in the Ohio Country, 1780–1825* (Kent, OH, 1986), 23; TJ to JM, 20 June 1787, *Papers of Jefferson*, 11: 481.
41. AH to Arthur St. Clair, 19 May 1790, *Papers of Hamilton*, 6: 421.
42. GW to Duane, 7 Sept. 1783, in Fitzpatrick, ed., *Writings of Washington*, 27: 140.

Nothing worked out as the Federalists and other leaders hoped. The Americans' desire for land was too great and the authority of the central government too weak to control the westward scramble. The result was decades of continual bloody warfare over possession of the newly acquired Western territories.

Prior to the Revolution the British crown had tried to control the Americans' movement into the West, especially with the Proclamation of 1763, and it had been no more successful than the Federalists were to be. Land companies sprang up and began staking claims to land in the Ohio Valley. By the time of the Revolution Kentucky had already become an incredible patchwork of conflicting land claims. The break from English authority worsened the disorder in the West. It threw people back upon themselves and their own individual interests. As one Western settler put it, "When without a king, [one] doeth according to the freedom of his own will." Land claims multiplied and, said one observer, were "so laid one upon another that scarcely any body knows who is safe."[43]

The Western settlers were as defiant of the new American authorities in the East as they had been of the British crown. Various separatist movements sought to take control of public lands and set up illegal governments within several of the states—notably in western Virginia, Vermont, the Wyoming valley, and western North Carolina. By the end of the War for Independence the earlier migrations had become a flood. One observer in 1785 thought the movement westward was so great that it seemed "as if the old states would depopulate, and the inhabitants be transported to the new."[44] By 1790 Tennessee had well over thirty-five thousand settlers, while Kentucky had more than double that number, stimulated in part by John Filson's popular 1784 account of the "Present State of Kentucke." Both territories were rapidly growing, and land-hungry squatters were already spilling north of the Ohio River in a scattered and unauthorized manner.

The Confederation Congress tried to bring some order out of this chaos. In the early 1780s the various states with claims to the West finally ceded to the Confederation their separate rights to the Western lands. In return, the United States pledged to use the revenues from sales of this national domain for the common benefit of the country and promised to see that the Western settlements would eventually be admitted to the Union as republican states equal in rights to the thirteen original states.

43. Eric Hinderaker, *Elusive Empires: Construction Colonialism in the Ohio Valley, 1673–1800* (Cambridge, UK, 1997), 193, 194; *National Gazette*, I (November 1791), in Eugene L. Schwaab, ed., *Travels in the Old South* (Lexington, KY, 1973), 1: 58.

44. Reginald Horsman, *The Frontier in the Formative Years, 1783–1815* (Albuquerque, 1975), 5–6.

The original plan for the trans-Appalachian West was embodied in the Ordinance of 1784 that was drawn up by a committee headed by Jefferson. This plan divided the West into a grid of sixteen states with straight-line boundaries that took no account of the region's complicated geographical contours.

Although Jefferson's abstract Enlightenment plan did not survive, it nevertheless set the pattern for the future development of the West. Perhaps more than anything else, it expressed the American leaders' desire that settlement of the West be neat and orderly. Certainly the Land Ordinance of 1785 by which the Confederation established a comprehensive system for the survey and sale of land in the West likewise revealed a preoccupation with regularity and order.[45]

The land north of the Ohio River and west of the Appalachians was to be surveyed and marked off in a rectangular pattern—with east-west baselines and north-south ranges—before any of it was sold. This territory was to be divided into townships six miles square, with each township in turn cut up into thirty-six numbered sections of 640 acres each. Land was to be sold at auction, but the minimum price was set at one dollar per acre, and no one could buy less than a section of 640 acres, which meant that a very substantial sum was needed for any purchase. In each township Congress retained four sections for future sale and set aside one other for the support of public education. Although only seven ranges were actually surveyed in southeastern Ohio, this policy of surveying in rectangular units became the basis of America's land system.

Those who devised this system assumed that development of the West would be centrally controlled, that settlement would be tightly clustered, and that the relatively high price for land would keep out poor, lazy, Indian-hating squatters. Congress hoped that the Western purchasers would be industrious market-oriented farmers who would respect the gradually moving boundary between the white settlers and the Indians. By following these regular procedures of compact settlement, said Washington, wildcat land jobbers and hustlers would be restrained, peace would be maintained with the Indians, and more useful types of citizens would be encouraged to migrate.[46] Not only would enterprising and commercially minded settlers be willing to buy the land that would produce the revenue the United States required, but such civilized settlers would also bring to the West much-needed order and enlightenment. Desiring that the Western settlers be properly educated, Congress mandated the setting aside land for public schools.

45. John Stilgoe, *Common Landscape of America, 1580 to 1845* (New Haven, 1982), 102–3.
46. GW to James Duane, 7 Sept. 1783, *Washington: Writings*, 536–38.

Many Eastern leaders were leery of encouraging Western settlement anyhow, which is why many Federalists like Hamilton hoped that the West would be settled mostly by immigrants from abroad. Many Easterners had an uneasy sense that the Western settlers were apt to drift away from civilization and union with the United States. As John Jay warned in 1787, "the Western Country will one Day give us trouble—to govern them will not be easy."[47]

Even when the Confederation Congress realized in 1787 that sales to individuals by auction were not going well, they continued to cling to the hope that someone would pay money for the Western land. In desperation it turned to Eastern speculators who all through the 1780s had concocted schemes for making profits out of undeveloped tracts of land in the West. In 1787 Congress was convinced by the lobbying efforts of Manasseh Cutler, a New England minister, that the Ohio Company—a joint-stock company made up of former Continental Army officers—might be able to supply the kinds of enterprising settlers, presumably New Englanders, and the money the United States needed. Thus for a million dollars Congress transferred to the private hands of the Ohio Company a large chunk of its Western land—1,500,000 acres west of the previously drawn seven ranges that ran north of the Ohio River. As part of the deal, the Ohio Company was given an option to apply for an additional 4,500,000 acres in the Ohio territory for a newly formed Scioto Company, the brainchild of William Duer, the secretary of the Confederation's Board of Treasury and later assistant secretary in Hamilton's Treasury Department.

Congress's sale of land encouraged other speculators to bid for land north of the Ohio, the biggest being John Cleves Symmes, a prominent New Jersey judge. Symmes acquired from Congress 1,000,000 acres in the southwestern corner of the present state of Ohio where Cincinnati was founded. The last major speculative group involved in the Ohio lands in the eighteenth century was the Connecticut Land Company, which purchased a huge tract of 3,000,000 acres of the lands near present-day Cleveland that the state of Connecticut had reserved for itself when it ceded its claims to the Confederation, the so-called Western Reserve.

Like most of the other speculators, the associates in the Connecticut Land Company were wealthy Eastern gentlemen who had no intentions of emigrating to the West. In an economy lacking sophisticated alternatives for investment, these gentlemen-speculators simply hoped to establish a landed basis to secure their aristocratic aspirations. Indeed, in the 1780s and

47. Cayton, *Frontier Republic*, 23; Kenneth R. Bowling, *The Creation of Washington, D.C.: The Idea and Location of the American Capital* (Fairfax, VA, 1991), 11.

1790s many members of the would-be Federalist aristocracy often tried their best to live up to the classical image of being disinterested leaders standing above the marketplace of interests by getting involved in land speculation. During these years many merchants, including Robert Morris, George Clymer, William Bingham, Elbridge Gerry, George Cabot, and others, followed the earlier example of John Hancock and Henry Laurens and retired from business and sought to emulate the English landed gentry, often in order to pursue public careers. Indeed, establishing a seat in the country became something of a mania among wealthy gentlemen in the early Republic, especially among the New England gentry.[48]

When Morris, who had been one of the wealthiest merchants in America, became a United States senator from Pennsylvania in 1789, he had already shifted much of his capital into speculative land—something that seemed more respectable than trade—and was desperately trying to set himself up as a disinterested aristocrat. In the Senate he was especially anxious to win the approval of the South Carolina nabobs Pierce Butler and Ralph Izard, who seemed to have "a particular antipathy" to him because of his mercantile background. When the Carolina senators haughtily expressed their contempt for vulgar money-making, Morris—to the astonishment of listeners—did "likewise": he gave himself "Compliments on his manner & Conduct in life,... and the little respect he paid to the common Opinions of People." Like the classical republican aristocrat he aspired to be, he was proud of "his disregard of money." For Morris, as for other would-be aristocrats, disregarding money eventually proved to be fatal.[49]

Probably the most successful land speculator in these years was William Cooper, the father of the novelist James Fenimore Cooper. In the mid-1780s William Cooper and a partner bought up shares in a defunct land company that claimed tens of thousands of acres in the Otsego area in upstate New York. The legalities were incredibly complicated, and Cooper hired the best lawyer in New York, Alexander Hamilton, to untangle them. Before other claimants could act, Cooper began selling off the land to settlers and speculators and promoting development of the town he called Cooperstown. Every step of the way he gambled, risked all, and won. By the early 1790s he had become not only the richest man in Otsego County but also an international celebrity whose advice on the sale and settlement of frontier land was sought by aspiring speculators from as far away as Holland and France.

48. Tamara Platkins Thornton, *Cultivating Gentlemen: The Meaning of Country Life Among the Boston Elite, 1785–1860* (New Haven, 1989), 15–56.
49. H. E. Scudder, ed., *Recollections of Samuel Breck* (Philadelphia, 1877), 203; *Diary of Maclay*, 48, 73–74, 134.

Cooper's timing was perfect. In the aftermath of the Revolution people were ready to move to better themselves, particularly the Yankees of New England, where a rapidly increasing population made land more and more scarce and expensive. At the same time, the defeat of the British and their Iroquois allies forced the Indians westward or into Canada. This turned upstate New York into one of the fastest growing areas of the country. And so the settlers in the Otsego region increased in number and prospered, and they did so in no small part because of Cooper's particular methods of development.

The secret of Cooper's success as a land developer was to build up a critical mass of settlers as quickly as possible and to promote their enterprise. Unlike other speculative landlords, Cooper made available all of his best land at once and sold it at modest prices with long-term credit and as freeholds, not as tenancies, in order to get the settlers to work as hard as they could on land they owned outright. At the same time, he realized that he could not be an absentee landlord. He knew that he needed to live among his settlers, to patronize and encourage them, and to work to develop saleable products and their access to markets. Cooper's idea of development was to tap into each settler's own interest in improving himself and make that self-interest redound to the community's interest and his own. By "the simple measure of letting things take their own course," he said, "I find my interest and that of the whole community promoted."[50]

Cooper was not the only Federalist in the 1790s who sought to secure his social position by acquiring proprietary wealth in land. Some, like Rufus Putnam, James Mitchell Varnum, and the other Ohio Company associates from New England who in 1788 established Marietta at the confluence of the Muskingum and Ohio rivers, sought to escape from Eastern democracy and dreamed of creating civilized landed empires in the West. Others, like Henry Knox, secretary of war, and James Wilson, associate justice of the Supreme Court, remained in the cities of the East and simply speculated in land. Most of these land speculators had the same hopes as the federal government for the gradual, piecemeal, and regulated settlement of the West. Even if the speculators sold some of their land for low prices, they counted on subsequent settlers slowly filling in the territory surrounding the land they retained, which would raise its value and bring them the promised returns on their investments.

Everything was built on illusions. Most of the people moving west ignored the government's plans for neat and orderly settlement. They shunned the speculators' lands and refused to buy land at the expensive

---

50. Alan Taylor, *William Cooper's Town: Power and Persuasion on the Frontier of the Early American Republic* (New York, 1995), 101.

prices at which it was offered. In 1785 a defiant spokesman for the Ohio squatters declared that "all mankind...have an undoubted right to pass into every vacant country, and there to form their constitution, and that...Congress is not empowered to forbid them, neither is Congress empowered...to make any sale of the uninhabited lands to pay the public debt."[51] In desperation, the speculators lowered their prices, but because of rumors that Congress would soon be selling land in Ohio at twenty-five cents an acre, the settlers continually held out for better terms. By the early 1790s Symmes complained that the settlers in Ohio laughed in his face when he asked them for a dollar an acre for first-rate land. Symmes especially blamed "many land jobbers from Kentucky" who, instead of paying him, only made plans for "selling what they never had any intention of making their own." When he fell behind in his payments to the government, Symmes eventually had to give back much of the land he had purchased.[52]

The Scioto Company ended even more disastrously. The company was not interested in settlement but in speculation. It sent the poet Joel Barlow to France to sell land claims to French speculators who presumably would assume all the cost and risks of settlement. Barlow turned for help to an unscrupulous Englishmen who not only sold rights to land in the Ohio Valley that the company did not actually own but sold them to French artisans ill-equipped to be farmers. Five to six hundred French immigrants in 1790 eventually established a miserable settlement they called Gallipolis on the Ohio River almost fifty miles southwest of Marietta. Disease and Indians killed off or drove away most of the French settlers, and by 1806 there were only sixteen families remaining from the original immigrants. The Scioto Company itself had collapsed in 1792.

Both the government and the speculators misunderstood the settlers and the West. The speculators tended to borrow heavily, overextending themselves in the expectation of quicker returns from land sales than was possible. Because of Indian hostilities, there were never enough settlers willing to pay for land they could have for free. Congress tried sending troops to the Ohio Valley to burn the squatters' settlements, but the settlers simply rebuilt once the soldiers had left. To President Washington it

51. Alan Taylor, "Land and Liberty on the Post-Revolutionary Frontier," in David Thomas Konig, ed., *Devising Liberty: Preserving and Creating Freedom in the New American Republic* (Stanford, 1995), 89.

52. Timothy J. Shannon, "'This Unpleasant Business': The Transformation of Land Speculation in the Ohio Country, 1787–1820," in Jeffery P. Brown and Andrew R. L. Cayton, eds., *The Pursuit of Public Power: Political Culture in Ohio, 1787–1861* (Kent, OH, 1994), 23; Horsman, *Frontier in the Formative Years*, 42.

soon became clear that "anything short of a Chinese wall, or a line of troops" would not be enough to stop the swarming settlers.[53] Not only did the settlers squat on land they did not own, but they moved irregularly, chaotically, and unevenly, jumping from place to place, leaving huge chunks of unsettled land behind them. They refused to live in organized communities, but instead roamed and rambled like the Indians whose treaty rights they continually violated. Their isolated and scattered settlements tended to make them vulnerable to Indian raids, which in turn incited white retaliation. These cycles of Indian-settler violence drenched the West in blood.

Congress eventually realized that the kinds of respectable, law-abiding, and productive settlers it wanted would not be attracted to the West unless there was peace with the Indians and law and order in the territories. The original plans for colonial governments in the West expressed in the Ordinance of 1784 had left the settlers to govern themselves. But self-government in the West was no more orderly and no more free of self-interest than it was within the several states. Although Washington and other Eastern gentry often called these disorderly settlers "adventurers" and "banditti," the settlers were actually not much different in character from all those common folk whose ambitions, self-interestedness, and democratic excesses had caused problems in the state legislatures in the 1780s.

Just as gentry up and down the continent sought in the Constitution of 1787 a remedy for localist democratic excesses in the states, so too did gentry in the Congress seek some sort of solution for the localist democratic excesses in the West. As Richard Henry Lee, a Virginian much involved with congressional plans for the West, pointed out, something had to be done "for the security of property" in the West because "the greater part of those who go there" were "uninformed and perhaps licentious people."[54]

In 1787 the Confederation Congress concluded, first, that the number of states to be carved out of the Northwest would have to be reduced to not more than five but not fewer than three, which inevitably meant that each state would be larger than those Jefferson had proposed in 1784. But, more important, Congress realized that it would have to create what one congressman called "a strong-toned government" to discipline the disorderly populace of the West. At the same time, it would have to provide for a gradual process by which settlements could grow into states. The result was the Northwest Ordinance of 1787.

53. Richard White, *The Middle Ground: Indians, Empires, and Republics in the Great Lakes Region, 1650–1815* (Cambridge, UK, 1991), 419; Robert Kagen, *Dangerous Nation* (New York, 2006), 74.
54. Cayton, *Frontier Republic*, 25.

Apart from winning the War of Independence, this ordinance was the greatest accomplishment of the Confederation Congress. It created an entirely new notion of empire and at a stroke solved the problem of relating colonial dependencies to the central authority that Great Britain had been unable to solve in the 1760s and 1770s.

When the monarchies of early modern Europe claimed new dominions by conquest or colonization, they inevitably considered their new provincial additions as permanently peripheral and inferior to the metropolitan center of the realm. But the Northwest Ordinance, which became the model for the development of much of the Southwest, promised an end to such permanent second-class colonies. It guaranteed to the settlers basic legal and political rights and set forth the unprecedented principle that new states of the American empire settled in the West would enter the Union "on an equal footing with the original States, in all respects whatsoever." Settlers could leave the older states with the assurances that they were not losing their political liberties and that they would be allowed eventually to form new republics as sovereign and independent as the other older states of the Union. With such a principle there was presumably no limit to the westward expansion of the empire of the United States.[55]

Of course, this empire had little or no place for the Indian. Although Congress promised that "the utmost good faith shall always be observed towards the Indians, [and that] their lands and property shall never be taken from them without their consent," the ordinance itself took for granted that the destiny of the Northwest belonged with white American settlers.

These new Western settlements, the congressional leaders believed, would have to be prepared for eventual statehood in stages. In the initial stage of settlement each of the territories was to be governed dictatorially by a federally appointed governor, a secretary, and three judges. Only when the population of the territory reached five thousand would a representative assembly with a very restricted suffrage be permitted. Even then the governor was given an absolute veto over legislation and could prorogue or dissolve the assembly at will. Only when a territory attained a population of sixty thousand could it be admitted to statehood.

Despite its progressive promises, the Northwest Ordinance was actually quite reactionary and anti-populist. Its proposal for garrison governments with authoritarian leadership for the new Western colonies resembled nothing so much as those failed seventeenth-century English efforts at establishing military governments over the obstreperous colonists.

55. Hinderaker, *Elusive Empires*, 231; Peter S. Onuf, *Statehood and Union: A History of the Northwest Ordinance* (Bloomington, IN, 1987), 58–66.

The ordinance was in fact an indication of just how much of a problem democracy had become in the 1780s and how fearful Eastern leaders had become of the unruly Westerners.

THE NEARLY ONE HUNDRED THOUSAND Indians who occupied the trans-Appalachian West had very different ideas from the white Americans about how the land ought to be used.[56] Nothing preoccupied the Federalist administration more than having to deal with these native peoples.

At the end of the seventeenth century perhaps as many as 1.4 million Indians had inhabited the North American continent, with a quarter of a million or so occupying the territory east of the Mississippi; but since that time disease and warfare had drastically reduced their numbers.[57] By the end of the eighteenth century most of the Indians in New England seemed to have vanished; many had intermarried with whites or blacks and had lost much of their tribal identity. In New York many Indians had migrated into Canada, and only remnants were left in the state from the once formidable Six Nations of the Iroquois.[58] But in the Northwest there remained a variety of native peoples who were willing to fight to preserve their hunting grounds and their way of life. These included Delawares and Wyandots in what is now eastern and central Ohio, Shawnees in western Ohio and northern Indiana, Mingos, who had villages at Sandusky, and the great northern tribes of Ottawa and Chippewa, some of whom hunted south of Lake Erie. Farther west along the Wabash River were Miami bands of Wea and Piankashaw, and, finally, there were various tribes of the Illinois in Indiana. On the Southern frontiers the Indian presence was even more formidable. From the Carolinas to the Yazoo River were some fourteen thousand warriors, mainly Cherokees, Creeks, Choctaws, and Chickasaws.

For decades the colonists had continually tried to draw lines between themselves and the Indians, offering them bribes to surrender more and more of their lands as they relentlessly pushed them westward.

---

56. Estimates of Indian populations are notoriously difficult. In 1789 Secretary of War Knox estimated there were 19,000 Indian warriors in the West, 14,000 of them south and 5,000 north of the Ohio. He estimated that there were three women, children, and older persons for every warrior, thus a total of 76,000. His estimate of nonwarriors may be too low. Knox to GW, 15 June 1789, *Papers of Washington: Presidential Ser.*, 2: 494.

57. Peter Wood, "From Atlantic History to a Continental Approach," in Jack P. Greene and Philip D. Morgan, eds., *Atlantic History: A Critical Appraisal* (New York, 2009), 422.

58. Alan Taylor, *The Divided Ground: Indians, Settlers, and the Northern Borderland of the American Revolution* (New York, 2006).

Many of these native peoples believed that they could move no further and were increasingly determined to fight to protect their dwindling hunting grounds. Over the succeeding decades the Indians, with the support of the borderland European powers of Great Britain and Spain, sought to resist the persistent expansion westward of white Americans.[59]

Although many whites admired the Indians for their freedom, the Anglo-American idea of liberty and independence was very different from theirs. Where ordinary white American men conceived of freedom in terms of owning their own plot of cultivated agricultural land, Indian males saw liberty in terms of their ability to roam and hunt at will. Like many American gentry, these Indian warriors did not believe they should actually work tilling fields. They thought, as one missionary to the Oneida reported in 1796, that "to labour in cultivating the Earth is degrading to the character of Man 'who (they say) was made for War & hunting & holding councils & that Squaws & hedge-hogs are made to scratch the ground.'" Native women in fact performed a wide variety of tasks. They grew vegetables, gathered nuts and berries, prepared meat, cut firewood, carried water, made shoes and clothing, and often erected and furnished their houses. So backbreaking was the labor the native women performed for their families that white Americans could only conclude that Indian women were virtual slaves. Indeed, the notion of women farming seemed so unnatural to many European Americans that Northerners at least had a hard time acknowledging that the Indians practiced any agriculture at all.[60]

Ultimately, this denial that the Indians actually cultivated the land became the white Americans' justification for taking it from them. Drawing from the legal thinking of the eighteenth-century theorist Emmerich de Vattel, political leaders maintained that no people had a right to land that they did not farm. This was one of the most important of the cultural misunderstandings that divided white Americans from the native peoples. Whites expected Indians to become farmers, that is, to move to another

---

59. See Kohn, *Eagle and Sword*, 92.
60. Taylor, "Land and Liberty on the Post-Revolutionary Frontier," in Konig, ed., *Devising Liberty*, 81–108; Theda Perdue, "Native Women in the Early Republic: Old World Perceptions, New World Realities," and Daniel H. Unser Jr., "Iroquois Livelihood and Jeffersonian Agrarianism: Reaching Behind the Models and Metaphors," in Frederick E. Hoxie et al., eds., *Native Americans and the Early Republic* (Charlottesville, 1999), 103–22, 200–225; Lucy Eldersveld Murphy, "To Live Among Us: Accommodation, Gender, and Conflict in the Western Great Lakes Region, 1760–1832," in Andrew R. L. Cayton and Fredrika J. Teute, eds., *Contact Points: American Frontiers from the Mohawk Valley to the Mississippi, 1750–1830* (Chapel Hill, 1998), 270–303.

stage in the process of social development and become civilized, or to get out of the way of the white settlers.[61]

The achievement of American independence from Great Britain had been a disaster for the Indians. Many of the tribes in the Northwest and Southwest had allied with the British, and with the peace treaty they discovered that Great Britain had ceded sovereignty over their land to the United States. As one Wea speaker complained to their British ally upon learning of the treaty, "In endeavouring to assist you, it seems we have wrought our own ruin."[62] Because so many of the Indians had fought on the side of the British, Americans tended to regard as enemies even those Indians who had been their allies during the Revolution. By the 1780s many Western Americans shared the expectation of the Indian fighter George Rogers Clark that all the Indians would eventually be eliminated. A common view was, as one military toast on the frontier put it, "Civilization or death to all American savages."[63]

Conceiving itself as a composite of different peoples, the British Empire could somehow accommodate the existence of the Indians within its territory. But the new American Republic was different: it contained only citizens who presumably were all equal to one another. Since the United States could scarcely imagine the Indians as citizens equal to all other American citizens, it had to regard the various Indian peoples as members of foreign nations with which treaties had to be negotiated. Of course, most of the Indians themselves had no desire to become citizens of the American Republic.

In the 1780s the Confederation government had sought to assume control of Indian affairs and to establish peaceful relations with the Indians. Although the Confederation Congress repeatedly spoke of its desire to be just and fair with the Indians, it considered them as conquered nations. In several treaties between the Confederation government and some of the various nations or tribes in the mid-1780s, the United States attempted to establish more or less fixed boundary lines between whites and Indians in return for Indian cessions of rights to land. In the Southwest in a series of treaties with the Cherokees, Choctaws, and Chickasaws at Hopewell, South Carolina, in 1785–1786, the Confederation attempted to fix boundaries in order to head off hostilities between the Indians and the states of North Carolina and Georgia. In treaties dealing with the Northwest Territory the Indians abandoned their rights to what is now eastern and

61. Perdue, "Native Women in the Early Republic," in Hoxie et al., eds., *Native Americans and the Early Republic*, 115–19.
62. White, *Middle Ground*, 408.
63. Bernard W. Sheehan, "The Indian Problem in the Northwest: From Conquest to Philanthropy," in Hoffman and Albert, eds., *Launching the 'Extended Republic,'* 191.

southern Ohio. In the treaty of Fort Stanwix in 1784 spokesmen for the Six Nations ceded all their claims to land west of Niagara. At Fort McIntosh on the Ohio in 1785 delegates from the Delaware, Wyandot, Chippewa, and Ottawa agreed to be confined north of the Ohio River. And at Fort Finney in 1786 representatives of the Shawnee ceded their rights to lands east of the Great Miami River. Believing that America owned the lands by right of conquest, the United States offered the Indians no compensation for the ceded lands.

The Confederation government, however, was weak, and the states could ignore its treaties. Not only did the states go ahead and make their own agreements with the Indians, but white settlers and squatters continued to move onto lands presumably reserved for the native peoples. By 1787 many of the Indians had repudiated the treaties some of their members had been compelled to sign and attempted to form loose confederations in order to resist the white advance. At the same time, they continued to raid white settlements up and down the frontier.

With the creation of the new federal government in 1789 President Washington and Secretary of War Henry Knox were determined to change the government's policy in the West. Not only were growing numbers of scattered squatter communities north of the Ohio undermining the government's plans for gradual and well-regulated settlement of the West, but they were also stirring up warfare with the Indians into which the federal government would inevitably be drawn. And a general war with the Indians would be both inhumane and costly.

As early as 1783 Washington had noted that there was "nothing to be obtained by an Indian War but the soil they live on and this can be had by purchase at less expense."[64] Since peace in the West seemed essential to getting the new nation on its feet, the Washington administration aimed to return to the colonial practice of purchasing the Indians' land instead of claiming it by right of conquest. At the same time, the administration sought to save the Indians in the West from the kind of extinction that seemed to have occurred with most Indians in the East.

The administration's intentions could scarcely have been more enlightened—at least for the enlightened eighteenth century. "The Indians being the prior occupants possess the right of the Soil," declared Knox, who assumed responsibility for Indian affairs because Secretary of State Jefferson had not yet arrived from Paris. "It cannot be taken from them unless by their free consent, or by the right of Conquest in case of a just War—To dispossess them on any other principle would be a gross violation of the fundamental Laws of Nature and of that distributive justice

64. Kohn, *Eagle and Sword*, 94.

which is the glory of a nation." Outright coercion and the elimination of the natives by war, said Knox, would be prohibitively expensive, and "the blood and injustice" involved "would stain the character of the nation." Thus, he concluded, "both policy and justice unite" in dictating negotiation, not war, between the United States and the Indians.[65] The various tribes should be treated as foreign nations, and not as subjects of any particular state. The states, said Knox, had rights to land within their existing boundaries, but only the federal government could acquire the land of the Western territories and negotiate "treaties on the execution or violation of which depend peace or war." With such treaties the United States could both compensate the Indians for the lands they gave up and protect them in the lands they still retained.[66]

But the administration aimed to do more. Knox proposed a radical policy, which he hoped would prevent the Western Indians from vanishing. "How different would be the sensations of a philosophic mind to reflect that instead of exterminating a part of the human race by our modes of population," the American colonists had behaved differently. If only we white Americans "had imparted our Knowledge of cultivation, and the arts, to the Aboriginals of the Country," then the "future life and happiness" of the Indians might have been "preserved and extended." But in the past we thought it "impracticable to civilize the Indians of North America," an opinion, Knox added, "probably more convenient than just." Americans now lived in an enlightened age, however, and "the civilization of the Indians," though difficult, could be achieved. To deny the possibility, said Knox, was to suppose that the Indians' character was incapable of amelioration — "a supposition entirely contradicted by the progress of society from the barbarous ages to its present degree of perfection."[67]

In other words, the Indians could save themselves by giving up their culture and becoming farmers like the whites. The progress of history, moving to a higher stage of civilization, demanded it. You can be taught, Knox informed the Indians, "to cultivate the earth, and raise corn; to raise oxen, sheep, and other domestic animals; to build comfortable houses, and to educate your children." Thus the "savages" might be able to leap right into the third stage of social development. If they did not abandon hunting and gathering and become civilized, explained General Benjamin Lincoln of Massachusetts, they would "dwindle and moulder away, from causes perhaps imperceptible to us, until the whole race shall

65. Knox to GW, 15 June 1789, *Papers of Washington, Presidential Ser.*, 2: 491.
66. Knox to Washington, 7 July 1789, *Papers of Washington: Presidential Ser.*, 3: 134–41.
67. Knox to Washington, 7 July 1789, *Papers of Washington: Presidential Ser.*, 3: 134–41.

become extinct." American civilization "from its very nature must operate to the extirpation of barbarism.... Civilized and uncivilized people cannot live in the same territory, or even in the same neighborhood."[68]

Although by today's standards it was a perverse and ethnocentric policy, by the most liberal standards of the eighteenth century it was the only realistic alternative to the Indians' outright removal or destruction. For better or for worse, this was the policy that governed the best and most philanthropic of American thinking about the Indians for the next generation.

The first Indian treaty to be ratified by the U.S. Senate was negotiated with a Creek chief named Alexander McGillivray, an educated "half-breed" who was as worldly and wily as anyone on the frontier. When McGillivray and twenty-six chiefs arrived in New York in the summer of 1790 they were greeted with the largest crowd since the president's inauguration. Weeks of official dinners and ceremonies more lavish than anything European diplomats ever received were followed by an elaborate signing ceremony. According to an account kept by the feminist writer Judith Sargent Murray, the Creek chiefs, who had entered Federal Hall with "shrieks and yells,... ardently expressed their satisfaction" with the treaty by seizing the elbow of the president, who was dressed "in rich vestments of purple satin," and entwining their arms with his.

In the treaty the Creeks ceded two-thirds of the land claimed by Georgia but received in return a federal guarantee of sovereign control of the rest. In secret clauses of the treaty McGillivray received a trade monopoly and a position as agent of the United States with the rank of brigadier general in the U.S. Army and an annual salary of $1,200. Washington backed up the treaty with a proclamation forbidding any encroachment on the Creeks' territory. But a corrupt Georgia legislature undid both the president's proclamation and the Treaty of New York. As early as January 1790, six months before the treaty was signed, it had announced the sale to speculators, calling themselves the Yazoo companies, of over fifteen million acres of land belonging to the Creeks. Before the bribed Georgia legislators were done doling out many more millions of acres, which included most of present-day Alabama and Mississippi, they had created the greatest real estate scandal in American history. The consequences of this outrageous land deal reverberated through the next three presidential administrations.[69]

---

68. Knox to the Northwestern Indians, 4 Apr. 1792, in Reginald Horsman, "The Indian Policy of an 'Empire for Liberty,'" in Hoxie et al., eds., *Native Americans and the Early Republic*, 45–46; Taylor, *Divided Ground*, 278, 240.

69. Washington to the U.S. Senate, 4 Aug. 1790, Proclamation, 14 Aug. 1790, *Papers of Washington, Presidential Ser.*, 6: 188–96, 248–54; Joseph J. Ellis, *American Creation: Triumphs and Tragedies at the Founding of the Republic* (New York, 2007), 149–56.

The Yazoo land sale was a barefaced assertion of state sovereignty that undermined both the treaty with the Creeks and the federal government's claim to exercise sole authority over Indian affairs. Indeed, the administration's high-minded Indian policy was in shambles. Although the policy had the advantage of easing the consciences of those who supported it, it was totally out of touch with the realities on the Western frontier. White settlers in the West had no intention of accommodating the Indians, and they continued to push westward by the tens of thousands. As hostilities with the native peoples became increasingly fierce, the settlers called on the federal government for protection. Washington realized that unless the government stepped in with military force to stop the indiscriminate raiding and counter-raiding by whites and Indians, the entire West, especially the Northwest, would erupt in a general Indian war.

The army had been involved in the Northwest from the beginning; indeed, it alone represented the authority of the United States government in the West during the 1780s. Under the command of Josiah Harmar of Pennsylvania, troops had been sent to the area to build forts and drive off squatters with the hope of avoiding hostilities with the Indians. But in 1790 continued pressure from settlers finally compelled the federal government to authorize a presumably limited punitive expedition against some of the renegade Indians northwest of the Ohio. General Harmar led a force of some three hundred regulars and twelve hundred militia northward from Fort Washington (present-day Cincinnati) to attack Indian villages in the area of what is now Fort Wayne. Although the Americans burned Miami and Shawnee villages and killed two hundred Indians, they lost an equal number of men and were forced to retreat. This show of force by the United States had proved embarrassing, and the administration was determined not to rely on militia to the same extent again.

This initial failure increased the pressure on the government to try once more to convince the Indians of the futility of resistance. In 1791 General Arthur St. Clair, the territorial governor of the Northwest, led a motley and contentious collection of over fourteen hundred regulars, militia, and levies from Fort Washington against the Miami villages. It took St. Clair over a month to move one hundred miles northward, and on November 4, 1791, he and his troops were surprised and overwhelmed by about a thousand Indians from various tribes commanded by Miami chieftain Little Turtle, one of the most impressive Indian leaders of the period. The Americans suffered nearly a thousand casualties, including over six hundred killed. To mock the Americans' hunger for their land, the Indians stuffed the dead soldiers' mouths with soil. Because second-in-command General Richard Butler had once told the Indians that "this country belongs to the United States," they smashed his skull, cut up his heart into pieces for every tribe that had participated in the battle, and left his corpse to be eaten by animals. St. Clair's defeat was the worst the Indians ever inflicted on the U.S. Army in its entire history.[70]

This humiliation convinced the administration that partial remedies would no longer work in pacifying the Indians. The government overhauled the War Department, doubled the military budget, and created the professional standing army of five thousand regulars that many Federalists had long wanted. At the same time, the government sought to negotiate a new treaty with the Indians.

Encouraged by the British in Canada, who wanted a neutral barrier state erected in the Northwest, the Indians refused to accept any white settlements north of the Ohio River, which had been the declared boundary of Quebec in 1774, and the negotiations broke down. The Indians told the American negotiators that all they wanted was "a small part of our once great country.... Look back, and review the lands from whence we have been driven to this spot. We can retreat no farther, ... and we have therefore resolved to leave our bones in this small space to which we are now confined."[71] The British continued to supply the Indians with food and arms, rebuilt their old Fort Miami near the rapids of the Maumee River, near what is now Toledo in northwest Ohio, and urged the Indians to resist the Americans with force.

In the meantime the U.S. Army had been reorganized, renamed the Legion, and placed under the command of General Anthony Wayne, a former Revolutionary officer. Because Wayne was noted for his impetuosity ("Brave and nothing else," said Jefferson, the kind of man who might "run his head against a wall where success was both impossible and useless"), his appointment in 1792 was controversial.[72] But "Mad" Anthony Wayne was determined to vindicate President Washington's faith in him. Over the next two years he trained, disciplined, and inspired his troops and turned them into a battle-ready fighting force. In the summer of 1794 Wayne and his army of two thousand regulars and fifteen hundred Kentucky volunteers moved northward toward the newly constructed British Fort Miami, with instructions from Knox to "dislodge" the British garrison if necessary, but only if "it shall promise complete success."[73] After repulsing several Indian attacks in June 1794, Wayne's Legionnaires moved northward and on August 20 soundly defeated a force of over a thousand Indians at Fallen

---

70. Andrew R. L. Cayton, "'Noble Actors' upon 'the Theatre of Honour': Power and Civility in the Treaty of Greenville," in Cayton and Teute, eds., *Contact Points*, 254–55; Taylor, *Divided Ground*, 259.
71. Horsman, *Frontier in the Formative Years*, 45.
72. Kohn, *Eagle and Sword*, 125
73. Cayton, "'Separate Interests' and the Nation-State," 156.

Timbers, near present-day Toledo. Although Wayne refrained from attacking Fort Miami, he burned and pillaged Indian towns, crops, and British storehouses around the post. The British, unwilling to provoke a war with the United States, did nothing to aid their Indian allies.

Wayne's victory broke Indian resistance in the Northwest and destroyed British influence over the Indians, at least until the eve of the War of 1812. The Indians had no alternative but to seek peace, and in August 1795 in the Treaty of Greenville they ceded to the United States their lands in what is now southern and eastern Ohio, together with a strip of southeastern Indiana. Even within the lands the Indians retained, the Americans gained the rights to erect posts and to pass freely. The Indians in the Northwest acknowledged that they were to be dependent on "no other power whatever" except the United States, which the Wyandot Tarhe said they must from now on call "our father." As children, Tarhe told his fellow Indians, they were to be "obedient to our father; ever listen to him when he speaks to you, and follow his advice." But of course the father had patriarchal obligations as well: "Should any of your children come to you crying and in distress, have pity on them, and relieve their wants." By bestowing the name of "father" on the United States, some of the Indians assumed that the Americans were taking on the paternalistic role that the French and British had played. In this respect the Indians were no freer of illusions than America's white leaders.[74]

The outcome at Fallen Timbers made inevitable the British evacuation of the Northwest posts they had been occupying since the Revolution. In the treaty negotiated by John Jay in 1794 and ratified in 1795 Britain finally agreed to get out of American territory. The sending of Jay to England in turn frightened the Spanish with the possibility that the British and the Americans might collaborate to threaten Spanish possessions in the New World. Consequently, Spain suddenly decided to reach a long-delayed agreement with the United States. Washington sent to Spain Thomas Pinckney of South Carolina, who was serving as the American minister to Great Britain. In the treaty that Pinckney signed at San Lorenzo on October 27, 1794, Spain finally recognized American claims to the Florida boundary of the United States at the 31st parallel and to the free navigation of the Mississippi, including the right of Americans to deposit their goods at New Orleans. Both the controversial Jay's Treaty and Pinckney's Treaty thus secured the territorial integrity of the United

---

74. R. Douglas Hurt, *The Ohio Frontier: Crucible of the Old Northwest, 1720–1830* (Bloomington, IN, 1996), 139; Richard White, "The Fictions of Patriarchy: Indians and Whites in the Early Republic," in Hoxie et al., eds., *Native Americans and the Early Republic*, 82–83; Cayton, "'Noble Actors' upon 'the Theatre of Honour,'" in Cayton and Teute, eds., *Contact Points*, 255–69.

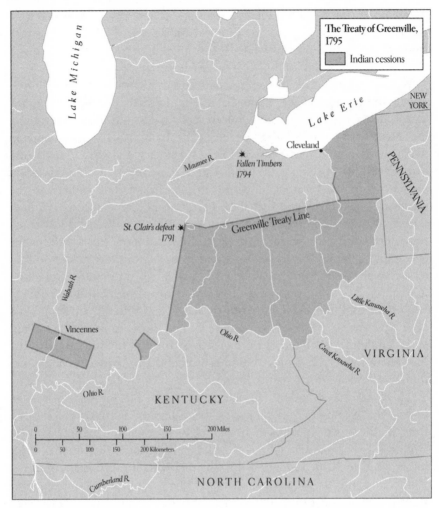

The Treaty of Greenville

States in a way the diplomacy of the Confederation had been unable to do. At the same time, the new federal government's actions strengthened the national loyalties of a region of the country that was intensely localist in outlook and that earlier had flirted with separation from the United States.

These achievements were the result in no small measure of the willingness of the Federalist government to create an army in the Northwest and to use it against the Indians. Not only did the U.S. Army's presence help to defend American settlements in the area, but it also contributed greatly to the process of integrating these Northwestern settlements into the nation. The army secured American land claims, protected new towns, developed communication and transportation networks, and provided cash and a reliable local market for the settlers' produce in the Northwest—all in all acting as an effective agent for an expansive new American empire that remained loyal to the national government in the East.[75]

That the U.S. Army was not similarly established in the Southwest profoundly affected the different development and loyalties of that region. Although the governor of the Southwest Territory, William Blount, pleaded with the national government for troops to deal with the Creeks and Cherokees, support was minimal. Whereas the Northwest had nearly three thousand regular federal troops by 1794, the Southwest possessed only two U.S. posts with seventy-five soldiers. With federal troops busy trying to put down the Indians in the Northwest, Secretary of War Knox advised Blount to negotiate treaties and pursue a strictly defensive policy toward the Southern Indians. But the settlers kept encroaching on the Indians' lands, usually in violation of treaties, and the Indians fought back. Settlers in Tennessee like Andrew Jackson were bitter at the federal government's neglect and its constant harping on the need to negotiate treaties with the Indians. "Treaties," declared Jackson in 1794, "answer No other Purpose than opening an Easy door for the Indians to pass through to Butcher our citizens." He warned that unless the federal government gave more aid to the Southwest the region would eventually have to separate "or seek a protection from some other Source than the present." Even after Tennessee was admitted to the Union in 1796, bitterness against the United States remained.[76]

ANTHONY WAYNE HAD TOLD James Madison as early as 1789 that there was no substitute for military victory in establishing the "Dignity, wealth, and Power" of the United States government, and events since that time had convinced many Federalists that Wayne was absolutely right. If only the United States had defeated the Indians earlier, said Judge Rufus Putnam in August 1794, it "would have given a weight and dignity to the Federal Government that would have tended to check the licentiousness and opposition to Government unfavorable in this

75. Cayton, "'Separate Interests' and the Nation-State," 53–54; Hinderaker, *Elusive Empires*, 244.
76. Robert V. Remini, *Andrew Jackson and His Indian Wars* (New York, 2001), 33; Cayton, "'Separate Interests' and the Nation-State," 61–65.

country."[77] It might even have prevented the events that became known as the Whiskey Rebellion.

In 1794 angry farmers in four counties of western Pennsylvania defied a federal excise tax on whiskey, terrorized the excise officers, robbed the mail, and closed the federal courts. Before everything was over, not only had some seven thousand western Pennsylvanians marched against the town of Pittsburgh and threatened its residents and the federal arsenal there, but rioting against the excise tax on whiskey had spread to the back-countries of Virginia and Maryland.

This so-called Whiskey Rebellion was the most serious domestic crisis the Washington administration had to face. It came at a frightening time. With the French Revolution creating havoc all over Europe and even threatening to spread to America, the Federalists came to fear that this insurrection in the West might actually lead to the overturning of America's government and the destruction of the Union. Although it was the largest incident of armed resistance to federal authority between the adoption of the Constitution and the Civil War, it was not the only such incident of rural insurgency; indeed, in the two decades following the Revolution the backcountry of states up and down the continent repeatedly erupted in protest, usually over shortages of money and credit among commercially minded farmers who needed both in order to carry on trade.[78]

The immediate sources of the uprising of 1794 lay in the decision of the Washington administration in 1790 to levy an excise tax on spirits distilled within the United States. Hamilton calculated that duties on foreign imports alone would not be sufficient to cover the revenue needs of his financial program and that some sort of additional tax would be necessary. The Constitution granted the federal government the authority to levy excise taxes, but many Americans bitterly resented such internal taxes, especially one levied by a far-removed central government. Customs duties were one thing; excise taxes were quite another. Customs duties were indirect taxes, paid at the ports on imported goods, often on luxuries. Most consumers were scarcely aware they were paying such taxes, blended as they were in the price of the goods. But payers of excise taxes knew only too well the burden of the tax. British on both sides of the

77. Cayton, "'Separate Interests' and the Nation-State," 53.
78. Terry Bouton, "A Road Closed: Rural Insurgency in Post-Independence Pennsylvania," *JAH*, 87 (2000), 855–87; Terry Bouton, *Taming Democracy: "The People," the Founders, and the Troubled Ending of the American Revolution* (New York, 2007); Alan Taylor, *Liberty Men and Great Proprietors: The Revolutionary Settlement on the Maine Frontier, 1760–1820* (Chapel Hill, 1990).

Atlantic had long resisted what the Continental Congress in 1775 called "the most odious of taxes."[79]

During the debate over the Constitution the Anti-Federalists had warned that granting the federal government the power to levy such internal taxes would result in hordes of excise men and military enforcement. Indeed, so hated were excise taxes that the first Congress in 1790 voted down Hamilton's bill. But after a renewed effort in 1791, with physicians endorsing the tax on the grounds that it would cut down on Americans' excessive drinking of hard liquor, the excise finally passed. Even Madison admitted that he saw no other way of raising the needed revenue.

Since Hamilton in *Federalist* No. 12 had warned "that the genius of the people will ill brook the inquisitive and peremptory spirit of excise laws," he knew that opposition would be intense. Although he had "long since learned to hold popular opinion of no value," he could scarcely have predicted the firestorm of controversy the tax aroused.[80] One North Carolina congressman simply assumed that the tax would never be enforced in the western counties of his state. Senator Maclay of Pennsylvania was particularly angry at the excise bill's attempt to organize the collection districts without regard to state lines. Like many other opponents of the Federalists, Maclay believed that Hamilton and his cronies were bent on eventually eliminating the states and the excise tax was a pretext for doing just that. Others thought that excise was simply another device for creating new offices to feed the administration's patronage machine. Still others believed that the tax was designed to make the obstreperous Scotch-Irish distillers in the backcountry feel the presence of the federal government.

No doubt the allegiance of these Westerners to the federal government, indeed, to any government, was suspect, but with good reason. The frontier settlers were far removed from the centers of government and continually felt that Eastern authorities did not care about protecting them from the Indians or helping them market their crops. Since the Western farmers had difficulty getting their perishable grain to market, they had commonly resorted to distilling that grain into the much more portable and less perishable form of alcohol. Although whiskey produced for home

79. Thomas P. Slaughter, *The Whiskey Rebellion: Frontier Epilogue to the American Revolution* (New York, 1986), 98. See also William Hogeland, *The Whiskey Rebellion: George Washington, Alexander Hamilton, and the Frontier Rebels Who Challenged America's Newfound Sovereignty* (New York, 2006).

80. Leland D. Baldwin, *Whiskey Rebels: The Story of a Frontier Uprising* (Pittsburgh, 1939), 68.

consumption was exempt from the tax, whiskey had become a necessary form of money for the cash-strapped Western areas.

While some western Pennsylvanians prevented enforcement of the tax by tarring and feathering and terrorizing excise collectors, others channeled their anger into extralegal meetings of protest. They sent petitions to Congress, organized assemblies and committees of correspondence, condemned the excise tax for being as unjust and oppressive as the Stamp Act of 1765, and ostracized everyone who favored or obeyed the excise law. Although many of the leaders of the opposition to the excise tax were themselves wealthy holders of important county or state positions, they certainly felt poorer and less influential than those in the Federalist establishment. Their spokesmen charged that the federal government was dominated by "aristocrats," "mercenary merchants," and "moneyed men" who were out to reverse the Revolution and deprive the common farmers of America of their liberty.

Because violence and protests in 1791 and 1792 spread through the frontier areas of every state south of New York, the Federalists in the East thought that all order and authority were being challenged and the integrity of the Union itself was threatened. America now had representative republican governments, the "friends of order" said, and there was no longer any need for extra-legislative popular meetings and protests. The citizens' role in politics was simply to vote for their rulers and representatives and let those who knew better run the government. Allowing the "rabble" and the "ignorant herd" to exercise authority, the Federalists said, would lead only to disorder and licentiousness. By defying the excise law, the Westerners—those "busy and restless sons of anarchy"— were in fact attempting "to bring us back to those scenes of humiliation and distress from which the new Constitution has so wonderfully extricated us."[81]

Because the resistance of the western Pennsylvanians took place "in the state in which is the immediate seat of government," Hamilton singled out the Pennsylvania backcountry for enforcement of the excise. Besides, it was the only Western region in the country where some officials were trying to enforce the law. In the backcountries of the other states there was no support whatsoever for the tax. In Kentucky President Washington could not even get anyone to accept the position of United States attorney—the officer who would have to prosecute evaders of the law.[82] If a test of national authority had to be made, better that it be made

81. Slaughter, *Whiskey Rebellion*, 133–34, 135.
82. Mary K. B. Tachau, *Federal Courts in the Early Republic: Kentucky, 1789–1816* (Princeton, 1978), 70–71.

in Pennsylvania, where the elite was divided. And the Federalists believed that a test was needed. It was "absolutely necessary," said Hamilton, "that a decided experiment should without delay be made of the energy of the laws, and of the government to put them in execution."[83] Although President Washington was less eager than Hamilton to use force, he agreed to issue a proclamation in September 1792 condemning the Westerners' challenges to authority and threatening strict enforcement of the excise tax.

Despite continued violence and protest against the excise in western Pennsylvania, the government did nothing in 1793 to back up the president's proclamation. But in 1794 the government proposed new excise taxes on snuff and sugar that aroused a renewed interest in the whiskey tax. In February the president reissued a proclamation expressing the government's determination to enforce the law in the West. The national government was increasingly fearful that settlers in Kentucky and western Pennsylvania were on the verge of breaking up the Union—perhaps with the aid and encouragement of British officials in Canada. Hamilton thought leniency toward the tax evaders had gone on long enough, and he concluded that "there was no choice but to try the efficiency of the laws in prosecuting with vigour delinquents and Offenders."[84]

These efforts at enforcement led to more violence and the massing of six thousand men in the Pittsburgh area who put on a threatening display of armed force. In August President Washington responded with yet another proclamation expressing his intention to call out the militia to maintain law and order. It was no longer a matter of putting down riots and mobs; eighteenth-century leaders were used to dealing with temporary outbursts of the people and did not usually panic when confronted with them. But the long-standing resistance to the law by the four counties of western Pennsylvania seemed much more serious. The rebels were invoking the example of revolutionary France, which had recently executed its king and unleashed the dogs of war and terror. These western Pennsylvanians hoisted their own flag, set up mock guillotines, erected their own extralegal courts, and talked of marching on the federal garrison in Pittsburgh to seize weapons. Some frightened gentry thought the rebels were actually going to march on Philadelphia, the nation's capital. The insurrection, concluded Attorney General William Bradford in August 1794, was part of "a well formed and regular plan for weakening and perhaps overthrowing the General Government."[85]

83. Slaughter, *Whiskey Rebellion*, 121.
84. Slaughter, *Whiskey Rebellion*, 177; AH to GW, 5 Aug 1794, *Papers of Hamilton*, 17: 52.
85. Kohn, *Eagle and Sword*, 159.

Despite Hamilton's desire for the immediate use of force, Washington hesitated. Instead, he sent a peace commission to negotiate with the rebels. Only with its failure in late August 1794 did he issue orders for the raising of fifteen thousand militia troops drawn from the states of New Jersey, Pennsylvania, Maryland, and Virginia—an army larger than any he had commanded during the Revolution. This excessive show of force was essential, the president declared, because "we had given no testimony to the world of being able or willing to support our government and laws."[86]

In the face of this large army all resistance in the West collapsed. The army arrested several men and paraded twenty rebels back to Philadelphia. Of these, only two were convicted of treason, and both were pardoned by the president. "An insurrection was announced and proclaimed and armed against, and marched against," jibed Jefferson, "but could never be found."[87] Still, many Federalists were satisfied with the results. The rebellion was a test of the government's strength, and the government had been successful. As Hamilton said on behalf of many Federalists, "The insurrection will do us a great deal of good and add to the solidity of every thing in this country."[88] In fact, so much did the rebellion redound to the benefit of the national government that some thought the Federalists were behind the entire uprising. Madison had no doubt that if the rebellion had not been so quickly put down the Federalists would have made "a formidable attempt...to establish the principle that a standing army was necessary for *enforcing the laws*."[89]

To Washington and other Federalists the rebellion had been a close-run thing. Although it had been suppressed, the threat of upheaval and disunion and the spread of French revolutionary ideas remained. "Certain self-created societies" were stirring up trouble everywhere. The insurrection, the president declared in his angry message to Congress in November 1794, had been "fomented by combinations of men, who careless of consequences...have disseminated, from an ignorance or perversions of fact, suspicions, jealousies, and accusations, of the whole Government." Rarely had the president displayed so much of his infamous

86. John C. Miller, *The Federalist Era, 1789–1801* (New York, 1960), 158; GW, Sixth Annual Address to Congress, 19 Nov. 1794, in Fitzpatrick, ed., *Writings of Washington*, 34: 28–30.

87. Miller, *Federalist Era*, 159; TJ to James Monroe, 26 May 1795, *Papers of Jefferson*, 28: 359.

88. Kohn, *Eagle and Sword*, 170; AH to Angelica Church, 23 Oct. 1794, *Papers of Hamilton*, 17: 340.

89. JM to James Monroe, 4 Dec. 1794, *Papers of Madison*, 15: 405–7; Baldwin, *Whiskey Rebellion*, 112.

temper publicly before, but he was seriously unsettled by the disorder that seemed linked to the chaos taking place in Revolutionary France. Organized opposition groups calling themselves Republicans or Democratic-Republicans and affirming their fraternal affiliation with atheistic Revolutionary France were challenging governmental authority all over America.[90]

The Whiskey Rebellion turned out to be among the least of the problems facing the Washington administration.

90. GW, Sixth Annual Message to Congress, 19 Nov. 1794, *Washington: Writings*, 893, 888.

# 4

# The Emergence of the Jeffersonian Republican Party

Opposition to the Federalist program was slow to develop. Since the only alternative to the new national government seemed to be disunity and anarchy, Alexander Hamilton and the Federalists were initially able to build their system without great difficulty. Besides, no one as yet could conceive of a legitimate opposition to government. Parties were considered a symptom of disease in the body politic, signs of partiality and self-interestedness in opposition to the general good. Republics, which were dedicated to the commonwealth, could have no place for an opposition party.[1]

During the first year of the new government (1789–1790), James Madison acted as congressional leader of those who were eager to counteract Anti-Federalist sentiment. For a time Madison seemed to be everywhere at once, speaking in the Congress, promoting legislation, and writing speeches for both the president and Congress. Because of his trust in Washington, he initially believed in a strong and independent executive. In the Congress he argued for the president's exclusive power to remove executive officials and worked to create a Treasury Department with a single head rather than a board that some congressmen favored.[2]

Hamilton in January 1790 was ready to present his first report to Congress. Fearful of being overawed by Hamilton's expertise, Congress requested that Hamilton's Report on the Public Credit be submitted in writing.

Once congressmen began to grasp the implications of the report, opposition quickly arose, especially to Hamilton's proposed handling of the domestic debt. Hamilton was not surprised. He knew that state and local interests would resist all efforts to strengthen national authority. But he was startled that his severest critic in the House of Representatives was his

---

1. Richard Hofstadter, *The Idea of a Party System: The Rise of Legitimate Opposition in the United States, 1780–1840* (Berkeley, 1969).
2. Stuart Leibiger, *Founding Friendship: George Washington, James Madison, and the Creation of the American Republic* (Charlottesville, 1999).

longtime ally James Madison. He and Madison had collaborated closely in the 1780s and had even written most of *The Federalist* together. Hamilton had thought that Madison desired a strong national government as much as he did. But now Madison seemed to be changing.

Madison had been a nationalist in the 1780s, but not, it was now becoming apparent, Hamilton's kind of nationalist. Madison was not opposed to funding the debt. He even suggested to Hamilton several forms of taxation, including an excise on liquor distilleries and a land tax, to supply revenue for extinguishing the debt.[3] But he had already emerged as a strong defender of the interests of Virginia and the South, often talking about the need for justice and equality among what he now referred to as a "Confederacy of States."[4] In settling the debt he wanted the government to discriminate somehow between the original and current holders of the government's bonds. Many of his Virginia constituents had heard stories of Northern speculators buying up the government's old securities at a fraction of their face value. They were angry that under Hamilton's funding plan the original purchasers of the securities would receive no compensation at all.

Hamilton wanted nothing to do with any sort of discrimination between original and current bondholders. Not only would administering such a discrimination become a nightmare, but refusing to pay the present holders of the securities their full face value would be a breach of contract and would harm the securities' capacity to serve as money. The secretary's views prevailed. On February 22, 1790, Madison's proposal was easily defeated in the House, thirty-six to thirteen.

The issue of the federal government's assumption of the states' debts, however, was not so easily disposed of. Only three states—Massachusetts, Connecticut, and South Carolina—owed nearly half the total state debts and were desperately anxious for assumption. Although some states were indifferent, several states—Virginia, Maryland, and Georgia—had already paid off a large proportion of their own debt and could hardly welcome paying federal taxes to retire the debts of the other states. Debate went on for six months, with some congressmen threatening that without assumption of the state debts there could be no Union. On June 2, 1790, the House of Representatives accepted a funding bill without assumption. The Senate responded by incorporating the assumption of state debts into the House bill. The Congress was deadlocked.

3. JM to AH, 19 Nov. 1789, *Papers of Hamilton*, 5: 525–26.
4. Kenneth R. Bowling, *The Creation of Washington, D.C.: The Idea and Location of the American Capital* (Fairfax, VA, 1991), 143.

THE DEADLOCK WAS EVENTUALLY BROKEN by a remarkable compromise. Congressman Richard Bland Lee of Virginia had previously hinted that assumption might be linked to the permanent location of the national capital.[5]

From the beginning the location of the federal government had been a problem. In 1776 no one had conceived that the Confederation Congress should have its own territory for its capital. During the Revolutionary War Congress had been forced repeatedly to migrate from place to place; in the 1780s it was still on the move, from Philadelphia to Princeton to Annapolis to Trenton and finally to New York. The Constitution had attempted to end the peripatetic existence of the new federal government by providing for the states to cede a district "not exceeding ten miles square" to be the permanent seat of the new national government. In this district Congress would have exclusive jurisdiction. Beyond that nothing else was specified.

The Southern states wanted the capital located on the Potomac; Washington was especially keen on having it near Alexandria and his plantation at Mount Vernon. The New England states and New York wanted to retain the capital in New York or someplace close by. Pennsylvania and the other middle states wanted it near Philadelphia or at least near the Susquehanna.

By June 1790 the Virginians were willing to support a temporary capital in Philadelphia in return for a permanent site being established on the Potomac. At the same time, Madison was becoming more fearful of the consequences of disunion and seemed reluctantly willing to accept the federal assumption of state debts. At a dinner arranged by Jefferson in late June 1790, Hamilton and Madison clinched a deal in which Southerners would accept the national assumption of state debts in return for having the permanent capital on the Potomac, the midpoint between Maine and Georgia. For ten years while that federal city was being built, Philadelphia was to be the temporary residence of the government.

The choice of a temporary residence was not surprising. After all, Philadelphia had been the meeting place of the First and Second Continental Congresses and the Constitutional Convention. It was also the largest city in the country, although not the fastest growing. (By 1810 New York would surpass it.) Prior to the Revolution it had been the major American entry port for thousands of European immigrants, mostly German, Scotch-Irish, and Irish, and would continue to be so in the 1790s, including such immigrants as French planters and blacks fleeing the revolution in Saint-Domingue (present-day Haiti), French refugees from the

5. Bowling, *Creation of Washington, D.C.*, 8.

revolution in France, and British and Irish refugees from Britain's coun-ter-revolutionary crackdown.

In 1790 Philadelphia's forty-five thousand diverse peoples lived in a giant triangle running two and a half miles along the Delaware River with the western tip of the triangle extending back about a mile on the High Street (renamed Market Street in 1790), which divided the city in two. In addition to being the site where the Declaration of Independence and the Constitution were written, Philadelphia was the commercial and cultural center of the United States. It housed the Bank of North America, the first bank in the country, and the American Philosophical Society and the Library Company, both of which had been established under Benjamin Franklin's leadership. It also contained Charles Willson Peale's Museum, which was the first popular museum of natural science and art in the nation. Philadelphia's Quaker heritage was everywhere, especially in making the city the national center for humanitarian reform, including the first society in the country promoting the abolition of slavery.

So fitting was Philadelphia as the nation's capital that some believed the government's temporary residence might be a lot longer than ten years. George Mason figured that it might take at least a half century for Congress to escape from the "Whirlpool of Philadelphia." Others thought the sectional cooperation expressed in the Compromise of 1790 could not last. "Southern and northern will often be the division of Congress," noted one observer. "The thought is disagreeable, but the distinction is founded in nature, and will last as long as the Union."[6]

THE COMPROMISE OF 1790—the location of the national capital in return for the federal assumption of state debts—showed that most congressmen were still willing to bargain for the sake of union. Nevertheless, some Southerners like James Monroe still had serious res-ervations about the compromise, believing that assumption would reduce "the necessity for State taxation" and thus would "undoubtedly leave the national government more at liberty to exercise its powers and increase the subjects on which it will act." One of those subjects might be slavery.[7]

The compromise was no sooner worked out than a new controversy arose over Hamilton's proposal in December 1790 to charter the Bank of the United States. With the Bank, opposition to the Federalist program

---

6. George Mason to TJ, 10 Jan 1791, *Papers of Jefferson*, 18: 484; Bowling, *Creation of Washington, D.C.*, 206.
7. James Roger Sharp, *American Politics in the Early Republic: The New Nation in Crisis* (New Haven, 1993), 37.

assumed a more strident and ideological character. Not only did the provision that the Bank was to reside in Philadelphia for its twenty-year life appear to threaten the promised move of the capital to the Potomac in 1800, but, more important, the creation of a national bank seemed to suggest that the United States was becoming a different kind of place from what many Americans wanted. Many Southerners in particular saw no need for banks. In their agricultural world banks seemed to create an unreal kind of money that benefited only Northern speculators. Even Northerners like Senator William Maclay regarded the Bank as "an Aristocratic engine" that could easily become "a Machine for the Mischievous purposes of bad Ministers."[8] Everywhere there was a sense that the Bank represented a new and frightening step toward centralizing national authority and Anglicizing America's government.

In the House of Representatives Madison launched a passionate attack against the bank proposal. He argued that the bank bill was a misguided imitation of England's monarchical practice of concentrating wealth and influence in the metropolitan capital, and, more important, that it was an unconstitutional assertion of federal power. The Constitution, he claimed, did not expressly grant the federal government the authority to charter a bank. But in February 1791 the bank bill passed over the objections of Madison and other Southerners, and Washington was faced with the problem of signing or vetoing it.

The president respected Madison's judgment and was deeply perplexed by the issue of constitutionality. He thus sought the advice of his fellow Virginians, Attorney General Edmund Randolph and Secretary of State Jefferson. Randolph offered a rambling argument against the bank bill's constitutionality, contending that the Tenth Amendment to the Constitution left all powers not specifically delegated to the Congress to the states or the people. Jefferson in his brief response took a similar position. Faced with such advice, Washington considered vetoing the bank bill and even went so far as to ask Madison to prepare a veto message. But first he wanted the opinion of his secretary of the treasury, who had devised the Bank.

Hamilton, with Randolph's and Jefferson's opinions before him, spent a week working out what became one of his most masterful state papers. He carefully refuted the arguments of Randolph and Jefferson and made a powerful case for a broad construction of the Constitution that resounded through subsequent decades of American history. He argued that Congress's authority to charter a bank was implied by the clause in Article I,

8. *The Diary of William Maclay and Other Notes on Senate Debates,* ed. Kenneth R. Bowling and Helen E. Veit (Baltimore, 1988), 347.

Section 8 of the Constitution that gave Congress the right to make all laws "necessary and proper" to carry out its delegated powers. Without such implied powers, Hamilton wrote, "the United States would furnish the singular spectacle of a *political society* without *sovereignty*, or of a people *governed* without *government*." That may have been Jefferson's ideal, but it was not Washington's. On February 25, 1791, the president signed the bank bill into law.[9]

This turn of events alarmed Madison and Jefferson. The Virginia legislature had already issued a series of resolutions protesting the federal assumption of state debts—protests that foreshadowed the state's later historic resolutions of 1798 against the Alien and Sedition Acts. In declaring the assumption law unconstitutional, the state noted the "striking resemblance" between Hamilton's financial system and the one that had been introduced in England in the early part of the eighteenth century. That English system, the Virginians declared, not only had "perpetuated upon the nation an enormous debt" but also had concentrated "in the hands of the executive, an unbounded influence, which pervading every branch of the government, bears down all opposition and daily threatens the destruction of everything that appertains to English liberty." The lesson for Americans was obvious: "The same causes produce the same effects." By creating "a large monied interest," the assumption law threatened to prostrate agriculture at the feet of commerce and to change the form of the federal government in a manner "fatal to the existence of American liberty."[10]

Hamilton saw at once the implications of these Virginia resolutions. He privately warned that they were "the first symptom of a spirit which must either be killed or will kill the constitution of the United States."[11] But his Federalist colleagues were confident that the prosperity the national government was bringing to the country would conquer all opposition.

YET OPPOSITION CONTINUED TO MOUNT. Indeed, Virginia's stand at the end of 1790 became the first major step in the development of an organized opposition designed to protect Southern agricultural interests

9. AH, "Opinion on the Constitutionality of the Bank," 23 Feb. 1791, *Papers of Hamilton*, 7: 98.
10. Virginia Resolutions on the Assumption of State Debts, 16 Dec. 1790, Henry Steele Commager, ed., *Documents in American History*, 4th ed. (New York, 1948), 155–56; Harry Ammon, "The Formation of the Republican Party in Virginia, 1798–1796," *Journal of Southern History*, 19 (1953), 292.
11. AH to John Jay, 13 Nov. 1790, *Papers of Hamilton*, 7: 149.

(including slavery) from Eastern commercial dominance. By early 1791 Jefferson was worried about the "heresies" that were being set forth in the press and began urging friends to support the agricultural interest and pure "republicanism" against the "stock-jobbers" in Congress. Soon Madison was describing the supporters of Hamilton's program not only as "speculators" but also as "Tories," a loaded term that evoked the opponents of the Revolution and the promoters of monarchy.[12] Madison's and Jefferson's comments were private, but by early 1791 the press boiled with talk of the dangers of monarchy and monocrats—talk that resonated well beyond the world of the Southern planters concerned with slavery: many Northern middling sorts were also anxious about the dangers of monarchy and the kind of aristocratic society that accompanied it.

Because Vice-President John Adams had pushed for titles in the Senate in 1789, some had labeled him a monarchist. Adams laid new claim to the title, as did his editor, John Fenno, by publishing in the *Gazette of the United States* in 1790 a series of essays called "Discourses on Davila." In these curious essays, ostensibly a commentary on the work of the seventeenth-century Italian historian Enrico Caterino Davila, Adams tried to justify his belief in the need for forms, titles, and distinctions in all societies, including republics.

Under these circumstances, with monarchy very much on people's minds, Jefferson suddenly and inadvertently found himself thrust into public prominence as a controversial defender of republicanism. In April 1791 he passed on an English copy of Thomas Paine's pamphlet *The Rights of Man* to a Philadelphia printer. Jefferson made the mistake, however, of including a covering note privately expressing his pleasure that "something is at length to be publickly said against the political heresies which have sprung up among us," by which he meant mainly Adams's "Discourses on Davila."[13]

When Jefferson's note was widely quoted in newspapers throughout the nation, he was embarrassed. Whether he wanted it or not, Jefferson was being associated in the public mind with resistance to the Hamiltonian system and perceived as a friend of the rights of man. His holiday trip with Madison in late May and June 1791 up the Hudson Valley in New York certainly convinced Hamilton and other Federalists that

---

12. Stanley Elkins and Eric McKitrick, *The Age of Federalism* (New York, 1993), 234; JM to TJ, 1 May 1791, *Papers of Jefferson*, 20: 337.

13. TJ to Jonathan B. Smith, 26 Apr. 1791, *Papers of Jefferson*, 20: 290. On the entire imbroglio over the unauthorized publication of Jefferson's note, see Julian Boyd's editorial discussion, "Rights of Man: The Contest of Burke and Paine . . . in America," *Papers of Jefferson*, 20: 268–90.

Jefferson and Madison were concocting an organized opposition to the government. At the same time, Jefferson noted that Hamilton was trying to qualify, but not repudiate, remarks in which he said that "the present government is not that which will answer the ends of society,... and that it will probably be found expedient to go into the British form."[14] Both Jefferson and Madison were coming to realize that Hamilton and the Federalists had an image quite different from their own of what the United States ought to become.

JEFFERSON AND MADISON had been good friends since 1779. Their shared passion for religious freedom had brought them together, and in the 1780s they had collaborated in pushing a number of bills through the Virginia assembly. When Jefferson was minister to France, they had kept up a regular correspondence, often in code. Now, however, their friendship deepened, grew more intensely political, and became more consequential for the history of the early Republic.[15] As John Quincy Adams once observed, "The mutual influence of these two mighty minds upon each other is a phenomenon, like the invisible and mysterious movements of the magnet in the physical world, and in which the sagacity of the future historian may discover the solution of much of our national history not otherwise easily accountable."[16]

It is not immediately obvious why the relationship was so intimate and long-lasting. The two men had markedly different temperaments. Jefferson was high-minded, optimistic, visionary, and often quick to grab hold of new and sometimes bizarre ideas. Although he could be a superb politician at times—acutely sensitive to what was possible and workable—he was also a radical utopian; he often dreamed of the future and was inspired by how things might be. Madison, by contrast, had a conservative strain that mingled with his own utopian thinking; he valued legitimacy and stability and was usually more willing than Jefferson to accept things as they were. He was often prudent and cold-eyed, if not pessimistic, analytical, and skeptical of radical schemes, especially if they might unleash popular passions. He never embraced an idea without questioning it, and he never possessed the kind of uncritical faith in the people that Jefferson had.

Both men were suspicious of governmental power, including the power of elected representative legislatures. But Jefferson's suspicion was based

14. TJ, Notes of a Conversation with AH, 13 Aug. 1791, *Papers of Jefferson*, 22: 38–39. On the Hudson Valley trip, see Boyd's editorial note, "The Northern Journey of Jefferson and Madison," *Papers of Jefferson*, 20: 434–53.

15. Adrienne Koch, *Jefferson and Madison: The Great Collaboration* (New York, 1964).

16. Introduction, *Republic of Letters*, 1–2.

on his fear of the unrepresentative character of the elected officials, that is, that the representatives might be too apt to drift away from the virtuous people who had elected them. Madison's suspicion, by contrast, was based on his fear that the elected officials were only too representative, only too expressive of the passions of their constituents. Jefferson worried about the rights of the majority; Madison worried about the rights of the minority.[17] As far as Jefferson was concerned, the people could do no wrong. When Madison was wringing his hands in the late 1780s over the turbulence of Shays's Rebellion, Jefferson was writing blithely from France about the value of the spirit of popular resistance to government and the need to keep it alive. "I like a little rebellion now and then," he said. Like a storm in the atmosphere, it cleared the air.[18]

In the 1780s the two men had had different ideas about politics and the character of the central government. Madison had been a fervent nationalist and had been eager to put down the states and create a strong central government. Jefferson, from his distant position in Paris, had not shared most of Madison's misgivings about democratic politics in the separate states. Although he had accepted the need for a new federal government, he continued to think of the United States as more of a decentralized confederation than Madison. Give the national government control over foreign policy and foreign trade, he urged, but leave all domestic affairs, including taxation, with the states. "To make us one nation as to foreign concerns, and keep us distinct in Domestic ones," he told Madison in 1786, "gives the outline of the proper division of powers between the general and particular governments."[19]

By 1792 Jefferson had not changed his views at all, but Madison had. For reasons that are still disputed, by 1792 he had become fearful of the very government he had done so much to create. No doubt his nationalism had never been as strong as Hamilton's, and no doubt his loyalty to Virginia had become more intense as he sensed a Northern bias in Hamilton's banking and funding system. But most important in his change of thinking was his growing realization that the new national government that Hamilton and the Federalists were erecting did not at all resemble the adjudicatory state that he had imagined in 1787. It was not a

17. For an excellent discussion of the differences between the two men, see Drew R. McCoy, *The Last of the Fathers: James Madison and the Republican Legacy* (Cambridge, UK, 1989), 45–64.

18. TJ to Abigail Adams, 22 Feb. 1787, Lester J. Cappon, ed., *The Adams-Jefferson Letters: The Complete Correspondence Between Thomas Jefferson and Abigail and John Adams* (Chapel Hill, 1959), 1: 173.

19. TJ to JM, 16 Dec. 1786, *Papers of Jefferson*, 10: 603.

judicial-like umpire they were creating but a modern European-type state with an elaborate bureaucracy, a standing army, perpetual debts, and a powerful independent executive—the very kind of monarch-like war-making state that radical Whigs in England had been warning about for generations. In his mind, as he recalled years later, he did not desert Hamilton, "Colonel Hamilton deserted me." "In a word," he told a young disciple, Nicholas Trist, near the end of his life, "the divergence between us took place—from his wishing to *administration*, or rather to administer the Government into what he thought it ought to be."[20]

Madison's growing realization that Hamilton held a different conception of the national government from his own was crucial in explaining his shift in thinking; but also important was his deep friendship with Jefferson. Although Madison was by far the more critical and questioning thinker, Jefferson, eight years Madison's senior, displayed an intellectual power that impressed his younger colleague. Jefferson knew more about more things and had read more books than any other American leader (except perhaps for John Adams), and, unlike Madison, he had lived in Europe and knew firsthand the great enlightened world beyond America.

For a variety of reasons, therefore, Madison tended to defer to his older friend, ready "always," he told him in 1794, to "receive your commands with pleasure."[21] Madison, however, was never so deferential as to avoid questioning some of the outlandish ideas that Jefferson was apt to put forward. In 1789, for example, Jefferson outlined for Madison his notion that no generation should be bound by the actions of its predecessors. Jefferson had picked up the idea during discussions in liberal Parisian circles and found it attractive, especially since he had become aware of how burdensome his own personal debts were. "One generation," he told Madison, "is to another as one independent nation to another." According to his elaborate but dubious calculations based on the demographic tables of the French naturalist the comte de Buffon, Jefferson deduced that a generation lasted about nineteen years. Therefore, he concluded, the "principle that the earth belongs to the living and not to the dead" meant that all personal and national debts, all laws, even all constitutions ought to expire every nineteen years.

20. N. P. Trist, Memoranda, 27 Sept. 1834, in Max Farrand, ed., *The Records of the Federal Convention of 1787* (New Haven, 1911, 1937), 3: 534; Michael Schwarz, "The Great Divergence Reconsidered: Hamilton, Madison, and U.S.–British Relations, 1783–89," *JER*, 27 (2007), 407–36. "Administration" was a loaded word for radical Whigs; it meant the active exercising of the prerogative powers of the king or the executive.

21. JM to TJ, 5 Oct. 1794, *Republic of Letters*, 857.

Madison's reply to this odd notion was a model of tact. After first complimenting Jefferson on the "many interesting reflections" his idea of generational autonomy suggested, Madison went on gently to demolish it for being "not in *all* respects compatible with the course of human affairs." He pointed out that some debts, like those created by the American Revolution, were actually incurred for the benefit of future generations. Moreover, to bring all constitutions and laws to an end every nineteen years would surely erode confidence between people and breed struggles over property that would unhinge the society. Still, he confessed that perhaps he had only the eye of an "ordinary Politician" that was unable to perceive "the sublime truths...seen thro' the medium of Philosophy."[22]

Madison knew his friend and knew that Jefferson's fanciful and exaggerated opinions were usually offset by his very practical and cautious behavior. As Madison later remarked, Jefferson had a habit like "others of great genius of expressing in strong and round terms, impressions of the moment."[23] Indeed, it was often the difference between Jefferson's impulsive opinions and his calculated behavior that led many critics to charge him with hypocrisy and inconsistency.

Perhaps it was the very innocence and impracticality of many of Jefferson's opinions—their utopianism—that attracted the more sober-minded and skeptical Madison. Jefferson's vision of a world free from coercion and war, free from the accumulated debts and regulations of the past, and free from corruption—this vision was an inspiring antidote to the prudential, mundane, and humdrum world of congressional politics that Madison often had to contend with. At any rate, Madison developed his own utopian views about the use of commercial restrictions in international relations and on this issue eventually became even more visionary than his mentor. But he was always the loyal protégé responsible for the dirty work in the collaboration. Since Jefferson did not like personal confrontations and polemical exchanges, he left it to Madison to write articles defending him in the press and to work out the details of their opposition to Hamilton's program.

As CRITICISM OF HAMILTON's financial policies and their support by "stock-jobbers" and "speculators" increased during 1791, defenders of the government retaliated. John Fenno had begun his staunchly Federalist newspaper the *Gazette of the United States* in 1789 with the hope of its becoming the official paper of the national government with the mission of supporting the Constitution and the national administration. But soon the

22. TJ to JM, 4 Feb. 1790, *Papers of Jefferson*, 16: 131–34.
23. Gordon S. Wood, *Revolutionary Characters: What Made the Founders Different* (New York, 2006), 110.

paper moved from simply celebrating the federal government to defending it from its critics. To those critics Fenno's publishing of Adams's "Discourses on Davila" was the last straw. The *Gazette* seemed to Jefferson to have become "a paper of pure Toryism, disseminating the doctrines of monarchy, aristocracy, and the exclusion of the influence of the people."[24]

Jefferson and Madison were concerned enough with the spread of what they took to be the anti-republican opinions of the *Gazette* to enter into negotiations with the poet Philip Freneau to edit a rival Philadelphia newspaper. After being offered a position as translator in the State Department and other promises of support, Freneau finally agreed. The first issue of his *National Gazette* appeared at the end of October 1791.[25] By early 1792 Freneau's newspaper was claiming that Hamilton's plans were part of a grand design to subvert liberty and establish aristocracy and monarchy in America. At the same time, Jefferson was hailed as the illustrious patriot who was defending liberty against Hamilton's system of corruption. Although there was no organized party as yet, something labeled the "republican interest" emerged in the Congress in 1791, with the Virginia delegation at its core.

Freneau and his newspaper were effectively altering the terms of the national debate. He portrayed the political conflict not as a contest between Federalists and Anti-Federalists but as a struggle between monocrats or aristocrats on one side and republicans on the other. As Hamilton recognized, these new terms were not at all favorable to the Federalists. It was one thing to cast the opponents of the Federalists as enemies of the Constitution and the Union; it was quite another to describe them as defenders of republicanism against monarchy and aristocracy. Yet to the Federalists' chagrin, Freneau's *National Gazette* could now openly declare that "the question in America is no longer between federalism and anti-federalism, but between republicanism and anti-republicanism." Since the press rarely published authentically signed pieces—most were anonymous or written under a pseudonym—the charges thrown about in the newspapers showed little restraint. When Freneau's paper bitterly attacked the Federalist government for slyly promoting monarchy and aristocracy and undermining republicanism, Hamilton eventually responded in Fenno's *Gazette of the United States* by assailing Jefferson directly. He labeled the secretary of state an intriguing incendiary plotting to destroy the Constitution and the authority of the national government.[26]

24. TJ to Thomas Mann Randolph Jr., 15 May 1791, *Papers of Jefferson*, 20: 416.
25. On this subject see Julian Boyd's editorial note, "Jefferson, Freneau, and the Founding of the *National Gazette*," *Papers of Jefferson*, 20: 718–53.
26. *National Gazette*, 20 Feb. 1792.

This political division quickly spread beyond the press. Although Americans were universally hostile to the idea of parties, observers in 1792 for the first time began to speak of parties in the Congress, with what Madison called the "Republican party" representing the eighteenth-century radical Whig or "country-opposition" of the people against the corrupt influence of the Federalist "court." Republicans began drawing on the libertarian ideas of the eighteenth-century British radical country-Whigs, ideas that had been integral to colonial American thinking in the years leading up to the Revolution.[27]

Jefferson was steeped in these ideas, but he found it difficult to lead an opposition. He was in an awkward position, to say the least. He had placed on the government's payroll an enemy of the administration of which he was an important member. Early in 1792 the secretary of state informed Washington of his desire to leave the government at the end of the president's first term. In the meantime, however, he sought to diminish Hamilton's influence. In February 1792 he tried to convince Washington that the post office ought to be put in the Department of State rather than in the Treasury Department where it originally resided. The treasury, he warned the president in a conversation, "possessed already such an influence as to swallow up the whole Executive powers, and...even the future Presidents (not supported by the weight of character which himself possessed) would not be able to make head against this department." He went on to accuse Hamilton of contriving "a system" of unproductive paper speculation that was poisoning the society and even the government itself.[28]

Indeed, even one of the chief perpetrators, Robert Morris, admitted that a "spirit of speculation infected all ranks" in the 1790s. Those speculative schemes involving the former assistant secretary of the treasury William Duer lent some support to the fears of corruption. Duer was a talented and energetic man, but, unlike Hamilton or Washington, he seemed to have little or no sense that his public responsibilities ought to precede his private interests. In the language of the age he appeared to have little or no virtue. Indeed, Duer epitomized the kind of gambling "stock-jobber" that Jefferson and Madison so feared. Although Duer departed the treasury after seven months, he presumably left with inside information that he tried to turn to his advantage by speculating in the federal debt and bank stock. Duer borrowed from a wide variety of people,

27. Lance Banning, *The Jeffersonian Persuasion: Evolution of a Party Ideology* (Ithaca, 1978), 126–78.
28. TJ's Memoranda of Conversations with the President, 1 Mar. 1792, *Papers of Jefferson*, 23: 184–87.

promising them ever increasing returns. When the speculative bubble finally burst in March 1792, investors big and small were badly hurt.

The collapse of Duer's schemes precipitated a financial panic—the first of its kind in American history—that some believed was so serious that it affected "private Credit from Georgia to New Hampshire." Suddenly, construction projects were halted, men were thrown out of work, and prices fell. One observer thought that the "revolution of property" was unprecedented.[29] Jefferson, who had little understanding of high finance, was convinced that "all that stuff called script, of whatever description, was folly or roguery."[30] Hamilton took a tough line in protecting the credit of the United States during the financial crisis, and Duer ended up in prison. Jefferson and Madison assumed, wrongly it turned out, that Hamilton himself was likewise involved in corruption, and they and their followers in the Congress tried to force the treasury secretary to resign.

By now Hamilton had come to realize that his former collaborator had joined with Jefferson to oppose all of his programs. By May 1792 he was convinced "that Mr. Madison cooperating with Mr. Jefferson is at the head of a faction decidedly hostile to me and my administration, and actuated by views in my judgment subversive of the principles of good government and dangerous to the union, peace and happiness of the Country."[31] Hamilton was horrified to learn that many congressmen wanted to undermine his funding system and even to repudiate the government's contracts of debt. He believed that Madison and especially Jefferson, whom he accused of wanting to become president, had attempted to make the national government so odious that they ran the risk of destroying the Union. In the opinion of Hamilton and other Federalists the future of the national government was in doubt. If all the states were as small as Maryland, New Jersey, or Connecticut, there would be little to fear. But, he thought, with a state as large and powerful as Virginia in opposition, could the government of the United States maintain itself? Hamilton insisted, perhaps too much so, that he was "*affectionately* attached to the Republican theory," meaning, as he said, that he had no vested interest in hereditary distinctions or the deprivation of equal political rights. That was true enough, but his idea of republicanism was certainly different from that of Madison and Jefferson.[32]

29. Bruce H. Mann, *Republic of Debtors: Bankruptcy in the Age of American Independence* (Cambridge, MA, 2002), 202, 194, 195.
30. TJ to Henry Remsen, 14 Apr. 1792, *Papers of Jefferson*, 23: 426.
31. AH to Edward Carrington, 26 May 1792, *Papers of Hamilton*, 11: 429.
32. AH to Edward Carrington, 26 May 1792, *Papers of Hamilton*, 11: 426–45.

At the same time, Jefferson himself was becoming increasingly alarmed at the direction of the federal government. In May 1792 he spelled out to Washington more fully than he had earlier his objections to Hamilton's paper schemes and the influence of his "corrupt squadron" in the Congress. The "ultimate object" of Hamilton's system, Jefferson wrote, was "to prepare the way for a change from the present republican form of government, to that of a monarchy, of which the English constitution is to be the model." If the great mass of the people did not rise up and support "the republican party," Jefferson warned, the Union itself might break apart. Although Jefferson wrote this in order to convince Washington that "the crisis" was so severe as to require the great man to stay on for a second term as president, he nevertheless sincerely believed what he wrote. This fear that the "Monarchical federalists" were using the new government "simply as a stepping stone to monarchy" became the basis of all his thinking in the 1790s and the central theme of the emerging Republican party.[33]

Washington tried to assure Jefferson that there was no design to create a monarchy. Instead, the president blamed most of the disturbances in the country on Freneau's paper. Yet, without revealing the source, Washington did ask Hamilton to respond to Jefferson's objections to the government's financial system.

In August 1792 in a fourteen-thousand-word document Hamilton answered Jefferson's arguments one by one and demonstrated his exceptional understanding of financial matters. He could not help assuming the exasperated tone of the sophisticated Wall Street lawyer explaining the intricacies of banks and credit to country bumpkins. He first pointed out that the debt was created not by the Federalist administration but by the Revolutionary War. If the opponents of the debt wanted it paid off, he said, then they ought to stop misrepresenting the measures of the government and depriving it of its ability to do just that. Hamilton went on to deny the charge that congressmen were corrupt because they were public creditors; indeed, he said, "it is a strange perversion of ideas, and as novel as it is extraordinary, that men should be deemed corrupt & criminal for becoming proprietors in the funds of their Country." He denied too that there was a conspiracy to transform America into a monarchy. He certainly was somewhat disingenuous in declaring that no one, as far as he knew, "contemplated the introducing into this country of a monarchy." But he did go on to ridicule the various fears of plots that the two different parties had—one fearing monarchy and the other fearing the overturning of the general government. "Both sides," he said, "may be equally wrong &

33. TJ to GW, 23 May 1792, *Papers of Jefferson*, 23: 535–40.

their mutual jealousies may be materially causes of the appearances which mutually disturb them, and sharpen them against each other."

Unfortunately, as Jefferson had pointed out, the division was assuming a sectional cast. "In the South," said Hamilton, "it is supposed that more government than is expedient is desired by the North. In the North, it is believed, that the prejudices of the South are incompatible with the necessary degree of Government and with the attainment of the essential ends of National Union." But happily, he said, most people in both sections favored "their true interest, UNION." Of course, Hamilton assumed that the Southern position was based on mere "theoretical prejudices," while the Northern position was based on "*great* and *substantial* national objects."[34]

To Washington's dismay, cabinet meetings had become increasingly acrimonious. As Jefferson later recalled, he and Hamilton were "daily pitted in the cabinet like two cocks."[35] At the end of August 1792 Washington wrote to both secretaries, urging "more charity for the opinions and acts of one another." He assumed that the differences between the two men were still merely personal, "for I cannot prevail on myself to believe that these measures are, as yet, the deliberate acts of a determined party." He appealed to his two cabinet officials to be less suspicious and more tolerant of one another. If "one pulls this way and another that," then the government "must inevitably be torn asunder," and "the fairest prospect of happiness and prosperity that ever was presented to man, will be lost— perhaps for ever!"[36]

Both men replied to Washington the same day. Each outlined his grievances against the other in order to justify his actions. Hamilton admitted that he had retaliated in the press against Jefferson. Indeed, his articles published during the latter half of 1792 in the *Gazette of the United States* actually attacked Jefferson by name and thus may have had the unintended effect of elevating Jefferson to leadership of the Republican opposition. One Federalist even labeled Jefferson the "Generalissimo" of the Republican armies, with Madison being relegated to the title of a mere "General."[37]

Hamilton believed that he had every justification for attacking Jefferson in the press. Jefferson from the beginning had formed a party "bent upon my subversion" and had created a newspaper with Philip Freneau as his

34. AH to GW, 18 Aug. 1792, *Papers of Hamilton*, 12: 228–58.
35. Ron Chernow, *Alexander Hamilton* (New York, 2004), 390.
36. GW to TJ, 23 Aug. 1792, *Papers of Jefferson*, 24: 317; GW to AH, 26 Aug. 1792, *Papers of Hamilton*, 12: 276–77.
37. Dumas Malone, *Jefferson and the Rights of Man* (Boston, 1951), 463–64, 477, 473.

agent in order "to render me and all the measures connected with my department as odious as possible." Undermining the nation's honor and credit, as Jefferson and his followers intended, would "bring the Government into contempt with that description of Men, who are in every society the only firm supporters of government."[38] Hamilton could not avoid thinking of society in a traditional hierarchical manner, with the proprietary gentry at the top being crucial to social order.

Jefferson replied with even more venom and self-pity than Hamilton. Although he had vowed never to interfere with the Congress, he had violated his resolution one time in the case of the assumption of state debts. He had been duped into it by Hamilton "and made a tool for forwarding his schemes, not then sufficiently understood by me." It was, he said, the biggest mistake of his political life. Jefferson then went on to describe his differences with Hamilton, differences that were not merely personal. "His system flowed from principles adverse to liberty, and was calculated to undermine and abolish the republic, by creating an influence of his department over the members of the legislature." Congressmen, Jefferson said, no longer spoke for the people; they were simply enriching themselves. The debt was a crucial point of difference between him and Hamilton. "I would wish the debt paid tomorrow; he wishes it never to be paid, but always to be a thing wherewith to corrupt and manage the legislature." Indeed, using influence was his mode of operation. How many sons, relatives, and friends of the legislators, asked Jefferson, had Hamilton provided for out of the thousand offices he had at his disposal? And he had the nerve, said Jefferson, to question the hiring of the newspaper editor Philip Freneau as a translator in the State Department. (Actually hiring Freneau had come to embarrass Jefferson, and he spent an inordinate amount of his letter justifying it.)

Jefferson's letter was more than three times as long as Hamilton's and was far more wide-ranging in its indictment of his enemy. He lashed out at Hamilton in every direction, charging that the treasury secretary's broad construction of the Constitution and his reliance on the general welfare clause were all part of his scheme of "subverting step by step the principles of the Constitution." Somewhat disingenuously, Jefferson claimed that he had done nothing to oppose Hamilton's schemes except to express dissent. Hamilton, he charged, had not been so innocent. The secretary of the treasury had continually interfered with Jefferson's department, discussing foreign affairs with the ministers of Britain and France, and had written hateful pieces against Jefferson in the press.

38. AH to GW, 9 Sept. 1792, *Papers of Hamilton*, 12: 348–49.

Did this not, Jefferson asked, harm "the dignity and even the decency of government"?

Rarely did Jefferson express as much anger in a letter as he did in this one. He promised to retire soon from his office, but he would not promise to give up the fight on behalf of the cause of republican freedom. "I will not suffer my retirement to be clouded by the slanders of a man whose history, from the moment when history can stoop to notice him, is a tissue of machinations against the liberty of the country which has not only received and given him bread, but heaped its honors on his head." Jefferson could not help but think of Hamilton, the bastard immigrant from the West Indies, as a parvenu who was something less than a native American. He never hated anyone more.[39]

THE ONE THING the two cabinet officers agreed upon was that Washington had to stay on as president. Washington wanted to retire in 1792. He felt old and tired, and he continued to worry about what people would think about his continuing in office when he had promised way back in 1783 to retire from public life. But everyone urged him to stay. Some Federalists like Robert Morris privately thought that four years was much too short a term for the president. They preferred a life term, and if not that, at least a twenty-one-year term.[40]

Even the Republicans wanted Washington to continue in office. Jefferson told him that he was the only man in the country thought to be above party.[41] Hamilton even used the ultimate argument on a man who was always anxious about his reputation—that retirement when he was so much needed would be "critically hazardous to your own reputation."[42]

Washington kept postponing a decision and thus tacitly agreed to stand for election for another term. When the electoral votes were counted in February 1793, Washington had once again received every electoral vote, the only president in American history to be so honored. John Adams received seventy-seven votes to fifty for Governor George Clinton of New York, and thus he remained as vice-president. Hamilton thought that Adams was far from perfect, but he was preferable to Clinton, who he said was "a man of narrow and perverse politics" and "opposed to national principles." Adams himself was outraged that Clinton should have received only twenty-seven votes fewer than he did. "Damn 'em, damn

39. TJ to GW, 9 Sept. 1792, *Papers of Jefferson*, 24: 351–59.
40. S.W. Jackman, "A Young Englishman Reports on the New Nation: Edward Thornton to James Bland Burges, 1791–1793," *WMQ*, 18 (1961), 93.
41. TJ, Notes of a Conversation with GW, 1 Oct. 1792, *Papers of Jefferson*, 24: 434.
42. AH to GW, 30 July 1792, *Papers of Hamilton*, 12: 137–38.

'em, damn 'em," he exclaimed to John Langdon of New Hampshire. "You see that an elective government will not do." No wonder people suspected Adams of monarchism.[43]

Aaron Burr, the senator from New York, apparently had canvassed for the vice-presidency but had received only one electoral vote—from South Carolina. Hamilton was not yet sure about Burr's character, but what he had heard suggested that "he is a man whose only political principle is, to *mount at all events* to the highest legal honours of the Nation and as much further as circumstances will carry him." Hamilton's biggest worry during the election had been that Adams, Clinton, and Burr would divide the votes of the North and allow Jefferson to sneak in as vice-president, which would have been "a serious misfortune." Jefferson, he said, was "a man of sublimated and paradoxical imagination—entertaining & propagating notions inconsistent with dignified and orderly Government."[44]

For their part Jefferson and Madison had sought to dampen Burr's candidacy, arguing that he was too inexperienced for the position. Although the Virginians praised Burr effusively, their opposition to his ambition never sat well with Burr, and he seethed over it.[45]

Washington hoped for less partisanship and more harmony in the government, but the worst was yet to come. By the end of 1792 Jefferson and most of his fellow Virginians in the House had become convinced that Hamilton was deep in corruption. In January 1793 they sponsored five resolutions calling for an accounting of the Treasury Department's affairs. They believed that Hamilton would never be able to answer them before the Congress adjourned in March, and thus the charges would fester for the rest of the year until Congress reconvened. But Hamilton outdid himself in answering his critics, and when the Virginia delegation, perhaps under the influence of Jefferson, pressed the House to censure Hamilton, the representatives refused by large majorities. At the same time, the congressional elections of 1792 suggested that many more of those dedicated to the Republican cause would sit in the Third Congress that would convene at the end of 1793.

YET THIS WAS NOT YET modern party politics. Politics in the 1790s retained much of its eighteenth-century character. It was still very much a personal and elitist business—resting on friendship, private alliances,

43. Milton Halsey Thomas, ed., *Elias Boudinot's Journey to Boston in 1809* (Princeton, 1955), 61 n.
44. AH to John Steele, 15 Oct. 1792, AH to Charles Cotesworth Pinckney, 10 Oct. 1792, *Papers of Hamilton*, 12: 568–69, 544.
45. Sharp, *American Politics in the Early Republic*, 58.

personal conversations, letter-writing, and intrigue. Such politics was regarded as the prerogative of notable gentry who presumably had sufficient reputations to gather supporters and followers. Because in America would-be aristocrats and gentlemen lacked any legal titles, their rank had to rest on reputation, on opinion, on having their claim to gentility accepted by the world. This was why eighteenth-century gentlemen, especially those who sought political leadership, so jealously guarded their reputations, or what they more commonly called their honor.

Honor was the value genteel society placed on a gentleman and the value that a gentleman placed on himself. Honor suggested a public drama in which men played roles for which they were either praised or blamed. It subsumed self-esteem, pride, and dignity and was akin to glory and fame. Gentlemen acted or avoided acting for the sake of their honor. Honor was exclusive, heroic, and aristocratic, and it presumed a hierarchical world different from the one that was emerging in America. Indeed, the eighteenth-century French philosopher Montesquieu, in his *Spirit of the Laws* (1748), had argued that honor was the animating principle of monarchy.

Since politics was still an aristocratic matter of individual loyalties and enmities, men had a hard time distinguishing between their status as gentlemen and their position as political leaders. Consequently, political struggles over policy often became personal struggles over reputation. Because reputation was a matter of public opinion, influencing that opinion became an essential aspect of politics. Hence personal insults, calumnies, and gossip were common weapons in these political battles over reputation. Gossip, said Fisher Ames, was an unfortunate fact of political life. "It is provoking," he lamented, "that a life of virtue and eminent usefulness should be embittered by calumny—but it is the ordinary event of the political drama."[46]

To deal with this sort of personal politics, gentlemen worked out sets of rituals and rules of conduct based on the importance they placed on their reputations. In defense against insult they resorted to a variety of measures: public posting in newspapers, the spreading of counter-gossip, and the writing of pamphlets or newspaper diatribes. Although the most extreme defense of one's reputation was to challenge the opponent to a duel, physical combat was not the most likely outcome in these ritualized struggles over honor. But the possibility that a political contest could end in an exchange of fire between two men gave an anxious edge to politics.

---

46. Joanne B. Freeman, *Affairs of Honor: National Politics in the New Republic* (New Haven, 2001), 8; Joanne B. Freeman, "Slander, Poison, Whispers, and Fame: Jefferson's 'Anas' and Political Gossip in the Early Republic," *JER*, 15 (1995), 25–57, quotation at 29.

Because the United States was still without firmly established institutions and structures of political behavior, this kind of personal gossip-laden politics meant that private relationships necessarily became intermingled with public affairs and vice versa. To attack a government policy was to attack a politician, which immediately called into question his reputation and honor. As William Plumer of New Hampshire complained, "It is impossible to censure measures without condemning men." This sort of politics based on personal alliances and animosities was difficult to manage and accounts for much of the volatility and passion of political life in the 1790s.[47] Although traditional gentry like John Jay continued to assume that "men may be hostile to each other in politics and yet be incapable of such conduct" in private, it was becoming increasingly difficult to behave magnanimously when so much seemed at stake.[48]

In this intimate world of competing gentlemen, political parties in any modern sense were slow to emerge. Because there were as yet no elaborate mechanisms for selecting candidates, raising money, and conducting campaigns, notable gentry used their personal reputations to gather supporters and followers. If a member of Congress found himself unable to be present in his district at election time, he might, as Madison did in 1790, write letters to influential friends or relatives and ask them to look after his interest. Gentlemen generally stood, not ran, for election, and canvassing for an office, as Burr was said to have done for the vice-presidency in 1792, was widely thought to be improper. Any interference with the right of each citizen to think and vote independently was anathema. A Connecticut congressman boasted that no one in his state had ever "solicited the suffrages of the freeman, for a place in the legislature." If anyone was ever foolish enough to try, "he may be assured of meeting with the general contempt and indignation of the people."[49]

With little competition for office, voter turnouts were often very low, sometimes fewer than 5 percent of the eligible electorate.[50] Gentlemen put great value on impartiality and disliked and feared parties as factious and self-seeking. "If I could not go to heaven but with a party," declared Jefferson in 1789, "I would not go there at all."[51] Given this deep-seated hostility to parties, it is not surprising that men found it difficult to draw up tickets of candidates and organize elections in any modern manner.

47. Freeman, *Affairs of Honor*, 69.
48. Jay to AH, 26 Nov. 1793, *Papers of Hamilton*, 15: 412–13.
49. Noble E. Cunningham, *The Jeffersonian Republicans: The Formation of Party Organization, 1789–1801* (Chapel Hill, 1957), 250.
50. Sharp, *American Politics in the Early Republic*, 67.
51. TJ to Francis Hopkinson, 13 March 1789, *Papers of Jefferson*, 14: 650.

Nevertheless, a Republican party of opposition was emerging, and men struggled to explain and justify what was happening. As one of the leaders of the Republican opposition, Madison had become convinced by September 1792 that a division into parties, "being natural to most political societies, is likely to be of some duration in ours." One party, he wrote publicly in 1792, was composed of those who "are more partial to the opulent than to the other classes of society; and having debauched themselves into a persuasion that mankind are incapable of governing themselves, it follows with them, of course, that government can be carried on only by the pageantry of rank, the influence of money and emoluments and the terror of military force." These Federalists, or members of what Madison called "the antirepublican party," expected the government to serve the interests of the few at the expense of the many and hoped that it would "be narrowed into fewer hands, and approximated to an hereditary form." Members of the other party, "the Republican party, as it may be termed," were those who believed "that mankind are capable of governing themselves" and hated "hereditary power as an insult to the reason and an outrage to the rights of man."[52]

In this essay, entitled "A Candid State of Parties," published in the *National Gazette* on September 26, 1792, Madison meant by parties not organized vehicles for recruiting candidates and winning elections but rather rough divisions of opinion manifested in Congress. In the face of the continual emphasis on the single interest of the public, men were reluctant to admit they might be members of a party. As late as 1794 the Virginia Republican congressman Nathaniel Macon wrote home, "It is said there are two parties in Congress, but the fact I do not positively know. If there are, I know that I do not belong to one."[53]

In these circumstances, of course, the emerging political division between the Federalists and the Republicans bore no resemblance to the party competition of modern American politics or to the politics of the antebellum period. Neither party accepted the legitimacy or existence of the other. Indeed, each believed that the other was out to destroy the country. The Federalists, whom John Adams defined in 1792 as "the Friends of the Constitution, order and good government," thought of themselves not as a party but as the legitimate administration that represented the whole people and the general good.[54] Only their Republican opponents were willing to describe themselves as a party, and they did so

---

52. JM, "A Candid State of Parties," 26 Sept. 1792, *Madison: Writings*, 530–32.
53. David Hackett Fischer, *The Revolution of American Conservatism: The Federalist Party in the Era of Jeffersonian Democracy* (New York, 1965), 51.
54. Richard H. Kohn, *Eagle and Sword: The Federalists and the Creation of the Military Establishment in America, 1783–1802* (New York, 1975), 198.

out of necessity, just as the colonists had created the Whig party to combat monarchical tyranny during the imperial crisis of the 1760s and 1770s.

Even so, some Republicans objected to the term "party"; they said they were better described as "a band of patriots," because they were looking after the good of the whole nation, not a part.[55] Because there was no legitimacy for organized opposition to the government, only the most appalling circumstances could justify the resort to a party as a means of collecting the will of the people. And that party had to be a temporary one; it would exist only as long as the threat from the dire circumstances persisted.

The organizers of the Republican party saw themselves in just such awful circumstances, indeed, in a situation resembling the 1760s and 1770s. They believed that monarchism was once again threatening liberty, and their party was justified as a means of arousing the people into resistance. If parties were divided "merely by a greediness for office, as in England," said Jefferson, then to participate in a party "would be unworthy of a reasonable or moral man." But where the difference was one "between the republicans and Monocrats of our country," then the only honorable course was to refrain from pursuing a middle line and "to take a firm and decided part," as any honest man would take against rogues.[56]

The Republican party began with the activities of notables at the center of government. Voting patterns in the First and Second Congresses (1789–1792) revealed shifting sectional splits that only gradually formed regular party divisions. Only in 1793 did consistent voting blocs in the Congress clearly emerge.[57]

But identification with the Republican cause involved more than the gentleman leaders in the Congress. In localities throughout much of the country, many ordinary people opposed to the established leadership or to the direction of affairs began organizing themselves and voicing their dissent. The sudden mushrooming of these Democratic-Republican Societies outside of the regular institutions of government frightened many people. Their seeming connection with the French Revolution and the Whiskey Rebellion and President Washington's criticism doomed them to a brief two-year existence.

The organizing of these Democratic-Republican Societies began in April 1793, sparked by growing popular enthusiasm for the revolutionary

55. Sharp, *American Politics in the Early Republic,* 64.
56. TJ to William Branch Giles, 31 Dec. 1795, *Papers of Jefferson,* 28: 566.
57. John F. Hoadley, "The Emergence of Political Parties in Congress, 1789–1803," *American Political Science Review,* 74 (1980), 757–79.

ideas of France. Some Germans in Philadelphia formed a Democratic-Republican Society in order to urge citizens to be vigilant in watching over their government. This group inspired the creation of the Democratic Society of Pennsylvania, which in turn sent a circular letter calling for the formation of similar societies throughout the country. By the end of 1794 no fewer than thirty-five and perhaps many more of these popular organizations had been created, scattered from Maine to South Carolina. They were often composed of self-made entrepreneurs, mechanics and manufacturers, small-time merchants, farmers, and other middling people, angry at the aristocratic pretensions of many of the Federalist gentry. The organizations issued resolutions and addresses; they denounced the Federalists and supported Republican candidates and causes everywhere; and they communicated with one another in the way the committees of correspondence of the 1760s and 1770s had.[58]

These societies were more radical and outspoken than elite leaders like Jefferson and Madison, who tended to keep well clear of them. They represented a democratic future that few American leaders could yet accept or even envision. They challenged the older world of deferential political leadership and called for the people's participation in the affairs of government beyond merely periodically casting their votes. They told the people to shed their habitual awe of their so-called betters and to think and act for themselves. They adopted the French Revolutionary address of "Citizen" and resolved no longer to address their correspondents as "Sir" or use the phrase "Your humble servant" to close their letters. They took the notion of the sovereignty of the people literally and believed that the people had a continual right to organize and protest against even the actions of their own elected representatives.

But these Democratic-Republican Societies also met widespread resistance. Most American political leaders continued to abhor such extralegal activity, for it seemed to undermine the very idea of a legal representative government. "Undoubtedly the people is sovereign," opponents of the Democratic-Republican Societies declared, "but this sovereignty is in the whole people, and not in any separate part, and cannot be exercised, but by the Representatives of the whole nation."[59] Although Jefferson and other Republican leaders were reluctant to endorse these popular societies openly for fear of being thought seditious, the societies

---

58. Matthew Schoenbacher, "Republicanism in the Age of the Democratic Revolution: The Democratic-Republican Societies of the 1790s," *JER*, 18 (1998), 237–62; Albrecht Koschnik, *"Let a Common Interest Bind Us Together": Associations, Partisanship, and Culture in Philadelphia, 1775–1840* (Charlottesville, 2007), 22–40.

59. Koschnik, *"Let a Common Interest Bind Us Together,"* 31–32.

themselves had no such reluctance in endorsing the Republican leaders. "May the patriots of '76 step forward with Jefferson at their head and cleanse the country of degeneracy and corruption," went one Kentucky toast in 1795.[60] Although these societies did not generally manage elections, nominate tickets, or seek control of offices, they did set forth ideas that made people of different areas and different social groups feel they were part of a common Republican cause. Thus, even though they became associated in many people's minds with the Whiskey Rebellion and disappeared as quickly as they had arisen, they foreshadowed the democratic world that was coming and contributed greatly to what held the Republican party together.

THE EMERGING REPUBLICAN PARTY comprised a wide variety of social groups. Foremost were the Southern landowners who were becoming conscious of the distinctiveness of their section and increasingly estranged from the commercial and banking world that Hamilton's system seemed to be promoting. They were surprised by the promotion of Hamilton's system, for they had expected to have greater control over the fate of the country than the Federalist program seemed to allow. At the outset of the new national government, they had had every reason to believe that the future belonged to them.

In 1789 the South dominated the nation. Close to half the population of the United States lived in the five states south of the Mason-Dixon Line. With a population of nearly seven hundred thousand, Virginia was by far the most populous state in the Union, almost double the size of its nearest competitor, Pennsylvania; in fact, by itself Virginia constituted a fifth of the nation. It was, as Patrick Henry declared in 1788, "the most mighty State in the Union." It surpassed every other state, he said, not only "in number of inhabitants" but "in extent of territory, felicity of position, and affluence and wealth."[61]

The population of nearly all of the Southern states was growing rapidly. Since the end of the French and Indian War in 1763, the white population had tripled in North Carolina and quadrupled in South Carolina and Georgia. Nearly everyone in the country in 1789 assumed that Southern migrants would be the principal settlers of the new lands of the West.

Although the entire Republic remained rural and still primarily devoted to agriculture, nowhere was it more rural and agricultural than

60. Eugene Perry Link, *Democratic-Republican Societies, 1790–1800* (New York, 1942), 133.
61. Richard Labunski, *James Madison and the Struggle for the Bill of Rights* (New York, 2006), 291–92.

in the South. Nearly the whole population of the South was engaged in growing staple crops for international markets, with relatively few people being involved in the internal trade and manufacturing that were rapidly emerging in the Northern states. Planters in Virginia and Maryland still produced many hogsheads of tobacco for sale abroad, though not as many as they had in the colonial period. Since tobacco was not a very perishable crop and had direct markets abroad in Glasgow and Liverpool, there had been no need for processing and distribution centers, and consequently the colonial Chesapeake had developed no towns or cities to speak of.[62] But tobacco was a crop that depleted the soil, and in the late colonial period many farmers in the Upper South, including Washington, had begun turning to wheat, corn, and livestock for export or for local consumption. Because wheat and other foodstuffs were perishable and required diverse markets, they needed central facilities for sorting and distributing, which on the eve of the Revolution contributed to the rapid growth of towns such as Norfolk, Baltimore, Alexandria, and Fredericksburg. In the Lower South rice and indigo for the dying of textiles were the principal staples; in 1789 cotton was not as yet a major crop.

Most important in distinguishing the Southern states from the rest of the country was the overwhelming presence of African slaves. In 1790 black slaves constituted 30 percent of the population of Maryland and North Carolina, 40 percent of that of Virginia, and nearly 60 percent of that of South Carolina. The Southern states held well over 90 percent of the country's slaves. They served their masters' every need, from making hogsheads and horseshoes to caring for gardens and children. The planters' reliance on the labor of their slaves inhibited the growth of large middling groups of white artisans, who were increasingly emerging in the Northern states.

Although most Southern planters were becoming more conscious of their distinctiveness, mostly because of their slaveholding, some Virginians did not as yet think of themselves as Southerners. Washington, for example, in the late 1780s regarded Virginia as one of "the middle states" and referred to South Carolina and Georgia as the "Southern states."[63] But other Americans were already aware of the sectional differences. In June 1776 John Adams had believed that the South was too aristocratic for the kind of popular republican government he had advocated in his *Thoughts on Government*, but he was relieved to see "the pride of the

---

62. Carville Earle and Ronald Hoffman, "Urban Development in the Eighteenth-Century South," *Perspectives in American History*, 10 (1976), 67.
63. John Richard Alden, *The First South* (Baton Rouge, 1961), 9.

haughty" brought down "a little" by the Revolution.[64] An English traveler likewise thought that the Virginia planters were "haughty"; in addition, they were "jealous of their liberties, impatient of restraint, and can scarcely bear the thought of being controuled by any superior power." By 1785 Stephen Higginson, Boston merchant and one of the Federalist leaders of Massachusetts, had become convinced that "in their habits, manners and commercial Interests, the southern and northern States are not only very dissimilar, but in many instances directly opposed."[65]

Jefferson agreed, and in 1785 he outlined to a French friend his sense of the differences between the people of the two sections, which, following the intellectual fashion of the age, he attributed mostly to differences of climate. The Northerners were "cool, sober, laborious, preserving, independent, jealous of their own liberties, and just to those of others, interested, chicaning, superstitious and hypocritical in their religion." By contrast, said Jefferson, the Southerners were "fiery, voluptuary, indolent, unsteady, independent, zealous for their own liberties but trampling on those of others, generous, candid, without attachment or pretensions to any religion but that of the heart." Jefferson thought that these characteristics grew "weaker and weaker by gradation from North to South and South to North," with Pennsylvania being the place where "the two characters seem to meet and blend, and form a people free from the extremes both of vice and virtue." Despite his sensitivity to the differences, however, Jefferson and most other planters scarcely foresaw how dissimilar the two sections would become over the next several decades.[66]

At first the new Republican party seemed to be exclusively a Southern party, with most of its leaders, including Jefferson and Madison, being members of the slaveholding aristocracy. Indeed, some historians have contended that the Republican party was designed mainly to protect slavery from an overweening federal government.[67] Certainly, there were some Southerners, especially by the second decade of the nineteenth century, who feared the power of the federal government precisely because of what it might do to the institution of slavery.

64. Gordon S. Wood, *The Creation of the American Republic, 1776–1787* (Chapel Hill, 1969), 97 n.
65. Carl Bridenbaugh, *Seat of Empire: The Political Role of Eighteenth-Century Williamsburg* (Williamsburg, 1950), 10; Higginson to JA, 8 Aug. 1785, in J. Franklin Jameson, ed., "Letters of Stephen Higginson, 1783–1804," *American Historical Association, Annual Report for 1896* (Washington, DC, 1897), 1: 728.
66. TJ to Marquis de Chastellux, 2 Sept. 1785, *Jefferson: Writings*, 826–27.
67. See, for examples, Joseph J. Ellis, *American Creation: Triumphs and Tragedies at the Founding of the Republic* (New York, 2007), 163–204; Robin L. Einhorn, *American Taxation, American Slavery* (Chicago, 2006), 151–55, 184–99, 251–55.

Yet paradoxically these slaveholding aristocratic leaders of the Republican party were the most fervent supporters of liberty, equality, and popular republican government in the nation. They condemned the privileges of rich speculators and moneyed men and celebrated the character of ordinary yeoman farmers, who were independent and incorruptible and "the surest support of a healthy nation." Unlike many Federalist gentry in the North, these Southern gentry retained the earlier Whig confidence in what Jefferson called the "honest heart" of the common man.[68]

Part of the faith in democratic politics that Jefferson and his Southern colleagues shared came from their relative isolation from it. With the increasing questioning of black slavery in the North and throughout the world, many white yeoman small farmers in the South found a common solidarity with large plantation owners. They tended more or less faithfully to support the leadership of the great slaveholding planters. As a result, the great Southern planters never felt threatened by the democratic electoral politics that was undermining people's deference to the "the better sort" in the North. The more established the leadership, in other words, the less reason the Southern leaders had to doubt republican principles or the power of the people.[69]

In the North, especially in the rapidly growing middle states, ambitious individuals and new groups without political connections were finding that the Republican party was the best means for challenging entrenched leaders who were more often than not Federalists. Therefore the Republican party in the North differed sharply from its Southern branch, which made the national party an unstable and incongruous coalition from the outset. In the South the Republican opposition to the Federalist program was largely the response of rural slaveholding gentry who were committed to a nostalgic image of independent free-holding farmers and fearful of anti-slavery sentiments and new financial and commercial interests emerging in the North.

In the North, however, the Republican party was the political expression of new egalitarian-minded social forces released and intensified by the Revolution. Of course, individuals had a variety of motives for joining the Republican party or voting for Republican candidates. Often those attracted to the Republican cause were minority groups, like the Baptists in Massachusetts and Connecticut who were eager to challenge the Federalist-dominated Congregational religious establishment. Many others, such as those of Scots-Irish or German heritage, sympathized with the

68. TJ, *Notes on the State of Virginia*, ed. William Peden (Chapel Hill, 1955), 164–65.
69. Richard Buel Jr., *Securing the Revolution: Ideology in American Politics, 1789–1815* (Ithaca, 1972), 72–90.

Republicans simply because they did not like the kind of Anglophiles who were Federalists. But most supportive of the Republican party in the North were those enterprising and rapidly increasing middling people resentful of the pretensions and privileges of the entrenched Federalist elites. These included ambitious commercial farmers, artisans, manufacturers, tradesmen, and second- and third-level merchants, especially those involved in newer or marginal trading areas. As the headstrong Massachusetts Federalist the Reverend Jedidiah Morse pointed out, these Northern Republicans were those who "most bitterly denounce as aristocrats all who do not think as they do."[70] "Aristocrat" indeed had become the pejorative term that best described the enemy of the Northern Republicans. These middling sorts had every reason to support the party that favored minimal government, low taxes, and hostility to monarchical England.

In May 1793 Jefferson offered his own description of the Federalists and Republicans. On the Federalist side, rife with "old tories," were the "fashionable circles" in the major port cities, merchants trading on British capital, and paper speculators. On the other Republican side, he said, were merchants trading on their own capital, Irish merchants, and "tradesmen, mechanics, farmers, and every other possible description of our citizens."[71] Jefferson's description can hardly explain the extent of popular support from ordinary folk that the Federalists commanded in the 1790s, but it does suggest the aspiring and upwardly mobile character of the Republican cause in the North.[72]

Because wealthy Federalist merchants dominated the lucrative imported dry goods trade with Great Britain, less well established merchants were forced to find trade partners wherever they could—the European continent, the West Indies, or elsewhere. When the arriviste merchant John Swanwick of Philadelphia was denied access both to the highest social circles of the city and to the established British trade routes, he knew how to get back at his Federalist tormentors. He found prosper-

---

70. Charles Warren, *Jacobin and Junto: Early American Politics as Viewed in the Diary of Dr. Nathaniel Ames, 1758–1822* (New York, 1931), 53.

71. TJ to JM, 13 May 1793, *Papers of Jefferson*, 26: 26.

72. Two years later, in 1795, Jefferson did attempt to explain how the "trifling" membership in the Federalist party, or "the Anti-republican party," as he called it, could have the "appearance of strength and numbers." The Federalists, he said, "all live in cities, together, and can act in a body readily and at all times; they give chief employment to the newspapers, and therefore have most of them under their control." Although the Republicans outnumbered the Federalists by five hundred to one, Jefferson thought that "the Agricultural interest is dispersed over a great extent of country, have little means of intercommunications with each other," and was vulnerable to the Federalists' unity. TJ, "Notes on the Letter of Christopher Daniel Ebeling," after 15 Oct. 1795, *Jefferson Papers*, 28: 509.

ous markets in China, India, Germany, France, and parts of southern Europe and became an enthusiastic member of the Pennsylvania Republican party. His defeat of an ultra-Federalist in the 1792 election to the Pennsylvania assembly was viewed as a setback for "the aristocrats" of the state and a victory for middling export merchants and rising entrepreneurs. Swanwick's election to Congress in 1794 as the first Republican congressman from Philadelphia was even more stunning. His victory convinced Madison that the tide was turning toward the Republicans in the North.[73]

Even Federalist-dominated New England had its share of "Republican-merchants." Many, like the Crowninshields of Salem, found a niche in trade with the French empire and the Far East and naturally resented the Federalist mercantile elite that commanded the profitable trade with Great Britain.[74] Elsewhere in New England those whose profits depended on trade with France, and not England, challenged Federalist control of the maritime towns. But in the 1790s these challengers were generally weak and marginal. There was, for example, only one Democratic-Republican Society of any importance in New England in 1794.[75] Federalist gentry and mercantile elites involved in the British import trade dominated New England to an extent not duplicated in other sections of the nation, which made New England the center of Federalism.

Even the artisans in New England, who in other places became Republicans, remained bound to the Federalist cause. From 1793 to 1807 New England's interests and prosperity were almost entirely absorbed in overseas trade. Indeed, investors put five to six times more money into mercantile enterprises than they did into industrial businesses. Consequently, the New England artisans often found themselves too closely tied into patronage-client relationships with the import merchants to develop as sharp a sense of their separate interests as that possessed by artisans and craftsmen elsewhere in the country. Since many of these New Englanders were involved in the building of ships and maritime equipment used in overseas trade, they inevitably became especially supportive of Hamilton's program and its reliance on the British import trade. As a consequence, the Republicans discovered that they were less able to recruit artisans and other middling sorts in the urban ports of New England than

73. Roland M. Baumann, "John Swanwick," *Pa. Mag. of Hist. and Biog.*, 97 (1973), 131–82, quotation at 142; Richard G. Miller, *Philadelphia—The Federalist City: A Study of Urban Politics, 1789–1801* (Port Washington, NY, 1976), 84–86.
74. Paul Goodman, *The Democratic-Republicans of Massachusetts: Politics in a Young Republic* (Cambridge, MA, 1964), 108–14.
75. Link, *Democratic-Republican Societies*, 63.

they were elsewhere. In the eyes of many people in the 1790s the Federalist party, such as it was, seemed to be mostly confined to New England.[76]

Outside of New England the situation was different. In the Mid-Atlantic States most artisans and manufacturers became Republicans. This development was unexpected. At the outset of the 1790s it seemed evident that most artisans throughout the country would be firm supporters of the Federalists. After all, during the debate over the Constitution in 1787–1788 artisans and manufacturers up and down the continent had been ardent Federalists. They had strongly favored the new Constitution and had looked forward to a strong national government that could levy tariffs and protect them from competitive British manufactured imports. Congress's first tariff act of 1789 listed a number of goods for protection, including beer, carriages, cordage, shoes, sugars, snuff, and tobacco products. Yet most of the manufacturers soon became dissatisfied with the government's measures, believing that the duties levied on foreign imports were too low and not sufficiently protective of their businesses. Secretary of the Treasury Hamilton seemed more interested in producing revenue to finance the federal debt than in offering protection to mechanics and manufacturers. Hamilton, of course, did not foresee the future any better than the other Founders; but by not supporting artisans and manufacturers, who were the budding businessmen of the future, he made his biggest political mistake. It cost the Federalists dearly.

Not only did the Federalists refuse to levy heavy protective tariffs, but they began taxing the artisans' products directly. When in 1794 Hamilton and the Washington administration resorted to placing excise taxes on American goods, artisans and manufacturers, especially in the Mid-Atlantic States, became alarmed. The federal government initially taxed snuff, refined sugar, and carriages, and implied that excise taxes on other goods might follow. In Philadelphia, large-scale manufacturers of tobacco and sugar organized a protest of hundreds of artisans and tradesmen against the excise taxes in May 1794. The federal excise taxes directly affected 15 percent of the manufacturers in the city and indirectly affected many more. Spokesmen for the manufacturers argued that these "infant industries" needed the "fostering care of government" and condemned the excise taxes as unrepublican. Instead of taxing industry and the new

76. Gary J. Kornblith, "Artisan Federalism: New England Mechanics and the Political Economy of the 1790s," in Ronald Hoffman and Peter J. Albert, eds., *Launching the "Extended Republic": The Federalist Era* (Charlottesville, 1996), 249–72; Lisa B. Lubow, "From Carpenter to Capitalist: The Business of Building in Postrevolutionary Boston," in Conrad Edrick Wright and Katheryn P. Viens, eds., *Entrepreneurs: The Boston Business Community, 1700–1850* (Boston, 1997), 195–96.

kind of entrepreneurial property that was emerging, the government, they argued, ought to be taxing landed and proprietary wealth.

But the Federalists, concentrating on the support of established gentry and of merchants involved in importing goods from abroad, ignored the pleas of the artisans and tradesmen. Despite his report on manufacturing, Hamilton thought that Americans were, "and must be for years, rather an Agricultural than a manufacturing people." Other Federalists agreed. The rich New England merchant and devout Federalist Stephen Higginson dismissed all American manufacturing as "of no consequence" and did all he could to stifle the efforts of artisans to organize. Although many Federalist gentlemen regarded these protesting Philadelphia artisans and mechanics as "the lower class of people" who were "ignorant but harmless," some of the manufacturers were in fact very wealthy, their incomes nearly equaling those of the richest gentlemen in the city.[77] Overall, of course, the Republicans in the North tended to have less wealth than the Federalists; during the 1790s the Republican candidates in Philadelphia, for example, possessed about half the mean wealth of the Federalist candidates.[78] But they were not the poor, and they were anything but inconsequential.

The Northern Republicans were thus supported by a variety of social interests, ranging from fairly wealthy manufacturers and entrepreneurs to journeymen-employees and common laborers. During the 1790s these mostly middling sorts increasingly came together in angry reaction to the contempt in which they were held by the Federalist gentry. The Federalists resisted every attempt by Northern artisans to organize, lest their success, as one Federalist writer put it, "excite similar attempts among all other descriptions of persons who live by manual labor."[79]

These rising Northern workers and entrepreneurs were in fact the principal contributors to the capitalist world that the Southern Republicans were coming to fear. Hamilton and the few stockjobbers, speculators, and wealthy merchants who supported his financial program could never by themselves have created the middling commercial world that was emerging in the Northern states. To be sure, it was the Federalists' stable political structure and Hamilton's financial program that made

77. AH, Conversations with George Beckwith, Oct. 1789, *Papers of Hamilton*, 5: 483; Roland M. Baumann, "Philadelphia's Manufacturers and the Excise Taxes of 1794," *Pa. Mag. of Hist. and Biog.*, 106 (1982), 17–18, 20, 22, 33; Link, *Democratic-Republican Societies*, 77.

78. Andrew Shankman, *Crucible of American Democracy: The Struggle to Fuse Egalitarianism and Capitalism in Jeffersonian Pennsylvania* (Lawrence, KS, 2004), 62.

79. Alfred F. Young, *The Democratic Republicans of New York: The Origins, 1763–1797* (Chapel Hill, 1967), 407.

economic development possible; but ultimately it was ordinary business-minded artisans and commercial farmers in the North who most fully exploited that political structure and that financial program to create the burgeoning capitalist economy of the early Republic. Although many of these Northern artisans and farmers became supporters of the Republican party, the Southern leaders of that party, Jefferson and Madison, scarcely understood the diverse social and sectional character of their followers.

What held these diverse and ultimately incompatible sectional and social elements together was a comprehensive and common ideology. This Republican ideology, involving a deep hatred of overgrown central power and a fear of the political and financial mechanisms that sustained such power—inflated executive authority, high taxes, standing armies, and perpetual debts—had been inherited from the English radical Whig "country-opposition" tradition that had been sharpened and American-ized during the Revolution. In the 1790s this ideology was given height-ened relevance by the monarchical-like policies of the Federalist administration.

To those steeped in this radical Whig ideology, Hamilton's system threatened to re-create the kind of government and society that many Americans thought they had destroyed in 1776. Such a hierarchical soci-ety, based on patronage connections and artificial privilege and supported by a bloated executive bureaucracy and a standing army, would in time, the Republicans believed, destroy the integrity and independence of the republican citizenry. Hamilton's federal program, including funding the Revolutionary debt, assuming the state debts, adopting excise taxes, estab-lishing a standing army, and creating a national bank, seemed to be remi-niscent of what Sir Robert Walpole and other ministers had done in England earlier in the century. Hamilton appeared to be using his new economic system to create a swelling phalanx of what Jefferson called "stock-jobbers and king-jobbers" in order to corrupt Congress and build up executive power at the expense of the people in the way eighteenth-century British ministers had done.

Once the Republicans grasped this ideological pattern, all the Federalist measures fell into place. The elaborate pageantry of the "court," the aris-tocratic talk of titles, the enlargement of the military, the growth of taxes, especially excise taxes, the reliance on the monarchical president and an aristocratic Senate—all these pointed toward a systematic plan, as Caro-line County of Virginia declared in 1793, of "assimilating the American government to the form and spirit of the British monarchy." Most basic and dangerous of all was the Federalist creation of a huge perpetual fed-eral debt, which, as New York governor George Clinton explained, not only would poison the morals of the people through speculation but would also "add an artificial support to the administration, and by a species of bribery enlist the monied men of the community on the side of the measures of the government.... Look to Great Britain." In the eyes of the Republicans it was the struggle against the corrupt monarchism of the 1760s and 1770s all over again.[80]

80. Banning, *Jeffersonian Persuasion*, 213.

# 5

# The French Revolution in America

The French Revolution began in 1789 at the very moment that the new American national government was getting under way. When the meeting of the Estates-General in May 1789 was followed by the formation of the French National Assembly in June, the fall of the Bastille in July, and the Declaration of the Rights of Man and Citizen in August 1789, Americans could only conclude that France was well on its way to emulating their own revolution. Most Americans gratefully recalled how France had come to their aid during their revolutionary struggle with Great Britain. Now Americans were repaying that debt by spreading the spirit of liberty abroad. Indeed, they hoped that their revolutionary ideals would eventually extend throughout the entire world.

The liberal nobleman the Marquis de Lafayette, who in 1777 at the age of twenty had joined Washington's army, certainly saw the insurrection of July 1789 as a response to American principles. After assuming leadership of the Paris National Guard in July 1789, Lafayette sent Washington the key to the Bastille as a token of his gratitude for having been taught what freedom was during his participation in the American Revolution. And it was right that he did so, declared Thomas Paine, for the idea "that the principles of America opened the Bastille is not to be doubted."[1] That France followed its Declaration of Rights with a written constitution in 1791 only convinced most Americans that they had become the instigator of an international liberal revolution.

At first, American enthusiasm for the French Revolution was almost unanimous. Federalists like John Jay and John Marshall were just as fervent in support of France's liberal reforms in 1789 as future Republicans like Thomas Jefferson and William Maclay. Even most of the conservative New England clergy initially welcomed what was happening in France. "We were all strongly attached to France—scarcely any man

1. Stanley Elkins and Eric McKitrick, *The Age of Federalism* (New York, 1993), 309.

more strongly than myself," recalled John Marshall. "I sincerely believed human liberty to depend in a great measure on the success of the French Revolution."[2]

During the July 1790 celebration in Paris of the first anniversary of the storming of the Bastille, John Paul Jones and Thomas Paine carried American flags symbolizing the connection between the two revolutions. Governor Harry Lee of Virginia was so excited by the French Revolution that he thought of emigrating to France and joining the cause; George Washington helped talk him out it. Even as the French Revolution became more radical, with the Revolutionary government launching a preemptive war against monarchical Europe in April 1792—a war that would not end until the peace of 1815—American support remained strong.

The European monarchies soon struck back. In August 1792 an Austrian and Prussian army together with some French aristocratic émigrés invaded France to put down the Revolution. When Americans learned that the French in September 1792 had stopped the Austrian and Prussian invaders at Valmy, one hundred miles east of Paris, and then had declared France a republic, they were thrilled. At last France had become a sister republic, joining America in a common struggle against the forces of monarchism.

Some Americans began wearing French tricolored cockades and singing French revolutionary songs. Revolutionary France reciprocated by bestowing honorary French citizenship on several Americans—George Washington, Thomas Paine, Alexander Hamilton, and James Madison—for courageously upholding the cause of liberty. Throughout the winter of 1792–1793 Americans celebrated the victory at Valmy up and down the continent with bells, illuminations, and parades; indeed, nearly everyone in the Western world, including Goethe, who was present at the battle, soon realized that the revolutionary enthusiasm of the French army at Valmy represented, in Goethe's words, the beginning of "a new epoch in the history of the world." The January 24, 1793, celebration in Boston, which was the center of conservative Federalism, was the most elaborate festival of all, involving thousands of citizens; in fact, it was the largest public celebration that had ever been held in North America.[3]

2. Elkins and McKitrick, *Age of Federalism*, 310; Philipp Ziesche, "Gouverneur Morris, Thomas Jefferson, and the National Struggle for Universal Rights in Revolutionary France," *JER*, 26 (2006), 419–47.

3. William Doyle, *The Oxford History of the French Revolution* (Oxford, 1989), 193; Simon F. Newman, *Parades and the Politics of the Street: Festive Culture in the Early American Republic* (Philadelphia, 1997), 124–25.

So popularly exuberant were these civic celebrations of "liberty and equality" in the winter of 1792–1793 that many Federalists became alarmed and began tempering their initial enthusiasm for the French Revolution. Actually, like Edmund Burke in England, some Federalists had expressed doubts at the outset about the course of the French Revolution and had pointed out its difference from the American Revolution. As early as 1790, members of the Senate, whose chamber was decorated with giant portraits of King Louis XVI and Marie Antoinette, were reluctant to receive any communications at all from the French National Assembly. When the French had learned of the death of Benjamin Franklin in 1790, they, unlike Americans, were quick to eulogize the great scientist and diplomat. In addition to declaring three days of mourning—the first such honor paid a foreigner in French history—the French National Assembly proposed to the American government that the people of "the two nations connect themselves by a mutual affection" in the interests of liberty. Many Federalists, however, were not all that eager to honor Franklin, who had become identified with democratic principles and with France; and in the clumsy politics of mourning that followed his death, the Senate received the proposal of the French National Assembly with what Senator Maclay called amazing "Coldness." Maclay could only wonder what the "French Patriots" would think "when they find that we, cold as Clay, care not a fig about them, Franklin, or Freedom."[4]

In other words, some Federalists were already prepared by events in America to think the worst about what was happening in France. Since at least the 1780s many members of the elite had become increasingly anxious about the growth of popular power in America and the licentious tendencies of the American Revolution. Had not the Constitution of 1787 and the new national government been created in part at least to control these democratic tendencies? Now some Federalists began to see in France the terrifying possibilities of what might happen in America if popular power were allowed to run free. The rioting in Paris and elsewhere, the horrific massacres in September 1792 of over fourteen hundred prisoners charged with being enemies of the Revolution, the news that Lafayette had been deserted by his troops and his allies in the Assembly and had fled France—all these events convinced the Federalists that the French Revolution was sliding into popular anarchy.

American enthusiasm for the French Revolution seemed to be quite capable of dragging the United States into the same kind of popular anarchy. After describing the horrors and butchery taking place in Paris,

4. Larry E. Tise, *American Counterrevolution: A Retreat from Liberty, 1783–1800* (Mechanicsburg, PA, 1998), 4–6.

Federalist George Cabot of Massachusetts asked anxiously, "Will not this, or something like it, be the wretched fate of our country?"[5]

When Americans learned that the thirty-eight-year-old king Louis XVI, the ruler who had helped them win their independence from the British a decade earlier, had been executed for treason on January 21, 1793, and that the French Republic had declared war on England on February 1, 1793, their division into Federalists and Republicans intensified. The meaning of the French Revolution now became entwined in the quarrel that Americans were having among themselves over the direction of their own revolution.

WHILE THE FEDERALISTS EXPRESSED HORROR at what was happening in France, Republicans everywhere applauded the abolition of the French monarchy, and some of them even welcomed the execution of America's former benefactor Louis XVI. Jefferson had no qualms about the king's trial and execution; Louis, he said, ought to be punished "like other criminals." James Monroe dismissed the regicide as merely an incidental contribution "to a much greater cause." The Republican *National Gazette* even joked about it—"Louis Capet has lost his Caput."[6]

While Jefferson and the Republicans tied the fate of the American Revolution to the success of the French Revolution, the Federalists were determined to distinguish them from one another. "Would to Heaven that the comparison were just," said Hamilton in May 1793. "Would to heaven that we could discern in the Mirror of French affairs, the same humanity, the same decorum, the same gravity, the same order, the same dignity, the same solemnity, which distinguished the course of the American Revolution." But unfortunately, he said, there was no "real resemblance" between the two revolutions—their "difference is no less great than that between Liberty and Licentiousness."[7] For the remainder of the decade, if not for the next two centuries, it became impossible for Americans to think of one revolution without the other—if only to contrast what many Americans described as their sober and conservative Revolution with the radical and chaotic French Revolution.

Most Federalists were convinced that the radical popular and egalitarian principles of the French Revolution threatened to corrupt American

5. Charles Warren, *Jacobin and Junto: Early American Politics as Viewed in the Diary of Dr. Nathaniel Ames, 1758–1822* (New York, 1931), 51.
6. TJ to Joseph Fay, 18 March 1793, *Papers of Jefferson*, 25: 402; Jay Winik, *The Great Upheaval: America and the Birth of the Modern World, 1788–1800* (New York, 2007), 463; Charles D. Hazen, *Contemporary American Opinion of the French Revolution* (1897; Gloucester, MA, 1964), 257.
7. AH to _____, 18 May 1793, *Papers of Hamilton*, 16: 475–76.

society and turn it into a wild and licentious democracy. They charged that the theories of Voltaire, Rousseau, and Condorcet and atheistic Jacobinical thinking were infecting the moral and religious culture of Americans. The principles of the French Revolution, they warned, would "destroy us as a society" and were "more to be dreaded in a moral view than a thousand yellow fevers in a physical." Better that the United States be "erased from existence than infected with French principles," declared a rather hysterical young Oliver Wolcott Jr.[8] For many frightened Federalists, Revolutionary France became a scapegoat for all that they found wrong with America.

Yet some of the more insightful Federalists knew better. Some realized that France was not actually the source of America's democratic troubles; the real source, they knew, lay within America itself. Although these Federalists could scarcely comprehend the extent to which their revolution had accelerated powerful underlying demographic and economic forces, they realized only too well that the democracy and equality that were afflicting America were the consequences of the American Revolution, not the French Revolution. Like the young lawyer Joseph Dennie, who would eventually become editor of the Port Folio, one of the most genteel magazines in America, the Federalists respected the "old whigs of 1775," but they also realized that these Whigs had unleashed dynamic popular movements that were spreading everywhere. It was the principles of the American Revolution, and not French influence, Dennie told his parents early in 1793, that "gave Tars and Tailors a civic feast and taught the rabble that they were viceroys."[9]

The parading, huzzahing, and rioting by the lower orders that had long been part of Anglo-American life in the 1790s took on a new, more alarming character. To Federalists anxious about the weakness of the new national government, the ever more frequent popular celebrations and festivals on behalf of liberty and equality seemed to be agencies of the emerging Republican party and thus a threat to public order.

This sense of threat was new. During most of the eighteenth century most elites had condescendingly dismissed these popular rites and rituals as the rabble simply letting off steam. Usually these popular celebrations had tended to reinforce the existing structures of authority even as they sometimes defied them. In fact, it was the awesomeness of personal and social authority in earlier times that had compelled common people to resort to mock ceremonies and rituals as a means of dealing with their humiliations and resentments. Such brief saturnalian transgressions of

8. Hazen, American Opinion of the French Revolution, 276, 277.
9. Newman, Parades and the Politics of the Street, 125.

the society's rules had momentarily allowed humble people to release in a controlled fashion their pent-up anger. Consequently, the use of effigies and role reversals, in which boys, apprentices, and servants became kings for a day, often had worked not to undermine but to reaffirm the existing hierarchy of society.

But Federalist elites could not be as complacent about these popular rites and rituals as their eighteenth-century colonial predecessors had been. The lower orders were not as lowly as they used to be; they were now composed of tens of thousands of those who referred to themselves as "middling sorts"—artisans, small farmers, shopkeepers, petty merchants, all those who made up the bulk of the Northern Republican party. And the Republicans seemed not at all interested in reaffirming the existing structure of authority; they meant to destroy it and bring down all of the "aristocrats" who hitherto had dominated it. This linked them with their fellow revolutionaries across the Atlantic.

The theater became a favorite site for expressing popular feelings on behalf of the French and against the English. When an actor appeared on the stage in Philadelphia in the 1790s wearing a British uniform, he was roundly booed and hissed by the middling and lower social ranks in the gallery. In vain did the actor protest that he was merely playing the part of a coward and bully. Audiences in Philadelphia, especially those in the gallery, demanded under threat of violence that the orchestras play the popular French revolutionary song "Ça Ira." Sometimes the passion for the French spilled over into actual violence. A Boston audience, for example, concluded that the portrayal of a comic French character in a British play was "a libel on the character of the whole French nation" and took out its anger by demolishing the theater. Theater managers else-where knew enough to alter lines that might be offensive to Francophiles in the audience.[10]

The French Revolution seemed to be speaking for angry and aggrieved peoples everywhere. Its assault on aristocracy only confirmed that the Republicans' struggle against Federalist monarchism and aristocracy had worldwide implications. And no Republican was a more ardent supporter of the French Revolution than the party's emergent leader, Thomas Jefferson.

As minister to France in the 1780s, Jefferson had been involved in the French Revolution from the outset. As early as 1788 he was convinced

---

10. Susan Branson, *These Fiery Frenchified Dames: Women and Political Culture in Early National Philadelphia* (Philadelphia, 2001), 109; Heather Nathans, *Early American Theater from the Revolution to Thomas Jefferson: Into the Hands of the People* (Cambridge, UK, 2003), 79–81.

that the French nation, as he told Washington, had been "awakened by our Revolution." Throughout the period of 1787–1789 he remained close to Lafayette and the other liberal aristocrats who were eager to reform the French monarchy. He sometimes met with them in his own house and advised them on constitutional politics and procedures; he even drew up a charter that might be presented to the king, and he revised Lafayette's draft of a declaration of rights. He was not disturbed by the fall of the Bastille in July 1789; he still recognized, as he had said in response to Shays's Rebellion in 1787, that the tree of liberty had to be watered from time to time with the blood of tyrants and patriots. Before he returned from France in the early fall of 1789, he expressed his confidence in the course of the French Revolution, a confidence he never entirely lost. He was a thorough Francophile. In his Philadelphia house in the early 1790s he sought to re-create his Paris residence of the 1780s, with a French housekeeper, a French coachman, French wine, French food, French paintings, and French furniture—all of which was bound to seem sinister to Federalists.[11] As a British dinner partner observed in 1792, Jefferson in conversation was "a vigorous stickler for revolutions and for the downfall of an aristocracy.... In fact, like his friend T. Payne, he cannot live but in a revolution, and all events in Europe are only considered by him in the relation they bear to the probability of a revolution to be produced by them."[12]

For Jefferson the stakes involved in the French Revolution could not have been higher. Not only did Jefferson believe that the success of the French Revolution would determine the fate of America's own Revolution, but if the French Revolution succeeded, he said, "it would spread sooner or later all over Europe." But if it failed, America was very apt to retreat "to that kind of Halfway-house, the English constitution," and the "revival of liberty" everywhere in the world would be seriously set back.[13]

Jefferson, to be sure, deplored the loss of the tens of thousands of people guillotined and killed in France's revolutionary frenzy, 85 percent of whom were commoners; nevertheless, he believed that these executions and killings were necessary. "The liberty of the whole earth was depending on the issue of the contest," he said in January 1793, "and...rather than it should have failed, I would have seen half the earth desolated. Were there but an Adam and an Eve left in every country, and left free, it

11. Annette Gordon-Reed, *The Hemingses of Monticello: An American Family* (New York, 2008), 468–69.
12. S. W. Jackman, "A Young Englishman Reports on the New Nation: Edward Thornton to James Bland Burges, 1791–1793," *WMQ*, 18 (1961), 110.
13. TJ to George Mason, 4 Feb. 1791, *Papers of Jefferson*, 19: 241.

would be better than as it is now."[14] He grew warm whenever he thought about all those European tyrants, those "scoundrels," who were attacking France and resisting the spread of the French Revolution; he could only hope that France's eventual triumph would "bring at length kings, nobles and priests to the scaffolds which they have been so long deluging with human blood." Extreme as these sentiments may seem, they were, Jefferson believed, "really those of 99 in an hundred of our citizens."[15]

By 1795 he was looking forward to an imminent French invasion of England. So sure was he of French success that he was tempted, he said, to leave Monticello and travel to London the following year in order to dine there with the victorious French general and "hail the dawn of liberty and republicanism in that island."[16]

Even after the Revolution had turned into a Napoleonic dictatorship, Jefferson never lost faith that it might eventually result in the establishment of a free French republic. Bad as Napoleon might be, the Bourbon and Hanoverian kings were worse. Throughout his public life, his affection for France and his hatred of England never dimmed. France, he said, was the Americans' "true mother country, since she has assured to them their liberty and independence." The British, on the other hand, were "our natural enemies, and...the only nation on earth who wished us ill from the bottom of their souls." That nation, Great Britain, he said in 1789, "has moved heaven, earth and hell to exterminate us in war, has insulted us in all her councils in peace, shut her doors to us in every port where her interests would admit it, libeled us in foreign nations, [and] endeavored to poison them against the reception of our most precious commodities."[17]

Jefferson seems to have generated his identity as an American from his hatred of England—understandably so, since the Americans and the English had once been one people but were now presumably two. Indeed, the fact that America's sense of itself as a nation was created and sustained by its antagonism to Great Britain decisively affected both the country's unity and its relation to the rest of the world over the coming decades.

FRANCE'S DECLARATION OF WAR against England on February 1, 1793, seemed to compel Americans to choose sides.

14. TJ to William Short, 3 Jan. 1793, *Papers of Jefferson*, 25: 14.
15. TJ to Tench Coxe, 1 May 1794, *Papers of Jefferson*, 28: 67.
16. TJ to William Branch Giles, 27 April 1795, *Papers of Jefferson*, 28: 337.
17. John C. Miller, *The Federalist Era, 1789–1801* (New York, 1960), 127; TJ to William Carmichael, 15 Dec. 1787, *Papers of Jefferson*, 12: 424; TJ to JM, 28 Aug. 1789, *Republic of Letters*, 629.

Jefferson and his Republican followers were naturally sympathetic to "our younger sister," the new French republic.[18] The position of Hamilton and the Federalists was more complicated. Certainly, many of the Federalists and especially Hamilton admired Great Britain and its institutions, and the increasing radicalism of the French Revolution made them even more fervent supporters of England as a bastion of stability in a world that was going mad. In addition, Hamilton in 1793 was still largely concerned with maintaining good commercial relations with Britain, since the duties from that trade were necessary for the success of his financial program. Ultimately, however, for all their differing sympathies for the two belligerents, both Jefferson and Hamilton remained convinced that the United States had to remain neutral in the European war.

How to maintain this neutrality? What were the nation's obligations under the French treaties of 1778? Did the alliance with France require the United States to defend the French West Indies? Should the United States recognize the new French republic and receive its minister, Citizen Edmond Charles Genet, already en route to Philadelphia? Although Hamilton argued that the terms of the French treaties should be "temporarily and provisionally suspended" on the grounds that the outcome of the French civil war was still in doubt, Washington decided that the treaties were still in effect and that Genet would be received, which would make the United States the first nation in the world to recognize the new French republic. But Jefferson, like Hamilton, did not want the United States to be bound by the French treaties in any way that would endanger the nation's security. Thus both advisors recommended that the president issue a proclamation of neutrality, which he did on April 22, 1793. The proclamation did not use the word "neutrality," but it did urge Americans to "pursue a conduct friendly and impartial towards the belligerent powers." Jefferson had not realized that Edmund Randolph had slipped the word "impartial" into the final draft.[19]

Despite his desire to avoid a war, Jefferson was aware that such a policy of "fair neutrality," as he told Madison in April 1793, "will prove a disagreeable pill to our friends, tho' necessary to keep us out of the calamities of a war."[20] With his Republican followers enthusiastic in support of

18. Donald J. Ratcliffe, *Party Spirit in a Frontier Republic: Democratic Politics in Ohio, 1793–1821* (Columbus, OH, 1998), 20; Alfred F. Young, *The Democratic Republicans of New York: The Origins, 1763–1797* (Chapel Hill, 1967), 363; Dumas Malone, *Jefferson and the Ordeal of Liberty* (Boston, 1962), 71.

19. Richard Buel Jr., *Securing the Revolution: Ideology in American Politics, 1789–1815* (Ithaca, 1972), 42–43.

20. TJ to JM, 28 April 1793, *Papers of Jefferson*, 25: 619.

France, Jefferson was embarrassed by the policy of neutrality that he had supported, especially since France and the United States had an alliance dating from 1778; consequently he immediately began to distance himself from the proclamation. Jefferson, who, as one British observer noted, had "a degree of finesse about him, which at first is not discernable," took great pains to tell his friends that he had not written the proclamation, explaining that at least he had been able to have the word "neutrality" omitted from it.[21] Yet this Jeffersonian nicety scarcely satisfied the most avid Republicans.

Although most Republicans had no desire to go to war, they were not at all willing to remain impartial. "The cause of France is the cause of man," declared Hugh Henry Brackenridge, a Republican leader of western Pennsylvania, "and neutrality is desertion." Other Republicans agreed; everywhere they held public dinners and civic feasts to celebrate French victories in Europe.[22] Some Republicans even rejected the aristocratic queues, knee britches, and silver-buckled shoes of the Federalists and began adopting the cropped hairstyle and sans-culotte dress of the French revolutionaries.[23] The Republican press heatedly condemned the proclamation and declared that the great mass of the people was outraged at the ingratitude shown to America's former revolutionary ally.

Although Madison was not given to outbursts of emotion, even he thought the proclamation was "a most unfortunate error" that wounded the national honor by seeming to disregard America's obligations to France and provoked "popular feelings by a seeming indifference to the cause of liberty." Madison was as much of a liberal enthusiast for the French Revolution as his friend Jefferson. He had no qualms about accepting honorary French citizenship and did so with a hearty cosmopolitan declamation against "those prejudices which have perverted the artificial boundaries of nations into exclusions of the philanthropy which ought to cement the whole into one great family." He went on to tell Jefferson that the president's issuing of the proclamation not only usurped the prerogative of the Congress in violation of the Constitution but also had "the appearance of being copied from a Monarchical model." Still, Madison was very cautious in criticizing Washington himself, suggesting that the president "may not be sufficiently aware of the snares that may be laid for his good intentions by men whose politics at bottom are very

21. Joanne B. Freeman, *Affairs of Honor: National Politics in the New Republic* (New Haven, 2001), 45.
22. John C. Miller, *The Federalist Era, 1789–1801* (New York, 1960), 130; Jackman, "A Young Englishman Reports on the New Nation," 119.
23. Ratcliffe, *Party Spirit in a Frontier Republic*, 94.

different from his own." He told Jefferson, however, that if the president continued to conduct himself in the same manner, he would suffer more criticism that would permanently harm his reputation and that of the government.[24]

In an effort to win support for the proclamation, Hamilton in the summer of 1793 wrote seven powerfully argued newspaper essays under the name "Pacificus." These became the classic constitutional justification of the president's inherent authority over foreign affairs. Hamilton contended that not only did the United States have the right to declare its neutrality, but the president was the proper official to make such a declaration, since the executive department was the "organ of intercourse between the Nation and foreign Nations." Moreover, the United States had no obligation under the 1778 treaties to come to the aid of France, since those treaties provided for only a defensive alliance and France was engaged in an offensive war. Besides, said Hamilton, the great contrast between the situation of France and that of the United States by itself rendered foolish any obligation to go to France's aid.

"The United States," wrote Hamilton, "are a young nation." (Note the use of the plural verb, which remained common usage until after the Civil War.) Hamilton went on to express the basic assumption of relative American weakness that lay behind all his policies. "Their population though rapidly increasing, still small—their resources, though growing, not great; without armies, without fleets—capable from the nature of their country and the spirit of its inhabitants of immense efforts for self-defense, but little capable of those external efforts which could materially serve the cause of France." Finally, Hamilton dismissed the idea that gratitude should dictate America's helping France. Gratitude, he said, should have no bearing on relations between states; national interest ought to be the only consideration. France, after all, came to America's aid in 1778 only out of its own national interest in defeating Britain.[25]

Jefferson, believing that American neutrality was coming to mean "a mere English neutrality," was alarmed at the influence Hamilton's writings were having.[26] "Nobody answers him," he warned Madison, "and his

24. JM to TJ, 19 June 1793, 13 June 1793, *Papers of Madison*, 15: 31, 29; JM to the Minister of the French Republic, April 1793, *Republic of Letters*, 778.

25. AH, Pacificus No. I, 29 June 1793, Pacificus No. II, 3 July 1793, Pacificus No. III, 6 July 1793, Pacificus No. IV, 10 July 1793, Pacificus No. V, 13–17 July 1793, Pacificus No. VI, 17 July 1795, Pacificus No. VII, 27 July 1793, *Papers of Hamilton*, 15: 33–43, quotation at 38; 55–63; 65–69; 82–86; 90–95; 100–106, quotation at 103; 130–35.

26. James Roger Sharp, *American Politics in the Early Republic: The New Nation in Crisis* (New Haven, 1993), 79.

doctrine will therefore be taken for confessed. For god's sake, my dear Sir, take up your pen, select the most striking heresies, and cut him to pieces in the face of the public. There is nobody else who can and will enter the lists with him."[27]

Madison with great reluctance agreed to reply, unsure that he could match the secretary of the treasury in knowledge or energy. He found the task, he confessed, "the most grating one I ever experienced."[28] And the resultant "Helvidius" essays, published in August and September 1793, revealed his difficulty. Madison knew he would have to set forth some intricate details, but he assumed, as most essayists of the 1790s did, that "none but intelligent readers will enter into such a controversy, and to their minds it ought principally to be accommodated." He avoided the larger questions involving America's neutrality and focused instead on the constitutional limits of executive power, thus contributing further to what would become the peculiar American tendency to discuss political issues in constitutional terms—a tendency that had the effect of turning quarrels over policy into contests over basic principles. In an uncharacteristically long-winded argument Madison concluded that "Pacificus" could only have borrowed his peculiar notions of executive power from *royal prerogatives* in the *British government.*"[29] Each of the two American parties was now unambiguously identified with one or the other of the two great belligerents.

THE ACTIVITIES IN AMERICA of the twenty-nine-year-old French minister Citizen Edmond Charles Genet further excited public opinion—his title a sign of the new egalitarian order in France. No one could have been more ill suited for his diplomatic mission. As the minister of one of the two most powerful nations in the world, Genet was cocky, impulsive, and headstrong, with little or no understanding of the American government he was supposed to deal with. He landed in Charleston, South Carolina, in April 1793, and in his monthlong journey north to Philadelphia he was everywhere greeted with warmth and enthusiasm. Americans sang the "Marseillaise," waved the French revolutionary flag, and passed liberty caps around. Some Federalists thought the French Revolution was being brought to America. Late in his life John Adams still vividly recalled the frenzied atmosphere of "Terrorism, excited by Genet," that ran through the nation's capital in the late spring of 1793. "Ten thousand People in the Streets of Philadelphia, day after day,

27. TJ to JM, 7 July 1793, *Papers of Jefferson*, 26: 444.
28. JM to TJ, 30 July 1793, *Papers of Madison*, 15: 48.
29. JM to TJ, 22 July 1793, and "Helvidius" No. 1, 24 Aug 1793, *Papers of Madison*, 15: 47, 72.

threatened to drag Washington out of his House and effect a Revolution in the Government, or compel it to declare War in favour of the French Revolution, and against England."[30]

Genet was instructed to get the Americans to recognize their treaty obligations and allow the outfitting of French privateers in American ports. He was also to seek American assistance in the conquest of Spanish and British possessions in America and help to expand what the French revolutionary government called the "Empire de la Liberté."[31] When he was in Charleston, he began organizing filibustering expeditions against the Spanish in the Southwest. He even told his government that he planned to "excite the Canadians to free themselves from the yoke of England." He persuaded the French immigrant and naturalist André Michaux to abandon his plans to travel overland to the Pacific, which had been supported by Jefferson and the American Philosophical Society, and instead aid his native France by joining up with George Rogers Clark and Benjamin Logan in Kentucky and using soldiers they recruited to attack the Spanish in Louisiana. If this impetuous French minister had his way, America would soon be at war with both Great Britain and Spain.[32]

Seeing himself as a revolutionary agent on behalf of the international cause of liberty, Genet mistook the enthusiastic welcome he received in America as a license to promote the French Revolution in any way he could; indeed, initially Jefferson seems to have encouraged Genet in his ambitious plans to gather armies on American soil in order to attack Spanish possessions in the West and Florida. When Michaux changed his plans in order to rendezvous with Clark and the Kentuckian soldiers, Jefferson more or less supported him, but he informed Genet that Michaux had to travel as a private citizen and not as a French consul, as Genet wanted. The secretary of state warned Genet that if Michaux and the Kentucky soldiers were caught taking up arms against a friendly country, they might be hanged. "Leaving out that article," he blithely told Genet, he "did not care what insurrection should be excited in Louisiana."[33]

Genet met with some of the nascent Democratic-Republican Societies and was rumored to have been appointed president of one of them. At the same time, the brash young minister began recruiting American seamen,

---

30. JA to TJ, 30 June 1813, in Lester J. Cappon, ed., *The Adams-Jefferson Letters: The Complete Correspondence Between Thomas Jefferson and Abigail and John Adams* (Chapel Hill, 1959), 2: 346–47.
31. "The Recall of Edmond Charles Genet," *Papers of Jefferson*, 26: 686.
32. Malone, *Jefferson and the Ordeal of Liberty*, 104.
33. TJ, Notes of Cabinet Meeting and Conversations with Edmond Charles Genet, 5 July 1793, *Papers of Jefferson*, 26: 438.

commissioning and arming American ships as privateers, and setting up prize courts in American ports—all to the increasing discomfort of Secretary of State Jefferson. Genet even outfitted a captured British ship, the *Little Sarah*, in an American port and, in deliberate defiance of Washington's request, sent it to sea as a French privateer—the *Petite Democrate*. The French minister threatened to appeal directly to the people if the government protested.[34]

Ignoring Washington's instructions not to allow the captured ship to sail was one thing; suggesting that he might go over the head of the president to the American people was quite another. When Washington learned of Genet's actions and plans, he became furious. "Is the Minister of the French Republic to set the Acts of this Government at defiance, *with impunity*? and then threaten the Executive with an appeal to the People?" the president asked in astonishment. "What must the world think of such conduct, and of the Government of the U. States in submitting to it?"[35]

In the end Genet undid himself. Those Federalists opposed to the French Revolution, led by Hamilton, John Jay, and Rufus King, exploited the French minister's diplomatic blunders both to win support for the government's policy of neutrality and to discredit and weaken the Republican opposition. By spreading rumors of Genet's actions, the Federalists aroused public opinion and succeeded in transforming a diplomatic incident into a major public controversy. In meetings in New York, New Jersey, Delaware, Maryland, and Virginia, the Federalists sponsored resolutions condemning Genet and defending the president.

All these Federalist efforts to weaken public sympathy for the French Revolution alarmed the Republican leaders. Such efforts seemed further evidence of the Hamiltonian march toward monarchism. Madison thought the Federalists were trying to use "public veneration for the President" to promote "an animosity between America & France" in order to dissolve "their political & commercial union." This, said Madison, would be followed by a "connection" with Great Britain, and "under her auspices" the United States would move "in a gradual approximation towards her Form of Government."[36]

In response to these fears the Republicans began organizing their own party meetings. In some of their celebrations the Republicans even toasted the radical Jacobins, who had taken over the French government,

34. Harry Ammon, "The Genet Mission and the Development of American Political Parties," *JAH*, 52 (1966), 725–41; Harry Ammon, *The Genet Mission* (New York, 1973).
35. Elkins and McKitrick, *Age of Federalism*, 351.
36. JM to Archibald Stuart, 1 Sept. 1793, *Papers of Madison*, 15: 88.

and they displayed models of the guillotine that the Jacobins were using to eliminate their enemies; indeed, in Paris it was on average cutting off more than two heads a minute. In the face of all the revolutionary bloodshed, Jefferson remained supportive of the French revolutionary cause, believing that it was all that kept America from undoing its own revolution.

As a member of the government that was being subverted by the French minister, Jefferson was in an increasingly awkward position. He kept trying to draw nice distinctions between his being the secretary of state while at the same time being the behind-the-scenes leader of the Republican opposition. When told by Genet of plans to arm the Canadians and the Kentuckians for expeditions against British and Spanish territories in the New World, he confided to his diary that Genet had "communicated these things to me not as Secy. of state, but as Mr. Jeff."[37] When he had to, Jefferson knew how to split hairs.

To influence public opinion effectively, the Republican leaders eventually came to realize that they would have to concede much of the Federalist position. They saw that the president was universally respected, that neutrality was overwhelmingly desired, and that Genet had to go.[38] "He will sink the republican interest if they do not abandon him," Jefferson warned Madison in August 1793. The Republicans had to approve the policy of neutrality "unequivocally," he said, and had to stop caviling about who constitutionally was to declare it. "In this way we shall keep the people on our side by keeping ourselves in the right." This was one of the many times Jefferson had a shrewder sense of public opinion than did his colleague Madison.[39]

Jefferson's acute political sensitivity to the will of the people revealed in this incident kept his personal animosities and revolutionary passions from getting out of hand. Perhaps even more crucial in dampening the extreme partisanship of both the Federalist and Republican leaders was Washington. The president used his immense prestige and good judgment repeatedly to restrain fears, limit intrigues, and stymie opposition that otherwise might have escalated into violence. Despite the intense partisan feelings that existed throughout the country, Washington never

37. TJ, Notes of Cabinet Meeting and Conversations with Edmond Charles Genet, 5 July 1793, *Papers of Jefferson*, 26: 438.
38. In August 1793 Washington asked France for Genet's recall, but when the French government complied, Genet, as a Girondin appointee, decided that his life might be in danger back in France, where the Jacobins had taken over. So he married the daughter of Governor George Clinton of New York, settled near Albany, and became an American citizen.
39. TJ to JM, 3 Aug., 11 Aug. 1793, *Papers of Jefferson*, 26: 606, 652.

entirely lost the respect of all the party leaders, and this respect allowed him to reconcile, resolve, and balance the clashing interests. Jefferson scarcely foresaw the half of Washington's influence when he remarked as early as 1784 that "the moderation and virtue of a single character has probably prevented this revolution from being closed, as most others have been, by a subversion of that liberty it was intended to establish."[40]

THE DISMISSAL OF GENET did not end the international problems facing the United States. During the Revolution the United States had strenuously promoted the most liberal principles concerning commerce on the high seas in wartime—namely, that free ships made free goods and that neutrals had the right to carry non-contraband goods into ports of belligerents. These principles, which were to plague Anglo-American relations for the next two decades, were very much a part of the American Revolution.

Just as liberal Americans in 1776 had sought a new kind of domestic politics that would end tyranny, so too had they sought a new kind of international politics that would promote peace among nations and, indeed, might even see an end to war itself. The American Revolution had been centrally concerned with power—not only power within a government but power among governments in their international relations. Throughout the eighteenth century liberal intellectuals had looked forward to a newly enlightened world in which corrupt monarchical diplomacy, secret alliances, dynastic rivalries, and balances of power would be eliminated. In short, they had hoped for nothing less than the abolition of war and the beginning of a new era of peaceful relations among nations.

Monarchy and war were thought to be intimately related. Indeed, as young Benjamin Lincoln Jr., declared, "Kings owe their origin to war."[41] The internal needs of monarchies—the requirements of their bloated bureaucracies, their standing armies, their marriage alliances, their restless dynastic ambitions—lay behind the prevalence of war. Eliminate monarchy and all its accouterments, many Americans believed, and war itself would be eliminated. A world of republican states would encourage a new, peace-loving diplomacy—one based on the natural concert of the commercial interests of the people of the various nations. If the world's peoples were left alone to exchange goods freely among themselves—without the corrupting interference of selfish monarchical courts, irrational dynastic rivalries, and the secret double-dealing diplomacy of the past—then, it was hoped, international politics would become republi-

40. TJ to GW, 16 April 1784, *Papers of Jefferson*, 7: 106–7.
41. "The Free Republican," Boston *Independent Chronicle*, 8 Dec. 1785.

canized, pacified, and ruled by commerce alone. Old-fashioned diplomats might no longer be necessary. This was the enlightened dream of liberals everywhere, from Thomas Jefferson to Immanuel Kant.

Suddenly in 1776, with the United States isolated and outside the European mercantile empires, Americans had both an opportunity and a need to put into practice these liberal ideas about international relations and the free exchange of goods. Thus commercial interest and revolutionary idealism blended to form a basis for American thinking about foreign affairs that has lasted even to the present.

"Our plan is commerce," Thomas Paine had told Americans in 1776, "and that, well attended to, will secure us the peace and friendship of all Europe; because it is the interest of all Europe to have America a free port." There was no need for America to form any partial political connections with any part of Europe. Such traditional military alliances were the legacies of monarchical governments, and they only led to war. "It is the true interest of America," said Paine, "to steer clear of European contentions." Trade between peoples alone would be enough. Indeed, for Paine and other enlightened liberals, peaceful trade among the people of the various nations became the counterpart in the international sphere to the sociability of people in the domestic sphere. Just as enlightened thinkers like Paine and Jefferson foresaw republican society held together solely by the natural affection of individuals one to another, so too did they envision a world of these republican societies held together by the natural interest of nations in trading with one another. In both the national and international spheres monarchy and its intrusive institutions and monopolistic ways were what prevented a natural harmony of people's feelings and interests.[42]

Americans had first expressed these "Liberal Sentiments," as John Adams called them, during discussions over the proposed treaty with France at the time of Independence. There was a hope then, Adams said in 1785, that "the increasing liberality of sentiments among philosophers and men of letters, in various nations," might lead to "a *reformation*, a kind of *protestantism*, in the commercial system of the world."[43] Many in the Continental Congress in 1776 had attempted to implement these hopes by devising a model treaty that would be applied to France and eventually to other

42. Paine, "Common Sense" (1776), in Philip S. Foner, ed., *The Complete Writings of Thomas Paine* (New York, 1969), 1: 20, 21; David M. Fitzsimons, "Tom Paine's New World Order: Idealistic Internationalism in the Ideology of Early American Foreign Relations," *Diplomatic History*, 19 (1995), 569–82.

43. Gerald Stourzh, *Alexander Hamilton and the Idea of Republican Government* (Stanford, 1970), 146.

nations—a treaty that would avoid the traditional kinds of political and military commitments and focus instead exclusively on commercial connections.[44] The model treaty, drafted mainly by John Adams in July 1776, promised the greatest amount of commercial freedom and equality possible, which, if widely achieved, would eliminate the tensions and conflicts of world politics. Were the principles of the model treaty "once really established and honestly observed," John Adams later recalled, "it would put an end forever to all maritime war, and render all military navies useless."[45]

Absolute reciprocity in trade was the guiding principle of the treaty. In duties and trade restrictions foreign merchants would be treated as one's own nationals were treated. Even in wartime trade was to be kept flowing. Indeed, a major idea of the treaty was to lessen the impact of war on civilians. Neutral nations would have the right to trade with and carry the goods of the belligerent nations—the right expressed in the phrase "free ships make free goods."

In retrospect the naïveté of the Revolutionary Americans seems astonishing. They were desperate for an alliance with France, yet they were willing to offer Louis XVI's government very little in return. Since political and military cooperation with France was to be avoided at all costs, the model treaty promised only that in case the commercial alliance between the United States and France led to a French war with Great Britain, then the United States would not assist Britain in the war!

In the end the Americans' dream was not fully realized. Although they did sign a commercial treaty with France that contained the free trade principles they had wanted, they also had to agree to a traditional political and military alliance with France that obligated the United States to guarantee "from the present time and forever...the present Possessions of the Crown of France in America as well as those it may acquire by the future Treaty of peace."[46] Many Americans, including John Adams, came out of their experience with European diplomacy with their enlightened ideas very much in doubt. "No facts are believed but decisive military conquests," Adams warned in 1780; "no arguments are seriously attended to in Europe but force." Given this reality, a balance of power might be useful after all.[47]

44. JA, March–April 1776, *Diary and Autobiography*, 2: 236.
45. Burton Spivak, *Jefferson's English Crisis: Commerce, Embargo, and the Republican Revolution* (Charlottesville, 1979), 1; Robert W. Tucker and David C. Hendrickson, *Empire of Liberty: The Statecraft of Thomas Jefferson* (New York, 1990), 56.
46. Tucker and Hendrickson, *Empire of Liberty*, 53.
47. JA to BF, 17 Aug. 1780, in Felix Gilbert, *To the Farewell Address: Ideas of Early American Foreign Policy* (Princeton, 1961), 86; Fitzsimons, "Tom Paine's New World Order"; Robert Kagan, *Dangerous Nation* (New York, 2006), 59.

Despite these doses of realism, however, the Americans' enlightened dream of a new world order based on commerce was not lost, and the signing of a peace treaty with Britain in 1783 seemed to make possible the revival of the dream. In 1784 the United States authorized a diplomatic commission composed of Jefferson, Adams, and Franklin to negotiate commercial treaties with sixteen European states based on the liberal principles of a revised model treaty. The hope was to have America, in the commissioners' words, lead the way to an "object so valuable to mankind as the total emancipation of commerce and the bringing together all nations for a free intercommunication of happiness."[48]

Only three states, however—Sweden, Prussia, and Morocco, peripheral powers with little overseas trade—agreed to sign liberal treaties with the United States. Most European states were indifferent to the Americans' ideas. They simply were ignorant of the importance of American commerce, said Jefferson, who had been instrumental in drawing up the new model treaty. Even someone as hardheaded as Washington reflected "with pleasure on the probable influence that commerce may hereafter have on human manners and society in general," even leading perhaps to an end of "the devastation and horrors of war."[49]

But it was Jefferson and Madison, among the Revolutionary leaders, who clung longest to the belief in the power of American trade to bring about changes in international behavior, indeed, to make commercial sanctions a substitute for the use of military force. This confidence in American commerce, which harked back to the non-importation policies against Britain in the 1760s and 1770s, became the basic premise of the Republican party's approach to international politics. It underlay Republican policies and thinking about the world well into the early decades of the nineteenth century. Jefferson and Madison never lost hope that the United States might be able to bring about a world in which war itself would no longer be necessary.

SINCE THE PRINCIPAL OBSTACLE to their hopes was Great Britain, the Republican leaders aimed to use the power of American commerce to convince Britain to change its policies. Yet Jefferson and Madison were not merely interested in opening up British ports to American trade. For the Republicans the economics of America's relationship with Britain was always less important than the politics of it. What they really wanted was to destroy Britain's commercial hegemony in the world and end America's commercial, and hence political, dependence on the former

48. American Commissioners to De Thulemeir, 14 March 1785, *Papers of Jefferson*, 8: 28.
49. GW to Lafayette, 15 Aug. 1786, in Fitzpatrick, ed., *Writings of Washington*, 28: 520.

mother country; and they were willing to compromise America's commercial prosperity to bring about this crucial end.

In 1789 Madison had sought unsuccessfully to levy discriminatory tariffs on British imports in order to force Britain to open its ports in the West Indies and Canada to American shipping. Although the British West Indies remained legally closed, American merchants continued to trade illegally with them. Indeed, American commerce with Britain was flourishing; three-quarters of all American exports and imports were exchanged with the former mother country.[50] Precisely because of all this trade, the Republican leaders thought the British were susceptible to American pressure; the time seemed ripe for using trade restrictions to break up Britain's navigation system. Relying on the arguments set forth by Jefferson in his December 1793 report to Congress on the state of America's foreign commerce, Madison in January 1794 introduced resolutions in the House calling for commercial reciprocity with all nations with which the United States did not have commercial treaties, the only important one, of course, being Great Britain. If that reciprocity were not forthcoming, the United States would retaliate with tariffs and trade restrictions against a nation that had already showed its hostility toward the United States by refusing to vacate American territory.

Although trade with America constituted only one-sixth of Britain's total commerce, the Republican leaders nevertheless assumed that American trade was absolutely vital to Great Britain. If Americans ceased buying luxuries from Britain, British manufacturers would be thrown out of work, riots would follow, and the British government would be compelled to capitulate. The Republican leaders did not expect their commercial retaliation to result in war. "If it does," said Jefferson, "we will meet it like men: but it may not bring on war, and then the experiment will have been a happy one." And America will have given "the world still another useful lesson, by shewing to them other modes of punishing injuries than by war, which is as much a punishment to the punisher as the sufferer."[51]

Naturally, the Federalists opposed these measures, which would have unsettled the economy and undermined Hamilton's entire financial program. Financing the funded national debt depended on the customs duties levied on foreign imports, most of which were British. Indeed, it was the extraordinary growth of federal customs revenue in the 1790s that enabled the state governments to lower their taxes, which of course enhanced the reputation of the Washington government.

50. Elkins and McKitrick, *Age of Federalism*, 131.
51. TJ to Tench Coxe, 1 May 1794, *Papers of Jefferson*, 28: 67.

In the Congress William Loughton Smith of South Carolina and Fisher Ames of Massachusetts took the lead in exposing the harmful consequences of destroying trade with Great Britain. American producers and consumers would suffer far more than the British from these proposed trade restrictions. No American merchant, no trading state in the Union, favored Madison's measures, said Ames in the Congress. We are asked "to engage in a contest of self-denial. For what?" In a letter in January 1794 Ames went on to inform his friend Christopher Gore of the progress of the debate and the strange nature of the Republicans' thinking. "The ground is avowedly changed," he told Gore. "Madison & Co. now avow that the political wrongs are *the* wrongs to be cured by commercial restrictions." In other words, "in plain English," the Republicans "set out with a tale of restrictions and injuries on our commerce." When that was "refuted solidly," and they were "pressed for a pretext," they declared "that we will make war, not for our commerce, but with it; not to make our commerce better, but to make it nothing, in order to reach the tender sides of our enemy, which are not to be wounded in any other way."[52]

In his response to the Federalists' arguments the best that Madison could do was emphasize the great political danger that America's extraordinary dependence on British trade and capital posed for the fledgling republic. That dependence, he told the Congress in January 1794, created an "influence that may be conveyed into the public councils...and the effect that may finally ensue on our taste, our manners, and our form of Government itself." In Republican eyes the Revolution against the British monarchy was far from over: a decade after the treaty of peace, England and English ways still seemed capable of destroying the young Republic.[53]

British actions certainly appeared to support this Republican view of a deep-seated monarchical antagonism toward the United States. Before the debate over trade restrictions could be resumed in March 1794, news arrived of the new British policy to seize all American ships trading with the French West Indies. Not only had over 250 American ships already been seized and American sailors mistreated, but also rumor spread that Sir Guy Carleton, the governor-general of Canada, had made an inflammatory speech inciting the Indians in the Northwest against the Americans.

In response, Congress immediately passed a thirty-day embargo on all shipping. War with Britain seemed inevitable. Even many Federalists were angry at English arrogance; Hamilton himself was ready to fight if

---

52. Elkins and McKitrick, *Age of Federalism*, 386; Ames to Christopher Gore, 28 Jan. 1794, in W. B. Allen, ed., *The Works of Fisher Ames* (Indianapolis, 1983), 2: 1028.
53. Elkins and McKitrick, *Age of Federalism*, 384–86.

necessary. "To be in a condition to defend ourselves, and annoy any who may attack us," he told the president, "will be the best method of securing our peace."[54]

The Federalists' approach to the crisis with Britain was to arm in preparation for war while attempting to negotiate peace. This policy grew out of their basic understanding of the world and the United States' role in it. Hamilton and most Federalists never accepted the premise of the most utopian Republican thinking—that once the European monarchies were eliminated and republics established, peace and the free flow of commerce would reign throughout the world. Hamilton saw the world made up of competing nation-states, with republics being no more peace-loving than monarchies. The sources of war, he said, did not lie in the needs of funding systems, bureaucracies, and standing armies, as the Republicans assumed; they lay in the natural ambitions and avarice of all human beings. "The seeds of war," he wrote in 1795, "are sown thickly in the human breast."[55] Although in such a hostile world commerce admittedly had a "softening and humanizing influence," the only real way for a nation to guarantee peace was to prepare for war.[56]

Unfortunately, said Hamilton, the United States, though growing, was not yet strong enough to assert itself as an equal in international affairs. But give the country time, perhaps as much as forty or fifty years, and it would be as powerful as any nation in the world. In the meantime the United States needed to maintain its credit and prosperity through trade with Great Britain. When British actions threatened that relationship in the spring of 1794, the Federalists prepared for war but, conscious of American weakness, hoped for negotiations.

The Federalists proposed raising between fifteen and twenty thousand troops, fortifying harbor defenses, and establishing a naval force. The Republicans were bitterly opposed to these military measures, which seemed to be part of a Federalist plot to build up the executive at the expense of the people's liberty. Had not Madison warned in his "Helvidius" essays that war was "the true nurse of executive aggrandizement"? "In war," he had said, "the public treasures are to be unlocked, and it is the executive hand which is to dispense them. In war the honors and emoluments of office are to be multiplied; and it is the executive patronage under which they are to be enjoyed. It is in war, finally, that laurels are to be gathered, and it is the executive brow they are to encircle."[57]

54. AH to GW, 8 Mar. 1794, *Papers of Hamilton*, 16: 134.
55. Hamilton, Defense of the Funding System, July 1795, *Papers of Hamilton*, 19: 56.
56. AH, "To Defence No. XX," 23–24 Oct. 1795, *Papers of Hamilton*, 19: 332.
57. JM, "Helvidius," No. 4, 14 Sept. 1793, *Papers of Madison*, 15: 108.

Fear of the way war could transform a republican government was fundamental to Republican thinking. James Monroe believed that the Federalist military measures were designed to create a military establishment that would suppress the Republican opposition to the government and were thus a far greater danger to the public liberty "than any now menac'd from Britain."[58] If America had to fight, the Republicans preferred to do it with privateers and militia.

News that Britain had changed its policy and had ceased its wholesale seizure of American shipping to the West Indies eased the crisis and gave the Federalists an opportunity to try negotiations. Washington took advantage of the apparent change in British attitude to name Chief Justice John Jay as a special envoy to Great Britain in order to head off war. It was one of Washington's most courageous actions as president.

The Republicans were outraged at Jay's appointment and the possibility of a negotiated treaty. They believed that the Federalists were conspiring to deny the popular will of the House of Representatives by using the treaty-making powers of the president and Senate to settle the British crisis. But they predicted that the Federalists would not get away with this ploy. Not only were "the Democratic Societies...beginning to open their batteries upon it," but, Madison told Jefferson on May 11, 1794, most Americans were furious as well. Indeed, the response to Jay's appointment, he said, was "the most powerful blow ever suffered by the popularity of the President."[59]

Yet scarcely two weeks later Madison was moaning to Jefferson, who had retired as secretary of state at the end of 1793, that all the Republicans' attempts to attack Britain "thro' her commerce" were defeated and that the president's policy "to supplicate for peace and, under the uncertainty of success, to prepare for war by taxes & troops" was carrying the day. In fact, Madison now saw more clearly than ever before that the presidency was the principal source of governmental power. "The influence of the Executive on events, the use made of them, and public confidence in the President," he told Jefferson, "are an overmatch for all the efforts Republicanism can make." All his Republican colleagues in the Congress were confused and dismayed.[60]

The outbreak of the Whiskey Rebellion in the summer of 1794 only aggravated these Republican fears of enhanced executive power. Madison said the talk in Philadelphia was running "high for a standing army to

58. James Monroe to TJ, 16 Mar. 1794, in S. M. Hamilton, ed., *The Writings of James Monroe* (New York, 1898), 1: 286–88.
59. JM to TJ, 11 May 1794, *Papers of Madison*, 15: 327–28.
60. JM to TJ, 25 May 1794, *Papers of Madison*, 15: 337–38.

enforce the laws." He had "no doubt that such an innovation will be attempted in earnest during the session [of Congress], if circumstances should be favorable." But he admitted that the president would probably not take such a step.[61]

If the suppression of the Whiskey Rebellion strengthened the popularity of the Washington administration, the treaty that Jay brought back to the United States in 1795 had the opposite effect. It invigorated the Republican party and initially turned much of the country against the Federalists. In the treaty Britain finally agreed to evacuate the Northwest posts, to open the British West Indies to some American trade in ships of small tonnage that could not easily or profitably sail the Atlantic (but at the price of forbidding American re-export of some tropical produce, including cotton), and to set up joint arbitration commissions to settle the unresolved issues of pre-war debts, boundaries, and compensation for illegal naval seizures of goods.

Although the treaty did not explicitly compel Americans to abandon their principles of freedom of the seas and neutral rights that they had supported since 1776—the idea of free ships, free goods, and the narrow definition of contraband—it did so implicitly. (Jay agreed, for example, to allow the English seizure of enemy food as contraband.) Although the treaty declared that none of its provisions should violate previously established treaties, its abandonment of long-standing liberal principles of neutral rights seemed to betray the Franco-American alliance of 1778, which had specifically recognized these liberal principles. Not only did the treaty tacitly accept British notions of neutral rights, but it also forbade the United States from discriminating against British trade for ten years, thus surrendering the one great weapon the Republicans were counting on to weaken the former mother country's hold on American commerce and society.

The Republicans were opposed to the treaty even before they learned of its terms. The very idea of the United States arranging any sort of friendly connection with Great Britain was detestable to the Republicans, who believed anything that favored the British monarchy necessarily undermined the French revolutionary cause. Some Republicans even suggested that the more favorable the treaty, the worse it might be for the Republican party.

The terms of the treaty were kept secret for months while the Senate considered it. After throwing out the article that limited American trade to the British West Indies (with the expectation that it could be renegotiated), the Senate on June 24, 1795, finally ratified the treaty by the barest two-thirds majority required. Acceptance was now left up to Washington.

---

61. JM to TJ, 16 Nov. 1794, *Republic of Letters*, 859.

When the terms of the treaty were prematurely leaked to the press, the country went wild. Jay was burned in effigy in Philadelphia, New York, Boston, and Lexington, Kentucky; in Charleston the public hangman burned copies of the treaty. Hamilton was stoned in New York when he tried to speak in favor of the treaty. Petitions and resolutions from every state inundated the president, all begging and even demanding that he refuse to sign the treaty. When resolutions from some states even threatened secession, Washington expressed concern over the possibility "of a separation of the Union into Northern & Southern."[62] Although the Federalists attempted to match the Republicans in organizing meetings and petitions, they were most effective in the press, Hamilton himself becoming what Jefferson described as a "host within himself" and "a colossus to the anti republican party."[63]

Washington regarded the growing popular opposition as all the more reason to sign the treaty and put an end to these threats to his government. In light of the Whiskey Rebellion, the spread of the Democratic-Republican Societies, and the increasing attacks on him personally, Washington could only conclude that more was involved than just the treaty with Britain. The future of an ordered society in the United States seemed at stake. When he learned that his new secretary of state, Edmund Randolph, who had replaced Jefferson, had communicated indiscreetly with the French minister Joseph Fauchet, he abruptly decided to accept the treaty without the further delay that Randolph had advocated.

Washington's signature in August 1795, however, did not end the public clamor. Most Republicans remained adamant in opposition. They criticized Washington as never before, charging him with violating the spirit of republicanism and promoting English-style corruption. Detractors accused Washington of being "the head of a British faction," an embezzler of public funds, a military incompetent, a "usurper with dark schemes of ambition," and even a traitor who had actually "labored to prevent our independence."[64] Some hotheads called for the president's impeachment. Jefferson dismissed the treaty out of hand and remained confident that the popular branch of the government, the House of Representatives, which controlled the appropriation of funds needed to implement the treaty, "will oppose it as constitutionally void...and thus rid us of this infamous act, which is really nothing more than a treaty of

---

62. Sharp, *American Politics in the Early Republic*, 119.
63. TJ to JM, 21 Sept. 1795, *Republic of Letters*, 897.
64. Marcus Daniels, *Scandal and Civility: Journalism and the Birth of American Democracy* (New York, 2009), 138–44; Barry Schwartz, *George Washington: The Making of an American Symbol* ((New York, 1987), 67–68.

alliance between England and the Anglomen of this country against the legislature & people of the United States."[65]

When in March 1796 the House called on the president to send it all the papers involved in the treaty negotiations, Washington refused, saying that treaties duly ratified by the Senate and signed by the president were the supreme law of the land. Recognition of any role for the House not only "would be to establish a dangerous precedent" but also would be unconstitutional. The Constitutional Convention over which he had presided, he said, had "explicitly rejected" the House's role in treaty-making.[66] Nevertheless, Madison and the Republicans in the Congress refused to back down and pushed to destroy the treaty once and for all. With both parties caucusing and disciplining their members, partisanship was at an all-time high.

Eventually, however, growing support for the treaty in the nation at large began to make itself felt, and following a stirring speech by a very ill Fisher Ames in April 1796 the Republicans were unable to muster a majority for their cause. This was a stunning defeat for Madison, who contemplated retiring from the House and returning to Virginia. His earlier friendship with the president was over. Washington never forgave him for his attempts to undermine the treaty and never consulted him again.

Already, a series of developments throughout the country were reinforcing support for the Federalists and their policies. With the appearance of the first part of Thomas Paine's *Age of Reason* in 1794 Protestant ministers and other conservatives, who had initially welcomed the French Revolution, became increasingly alarmed at the threats that the upheaval in France had come to pose for revealed religion. Paine's book, which went through eight American editions in 1794, seven in 1795, and two in 1796 (making it the most widely published religious work in eighteenth-century America), attacked the scriptural truth of the Bible and all organized religion. Its publication set off a flood of similar radical anti-religious works, including Baron Holbach's *Christianity Unveiled* and *Common Sense; or, Natural Ideas Opposed to Supernatural*, Count Volney's *Ruins; or, Meditations on the Revolution of Empires*, William Godwin's *Enquiry Concerning Political Justice*, the first edition in translation of Voltaire's *Dictionnaire philosophique*, and the second part of Paine's *Age of Reason*, in which Paine declared that "of all the systems of religion that were ever

65. TJ to James Monroe, 6 Sept. 1795, TJ to Edward Rutledge, 30 Nov. 1795, *Papers of Jefferson*, 28: 542.

66. GW to the House of Representatives, 30 March 1796, in Fitzpatrick, ed., *Writings of Washington*, 35: 3, 5.

invented, there is none more derogatory to the Almighty, more unedify-
ing to man, more repugnant to reason, and more contradictory in itself,
than this thing called Christianity."

Paine's inexpensive work sold widely—Benjamin Franklin Bache,
grandson of his namesake and virulent foe of the Federalists, sold fifteen
thousand copies of the second part of the *Age of Reason* in his Philadelphia bookstore—and it was read by huge numbers and discussed in taverns and on street corners everywhere. College students at Harvard, Yale,
and Princeton, infected with what was recalled as an "infidel and irreli-
gious spirit," especially liked Paine's work and enjoyed throwing its heresies in the faces of their bewildered clerical teachers.[67]

Since no one known to Americans was more identified with the turmoil in France than Thomas Paine, his "blasphemous" ideas were seen as
the by-products of the French Revolution and what Noah Webster called
its "atheistic attacks on Christianity." The orthodox Christian clergy suddenly lost their earlier enthusiasm for the French Revolution and in
1794–1796 turned on Paine, the Revolution, and the Republican party
with a vengeance. All at once the Federalist leaders discovered that they
had acquired important clerical allies in their struggle with the revolu-
tionary-minded Republicans. "Tom Paine," Fisher Ames noted, "has kindly
cured our clergy of their prejudices."[68]

MORE LAY BEHIND THE REVIVAL of the Federalists than the support given them by frightened clergymen. Circumstances everywhere in
America were better, and the pursuit of happiness for more people had
never seemed more promising. By 1795–1796, with General Anthony
Wayne's victory over the Indians in August 1794 and the imminent British
return of the Northwest posts, Americans were ready and eager to exploit
the territory north of the Ohio River. Towns were sprouting up all over
Kentucky, and wagonloads of consumer goods from the East were pouring over the Appalachian Mountains into the Ohio Valley.[69]

At the same time, the situation in the Southwest was dramatically
transformed. In 1791 the ideals of liberty and equality coming out of the
French Revolution had spread across the Atlantic to the rich French

67. TP, *The Age of Reason* (1794), in Philip Foner, ed., *The Complete Writings of Thomas
    Paine* (New York, 1969), 1: 600; Russell Blaine Nye, *The Cultural Life of the New
    Nation, 1776–1830* (New York, 1960), 214; Daniels, *Scandal and Civility*, 242–49.
68. Gary B. Nash, "The American Clergy and the French Revolution," WMQ, 22 (1965),
    402–12; Henry May, *The Enlightenment in America* (New York, 1976), 258.
69. Elizabeth A. Perkins, "The Consumer Frontier: Household Consumption in Early
    Kentucky," JAH, 78 (1991–92), 486–510.

sugar colony of Saint-Domingue and inspired a bloody slave revolt, led by Toussaint L'Ouverture, that lasted a dozen years. Before this rebellion ended in 1804 with the establishment of the republic of Haiti, thousands of refugees, whites and free and enslaved blacks alike, had fled to other Caribbean islands and to cities in North America, including New Orleans. Spanish officials became increasingly apprehensive that revolutionary sentiments might spread to Louisiana. After all, most of the six thousand people in New Orleans were French, France having owned Louisiana until 1763, and Spanish military authority in the colony was notoriously weak.

Indeed, the Spanish authorities in Louisiana were so feeble and so fearful of American filibustering activities, especially those threatened by George Rogers Clark of Kentucky, that they thought they had better come to terms with the United States in the West or else lose everything. When it seemed possible that the Federalist government might even ally with Britain and threaten the entire Spanish Empire, the Spanish government finally decided to reverse a decade's opposition to American demands in the Southwest. Suddenly Spain was willing to settle the boundary of its territories of Florida and Louisiana at the 31st parallel, forsaking the Yazoo lands, and to open up the Mississippi to American navigation.

In October 1795 the newly appointed American ambassador to Spain, Thomas Pinckney, former governor of South Carolina and cousin of Charles Pinckney, who had attacked Jay's plans in 1786 to sell out the Westerners, signed the Treaty of San Lorenzo that gave the Americans pretty much all they had wanted. When news of Pinckney's Treaty reached Kentucky, people were ecstatic. The Federalist administration had achieved a great diplomatic success and had immediately made the West far more attractive to both settlers and land speculators. Navigation of the Mississippi, observed Robert Morris, who always had his eye out for a good deal, "doubles or trebles the value of lands bordering upon the Western Waters of the Ohio."[70]

But most important in stimulating support for Federalism in the mid-1790s was the increasing growth of American prosperity. Hamilton's financial program was working wonders. The federal government's assumption of the states' war debts had indeed reduced the states' need to tax their citizens, and the states lowered their taxes to between 50 and 90 percent of what they had been in the 1780s. By the mid-1790s the burden of taxation in the states had returned to pre-Revolution levels, which were

70. Elkins and McKitrick, *Age of Federalism*, 842n.

considerably lower than those of the European nations. By 1795 some states had done away with poll taxes and other direct taxes altogether.[71]

With more money to spend, Americans were consuming more. The value of American imported consumer goods went from $23,500,00 in 1790 to $63,000,000 in 1795. Thanks in part to Jay's Treaty, America was well on its way to becoming Britain's best customer. Americans were selling more goods abroad too. The value of domestic exports rose rapidly—the price of a bushel of wheat exported from Philadelphia more than doubled between 1792 and 1796. The war in Europe created an ever expanding demand for American products, especially food, and opened up new opportunities for American neutral shipping.

American ships spanned the world. They had reached China in 1783 and were now sailing all over the Pacific—to Hawaii, Indonesia, Indochina, the Philippines, and India. The *Benjamin* out of Salem, Massachusetts, in 1792–1793 made a prosperous nineteen-month voyage to the Cape of Good Hope and the Isle de France. It was no easy voyage. The ship's captain, Nathaniel Silsbee (later senator from Massachusetts), had to carefully select ports, decide on cargos, and judge freight costs, and at the same time avoid British and French warships. Although Silsbee was only nineteen, he had been at sea for five years; his first mate was aged twenty, and his clerk was eighteen. The ship went out with a mixed cargo of hops, saddlery, window glass, mahogany boards, tobacco, and Madeira wine and brought back goods that returned almost a 500 percent profit to their owner, Elias Hasket Derby.[72]

"The wars of Europe," declared the *Columbian Centinel* in May 1795, "...rain riches upon us; and it is as much as we can do to find dishes to catch the golden shower." Shippers increased their profits threefold between 1792 and 1796, which in turn stimulated an extraordinary increase in shipbuilding. More ships needed more lumber, more canvas, more rope, more tar, and more workers. Daily wages for both ship carpenters and laborers in Philadelphia doubled between 1790 and 1796.

This "golden shower" of prosperity inevitably diluted much of the Republican opposition to Federalist policies. "The farmers are so intent on improving the means of getting rich," the Federalists noted with glee, "that they can hardly be got to lend an ear to any political subject, however interesting."[73] By the end of 1795 the three dozen or more Democratic-Republican Societies

---

71. Max M. Edling and Mark D. Kaplanoff, "Alexander Hamilton's Fiscal Reform: Transforming the Structure of Taxation in the Early Republic," WMQ, 61 (2004), 712–44.

72. Samuel Eliot Morison, *The Maritime History of Massachusetts, 1783–1860* (Boston, 1961), 73–74.

73. Elkins and McKitrick, *Age of Federalism*, 441, 842–43, 443.

that had emerged in 1793–1794 to support the Republican cause and challenge the Federalists had disappeared as suddenly as they had arisen.

Part of the reason for the disappearance of the Democratic-Republican Societies was the Federalists' ability to hold them responsible for the Whiskey Rebellion. In his November 1794 message to Congress Washington had condemned "certain self-created societies" for fomenting the rebellion. The president's reference put the societies on the defensive and precipitated a debate in Congress over the right of associations to influence the people's representatives. Although such societies might be necessary in a monarchy, said the Federalists, a republic that had numerous elected officials had no need of them. But America, the Republicans replied, had all sorts of private associations of people. The Baptists and Methodists, for example, might be termed self-created societies.

No one denied the right of people to form various associations, the Federalists retorted. It was what they did with these associations that was at issue. "Private associations of men for the purpose of promoting arts, sciences, benevolence or charity are very laudable," declared Noah Webster, but associations formed for political purposes were "dangerous to good government." Ambitious and desperate citizens had used the Democratic-Republican Societies to attack government with smears and slanders and had brought the authority of the governing officials into disrepute. "Citizens," declared Fisher Ames, who made the most powerful congressional speech against the political clubs, "have thus been led by calumny and lies to despise their Government and its Ministers, to dread and to hate it, and all concerned in it."[74]

The Federalists assumed in traditional eighteenth-century fashion—and it was an assumption they never lost—that no free government could long exist without the people's confidence in the private character and respectability of the governing officials; indeed, they believed that without their personal credibility the weak national government might not have been able to sustain itself at all. Given the fierceness with which the Federalists were being criticized, many of them may have wondered whether they themselves had sufficient character and respectability left to command the people's trust. But they had a trump card in the president's unquestioned reputation for virtue, and they played it over and again with particular effectiveness.

74. [Noah Webster], *The Revolution in France, Considered in Respect to Its Progress and Effects* (New York, 1794), in Ellis Sandoz, ed., *Political Sermons of the Founding Era, 1750–1805* (Indianapolis, 1991), 1279; *Annals of Congress*, 3rd Congress, 2nd session, IV, 929; Albrecht Koschnik, "The Democratic Societies of Philadelphia and the Limits of the American Public Sphere, circa 1793–1795," *WMQ*, 58 (2001), 615–36.

Madison thought he saw how the Federalists were using the president's popularity for "party-advantage." "The game," he explained in a letter to Monroe in December 1794, "was to connect the democratic Societies with the odium of the insurrection—to connect the Republicans in Congress with those Societies—to put the President ostensibly at the head of the other party, in opposition to both." Such efforts, he believed, could only wound the president's popularity; indeed, he thought that Washington's mention of "certain secret societies" in his message to Congress was "perhaps the greatest political Error of his life." But Madison was not yet prepared to criticize the president directly or to admit that his own efforts on behalf of the Republican party were also a "game."[75] Political parties in any modern sense were still unacceptable to most Americans.

EVEN POLITICS IN ANY MODERN SENSE was not possible. Because Federalists and Republicans alike fervently believed that the very existence of the United States as an independent republic was directly related to the conflict between Great Britain and revolutionary France, some public officials in the 1790s were led into extraordinarily improper diplomatic behavior. Indeed, in this era of revolutionary passions and hatreds, proper and conventional diplomatic behavior from anyone may have been too much to expect.

In 1789–1790 Alexander Hamilton carried on private discussions with Major George Beckwith, who was acting as agent of the British government in the absence of a regular minister. He suggested to Beckwith that he, as secretary of the treasury, might be a better channel of communication to the administration than the secretary of state. He went on to tell the British agent that he "always preferred a Connexion with you, to that of any other Country, *We think in English*, and have a similarity of prejudices, and of predilections."[76] When in 1791 Jefferson as secretary of state greeted the first British minister, George Hammond, with unusually abrupt hostility, Hammond turned to Secretary of the Treasury Hamilton for discussions of Anglo-American affairs.

Jefferson and other Republican officials, of course, behaved with France as Hamilton did with England. Jefferson misled the French minister Genet into thinking that France would receive more support from the United States government than in fact it was willing to give. But the impropriety of Jefferson's diplomatic behavior was nothing compared to that of his fellow Virginians, Edmund Randolph and James Monroe.

---

75. JM to James Monroe, 4 Dec. 1794, *Papers of Madison*, 15: 406–7; Elkins and McKitrick, *Age of Federalism*, 487–88.
76. AH, Conversation with George Beckwith, Oct. 1789, *Papers of Hamilton*, 5: 383.

Secretary of State Randolph was never happy with Hamilton's influence in the administration or with Jay's mission to England, and he conveyed his unhappiness to Genet's successor as French minister, Joseph Fauchet. One of Fauchet's dispatches to the French government was intercepted at sea by a British warship and in the summer of 1795 was turned over to Oliver Wolcott, the new secretary of the treasury. Fauchet revealed that he had learned in conversations with Randolph that some members of the Federalist government were bent on absolute power; he suggested that they might have instigated the Whiskey Rebellion as a pretext for misleading the president and giving energy to the government. Worse still, Fauchet went on with an ambiguous reference to thousands of dollars that Randolph had requested from France—a reference that most assumed involved a bribe, mistakenly, it turned out.

When Washington confronted Randolph with Fauchet's letter, the secretary of state immediately resigned, and then spent several months preparing a lengthy *Vindication* that did little to salvage his reputation. Randolph was not guilty of treason, as some high Federalists such as Secretary of War Timothy Pickering charged, but he was certainly guilty of stupidity and impropriety.[77]

James Monroe was likewise guilty of foolish behavior and even more partisan indiscretion during the two years, 1794 to 1796, when he was minister to France. He made no secret of his sympathies for "the fortitude, magnanimity, and heroic valor" of the French forces warring against Britain. He undermined his own government's policies in every way, assuming, as he repeatedly told the French, that the interests of the United States were identical to those of her sister republic. He proposed that the United States make a $5 million loan to France, confident, he said, that the American people "would cheerfully bear a tax, the product of which was to be applied in aid of the French Republic."[78] Monroe kept advocating military action against Britain and continually downplayed the fact that Jay was in England trying to avoid war. When the Jay Treaty was published, Monroe was so personally opposed to it that he could never adequately explain it to the French on behalf of the government he represented. He even intimated to French officials that the election of Jefferson in 1796 would solve everything.

When some of Monroe's private views expressed to fellow Republicans back home came to light, he was recalled. That Monroe as minister should have persisted so long opposing the government he represented is

77. Gerard H. Clarfield, *Timothy Pickering and the American Republic* (Pittsburgh, 1980), 160–61; Elkins and McKitrick, *Age of Federalism*, 838.
78. Elkins and McKitrick, *Age of Federalism*, 500.

a measure of the high stakes involved. For Monroe and other Republicans the future of liberty itself seemed to rest on French success. Such ideological passions made ordinary politics impossible.

BY EARLY 1796, President Washington had had enough. He was determined to escape the "serious anxiety...troubles and perplexities of office." Having a thin skin and always acutely concerned with his reputation, he had suffered deeply from the criticism leveled at him. He had been "accused of being the enemy of one Nation, and the subject to the influence of another." Every act of his administration, he said, had been tortured and misrepresented, and he himself had been vilified "in such exaggerated, and indecent terms as could scarcely be applied to a Nero; a notorious defaulter; or even to a common picket-pocket."[79] He was sixty-four and tired, he said, in both body and mind.

As in the case of his career as commander-in-chief, Washington's most important act as president was his giving up the office. The significance of his retirement from the presidency is easily overlooked today, but his contemporaries knew what it meant. Most people assumed that Washington might be president as long as he lived, that he would be a kind of elective monarch like the king of Poland. Hence his retirement from the presidency enhanced his moral authority and set a precedent for future presidents. But it also did more: that the chief executive of a state should willingly relinquish his office was an objective lesson in republicanism at a time when the republican experiment throughout the Atlantic world was very much in doubt.

Before Washington left office he wanted to say some things to "the Yeomanry of this Country" and "in language that was plain and intelligible to their understanding."[80] When he had thought of retiring in 1792, he had had Madison prepare a draft of a valedictory address. Now he altered that draft and gave the revision to Hamilton to rework into an address. Hamilton prepared two versions, one containing more of his own inclinations than Madison's. Washington preferred that one, believing it "more dignified...and [containing] less egotism."[81]

Despite all this collaboration, the final document very much represented the president's ideas about what his administration had experienced; it also expressed his deep anxiety about the future of the new nation. After some more editing by Washington, his Farewell Address was

79. John Ferling, *The First of Men: A Life of George Washington* (Knoxville, 1988), 465–66; GW to TJ, 6 July 1796, *Papers of Jefferson*, 29: 142–43.
80. GW to AH, 25 Aug. 1796, *Papers of Hamilton*, 20: 308.
81. Ferling, *First of Men*, 466.

given to the press and published on September 19, 1796. The president never delivered it orally.

This document became one of the great state papers of American history, often read in classrooms and elsewhere well into the twentieth century. Indeed, speakers and writers at the time, both Federalists and Republicans, urged that the Farewell Address be read by all Americans. It seemed that significant to the future of the nation.

Washington's major theme was the importance of the Union, which alone made Americans "one people." The national Union, he told his fellow countrymen, was what insured "your real independence." The national government was the main "support of your tranquillity at home, your peace abroad; of your safety; of your prosperity; of that very Liberty which you value so highly." He appealed to his fellow citizens to forget what divided them and to concentrate on the "sacred ties" that bound them together—their similarity of religion, manners, and political principles and, above all, their common participation in the Revolutionary cause. Although the different sections had different interests, they blended together into "an indissoluble community of Interest as *one Nation.*" It was true, he said, that theorists had doubted whether a republican government could embrace a large territory. But let us try the experiment, he urged.

Most dangerous to this experiment in an extended republic, he declared, was the spirit of party and faction that had recently arisen to unsettle American politics. Parties were the tools that "cunning, ambitious and unprincipled men" used "to subvert the Power of the People and to usurp for themselves the reins of Government." The spirit of party agitated the community with ill-founded jealousies and false alarms; it turned one part of the society against another; it even fomented riots and insurrections; and it offered the opportunity for foreigners to influence and corrupt the government itself. In all of these warnings Washington was, of course, thinking of the recent events of his administration. He conceded a possible role for this spirit of party in monarchies, but popularly elective republics had to be constantly vigilant against its rise.

Probably nothing in Washington's Address reveals the traditional nature of his thinking about politics more than this lengthy heartfelt condemnation of parties. Of course, he was striking out against the Republican party without conceding that the Federalists, of whom he was the leader, were in any way a party. This was not confused hypocrisy on Washington's part, but simply an example of how much conventional thinking continued to abhor partisan division in the state. Washington always sincerely saw himself as acting above partisan passions and, of course, could scarcely have imagined the nineteenth-century development of political parties normally contesting with one another.

After stressing the importance of religion, morality, a general diffusion of knowledge, and public credit, Washington concluded his valedictory with a long discussion of foreign policy. Here again he had recent experience, especially the behavior of the Republican party, very much in mind. He urged that the United States avoid all "permanent, inveterate antipathies" and all "passionate attachments" to particular nations. He was especially concerned that relatively small and weak nations, like the United States, not become satellites of great and powerful nations. Like many other Americans, including many Republicans, he advocated the extending of commercial relations to foreign nations and having "as little *political* connection as possible." America was in a fortunate situation, separated by an ocean from the vicissitudes of European politics to which it had very little, if any relation. Although "temporary alliances" with foreign nations might be necessary in "extraordinary emergencies," it was America's "true policy to steer clear of permanent Alliances with any portion of the foreign world." It was "folly in one Nation to look for disinterested favors from another."[82]

Beneath Washington's idealistic picture of America as a uniquely situated experiment in republicanism lay a strong base of realism. All these principles, he said, were what had guided the policies of his own administration, in particular the Proclamation of Neutrality of 1793. All he ever wanted for America, he declared, was time for its institutions to settle and mature, time for it to progress in strength and become master of its own fortunes.

He ended by looking forward to the sweet enjoyment of retirement under the benign influence of the free government that he had done so much to bring about. And he surely yearned for an end to the partisan fighting that marred the last years of his presidency. As anxious as he was about the future, he scarcely foresaw how unsettled and disturbing, and how partisan, the remaining years of the 1790s and of his life would be.

82. GW, Farewell Address (1796), *Washington: Writings*, 962–77.

# 6

# John Adams and the Few
# and the Many

Except for the era of the Civil War, the last several years of the eighteenth century were the most politically contentious in United States history. With no George Washington in office to calm the emotions and reconcile the clashing interests, sectional antagonisms became more and more bitter. Some leaders began predicting a French invasion of the United States and envisioned once again a breakup of the Union. As the Federalist and the Republican parties furiously attacked each other as enemies of the Constitution, party loyalties became more intense and began to override personal ties, as every aspect of American life became politicized. People who had known one another their whole lives now crossed streets to avoid confrontations. Personal differences easily spilled into violence, and fighting erupted in the state legislatures and even in the federal Congress. By 1798 public passions and partisanship and indeed public hysteria had increased to the point where armed conflict among the states and the American people seemed likely. By the end of the decade, in the opinion of the British foreign secretary, the "whole system of American Government" seemed to be "tottering to its foundations."[1]

DURING THE PRESIDENTIAL ELECTION OF 1796 few Americans foresaw how bad things would become. With Washington retired, for the first time political leaders were confronted with the prospect of actually choosing someone to be president, and no one was sure how this should be done. According to the Constitution, presidents were elected by the Electoral College, in which each state had the same number of electors as it had congressmen and senators. The Electoral College had been the product of long agonizing debate in the Constitutional Convention. Some delegates, including James Wilson, had proposed direct election by the people. But others wondered, once Washington had served, how the

1. Manning J. Dauer, *The Adams Federalists* (Baltimore, 1953), 241; Marshall Smelser, "The Federalist Era as an Age of Passion," *American Quarterly*, 10 (1958), 391–419.

people would know whom to vote for outside of the notables in their own state. The delegates, of course, did not anticipate political parties that would propose tickets or mass media that would create national celebrities. Other delegates suggested that Congress, which would know who was qualified nationally, should elect the president. But when it was pointed out that this would make the president dependent on the Congress, others suggested that the president be elected for a single term of seven years and not be eligible for re-election: by not having to seek re-election, the president would not have to kowtow to the Congress. Others, however, feared that seven years was too long a term. And so the debate went, until someone suggested creating an alternative Congress of independent electors that would have the sole and exclusive responsibility for electing the president every four years. Thus the Electoral College was born.

By 1796, with the admission to statehood of Vermont, Kentucky, and Tennessee, the electors totaled 138. The states could select their electors in any way they chose, and the electors were free to vote for any two people they wished, as long as one of them was from outside the state. The man who received the highest majority of votes was president; the second highest, vice-president. If no one received a majority of electoral votes, then the House of Representatives voting by state congressional delegations with each delegation having but a single vote was to select the president from those candidates with the five highest numbers of electoral votes.

After Washington, this elaborate two-stage procedure was probably how most Framers expected the electoral process would normally work. Because they assumed that worthy presidential candidates might not be known outside of their state or region, they thought that the Electoral College, which favored the large states, would act as a nominating body. The electoral votes would be scattered, and no one, it was assumed, would receive a majority of them; thus from the five men with the highest number of electoral votes, the House would make the final selection of the president. The unanticipated development of parties undermined these expectations.

But not at once. Parties in 1796 were still distasteful, and most people were reluctant to put party loyalties ahead of regional, state, or personal loyalties. Hence the leading contenders for the presidency—John Adams and Thomas Jefferson—had to appear as if they were indifferent to the office. In 1796 they did not openly campaign but instead remained secluded on their farms, making no statements and offering no hints of their intentions. Although Adams saw himself as the "heir apparent" and believed his "succession" was likely, he knew as well as Jefferson that the ideal character for the presidency had to be called to the office.[2]

2. James Roger Sharp, *American Politics in the Early Republic: The New Nation in Crisis* (New Haven, 1993), 142.

It was thus left to friends and allies to promote a man's candidacy. Most Federalists thought that Adams deserved the presidency, but, of course, they wanted a Federalist sympathizer for vice-president as well. Thomas Pinckney of South Carolina, the negotiator of the treaty with Spain, was most talked about, but not everyone knew who he was. Pinckney himself was in the middle of the Atlantic on his way home from Europe and knew nothing of the promotion of his candidacy for high office. Hamilton actually thought that Pinckney was more suitable for the presidency than Adams (he had "a temper far more discreet and conciliatory"). But whether Adams or Pinckney, Hamilton was at least clear about one thing: "all personal and partial considerations must be discarded, and every thing must give way to the great object of excluding Jefferson."[3]

Other Federalists were equally appalled at the prospect of Jefferson's becoming president or even vice-president. Jefferson as president, said Oliver Wolcott Jr., the Connecticut Federalist who had replaced Hamilton as secretary of the treasury in 1795, would "innovate upon and fritter away the Constitution." But, continued Wolcott, Jefferson as vice-president might even be worse than if he were president: "he would become the rallying point of faction and French influence" and "without any responsibility, he would...divide, and undermine, and finally subvert the rival administration."[4] Better to support Pinckney as president, some Federalists declared, than to see Jefferson in any office, even if it cost Adams the presidency.

Adams picked up some of this Federalist gossip and was furious. The idea of Pinckney's becoming president ahead of him violated the natural hierarchy of society and the very meaning of the Revolution. "To see such...an unknown being as Pinckney, brought over my head, and trampling on the bellies of hundreds of other men infinitely his superiors in talents, services, and reputation, filled me with apprehensions for the safety of us all."[5]

For the Republicans, Jefferson was the most obvious person to be president. But they were even more confused and divided than the Federalists over the choice of vice-president. Some wanted Pierce Butler of South Carolina. Others mentioned John Langdon of New Hampshire. And still

3. Joseph Charles, "Hamilton and Washington: The Origins of the American Party System," WMQ, 12 (1955), 414–15; AH to _____, 8 Nov. 1796, Papers of Hamilton, 20: 376–77; AH, Letter from Alexander Hamilton, Concerning the Public Conduct and Character of John Adams, Esq. President of the United States, 24 Oct. 1800, Papers of Hamilton, 25: 195.
4. Sharp, American Politics in the Early Republic, 149.
5. Joanne B. Freeman, "The Presidential Election of 1796," in Richard Alan Ryerson, ed., John Adams and the Founding of the Republic (Boston, 2001), 148.

others suggested Robert R. Livingston or Aaron Burr of New York. Burr, who was especially charming and well connected, actually had his eyes on the presidency and was willing to cultivate Federalist votes to get it. Burr's personal maneuvering made many believe that he was "unsettled in his politics" and thus likely to "go over to the other side."[6]

In the end personal ambitions, local interests, sectional ties, and personal friendships tended to override national party loyalties, making the final election a confused and chaotic affair. Thus the rudimentary efforts of party caucuses to designate a suitable pair of candidates had less effect than many wanted. With the electors in each state chosen in a variety of ways and free to vote for whomever they wished, the electoral system inhibited the capacity of the parties to organize presidential and vice-presidential tickets.

The Constitution provided for the electors to select any two candidates that suited them, even if they were from opposing parties. So in Pennsylvania one elector voted for both Jefferson and Pinckney. In Maryland an elector voted for Adams and Jefferson. And all the electors of South Carolina voted for both Jefferson and Pinckney. Despite these examples of crossing party lines, however, eight of sixteen states did vote a straight Adams-Pinckney or Jefferson-Burr ticket. Yet, as the vote of the South Carolina electors suggests, the election in fact reflected more of a sectional than a party split.

In the end Adams received seventy-one electoral votes, mostly from New England and New York and New Jersey. Jefferson was next with sixty-eight, all from Pennsylvania and the states in the South. Pinckney received fifty-nine votes and Burr thirty. The remaining forty-eight votes were scattered among nine men, including Samuel Adams, who received fifteen electoral votes from Virginia as an expression of that state's mistrust of Burr—something Burr never forgave.

Initially, the election of the Federalist John Adams as president and the Republican Thomas Jefferson as vice-president seemed to promise an end to factionalism and a new era of goodwill. Jefferson and Adams had been friends during the Revolution, and the results of the electoral contest, together with Jefferson's expressed willingness to serve as vice-president under the more senior Adams, suggested to both men the possibility not only of renewing the friendship but also of restoring the Founders' dream of nonpartisan government. Others had the same hope—that somehow the two men would detach themselves from their respective factions and end what one observer called the "prevailing spirit of jealousy and party."[7]

---

6. Joanne B. Freeman, *Affairs of Honor: National Politics in the New Republic* (New Haven, 2001), 217–18; Sharp, *American Politics in the Early Republic,* 147.

7. Sharp, *American Politics in the Early Republic,* 158.

John Adams came to the presidency much opposed to what he repeatedly called "that fiend, the Spirit of Party."[8] As a good radical Whig, he had always valued independence, not only the independence of America from Great Britain and the independence of one part of the government from another, but also the independence of one man from another; indeed, he always prided himself on his own independence. He defied his father in choosing a career as a lawyer rather than as a clergyman. He defied many of his fellow patriots in 1774 by defending loyalist victims of a mob in the aftermath of the so-called Boston Massacre.[9] While in Europe negotiating the peace in the early 1780s, he defied both Congress and his colleagues in doing what he thought was best for the United States and New England. He repeatedly expressed fears of being under obligation to other people, and he seemed to take a stubborn pride in the snubs and sneers that he often received for his cantankerous and outspoken opinions. "Popularity," he told James Warren in 1787, "was never my Mistress, nor was I ever, or shall I ever be a popular Man." His classical heroes were Demosthenes and Cicero, whose achievements came in the teeth of their defeats, their unpopularity, and their loneliness. "I must think myself independent, as long as I live," he said. "The feeling is essential to my existence."[10]

That feeling was expressed in his political and constitutional theories. Adams was always interested in constitutionalism and the proper structuring of government. Indeed, none of the Revolutionaries took the science of politics more seriously. At the moment of Independence and constitution-making in 1776, his pamphlet, *Thoughts on Government*, became the most influential work guiding the framers of the new state republics. In 1780 he took the lead in drafting the Massachusetts constitution, widely regarded as the most consequential state constitution of the Revolutionary era. And in 1787–1788 when he was abroad serving as first minister to Great Britain he sought to translate what he had learned into some basic principles of political science applicable to all peoples at all times. The result was his three-volume work *Defence of the Constitutions of Government of the United States*, a bulky, disordered conglomeration of political glosses on the single theme of mixed or balanced government.

By 1787 Adams had lost whatever confidence he had once possessed at the time of Independence in the capacity of the American people to make

8. Stanley Elkins and Eric McKitrick, *The Age of Federalism* (New York, 1993), 535.
9. Actually, Samuel Adams and some other Boston patriots were eager for Adams to take on the defense of the soldiers, perhaps in an effort to protect the reputation of Boston in the empire. Hiller B. Zobel, *The Boston Massacre* (New York, 1970), 220–21.
10. Gordon S. Wood, *The Creation of the American Republic, 1776–1787* (Chapel Hill, 1969), 581; Peter Shaw, *The Character of John Adams* (Chapel Hill, 1976), 318.

themselves into a benevolent and virtuous people. Americans, he now concluded, had "never merited the Character of very exalted Virtue," and it was foolish to have "expected that they should have grown much better."[11] Life everywhere was a struggle for superiority. In this struggle only a few made it to the top, and once there, these aristocratic few, who were rarely the most talented or virtuous, would seek only to stabilize and aggrandize their position by oppressing those below them. Those on the bottom of society, driven by the most ambitious, would in turn seek only to ruin and replace the few aristocratic social leaders they hated and envied.

Hence arose, said Adams, an inevitable social division between the few and the many, between gentlemen and commoners, between "the rich and the poor, the laborious and the idle, the learned and the ignorant," between those who had attained superiority and those who aspired to it. Grounded as it was in the irrational passions of people, this division could be neither stable nor secure. This struggle for superiority existed everywhere, even in egalitarian, republican America. Indeed, argued Adams, almost a half century before Tocqueville made the same penetrating observation, Americans were more driven by the passion for distinction, by the desire to set themselves from one another, than other peoples. In a republican society devoted to equality "there can be no subordination." A man would see his neighbor "whom he holds his equal" with a better coat, house, or horse. "He cannot bear it; he must and will be on a level with him." America, Adams concluded, had thus become "more Avaricious than any other Nation."[12]

Adams's political solution to this ceaseless scramble for place and prestige was a mixed or balanced government. Education, religion, superstition, oaths—none of these devices could control human appetites and passions. "Nothing," he told Jefferson in 1787, "but Force, and Power and Strength can restrain them." Nothing "but three different orders of men, bound by their interests to watch over each other, and stand the guardians of the laws" could maintain social peace.[13]

Constitution-makers, said Adams, must provide separate chambers in the legislature for those at the top and those on the bottom of the society, for the aristocracy and for the democracy. They must segregate and balance the two warring social elements in a bicameral legislature and erect an independent executive who would share in the law-making and mediate the basic social struggle between the few and the many.

11. JA to James Warren, 9 Jan. 1787, in Worthington C. Ford, ed., *Warren-Adams Letters* (Mass. Hist. Soc., *Coll.*, 72–73 [1917, 1925]), 2: 280.
12. Wood, *Creation of the American Republic*, 574.
13. Wood, *Creation of the American Republic*, 575.

Although Adams's idea of mixed or balanced government resembled the traditional theory that went back to the ancient Greeks, he gave it a new twist. In 1776 most Americans, like most eighteenth-century English Whigs, had assumed that the basic struggle in English history had always been between the crown and the people, between the king and the House of Commons, between the royal governors and the colonial assemblies. In this perennial conflict the aristocracy sitting in the House of Lords and the various colonial councils had played a mediating or balancing role in the famous mixed English constitution and in each of its miniature colonial counterparts. Now in the 1780s Adams, like some other Americans and especially like the Swiss writer on the English constitution Jean Louis De Lolme, recast the basic struggle and turned it into one between ordinary people and the aristocracy, between commoners and gentry, and between the lower and the upper houses of a bicameral legislature. In this new social conflict the executive, the monarchical element in this mixed constitution, became the balancer or mediator. Adams's image of the government was a set of two scales held by a third hand, which was the executive.[14]

With a veto power over all legislation such as that theoretically held by the British monarch, the executive could throw its weight against the irrational and oppressive measures of either branch of the legislature, especially against the usurpations of the aristocracy segregated in the upper house. "If there is one certain truth to be collected from the history of all ages," argued Adams in his *Defence*, it was "that the people's rights and liberties, and the democratical mixture in a constitution, can never be preserved without a strong executive."[15]

For all his theoretical emphasis on the importance of the executive in government, Adams had never actually served as an executive in any organization. He had never been a governor, or a cabinet officer, or a military commander. Even as vice-president he had not been involved in the discussions and decisions of the Washington administration. Yet now he was the chief executive of the United States, able to put his ideas of a balanced constitution to the test.

It would not prove easy. Adams had little of Washington's prestige, and that distinction between him and his illustrious predecessor became the scourge of his life. Every time he heard Washington praised as the savior of the country he squirmed with irritation and envy. Added to his woes was his reputation for favoring monarchism that bred suspicion of his

---

14. David Lieberman has edited a new edition of Jean Louis De Lolme's *Constitution of England; or, An Account of the English Government* (Indianapolis, 2007).
15. JA, *Defence*, in Wood, *Creation of the American Republic*, 578.

presidency. He had so often praised the English constitution (that "most stupendous fabric of human invention"), and in his writings so often emphasized the "monarchical" element in his balanced constitution, and so often talked of America's having become a "monarchical republic" because of its single strong president that his commitment to republicanism was always mistrusted. His fellow Americans had good reason to believe that he had absorbed too much English royal thinking during his mission to the Court of St. James's in the 1780s.

ADAMS'S SIMPLE-MINDED CONSTITUTIONAL REMEDY of bicameral legislatures may have been disproportionate to the unruly and dynamic social circumstances he described, but he was not wrong in his contention that American society was divided between the few and the many. In fact, that was how many Americans in the 1790s had come to describe their society, as a contest between "democrats" and "aristocrats," which were the derogatory terms that the two emerging parties of Federalists and Republicans commonly used to label one another.

Although Jefferson could privately call himself and others like him "natural aristocrats," most Federalists were not at all happy with being called "aristocrats." While John Adams in his honest, blunt way was elevating the contest between the few and the many into his elaborate science of politics, most of his fellow Federalists were vainly trying to deny publicly that there was any difference at all between themselves and ordinary folk. The Revolution had turned "aristocrat" into a pejorative term or worse—the enemy of all good republicans and liberal reformers. Thus labeling one's opponent an aristocrat was good rhetorical strategy, and all the more effective in light of the way in which the French revolutionaries were demonizing their privileged aristocrats as being even beyond the pale of citizenship, something they were underlining in blood.[16] If the Federalists were willing to be recognized as distinctive at all, they wanted to be thought of as the rightful rulers of the society, as disinterested leaders beset by hordes of Jacobinical sans-culottes who were out to destroy all harmony and order in the society.

The Northern Republicans, of course, were only too eager to label the Federalists—all those landed gentlemen, rich merchants, wealthy lawyers, and other well-to-do professionals—as "aristocrats" who "fancy themselves

---

16. On the way in which the French revolutionaries cast their social struggle, see Sarah Maza, "The Social Imagery of the French Revolution: The Third Estate, the National Guard, and the Absent Bourgeoisie," in Colin Jones and Dror Wahrman, eds., *The Age of Cultural Revolutions: Britain and France, 1750–1820* (Berkeley, 2002), 106–23.

to have a right of pre-eminence in every thing."[17] In fact, they were merely puffed-up phonies whose claims of disinterested superiority had no basis in reality. Most of those who made up the Northern Republican party may have been middling people, but they thought the Revolution with its republican emphasis on merit as the only criterion of leadership gave them as much right to govern and exert authority as the so-called better sort of Federalists. These ordinary men supported the Republican party and opposed Great Britain not because they had necessarily thought through all the particular issues and policies dividing them from the Federalists, but because they hated what they thought the Federalists and the monarchical spirit of Great Britain had come to stand for. Ultimately, as with all politics, there was a deep emotional basis to the ideological party division.

The Federalists tried to retaliate by calling their Republican opponents "democrats," a term that in the past had suggested the licentiousness of the common people, but one that was now acquiring a more positive connotation. Indeed, the Republicans began to wear the hitherto derogatory term of "democrat" as a badge of honor.

The experience of three middling individuals who became ardent Republicans—William Findley of Pennsylvania, Jedediah Peck of New York, and Matthew Lyon of Vermont—may help illuminate the kinds of social feelings involved in the contest between the Federalists and the Republicans, or at least between the Federalists and Northern Republicans. These three individuals might be considered as stand-ins for tens of thousands of other common folk.

Although the conflict these individuals had with their Federalist opponents was described by them as "democrats" versus "aristocrats," it was not quite a "class conflict" as the term is often understood today. To be sure, it was an important social conflict, but not one of an oppressed working class taking on an exploitative bourgeoisie or moneyed men, as some historians have contended.[18] Indeed, if either contestant represented the "bourgeoisie," it was the so-called middling "democrats," men such as Findley, Peck, and Lyon. Although the contestants in this social struggle knew each other well, often dined with one other, and had a great deal in common, they nevertheless were engaged in a social struggle that revealed much of what America from its earliest days had been about

17. Debate in the New York Ratifying Convention, 17 June–26 July 1788, in Bernard Bailyn, ed., *The Debate on the Constitution* (New York, 1993), 2: 761.

18. Michael Merrill and Sean Wilentz, eds., *The Key of Liberty: The Life and Democratic Writings of William Manning, "A Laborer," 1747–1814* (Cambridge, MA, 1993); Michael Merrill, "Putting Capitalism in Its Place: A Review of Recent Literature," *WMQ*, 52 (1995), 315–26.

and would continue to be about—the difficulty would-be aristocrats had setting themselves off from those just below them.

WILLIAM FINDLEY CAME TO AMERICA from northern Ireland in 1763, at age twenty-two.[19] Apparently trained as a weaver, this Scots-Irish immigrant tried his hand at schoolteaching before buying a farm in 1768 in Cumberland (later Franklin) County, Pennsylvania. He joined the Revolutionary movement, moved through the ranks of the militia to a captaincy, and became a political officeholder, eventually a representative from Westmoreland County near Pittsburgh. Findley was the prototype of a later professional politician and was as much a product of the Revolution as were the more illustrious patriots like John Adams or Alexander Hamilton. He had no lineage to speak of, he had attended no college, and he possessed no great wealth. He was completely self-taught and self-made, but not in the manner of a Benjamin Franklin who acquired the sophisticated attributes of a gentleman. Findley's origins showed, and conspicuously so. In his middling aspirations, middling achievements, and middling resentments, he represented far more accurately what America was becoming than did cosmopolitan gentlemen like Benjamin Franklin and Alexander Hamilton.

In the 1780s this red-faced Scots-Irishman became one of the most articulate spokesmen for the debtor–paper money interests that lay behind the political turbulence and democratic excesses of the decade. As a representative from the West in the Pennsylvania state legislature in the 1780s, Findley embodied that rough, upstart, individualistic society that the Pennsylvania gentry, such as Hugh Henry Brackenridge, Robert Morris, and James Wilson, both scorned and feared.[20]

Hugh Henry Brackenridge, born in 1748, was seven years younger than Findley. As the son of a poor Scottish farmer, he too had humble origins. At the age of five, Brackenridge immigrated to Pennsylvania with his family. But his parents gave him a grammar school education and sent him to the College of New Jersey (Princeton), which upon his graduation in 1771 turned him into a gentleman. In 1781 he moved to western Pennsylvania because he thought that the wilds of Pittsburgh offered greater opportunities for advancement than crowded Philadelphia. As the only

19. On Findley, see John Caldwell, *William Findley from West of the Mountains: A Politician in Pennsylvania, 1783–1791* (Gig Harbor, WA, 2000); and Caldwell, *William Findley from West of the Mountains: Congressman, 1791–1821* (Gig Harbor, WA, 2001).

20. Jerry Grundfest, *George Clymer: Philadelphia Revolutionary, 1739–1813* (New York, 1982), 141.

college-educated gentleman in the area, he saw himself as an oasis of cultivation. Wanting to be "among the first to bring the press to the west of the mountains," he helped to establish a newspaper in Pittsburgh for which he wrote poetry, bagatelles, and other things.[21] Missing no opportunity to show off his learning, this young, ambitious, and pretentious Princeton graduate was just the sort of person to drive someone like William Findley to distraction.

Findley was already a member of the state legislature in 1786 when Brackenridge decided that he too would like to be a legislator. Brackenridge ran for election and won by promising his western constituents that he would look after their particular interests, especially in favoring the use of state certificates of paper money in buying land. But then his troubles began. In the state capital in Philadelphia he fell in with the well-to-do crowd around Robert Morris and James Wilson, who had cosmopolitan tastes more to his liking. Under the influence of Morris, Brackenridge not only voted against the state certificates he had promised to support but came to identify himself with the eastern establishment. He actually had the nerve to write in the *Pittsburgh Gazette* that the "eastern members" of the assembly had singled him out among all the "Huns, Goths and Vandals," who usually came over the mountains to legislate in Philadelphia, and had complimented him on his "liberality." But it was at a dinner party at Chief Justice Thomas McKean's house in December 1786, at which both he and Findley were guests, where he made his most costly mistake. One guest suggested that Robert Morris's support for the Bank of North America seemed mainly for his own personal benefit rather than for the benefit of the people. To this Brackenridge replied loudly, "The people are fools; if they would let Mr. Morris alone, he would make Pennsylvania a great people, but they will not suffer him to do it."[22]

Most political leaders already knew better than to call the people fools, at least in public, and Findley saw his chance to bring Brackenridge down a peg. He wrote an account of Brackenridge's statement in the *Pittsburgh Gazette* and accused him of betraying the people's trust by his vote against the state certificates. It was all right, said Findley sarcastically, for a representative to change his mind if he had not solicited or expected the office, "which is the case generally with modest, disinterested men." But for someone like Brackenridge who had openly sought the office and had

21. Claude M. Newlin, *The Life and Writings of Hugh Henry Brackenridge* (Princeton, 1932), 71.
22. Newlin, *Brackenridge*, 80–81, 78; Russell J. Ferguson, *Early Western Pennsylvania Politics* (Pittsburgh, 1938), 66–69.

made campaign promises—for Brackenridge to change his vote could only arouse the "indignation" and "contempt" of the people.

Brackenridge vainly tried to reply. He sought to justify his change of vote on the classic republican grounds that the people could not know about the "complex, intricate and involved" problems and interests involved in law-making. Only an educated elite in the assembly, said Brackenridge, possessed the "ability to be able to distinguish clearly the interests of a state."[23]

But the more Brackenridge tried to explain, the worse his situation became, and he never fully recovered from Findley's attack. The two men crossed swords again in the election to the state ratifying convention in 1788, and Brackenridge as an avowed Federalist lost to the Anti-Federalist Findley. Brackenridge then abandoned politics for the time being and turned his disillusionment with the vagaries of American democracy into his comic masterpiece, *Modern Chivalry*.

In this rambling picaresque novel, written piecemeal between 1792 and 1815, Brackenridge vented all his anger at the social changes taking place in America. His hero and spokesman in his novel was a classic figure ("his ideas were drawn chiefly from what may be called the old school; the Greek and Roman notions of things"). Nothing was more foolish, declared his classic hero, than the people's raising of the ignorant and the unqualified—weavers, brewers, and tavern keepers—into public office. "To rise from the cellar to the senate house, would be an unnatural hoist. To come from counting threads, and adjusting them to the splits of a reed, to regulate the finances of a government, would be preposterous; there being no congruity in the case.... It would be a reversion of the order of things."

This "evil of men seeking office for which they are not qualified" became "the great moral" of Brackenridge's novel. Yet precisely because he himself was a product of social mobility, Brackenridge never lost his faith in republicanism and never fully accepted the Federalist belief in social hierarchy.

In trying to put the best face on what was happening, Brackenridge had the character of a conjuror in his story explain that there was "in every government a patrician class, against whom the spirit of the multitude naturally militates: And hence a perpetual war; the aristocrats endeavouring to detrude the people, and the people contending to obtrude themselves. And it is right it should be so," the conjuror said; "for by this fermentation, the spirit of democracy is kept alive." Since there seemed nothing anyone could do about this "perpetual war,"

---

23. Newlin, *Brackenridge*, 79–80; Ferguson, *Early Western Pennsylvania*, 70–72.

Brackenridge had to accept the fact that "the common people are more disposed to trust one of their own class, than those who may affect to be superior." In the end, unable to repudiate the people, and convinced that the "representatives must yield to the prejudices of their constituents even contrary to their own judgments," Brackenridge became a moderate Jeffersonian Republican.[24]

Federalists like Robert Morris and James Wilson were not so forgiving of the spirit of democracy as Brackenridge turned out to be, and because they flaunted their patrician superiority more fully than Brackenridge, Findley was even more determined to knock them off their high horses. During the debate over the re-chartering of the Bank of North America in the Pennsylvania assembly in 1786, Findley accused Morris of having a selfish interest in the bank and using it to acquire wealth for himself. The supporters of the bank were its directors or stockholders and thus had no right to claim that they were impartial umpires only deciding what was good for the state.

Findley and his fellow western opponents of the bank, however, had no desire to establish themselves as disinterested politicians. All they wanted was to hear no more spurious patrician talk of virtue and disinterestedness. They had no objection to Morris's and the other shareholders' interest in the bank's re-chartering. "Any others in their situation ... would do as they did." Morris and the other legislators in favor of the bank, said Findley, "have a right to advocate their own cause, on the floor of this house." But then they could not protest when others came to realize "that it is their own cause they are advocating; and to give credit to their opinions, and to think of their votes accordingly." Indeed, said Findley, in one of the most remarkable anticipations of modern politics made during this period, such open promotion of interests promised an end to what he now regarded as the archaic idea that political representatives should simply stand and not run for election. When a candidate of the legislature "has a cause of his own to advocate," said Findley, "interest will dictate the propriety of canvassing for a seat."

With this simple remark Findley was challenging the entire classical tradition of disinterested public leadership and setting forth a rationale for competitive democratic interest-laden politics that has never been bettered; it was in fact a rationale that would come to dominate the reality if not the professed standard of American politics. Such a conception of politics meant that politically ambitious middling men—like Findley—with interests and causes to promote could now legitimately run and

24. Hugh Henry Brackenridge, *Modern Chivalry*, ed. Claude M. Newlin (New York, 1937), 53, 14, 611, 19, 449.

compete for electoral office. These politicians would thus become what Madison in *Federalist* No. 10 had most feared—parties who were at the same time judges in their own causes. With just such simple exchanges was the traditional political culture gradually transformed.[25]

Findley's tangle with James Wilson, the Scottish graduate of St. Andrews, came in the Pennsylvania ratifying convention. Findley believed that Wilson and the other genteel supporters of the Constitution thought they were "born of a different race from the rest of the sons of men" and "able to conceive and perform great things."[26] But he knew better, and he deeply resented the contemptuous way he was treated in the ratification debates. When the Philadelphia gentry were not laughing at him when he rose to speak, they repeatedly made snide and sarcastic comments about his arguments. The crucial moment came when Findley claimed that Sweden had declined when it ceased using jury trials. Wilson, who was one of the leading lawyers in the state, and Thomas McKean, the state's chief justice, immediately challenged Findley to prove that Sweden had ever had jury trials.

These learned lawyers assumed that this hick from the west did not know what he was talking about. Wilson haughtily declared that "he had never met with such an idea in the course of his reading." Findley had nothing to say at the moment but promised to answer the scoffing. When the convention assembled several days later, Findley brought with him two sources that confirmed that Sweden at one time did have jury trials. One of the sources was the third volume of William Blackstone's *Commentaries*, the bible for all lawyers. Embarrassed, McKean had the good sense to remain silent, but Wilson could not. "I do not pretend to remember everything I read," he sneered. "But I will add, sir, that those whose stock of knowledge is limited to a few items may easily remember and refer to them, but many things may be overlooked and forgotten by someone who has read an enormous number of books." Wilson went on to claim that someone as well read as he had forgotten more things than someone like Findley had ever learned.[27]

25. Mathew Carey, ed., *Debates and Proceedings of the General Assembly of Pennsylvania on the Memorials Praying a Repeal or Suspension of the Law Annulling the Charter of the Bank* (Philadelphia, 1786), 19, 64, 66, 87, 128, 21, 130, 38, 15, 72–73.

26. [Findley], "Letter by an Officer of the Late Continental Army," Philadelphia *Independent Gazette*, 6 Nov. 1787, in Herbert J. Storing, ed., *The Complete Anti-Federalist* (Chicago, 1981), 3: 95.

27. Merrill Jensen and Robert A. Becker, eds., *The Documentary History of the First Federal Elections, 1788–1790* (Madison WI, 1976), 2: 528–32, 551; Caldwell, *William Findley: Politician*, 166–68; Owen S. Ireland, *Religion, Ethnicity, and Politics: Ratifying the Constitution in Pennsylvania* (University Park, PA, 1995), 99–101.

Such expressions of arrogance only intensified the anger of middling men like Findley. Unlike many of the Revolutionary leaders, such as John Adams, who came from ordinary backgrounds but attended college and became acculturated to gentry standards, Findley continued to identify himself as a "democrat." He eventually became a dedicated Jeffersonian Republican determined to expose the phoniness of the aristocratic claims of men like Wilson. "The citizens," he wrote in 1794, by which he meant common citizens like himself, "have learned to take a surer course of obtaining information respecting political characters," particularly those who pretended to disinterested public service. They had learned to inquire "into the local interests and circumstances" of such characters and to point out those with "pursuits or interests" that were "inconsistent with the equal administration of government." Findley had seen the gentry up close, so close in fact that all the sense of awe and mystery that had hitherto surrounded aristocratic authority vanished.[28]

Findley went on to have a lengthy career in Congress, more or less subverting Madison's hope in 1787 that the elevated and extended nature of the national republic would filter out his likes. He represented the western country of Pennsylvania in the Second through the Fifth Congresses (1791–1799) and again in the Eighth through the Fourteenth (1803–1817). Findley always saw himself as a spokesman for ordinary citizens. He opposed Hamilton's financial program and the excise tax on whiskey and favored selling western land in small parcels so as to benefit small farmers rather than large speculators. As a good Jeffersonian Republican, Findley favored free public education and states' rights, but unlike his party's leaders he opposed slavery. Because he became the longest-serving member of Congress, he was designated the "Father of the House" just before he retired from Congress in 1817; he was the first congressman awarded this honorary title.

JEDEDIAH PECK ALSO SAW the would-be aristocracy up close and became equally aware of how superficial its genteel claims could be. He began his political career as an ally of Federalist William Cooper, the great landlord of Otsego County in New York. Once he came to realize, however, that Cooper, for all his aristocratic pretensions, was no different from him, he turned against his patron and became a fiery Republican.

Cooper had wanted to become an aristocratic patriarch, but like many other Federalists he never acquired enough gentility to pull it off. He found himself continually scrambling to make money, and the

---

28. William Findley, *A Review of the Revenue System Adopted at the First Congress Under the Federal Constitution* (Philadelphia, 1794), 117.

more he scrambled the less he was able to fulfill a Federalist image of leisured gentility. Cooper certainly sought to display his wealth as aristocratically as he could. He bought a carriage, erected his substantial Manor House in the midst of the primitive village of Cooperstown, stocked it with books, and supplied it with indentured servants and slaves. Yet at every turn he betrayed his lowly origins, his crude manners, and his unenlightened temperament. The wooden unornamented Manor House, as his son the author James Fenimore Cooper recalled with embarrassment, was "low and straggling." Cooper had to hire men to walk alongside his pretentious carriage to keep it from jolting on the uneven rocky roads of the county. He never learned to keep a proper gentlemanly distance from the common settlers of his village; he not only jostled and joked with them but wrestled them. He could not even remain superior to his servants: one of them could write better than he could.

More than anything, Cooper yearned to be a father to his people. To do so, however, he needed political authority commensurate with his social position and wealth. When Otsego became a New York county in 1791, Cooperstown became the county seat, and Cooper became the county's first judge, a powerful and influential position. In 1794 he was elected to the U.S. Congress, narrowly defeated in 1796, but re-elected in 1798. From a distance Cooper appeared to have had the county pretty much in his pocket (Jefferson called him "the Bashaw of Otsego") and to have become the dominant patriarchal political figure he longed to be. But in fact he was more confused, more vulnerable, and less powerful than he appeared. Cooper never fitted the Federalist ideal of a learned, wise, and genteel leader; he never came close to possessing the self-assurance and politeness of someone like John Jay. Cooper was caught up in a dynamic democratic frontier world that was rapidly undermining everything the Federalists stood for.

Representative of that new democratic world was Jedediah Peck. Peck was born in 1748 in Lyme, Connecticut, one of thirteen children of a lowly farmer. He essentially taught himself to read, mostly by reading the Bible over and over. He served in the Continental Army as a common soldier, developing a latent resentment of aristocratic pretension. After the war Peck was one of the early migrants to the Otsego area. He became a jack-of-all-trades, trying his hand at farming, surveying, carpentry, and millwrighting; he even traveled about as an evangelical preacher unaffiliated with any denomination before he became Cooper's protégé. Although Peck's origins were not all that different from Cooper's, he acquired little of Cooper's wealth and none of his need for Federalist gentility. One of his contemporaries described Peck as "illiterate but a shrewd cunning man....He had not talent as a preacher or speaker; his language was low and he spoke with a drawling, nasal twang, so that on public speaking he was almost unintelligible."[29]

Peck had begun as a Federalist, securing a county judgeship with Cooper's influence. But in 1796 he turned to electoral politics and in a raucous populist campaign sought a seat in the New York senate. Writing in the Otsego newspaper as "A Ploughjogger," Peck identified with "my brother farmers, mechanicks and traders." He apologized for his misspellings and his simple style, for he knew his brother commoners would forgive him. He especially attacked the "intriguing set" of lawyers who, he said, "have wooled up the practices of the laws in such a heap of formality on purpose so that we cannot see through their entanglement to oblige us to employ them to untangle them, and if we go to them for advice they will not say a word without five dollars." All this demagoguery infuriated the gentry elite of the county, and they retaliated by calling Peck an "ambitious, mean, and groveling demagogue," who resembled a frog, an "insignificant animal that just so vainly imagined its little self swelled, or about to be, to the size of an ox."[30]

Although Peck did not win this particular election, the attacks on him made him a popular hero among the small and middling people of the county. As a result, he was repeatedly elected as a Republican member of the New York state legislature, serving in the assembly for six years between 1798 and 1804, and in the state senate for five years between 1804 and 1808. He became the defender of the common farmers and other laboring people against privileged lawyers and leisured aristocrats. Sick and tired of Federalist criticism that he was unrefined and had not read Montesquieu, Peck turned his deficiencies back on his critics. He took to ridiculing pretentious book-learning, genteel manners, and aristocratic arrogance and, to the amazement of Cooper and other Federalist gentry, won popularity in the process. Unlike the Federalists, who stood for office by writing each other letters and lining up influential gentlemen as supporters, Peck and other Republicans in the region began promoting their own candidacies and campaigning for office openly. They used the newspapers to reach out to other common people in order to challenge the Federalist assumption that only well-to-do

29. Alfred F. Young, *The Democratic Republicans of New York: The Origins, 1763–1797* (Chapel Hill, 1967), 509–10.

30. Young, *Democratic Republicans of New York*, 511–12; Alan Taylor, *William Cooper's Town: Power and Persuasion on the Frontiers of the Early American Republic* (New York, 1995), 245–46.

educated gentlemen were capable of exercising political authority. Cooper, like other Federalists, saw all his aristocratic dreams endangered by the demagogic behavior of Peck, and he began to try to stifle these new kinds of democratic writings and actions.[31]

The Federalist gentry could scarcely oppose social mobility since most of them were themselves the product of it. Indeed, many of the Revolutionary leaders in the 1760s and 1770s had expressed the same kind of resentment of arrogant aristocrats as Findley and Peck were voicing in the 1790s. As a young man John Adams had wondered "who are to be understood by the better Sort of People" and had concluded that there was "no Difference between one Man and another, but what real Merit creates." He was thinking of the royal official Thomas Hutchinson and his genteel crowd, with their "certain Airs of Wisdom and Superiority," and their "Scorn and Contempt and turning up of the Nose," and he felt passionately that they were no better than he was.

But Adams's remedy for his resentment had not been to celebrate his plebeian origins, as Peck did, but instead to outdo Hutchinson and his aristocratic crowd at their own genteel game. Although Adams began his career, like Peck, writing as a hick farmer, "Humphrey Ploughjogger," in order to do battle on behalf of all those ordinary humble people who were "made of as good Clay" as the so-called "great ones of the World," he had no intention of remaining one of those humble people. Instead, Adams had determined to become more learned, more refined, and, most important, more virtuous and public-spirited than Hutchinson and his ilk, who lived only by their lineage. Let the people decide who are the better sort, said Adams, in his naïve and youthful republican enthusiasm; they would be the best judges of merit.[32]

Many of the Republican upstarts of post-Revolutionary America were behaving quite differently. Benjamin Franklin in the 1730s had made fun of all those ordinary folk—mechanics and tradesmen—who found themselves "by their Industry or good Fortune, from mean Beginnings...in Circumstances a little more easy" and sought to become gentlemen when they were not really ready for the status. It was, said Franklin, "no easy Thing for a Clown or a Labourer, on a sudden to hit in all respects, the natural and easy Manner of those who have been genteelly educated: And 'tis the Curse of *Imitation*, that it almost always either under-does or over-does." Such men, said Franklin, were "Molatto Gentlemen,"

---

31. Taylor, *William Cooper's Town*, 244–46. As Taylor points out in his brilliant book, James Fenimore Cooper's novel *The Pioneers* is based on the experience of his father.
32. Gordon S. Wood, *The Radicalism of the American Revolution* (New York, 1992), 237–38.

possessing genteel desires and aspirations but lacking the talent and politeness to pull it off.[33]

But a new generation of ambitious commoners was moving in a very different world. They had the advantage of a post-Revolutionary republican climate that celebrated equality in a manner that Franklin's earlier generation had never quite known. To be sure, large numbers of middling sorts were buying and reading etiquette manuals in order to become polite and genteel, but many more were acting like Franklin's "Molatto Gentlemen," indeed, even flaunting their lowly origins and their plebeian tastes and manners, and getting away with it. No one was more representative of this kind of parvenu than Matthew Lyon.

LYON HAD ARRIVED IN AMERICA from Ireland in 1764 as a fifteen-year-old indentured servant. He had been bound to a dealer in pork, who sold him to another master for a "yoke of bulls." In 1773 he bought land in what became Vermont, and the following year migrated there and fell in with Ethan Allen and his brothers. Lyon was an ambitious scrambler who seized every opportunity for personal advancement offered by the Revolution, whether it was the confiscation of Loyalist lands or the creation of an independent Vermont. He founded the Vermont town of Fair Haven and served for well over a decade in the state assembly. He built saw, grist, and paper mills, an iron foundry, a blast furnace, and a tavern. Before he was done he had become a leader in the Vermont assembly and one of the richest entrepreneurs and manufacturers in Vermont, if not in all New England. Inevitably, he became a fervent Republican.

But for all of his wealth Lyon was always just an "ignorant Irish puppy" in the eyes of educated gentlemen like Nathaniel Chipman. It was not that Chipman himself came from a genteel background. Far from it: he was the son of a Connecticut blacksmith and farmer. But he had graduated from Yale College in 1777, and in his mind that made all the difference between him and the likes of Matthew Lyon. Like so many of the Revolutionary leaders Chipman was the first of his family to go to college and become a full-fledged gentleman. After resigning his commission in the Revolutionary army in 1778 because he lacked the income "to support the character of a gentleman" and "an officer," Chipman followed many other Connecticut migrants, including Lyon, up the Connecticut River to Vermont, where he thought his college degree and his legal education at Litchfield Law School might go further. "I shall indeed be *rara avis* in *terris*," he joked to a friend in 1779, "for there is not an attorney in

---

33. BF, "Blackamore, on Molatto Gentlemen," 1733, *Franklin: Writings*, 219; Albrecht Koschnik, "Political Conflict and Public Contest: Rituals of National Celebration in Philadelphia, 1788–1815," *Penn. Mag. of Hist. and Biog.*, 118 (1994), 209.

the state. Think…think what a figure I shall make, when I become the oracle of law to the state of Vermont."

Although there was a good deal of self-protective humor in these reve-lations of ambition to a close friend, there is no doubt Chipman was seri-ous about rising rapidly in government, eventually even becoming a member of the Confederation Congress, then the highest national office in the land. All his joshing about the "many steps" he had to mount to attain "that pinnacle of happiness.…First, an attorney; then a selectman; a huffing justice; a deputy; an assistant; a member of Congress"—only points up his arrogant expectation that such offices naturally belonged to educated gentlemen like himself. It was just as inevitable that Chipman became a Federalist as Lyon had become a Republican.[34]

Naturally, Lyon deeply resented someone like Chipman. He regarded him and his fellow lawyers as "professional gentlemen" and "aristocrats" who used their knowledge of the rigmarole of the common law on behalf of former Loyalists, New York landlords, and other "over-grown land jobbers in preference to the poorer sort of people." However big a manufacturer and however rich he became, Lyon was not wrong in claiming to represent the poorer sort of people, for emotionally and traditionally he remained one of them. From his perspective the struggle between Federalists like Chipman and Republicans like himself was indeed, as he said echoing John Adams, "a struggle…between the aristocrats and the democrats." In 1793 Lyon formed a newspaper, the *Farmer's Library*, which opposed Hamilton's financial pro-gram and promoted the French Revolution. At the same time, he missed no opportunity to label Chipman and his family "tories" and "aristocrats."[35]

The ironies of being called an "aristocrat" were not lost on Chipman and his family. "Nathaniel Chipman an aristocrat!" said his brother in amazed disbelief. "This must sound very oddly…to all those who have witnessed his plain, republican manners, habits, and sentiments." Yet in the levels below levels of post-Revolutionary American egalitarianism, Chipman was in fact as much of an aristocrat as Vermont was to know, and Lyon, especially because he was wealthier than Chipman, deeply resented being made to feel his inferior.[36]

Although Lyon was a member of the state legislature, he spent the greater part of the 1790s trying to get elected to the United States Congress and was finally successful in 1797. He arrived in Philadelphia seething

---

34. Daniel Chipman, *The Life of Hon. Nathaniel Chipman…with Selections from His Miscellaneous Papers* (Boston, 1846), 33, 29, 30, 31–32.
35. Aleine Austin, *Matthew Lyon: "New Man" of the Democratic Revolution, 1749–1822* (University Park, PA, 1981), 46, 45.
36. Chipman, *Life of Nathaniel Chipman*, 110.

with rage at the aristocratic Federalist world. He immediately began ridiculing the customary ceremonies involved in the House's replying to an address of the president. He did not wish, he declared, to take any part in "such a boyish piece of business." In reaction, the Federalists missed no opportunity to make fun of his behavior and his origins, both in the Congress itself and in the press. Chipman, at that time one of Vermont's senators, hoped that Lyon was making so "incredulous a figure" that he would embarrass his fellow Republicans. The Federalists called him "ragged Matt, the Democrat," a "beast" that ought to be caged, the "Lyon" that was captured in the bogs of Hibernia. He was an Irishman, they said, who did not have real American blood in him. It was left to William Cobbett, the acerbic Federalist editor of *Porcupine's Gazette*, however, to deliver the most devastating attack of all on Lyon. Among other derisive and satirical comments, Cobbett brought up the fact that Lyon had been court-martialed for cowardice during the Revolutionary War and had been forced to wear a wooden sword as punishment. This was something neither Lyon nor the Federalists were apt to forget.[37]

On January 30, 1798, during a brief recess in the Congress, Lyon was telling a group of his fellow congressmen that the conservative people of Connecticut needed someone like him to come in with his newspaper and turn them into Republicans. Federalist Roger Griswold of Connecticut interrupted to tell Lyon that if he were going to go into Connecticut, he had better wear his wooden sword, whereupon a furious Lyon spat in Griswold's face. Many members were aghast at Lyon's behavior but were even more appalled by the "outrageous" and "indecent" defense he offered for it: he was reported in the papers to have said, "I did not come here to have my——kicked by everybody." When the Federalists urged that Lyon be expelled from the House for "gross indecency," the Republicans rallied to his defense and prevented the two-thirds majority needed for expulsion.

Frustrated, Griswold wanted to avenge his honor. Had he considered Lyon his equal, he might have challenged him to a duel; instead, two weeks after having been spat upon, he assaulted and began caning Lyon in the House chamber. Lyon responded by grabbing a pair of fireplace tongs, and the two men ended up wrestling on the floor of the House of Representatives. Many were horrified, and some concluded that Congress had become no better than a "tavern," filled with "beasts, and not gentlemen."[38] More than words ever could, this extraordinary incident of

37. Austin, *Matthew Lyon*, 91, 95; J. Fairfax McLaughlin, *Matthew Lyon: The Hampden of Congress* (New York, 1900), 500.
38. *Annals of Congress*, 5th Congress, 2nd session (Feb. 1798), VII, 955–1067.

two congressmen wrestling on the floor of the House revealed the intensity of partisan antagonism and the emergence of new men into politics.

But THE SOCIAL STRUGGLE that underlay the political conflict between Federalists and Republicans in the Northern states in the 1790s was not simply a matter of new middling sorts of men challenging the established order. It was also a matter of the established aristocratic order being too feeble to resist these challenges. The persistent problem of American society—the weakness of its would-be aristocracy, at least in the North—became more glaringly evident in the 1790s. Too many of the Federalists, like William Cooper, lacked the attributes of gentility and seemed scarcely distinguishable from the middling sorts who were challenging them.

In eighteenth-century America it had never been easy for gentlemen to play the role of disinterested public servants who were supposed to sacrifice their private interests for the sake of the public. The problem had become especially apparent during the Revolution. General Richard Montgomery, who in 1775 led a fatal ill-fated expedition to Quebec, continually complained about the lack of discipline among his troops. If only "some method" could be found of "engaging *gentlemen* to serve," he said, the soldiers would become "more tractable," since "that class of men" presumably commanded deference from commoners. But many gentlemen had chosen not to serve, since as officers they had to serve without pay.[39]

The same had been true of many of the Revolutionary leaders serving in the Continental Congress, especially those of "small fortunes." They had grumbled repeatedly over the burdens of office and had begged to be relieved from those burdens in order to pursue their private interests. Periodic temporary retirement from the cares and turmoil of office to one's country estate for refuge and rest was acceptable classical behavior. But too often America's political leaders, especially in the North, had to retire, not to relaxation in the solitude and leisure of a rural retreat, but to the making of money in the busyness and bustle of a city law practice.[40]

In short, America's would-be gentlemen had a great deal of trouble maintaining the desired classical independence and freedom from business and the marketplace that philosophers like Adam Smith thought necessary for political leadership. Smith in his *Wealth of Nations* (1776) had praised the English landed gentry for being particularly qualified for

39. Christopher Clark, *Social Change in America: From the Revolution Through the Civil War* (Chicago, 2006), 55.

40. Jack N. Rakove, *The Beginnings of National Politics: An Interpretative History of the Continental Congress* (New York, 1979), 216–39; George A. Billias, *Elbridge Gerry: Founding Father and Republican Statesman* (New York, 1976), 138–39.

disinterested political leadership. This was because their income came from the rents of tenants, which, said Smith, "costs them neither labour nor care, but comes to them, as it were, of its own accord, and independent of any plan or project of their own."[41]

In America there were not many gentry who were capable of living in such a manner. Of course, large numbers of Southern gentry-planters enjoyed leisure based on the labor of their slaves, but most Southern planters were not as removed from the day-to-day management of their estates as their counterparts among the English landed gentry. Since they had slaves, not rent-paying tenants, their overseers were not comparable to the bailiffs or stewards of the English gentry. Thus the planters, despite their aristocratic poses, were often busy, commercially involved men. Their livelihoods were tied directly to the vicissitudes of international trade, and they always had an uneasy sense of being dependent on the market. Still, the great Southern planters at least approached the classical image of disinterested gentlemanly leadership, and they made the most of this image throughout the Revolutionary era and beyond. Virginia especially contributed a galaxy of leaders, including George Washington, Thomas Jefferson, James Madison, James Monroe, Patrick Henry, and George Mason—slaveholders all.[42]

For the Northern gentry the problems of maintaining their independence from the marketplace were particularly acute. Northern gentry-leaders were never able to duplicate the degree of self-confidence and noblesse oblige that characterized even the Southern gentry, let alone the English aristocracy. More and more of the Federalist officeholders found that their property, or their proprietary wealth, did not generate enough income for them to ignore or neglect their private affairs. Consequently, they either had to exploit their offices for profit or had to absent themselves from their public responsibilities.

Although the First Congress granted members of both houses a salary of six dollars a day—a radical act for the age: members of the British Parliament did not receive salaries until 1911—paying congressmen and other federal officers salaries was never enough. Too often private interests had to trump the official's public duty. At a crucial moment during the debate over the assumption of state debts, Federalist congressman Theodore Sedgwick of Massachusetts complained about absences. Thomas Fitzsimmons and George Clymer, he said, were absorbed in their private

41. Adam Smith, *An Inquiry into the Nature and Causes of the Wealth of Nations*, ed. R. H. Campbell and A. S. Skinner (xi, par. 8) (Oxford, 1976), 1: 265.
42. See William R. Taylor, *Cavalier and Yankee: The Old South and American Character* (New York, 1961).

affairs in Philadelphia, while Jeremiah Wadsworth of Connecticut "has thought it more for his interests to speculate than to attend his duty in Congress, and is gone home."[43]

New England Federalists, precarious aristocrats that they were, complained ceaselessly of "the continued disgrace of starving our public officers." Fisher Ames thought that "such a sum should be paid for service as was sufficient to command men of talents to perform it. Anything below this was parsimonious and unwise." Good men, he said, would not take up the public burden; or, as Oliver Wolcott Jr. put it, in words that by themselves repudiated the classical tradition of public service, "good abilities command high prices at market." Although the federal administration had more than enough applicants for its lower and middling offices, by the mid-1790s it was having trouble filling its highest offices. In 1795 South Carolina Federalist William Loughton Smith charged in the House of Representatives that Jefferson, Hamilton, and Henry Knox had all resigned from the cabinet "chiefly for one reason, the smallness of the salary." Although this was not true for Jefferson, both Knox and Hamilton did have trouble maintaining a genteel standard of living on their government salaries.[44]

Hamilton's scrupulousness over the issue reveals the dilemma that personal interests could pose for those who wanted to hold public office. There is no doubt that Hamilton left the treasury early in 1795 in order to return to Wall Street and earn some money for his family. Since he was out of office and short of funds, his close friend Robert Troup pleaded with him to get involved in business, especially in speculative land schemes. Everyone else was doing it, said Troup. "Why should you object to making a little money in a way that cannot be reproachful? Is it not time for you to think of putting yourself in a state of independence?" Troup even joked to Hamilton that such money-making schemes might be "instrumental in making a man of fortune—I may say—a gentleman of you. For such is the present insolence of the World that hardly a man is treated like a gentleman unless his fortune enables him to live at his ease."

Although he knew that many Federalists were using their governmental connections to get rich, Hamilton did not want to be one of them. "Saints,"

---

43. *The Diary of William Maclay and Other Notes on Senate Debates*, ed. Kenneth R. Bowling and Helen E. Veit (Baltimore, 1988), 141; Jack N. Rakove, "The Structure of Politics at the Accession of George Washington," in Richard Beeman et al., eds., *Beyond Confederation: Origins of the Constitution and American National Identity* (Chapel Hill, 1987), 283.

44. Leonard D. White, *The Federalists: A Study in Administrative History* (New York, 1948), 271, 292, 301.

he told Troup, might get away with such profit-making, but he knew he would be denounced by his Republican opponents as just another one of those "speculators" and "peculators." He had to refuse "because," as he sardonically put it, "there must be some public fools who sacrifice private to public interest at the certainty of ingratitude and obloquy—because my vanity whispers I ought to be one of those fools and ought to keep myself in a situation the best calculated to render service."[45] Hamilton clung long and hard to the classical conception of leadership.

Many of those Federalist aristocrats who sought to live up to the classical ideal sooner or later fell on hard times. Federalist congressman Joshua Coit of Connecticut found that his attempt to achieve "Independence" and real gentility by living off a nine-hundred-acre livestock farm was "utopian" and beyond his means. Even wealthy Christopher Gore, the first district attorney for Massachusetts and later one of the commissioners in London dealing with the issues of Jay's Treaty, discovered that he did not have sufficient proprietary wealth to realize his genteel dreams of living without having to work. Fisher Ames thought that Gore would have to forgo retiring to his Waltham estate for a while and take up his law practice once again if he were to keep up the style of life appropriate to a gentleman of his rank. "A man may not incline to take a certain degree on the scale of genteel living," Ames told Gore, "but having once taken it he must maintain it."[46]

By the late 1790s in Philadelphia, contemporaries noted, many of "those who call themselves Gentlemen" had gone bankrupt and thus had destroyed that paternalistic "Confidence in men of reputed fortunes and prudence as used to exist." Federalists who had sought to establish their genteel independence by acquiring landed estates could not fulfill their ambitions of emulating the English landed aristocracy. Since land in the New World was a far riskier investment than it was in England, failure was common; and many prominent Federalists such as Henry Knox, James Wilson, William Duer, and Robert Morris ended their careers in bankruptcy or in some cases in debtors' prison.[47]

45. Troup to AH, 31 March 1795, AH to Troup, 13 April 1795, *Papers of Hamilton*, 18: 310, 329.

46. Chester McArthur Destler, *Joshua Coit: American Federalist, 1758–1798* (Middletown, CT, 1962), 64; Fisher Ames to Christopher Gore, 5 Oct. 1802, in W. B. Allen, ed., *Works of Fisher Ames* (Indianapolis, 1983), 2: 1438; Tamara Platkins Thornton, *Cultivating Gentlemen: The Meaning of Country Life Among the Boston Elite, 1785–1860* (New Haven, 1989), 31.

47. Ethel E. Rasmusson, "Democratic Environment—Aristocratic Aspiration," *Penn. Mag. of Hist. and Biog.*, 90 (1966), 155–82; Bruce H. Mann, *Republic of Debtors: Bankruptcy in the Age of American Independence* (Cambridge, MA, 2002), 187–220. On Federalist dreams of Western empires, see Andrew R. L. Cayton, *The Frontier Republic: Ideology and Politics in the Ohio Country, 1780–1825* (Kent, OH, 1986), 12–32.

At the new government's outset Benjamin Rush put his finger on the peculiar problem of the aristocracy in America. Many, said Rush in 1789, had expressed doubts about the appointment of James Wilson to the Supreme Court because of "the deranged state of his Affairs." Rush admitted as much to John Adams. "But where," he asked, "will you find an American landholder free from embarrassments?" It was a fact of American life that too many of its wealthy gentry, at least in the North, could not live up to their pretensions of aristocratic status.[48]

In such circumstances it became increasingly difficult to find gentlemen willing to sacrifice their private interests in order to hold public office. After Henry Knox retired, President Washington had to go to his fourth choice for secretary of war, James McHenry, and to replace Randolph as secretary of state he had to go to his seventh choice, Timothy Pickering. Most of the gentry in America, in the Northern states at least, simply did not have the wherewithal to devote themselves exclusively to public service. This weakness was the Federalists' dilemma. They believed that they and their kind had a natural right to rule. All history, all learning, said so; indeed, the Revolution had been largely about securing the right of the natural aristocracy of talent to rule. But if their wealth were not sufficient for them to govern, what did that mean? Would that justify the opening of opportunities in government for new men, ordinary men, who seemed to the gentry to be less scrupulous in using government to make money and promote their private interests? In the eyes of the Federalist aristocracy these new middling men such as William Findley, Jedediah Peck, and Matthew Lyon were not supposed to be political leaders; their presence violated the natural order of things. They were not well educated; they were illiberal, ill-bred, and without any cosmopolitan perspective. They were "men, who," in the opinion of Oliver Wolcott Jr., "possessed neither capital nor experience" and not even the inclination to be virtuous or disinterested.[49]

Ironically, only the South—which provided much of the leadership of the pro-democratic Republicans opposed to the aristocratic Federalists—was able to maintain a semblance of a traditional leisured patriciate. But the Republican leaders, Madison and Jefferson, never really appreciated the character of the democratic and egalitarian forces they and their fellow Southern slaveholding Republicans were unleashing in the North.

48. BR to JA, 22 April 1789, in Maeva Marcus and James R. Perry et al., eds., *The Documentary History of the Supreme Court of the United States, 1789–1800* (New York, 1985), 1: 613.
49. David T. Gilchrist, ed., *The Growth of the Seaport Cities, 1790–1825* (Charlottesville, 1967), 119; Ethel E. Rasmusson, "Democratic Environment—Aristocratic Aspiration," *Penn. Mag. of Hist. and Biog.*, 90 (1966), 155–82.

ARISTOCRACY MAY HAVE BEEN unusually weak in America, especially in the Northern states, but some members of this aristocracy continued to cling to what they considered its distinctive manners and customs.
Indeed, the more rapidly their aristocratic rank was being undermined by
fast-moving social developments, the more insistent some of them were
in claiming its prerogatives and privileges. Although the emergence of
the Federalists and Republicans as political parties in the 1790s steadily
eroded the personal character of politics, the aristocratic concept of honor
still remained strong. Many of the leading figures continued to struggle
with the various ways of defending their honor in a world where the concept was fast becoming irrelevant.

The manner in which Jefferson handled publication of a notorious letter he had sent to his Italian friend Philip Mazzei reveals how the politics
of reputation could work. Jefferson had written the letter in 1796 in the
aftermath of the heated controversy over the Jay Treaty, and in it he
expressed his deep disappointment with the Washington administration.
"An Anglican monarchical, and aristocratical party," he told Mazzei, was
trying to subvert the Americans' love of liberty and republicanism and
turn the American government into something resembling the rotten
British monarchy. "It would give you a fever," wrote Jefferson, "were I to
name to you the apostates who have gone over to these heresies, men
who were Samsons in the field and Solomons in the council, but who
have had their heads shorn by the harlot England." Mazzei translated the
political portion of this letter into Italian and published it in a Florentine
newspaper. A French newspaper picked it up, and this French version,
translated back into English, appeared in the American press in
May 1797.[50]

Since most people assumed that Jefferson was defaming Washington,
America's great hero, the Federalists were delighted with the letter and
missed no opportunity to publicize it, even having it read in the House of
Representatives. "Nothing but treason and insurrection would be the
consequence of such opinions," declared one Federalist congressman.[51]

Jefferson was deeply embarrassed by the revelation of the letter. At first
the vice-president thought that in defense of his reputation he must "take
the field of the public papers"; but he soon realized, as he explained to
Madison, that any response would involve him in endless explanations
and would bring on "a personal difference between Genl. Washington
and myself," not to mention embroiling him "with all those with whom
his character is still popular, that is to say, nine tenths of the people of the

---

50. TJ to Mazzei, 24 April 1796, in Ford, ed., *Writings of Jefferson*, 7: 72–78.
51. Dumas Malone, *Jefferson and the Ordeal of Liberty* (Boston, 1962), 366.

U.S."[52] Madison agreed that silence was probably Jefferson's best alternative. Among those the vice-president consulted, only James Monroe urged him to reply publicly, as he himself was doing in an angry response to his embarrassing recall from France.

Monroe was a militant Republican and as a veteran of the Revolutionary War much more committed to the code of honor than either Jefferson or Madison. In 1798 he was angered by President John Adams's reference to him as "a disgraced minister, recalled in displeasure for misconduct," and he wrote to Madison for advice on how to respond within the code of honor. Monroe believed he could not simply ignore Adams's insult, for "not to notice it may with many leave an unfavorable impression agnst me." Yet a personal challenge to a duel seemed impossible, since Adams was "an old man and President." He could not simply request an explanation for his recall from France, because he had already done that. Perhaps he could write a pamphlet and attack Adams, "ridicule his political career, shew it to be the consummation of folly & wickedness." In response, Madison suggested that if Monroe were to do anything in the present heated atmosphere of partisanship, he ought to compose "a temperate & dignified animadversion published with your name to it."[53]

Although Madison never fought a duel, he was well aware of the code of honor involved in these personal confrontations. He criticized Roger Griswold, for example, for not challenging Lyon to a duel. If Griswold had been "a man of the sword" he would never have allowed the House to intervene in his conflict with Lyon. "No man," he said, "ought to reproach another with cowardice, who is not ready to give proof of his own courage."[54]

Hamilton, as a Revolutionary War veteran, was very much a man of the sword—as a confrontation he had with Monroe in 1797 showed. Five years earlier, in 1792, Hamilton when he was secretary of the treasury had engaged in adultery with a woman named Maria Reynolds and had actually paid blackmail to her husband in order to keep the affair quiet. When privately challenged in 1792 by several suspicious congressmen, including Senator James Monroe, for misusing treasury funds, Hamilton confessed to the affair and the blackmail, which had nothing to do with treasury business. The congressmen, who were embarrassed by this

52. TJ to JM, 3 Aug. 1797, *Republic of Letters*, 985.
53. Monroe to JM, 8 June 1798, JM to Monroe, 9 June 1798, *Papers of Madison*, 17: 145–46, 149.
54. JM to TJ, 18 Feb 1798, *Papers of Madison*, 17: 82; Freeman, *Affairs of Honor*, 174; Joanne B. Freeman, "Dueling as Politics: Reinterpreting the Burr-Hamilton Duel," *WMQ*, 53 (1996), 299.

revelation, seemed to accept Hamilton's explanation and dropped their investigation.

Rumors of Hamilton's involvement with the Reynoldses circulated over the next several years, but it was not until 1797 that James Thomson Callender, a Scottish refugee and one of the new breed of unscrupulous journalists who were spreading scurrility everywhere, used documents that he had acquired to charge Hamilton publicly with speculating in treasury funds. Although it was probably John Beckley, a loyal Republican and recently dismissed clerk of the House of Representative, who had supplied Callender with the documents, Hamilton suspected that it was Monroe, and he pressed Monroe to make a public statement avowing his belief in Hamilton's explanation of five years earlier. The quarrel between the two men became so heated that only an exchange of letters and some complicated negotiations, including the intervention of Aaron Burr, averted a duel. The code of honor, however, required that Hamilton defend his reputation somehow, and therefore he published a lengthy pamphlet laying out all the sordid details of the affair with Mrs. Reynolds. Better to be thought a private adulterer than a corrupt public official. The pamphlet was a disastrous mistake, and it led Callender to gloat that Hamilton had done himself more damage than "fifty of the best pens in America could have said against him."[55]

Hamilton was unusually intense and thin-skinned and sensitive to any criticism, but his experience with Monroe in 1797 was not unusual. Dueling was part of the politics of the day—a sign of how much aristocratic standards still prevailed even as the society was becoming more democratic. Men engaged in duels were not simply trying to maim or kill their adversaries; instead, they were seeking both to display their bravery, military prowess, and willingness to sacrifice their lives for their honor and to conduct partisan politics. Dueling was part of an elaborate political ritual designed to protect reputations and affect politics in what was still a very personal aristocratic world.

The challenges and responses and the negotiations among principals and their seconds and friends often went on for weeks or even months. The duels were often timed for political effect, and their complicated procedures and public exchanges in newspapers were calculated to influence a broad public. There were many duels, most of which did not end in exchanges of gunfire. In New York City between 1795 and 1807, for example, there were at least sixteen affairs of honor, though few resulted in anyone's death. Hamilton was the principal in eleven affairs of honor

---

55. Thomas J. Fleming, *Duel: Alexander Hamilton, Aaron Burr, and the Future of America* (New York, 1999), 21.

during his lifetime, but he actually exchanged fire in only one—his last, fatal duel with Aaron Burr.[56]

During the 1790s this politics of reputation and individual character was rapidly being eroded in a number of ways, especially through the growth of political parties and the proliferation of scandal-mongering newspapers that were reaching out to a new popular readership. Indeed, the clash between an older aristocratic world of honor and the emerging new democratic world of political parties and partisan newspapers lay behind much of the turbulence and passion of the 1790s. Under these changing circumstances newspapers became weapons of the new political parties, to be used to discredit and demolish the characters of the opposing leaders in the eyes of unprecedented numbers of new readers. Since the lingering code of honor was designed for gentlemen dealing personally with one another, it was incapable of handling the new problems created by an ever growing and more vituperative popular press, especially in a time of great crisis.

With the inauguration of John Adams as president and the spread of the French Revolution throughout the Western world, America was heading for just that kind of crisis.

56. Freeman, *Affairs of Honor*, 167.

# 7

# The Crisis of 1798–1799

When the French learned of Jay's treaty with Great Britain, they immediately began seizing American ships and confiscating their cargoes. Actually, ever since the European war had broken out in 1793, the French treatment of American neutral shipping had not been all that different from that of the British, despite the stipulations of "free ships, free goods" in the French-American treaty of 1778. But throughout all its erratic seizing of American ships France at least had pretended to respect American neutral rights.

The Federalists were primed to be suspicious of anything France did. The president's son John Quincy Adams, minister to the Netherlands, which had recently become a French satellite, fed Federalist fears. France, he reported to his father in 1796, was working to undermine the Federalists and bring about the "triumph of the French party, French principles, and French influence" in American affairs. France believed that "the *people* of the United States had but a feeble attachment to their government and will not support them in a contest with that of France." Young Adams even suggested that France planned to invade the South and with the support of sympathizers there and in the West break up the Union and create a puppet republic. Revolutionary France and its armies were, after all, doing just that—setting up puppet regimes—throughout Europe. Such a conspiratorial and fearful atmosphere seemed to make any sort of normal diplomatic relations impossible.[1]

In 1797, after Adams's presidential victory, France abandoned its earlier efforts to divide Americans politically and decided to confront the United States directly. Not only did France's Directory government refuse to receive Thomas Pinckney's elder brother Charles Cotesworth Pinckney, whom Washington had sent to Paris to replace Monroe, but it also announced that all neutral American ships carrying British goods were now liable to seizure and that all American sailors impressed onto British ships would be treated as pirates.

---

1. Richard H. Kohn, *Eagle and Sword: The Federalists and the Creation of the Military Establishment in America, 1783–1802* (New York, 1975), 205–6.

In response, President Adams called a special session of Congress for May 1797, the first president to do so. After Adams urged a buildup of American military forces, especially the navy, Congress authorized the president to call up eighty thousand militiamen, provided for harbor fortifications, and approved the completion of three frigates still on the ways. At the same time, the president criticized the French for trying to divide the people of the United States from their government, declaring that "we are not a degraded people, humiliated under a colonial spirit of fear and sense of inferiority, fitted to be the miserable instruments of foreign influence."[2] By the middle of 1797 the United States and France were on the verge of war with one another in much the same way that the United States and Britain had been in 1794. Since Washington had earlier headed off war with Britain by sending Jay on his diplomatic mission, Adams decided to follow his predecessor's example and send a similar mission to France.

At first, Adams toyed with the idea of sending Madison, but his cabinet, composed of Washington appointees Timothy Pickering (State), Oliver Wolcott Jr. (Treasury), and James McHenry (War), was decidedly hostile to this suggestion. Hamilton, on the other hand, favored sending Madison, confident that Madison would be unwilling to sell out the United States to France. America, Hamilton believed, still needed peace; it was not yet mature or strong enough for out-and-out war with any of the European states. But other Federalists wanted no capitulation to French pressure; the extreme hard-liner Pickering, in fact, urged a declaration of war against France and an American alliance with Britain.[3]

For their part, the Republican leaders doubted that France wanted war with the United States and urged that America delay any action. They were not at all eager to get involved in peace-making efforts with France that might mean endorsing the Jay Treaty with Great Britain. Jefferson and other Republicans believed that a French invasion of Britain was imminent and that its success would solve all the problems. Since the coalition massed against the revolutionary regime had fallen apart, France now dominated Europe. Napoleon had defeated the Austrians in Italy and looked to crush France's one remaining enemy. It was rumored that the Dutch, in their French-dominated Batavian Republic, were preparing an invasion force. In fact, fourteen hundred French banditti did manage to land on the British coast, though they were quickly surrounded by local militia.

2. James Roger Sharpe, *American Politics in the Early Republic: The New Nation in Crisis* (New Haven, 1993), 167.
3. Aaron N. Coleman, "'A Second Bounaparty?' A Reexamination of Alexander Hamilton During the Franco-American Crisis, 1796–1801," *JER*, 28 (2008), 199.

Britain seemed quite plausibly to be on the verge of collapse. Bread was scarce and famine threatened. Mutinies rocked the Royal Navy. Stocks on the British exchange fell to a record low, and the Bank of England was forced to suspend gold payments to private persons. General Cornwallis, the Yorktown loser who had become governor-general of British India, was deeply alarmed. "Torn as we are by faction, without an army, without money, trusting entirely to a navy whom we may not be able to pay, and on whose loyalty, even if we can, no firm reliance is to be placed, how," he asked, "are we to get out of this accursed war without a Revolution?"[4]

To Jefferson and the Republicans, war with France was inconceivable and had to be avoided at almost any cost. War would play into the hands of the Federalist "Anglomen" in America and destroy the republican experiment everywhere. In this confusing and emotional atmosphere Adams appointed a three-man commission to France to negotiate peace — Charles Cotesworth Pinckney, the minister whom the French had refused to receive; John Marshall, a moderate Virginia Federalist; and Elbridge Gerry, Adams's quirky Massachusetts friend who was even more anti-party than Adams himself.

The French foreign minister, Charles Maurice de Talleyrand-Périgord, was, like Jefferson, known for his finesse and his ability to hide his feelings. At this moment he was in no hurry to negotiate with the United States and did not believe he had to. America posed no threat to France, he thought, and most of its people seemed to be sympathetic to the French cause. In fact, Jefferson had been advising French diplomats in America that delay was the best line for the French to take, because, as he and many others assumed, the war between monarchical Britain and revolutionary France would not last much longer. France would conquer Britain as it had conquered other nations in Europe.

The Directory in charge of the French government, however, was not as strong as its army's victories on the Continent suggested. Not only was its authority shaky and increasingly dependent on the army, but it was desperate for funds and showed no interest in anything except extracting money from its client states and puppet republics. Thus when the American envoys arrived in Paris in October 1797, they were met with a series of humiliating conditions before negotiations could even begin. Agents of Talleyrand and the Directory, later referred to as "X, Y, and Z" in dispatches published in America, demanded that the American government apologize for President Adams's hostile May 1797 speech to Congress and assume responsibility for any outstanding French debts and

4. Ben Wilson, *The Making of Victorian Values: Decency and Dissent in Britain, 1789–1837* (New York, 2007), 30.

indemnities owed to Americans. At the same time, these French agents insisted that the United States make a "considerable loan" to France and give to Talleyrand and the Directory a large sum of money for their "private use," that is, a substantial bribe of fifty thousand pounds. Only then might the French government receive the American commissioners.

These requests were followed by scarcely veiled threats. America's neutrality, the French agents said, was no longer possible: all nations must aid France or be treated as enemies. In April 1798, after months of further discussions, a disgusted Marshall and Pinckney returned to the United States. Gerry, fearful that a war with France would "disgrace republicanism & make it the scoff of despots," remained behind.[5]

In the meantime, France decreed that any neutral ship carrying any English product could be seized—in effect denying that free ships meant free goods and claiming the right to confiscate virtually all American ships on the high seas. The president had received the dispatches that Marshall had written describing the XYZ Affair and the collapse of negotiations with France. Without revealing the dispatches, Adams informed Congress in March 1798 of the failure of the diplomatic mission and called for arming America's merchant vessels.

Knowing nothing of the contents of the dispatches, Vice-President Jefferson was furious at what he took to be the president's rash and irrational behavior. He thought that Adams's message was "almost insane" and believed that the administration's refusal to make the dispatches public was a cover-up. He continued to urge his Republican friends in Congress to delay any further moves toward war. "If we could but gain this season," he told Madison, "we should be saved."[6]

The country teemed with rumors of war. In January 1798 a Federalist measure in Congress to fund the diplomatic missions abroad led to a proposal by Republican congressman John Nicholas of Virginia that the whole diplomatic establishment be cut back, and perhaps eventually eliminated altogether. The executive had too much power already, Nicholas said, and needed to be reduced. This set off a six-week debate that released all the partisan suspicion and anger that had been building up since the struggle over the Jay Treaty. "The legislature is as much divided and the parties in it as much embittered against each other as it is possible to conceive," concluded Senator James Ross of Pennsylvania.[7] It may not have seemed possible, but things got worse.

5. George A. Billias, *Elbridge Gerry: Founding Father and Republican Statesman* (New York, 1976), 274.
6. TJ to JM, 29 March 1798, *Republic of Letters*, 1030.
7. Stephen G. Kurtz, *The Presidency of John Adams: The Collapse of Federalism, 1795–1800* (New York, 1957), 293.

The Republicans called for the release of the commission's dispatches, unaware of how damaging they were to their cause. When the country finally learned of the humiliations of the XYZ Affair in April 1798, it went wild with anger against the French. Publication of the dispatches, Jefferson told Madison, "produced such a shock on the republican mind as has never been seen since our independence." Particularly embarrassing were the French agents' references to the "friends of France" in the United States, implying that there was a kind of fifth column in the country willing to aid the French. Many of the Republican party's "wavering characters," Jefferson complained, were so anxious "to wipe out the imputation of being French partisans" that they were going over in droves to "the war party."[8]

The Federalists were ecstatic. "The Jacobins," as Fisher Ames and many other Federalists usually labeled the Republicans, "were confounded, and the trimmers dropt off from the party like windfalls from an apple-tree in September."[9] Even "out of doors," reported Secretary of State Pickering, "the French Devotees are rapidly quitting the worship of their idol." "In this state of things," groaned Jefferson, the Federalists "will carry what they please." Over the remainder of 1798 and into 1799 the Federalists won election after election, most surprisingly even in the South, and gained control of the Congress.[10]

The president and his ministers, as a rather astonished Fisher Ames pointed out, had become at last "decidedly popular."[11] Ames was astonished because in the Federalist scheme of things the Federalists were not supposed to become popular until American society developed further and became more mature and hierarchical. But the French played into Federalist hands. The American envoys' reply to the French demand for a bribe, as a newspaper colorfully put it, was "Millions for defense but not one cent for tribute!" It became their rallying cry. (Pinckney actually had said, "It is no, no, not a sixpence!") When Marshall arrived back in the United States, he was hailed as a national hero who had refused to be intimidated and bribed. Patriotic demonstrations spread everywhere, and the Federalists' long opposition to the French Revolution seemed to be finally vindicated. Plays and songs acclaimed the Federalists and the president as patriots and heroes. "Hail Columbia," written by a Philadelphia lawyer, Joseph Hopkinson, and set to the tune of "The President's

8. TJ to JM, 6, 19 April 1798, *Republic of Letters*, 1035, 1039.
9. Ames to Gore, 18 Dec. 1798, *Works of Fisher Ames* (1854), ed. W. B. Allen (Indianapolis, 1983), 2: 1302.
10. Stanley Elkins and Eric McKitrick, *The Age of Federalism: The Early American Republic, 1788–1800* (New York, 1993), 588.
11. Ames to H. G. Otis, 23 April 1798, *Works of Ames*, ed. Allen, 2: 1275.

March," became an instant hit. Theater audiences that earlier had rioted on behalf of the French now sang the praises of President Adams. In one case the audience demanded that the orchestra play "The President's March" six times before it was satisfied.

Most impressive were the complimentary addresses that poured in upon the president—hundreds of them, from state legislatures, town meetings, college students, grand juries, Masonic lodges, and military companies. They congratulated the president on his stand against the French; some even warned that false patriots "who called themselves Americans" were "endeavoring to poison the minds of the well-meaning citizens and to withdraw from the government the support of the people."[12] President Adams, giddy with such unaccustomed popularity, responded to them all, sometimes with bellicose sentiments against France and charges of disloyalty among the Republicans that left even some Federalists uneasy. The president took the responsibility of answering the many addresses so seriously that his wife feared for his health; but he himself was never happier than during these months lecturing his countrymen on the basics of political science.

Adams had called for a day of fasting and prayer on May 9, 1798, and the orthodox clergy in the North and the Middle States responded with support for the Federalist cause, especially since most of the rapidly expanding dissenting Baptists and Methodists favored the Republicans. The traditional Congregational, Presbyterian, and Episcopalian clergy clearly saw their fight against infidelity linked to the Federalist fight against France and the Jacobins in America's midst. Jedidiah Morse, author of the best-selling *American Geography* (1789) and Congregational minister in Charlestown, Massachusetts, spread the theory that the French Revolution was part of an international conspiracy to destroy Christianity and all civil government. Drawing on the anti-Jacobin work of the Scot John Robison, *Proofs of a Conspiracy Against All the Religions and Governments of Europe* (1798), Morse traced this conspiracy back to a central European society of freethinkers called the Bavarian Illuminati who had infiltrated Masonic organizations in Europe. Morse claimed that the French were now conspiring to use the Jeffersonian Republicans to subvert America's government and religion.

Preposterous as these conspiratorial notions may seem, at the time they were believed by a large number of distinguished and learned American clergymen, including Timothy Dwight, president of Yale College, and David Tappan, Hollis Professor of Divinity at Harvard. Not only were

12. James Morton Smith, *Freedom's Fetters: The Alien and Sedition Acts and American Civil Liberties* (Ithaca, 1956), 97.

these beliefs in plots and plotters a measure of the Federalists' fear that American society was badly deteriorating, but such conspiratorial notions were often the only means by which enlightened people in the eighteenth century could explain a concatenation of complicated events.

The question they asked of an event was not "how did it happen?" but rather "who did it?" The French Revolution and the upheavals in America seemed so convulsive, so complicated, and so awesome that many could scarcely comprehend their causes. But if human agents were responsible for all the tumult, they could not be a small group of plotters like those several British ministers who in the 1760s and 1770s had conspired to oppress the colonists. They had to be part of elaborately organized secret societies like the Bavarian Illuminati involving thousands of individuals linked by sinister designs. Many Americans seriously believed that such conspiracies were behind the momentous events of the 1790s.

On the day President Adams appointed for fasting and prayer, people spread rumors that a plot was afoot to burn Philadelphia, compelling many residents to pack their belongings while the longtime Pennsylvania governor, Thomas Mifflin, took steps to thwart the plot. At the same time, riots and brawling broke out in the capital between supporters of Britain and those of France, and mobs attacked Republican newspaper editors. Federalists in the Congress warned of resident aliens who were plotting "to completely stop the wheels of Government, and to lay it prostrate at the feet of its external and internal foes." Speaker of the House Jonathan Dayton of New Jersey announced that France was preparing to invade the United States, and the Federalist press, citing "authentic information" from Europe, confirmed this rumor.[13]

Congress responded to the president's call by sanctioning a Quasi-War, or what Adams called "the half war with France."[14] It laid an embargo on all trade, and formally abrogated all treaties, with France. It allowed American naval vessels anywhere on the high seas to attack armed French ships that were seizing American merchant vessels. In addition to laying plans for building up the army, Congress authorized the acquisition of sloops and galleys for the protection of the shallow coastal waters and approved the building of fifteen warships. The budget for the navy reached $1.4 million, more naval spending in the one year of 1798 than in all previous years combined. To supervise the new fleet, Congress created an independent Navy Department, with Benjamin Stoddard of Maryland as

13. Smith, *Freedom's Fetters*, 103; Alexander DeConde, *The Quasi-War: The Politics and Diplomacy of the Undeclared War with France, 1797–1801* (New York, 1966), 82.
14. DeConde, *The Quasi-War*, 328.

its first secretary. To all these Federalist measures the Republicans put up a spirited resistance, and all passed by only narrow margins.[15]

The Republicans disavowed Madison's idea of the 1780s that the legislative branch had a natural tendency to encroach upon the executive. Quite the contrary, declared Albert Gallatin, the brilliant Swiss-born congressman from Pennsylvania, who, following Madison's retirement from Congress in 1797, had become the Republicans' leader. The history of Europe over the previous three centuries, said Gallatin, showed that executives everywhere greatly increased their power at the expense of the legislatures; the result always had been "prodigality, wars, excessive taxes, and ever progressive debts." And now the same thing was happening in America. The "Executive Party" was fomenting the crisis only to "increase their power and to bind us by the treble chain of fiscal, legal and military despotism."[16] Although not native to America, Gallatin had absorbed the eighteenth-century enlightened fear of high taxes, standing armies, and bloated executive authority as thoroughly as Jefferson or any other radical Whig.

The Federalists were frightened not merely by the prospect of war with France but, more important, by the way it might spark a civil war in the United States. It was the brutal and insidious manner that revolutionary France was dominating Europe and what this might mean for America that really unnerved them. France, the Federalists said, not only had annexed Belgium and parts of Germany outright but, more alarming, had used native collaborators to create revolutionary puppet republics in the Netherlands, Switzerland, and much of Italy. Might not something similar occur in America? Federalists wondered. In the event of a French invasion might not all the French émigrés and Jacobinical sympathizers in the country become collaborators?[17]

"Do we not know," said Congressman Harrison Gray Otis of Massachusetts, who was far from the most extreme of the Federalists, "that the French nation have organized bands of aliens as well as their own citizens, in other countries, to bring about their nefarious purposes[?]...By these means they have overrun all the republics in the world but our

15. DeConde, *The Quasi-War*, 90–91; Marshall Smelser, *The Congress Founds the Navy, 1787–1798* (Notre Dame, IN, 1959), 150–59; Ian W. Toll, *Six Frigates: The Epic History of the Founding of the U.S. Navy* (New York, 2006), 101, 105–6; George C. Daughan, *If by Sea: The Forging of the American Navy from the Revolution to the War of 1812* (New York, 2008).

16. E. James Ferguson, ed., *Selected Writings of Gallatin* (Indianapolis, 1967), 137; David McCullough, *John Adams* (New York, 2001), 499.

17. Richard Buel Jr., *America on the Brink: How the Political Struggle over the War of 1812 Almost Destroyed the Young Republic* (New York, 2005), 17.

own....And may we not expect the same means to be employed against this country?" Were not the French victories in Europe due to France's elaborate system of supporters and spies? Did not the mysterious voyage to France on June 13, 1798, of Dr. George Logan, an ardent Philadelphia Republican, suggest that he intended to contact the French government in order to bring about "the introduction of a French army, *to teach us the genuine value of true and essential liberty*"? And did not a Republican newspaper's publication of a letter from Talleyrand to the State Department before the U.S. government released the text suggest that France had a direct line to its American agents, many of whom were editors? And were not these editors immigrant aliens, and were they not using their papers to stir up popular support for the Jacobinical cause?[18]

By 1798 the Federalists were convinced that they had to do something to suppress what they believed were the sources of Jacobin influence in America—the increasing numbers of foreign immigrants and the scurrilous behavior of the Republican press.

IN DESPERATION MANY FEDERALISTS resorted to a series of federal acts dealing with the problems they perceived—the so-called Alien and Sedition Acts. However justified they may have been in enacting them, in the end these acts turned out to be a disastrous mistake. Indeed, the Alien and Sedition Acts so thoroughly destroyed the Federalists' historical reputation that it is unlikely it can ever be recovered. Yet it is important to know why they acted as they did.

Because the Federalists believed, in the words of Congressman Joshua Coit of Connecticut, that "we may very shortly be involved in war" with France, they feared that the "immense number of French citizens in our country," together with the many Irish immigrants who came filled with hatred of Great Britain, might become enemy agents. One way of dealing with this threat was to restrict the naturalization of immigrants and the rights of aliens. Unfortunately, this meant challenging the Revolutionary idea that America was an asylum of liberty for the oppressed of the world.

It was ironic that the Federalists should have become frightened by the new immigrants of the 1790s. At the beginning of the decade it was the Federalists, especially Federalist land speculators, who had most encouraged foreign immigration. By contrast, the Jeffersonian Republicans had tended to be more cautious about mass immigration. Since the

18. Marilyn C. Baseler, *"Asylum for Mankind": America, 1607–1800* (Ithaca, 1998), 272; Smith, *Freedom's Fetters*, 64, 31, 66, 102; *Annals of Congress*, 5th Congress, 2nd session (April 1798), VIII, 1427; (June 1798), VIII, 1987–89.

Republicans believed in a more active hands-on role for people in politics than did the Federalists, they had worried that immigrants might lack the necessary qualifications to sustain liberty and self-government. In his *Notes on the State of Virginia* (1785), Jefferson had expressed concern that too many Europeans would come to America with monarchical principles, a development that was apt to make the society and its laws "a heterogeneous, incoherent, distracted mass." By relying instead on a natural increase of the population, America's government, said Jefferson, would become "more homogeneous, more peaceable, more durable."[19]

Still, most Americans accepted the idea that America represented an asylum for the oppressed of the world, and during the 1790s nearly one hundred thousand immigrants poured into the United States.[20] During the debates in the Congress over naturalization, Americans struggled with their desire to welcome these immigrants on one hand and their fears of being overwhelmed by un-American ideas on the other.

The radical Revolutionary commitment to voluntary citizenship and expatriation—the idea that a person could disavow his subject status and become a citizen of another country—aggravated this dilemma. Unlike the English, who clung to the idea of perpetual allegiance—once an Englishman always an Englishman—most Americans necessarily accepted the right of expatriation. But they worried that naturalized citizens who had sworn allegiance to the United States might later transfer their loyalty to another country. And they were troubled by American expatriates who wanted to be readmitted to the United States as citizens. With these kinds of examples America's concept of volitional citizenship seemed alarmingly capricious and open to abuse.[21]

Although Congress in 1790 passed a fairly liberal naturalization act requiring only two years of residency for free white persons, it soon changed its mind under the impact of the French Revolution. Both Federalists and Republicans backed the Naturalization Act of 1795, which extended the time of residency to five years and required aliens seeking citizenship to renounce any title of nobility they may have held and to provide proof of their good moral character and their devotion to the Constitution of the United States.

19. TJ, *Notes on the State of Virginia*, ed. William Peden (Chapel Hill, 1955), 84–85; Basler, "*Asylum for Mankind*," 248–51.

20. Hans-Jürgen Grabbe, "European Immigration to the United States in the Early National Period, 1783–1820," in Susan E. Klepp, ed., *The Demographic History of the Philadelphia Region, 1600–1860*, American Philosophical Society, *Proc.*, 133 (1989), 190–214.

21. Baseler, "Asylum for Mankind," 243–55; James H. Kettner, *The Development of American Citizenship, 1608–1870* (Chapel Hill, 1978), 269–74.

It was not long, however, before the Federalists realized that most of the immigrants, especially those whom Harrison Gray Otis labeled the "hordes of wild Irishmen," posed a distinct threat to the kind of stable and hierarchal society they expected America to become. By 1798 the Federalists' earlier optimism in welcoming foreign immigration was gone. Since these masses of new immigrants with their disorderly and Jacobinical ideas were "the grand cause of all our present difficulties," the Federalists concluded, in the most pessimistic refrain—one that virtually repudiated one of the central tenets of the Revolution—"let us no longer pray that America may become an asylum to all nations."[22]

Some extreme Federalist congressmen, such as Robert Goodloe Harper of South Carolina, thought that "the time is now come when it will be proper to declare that nothing but birth shall entitle a man to citizenship in this country."[23] Although most congressmen thought Harper's proposal went too far, they did eventually enact a fairly radical naturalization act. The Naturalization Act of June 18, 1798, extended the period of residence required before an alien could apply to become a citizen from five to fourteen years, compelled all aliens to register with a district court or an agent appointed by the president within forty-eight hours of arrival in the United States, and forbade all aliens who were citizens or subjects of a nation with which the United States was at war from becoming American citizens.

The Federalists also laid plans for dealing with the aliens who were already in the country. Even the Republicans feared some aliens. Consequently, they had no serious objection to restraining enemy aliens during wartime and, mainly in order to prevent worse legislation, virtually took over the passage of the Alien Enemies Act of July 6, 1798—an act that is still on the books. But the Federalists wanted an even wider-ranging law to deal with aliens in peacetime as well as wartime, because, as Abigail Adams put it, even though the United States had not actually declared war against France, nonetheless, "in times like the present, a more careful and attentive watch ought to be kept over foreigners." The resultant Alien Friends Act of June 25, 1798, which Jefferson labeled "a most detestable thing...worthy of the 8th or 9th century," gave the president the power to expel, without a hearing or even giving reasons, any alien whom the president judged "dangerous to the peace and safety of the United States." If such aliens failed to leave the country, they could be imprisoned for up to three years and permanently barred from

22. Baseler, "Asylum for Mankind," 255–70; Smith, *Freedom's Fetters*, 24.
23. Smith, *Freedom's Fetters*, 27; *Annals of Congress*, 5th Congress, 2nd session, VIII, 1567–68.

becoming citizens. This extraordinary act was temporary and was to expire in two years.[24]

The Alien Friends Act and the Naturalization Act met strenuous opposition from the Republicans, especially from the New York congressmen Edward Livingston and Albert Gallatin. Denying that a French invasion was imminent, the Republicans argued that the measures were unnecessary. They declared that the state laws and courts were more than capable of taking care of all aliens and spies in the country. They claimed that the acts were unconstitutional, first, because Article V of the Constitution, made with the slave trade in mind, prevented Congress prior to 1808 from prohibiting "the Migration or Importation" of persons coming into the United States, and, second, because the acts gave the president arbitrary power. Gallatin in particular argued that the Alien Friends Act violated the Fifth Amendment's guarantee that "no person shall be deprived of his life, liberty, or property, without due process of law," pointing out that this right extended to every "person," not just to citizens.[25]

Federalists, fearful, as Harrison Gray Otis put it, of "an army of spies and incendiaries scattered through the continent," brooked no interference with their plans.[26] Nevertheless, some of the Federalists were uneasy over the severity of the measures, especially those with large immigrant populations in their states, and the Naturalization Act and Alien Friends Act passed by only narrow margins. Still, most Federalists were pleased that the new measures would in the future deprive aliens from influencing America's elections. Adams much later justified to Jefferson his signing of the Alien Friends bill on the grounds that "we were then at War with France: French Spies then swarmed in our Cities and in the Country....To check them was the design of this law. Was there ever a Government," he asked Jefferson, "which had not Authority to defend itself against Spies in its own Bosom?"[27]

RESTRICTING NATURALIZATION and restraining aliens were only partial solutions to the crisis the Federalists saw threatening the security of the country. Equally important was finding a way of dealing with the immense power over public opinion that newspapers were developing in the 1790s. In fact, the American press had become the most important instrument of democracy in the modern world, and because the Federalists were fearful of too much democracy, they believed the press had to be restrained.

24. Smith, *Freedom's Fetters*, 53, 438–40.
25. *Annals of Congress*, 5th Congress, 2nd session (June 1798), VIII, 1956.
26. Smith, *Freedom's Fetters*, 82.
27. JA to TJ, 14 June 1813, in Lester J. Cappon, ed., *The Adams-Jefferson Letters: The Complete Correspondence Between Thomas Jefferson and Abigail and John Adams* (Chapel Hill, 1959), 2: 329.

With the number of newspapers more than doubling in the 1790s, Americans were rapidly becoming the largest newspaper-reading public in the world. When the great French observer of America Alexis de Tocqueville came to the United States in 1831 he marveled at the role newspapers had come to play in American culture. Since, as he noted, there was "hardly a hamlet in America without its newspaper," the power of the American press made "political life circulate in every corner of that vast land." The press's power, Tocqueville suggested, flowed from the democratic nature of the society. An aristocratic society, such as that promoted by the Federalists, was tied together by patronage and personal connections. But when these ties disintegrated, which is what happened when the society became more democratic, then, said Tocqueville, it became impossible to get great numbers of people to come together and cooperate unless each individual could be persuaded to think that his private interests were best served by uniting his efforts with those of many other people. "That cannot be done habitually and conveniently without the help of a newspaper," Tocqueville concluded. "Only a newspaper can put the same thought at the same time before a thousand readers."[28]

Madison was one of the first to see the important role of newspapers in creating public opinion. Near the end of 1791 he revised some of his thinking in *Federalist* Nos. 10 and 51 and argued now that the large extent of the country was a disadvantage for republican government. In a huge country like the United States, not only was ascertaining the real opinion of the public difficult, but what opinion there was could be more easily counterfeited, which was "favorable to the authority of government." At the same time, the more extensive the country, "the more insignificant is each individual in his own eyes," which was "unfavorable to liberty." The solution, said Madison, was to encourage "a general intercourse of sentiments" by whatever means—good roads, domestic commerce, the exchange of representatives, and "particularly *a circulation of newspapers through the entire body of the people*."[29]

Even as Madison wrote, the press itself was changing. It began shedding its traditional neutral role of providing advertising, mercantile information, and foreign news to its readers. Editors such as John Fenno and Philip Freneau no longer saw themselves as mere tradesmen earning a living, as printer Benjamin Franklin had in the colonial era; instead, they became political advocates and party activists. During the course of the 1790s, these partisan editors, many of them immigrants, and their

28. Alexis de Tocqueville, *Democracy in America*, ed. J. P. Mayer (Garden City, NY, 1966), 185–86, 517.
29. JM, "Public Opinion," 19 Dec. 1791, *Madison: Writings*, 500–501.

newspapers became essential to the emerging national parties of the Federalists and especially the Republicans.

In the generation following the Revolution, over three hundred thousand British and Irish immigrants entered the United States. Many were political or religious refugees, radical exiles driven from Britain and Ireland because of their dissenting beliefs, including the English Unitarian Joseph Priestley and the militant Irish Catholic brothers Mathew and James Carey. Since many of these radical exiles were writers, printers, and editors, they inevitably ended up in America creating or running newspapers. Indeed, they contributed in disproportionate numbers to the rapid growth of the American press. In the several decades following the end of the Revolutionary War, twenty-three English, Scottish, and Irish radicals edited and produced no fewer than fifty-seven American newspapers and magazines, most of which supported the Republican cause in the politically sensitive Middle States.[30] Since in the early 1790s over 90 percent of newspapers had generally supported the Federalists, this surge of Republican papers represented a remarkable shift in a short period of time.[31]

These partisan newspapers gave party members, especially those of the opposition Republican party, a sense of identity and a sense of belonging to a common cause. Since there were no modern party organizations, no official ballots, and no lists of party members, newspaper subscriptions and readership often came to define partisanship; newspaper offices even printed party tickets.[32]

As these newspapers grew in number and partisanship, they became increasingly accessible to more ordinary people. Of course, by modern standards the circulation of individual newspapers remained small—from a few hundred to a few thousand for the most successful of the urban papers. Yet because they were often available in taverns and

---

30. Paul Starr, *The Creation of the Media: Political Origins of Modern Communications* (New York, 2004), 80.
31. Michael Durey, *Transatlantic Radicals and the Early American Republic* (Lawrence, KS, 1997). Of the 219 political refugees Durey has studied, 152 were Irish (69 percent), 49 English (23 percent), and 18 Scottish (8 percent)—proportions, says Durey, that probably reflect the relative intensity of political conflict in each of the countries in the 1790s. In England the peak years of emigration were 1793 and 1794, suggesting that the exiles were the victims of the first wave of the English government's repression that culminated in the treason trials of 1794. The main phase of Scottish radical emigration to the United States came in 1794–1795 in the aftermath of the Watt conspiracy in Edinburgh. And in Ireland the vast majority of radicals fled into exile after the 1798 Wexford Rising.
32. Jeffrey L. Pasley, *"The Tyranny of the Printers": Newspaper Politics in the Early American Republic* (Charlottesville, 2001), 1–47.

other public places and were sometimes read aloud to groups, they did manage to reach ever larger numbers of people. By the end of the decade some claimed that newspapers were entering three-quarters of American homes.[33]

No editor did more to politicize the press in the 1790s than Benjamin Franklin Bache, Franklin's grandson. Bache, called "Lightning-Rod Junior" by the Federalists, was the most prominent of the Republican editors, and he took the lead in arguing for a new and special role for the press in a popular republic. In 1793 Bache's paper, the *General Advertiser* (later the *Aurora*), claimed that the press provided "a constitutional check upon the conduct of public servants." Since public opinion was the basis of a republic, and newspapers were the principal and in some cases the only organ of that opinion, the press in America, said Bache, needed to become a major participant in politics. Because the people could not always count on their elected representatives to express their sentiments, newspapers and other institutions outside of government had responsibilities to protect the people's liberties and promote their interests.

Of course, nothing could be more different from the Federalists' view of the people's relationship to their republican governments. They assumed in traditional English fashion that once the people had elected their representatives, they should remain quiet and uninvolved in politics until the next election. But Bache's *Aurora* and other Republican newspapers in the 1790s set about educating the people in their new obligations as citizens. In order to get people to throw off their traditional passivity and deference and become engaged in politics, the Republican editors urged people to change their consciousness. They relentlessly attacked aristocratic pretension and privilege and classical deference and decorum and implored the people to cast off their sense of inferiority to the "well-born" and their so-called betters and elect whomever they wished to the offices of government, including men like William Findley, Jedediah Peck, and Matthew Lyon.

"In Representative Governments," these Republican editors declared, "the people are masters, all their officers from the highest to the lowest are servants to the people." And the people should be able to elect men "not only *of* ourselves, but as much as possible *as* ourselves, Men who have the same kind of interests to protect and the same dangers to avert." How could a "freeman," they asked, trust any leader "who boldly tells the world, that there are different grades and castes in every society,

33. Donald H. Stewart, *The Opposition Press of the Federalist Period* (Albany, 1969), 13; Richard D. Brown, *Knowledge Is Power: The Diffusion of Information in Early America, 1700–1865* (New York, 1989).

arising from natural causes, and that these grades and castes must have a separate influence and power in the government, in order to preserve the whole"? For too long the "great men" of the Federalist party had looked "upon the honest laborer as a distinct animal of an inferior species." Above all, the Republican editors attacked the leisured gentry as drones and parasites feeding on the labor of the common people. Such leisured gentlemen — who were "for the most part merchants, speculators, priests, lawyers and men employed in the various departments of government" — obtained their wealth either by inheritance or "by their *art* and *cunning*."[34]

In just these ways did the Republican newspapers meet the emotional needs of thousands upon thousands of aspiring middling sorts, especially in the Northern states, who for so long had resented the condescending arrogance of the so-called better sort, or the "prigarchy," as one Northern Republican labeled the Federalists.[35] Even a Republican paper in the tiny town of Cincinnati, Ohio, filled its pages with hopeful lessons from the French Revolution that "sufficiently proved that generals may be taken from the ranks, and ministers of state from the obscurity of the most remote village."[36]

By contrast with this extensive Republican use of the press, the Federalists did little. Presuming that they had a natural right to rule, they had no need to stir up public opinion, which was what demagogues did in exploiting the people's ignorance and innocence.[37] Federalist editors and printers of newspapers like John Fenno and his *Gazette of the United States* did exist, but most of these supporters of the national government were conservative in temperament; they tended to agree with the Federalist gentry that artisan-printers had no business organizing political parties or engaging in electioneering.[38]

Even the most successful printer-editor associated with the Federalist cause, William Cobbett, had very little to do with party politics. Although Cobbett was himself a British émigré who arrived in the United States in 1792, he shared none of the radical politics of his fellow émigrés. Indeed, he loved his homeland and always portrayed himself as a simple British

34. Joyce Appleby, *Capitalism and a New Social Order: The Republican Vision of the 1790s* (New York, 1984), 66, 69, 75; Stewart, *Opposition Press*, 389, 390.

35. Charles Warren, *Jacobin and Junto; or, Early American Politics as Viewed in the Diary of Dr. Nathaniel Ames, 1758–1822* (New York, 1931), 71.

36. Donald J. Ratcliffe, *Party Spirit in a Frontier Republic: Democratic Politics in Ohio, 1793–1821* (Columbus, OH, 1998), 20.

37. Richard Buel Jr., *Securing the Revolution: Ideology in American Politics, 1789–1815* (Ithaca, 1972), 99.

38. Pasley, *"Tyranny of the Printers,"* 231.

patriot who admired all things British. What made him appear to be a supporter of the Federalists was his deep and abiding hatred of the French Revolution and all those Republicans who supported it. He actually had no great affection for the United States and never became an American citizen. He thought the country was "detestable...good for getting money" and little else, while its people were "a cheating, sly, roguish gang."[39] He supported the Federalists indirectly by attacking the Republicans, whose "rage for equality" he ridiculed.

Cobbett was especially effective in mocking the hypocrisy of the liberty-loving Southern Republicans who were slaveholders. "After having spent the day in singing hymns to the Goddess of Liberty," he wrote in his 1795 pamphlet, *A Bone to Gnaw, for the Democrats*, "the virtuous Democrat gets him home to his peaceful dwelling, and sleeps, with his *property* secure beneath his roof, yea, sometimes in his very *arms*; and when his '*industry*' has enhanced its value, it bears to a new owner the proofs of his Democratic Delicacy!" Such earthy sarcasm and fiery invective were unmatched by any other writer of the period. Sometimes Cobbett's nastiness and vulgarity embarrassed even the Federalists.[40]

Since Cobbett was much more anti-French and pro-British than pro-Federalist, he never played the same role in organizing the Federalist party that Bache played in creating the Republican party. What Cobbett did do, however, was legitimize many latent American loyalties to the former mother country. "After all," he wrote, "our connexions are nearly as close as those of Man and Wife (I avoid," he said, "the comparison of Mother and Child, for fear of affecting the nerves of some delicate constitutions.)" Reading Cobbett, many Federalists felt they could at last express their long-suppressed affection for England openly and without embarrassment, especially as England had emerged as the champion of the European counter-revolution, opposed to all the frenzy and madness coming out of France.[41]

All aspects of American culture—parades, songs, art, theater, even language—became engines of one party or another promoting France or Britain. The Republicans attacked the English-dominated theater and, according to Cobbett, prohibited the use of all such words as "your majesty, My Lord, and the like," and the appearance onstage of all "silks, gold lace, painted cheeks, and powdered periwigs." They sang the new song attributed

39. Marcus Daniel, *Scandal and Civility: Journalism and the Birth of American Democracy* (New York, 2009), 295.
40. William Cobbett, *Peter Porcupine in America: Pamphlets on Republicanism and Revolution*, ed. David A. Wilson (Ithaca, 1994), 95, 113, 108.
41. Cobbett, *Peter Porcupine in America*, 117.

to Joel Barlow, "God Save the Guillotine," to the tune of "God Save the King." They pulled down all remnants of Britain and royalty, including a statue of William Pitt, Lord Chatham, which Americans themselves had erected during the imperial crisis, and destroyed images of the executed French king Louis XVI, who had helped America win the Revolution.[42]

When the Republicans began wearing the French tricolor cockade to show their support for the French Revolution, the Federalists labeled it "that emblem of treason" and in retaliation adopted a cockade of black ribbon, four inches in diameter and worn with a white button on a hat. Passions ran so high that some church services in 1798 ended in fisticuffs when several Republicans dared to show up wearing French cockades. According to one person's recollection, even ladies would "meet at the church door and violently pluck the badges from one another's bosoms." To some frightened observers society seemed to be breaking up. "Friendships were dissolved, tradesmen dismissed, and custom withdrawn from the Republican party," complained the wife of a prominent Republican in Philadelphia. "Many gentlemen went armed."[43]

It was the newspapers that became the principal instruments of this partisan warfare. While the Federalist press accused the Republicans of being "filthy Jacobins" and "monsters of sedition," the Republican press denounced the Federalists for being "Tory monarchists" and "British-loving aristocrats" and the president for being "a mock Monarch" who was "blind, bald, toothless, querulous" and "a ruffian deserving of the curses of mankind." By the late 1790s both President John Adams and Vice-President Thomas Jefferson came to believe that they had become the victims, in Adams's words, of "the most envious malignity, the most base, vulgar, sordid, fish-woman scurrility, and the most palpable lies" that had ever been leveled against any public official.[44]

BECAUSE THE FEDERALISTS were in charge of the government in the 1790s, they were the ones most frightened by the vituperation of the Republican press. It was one thing to libel private individuals; it was quite another thing to libel someone in public office. Such libels were doubly serious, indeed, under the common law were seditious, because they called into question the officeholders' authority to rule. Even Republican Thomas McKean, chief justice of the Pennsylvania Supreme Court, agreed. Libels against public officials, McKean declared, involved "a

42. Cobbett, *Peter Porcupine in America*, 89–118.
43. Warren, *Jacobin and Junto*, 85, 82, 86; DeConde, *The Quasi-War*, 82.
44. Smith, *Freedom's Fetters*, 116; John C. Miller, *The Federalist Era, 1789–1801* (New York, 1960), 233; Warren, *Jacobin and Junto*, 96.

direct tendency to breed in the people a dislike of their governors, and incline them to faction and sedition."[45]

Because politics was still personal, the honor and reputation of the political leaders seemed essential to social order and stability. Indeed, it was difficult in this early modern world for men to conceive of anyone becoming a political leader who did not already have an established social superiority. The reasons seemed obvious to many American leaders at the time, both Federalists and Republicans alike. Since early modern governments lacked most of the local coercive powers of a modern state—a few constables and sheriffs scarcely constituted a police force—officeholders had to rely on their social respectability and their reputation for character to compel the obedience of ordinary people and maintain public order. It is not surprising, therefore, that public officials should have been acutely sensitive to criticism of their private character. "Whatever tends to create in the minds of the people, a contempt of the persons who hold the highest offices in the state," declared conventional eighteenth-century wisdom, whatever convinced people that "subordination is not necessary, and is no essential part of government, tends directly to destroy it."[46]

In the Federalists' eyes much of the Republican press in the 1790s was indeed creating contempt for authority and undermining the due subordination of society. President Adams was especially vulnerable to criticism. Lacking Washington's popularity and stature, Adams was ill equipped to play the role of the republican monarch, and efforts to bolster his authority with formal ceremonies and elaborate rituals only made him seem absurd and open to ridicule, which the Republican press was more than willing to supply.[47]

If the Republicans' smear campaigns had been read by gentlemanly elites alone, they might have been tolerable to the Federalists. But, instead, the Republicans' slanders against public officials were reaching down to new popular levels of readers. The Federalist attitude to published materials was similar to that of the attorney general of Great Britain. When the radical scientist Thomas Cooper, who would soon emigrate to the United States, sought to respond in print to an attack by Edmund Burke, he was warned by the British attorney general to publish his work in an expensive

45. Norman L. Rosenberg, *Protecting the Best Men: An Interpretative History of the Law of Libel* (Chapel Hill, 1986), 77. In *New York Times Co. v. Sullivan* (1964) the Supreme Court decided just the opposite was the law. Not only could the press legally criticize public officials, but it could even make false statements about the conduct of public officials as long as no "actual malice" was intended. This broad version of freedom of the press exists nowhere else in the world.

46. Gordon S. Wood, *The Radicalism of the American Revolution* (New York, 1992), 86.

47. Buel, *Securing the Revolution*, 156.

edition, "so as to confine it probably to that class of readers who may consider it coolly." If it were to be "published cheaply for dissemination among the populace," declared this law officer of the crown, "it will be my duty to prosecute."[48] In other words, more important than what one said was to whom it was said. Anything that undermined the public's confidence in their leaders' capacities to rule was by that fact alone seditious.

It was bad enough that the Republican newspapers' slanderous and malicious attacks on federal officials were reaching out to a new popular readership, but, equally alarming to many Federalists, like the Reverend Samuel Miller, whose *Brief Retrospect of the Eighteenth Century* was an elaborate compendium of the Enlightenment, these newspapers had fallen into "the hands of persons destitute at once of the urbanity of gentlemen, the information of scholars, and the principles of virtue."[49] This helped explain why the Republicans' writings had become so vulgar and vituperative. The politics of honor made it difficult to deal with muckraking by social inferiors. Newspaper criticism from the likes of James Madison or James Monroe could be handled by the code of honor. But criticism from the likes of Matthew Lyon or William Duane or James Callender was another matter altogether. Such Republican editors and writers were not gentlemen and in many cases were not even American citizens.

The Federalists concluded that these upstart scandalmongers were destroying the character of the country's political leaders and undermining the entire political order. Believing, as George Cabot of Massachusetts put it, that "no free government, however perfect its form and virtuous its administration, can withstand the continued assaults of unrefuted calumny," they sought to limit the national effectiveness of the muckrakers in the only way possible outside of the code of honor—by making seditious libel a federal crime.[50]

Americans believed in freedom of the press and had written that freedom into their Bill of Rights. But they believed in it as Englishmen did. Indeed, the English had celebrated freedom of the press since the seventeenth century, but they meant by it, in contrast with the French, no prior restraint or censorship of what was published. Under English law, people were nevertheless held responsible for what they published. If a person's publications were slanderous and calumnious enough to bring public officials into disrepect, then under the common law the publisher could be prosecuted for seditious libel. The truth of what was published was no

48. Appleby, *Capitalism and a New Social Order*, 60.
49. Samuel Miller, *A Brief Retrospect of the Eighteenth Century* (New York, 1803), 2: 254–55.
50. Kohn, *Eagle and Sword*, 200; Joanne B. Freeman, *Affairs of Honor: National Politics in the New Republic* (New Haven, 2001), xvii–xviii.

defense; indeed, it even aggravated the offense. Furthermore, under the common law judges, not juries, had the responsibility to decide whether or not a publication was seditious. Although this common law view of seditious libel had been challenged and seriously weakened by John Peter Zenger's trial in New York in 1735, it had never been fully eradicated from American thinking or practice in the state courts.

Federalists wanted such a sedition law for the national government. The Sedition Act of July 14, 1798, which Vice-President Jefferson said was designed for the "suppression of the whig presses," especially Bache's *Aurora*, made it a crime to "write, print, utter or publish . . . any false, scandalous, and malicious writing or writings against the Government of the United States, or either House of the Congress of the United States, with intent to defame the said government, or either house of the said Congress, or the President, or to bring them . . . into contempt or disrepute, or to excite against them, or either or any of them, the hatred of the good people of the United States." (Significantly, the office of vice-president was not protected by the act.) The punishment was a fine not exceeding two thousand dollars and imprisonment not exceeding two years.[51] Compared to the harsh punishments Britain had meted out in its sedition trials of 1793–1794—individuals transported to Australia for fourteen years for expressing the slightest misgivings about the war with France—the American punishments for seditious libel were tame.

The sedition bill nevertheless left the Republicans aghast. It was one thing to repress aliens; it was quite another to repress the country's own citizens. But radical Federalists like Robert Goodloe Harper thought that some citizens had become as dangerous as aliens. "There existed," he said, "a domestic—what shall I call it?—a conspiracy, a faction leagued with a foreign Power to effect a revolution or a subjugation of this country, by the arms of that foreign Power." Republican calls to the citizens to resist this legislation only confirmed the Federalist fears of "the contagion of the French mania." The evidence was everywhere, said Harrison Gray Otis, of "the necessity of purifying the country from the sources of pollution."[52]

The Federalist congressmen seemed almost demonic in the intensity of their passion. Even Hamilton became alarmed at the hasty vigor with which the Federalists in the Congress were moving. Slow down, he urged. "Let us not establish a tyranny. Energy is very different thing from violence." By pushing things to an extreme too fast, he warned, the congressional Federalists might end up strengthening the Republicans.[53]

51. TJ to JM, 26 April 1798, *Republic of Letters*, 1042; Smith, *Freedom's Fetters*, 441–42.
52. *Annals of Congress*, 5th Congress, 2nd session (June 1798), VIII, 2024–25, 2017–18.
53. AH to Wolcott, 29 June 1798, *Papers of Hamilton*, 21: 522.

Ironically, the Sedition Act was actually a liberalization of the common law of seditious libel that continued to run in the state courts. Under the new federal statute, which resembled the liberal argument Zenger's lawyer had used, the truth of what was said or published could be admitted as a defense, and juries could decide not only the facts of the case (did so-and-so publish this particular piece?) but the law as well; in other words, the jury could decide whether the defendant was guilty or not guilty of having written something libelous and seditious. Neither truth as a defense nor juries' deciding the law was allowed under the American common law. Indeed, some Federalists believed that the national government did not even need a statute to punish seditious libel; they claimed that the common law of crimes ran in the federal courts and could be used to prosecute cases of seditious libel.

Despite these liberal elements, however, the bill passed the House by only forty-four to forty-one. It was due to expire on March 3, 1801, the day before the end of the Adams administration. However disastrously this act turned out for the Federalists' reputation, at the time it seemed to many of them to be necessary for the protection of the country.

EVEN BEFORE THE ALIEN FRIENDS ACT was passed, anxious Frenchmen, including the noted French philosophe Constantine François Chasseboeuf, comte de Volney, prepared to leave the country for France. Following the act's passage, more than a dozen shiploads sailed for France or Saint-Domingue. Many who did not flee the country were kept under surveillance by the ultra-suspicious secretary of state, Timothy Pickering. When Médéric Louis Elie Moreau de St. Méry, a refugee from the Reign of Terror, who in 1794 had established a bookstore in Philadelphia, asked why he was on the president's list for deportation, he was told of President Adams's blunt reply: "Nothing in particular, but he's too French."[54] In the end, because so many foreigners left before the act was enforced and because of the president's strict interpretation of the statute, the Federalist government never actually deported a single alien under the auspices of the Alien Act.

It was another story with the Sedition Act. The government arrested twenty-five persons and brought seventeen indictments of seditious libel against Republican journalists and editors (fourteen under the Sedition Act itself), of which ten resulted in conviction and punishment. So fearful were the Federalists of pro-French fifth column activities by the Republican editors that they could not even wait for the statute to be

---

54. Kenneth Roberts and Anna M. Roberts, eds., *Moreau de St. Méry's American Journey*, 1793–1798 (New York, 1947), 253.

passed. Three weeks before President Adams signed the Sedition Act into law, the government arrested Benjamin Franklin Bache, charging him with seditious libel under the common law. In vain did Bache's attorneys argue before District Judge Richard Peters that the common law of crimes did not run in the federal courts. Judge Peters thought otherwise and set bail at two thousand dollars, but Bache died of yellow fever in September 1798 before he could be tried.

The Federalists, again under the zealous leadership of Secretary of State Pickering, went after the other leading Republican newspaper editors. Three of those convicted were refugees from British repression in the 1790s—Thomas Cooper, the English lawyer and scientist who turned to journalism in the late 1790s; James Callender, the Scottish radical who had stirred up the Reynolds affair against Hamilton; and William Duane, the American-born but Irish-bred publisher who took over the *Aurora* upon Bache's sudden death in 1798. Cooper's trial took place in Philadelphia before Supreme Court Justice Samuel Chase. In his charge to the jury, Chase set forth the Federalists' rationale for the Sedition Act. "If a man attempts to destroy the confidence of the people in their officers, their supreme magistrate, and their legislature," Chase declared, "he effectively saps the foundation of the government." Cooper was found guilty, fined four hundred dollars, and sentenced to six months in the local prison.[55]

Chase was even more vindictive in the trial of Callender, badgering the defense attorneys and forbidding them from calling witnesses. Again the jury found Callender guilty, and Chase fined him two hundred dollars and sentenced him to nine months in jail. The severest sentence under the Sedition Act was imposed on David Brown, a semi-literate commoner and itinerant political agitator who had traveled to over eighty Massachusetts towns writing and lecturing against the Federalists. Brown directed his message at middling and lower sorts of "Farmers, Mechanicks, and Labourers" and emphasized the "struggle between the laboring part of the community and those lazy rascals" who did not have to work for a living.

In the fall of 1798 Brown rambled into Dedham, Massachusetts, the hometown of the arch-Federalist Fisher Ames, who described Brown as "a vagabond ragged fellow," a "wandering apostle of sedition," who gave speeches "telling everybody the sins and enormities of the Government." Brown's speeches apparently incited the Republicans in the town into erecting a liberty pole that contained an inscription denouncing the

55. Edward J. Larson, *A Magnificent Catastrophe: The Tumultuous Election of 1800, America's First Presidential Campaign* (New York, 2007), 77.

Federalists and their actions. The Federalists were outraged, calling the liberty pole "a rallying point of insurrection and civil war," and they had Brown and Benjamin Fairbanks, a very substantial citizen of the town, arrested and tried for sedition with Associate Justice Samuel Chase again presiding. Both indicted men pled guilty. Chase, who was becoming even more notorious for his Federalist partisanship, let Fairbanks off with a five-dollar fine and six hours of imprisonment, but because Brown had "attempted to incite the uninformed part of the community," Chase sentenced him to eighteen months' imprisonment and a fine of $480—an extraordinary punishment that was a measure of the Federalists' fears, in Ames's words, of "the tendencies of democracy to anarchy."[56]

The Federalist administration also indicted Matthew Lyon and Jedediah Peck. Lyon was actually the first person put on trial for violating the Sedition Act. But his conviction and the punishment (four months in jail and a thousand-dollar fine) backfired and turned Lyon into a Republican martyr. From his jail cell not only did Lyon continue to write on behalf of the Republican cause, but he also ran a successful campaign for reelection to Congress, the first prisoner in American history to do so.

The government had more trouble with Peck. Judge Cooper in Otsego County had Peck arrested for circulating petitions against the Alien and Sedition Acts and had him taken in irons to New York City for trial. But when the government realized that prosecuting this Revolutionary War veteran only increased Republican strength in his New York county, it dropped the case.

The short-term success of the Federalist Sedition Act in shutting down several Republican newspapers scarcely justified the long-term consequences of the government's actions. Republican editors were not cowed; indeed, the number of new Republican newspapers increased dramatically between 1798 and 1800. Just as printers increasingly came to see themselves as political professionals, making a living out of politics, so did many Federalists reluctantly come to realize that seditious libel made a very poor political weapon for putting down faction in the kind of democratic society America, at least in its Northern parts, was rapidly becoming.[57]

STILL, EXPELLING ALIENS and stopping the flow of scurrilous writings were only parts of a larger Federalist program for saving the Republic from the scourge of Jacobinism. There remained what many Federalists

---

56. Smith, *Freedom's Fetters*, 258–68; Warren, *Jacobin and Junto*, 107–10; Ames, "Laocoon 1," April 1799, *Works of Ames*, ed. Allen, 1: 192–93,196.
57. Pasley, *"Tyranny of the Printers,"* 126–31.

thought was the likelihood of a French army invading the United States. Under this threat of invasion Congress began beefing up the country's military forces. It levied new taxes on land, houses, and slaves. In addition to its naval buildup, it authorized a dramatic enlargement of the military establishment. At last, many Federalists believed they would have the standing army that they had long yearned for. Without an army, they believed, the United States could scarcely qualify as a modern nation: it would lack the most important attribute of a modern state—the ability to wage war. Some Federalists even thought that this army might be profitably used in other ways than simply against the French.

After the suppression of the Whiskey Rebellion, the country in 1796 had settled on a peacetime army of about three thousand men. Although this regular army was simply a constabulary force strung out in forts along the frontier, even it aroused anxieties among many Americans fearful of any semblance of a "standing army." Most Republicans thought the state militias were more than able to handle any military crises. War produced armies, debts, taxes, patronage, and a bloated executive power, and these, said James Madison, "are the known instruments for bringing the many under the domination of the few."[58] The best way to avoid war was not to build up the country's military forces; that only made war inevitable. Instead, the nation ought to negotiate, avoid provocations, and look for peaceful alternatives to fighting.

Suddenly under threat of a French invasion, the Federalists were in a position to counter what they regarded as this milksop Republican approach to foreign policy and achieve the kind of military establishment that would make the United States the equal of the European states. Most Federalists assumed that possessing a strong military force not only was an essential feature of a real nation-state but was as well the best means of preventing war. "Can a Country," asked Theodore Sedgwick in 1797, "expect to repel invasion and interruption by declaring they not only never will fight; but never will prepare either by Land or water, an effectual defence?"[59]

In the frenzied atmosphere of 1798, the Congress enlarged the regular army by twelve regiments and six troops of dragoons, creating what was called a "New Army" of twelve thousand men to be organized at once. At the same time, Congress created a "Provisional Army" of ten thousand men, which the president could activate in case of actual war or invasion or even the "imminent danger" of invasion. The rumor that France was

58. JM, "Political Observations" (1795), in Marvin Meyers, ed., *The Mind of the Founder: Sources of the Political Thought of James Madison* (Indianapolis, 1973), 287.
59. Kohn, *Eagle and Sword*, 223.

going to use blacks from Saint-Domingue to invade and foment slave rebellions in the South even led to Federalist gains in the Southern states in the 1798 elections.

Although this military force was smaller than Hamilton wanted, it was much larger than President Adams thought necessary. Like many of his English ancestors, the historically minded Adams disliked armies, which could manage coups and create despotisms, but liked navies, which were usually away at sea. Thus he favored the new Navy Department that was created at the same time the army was augmented. Besides, unlike most of his Federalist colleagues, the president doubted that France could ever invade the United States. He realized that the United States might be drawn into a full-scale war, but he himself would never push for it. Consequently, he never recommended that Congress enlarge the army; Hamilton, he believed, was responsible for that. Indeed, the way Adams tended to recall the events of 1798, and sometimes even the way he acted at the time, was almost as if he were not the chief executive at all.

Adams in 1798 had the sense that there was "too much intrigue in this business" of the army and its leadership, and with good reason.[60] In many respects this grandiose military force was peculiarly Hamilton's. Certainly no one wanted the United States to become a European-like state more passionately than did Hamilton, and he had shown a willingness to employ the army for internal purposes. In 1783 he had even urged Washington to use the army to pressure Congress into strengthening public finances, which had led General Washington to warn his high-strung aide that the army was "a dangerous instrument to play with."[61]

Although Hamilton had been out of office and practicing law in New York since 1795, he had remained immensely influential with Adams's cabinet and other Federalists. He saw in this crisis with France an opportunity both to redeem his reputation and, more important, to realize some of his vision of what the nation ought to become. In the spring of 1798 he dashed off a seven-part series of newspaper essays calling for the creation of a huge army to resist the imperialistic plans of the French and accusing the weak-kneed Republicans of appeasement. When some Federalists tried to lure him back into government with offers of a Senate seat from New York or the position of secretary of war, he resisted. He had his sights on a bigger role for himself: the effective commander-in-chief of the new army.

To be in charge of all the American armies seemed to Hamilton like a dream fulfilled. Instead of having to wait patiently for time and social development to turn America into a modern state, he could take advantage

60. Kohn, *Eagle and Sword*, 604.
61. Chernow, *Hamilton*, 179.

of the crisis with France and short-circuit the process. The army was central to his plans, both at home and abroad. With some justification, the Republicans believed that Hamilton intended to use the army against them. Sincerely fearing that a fifth column within the United States was willing to aid an invading French army, Hamilton certainly was eager to suppress any domestic insurrection with a massive show of force. When rumors spread that Jefferson's and Madison's home state was arming, he seemed prepared to "put Virginia to the Test of resistance."[62]

When an armed uprising of Germans led by John Fries actually occurred in several southeastern Pennsylvania counties early in 1799, Hamilton told the secretary of war not to err by sending too few troops. "Whenever the Government appears in arms," he wrote, "it ought to appear like a *Hercules*, and inspire respect by the display of strength."[63] He thought that a respectable standing army would enable the United States both "to subdue a *refractory* & powerful *state*" such as Virginia and to deal independently and equally with the warring powers of Europe. President Adams did respond to the Fries uprising with five hundred militiamen at a cost of eighty thousand dollars. The so-called rebellion was put down with no injuries.[64]

A strong military establishment seems to have been just the beginning of Hamilton's future plans for strengthening the Union. He wanted as well to extend the judiciary, to build a system of roads and canals, to increase taxes, and to amend the Constitution in order to subdivide the larger states.[65]

Beyond the borders of the United States his aims were even more grandiose. He thought the war with France would enable the United States, in cooperation with Britain, to seize both Florida and Louisiana from Spain — in order, he said, to keep them out of the hands of France. At the same time, he held out the possibility of helping the Venezuelan patriot Francisco de Miranda to liberate South America. In all these endeavors, he told the American minister in Britain, Rufus King, America should be "the principal agency," especially in supplying the land army. "The command in this case would very naturally fall upon me — and I hope I should disappoint no favorable anticipation."[66]

---

62. AH to Theodore Sedgwick, 2 Feb. 1799, *Hamilton: Writings*, 914.
63. AH to James McHenry, 18 March 1799, *Papers of Hamilton*, 22: 552–53.
64. AH to Sedgwick, 2 Feb. 1799, *Papers of Hamilton*, 22: 453; Thomas P. Slaughter, "'The King of Crimes': Early American Treason Law, 1787–1860," in Ronald Hoffman and Peter J. Albert, eds., *Launching the "Extended Republic": The Federalist Era* (Charlottesville, 1996), 96–97. Fries and two others were convicted of treason and sentenced to death, but President Adams pardoned them, even in the face of opposition from many Federalists.
65. AH to Jonathan Dayton, Oct.–Nov. 1799, *Papers of Hamilton*, 23: 599–604.
66. AH to Rufus King, 22 Aug. 1798, *Papers of Hamilton*, 22: 154–55.

As Fisher Ames later pointed out, Hamilton had never wanted power, popularity, or wealth; the only thing he ever craved was military fame and glory, not just for himself but for the country as well. "He was qualified, beyond any man of the age," said Ames, "to display the talents of a great general."[67]

But in 1798 America already had a great general, in retirement at Mount Vernon. If he were to realize his dreams, Hamilton knew that he would have to convince Washington to buckle on his sword and become Hamilton's aegis once again, as he had during his presidency. But the current president would be a problem. President Adams had no hesitation in commissioning Washington as "Lieutenant General and commander in Chief of all the Armies raised or to be raised for the service of the United States," and in July 1798 he did so, even before he received Washington's permission. Adams was not at all eager to make Hamilton second in command, which was what the High Federalists in his cabinet were plotting. Other officers from the Revolution had been senior to Colonel Hamilton, namely Henry Knox and Charles Cotesworth Pinckney.

How to sort out the order of command? Since Knox declared that he would not serve under Pinckney or Hamilton, Adams favored Knox as next in command to Washington; but Hamilton said he would not serve under Knox. For his part Washington wanted Hamilton as second in command and threatened to resign if the bickering continued. The president, finally outmaneuvered by both his cabinet and Washington, reluctantly had to accede to Hamilton's becoming major general and second in command to Washington. He was furious that he had been compelled to promote this foreigner, Hamilton, a man who was "the most restless, impatient, indefatigable and unprincipled Intriguer in the United States, if not in the world."[68] Soon, however, he would get his revenge on Hamilton and the whole crowd of Hamiltonians.

Hamilton had his army, and he had Washington as his aegis. Hamilton told Washington in May 1798 that he was convinced that the Republicans intended "to *new model* our constitution under the *influence* or *coercion* of France," and in substance, if not in name, "to make this Country a province of France."[69] Washington more or less agreed. Although he doubted that the French were capable at present of invading the country, he was sure that the Republicans were up to no good. Believing as he did that organized party opposition was pernicious, he concluded that the beleaguered Federalists were simply "the Friends of Government" trying

67. Ames, Sketch of the Character of Alexander Hamilton, July 1804, *Works of Ames*, ed. Allen, I: 518.
68. JA, *Boston Patriot*, 10 June 1809, Adams, ed., *Works*, 9: 305–6.
69. AH to GW, 19 May 1798, *Papers of Hamilton*, 21: 467.

to defend a Constitution that the French party of Republicans would use every means to "subvert" and turn into "a mere cipher."[70] The former president knew he could not remain an unconcerned spectator of France's attempt to do what Britain had once tried to do—deprive America of its rights. Although Washington, as he had repeatedly in the past, expressed his reluctance to resume public office and wondered whether becoming commander-in-chief would not be considered "a restless Act, evincive of my discontent in retirement," he was far more eager in 1798 to step back into the breach and do his duty than he ever had been before. It indicated just how seriously he took the crisis in 1798.[71]

With President Adams expressing a distinct lack of enthusiasm for the whole project, organizing the army did not go well. In November 1798 Hamilton met with Washington and Pinckney in Philadelphia to appoint the officers and to recruit the troops. Because the army was designed not only to resist the French but presumably to put down domestic insurrections, and even political opposition, the officers had to be both talented and scrupulously Federalist; thus the process of appointment was slow. The chain of command was garbled, with Hamilton giving orders to his ostensible superior, the secretary of war, and the recruiting and supplying of the soldiers suffered from delays and confusion, with Hamilton bickering over the most trivial details, including how the soldiers' hats should be cocked. More dismaying, Washington's willingness to participate in the creation of the army began to cool; eventually the former president gave up on the project and returned to Mount Vernon thoroughly disillusioned with what was happening in the country. By the time the New Army disbanded in May 1800, it had become a joke.

EVEN BEFORE THE PASSAGE of the Alien and Sedition Acts, some Southern Republicans were thinking of ways to protect both liberty and the sectional interests of the South from the growing power of the national government. In the spring of 1798 John Taylor, who was rapidly becoming the conscience of the Republican party, wrote Monroe and Jefferson about his fears. Unless the Federalists were stopped, Taylor said, "the southern states must lose their capital and commerce—and...America is destined to war—standing armies—and oppressive taxation." Taylor even raised the possibility that some of the Southern states might secede from the Union. In response, Jefferson tried to calm Taylor down. Federalist dominance was unnatural and only temporary. "A little patience," Jefferson wrote in his famous letter of June 4, 1798, "and we shall see the reign of the witches

70. GW to Lafayette, 25 Dec. 1798, *Papers of Washington: Retirement Ser.*, 3: 281–82.
71. GW to McHenry, 4 July 1798, *Papers of Washington: Retirement Ser.*, 2: 378.

pass over, their spells dissolved, and the people recovering their true sight, and restoring their government to its true principles."[72]

With the passage of the Alien and Sedition Acts in the summer of 1798, however, Jefferson changed his tune, especially as he saw the Federalists resorting to all sorts of insidious devices to sustain their popularity. The usually sanguine vice-president despaired. He thought that if these laws were accepted by the American people, Congress would next allow the president to serve for life, which would be the first step toward making the office hereditary, and then it would establish the Senate for life. Some Federalists, he believed, even wanted to restore George III over the American people. He thought the Federalists' attack on freedom of the press was the prelude to an attack on freedom of religion; the denial of the press's freedom "had given to the clergy a very favorite hope of obtaining an establishment of a particular form of Christianity thro' the U.S." With some justification, he even feared that "our Buonaparte" Hamilton and the new army might invade Virginia in order to suppress dissent.[73] In fact, the Republicans in general were as frightened by what they described as the Federalists' moves toward monarchy and a war with France as the Federalists were by what they described as the Republicans' radical efforts to collaborate in bringing the French Revolution to America.

With both the Federalists and the Republicans having legitimate reasons for their fears, their extreme partisanship divided the country more deeply than at any time since 1776. A Federalist newspaper in Virginia predicted an "ultimate appeal to arms by the two great parties." Republican William Branch Giles of Virginia hoped "to see a separation of this state, from the General-Union."[74]

With the Congress under the control of the Federalists, the vice-president and both Southern and some Northern Republicans thought the federal government had become in effect a "foreign jurisdiction," and they began to look to the states as the best means of resisting Federalist tyranny. While Jefferson believed that the federal government had become "more arbitrary, and has swallowed more of the public liberty than even that of England," he thought that "our state governments are the *very best in the world* without exception or comparison."[75] There in

72. Sharp, *American Politics in the Early Republic*, 188; TJ to Taylor, 4 June 1798, *Papers of Jefferson*, 30: 389.

73. TJ to Stevens Thomson Mason, 11 Oct. 1798, to Thomas Mann Randolph, 4 Feb. 1800, *Papers of Jefferson*, 30: 560; 31: 360; TJ to BR, 23 Sept. 1800, *Jefferson: Writings*, 1081–82.

74. Douglas R. Egerton, *Gabriel's Rebellion: The Virginia Slave Conspiracies of 1800 and 1802* (Chapel Hill, 1993), 37.

75. Sharp, *American Politics in the Early Republic*, 188; TJ to Taylor, 26 Nov. 1798, *Papers of Jefferson*, 30: 589.

the states was where integrity and the solution to America's problems could be found.

Madison, retired from Congress since 1797, was urged to run for election to the Virginia legislature. As one Republican told James Monroe, it was "highly important, at this moment and will be more so every day, to pay particular attention to the State Legislatures, and to get into them men of respectability." Before Madison took office in the Virginia legislature in 1799, he and Jefferson thought they had to do something to combat the Federalist actions. Believing, as Madison put it, that the Federalists were seeking to create a consolidated government and "transform the present republican system of the United States, into an absolute, or at best a mixed monarchy," the two Republican leaders quietly plotted to use the state legislatures as the most effective instrument for combating the constitutionality of the Alien and Sedition Acts. Because they intended to set forth radical constitutional ideas about the nature of the Union, they wanted their authorship to remain unknown except to the men who would actually introduce their legislative resolutions. Although Madison and Jefferson were not primarily thinking about protecting slavery in 1798, their ideas—"the spirit of '98"—certainly laid the basis for the nullification and states' rights doctrines later used to defend slavery and Southern distinctiveness in the period leading up to the Civil War.[76]

In his draft of state resolutions, which was intended for the Virginia legislature but instead ended up in that of Kentucky, Jefferson described the Constitution as "a compact" among the several states, with each state retaining final authority to declare acts of the federal government that exceeded its delegated powers, in this case, the Alien and Sedition Acts, "void & of no force" within that state's jurisdiction. Jefferson labeled this remedy for abusive federal actions "nullification," but, fortunately for his subsequent reputation, the Kentucky legislature edited out this inflammatory term when it adopted Jefferson's draft in a set of resolves issued in November 1798.[77]

The resolutions drafted by Madison and issued by the Virginia legislature in December 1798 were somewhat less radical than Jefferson's, especially in their conception of the compact as the consequence of the collective action of the people in each state; indeed, Madison seems to have thought of his resolutions as protests rather than as acts of nullification. He objected in particular to Jefferson's idea that the state legislature could declare unconstitutional acts null and void. "Have you ever

76. Sharp, *American Politics in the Early Republic*, 194; JM, Virginia Resolutions Against the Alien and Sedition Acts, 21 Dec. 1798, *Madison: Writings*, 590.

77. TJ's Draft of Kentucky Resolutions of 1798, before 4 Oct. 1798, *Papers of Jefferson*, 30: 531–32, 536–41.

considered thoroughly the distinction between the power of the *State*, & that of *the Legislature*, on questions relating to the federal pact?" Madison asked his friend. Since Madison believed that the state, by which he meant the people themselves, was "the ultimate Judge of infractions," the legislature had no business exercising such an authority; it belonged to a constitutional convention, since that was "the organ by which the Compact was made." Unlike Jefferson, who was out of the country in 1787–1788, Madison was there at the creation, and he never forgot that the Constitution was ratified by state conventions, not state legislatures. In America, unlike England, he said, "the people, not the government, possess the absolute sovereignty. The legislature, no less than the executive, is under limitations....Hence, in the United States, the great and essential rights of the people are secured against legislative as well as executive ambition."[78]

Both the Kentucky and Virginia legislatures called upon the other states to join them in declaring the Alien and Sedition Acts unconstitutional, but none of the other fourteen state legislatures followed.[79] Although four Southern states took no action at all, nine Northern states decisively rejected the resolutions, most of them declaring that the judiciary, and not the state legislatures, was the proper body to determine the constitutionality of acts of Congress. By August 1799 Jefferson was contemplating even more radical action. If the people did not soon change the direction and tone of the national government, he told Madison, Virginia and Kentucky ought "to sever our selves from that union we so much value, rather than give up the rights of self government which we have reserved, and in which alone we see liberty."[80] Although secession was being openly discussed, neither Jefferson nor Madison was willing to advocate force to bring it about.

Instead, the Republican leaders sought to have the Kentucky and Virginia legislatures answer the objections of the other states and reaffirm

---

78. JM to TJ, 29 Dec. 1798, *Papers of Jefferson*, 30: 606; JM, Report on the Alien and Sedition Acts, 7 Jan. 1800, *Madison: Writings*, 608–62.

79. For traditional accounts of the Virginia and Kentucky Resolutions, see Philip G. Davidson, "Virginia and the Alien and Sedition Laws," *AHR*, 36 (1931), 336–42; and Adrienne Koch and Harry Ammon, "The Virginia and Kentucky Resolutions: An Episode in Jefferson's and Madison's Defense of Civil Liberties," *WMQ*, (1948), 145–76. Both accounts deny that Virginia was arming. Sharp, *American Politics in the Early Republic*, 187–207, offers a persuasive argument that Virginia was indeed preparing for a violent confrontation with the federal government. In a more recent study William J. Watkins Jr., *Reclaiming the American Revolution: The Kentucky and Virginia Resolutions and Their Legacy* (New York, 2004), 24, contends that Virginia was not arming to confront the federal government but only trying to upgrade its neglected defenses, primarily in response to increased Indian attacks in the West.

80. TJ to JM, 23 Aug. 1799, *Republic of Letters*, 1119.

the sentiments of the original resolutions. With some advice from Jefferson, the Kentucky legislature in November 1799 repeated its opposition to the Alien and Sedition Acts and declared "a Nullification of those acts by the States to be the rightful remedy."[81] Even with this provocative word included, the legislature's resolve was much more conciliatory and much less extreme than the secessionist views Jefferson had expressed in letters several months earlier.

For his part Madison on January 7, 1800, issued a notable committee report to the Virginia assembly in which he defended the earlier resolutions and warned that the Federalist plans for a consolidation would "transform the republican system of the United States into a monarchy." If the federal government extended its "power to every subject falling within the idea of the 'general welfare,'" the discretionary and patronage authority of the executive would be greatly expanded; this in turn would lead to insidious efforts by the chief magistrate to manipulate his repeated re-election or to increasingly corrupt and violent elections, to the point where "the public voice itself might call for an hereditary in place of an elective succession." In addition to denying the Federalist contention that the common law—"a law of vast extent and complexity, and embracing almost every possible subject of legislation"—ran in the federal courts, Madison made a powerful case for a strict construction of the Constitution, particularly its "necessary and proper" clause that Hamilton had exploited so effectively.

Finally, he offered a brilliant defense of the freedoms described in the First Amendment, especially freedom of the press. Elective republican governments, which were responsible to the people, required, said Madison, "a greater freedom of animadversion" than hereditary monarchies. This meant "a different degree of freedom, on the use of the press"; indeed, despite the excesses of scurrility and slander, popular governments needed newspapers for "canvassing the merits and measures of public men.... To the press alone, chequered as it is with abuses," he concluded, "the world is indebted for all the triumphs which have been gained by reason and humanity, over error and oppression."[82]

SUDDENLY, SEVERAL DEVELOPMENTS worked to calm this fearful and frenzied climate. British admiral Horatio Nelson's naval victory over the French at the Battle of the Nile in October 1798 essentially destroyed the possibility of a French invasion of either England or America. With the threat of a French invasion gone, the Federalists lost

81. John Breckinridge to TJ, 13 Dec. 1799, *Papers of Jefferson*, 30: 266.
82. JM, Report on the Alien and Sedition Acts, 7 Jan. 1800, *Madison: Writings*, 646–47.

much of the rationale for their program. But more important in reducing the sense of crisis was the bold and courageous but bizarre action of President John Adams.

Adams's presidency had been extraordinarily contentious, and Adams was never in command of his own cabinet, let alone the government. Indeed, he seemed to many to be escaping from the troubles of the capital in Philadelphia by spending more and more time at his home in Quincy, Massachusetts. This short, stout, and sensitive man had been much too honest, impulsive, and passionate to handle the growing division among the Federalists over Hamilton's ascendancy and the military buildup. Despite all the importance his political theory gave to the executive in a balanced government, he was temperamentally ill equipped to be Washington's successor as president. He shared little of the Hamiltonian dream of turning the United States into a European-like state with a huge bureaucracy and a massive army with the capacity to wage war; indeed, Adams had been the author of the model treaty of 1776, and his ideas about foreign policy and war were closer to Jefferson's than Hamilton's. And Adams certainly had none of the personal Benjamin Franklin–like talents needed to deal with the intense, meddling, and high-strung personalities around him. But he was intelligent and patriotic, and he increasingly sensed that he had to do something to end the crisis.

In November 1798 he returned to Philadelphia from one of his many long vacations in Quincy determined once and for all to take command of his administration. Aware of Hamilton's grand military ambitions and machinations and learning from various sources that the French government was finally ready to reach an accommodation with the United States, Adams decided, without consulting anyone, including his own cabinet, to send a new mission to France. On February 18, 1799, he informed Congress that he had appointed William Vans Murray as minister plenipotentiary to make peace with France. Although Murray was a former Federalist congressman from Maryland and presently minister to the Batavian Republic, he was not a major figure among the Federalists; but Adams had known and liked him in London in the 1780s, and for Adams that was enough. All things considered, it was a strange way for a president to behave.

Most Federalists were stunned by Adams's action. While many seethed with "surprise, indignation, grief & disgust," others thought the president had lost his mind.[83] Under immense pressure from the High Federalists, including meetings that ended in undignified shouting matches, Adams

83. John Ferling, *Adams vs. Jefferson: The Tumultuous Election of 1800* (New York, 2004), 121.

was forced to make some concessions. He agreed to add two more envoys to join Murray—Chief Justice Oliver Ellsworth and William Davie, the governor of North Carolina—and to delay the departure of the mission until the French gave more assurance that it would be received, which they did in August 1799. In the meantime Congress had adjourned at the end of February 1799 without further expanding the army, and Adams had gone back home to Quincy, where he remained angrily secluded for the next seven months.

The High Federalists, led by Secretary of State Pickering, were furious. With all their plans for the army and the suppression of the Republicans in disarray, they plotted to undermine the mission to France. Only when his new secretary of the navy, Benjamin Stoddard, who was not part of the Hamiltonian gang, warned Adams of the "artful, designing men" in the cabinet working against him did the morose and irritable president reluctantly return to the capital. In October 1799 Hamilton, whose own high-strung temperament was being stretched to the breaking point, made a last-ditch effort to delay the mission by arrogantly lecturing the president on European politics and the likelihood of Britain's restoring the Bourbons to the French throne. "Never in my life," Adams recalled, "did I hear a man talk more like a fool."[84] (Of course, in 1814–1815 Britain and its allies actually did restore the Bourbon king Louis XVIII to the French throne.) Finally, by early November 1799, Adams was able to get his envoys off to Paris.

Adams's awkwardly independent action irreparably divided the Federalist leadership between the moderates who supported the president and the extremists or "ultras" who supported Hamilton—seriously endangering Federalist prospects for the upcoming presidential election in 1800. Once the Federalist caucus had nominated Adams and Charles Cotesworth Pinckney for president and vice-president in May 1800 (without, however, determining which person should have which office), the president felt strong enough politically to do what he should have done long before—dismiss the Hamiltonians in his cabinet, McHenry and Pickering. In one of his all too common fits of rage, Adams told McHenry that Hamilton, whom he called "the greatest intriguant in the World—a man devoid of every moral principle—a Bastard," was the source of all the Federalists' problems and that Jefferson was an "infinitely better" and "wiser" man.[85] Learning of Adams's tirade, and especially the reference to his illegitimacy, a deeply dispirited Hamilton concluded that the president

84. JA, 1809, *Papers of Hamilton*, 23: 546–47; Sharp, *American Politics in the Early Republic*, 213.
85. JA to James McHenry, 31 May 1800, *Papers of Hamilton*, 24: 557.

was "more mad than I ever thought him," and because of his praise of Jefferson perhaps "as wicked as he is mad."[86]

Abandoning all sense of prudence and perspective, Hamilton and some other High Federalists began working to find some alternative to Adams as president, perhaps by electing Pinckney over Adams, or even by calling Washington out of retirement. With his dreams of making the United States a great nation falling apart all around him, Hamilton finally exploded. If he could not instigate a duel with the president to defend his honor, then he would publish a letter that would destroy the president and promote Pinckney's candidacy, all in "the shape of a *defence of my self*"—a delicate task that was beyond his angry mood.[87] In the summer and fall of 1800 he wrote a fifty-four-page privately published *Letter from Alexander Hamilton, Concerning the Public Conduct and Character of John Adams, Esq. President of the United States.*

In this work, which apparently was originally intended to circulate only among select Federalists, including Federalist electors, Hamilton described Adams's career in detail, praising here and there but mostly criticizing the man for his "eccentric tendencies," his "distempered jealousy," his "extreme egotism," his "ungovernable temper," and his "vanity without bounds." He also attempted to answer Adams's "virulent and indecent abuses" of himself, especially Adams's charge that he was "the leader of a British Faction." In his counter-charge Hamilton said that Adams, with his many "paroxysms of anger," had undone everything that Washington had established in his presidency, and if he were to continue as president, he might bring the government to ruin. Despite saying that he had "the unqualified conviction of [Adams's] unfitness" for the office, Hamilton ended his diatribe strangely enough by supporting the president's re-election. Apparently he was hoping for some sort of combination of electoral votes that would result in a Pinckney victory.[88]

Republicans published excerpts of the leaked *Letter* in newspapers, a far from dignified forum, which compelled a horrified Hamilton to release the whole to the press. Although the *Letter* was not entirely wrong in its assessment of Adams's quirky temperament, when widely circulated, it became a disaster both for Hamilton personally and for the Federalist party. The Federalists were appalled, and the Republicans were gleeful. It was ironic, to say the least, that Republican editors were going to prison for saying some of the very things about the president that Hamilton said

---

86. AH to McHenry, 6 June 1800, *Papers of Hamilton*, 24: 573.
87. AH to Oliver Wolcott, 3 Aug. 1800, *Papers of Hamilton*, 25: 54; Freeman, *Affairs of Honor*, 119.
88. AH, *Papers of Hamilton*, 25: 186–234; Ferling, *Adams vs. Jefferson*, 142–43.

in his pamphlet. Although Hamilton's *Letter* may not by itself have prevented Adams's re-election, its appearance was evidence of the deep division among the Federalists that made Jefferson's election as president more or less inevitable.

That division was brought about by Adams's decision to send a new mission to France, the issue that Hamilton most dwelled on in his *Letter*. Adams, always ready to bemoan his country's neglect of his achievements, considered this decision to try once again to negotiate with France, as he never tired of telling his correspondents, to be "the most disinterested, prudent, and successful conduct in my whole life."[89] This controversial decision may have been precipitate and injudicious, as Hamilton claimed it was, but it did effectively end the war crisis; and thus it undermined the attempts of the extreme Federalists to strengthen the central government and the military establishment of the United States. After months of negotiations, France, under First Consul Napoleon Bonaparte, who would soon make himself emperor, agreed to terms and in 1800 signed the Treaty of Mortefontaine with the United States that brought the Quasi-War to a close and suspended the Franco-American treaty of 1778, thus freeing America from its first of what Jefferson would refer to as "entangling alliances." Unfortunately for Adams, word of the ending of the conflict did not reach America until the Republicans had won the presidency.[90]

89. Freeman, *Affairs of Honor*, 111; Stephen G. Kurtz, *The Presidency of John Adams: The Collapse of Federalism, 1795–1800* (Philadelphia, 1957), 373.
90. Samuel Flagg Bemis, A *Diplomatic History of the United States*, 3rd ed. (New York, 1953), 125.

# 8

# The Jeffersonian Revolution of 1800

Born in reaction to the popular excesses of the Revolution, the Federalist world could not endure. The Federalists of the 1790s stood in the way of popular democracy as it was emerging in the United States, and thus they became heretics opposed to the developing democratic faith. To be sure, they believed in popular sovereignty and republican government, but they did not believe that ordinary people had a direct role to play in ruling the society. They were so confident that the future belonged to them, that the society would become less egalitarian and more hierarchical, that they treated the people with condescension and lost touch with them. "They have attempted," as Noah Webster observed, "to resist the force of public opinion, instead of falling into the current with a view to correct it. In this they have manifested more integrity than address."[1] Indeed, they were so out of touch with the developing popular realities of American life, and their monarchical program was so counter to the libertarian impulses of America's republican ideology, that they provoked a second revolutionary movement that threatened to tear the Republic apart.

Only the electoral victory of the Republicans in 1800 ended this threat and brought, in the eyes of many Americans, the entire revolutionary venture of two and a half decades to successful completion. Indeed, "the Revolution of 1800," as the Republican leader and third president of the United States, Thomas Jefferson, later called it, "was as real a revolution in the principles of our government as that of 1776 was in its form."[2] He and his Republican party took over the presidency and both houses of the Congress in 1801 with a worldview that was fundamentally different from that of the Federalists. Not only were the Republicans opposed to

---

1. David Hackett Fischer, *The Revolution of American Conservatism: The Federalist Party in the Era of Jeffersonian Democracy* (New York, 1965), 151–52.
2. TJ to Spencer Roane, 6 Sept. 1819, in Ford, ed., *Writings of Jefferson*, 10: 140; Susan Dunn, *Jefferson's Second Revolution: The Electoral Crisis of 1800 and the Triumph of Republicanism* (Boston, 2004), 274.

traditional monarchies with their bloated executives, high taxes, oppressive debts, and standing armies and in favor of republics with the least government possible, but they also dreamed of a world different from any that had ever existed, a world of democratic republics in which the scourge of war would at last be eliminated and peace would reign among all nations. It is not surprising that Jefferson's election helped to convince a despairing Alexander Hamilton, the brilliant leader of the Federalists, who more than anyone had pursued the heroic dreams of the age, "that this American world was not meant for me."[3]

JEFFERSON PERSONIFIED this revolutionary transformation. His ideas about liberty and democracy left such a deep imprint on the future of his country that, despite persistent attempts to discredit his reputation, as long as there is a United States he will remain the supreme spokesman for the nation's noblest ideals and highest aspirations.

Yet Jefferson himself was the most unlikely of popular radicals. He was a well-connected and highly cultivated Southern landowner who never had to scramble for his position in Virginia. The wealth and leisure that made possible his great contributions to liberty and democracy were supported by the labor of hundreds of slaves. He was tall—six feet two or three—and gangling, with a reddish freckled complexion, bright hazel eyes, and copper-colored hair, which he tended to wear unpowdered in a queue. Unlike his fellow Revolutionary John Adams, whom he both fought and befriended for fifty years, he was reserved, self-possessed, and incurably optimistic, sometimes to the point of quixoticism. Although he could be shrewd and practical, his sense of the future was sometimes skewed. As late as 1806, for example, he believed that Norfolk, Virginia, would soon surpass New York as a great commercial city and would probably in time become "the greatest sea-port in the United States, New Orleans perhaps excepted."[4] He disliked personal controversy and was always charming in face-to-face relations with both friends and enemies. But at a distance he could hate, and thus many of his opponents concluded that he was two-faced and duplicitous.

He was undoubtedly complicated. He mingled the loftiest visions with astute backroom politicking. He spared himself nothing and was a compulsive shopper, yet he extolled the simple yeoman farmer who was free from the lures of the marketplace. He hated the obsessive money-making,

3. AH to Gouverneur Morris, 29 Feb. 1802, *Papers of Hamilton*, 25: 544.
4. John Melish, *Travels Through the United States of America, in the Years 1806 and 1807, and 1809, 1810, and 1811* (London, 1815), 149.

the proliferating banks, and the liberal capitalistic world that emerged in the Northern states in the early nineteenth century, but no one in America did more to bring that world about. Although he kept the most tidy and meticulous accounts of his daily transactions, he never added up his profits and losses. He thought public debts were the curse of a healthy state, yet his private debts kept mounting as he borrowed and borrowed again to meet his rising expenditures. He was a sophisticated man of the world who loved no place better than his remote mountaintop home in Virginia. This slaveholding aristocrat ended up becoming the most important apostle for liberty and democracy in American history.

Jefferson's narrow victory in the presidential election of 1800 confirmed the changing course of national developments. Jefferson received seventy-three electoral votes to the sixty-five of the Federalist candidate, John Adams. For several weeks even that close victory was in doubt. Because the original Constitution did not state that the electors had to distinguish between their votes for president and those for vice-president, both Jefferson and the Republican vice-presidential candidate, Aaron Burr, had received the same number of electoral votes. Because of this tie, the election, according to the Constitution, was to be thrown into the House of Representatives, where each state congressional delegation would have a single vote. The newly elected Republican-dominated Congress would not be seated until December 1801. Suddenly, there loomed the possibility that the lame-duck Federalists in the Congress would be able to engineer the election of Aaron Burr as president.

Many Federalists wanted to do just that, including John Marshall, whom John Adams in the waning days of his administration had appointed chief justice of the United States. Marshall did not know Burr at all, but he did know Jefferson, his cousin, and he had "almost insuperable objections" to Jefferson's character.[5] Marshall feared what the Republican leader would do to the authority of the nation and the presidency, to the Federalist commercial and banking systems, and to American foreign policy. Federalists figured that Jefferson was a doctrinaire democrat who wanted to take the country back to something resembling the Articles of Confederation, and that he was in the pocket of France and would likely go to war with Great Britain. Burr posed no such threat. Some of the Federalists thought that they might work out a deal with Burr. The country was on the verge of a constitutional crisis.

DURING THE EARLY 1790s Aaron Burr had been one of the most promising leaders in American politics. He had been a member of the

5. Albert J. Beveridge, *The Life of John Marshall* (Boston, 1916), 2: 537.

United States Senate from New York, and in the election of 1796 he had received thirty electoral votes for president. He seemed to have everything a gentleman could want—looks, charm, extraordinary abilities, a Princeton education, distinguished Revolutionary service, and, above all, a notable lineage. John Adams said that he had "never known, in any country, the prejudice in favor of birth, parentage, and descent more conspicuous than in the instance of Colonel Burr." Unlike most of the other Revolutionary leaders, who were the first in their families to attend college, Burr was the son of a president of Princeton and the grandson of another Princeton president—Jonathan Edwards, the most famous theologian in eighteenth-century America—and, said Adams, he "was connected by blood with many respectable families in New England."[6] This presumption that he was already an aristocrat by blood separated Burr from most of the other leaders of the Revolutionary generation. He always had an air of superiority about him, and he always considered himself to be more of a gentleman than other men.[7]

He certainly sought to live the life of an eighteenth-century aristocratic gentleman. He had the best of everything—fine houses, elegant clothes, lavish coaches, superb wines. His sexual excesses and his celebrated liberality flowed from his traditional European notions of gentility. Since real gentlemen were not supposed to work for a living, he could not regard his law practice, or indeed even money—that "paltry object"—with anything but distaste.[8] Like a perfect Chesterfieldian gentleman, he almost never revealed his inner feelings. In several respects he was highly enlightened, especially in his opposition to slavery (despite owning slaves himself) and in his advanced position on the role of women.[9]

The great flaw in Burr's desire to be an eighteenth-century aristocrat was that he lacked the money to bring it off. Money was "contemptible," he said.[10] Despite being one of the most highly paid lawyers in New York, he was perpetually in debt and often on the edge of bankruptcy because of his lavish living. He borrowed over and over and created complicated structures of credit that always threatened to come crashing down. It was this insecure financial situation coupled with his grandiose expectations that led to his wheeling and dealing and self-serving politics.

---

6. James Parton, *The Life and Times of Aaron Burr* (New York, 1858), 1: 235.
7. Milton Lomask, *Aaron Burr* (New York, 1979, 1982), 1: 37, 44.
8. Matthew L. Davis, *Memoirs of Aaron Burr* (New York, 1836), 1: 297.
9. For a modern defense of Burr, see Nancy Isenberg, *Fallen Founder: The Life of Aaron Burr* (New York, 2007).
10. Davis, *Memoirs of Burr*, 1: 297.

Burr could easily have become a Federalist. He viewed politics largely in traditional terms—as contests between "great men" and their followers, tied together by strings of interest and influence. He expected that someone with his pedigree and talent was owed high office as a matter of course, and that naturally public office was to be used to maintain his position and influence. Beyond what politics could do for his friends, his family, and him personally, it had little emotional significance for him. Politics, as he once put it, was "fun and honor & profit."[11]

Of course, other politicians of the early Republic viewed politics in much the same way as Burr did, especially in New York with its family-based factions of Clintons, Livingstons, Van Rensselaers, and Schuylers. Yet no other political leader of his prominence ever spent so much time and energy so blatantly scheming for his own personal and political advantage. And no one of the other great Revolutionary statesmen was so immune to the ideology and the values of the Revolution as Burr was.

Burr certainly had little of the aversion to the use of patronage, or what was often called "corruption," that a Revolutionary ideologue like Jefferson had. Burr was utterly shameless in recommending anyone and everyone for an office—even in the end himself. Jefferson recalled that he had first met Burr when Burr was senator from New York in the early 1790s, and he mistrusted him right away. He remembered that when both the Washington and Adams administrations were about to make a major military or diplomatic appointment, Burr came quickly to the capital "to shew himself" and to let the administration know, in Jefferson's words, "that he was always at market, if they had wanted him." Burr's zealousness over patronage was crucial in eventually convincing Jefferson that Burr was not Jefferson's kind of Republican.[12]

For Burr, befriending people and creating personal loyalties and connections was the way politics and society worked. Aristocrats were patrons, and they had clients who were obliged to them. Hence Burr sought to patronize as many people as he could. His celebrated liberality and generosity grew out of this need. Like any "great man" of the age, he even patronized young artists, including New York painter John Vanderlyn, whom he sent on a grand tour of Europe.

Most of Burr's surviving correspondence deals either with patronage and influence or with speculative money-making schemes. Many of

11. Burr to Aaron Ward, 14 Jan. 1832, in Mary-Jo Kline et al., eds., *Political Correspondence and Public Papers of Aaron Burr* (Princeton, 1983), 2: 1211.
12. TJ, Anas (1804), *Jefferson: Writings*, 693; Mary-Jo Kline, "Aaron Burr as a Symbol of Corruption in the New Republic," in Abraham S. Eisenstadt et al., eds., *Before Watergate: Problems of Corruption in American Society* (Brooklyn, 1978), 71–72.

his letters were the hastily scribbled notes of a busy man who did not have the time or the desire to put much on paper. They were for the moment and, unlike the letters of the other Founders, were rarely written with a future audience in mind. Indeed, he once warned his law clerks, "Things written remain."[13] He was always worried that his letters might "miscarry," and thus he tried to avoid saying anything in them too implicating. "If it were discreet to write plainly," he said at one point, but in his conspiratorial world it was rarely possible to write plainly. He repeatedly appended warnings to his letters: "Say nothing of this to any other person," or "Let no suspicion arise that you have any knowledge of these matters," or "The recommendation must not appear to have been influenced by me," or "You & I should not appear to act in concert."[14]

But the peculiar character of Burr's correspondence goes beyond his preoccupation with haste and secrecy. Burr never developed any ideas about constitutionalism or governmental policy in the way the other Revolutionary statesmen did, because, in truth, he was not much concerned about such matters. If he had an idea about the new federal Constitution of 1787, he left no record of it. Nor did he have much to say about the Federalists' great financial program of the early 1790s. Although he mentioned Hamilton's plan for a national bank at one point in 1791—the year he was elected to the U.S. Senate—he confessed he had not read Hamilton's arguments.[15] Burr had "*no theory*," it was said; he was "a mere matter of fact man." He seems not to have cared much what posterity thought of him. Burr, said Hamilton, in his most damning indictment, "never appeared solicitous for fame."[16]

Burr never pretended to be public-spirited in the fulsome way that Washington, Jefferson, Adams, Madison, Hamilton, and other Founders did. There was nothing self-righteous and hypocritical about him. Perhaps because he was so sure of his aristocratic lineage, he did not have the same emotional need the other Revolutionary statesmen had to justify a gentlemanly status by continually expressing an abhorrence of corruption and a love of virtue.

13. Lomask, *Burr*, 1: 87.
14. Burr to William Eustis, 20 Oct. 1797, to Charles Biddle, 14 Nov. 1804, to John Taylor, 22 May 1791, to Peter Van Gaasbeek, 8 May 1795, to James Monroe, 30 May 1794, to Jonathan Russell, 1 June 1801, to Théophile Cazenove, 8 June 1798, all in Kline et al., eds., *Papers of Burr*, 1: 316; 2: 897; 1: 82, 211, 180; 2: 601; 1: 344.
15. Burr to Theodore Sedgwick, 3 Feb. 1791, in Kline et al., eds., *Papers of Burr*, 1: 68.
16. Theodore Sedgwick to AH, 10 Jan. 1801, AH to James A. Bayard, 16 Jan. 1801, AH to Bayard, 16 Jan. 1801, *Papers of Hamilton*, 25: 311, 321, 320, 323.

In the early 1790s Burr could have gone in several different directions; only a series of accidents and his own trimming temperament had thrown him into the Republican party. He opposed Jay's Treaty and championed the Democratic-Republican Societies against Washington's criticism. When his efforts to become vice-president in 1796 did not pan out, he lost interest in his Senate seat; he stopped attending the sessions and devoted his attention to making money through speculation. Because there were more opportunities for money-making in the state legislature than in the Congress, he entered the New York assembly in the hope of aiding his business associates and restoring his personal fortune. He pushed for tax exemptions, bridge and road charters, land bounties, alien rights to own land—any scheme in which he and his friends had an interest. His manipulation of the Manhattan Company in 1798–1799, where he used a state charter to provide water for the city of New York as a cover for the creation of a bank, was only the most notorious of his self-interested shenanigans.

Burr's political skills were extraordinary. He developed remarkably modern hands-on techniques for organizing the Republican party and getting out the vote. Eventually he built such a strong political machine in New York that he was able to carry the state assembly for the Republicans in the spring elections of 1800. Artisans and other workers in New York City were especially angry at Hamilton and the Federalists' general neglect of their interests, and in the election to the assembly they supported the Republicans by a two-to-one margin.

Since the New York legislature chose the presidential electors, the Republican presidential candidates would be assured of all twelve of New York's electoral votes later that year. The frightening prospect that Jefferson might become president led a desperate Hamilton to urge Governor John Jay to change retroactively the state's electoral rules and reverse the results, telling Jay that "in times like these in which we live, it will not do to be overly scrupulous." It was imperative, he said, "to prevent an *Atheist* in Religion and a *Fanatic* in politics from gaining possession of the helm of the State." Jay never replied, writing on the back of Hamilton's letter, "Proposing a measure for party purposes which it would not become me to adopt."[17]

SINCE THE REPUBLICANS had known that New York would make all the difference in the presidential election of 1800, they had made Burr their candidate for vice-president. No Republican, however, expected him to get the same number of electoral votes as Jefferson.

---

17. AH to John Jay, 7 May 1800, *Papers of Hamilton*, 24: 464–67.

In the House of Representatives nine states were needed for election. Although the Federalists had a majority of congressmen in this lame-duck Congress, they controlled only six state delegations; the Republicans controlled eight. The congressional delegations of two states, Vermont and Maryland, were evenly divided between the two parties. The prospect loomed that no president might be elected in time for the inauguration on March 4, 1801. All sorts of plans flew about—ranging from Federalist ideas of the Federalist-dominated Congress selecting an interim president to Republican ideas of holding a new election. Symptomatic of their contrasting situations, the Federalists relied on legalistic and constitutional manipulations, while the Republicans generally relied on their faith in the people, creating what one scholar has called the "plebiscitarian principle" of the presidency—the notion that the presidency rightfully belongs to the candidate whose party has won an electoral mandate from the voters. Jefferson himself came to describe the presidency in these terms: It was the "Duty of the Chief magistrate...," he said, "to unite in himself the confidence of the whole people" in order to "produce an union of the powers of the whole, and point them in a single direction, as if all constituted but one body & one mind."[18]

Federalists thought they might be able to convince some congressmen to throw the election to Burr. Indeed, so great was the Federalists' fear of Jefferson that many of them thought that simply electing Burr was the best way of keeping Jefferson out of the presidency. Burr, said Federalist Theodore Sedgwick of Massachusetts, was a much safer choice than Jefferson. Burr was no democrat, he was not attached to any foreign nation, and he was not an enthusiast for any sort of theory. He was just an ordinary selfish, interested politician who would promote whatever would benefit him. Burr's "very selfishness," said Sedgwick, was his saving grace. Burr had personally benefited so much from the Federalists' national and commercial systems, said Sedgwick, that he would do nothing to dismantle them.[19]

Hamilton, for one, disagreed violently. To him (and to Jefferson too), Burr's reputation for "selfishness" was precisely the problem. Burr may have represented what most American politicians would eventually become—pragmatic, get-along men—but to Hamilton and Jefferson he

18. Bruce Ackerman, *The Failure of the Founding Fathers: Jefferson, Marshall, and the Rise of Presidential Democracy* (Cambridge, MA, 2005), 85; TJ to John Garland Jefferson, 25 Jan. 1810, *Papers of Jefferson: Retirement Ser.*, 2: 183.
19. Theodore Sedgwick to AH, 10 Jan. 1801, *Papers of Hamilton*, 25: 311–12; James H. Broussard, *The Southern Federalists, 1800–1816* (Baton Rouge, 1978), 33.

violated everything they had thought the American Revolution had been about. There was "no doubt" in Hamilton's mind that "upon every virtuous and prudent calculation" Jefferson was to be preferred to Burr. It was a matter of character, he said: Burr had none, and Jefferson at least had "pretensions to character."[20]

When it seemed likely that the election would end in a tie, Hamilton spared no energy in trying to convince his fellow Federalists to support Jefferson over Burr. Over five or six weeks in December 1800 and January 1801, he wrote letter after letter in a frantic campaign to prevent Burr from becoming president. "For heaven's sake," he pleaded with Sedgwick, "let not the Federal party be responsible for the elevation of this Man." "Burr," he told his correspondents over and over, "is sanguine enough to hope every thing—daring enough to attempt every thing—wicked enough to scruple nothing."[21] Hamilton preferred Jefferson even though they were personal enemies; indeed, he said, "if there be a man in the world I ought to hate, it is Jefferson." And he knew too that the opposite was true with Burr: he had always gotten along well with him personally. But, said Hamilton, his personal relations should not count in this matter. The country's survival was at stake, and "the public good," he insisted, "must be paramount to every private consideration."[22]

Burr did little during the crisis to disabuse people of his reputation for selfishness. Although he did not campaign for the presidency and never approached the Federalists, neither did he announce that he would refuse the presidency and resign the office if he should be elected. Many Republicans would never forgive him for his unwillingness to sacrifice himself for the cause; they assumed that he had intrigued against Jefferson. That he had not done, but he was certainly angry with many of the Republicans, especially those from Virginia who had deceived him in 1792 and 1796.

Over the course of several days in mid-February 1801 the House voted thirty-five times with no majority. Inauguration day, March 4, drew ever closer. Republican newspapers talked of military intervention. The governors of Virginia and Pennsylvania began preparing their state militias for action. Mobs gathered in the capital and threatened to prevent any president from being appointed by statute. On February 15 Jefferson wrote

20. AH to Oliver Wolcott Jr., 16 Dec. 1800, to Gouverneur Morris, 24 Dec. 1800, *Papers of Hamilton*, 25: 257, 272.
21. AH to Theodore Sedgwick, 22 Dec. 1800, to Harrison Gray Otis, 23 Dec. 1800, to Gouverneur Morris, 24 Dec. 1800, *Papers of Hamilton*, 25: 270, 271, 272.
22. AH to Gouverneur Morris, 26 Dec. 1800, *Papers of Hamilton*, 25: 275.

Governor James Monroe of Virginia that the Republicans had warned the Federalists that any statutory naming of a president would lead to the arming of the Middle States and the prevention of any "such usurpation." Moreover, the Republicans threatened to call a new constitutional convention, which, said Jefferson, gave the Federalists "horrors; as in the present democratical spirit of America, they fear they should lose some of the favourite morsels of the constitution."[23]

Finally Congressman James Bayard, a moderate Federalist from Delaware, received from General Samuel Smith, a Republican from Maryland, what Bayard took to be firm assurances from Jefferson that he would preserve the Federalist financial program, maintain the navy, and refrain from dismissing subordinate Federalist officeholders except for cause. Although Jefferson declared that he would not go into the presidency "with my hands tied," and Smith later said that these assurances were his opinion only, Federalists in Congress thought they had a deal with Jefferson.[24] On February 17, 1801, some Federalist delegations abstained from voting, and on the thirty-sixth ballot Jefferson was finally elected president, receiving the vote of ten states to four for Burr, with two states blank.

To avoid a repetition of this electoral impasse, the country adopted the Twelfth Amendment to the Constitution, which allowed the electors to designate their presidential and vice-presidential choices separately in their ballots. This amendment turned the Electoral College from a decision-making body to a device for apportioning votes. It also signaled that presidential politics had become popular in a way the Founders in 1787 had not anticipated.[25]

Although the Republican *Aurora* declared that Jefferson's election meant that "the Revolution of 1776, is now, and for the *first* time arrived at its completion," the confused electoral maneuvering makes it difficult to see the bold and revolutionary character of the event.[26] It was one of the first popular elections in modern history that resulted in the peaceful transfer of power from one "party" to another. Jefferson's inauguration, as one sympathetic observer noted, was "one of the most interesting scenes, a free people could ever witness. The changes of administration, which in every government and in every age have most generally been epochs of

23. TJ to Monroe, 15 Feb. 1801, *Papers of Jefferson*, 32: 594.
24. TJ to Monroe, 15 Feb. 1801, *Papers of Jefferson*, 32: 594.
25. Tadahisa Kuroda, *The Origins of the Twelfth Amendment: The Electoral College in the Early Republic, 1787–1804* (Westport, CT, 1994).
26. Ackerman, *Failure of the Founding Fathers*, 107.

confusion, villainy and bloodshed, in this our happy country take place without any species of distraction, or disorder."[27]

At the outset Jefferson himself struck a note of conciliation: "We are all republicans—we are all federalists," he declared in his inaugural address—an expression of his traditional desire, shared by some other Republicans, to get rid of unnecessary party designations. The chasm that the Federalists had created between the federal government and the people was now closed, and there was no real need any longer for the Republican party. Because the Republicans believed that they were "the people," they were willing to absorb many Federalists into their cause, thus reinforcing the sense of continuity with the 1790s.

Consequently, the Jeffersonian "Revolution of 1800" has blended nearly imperceptibly into the main democratic currents of American history. Jefferson himself was sensible of his inability to accomplish "all the reformation which reason would suggest and experience approve." He was not free to do whatever he thought best, he said; he realized how difficult it was "to advance the notions of a whole people suddenly to ideal right," and he concluded "that no more good must be attempted than the people will bear."[28] Still, when compared to the consolidated heroic European-like state that the Federalists tried to build in the 1790s, what Jefferson and the Republicans did after 1800 proved that a real revolution—as real as Jefferson said it was—had taken place.[29]

IN HIS INAUGURAL ADDRESS the fifty-seven-year-old Thomas Jefferson contemplated "a rising nation, spread over a wide and fruitful land, traversing all the seas with the rich productions of their industry, engaged in commerce with nations that feel power and forget right, advancing rapidly to destinies beyond the reach of mortal eye." America, he said, was "the world's best hope," and it possessed "the strongest Government on earth." It was "a chosen country, with room enough for our descendents to the thousandth and thousandth generation." He believed

27. Mrs. Samuel Harrison Smith (Margaret Bayard), *Forty Years of Washington Society*, ed. Gaillard Hunt (London, 1906), 25.

28. TJ to Dr. Walter Jones, 31 March 1801, in L and B, eds., *Writings of Jefferson*, 10: 255–56.

29. Since Henry Adams, most historians have played down the radical character of Jefferson's election in 1800. But see Jeffrey L. Pasley, "1800 as a Revolution in Political Culture: Newspapers, Celebrations, Voting and Democratization in the Early Republic," in James Horn, Jan Ellen Lewis, and Peter S. Onuf, eds., *The Revolution of 1800: Democracy, Race, and the New Republic* (Charlottesville, 2002), 121, 52.

that the spirit of 1776 had finally been fulfilled and that the United States could at last become a beacon of liberty for the world. "A just and solid republican government" of the kind he sought to build, he said, "will be a standing monument & example for the aim & imitation of the people of other countries." The American Revolution was a world-historical event, something "new under the sun," he told the radical scientist Joseph Priestley. It had excited the minds of "the mass of mankind," he said, and its "consequences will ameliorate the condition of man over a great portion of the globe." No wonder Jefferson became the fount of American democracy, for he set forth at the outset of his presidency a body of American ideas and ideals that have persisted to this day.[30]

Believing that most of the evils afflicting human beings in the past had flowed from the abuses of inflated political establishments, Jefferson and the Republicans in 1800 deliberately set about to carry out what they rightly believed was the original aim of the Revolution: to reduce the overweening and dangerous power of government. Both Jefferson and his fellow Republicans wanted to form a national republic based on the eighteenth-century country-Whig opposition ideology that held that the smaller the government, the better. Jefferson had not initially much liked the Constitution. He thought the president was "a bad edition of a Polish king." In fact, he thought that three or four new articles added "to the good, old, and venerable fabrick" of the Articles of Confederation would have sufficed.[31] In 1801 he and his fellow Republicans were in a position to ensure that the United States would continue to be spoken of in the plural, as a union of separate sovereign states, which remained the case through the entire antebellum period. In short, they aimed to make the central government's authority resemble that of the old Articles of Confederation rather than that of the European-type state that the Federalists had sought to build. To do so, Jefferson and his colleagues had to create a general government that could rule without the traditional attributes of power.

From the outset Jefferson was determined that the new government would spurn even the usual rituals of power. At the very beginning he set a new tone of republican simplicity that was in sharp contrast to the stiff formality and regal ceremony with which the Federalists had surrounded the presidency. No elaborately ornamented coach drawn by four or six horses for Jefferson: the president-elect walked from his boardinghouse

---

30. TJ, First Inaugural Address, 4 March 1801, TJ to Dickinson, 6 March 1801, TJ to Priestley, 21 Mar. 1801, *Jefferson: Writings*, 493–96, 1084, 1086.
31. TJ to JA, 13 Nov. 1787, *Papers of Jefferson*, 12: 351.

on New Jersey Avenue to his inauguration without any fanfare whatsoever. He immediately sold the coaches, horses, and silver harnesses that President Adams had used and kept only a one-horse market cart.

That day in March 1801 on which he became president, he said, "buried levees, birthdays, royal parades, and the arrogation of precedence in society by certain self-stiled friends of order, but truly stiled friends of privileged orders."[32] Since the Federalist presidents Washington and Adams, like the English monarchs, had delivered their addresses to the Congress "from the throne," Jefferson chose to deliver his message in writing to which no formal answer from the Congress would be expected; this set a precedent that was not broken until the presidency of Woodrow Wilson. Unlike Washington and Adams, Jefferson ("his Democratic majesty," as one person called him) made himself easily accessible to visitors, all of whom, no matter how distinguished, he received, as the British chargé reported, "with a most perfect disregard to ceremony both in his dress and manner." His dress was often informal, he sometimes greeted guests in carpet slippers, and he wore his hair, said one observer, "in negligent disorder, though not ungracefully."[33]

At American state occasions President Jefferson, to the shock of foreign dignitaries, replaced the protocol and the distinctions of European court life with the egalitarian rules of what he called "pell-mell" or "next the door," which essentially meant, sit wherever one wanted. His treatment of the new pompous minister from Great Britain, Anthony Merry, became notorious. Not only did Jefferson greet Merry in his usual casual manner, but he added to the minister's astonishment at a dinner by paying no attention to Merry and his wife's rank in seating and by inviting the French minister to the same dinner, even though the two countries were at war. After this experience, Merry never accepted another invitation to dine with the president.

While Jefferson's gentlemanly tastes scarcely allowed for any actual leveling in social gatherings, his symbolic transformation of manners at the capital reflected changes that were taking place in American society. For the Republican revolution brought to the national government men who, unlike Jefferson, did not have the outward manners of gentlemen, who did not know one another, and who were decidedly not at home in polite society. Over half the members of the Republican-dominated Seventh Congress that convened in December 1801, for example, were new.[34]

32. Dumas Malone, *Jefferson the President: First Term, 1801–1805* (Boston, 1970), 388.
33. Malone, *Jefferson the President: First Term*, 383, 93.
34. James Sterling Young, *The Washington Community, 1800–1828* (New York, 1966), 90.

The British envoy in Washington wondered how long such a system of ordinary men with humble occupations promoting the "low arts of popularity" could last. "The excess of the democratic ferment in this people is continuously evinced by the dregs having got to the top."[35]

THE REMOVAL OF THE NATIONAL CAPITAL in 1800 from Philadelphia to the rural wilderness of the Federal City on the Potomac accentuated the transformation of power. It dramatized the Republicans' attempt to separate the national government from intimate involvement in the society. "Congress were almost overawed by the city [of Philadelphia]," recalled Matthew Lyon of his experiences as a congressman in the 1790s; "measures were dictated by that city." Lyon even referred to the sources of influence as "a commanding lobby," one of the first instances of the term being used in this modern sense. Other congressmen had also feared the influence of Philadelphia's lobbyists. "We talk of our independence," Nathaniel Macon of North Carolina reminded his congressional colleagues, "but every man in Congress, when at Philadelphia, knew that city had more than its proportional weight in the councils of the Union." To prevent this kind of social and commercial pressure, many of the Republicans aimed to erect the very kind of government that Hamilton in *Federalist* No. 27 had warned against, "a government at a distance and out of sight" that could "hardly be expected to interest the sensations of the people."[36]

The new capital, as a British diplomat noted, was "like no other in the world." It was surrounded by woods, its streets were muddy and filled with tree stumps, its landscape was swampy and mosquito infested, and its unfinished government buildings stood like Roman ruins in a deserted ancient city. Although one could easily get mired in the red mud of Pennsylvania Avenue, "excellent snipe shooting and even partridge shooting was to be had on each side of the main avenue and even close under the wall of the Capitol."[37] Cows grazed on the Mall, and Pierre L'Enfant's splendid squares were used as vegetable gardens. Not a single merchant house stood in the city, nor anything in the way of clubs or theaters. Land

35. Dumas Malone, *Jefferson the President: Second Term, 1805–1809* (Boston, 1974), 568.
36. Jeffrey L. Pasley, "Private Access and Public Power: Gentility and Lobbying in the Early Congress," in Kenneth R. Bowling and Donald R. Kennon, eds., *The House and Senate in the 1790s: Petitioning, Lobbying, and Institutional Development* (Athens, OH, 2002), 74–76.
37. Richard Beale Davis, ed., *Jeffersonian America: Note on the United States of America Collected in the Years 1805–6–7 and 11–12 by Sir Augustus John Foster, Bart.* (San Marino, CA, 1954), 49.

auctions were held, but few bids were made. Washington's hopes for a national university in the city went begging. The Potomac was dredged, bridges were built, but still no trade, no business, came to the capital. The bulk of the tiny population seemed to be on poor relief.

The Federal City remained such a primitive and desolate village that, in the words of the secretary of the British legation, "one may take a ride of several hours within the precincts without meeting a single individual to disturb one's meditations."[38] Since houses were scattered and had no street numbers and the few existing roads had no lamps and often trailed off into cow paths, people easily got lost. If it had been completed, the Capitol would have been imposing, but the Senate and House chambers stood in unfinished isolation, joined by only a covered boardwalk. Inside the Capitol, the design and workmanship were so poor that columns split, roofs leaked, and portions of the ceilings collapsed. Still, Jefferson lived with the hope, as he said in 1808, that "the work when finished will be a durable and honorable monument of our infant republic, and will bear favorable comparison with the remains of the same kind of the ancient republics of Greece and Rome."[39]

The "President's Palace," as the White House was originally called, was the largest house in the country and, because of Washington's influence, was as impressive as the Capitol, but it was equally unfinished. For years its grounds resembled a construction site with workmen's shacks, privies, and old brick-kilns scattered about, so cluttered, in fact, that visitors to the President's House were always in danger of falling into a pit or stumbling into a heap of rubbish. Because of the unwillingness of the parsimonious Republican Congress to spend money, everything in the capital remained unfinished, complained the English-trained architect Benjamin Latrobe, who had migrated to the United States in 1796 and had become surveyor of public buildings under Jefferson.[40]

In other words, this new and remote capital, the city of Washington in the District of Columbia, utterly failed to attract the population, the commerce, and the social and cultural life that were needed to make what its original planners had boldly expected, the Rome of the New World. Instead of acquiring the population of one hundred sixty thousand that one of the city's commissioners had predicted "as a matter of course in a few years," Washington remained for the next two decades an out-of-the-way village of less than ten thousand inhabitants whose principal business

38. Davis, ed., *Jeffersonian America*, 8.
39. Malone, *Jefferson the President: Second Term*, 540.
40. Young, *Washington Community*, 46; William Seale, *The President's House* (Washington, DC, 1986), 47–50.

was the keeping of boardinghouses.⁴¹ Situated on a marsh, the Federal City fully deserved the many jibes of visitors, including that of the Irish poet Thomas Moore:

> This fam'd metropolis, where fancy sees
> Squares in morasses, obelisks in trees;
> Which traveling fools and gazetteers adorn
> With shrines unbuilt and heroes yet unborn,
> Though nought but wood and [Jefferson] they see,
> Where streets should run and sages *ought* to be!⁴²

THE REPUBLICANS IN FACT meant to have an insignificant national government. The federal government, Jefferson declared in his first message to Congress in 1801, was "charged with the external and mutual relations only of these states." All the rest—the "principal care of our persons, our property, and our reputation, constituting the great field of human concerns"—were to be left to the states, which Jefferson thought were the best governments in the world.⁴³ Such a limited national government meant turning back a decade of Federalist policy in order to restore what Virginia Republican theorist John Taylor called the "pristine health" of the Constitution. The Sedition Act was allowed to lapse, and a new liberal naturalization law was adopted. Because of what Jefferson called the Federalist "scenes of favoritism" and "dissipation of treasure," strict economy was ordered to root out corruption.⁴⁴

The inherited Federalist governmental establishment was small even by eighteenth-century European standards. In 1801 the headquarters of the War Department, for example, consisted of only the secretary, an accountant, fourteen clerks, and two messengers. The secretary of state had a staff consisting of a chief clerk, six other clerks (one of whom ran the patent office), and a messenger. The attorney general did not yet even have a clerk. Nevertheless, in Jefferson's eyes, this tiny federal bureaucracy had become "too complicated, too expensive," and offices under the Federalists had "multiplied unnecessarily."⁴⁵

The number of offices had certainly grown over the previous decade. The listing of offices in the early 1790s took up only eleven pages; ten

41. Young, *Washington Community*, 23.
42. Thomas Moore, *Epistles, Odes, and Other Poems* (Philadelphia, 1806), 154.
43. TJ, First Annual Message, 8 Dec. 1801, *Jefferson: Writings*, 504.
44. Noble E. Cunningham Jr., *The Process of Government Under Jefferson* (Princeton, 1978), 22.
45. TJ, First Annual Message, 8 Dec. 1801, *Jefferson: Writings*, 504.

years later the roll filled nearly sixty pages.[46] Everywhere in the previous Federalist administrations, Jefferson saw "expenses...for jobs not seen; agencies upon agencies in every part of the earth, and for the most useless or mischievous purposes, and all of these opening doors for fraud and embezzlement far beyond the ostensible profits of the agency."[47] Thus the roll of federal officials had to be severely cut back. All tax inspectors and collectors were eliminated, which shrank the number of treasury employees by 40 percent. The diplomatic establishment was reduced to three missions—in Britain, France, and Spain. If Jefferson could have had his way, he would have gotten rid of all the foreign missions. Like other enlightened believers in the possibility of universal peace, he longed to have only commercial connections with other nations.[48]

The Republicans were determined to destroy the Federalist dream of creating a modern army and navy. When Jefferson learned early in 1800 of Napoleon's coup d'état of November 1799 that overthrew the French Republic, he did not draw the lesson the Federalists did: that too much democracy led to dictatorship. Instead, he said, "I read it as a lesson against standing armies."[49] After he took office, he made sure that the military budget was cut in half. Since the armed forces had been the largest cause of non-debt-related spending in the 1790s, amounting to nearly 40 percent of the total federal budget, this action meant a severe decrease in the overall expenditures of the national government.

Because the officer corps of the army was Federalist-dominated, it needed to be radically reformed, with the most partisan Federalist officers dismissed and the rest made loyal to the Republican administration. Although Jefferson in the 1790s had opposed the creation of a military academy, he now favored the establishment of one at West Point as a means of educating Republican army officers, especially those whose families lacked the wealth to send their sons to college. The Military Peace Establishment Act of 1802 that laid the basis for Jefferson's reform of the army gave the president extraordinary powers over the new academy and the Corps of Engineers charged with its operation.[50]

Until it could be thoroughly "republicanized," the army, stationed in the West, was left with three thousand regulars and only 172 officers. The

46. Malone, *Jefferson the President: First Term*, 69.
47. Cunningham, *Process of Government Under Jefferson*, 22.
48. Malone, *Jefferson the President: First Term*, 386.
49. TJ to Samuel Adams, 26 Feb. 1800, *Papers of Jefferson*, 31: 395.
50. Theodore J. Crackel, *Mr. Jefferson's Army: Political and Social Reform of the Military Establishment, 1801–1809* (New York, 1987); Robert M. S. McDonald, *Thomas Jefferson's Military Academy: The Founding of West Point* (Charlottesville, 2004).

state militias were enough for America's defense, said Jefferson. Although the navy's war machine consisted of only a half-dozen frigates, Jefferson wanted to replace this semblance of a standing navy with several hundred small, shallow-draft gunboats, which were intended simply for inland waters and harbor defense. They would be the navy's version of the militia, unquestionably designed for defense of the coastline and not for risky military ventures on the high seas. Such small, defensive ships, said Jefferson, could never "become an excitement to engage in offensive maritime war" and were unlikely to provoke naval attacks from hostile foreign powers.[51] The kind of permanent military establishment the Federalists had desired was both expensive and, more important, a threat to liberty.

Since Hamilton's financial program had formed the basis of the heightened political power of the federal government, it above all had to be dismantled—at least to the extent possible. It mortified Jefferson that his government inherited "the contracted, English, half-lettered ideas of Hamilton. . . . We can pay off his debt in 15 years, but we can never get rid of his financial system." But something could be done. All the internal excise taxes the Federalists had designed to make the people feel the energy of the national government were eliminated. For most citizens the federal presence was reduced to the delivery of the mail. Such an inconsequential and distant government, noted one observer in 1811, was "too little felt in the ordinary concerns of life to vie in any considerable degree with the nearer and more powerful influence produced by the operations of the local governments."[52]

ALTHOUGH JEFFERSON'S EXTREMELY ABLE secretary of the treasury, Albert Gallatin, persuaded the reluctant president to keep the Bank of the United States, the government was under continual pressure to reduce the Bank's influence, especially from state banking interests. When the Bank of the United States was chartered in 1791, there were only four state banks; but since then their numbers had grown and were continuing to grow dramatically, twenty-eight by 1800, eighty-seven by 1811, and 246 by 1816. Despite the hopes of some Federalists that the branches of the BUS might absorb the state banks, that had not happened. In 1791 Fisher Ames had predicted that "the state Banks will

51. Ian W. Toll, *Six Frigates: The Epic History of the Founding of the U.S. Navy* (New York, 2006), 285.
52. TJ to Pierre-Samuel du Pont de Nemours, 18 Jan. 1802, in Ford, ed., *Writings of Jefferson*, 8: 127; Davis, ed., *Jeffersonian America*, 3.

become unfriendly to that of the U.S. Causes of hatred & rivalry will abound. The state banks...may become dangerous instruments in the hands of state partisans."[53] Ames was correct. The proliferating state banks resented the restraints the BUS was able to place on their ability to issue paper money, and from the beginning they sought to weaken or destroy it.

Then as now banking remained a mysterious business for many Americans. Many of the Southern planters scarcely understood banking, and those Northern gentry who lived off salaries or proprietary wealth such as rents and interest from money out on loan were not much more knowledgeable. The only real money, of course, was specie or gold and silver. But since there was never enough specie and it was unwieldy to carry, the banks issued pieces of paper (that is, made loans) in their own names, promising to pay gold and silver to the bearer on demand. Yet most people, confident that the bank could redeem their notes at any time, did not bother to have them redeemed and instead passed the notes on to one another in commercial exchanges. The banks soon realized they could lend out two, three, four, or five times in paper notes the amount of gold and silver they had in their vaults to cover these notes. Since the banks made money from these loans, they had a vested interest in issuing as many notes as they could.

Opposition to the Bank of the United States came from two principal sources: from Southern agrarians like Jefferson who never understood banks and hated them, and from the entrepreneurial interests of the state banks who did not like their paper-issuing abilities restrained in any way. In 1792 Jefferson was so angry at Hamilton that he told Madison that the federal government's chartering of the BUS, which it had no right to do, was "an act of *treason*" against the states, and anyone who tried to "act under colour of the authority of a foreign legislature" (that is, the federal Congress) and issue and pass notes ought to be "adjudged guilty of high treason and suffer death accordingly, by the judgment of the state courts." Obviously this was one of those times that Madison was referring to when he said that Jefferson, like other "men of great genius," had a habit of "expressing in strong and round terms, impressions of the moment." Jefferson never really accepted the idea of a bank ("a source of poison and corruption") or the paper it issued. Such paper, he said, was designed "to enrich swindlers at the expense of the honest and industrious part of the

53. Ames to AH, 31 July 1791, *Papers of Hamilton*, 8: 590; Richard Sylla, John B. Legler, and John J. Wallis, "Banks and State Public Finance in the New Republic," *Journal of Economic History*, 47 (1987), 391–403.

nation." He could not comprehend how "legerdemain tricks upon paper can produce as solid wealth or hard labor in the earth. It is vain for common sense to urge that *nothing* can produce but *nothing*."[54]

But the more important enemies of the BUS were the state banks. By regularly redeeming the outstanding notes of the state banks, the BUS had checked their ability to issue notes too far in excess of what they could cover with specie, that is, their reserves; and this had become a deep source of anger. In addition, the state banks resented the monopolistic position the BUS had in holding the national government's deposits and condemned it for being Federalist and British-dominated. Jefferson agreed. If they had to exist, then, as he told Gallatin in 1803, he was "decidedly in favor of making all the banks republican by sharing [the federal government's] deposits amongst them in proportion to the dispositions they show," by which he meant their loyalty to the Republican cause.[55] When the twenty-year charter of Hamilton's BUS was about to expire in 1811, it was not surprising that these state banks were determined that it would not be renewed.

Despite the opposition of President Jefferson and later President Madison to the BUS, Gallatin, who knew something about banks and had created in 1793 a state bank for Pennsylvania modeled on the BUS, urged that the Bank of the United States be issued a new charter. He knew that the issue was tricky, that the Virginia Republicans regarded the Bank as a British bank, and he worried that the question might become "blended with or affected by... extraneous political considerations." As early as 1808 the Bank applied for renewal of its charter, and Gallatin earnestly supported the application, offering to enlarge the number of stockholders so as to include fewer foreigners. Congress delayed dealing with the issue until 1811. By this time the radical Republican press was excoriating Gallatin for showing "alarming symptoms in the English style."[56] Despite Gallatin's enthusiastic backing of a new charter for the BUS, the Congress by the closest of votes denied the re-chartering, and the state banks had their victory and the national government's deposits. Gallatin warned

54. Bray Hammond, *Banks and Politics from the Revolution to the Civil War* (Princeton, 1957), 188, 196, 189; TJ to JM, 1 Oct. 1792, *Republic of Letters*, 740; Gordon S. Wood, *Revolutionary Characters: What Made the Founders Different* (New York, 2006), 110; TJ to Col. Charles Yancey, 6 Jan. 1816, in Paul Ford, ed., *Works of Thomas Jefferson: Federal Edition* (1904–05), 11: 494.

55. Howard Bodenhorn, *State Banking in Early America: A New Economic History* (New York, 2003), 14.

56. Raymond Walters Jr., *Albert Gallatin: Jeffersonian Financier and Diplomat* (New York, 1957), 237, 239.

that the switch to the state banks would be "attended with much individual, and probably with no inconsiderable public injury," and questioned "why an untried system should be substituted to one under which the treasury business had so long been conducted with perfect security," but all to no avail.[57]

Although Gallatin later blamed the defeat more on the Republican ideologues than on pressure from the state banks, the result was that the federal government distributed its patronage among twenty-one state banks and thus effectively diluted its authority to control either the society or the economy.

With the demise of the BUS, America suddenly went wild in creating new banks. Seventy-one banks, including the BUS, had been created in the two decades between 1790 and 1811. In the next five years 175 additional state-chartered banks were established. These banks, unlike the original Bank of North America or the BUS, were not just sources of credit for government, not just commercial banks, handling short-term credit for merchants, but banks for all the different economic interests of the society that wanted easy, long-term credit—mechanics and farmers as well as governments and merchants. In 1792 the Massachusetts legislature had required the second state bank it created to lend at least 20 percent of its funds to citizens living outside of the city of Boston in order that the bank "shall wholly and exclusively regard the agricultural interest."[58] The state charter setting up the Farmers and Mechanics Bank of Philadelphia in 1809 had stipulated that a majority of the directors be "farmers, mechanics, and manufacturers actually employed in their respective professions." Many new charters had similar requirements.[59]

And these banks were to be located not merely in the large urban centers such as Philadelphia or Boston but also in such outlying areas as Westerly, Rhode Island, where a new bank established in 1800, called Washington Trust, justified itself by declaring that existing state banks in Providence, Newport, and Bristol were "too remote or too confined in their operations to diffuse their benefits so generally to the country as could be wished." By 1818 the tiny state of Rhode Island, one of the most

---

57. Albert Gallatin to William H. Crawford, 30 Jan. 1811, in E. James Ferguson, ed., *Selected Writings of Albert Gallatin* (Indianapolis, 1967), 277.

58. Pauline Maier, "The Debate over Incorporations: Massachusetts in the Early Republic," in Conrad Edick Wright, ed., *Massachusetts and the New Nation* (Boston, 1992), 111; J. Van Fenstermaker, *The Development of American Commercial Banking, 1782–1837* (Kent, OH, 1965), 4–14.

59. Hammond, *Banks and Politics*, 145, 165; Charles G. Steffen, *The Mechanics of Baltimore: Workers and Politics in the Age of Revolution* (Urbana, IL, 1984), 192–95.

commercially advanced in the nation, had twenty-seven banks. In 1813 the Pennsylvania legislature in a single bill authorized incorporation of twenty-five new banks. After the governor vetoed this bill, the legislature in 1814 passed over the governor's veto another bill incorporating forty-one banks. As early as 1793 John Swanwick of Philadelphia had envisioned banks sprouting up in all the provincial towns of the state. "Their number will be so far multiplied," he told the Pennsylvania legislature, "that it will be no longer a favor to obtain discounts." By the end of the second decade of the nineteenth century it seemed to one observer that nearly every village in the country had a bank; wherever there was a church, a tavern, and a blacksmith, one could usually find a bank as well. By 1818 Kentucky had forty-three new banks, two of them in towns that had fewer than one hundred inhabitants.[60]

It was the proliferation of these state-chartered banks and their issuing of notes that enabled the states to have paper money after all—despite the Constitution's prohibition in Article I, Section 10 against the states themselves issuing bills of credit.[61] Indeed, since, unlike today, the federal government did not issue any paper money, without these increasing bank notes (that is, credit) the society could never have commercialized as rapidly as it did. By 1815 over two hundred banks had deposits and note liabilities of about $90 million backed by only $17 million of specie.[62] In 1808 the Farmers' Exchange Bank of Gloucester (now Glocester), Rhode Island, emitted over $600,000 in paper; it had, however, only $86.45 in specie to support these notes. This was too much, even for Rhode Island, which had a notorious reputation for excessive paper emissions or loose credit; and in 1809 the state legislature closed the bank, making it the first bank to fail in United States history.[63]

The American economy floated on paper. "The circulation of our country," Senator James Lloyd of Massachusetts declared in 1811, "is at present emphatically a paper circulation; very little specie passes in exchange between individuals." With this extraordinary multiplication of banks, entrepreneurial farmers in the backcountry had the money and

---

60. Hammond, *Banks and Politics*, 147; Pennsylvania *General Advertiser*, 16 Feb. 1793; Richard Gabriel Stone, *Hezekiah Niles as an Economist* (Baltimore, 1933), 94–95; Fenstermaker, *American Commercial Banking*, 8.

61. In *Briscoe v. Bank of the Commonwealth of Kentucky* (1837) the Supreme Court determined that Article 1, Section 10, prohibiting the states from issuing paper money, did not apply to the banks chartered by the states.

62. Hammond, *Banks and Politics*, 188, 196.

63. Jane Kamensky, *The Exchange Artist: A Tale of High-Flying Speculation and America's First Banking Collapse* (New York, 2008), 9, 160.

the sources of credit they had long desired, and the agrarian unrest that had troubled the rural areas in the aftermath of the Revolution tended to subside. Indeed, Americans had created a modern financial system that was the equal of any in the world. According to two economic historians, the United States in the early nineteenth century became "history's most successful emerging market, attracting the capital of investors in older nations seeking higher returns."[64]

REPUBLICANIZING THE BANKING SYSTEM may have become important to Jefferson, but shrinking the debt was far more crucial: it went to the heart of the Republicans' conception of government. Precisely because Hamilton had regarded the permanent federal debt as a principal source of support for the national government, Jefferson and the Republicans were determined to pay it off—and quickly. More important, they regarded the ability of governments to borrow money as the major means by which nations carried on war, something they wished to avoid. In 1798 Jefferson actually thought of amending the Constitution by "taking from the federal government the power of borrowing." He knew "that to pay all proper expences within the year would, in case of war, be hard on us." But the alternative was worse, "ten wars instead of one. For wars would be reduced in that proportion."[65] But in 1801 he knew such a proposal would be controversial, and the same end could be accomplished by severe economy.[66] Each year of his presidency he habitually called for further reductions in the debt. If the public debt were not extinguished, he warned Gallatin in 1809, "we shall be committed to the English career of debt, corruption and rottenness, closing with revolution. The discharge of the debt, therefore, is vital to the destinies of our government."[67]

By 1810, even with the $15 million in cash and claims spent on the Louisiana Purchase, the Republicans had reduced the federal debt to half of the $80 million it had been when they took office. Jefferson was obsessed with the power of debt. It was not only a matter of preventing a present generation from burdening its descendants or of reducing the wherewithal of waging war. He also wanted to destroy what he considered

---

64. Hammond, *Banks and Politics*, 189; Peter L. Rousseau and Richard Sylla, "Emerging Financial Markets and Early US Growth," *Explorations in Economic History*, 42 (2005), 1–26, quotation at 20–21.

65. TJ to Taylor, 26 Nov. 1798, *Papers of Jefferson*, 30: 589.

66. Herbert E. Sloan, *Principle and Interest: Thomas Jefferson and the Problem of Debt* (New York, 1995), 196.

67. TJ to Gallatin, 11 Oct. 1809, in Ford, ed., *Writings of Jefferson*, 9: 264.

an insidious and dangerous instrument of political influence. Eliminating the public debt was part of his ultimate desire to create an entirely new kind of government, one without privilege or patronage.

Perhaps nothing illustrates Jefferson's radical conception of government better than his problems with patronage. In the radical Whig-country view of politics, patronage—appointing people to office and creating clients—was corruption. Jefferson believed that Hamilton, like all the eighteenth-century English ministers of the crown, had built support for his program by essentially buying people off—giving them offices or other favors. When Jefferson assumed the presidency in 1801, he was determined to do things differently, to create a republican government that was free of corruption.

The problem was that not all Republicans took his assault on patronage as seriously as he did. Many of them, alarmed by his suggestion in his inaugural address that "we are all republicans, we are all federalists," thought that he might not thoroughly oust the enemy. Some were reluctant to join a government in which they might have few sources of influence. With the slashing reductions contemplated for the navy, for example, Jefferson had to go to his fifth choice before he got Robert Smith of Maryland to serve as secretary of the navy. Jefferson tried to assure his colleagues that the conciliatory words in his inaugural address referred only to the large body of Federalists, not their leaders. But the Republicans wanted more than just a few officers removed. "Elective government would then be contemptible indeed," declared William Duane's *Aurora*, "if a change of a few superior individuals, without regard to the virtues or integrity of subordinate agents, were to be the only consequences."[68]

Jefferson felt beleaguered by this sort of pressure. "It is the business of removal and appointment," Jefferson grumbled to John Dickinson in June 1801, "which presents the serious difficulties. All others compared with these, are as nothing." Time and again the president found himself caught between his conscientious determination to avoid anything resembling Hamilton's corruption and the pressing demands of his fellow Republicans that he give them the offices they deserved. In his reply to a group of New Haven merchants in July 1801 he suggested the Republicans were owed at least "a proportionate share in the direction of the public affairs," by which he seems to have meant about one-half the offices. His Republican colleagues, however, interpreted the phrase to mean something closer to three-quarters, and this became the rule. The

68. Noble Cunningham Jr., *The Jeffersonian Republicans in Power: Party Operations, 1801–1809* (Chapel Hill, 1963), 17.

Federalists were furious and castigated the president for being "the head of a party & not of the nation." No wonder that Jefferson complained that the removal and appointment of officeholders was the heaviest burden of his presidency.[69]

Of course, once the Federalists were replaced by Republicans, there was no further need for the Republicans to compromise on this issue of patronage, and removals from office for political reasons came to an end. Under Jefferson and his Republican successors, James Madison, James Monroe, and John Quincy Adams, the holders of federal government appointments became a permanent officialdom of men grown old in their positions.

Still, many Republican congressmen remained eager to isolate themselves from all executive influence in their desire to prevent the Congress from becoming "a corrupt, servile, dependent and contemptible body" like the British House of Commons. With Jefferson himself being "averse to giving contracts of any kind to members of the Legislature," Congress in 1808 explicitly forbade this practice in order to maintain, as one Virginia congressman put it, "the purity of the Representative body."[70] Despite this legislative isolation, however, Jefferson was able personally to direct Congress and the Republican party to an extraordinary degree. He used a combination of his initial patronage and some improvised forms of political influence — in particular his use of confidential legislative agents and his weekday legislative dinner parties with congressmen, usually eight in number with no women present.

As Federalist Manasseh Cutler observed in 1802, Jefferson held no levees but instead held dinners for the congressmen in rotation. "Strange" as it seemed, said Cutler, "(if anything done here can be strange) only Federalists or only Democrats are invited at the same time." The idea, as Jefferson explained in 1806, was to bring congressmen and the president together to "know one another and have opportunities of little explanations of circumstances, which, [if] not understood might produce jealousies and suspicions injurious to the public interest." Of course, as the numbers of Federalists in Congress declined, fewer of them needed to be invited to dinner.[71]

69. Cunningham, *Jeffersonian Republicans in Power*, 23–29; Broussard, *Southern Federalists*, 44.

70. Leonard D. White, *The Jeffersonians: A Study in Administrative History, 1801–1829* (New York, 1951), 81.

71. Jon Kukla, *Mr. Jefferson's Women* (New York, 2007), 185; Merry Ellen Scofield, "The Fatigues of His Table: The Politics of Presidential Dining During the Jefferson Administration," *JER*, 26 (2006), 449–69.

Yet Jefferson's personal influence and his notable achievements as president cannot obscure the remarkable transformation in the traditional meaning of government that the Republican revolution of 1800 created. During the opening decades of the nineteenth century, especially after Jefferson retired from the presidency, the United States government was weaker than at any other time in its history. Foreign immigrants were astonished that the national "government" in America made "no sensation." "It is round about you like the air," said a startled William Sampson fresh from Ireland, "and you cannot even feel it."[72]

THE JEFFERSONIAN REVOLUTION was an extraordinary and unprecedented experiment in governing without the traditional instruments of power. Governments in the early nineteenth century were not supposed to cut taxes, shrink their bureaucracies, pay off their debts, reduce their armed forces, and diminish their coercive power. No government in history had ever voluntarily cut back its authority. With such a diminished and weakened government, how would the society hold together? Jefferson and the other Republican leaders had an answer, an enlightened answer that makes their political experiment one of the most idealistic in American if not world history. They imagined that people's natural sociability and willingness to sacrifice their selfish interests for the sake of the whole would be sufficient social adhesives. And if these republican ideas could spread, perhaps the world itself would become a different place.

But for Hamilton and the Federalists these imaginings were nothing but "pernicious dreams." By abandoning monarchical ceremonies and rituals, force, and governmental corruption—the main instruments by which eighteenth-century governments had held their turbulent societies together and ruled—the Republicans, said a disgruntled Hamilton, were offering "the bewitching tenets of the illuminated doctrine, which promises men, ere long, an emancipation from the burdens and restraints of government." As early as 1794 Hamilton had been alarmed by the extraordinarily utopian idea coming out of the French Revolution "that but a small portion of power is requisite to Government." And some radicals believed that "even this is only temporarily necessary" and could be done away with once "the bad habits" of the ancien régime were eliminated. Unfortunately, said Hamilton, there were wishful thinkers in both France and America who assumed that, "as human nature shall refine and ameliorate by the operation of a more enlightened plan" based on

---

72. Maxwell H. Bloomfield, *American Lawyers in a Changing Society, 1776–1876* (Cambridge, MA, 1976), 37.

common moral feelings and the spread of affection and benevolence, "government itself will become useless, and Society will subsist and flourish free from its shackles."

With all the "mischiefs...inherent in such a wild and fatal a scheme," Hamilton had hoped that the Republican "votaries of this new philosophy" would not push it to its fullest. But now the new Jefferson administration was trying to do just that. "No army, no navy, no *active* commerce—national defence, not by arms but by embargoes, prohibition of trade &c.—as little government as possible." These all added up, said Hamilton in 1802, to "a most visionary theory." Because of the grandiose nature of these Jeffersonian pipe dreams, the Federalists never tired of ridiculing the Republicans for walking with their heads in the clouds trying to extract sunbeams from cucumbers.[73] Jefferson, the philosophical visionary, may have been ideally suited to be a college professor, they said, but he was not suited to be the leader of a great nation.[74]

PERHAPS THE MOST RADICAL CHANGE resulting from the Jeffersonian election of 1800 was in politics. Popular voting took on a significance that it had never quite had before, and the increased numbers of contested elections for both federal and state officials sent the turnout of voters skyrocketing. In many places, especially in the North, the participation of eligible voters went from 20 percent or so in the 1790s to 80 percent or more in the first decade of the nineteenth century. At the same time, states that had not already done so began to expand the franchise by eliminating property qualifications or transforming the requirement into the mere paying of taxes. Of course, the enhanced importance of voting and the increase in electoral competition made suffrage exclusions as important as suffrage expansions. Delaware, Kentucky, Maryland, and New Jersey, which earlier had had no racial restrictions, now confined voting exclusively to white adult males. With the exception of a brief period in New Jersey (1790–1807) no state granted women the suffrage. By modern standards the system was far from democratic, but by the standards of the early nineteenth century America possessed the most popular electoral politics in the world.[75]

---

73. See especially David Daggett, *Sun-Beams May Be Extracted from Cucumbers, but the Process Is Tedious* (New Haven, 1799).

74. AH to Rufus King, 3 June 1802, *Papers of Hamilton*, 26: 14; AH, "Views on the French Revolution," (1794), *Papers of Hamilton*, 26: 739–40.

75. Chilton Williamson, *American Suffrage: From Property to Democracy, 1760–1860* (Princeton, 1960); Alexander Keyssar, *The Right to Vote: The Contested History of Democracy in the United States* (New York, 2000). Philip Lampi's Collection of

For the Federalists the Republican victory in 1800 was bewildering. It was not just the loss of the presidency and the Congress that disturbed them; it was what Jefferson's election represented socially and culturally that was so frightening. Since "the Degradation of our Nation and the corruption of the public mind & of the Morals of Individuals are constantly increasing," it seemed to Federalists like Christopher Gore of Massachusetts that the America they envisioned was coming to an end.[76] Because the Federalists did not think of themselves as a party but rather as natural leaders who possessed superior social and cultural credentials, at first they did not think of the contest with the Republicans as one party against another. It was instead "a war of principles,...a contest between the tyranny of Jacobinism, which confounds and levels every thing, and the mild reign of rational liberty."[77]

The Federalists' world was dramatically changing, and they were understandably alarmed. Vulgarity seemed to be spreading everywhere, and in their minds upstarts and demagogues and Jacobins had taken over the reins of government. "We are sliding down into the mire of a democracy, which pollutes the morals of the citizens before it swallows up their liberties," wrote a deeply pessimistic Fisher Ames.[78]

Not all Federalists were as depressed as Ames, but most were confused and unsure of what to do. They could not understand how so many uneducated and illiterate men were gaining elective office at the expense of men of talent and education.[79] They had tried satire and ridicule, as Noah Webster had by mocking the middling sort of politician in pursuit of office: "I will run about streets," he had his character declaim, "take every body by the hand, squeeze it hard, and look sweet." But such

---

American Election Data, 1787–1825, for presidential, congressional, gubernatorial, and state legislative elections revolutionizes historians' understanding of the development of democracy in the early Republic; it is available online via the American Antiquarian Society's Web page: "A New Nation Votes: American Election Returns, 1787–1825."

76. James M. Banner Jr., *To the Hartford Convention: The Federalists and the Origins of Party Politics in Massachusetts, 1789–1815* (New York, 1970), 39.

77. William C. Dowling, *Literary Federalism in the Age of Jefferson: Joseph Dennie and the Port Folio, 1801–1812* (Columbia, SC, 1999), 6.

78. Fisher Ames, "The Mire of Democracy" (Nov. 1805), in Lewis P. Simpson, ed., *The Federalist Literary Mind: Selections from the Monthly Anthology and Boston Review, 1803–1811* (Baton Rouge, 1962), 54.

79. Albrecht Koschnik, "Young Federalists, Masculinity, and Partisanship During the War of 1812," in Jeffery L. Pasley, Andrew W. Robertson, and David Waldstreicher, eds., *Beyond the Founders: New Approaches to the Political History of the Early Republic* (Chapel Hill, 2004), 166–68.

mocking had no effect. What was most socially alarming about the new style of popular campaigning, said Webster, was that it could make a "SOMEBODY" out of a "MR. NOBODY."[80]

As heirs of the republican Revolution, which in some sense was all about making somebodies out of nobodies, the Federalists were confused. Since they believed that the people should be the fount of government, they found it difficult to oppose the Republicans' efforts to have as many offices as possible made elective. As an Ohio Federalist lamented, to oppose elections would be used "by our enemies, as an evidence of an encroachment on the privileges of the people."[81] With no real alternative to the people's will, the Federalists inevitably surrendered the national ruling authority in 1801 without a fight—and it was their willingness to surrender that made the historic transition so peaceful. But they certainly did not regard the transfer of power from one party to another as normal in any modern sense. Because the older Federalist leaders considered themselves gentlemen for whom politics should not be an exclusive concern or vocation, many, including John Jay, George Cabot, and Charles Cotesworth Pinckney, echoed Joseph Addison's Cato: "When vice prevails, and impious men bear sway,/ The post of honor is a private station," and retired to their professions and private lives to await what they assumed would soon be the people's desperate call for the return of the "wise and good" and the "natural rulers."[82]

But the popular reaction to the Republican revolution did not come. Many gentlemen of property and standing who earlier might have felt an obligation of their rank to participate in public affairs now stayed home and advised others to do the same, rather than have your "character bandied about through so many counties." Even as early as 1797 Hamilton had begun questioning the classical imperative that men like him, men who were not independently wealthy, had an obligation to assume public office. In America "the pecuniary emolument is so inconsiderable as to amount to a sacrifice to any man who can employ his time with advantage in any liberal profession," he told his Scottish uncle. "The opportunity of doing good, from the jealousy of power and the spirit of faction, is too small in any station to warrant a long continuance of private sacrifices." With the spread of such sentiments a world was coming to an end.[83]

80. Isenberg, Fallen Founder, 145.
81. Donald J. Ratcliffe, Party Spirit in a Frontier Republic: Democratic Politics in Ohio, 1793–1821 (Columbus, OH, 1998), 81.
82. Linda K. Kerber, Federalists in Dissent: Imagery and Ideology in Jeffersonian America (Ithaca, 1970), 162; Fischer, Revolution of American Conservatism, 26.
83. Fischer, Revolution of American Conservatism, 32; AH to William Hamilton, 2 May 1797, Papers of Hamilton, 21: 78.

In 1803 President Timothy Dwight of Yale told his graduates to "never look either for subsistence, or for character, to popular suffrage, or governmental appointment, to public salaries, or official perquisites."[84] But others who wanted a successful political career and were convinced that Federalism could never come back, like John Quincy Adams, the son of the former president, and William Plumer, senator and later governor of New Hampshire, eventually joined the Republican movement. Young Adams concluded as early as 1802 that the Jefferson administration had "the support of a much stronger majority of the people throughout the Union than the former administrations ever possessed." The Federalist system, he said, had been "completely and irrevocably abandoned and rejected by the popular vote. It never can and never will be revived."[85]

Nevertheless, others, like Robert Goodloe Harper of South Carolina and James A. Bayard of Delaware, clung to their Federalist principles and their minority status in the Congress or in their state governments. Still others, like Fisher Ames, urged their colleagues to "entrench themselves in the State governments and endeavour to make State justice and State power a shelter of the wise, and good, and rich."[86] And still others, like Timothy Pickering, secretary of state under Adams, and Roger Griswold, congressman and later governor of Connecticut, dreamed of revenge and fomented separatist plots in New England. Yet most thoughtful Federalists knew that separation of the Northeastern states from the Francophiles in the rest of the country was no solution to the problems of America; for, as George Cabot of Massachusetts put it, the source of the evils afflicting America ultimately lay not in the Southern states or in Revolutionary France but "in the political theories of our country and in ourselves."[87]

STUNNED BY THE JEFFERSONIAN TAKEOVER, many Federalists sensed that they had to change their ways. Their party, they said, lacked the kind of organization and newspaper support the Republicans possessed. And with Washington's death in December 1799 they seemed to have no leader. "The Federalists scarcely deserve the name of a party," lamented Fisher Ames in 1800. "Their association is a loose one—formed

---

84. Steven J. Novak, *The Rights of Youth: American Colleges and Student Revolt, 1798–1815* (Cambridge, MA, 1977), 55.
85. White, *The Jeffersonians*, 13.
86. Marshall Foletta, *Coming to Terms with Democracy: Federalist Intellectuals and the Shaping of an American Culture* (Charlottesville, 2001), 30.
87. Winfred E. A. Bernard, *Fisher Ames: Federalist and Statesman, 1758–1808* (Chapel Hill, 1965), 341.

by accident and shaken by every prospect of labour or hazard."[88] While the Republicans were busy drawing up tickets and using all sorts of imaginative techniques to get out the vote, the Federalist gentry were writing letters to one another and addressing their political pamphlets to "the *substantial* (not the *people*) citizens."[89] The Federalists had no organized nominating process and often had multiple candidates for the same office who competed against each other, which allowed Republicans to win with less than a majority. Many of the old-school Federalists simply shook their heads and wrung their hands over the Republicans' electoral successes. But in the aftermath of Jefferson's election some Federalists sought to do things differently.

The election of 1800 had a cathartic effect on many Federalists. It broke the tension between the politics of honor and the politics of party and prepared the way for the expansion of democratic politics. With the spread of popular politics, many of the Federalists, especially the younger ones, reluctantly concluded that if they were to win back power they would have to swallow their pride and adopt some of the electioneering techniques of the Republicans. Many now accepted the fact that they were indeed a party—to be sure, not a self-interested faction like the Republicans, but a party of principle. Beginning first in New York in 1801, groups of Federalist activists created networks of caucuses and committees in each state that reached down to the localities. These Federalist caucuses and committees picked candidates, disciplined party members, and organized for elections, just as the Republicans had been doing.

The Federalist party created legislative programs and formed its own self-created societies to rival those of the Republican Tammany Societies. Most notable were the hundreds of Washington Benevolent Societies, which were ostensibly charitable organizations but in reality arms of the party. Some Federalists were now as determined to mobilize the people as the Republicans. "We must court popular favor," concluded Theodore Sedgwick of Massachusetts, "we must study public opinion, and accommodate measures to what it is and still more what it ought to be."[90]

Of course, many other Federalists, especially old-school Federalists, resisted these efforts to become a party. They saw themselves as the wise, natural rulers of the society, and thus found it virtually impossible to

---

88. Ames to Oliver Wolcott, 3 Aug. 1800, *Works of Fisher Ames* (1854), ed. W. B. Allen (Indianapolis, 1983), 2: 1368.
89. Broussard, *Southern Federalists*, 308.
90. Banner, *To the Hartford Convention*, 133–34; Albrecht Koschnik, *"Let a Common Interest Bind Us Together": Associations, Partisanship, and Culture in Philadelphia, 1775–1840* (Charlottesville, 2007), 3–4, 153–83.

conceive of themselves as an opposition party. Parties were factious and seditious, and they wanted no part of them. Many of the older Federalists refused to electioneer or campaign for office and, like Gouverneur Morris, indignantly condemned "those brawlers, who make popularity a trade."[91]

No doubt these traditional views of politics hampered the ability of the Federalists to organize themselves. The party organization in Massachusetts, for example, remained strictly secret and designed only to carry out the decisions of its Boston leaders rather than mobilizing the statewide populace in the way the Republicans were doing. Not just the Federalists but many Republicans as well found it hard to accept the existence of competing parties.

Despite appearances to the contrary—the party designations, the caucuses, and the many contested elections—this was not quite yet a modern party system. There were no nominating conventions, no formal platforms, no party chairmen, no national party committees, and, most important, no intellectual justification for party competition. Old ideals of the unity of the public interest died hard. Even Republican governor Elbridge Gerry of Massachusetts, of gerrymandering fame, came out against parties in 1810, declaring that "a house divided against itself cannot stand," and urging each citizen to "determine for himself to relinquish the party system."[92]

Yet popular party politics of a new and distinctive sort did emerge, a kind of "celebratory politics," as one historian has called it.[93] Party tickets, party principles, and party loyalties developed, and partisan political activists sought to use every means they could to drum up popular support for their candidates. Anything and everything that was part of everyday popular culture—holidays, parades, barbecues, songs, sermons, toasts, funerals, militia meetings, and every conceivable form of print—was turned to partisan causes. The Republicans made the Fourth of July, with its celebration of Jefferson's egalitarian Declaration of Independence, the paramount national holiday and used it to promote their party. The Federalists retaliated with celebrations of Washington's birthday and any other local holiday, such as New York's Evacuation Day, that they could employ to their advantage.

Newspapers, which had begun to form the basis for party organization and identity in the 1790s, continued to grow in numbers and political

91. Fischer, *Revolution of American Conservatism*, 86.
92. Ronald P. Formisano, *The Transformation of Political Culture: Massachusetts Parties, 1790s–1840s* (New York, 1983), 74.
93. David Waldstreicher, *In the Midst of Perpetual Fetes: The Making of American Nationalism* (Chapel Hill, 1997), 216.

significance in response to the competitive partisan atmosphere. Despite the arrests of printers and editors under the Sedition Act, the number of Republican newspapers suddenly exploded in 1800—with eighty-five Republican papers published in that year, two-thirds more than had existed before the act. All these partisan papers tended to create an informal network that connected Republicans throughout the country. News originating from William Duane's Philadelphia *Aurora*, the ideological center of the party, could reach Pittsfield, Massachusetts, or Raleigh, North Carolina, in only a few days. Not surprisingly, people in both parties became convinced that the Republicans owed their massive victory in 1800 to the power of their greatly expanded and openly partisan press. A "mighty wave of public opinion," said Jefferson in 1801, had rolled over the country.[94]

Stimulated by the Republicans' success, the Federalists sought to create rival newspapers. In 1801 Hamilton raised ten thousand dollars in just a few weeks and launched the flagship New York *Evening Post*. During the first decade of the nineteenth century the Federalists created dozens of papers, "igniting" what one historian has called "a journalistic arms race with the Republicans." They now knew more clearly than ever before, as Fisher Ames put it, that "public opinion must be addressed; must be purified from the dangerous errors with which it is infected; and, above all, must be aroused from the prevailing apathy."[95]

BY THE EARLY DECADES of the nineteenth century Americans had come to realize that public opinion, "that invisible guardian of honour—that eagle-eyed spy on human actions—that inexorable judge of men and manners—that arbiter, whom tears cannot appease, nor ingenuity soften and from whose terrible decisions there is no appeal," had become "the vital principle" underlying American government, society, and culture.[96]

94. Pasley, "1800 as a Revolution in Political Culture," in Horn et al., eds., *The Revolution of 1800*, 132–33; Jeffrey L. Pasley, *"The Tyranny of Printers": Newspaper Politics in the Early American Republic* (Charlottesville, 2001), 126, 153–75; TJ to Priestley, 21 March 1801, *Jefferson: Writings*, 1086.

95. Pasley, *"Tyranny of Printers,"* 236; Ames to Christopher Gore, 13 Dec. 1802, *Works of Ames*, ed. Allen, 2: 1445–46. See Charles G. Steffen, "Newspapers for Free: The Economies of Newspaper Circulation in the Early Republic," *JER*, 23 (2004), 381–419.

96. William Crafts Jr., *An Oration on the Influence of Moral Causes on National Character, Delivered Before the Phi Beta Kappa Society, on Their Anniversary, 28 August, 1817* (Cambridge MA, 1817), 5–6; Tunis Wortman, *A Treatise Concerning Political Enquiry, and the Liberty of the Press* (New York, 1800), 180.

Nearly every educated person in the Anglo-American world believed in the power of public opinion and talked endlessly about it. Indeed, men were so preoccupied with their reputations and their honor precisely because of their intense concern for the judgment of others. By the word "public," like the word "society," however, eighteenth-century gentlemen usually had meant "the rational part of it" and not "the ignorant vulgar."[97] When Madison in 1791, echoing David Hume and others, said that public opinion was "the real sovereign" in any free government, he still conceived of it as the intellectual product of limited circles of "those philosophical and patriotic citizens who cultivate their reason." Which is why he came to fear that the large extent of the United States made the isolated individual insignificant in his own eyes and made easier the fabricating of opinion by a few.[98] Other Americans, however, were coming to see in the very breadth of the country and in the very insignificance of the solitary individual the saving sources of a general opinion that could be trusted.

The Sedition Act of 1798 marked a crucial point in the development of the American idea of public opinion. Its passage provoked a debate that went far beyond the issue of freedom of speech or freedom of the press; it eventually involved the very nature of America's intellectual life. The debate, which spilled into the early years of the nineteenth century, drew out the logic of America's intellectual experience since the Revolution, and in the process it undermined the foundations of the elitist eighteenth-century classical world on which the Founders had stood.

In the Sedition Act of 1798 the Federalists had thought they were being generous by changing the common law conception of seditious libel and enacting the Zenger defense into law. They not only allowed juries to determine what was seditious, but they made truth a defense, stating that only those statements that were "false, scandalous, and malicious" would be punished. But staunch Republican polemicists would have no part of this generosity. In the debate over the sedition law the Republican libertarian theorists, including George Hay of Virginia and Tunis Wortman of New York, rejected both the old common law restrictions on the liberty of the press and the new legal recognition of the distinction between truth and falsity of opinion that the Federalists had incorporated into the Sedition Act. While the Federalists clung to the eighteenth century's

97. Gordon S. Wood, "The Democratization of Mind in the American Revolution," in *Leadership in the American Revolution: Library of Congress Symposia in the American Revolution* (Washington, DC, 1974), 67; this article has an extended analysis of public opinion (63–89), from which this discussion is drawn.

98. JM to BR, 7 March 1790, *Papers of Madison*, 13: 93; JM, "Public Opinion," 19 Dec. 1791, *Madison: Writings*, 500–501.

conception that "truths" were constant and universal and capable of being discovered by enlightened and reasonable men, the Republican libertarians argued that opinions about government and governors were many and diverse and their truth could not be determined simply by individual judges and juries, no matter how reasonable such men were. Hence, they concluded that all political opinions—that is, words as distinct from overt acts—even those opinions that were "false, scandalous, and malicious," ought to be allowed, as Jefferson put it, to "stand undisturbed as monuments of the safety with which error of opinion may be tolerated where reason is left free to combat it."[99]

The Federalists were dumbfounded. "How…could the rights of the people require a liberty to utter falsehood?" they asked. "How could it be right to do wrong?"[100] It was not an easy question to answer, neither then nor later. "Truth," the Federalists said, "has but one side and listening to error and falsehood is indeed a strange way to discover truth." Any notion of multiple and varying truths would produce "universal uncertainty, universal misery," and "set all morality afloat." People needed to know the "criterion by which we may determine with certainty, *who are right, and who are wrong.*"[101]

Most Republicans felt they could not deny outright the possibility of truth and falsity in political beliefs, and thus they fell back on a tenuous distinction, developed by Jefferson in his first inaugural address, between principles and opinions. Principles, it seemed, were hard and fixed, while opinions were soft and fluid; therefore, said Jefferson, "every difference of opinion is not a difference of principle." The implication was, as Benjamin Rush suggested, that individual opinions did not count as much as they had in the past, and for that reason such individual opinions could be permitted the freest possible expression.[102]

---

99. [George Hay], *An Essay on the Liberty of the Press* (Philadelphia, 1799), 40; TJ, Inaugural Address, 4 March 1801, *Jefferson: Writings*, 493.

100. Richard Buel Jr., *Securing the Revolution: Ideology in American Politics, 1789–1815* (Ithaca, 1972), 252.

101. John C. Miller, *The Federalist Era, 1789–1801* (New York, 1960), 232; Isaac Chapman Bates, *An Oration, Pronounced at Northampton, July 4, 1805* (Northampton, MA, 1805), 6–7, 15.

102. TJ, Inaugural Address, 4 March 1801, *Jefferson: Writings*, 493; BR to TJ, 12 March 1801, *Letters of Rush*, 2: 831. Of course, the new liberal idea of freedom of the press did not immediately take hold. As late as 1813, for example, Chief Justice James Kent of the New York Supreme Court still clung to the notion that "individual character must be protected, or social happiness and domestic peace are destroyed," and upheld a libel charge against a printer in the state of New York. Donald Roper, "James Kent and the Emergence of New York's Libel Law," *American Journal of Legal History*, 17 (1973), 228–29.

What ultimately made such distinctions comprehensible was the Republicans' assumption that opinions about politics were no longer the monopoly of the educated and aristocratic few. Not only were true and false and even malicious opinions equally to be tolerated, but everyone and anyone in the society should be equally able to express them. Sincerity and honesty, the Republican polemicists argued, were far more important in the articulation of ultimate political truth than learning and fancy words that had often been used to deceive and dissimulate. Truth was actually the creation of many voices and many minds, no one of which was more important than another and each of which made its own separate and equally significant contribution to the whole. Solitary opinions of single individuals may now have counted for less, but in their statistical collectivity they now added up to something far more significant than had ever existed before, something that the New York Republican Tunis Wortman referred to as "the extremely complicated term *Public Opinion*."[103]

Because American society was not the kind of organic hierarchy with "an intellectual unity" that the Federalists had wanted, public opinion in America, argued Wortman, the most articulate of the new Republican libertarians, could no longer be the consequence of the intellectual leadership of a few learned gentlemen. General public opinion was simply "an aggregation of individual sentiments," the combined product of multitudes of minds thinking and reflecting independently, communicating their ideas in different ways, causing opinions to collide and blend with one another, to refine and correct each other, leading toward "the ultimate triumph of Truth." Such a product, such a public opinion, could be trusted because it had so many sources, so many voices and minds, all interacting, that no privileged individual or group could manipulate or dominate the whole.[104] Like the example of religious diversity in America, a comparison many drew upon to explain their new confidence in public opinion, the separate opinions allowed to circulate freely would by their very differentness act, in Jefferson's word, as "a Censor" over each other and the society—performing the role that the ancients and early eighteenth-century Augustan Englishmen had expected heroic individuals and satiric poets to perform.[105]

---

103. Wortman, *Treatise Concerning Political Enquiry*, 118.
104. Wortman, *Treatise Concerning Political Enquiry*, 118–19, 122–23, 155–57.
105. TJ to JA, 11 Jan. 1816, in Lester J. Cappon, ed., *The Adams-Jefferson Letters: The Complete Correspondence Between Thomas Jefferson and Abigail and John Adams* (Chapel Hill, 1959), 2: 458.

This vast, impersonal, and democratic idea of public opinion soon came to dominate all of American intellectual life. In all endeavors — whether art, language, medicine, or politics — connoisseurs, professors, doctors, and statesmen had to give way before the power of the collective opinion of the people. This conception of public opinion, said Federalist Theodore Sedgwick in disgust, "is of all things the most destructive of personal independence and of that weight of character which a great man ought to possess."[106] But no matter, it was the people's opinion, and it could be trusted because no one controlled it and everyone contributed to it. "Public opinion," said Harvard professor Samuel Williams, "will be much nearer the truth, than the reasoning and refinements of speculative and interested men." Even in matters of artistic taste, declared Joseph Hopkinson before the Pennsylvania Academy of the Fine Arts in 1810, "public opinion has, in more instances than one, triumphed over critics and connoisseurs." Of course, the Federalists warned that a government dependent exclusively on public opinion was a mere "democracy," in which "opinion shifts with every current of caprice."[107] But there was no turning back. In no country in the world did public opinion become more awesome and powerful than it did in increasingly democratic America.

BECAUSE OF THIS RELENTLESS DEMOCRATIZATION, the Federalists were never again able to gather the kind of national electoral strength they had had in the 1790s. In the off-year election of 1802 the Republicans increased their strength in the Congress. In 1804 the Federalists put up Charles Cotesworth Pinckney of XYZ fame for president, but he was able to garner only 14 to Jefferson's 162 electoral votes. Jefferson took the electoral votes of all the states, except those of Connecticut and Delaware and two from Maryland. Even Massachusetts went for Jefferson. In 1808 Pinckney did better with 47 to Madison's 122 electoral votes. Although the Federalists continued to put up presidential candidates through the election of 1816, their electoral strength was continually weak and confined to New England. But even in their New England stronghold cracks began to appear. The Republicans began winning

---

106. Wortman, *A Treatise Concerning Political Enquiry*, 180; Richard E. Welch Jr., *Theodore Sedgwick, Federalist: A Political Portrait* (Middletown, CT, 1965), 211.

107. Samuel Williams, *The Natural and Civil History of Vermont* (Walpole, NH, 1794), 2: 394; Joseph Hopkinson, *Annual Discourse, Delivered Before the Pennsylvania Academy of the Fine Arts* (1810), in Gordon S. Wood, ed., *The Rising Glory of America, 1760–1820*, rev. ed. (Boston, 1990) 333; Ames, "The Mire of Democracy," in Simpson, ed., *Federalist Literary Mind*, 54.

local elections, and by 1807 Massachusetts had more Republican than Federalist congressmen.

The party slowly withered. It was much too tainted with aristocracy and New England sectionalism to carry on as a national party. In the new Western states it virtually disappeared. One Republican reported from Ohio after the 1804 election that the Federalists "have dwindled to a number so inconsiderable that they are altogether silent on Politics."[108] Consequently, many Federalist gentry turned from party politics to the construction of civic institutions that could influence the culture—private libraries, literary and historical societies, art academies, and professional associations. By 1820 their party had become too weak even to nominate a presidential candidate, although the cultural authority of the Federalists, especially in New England, had grown substantially.[109]

At first the Republicans were remarkably united. In 1804 the Republican congressional caucus nominated Jefferson for president and sixty-seven-year-old George Clinton of New York for vice-president; no one at the meeting supported Vice-President Burr. By 1808 the party was faced with three candidates for the presidency—Secretary of State Madison, who was presumed to have Jefferson's backing, Vice-President Clinton, who had strong support in New York and Pennsylvania, and James Monroe, who had recently returned from his ministry in England and had the backing of John Randolph of Virginia. Although Madison won the support of the congressional caucus (with Clinton as the vice-presidential candidate again), the supporters of Monroe and Clinton refused to recognize the right of the caucus to nominate candidates.

It was obvious that the Republican party was coming apart. Since its creation, its unity had rested on the threat the Federalists had posed to the principles of free and popular government; thus the decline of the Federalists meant that the Republicans began, in Jefferson's words, to "schismatize among themselves."[110] A variety of Republican factions and groups arose in Congress and in the several states. These divisions were organized around particular individuals (the "Burrites," the "Clintonians"), around political and social distinctions (the "Pennsylvania Quids," the "Malcontents"), around states or sections (the "Old Republicans" of the South), and sometimes around ideology ("the Principles of '98," the "Invisibles," the "War Hawks").

108. Ratcliffe, *Party Spirit in a Frontier Republic*, 86.
109. Koschnik, "*Let a Common Interest Bind Us Together*," 184–227; Foletta, *Coming to Terms with Democracy*.
110. Richard E. Ellis, *The Jeffersonian Crisis: Courts and Politics in the Young Republic* (New York, 1971), 234.

The Republicans disagreed over multitudes of issues, but mainly over the degree to which the state and federal governments represented the people. Sometimes the moderate Republicans even sounded like Federalists, appealing, as Thomas McKean's Pennsylvania "Quids" did in 1805, to the fact that "the best and wisest men in the community" were opposed to the "mad schemes" of the radicals, who in any case were little more than "backwoods bumpkins."[111] Unlike the Federalists, however, these moderate Republicans expressed no doubt about democracy and the sacredness of the will of the people. It was all part of the process of learning just how far republican equality could be carried. Of course, many individual politicians continued to pride themselves on their independence from factions and influence of any sort, and "party" still remained a disrespectful word. In fact, until the Jacksonian era nothing approaching a stable party system developed in Congress.

111. Andrew Shankman, *Crucible of American Democracy: The Struggle to Fuse Egalitarianism and Capitalism in Jeffersonian Pennsylvania* (Lawrence, KS, 2004), 146, 147.

# 9

# Republican Society

The Jeffersonian revolution and all that it meant socially and culturally were driven by the same dynamic forces that had been at work since at least the middle of the eighteenth century—population growth and movement and commercial expansion.[1] By 1800 5,297,000 people lived in the United States, one-fifth of whom were black slaves. Since most adult whites married at early ages, fertility rates were high, with over seven births per woman being the average, nearly double that of the European states.[2] After 1800 this fertility rate began to decline as people became more conscious of their ability to create prosperity for themselves and their children by limiting the size of their families. Nevertheless, the population as a whole continued to expand dramatically, doubling every twenty years or so, twice the rate of growth of any European nation.

At the pace America was growing, one observer predicted that the country would contain 860 million people by the middle of the twentieth century.[3] Americans marveled at the fact that by 1810 the United States, numbering over seven million people, was nearly as populous as England and Wales had been in 1801.[4] And it was a remarkably young population:

1. In the opening chapters of his classic account of the Jefferson and Madison administrations, Henry Adams exaggerated the traditional and static character of American society in 1800 in order to contrast it with a more modern and dynamic America at the end of Madison's presidency in 1817. But America in 1800 was already an energetic and enterprising society and anything but stable. The roots of the extraordinary changes taking place in this period lay in the Revolution, not in Jefferson's election. For a necessary corrective to Adams, see Noble E. Cunningham, *The United States in 1800: Henry Adams Revisited* (Charlottesville, 1988.) For a justification of Adams's approach, see Garry Wills, *Henry Adams and the Making of America* (Boston, 2005).
2. Herbert S. Klein, *A Population History of the United States* (Cambridge, UK, 2004), 77. The fertility of black women was equally high.
3. Ralph H. Brown, *Mirror for Americans: Likeness of the Eastern Seaboard, 1810* (New York, 1943), 30.
4. *Niles' Weekly Register*, 1 (1811–12), 10.

in 1810 36 percent of the white population was under the age of ten, and nearly 70 percent was under the age of twenty-five.

It was also a population on the move as never before. While the sparse population of the new state of Tennessee (1796) multiplied tenfold between 1790 and 1820, New York's already considerable population more than quadrupled, much of it spilling into the western parts of the state; in the single decade between 1800 and 1810 New York added fifteen new counties, 147 new towns, and 374,000 new inhabitants. "The woods are full of new settlers," remarked a traveler in upstate New York in 1805. "Axes were resounding and the trees literally were falling about us as we passed." Although nine-tenths of the country's population in 1800 still lived east of the Alleghenies, increasing numbers of Americans were crossing the mountains into the West—to the dread of many Federalists. As the high-toned Federalist Gouverneur Morris warned, the backcountry folk were crude and unenlightened and were "always most adverse to the best measures."[5]

Before the Revolution the territory of Kentucky had contained almost no white settlers. By 1800 it had become a state (1792) and grown to over 220,000; at that point not a single adult Kentuckian had been born and grown up within the state's borders. And these burgeoning Westerners were prospering. Despite the poor roads and the prevalence of simple log cabins, observed a traveler in 1802, one could not find "a single family without milk, butter, smoked or salted meat—the poorest man has always one or two horses." By 1800 most of the major cities of the future Midwest had already been founded—St. Louis, Detroit, Pittsburgh, Cincinnati, Lexington, Erie, Cleveland, Nashville, and Louisville.[6]

When the defeat of the Indians at Fallen Timbers in 1794 and the Treaty of Greenville in 1795 opened up the southern two-thirds of the present state of Ohio to white settlement, people began pouring into the region. Between 1800 and 1810 Ohio gained statehood (1803) and grew from 45,000 inhabitants to over 230,000. Cincinnati was already being called "the Great Emporium of the West." By 1820, only thirty-two years after the first permanent white settlers arrived, Ohio had a population of over a half million people and was the fifth-largest state in the Union. The state was creating so many new towns that Ohioans complained they

---

5. Edward J. Nygren and Bruce Robertson, eds., *Views and Visions: American Landscape Before 1830* (Washington, DC, 1986), 37; Max Farrand, ed., *The Records of the Federal Convention of 1787* (New Haven, 1911, 1937), 1: 583.

6. Cunningham, *United States in 1800*, 6; Richard C. Wade, *The Urban Frontier: Pioneer Life in Early Pittsburgh, Cincinnati, Lexington, Louisville, and St. Louis* (Chicago, 1959); Harriet Simpson Arnow, *Flowering of the Cumberland* (Lexington, KY, 1963), 90.

had run out of names for them. Gazetteers in America, it was said, could not keep up with the "very frequent changes" in the dividing of territories and naming of places "which are almost daily taking place": it was a problem "peculiar to a new, progressive and extensive country."[7]

In 1795 the population west of the mountains had been only 150,000; by 1810 it was more than a million.[8] The Americans, said the British traveler Isaac Weld, were a restless people, always on the lookout for something better or more profitable. They "seldom or ever consider whether the part of the country to which they are going is healthy or otherwise.... If the lands in one part... are superior to those in another in fertility; if they are in the neighborhood of a navigable river, or situated conveniently to a good market; if they are cheap and rising in value, thither the American will gladly emigrate, let the climate be ever so unfriendly to the human system."[9]

Lucy Fletcher Kellogg's father, like many other American farmers, traded goods, ran a brickyard, kept a tavern, and was always on the move. Her parents had a farm in Sutton, Massachusetts, she recalled in her memoir, but "in accordance with the instincts of New England people, they must sell the farm and move to New Hampshire or some other new place." The father of Joseph Smith, the founder of Mormonism, moved his family seven times in fourteen years. Others moved at least three or four times in a lifetime, selling their land to new settlers at a profit each time; "they are," it was noted, "very indifferent ploughmen" anyway. Americans had a reputation among the Spanish of being able to travel "200 leagues with no other aids than a sack of cornmeal and flask of powder."[10]

The country still remained overwhelmingly rural and agricultural—a puzzling condition that seemed to violate the widely accepted theories of social development. An expanding population was presumably the force that compelled a society to move from one stage of civilization to another. But that was not happening in America.

7. *Monthly Magazine*, 1 (1799), 129.
8. *Monthly Magazine*, 1 (1799), 129; William A. Schaper, *Sectionalism and Representation in South Carolina* (1901; New York, 1968), 139.
9. Curtis P. Nettels, *The Emergence of a National Economy, 1775–1815* (New York, 1962), 158–59.
10. Andrew R. L. Cayton, The *Frontier Republic: Ideology and Politics in the Ohio Country, 1780–1825* (Kent, OH, 1986), 116; Lucy Fletcher Kellogg, in Joyce Appleby, ed., *Recollections of the Early Republic: Selected Autobiographies* (Boston, 1997), 145, 147; Malcolm J. Rohrbough, *The Trans-Appalachian Frontier: People, Societies, and Institutions, 1775–1850* (New York, 1978), 36–37, 96–97; Noel M. Loomis, "Philip Nolan's Entry into Texas in 1800," in John Francis McDermott, ed., *The Spanish in the Mississippi Valley, 1762–1804* (Urbana, IL, 1974), 120.

During the early nineteenth century nineteen out of twenty Americans continued to live in rural places, that is, unincorporated sites with fewer than twenty-five hundred inhabitants. In 1800 nearly 90 percent of the labor force was still engaged in farming. Even the more urbanized areas of New England and the Mid-Atlantic had 70 percent of their workers on farms. In 1800 only thirty-three towns claimed a population of twenty-five hundred or more, and only six of these urban areas had populations over ten thousand.[11] By contrast, in 1801 one-third of people in England lived in cities, and only 36 percent of English workers engaged in agriculture.

If the United States were eventually to become a fiscal-military state capable of taking on the European powers, this was not the way to go about it. A rural, underdeveloped society preoccupied with farming was not one that could sustain a European-type war-making capacity, and it was not at all what many Federalists had wanted or expected. The Federalists had thought that America's rapid multiplication of people would force the country to develop the same sorts of civilized urban institutions, the same kinds of integrated social hierarchies and industrial centers, the same types of balanced economies in which manufacturing was as important as farming, the same sorts of bureaucratic governments that made the states of Europe, at least before the accursed French Revolution erupted, so impressive, so powerful, and so civilized. They assumed that American society would eventually become more like that of Europe and that what Franklin had once called the "general happy Mediocrity" of America would gradually disappear.[12]

But the opposite was happening. Not only was American social mediocrity spreading at an alarming rate, but more and more Americans were taking advantage of the availability of land in America and living apart from all traditional social hierarchies—especially in the new Western areas, where, in the words of George Clymer of Philadelphia, there were "no private or publick associations for the common good." Indeed, conservatives asked, could the frontier areas even "be called society where every man is for himself alone and has no regard for any other person farther than he can make him subservient to his own views"?[13]

11. James L. Huston, *Securing the Fruits of Labor: The American Concepts of Wealth Distribution, 1765–1900* (Baton Rouge, 1998), 89; Adna Ferrin Weber, *The Growth of Cities in the Nineteenth Century: A Study in Statistics* (New York, 1969), 40–47; Philip Abrams and E. A. Wrigley, eds., *Towns in Society: Essays in Economic History and Historical Sociology* (Cambridge, UK, 1978), 247–48.

12. Franklin, "Information to Those Who Would Remove to America," (1784), *Franklin: Writings*, 975.

13. Jerry Grundfest, *George Clymer: Philadelphia Revolutionary, 1739–1813* (New York, 1982), 141; Lucius Versus Bierce, *Travels in the Southland, 1822–1823: The Journal of Lucius Versus Bierce*, ed. George W. Knepper (Columbus, OH, 1966), 103.

Settlers on the move had little respect for authority. A mobile population, one Kentuckian told James Madison in 1792, "must make a very different mass from one which is composed of men born and raised on the same spot.... They see none about them to whom or to whose families they have been accustomed to think themselves inferior." In these new Western territories, where "society is yet unborn," where "your connections and friends are absent, and at a distance," and where there was "no distinction assumed on account of rank or property," it was difficult to put together anything that resembled a traditional social order, or even a civilized community. Kentucky, like all frontier areas, travelers noted, was "different from a staid and settled society.... A certain loss of civility is inevitable." Yet to some "plain, poor" Yankees from New England like Amos Kendall, Lexington, Kentucky, was already too aristocratic and stratified for their tastes, and they continued to look westward for opportunities.[14]

The changes, especially outside of the South, seemed overwhelming. America, noted a French observer, was a "country in flux; that which is true today as regards its population, its establishments, its prices, its commerce will not be true six months from now."[15] Americans appeared to love liberty too much. They "dread everything that preaches constraint," concluded another foreign observer. "Natural freedom... is what pleases them."[16]

Although many Americans, including Jefferson, celebrated the freedom that such weak social constraints offered, most Federalists were horrified by what was happening, dismayed and disillusioned by all the licentious changes and breakdowns of authority. Perhaps no Federalist was more troubled than William Cooper of Otsego County, New York. Cooper had once imagined becoming a genteel patriarch, but his design soon began collapsing all about him. The settlers of Cooperstown grew in numbers and diversity and became strangers to Cooper and to one another. His town was increasingly racked by lawsuits, bankruptcies, disobedient servants, vandalism, thefts, and incidents of violence and arson. Cooper himself was caned in a Cooperstown street in 1807, imparting to

14. Patricia S. Watlington, *The Partisan Spirit: Kentucky Politics, 1779–1792* (New York, 1972), 46; Morris Birkbeck, *Letters from Illinois* (London, 1818), 14; Rohrbough, *Trans-Appalachian Frontier*, 55; William C. Preston, *Reminiscences*, quoted in Charles L. Sanford, ed., *Quest for America, 1810–1824* (New York, 1964), 26; Donald B. Cole, "A Yankee in Kentucky: The Early Years of Amos Kendall, 1789–1828," Mass. Hist. Soc., *Proc.*, 109 (1997), 31.

15. Joyce Appleby, *Inheriting the Revolution: The First Generation of Americans* (Cambridge, MA, 2000), 6.

16. Johann David Schoepf, *Travels in the Confederation, 1783–1784* (Philadelphia, 1911), 1: 238–39.

him and his family a growing dread that anarchy and chaos were all about them.

By the time his political world was disintegrating, Cooper had concluded that the gentility he had so relentlessly sought was beyond his grasp and that he must look to his five sons and two daughters to finish what he had begun. But in 1800 his cherished elder daughter, Hannah, died in a fall from a horse. He sent William Jr. to Princeton, where the boy became a dissipated dandy, spending lavishly on clothes, wines, and cigars before being expelled in 1802 on suspicion of setting a fire that burned Nassau Hall. He next sent James to Yale, where the future novelist ran up debts and behaved as foolishly as his brother had: in 1805 he too was expelled—for fighting and using gunpowder to blow off his opponent's dormitory door; James then ran off and joined the navy. After William Cooper died in 1809, his children thought they could continue to live extravagantly. But Cooper's great wealth was more apparent than real, and within fifteen years his entire estate was gone, eaten up by debts, failed speculations, unpaid mortgages, and legal suits.

The Cooper family was devastated. Ill equipped to deal with financial problems, four of the Cooper sons succumbed to some combination of stress and high living during the next decade and one by one died prematurely—all in their thirties. By 1819, a decade after the father's death, only two children were left—the second daughter, Ann, and James, the future novelist. The family property in Cooperstown was bought up by a new breed of upstart, William Holt Averell, the son of a Cooperstown shoemaker and a shrewd hard-nosed capitalist who would have nothing to do with wasteful spending on gentility: he trained his sons to be businessmen, not gentlemen, and succeeded where Cooper had failed.

ALTHOUGH AMERICANS, compared to Englishmen, had never been very respectful of authority, the Revolution seemed to have emboldened many of them to challenge all hierarchy and all distinctions, even those naturally earned. Middling men began asserting themselves as never before. As one foreigner noted, "The lowest here...stand erect and crouch not before any man."[17] After the Revolution Bostonians stopped using the designations of "yeoman" and "husbandman" and began recording the occupational titles among artisans less and less. All adult white males began using the designation of "Mr.," which had traditionally belonged exclusively to the gentry. Even the city council of Charleston,

---

17. Christopher Clark, *Social Change in America: From the Revolution Through the Civil War* (Chicago, 2006), 79.

South Carolina, felt sufficient egalitarian pressure to abolish the titles of "Esq." and "His Honor."[18]

By what right did authority claim obedience? This was the question now being asked of every institution, every organization, every individual. It was as if the Revolution had set in motion a disintegrative force that could not be stopped.

European travelers, especially those from England, were, of course, those most dismayed by the society of the new Republic, and much of their criticism was devastating. Many Europeans regarded the English as wild and liberty-loving, but by comparison the licentious Americans made the English seem stable and staid. Many Americans naturally tried to discount this criticism, but for the Federalists most of it was only too true. How could they not agree with foreign critics who declared that in the United States "liberty and equality level all ranks"?

One of the most colorful and censorious of these foreigners was Charles William Janson, an English immigrant who spent more than a dozen years between 1793 and 1806 trying to understand the people of this new country, who by 1806 were, he said, "the only remaining republicans in the civilized world." Janson said that he had come to America "with an intention of passing a considerable part of his life there," but a series of land-speculating and business failures eventually drove him back to England. American customs and manners, he concluded in his book *The Stranger in America* (1807), were "in every respect uncongenial to English habits, and to the tone of an Englishman's constitution." Yet his account of the emerging nature of America's character was no more disparaging and despairing than the accounts of many Federalists, who were equally fearful of the brutality and vulgarity the new republican society seemed to be breeding. By the early nineteenth century Janson was not the only one in America who felt that he was a stranger in the land.[19]

Janson's views of America's democratic society, where the meanest and most ignorant people "consider themselves on an equal footing with the best educated people in the country," were actually no more severe than those of Joseph Dennie, whom Janson quoted. The Boston-born and Harvard-educated Dennie was the editor of the *Port Folio*, the most influential and longest-lasting literary journal of its day and the most distinguished

18. Lawrence W. Towner, "The Indentures of Boston's Poor Apprentices: 1734–1805," Colonial Society of Massachusetts, *Publications*, 43 (1956–1963), 427; Philip S. Foner, ed., *The Democratic-Republican Societies, 1790–1800: A Documentary Sourcebook of Constitutions, Addresses, Resolutions, and Toasts* (Westport, CT, 1976), 10.

19. Charles William Janson, *Stranger in America* (London, 1807), ed. Carl S. Driver (New York, 1935), xxiii–iv.

Federalist publication in the age of Jefferson. In 1803 in one of his early issues Dennie wrote with more valor than discretion that "a democracy is scarcely tolerable at any period of national history. Its omens are always sinister....It was weak and wicked in Athens. It was bad in Sparta, and worse in Rome. It has been tried in France, and has terminated in despotism. It was tried in England, and rejected with the utmost loathing and abhorrence. It is on its trial here, and the issue will be civil war, desolation, and anarchy." For these comments Dennie was hauled into court as a factious and seditious person, though eventually acquitted.[20]

But Dennie and other Federalists soon came to realize that democracy in America was not going to end, as it had elsewhere, in anarchy leading to dictatorship and despotism. Instead, American democracy, driven by the most intense competitiveness, especially for the making of money, was going to end in orgies of getting and spending. Too many of the American people seemed absorbed in the selfish pursuit of their own interests, buying and selling like no other people in the world. Federalist literati and others were appalled by what seemed to be the sudden emergence of thousands upon thousands of hustling "businessmen," which was the term that soon came into favor—appropriately enough, for the whole society seemed absorbed in business. "Enterprise," "improvement," and "getting ahead" were everywhere extolled in the press. "The voice of the people and their government is loud and unanimous for commerce," said a disgruntled and bewildered Dr. Samuel Mitchill in 1800. "Their inclination and habits are adapted to trade and traffic," declared this professor of natural history at Columbia College, who knew so much that he was called "a living encyclopedia" and "the walking library." "From one end of the continent to the other," said Mitchill, "the universal roar is Commerce! Commerce! at all events, Commerce!"[21]

Although nearly all Americans lived in rural places and were engaged in farming, most of them, as Professor Mitchill correctly perceived, were by 1800 much involved in commerce and the exchange of goods. The extent of their commercial involvement has been a matter of some debate among historians. Some have suggested that many eighteenth-century farmers, especially in New England, were pre-modern and anti-capitalist in their outlook. These farmers, these historians contend, were mainly engaged in household modes of production in which they sought not to

20. Janson, *Stranger in America*, 423–24, 311, 20, 86; William C. Dowling, *Literary Federalism in the Age of Jefferson: Joseph Dennie and The Port Folio, 1801–1811* (Columbia, SC, 1999), 1.
21. Samuel L. Mitchill, *An Address to the Citizens of New York* (New York, 1800), 23; Joseph Kastner, *A Species of Eternity* (New York, 1977), 195.

maximize profits but only to satisfy their family needs and maintain the competency and independence of their households. They sought land not to increase their personal wealth but to provide estates for their lineal families. Rather than relying on extended markets, these husbandmen tended to produce goods for their own consumption or for exchanges within their local communities.[22]

While eighteenth-century farmers may have been less commercial than they would become in the nineteenth century, they certainly knew about trade and commerce. Many, if not most, at least occasionally brought "surpluses" to markets beyond their neighborhoods—selling tobacco and other staples to Britain, sending wheat and other foodstuffs to Europe, and exporting lumber and livestock to the West Indies. In other words, from the beginning of the seventeenth century colonial Americans exchanged goods and knew about marketplaces; but, in New England at least, many farmers may not have participated in what economists call a true market economy. Only when the market became separated from the political, social, and cultural systems constraining it and became itself an agent of change, only when most people in the society became involved in buying and selling and began to think in terms of bettering themselves economically—only then did Americans begin to enter a market economy.

Economic historian Winifred Barr Rothenberg has dated the emergence of this market economy in New England in the several decades following the American Revolution. She has discovered that market integration, the price convergence of commodities, and the development of capital markets in rural New England took place in this period—brought about by the impersonal exchanges of the farmers themselves. In the 1780s and 1790s farmers were lending more money more often to ever more scattered and distant debtors and shifting more of their assets away from cattle and implements toward liquid and evanescent forms of wealth. At the same time as interest rates, or the price of money, began to float free from their ancient and customary restraints, agricultural productivity of all sorts began to increase rapidly. By 1801, for example, the output of grains in a sample of Massachusetts towns was nearly two and a half times what it had been in 1771. Only when these farmers increased their

22. James A. Henretta, *The Origins of American Capitalism: Selected Essays* (Boston, 1991); Allan Kulikoff, *The Agrarian Origins of American Capitalism* (Charlottesville, 1992); Christopher Clark, *The Roots of Rural Capitalism: Western Massachusetts, 1780–1860* (Ithaca, 1990). For analyses of the "transition to capitalism" debate, see Gordon S. Wood, "Inventing American Capitalism," *New York Review of Books* (9 June 1994), 44–49; and Wood, "The Enemy Is Us: Democratic Capitalism in the Early Republic," in Paul A. Gilje, ed., *Wages of Independence: Capitalism in the Early Republic* (Madison, WI, 1997), 137–53.

productivity to the point where an increasing proportion of them could engage in manufacturing and at the same time provide a home market for that manufacturing—only then could the takeoff into capitalistic expansion take place.[23]

Since this remarkable increase in labor productivity occurred well before the availability of any new farm machinery or any other technological change, it can be explained only by the more efficient use and organization of labor. In 1795 a Massachusetts physician noted the changes taking place among the farmers of his little town. "The former state of cultivation was bad, but is much altered for the better," he said. "A spirit of emulation prevails among the farmers. Their enclosures, which used to be fenced with hedge and log fences, are now generally fenced with good stone wall," a sure sign, he suggested, that the farmers were using their land more intensively and more productively.[24] Farmers were becoming more productive because they glimpsed the prospect of improving their standard of living by consuming luxury goods that hitherto only the gentry had consumed—feather instead of straw mattresses, pewter instead of wooden bowls, and silk instead of cotton handkerchiefs.

"Is not the Hope of one day being able to purchase and enjoy Luxuries a great Spur to labour and Industry?" Benjamin Franklin had asked in 1784—a question that flew in the face of age-old wisdom. For centuries it was assumed that most people would not work unless they had to. "Everybody but an idiot," declared the enlightened English agricultural writer Arthur Young, in a startling summary of this traditional view, "knows that the lower class must be kept poor or they will never be industrious."[25] But farmers now were working harder, not, as conventional thinking would have it, out of poverty and necessity, but in order to increase their purchase of luxury goods and become more respectable.

23. Rothenberg, whose book is based on empirical data drawn from account books, probate inventories, and tax valuations, argues that an authentic market economy exists wherever buyers and sellers are in such free exchange with one another over a region that the prices of the same goods tend to converge. In other words, a market economy, Rothenberg concludes, emerged in rural New England only when the prices of farm commodities, farm labor (or wages), and rural savings (or interest), came to be set, not by custom or by government, but by the impersonal exchanges of the market. Winifred Barr Rothenberg, *From Market-Places to a Market Economy: The Transformation of Rural Massachusetts, 1750–1850* (Chicago, 1992), 124, 220, 243, 101.

24. J. M. Opal, *Beyond the Farm: National Ambitions in Rural New England* (Philadelphia, 2008), 53.

25. BF to Benjamin Vaughn, 26 July 1784, in Albert Henry Smyth, ed., *The Writings of Benjamin Franklin* (New York, 1905–1907), 9: 243–44; Derek Jarrett, *England in the Age of Hogarth* (London, 1974), 79–80.

ALTHOUGH MOST FEDERALISTS and even some Republican elites like Professor Mitchill, who later became a Republican congressman and U.S. senator from New York, were frightened by the growing mania for commerce and money, believing that it resembled people's being at war with one another, most of the farmers and businessmen themselves welcomed this competitive scramble. Some of them, in the Northern states at least, used the competitive vehicle of the Republican party to challenge the static Federalist establishment. But others sensed, as John Adams had, that competition arose out of the egalitarianism of the society as people sought not just to keep up with the Joneses but to get ahead of them. And they came to see that a spirit of emulation was good for prosperity.

Americans were in fact using competition to democratize ambition and make it the basis for a new kind of middling society. Other societies, said Noah Webster, trained their children in the occupations of their parents. But this European practice "cramps genius and limits the progress of national improvement." Americans celebrated the "ambition and fire of youth" and allowed genius to express itself. Many cultures feared the expression of ambition because it was an aristocratic passion that belonged to the Macbeths of the world—great-souled individuals who were apt to be dangerous. Americans, however, need not have this fear, at least not to the same extent. In a republic ambition should belong to everyone, and, said Webster, it "should be governed, rather than repressed."[26]

Elkanah Watson was eager to exploit this popular characteristic of American culture. Watson, the son of a Plymouth, Massachusetts, artisan and representative of the new breed of hustlers springing up everywhere, discovered that the earlier aristocratic and philosophical techniques of stimulating agricultural reform through scientific societies of gentleman-farmers would not work in America. Because Americans were too independent for such learned paternalism, Watson in 1810 devised for Berkshire County in western Massachusetts what soon became the familiar American county fair, with exhibitions, music, dancing, singing, and prizes awarded for the best crops and the biggest livestock. In 1812 "the female part of the community in a spirit of honorable competition" was allowed to demonstrate cloth, lace, hats, and other products of domestic manufacturing. Women began hanging their prizewinning certificates on the walls of their homes, where "they excite the envy of a whole neighbourhood." Indeed, said Watson, producing "some tincture of envy" was crucial in calling forth "more extended efforts" by the farmers and their wives. The fairs, which Watson claimed were "original and peculiar,"

26. Opal, *Beyond the Farm,* 75.

were designed "to excite a lively spirit of competition" by exploiting the desire for "personal ambition" that he claimed was characteristic of all Americans. Watson knew, as the enlightened gentry apparently did not, that society had to be dealt with "in its actual state of existence,—not as we could wish it." One of his fairs, he said, produced "more *practical good*" and more actual agricultural improvement "than *ten* studied, wire-drawn books" written by "scientific gentlemen farmers" settled in their Eastern cities. The only way of achieving public benefits in agriculture and domestic manufacturing, said Watson, was to create "a system congenial to *American habits*, and the state of *our society*," and to incite the farmers' "self-love,—self-interest, combined with a natural love of country." Watson thought that his county fairs had produced "a general strife" among farmers and had done much to awaken the slumbers of husbandry in the United States.[27]

Teachers in New England developed a new pedagogy based on ambition and competition instead of the traditional resort to corporal punishment. Many of the new academies that were springing up all over New England were doing with schoolchildren what Elkanah Watson was doing with his farmers and his county fairs—exciting among them "a spirit of emulation." A schoolmaster in a tiny Massachusetts town discovered that he could get his male students to study hard by raising "their ambition to such a pitch that that their greatest thought was, who would perform the best." Even the young women in the Litchfield Female Academy lived in a highly competitive atmosphere, with the girls repeatedly and publicly pitted against one another for awards, prizes, and credit marks. "Ambition has been raised to an uncommon degree, and our exertions have been wonderfully answered," declared one of their teachers. Encouraging young people of all ranks to be ambitious in this manner was bound to have a powerful effect on the society.

Many, of course, continued to urge patience and contentment with one's lot and to raise fears that too much stress on ambition could arouse envy and other harmful passions. "A degree of emulation, among literary institutions, is proper," warned a Calvinist preacher. "But when it goes to pull down one, in order to build another up, it is wrong." Despite these

27. Elkanah Watson, *Address of Elkanah Watson, Esq.. Delivered before the Berkshire Agricultural Societ y... 7th October, 1814* (Pittsfield, MA, 1814), 4, 7; Elkanah Watson, *History of the Rise, Progress, and Existing State of Modern Agricultural Societies on the Berkshire System, from 1807 to Establishment of the Board of Agriculture in the State of New York, January 10, 1820* (Albany, 1820), 114, 126, 132, 142, 145, 160, 168n, 169, 177–78, 182; Winslow C. Watson, ed., *Men and Times of the Revolution; or, Memoirs of Elkanah Watson...from the year 1777 to 1842* (New York, 1857), 425, 426–27, 428.

sorts of misgivings, however, the traditional way of doing things could scarcely stand against the newly awakened sense of ambition among so many common folk.[28]

Competition existed everywhere in America, even in the South, where it took a different form. Many Southern planters, even though they were good Jeffersonian Republicans, were just as contemptuous of crass money-making as Northern Federalists, but they did enjoy competing with one another. Of course, they valued hierarchy but, being uncertain of their position in it, were always eager to assert their abilities and status, often through horse racing, cockfighting, gambling, and dueling.

Many Southern gentlemen possessed hair-trigger tempers and were acutely sensitive to any perceived insult, however slight.[29] In 1806 Andrew Jackson, son of Scots-Irish immigrants from northern Ireland, a sometime congressman and U.S. senator from Tennessee, and a great lover of horse racing and cockfighting, ended up killing a man in a duel that began with a quarrel over a horse race wager. Duels growing out of the most trivial causes were not uncommon, especially on the frontier, where honor and gentlemanly status were especially vague and fluid and Celtic pride and touchiness were everywhere. Since Southerners bet on everything, they bet on the outcome of duels. In Nashville bets were freely made on Jackson's duel, mostly against Jackson since his opponent was considered the better shot. Jackson took a bullet that remained lodged in his chest for the rest of his life.

So barbarous was the fighting among commoners in the South that some observers, including New England Federalists and visiting foreigners, thought the white Americans' behavior was "worthy of their savage neighbors."[30] Men on the frontier often fought with "no holds barred," using their hands, feet, and teeth to disfigure or dismember each other until one or the other surrendered or was incapacitated. "Scratching, pulling hair, choking, gouging out each other's eyes, and biting off each other's noses" were all tried, recalled Daniel Drake, growing up in late eighteenth-century Kentucky. "But what is worse than all," observed the

28. Opal, *Beyond the Farm*, 96–125, esp. 118, 101, 111–13, 120; Rena L. Vassar, ed., "The Life or Biography of Silas Felton Written by Himself," American Antiquarian Society, *Proc.*, 69 (1959), 140.

29. Bertram Wyatt-Brown, *Southern Honor: Ethics and Behavior in the Old South* (New York, 1982); Jack K. Williams, *Dueling in the Old South: Vignettes of Social History* (College Station, TX, 1980).

30. Marquis de Chastellux, *Travels in North America in the Years 1780, 1781 and 1782*, ed. Howard C. Rice Jr., (Chapel Hill, 1963), 2: 601; Elliot J. Gorn, " 'Gouge and Bite, Pull Hair and Scratch': The Social Significance of Fighting in the Southern Backcountry," *AHR*, 90 (1985), 18–43; Rhys Isaac, *The Transformation of Virginia, 1740–1790* (Chapel Hill, 1982), 98–104.

English traveler Isaac Weld, "these wretches in their combat endeavor to their utmost to tear out each other's testicles."[31]

Most of these practices of rough-and-tumble fighting had been brought over from the Celtic borderlands of the British Isles—Scotland, Ireland, Wales, and Cornwall. Indeed, some historians have persuasively argued that most of the characteristics of the Southern "rednecks"—including their indolence, the making of "moonshine," fiddling and banjo-playing, chewing tobacco, hunting, and hog-raising—can be traced back to their Celtic ancestors. This is especially true, they say, of the hot-headedness and propensity to personal violence of backcountry Southern "crackers," with someone like Andrew Jackson being a prime representative.[32]

But what were occasional practices of personal violence in Britain became a unique fighting style in the American South, and gouging out the eyes of one's opponent became the defining element of that style. Although the acerbic Englishman Charles Janson may have been exaggerating in claiming that "this more than savage custom is daily practiced among the lower classes in the southern states," he was not wrong in suggesting that it was common. Not only had the Reverend Jedidiah Morse in his *American Geography* confirmed the prevalence of the practice of gouging, but many early nineteenth-century travelers besides Janson witnessed examples of these gouging matches.[33]

The fighters became heroes in their local communities, and their success in these rough-and-tumble matches generated its own folklore. Eventually these matches became part of the exaggerated boasting and bombast that came to characterize Southwestern humor. At the same time, the prevalence of such personal violence convinced many observers, Federalists and European travelers alike, that as Americans moved westward and down the Ohio River they were losing civilization and reverting to savagery.[34]

Barbarism was not confined to the rural South and Southwest but seemed to be spreading even to the urban North and Northeast. Philadelphia in the 1790s was full of cockfighting, gambling, and quarreling that often led to fistfights.[35] Despite all the rhetoric promoting politeness and

31. Daniel Drake, *Pioneer Life in Kentucky: A Series of Reminiscential Letters*, in Joyce Appleby, ed., *Recollections of the Early Republic: Selected Autobiographies* (Boston, 1997), 64; Gorn, " 'Gouge and Bite,' " 23–25.

32. Grady McWhiney, *Cracker Culture: Celtic Ways in the Old South* (Tuscaloosa, 1988); David Hackett Fischer, *Albion's Seed: Four British Folkways in America* (New York, 1989).

33. Janson, *Stranger in America*, 307–8; Gorn, " 'Gouge and Bite,' " 31–36.

34. Kenneth S. Lynn, *Mark Twain and Southwestern Humor* (Boston, 1960), 23–72.

35. Kenneth Roberts and Anna M. Roberts, eds., *Moreau de St. Méry's American Journey, 1793–1798* (Garden City, NY, 1947), 328–29, 333.

civility, Americans by 1800 were already known for pushing and shoving each other in public and for their dread of ceremony. Foreigners thought the Americans' eating habits were atrocious, their food execrable, and their coffee detestable. Americans tended to eat fast, often sharing a common bowl or cup, to bolt their food in silence, and to use only their knives in eating. Everywhere travelers complained about "the violation of decorum, the want of etiquette, the rusticity of manners in this generation."[36]

ALL THIS VULGARITY was changing the character of political leadership. With self-interested behavior becoming so common, the classical republican conception of governmental leadership that the Founders had extolled was rapidly losing its meaning. It became increasingly clear that society could no longer expect men to sacrifice their time and money—their private interests—for the sake of the public. It was said that John Jay had hesitated to accept a position in the new federal government because he was "waiting to see which Salary is best, that of Lord Chief Justice or Secretary of State." If this were the case with someone as wealthy and prominent as Jay, public office could no longer be regarded merely as a burden that prominent gentlemen had an obligation to bear. If anything, holding office was becoming the source of that wealth and social authority.[37]

Many Americans of the early Republic, with varying degrees of reluctance or enthusiasm, came to believe that what they once thought was true was no longer true. Government officials were no longer to play the role of umpires, standing above the competing interests of the marketplace and making impartial judgments about what was good for the whole society. The democratic nightmare that had been first experienced in the 1780s was becoming all too pervasive and real. Elected officials were bringing the partial, local interests of the society, and sometimes even their own interests, right into the workings of government. The word "logrolling" in the making of laws (that is, the trading of votes by legislators for each other's bills) began to be used for the first time, to the bewilderment

---

36. *The Journal of William D. Martin: A Journey from South Carolina to Connecticut in the Year 1809*, ed. Anna D. Elmore (Charlotte, SC, 1959), 8–9; Ester B. Aresty, *The Best Behavior: The Course of Good Manners—From Antiquity to the Present as Seen Through Courtesy and Etiquette Books* (New York, 1970), 189–90, 229; *North American Review*, 1 (1815), 20.

37. Samuel A. Otis to John Langdon, [16–22] Sept. 1789, in Maeva Marcus and James R. Perry et al., eds., *The Documentary History of the Supreme Court of the United States* (New York, 1985), 1: 661. Part 2 of this volume is full of the awkward letters of men who desired appointment to the Supreme Court but were culturally inhibited from expressing their desires too boldly.

of the Federalists. "I do not well understand the Term," said an Ohio Federalist, "but I believe it means bargaining with each other for the little loaves and fishes of the State."[38]

Under such circumstances partisanship and parties—using government to promote partial interests—became increasingly legitimate. As property as a source of independence and authority gave way to an entrepreneurial idea of property, as a commodity to be exchanged in the marketplace, the older proprietary qualifications for officeholding and the suffrage existing in many of the states lost their meaning and soon fell away. Property that fluctuated and changed hands so frequently was no basis for the right to vote. When Republicans, such as those of New York in 1812, claimed that the mere owning of property was no "proof of superior virtue, discernment or patriotism," conservative Federalists had no answer.[39] In state after state the Democratic-Republicans successfully pushed for an expansion of the suffrage. By 1825 every state but Rhode Island, Virginia, and Louisiana had achieved universal white manhood suffrage; by 1830 only Rhode Island, which had once been the most democratic place in North America, retained a general freehold qualification for voting.

The expansion of the suffrage and the celebration of ordinary people meant that ordinary people might even become government officials, as many increasingly did in the Northern states in the early decades of the nineteenth century. Republican leaders in the North repeatedly appealed to mechanics, laborers, and farmers to elect men of their own kind. "Does a nobleman . . . know the wants of the farmer and the mechanic?" asked a New York broadside in 1810. "If we give such men the management of our concerns, where is our INDEPENDENCE and FREEDOM?" Republican spokesmen warned the common people not to elect "men whose aristocratic doctrine teaches that the rights and representative authority of the people are vested in a few proud elites" and used the Revolutionary idea of equality to justify electing ordinary men to office. To the surprise of many, Jonathan Jamison of Indiana Territory, a former clerk in the Land Office, openly and successfully campaigned for office in 1809 and continued to use his new brand of popular politics to become the state's first governor when Indiana was admitted to the Union in 1816.[40]

Even parts of the South, as a North Carolinian complained in 1803, were not immune from the new egalitarian politics. "The charge of

---

38. Donald J. Ratcliffe, *Party Spirit in a Frontier Republic: Democratic Politics in Ohio, 1793–1821* (Columbus, OH, 1998), 79.
39. Harvey Strum, "Property Qualifications and Voting Behavior in New York, 1807–1816," *JER*, 1 (1981), 359.
40. Strum, "Property Qualifications," 367.

aristocracy, fatal in America, was pressed against him," he explained, in accounting for the defeat of former governor and Federalist-leaning William Davie in his 1803 bid for Congress, "and the radicalism of the people caused a revolt against their ancient leader." Naturally the Old Republican John Randolph was disgusted at what was happening. The affairs of the nation, he told his fellow congressmen, had been "committed to Tom, Dick, and Harry, the refuse of the retail trade of politics."[41]

Even when political candidates were not ordinary, many now found it advantageous to pose as such. In the campaign for governor of New York in 1807 Daniel Tompkins, successful lawyer and graduate of Columbia College, was portrayed as a simple "Farmers Boy" in contrast to his opponent, Morgan Lewis, who was an in-law of the aristocratic Livingston family. Of course, the New York Federalists in 1810 tried to combat Tompkins and the Republicans with their own plebeian candidate, Jonas Platt, "whose habits and manners," said the Federalists, "are as plain and republican as those of his country neighbors." Unlike Tompkins, Platt was not "a city lawyer who rolls in splendor and wallows in luxury."[42] In trying to out-popularize the Republicans, however, the Federalists could only ultimately lose, for most Republicans, in the North at least, did in fact come from lower social strata than the Federalists.

The common people increasingly seemed to want unpretentious men as their rulers, men who never went to college and never put on airs. Such a man was Simon Snyder, son of a poor mechanic in Lancaster, Pennsylvania. Snyder began his career as a tanner and scrivener and acquired what education he had by attending night school taught by a Quaker. He eventually became a storekeeper, mill owner, and successful businessman, so successful in fact that he was soon appointed justice of the peace and judge of the Court of Common Pleas of Northumberland County, Pennsylvania. Entering the Pennsylvania assembly in 1797, Snyder moved up to become the speaker of the state's house of representatives in 1802 and then governor in 1808, but he never shed his lowly origins. When he was elected governor, he refused an honor guard at his inauguration. "I hate and despise all ostentation—pomp and parade as anti-democratic...," he said. "I should feel exceedingly awkward" with such pretension. When opponents mocked Snyder's obscure origins and called him and his followers "clodhoppers," he and his supporters quite shrewdly picked up the epithet and began proudly wearing it. Being a

41. Griffith J. McRee, *Life and Correspondence of James Iredell* (New York, 1857–1858), 2: 160; Norman K. Risjord, *The Old Republicans: Southern Conservatism in the Age of Jefferson* (New York, 1965), 57.
42. Strum, "Property Qualifications," 350, 369.

clodhopper in a society of clodhoppers was the source of much of Snyder's political success. The snobbish Philadelphia-based American Philosophical Society responded to Snyder's election by quietly dropping the
office of patron, which the incumbent governor had always held.[43]

Feelings of equality spread throughout Northern society and even began
to be expressed in dress. Unlike in the eighteenth century, when gentlemen
often wore varied and colorful clothes, nineteenth-century men began dressing alike, in black coats and pantaloons, as befitting solid and substantial
businessmen who considered themselves the equals of every other man.[44]

By the first decade of the nineteenth century many gentlemen like
Benjamin Latrobe, President Jefferson's surveyor of public buildings,
thought that democracy was getting out of hand. Although Latrobe was a
good Republican, he nonetheless complained in 1806 to the Italian
patriot Philip Mazzei that too many representatives in America's national
government resembled their constituents and were ignorant and
"unlearned." Philadelphia and its suburbs sent to the Congress not a single man of letters. One congressman was indeed a lawyer, "but of no
eminence." Another congressman, said Latrobe, was a clerk in a bank,
and "the others are plain farmers." From the county was sent a blacksmith
and from just over the river a butcher.[45]

The butcher Latrobe referred to was probably the congressman who
used his generous congressional franking privileges in Washington to
send his linen home for laundering. It was not much of an abuse, critics
said, since the butcher-congressman "was known to change his shirt only
once a week." When invited to President Jefferson's dinner at the White
House, the butcher, noted a British witness, "observing a leg of mutton of
a miserably lean description,... could not help forgetting the legislator for
a few moments, expressing the feelings of his profession and exclaiming
that at his stall no such leg of mutton should ever have found a place."[46]

Latrobe believed that the "ideal rank" of gentlemen "which manners
has established" had virtually disappeared, even in the city of Philadelphia.

43. Andrew Shankman, Crucible of American Democracy: The Struggle to Fuse
    Egalitarianism and Capitalism in Jeffersonian Pennsylvania (Lawrence, KS, 2004),
    199, 153; Sean Wilentz, The Rise of American Democracy: Jefferson to Lincoln (New
    York, 2005), 123.
44. Michael Zakim, Ready-Made Democracy: A History of Men's Dress in the American
    Republic, 1760–1860 (Chicago, 2003).
45. Benjamin Latrobe to Philip Mazzei, 19 Dec. 1806, in Margherita Marchione et al.,
    eds., Philip Mazzei: Select Writings and Correspondence (Prato, Italy, 1983), 439.
46. Richard Beale Davis, ed., Jeffersonian America: Notes on the United States of America
    Collected in the Years 1805–6–7 and 11–12 by Sir Augustus John Foster, Bart. (San
    Marino, CA, 1954), 56.

Latrobe admitted that there were "solid and general advantages" to this kind of egalitarian society. "But to a cultivated mind, to a man of letters, to a lover of the arts," in other words, to someone like him, "it presents a very unpleasant picture." American society, based as it was on "the freedom which opens every legal avenue to wealth to everyone individually," made "all citizens rivals in the pursuit of riches," which in turn weakened the ties that bound them to one another and rendered them indifferent as to how they made their money.[47]

THE SPREAD OF EQUALITY and changing conceptions of political leadership generated intense partisan passions. The Federalists and the Jeffersonian Republicans may not have been modern parties, but they increasingly acted like parties, and they produced powerful loyalties among large numbers of the population, especially among the Republicans. In 1809 the Republican minister William Bentley in Salem, Massachusetts, declared that the "parties hate each other as much as the French and English hate each [other] in time of war." Families broke up over politics, and employers dismissed their employees because of party differences. Political passions, noted an English visitor, even reached into the grave. In 1808 Jeffersonian Nathaniel Ames refused to attend the funeral of his brother Fisher Ames after the Massachusetts Federalists "snatched" the "putrid corpse" and turned the burial into one of their "political funerals."[48] In Ohio in 1804 Republican animosity toward the Federalists led some of them to want to change the names of Hamilton and Adams counties—"republicanism... run mad," admitted a moderate Republican. The Federalists' feelings ran just as high. Upon learning of the death of a Republican, a Federalist in 1808 exclaimed, "Another God Damned Democrat has gone to Hell, and I wish they were all there."[49]

Partisanship sometimes resulted in violence. "Three-fourths of the duels which have been fought in the United States were produced by political disputes," claimed a South Carolinian in 1805; such fights were inevitable as long as "party violence is carried to an abominable excess."[50] But since dueling required the participants to think of themselves as

47. Latrobe to Mazzei, 19 Dec. 1806, in Marchione et al., eds., *Mazzei: Writings*, 439.
48. David Hackett Fischer, *The Revolution of American Conservatism: The Federalist Party in the Era of Jeffersonian Democracy* (New York, 1965), 183; Charles Warren, *Jacobin and Junto; or, Early American Politics as Viewed in the Diary of Dr. Nathaniel Ames, 1758–1822* (New York, 1931), 223.
49. Ratcliffe, *Party Spirit in a Frontier Republic*, 82; Chilton Williamson, *American Suffrage: From Property to Democracy, 1760–1860* (Princeton, 1960), 161.
50. Appleby, *Inheriting the Revolution*, 43.

gentlemanly equals, many Federalists often resorted to caning their Republican enemies.

During an 1807 election campaign in Albany, New York, a Republican meeting issued a resolution on April 17 questioning the integrity of General Solomon Van Rensselaer, a prominent Federalist. On April 21 Van Rensselaer sought out Elisha Jenkins, the author of the provocative resolution, and beat him with a heavy cane and then stomped on him with his feet. Partisans on each side joined in the fray and turned the city, according to one observer, into "a tumultuous *sea of heads*, over which clattered a forest of canes; the vast body, now surging this way, now that, as the tide of combat ebbed or flowed." Nine days later an Albany newspaper gave thanks for the end of an election campaign that had resulted in violence that was "little short of insurrection and blood."[51]

The most well known episode of partisan violence in the period took place in Massachusetts in 1806 when the state was torn apart for months by what was called a "political murder." Benjamin Austin, a prominent and zealous Republican editor, noted for his sharp tongue and his vigorous attacks on the Federalists, made some public reference to "a damned Federalist lawyer." In response, that lawyer, a young man named Thomas O. Selfridge, arrogantly called for a retraction and, when Austin ignored him, publicly posted Austin as "a coward, a liar, and a scoundrel." To revenge this insult to his father, Austin's son, an eighteen-year-old senior at Harvard, sought out Selfridge in the streets of Boston and struck him with a cane; Selfridge pulled a pistol he had been carrying and shot and killed the young man. Selfridge quickly turned himself in, in order, as he later said, "to escape into prison to elude the fury of democracy." Selfridge's trial, at which he was finally acquitted, further inflamed partisan passions. Selfridge himself added to the ugly atmosphere by publishing an extraordinarily offensive pamphlet. The hostility the case aroused lingered on for years.[52]

BUT IT WAS NOT JUST PARTISAN POLITICS that generated violence. Personal violence was more common in America than it was in England. During the second half of the eighteenth century, Pennsylvania's murder rate was twice that of London. In the newer counties of Pennsylvania assaults in the 1780s and 1790s made up over 40 percent of all allegations

51. Alan Taylor, *William Cooper's Town: Power and Persuasion on the Frontier of the Early American Republic* (New York, 1995), 367–68.

52. Warren, *Jacobin and Junto*, 183–214; Saul Cornell, *A Well-Regulated Militia: The Founding Fathers and the Origins of Gun Control in America* (New York, 2006), 113–17.

coming before grand juries. Complaints of personal violence in the state rose precipitously in the decades following the Revolution. Homicide rates in the Chesapeake and in the backcountry of the South reversed a century of decline and increased dramatically among both blacks and whites in the turbulent decades following the Revolution. In 1797 New York City saw a sudden rise in its homicide rate. During the twenty-six years between 1770 and 1796 the city experienced only seventeen homicides, including four that occurred during the chaotic years of 1783–1784 following the British evacuation. In 1797 the number of homicides went up and stayed there over the subsequent decades, resulting in a total of eighty homicides in the eighteen years between 1797 and 1815, including eleven in the single year of 1811. Equally alarming, especially to New Yorker Samuel L. Mitchill, was the high suicide rate in the city. Between 1804 and 1808 seventy-five adults killed themselves—a consequence, Mitchill concluded, of something "morbid in the mental constitution of the people."[53]

By the late 1790s Americans sensed latent violence everywhere. News of reciprocal brutality and violence between whites and Indians on the frontiers gave people the uneasy sense that civility in America was becoming paper-thin and could be punctured by acts of barbarism at any time. Incidents of multiple family murders dramatically increased, with one of them becoming the basis for Charles Brockden Brown's novel *Wieland*.[54] Even civilized and stable areas in New England seemed to be regressing. In 1796 and 1799 local authorities in rural areas of Massachusetts and Connecticut independently indicted two elderly men for bestiality, a crime that had not been prosecuted in New England for nearly a century.[55] By modern standards murder was still rare, but nevertheless Americans expressed a fascination with horrific murders, especially those of passion. News of notorious trials of domestic violence, including cases of

---

53. G. S. Rowe and Jack D. Marietta, "Personal Violence in a 'Peaceable Kingdom': Pennsylvania, 1682–1801," in Christine Daniels and Michael V. Kennedy, eds., *Over the Threshold: Intimate Violence in Early America* (New York, 1999), 24–27; Eric H. Monkkonen, *Murder in New York City* (Berkeley, 2001); Historical Violence Database, http://cjrc.ose.edu/hvd; Alan David Aberbach, *In Search of An American Identity: Samuel Latham Mitchill, Jeffersonian Nationalist* (New York, 1988), 187.
54. Neil K. Fitzgerald, "Towards an American Abraham: Multiple Parricide and the Rejection of Revelation in the Early National Period…" (M.A. thesis, Brown University, 1971), 8–9.
55. Doron Ben-Atar and Richard D. Brown, "Darkness in New Light New England: Punishing Bestial Acts in the 1790's," unpublished paper presented at the American Historical Association Convention, 5 Jan. 2008, and cited with permission of the authors.

fathers raping their daughters, like the case of Ephraim Wheeler in western Massachusetts in 1805, were deeply unsettling and often blended into the partisan atmosphere of the time. Wheeler's execution for his crime, for example, became a means by which the Massachusetts Republicans could accuse the Federalists in power of being proponents of "the sanguinary principles of a monarchical system."[56]

Urban rioting became more prevalent and destructive. Street, tavern, and theater rowdiness, labor strikes, racial and ethnic conflicts—all increased greatly after 1800. Of course, mobbing and rioting had been common in the eighteenth century, but these nineteenth-century mobs were different. They were uncontrolled and sometimes murderous, and no longer paid tribute to paternalism and hierarchy as the relatively restrained mobs of the eighteenth century had done. Unlike the earlier colonial mobs, which were often made up of a cross-section of the community more or less under the control of elites, the mobs and gangs of the early Republic were composed of mostly unconnected and anonymous lowly people, full of class resentment, and thus all the more frightening. Indeed, Republicans in New York City played upon such resentment in 1801 by telling people in election handbills that the Federalist mayor "hates you; from his own soul he hates you...; do your duty and...you will get rid of a mayor who acts as if he thought a poor man had no more right than a horse."[57]

The growing urban societies appeared to have lost all sense of cohesion and hierarchy; they had become, in the words of a longtime New York police magistrate, but "a heterogeneous mass" of men with "weak and depraved minds" and an "insatiable appetite for animal gratification." Indeed, the population of the cities was now "so numerous that the citizens are not all known to each other," thus allowing "depredators [to] merge in the mass, and spoliate in secret and safety." Mounting fear of disorder compelled New York City to increase the numbers of watchmen from fifty in 1788 to 428 by 1825, which was nearly double the proportionate growth in population; and still the murderous rioting continued.[58]

The most serious rioting in the period took place in Baltimore during the opening weeks of the War of 1812. Since Baltimore was the fastest-growing city in the United States(its population of 46,600 in 1810 made

56. Roger Lane, *Murder in America* (Columbus, OH, 1997), 82–84; Irene Q. Brown and Richard D. Brown, *The Hanging of Ephraim Wheeler: A Story of Rape, Incest, and Justice in Early America* (Cambridge, MA, 2003), 260.

57. Paul A. Gilje, *The Road to Mobocracy: Popular Disorder in New York City, 1763–1834* (Chapel Hill, 1987), 123–288; Howard B. Rock, *Artisans of the New Republic: The Tradesmen of New York City in the Age of Jefferson* (New York, 1979), 59.

58. Gilje, *Road to Mobocracy*, 268, 274, 279.

it the third-largest city in the country), it was being torn apart in every conceivable way—by politics, class, religion, ethnicity, nativist fears of immigration, and race. Between 1790 and 1810 the city's percentage of blacks grew from 12 percent to 22 percent, with the proportion of free blacks among the African American population growing even faster, from 2 percent to 11 percent of the total population. Anglicans of English ancestry, Scotch-Irish Presbyterians, German Lutherans, and large numbers of Irish Catholics jostled with one another, all trying to fend off the astonishing growth of the Methodists. The occupational makeup of the city was less diverse but still mixed. Mechanics composed half the population, and merchants made up 15 percent. As masters turned into employers and journeymen became employees, the mechanics were at each other's throats, especially as the master-employers began replacing the skilled journeymen with unskilled laborers, many of them blacks. Draymen, dock workers, sailors, and laborers, constituting perhaps another 15 percent of the population, composed the lowest ranks of the city's society. The Republican-dominated city was a tinderbox, not needing much to touch it off.[59]

The rioting, which began on June 22, 1812, was sparked by the declaration of war against Great Britain and the long-existing division between the city's Federalists and Republicans. A mob of thirty to forty Republican stalwarts dismantled the offices of a much-hated Federalist newspaper, which had been publishing vicious attacks on the Republicans and their unnecessary war. When the mayor, himself a Republican, tried to intervene, he was told by members of the mob that they knew him "very well, no body wants to hurt you; but the laws of the land must sleep, and laws of nature and reason prevail; that house is the Temple of Infamy; it is supported with English gold, and it must and shall come down to the ground."[60] This mob behaved in a traditional eighteenth-century manner, enforcing what it took to be natural standards of the community; indeed, according to a newspaper account, the members of the mob went about tearing down the building in a workman-like way, "as regularly as if they contracted to perform the job for pay."[61]

This traditional mob action seemed to unleash emotions throughout the city. Protestants and Catholics and whites and blacks turned on one another. But it was the Federalists who aroused the most anger. On July 27, 1812, the Federalists, some of whom were ensconced in a house with guns and powder, issued their newspaper once again. This provoked another

59. Seth Rockman, *Scraping By: Wage Labor, Slavery, and Survival in Early Baltimore* (Baltimore, 2009).

60. Donald R. Hickey, *The War of 1812: A Forgotten Conflict* (Urbana, IL, 1989), 59.

61. Paul A. Gilje, *Rioting in America* (Bloomington, IN, 1996), 60–63.

Republican mob, largely composed of militant journeyman mechanics unrestrained by master artisans and other social superiors. The two dozen Federalists in the house were mostly members of Maryland's elite, and they included two Revolutionary War generals; they thought that if they stood firm, the riffraff in front of their house would defer to their betters and melt away. The Federalists first fired warning shots, but when the mob persisted and stormed the house, they fired and killed two persons. When the mob set up a cannon in front of the house, the city authorities finally acted and negotiated the surrender of the Federalists.

The Federalists requested that they be taken to the jail in carriages—their usual aristocratic mode of transportation—but the mob wanted them conveyed in carts, the way criminals were transported. The Republican authorities finally insisted that they walk to the jail, where presumably they would be safe. But the Republican mob was not satisfied. The next night it attacked the lightly guarded jail and beat the Federalist prisoners, some of them senseless, stabbing them and tearing off their genteel clothes, the most conspicuous symbol of their aristocratic status. One Revolutionary War veteran, General James N. Lingan, died of his wounds, and the other, Henry "Light Horse Harry" Lee, the father of Robert E. Lee and the celebrated eulogist of Washington, was crippled and never fully recovered. James Monroe was alarmed enough by the mobbing to warn President Madison of the "danger of a civil war, which may undermine our free system of government."[62]

Still, the threat of mobbing in Baltimore continued. In early August the Federalists tried to send their newspaper through the mail to Baltimore; but when crowds threatened the U.S. Post Office, the city's magistrates had enough, and the militia dispersed the mob.[63]

The summer's bloody rioting in Baltimore, the worst in the history of the early Republic, was over, but mobbing was not. Mobs became more ferocious, more willing to engage in personal violence, and more ready to burn property than dismantle it. Such mobs were now prepared to act without elite participation or sanction, indeed, even to act *against* elites precisely because they *were* elites. By the second decade of the nineteenth century more and more political leaders were understandably calling for

---

62. James Monroe to JM, 4 Aug. 1812, *Papers of Madison: Presidential Ser.*, 5: 114.

63. Gilje, *Rioting in America*, 60–63; Charles G. Steffen, *The Mechanics of Baltimore: Workers and Politics in the Age of Revolution, 1763–1812* (Urbana, IL, 1984), 243–50; Hickey, *War of 1812*, 52–71; Frank A. Cassell, "The Great Baltimore Riot of 1812," *Maryland Historical Magazine*, 70 (1975), 241–59; Donald R. Hickey, "The Darker Side of Democracy: The Baltimore Riots of 1812," *Maryland Historian*, 7 (1976), 1–19; Paul A. Gilje, "The Baltimore Riots of 1812 and the Breakdown of the Anglo-American Mob Tradition," *Journal of Social History*, 13 (1979), 547–64.

the creation of professional police forces to curb the increasing urban disorder. The social authority and the patronage power of individual magistrates and gentry were no longer able to keep the peace.

ONE EXPLANATION OFTEN OFFERED at the time for all this violence was the sudden rise in the drinking of hard liquor. Both the rough-and-tumble fighters and members of the urban mobs were often drunk. But such ordinary and lowly people were not the only ones drinking too much. The distinguished physician and professor of materia medica at Columbia College Dr. David Hosack complained that forty of the hundred physicians in New York City were drunkards. Even the misbehavior of children was blamed on too much alcohol. Charles Janson reported that he often had, "with horror, seen boys, whose dress indicated wealthy parents, intoxicated, shouting and swearing in the public streets."[64]

Certainly the American consumption of distilled spirits was climbing rapidly during this period, rising from two and a half gallons per person per year in 1790 to almost five gallons in 1820—an amount nearly triple today's consumption and greater than that of every major European nation at that time. If the 1,750,000 slaves, who did not have much access to alcohol, are excluded from these figures of 1820, then the Americans' per capita consumption was even more remarkable—higher than at any other time in American history.

From the beginning of the Republic American grain farmers, particularly those of Celtic origin in western Pennsylvania, Kentucky, and Tennessee, had found it easier and more profitable to distill, ship, and sell whiskey than to try to ship and sell the perishable grain itself. Consequently, distilleries popped up everywhere, their numbers growing rapidly after the 1780s, reaching ten thousand by 1810. In 1815 even the little town of Peacham, Vermont, with a population of about fifteen hundred persons, had thirty distilleries. According to Samuel L. Mitchill in 1812, American stills were producing 23,720,000 gallons of "ardent spirits" a year—an alarming amount, said Mitchill, that was turning freedom into "rudeness and something worse." He estimated that some workers in the country were consuming up to a quart of hard liquor every day.[65]

Distilling whiskey was good business because, to the astonishment of foreigners, nearly all Americans—men, women, children, and sometimes even babies—drank whiskey all day long. Some workers began drinking before breakfast and then took dram breaks instead of coffee breaks. "Treating" with drink by militia officers and politicians was considered

64. Janson, *Stranger in America*, 304.
65. Samuel L. Mitchill, *Emporium*, 1 (1812), 74; Aberbach, *American Identity: Samuel Latham Mitchill*, 189.

essential to election. During court trials a bottle of liquor might be passed among the attorneys, spectators, clients, and the judge and jury.

Whiskey accompanied every communal activity, including women's quilting bees. But since manliness was defined by the ability to drink alcohol, men were the greatest imbibers. And taverns, unlike tea parties and assemblies, were exclusively male preserves. Taverns existed everywhere; indeed, most towns, even in staid New England, had more taverns than churches. By 1810 Americans were spending 2 percent of their personal income on distilled spirits, a huge amount at a time when most people's income went to the basic needs of food and shelter. One quarter of the total sales of an ordinary New Hampshire store was alcohol.[66]

The social consequences of all this drinking were frightening—absenteeism, accidental deaths, wife-beating, family desertion, rioting, and fighting. Dr. Benjamin Rush, who was a temperance reformer, outlined a number of diseases that he believed were aggravated by heavy drinking, including fevers of all sorts, obstructions of the liver, jaundice, hoarseness that often terminated in consumption, epilepsy, gout, and madness. In addition to diseases, said Rush in 1805, poverty and misery, crimes and infamy, were "all the natural and usual consequences of the intemperate use of ardent spirits." Washington, who himself had a distillery, thought as early as 1789 that distilled spirits were "the ruin of half the workmen in this Country." "The thing has arrived to such a height," declared the Greene and Delaware Moral Society in 1815, "that we are actually threatened with becoming a nation of drunkards."[67]

EXCESSIVE DRINKING MIGHT HAVE AGGRAVATED much of America's licentious behavior, but many observers believed the ultimate source of the social disorder lay with the family. Charles Janson, for example, thought that all the intoxicated boys he had seen resulted from indulgent parents' allowing their children to do whatever they wanted. John Adams went further and held parents responsible for all the social and political disorder in America. "The source of revolution, democracy, Jacobinism . . . ,"

66. W. J. Rorabaugh, *The Alcoholic Republic: An American Tradition* (New York, 1979) 89, 17.

67. Rorabaugh, *Alcoholic Republic*, 3–21, 87; Ian R. Tyrell, *Sobering Up: From Temperance to Prohibition in Antebellum America, 1800–1860* (Westport, CT, 1979), 3–32; Randolph A. Roth, *The Democratic Dilemma: Religion, Reform, and the Social Order in the Connecticut River Valley of Vermont, 1791–1850* (Cambridge, UK, 1987), 48; Elizabeth Cometti, ed., *Seeing America and Its Great Men: The Journals and Letters of Count Francesco dal Verme, 1783–1784* (Charlottesville, 1969), 15; BR, "The Effects of Ardent Spirits upon Man," in Dagobert D. Runes, ed., *The Selected Writings of Benjamin Rush* (New York, 1947), 340.

he told his son in 1799, "has been a systematical dissolution of the true family authority." Patriarchy was in disarray, and that had affected all authority, including that of government. In fact, said Adams, "there can never be any regular government of a nation without a marked subordination of mother and children to the father."[68]

Without clearly understanding what was happening, fathers, husbands, ministers, masters, and magistrates—patriarchy everywhere—felt their authority draining away. Stephen Arnold's trial for beating his adopted daughter to death attracted so much attention in upstate New York in 1805 precisely because people had become unsure of the proper relationship of children to their parents.[69]

The spectacular movement of people did not help matters any. Strangers were now everywhere, and no one was quite certain of who owed deference to whom. Children in greater numbers left their homes for new land, in most cases never to see their parents again. Because so many of their male citizens had set out in search of new opportunities in Vermont, Maine, or the West, the older states of Massachusetts, Connecticut, and Rhode Island had a majority of females—which may help account for their relative Federalist stability. But even in New England more sons and daughters asserted their independence from their parents in courtship and in choosing their marriage partners. Daughters in wealthy families tended to delay marriage, to marry out of birth order, or to remain single—all of which imply less parental involvement and greater freedom of choice for young women in marriage.

The Revolutionary War had relaxed the traditional norms of sexual behavior, particularly in the city of Philadelphia, which had been occupied by British soldiers. Not only did more women leave their marriages than ever before, but in the post-Revolutionary period the rate of bastardy nearly doubled, accompanied by a noticeable increase in prostitution and adultery, involving all ages and all social classes.[70] With the dramatic slackening of laws against moral offenses in post-Revolutionary America, women began to experience unprecedented social and sexual freedom. Indeed, this new freedom accounts for the sudden flood of didactic novels and pedagogical writings warning of the dangers of seduction and female sexuality. Novels, such as Susanna Rowson's *Charlotte Temple*

68. Page Smith, *John Adams* (Garden City, NY, 1962), 2: 1016–17.
69. Alan Taylor, " 'The Unhappy Stephen Arnold': An Episode of Murder and Penitence in the Early Republic," in Ronald Hoffman, Mechel Sobel, and Fredrika J. Teute, eds., *Through a Glass Darkly: Reflections on Personal Identity in Early America* (Chapel Hill, 1997), 105.
70. Clare A. Lyons, *Sex Among the Rabble: An Intimate History of Gender and Power in the Age of Revolution, Philadelphia, 1730–1830* (Chapel Hill, 2006), 188–353.

(1791), Samuel Relf's *Infidelity* (1797), and Sally Wood's *Darval* (1801), assumed the responsibility of policing female sexuality that hitherto had been left to parents and legal authorities. Some physicians like Dr. Rush even began warning that guilt resulting from adultery, or any failure to control the passions, almost always ended in insanity. Leaders in the early Republic offered so many prescriptions for discipline precisely because there were so many frightening examples of disorder and indiscipline.[71]

For many observers it seemed as if sexual passions were running amuck. Premarital pregnancies dramatically increased, at rates not reached again until the 1960s. In some communities one third of all marriages took place after the woman was pregnant. Between 1785 and 1797 Martha Ballard, a midwife in Lincoln County, Maine, delivered 106 women of their first babies; forty, or 38 percent, were conceived out of wedlock. All these statistics suggest that many sons and daughters were selecting their mates without waiting for parental approval.[72]

Everywhere traditional subordinations were challenged and undermined. America "is the place where old age will not be blindly worshipped," promised one writer in 1789. Aged persons began to lose much of the respect they had commanded, and young people began asserting themselves in new ways. Seating in the New England meetinghouses by age was abandoned in favor of wealth. For the first time, American state legislatures began requiring that public officials retire at a prescribed age, usually sixty or seventy. By 1800 people were representing themselves as younger than they actually were, something not done earlier. At the same time, male dress, especially wigs, powdered hair, and knee-breeches that had earlier tended to favor older men (the calves being the last to show age), began giving way to styles, particularly hairpieces and trousers, that flattered young men. In family portraits the fathers traditionally had stood dominantly above their wives and children; now, however, they were more often portrayed alongside their families—a symbolic leveling.[73]

71.  Karen A. Weyler, *Intricate Relations: Sexual and Economic Desire in American Fiction, 1789–1814* (Iowa City, 2004), 24.

72.  Ellen K. Rothman, "Sex and Self-Control: Middle-Class Courtship in America, 1770–1870," in Michael Gordon, ed., *The American Family in Social-Historical Perspective* (New York, 1983), 394–95; Daniel Scott Smith, "Parental Power and Marriage Patterns: An Analysis of Historical Trends in Hingham, Massachusetts," *Journal of Marriage and the Family*, 35 (1973), 419–28; Daniel Scott Smith and Michael S. Hindus, "Premarital Pregnancy in America, 1640–1971," *Journal of Interdisciplinary History*, 5 (1975), 561; Laurel Thatcher Ulrich, *A Midwife's Tale: The Life of Martha Ballard, Based on Her Diary, 1785–1822* (New York, 1990), 155–56.

73.  *American Museum*, 7 (1790), 306; David Hackett Fischer, *Growing Old in America* (New York, 1977), 77–112; Zakim, *Ready-Made Democracy*.

YOUTHS' DEFIANCE OF TRADITIONAL AUTHORITY and hierarchy showed up dramatically in the colleges. It began on the eve of the Revolution when Harvard and Yale abandoned the ranking of entering students on the basis of their families' social position and estate. Then in the aftermath of the Revolution distinctions between upper and lower classmen began to break down. And as the Revolutionary message of liberty and equality spread throughout the country, all distinctions were brought into question.

As Samuel Stanhope Smith of Princeton explained in 1785 to Charles Nisbet, who was about to leave Scotland to become the first president of Dickinson College in Pennsylvania, "our freedom certainly takes away the distinctions of rank that are so visible in Europe; and of consequence takes away, in the same proportion, those submissive forms of politeness that exist there." Although suitably warned, Nisbet was nevertheless stunned by what he presumed the Revolution on behalf of liberty had done to American society. It had created "a new world...unfortunately composed...of discordant atoms, jumbled together by chance, and tossed by unconstancy in an immense vacuum." Nisbet had bumbled into a society that "greatly wants a principle of attraction and cohesion."[74]

The unruly students Nisbet encountered only deepened his despair. Indeed, when college students, like those of the University of North Carolina in 1796, could debate the issue of whether "the Faculty had too much authority," then serious trouble could not be far away.[75]

Between 1798 and 1808 American colleges were racked by mounting incidents of student defiance and outright rebellion—on a scale never seen before or since in American history. At Brown in 1798 the students protested commencement speaking assignments and the price of board and brought the college to a halt. Eventually, Jonathan Maxey, the president of Brown, was forced to sign a "Treaty of Amity and Intercourse" with the rebellious students, offering amnesty to the protesters and establishing procedures for legitimate protest. At Union College in 1800 students petitioned that a professor be fired. Although the authorities dismissed the petition, the professor resigned, giving the students a victory.[76]

These incidents only foreshadowed much more extensive and violent student protests. In 1799 University of North Carolina students beat the

---

74. Steven J. Novak, *The Rights of Youth: American Colleges and Student Revolt, 1798–1815* (Cambridge, MA, 1977), 12–13, 14; Charles Nisbet (1787), quoted in Samuel Miller, *Memoir of the Rev. Charles Nisbet, D.D., Late President of Dickinson College, Carlisle* (New York, 1840), 167.
75. Novak, *The Rights of Youth*, 14.
76. Novak, *The Rights of Youth*, 17–18.

president, stoned two professors, and threatened others with injury. In 1800 conflicts over discipline broke out at Harvard, Brown, William and Mary, and Princeton. In 1802 the rioting became even more serious. Williams College was under siege for two weeks. According to a tutor, Yale was in a state of "wars and rumors of wars." After months of student rioting, Princeton's Nassau Hall was mysteriously gutted by fire; the students, including William Cooper's eldest son, were blamed for setting it aflame. As with other sorts of rioting, alcohol was often present. One student informed the president of Dartmouth that "the least quantity he could put up with ... was from two to three pints daily."[77]

Finally, college authorities tightened up their codes of discipline. But repression only provoked more student rebellions. In 1805 forty-five students, a majority of the total enrollment, withdrew from the University of North Carolina in protest over the new disciplinary rules, crippling the university. In 1807 Harvard students rioted over rotten cabbage and the general quality of food served in the commons; but, as a professor noted, complaining about the food was merely "the spark to set the combustibles on fire." When the Harvard Corporation expelled twenty-three of the rebels, nearly two dozen other sympathetic students refused to return to the college. In the same year, student unrest at Princeton led to rioting and the calling out of the local town militia. Fifty-five students out of the 120 attending the college were expelled. In 1808 a student insurrection closed Williams for a month and forced the college to recruit a new faculty. Finally, college authorities up and down the continent began getting together and blacklisting the rebellious students, preventing them from enrolling in another college.[78]

People had a wide variety of explanations for the extraordinary student unrest. Some thought the students had read too much William Godwin and Thomas Paine and that French revolutionary principles of Jacobinism and atheism had infected their young minds. Others assumed that all these rich sons of elites were spoiled brats with too much money to spend, especially on whiskey and rum. Others reasoned that these mostly Federalist sons of the Founding generation were simply anxious to assert their manhood and prove their patriotism, citing especially the Quasi-War of 1798 for leaving these young men "panting for war." Others believed that the rebellious students were simply reliving their fathers' Revolution. As a Brown student wrote of the 1800 uprising: "Nothing but riot and confusion! No regard paid to superiors. Indeed, Sir, the Spirit of '75 was displayed in its brightest colors."[79]

77. Novak, *The Rights of Youth*, 20–21; Rorabaugh, *Alcoholic Republic*, 139.
78. Novak, *The Rights of Youth*, 28.
79. Novak, *The Rights of Youth*, 45, 57.

But still others supposed that the student disorder came from deeper evils in the society, from everything that the Jeffersonian Republican takeover of the government in 1801 had come to represent socially and culturally. It came, as the president of the University of Vermont declared in 1809,

> from deficiencies in modern, early parental discipline; from erroneous notions of *liberty* and equality; from the spirit of revolution in the *minds* of men, constantly progressing, tending to a relinquishment of all *ancient* systems, discipline and dignities; from an increasing desire to *level* distinctions, traduce authority and diminish restraint; from licentious political discussions and controversies.[80]

THE REVOLUTION HAD REPRESENTED an attack on patriarchal monarchy, and that attack began to ramify throughout the society. In vain did conservatives complain that too many people had been captivated by "false ideas of liberty." By collapsing all the different dependencies in the society into either freemen or slaves, the Revolution made it increasingly impossible for white males to accept any dependent status whatsoever. They were, as they told superiors who paternalistically tried to intervene in their private affairs, "free and independent."[81] Servitude of any sort in the early Republic suddenly became anomalous and anachronistic. In 1784 in New York a group, believing that indentured servitude was "contrary to...the idea of liberty this country has so happily established," released a shipload of immigrant servants and arranged for public subscriptions to pay for their passage. As early as 1775 in Philadelphia the proportion of the workforce that was unfree—composed of servants and slaves—had already declined to 13 percent from the 40 to 50 percent that it had been in the middle of the eighteenth century. By 1800 less than 2 percent of the city's labor force remained unfree. It was not long before indentured servitude, which had existed for centuries, disappeared altogether.[82]

With the republican culture talking of nothing but liberty, equality, and independence, maintaining even hired servants who worked for

---

80. Novak, *Rights of Youth*, 76.
81. Lyons, *Sex Among the Rabble*, 225.
82. William Miller, "The Effects of the American Revolution on Indentured Servitude," *Pennsylvania History*, 7 (1940), 136; Sharon V. Salinger, "Artisans, Journeymen, and the Transformation of Labor in Late Eighteenth-Century Philadelphia," *WMQ*, 40 (1983), 64–66; Steven Rosswurm, *Arms, Country, and Class: The Philadelphia Militia and "Lower Sort" During the American Revolution, 1775–1783* (New Brunswick, NJ, 1987), 16.

wages became a problem. Eighteenth-century advice manuals had not devoted much space to the proper behavior of masters toward servants, since dependency and servitude had been taken for granted. But the new nineteenth-century masters, especially those in middling circumstances, had become self-conscious about the relationship and needed advice on how to treat people who were supposed to be their inferiors in a culture that prized equality. "Servitude being established contrary to the natural rights of man," declared one such manual in 1816, "it ought to be softened as much as possible, and servants made to feel their condition as little as may be." Many middling masters were not all that sure of their own status, yet they had to deal with servants who may have not been all that different in origin. Hence they needed advice on how to talk to their servants, how to ask them to do tasks, and how to maintain a distance, without being unkind or contemptuous toward them.[83]

Controlling or even finding servants was difficult in this egalitarian atmosphere. With some Americans concluding that the practice of keeping servants was "highly anti-republican," servants resisted the implications of the status. They refused to call their employers "master" or "mistress"; for many the term "boss," derived from the Dutch word for master, became a euphemistic substitute. A minister in Maine favored the euphemism "help" applied to a domestic maid he admired because, unlike the word "servant," it implied "a sense of independence and a hope of rising in the world"—something that the young woman and many other Americans were increasingly capable of doing.[84]

With the disappearance of indentured servitude, black slavery became more conspicuous and more peculiar than it had been in the past, and hired white servants resisted any identification with black slaves. A foreign traveler was startled to discover that a white female domestic refused to admit that she was a servant and that she lived in her master's home. She was simply "help," and she only "stayed" in the house. "I'd have you know, *man*," she indignantly told this foreigner, "that I am no *sarvant*; none but *negers* are *sarvants*." White servants often demanded to sit at the table with their masters and mistresses, justifying their demand by claiming they lived in a free country, and that no freeborn American should be treated like a servant. William Cooper's daughter-in-law could not believe

83. C. Dallett Hemphill, *Bowing to Necessities: A History of Manners in America, 1620–1860* (New York, 1999), 83.
84. *American Museum*, 11 (1792), 84; Daniel E. Sutherland, *Americans and Their Servants: Domestic Service in the United States from 1800 to 1920* (Baton Rouge, 1981), 125–26; Richard S. Pressman, "Class Positioning and Shays' Rebellion: Resolving the Contradictions of *The Contrast*," *Early American Literature*, 21 (1986), 95; Appleby, *Inheriting the Revolution*, 132.

the bold behavior of servants. She blamed it all on notions of "Yankee dignity and ideas of Liberty—which is insolence only." Since early nineteenth-century Yankees were not at all eager to become someone's flunky, Bostonian Harrison Gray Otis had to make do with a series of French-speaking Germans, who soon picked up New England ways and rebelled at being servants. In 1811 John Jay's son, in a common complaint, reported that his uncle was having problems with his servants, who had "become more and more ungovernable."[85]

Since the slave-ridden South scarcely needed hired servants, the servant problem was largely confined to the North. Desperate would-be masters in several Northern cities were eventually compelled to form organizations for the encouragement of faithful domestic servants. These organizations were especially designed to reduce the servants' incessant mobility and eliminate the insidious practice of masters' enticing someone else's servant to join their household. Despite all these efforts, however, the problem of getting and keeping good servants persisted and would continue to bother many Americans throughout the nineteenth century.

Because of the servant problem, Americans in the 1790s began to build hotels as public residences. The New York City Hotel, built in 1794, contained 137 rooms and many public spaces. These hotels combined both eating and lodging, provided private sleeping quarters, prohibited tipping, and were often occupied by permanent boarders. Many found this arrangement cheaper than setting up a household with servants who were so hard to acquire and deal with. Foreigners found such hotels and boardinghouses to be peculiarly American institutions.[86]

BY THE EARLY NINETEENTH CENTURY much of what remained of traditional eighteenth-century hierarchy was in shambles—broken by

85. Janson, *Stranger in America*, 88; M. J. Heale, "From City Fathers to Social Critics: Humanitarianism and Government in New York, 1790–1860," *JAH*, 63 (1976), 26–27; Nancy F. Cott, *The Bonds of Womanhood: "Woman's Sphere" in New England, 1780–1835* (New Haven, 1977), 28–30, 49; Taylor, *William Cooper's Town*, 379; Samuel Eliot Morison, *Harrison Gray Otis, 1765–1848: The Urbane Federalist* (Boston, 1969), 533; Strum, "Property Qualifications," 371.

86. David John Jeremy, ed., *Henry Wansey and His American Journal, 1794* (Philadelphia, 1970) 99; Douglas T. Miller, *Jacksonian Aristocracy: Class and Democracy in New York, 1830–1860* (New York, 1967), 5–7; Arthur M. Schlesinger Sr., *Learning How to Behave: A Historical Study of Etiquette Books* (New York, 1946), 82; Doris Elizabeth King, "The First-Class Hotel and the Age of the Common Man," *Journal of Southern History*, 23 (1957), 173–88; Sharon V. Salinger, *Taverns and Drinking in Early America* (Baltimore, 2002), 244–46; A. K. Sandoval-Strauss, *Hotel: An American History* (New Haven, 2007).

social and economic changes and justified by the republican commitment to equality. No longer were apprentices simply dependents within a family; they had become trainees within a business that was increasingly conducted outside the household. A master became less of a patriarch in the craft and more of an employer, retail merchant, or businessman. Artisans did less and less "bespoke" or made-to-order work for particular patrons and instead produced more and more ready-made goods for mass distribution to impersonal markets of consumers. Cabinetmakers began stocking warehouses with a variety of pieces of furniture for ready sale in a modern manner. Impersonal cash payments of wages replaced the older paternalistic relationship between masters and journeymen, which resulted in these free wage-earners moving about in increasing numbers. Six months, for example, was the average time of employment for journeymen in one Philadelphia cabinet shop between 1795 and 1803.[87]

Although both masters and journeymen tried to maintain the traditional fiction that they were bound together for the "good of the trade," they increasingly saw themselves as employers and employees with different interests. Observers applauded the fact that apprentices, journeymen, and masters of each craft had marched together in the federal procession in Philadelphia on July 4, 1788, yet some tensions and divergence of interests were already visible. By the 1780s and 1790s some journeymen in various crafts were organizing themselves against their masters' organizations, banning their employers from their meetings, and declaring that "the interests of the journeymen are separate and in some respects opposite of those of their employers."[88]

In the eighteenth century artisans had participated in strikes, but these were strikes of the whole craft against the community, a withholding of their services or goods until some communal restriction on their craft was removed. Now, however, the strikes were within the crafts themselves, pitting journeyman-employees against their master-employers until their wages or other working conditions of the employees were improved. In 1796 in Philadelphia journeyman cabinetmakers successfully struck for a wage hike, which came out to be about a dollar a day and included a provision for cost-of-living increases. To add to worker solidarity, journeymen in one craft and city began calling on journeymen in other crafts

87. Sharon V. Salinger, *"To Serve Well and Faithfully": Labor and Indentured Servants in Pennsylvania, 1682–1800* (Cambridge, 1987), 154, 156–57; Charles F. Montgomery, *American Furniture: The Federal Period* (New York, 1966), 14.

88. Eric Foner, *Tom Paine and Revolutionary America* (New York, 1976), 39; Salinger, *"To Serve Well and Faithfully,"* 167–68; Sean Wilentz, *Chants Democratic: New York City and the Rise of the American Working Class, 1788–1850* (New York, 1984), 58.

and cities to come together in a union to protect their mutual interests against hostile masters. Between 1786 and 1816 at least twelve major strikes by various journeyman craftsmen occurred—the first major strikes by employees against employers in American history.[89]

Despite these early incidents of clashing interests, however, the modern separation between employers and wage-earning employees came slowly. During the first several decades of the early Republic both masters and journeymen still tended to combine as artisans with similar concerns for the trade. At the outset most journeymen could look forward to becoming masters. In 1790 87 percent of the carpenters in Boston were masters, and most of the journeymen present in the city that year eventually became masters.[90] In addition, masters and journeymen were brought together by their common status as tradesmen who worked with their hands. If anything, the contempt in which their labor had traditionally been held by the aristocratic gentry compelled their collaboration. So even those who differed from one other as greatly as did Walter Brewster, a young struggling shoemaker of Canterbury, Connecticut, and Christopher Leffingwell, a well-to-do manufacturer of Norwich, Connecticut, who owned several mills and shops and was the town's largest employer, could join forces in the 1790s in a political movement on behalf of artisans against lawyers and other Connecticut gentry. Given their common lowliness as workers involved in manual trades, men like Brewster and Leffingwell were natural allies, and they understandably identified their "laboring interest" with "the general or common interest" of the whole state.[91]

In time, of course, the distinction between rich capitalist employers and poor wage-earning journeymen-employees would become more conspicuous. By 1825 in Boston, for example, 62 percent of all carpenters in the city had become property-less employees; and only about 10 percent of the journeymen in that year were able to rise to become masters.[92] By the third decade of the nineteenth century most of the crafts had begun splitting into the modern class division between employers and employees. But in the 1790s large-scale manufacturers like Leffingwell and small craftsmen like Brewster still shared a common resentment of a genteel aristocratic world

89. Montgomery, *American Furniture*, 22–23; Ian M. G. Quimby, "The Cordwainers Protest: A Crisis in Labor Relations," *Winterthur Portfolio*, 3 (1967), 83–101.

90. Lisa B. Lubow, "From Carpenter to Capitalist: The Business of Building in Postrevolutionary Boston," in Conrad Edrick Wright and Katheryn P. Viens, eds., *Entrepreneurs: The Boston Business Community, 1700–1850* (Boston, 1997), 195.

91. James P. Walsh, "'Mechanics and Citizens': The Connecticut Artisan Protest of 1792," *WMQ*, 62 (1985), 66–89.

92. Lubow, "From Carpenter to Capitalist," in Wright and Viens, eds., *Entrepreneurs*, 206, 207.

that had humiliated them from the beginning of time. For the same reason Joseph Williams, a mule-trader, took up the same political cause of artisans and manufacturers as Brewster and Leffingwell. Although Williams was the richest man in Norwich and as a merchant had interests that were different from those of artisans and manufacturers, he nevertheless identified with their loathing of the Federalist aristocracy of Connecticut.[93]

Despite all the apparent differences between wealthy mule-merchants, small shoemakers, and big manufacturers, socially and psychologically they were all middling sorts with occupations—sharply separated from gentlemen-aristocrats who did not seem to have to work for a living. In the eighteenth century, writes the premier historian of the emerging middle class in America, "the important hierarchal distinction was the one that set off the several elites from everyone else." Thus in comparison with the great difference between the gentry and ordinary people, "differences between artisans and laborers were of no real consequence. The effect, needless to say," says historian Stuart M. Blumin, "was to identify middling people much more closely with the bottom of the society than with the top." What tied these disparate middling artisans and laborers together was their common involvement in manual labor. Mechanics and tradesmen considered "the farmers in the country" as "brethren," for they "get their living as we do, by the labour of their hands."[94]

In the decades following the Revolution these middling workers in the Northern parts of the country—farmers, artisans, laborers, and proto-businessmen of all sorts—released their pent-up egalitarian anger at all those "aristocrats" who had scorned and despised them as narrow-minded, parochial, and illiberal—and all because they had "not snored through four years at Princeton." They urged each other to shed their earlier political apathy and "keep up the cry against Judges, Lawyers, Generals, Colonels, and all other designing men, and the day will be our own." They demanded that they do their "utmost at election to prevent all men of talents, lawyers, rich men from being elected."[95] In the 1790s they organized themselves in Democratic-Republican Societies, and eventually

93. Walsh, " 'Mechanics and Citizens,' " 66–89.
94. Stuart M. Blumin, *The Emergence of the Middle Class: Social Experience in the American City, 1760–1900* (Cambridge, UK, 1989), 33–34; Lubow, "From Carpenter to Capitalist," in Wright and Viens, eds., *Entrepreneurs*, 185.
95. George Warner, *Means for the Preservation of Political Liberty: An Oration Delivered in the New Dutch Church, on the Fourth of July, 1797* (New York, 1797), 13–14; Alfred Young, "The Mechanics and the Jeffersonians: New York, 1789–1801," *Labor History*, 5 (1964), 274; Donald H. Stewart, *The Opposition Press of the Federalist Period* (Albany, 1969), 389; Richard E. Ellis, *Jeffersonian Crisis: Courts and Politics in the Young Republic* (New York, 1971), 173.

they came to constitute the bulk of the Republican party in the North. By the end of the second decade of the nineteenth century, these ordinary working men had transformed what it meant to be a gentleman and a political leader.

Although Jefferson was an aristocratic slaveholder, it was his political genius to sense that the world of the early Republic ought to belong to people who lived by manual labor and not by their wits. Cities, he believed, were dangerous and promoted dissipation precisely because they were places, he said, where men sought "to live by their heads rather than their hands."[96] But Jefferson was only expressing the views of his many Northern followers. In the decades following the Revolution living by one's head became equated with leisure, which was labeled idleness and subjected to the most scathing criticism—criticism that went well beyond anything experienced in England or Europe in these years.

Angry Democratic-Republicans, including Matthew Lyon, who moved to Kentucky and served as congressman there from 1803 to 1811, accused all those gentlemen who were "not...under the necessity of getting their bread by industry" of living off "the labour of the honest farmers and mechanics." Those who "do not labor, but who enjoy in luxury, the fruits of labor," these Republicans charged, had no right to "finally decide all acts and laws" as they had in the past. At the same time as the Northern Republicans assaulted the gentry's idleness and capacity to govern, they emphasized and honored the significance and dignity of labor, which aristocrats traditionally had held in contempt.[97]

Having to work for a living became the identifying symbol for all those common middling sorts championed by Jefferson and the other Republican leaders. America's political and social struggle, said William Manning, an uneducated New England farmer speaking as "a Labourer" on behalf of many Northern Republicans, was between the many and the few; it was based on "a Conceived Difference of Interest Between those that Labour for a Living and those that git a Living without Bodily Labour." Those who did not have to do bodily work were "the merchant, phisition, lawyer & divine, the philosipher and school master, the Juditial &

96. TJ to David Williams, 14 Nov. 1803, in L and B, eds., *Writings of Jefferson*, 10: 431.
97. Ruth Bogin, *Abraham Clark and the Quest for Equality in the Revolutionary Era, 1774–1794* (East Brunswick, NJ, 1982), 32; Abraham Bishop, *Proofs of a Conspiracy Against Christianity and the Government of the United States* (Hartford, 1802), 20; Jerome J. Nadelhaft, "'The Snarls of Invidious Animals': The Democratization of Revolutionary South Carolina," in Ronald Hoffman and Peter J. Albert, eds., *Sovereign States in an Age of Uncertainty* (Charlottesville, 1981), 77; Aleine Austin, *Matthew Lyon: "New Man" of the Democratic Revolution, 1749–1822* (University Park, PA, 1981), 274, 67; Stewart, *Opposition Press of the Federalist Period*, 390.

Executive Officers, & many others." These "orders of men," once they had attained their life of "ease & rest" that "at once creates a sense of superiority," wrote Manning in phonetic prose that was real and not some gentleman's satiric ploy, tended to "asotiate together and look down with two much contempt on those that labour." Although "the hole of them do not amount to one eighth part of the people," these gentry had the "spare time" and the "arts & skeems" to combine and consult with one another. They had the power to control the electorate and the government "in a veriaty of ways." Some voters they flattered "by promise of favors, such as being customers to them, or helping them out of debt, or other difficultyes; or help them to a good bargain, or treet them or trust them, or lend them money, or even give them a little money"—anything or everything if only "they will vote for such & such a man." Other voters the gentry threatened: "'if you don't vote for such & such a man,' or 'if you do' and, 'you shall pay me what you owe me,' or 'I will sew you'—'I will turne you out of my house' or 'off of my farm'—'I wont be your customer any longer.'...All these things have bin practised & may be again." This was how the "few" exerted influence over the many.

Those who "live without Labour" (the phrase that Manning used over and over to identify the gentry) managed the government and laws, making them as "numerous, intricate and as inexplicit as possible," controlled the newspapers, making them as "costly as possible," and manipulated the banks and credit, so as to make "money scarse," especially since "the interests and incomes of the few lays chiefly in money at interest, rents, salaryes, and fees that are fixed on the nominal value of money." In addition these "few," by which he meant the Federalists of New England, were "always crying up the advantages of costly collages, national academyes & grammer schools, in order to make places for men to live without work, & so strengthen their party." In fact, wrote Manning in 1798, "all the orders of men who live without Labour have got so monstrously crouded with numbers & made it fashanable to live & dress so high, that Labour & produce is scarse." Manning ended his lengthy diatribe against all gentlemen of leisure by proposing to form "a Society of Labourers to be formed as near after the order of Cincinnati as the largeness of their numbers will admit of."[98]

Some historians have thought of Manning as just a simple farmer in his little developing town of Billerica, Massachusetts. But in fact he was

98. Samuel Eliot Morison, ed., "William Manning's The Key of Libberty," WMQ, 13 (1956), 202–54. Michael Merrill and Sean Wilentz have edited a modern edition of The Key of Liberty: The Life and Democratic Writings of William Manning: "A Laborer," 1747–1814 (Cambridge, MA, 1993), but unfortunately they have corrected all his phonetic spelling.

much more of a middling sort—an improver and a small-time entrepreneurial hustler, or what later would be called a petty businessman. He ran a tavern off and on, erected a saltpeter works making gunpowder during the Revolutionary War, helped build a canal, bought and sold land, constantly borrowed money, and urged the printing of money by state-chartered banks, seeking (not very successfully, it seems) every which way to better his and his family's condition. By themselves Manning's commercial activities may not be much, but multiply them many thousand-fold throughout the society and we have the makings of an expanding commercial economy.

If anyone in the North was opposed to the developing market society, it was not the likes of Manning and other Northern Republicans; in fact, it was many of the traditional-minded Federalists who tried to stand in the way of the middling paper-money world that was taking over the society of the North. But the passions that divided Republicans and Federalists went beyond economic issues and political ideas. Manning and the Northern Republicans knew only too well the kind of society the Federalists favored—a hierarchical one held together by patronage and connections and dominated by a leisured few who used the mysteries of the law and their proprietary wealth to lord it over the many. The Democratic-Republicans feared and hated the English monarchy so much because it symbolized that kind of privileged aristocratic society.

MOCKING IDLENESS AND TURNING LABOR into a badge of honor made the South, with its leisured aristocracy supported by slavery, seem even more anomalous than it had been at the time of the Revolution, thus aggravating the growing sectional split in the country. Many Southern aristocrats began emphasizing their cavalier status in contrast to the money-grubbing northern Yankees. They were fond of saying that they were real gentlemen, a rare thing in America.

But even the Southern cavaliers were not entirely immune to the changing culture. Indeed, so prevalent did the scorn of gentlemanly leisure become that some Southern slaveholding aristocrats felt compelled to identify themselves with hard work and productive labor. As good Jeffersonian Republicans, some of these Southern planters contended that they, like the ordinary working people in the North, were involved in productive labor in contrast to all those Northern Federalist professionals, bankers, speculators, and moneyed men who never grew or made a single thing.

The Southerners could even respond to the marvelous manner in which Parson Mason Weems, author of the most popular biography of George Washington ever written, turned the aristocratic father of his country into someone who worked as diligently for a living as an ordinary mechanic. By conceiving of Washington as an industrious businessman, Weems spoke for the new rising generation of middling entrepreneurs and others eager to get ahead. He was determined, he said, to destroy the "notion, from the land of lies," which had "taken too deep root among some, that 'labour is a low-lived thing, fit for none but poor people and slaves! and that dress and pleasure are the only accomplishments for a gentleman!'" Weems urged all the young men who might be reading his book, "though humble thy birth, low thy fortune, and few thy friends, still think of Washington, and HOPE."[99]

Of course, since more than anyone in the society the Southern slave-holding aristocrats depended on the labor of others, honoring themselves as workers was awkward, to say the least. In fact, once the planters invoked this celebration of productive labor, they discovered it could be readily turned against them. Professional lawyers in Virginia, struggling to gain control of the county courts from gentlemen-amateurs, accused the planter-aristocrats of being men raised to no "pursuit of honest industry." All a member of this idle gentry had ever done, charged the lawyers, was "learned to dress, to dance, to drink, to smoke, to swear, to game; con-tracted a violent passion for the very rational, elegant and humane plea-sures of the turf and the cock-pit, and was long distinguished for the best horses and game-cocks in the country." Then again, the lawyers found themselves open to the same accusation: that they were unproductive parasites who lived off the cares and anxieties of others.[100] Everyone in America, it seemed, was expected to be a worker or businessman—an expectation that was not matched to the same extent by any other country in the world.

THE CULTURE WAS CHANGING RADICALLY, especially in the North, and many Americans, older generations in particular, became frightened that the young Republic was caught up in a carousal of getting and spend-ing. As Benjamin Rush lamented in 1809, the values of the Founders were being replaced by the "love of money."[101] Too many of the American

---

99. Mason L. Weems, *The Life of Washington* (1809), ed. Marcus Cunliffe (Cambridge, MA, 1962), 203–14.

100. A. G. Roeber, *Faithful Magistrates and Republican Lawyers: Creators of Virginia Legal Culture, 1680–1810* (Chapel Hill, 1981), 247, 251; Bogin, *Abraham Clark*, 32; Austin, *Matthew Lyon*, 64.

101. Dowling, *Literary Federalism*, 15; George W. Corner, ed., *Autobiography of Benjamin Rush* (Princeton, 1948), 338.

people seemed absorbed in the selfish pursuit of their own interests. Americans, in what Federalist Joseph Dennie called this "penny-getting pound-hoarding world," were always looking to bargain; they treated everything they owned, even their homes, as merchandise.[102] English travelers were stunned to see Americans selling their landed estates in order to go into trade—the reverse of what Englishmen sought to do. Nothing was beyond the lure of cash. In the heart of Federalist New England an enterprising Yankee even saw a way to make money out of the gruesome Baltimore riots. Within weeks after the riots, this New Haven hustler established a museum exhibit of the "*Cruelties of the Baltimore MOB*" in "a group of WAX FIGURES as large as life" and charged twenty-five cents admission.[103]

Many, of course, even some Federalists, wanted to put the best face on what was happening. In his publications President Timothy Dwight of Yale, for example, was eager to counter foreign criticism of American materialism, and thus in his published comments, though not in his private notes, he always tried to emphasize the positive aspects of American behavior. Americans may have been restless adventurers, he wrote in his *Travels in New England and New York*, but they were also enterprising and versatile, "ready when disappointed in one kind of business to slide into another, and fitted to conduct the second, or even a third, or fourth, with much the same facility and success as if they had been bred to nothing else."[104]

James Sullivan, a Maine-born lawyer who became Republican governor of Massachusetts in 1807, tried to justify all the scrambling for money, especially since most of the hustlers were members of his own party. In an extraordinary argument that marked the passing of the aristocratic passions of power and glory and the coming of the harmless and humdrum interests of ordinary money-making, Sullivan suggested that a man who sought only to acquire property "is not, perhaps, the good man for whom 'one would dare to die'; but he is a character whom no one need to fear." Indeed, by advancing his own particular interest in an innocuous piecemeal way, he even "advances the interest of the public." Sullivan was celebrating the fact that the older aristocratic world of the great-souled and ambitious Hamiltons and Burrs, who were heroic but dangerous, was giving way to a new

102. Leary, "Dennie on Franklin," in J. A. Leo Lemay and P. M. Zall, eds., *Benjamin Franklin's Autobiography* (New York, 1986), 244.
103. Charles Royster, *Light-Horse Harry Lee and the Legacy of the American Revolution* (New York, 1981), 168.
104. Timothy Dwight, *Travels in New England and New York*, ed. Barbara Miller Solomon (Cambridge, MA, 1969), 3: 372.

world of ordinary middling businessmen, who were mundane but safe. Ambition, which hitherto had been associated with the desire for aristocratic distinction, was becoming tamed and domesticated. Common people were now capable of ambition—the desire for improvement or gain—without necessarily being thought selfish or self-seeking, an endorsement of a peculiar kind of success that had extraordinary cultural power.[105]

Many others, however, were frightened and confused by what seemed to be a whole society being taken over by money-making and the pursuit of "soul-destroying dollars." Too many were racing ahead in search of success without regard for the collective good or for those who failed and were left behind. Literati of varying tastes—ranging from Philip Freneau to Charles Brockden Brown to Washington Irving—filled the air with satirical complaints or hand-wringing analyses of what was happening. "This is a nation of peddlers and shopkeepers," Brown complained of his countrymen in 1803. "Money engrosses all their passions and pursuits." Such imaginative writers wanted nothing to do with men, as one Baltimore editor put it, "who are immersed in business, whose souls are exclusively devoted to the pursuit of riches, who suffer no ideas to intrude upon their speculations, or to disturb their calculations on exchange, insurance, and bank stock."[106] Although authors, professors, and poets were eager to be patriotic, many of them feared that a society so absorbed in business and money-making not only would contribute nothing to the arts and the finer things of life but would eventually fall apart in an orgy of selfishness.

At the outset of his presidency in 1802 Jefferson told the newly arrived immigrant Joseph Priestley that the theologian-scientist had become part of a grand experiment in freedom, an experiment in which Americans were "acting for all mankind." Precisely because Americans enjoyed liberties denied the rest of mankind, said Jefferson, they had "the duty of proving what is the degree of freedom and self-government in which a society may venture to leave its individual members." By the end of Jefferson's administration in 1809 some Americans, mostly Federalists, thought the experiment was failing, that the degree of freedom left to individuals had already gone too far.[107]

---

105. [James Sullivan], *The Path to Riches: An Inquiry into the Origin and Use of Money; and into the Principles of Stocks and Banks* (Boston, 1792), 6. On this point of interests versus passions and the taming of ambition, see Albert O. Hirschman, *The Passions and the Interests: Political Arguments for Capitalism Before Its Triumph* (Princeton, 1977); and J. M. Opal, *Beyond the Farm: National Ambitions in Rural New England* (Philadelphia, 2008).

106. Steven Watts, *The Republic Reborn: War and the Making of Liberal America, 1790–1820* (Baltimore, 1987), 186; Dowling, *Literary Federalism*, 15, 64.

107. TJ to Joseph Priestley, 19 June 1802, in L and B, eds., *Writings of Jefferson*, 10: 324–25.

# 10

# The Jeffersonian West

Alexander Hamilton always faced east, toward Europe. By contrast, Thomas Jefferson faced west, toward the trans-Appalachian territory and even the lands beyond the Mississippi. Although Jefferson himself never traveled beyond the Blue Ridge Mountains, he was obsessed with the West. He always had, as he said in 1781, "a peculiar confidence in the men from the Western side of the mountains."[1] Only by moving westward, Jefferson believed, could Americans maintain their republican society of independent yeoman farmers and avoid the miseries of the concentrated urban working classes of Europe. Indeed, an expansive West was capable of redeeming the nation if its Eastern sections should ever become corrupt. "By enlarging the empire of liberty," said Jefferson, "we multiply its auxiliaries, and provide new sources of renovation, should its principles at any time degenerate in those portions of our country which gave them birth."[2]

Jefferson was the most expansion-minded president in American history, a firm believer in what might be called demographic imperialism. As early as 1786 he thought the United States might become "the nest from which all America, North and South, is to be peopled," creating what he referred to more than once as an "empire of liberty." "Empire" for him did not mean the coercive domination of alien peoples; instead, it meant a nation of citizens spread over vast tracts of land. Yet the British Empire had given enough ambiguity to the term to lend some irony to Jefferson's use of it.[3]

1. TJ to J.P.G. Muhlenberg, 31 Jan. 1781, *Papers of Jefferson*, 4: 487; Reginald Horsman, "The Dimensions of an 'Empire of Liberty': Expansionism and Republicanism," *JER*, 9 (1989), 6. On the Jeffersonian West, see François Furstenberg, "The Significance of the Trans-Appalachian Frontier in Atlantic History," *AHR*, 113 (2008), 647–77.

2. Merrill D. Peterson, *Thomas Jefferson and the New Nation: A Biography* (New York, 1970), 773.

3. TJ to Archibald Stuart, 25 Jan. 1786, to George Rogers Clark, 25 Dec. 1780, *Papers of Jefferson*, 9: 218; 4: 237. On the different meanings of empire in the late eighteenth century, see Gerald Stourzh, *Alexander Hamilton and the Idea of Republican Government* (Stanford, 1970), 189–95.

Although the United States was by 1801 hemmed in by Britain and Spain on America's northern and southern frontiers and by Indians in the West, "it was impossible," Jefferson told Governor James Monroe of Virginia in 1801, "not to look forward to distant times, when our rapid multiplication will expand itself beyond those limits, and cover the whole northern, if not the southern continent, with a people by similar laws."[4] The vision was not just Jefferson's. The inhabitants of this empire, wrote Thomas Hutchins, America's first geographer, in 1784, "far from being in the least danger from the attacks of any other quarter of the globe, will have it in their power to engross the whole commerce of it, and to reign not only lords of America, but to possess, in the utmost security, the dominion of seas throughout the world, which their ancestors enjoyed before them."[5]

Foreign observers could only shake their heads in amazement at the numbers and the speed of the Americans migrating to the West. "Old America," said the recent English immigrant Morris Birkbeck, "seems to be breaking up and moving westward."[6] The settlers created a great triangular wedge of settlement reaching to the Mississippi River. Its northern side ran from New York along the Ohio River, its southern side from east Georgia through Tennessee, and the sides met at the apex, St. Louis. Within this huge triangle of settlement people distributed themselves haphazardly, with huge pockets remaining virtually vacant or sparsely inhabited by Indians.[7]

National leaders expected American westward migration, but not the way it was happening. The carefully drawn plans of the 1780s for the orderly surveying and settlement of the West were simply overwhelmed by the massive and chaotic movement of people. "We rush like a comet into infinite space," declared a despairing Fisher Ames. "In our wild career, we may jostle some other world out of its orbit, but we shall, in every event, quench the light of our own."[8]

4. TJ to Monroe, 24 Nov. 1801, *Jefferson: Writings*, 1097.
5. Andro Linklater, *Measuring America: How an Untamed Wilderness Shaped the United States and Fulfilled the Promise of Democracy* (New York, 2002), 76.
6. Andrew R. L. Cayton, The *Frontier Republic: Ideology and Politics in the Ohio Country, 1780–1825* (Kent, OH, 1986), 116; Henry Wansey, *The Journal of an Excursion to the United States of North America in the Summer of 1794* (New York, 1969), 183; J. M. Opal, *Beyond the Farm: National Ambitions in Rural New England* (Philadelphia, 2008), 45.
7. Malcolm J. Rohrbough, *The Trans-Appalachian Frontier: People, Societies, and Institutions, 1775–1850* (New York, 1978), 89–156.
8. Ames to Christopher Gore, 3 Oct. 1803, *Works of Fisher Ames* (1854), ed. W. B. Allen (Indianapolis, 1983), 2: 1462.

Many settlers ignored land ordinances and titles, squatted on the land, and claimed preemptive rights to it. From 1800 on Congress steadily lowered the price of Western land, reduced the size of purchasable tracts, and relaxed the terms of credit for settlers in ever more desperate efforts to bring the land laws into line with the speed with which the lands were being settled. People moved into the area the Indians had ceded in the Treaty of Greenville and then spread north from the Ohio Valley into the valleys of Indiana and Illinois. Congress created new territories in Indiana (1800), Michigan (1805), and Illinois (1809). In the South people in the Mississippi Territory (created in 1798) moved along the river from Vicksburg toward Spanish-held New Orleans.

ALTHOUGH BOTH THE RAPIDLY SETTLED NORTHWEST and the Southwest territories were overwhelmingly Jeffersonian Republican in their politics, they tended to create very different kinds of places from one another. That difference essentially flowed from the existence of slavery in one area and not in the other.[9]

But not immediately. Most of the early migrants that initially spilled over the Appalachian Mountains to the West, whether from the North or the South, traveled with only the labor of their families to help them get on their feet. The first waves of ordinary settlers to the frontier, whether to Kentucky and Tennessee or to Ohio and Indiana, generally began by building a small lean-to house before they turned to the crucially important tasks of clearing the land and planting crops. They felled some trees with axes and killed others by girdling them. They burned so much brush and scrub that smoky hazes often hung over the land for months or even years on end. While the women saw to all the gardening, cooking, sewing, and housekeeping, the men plowed the land and planted the marketable crops, in the Northwest, mainly corn and wheat, with whiskey a major by-product; in the Southwest, corn, tobacco, and eventually cotton were the major crops. For both areas hogs and cattle were the principal livestock.

With crops planted, the pioneers began building more substantial houses—usually cabins built of notched logs designed to shelter households that averaged five to seven persons. The roofs of these primitive homes were clapboard, and the floors were dirt, which meant that vermin and the lack of cleanliness were taken for granted—a sure sign in the eyes

9. Stanley Elkins and Eric McKitrick, "A Meaning for Turner's Frontier: Part I: Democracy in the Old Northwest," and "A Meaning for Turner's Frontier: Part II: The Southwest Frontier and New England," *Political Science Quarterly*, 69 (1954), 321–53, 565–602.

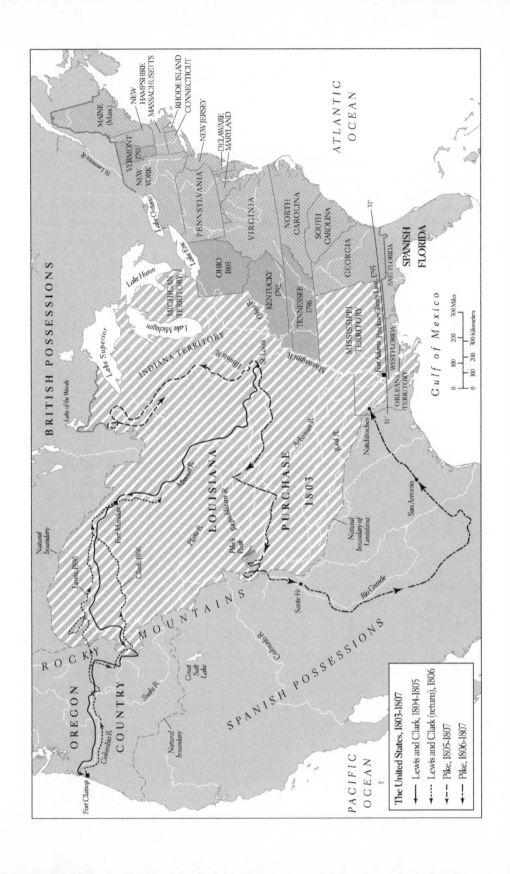

The United States, 1803–1807

— Lewis and Clark, 1804–1805
---- Lewis and Clark (return), 1806
—·— Pike, 1805–1807
—··— Pike, 1806–1807

BRITISH POSSESSIONS

ATLANTIC OCEAN

NEW HAMPSHIRE
MASSACHUSETTS
RHODE ISLAND
CONNECTICUT
MAINE (Mass.)
VERMONT 1791
NEW YORK
NEW JERSEY
DELAWARE
MARYLAND
PENNSYLVANIA
VIRGINIA
NORTH CAROLINA
SOUTH CAROLINA
GEORGIA

St. Lawrence R.
Lake Ontario
Lake Erie
Lake Huron
Lake Superior
Lake Michigan
Lake of the Woods

OHIO 1803
MICHIGAN TERRITORY
INDIANA TERRITORY
KENTUCKY 1792
TENNESSEE 1796
MISSISSIPPI TERRITORY

Ohio R.
Illinois R.
St. Louis
Mississippi R.
Missouri R.
Platte R.
Republican R.
Arkansas R.
Red R.

LOUISIANA PURCHASE 1803

Fort Adams, Pinckney Treaty Line, 1795
WEST FLORIDA
EAST FLORIDA
31°
SPANISH FLORIDA
ORLEANS TERRITORY
31°
Natchitoches

Gulf of Mexico

0 100 200 300 Miles
0 100 200 300 Kilometers

San Antonio
Rio Grande
Sante Fe
Colorado R.
Great Salt Lake
Snake R.

SPANISH POSSESSIONS

Natural boundary of Louisiana
Natural boundary
Natural boundary

ROCKY MOUNTAINS

Lewis, 1806
Fort Mandan
Clark, 1806
Pike's Peak

OREGON COUNTRY
Columbia R.
Fort Clatsop

PACIFIC OCEAN

of Eastern observers that the occupants weren't quite civilized.[10] Diets were limited, with lots of hominy. Coffee and tea were available in Pittsburgh in 1807 but were very expensive. What the new settlers most wanted was access to rivers and the laying out of roads so they could market some of their produce.[11]

In the Old Northwest the early settlers resisted the claims of absentee speculators and landlords and were remarkably successful in establishing their small independent farms throughout the region. But the situation in the Old Southwest was different. The early pioneers there were soon overwhelmed by substantial planters who came west with slaves in ever increasing numbers. As early as 1795 slaves had come to constitute more than 20 percent of the population of Middle Tennessee. Since these slaveholding settlers were men of means, they quickly bought out those who had preceded them or purchased new land in the most accessible and desirable areas. By 1802 slaveholders had already established large plantations in the rich valleys of the Cumberland in Middle Tennessee. With the development of cotton as the major staple of the Southwest, slavery flourished. But where the growing season was too short for cotton, as in the northern counties of West Tennessee, the number of slaves remained small. Since slavery and cotton went together, the big slaveholding cotton planters dominated both the economy and government. In both the Southwest and the Northwest, however, the top political positions tended to be captured by those who had initially achieved some military glory, like William Henry Harrison and Andrew Jackson.[12]

Although slavery and the society and economy it bred were what ultimately separated the Southwest from the Northwest, it was not obvious at the outset that the Northwest would remain free of slaves—despite the

---

10. Kathleen M. Brown, *Foul Bodies: Cleanliness in Early America* (New Haven, 2009).
11. Steven F. Miller, "Plantation Labor Organization and Slave Life on the Cotton Frontier: The Alabama-Mississippi Black Belt, 1815–1840," in Ira Berlin and Philip D. Morgan, eds., *Cultivation and Culture: Labor and the Shaping of Slave Life in the Americas* (Charlottesville, 1993), 155–69; Andrew R. L. Cayton, *Frontier Indiana* (Bloomington, 1996), 183–87; Thomas P. Abernethy, *From Frontier to Plantation in Tennessee: A Study in Frontier Democracy* (Chapel Hill, 1932), 146–51; Harriette Simpson Arnow, *Seedtime on the Cumberland* (Lexington, KY, 1960), 247–81; Rohrbough, *The Trans-Appalachian Frontier*; Solon J. Buck and Elizabeth Hawthorn Buck, *The Planting of Civilization in Western Pennsylvania* (Pittsburgh, 1939), 333, 346–47.
12. Adam Rothman, *Slave Country: American Expansion and the Origins of the Deep South* (Cambridge, MA, 2005); Abernethy, *From Frontier to Plantation in Tennessee*, 208; Robert E. Corlew, *Tennessee: A Short History* (Knoxville, 1969, 1981), 209, 210.

declaration in the Northwest Ordinance that "there shall be neither slavery nor involuntary servitude" in the territory.[13]

Many of the migrants to the area immediately north of the Ohio River were from the Upper South and were eager to introduce slavery to the Northwest Territory. William Henry Harrison, the son of a prominent slaveholding Virginia family, was the most influential of these advocates for bringing slavery to the Northwest. In 1791 at age nineteen Harrison abandoned a career in medicine and received a commission in the army. He proved invaluable as an aide to General Anthony Wayne at the battle of Fallen Timbers in 1794, and a year later he married the daughter of the speculator John Cleves Symmes. In 1798 he became registrar of the Land Office in Cincinnati, and, using his influence with his friend Robert Goodloe Harper of South Carolina, the Federalist chairman of the House Committee on Ways and Means, he was soon appointed secretary of the Northwest Territory by President John Adams. Within a year Harrison had won election as the territory's delegate to Congress. In 1800 the Northwest Territory was divided into two parts, the territory of Ohio and the Indiana Territory, of which the twenty-eight-year-old Harrison was appointed governor. He accepted, but only after receiving assurances that if Thomas Jefferson became president, he would be retained in office. No one in the West was more assiduous in cultivating patrons and moving up in the governmental hierarchy than Harrison.[14]

In 1803 Harrison and his pro-slavery allies in Indiana petitioned Congress to waive the ordinance's prohibition against slavery for at least ten years. When Congress tabled the petition, Indiana's pro-slavery settlers circumvented the restriction; and after the territory acquired its legislature in 1804, it passed laws that sustained a de facto form of black slavery. By 1810 there were 630 blacks in Indiana, most of whom were indentured servants serving for long terms or for life.[15]

But many settlers in the Indiana Territory were opposed to both Harrison and slavery; they argued that slavery made men haughty and proud and that the institution not only sustained a leisured aristocracy but also inhibited the immigration of non-slaveholders. In 1809 the territory of Indiana was divided in two, and Illinois Territory was created. This reduced Harrison's influence in Indiana and allowed the anti-slave forces

13. Paul Finkelman, "Slavery and the Northwest Ordinance: A Study in Ambiguity," *JER*, 6 (1986), 343–70; and Finkelman, "Evading the Ordinance: The Persistence of Bondage in Indiana and Illinois," *JER*, 9 (1989), 21–51.
14. Freeman Cleaves, *Old Tippecanoe: William Henry Harrison and His Time* (New York, 1939), 9–32.
15. Cayton, *Frontier Indiana*, 188–92, 246–47.

under the leadership of populist Jonathan Jennings to gain strength in the territory. In 1809 the New Jersey–born Jennings, who liked to campaign as the common man, sometimes stopping and helping pioneers repair their cabins or cut wood, defeated Harrison's candidate, Thomas Randolph, the territorial attorney general, in a close contest for territorial delegate to Congress.

In Washington, where he served three terms, Jennings fought to eliminate property qualifications for voting and to do away with the arbitrary and "monarchical" system of territorial government that had been established by the Northwest Ordinance of 1787, a system, said Jennings, that was "little reconcilable to the principles which governed the institutions of the different States of the Union." By seeking at every turn to undermine Harrison's influence in Indiana Territory, Jennings provoked Harrison into labeling him as that "poor animal who represents us." When Jennings's allies finally took control of the territorial legislature in 1810, they revoked the laws that maintained de facto slavery in the territory and repudiated the closed system of patronage politics that Harrison and his cronies had used to maintain their power. By exploiting democratic and anti-aristocratic rhetoric, Jennings in 1816 became Indiana's first state governor.[16]

Among the most effective arguments the anti-slave forces in Indiana invoked was the example of the incredibly speedy settlement of Ohio. Ohio's rapid growth convinced many leaders that prohibiting slavery was the best means of enticing the proper kinds of non-aristocratic settlers to migrate westward. Indeed, the area north of the Ohio River was settled largely by swarming numbers of anti-slave Yankees from New England. Many of them came to Ohio via New York and continued to push westward into the northern parts of Indiana and Illinois, bringing their communal spirit and their place names with them; towns named Cambridge, Lexington, Springfield, and Hartford were scattered throughout the states of New York, Ohio, Indiana, Illinois, and Michigan.

16. Cayton, *Frontier Indiana*, 247–52; Patrick J. Furlong, "Jonathan Jennings," *American National Biography* (New York, 1999), 11: 951–52; Reginald Horsman, *The Frontier in the Formative Years, 1783–1815* (New York, 1970), 92. Although Harrison himself ran a populist campaign for the presidency in 1840, using hard cider and a log cabin as his symbols to hide his aristocratic Virginia background, he had not forgotten what Jennings had done to him. In his inaugural address as president, Harrison called attention to this "old trick of those who would usurp the government of their country. In the name of democracy they speak, warning the people against the influence of wealth and the dangers of aristocracy. History, ancient and modern, is full of such examples."

Because most of the settlers in the Northwest Territory were small farmers, their society tended to be more democratic and egalitarian than the society of the Southwest, dominated as it was by slaveholding planters. To be sure, landholding in Ohio could be just as oligarchic as that in the South and Southwest: the top 1 percent of Ohio landowners, for example, owned 23 percent of the land.[17] But, unlike in the South and Southwest, social and economic authority in the Northwest did not automatically translate into political authority.

Ohio's first congressman, Jeremiah Morrow, who served as a Republican in the House from 1803 to 1813, was not one of the state's great landowners. Unlike those Federalist magnates who possessed five-thousand-acre spreads, Morrow had a mere 385 acres, which, to the amazement of foreign visitors, he worked himself when he was back home from Congress. The large landowners in Ohio tended to be speculators who were in control of neither the economy nor the government. Because of competition, these speculators usually were forced to sell their lands not only as quickly as possible but also much more cheaply than they wished. These Ohio grandees were always vulnerable to having their unimproved lands taxed and to being challenged by other parvenu speculators; and, unlike the planters of the Southwest, they did not have dozens of slaves to set themselves off from the other landowners in the state.

But perhaps more important, not everyone in Ohio was a farmer. Indeed, the hundreds of multiplying small towns in the Northwest created a dizzying variety of occupations that made farming, and the growing of corn and wheat, seem to be an avocation rather than the basis for the economy. Newspapers proliferated in the Northwest in a way they did not in the Southwest, or even in the Old South. Before any state had been formed in the Northwest Territory, the area already had thirteen newspapers. By contrast, North Carolina, although over a century older than the Northwest Territory and with a population of nearly half a million, had only four newspapers. By the second decade of the nineteenth century Ohio had more than twice as many newspapers per capita as Georgia.[18]

Most of the capital in the Old Southwest was tied up in slaves and not, as in the Old Northwest, in land or manufacturing or other businesses; and those planters with the most human capital were the ones most able to move to the choice lands in the West and most capable of dominating

17. Donald J. Ratcliffe, *Party Spirit in a Frontier Republic: Democratic Politics in Ohio, 1793–1821* (Columbus, OH, 1998), 102.
18. Joyce Appleby, *Inheriting the Revolution: The First Generation of Americans* (Cambridge, MA, 2000), 103.

the commercial life of the area. The slave economy of the Old Southwest produced a single staple crop, cotton, whose credit and marketing systems tended to breed hierarchical structures of authority. Since small cotton farmers needed the patronage of the large planters with access to capital and markets, they inevitably deferred to them both socially and politically. The early nineteenth-century Southwest frontier, in other words, was not all that different from the Old South of the eighteenth century. Like tobacco in the eighteenth-century Upper South, cotton was a non-perishable product with a limited number of markets, mostly overseas. Since cotton did not need elaborate storage and handling facilities, marketing it did not produce towns or other distribution centers.[19] Consequently, life in the Old Southwest did not revolve around towns or villages, as in the Old Northwest, but around plantations.[20]

By contrast, the economy of Ohio in the Old Northwest was diverse, with a variety of markets and no simple distribution system for the region's many products, resulting in a proliferation of towns. Ohio's political structure also differed from that of the territories and states of the Old Southwest. Unlike the county courts of the South and Southwest, the county commissions in Ohio were not self-perpetuating bodies but were under the elective control of local people. In addition, they shared authority with a hodgepodge of overlapping jurisdictions of towns, school districts, and other subdivisions, all of which produced a profusion of elective offices.[21] In fact, with so many political offices available, everyone seemed to run for one of them at one time or another. One hundred sixteen men ran for Hamilton County's seven seats in Ohio's third territorial assembly, and ninety-nine men ran for its ten seats in the constitutional convention of 1802. In 1803 twenty-two candidates ran for the office of the first state governor. No wonder the Federalists complained that "few Constitutions were ever so bepeopled…throughout" as was the Ohio constitution of 1802.[22]

STILL, THE SOUTHWEST WAS HARDLY STATIC, and despite the hierarchical influence of slavery on the society, many thought the region was

---

19. Jacob M. Price, "Economic Function and the Growth of American Port Towns in the Eighteenth Century," *Perspectives in American History*, 8 (1974), 123–86; Carville Earle and Ronald Hoffman, "Urban Development in the Eighteenth-Century South," *Perspectives in American History*, 10 (1976), 7–78.
20. Rohrbough, *The Trans-Appalachian Frontier*, 140.
21. Elkins and McKitrick, "A Meaning for Turner's Frontier," 572.
22. Stanley Elkins and Eric McKitrick, *Age of Federalism* (New York, 1993), 335; Ratcliffe, *Party Spirit in a Frontier Republic*, 61, 74.

anything but stable. People in the Southwest were on the move, many of them in the 1790s pushing down the Mississippi toward the Spanish-held port city of New Orleans, which was becoming increasingly important to all Western Americans. Of course, New Orleans had always been on the mind of any American concerned about the West. Even Hamilton in 1790 thought that when the United States grew stronger and the American people were able to make good "our pretensions," we would not "leave in the possession of any foreign power the territories at the mouth of the Mississippi, which are to be regarded as the key to it."[23] In the Treaty of San Lorenzo in 1795 the Americans had secured from Spain the right of depositing their goods in New Orleans and thus access to the larger commercial world through the Gulf of Mexico.

With this treaty Spain was trying to prevent an American takeover of its empire, but perhaps it was only postponing the inevitable. Jefferson and other Americans believed that Spain's hold on its North American empire was so weak that it was only a matter of time before the various pieces of that empire—New Orleans, East and West Florida, maybe even Cuba—fell like ripe fruit "piece by piece" into American hands.[24] As early as 1784 James Madison predicted that the safety of Spain's "possessions in this quarter of the globe must depend more upon our peaceableness than her own power."[25] America need only wait and let its phenomenal demographic growth and movement take care of things.

Because of Spain's weakness, its possessions on the continent were no problem for Jefferson; but the dynamic nation of England was a different matter altogether. Jefferson could not tolerate any additional English presence on the continent. During the Nootka Sound controversy in 1790, when an incident between England and Spain off the west coast of Vancouver Island threatened a war between the two European powers that bordered the United States, the Washington administration was deeply disturbed. By attempting to set up a base in Nootka Sound, the British had encroached on territory on the Pacific coast that the Spanish had regarded for centuries as exclusively theirs. When the Spanish seized and arrested the British intruders, Great Britain was prepared to retaliate. The U.S. government and especially Secretary of State Jefferson were apprehensive that Britain might use the conflict to seize all the Spanish possessions in North America, which would pose a danger to the security and even the independence of the new Republic.

23. AH to GW, 15 Sept. 1790, *Papers of Hamilton*, 7: 51–53.
24. TJ to Archibald Stuart, 25 Jan. 1786, *Papers of Jefferson*, 9: 218.
25. JM to TJ, 20 Aug. 1784, *Republic of Letters*, 339.

What if the British requested permission to cross American territory to engage the Spanish in the West? What should the American response be? These were the questions that President Washington asked of his advisors. Washington was also worried that if war broke out between Spain and Britain, Spain's ally France might get involved. Despite America's alliance with France, Secretary of State Jefferson was willing to use American neutrality in the conflict between Spain and Britain to bargain for either Britain's withdrawal from the Northwest posts or Spain's opening up the Mississippi to American commerce. He expressed a willingness to go to war with Spain to acquire Florida and the rights to the Mississippi or, more important, even with Britain to prevent the former mother country from taking over Spain's possessions.

In the end further conflict was averted. When France, preoccupied with its Revolution, declined to help Spain, the Spanish government backed down and in the Nootka Sound Convention of 1790 agreed to recognize the right of England to trade and settle in the unoccupied territory that it had formerly claimed was exclusively Spanish. When in 1819 Spain ceded its rights to the Oregon Country to the United States, the stage was set for a competition between the two English-speaking nations for control of this far northwest piece of the continent. Partly as a result of the Nootka Sound controversy, Great Britain came to realize that having an accredited minister in the United States capital might be in its interest after all, and it sent George Hammond, who arrived in October 1791.

Spanish officials were well aware of America's demographic growth and became more and more fearful of American encroachment. Suddenly in October 1800 Spain decided, under pressure from Napoleon, who was now in charge of the French Republic, to cede Louisiana back to France in the secret Treaty of San Ildefonso. Spain believed that France, as the dominant European power, would be better able to maintain a barrier between the Americans and the silver mines of Mexico.

In the meantime, France, under Napoleon's leadership, had developed a renewed interest in its lost North American empire. Not only could French possession of Louisiana counter British ambitions in Canada, but, more important, Louisiana could become a dumping ground for French malcontents and a source for provisioning the lucrative French sugar islands in the Caribbean—Martinique, Guadeloupe, and especially Saint-Domingue.

Sugar was important to France. Processed in France and sold throughout Europe, sugar accounted for nearly 20 percent of France's exports. And 70 percent of France's sugar supply came from the single colony of Saint-Domingue. Napoleon knew that if France's imperial ambitions were to be realized, the slave rebellion in Saint-Domingue led by

Toussaint L'Ouverture would have to be put down and the island recovered for France. In 1801 Napoleon sent his brother-in-law General Charles Victor Emmanuel Leclerc with an enormous force of forty thousand troops to recover Saint-Domingue and reinstate the ancien régime slave system that had made the island so profitable for France.

It was one of the greatest mistakes Napoleon ever made, as he himself later admitted. By 1802 most of the French troops had been killed or had succumbed to yellow fever, including Leclerc himself, and only two thousand remained healthy. Before the rebellion that had begun in 1791 ended in 1803 followed by the declaration of Haitian independence on January 1, 1804, some three hundred fifty thousand Haitians of all colors had died along with as many as sixty thousand French soldiers. Since Louisiana was supposed to supply goods to Saint-Domingue, the loss of that rich island suddenly made Louisiana dispensable. Already Napoleon was turning his eyes back toward Europe and to a renewal of the war with Great Britain, for which he needed money.

But Americans did not yet know of this turn of events. In 1802 all they heard were rumors that Napoleon had induced Spain to retrocede Louisiana to France, including, as many thought, both East and West Florida. For the Americans, and especially for President Jefferson, nothing could have been more alarming. It was one thing for a feeble and decrepit Spain to hold Louisiana; "her possession of the place," said Jefferson, "would hardly be felt by us." But it was quite another for a vigorous and powerful France to control what Jefferson called "the one single spot" on the globe, "the possessor of which is our natural and habitual enemy." Since that one single spot, New Orleans, was fast becoming the outlet for the produce of more than half of America's inhabitants, in French hands, said Jefferson, it would become "a point of eternal friction with us." Indeed, Jefferson told the American minister in France, Robert R. Livingston, "the day that France takes possession of New Orleans... seals the union of two nations, who, in conjunction, can maintain exclusive possession of the ocean. From that moment, we must marry ourselves to the British fleet and nation."[26]

For someone like Jefferson who hated the British with a passion matched by no other American, this was an extraordinary statement, but one that he knew Livingston would pass on to Napoleon and French officials. Probably Jefferson was never serious about an Anglo-American military alliance but hoped that Napoleon would see the light and realize that such an alliance was not in the interest of either France or the United

---

26. TJ to Robert R. Livingston, 18 April 1802, *Jefferson: Writings*, 1104–7.

States.[27] If France insisted on taking possession of Louisiana, however, "she might perhaps be willing to look about for arrangements which might reconcile it to our interests. If anything could do this," the crafty president told Livingston in April 1802, "it would be the ceding to us the island of New Orleans and the Floridas." He thought France might be willing to sell these territories for $6 million, and he sent his good and trusted friend James Monroe to Paris to help Livingston clinch the deal.[28]

Only Monroe had enough confidence in his intimacy with his fellow Virginians, President Jefferson and Secretary of State James Madison, to allow him and Livingston to exceed their instructions and pay $15 million for all of Louisiana, some nine hundred thousand square miles of Western land.

When he learned of the acquisition Jefferson was ecstatic. "It is something larger than the whole U.S.," he exclaimed, "probably containing 500 million acres." Not only did the acquisition of Louisiana fulfill the president's greatest dream of having sufficient land for generations to come of his yeoman farmers, his "chosen people of God," but, he said, it also "removes from us the greatest source of danger to our peace." Neither France nor Britain could now threaten New Orleans and America's Mississippi outlet to the sea. The fact that East and West Florida remained with Spain was of little concern, "because," said Jefferson, "we think they cannot fail to fall in our hands."[29]

The purchase of Louisiana was the most popular and momentous event of Jefferson's presidency. Not only did it end the long struggle for control of the Mississippi's outlet to the sea, but it also, as Jefferson exulted, freed America from Europe's colonial entanglements and prepared the way for the eventual dominance of the United States in the Western Hemisphere.

Most Federalists saw it differently; indeed, they were aghast at the purchase. Louisiana, declared Fisher Ames of Massachusetts, was "a great waste, a wilderness unpeopled with any beings except wolves and wandering Indians." He thought the deal was a disaster. "We are to spend money of which we have too little for land of which we already have too much." It was simply a device by which "Imperial Virginia" could spread its

27. Lawrence S. Kaplan, *Jefferson and France: An Essay on Politics and Political Ideas* (New Haven, 1967), 101.
28. TJ to Robert R. Livingston, 18 April 1802, *Jefferson: Writings*, 1104–7.
29. Jon Kukla, *A Wilderness So Immense: The Louisiana Purchase and the Destiny of America* (New York, 2003), 287, 289.

slaveholding population westward in order to remain "arbitress" of the whole nation.

Although Alexander Hamilton favored the purchase, without granting Jefferson any credit for it, he was worried about what the addition of such a great extent of territory would mean for the integrity of the United States. Could the people of Louisiana, with such differences of culture, religion, and ethnicity, be made "an integral part of the United States," or would the territory have to remain a permanent colony of the United States?[30]

Many Federalists fretted that this expansion of the nation would enhance the slaveholding South at the expense of the Northeast. "The Virginia faction," observed Stephen Higginson of Massachusetts, "have certainly formed a deliberate plan to govern and depress New England; and this eagerness to extend our territory and create new States is an essential part of it."[31] Some of these Federalists, led by former secretary of state Timothy Pickering and Connecticut's Roger Griswold, revived the 1780s idea of breaking away and forming a separate confederacy of New England and New York. Hamilton's adamant opposition to such a scheme, however, essentially killed it, at least for the time being. "Dismemberment of our Empire," Hamilton told one prominent New England Federalist the night before his fatal duel with Aaron Burr in July 1804, offered "no relief to our real Disease; which is DEMOCRACY."[32]

With their conception of the United States as a loosely bound confederation of states, the Democratic-Republicans had no problem with the addition of this huge expanse of territory. "Who can limit the extent to which the federative principle may operate effectively?" asked Jefferson in his second inaugural address in March 1805. Jefferson's "empire of liberty" was always one of like principles, not of like boundaries. As long as Americans believed in certain ideals, he said, they remained Americans, regardless of the territory they happened to occupy.[33]

In 1799, for example, the famous pioneer Daniel Boone moved his extended family from Kentucky to Missouri—into Spanish territory!— without any sense that he had become less American. The Spanish government had simply promised ample portions of cheap land for him and

30. Kukla, A Wilderness So Immense, 292, 291.
31. Higginson to Timothy Pickering, 22 Nov. 1803, "Letters of Stephen Higginson, 1783–1804," Annual Report of the American Historical Association for the Year 1896 (Washington, DC, 1897), 1: 837.
32. AH to Theodore Sedgwick, 10 July 1804, Papers of Hamilton, 26: 309.
33. TJ, Second Inaugural, 4 Mar. 1805, Jefferson: Writings, 519.

his family, and that was enough, not just for him but for countless other Americans who moved into Spanish-owned territory, including Texas, in search of cheap land. Boone later said that he would never have settled outside the United States "had he not firmly believed it would become a portion of the American republic." Maybe so: Jefferson certainly welcomed this movement of Americans into lands owned by Spain, since "it may be the means of delivering to us peaceably what may otherwise cost us a war."[34]

The president often expressed a strange idea of the American nation. At times he was remarkably indifferent to the possibility that a Western confederacy might break away from the Eastern United States. What did it matter? he asked in 1804. "Those of the western confederacy will be as much our children & descendents as those of the eastern."[35] This relaxed attitude toward a precisely bounded territory as a source of nationhood was different from that of the European nations. For Jefferson and many other Republicans, this peculiar conception of nationhood made ideology a more important determinant of America's identity than occupying a particular geographical space.

Despite Jefferson's great enthusiasm for the purchase, he hesitated to send the treaty to the Senate for ratification. Being a firm believer in limited government and strict construction of the Constitution, Jefferson doubted that the federal government had the constitutional right either to acquire foreign territory or, more important, to incorporate it into the Union. For seven weeks he worried about the issue and tinkered with the idea of amending the Constitution. Only when Livingston and Monroe informed him in August 1803 that Napoleon was having second thoughts about the deal did he reluctantly agree to send the treaty to the Senate without mentioning his constitutional misgivings. Better to pass over them in silence, he said, than to attempt to justify the purchase by invoking a broad construction of the Constitution.

The Senate complied with Jefferson's wishes, but the more unruly and rambunctious House of Representatives, which had to implement the treaty financially, opened up the constitutional issues that Jefferson had hoped to avoid. Although they remained firm believers in states' rights and strict construction, many House Republicans were forced to invoke, as Hamilton had in the 1790s, the "necessary and proper" clause of the Constitution to justify the government's acquisition of Louisiana. Even

34. John Mack Faragher, *Daniel Boone: The Life and Legend of an American Pioneer* (New York, 1992), 174–75.
35. TJ to Joseph Priestley, 29 Jan. 1804, *Jefferson: Writings*, 1142.

though the Republicans enjoyed a three-to-one majority in the House, the supporters of the purchase were able to carry their first procedural bill by a margin of only two votes, fifty-nine to fifty-seven.

It was certainly ironic that some Republicans talked like Federalists, but too much can be made of that. More impressive is the seriousness with which Jefferson and the other Republicans took their constitutional scruples. Although they wanted this addition of Western territory in the worst way, they nevertheless worried and hesitated to the point where they almost lost it.

In Article III of the treaty the United States committed itself to incorporating the inhabitants of the ceded territory into the Union "as soon as possible." But most Americans believed that this would not be easy, either constitutionally or culturally. Like the Federalists, Jefferson knew that this new territory was composed of people who were quite different from those of the United States, in religion, race, and ethnicity. Because these former subjects of France and Spain were accustomed to authoritarian rule and unfamiliar with self-government, "the approach of such a people to liberty," the Republicans said, "must be gradual." Consequently, the administration thought that until the people of Louisiana were ready for democracy America might have to continue to rule them arbitrarily. The president was given far more power to rule in Louisiana than was the case in the other territories, leading some critics to charge that the administration had created in Louisiana "a government about as despotic as that of Turkey in Asia."[36]

In March 1804 Congress divided the Louisiana Purchase by a line that is now the northern border of the present state of Louisiana. While the vast and little-known region to the north became the District of Louisiana with St. Louis as its capital and with the notorious General James Wilkinson as its governor, the southern part became the Territory of Orleans with New Orleans as its capital.[37] The borders with Spanish territory were unclear, and although a buffer zone between Louisiana and Texas was created, boundary disputes between the Americans and the Spanish were both inevitable and exploitable by adventurers, runaway slaves, and troublemakers of all sorts.

The first governor of the Territory of Orleans was twenty-nine-year-old William Claiborne, who at twenty-one had been a judge of the Tennessee state supreme court and most recently was governor of the Mississippi

---

36. Kukla, *A Wilderness So Immense*, 311–13; Alexander DeConde, *This Affair of Louisiana* (New York, 1976), 212.

37. William E. Foley, *A History of Missouri*, vol. 1, 1673–1820 (Columbia, MO, 1971), 63–119.

Territory. Because of doubts about the capacity of the French and Spanish people of Orleans for self-rule, Claiborne was given nearly dictatorial powers over them, even though he did not speak their languages, share their religion, or comprehend their customs and society. Not surprisingly, Claiborne found dealing with the diversity of the new territory to be his "principal difficulty."[38]

Since Claiborne, like nearly all white Americans, was used to a black-white, slave-free dichotomy, he found it especially difficult to understand the division of Louisiana society into at least three castes—black, free colored, and white. Could the free colored population be armed and participate in the militia? Could they become citizens? Fisher Ames's warning that Louisiana society was simply a *"Gallo-Hispano-Indian omnium gatherum* of savages and adventurers" whose morals could never be "expected to sustain and glorify our republic" frightened many Americans.[39]

Not only did the large numbers of Americans moving into Orleans have to adapt their common law to the European civil law, but they had to make their way into a multi-racial, multi-ethnic, and Catholic-dominated society unlike anyplace else in the United States. Fearing the unruly slaves being brought from the rebellious colony of Saint-Domingue, Congress in 1804 forbade the importation of slaves from abroad into Orleans. This restriction assumed that the domestic slave trade could supply the territory's needs and thereby offset the influence of the French and Spanish slaves and what the Americans believed were the pernicious racial attitudes of the French and Spanish residents.

Franco-Spanish slavery was different from Anglo-American slavery. Manumission and the slave's right to self-purchase were easier; indeed, to the consternation of many white Americans, between 1804 and 1806 nearly two hundred slaves in Orleans purchased their own freedom. By 1810 free blacks composed about 20 percent of the population of the city of New Orleans.[40] Consequently, the numbers of free blacks, interracial marriages and unions, and people of mixed race were much greater than elsewhere in the American South. Despite these differences, however, the territory of Orleans, or what became Louisiana, gained statehood in 1812, less than a decade after the Louisiana Purchase.

Over the decades following 1803, Americans tried with mixed success to bring this polyglot society and its permissive interracial mixing into line

---

38. Kukla, *A Wilderness So Immense*, 323.
39. Fisher Ames to Thomas Dwight, 31 Oct. 1803, *Works of Ames*, ed. Allen, 2: 1468–69.
40. Peter J. Kastor, *The Nation's Crucible: The Louisiana Purchase and the Creation of America* (New Haven, 2004), 66; Rothman, *Slave Country*, 101–2.

with the binary racial culture prevailing throughout the rest of America. In the nineteenth century most Americans retained an image of New Orleans as an exotic place of loose morals and rampant miscegenation, and thus they learned little or nothing from this remarkable multi-cultural and multi-racial addition to the United States.

JEFFERSON WAS EAGER to take advantage of the hazy boundaries of the Louisiana Territory. He thought that the western border went all the way to the Rio Grande and was convinced that West Florida on the eastern border was part of the Louisiana Purchase. The American negotiators, Livingston and Monroe, certainly had argued that Louisiana extended eastward to the Perdido River (the present western boundary of Florida), and they had backed up their argument by showing that France had claimed such a border for Louisiana prior to 1763.[41] When Livingston asked the French foreign minister about the "East bounds of the Territory ceded to us," the wily Talleyrand replied, "I can give you no direction; you have made a noble bargain for yourselves and I suppose you will make the most of it."[42]

They did make the most of it—at the expense of Spain. The Republicans' policy was simple: Claim West Florida as part of Louisiana (pointing out that that was how France had defined it) and then offer to forgo the use of force if Spain would sell both East and West Florida to the United States. Since, as Monroe pointed out, in what was conventional wisdom among most American leaders, America was "a rising and Spain a declining power," the Floridas were sooner or later going to fall to the United States anyhow; thus it was in Spain's interest to sell them now. In 1804 Congress passed the Mobile Act that extended the federal revenue laws to all territory ceded by France, including West Florida, which Spain considered to be its territory. The act vested the president with discretionary authority to take possession of the Mobile area "whenever he shall deem it expedient."[43]

Spain called this act an "atrocious libel" and sought French backing for its position. Although Monroe and others recommended that the United States simply seize the disputed territory, Jefferson reluctantly decided to wait for circumstances to ripen. Yet at the same time he was eager to "correct the dangerous error that we are a people whom no

41. J.C.A. Stagg, *Borderlines in Borderlands: James Madison and the Spanish-American Frontier, 1776–1821* (New Haven, 2008), 39, 41.

42. Livingston to JM, 20 May 1803, *Papers of Madison: Secretary of State Ser.*, 5: 19.

43. DeConde, *This Affair of Louisiana*, 215, 216.

injuries can provoke to war," and in his December 1805 message to the Congress he came close to calling for a declaration of war against Spain. To the amazement of foreign observers, the aggressive young country with little or no military establishment seemed to have no doubt that it was destined, in the words of a French diplomat, "to devour the whole of North America."[44]

It seemed as if America could not acquire territory fast enough. When in early 1806 Jefferson requested $2 million from Congress to help obtain the Floridas, Senator Stephen Bradley of Vermont proposed an amendment to give the president authority to acquire not only West and East Florida but also Canada and Nova Scotia, by purchase or "otherwise," by which he meant military means. The amendment gained some support but was defeated. The "Two Million Dollar Act," as it was called, was bitterly opposed by John Randolph, the Virginia spokesman for the States' Rights Principles of 1798, largely because the money was to be paid to France, which presumably would influence Spain to surrender the Floridas. Randolph "considered it a base prostration of the national character, to excite one nation by money to bully another out of its property," and he used this incident to break decisively with Jefferson.[45]

Although Randolph was not opposed to American expansion but only to the administration's unbecoming and secret maneuvering, others were being made uneasy by the constant pressure for acquiring territory. Senator Samuel Mitchill of New York said the United States was caught up in "a land mania." First it was Louisiana, "a world without bounds, without limits." Now "we must buy more—we must have the Floridas. What next?" he asked. "Why all the Globe—why this rage—Have we an inhabitant for every acre?"[46]

After several years of rumors, plots, and threats of war, a group of American settlers in the summer of 1810 rebelled against what remained of Spanish rule in West Florida. Believing they were justified by Napoleon's takeover of the Bourbon regime in Spain, the rebels marched on the fort at Baton Rouge, declared themselves to be the independent Republic of West Florida, and requested annexation by the United States. Despite protests from the European powers, the Madison administration

44. DeConde, *This Affair of Louisiana*, 218, 225, 214; TJ to JM, 18 Sept. 1805, *Republic of Letters*, 1387.

45. Randolph, *Annals of Congress*, 9th Congress, 1st session (April 1806), 947.

46. Reginald Horsman, "The Dimensions of an 'Empire of Liberty': Expansionism and Republicanism," *JER*, 9 (1989), 11; Everett S. Brown, ed., *William Plumer's Memorandum of Proceedings in the United States Senate, 1803–1807* (New York, 1923), 401.

proclaimed the annexation of West Florida and then made the region part of the Territory of Orleans, defending its controversial actions as the delayed carrying out of the purchase of Louisiana. Three years later, in 1813, American troops occupied the last remaining piece of West Florida, the Mobile district that ran to the Perdido River.

From the outset Jefferson had had his eye on not only all the rest of the Floridas but also Cuba, Mexico's provinces, and Canada. When all of these territories became part of the United States, he said, "we should have such an empire for liberty as she has never surveyed since the creation." It was America's destiny. He was "persuaded no constitution was ever before so well calculated as ours for extensive empire and self government."[47]

JEFFERSON HAD BEEN FASCINATED with expansion into the West from an early age. He had read everything he could about the region and was probably the best-informed American on the territory beyond the Mississippi. When the Revolutionary War ended in 1783, he was already dreaming of explorations to the Pacific. In 1783 he asked the Revolutionary War hero George Rogers Clark to lead a privately sponsored expedition to explore the West, but Clark declined. When Jefferson was minister to France he encouraged the extravagant and ill-fated hopes of Connecticut-born John Ledyard to cross Siberia and reach the western coast of North America; from there Ledyard was supposed to travel east across the continent to the Atlantic. Ledyard reached Siberia but was arrested by Catherine the Great in 1788, brought back to Moscow, and expelled from the country. While in Egypt, he continued to write Jefferson about the value of travel in correcting the errors of historians; he died during a voyage up the Nile in 1789 at age thirty-seven.[48]

Later as secretary of state in the Washington administration Jefferson supported several plans for expeditions up the Missouri, including backing the plans of the French immigrant and naturalist André Michaux to journey to the Pacific; these went nowhere when Michaux got caught up in Citizen Genet's shenanigans. In 1792 an American sea trader from Rhode Island, Captain Robert Gray, discovered and named the Columbia River, and after the Nootka Sound controversy Captain George Vancouver of the British navy and the Canadian trader Alexander Mackenzie

47. TJ to JM, 27 April 1809, *Republic of Letters*, 1586; Andrew McMichael, *Atlantic Loyalties: Americans in Spanish West Florida, 1785–1810* (Athens, GA, 2008).

48. Edward G. Gray, *The Making of John Ledyard: Empire and Ambition in the Life of an Early American Traveler* (New Haven, 2007).

began staking British claims to the northwest portion of the continent and threatening to take complete control of the fur trade in the Columbia River area. In 1792–1793 Mackenzie in fact made the first crossing of the continent north of Mexico, at least by a white man.

Mackenzie's account of his expedition published in 1801 was apparently what jogged President Jefferson into action. Well before he had any inkling that America would purchase the whole Louisiana Territory, the president laid plans for an ostensibly scientific but also a covert military and commercial expedition into the Spanish-held trans-Mississippi West. "The idea that you are going to explore the Mississippi has been generally given out," Jefferson informed the leader of the expedition. "It satisfies public curiosity and masks sufficiently the real destination," which was the Pacific.[49]

To lead this Western expedition, Jefferson in 1802 selected his private secretary, Meriwether Lewis, an army veteran. Lewis had volunteered for a Jefferson-planned expedition of 1793 that never came off and undoubtedly had conveyed to Jefferson in numerous conversations his desire to explore the West. It was an excellent choice. As Jefferson explained to Dr. Benjamin Rush, "Capt. Lewis is brave, prudent, habituated to the woods, & familiar with Indian manners & character." Although Lewis was "not regularly educated," he knew enough about nature to select and describe flora and fauna that were new. And what he did not know he could learn. Jefferson sent Lewis off to Philadelphia for crash courses in astronomy, natural history, medicine, map-making, lunar navigation, and ethnology with several scientific experts. He was told to learn all he could about the Indians, from their sexual habits to their feelings of melancholy and tendencies to suicide.[50]

Lewis wanted a co-commander and selected his old army friend William Clark, younger brother of the Indian fighter George Rogers Clark, who had declined Jefferson's earlier request to lead an expedition. Clark was four years older than Lewis and had been Lewis's immediate superior for a time, but in 1796 he had resigned his captain's commission and was engaged in family business in the Ohio Valley when he received Lewis's invitation. Since the army regulations for the expedition provided for only a lieutenant as the second officer, Clark did not get his captain's commission back. But Lewis was determined that Clark be treated as

---

49. TJ to Meriwether Lewis, 15 July 1803, in Ford, ed., *Writings of Jefferson*, 8: 199–200.
50. Stephen E. Ambrose, *Undaunted Courage: Meriwether Lewis, Thomas Jefferson, and the Opening of the American West* (New York, 1996), 79; William H. Goetzmann and William N. Goetzmann, *The West in the Imagination* (New York, 1986), 7.

his equal and kept the lieutenancy a secret from the men of the expedition.[51]

Having co-commanders was an extraordinary experiment in cooperation, in violation of all army ideas of chain of command, but it worked. Lewis and Clark seem never to have quarreled and only rarely disagreed with one another. They complemented each other beautifully. Clark had been a company commander and had explored the Mississippi. He knew how to handle enlisted men and was a better surveyor, map-maker, and waterman than Lewis. Where Lewis was apt to be moody and sometimes wander off alone, Clark was always tough, steady, and reliable. Best of all, the two captains were writers: they wrote continually, describing in often vivid and sharp prose much of what they encountered—plants, animals, people, weather, geography, and unusual experiences.

So much about the land beyond the Mississippi remained unknown or wrongly understood that no one could prepare fully for what lay ahead. Although Jefferson had the most extensive library in the world on the geography, cartography, natural history, and ethnology of the American West, he nevertheless assumed in 1800 that the Rockies were no higher than the Blue Ridge Mountains, that mammoths and other prehistoric creatures still roamed along the upper Missouri among active volcanoes, that a huge mile-long mountain of pure salt lay somewhere on the Great Plains, that the Western Indians may have been the lost tribes of Israel or wandering Welshmen, and, most important, that there was a water route, linked by a low portage across the mountains, that led to the Pacific—the long-sought northwest passage.

Lewis and Clark set out from St. Louis on May 14, 1804, with forty or so men, including Clark's black slave, York. They traveled up the Missouri and by October reached the villages of the Mandan Indians, in present-day North Dakota, where they decided to spend the winter of 1804–1805.

Since fur traders had penetrated this far up the Missouri, the expedition had not yet covered completely unknown ground. Lewis and Clark spent time during this first stage of the journey dealing with some disciplinary problems and the death of a sergeant from appendicitis—the only member of the company to die on the journey. Although they had a nearly violent confrontation with the Teton Sioux in present-day South Dakota, most of the time the captains left the Indians they met more bewildered than angry.

The translation problems were immense. The Indians would speak to an Indian in the expedition who then spoke to someone who could only

---

51. Landon Y. Jones, *William Clark and the Shaping of the West* (New York, 2004).

speak French who then passed on what he heard to someone who understood French but also spoke English. Only then could Lewis and Clark finally find out what the Indians had originally said. Their reply, of course, had to repeat the process in reverse. Laborious as conversation with the Indians was, Lewis and Clark worked out an elaborate ceremony for all the Indian tribes they encountered, informing them that the United States had taken over the territory and that their new father, "the great Chief the President," was "the only friend to whom you can now look for protection, or from whom you can ask favours, or receive good councils, and he will take care to serve you, & and not deceive you."[52] After what became the standard speech to the Indians, the captains distributed presents—beads, brass buttons, tomahawks, axes, moccasin awls, scissors, and mirrors, as well as U.S. flags and medals with Jefferson's visage.

The Corps of Discovery, as the expedition was called, spent the winter of 1804–1805 in a fort it constructed near the Mandan villages. In April 1805 Lewis and Clark sent back their heavy keelboat and some enlisted men to St. Louis along with a written report, a map, and some botanical, mineral, and animal specimens to be delivered to President Jefferson. Joining the party now was the Shoshone woman Sacagawea with her husband, Toussaint Charbonneau, a French-Canadian river man, and their infant son. Sacagawea and Charbonneau were to prove invaluable as translators during the next stages of the journey. In addition, the presence of Sacagawea and her baby was a sign to the Indians met by the Corps that the explorers came in peace.

In six canoes and two pirogues the Corps of thirty-three set out on April 7, 1805, to proceed up the Missouri to the Rockies. Even though Lewis, as he wrote in his journal, was about "to penetrate a country at least two thousand miles in width, on which the foot of civillized man had never trodden, the good or evil it had in store for us was for experiment yet to determine," he could not have been happier. "This little fleet," he said, "altho' not quite so rispectable as those of Columbus or Capt. Cook, were still viewed by us with as much pleasure as those deservedly famed adventurers ever beheld theirs; and I dare say with quite as much anxiety for their safety and preservation."[53]

Despite his happiness in getting his expedition going once again in April 1805, Lewis scarcely realized how arduous the rest of the journey to the Pacific would be. It took the party four months just to get to the

---

52. Ambrose, *Undaunted Courage*, 156–57.
53. Ambrose, *Undaunted Courage*, 212.

Rockies, including a monthlong portage around the Great Falls of the Missouri. The men suffered badly from eating their virtually all-meat diet. Lewis tended to give the ailing soldiers some of the fifty dozen pills that Dr. Benjamin Rush had prescribed for the journey. Generally referred to as "Thunderclappers," the pills were composed of a variety of drugs, each of which was a powerful purgative.

By the time the party reached the Continental Divide on the present Montana–Idaho border in August 1805, Lewis (who turned thirty-one on August 18) realized that there would be no simple portage to the waters of the Columbia. Although the commanders did not know it, they could scarcely have picked a more difficult place to cross the Rockies. From Sacagawea's Shoshone tribe the expedition got guides and horses for the journey across what one sergeant called "the most terrible mountains I ever beheld."[54] The crossing of Lolo Pass in the Bitterroots was the expedition's worst experience. Beset by snow and hail, exhausted and half-starved, the men killed their horses and drank melted snow for nourishment. Yet the expedition made 160 miles in eleven days, an incredible feat.

On September 22, 1805, the party finally reached the country of the Nez Percé Indians on the Clearwater River in Idaho, where it built canoes for the trip down the Clearwater, the Snake, and the Columbia to the Pacific. On November 7, 1805, though the group was still in the estuary of the Columbia, Clark described what he saw: "*Ocian in view*! O! the joy!...Ocian 4142 Miles from the Mouth of *Missouri* R."[55]

The men built Fort Clatsop on the south side of the Columbia estuary, where the captains spent a long wet winter writing descriptions of nature and the Indians and making a map. In March 1806 they began their return, and spent a month with the Nez Percé waiting for the snow to melt in the Rockies. After crossing the mountains, Lewis and Clark separated. Lewis explored the Marias River in present Montana while Clark traveled down the Yellowstone River. On their trip Lewis and his men ran into a party of Blackfoot Indians, who tried to steal their horses. In the only real violence of the expedition, Lewis and his men killed two of the Indians and were lucky to escape with their lives.

Reunited in North Dakota, the captains revisited the Mandan villages where they had wintered in 1804–1805. They left Sacagawea and her husband and child with the Mandans and moved rapidly down the Missouri to St. Louis, arriving on September 23, 1806. From the time they had

54. James P. Ronda, *Lewis and Clark Among the Indians* (Lincoln, NE, 1984), 157.
55. Ambrose, *Undaunted Courage*, 305.

originally set out from St. Louis, they had been gone two years and four months. Nearly everyone had given them up for lost—except Jefferson.

The Lewis and Clark expedition was the greatest adventure of exploration in American history. But it was more than that. In addition to opening up a fur-trading empire in the West and strengthening America's claim to the Oregon Country, the explorers had brought back a wealth of scientific information. They had discovered and described 178 new plants and 122 species and subspecies of animals. By systematically recording all they had seen, they introduced new approaches to exploration that affected all future expeditions. Their marvelous journals influenced all subsequent writing on the American West.

Unfortunately, however, the explorers were unable to get their manuscripts ready for publication. Lewis, who was appointed governor of the Louisiana Territory, became involved in establishing a fur company and other get-rich schemes and apparently began drinking heavily, taking drugs, and running up debts. He was so deeply depressed that on a trip back from St. Louis to Washington in 1809 he committed suicide. He was thirty-five.

Clark tried to pick up the pieces, and he persuaded Nicholas Biddle, a precocious young Philadelphian, to edit the journals. In 1814 Biddle, the future president of the Second Bank of the United States, published a narrative account of the journey that omitted most of the material on the flora and fauna. Because Biddle's *History of the Expedition Under the Commands of Captains Lewis and Clark* was for the next ninety years the only printed account of the expedition based on the journals, Lewis and Clark received no credit for most of their discoveries in nature. Others renamed the plants, animals, birds, and rivers that they had discovered and named, and these later names, not Lewis's and Clark's, were the ones that have survived.[56]

One person who hoped to benefit from the expedition was the fur trader and businessman John Jacob Astor. In 1808 Astor established a trans-continental fur company that aimed to control all the Indian trade

---

56. In 1893 Dr. Elliott Coues published a new annotated edition of Biddle's *History* in which he identified many of the plants and animals mentioned in the text. But it was not until Reuben Gold Thwaites, director of the State Historical Society of Wisconsin and an experienced documentary editor, published in 1904–1905 his multi-volume edition of the *Original Journals of the Lewis and Clark Expedition* that the world discovered what Lewis and Clark and their subordinates had actually written. These earlier editions have been superseded by the thirteen-volume edition edited by Gary Moulton, *The Journals of the Lewis and Clark Expedition* (Lincoln, NE, 1987–2001).

from the Northwest. He set up routes from upstate New York through the Great Lakes, up the Missouri River, and across the Rocky Mountains to a northwestern post on the Pacific Ocean. He named the post Astoria, and in 1811 it became the first American settlement in the Oregon Country. Although the conflict with Great Britain culminating in the War of 1812 undid many of Astor's plans, his ventures did help to maintain American interests in the Northwest while Astor himself turned his attention to New York real estate.

Once the Lewis and Clark expedition had tracked the Northwest, the Southwest of the continent remained to be explored, even though much of it was Spanish territory. Several American expeditions in 1804 and 1805 looked for the elusive source of the Red River and created trouble with the Spanish. After having explored the Mississippi to its source in 1805, Lieutenant Zebulon Pike in 1806 led an expedition up the Arkansas River into what is now Colorado. Pike tried but was unable to reach the summit of the fourteen-thousand-foot peak that bears his name. His party was eventually captured by Spanish troops and brought to Santa Fe and then Chihuahua in Mexico before being sent under guard through Mexico to an American border post at Natchitoches in the northwest corner of present-day Louisiana.[57]

Since Pike's expeditions had been ordered by General James Wilkinson, governor of the Louisiana Territory and commander-in-chief of the United States Army, Pike's fame was tainted by Wilkinson's reputation for intrigue and shady dealing. Indeed, the borders of the new Louisiana Territory were so vague, Spain's hold on the East and West Florida and Texas was so weak, and the rough and unruly frontier inhabitants were so captivated by dreams of America's inevitable expansion that adventurers, filibustering expeditions, and rumors of plots and conspiracies flourished throughout Orleans and the Southwest.

THE MOST GRANDIOSE of these schemes was that of 1806–1807 involving Aaron Burr, Jefferson's former vice-president, and General Wilkinson. Wilkinson's involvement is explicable: he was a notorious schemer and plotter and was rumored, correctly, to be in the pay of the Spanish government. It is Burr's participation that is astonishing, and it has captivated the imagination of Americans for over two hundred years. Indeed, Burr has become the most romanticized and vilified historical character in American literature. He has been the subject of countless

57. William H. Goetzmann, *Army Exploration in the American West, 1803–1863* (New Haven, 1959).

poems, songs, sermons, and semi-fictional popular biographies, and the central figure in nearly three dozen plays and more than four dozen novels. Despite all his hustling and scheming, however, it is doubtful that Burr would ever have become embroiled in his mysterious adventures in the West if he had not become alienated from the Jefferson administration and had not killed Alexander Hamilton in a duel.

Because of his passive behavior during the electoral deadlock in 1801, Vice-President Burr at once created doubts about his loyalty to the Jefferson administration. Jefferson did not ask his opinion on appointments to the cabinet and instead turned to Governor George Clinton of New York for advice and then appointed few of Burr's followers to offices. Burr in turn began to defend Federalist policies and, to the consternation of Republican leaders, even participated in a Federalist celebration of Washington's birthday.

As Burr's ties to the administration eroded, the Republicans in New York divided between the Burrites and the supporters of Governor Clinton and his nephew DeWitt Clinton. In 1802 the leading Republican journalist in the state, James Cheetham, a convert to the Clintonians, accused Burr of conniving to win the presidency for himself in the election of 1800. The charges had a devastating effect on Burr's reputation among Republicans everywhere. By 1804 the Republican congressional caucus gave him not a single vote as the vice-presidential candidate on the ticket and replaced him with George Clinton.

After a long and futile interview with Jefferson in January 1804, in which Burr apparently asked for an appointment, Burr decided to run for governor of New York against the Republican candidate backed by the Clinton and Livingston families. Frustrated at losing the race despite some Federalist support, Burr, according to one of his close friends, was "determined to call out the first man of any respectability concerned in the infamous publications concerning him."[58] Hamilton had opposed Burr's candidacy, and he became that man. According to an Albany physician, Hamilton at a dinner party had expressed "a still more despicable opinion" of Burr than simply saying that he was "a dangerous man."[59] When Hamilton passed up an opportunity to disown this particular incident with some evasive remarks, the exchanges between the two men got out of hand. Finally, his anger fully aroused, Burr "required a General disavowal of any intention on the part of Genl Hamilton in his various

58. Editorial note, Mary-Jo Kline and Joanne Wood Ryan, eds., *Political Correspondence and Public Papers of Aaron Burr* (Princeton, 1983), 2: 882.
59. Milton Lomask, *Aaron Burr* (New York, 1979, 1982), 1: 347.

conversations to convey impressions derogatory to the honor of M. Burr." When Hamilton refused to make this sort of blanket denial, Burr challenged him to a duel.[60]

Hamilton reluctantly accepted Burr's challenge, and the two men met in Weehawken, New Jersey, on July 11, 1804. Hamilton's death from his wounds the next day released an outpouring of mourning, and Burr, shocked by the response to Hamilton's death, was forced to flee New York to the island home of Pierce Butler off the coast of Georgia. With warrants out for his arrest, the vice-president had become a fugitive from justice.

Already Burr was thinking of some exploit in the West that might recoup his reputation and his fortune. As war between the United States and Spain became more and more likely and the uproar in New York died down, Burr met with General Wilkinson many times in Washington during the winter of 1804–1805 and pored over maps of the Floridas and Texas. He seemed to think that the military officers in the West were so estranged from the Republican administration that they could be recruited to do most anything. In December 1804 General John Adair, a Kentucky speculator, wrote Wilkinson that his Kentuckians were "full of enterprise" and ready to move. "Mexico glitters in our Eyes—the word is all we wait for."[61] At the same time, Burr was trying to get British financial and naval backing for his schemes—support which the British refused to give. In the spring of 1805 he traveled down the Ohio and Mississippi and conferred with friends and others, including Andrew Jackson in Nashville and Wilkinson in St. Louis. Although the war with Spain never broke out, Burr in the summer of 1806 led sixty or so men and half a dozen flatboats down the Mississippi toward New Orleans.

Since Burr said so many different things to so many different people, his ultimate aim has never been entirely clear. Did he simply intend to lead Americans in a filibustering expedition to take over West Florida or Texas from Spain? Or did he actually mean to separate the West from the Union and create his own empire? As conflicting rumors flew about, federal officials in Kentucky in the late fall of 1806 charged Burr with plotting a military expedition against Mexico, but a sympathetic grand jury refused to indict him. With the Jefferson administration becoming more and more concerned with Burr's activities in the West, Wilkinson decided to save himself by betraying Burr. In November 1806 he warned President Jefferson of "a deep, dark, and wide-spread conspiracy" and ordered Burr

60. Lomask, Aaron Burr, 1: 350.
61. Lomask, Aaron Burr, 2: 45.

arrested.[62] Constitutionally scrupulous as always, Jefferson worried about whether the president had the authority to call out the regular armed forces to put down a domestic attempt to dismember the Union, so he asked Congress for legislation giving him that authority.

After being arrested, Burr was paroled. He then sought to flee to Spanish territory but was seized and brought to Virginia. In 1807 he was indicted for treason and brought to trial in the U.S. Circuit Court in Richmond, Virginia, with Chief Justice John Marshall as the presiding judge. Unfortunately for Burr, Jefferson had already told Congress that Burr's "guilt is placed beyond question."[63] Earlier Jefferson had been rather casual about the separation of the West from the Union; but in those cases he had assumed that the Western areas, namely Kentucky and Tennessee, were full of Americans who believed in American principles and therefore were citizens not much tempted by disunionist schemes. But Burr threatened the separation of New Orleans, which was not yet filled with Americans, and that made a difference.

Determined to see Burr found guilty of treason, Jefferson worked hard for his conviction.[64] Marshall's decisions during the trial and his strict definition of treason frustrated Jefferson. Burr was eventually found not guilty, but his political career was ruined. He fled the country in disgrace, only returning years later to live out the remainder of his life in obscurity.

JEFFERSON'S WEST WAS, of course, still inhabited by Indians, who were as fascinating to him as the West itself. Although Jefferson has been much criticized for his lack of modern ethnographic sympathy, he was actually a more sensitive ethnographer than most of his contemporaries. No other president in American history was as interested in the indigenous people as Jefferson. He collected every scrap of information about them—their bodies, their orations, their habits, their languages; in fact, he spent most of his life collecting and studying Indian vocabularies.[65]

---

62. Lomask, *Aaron Burr*, 2: 172.
63. TJ, Message to Congress, 22 Jan. 1807, *Jefferson: Writings*, 532. John Adams made the obvious point. Even if Burr's guilt was "as clear as the Noon day Sun," he told Benjamin Rush in February 1807, "the first Magistrate ought not to have pronounced it so before a Jury had tried him." Leonard W. Levy, *Jefferson and Civil Liberties: The Darker Side* (Cambridge, MA, 1963), 71.
64. On the trial from Burr's point of view, see Isenberg, *Fallen Founder*, 319–65.
65. Unfortunately, most of Jefferson's thirty years of work on Indian vocabularies was stolen during his move back to Monticello at the end of his presidency. Dumas Malone, *Jefferson and His Time: The Sage of Monticello* (Boston, 1981), 4–5.

Jefferson's obsession with the Indians was shared by most of his fellow Americans. Indeed, never before in American history had the Indian become so central to the hopes and dreams of educated white Americans. And never before was the Indian so admired and celebrated as he was by Jefferson's generation. Since this was the generation that essentially destroyed the society and culture of those Indians living east of the Mississippi, this fixation becomes all the more curious and ironic. It actually grew out of the Americans' nervousness over their New World habitat. Americans of the early Republic were informed by the best scientific authorities of the Western world that the American natural environment was deleterious to all animal life. There was in fact something terribly wrong—something inherent in nature itself—that made the climate of the New World harmful to all living creatures, including the Indians, who were the only humans native to the New World.[66]

This was not the conclusion of a few crackpots or of some fanatic European aristocrats eager to malign American republicanism. It was the conclusion of the greatest naturalist of the Western world, the French scientist George Louis Leclerc, comte de Buffon. In the rambling thirty-six volumes of his *Natural History* published between 1749 and 1800, Buffon presented a profoundly pessimistic but scientifically grounded picture of the American environment. There was in the New World, Buffon wrote, "some combination of elements and other physical causes, something that opposes the amplification of animated Nature."[67]

The American continents, said Buffon, were newer than those of the Old World. They had, it seemed, only recently emerged from the flood and had not as yet properly dried out. The American air was more humid than that of the older continents. Its topography was more irregular, its weather more variable, its forests and miasmic swamps more extensive. In short, America had an unhealthy climate in which to live.

Animals in the New World, said Buffon, were underdeveloped—smaller than those of the Old World. America did not have any lions. The

66. For a fuller analysis of this issue of America's climate, see Gordon S. Wood, "Environmental Hazards, Eighteenth-Century Style," in Leonard J. Sadosky et al., eds., *Old World, New World: America and Europe in the Age of Jefferson* (Charlottesville, forthcoming), from which this discussion is drawn.

67. Buffon, *Natural History, General and Particular*, in Henry Steele Commager and Elmo Giordanetti, eds., *Was America a Mistake? An Eighteenth-Century Controversy* (New York, 1967), 60; Gilbert Chinard, "Eighteenth-Century Theories on America as a Human Habitat," American Philosophical Society, Proc., 91 (1947), 25–57; Antonello Gerbi, *The Dispute of the New World: The History of a Polemic, 1750–1900* (Pittsburgh, 1973); Philippe Roger, *The American Enemy: A Story of French Anti-Americanism* (Chicago, 2005), 1–29.

American puma was scarcely a real lion; it did not even have a mane, and "it is also much smaller, weaker, and more cowardly than the real lion." The New World had no elephants; in fact, no American wildlife could be compared to the elephant in size or shape. The best that America had, Buffon wrote sarcastically, was the tapir of Brazil, but "this elephant of the New World" was not bigger than "a six-month-old calf." All the American animals were "four, six, eight, and ten times" smaller than those of the older continents. Even the domestic animals introduced to America from Europe tended to shrink and dwindle under the influence of the New World's climate.[68]

Buffon's conclusion about the environment was stark and frightening. "Living nature," he wrote, "is thus much less active there, much less varied, and we may even say, less strong." To learn that the peculiar American habitat had affected animal life was unsettling, but to learn that the environment of the New World was also unhealthy for humans was truly alarming. Buffon claimed that the American environment was responsible for the apparently retarded development of the native Indians, who seemed to be wandering savages stuck in the first stage of social development without any structured society. The Indians, Buffon said, were like reptiles; they were cold-blooded. Their "organs of generation are small and feeble." The natives of the New World had no hair, no beards, no ardor for their females. Their social bonds were weak; they had very few children and paid little attention to those they had. In some way this strange, moist climate of the New World had devastatingly affected the physical and social character of the only humans native to it. The outlook for humans of the Old World transplanted to this forbidding environment was therefore not a happy one.[69]

It is difficult to appreciate the extent of European ignorance about the Western Hemisphere, even as late as the eighteenth century. Since Alexander von Humboldt had not yet made his journeys and published his findings, even educated Europeans had strange ideas about the New World. Of course, at the beginning Europeans had expected the climate of America to be similar to that of the Old World. Indeed, "climate" was described, as, for example, in Jedidiah Morse's *American Geography* (1796), as a belt of the earth's surface between two given parallels of latitude. People assumed that places that were the same distance from the

---

68. Gerbi, *Dispute of the New World*, 4; Buffon, *Natural History*, in Commager and Giordanetti, eds., *Was America a Mistake?*, 53, 60.
69. Buffon, *Natural History*, in Commager and Giordanetti, eds., *Was America a Mistake?*, 60, 61.

poles or the equator would have the same climate and were surprised to find the contrary. The latitude of London was north of Newfoundland; that of Rome was nearly the same as New York City. Yet the climates of these places on the same latitude were very different. It was out of this sense of difference between the Old and New Worlds and the hearsay it generated that Buffon fabricated his scientific conclusions.[70]

The great naturalist's theories about the New World were taken up by others, including Corneille de Pauw, the Abbé Raynal, and the Scottish historian William Robertson, and through such writers they entered the popular thinking about America in the late eighteenth century.[71] Naturally those Americans who became aware of Buffon's findings were alarmed. If Buffon's scientific claims were true, then the chances for the success of the new American republican experiment were not good, and the predictions of pessimistic Europeans about the future of the New World would be proved correct. For many eighteenth-century Englishmen and Europeans the term "American" often had conjured up images of unrefined if not barbarous persons, degenerate and racially debased mongrels living amidst African slaves and Indian savages thousands of miles from civilization. Hessian soldiers arriving in New York in 1776 had been surprised to find that there were actually many white people in the New World.[72] Now the best scientific theories of the day seemed to reinforce these popular European images of the degeneracy of the New World.

Of course, most Americans in the generation following the Revolution did not let these English and European charges seriously dampen their optimism and enthusiasm for the future. Instead, they reacted with indignant dismissal, exaggerated boasting, or extensive scientific comparison. Perhaps it was true, conceded Jefferson, that America had twice as much rain as Europe, but in America, he said, it fell "in half the time."[73]

---

70. Karen Ordahl Kupperman, "The Puzzle of the American Climate in the Early Colonial Period," *AHR*, 87 (1982), 1262–89.

71. Durand Echeverria, *Mirage in the West: A History of the French Image of American Society to 1815* (Princeton, 1957).

72. Stanley Weintraub, *Iron Tears: America's Battle for Freedom, Britain's Quagmire, 1775–1783* (New York, 2005), 65; Stacy Schiff, *A Great Improvisation: Franklin, France, and the Birth of America* (New York, 2005), 169. T. H. Breen, "Ideology and Nationalism on the Eve of the American Revolution: Revisions Once More in Need of Revising," *JAH*, 84 (1997), 29–32; Stephen Conway, "From Fellow-Nationals to Foreigners: British Perceptions of the Americans, circa 1739–1783," *WMQ*, 59 (2002), 65–100.

73. TJ to C. F. de C. Volney, 8 Feb. 1805, *Jefferson: Writings*, 1155.

Yet some Americans seemed to have an underlying anxiety that the European critics might be right after all. There did seem to be something peculiar about America's climate. The same regions with temperatures well below zero in winter could swelter in heat close to one hundred degrees Fahrenheit in the summer; also, swings of forty degrees Fahrenheit in twenty-four hours were not uncommon. No place in Europe had these sorts of radical variations in temperature. The American climate did seem to have more moisture. Humidity was often high, and heavy rainfall alternated with an unusual number of sunny cloudless days. Some speculated that these peculiarities were due to the existence of so much uncultivated land with so many dense forests in America. Europe's climate had once been like America's, it was thought, but once most of its trees had been cut down, its climate had changed.

The devastating epidemics of yellow fever that erupted in American cities during this period, beginning with the catastrophe in Philadelphia in 1793 (which killed 10 percent of the population), were not duplicated elsewhere in the Western world. This led some Americans, including Jefferson, to conclude that the disease was indeed "peculiar to our country." Because the sun rarely shone in the middle and northern parts of Europe, the Europeans could "safely build cities in solid blocks without generating disease." But America's unusual atmosphere—the cloudless skies and the intense heat and humidity—fermented the garbage and filth in America's cities, creating putrefaction that released effluvia and morbific fluids that bred disease; thus in America, said Jefferson, "men cannot be piled on one another with impunity." He hoped that some good might come out of these epidemics of yellow fever: Americans might be inhibited from building the sorts of huge sprawling cities that existed in Europe.[74]

Although America's cities were scarcely crowded or dirty by European standards, many Americans decided that their unusual climate required their cities to be designed differently from those in the Old World. Urban renewal in the early Republic was born out of these concerns. Jefferson was especially worried about New Orleans, which promised to become "the greatest city the world had ever seen. There is no spot on the globe," he said, "to which the produce of so great an extent of fertile country must necessarily come." But unfortunately at the same time "there is no spot where yellow fever is so much to be apprehended." He decided that New Orleans and other American cities had "to take the chequer board" for a

---

74. TJ to BR, 12 Sept. 1799, *Papers of Jefferson*, 31: 183–84; Edwin T. Martin, *Thomas Jefferson: Scientist* (New York, 1952), 131–47.

plan, with "the white squares open and unbuilt for ever, and planted with trees."[75]

Not just Jefferson but many other leading intellectuals of the day, such as Benjamin Rush, Noah Webster, Samuel L. Mitchill, and Benjamin Latrobe, also concocted plans for cleaning and renovating America's cities. But Dr. Charles Caldwell, a Philadelphia physician, was the one who drew up the most elaborate plans for urban renewal to deal with the effluvia that presumably caused yellow fever. Caldwell thought all of America's cities, which were simply "vast factories of this febrile poison," would have to be rebuilt in accord with the country's unusual climate—requiring lofty buildings, lots of squares, and many trees, especially Lombardy poplars, which were the best kind of tree for soaking up the miasma and emitting vital air.

Caldwell seems to have conceded that the Europeans were correct in their judgment about America's climate. Instead of denying the Europeans' charges, he turned them around by claiming that America's climate was simply more stupendous than any other. "Nature," he said in an oration in 1802, "was more gigantic in her operations" in America. "Compared to our own, how humble are the mountains, rivers, lakes, and cataracts of the Old World." It stood to reason, he said, that America had bigger and more powerful diseases than other places. "Our diseases are not only more frequent but aspire to the same scale of greatness with our other phenomena."[76]

Americans' preoccupation with the climate that was causing these diseases grew out of their Enlightenment assumption that people were the products of experience and external circumstances. Since, as most people believed, humans had all sprung from the same origin, as recorded in Genesis, only the effects of the environment through time could account for the obvious differences among them. Even skin color was explained in environmental terms. Many believed that the Negro's blackness came from the intense African sun—that somehow the African's skin had

75. TJ to Governor William Henry Harrison, 27 Feb. 1803, in L and B, eds., *Writings of Jefferson*, 10: 368; Governor William C. C. Claiborne, 7 July 1804, in Merrill Peterson, ed., *The Portable Jefferson* (New York, 1975), 499–500; TJ to Benjamin Rush, 12 Sept. 1799, *Papers of Jefferson*, 31: 183–84.

76. Charles Caldwell, *Medical and Physical Memoirs: Containing, Among Other Subjects, a Particular Enquiry into the Origin and Nature of the Late Pestilential Epidemics of the United States* (Philadelphia, 1801), 46, 51, 64, 117; Caldwell, *An Oration on the Causes of the Difference, in Point of Frequency and Force, Between the Endemic Diseases of the United States of America, and Those of the Countries of Europe* (Philadelphia, 1802), 5–9, 13, 16, 18, 32.

become scorched. In the peculiar climate of America, some Americans thought, the African Americans' skin would gradually become lighter, perhaps eventually white. The South Carolina historian David Ramsay, who believed that "all mankind [was] originally the same and only diversified by accidental circumstances," claimed that "in a few centuries the negroes will lose their black color. I think now they are less black in Jersey than Carolina."[77]

All this emphasis on the power of climate had ominous implications for Americans. If the climate of the New World were powerful enough to create peculiar American diseases or to affect the color of people's skins, then Buffon's charges were very serious indeed. In fact, they lay behind the only book Thomas Jefferson ever wrote.

In his *Notes on the State of Virginia* (first published in a French edition in 1785; the first American edition appeared in 1787, with two more in 1800 and five new editions in 1801), Jefferson systematically attempted to answer the famous theories of Buffon; in fact, he requested that one of the first copies of his book be delivered directly to the great naturalist. The parts of the book that today are often skipped over or eliminated entirely in modern abbreviated editions—the tables and statistics about animals that Jefferson compiled in Query VI—are precisely those parts that Jefferson considered central to his work.

Side by side in order of volume Jefferson listed the animals of the Old and New Worlds, accompanied by the weights of each in pounds and ounces. In almost every case the American animal is bigger. If the European cow weighed 763 pounds, the American cow was 2,500 pounds. If the European bear weighed 153.7 pounds, then the American bear weighed 410 pounds. As Jefferson described the various American animals—the moose, the beaver, the weasel, the fox—and found them all equaling or bettering their European counterparts, he got carried away with excitement and even brought in the prehistoric mammoth to offset the Old World elephant. He even matched Buffon's sarcastic reference to the tapir, "the elephant of America," being but the size of a small cow. "To preserve our comparison, I will add that the wild boar, the elephant of Europe, is little more than half that size."

Jefferson scarcely hid his anger at Buffon's charges, and he raised question after question about the sources of the famous naturalist's data. Who were those European travelers who supplied the information about America's animals? Were they real scientists? Was natural history the object of

---

77. Ramsey to TJ, 3 May 1786, *Papers of Jefferson*, 9: 441.

their travels? Did they measure or weigh the animals they speak of? Did they really know anything at all about animals? Jefferson's conclusion was clear: Buffon and the other European intellectuals did not know what they were talking about.[78]

Jefferson was not someone who liked personal confrontations, but when he went to France in the 1780s as American minister he prepared himself for his first meeting with Buffon by taking with him "an uncommonly large panther skin." He was introduced to Buffon, the curator of King Louis XVI's cabinet of natural history, as someone who had combated several of Buffon's theories. Jefferson did not hesitate in pressing Buffon about his ignorance of American animals. He especially stressed the great size of the American moose and told Buffon that it was so big that a European reindeer could walk under its belly. Finally, in exasperation, the eminent European naturalist promised that if Jefferson could produce a single specimen of the moose with foot-long antlers, "he would give up the question."[79]

That was all Jefferson needed, and he went busily to work, writing friends in America, imploring them to send him all the skins, bones, and horns they could find, or better still, entire stuffed animals. Governor John Sullivan of New Hampshire took the most trouble of anyone, for he was commissioned to get the moose that was to demolish Buffon's theories once and for all. Sullivan sent a virtual army into the northern wilderness of New Hampshire and even cut a twenty-mile road through the woods to drag it out. By the time the specimen arrived in Portsmouth to be readied for its transit across the Atlantic, it was half rotten and had lost all its hair and head bones. So Sullivan sent along to Paris the horns of some other animal, blithely explaining to Jefferson that "they are not the horns of this Moose but may be fixed on at pleasure."[80]

Understandably, Jefferson was not entirely happy with the impression his bones and skins were making on Buffon. Although he asked his correspondents in America to send him the biggest specimens they could find, he continually apologized to Buffon for their smallness. Apparently, however, the specimens convinced Buffon of his errors, for according to Jefferson, the French naturalist promised to set these things right in his next volume; but he died before he could do so.[81]

78. TJ, *Notes on the State of Virginia*, ed. William Peden (Chapel Hill, 1955), 43–58, quotation at 55.
79. Gerbi, *Dispute of the New World*, 264.
80. John Sullivan to TJ, 16 April 1787, *Papers of Jefferson*, 11: 296.
81. TJ to Buffon, 1 Oct. 1787, *Papers of Jefferson*, 12: 194; Martin, *Jefferson: Scientist*, 187.

Jefferson continued to be interested in the size of American animals. In 1789 he urged the president of Harvard to encourage the study of America's natural history in order "to do justice to our country, it's productions, and it's genius." In the mid-1790s on the basis of some fossil remains, probably belonging to a prehistoric sloth, he concocted the existence of a huge super-lion, three times bigger than the African lion, and presented his imagined beast to the scientific world as the Megalonyx, "the great claw."[82]

The most exciting scientific find of the period was Charles Willson Peale's exhumation in 1801 near Newburgh, New York, of the bones of the mastodon, or mammoth. Peale displayed his mammoth in his celebrated museum and in 1806 painted a marvelous picture of what was perhaps the first organized scientific exhumation in American history. Peale's discovery electrified the country and put the word "mammoth" on everybody's lips. A Philadelphia baker advertised the sale of "mammoth bread." In Washington a "mammoth eater" ate forty-two eggs in ten minutes. And under the leadership of the Baptist preacher John Leland, the ladies of Cheshire, Massachusetts, late in 1801 sent to President Jefferson a "mammoth cheese," six feet in diameter and nearly two feet thick and weighing 1,230 pounds. The cheese was produced from the milk of nine hundred cows at a single milking, with no Federalist cows being allowed to participate. The president welcomed this gift from the heart of Federalism as "an ebullition of the passion of republicanism in a state where it has been under heavy persecution."[83]

Others besides Jefferson wrestled with the problem of America's environment. Indeed, at times it seemed as if the entire American intellectual community was involved in examining the creatures and the soil and climate of America. The Scottish-born self-made naturalist Alexander Wilson filled his remarkable nine-volume *American Ornithology* (1808–1814) with corrections of Buffon, who, said Wilson, committed error after error "with equal eloquence and absurdity."[84] Calls went out everywhere for information about the American habitat. Was the climate really wetter

82. TJ to Joseph Willard, 24 Mar. 1789, *Papers of Jefferson*, 14: 699; to Bishop James Madison, 1 Apr. 1798, *Papers of Jefferson*, 30: 236; to Palisot de Beauvois, 25 Apr. 1798, *Papers of Jefferson*, 30: 293–97; American Philosophical Society, *Trans.*, 4 (1799), 246–60.

83. Charles Coleman Sellers, *Mr. Peale's Museum: Charles Willson Peale and the First Popular Museum of Natural Science and Art* (New York, 1980), 146–47; C. A. Browne, "Elder John Leland and the Mammoth Cheshire Cheese," *Agricultural History*, 18 (1944); L. H. Butterfield, "Elder John Leland, Jeffersonian Itinerant," American Antiquarian Society, *Proc.*, 62 ((1952).

84. Joseph Kastner, *A Species of Eternity* (New York, 1977), 190–91.

than that of Europe, and if so, could anything be done about it? Charles Brockden Brown abandoned his novel-writing career in order to devote his energies to translating the comte de Volney's disparaging *Tableau du climat et du sol des États-Unis d'Amérique* (A *View of the Soil and Climate of the United States of America*), even though a London translation was readily available. In his notes to his new translation Brown wanted to refute Volney's claim that America's climate was responsible for America's inability to produce a decent artist or writer.[85]

Clergymen in such obscure places as Mason, New Hampshire, faithfully compiled meteorological and demographic records, and otherwise exclusively literary journals such as the *Columbia Magazine* and the *North American Review* published periodic weather charts sent from distant correspondents in Brunswick, Maine, and Albany, New York. Indeed, temperature-taking became everyone's way of participating in the fact-gathering of enlightened science. Between 1763 and 1795 Ezra Stiles, president of Yale, filled six volumes with his daily temperature and weather readings. Every intellectual felt the need to present a paper to some philosophical society on the subject of America's climate. The *Transactions* of the American Philosophical Society for the single year of 1799 contained no less than six articles on the topic.

All these writings and all this temperature-taking showed that Americans were actually changing their climate. By cutting down forests and filling in swamps, they were moderating the extreme temperatures that had existed decades earlier. If Americans could change the weather, then they could change anything, or so they hoped.

AMIDST ALL THE DISCUSSION and debate, the issue finally came back to the Indian. Had America's climate actually retarded the development of the only people native to the New World? Jefferson's lifelong defense of the prowess and virtue of the Indian grew out of this passionate desire to protect the American environment against European aspersions. Buffon was wrong, he wrote; the Indian "is neither more defective in ardor, nor more impotent with his female, than the white reduced to the same diet and exercise." The difference between the native peoples of America and Europeans was "not a difference of nature, but of circumstance." There were good reasons why Indian women bore fewer children than whites, why the Indians' hands and wrists were small, why they had less hair on their bodies; and those reasons, said Jefferson, had nothing to

85. Cecelia Tichi, "Charles Brockden Brown, Translator," *American Literature*, 44 (1972), 1–12.

do with America's soil or climate. For Jefferson the Indian had to be "in body and mind the equal of the white man." He could readily doubt the capacities of blacks, who after all came from Africa, but he could never admit any inferiority in the red men, who were products of the very soil and climate that would mold the people of the United States.[86]

The Reverend James Madison, president of the College of William and Mary and a second cousin of the famous Founder, had much more hope for the assimilation of the Indian than of the African into white society. He told Jefferson of reports of an Indian near Albany who had gradually whitened in the past two years. But he knew of no African changing color. "It seems as if Nature had absolutely denied to him the Possibility of ever acquiring the Complexion of the White."[87] (Of course, Jefferson might have reminded the Reverend Madison of all those slave children who were becoming whiter as a consequence of what Jefferson called "the perpetual exercise of the most boisterous [meaning coarse or savage] passions" between the white planters and their African slaves.)[88]

The Indian, admitted Jefferson, was at an earlier stage—the hunting and gathering stage of development; but this was not from a lack of native genius, only a lack of cultivation. Yet what if the American environment were strong enough to prevent that process of cultivation and refinement from operating? What if the environmental conditions that kept the native peoples from advancing worked to make the transplanted whites more Indian-like? Instead of progressing along through the successive stages of civilization, Americans might degenerate to a cruder and more savage state.

Some Americans thought that such a regression was actually taking place in the frontier areas—where whites responded to brutal Indian atrocities with even more bloody atrocities of their own. Tales were told of "white savages" who bashed Indian children and cut off the limbs and severed the heads of their Indian victims. Americans had long been fearfully fascinated with stories of these "white savages," of white men apparently abandoning civilization and adopting scalping and other violent

---

86. TJ, *Notes on Virginia*, ed. Peden, 58–62; TJ to Chastellux, 7 June 1785, *Papers of Jefferson*, 8: 184–86.

87. Rev. James Madison to TJ, 28 Dec. 1786, *Papers of Jefferson*, 10: 643.

88. TJ, *Notes on Virginia*, ed. Peden, 162. In 1798 Jefferson's protégé William Short offered Jefferson what he believed was the best solution to America's racial predicament—racial mixing. Jefferson, who regarded miscegenation as a degradation of the whites, ignored Short's suggestion. Annette Gordon-Reed, *The Hemingses of Monticello: An American Family* (New York, 2008), 536–39.

Indian ways. In the early Republic this fascination took on a heightened importance. Was America advancing from rudeness to refinement, as the Revolutionaries had hoped, or was the move westward actually turning the civilizing process around?[89]

"The manner in which the population is spreading over this continent has no parallel in history," declared an anxious New England analyst of what was taking place in early nineteenth-century America. Usually the first settlers of any country were barbarians who gradually in time became cultivated and civilized. "The progress has been from ignorance to knowledge, from the rudeness of savage life to the refinements of polished society. But in the settlement of North America the case is reversed. The tendency is from civilization to barbarism." By moving to the West, cultivated Easterners were losing their politeness and refinement. "The tendency of the American character is then to degenerate, and to degenerate rapidly; and that not from any peculiar vice in the American people, but from the very nature of a spreading population. The population of the country is out-growing its institutions."[90]

Jefferson himself realized that the West was more barbaric than the East; in fact, he thought that the United States contained within itself all the stages of social development, "from the infancy of creation to the present day.... Let a philosophic observer," he said,

> commence a journey from the savages of the Rocky Mountains, eastwardly towards our sea-coast. These he would observe in the earliest stage of association living under no law but that of nature, subsisting and covering themselves with the flesh and skins of wild beasts. He would next find those on our frontiers in the pastoral state, raising domestic animals to supply the defects of hunting. Then succeed our own semi-barbarous citizens, the pioneers of the advance of civilization, and so in his progress he would meet the gradual shades of improving man until he would reach his, as yet, most improved state in our seaport towns.[91]

Still, was the fact that the Indian remained in the earliest stage of social development the fault of the natural environment? Was the New World's climate destined to turn white Americans into Indians, or at least prevent them from progressing? These sorts of nervous questions underlay the extraordinary concern that Jefferson and other educated Americans had

89. Bernard W. Sheehan, *Seeds of Extinction: Jeffersonian Philanthropy and the American Indian* (New York, 1974), 201–7.

90. *Panoplist and Missionary Herald*, 14 (1818), 212–13.

91. TJ to William Ludlow, 6 Sept. 1824, *Jefferson: Writings*, 1496–97.

for the fate of the Indian in the early Republic. If the Indian could not be civilized, that is, assimilated and turned into something resembling white farmers, then perhaps the natural environment of the New World was too strong and too impervious to cultural and social reform, suggesting that white men living in such a powerful natural habitat could not become fully civilized either. This unease that Buffon and his followers might be proved right after all lent a sense of urgency to the Jeffersonians' philan-thropic efforts to civilize the Indian.

Of course, these efforts, like those of the Washington administration, gave no recognition whatsoever to the worth or integrity of the Indians' own existing culture. In the minds of many early nineteenth-century whites, enlightened civilization was still too recent, too precarious, for them to treat it as simply an alternative culture or lifestyle. Only later, only when the Indians' culture had been virtually destroyed, could white Americans begin to try to redeem the tragedy that had occurred.

Jefferson, like Secretary of War Henry Knox before him, had no doubt of the superiority of white agricultural society to the "savage" state of the native peoples of America. In his first annual message to Congress in December 1801 Jefferson made clear that he would continue what he took to be the successful efforts of his predecessors to introduce among "our Indian neigh-bors...the implements and the practice of husbandry, and of the household arts." The Indians, he said, were "becoming more and more sensible of the superiority of this dependence [on husbandry] for clothing and subsistence over the precarious resources of hunting and fishing." Some Indians, he added, were even experiencing "an increase in population."[92]

Jefferson, of course, never questioned that the Indians might not want to become civilized and participate in the progressive course of history. In his mind and in the minds of most enlightened Americans, his intentions were always pure. "We will never do an unjust act towards you," he told a visiting delegation of Northwestern Indians in 1809 just before he left the presidency. "On the contrary we wish you to live in peace, to increase in numbers, to learn to labor as we do, and furnish food for your ever increasing numbers, when the game shall have left you. We wish to see you possessed of property and protecting it by regular laws. In time you will be as we are; you will become one people with us. Your blood will mix with ours; and will spread, with ours, over this great land."[93]

---

92. TJ, First Annual Message, 8 Dec. 1801, *Jefferson: Writings*, 501.
93. TJ to the Chiefs of the Wyandots, Ottawas, Chippewas, Powtewatamies, and Shawanese, 10 Jan. 1809, in L and B, eds., *Writings of Jefferson*, 16: 464; Anthony F. C. Wallace, *Jefferson and the Indians: The Tragic Fate of the First Americans* (Cambridge, MA, 1999).

Jefferson's policy toward the Indians was tragically simple: let the natural demographic growth and movement of white Americans take their course. The dynamic white settlers would surround the Indians and circumscribe their hunting grounds and thus pressure them into taking up farming, which would not require large tracts of land. Therefore the remainder of their hunting grounds could be ceded piecemeal to the United States. But even before the assimilation and incorporation of the Indians had taken place, Jefferson jumped at every opportunity to get the land that was destined to belong to American farmers. He and his successor, President James Madison, negotiated fifty-three treaties of land cession with various tribes.

Although the Cherokees in the Southwest made extraordinary progress in developing white ways—living in houses and relying on agriculture and not game for their food—for the most part the Jeffersonian program of Indian acculturation was a disaster. Indian society and culture tended to disintegrate as they came in contact with white civilization. Commerce with the whites, especially the trade in liquor, corrupted the Indians and destroyed their independence; and diseases, especially smallpox, were devastating. In 1802 three-quarters of the tribes along the Mississippi and Missouri Rivers perished from disease.

So confident were Jefferson and other enlightened Americans in the capacity of people to reinvent themselves and become civilized that none of them had any capacity whatsoever to comprehend the terrible human cost involved in destroying a way of life. They always thought they were acting in the best long-run interests of the native peoples.

Before long many of the philanthropists most concerned for the fate of the Indians were urging that removing them from immediate proximity to the whites and slowing down the process of assimilation were the only means of saving them from extinction. Thus the way was prepared for the wholesale removal of the Indians that took place under President Andrew Jackson—lending a humanitarian justification for what most white settlers wanted anyhow: to get rid of the Indians and take their lands.[94]

The encounter between the two incompatible cultures was a tragedy from beginning to end. Although Jefferson and other Americans continued to talk about incorporating the Indian into mainstream American life, in their hearts they knew better; and much of their writing about the Indians took on an elegiac tone, as if they realized that the native peoples

---

94. Sheehan, *Seeds of Extinction*.

were already doomed. They knew that the Indians represented much of what they themselves valued—a respect for human dignity and a passion for human freedom. These were values that Americans also came to identify with the West. Americans never lost the sense that the Indian and America's West were inextricably bound together.

# 11

# Law and an Independent Judiciary

In 1801 the Republicans had taken control of two-thirds of the federal government—the presidency and the Congress—but the judiciary remained in the hands of the Federalists. The Federalist grip on the judiciary more than rankled Jefferson and his Republican colleagues; it enraged them. Most extreme Republicans never liked the judiciary anyway. It was the least popular part of both the state and federal constitutions and the institution relied upon by those who most scorned and feared the people. Most judges were appointed, not elected by the people, and often, as in the case of the federal judges, with tenure during good behavior. With its robes, court ceremonies, and elevated benches, the judiciary seemed to be the branch of government that was essentially unrepublican. Consequently, some of the most rabid Republicans would have liked to do away with the judiciary altogether.

This popular antagonism toward the judiciary had deep roots in the history of colonial America. Judges in the colonies had not gained their independence in the aftermath of the Glorious Revolution of 1688–1689 as those in the mother country had. Prior to the eighteenth century the English common law courts had been regarded as servants of the crown, and judges held their offices at royal pleasure. As a consequence of the Glorious Revolution and the Act of Settlement of 1701, however, royally appointed judges in the mother country had won tenure during good behavior. But in most colonies judges had continued to hold office at the pleasure of the crown. Many colonists had resented this dependence of the courts on the crown and thus had tended to identify the judges, or magistrates, as they were often called, with the much resented royal governors, or chief magistrates.

The colonists had not usually regarded the judiciary as an independent entity or even as a separate branch of government. Indeed, they had often considered the colonial courts to be essentially political bodies, as magistracies that performed numerous administrative and executive tasks. The colonial courts in most colonies had assessed taxes, granted licenses, overseen poor relief, supervised road repairs, set prices, upheld moral standards, and all in all monitored the localities over which they presided.[1] Consequently, it is not surprising that many colonists had concluded that there were really "no more than two powers in any government, viz. the power to make laws, and the power to execute them; for the judicial power is only a branch of the executive, the CHIEF of every country being the first magistrate." Even John Adams in 1766 had regarded "the first grand division of constitutional powers" as "those of legislation and those of execution," with "the administration of justice" resting in "the executive part of the constitution."[2] The colonial judges therefore had borne much of the opprobrium attached to the royal governors and often had been circumscribed by the power of popular juries to an extent not found in England itself.

Since Americans had become convinced that the dependence of the judges on executive caprice was, in the words of William Henry Drayton of South Carolina, "dangerous to liberty and property of the subject," they sought to end that dependence at the Revolution.[3] Most of the Revolutionary state constitutions of 1776–1777 took away the traditional power of the governors to appoint judges and gave it to the legislatures. The judges' tenure clearly no longer depended on the pleasure of the chief magistrate. These changes in the judiciary's status often were justified by reference to the doctrine of separation of powers made famous in the eighteenth century by Montesquieu—that, as the Virginia constitution of 1776 asserted, "the legislative, executive, and judiciary departments shall be separate and distinct, so that neither exercise the powers properly belonging to the other."

This separation of the judges from their customary magisterial connection made them independent of the governors, but they were not yet independent of the people or their representatives in the state legislatures. In some of the states the legislatures elected the judges for a prescribed number of years—annually in Rhode Island, Connecticut, and Vermont—which was bound to make the judges feel dependent. When the assembly of Rhode Island, for example, did not like the behavior of

---

1. William E. Nelson, *Americanization of the Common Law: The Impact of Legal Change on Massachusetts Society, 1760–1830* (Cambridge, MA, 1975), 14–16; Hendrik Hartog, "The Public Law of a County Court: Judicial Government in Eighteenth-Century Massachusetts," *American Journal of Legal History*, 20 (1976), 321–23.

2. [Anon.], *Four Letters on Interesting Subjects* (Philadelphia, 1776), 21; [Adams], *Boston Gazette*, Jan. 27, 1766, in Adams, ed., *Works*, 3: 480–82. Thomas Paine, who was likely the author of *Four Letters*, was still contending in his *Rights of Man, Part Second* (1792), that "the judicial power, is strictly and properly the executive power of every country." Philip Foner, ed., *The Complete Writings of Thomas Paine* (New York, 1969), 1: 388.

3. William Henry Drayton, *A Letter from Freeman of South-Carolina* (Charleston, 1774), 10.

the state's supreme court in 1786, it simply elected a new court the following year. But even in those states that granted judges tenure during good behavior, the legislatures controlled the judges' salaries and fees and the power of removal, usually by the simple address of a majority of the legislature. Of the thirteen original states only three—Virginia, North Carolina, and New York—gave a measure of independence to their judges, but only a measure: in Virginia and North Carolina the legislatures elected the judges, and in New York judges had to retire at age sixty.[4]

Because the American Revolutionaries had so closely identified the judges with the much hated magisterial power, they sought in 1776 not to strengthen the judiciary but to weaken it. They especially feared the seemingly arbitrary discretionary authority that colonial judges had exercised. That discretion had flowed from the fact that the colonists' laws came from many different and conflicting sources. The colonial judges accepted many parliamentary statutes, but not all; they recognized much of the body of unwritten common law, but not all; and they had to reconcile what they accepted of the English common law with their own colonial statutes.

Because of these different sources of metropolitan and provincial law, the ability of colonial judges to pick and choose the appropriate law had often been much greater than that exercised by judges in England itself.[5] The result, as Jefferson put it in 1776, was that Americans had come to view judicial activity as "the eccentric impulses of whimsical, capricious designing men." Inevitably, most Americans in 1776 had come to believe that their popularly elected legislatures could be better trusted than judges to dispense justice, in Jefferson's words, "equally and impartially to every description of men."[6]

Coupled with this dislike of the judiciary was an equally intense popular dislike of lawyers. By the middle of the eighteenth century lawyers had achieved a measure of stability and some distinction as a profession. But the Revolution disrupted these developments. Many of the most prominent lawyers were Loyalists who fled the country or were disbarred. With the loss of as much as a quarter of the colonial legal profession, opportunities opened up for all sorts of legal sharpers and pettifoggers. All this in turn made the democratic middling forces released by the Revolution even more hostile toward lawyers, especially since lawyers were growing in number four times faster than the general

---

4. Gerhard Casper, "The Judiciary Act of 1789 and Judicial Independence," Maeva Marcus, ed., *Origins of the Federal Judiciary: Essays on the Judiciary Act of 1789* (New York, 1992), 284.

5. Gordon S. Wood, "The Origins of Judicial Review," *Suffolk Law Review*, 22 (1988), 1293–307.

6. TJ to Edmund Pendleton, 26 Aug. 1776, *Papers of Jefferson*, 1: 505.

population.[7] In the eyes of many average Americans and popular radicals, the most famous being editor Benjamin Austin of Massachusetts, lawyers became responsible for everything that was wrong in the society. They were simply locusts who enriched themselves by living off the disputes and distresses of ordinary folk. In 1786 even Braintree, Massachusetts, the hometown of the former attorney John Adams, passed a resolve to "crush... that order of Gentlemen denominated Lawyers."[8]

Since lawyers flourished by manipulating the arcane and intricate mysteries of the common law, they were best dealt with by eliminating or reforming the common law—that body of unwritten rules, practices, and precedents drawn from centuries of English jurisprudence. Although the Revolutionary leaders—many of them attorneys themselves—could scarcely be opposed to lawyers, some of them were interested in simplifying the common law and in bringing it into line with American conditions. Not only did they hope to create certainty out of uncertainty, but, more important, they were eager to circumscribe the much resented judicial discretion that had been exercised by the royal courts. By having the new state legislatures write down the laws in black and white, some of the Revolutionaries aimed to turn the judge into what Jefferson hoped would be "a mere machine."[9]

The solution was codification—that is, relying exclusively on statutes and not on the unwritten common law. Indeed, throughout Western and Central Europe in the last half of the eighteenth century codification of the law became a central reform of all enlightened statecraft. Continental rulers everywhere sought to rationalize their legal systems, to make law scientific, to extend it in a vernacular language evenly over their territories, and to put an end to the earlier jumble of customs, privileges, and local rights. Eventually these efforts at legal codification were at least partially successful in Bavaria, Prussia, and Austria, and most fully successful with the Civil Code of Napoleonic France.[10]

Although the eighteenth-century English remained committed to the complexities and obscurities of their common law, even they attempted

---

7. Anaton-Hermann Chroust, *The Rise of the Legal Profession in America* (Norman, OK, 1965), 2: 5–15; George Dargo, *Law in the New Republic: Private Law and the Public Estate* (New York, 1983), 49–59; Lawrence M. Friedman, *A History of American Law* (New York, 1973), 276–81.
8. Chroust, *Rise of the Legal Profession in America*, 2: 28.
9. TJ to Pendleton, 26 Aug. 1776, *Papers of Jefferson*, 1: 505.
10. Marc Raeff, "The Well-Ordered Police State and the Development of Modernity in Seventeenth- and Eighteenth-Century Europe: An Attempt at a Comparative Approach," *AHR*, 80 (1975), 1221–43; David Lieberman, "Codification, Consolidation, and Parliamentary Statute," in John Brewer and Eckhart Hellmuth, eds., *Rethinking Leviathan: The Eighteenth-Century State in Britain and Germany* (London, 1999), 359–90.

some systemization of their laws. In 1731 through parliamentary statute they established English rather than Latin as the language of legal practice and legal authority and for the first time began treating law as a subject to be taught in universities. At the same time, British jurists sought to summarize what they believed about their law in a comprehensive and methodical manner. William Blackstone's *Commentaries on the Laws of England* (1765–1769) was only the most famous of these efforts to reduce the English laws to a system. Everywhere in Great Britain in the last half of the eighteenth century there was talk of rationalizing and humanizing the absurd and barbarous notions of justice that had existed in the past. Existing statutes should be consolidated, and law-making or legislation should be made into a science for the improvement of society. Despite all this talk of legal reform, however, the complicated and largely untidy common law continued to remain for most English jurists the foundation of the entire legal structure.

As Americans became aware of the legal reform that was taking place in the mother country and elsewhere in Europe, they became increasingly frustrated with their confused hodgepodge of barbarous and antiquated laws. "I knew," Jefferson recalled in his autobiography, "that our legislation under the regal government had many very vicious points which urgently required reformation."[11] The break from Great Britain in 1776 at last gave him and other reformers the opportunity to simplify and clarify the unwritten nature of the common law and reduce the ability of judges to pick and choose what was law.

In 1776 most of the states agreed to retain as much of the English common law as was applicable to their circumstances, until it should be altered by future legislative acts. Nearly all the states thus began weeding out archaic English laws and legal technicalities and codifying parts of the common law. Society, it was said, often with ample quotations from the eighteenth-century Italian legal reformer Cesare Beccaria, needed "but few laws, and these simple, clear, sensible, and easy in their application to the actions of men."[12] Only through scientific codification and strict judicial observance of what William Henry Drayton of South Carolina called in 1778, quoting Beccaria, "the letter of the law" could the people be protected from becoming "slaves to the magistrates."[13]

11. TJ, Autobiography (1821), *Jefferson: Writings*, 32.
12. "On the Present States of America," 10 Oct. 1776, in Peter Force, ed., *American Archives*, 5th Ser. (Washington, DC, 1837–46), 2: 969.
13. Drayton, Speech to General Assembly of South Carolina, Jan. 20, 1778, in Hezekiah Niles, ed., *Principles and Acts of the Revolution in America* (New York, 1876), 359. For a discussion of the confused state of colonial law and the prevalence of judicial discretion, see Gordon S. Wood, *The Creation of the American Republic, 1776–1787* (Chapel Hill, 1969), 291–305.

The Revolutionaries aimed to modernize state power, and thus their new state assemblies began legislating in a programmatic manner—creating institutions, organizing taxes, reforming the legal system, printing money—and in the process doubling and tripling their output of statutes. Not only did modern commercial policy and the need for improvement of all sorts demand new legislation, but the Revolutionary desire for legal reform and codification also required the enactment of an increasing number of laws.

But within a decade following the Declaration of Independence many Revolutionaries began to realize that all their law-making and all their plans for legal reform and simplification were not working out as they had hoped. Many statutes were enacted and many laws were printed, but rarely in the way reformers like Jefferson and Madison had expected. Unstable, annually elected, and logrolling democratic legislatures broke apart well-thought-out plans for comprehensive legal codes and passed statutes in such confused and piecemeal ways that the purposes of simplicity and clarity were defeated; "for every new law...," complained a South Carolinian, "acts as rubbish, under which we bury the former."[14] Not only did the laws proliferate in ever-increasing numbers, but also many of the new statutes were poorly drafted and filled with inaccuracies and inconsistencies. As jurist St. George Tucker recalled, every attempt by Virginians to systemize and clarify their laws was "the parent of new perplexities, by the introduction of new laws; and the re-enaction, omission, or suspension of former acts, whose operation is thus rendered *doubtful*, even in the most important cases."[15] The multiplicity, mutability, and injustices of all this legislation meant that judicial discretion, far from diminishing, became more prevalent than it had been before the Revolution, as judges tried to bring some order out of the legal chaos.

By relying more and more on judicial interpretation, the American states were replicating British developments that had taken place a generation earlier. Of course, English common law judges had always

14. [Anon.], *Rudiments of Law and Government, Deduced from the Law of Nature* (Charleston, SC, 1783), 35–37.

15. St. George Tucker, *Blackstone's Commentaries: With Notes of Reference to the Constitution and Laws of the Federal Government and of the Commonwealth of Virginia* (Philadelphia, 1803), I, pt. 1, xiii. Of course, this proliferation of statutes in the early Republic was nothing compared to what has taken place in modern times. The *Digest of 1798*, the first codification of laws of the state of Rhode Island, for example, consisted of a single volume of 652 pages. By contrast, the *General Laws of the State in 1998* consisted of thirty volumes with over twenty-one thousand pages of text. Patrick T. Conley, ed., *Liberty and Justice: A History of Law and Lawyers in Rhode Island, 1636–1998* (East Providence, 1998), 11.

exercised an extraordinary degree of discretion in interpreting the law, especially in setting aside the bylaws of corporations that were repugnant to the prerogatives of the king or to what many took to be the mysterious common law of the land.[16] Even with the development of parliamentary sovereignty in the eighteenth century, English judges continued to interpret and construe parliamentary statutes in such a way as to fit them into the entire legal structure.[17] Thus eighteenth-century English common law judges, despite having to acknowledge the sovereign law-making authority of Parliament, were left with an extraordinary amount of room for statutory interpretation and construction. In the mid-eighteenth century that traditional discretionary judicial duty was greatly enhanced by both William Blackstone and especially Lord Mansfield, the chief justice of the Court of King's Bench between 1756 and 1788. Both British jurists, confronted with a multitude of inconsistent and contradictory parliamentary statutes, carved out a huge interpretative role for British judges as they sought to bring the law into accord with equity, reason, and good sense.[18]

In the decades following the Revolution, Americans confronted with a similar "prolixity in our laws" used these British examples of judicial flexibility and creativity and expanded them.[19] Even before the Revolution, as Edmund Burke pointed out in 1775, the colonists had turned Blackstone's *Commentaries* into an American best seller, buying more copies per capita than the English themselves. What Americans wanted from Blackstone was not his emphasis on legislative sovereignty but rather his understanding that the law was reasonable and predictable and that the courts had a responsibility to make it so.

By the 1780s many Americans were already having serious second thoughts about their earlier confidence in their popularly elected legislatures and were beginning to re-evaluate their former hostility to judicial power and discretion. When particular statutes had to be enacted for every circumstance, said Connecticut clergyman Moses Mather in 1781, the laws proliferated and led to a confusion that wicked men could exploit for their private advantage. All the legislatures really should do was enact

16. Mary Sarah Bilder, "The Corporate Origins of Judicial Review," *Yale Law Journal*, 116 (2006), 502–66 (I owe this reference to Bruce H. Mann); Philip Hamburger, *Law and Judicial Duty* (Cambridge, MA, 2008).

17. W. M. Geldart, *Elements of English Law*, 6th ed., rev. William Holdsworth and H. G. Hanbury (London, 1959).

18. David Lieberman, *The Province of Legislation Determined: Legal Theory in Eighteenth-Century Britain* (Cambridge, UK, 1989), 13, 28.

19. "The Free Republican," Boston *Independent Chronicle*, 26 Jan. 1786.

a few plain general rules of equity and leave their interpretation to the courts. "Indeed," said Mather, "where civil justice is to be administered not by particular statutes, but by the application of general rules of equity, much will depend upon the wisdom and integrity of the judges."[20] This was a far cry from the Beccarian reformist sentiments of 1776 and represented the extent to which experience since the Declaration of Independence with the "excesses of democracy" had changed the thinking of some Americans.

By the 1780s many American leaders had concluded that their popular state assemblies not only were incapable of simplifying and codifying the law but, more alarming, had also become major threats to individual liberties and the property rights of minorities, and the principal source of injustice in the society.[21] Although James Madison had counted on the new federal government's becoming an impartial umpire that would mitigate the problem of unjust legislation by the states, other leaders reasoned that if such impartial judicial-like umpires were needed, then why not rely on judges themselves? Indeed, many gentry in the aftermath of the Revolution looked to the once feared judiciary as a principal means of restraining the rampaging and unstable popular legislatures. As early as 1786 William Plumer, a future U.S. senator and governor of New Hampshire, concluded that the very "existence" of America's elective governments had come to depend upon the judiciary: "that is the only body of men who will have an effective check upon a numerous Assembly."[22]

In the massive rethinking that took place in the 1780s, nearly all parts of America's governments were reformed and reconstituted, often justified by ingenious manipulations of Montesquieu's doctrine of the "separation of powers." But the part of government that benefited most from this rethinking was the judiciary. In the decade following the Declaration of Independence the position of the judiciary in American life began to be transformed—from the much scorned and insignificant appendage of crown authority into what Americans increasingly called one of "the three capital powers of Government," from minor magistrates identified with the colonial executives into an equal and independent part of a modern tripartite government.[23]

20. Moses Mather, *Sermon, Preached in the Audience of the General Assembly...on the Day of Their Anniversary Election, May 10, 1781* (New London, 1781), 7–8.
21. Charleston *State Gazette of South Carolina*, 8 Sept. 1784.
22. Lynn W. Turner, *William Plumer of New Hampshire, 1759–1850* (Chapel Hill, 1962), 34–35.
23. Address of Massachusetts Convention (1780), in Oscar and Mary Handlin, eds., *The Popular Sources of Political Authority: Documents on the Massachusetts Constitution of 1780* (Cambridge, MA, 1966), 437.

It was a remarkable transformation, taking place as it did in such a relatively short period of time. And it was all the more remarkable because it flew in the face of much conventional eighteenth-century wisdom. Getting Americans to believe that judges appointed for life were an integral and independent part of their democratic governments—equal in status and authority to the popularly elected executives and legislatures—was no mean accomplishment. Such a change in thinking was a measure of how severe the crisis of the 1780s really was and how deep the disillusionment with popular legislative government in the states had become since the idealistic confidence of 1776—at least for those who became Federalists.

THE CONVENTION THAT CREATED the Constitution of 1787 was committed to an independent federal judiciary. The delegates agreed rather easily on an appointed judiciary serving for life during good behavior with a guaranteed salary and removal only by impeachment. No single state constitution had granted that degree of independence to its judiciary; indeed, in 1789 most state judges remained remarkably dependent on the popular legislatures, which in nearly all the states, like the House of Lords in England, retained some appellate authority in adjudication.[24]

Although the convention wanted an independent judiciary, it had difficulty in prescribing a court system for the new nation. Some of the delegates, especially those from South Carolina, wanted no separate national court system at all (with the exception of a single supreme court) and urged that all federal cases be tried in the existing state courts with the right of appeal to the federal Supreme Court. Others believed that the state courts could not be trusted to execute federal laws. Ultimately in Article III of the Constitution the convention delegates put many of the problems off to the future. They created a Supreme Court to be appointed by the president with the advice and consent of the Senate but only allowed for "such inferior courts as the Congress may from time to time ordain and establish." Whether Congress was actually required to establish inferior courts was not at all clear. The Constitution did declare, however, that among other things "the Judicial Power shall extend...to Controversies between Citizens of the different States."

When the first Congress convened in April 1789, the Senate immediately established a committee to draft a judiciary bill, chaired by Oliver

24. Wilfred J. Ritz, *Rewriting the History of the Judiciary Act of 1789: Exposing Myths, Challenging Premises, and Using New Evidence*, ed. Wythe Hold and L.H. LaRue (Norman, OK, 1990), 36; D. Kurt Graham, "The Lower Federal Courts in the Early Republic: Rhode Island, 1790–1812" (Ph.D. diss., Brown University, 2002).

Ellsworth, an experienced jurist from Connecticut who had sat on the Continental Congress's Committee on Appeals and had been a member of the Constitutional Convention. Article III of the Constitution allowed the committee a wide variety of options. If lofty-minded Federalists like Alexander Hamilton had had their way, Congress would have established national judicial districts that cut through state lines and were staffed by squadrons of federal judges with full authority to carry national law into every corner of the land. At the other extreme were those Anti-Federalists who wanted to rely on the state courts to enforce federal law, allowing any separate federal courts to possess only admiralty jurisdiction.

Ellsworth and his committee wanted a separate federal court system. At the same time, however, they were well aware of the fears of a national judiciary that the Anti-Federalists had aroused during the ratification debates, especially fears of a national judiciary that omitted certain common law rights like trial by jury. Since Section 25 of the judiciary bill the committee drafted allowed for the overturning of state laws and state court rulings if they conflicted with federal treaties, statutes, or the Constitution, many Southerners feared it. Although some may have been worried about federal judges' interfering with slavery, most were apprehensive that inferior federal courts might try to overrule state court decisions that forestalled payment of debts to British creditors required by the peace treaty of 1783.[25] The possibility of conflict between the new federal government and the states was thus very great. One congressman even warned that the creation of a federal judiciary would lead to civil war.

The resultant Judiciary Act passed in September 1789 was an ingenious bundle of compromises that allayed many of the Anti-Federalist suspicions. Passage of the act was aided considerably by the fact that Congress at the same time was enacting a series of amendments to the Constitution that became the Bill of Rights, especially the Sixth and Seventh Amendments that protected people's right to jury trials. In the end the Judiciary Act created an innovative three-tiered hierarchical federal court structure, consisting of the Supreme Court, circuit courts, and district courts, that has remained the basis for the court system to this day.

25. This happened in 1792 in Rhode Island in *Champion and Dickason v. Casey*. Two of Silas Casey's English creditors brought suit in federal circuit court that Rhode Island's 1791 statute exempting Casey from his debts for three years was a violation of the contract clause in Article I, Section 10 of the Constitution. The decision in favor of the plaintiffs, says the premier historian of Rhode Island's past, was "the first instance in American history where a federal court struck down a state statute for violating the Constitution of the United States." Patrick T. Conley, *First in War, Last in Peace: Rhode Island and the Constitution, 1786–1790* (Providence, 1987), 44.

ALTHOUGH THE ACT ESTABLISHED the judiciary as one of the three essential branches of the federal government, it nevertheless allowed the existing state courts concurrently to exercise federal jurisdiction. Indeed, at first there was a good deal of overlap between federal and state judicial offices. In Rhode Island, for example, the U.S. district attorney, Ray Green, between 1794 and 1797 was at the same time the state's attorney general. Only gradually during the 1790s did the states begin to pass laws prohibiting members of the state legislatures and other state officers from simultaneously holding federal positions. Until the national government got on its feet, the federal court system necessarily had to rely heavily on the states to carry on its business. Not only did federal judicial officials have to use state buildings for their activities, the Judiciary Act of 1789 also allowed state officials to arrest federal offenders, accept federal bail money, and detain all prisoners committed under the authority of the United States. Moreover, in all of the federal judicial districts, which coincided with the boundaries of the states (except for Virginia and Massachusetts, which each had two districts), the fee schedules, modes of selecting jurors, and the qualifications of admitting lawyers to the federal bar were patterned after state practice. Each of the district courts, which formed the lowest level of the federal judicial system, had to have a local resident as its judge, someone who necessarily would be familiar with local people and local practices.[26]

According to the Judiciary Act of 1789 these local district courts were to have jurisdiction over admiralty cases, petty crimes, and revenue collection. At the next level of the federal system were three circuit courts, catering to the three regions of the country, North, Middle, and South, each composed of three judges—the local district judge and two Supreme Court justices riding circuit twice a year, which the justices came to find increasingly intolerable. (In 1793 Congress reduced the number of judges for the circuit courts from three to two, thus somewhat easing the burden of travel for the Supreme Court justices.) These circuit courts were to be the major national trial courts with jurisdiction over important crimes, over cases involving out-of-state or foreign citizens, and over appeals from the district courts in admiralty cases. In those cases where the amount in question was more than five hundred dollars and there was diversity of citizenship, that is, the litigants were from different states, the federal circuit courts had "concurrent cognizance" with the state courts. Thus out-of-state litigants were able to remove their cases from what were often seen as the prejudiced state courts to the more neutral federal courts.

26. Dwight F. Henderson, *Courts for a New Nation* (Washington, DC, 1971), 30.

At the top was the Supreme Court of six justices to convene twice a year in the national capital for two-week terms. Because most of the work of the justices was to take place on the road in the circuit courts, the Supreme Court initially was not expected to do much; indeed, up to 1801 the Court heard a total of only eighty-seven cases.[27] In addition to possessing some original jurisdiction, the Supreme Court was granted appellate authority, including that over questions of federal law that had been decided in the state courts and in the federal circuit courts. Exactly what kinds of law— whether the civil and criminal common law, state statutes, or only federal statutes—ran in this federal system was left vague. Certainly most Federalists expected the federal judiciary to exercise the broadest possible jurisdiction, including that of the common law of crimes.[28]

Because Washington believed that the administration of justice was "the strongest cement of good government," he sought for the courts only "the fittest characters to expound the laws and dispense justice," by which he meant men with established social and political positions.[29] He thus appointed as chief justice his wealthy friend from New York, John Jay, who formerly had served as president of the Continental Congress, peace commissioner in Paris in the early 1780s, and secretary of foreign affairs under the Confederation. Likewise, Washington's appointments of associate justices were distinguished political figures with Federalist sympathies drawn from various sections of the country, appropriate to the circuit courts; these included John Rutledge of South Carolina, James Wilson of Pennsylvania, William Cushing of Massachusetts, and James Iredell of North Carolina, which had finally ratified the Constitution on November 21, 1789. Most of these judges still maintained a traditional magisterial notion of their judicial offices.

Traditionally, judges in the eighteenth century had been appointed to the courts because of their social and political rank, not because of their legal expertise; many were not even legally trained. They were expected to exercise a broad, ill-defined magisterial authority befitting their social position; they were considered members of the government and remained intimately involved in politics. In the colonial period Thomas Hutchinson of Massachusetts, for example, who was no lawyer, had been chief justice of the superior

27. Julius Goebel, *Antecedents and Beginnings to 1801: History of the Supreme Court of the United States* (New York, 1971).
28. Ritz, *Rewriting the History of the Judiciary Act of 1789*, 22–23; Stephen B. Presser, *The Original Misunderstanding: The English, the Americans, and the Dialectic of Federalist Jurisprudence* (Durham, 1991), ch. 6.
29. William R. Casto, *The Supreme Court in the Early Republic: The Chief Justiceships of John Jay and Oliver Ellsworth* (Columbia, SC, 1995), 55.

court, lieutenant governor, a member of the council or upper house, and judge of probate of Suffolk County of Massachusetts, all at the same time.

Similar traditional conceptions of the judiciary were carried into the Revolution and early Republic. During the Revolution Thomas McKean sat as a delegate to the Continental Congress from Delaware and even served as president of the Congress while continuing to be chief justice of the Pennsylvania Supreme Court. In Connecticut in the early nineteenth century, Jonathan Brace was simultaneously a member of the Connecticut council (the state's upper house), judge of the county court, judge of the probate court, state's attorney from Hartford, and judge of the city court.[30] The Virginia Plan at the Constitutional Convention of 1787 proposed that the national executive join with several members of the national judiciary to constitute a "council of revision" to oversee all legislation passed by the Congress and each state legislature. While this proposal, modeled on New York's similar council, was not finally approved by the convention, the mere fact that Madison, Wilson, and others vehemently defended this combination suggests that many leaders continued to think of judges as political magistrates rather than as legal experts separated from politics.

The same kind of traditional thinking influenced the appointments and behavior of the new federal judges in the 1790s. Washington was certainly much less interested in the judicial experience of his appointees than he was in their political character. Although Jay had been chief justice of New York, he had served only a few weeks in that office. Iredell had less than six months of previous judicial experience before being named to the Supreme Court, and Wilson had never served as a state judge.[31] Of the twenty-eight men who sat on the federal district courts in the 1790s, only eight had held high judicial office in their states, but nearly all of them had been prominent political figures.[32] They saw their service on the court as simply an extension of their general political activity; some of them even continued to exercise political influence, write political articles for newspapers, and pass on Federalist patronage in their districts while sitting on the bench.

Probably the most conspicuous example of the judges' magisterial behavior in the 1790s was the political character of their charges to grand juries. These charges were not simply narrow treatises on the niceties of the law; they were broad pronouncements on politics, often printed in the newspapers and then reprinted and spread throughout the land. The Federalist judges

30. Henry J. Friendly, "The Historic Basis of Diversity Jurisdiction," *Harvard Law Review*, 41 (1928), 498.

31. Casto, *Supreme Court in the Early Republic*, 66.

32. Carl E. Prince, *The Federalists and the Origins of the U.S. Civil Service* (New York, 1977), 242–47.

took advantage of these ceremonial occasions to instruct citizens on their duties and responsibilities to support the fledging national government and to criticize those who seemed to be opposed to the Federalist administration.[33] At first, this sort of political behavior did not strike most people as unconventional; colonial judges had often charged juries with lectures on politics.[34] Such practices were merely an aspect of the pre-modern magisterial character of the eighteenth-century courts. During the trials of the rebels in the Whiskey Rebellion, for example, no one objected to Justice William Paterson's explicit directions to the jury to find the defendants guilty. With respect to the defendant's intention, Justice Paterson declared, "there is not, unhappily, the slightest possibility of doubt....The crime is proved." Such directions were still considered customary in the late eighteenth century.[35]

Thus it is understandable that the irascible and abrasive Samuel Chase of Maryland, appointed to the Supreme Court in 1796, saw nothing wrong with his politicking openly on behalf of the Federalist cause while sitting on the bench. Indeed, he, along with Bushrod Washington, his colleague on the Supreme Court, even openly campaigned for the re-election of President Adams in 1800. Chase was only doing what he thought his position as a political authority and magistrate justified.

Because many people in the 1790s continued to regard the federal judges as political magistrates, the early Congresses assigned a surprisingly large number of non-judicial responsibilities to them, including conducting the census and serving on commissions to reduce the public debt. In nearly all cases the judges willingly accepted these administrative responsibilities.[36] Hamilton summed up the traditional view in 1802 by pointing out that judges were ex officio conservators of the peace and were expected to do more than merely adjudicate. Their duties were twofold, "judicial and ministerial," and the ministerial duties were "performed out of Court and often without reference to it."[37]

33. Ralph Lerner, *The Thinking Revolutionary: Principle and Practice in the New Republic* (Ithaca, 1987), 91–136; Casto, *Supreme Court in the Early Republic*, 126–29.

34. George L. Haskins and Herbert A. Johnson, *Foundations of Power: John Marshall, 1801–1815: The History of the Supreme Court of the United States of America* (New York, 1981), 395.

35. Casto, *Supreme Court in the Early Republic*, 164; Thomas P. Slaughter, "'The King of Crimes': Early American Treason Law, 1787–1860," in Ronald Hoffman and Peter J. Albert, eds., *Launching the "Extended Republic": The Federalist Era* (Charlottesville, 1996), 91.

36. Administrative Duties of the Judges, in Maeva Marcus et al., eds., *The Documentary History of the Supreme Court of the United States, 1789–1800* (New York, 1992), 4: 723–29.

37. AH, "The Examination," 23 Feb 1802, *Papers of Hamilton*, 25: 531–32.

Almost immediately after appointing Jay as chief justice, Washington sought his diplomatic advice on the Nootka Sound crisis in 1790, and Jay had no inhibitions about giving it in writing. He had after all served simultaneously as secretary of state and chief justice of the Supreme Court while waiting for Jefferson's return from France in 1789. Chief Justice Jay likewise responded in writing when Secretary of the Treasury Hamilton asked him for a draft of a neutrality proclamation in April 1793. Jay later worked his ideas about American neutrality into a grand jury charge, which was published in the newspapers and which the government sent abroad as a formal explanation of its position.[38] Although Jay's appointment as a special envoy to Britain in 1794 to prevent an impending war aroused some opposition in the Senate, most officials saw nothing inappropriate in the chief justice performing such a diplomatic mission. Later in 1799 Chief Justice Oliver Ellsworth headed the mission sent to negotiate the end of the Quasi-War with France. Indeed, throughout his tenure as chief justice, Ellsworth repeatedly offered advice to the Federalist administration on political matters and even on matters involving criminal prosecutions.[39]

In fact, the Federalists hoped that the federal courts might help to break down state loyalties and nationalize the society. Federal law under the Constitution, unlike that of the Confederation, would penetrate the membrane of state sovereignty and operate directly on individuals—one of the most radical features of the new national government. Senator William Paterson, later an associate justice of the Supreme Court, said during the drafting of the Judiciary Act in 1789 that he expected the federal courts to "carry law" to the people, "to their Homes, to their very Doors," so that "we shall think, and feel, & act as one People."[40]

But given the strong loyalty most Americans had to their separate states, this expansion of the authority of the federal courts had to be done carefully. Chief Justice Jay knew only too well that "the federal Courts had Enemies in all who fear their Influence on State Objects." Thus contradictory opinions by the circuit courts, circuit-riding in general, and other problems with the federal courts "should be corrected quietly," for, as Chief Justice Jay told New York senator Rufus King in 1793, if the "Defects were all exposed to public View in striking Colors, more Enemies would arise, and the Difficulty of mending them increased."[41]

38. Casto, *Supreme Court in the Early Republic*, 74–75.
39. Casto, *Supreme Court in the Early Republic*, 116, 178–79.
40. William Paterson Notes on Judicial Bill Debate, 22 June 1789, Marcus et al., eds., *Documentary History of the Supreme Court*, 4: 410–12, 414–16.
41. Jay to Rufus King, 22 Dec. 1793, in Marcus et al., eds., *Documentary History of the Supreme Court*, 2: 434–35; Graham, "The Lower Federal Courts in the Early Republic," ch. 2.

Out of fear that the state courts might undermine national authority, the Federalists drafted the Judiciary Act of 1789 in such a way as to make it more likely that the initial filing of federal cases would be done in federal trial courts rather than in state courts. This lessened the need for federal appellate review of state court decisions, particularly decisions involving suits of British creditors, which might have led to nasty conflicts between the federal and state judiciaries. Just such a British debt case, *Ware v. Hylton*, which had begun in a federal court, reached the Supreme Court in 1796. The Court decided that the supremacy clause of the Constitution provided that treaties of the United States overrode a Virginia state law—an important precedent for establishing national authority. In that same year, 1796, the Court in *Hylton v. United States* ensured that the new federal government would have taxing power broad enough to meet its needs, again by defeating a Virginia case against a federal carriage tax. This case was an important enough precedent for the federal government's ability to extract revenue from its citizens that Alexander Hamilton temporarily left his private law practice to argue the case before the Court on behalf of the government; this was the only time he ever appeared before the Court.

With these decisions the Federalist-dominated Court revealed its desire to declare that the United States formed a single nation of one people. In *Chisholm v. Georgia* (1793), however, the Court overreached itself. It decided that the state of Georgia was not immune from suits by citizens of another state. This decision represented such a serious assault on state sovereignty that it could not stand; even Federalists in Massachusetts were appalled by it. Many of the state legislatures called for a constitutional amendment to overturn the *Chisholm* decision and prevent states from being sued by foreigners or by citizens of another state. The result was adoption in 1798 of the Eleventh Amendment to the Constitution, which declared that "the Judicial power of the United States shall not be construed to extend to any suit in law or equity, commenced or prosecuted against one of the United States by Citizens of another State, or by Citizens or Subjects of any Foreign State."[42]

Although most Federalists were not bent on abolishing the states and all state sovereignty, they were eager to ensure that the national government had sufficient authority to govern. During the trials of the rebels in the Whiskey and Fries rebellions, the federal courts offered a broad

42. In its ratifying convention in 1790 Rhode Island had anticipated the problem of individuals suing the state and had recommended that such cases be removed from federal jurisdiction. Patrick T. Conley, *Rhode Island in Rhetoric and Reflection: Public Addresses and Essays* (East Providence, 2002), 92.

"constructive" interpretation of treason in the Constitution by contending that mere armed opposition to a statute was equivalent to the levying of war against the United States. If the object of the insurrection was "to suppress the excise offices and to prevent the execution of an act of Congress, by force and intimidation," declared Justice Paterson in the trial of the Whiskey rebels, "the offence in legal estimation is high treason; it is an usurpation of the authority of government; it is high treason by levying of war." It did not matter to Paterson that the prosecution had failed to produce two witnesses to the defendant's overt acts. The Federalists meant to put down disorder. The same thinking governed the trial of the Fries rebels of 1799. Although John Fries and a mob did rescue eighteen men from a federal marshal and his deputies, no shots were fired, and the prisoners later made their way unescorted to Philadelphia, where they gave themselves up to the law. Nevertheless, Fries was charged and twice convicted of treason for levying war against the United States. Defining riot and rescue as treason was a stretch—a *novel experiment*," said the defense attorneys—but in the atmosphere of 1799 the Federalists were frightened.[43]

Equally important in strengthening the authority of the federal government were the Federalists' efforts to create a bankruptcy law for the nation. The main purpose behind the uniform national bankruptcy law of 1799 was the Federalist desire, as Congressman James Bayard of Delaware put it, to "unite and naturalize the United States, and...cement together the different parts of the Union, and connect more closely the nation with the Federal Government."[44]

Perhaps most important of the Federalists' attempts to bolster national authority in the 1790s was their claim that the federal courts had jurisdiction over common law crimes. The Federalists contended that the federal courts could use something called an American common law—a body of precedents and practices drawn from the unwritten English common law and adapted to American conditions—to punish crimes against the United States and its government even in the absence of specific federal criminal statutes.

43. Bradley Chapin, *The American Law of Treason: Revolutionary and Early National Origins* (Seattle, 1964); Slaughter, "'The King of Crimes,'" in Hoffman and Albert, eds., *Launching the "Extended Republic,"* 93–94, 97–108.

44. In 1800 the Federalist-dominated Congress finally passed a complicated and much contested bankruptcy act, which the Republicans correctly saw as just another Federalist scheme to extend executive patronage and consolidate the Union. In 1801 the Republicans immediately repealed the act. Not until 1841 did the federal government enact another bankruptcy law, and it lasted only a year. Bruce H. Mann, *Republic of Debtors: Bankruptcy in the Age of American Independence* (Cambridge, MA, 2002), 214, 215.

Chief Justice John Jay's first charge to a grand jury in the spring of 1790 staked out a large area of national common law jurisdiction. He told the jurors that their duty extended "to the enquiry and presentment of all offences of every kind, committed against the United States," by which he seems to have meant virtually any example of wrongdoing against the nation or its government whether proscribed by a federal criminal statute or not.[45] In 1793 Justice James Wilson in a grand jury charge went even further in expanding the federal courts' jurisdiction by claiming that the law of nations was part of what he called the "common law" of the United States.

In the 1790s most Federalist judges scarcely doubted the existence of a federal common law of crimes adapted to American circumstance. In fact, they assumed that no national government could rightly call itself a real government if it lacked the legal means of protecting itself by judicial proceedings alone. As Chief Justice Ellsworth declared in 1799, acts that were "clearly destructive of a government or its powers, which the people have ordained to *exist*, must be criminal." It was not necessary to particularize these criminal acts by legislative statute, said Ellsworth, "because they are readily perceived, and are ascertained by known and established rules; I mean the maxims and principles of the common law of our land."[46]

Probably no Federalist conception in the 1790s seemed to the Republicans more threatening in its implications than this notion that the common law of crimes ran in the federal courts. The common law, as the Republicans pointed out, "was a complete system for the management of all the affairs of a country. It...went to all things for which laws are necessary." Common law jurisdiction relating to crimes, said Madison, "would confer on the judicial department a discretion little short of legislative power." If the federal courts could use the "vast and multifarious" body of the common law to control American behavior, then, concluded Madison in his famous report of January 1800 to the Virginia assembly, the courts alone might "new model the whole political fabric of the country."[47]

Although the federal judges denied that they were newly modeling the whole political fabric of the country, they did attempt to use the common law to expand national authority in a variety of ways. During the trials of the rebels in the Whiskey and Fries rebellions, the federal courts used the

45. Presser, *Original Misunderstanding*, 68–69.
46. Presser, *Original Misunderstanding*, 90.
47. Casto, *Supreme Court in the Early Republic*, 150, 156–57; JM, Report on the Alien and Sedition Acts, 7 Jan. 1800, *Madison: Writings*, 640.

federal common law to justify the federal government's trying and punishing the rebels' violations of state law and state practices. "Although, in
ordinary cases, it would be well to accommodate our practice with that of
the state," declared District Judge Richard Peters in the trial of the Whiskey rebels, "yet the judiciary of the United States should not be fettered
and controlled in its operations, by a strict adherence to state regulations
and practice."[48]

When some of the Federalists began claiming that the federal courts
could use the criminal common law to punish seditious libel even without
a sedition act, the Republicans became truly alarmed. The claim that the
federal judiciary could use the common law to punish crimes, Jefferson
declared in 1799, was the "most formidable" doctrine that the Federalists
had ever set forth. He told Edmund Randolph that all that the Federalist
monocrats and aristocrats had done to tyrannize over the people—creating
the Bank, Jay's Treaty, even the Sedition Act of 1798—were "solitary, inconsequential timid things in comparison with the audacious, barefaced and
sweeping pretension to a system of law for the US without the adoption of
their legislature, and so infinitely beyond their power to adopt."[49] If the
Federalists were ever able to establish this doctrine, Jefferson believed that
the state courts would be put out of business. As far as he was concerned,
there could be no law that existed apart from the popular will of the nation.
And since that will had never established the common law for the United
States, and indeed had no right to do so anyway for such a limited government, the federal government contained no such common law.[50]

WITH GOOD REASON, the Jeffersonian Republicans had become
convinced by 1800 that the national judiciary had become little more
than an agent for the promotion of the Federalist cause. Some Federalists
in 1798–1799 had thought that the army might be used to put down the
states, but shrewder Federalists knew better. "It is impossible, in this
country, to render an army an engine of government," Secretary of the
Treasury Oliver Wolcott Jr. told Fisher Ames in December 1799; "there is
no way to combat the state opposition but by an efficient and extended
organization of judges, magistrates, and other civil offices."[51]

Nothing seemed to give pause to the Federalist plans to control the
judiciary—not even the election of Republicans to the presidency and

---

48. Presser, *Original Misunderstanding*, 103.

49. TJ to Edmund Randolph, 18 Aug. 1799, *Jefferson: Writings*, 1066.

50. TJ to Randolph, 18 Aug. 1799, *Jefferson: Writings*, 1066–68.

51. Oliver Wolcott Jr. to Fisher Ames, 29 Dec. 1799, in Haskins and Johnson, *Foundations of Power: Marshall*, 121.

the Congress in 1800; indeed, the election results only made the Federalists more desperate to hold on to the courts. If a free government could not tolerate a standing army to hold itself together, then, said the Federalists, the only thing left was "a firm, independent, and extensive Judiciary."[52]

Although the Federalists had lost the election in the late fall of 1800, the new Republican administration did not take office until March 1801, and the new Congress would not be seated until December 1801 (not changed until the Twentieth Amendment adopted in 1933 eliminated the December to March lame-duck session of Congress). In February 1801, less than three weeks before its expiration, the lame-duck Federalist-controlled Congress passed a new judiciary act, which was designed to further consolidate national judicial authority. The act eliminated circuit court duty for the justices of the Supreme Court by creating six new circuit courts with sixteen new judges. It broadened the original jurisdiction of the circuit courts, especially in cases involving land titles, and provided for the easier removal of litigation from state to federal courts. It also recognized that the common law of crimes ran in the federal courts. On the assumption that the work of the Supreme Court would be lessened, the Federalist Congress reduced the Court's membership from six to five justices with the next vacancy. This meant that Jefferson would be prevented from naming a Supreme Court justice until two vacancies occurred.[53]

To add insult to injury, John Adams, before surrendering the presidency to Jefferson, appointed a number of Federalist judges to this newly enlarged federal judiciary, including incumbent Secretary of State John Marshall as chief justice of the United States. The act also provided for numerous offices of clerks, marshals, attorneys, and justices of the peace to which deserving Federalists were quickly appointed. Because Adams signed the commissions of many of these appointments on the eve of Jefferson's inauguration, the new Federalist appointees were labeled "midnight judges."[54]

Although the Federalists had been considering reform of the judiciary for some while, this last-minute action seemed desperate and designed to perpetuate their cause in spite of the popular will. Some Federalists admitted as much. Since the Federalists with the Republicans' victory "are about to experience a heavy gale of adverse wind," Gouverneur

---

52. Boston *Columbia Centinel*, 14 Jan. 1801, quoted in Graham, "The Lower Federal Courts in the Early Republic," ch. 2.

53. Kathryn Turner, "Federalist Policy and the Judiciary Act of 1801," WMQ, 22 (1965), 3–32.

54. Kathryn Turner, "Midnight Judges," *University of Pennsylvania Law Review*, 109 (1961), 494–523.

Morris explained, "can they be blamed for casting many anchors to hold their ship through the storm?"[55]

WHEN THE REPUBLICANS TOOK OVER the elective branches of the national government in 1801, it was inevitable that they would turn their attention to the judiciary. Jefferson believed that the Federalists had "retired into the judiciary as a stronghold . . . , and from that battery all the works of republicanism are to be beaten down and erased."[56] To complete the Republican "revolution," therefore, as Virginia congressman William Branch Giles told Jefferson, "the enemy" had to be routed from "that strong fortress."[57]

To the most extreme Republicans like Giles it was outrageous and anti-republican that the federal judges remained free of popular control under some sort of "misapplied idea of 'independence.'" These zealous Democratic-Republicans would be satisfied with nothing less than "an absolute repeal of the whole Judiciary and terminating the present officers and creating a new system."[58] But Jefferson was more cautious. Realizing that there were many Republicans who valued an independent judiciary and even some who liked the features of the new Federalist Judiciary Act of 1801, he moved slowly at first. He knew that removing the Federalist judges would pose problems. Since their lifetime appointments were in "the nature of freeholds," it was "difficult," he said, "to undo what is done." But at least he could appoint Republicans as other important officers of the courts who served at the pleasure of the president—the U.S. district attorneys who prosecuted the government cases and the marshals who selected the juries and executed the courts' sentences. These officers would become "the only shield" protecting the people from the Federalist judges.[59]

Despite his sense of the difficulties involved, however, Jefferson had no doubt that the Federalist Judiciary Act of 1801 was a "parasitical plant engrafted at the last session on the judiciary body," a plant that had to be lopped off.[60] After a long and bitter debate in the Congress, the Republicans in 1802 repealed the Federalist law, thus at a stroke destroying the newly created circuit courts and for the first and only time in United

55. Richard E. Ellis, *The Jeffersonian Crisis: Courts and Politics in the Young Republic* (New York, 1971), 15.
56. Dumas Malone, *Jefferson the President: First Term, 1801–1805* (Boston, 1970), 458.
57. Malone, *Jefferson the President: First Term*, 116.
58. Ellis, *Jeffersonian Crisis*, 20–21.
59. TJ to JM, 26 Dec. 1800, *Republic of Letters*, 1156; Ellis, *Jeffersonian Crisis*, 33; Haskins and Johnson, *Foundations of Power: Marshall*, 152.
60. Malone, *Jefferson the President: First Term*, 119.

States history revoking the tenure of federal judges as well. Of course, the Republicans said that they were not legislatively removing the judges, which would be a violation of their tenure during good behavior and thus unconstitutional, but they were simply abolishing the courts. Federalist Justice Samuel Chase was not amused. "The distinction of taking the Office from the Judge, and not the Judge from the Office," was, said Chase, "puerile and nonsensical."[61]

The Republicans then went on to amend the judicial system. Instead of three circuit courts there were now to be six, within each of which a justice of the Supreme Court was to serve on circuit twice a year with the various district judges. Instead of meeting two times a year for two weeks, the Supreme Court would meet only once a year for a term of four weeks. Since the Supreme Court had last met in December 1801, it could not legally reconvene until February 1803—a fourteen-month suspension that some Federalists believed might set a precedent for an even longer suspension, even virtual abolition, of the Court.[62] But Jefferson did not want to destroy the Court, only republicanize it. The repeal and the new Judiciary Act of 1802, the president declared, were designed to "restore our judiciary to what it was while justice & not Federalism was its object."[63]

Many were upset by these changes, which were designed to meet the most serious objections to the 1789 system. Even some moderate Republicans regretted the repeal of the 1801 Judiciary Act and the abolition of the new tier of federal circuit courts. Those involved in commerce especially had come to appreciate the integrity and efficiency of the federal courts in contrast to the state courts, where legally uneducated judges without secure tenure were not to be trusted to make even-handed judgments.[64]

Federalists saw the repeal as a threat to the Union itself. In May 1803 in a charge to a federal grand jury in Baltimore, Justice Samuel Chase assailed the Republicans for shaking the independence of the national judiciary to its foundations and threatening the security of all liberty and property. Many Federalists called for the Supreme Court to declare Congress's repeal of the Judiciary Act of 1801 null and void because it had rescinded the tenure of the new circuit judges and deprived them of their

---

61. Samuel Chase to John Marshall, 24 April 1802, in *Papers of Marshall*, 6: 110.
62. Graham, "The Lower Federal Courts in the Early Republic," ch. 2.
63. Ellis, *Jeffersonian Crisis*, 52.
64. Ellis, *Jeffersonian Crisis*, 49; Friendly, "Historic Basis of Diversity Jurisdiction," *Harvard Law Review*, 41 (1928), 483–510; Robert L. Jones, "Finishing a Friendly Argument: The Jury and the Historical Origins of Diversity Jurisdiction," *New York University Law Review*, 82 (2007), 997–1101.

salaries in violation of Article III, Section 1 of the Constitution. Others wanted the judges to ignore the act and go on strike. Still others were more pessimistic and predicted that armed resistance would be the only answer to the Republican assault on the judiciary.

For their part many of the Republicans were not satisfied with the mere repeal of the Judiciary Act of 1801 and the elimination of the new courts. Some, including President Jefferson, wanted the Constitution amended so that the president could remove any judge following a joint address of the majority of the Congress. But when this seemed too complicated, the Republicans fixed on impeachment for "high crimes and misdemeanors" as the best available constitutional device for getting rid of obnoxious Federalist judges. Although Jefferson complained that impeachment was "a *bungling way*" of dealing with the problem, he was reluctantly willing to give it a try.[65]

In 1804 the Republicans in the House of Representatives first impeached and the Senate convicted John Pickering, an alcoholic and probably insane judge of the federal district court of New Hampshire. Although Pickering had been violently partisan, he had committed no offense clearly recognized by the Constitution. As Senator William Plumer of New Hampshire pointed out, the Republicans were considering the "process of impeachment...in effect as a *mode of removal*, and not as a charge and conviction of high crimes and misdemeanors." Congressman John Randolph of Virginia, the Republican leader in the House, was reported to have said that the provision in the Constitution that judges shall hold their offices during good behavior was intended to guard them against the executive alone. It did not apply to the Congress, which should be able to remove them by majority vote.[66]

On the very day in March 1804 that the Senate found Pickering guilty, the House passed a resolution for the impeachment of Justice Samuel Chase, the most overbearing Federalist on the Supreme Court. Although Jefferson had urged privately that some action be taken against Justice Chase for his grand jury charge in Baltimore in 1803, it was Randolph who assumed full control of the impeachment of Chase.

Early in the new Republican-dominated Congress, Randolph emerged as chairman of the Ways and Means Committee and majority leader. Although he had his successes, a more unlikely leader can hardly be imagined. To be sure, he had some important credentials: he was a member of the most distinguished family in Virginia, a cousin of Thomas Jefferson, a close friend of the Speaker of the House, North Carolina congressman Nathaniel Macon, and a religiously devout Republican. But he was

65. Malone, *Jefferson the President: First Term*, 462.
66. Ellis, *Jeffersonian Crisis*, 75.

arrogant and belligerent, and not temperamentally suited for the compromising and deal-making required of a majority leader. He appeared in the House booted and spurred with a whip in hand, imitating what he assumed was the behavior of members of the British Parliament. He was pale, thin, and beardless with burning hazel eyes and a high piercing voice that he used with great effectiveness. He was a fascinating orator—an extemporaneous speaker, jumpy and excitable as a young filly, and quick to put men down with wit and sarcasm. His opponents in the House fumed and eventually wilted when he pointed his long bony finger at them and verbally abused them. Randolph saw corruption everywhere and was devoted to the Republican ideals of '98—"jealousy of the State Governments toward the General Government; a dread of standing armies; a loathing of public debt, taxes, and excises; tenderness for the liberty of the citizen; jealousy, Argus-eyed jealousy of the patronage of the President." He had little or no conception of the American nation: "when I speak of my country," he said, "I mean the Commonwealth of Virginia." When he took over the leadership of the Republicans' impeachment of Justice Chase in 1804 he had just turned thirty.[67]

Randolph was no more equipped to handle the impeachment of Chase than he was to be majority leader. He had no legal experience, and his emotional and sarcastic style of speaking was inappropriate for the august trial held in the Senate in February 1805. The Senate was draped in crimson and green and, according to one senator, "fitted up in a style beyond anything which has ever appeared in this country." Most of official Washington was present, along with a thousand or more spectators.[68]

There were eight articles of impeachment accusing Chase not only of criminal behavior but also of mistakes in procedure during one of his trials. The implications were ominous: if Chase were to be convicted for these mistakes, then in the future any judge could be easily removed by impeachment. Apparently, Randolph and some other Republicans hoped to follow up Chase's conviction with an attack on other justices of the Supreme Court. Many thought Chief Justice Marshall would be next. Marshall was certainly unnerved by the Chase impeachment. He wrote Chase on the eve of the trial expressing his apprehensions over the "modern doctrine…that a Judge giving a legal opinion contrary to the legislature is liable to impeachment." A much better and more humane way of handling these issues, he told Chase, would be for the legislature simply to reverse "those legal opinions deemed unsound by

67. Robert Dawidoff, *The Education of John Randolph* (New York, 1979), 30, 152–54.
68. Richard E. Ellis, "The Impeachment of Samuel Chase," in Michael R. Belknap, ed., *American Political Trials* (Westport, CT, 1981), 70.

the legislature." Thus "impeachment should yield to the appellate jurisdiction in the legislature."[69]

As it turned out, Randolph mishandled the trial and lost the support of
some of his fellow Republicans. Although Randolph and the House managers did get a simple majority of the Senate to convict Chase on three charges,
they could not muster the necessary two-thirds on any of them. (There were
twenty-five Republicans and nine Federalists in the Senate.) Not a single
senator voted for the article accusing Chase of procedural mistakes in one of
his trials. As much as they hated Chase, many Republican senators were
reluctant to convict him for acts that were not prohibited by any express and
positive laws—the very point of the Republicans' objection to the use of the
common law of crimes. They also realized that Chase's political behavior on
the bench, while excessive at times, was not all that unusual and was not
criminal. After all, many Republican state judges were likewise using their
courts for partisan purposes. The line between law and politics was still
thought hazy enough for many to be unsure of which was which.

Still, the Chase trial helped to clear the air. Chase himself changed his
behavior; from that moment until his death in 1811 he ceased engaging in
political controversy. Senator John Quincy Adams thought that the failure to convict Chase established that only actual crimes were impeach-
able offenses.[70]

Chase's acquittal effectively destroyed Randolph's reputation among
his fellow Republicans and drove him to the extremist edges of the party.
Although the Republicans' failure to convict Chase ended for the time
being their assault on the national judiciary, they did not abandon their
desire to make the judiciary more responsive to the nation. "Impeachment was a farce which will not be tried again," Jefferson said in 1807.
What was needed, he said, was "an amendment to the Constitution
which, keeping the judges independent of the Executive, will not leave
them so, of the nation." Republicans from some of the states proposed
several amendments that were variations on the English pattern—that
simple address of the Congress be sufficient for removal of judges.[71] But

69. John Marshal to Samuel Chase, 23 Jan. 1805, *Papers of Marshall*, 6: 347–48.
70. Presser, *Original Misunderstanding*, 157; Ellis, "Impeachment of Chase," in Belknap,
    ed., *American Political Trials*, 72–73; Andrew Shankman, *Crucible of American
    Democracy: The Struggle to Fuse Egalitarianism and Capitalism in Jeffersonian
    Pennsylvania* (Lawrence, KS, 2004), 85.
71. In England in the eighteenth century judges could be removed upon a simple
    address by both houses of Parliament to the crown. The Act of Settlement giving
    tenure to judges during good behavior applied only to the crown. See Saikrishna
    Prakash and Steven D. Smith, "How to Remove a Federal Judge," *Yale Law Journal*,
    116 (2006), 72–137.

these various proposals went nowhere. By the end of Jefferson's administration the Supreme Court was gaining in authority under Chief Justice John Marshall's careful leadership, especially since, as Gouverneur Morris reminded Marshall, "your Office being independent of popular whim, the Shafts of Malice cannot easily prevail."[72]

SIMILAR STRUGGLES BETWEEN the Federalists and Jeffersonian Republicans over the role of law and the judiciary in American life were also unfolding in the states. The increasing democratization of American society and politics made more and more leaders turn to the law and judges as restraints on the popular power expressed in the state legislatures. The Federalists had long since become convinced that the courts were essential in staving off "the confiscating avarice of Democracy."[73]

But it was too late: "equal rights" was the rallying cry almost everywhere against aristocratic judicial privilege and the mysteries of the common law. Indeed, so threatening and unsettling did the popular anti-aristocratic attacks on lawyers and judges become that even many Republicans eventually felt the need to come to the defense of the common law and an independent judiciary.

As the Federalists rapidly declined in influence during the first decade of the nineteenth century, the dominant Republicans began turning on one another. Jefferson had predicted that the Republicans would divide among themselves into different parties, and "whatever names the parties might bear, the real division would be into moderate and ardent republicanism."[74] The issue that most conspicuously divided the Republicans was the role of the judiciary.

Nearly all the states sought to reform the law and their judiciaries during the decades following the Revolution, and these efforts generated continual controversy. While the Federalists, often speaking for the static property interests of rentier groups, wanted a judiciary as independent as possible from popular control, the Republicans usually pushed for an elected judiciary, codification, if not elimination, of the common law, and legislative dominance over the judges.

By 1800 almost every state had problems with its judiciary, some more than others. As the governor of Pennsylvania complained, "The extension of Commerce and Agriculture, the increase of population, and the

72. TJ to Giles, 20 April 1807, in L and B, eds., *Writings of Jefferson*, 9: 191; Dumas Malone, *Jefferson the President: Second Term, 1805–1809* (Boston, 1974), 367–68; Gouverneur Morris to John Marshall, 26 June 1807, *Papers of Marshall*, 7: 54.
73. Ellis, *Jeffersonian Crisis*, 229.
74. Ellis, *Jeffersonian Crisis*, 234.

multiplication of Counties" had rendered the state's court system "no longer adequate to the regular and efficient administration of justice."[75] Consequently, judicial reforms of one sort or another became necessary. In some states like Kentucky and Ohio the radical Republicans, representing those common farmers most resentful of sophisticated legal processes, were able to accomplish much of their program of weakening the common law and of bringing the judiciary under the control of the people. Elsewhere, however, moderate Republicans, generally representing those who had the strongest entrepreneurial and market interests, came to realize the importance of the common law and an independent judiciary to economic development and began resisting the more radical popular demands.

Of all the struggles over the law and judiciary that took place in the states during the first two decades of the nineteenth century, probably the longest and most intense occurred in Pennsylvania, where there were factions within factions. Groups of radicals in Pennsylvania believed that the revolution on behalf of republicanism had not been carried far enough. The most extreme of these factions was led by Dr. Michael Leib, a Philadelphia physician and political activist, and William Duane, the editor of the *Aurora*. Leib, a founder of the German Republican Society who became a member of the state legislature, later a member of Congress, and eventually a U.S. senator, was totally committed to turning the poor and the common laborers of Pennsylvania into political actors. His commitment to the international republican revolution and the most extreme forms of majoritarian democracy was equally strong.

As long as the Federalists were the major enemy, different opposition groups in Pennsylvania, including artisans, entrepreneurs, and laborers of all sorts, had been able to combine under the rubric of the Republican party. But with Jefferson's victory in 1800 and the decline of the Federalists, the radicalism of Leib and Duane became more conspicuous. The Leib-Duane faction began attacking all social and economic distinctions, even those naturally earned, denouncing the role of gentlemen in politics, and promoting a "happy mediocrity of condition" in all things, including property.[76] These radicals, who came to be called the "Malcontents" or the "Jacobins," objected to the entire complex structure of America's federal and state governments, its separation of powers, and, in particular, its independent judiciaries. Leib and Duane and their

75. Governor to the Assembly, 21 Nov. 1800, "Papers of the Governors, 1785–1817," ed. George Edward Reed and W. W. Griest, *Pennsylvania Archives*, 4th Ser. (Harrisburg, 1900) 4: 460–461.

76. Shankman, *Crucible of American Democracy*, 80.

followers charged that the courts were not susceptible to popular control and that judges used the mysteries of the common law to enhance the privileges of the few at the expense of the many. By 1805 Leib's extremism led his more conservative Republican critics to compare him to Robespierre.[77]

To move against some Federalist members of the judiciary, Leib and Duane combined with other radicals in the state legislature led by Nathaniel Boileau, a graduate of Princeton and a descendant of Huguenot immigrants, and Simon Snyder, a self-made man who in 1802 became speaker of the house in the state legislature and in 1808 governor of the state. Their radical cause was reinforced by an Irish-born immigrant from England, John Binns, who, like others, had fled the British crackdown on advocates of French revolutionary republicanism. Binns established the Northumberland *Republican Argus*, which, along with Duane's *Aurora*, became an important mouthpiece for the reformers' campaign. These factions condemned the common law for its "abstruse and technical phrases," and for being "ill suited to the plain and simple nature of a Republican form of government," and urged the state house of representatives to order the judges to simplify it.[78]

Although this measure failed, the radical Republicans in the state legislature, like their colleagues in the federal Congress, turned to the process of impeachment as a means of removing obnoxiously partisan Federalist judges. The first victim was Alexander Addison, a hard-line Federalist and president of one of Pennsylvania's district courts of common pleas. Addison had helped suppress the Whiskey Rebellion and had furiously condemned the principles of the Virginia and Kentucky resolutions. In January 1803 the Pennsylvania house of representatives impeached him, with the radical Republicans arguing that his opposition to the will of the people, and not any criminal act, was sufficient grounds for impeachment. After a two-day trial, with Addison conducting his own defense in what one newspaper called "the most insolent, arrogant and overbearing" manner, the senate convicted him on a party vote, removed him from office, and forbade him from ever again holding judicial office in Pennsylvania.[79]

Addison's ouster scarcely satisfied the radical Republicans, and in 1805 they pressured the assembly to impeach three additional Federalists

---

77. Shankman, *Crucible of American Democracy*, 99, 141, 142.
78. Elizabeth K. Henderson, "The Attack on the Judiciary in Pennsylvania, 1800–1810," *Penn. Mag. of Hist. and Biog.*, 61 (1937), 113–36; Shankman, *Crucible of American Democracy*, 88.
79. Ellis, *Jeffersonian Crisis*, 157–70, quotation at 165.

who were members of the state supreme court. By now, however, many other Republicans believed that the assault on the judiciary was getting out of hand. With the Republicans breaking apart into radical and moderate wings, the state senate was unable to muster the necessary two-thirds vote for the conviction of the three Federalist judges. The moderates argued that the judges were "the bulwarks of a limited constitution, against legislative encroachments." Their power did not mean that they had any superiority over the legislature. "It implies nothing more than the people are superior to the legislature, and that the judiciary, as a coordinate branch of the government, charged with execution of certain powers, is bound to regard the will of the people, as expressed in the constitution, in preference to the will of the legislative body." It was the same argument Hamilton had made nearly twenty years earlier in *Federalist* No. 78.[80]

By now the struggle had widened into a full-scale debate over the future of the common law and the character of judges in Pennsylvania. Republican governor Thomas McKean, who had been chief justice of the state supreme court for two decades, was appalled at the ignorance and narrow-mindedness of the populists in the assembly. The radicals, he said, were urging the barring of lawyers from the courts, the eliminating of the common law (or "lawyers law," as they labeled it), and the substituting of untrained arbitrators for educated judges. But even more alarming, they were also contending that "all men of talents, lawyers, [and] rich men" were unqualified to sit in the legislature. These "clodhoppers," as McKean called them, could not comprehend that the law was "a science of great difficulty and endless complications" and required "a lifetime to understand it."[81]

With the radicals seemingly threatening "the destruction of our state Government," McKean was able to gather to his side many moderate Republicans, or "Quids," as Duane, the irascible editor of the *Aurora*, called them. ("Quids" after *tertium quid*: a "third something," neither Federalists nor, in Duane's opinion, true Republicans.) Perhaps McKean's principal supporter and most loyal ally was Alexander J. Dallas, U.S. district attorney who had been secretary of the Commonwealth of Pennsylvania in the 1790s. When the Republican party caucus dominated by the radicals denied McKean the gubernatorial nomination in 1805, McKean, Dallas, and other Quids combined with the Federalists to create

80. Shankman, *Crucible of American Democracy*, 133.
81. Ellis, *Jeffersonian Crisis*, 173, 163–64; James Headley Peeling, "Governor McKean and the Pennsylvanian Jacobins (1799–1808)," *Penn. Mag. of Hist. and Biog.*, 54 (1930), 320–54; Shankman, *Crucible of American Democracy*, 153.

a coalition ticket. The nature of the judiciary and the common law was the principal issue of the campaign.[82]

Dallas helped compose an address in 1805 that summarized the fears of the moderate Republicans that too much democracy was endangering Pennsylvania society. This address, widely distributed in newspapers and pamphlets, was one of the most comprehensive defenses of the judiciary and the common law made in these years. It contended that without the protection of the courts and the mysterious intricacies of the common law, "rights would remain forever without remedies and wrongs without redress." The people of Pennsylvania, the address declared, could no longer count on their popularly elected legislature to solve many of the problems of their lives. "For the varying exigencies of social life, for the complicated interests of an enterprising nation, the positive acts of the legislature can provide little fundamental protection alone."[83] These views represented a severe indictment of democracy.

McKean narrowly won the bitterly contested election for the governorship. Following a failed attempt to impeach McKean, the coalition between the Leib-Duane faction and the Snyderites began to break apart, especially as Snyder and his followers glimpsed the possibility of actually attaining the governorship if they moderated their message. While Leib, who was back in the state legislature after serving in the U.S. Congress, demanded that the state remove all English cases from state law and codify the entire common law, the Snyderites argued for much more piecemeal reform, with Nathaniel Boileau contending "it would not be practicable to reduce the common law at once into a text."

This conflict between these two popular reform factions broke new political ground in America. For the first time, no "aristocracy" was involved; both of the two contesting groups called themselves "democrats," and both spoke in the name of the common man.[84]

But the issue of the role of the courts versus the role of the legislature continued to plague Pennsylvania. "The acts of the legislature form but a small part of that code from which the citizen is to learn his duties, or the magistrate his power and rule of action," declared the presiding judge Moses Levy in the Pennsylvania cordwainers' trial of 1806. These legislative acts were simply the "temporary emanations of a body, the component members of which are subject to perpetual change," and they

82. Ellis, *Jeffersonian Crisis*, 174–81.
83. Ellis, *Jeffersonian Crisis*, 179; Michael Les Benedict, "Laissez-Faire and Liberty: A Re-Evaluation of the Meaning and Origins of Laissez-Faire Constitutionalism," *Law and History Review*, 3 (1985), 323–26; Shankman, *Crucible of American Democracy*, 145.
84. Shankman, *Crucible of American Democracy*, 175, 178.

applied "principally to the political exigencies of the day." Only the unwritten common law could supply what was legally needed. Only "that invaluable code" composed of ancient precedents and customs could ascertain and define, "with a critical precision, and with a consistency that no fluctuating political body could or can attain, not only the civil rights of property, but the nature of all crimes from treason to trespass." The conclusion was clear. Only the common law whose "rules are the result of the wisdom of ages" could adapt to the novel and shifting circumstances of modernity and regulate "with a sound discretion most of our concerns in civil and social life."[85]

Yet the Pennsylvania radicals continued to assault judges for their abuse of discretionary authority. "Judges," the popular radicals contended in 1807, "very often discover that the law, as written, may be made to mean something which the legislature never thought of. The greatest part of their decisions are in fact, and in effect, making new laws."[86]

Other states also experienced bitter clashes over the common law and the independence of the judiciary. Since opponents of the common law made much of its British origins, its defenders were hard put to find for the common law in America a basis other than ancient English precedents. Confronted with the argument that only the popularly elected legislature ought to make law, apologists for the common law contended that it also had popular will behind it. Just as statutes were binding because they were enacted with the consent of the legislature, "so these unwritten customs and regulations...," declared Jesse Root of Connecticut in 1798, "have the sanction of universal consent and adoption in practice."[87]

But the radical reformers would not agree with what to them seemed sophistry. Their every attempt to codify and eliminate the common law from the courts thus split the Republicans. Many moderate Republicans who had hitherto condemned the courts as aristocratic bastions of Federalist privilege came to appreciate them and their ability to secure all sorts of commercial property from the ravages of radical populists. Thus in state after state Republican parties began breaking apart over support of the judiciary and the protection of property, especially the new sorts of dynamic commercial property owned by rising Republican entrepreneurs

85. John R. Commons et al., eds., A Documentary History of American Industrial Society (Cleveland, 1919–1911), 3: 231–32; Christopher L. Tomlins, Law, Labor, and Ideology in the Early American Republic (Cambridge, UK, 1993), 133.
86. Shankman, Crucible of American Democracy, 195.
87. Morton J. Horwitz, The Transformation of American Law, 1780–1860 (Cambridge, MA, 1977), 21, 22.

and businessmen. What was important, however, was that the moderate Republicans were able to resist the radical positions without repudiating either the people or democratic politics.

In 1807 the most extreme Republicans in Massachusetts expected that the election of Republican James Sullivan as governor would at long last enable them to bring the state's judiciary to heel. Instead, Sullivan in his inaugural address defended the independence of the courts, declaring that "the Judicial department will invariably claim the first regard of patriotism. Upon its wisdom and purity, freedom, property and all the valuable possessions in civil society depend."[88] The burgeoning commercial economy of America made many Republicans like Sullivan as eager to defend the courts and property as the traditional proprietary-minded Federalists had been.

Everywhere moderate Republicans came to understand that a strong independent judiciary and a flexible common law were crucial, as one North Carolinian put in 1806, to meeting the needs of an "improving people, whose minds are expanding, whose wants are increasing, and whose relative situations are daily changing."[89] They came to see that the radical attempt to eliminate the common law entirely and to make the judiciary dependent on the legislatures or on the people endangered both private rights and economic progress. And everywhere they sought either to thwart or evade the assaults on the judiciary and common law.

When, for example, the Ohio legislature in 1806 directly prohibited the common law from running in the state's courts, the state's judges somehow found ways of bringing it back into effect. Judge Benjamin Tappan of the state's Fifth Circuit declared in 1817 that, despite the legislature's edict, the common law, "founded on the laws of nature and the dictates of reason," had to be maintained. "Not only is the common law necessarily in force here," said Tappan, who was the brother of the famous abolitionists Arthur and Lewis Tappan, "but... its authority is superior to that of the written laws; for it not only furnishes the rules and principles by which the statute laws are construed, but it ascertains and determines the validity and authority of them."

Of course, Tappan's reasoning in Republican-dominated Ohio aroused a storm of controversy, including a four-hundred-page rebuttal. Judge John McLean of the state supreme court was shrewder and more subtle. In the same year, 1817, he conceded that the common law of crimes did not exist in Ohio's courts. At the same time, however, this future U.S. Supreme Court justice could not hide his respect for the common law;

88. Ellis, *Jeffersonian Crisis*, 221.
89. Ellis, *Jeffersonian Crisis*, 246.

"for," he said, "if the common law were expressly repealed by statute, the shadow only would disappear—the life and spirit of it would remain."[90]

Thus in 1842 Justice McLean of the federal Supreme Court joined Justice Joseph Story's decision in *Swift v. Tyson* in affirming the authority of the federal courts to decide cases on the basis of "general principles and doctrines of commercial jurisprudence" and not on the basis of the decisional law of the state of New York. In this decision Story construed Section 34 (the Rules of Decision Act) of the Judiciary Act of 1789 in such a way as to grant the federal courts common law authority over a wide variety of civil disputes, some of which were actually outside the limits of Congress's legislative power. Although *Swift v. Tyson* was eventually overturned in 1938 in *Erie Railroad Co. v. Tompkins*, partly on the grounds that the doctrine set forth by Story was "an unconstitutional assumption of powers by the Courts of the United States," the *Swift* decision in 1842 indicated that the fast-moving, democratic, and commercial society of the early Republic had a need for the flexibility of the common law that could not be stifled.[91]

90. William T. Utter, "Ohio and the English Common Law," *Mississippi Valley Historical Review*, 16 (1929–1930), 328–31.
91. Although Justice Louise D. Brandeis declared in the Erie Railroad Co. decision (1938) that "there is no federal general common law," there still remains at present a specialized federal common law.

# 12

## Chief Justice John Marshall and the Origins of Judicial Review

Just as the Republican party was divided between its radical and moderate factions, so too was the Federalist party. And the most important moderate Federalist in 1801 was newly appointed Chief Justice John Marshall. Marshall had opposed the Alien and Sedition Acts and had been uneasy over Justice Chase's behavior. Yet like other Federalists he feared the democratic excesses of the Republicans, and in 1801 he set out to save the Supreme Court and the federal judiciary from these popular Republican passions. As chief justice he thought he might be able to drain some of the bitterness from the controversy over the judiciary. In doing so not only did he help to lay the basis for what came to be called judicial review, but he also contributed mightily to the development of an independent judiciary. More than any other single judge, Marshall helped to carve out an exclusive sphere of activity for the judiciary that was separate from politics and popular legislative power.

Marshall was born in what became the frontier county of Fauquier, Virginia, bordering the Blue Ridge Mountains. His father, Thomas Marshall, was descended from Welsh yeomanry, began as a surveyor, and rose to prominence as one of the largest landowners in the county. Marshall's father married an heir of the Randolphs, the most distinguished family in all of Virginia, and eventually became his county's first magistrate and its representative in the colonial assembly. The career of Marshall's father followed the pattern of another Welsh backcountry surveyor and farmer, Peter Jefferson, father of the future president. The resemblance of Marshall's background to that of his distant cousin and lifelong enemy Thomas Jefferson is remarkable.

Unlike Jefferson, however, Marshall never acquired the cultivated elegance of his Randolph forebears and in fact never shed the rough but genial manners of his frontier father. He had simple tastes and a common touch that Jefferson never had, a popular style that Jefferson snidely attributed to "his lax lounging manners." Marshall was unassuming and easygoing with a ready humor and twinkling black eyes. In fact, his extraordinary amiability was the source of much of his success. "I love his laugh," his colleague on the Court Joseph Story said of him; "it is too hearty for an intriguer."[1]

Although Marshall attended the College of William and Mary for only three months and never acquired the vast erudition of Jefferson, he certainly did not lack learning. Indeed, he was hardly the unlettered country lawyer relying on only native genius that he sometimes has been made out to be. Although he admitted that his legal learning was "not equal to that of many of the great masters in the profession," he did have an impressive knowledge of the common law that carried him far beyond Blackstone's *Commentaries on the Laws of England*, with which he had begun his studies. In addition, he was widely read in the classics and in English literature, especially Jane Austen.

Yet there is no doubt that his natural abilities were what most distinguished Marshall from other lawyers and jurists. "His head," said Senator Rufus King, "is the best organized of anyone I have known."[2] Marshall could grasp a subject in its whole and yet simultaneously analyze its parts and relate them to the whole. He could move progressively and efficiently from premise to conclusion in a logical and rigorous manner and extract the essence of the law from the mass of particulars. In the words of Justice Story, he had the remarkable ability to seize, "as it were by intuition, the very spirit of juridical doctrines." Even Jefferson acknowledged Marshall's talent, but he scarcely respected it. Jefferson told Story that "when conversing with Marshall, I never admit anything. So sure as you admit any position to be good, no matter how remote from the conclusion he seeks to establish, you are gone. So great is his sophistry you must never give him an affirmative answer, or you will be forced to grant his conclusion. Why, if he were to ask me whether it were daylight or not, I'd reply, 'Sir, I don't know, I can't tell.'"[3]

The enmity between the two cousins began during the Revolutionary War. Unlike Jefferson, Marshall saw military action and suffered with Washington at Valley Forge in the winter of 1777–1778. He apparently regarded Jefferson as a shirker. Marshall believed that his own service as a captain in the Continental Army had made a nationalist of him, confirming him "in the habit of considering America as my country, and Congress as my government." It also had convinced him that George Washington was "the greatest man on earth."[4]

1. Albert J. Beveridge, *The Life of John Marshall* (Boston, 1919), 4: 81.
2. Jean Edward Smith, *John Marshall: Definer of a Nation* (New York, 1996), 5.
3. Charles F. Hobson, *The Great Chief Justice: John Marshall and the Rule of Law* (Lawrence, KS, 1996), 15; R. Kent Newmyer, *John Marshall and the Heroic Age of the Supreme Court* (Baton Rouge, 2001), 80; *Diary and Letters of Rutherford B. Hayes*, ed. Charles R. Williams (Columbus, OH, 1922–1926), 1: 116.
4. Hobson, *The Great Chief Justice: Marshall*, 20.

After the war Marshall practiced law in Richmond and by the 1780s became the leader of the Virginia bar. He became involved in Virginia politics and in the 1780s served in the state assembly and briefly on the executive council of state. The high point of his early career, however, was his participation on behalf of the Constitution in the Virginia ratifying convention of 1788. Having helped to create the new national government, he remained throughout his life emotionally committed to it. Even when most Virginians moved into the Jeffersonian Republican ranks in the 1790s, Marshall remained a loyal Federalist.

Although his fellow Federalists urged him to get more involved in national politics, Marshall was reluctant to give up his lucrative law practice. Even his acceptance of an appointment by President John Adams to be one of the three envoys to negotiate the end of mounting hostilities with France in 1797 was apparently in part based on his desire to raise some Dutch loans for some land purchases. Marshall's dispatches to the United States during the XYZ Affair electrified the nation and made him an instant celebrity. The many toasts and banquets honoring him, coupled with the sudden revival of the declining fortunes of the Federalist party and pressure from George Washington, convinced Marshall to join Congress and later the Adams administration as secretary of state. By 1800 Jefferson thought that the spirit of "Marshallism" had come to dominate the Federalist party, at least in Virginia, and "nothing," Jefferson told James Monroe, "should be spared to eradicate" such a "spirit."[5]

Marshall's doubts about the Alien and Sedition Acts separated him from the most extreme Federalists and drew him closer to the beleaguered President Adams. Having lost the election of 1800, Adams was already a lame-duck president in January 1801 when he had the opportunity to appoint a new chief justice of the United States. His first choice was John Jay, who had served earlier as chief justice; the president consulted no one and even sent Jay's appointment to the Senate before getting Jay's approval. Oliver Wolcott thought that everyone considered the nomination "as having been made in one of those 'sportive' humors for which our Chief is distinguished." When Adams learned of Jay's refusal, he realized that he could not delay much longer and possibly allow his Republican successor the appointment. On January 21 Adams sent the name of his secretary of state, John Marshall, to the Senate, the very day the Federalist House passed the new Judiciary Act.

Not all Federalists were happy with Marshall's nomination. Theodore Sedgwick said that when Marshall was in the House in the late 1790s some members had "thought him temporizing, while others deemed him fool-

5. TJ to Monroe, 13 Apr. 1800, in L and B, eds., *Writings of Jefferson*, 19: 120.

ish." Sedgwick himself said that Marshall was "attached to pleasures, with convivial habits strongly fixed," and thus "he is indolent" with "a strong attachment to popularity," making him "disposed on all popular subjects to feel the public pulse." Nevertheless, after attempts by some Federalist senators to change the president's mind, the Senate finally confirmed forty-five-year-old Marshall as the new chief justice on January 27, 1801.[6]

WHEN JEFFERSON'S ELECTION STALLED in the House of Representatives in early January, Marshall tended to favor Burr over Jefferson, even though he knew nothing about Burr. He had "almost insuperable objections" to Jefferson's becoming president, he told Alexander Hamilton. Jefferson's prejudices in favor of France rendered him "totally unfit for the chief magistracy" of the United States. Jefferson, he said, will play to the popular House of Representatives, increase his personal power, and weaken the presidency. "He will diminish his responsibility, sap the fundamental principles of the government & become the leader of that party which is about to constitute the majority of the legislature....I cannot bring my self to aid Mr. Jefferson." Yet on March 4, 1801, only a bit over a month after he himself had been confirmed as chief justice of the United States, he had to administer the oath of office of president to this man he disliked so much. Awkward as the situation was, all he could do to show his displeasure was to turn his back on Jefferson while administering the oath.[7]

Although the Federalist Court between 1789 and 1801 had decided only sixty-three cases, it certainly had done much to establish its position in the national government. It had claimed that the criminal common law ran in the federal courts, and it had sought to carve out an expanded definition of treason against the United States in order to bolster federal authority. It had enlarged its jurisdiction at the expense of the state courts, protected vested rights against state intrusion, and asserted the supremacy of federal statutes over state law. Besides beginning the task of creating its rules of procedure, the Court had gone a long way toward working out its relationship with the lower federal courts and state judiciaries.

Despite its promising development as a Federalist institution, however, it still remained, in Hamilton's words, the "least dangerous" branch of the government and was far from having the final word on constitutional interpretation.[8] Congress had claimed to be an equally important

6. Kathryn Turner, "The Appointment of Chief Justice Marshall," WMQ, 17 (1960), 145, 155, 157.

7. Marshall to AH, 1 Jan 1801, *Papers of Marshall*, 6: 46–47; Editorial Note, ibid., 379.

8. AH, *Federalist* No. 78.

interpreter of the Constitution, and so had the states. As America became more democratic, the Supreme Court, like all courts, seemed increasingly aristocratic and vulnerable to popular attack. Finding able men to sit on it became more difficult. Between 1789 and 1801 twelve men had served on the Court. Five of them, including two chief justices, had resigned. The Court had trouble gathering a quorum, forcing cases to be carried over and occasionally sessions to be canceled entirely. Morale on the Court had become poor. John Jay, in declining Adams's offer of reappointment as chief justice, explained that the Court had none of the necessary "Energy, weight and Dignity" to support the national government and little likelihood of acquiring any.[9]

Marshall set out to remedy this situation. He sought to solidify the Court by cutting down on the previous practice of each justice issuing his own opinion seriatim, a practice that was customary in both the eighteenth-century English courts and American state courts. Instead, he convinced the associate justices in most cases to reach a collective decision (usually written by him), thus enhancing the Court's authority by having it speak with one voice.[10]

It was not that he imposed his opinions on his strong-minded colleagues. Instead, he turned the Court into "a band of brothers" and worked at building consensus through friendly discussion and more than an occasional glass of wine. The Court had a rule that it would indulge in wine-drinking only if it were raining. Marshall would look out the window on a sunny day and decide that wine-drinking was permissible since "our jurisdiction extends over so large a territory that the doctrine of chances makes it certain that it must be raining somewhere."[11]

During the first four years of Marshall's tenure, from 1801 to 1805, the Court handed down forty-six written decisions, all of them unanimous. Marshall participated in forty-two, and in each of these he wrote the opinion of the Court. Even after 1810, when there were more Republican than Federalist justices, Marshall continued his amiable dominance. Joseph Story, who had entered the Court in 1811 at the age of thirty-two as a Republican and a teetotaler, quickly succumbed to Marshall's charm and

9. John Jay to JA, 2 Jan. 1801, in Maeva Marcus et al., eds., *The Documentary History of the United States Supreme Court* (New York, 1992) 4:664; R. Kent Newmyer, *The Supreme Court Under Marshall and Taney* (Arlington Heights, IL, 1968), 26, 37.

10. Jefferson came to believe that this practice of justices issuing a single opinion instead of seriatim opinions was wrong-headed and the result of Lord Mansfield's influence on Marshall. TJ to Johnson, 27 Oct. 1822, in Paul L. Ford, ed., *The Works of Thomas Jefferson: Federal Edition* (New York, 1905), 12: 250.

11. Smith, *John Marshall*, 403.

wine-drinking and became a fervent supporter. All in all between 1801 and 1815 Marshall wrote 209 of the Court's 378 opinions.[12]

Ultimately Marshall's greatest achievement was maintaining the Court's existence and asserting its independence in a hostile Republican climate. He began by changing the lordly image of the Court. Under the Federalists the justices had tended to wear either individual academic gowns or robes of scarlet and ermine in imitation of the King's Bench of England—dress that one Republican senator called the "party-colored robes" of an oppressive judiciary.[13] By his example, Marshall induced his colleagues into wearing the plain black republican-style robes that the Virginia judges used.

This symbolic rejection of monarchism was only the first step in Marshall's efforts to escape from the partisan politics of the 1790s. He strenuously sought to reach some sort of accommodation with the other branches of the government, and at least up to the War of 1812 he tried as much as possible to avoid too direct a confrontation with the Republicans. All of his evasion and caution, as he later told Justice Story, was based on his quite sensible fear that the justices might be "condemned as a pack of consolidating aristocratics."[14]

In a series of decisions the Court retreated from some of the advanced positions the Federalists had tried to establish for the judiciary and federal law in the 1790s. Since the fiery partisan charges to grand juries by Federalist judges and justices, especially those of Justice Chase, had aroused the political passions of the Republicans, the chief justice quickly set about trying to change Federalist judicial behavior. He self-consciously refrained from injecting political statements in his grand jury charges and refused to have them published in the newspapers, "saying that he had laid it down as a rule from which he did not intend to depart."[15]

Since the Federalist claim that the English common law ran in the federal courts had aroused such intense Republican hostility, he suggested in 1800 that this was not the case and blamed the currency of "this strange & absurd doctrine" on "some frothy newspaper publications."[16] Yet this sly suggestion was a bit disingenuous, since Marshall denied the

---

12. George L. Haskins and Herbert A. Johnson, *Foundations of Power: John Marshall, 1801–1815*, vol. 2 of the Oliver Wendell Holmes Devise History of the Supreme Court of the United States (New York, 1981), 652.
13. Smith, *John Marshall*, 285–86.
14. Haskins and Johnson, *Foundations of Power: Marshall*, 74.
15. Editorial Note, United States Circuit Court for North Carolina (1803), *Papers of Marshall*, 6: 144.
16. Marshall to St. George Tucker, 27 Nov. 1800, *Papers of Marshall*, 6: 23.

presence only of "the common law of England" in the courts; he agreed that versions of an American common law existed in each state, which judges of both the state and federal courts could invoke. But even this was too exposed a position, and in several decisions between 1807 and 1811 Marshall's Court declared that "the jurisdiction of the courts of the United States depends, exclusively, on the constitution and laws of the United States."[17] Finally in *United States v. Hudson* (1812) the Court decided that the federal courts did not possess any criminal common law jurisdiction after all. Although this decision swept away a number of lower federal court precedents and reversed two decades of Federalist claims, it was probably inevitable. The issue, as the Court said, had been "long since settled in public opinion."[18]

Even in the 1807 trial of Aaron Burr, which Marshall regarded as "the most unpleasant case which has ever been brought before a Judge in this or perhaps in any other country which affected to be governed by laws," the chief justice subtly undermined earlier Federalist positions.[19] In his decision he rejected the broad definition of treason the Federalists had used in the 1790s in prosecuting the participants in the Whiskey and Fries rebellions and instead interpreted the Constitution's definition of treason narrowly. Speaking for the court, Marshall declared that conspiracy to levy war and actual levying of war against the United States were "distinct offenses," and "conspiracy is not treason." Planning to wage war, enlisting soldiers, even marching to a meeting place before an "actual assembling" of an army—these were not enough to constitute treason. In effect, Marshall ignored the arguments of the prosecution and the testimony of 140 witnesses and through his narrow interpretation of the law virtually determined by himself the outcome of the trials of Burr and his associates.[20]

The Republicans were furious. They enthusiastically supported their president who had brought the case to court and denounced Marshall for writing "a *Treatise* on the best way of committing treason without detection or punishment" and for "conniving in the escape of the traitor." By outlining the law in the way that he did to the jury, Marshall, the Republicans complained, had effectively usurped the jury's role and had undermined that sacred and popular institution. So angry were the Republicans

---

17. Smith, *John Marshall*, 284n.
18. Stephen B. Presser, *"The Original Misunderstanding": The English, the Americans, and the Dialectic of Federalist Jurisprudence* (Durham, 1991), 81, 97.
19. Marshall to Richard Peters, 23 Nov. 1807, *Papers of Marshall*, 7: 165.
20. Thomas P. Slaughter, "'The King of Crimes': Early American Treason Law, 1787–1860," in Ronald Hoffman and Peter J. Albert, eds., *Launching the "Extended Republic": The Federalist Era* (Charlottesville, 1996), 110–18; Joseph Wheelan, *Jefferson's Vendetta: The Pursuit of Aaron Burr and the Judiciary* (New York, 2005), 10.

with the decision that they overlooked the fact that Marshall had repudiated the English doctrine of constructive treason exploited by Federalists in the 1790s. All they could see in the decision was judicial arrogance and usurpation, and many vowed once again to reduce the Court "to its proper limits." For his part Jefferson thought the decision demonstrated "the original error of establishing a judiciary independent of the nation."[21] Although a Republican mob in Baltimore hanged Marshall in effigy, much of the furor over the Burr decision soon subsided.

At the very outset of his tenure as chief justice Marshall had revealed his strategy of retrenchment and conciliation and his genius for compromise while at the same time asserting the authority of the Court. He knew that the Republicans' takeover of the Congress and the presidency in 1801 posed a serious threat to the judiciary, and he meant to blunt that threat. Although some Federalists were urging Marshall and the Court to confront the Republicans directly and declare their 1802 repeal of the Judiciary Act of 1801 unconstitutional, Marshall realized that such a direct clash could seriously harm the Court. Already Republicans in Congress were daring the Court to try to disavow the repeal of the Judiciary Act. "If the Supreme Court shall arrogate this power to themselves, and declare our law to be unconstitutional, it will then behoove us to act," asserted Congressman John Nicholas of Virginia. "Our duty is clear."[22]

Some such legislative reprisal against the Court was precisely what Marshall was trying to avoid; yet he did not want simply to roll over and surrender to the Republican Congress. Hearing the case *Stuart v. Laird* in circuit court in 1802, he accepted the legitimacy of Congress's repeal of the Judiciary Act of 1801, a position later endorsed by the Supreme Court on appeal. If Marshall were to assert the Court's authority amid this Republican anti-judicial climate, he knew it had to be done subtly and obliquely. The case of *Marbury v. Madison* (1803) gave him the opportunity.

WILLIAM MARBURY was one of the "midnight judges" appointed at the last minute by President Adams to be a justice of the peace for the District of Columbia. Adams, however, left office before Marbury's commission could be delivered, and President Jefferson refused to deliver it. Marbury then brought suit in the Supreme Court seeking a writ of mandamus (a judicial command) requiring Secretary of State Madison to deliver his commission. (It was actually Secretary of State Marshall who had

---

21. Editorial Note, *United States v. Burr* (1807), *Papers of Marshall*, 7: 3–11, quotations at 9, 10; TJ to Eppes, 28 May 1807, in Ford, ed., *Writings of Jefferson*, 9: 67–68.
22. Smith, *John Marshall*, 313; Newmyer, *Marshall and the Heroic Age of the Supreme Court*, 157–75.

failed to deliver Marbury's commission on time, which made it awkward, to say the least, for Chief Justice Marshall to hear the case.) Many thought that the Court might openly challenge the authority of the president. But in a direct contest with the president the Marshall Court could only lose: if the Court refused to order Jefferson to deliver the commission, the Republicans would win by default; if, however, the Court did order the president to do so and he refused, the Court would be humiliated. The Court thus had to move in a roundabout way to assert its authority.

The Court's opinion set forth in 1803 answered several key questions. Was Marbury entitled to his commission? And if so, did the law afford him a remedy? Yes, answered Marshall to both questions. Marbury had a vested right in the office for the term fixed by statute, and the law had to provide a remedy for a violation of a vested legal right. The first officer of the nation, said Marshall, "cannot at his discretion sport away the vested rights of others." A collision with President Jefferson seemed imminent, but when Marshall asked and answered his third question he wisely evaded it. Was the remedy for this violation of Marbury's right a writ of mandamus issued by the Supreme Court? No, said Marshall. The Supreme Court could not issue such writs because Section 13 of the 1789 Judiciary Act authorizing that power was unconstitutional: Congress did not have the authority to alter the original jurisdiction of the Supreme Court contained in Section III of the Constitution.[23]

By posing the questions in this unusual order Marshall was able to make his point without having to suffer the consequences. As Jefferson and other Republicans pointed out, the Court in its final question disclaimed all cognizance of the case, but in the first two questions declared what its opinion would have been if it had had cognizance of it.[24]

Thus Marshall indirectly asserted the Court's role in overseeing the Constitution without the serious political repercussions that would have followed from a head-on collision with the Republicans. Since the American people regarded their written Constitution as "the fundamental and paramount law of the nation," wrote Marshall for the Court, then it followed that "a law repugnant to the Constitution," such as part of the 1789 Judiciary Act, "is void; and that courts, as well as other departments, are bound by that instrument."[25]

---

23. Despite Marshall's statement, the Congress, according to a distinguished constitutional scholar, had not added to the Court's original jurisdiction. See Akhil Reed Amar, *The American Constitution: A Biography* (New York, 2005), 232–33.

24. Dumas Malone, *Jefferson the President: First Term, 1801–1805* (Boston, 1970), 149.

25. *Marbury v. Madison* (1803), in William Cranch, ed., *U.S. Supreme Court Reports* (Washington, DC, 1804), 177.

Although Marshall's decision in *Marbury v. Madison* has since taken on immense historical significance as the first assertion by the Supreme Court of its right to declare acts of Congress unconstitutional, few in 1803 saw its far-reaching implications. Certainly most Republicans were not troubled by it. If Marshall wanted to circumscribe the power of his Court, as he did in the Marbury decision, then he had every right to do so. But, said Jefferson, the judiciary was not the only branch of the government that had the right to interpret the Constitution. The executive and legislature could too. To grant the courts the exclusive authority to decide what laws were constitutional, declared Jefferson in 1804, "would make the judiciary a despotic branch."[26]

Since Marshall had not explicitly claimed that the Court had an exclusive right and duty to interpret the Constitution, his assertion of judicial authority in the Marbury decision was limited and ambiguous. In fact, it was the only time in Marshall's long tenure as chief justice in which the Supreme Court declared an act of Congress unconstitutional; indeed, no other Supreme Court did so until the *Dred Scott* decision of 1857. Probably Marshall's *Marbury* decision can be best understood as another example of his policy of restraint and of getting the Court out of harm's way, even as he managed to lecture the president on the dereliction of his duty in not delivering Marbury his commission. Although the decision did make a major statement about the role of the judiciary in America's constitutional system, it did not and could not by itself create the practice of judicial review. Much more was involved.

SUBSEQUENT HISTORY has brought into question Alexander Hamilton's claim in the *Federalist* that the judiciary was the "weakest" branch of the new federal government.[27] The unelected, life-tenured judiciary grew remarkably strong, and at times became even bolder and more capable than the two elective branches in setting social policy. Certainly the federal judges, and especially the justices of the Supreme Court, precisely because they do not periodically have to face an electorate, have exercised an extraordinary degree of authority over America's society and culture. The Supreme Court not only sets aside laws passed by popularly elected legislatures but also interprets and construes the law with a freedom that sometimes is virtually legislative in scope. Nowhere else in the modern world do courts wield as much power in shaping the contours of life as the Supreme Court does in the United States.

26. Malone, *Jefferson the President: First Term*, 155.
27. AH, *Federalist* No. 78.

"Judicial review" is the usual name given to this sweeping judicial authority. But if judicial review means only the power of the Supreme Court to set aside legislative acts in violation of the Constitution, then the term is too narrow, for voiding legislation is only the most prominent part of broader manipulative or interpretative power exercised by the Court over wide areas of American life.[28]

Historians and constitutional scholars have often emphasized some early examples of judges restricting legislatures in the immediate aftermath of the Revolution. As a consequence of what some saw as legislative tyranny in the 1780s, judges in some states—New Jersey, Virginia, New York, and North Carolina, and perhaps in several others as well—gingerly and ambiguously began moving in isolated but important decisions to impose restraints on what these legislatures were enacting as law. They attempted to say to the legislatures, as Judge George Wythe of Virginia declared in 1782, "Here is the limit of your authority, and, hither, shall you go, but no further."[29] Yet cautious and tentative as they were, such attempts by the judiciary, like Wythe's opinion in Virginia, "to declare the nullity of a law passed in its forms by the legislative power, without exercising the power of that branch," were not easily justified; they raised, in the words of Wythe's Virginia colleague Judge Edmund Pendleton, "a deep, and important, and ... tremendous question, the decision of which might involve consequences to which gentlemen may not have extended their ideas."[30]

28. Some historians have claimed that the origins of the modern practice of judicial review can best be found, not in the Court of John Marshall, but in the history of the last century or so. Indeed, the term itself was apparently only coined by constitutional scholar Edward Corwin in 1910. For these revisionist studies, see Christopher Wolfe, *The Rise of Modern Judicial Review: From Constitutional Interpretation to Judge-Made Law* (New York, 1986); J. M. Sosin, *The Aristocracy of the Long Robe: The Origins of Judicial Review in America* (Westport, CT, 1989); Robert Lowry Clinton, *Marbury v. Madison and Judicial Review* (Lawrence, KS, 1989). William E. Nelson, *Marbury v. Madison: The Origins and Legacy of Judicial Review* (Lawrence, KS, 2000) is a sensible account.

29. *Commonwealth of Va. v. Caton and Others* (Nov. 1782), in Peter Call, ed., *Reports of Cases Argued and Decided in the Court of Appeals of Virginia* (Richmond, 1833), 4: 8. Philip Hamburger, *Law and Judicial Duty* (Cambridge, MA, 2008), emphasizes the degree to which English and colonial judges already exercised a broad judicial review based on their conventional assumptions about the hierarchal character of law and about the duty of judges to decide in accord with law. Hence, he contends, the American state judges who challenged legislative acts in the aftermath of the Revolution were doing nothing new. But, of course, many people thought the courts were doing something new and protested vehemently.

30. *Commonwealth of Va. v. Caton*, in Call, ed., *Reports*, 4: 17–18.

Even those who agreed that many of the laws passed by the state legislatures in the 1780s were unjust and even unconstitutional could not agree that judges ought to have the authority to declare such legislation void. Allowing unelected judges to declare laws enacted by popularly elected legislatures unconstitutional and invalid seemed flagrantly inconsistent with free popular government. Such judicial usurpation, said Richard Dobbs Spaight, delegate to the Constitutional Convention from North Carolina, was "absurd" and "operated as an absolute negative on the proceedings of the Legislature, which no judiciary ought ever to possess." Instead of being governed by their representatives in the assembly, the people would be subject to the will of a few individuals in the court, "who united in their own persons the legislative and judiciary powers," making the courts more despotic than the Roman decemvirate or of any monarchy in Europe.[31] "This," said a perplexed James Madison in 1788, "makes the Judiciary Department paramount in fact to the Legislature, which was never intended and can never be proper."[32]

Yet judicial review of some form did develop in these early decades of the new Republic. What was it? And how did it arise?

The first and most conspicuous source of something as significant and forbidding as judicial review lay in the idea of fundamental law and its embodiment in a written constitution. Almost all eighteenth-century Englishmen on both sides of the Atlantic had recognized something called fundamental law as a guide to the moral rightness and constitutionality of ordinary law and politics. Nearly everyone repeatedly invoked Magna Carta and other fundamental laws of the English constitution. Yet all these theoretical references to fundamental law could not have much day-to-day practical importance. For most this fundamental or natural law of the English constitution was seen as a kind of moral inhibition or conscience existing in the minds of legislators and others. It was so basic and primal, so imposing and political, that it was really enforceable only by the popular elective process or ultimately by the people's right of revolution. Eighteenth-century Englishmen had difficulty calling upon this fundamental law in their everyday political and legal business.[33]

The written constitutions of 1776–1777, however, gave Revolutionary Americans a concrete handle with which to grasp this otherwise insub-

31. Richard Spaight to James Iredell, 12 Aug. 1787, in Griffith J. McRee, *Life and Correspondence of James Iredell* (New York, 1857–1858), 2: 169–70.

32. Madison's Observations on Jefferson's Draft of a Constitution for Virginia, 1788, *Papers of Jefferson*, 6: 315.

33. J. W. Gough, *Fundamental Law in English Constitutional History* (Oxford, 1955, 1961), 186–90, 206, 214.

stantial fundamental law. Suddenly, with these written documents the fundamental law and the first principles that Englishmen had referred to for generations gained a new degree of explicitness and reality. The constitution in America, said James Iredell of North Carolina in 1787, had therefore become not "a mere imaginary thing, about which ten thousand different opinions may be formed, but a written document to which all may have recourse, and to which, therefore, the judges cannot witfully blind themselves."[34]

But were the judges to have an exclusive authority to examine these fundamental laws and to determine what was constitutional and what was not? All Americans agreed that the written constitution, as Edmund Pendleton conceded in 1782, "must be considered as a rule obligatory upon every department, not to be departed from on any occasion."[35] It was not immediately evident to Pendleton or to others, however, that the judiciary had any special or unique power to invoke this obligatory rule in order to limit the other departments of the government, particularly the legislatures. In other words, it was clear by the 1780s that legislatures in America were bound by explicitly written constitutions in ways that the English Parliament was not. But it was not yet clear that the courts by themselves were able to enforce those boundaries upon the legislatures.[36] Members of the Philadelphia Convention, according to Madison's notes, "generally supposed the jurisdiction given [to the Court] was constructively limited to cases of a Judiciary nature." Madison later admitted that "in the ordinary course of Government" the judiciary might interpret the laws and the Constitution, but surely, he said, it had no more right to determine the limits of the Constitution than did the executive or legislature. Both Jefferson and Madison remained convinced to the end of their lives that all parts of America's government had equal authority to interpret the fundamental law of the Constitution — all departments had what Madison called "a *concurrent* right to expound the constitution."[37]

And when the several departments disagreed in their understanding of the fundamental law, wrote Madison in *Federalist* No. 49, only "an appeal to the people themselves...can alone declare its true meaning,

34. James Iredell to Richard Spaight, 26 Aug. 1787, McRee, *Life of James Iredell*, 2: 172–76.
35. *Commonwealth of Va. v. Caton*, in Call, ed., *Reports*, 4: 17.
36. Iredell, "To the Public," 17 Aug. 1786, in McRee, *Life of Iredell*, 2: 147.
37. Max Farrand, ed., *The Records of the Federal Convention of 1787* (New Haven, 1911, 1937), 2: 430; JM, quoted in Maeva Marcus, "Judicial Review in the Early Republic," in Hoffman and Albert, eds., *Launching the "Extended Republic,"* 31; JM, "Helvidius No. II," 1793, in Guillard Hunt, ed., *The Writings of James Madison* (New York, 1900–1910), 6: 155; TJ to Spencer Roane, 6 Sept. 1819, *Jefferson: Writings*, 1425–28.

and enforce its observance." Written constitutions, including the Bill of Rights, remained for Jefferson and Madison a set of great first principles that the several governmental departments, including the judiciary, could appeal to in those extraordinary occasions of violation. But since none of these departments could "pretend to an exclusive or superior right of settling the boundaries between their respective powers," the ultimate appeal in these quasi-revolutionary situations had to be to the people themselves.[38]

In other words, many Revolutionaries and Founders still thought that fundamental law, even when expressed in a written constitution, was so fundamental, so different in kind from ordinary law, that its invocation had to be essentially an exceptional and delicate political exercise and not a part of routine judicial business.[39] This is why many of the delegates to the Philadelphia Convention in 1787 had regarded judicial nullification of legislation with a sense of awe and wonder, impressed, as Elbridge Gerry was, that "in some States, the Judges had actually set aside laws as being against the Constitution." This is also why many others in the Convention, including James Wilson and George Mason, wanted to join the judges with the executive in a council of revision (modeled on that of New York) and thus give the judiciary a double negative over the laws.[40] They considered that the power of the judges alone to declare unconstitutional laws void was too extreme, too exceptional, and too fearful an act to be used against all those ordinary unjust, unwise, and dangerous laws that were nevertheless not "so unconstitutional as to justify the Judges in refusing to give them effect."[41] This is also why some congressmen in 1792 debated establishing a regular procedure for federal judges to notify Congress officially when they declared a law unconstitutional—so nervous were they over the gravity of such an action.[42]

When the federal circuit court of Pennsylvania in 1792 in *Hayburn's Case* declared the federal Invalid Pension Act unconstitutional on the grounds that it violated the separation of powers, it did so in a hesitant and apologetic manner. What they did, the judges said, "was far from being pleasant. To be obliged to act contrary, either to the obvious directions of Congress, or to a constitutional principle, in our judgment equally

38. *Federalist* No. 49.
39. Sylvia Snowiss, *Judicial Review and the Law of the Constitution* (New Haven, 1990), 74.
40. Jeff Roedel, "Stoking the Doctrinal Furnace: Judicial Review and the New York Council of Revision," *New York History*, 69 (1988), 261–83.
41. Farrand, ed., *Records of the Federal Convention*, 1: 97, 73.
42. *Annals of Congress*, 2nd Congress, 1st Session (April, 1792), 3: 557.

obvious, excited feelings in us, which we hope never to experience again." Congress quickly modified the Pension Act in order to avoid the crisis that would result if the Supreme Court declared the act unconstitutional.[43] One newspaper that favored judicial review in *Hayburn's Case* nonetheless suggested that perhaps all the circuit court justices should be consulted before a law could be declared unconstitutional.[44]

Everyone thus sensed that setting aside legislative acts could be no ordinary matter. As Justice Samuel Chase said in *Hylton v. United States* (1796), if the constitutionality of a federal law had been "*doubtful,*" he would have been bound "to receive the construction of the legislature."[45] As late as 1800 in *Cooper v. Telfair* Associate Justices Bushrod Washington and William Paterson agreed that judicial review was an exceptional act, to be only infrequently exercised. "The presumption...must always be in favour of the validity of laws, if the contrary is not clearly demonstrated," declared Washington. For the Supreme Court "to pronounce any law void," said Paterson, there "must be a clear and unequivocal breach of the constitution, not a doubtful and argumentative implication."[46]

Thus for many Americans in the 1790s judicial review did exist, but it remained an extraordinary and solemn political action, akin to the interposition of the states suggested by Jefferson and Madison in the Kentucky and Virginia Resolutions of 1798–1799—something to be invoked only on the rare occasions of flagrant and unequivocal violations of the Constitution. It was not to be exercised in doubtful cases of unconstitutionality and was not yet accepted as an aspect of ordinary judicial activity.

THE IDEA OF FUNDAMENTAL WRITTEN LAW, important as it was, could not by itself have led to the development of America's judicial review. What in the final analysis gives significance to Americans' unusual notion of a constitution is not that it is written or that it is fundamental, but rather that it runs and is litigated in the ordinary court system. America's federal and state constitutions may be higher laws, special acts of the people in their sovereign capacity, but they are just like lowly legislative statutes in that they are implemented through the normal practice of adversarial justice in the regular courts.

43. Marcus, "Judicial Review," in Hoffman and Albert, eds., *Launching the "Extended Republic*," 36–37.
44. G. S. Rowe, "Judicial Tyrant and Vox Populi: Pennsylvanians View Their State Supreme Court, 1777–1799," *Penn. Mag. of Hist. and Biog.*, 118 (1994), 55.
45. *Hylton v. United States*, 3 Dallas 171 (1796).
46. *Cooper v. Telfair*, 4 Dallas 18 (1800).

Thus the source of judicial review lay not in the idea of fundamental law or in written constitutions, but in the transformation of this written fundamental law into the kind of law that could be expounded and construed in the ordinary court system. This transformation was made possible by Americans' exploiting the discretionary authority that English common law judges and their own colonial judges had always exercised.[47] American jurists were well aware of the complex set of rules for construing statutes that eighteenth-century English jurists, especially William Blackstone and Lord Mansfield, had created in order to fit the plethora of confused and ill-drafted parliamentary legislation into the body of the common law.[48] American judges took these rules—rules that Hamilton in *Federalist* No. 83 called "rules of *common sense*, adopted by the courts in the construction of the laws"—and applied them to both the state and federal constitutions. They in effect collapsed the earlier distinction between fundamental and ordinary law and turned constitutions into a species of statutes, super-statutes, no doubt, but statutes nonetheless. American judges could now construe the all-too-brief words of the Constitution in relation to subject matter, intention, context, and reasonableness, as if they were the words of an ordinary statute. The result was the beginning of the creation of a special body of textual exegeses and legal expositions and precedents that Americans have come to call constitutional law.

Considering the Constitution as a kind of law that was cognizable in the regular courts (and not, as in some other countries, in special constitutional courts) permitted American judges not only to expound and construe the Constitution according to existing rules of statutory construction but also to expect regular enforcement of the Constitution as if it were a simple statute.[49]

The implications of this transformation were momentous. Once the Constitution became a legal rather than a political document, judicial review, although not judicial supremacy, became inevitable.[50] The secret

47. On the common law courts' traditional authority and duty to distinguish between superior and inferior laws, see Mary Sarah Bilder, "The Corporate Origins of Judicial Review," *Yale Law Journal*, 116 (2006), 502–66; Philip Hamburger, *Law and Judicial Duty* (Cambridge, MA, 2008); and Gordon S. Wood, "The Origins of Judicial Review," *Suffolk Law Review*, 22 (1988), 1293–1307.

48. David Lieberman, *The Province of Legislation Determined: Legal Theory in Eighteenth-Century Britain* (Cambridge, UK, 1989), 16–20.

49. Gerald Gunther, "Judicial Review," in Leonard W. Levy, ed., *Encyclopedia of the American Constitution* (New York, 1986), 1055; Larry D. Kramer, *The People Themselves: Popular Constitutionalism and Judicial Review* (New York, 2004), 150, 155.

50. For the important distinction between judicial review and judicial supremacy, see Kramer, *The People Themselves*, 139–40, 143, 210.

of Marshall's success in his *Marbury* decision was his unquestioned assumption that the Constitution was simply a law.[51] Because, as he said, it was "emphatically the province and duty of the judicial department to say what the law is," treating the Constitution as mere law that had to be expounded and interpreted and applied to particular cases like a statute suggested that American judges had a special authority to interpret constitutions that other branches of the government did not possess.[52]

Jefferson would have none of this. For him the Constitution remained primarily a political document, and judges had no monopoly in interpreting it. Indeed, he believed that judges' ability to interpret any law ought to be strictly limited. Statutes ought to be precisely drawn, and judges ought to be bound by the letter of these statutes. "Relieve the judges from the rigour of text law, and permit them to wander into its equity," he said, "and the whole legal system becomes uncertain." Jefferson rejected out of hand the eighteenth-century "revolution" in jurisprudence that Blackstone and Mansfield had created in England, dismissing their efforts to construe the common law equitably and to broaden judicial discretion as dangerous to liberty. The goal of judges was supposed to be "to render the law more & more certain." The goal of Mansfield and Blackstone, according to Jefferson, had been the exact opposite. They intended "to render it more uncertain under pretense of rendering it more reasonable." Jefferson realized that these English advocates of judicial flexibility had a powerful influence on American judicial thinking and practice. Indeed, he believed there was "so much sly poison" in Mansfield's "seducing eloquence" that he wanted to forbid American courts from citing any English decisions rendered by the Court of the King's Bench since Mansfield acceded to the court. Jefferson never ceased complaining that "the honeyed Mansfieldism of Blackstone" had forced young Americans to slide into "toryism" to the point where they "no longer know what whigism or republicanism means."[53]

John Marshall thought exactly the opposite. He believed Mansfield to be "one of the greatest Judges who ever sat on any bench, & who has done more than any other to remove those technical impediments which grew out of a different state of society, & too long continued to obstruct the course of substantial justice." As the editor of the *Papers of John*

51. L. H. LaRue, *Constitutional Law as Fiction: Narrative in the Rhetoric of Authority* (University Park, PA, 1995), 56–69.
52. *Marbury v. Madison* (1803), in William Cranch, ed., *U.S. Supreme Court Reports* (Washington, DC, 1804), 177.
53. TJ to Phillip Mazzei, 28 Nov. 1785, to John Brown Cutting, 2 Oct. 1788, *Papers of Jefferson*, 9: 67–72; 13: 649; to JM, 17 Feb. 1826, *Jefferson: Writings*, 1513–14.

*Marshall* has pointed out, "Among all the various elements composing the deep-seated conflict between these two Virginians, not the least important was Jefferson's concern that an American Mansfield held the chief justiceship of the United States."[54]

ULTIMATELY, WHAT MADE ALL OF THIS new thinking about the judiciary comprehensible—what gave the judiciary equality with the legislative and executive branches in a tripartite system of government—was the Americans' peculiar conception of representation, that is, the unusual way that American people embodied themselves in the institutions of government. By the time the new federal judiciary was being established in 1789, some Federalists were even coming to regard judges as another kind of agent or representative of the people.

Such a remarkable conclusion followed from the logic of the Americans' conception that sovereignty—the final, supreme, and indivisible lawmaking authority in the state—remained with the people themselves. In England sovereignty rested in Parliament because it embodied the whole society, all the estates of the realm, within itself, but the sovereign American people were never eclipsed by their governments. They remained legally viable even after doling out bits and pieces of their power, but never all of it, to their various agents in the state and federal governments.

Only by conceiving of sovereignty as remaining with the people could Americans make sense of their new constitutional achievements such as federalism, that is, the remarkable division of power between central and provincial governments, the ideas of special constitution-making conventions, and the process of popular ratification of constitutions. This conception of sovereignty eventually made possible the emergence of unusual institutions and processes of later years, such as the primaries, referendums, recall of officials, and ballot initiatives introduced by Progressive reformers at the beginning of the twentieth century. It also made possible the idea that a judge was just another representative agent of the people.

In 1776 most Americans had initially thought of the lower houses of their new state legislatures as the exclusive embodiments of the people, which is why nearly all of them had been called the "house of representatives." During the following decade, partly as a result of the heavy criticism of their legislative abuses, the lower houses began to lose their exclusive authority as representatives of the people. Some Americans began to regard the upper houses, or senates, as being just as representative

---

54. Opinion, *Livingston v. Jefferson*, 5 Dec. 1811, *Papers of Marshall*, 7: 284; Hobson, *The Great Chief Justice: Marshall*, 37.

of the people as the lower houses. Originally, the senates had not been considered representative bodies at all. They were supposed to be composed of the wisest and most distinguished members of the society; consequently, even when they were elected, they presumably had no constituents.

It was soon apparent, however, that justifying a senate or upper house smacked of "aristocracy" and was too politically incorrect to be used publicly. Instead, those who wished to justify senates had to argue that they were simply "double representations" of the people. But if the people could be represented twice, then, of course, they could be represented in additional ways as well. As a result, many came to think of all elected officials, including senators and governors, as representatives of the people, and the term "house of representatives" became an awkward reminder that Americans had once thought of popular representation as the English had, as confined to the lower houses of their legislatures.

Regarding the legislatures as something less than a full embodiment of the people allowed the defenders of judicial authority, like Alexander Hamilton in *Federalist* No. 78, to suggest that judges were as much agents of the people as the members of the legislatures. Americans, said Hamilton, had no intention of allowing "the representatives of the people to substitute their *will* to that of their constituents." In fact, it was "far more rational to suppose, that the courts were designed to be an intermediate body between the people and the legislature, in order, among other things, to keep the latter within the limits assigned their authority." The authority of the judges to set aside acts of the legislatures, said Hamilton, did not "by any means suppose a superiority of the judicial to the legislative power. It only supposes that the power of the people is superior to both; and that where the will of the legislature declared in its statutes, stands in opposition to that of the people, declared in the constitution, the judges...ought to regulate their decisions by the fundamental laws, rather than by those which are not fundamental."[55]

In his "Lectures on Law" presented in 1790–1791 James Wilson (the first justice to take the oath of office as a member of the Supreme Court) expanded the logic of seeing all parts of the government as agents of the sovereign people. Some individuals call the legislature "the *people's representatives*," complained Wilson; they seem to imply by that term "that the executive and judicial powers are not connected with the people by a relation so strong, or near, or dear. But it is high time that we should chastise our prejudices," said Wilson, "and that we should look upon the

55. AH, *Federalist* No. 78.

different parts of the government with a just and impartial eye. The executive and judicial powers are now drawn from the same source, are now animated by the same principles, and are now directed to the same ends, with the legislative authority: they who execute, and they who administer the laws, are as much the servants, and therefore as much the friends of the people, as they who make them."[56]

Of course, only a minority as yet saw the judges as just another kind of servant of the people; but those that did were always ready to exploit the implication. Some even concluded that if the judges were really agents of the people, then they should be elected as other agents were. Although this logic would not be followed in actual practice until the middle decades of the nineteenth century, the Republican radical John Leland made this point explicitly as early as 1805. "The election of all officers, to fill all parts of the government," he said, "is the natural genius that presides over the United States.... If men are incompetent to elect their judges, they are equally incompetent to appoint others to do it for them." Judges should not be immune to the authority of the people. "A judicial monarch is a character as abhorrent as an executive or legislative monarch."[57]

In the succeeding decades many of the states, especially the new states of the West, began electing their judges. And today at least thirty-nine states elect their judges in one way or another. Certainly making the judiciary an equal part of a modern tripartite representative government in the early Republic helped to strengthen judicial authority and to justify judicial independence. This was perhaps the Federalists' greatest legacy.

ALTHOUGH MANY AMERICANS in the 1790s had come to accept most of the principles that made for an understanding of judicial review, that acceptance remained largely partisan—shared by most Federalists but not by most Republicans and probably not by the bulk of the American people.[58] To make judicial review something more than an instrument of the Federalist cause, something else was needed—some radical change in the character of adjudication, some separation of law from politics.

56. James Wilson, "Lectures on Law" (1790–1791), *The Works of James Wilson*, ed. Robert Green McCloskey (Cambridge, MA, 1967), 293.

57. William A. Robinson, *Jeffersonian Democracy in New England* (New Haven, 1916), 120.

58. For the widespread acceptance of judicial review in the 1790s, see William E. Nelson, "Changing Conceptions of Judicial Review: The Evolution of Constitutional Theory in the States, 1790–1860," *University of Pennsylvania Law Review*, 120 (1972), 1166, 1169–70; Marcus, "Judicial Review," in Hoffman and Albert, eds., *Launching the "Extended Republic,"* 25–53; Kramer, *The People Themselves*, 148.

If the higher law of the Constitution were to be brought down to the level of a lowly statute, and if setting aside statutes as unconstitutional were to be simply part of the routine business of legal interpretation and not an earthshaking political exercise, then it followed that the entire process of adjudication had to be removed from the passions and interests of politics and from legislative tampering. Somehow or other judges had to carve out for themselves an exclusive sphere of disinterested professional legal activity.

After 1800 this was precisely what happened. Judges shed their traditional broad and ill-defined political and magisterial roles that had previously identified them with the executive branch or chief magistracy and adopted roles that were much more exclusively legal. The practices of judges' politically haranguing juries from the bench and of justices' performing diplomatic missions while sitting on the Court were discontinued. Judges increasingly saw themselves as professional jurists, qualified only for hearing cases and interpreting the law.

As early as *Hayburn's Case* in 1792 the federal circuit court for the district of Pennsylvania protested Congress's Invalid Pension Act for violating the separation of powers. The act had given the judges of the United States circuit courts the administrative task of deciding the pension claims of veterans injured in the Revolutionary War. Their decisions, however, were subject to review and reversal by the secretary of war and the Congress. The circuit court, which comprised two Supreme Court justices and the district judge, refused to hear William Hayburn's petition for a pension and declared the Pension Act unconstitutional on the grounds that engaging in non-judicial activities that were subject to revision by other branches of government violated judicial independence. Although the judges apologized for their decision, they nonetheless expressed a clear understanding of their distinctive judicial status. No longer did they want to be considered as political magistrates with administrative responsibilities.[59]

With the spread of this kind of thinking judges increasingly limited their activities to the regular courts, which became more professional and less burdened by popular juries. Even at the outset the Supreme Court had avoided giving an opinion that did not arise out of actual litigation between parties. In 1790 Chief Justice John Jay refused a request from Secretary of the Treasury Hamilton for the Court to take a stand against Virginia's opposition to the federal assumption of state debts. Then again in 1793 the Court turned down President Washington's request for

---

59. Marcus, "Judicial Review," in Hoffman and Albert, eds., *Launching the "Extended Republic,"* 36–37.

extra-judicial opinions on matters relating to international law, neutrality, and the British and French treaties. Although some states continue to this day to give advisory opinions, these early refusals to offer advisory opinions helped to establish the Supreme Court and other federal courts as purely judicial bodies hearing particular litigated cases.[60]

Yet even after 1800 the withdrawal of judges from politics did not occur quickly. Of the ten justices that served between 1802 and 1823 on New York's supreme court, for example, four had tried to become governor and three had succeeded. The fact that New York's justices of the supreme court sat with the chancellor and governor on the state's peculiar council of revision (abolished in 1821) no doubt contributed to their greater political activity.

Despite these vestiges of an earlier era, more and more judges tended to avoid partisan politics and to pride themselves on their judicial expertise and impartiality. They supported the publishing of judicial opinions and the collecting of law reports. In 1798 Alexander J. Dallas published the first volume of cases decided by the Supreme Court of the United States, and in 1804 William Cranch began publication of his *Supreme Court Reports*. By the early nineteenth century the states themselves were busy publishing reports of their court decisions. By 1821 Justice Story estimated that more than 150 volumes of American reports already existed, "containing," he said, "a mass of decisions which evince uncommon ambition to acquire the highest professional character."[61]

Everywhere jurists published treatises and promoted the emergence of law as a science known best by trained impartial experts. The states tried to comply with this view by erecting new qualifications for entrance to the bar. New Hampshire required at least two years of practice before the Court of Common Pleas for admittance. In Delaware and Maryland three years of law study were needed followed by examinations. Universities added professors of law to their faculties, and some jurists called for the establishment of separate law schools to teach the new science of law. The most notable was that established by Tapping Reeve in Litchfield, Connecticut, in 1784. The founding of Harvard Law School followed in 1817. Yale's Law School grew out of the offices of New Haven lawyer Seth Staples in the 1810s.[62]

As jurists and lawyers became more professional and the law was increasingly regarded as a special science, the courts tried to avoid the most explosive

60. Charles Warren, *The Supreme Court in United States History* (Boston, 1937), 1: 52–53, 110–11.
61. Anaton-Hermann Chroust, *The Rise of the Legal Profession in America* (Norman, OK, 1965), 2: 75–77.
62. Chroust, *Rise of the Legal Profession*, 2: 36–37, 173–223.

and partisan political issues. Certainly that was the secret of much of the success of the Marshall Court in these years. Not only did the Court retreat from the advanced and exposed political positions that the Federalists had tried to stake out for the national judiciary in the 1790s, but it also sought at every turn, at least up to the War of 1812, to avoid serious confrontations with the Republicans. Even the Court's decision to issue a single anonymous "opinion of the Court" tended to dampen controversy and to give the impression of more consensus than existed in fact. In many of its decisions the Court sought to curtail governmental power—something that Marshall and other Federalists knew would be acceptable to many Republicans who were eager to expand the areas of individual freedom.

Prior to its decision in *McCulloch v. Maryland* in 1819, the Marshall Court did not attempt to build up the power of the federal government positively. That enhancement of governmental power would have aroused Republican hostility everywhere. Instead, it moved to reduce governmental power, not at the federal but at the state level. It declared a large number of *state* judicial interpretations and *state* laws invalid because they violated the national Constitution. In doing so it indirectly augmented the supremacy of the nation and its own authority as well. In a series of decisions beginning with *United States v. Peters* (1809) and *Fletcher v. Peck* (1810) and proceeding through *Martin v. Hunter's Lessee* (1816), the Supreme Court established its right to review and reverse decisions of state courts and state legislatures involving interpretations of federal law and the federal Constitution. At the same time, the Court's insistence on the rule of law binding the entire country worked to strengthen people's feeling of being citizens of the United States and not just their individual state.[63]

In the *Peters* case the Pennsylvania state legislature had ignored a federal district court decision and had claimed the right by itself to interpret federal law. In a powerful opinion Marshall declared that a state legislature could not annul the judgments of the courts of the United States in this way or else the Constitution would become "a solemn mockery." The nation, if it were to be one, had to have "the means of enforcing its laws by the instrumentality of its own tribunals." When Pennsylvania appealed to President Madison for help in resisting this judgment, Madison refused, fearing the effect it would have on the New England states that were resisting federal law.[64]

In the *Martin* case the Virginia Court of Appeals had refused to obey an earlier decision of the U.S. Supreme Court. But it also had denied the right of Congress in the Judiciary Act of 1789 to grant authority to the

---

63. Haskins, "Law Versus Politics," *University of Pennsylvania Law Review*, 130 (1981), 24.
64. Haskins and Johnson, *Foundations of Power: John Marshall*, 322–31.

Supreme Court to hear appeals from the state courts. In a masterful opinion written by Justice Joseph Story (with Marshall absenting himself because of a conflict of interest), the Court asserted the supremacy of the nation. It said that the people, not the states, had created the Constitution, and therefore they had the right to grant to the national government whatever powers they chose and to prevent the states from exercising powers they believed incompatible with the authority of the central government. From these premises the Court went on to declare that no state decision involving federal matters could be final. To enforce the supremacy clause of the Constitution and to maintain the uniformity of national law throughout the country, the Supreme Court had to have the ultimate authority to hear appeals from state courts on federal issues. This became the cornerstone of the American judicial system.

At the same time, following the test case *Fletcher v. Peck* (1810), the Court overturned a series of state laws that interfered with private contracts and thus violated Article I, Section 10 of the Constitution. The *Fletcher* case was the result of a twenty-year process of legal and political manipulations arising out of the Yazoo land scandal of the 1790s. In the early 1790s the corrupt Georgia legislature had sold thirty-five million acres of land to several Yazoo land companies for $500,000, the price adding up to something less than two cents an acre. In 1796 the outraged voters of Georgia elected a new legislature that voided the sale and burned all records of it. In the meantime, however, the speculative land companies had sold many acres to good faith buyers, many of whom were New Englanders. Confusion and lawsuits followed. The Jefferson administration tried to work out a compromise among the various interests, which enraged John Randolph, who, according to William Plumer, lashed out at everyone, "demo's and feds indiscriminately," in the most "coarse & vulgar" manner, charging everyone "with peculation, bribery, & corruption." By 1810 the Supreme Court had received a contrived case that sought to settle the whole matter, at least legally.[65]

In his opinion in the *Fletcher* case Marshall decided that the Georgia legislature's rescinding of a previous corrupt legislative sale of the Yazoo lands had violated the contract clause in Article I, Section 10 of the Constitution, and was thus invalid. The legislature's original sale, however corrupt, was in the nature of a contract that gave the buyers vested rights in the property, and no subsequent state law could divest those rights. Not only was this the first major Supreme Court decision to declare a state statute in violation

---

65. Everett Somerville Brown, ed., *William Plumer's Memorandum of Proceedings in the United States Senate, 1803–1807* (London, 1923), 269; C. Peter Magrath, *Yazoo: Law and Politics in the New Republic: The Case of Fletcher v. Peck* (New York, 1967).

of the Constitution, but Marshall also shrewdly stated that the Court had no business getting into the motives of the Georgia legislature, thus helping to underline the idea that law and politics were separate spheres.

In the *Fletcher* decision Marshall also argued that it was not simply "the particular provisions of the Constitution of the United States" that nullified the Georgia statute but also those "general principles which are common to our free institutions." The Court, he said, could draw upon these principles to protect individual property rights from the "sudden and strong passions" of the popular state legislatures. The Constitution, said Marshall, contained "what may be deemed a bill of rights for the people of each state." Justice William Johnson in a concurring opinion carried this point of fundamental principles much further. He agreed with Marshall that the state of Georgia did not have the power to revoke its grant once made. He agreed, however, not on the basis of the contract clause of the Constitution, but "on a general principle, on the reason and nature of things; a principle which will impose laws even on the Deity."[66]

These kinds of judicial appeals to reason and the nature of things became increasingly common in the early Republic. They grew out of the Americans' ambiguous and unusually instrumental attitude toward law that had its roots in the colonial period. Each of the states began developing its own non-statutory body of rules and procedures—its own common law. In place of the customs and technicalities of the English common law, the courts offered prudent and pragmatic regulations and justified them by what Connecticut jurist Jesse Root in 1798 called "the reasonableness and utility of their operation."[67] By the early decades of the nineteenth century some Americans regarded their common law as something that could be self-consciously created and manipulated, but of course only in a piecemeal fashion; indeed, some were even expanding Lord Mansfield's view that judges ought to be the chief agents of legal change. Only the courts, Zephaniah Swift, chief justice of the Connecticut supreme court, declared in 1810, "possess a discretion of shaping the rules...[and] furnishing remedies according to the growing wants, and varying circumstances of men,...without waiting for the slow progress of Legislative interference."[68]

Although most judges continued to deny that they made law in the way legislatures did, it became increasingly obvious that they did something

66. Carl Brent Swisher, *American Constitutional Development*, 2nd ed. (Cambridge, MA, 1954), 153–54; Haskins and Johnson, *Foundations of Power: John Marshall*, 597.

67. Morton J. Horwitz, *The Transformation of American Law, 1780–1860* (Cambridge, MA, 1977), 21

68. Horwitz, *Transformation of American Law*, 23.

more than simply discover it in the precedents and customs of the past. Indeed, many judges soon came to realize that they had the primary responsibility to make new law to meet new circumstances.[69] Judges could justify this extraordinary role for themselves only by claiming that they were pulling back from overt participation in politics and by designating as issues of law some particular things that were now within their special jurisdiction.[70]

Jurists and politicians in the early Republic began to draw lines around what was political or legislative and what was legal or judicial and to explain the distinctions by the doctrine of separation of powers. In his *Marbury* decision Marshall clearly drew this distinction. Some questions were political, he said; "they respect the nation, not individual rights," and thus were "only politically examinable." But questions involving the vested rights of individuals were different; they were in their "nature, judicial, and must be tried by the judicial authority."[71] By turning all questions of individual rights into exclusively judicial issues, Marshall appropriated an enormous amount of authority for the courts. After all, even Jefferson in 1789 had conceded the authority of judges, "kept strictly to their own department," to protect the rights of individuals. Of course, Jefferson had not anticipated Marshall's expansive notion of rights.[72]

Although Marshall had the extraordinary rhetorical ability to make everything he said seem natural and inevitable, his separation of law from politics would not have been possible without large numbers of influential people becoming increasingly disillusioned with the kind of legislative democracy that was emerging in the early Republic. This abhorrence of democratic politics and reliance on the judiciary were, of course, much easier for Federalists who were having more and more difficulty getting elected. As Virginia jurist St. George Tucker pointed out in his annotated edition of Blackstone's *Commentaries* of 1803, because the men of greatest talents, education, and virtue were not able to compete as well as others in the new scrambling, pushy, and interest-mongering world of popular electoral politics, they necessarily had to look to the law for security.[73]

---

69. William E. Nelson, *Americanization of the Common Law: The Impact of Legal Change on Massachusetts Society, 1760–1830* (Cambridge, MA, 1975), 172; Horwitz, *Transformation of American Law*, 23–26.

70. On this issue see Gordon S. Wood, "The History of Rights in Early America," in Barry Alan Shain, ed., *The Nature of Rights at the American Founding and Beyond* (Charlottesville, 2007), 233–57.

71. *Marbury v. Madison* (1803), in Cranch, ed., *U.S. Supreme Court Reports*, 166, 167;

72. TJ to JM, 15 March 1789, *Republic of Letters*, 587.

73. St. George Tucker, *Blackstone's Commentaries: With Notes of Reference to the Constitution and Laws of the Federal Government and of the Commonwealth of Virginia* (Philadelphia, 1803), I, pt. 1, xxv.

*George Washington* (1732–1799), by Gilbert Stuart. This portrait painted in 1797 was the one rescued by Dolley Madison in 1814 when the British burned the White House. Library of Congress.

*Alexander Hamilton* (1755–1804), by John Trumbull. Hamilton had a heroic vision of himself and the nation. As Gouverneur Morris said, "He was more covetous of glory than of wealth or power." With the growth of democracy, Hamilton rightly came to realize "that this American world was not meant for me." Library of Congress.

*John Adams* (1735–1826), by John Trumbull (1783). Oil on canvas, 77 x 61.6 cm (30 ⁵⁄₁₆ x 24 ¼ in.). Adams always felt neglected by his contemporaries, and, indeed, not until recently has he received the degree of attention as a Founder that he deserves. Harvard Art Museum, Fogg Art Museum, Harvard University Portrait Collection, Gift of Andrew Craigie to Harvard College, 1794, H73. Imaging Department © President and Fellows of Harvard College.

*Abigail Adams* (1744–1818), by Ralph Earl. Of all the wives of the leading Founders, Abigail was the most intelligent and most widely read. We are blessed with more than a thousand interesting letters between her and her husband. Fenimore Art Museum, Cooperstown, New York.

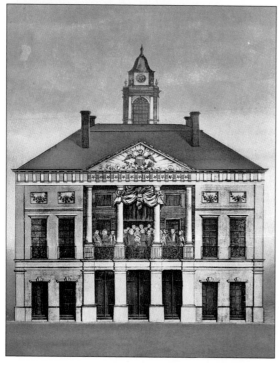

Federal Hall (1790). Originally the New York City Hall, the building was remodeled and enlarged by Pierre L'Enfant in 1788 to become the first capitol of the United States under the new federal Constitution and the site of Washington's first inauguration. It was torn down in the nineteenth century.

The Great Seal of the United States. The seal, which appears on the one-dollar bill, shows on the obverse side the coat of arms of the United States with a bald eagle holding thirteen arrows in its left talon and thirteen olive leaves in its right talon. The reverse side shows an unfinished pyramid and the eye of Providence together with several mottos drawn from Virgil. Library of Congress.

*Fisher Ames* (1758–1808), engraving after a portrait by Gilbert Stuart. Ames was a renowned Federalist orator and very influential in the Congress during much of the 1790s. Poor health forced him to leave Congress, but he continued to write against Jacobinism and Jeffersonian democracy. He died at age fifty-one in 1808. Image courtesy Darlington Memorial, Special Collections, University of Pittsburgh.

*John Jay* (1745–1829), by Rembrandt Peale and Raphaelle Peale. Few Americans contributed as much as Jay to the formation of the new nation. He not only helped draft the New York constitution and the treaty of peace with Britain, but he became as well president of the Continental Congress, secretary for foreign affairs under the Confederation, the first chief justice of the Supreme Court, and governor of New York. Courtesy of The Maryland Historical Society.

Washington reviewing the Western Army at Fort Cumberland, Cumberland, Maryland, after 1795. President Washington, believing that peace was achieved by being ready for war, always mistrusted the state militia and worked to create a regular national military establishment. Courtesy of Winterthur Museum.

*General Anthony Wayne* (1745–1796), by James Sharples, Sr. A former Revolutionary War general, Wayne had fallen on bad times and was deeply in debt. Washington's appointment of him in 1792 to reorganize the army was controversial but Wayne's success at Fallen Timbers vindicated the choice. Independence National Historical Park.

*John Quincy Adams* (1767–1848), by John S. Copley. In 1794 President Washington appointed the twenty-seven-year-old Adams as minister to The Hague, and his parents were elated. In 1809, however, when President Madison, a Republican, appointed him minister to Russia, many Federalists, including his parents, were upset.© 1796, Museum of Fine Arts, Boston.

Lyon-Griswold Brawl (1798). Outraged by this brawl on the floor of the House of Representatives, many concluded that Congress had become contemptible in the eyes of all "polite or genteel" societies. Library of Congress.

Amos Doolittle (1754–1832), *A New Display of the United States* (1799). Doolittle was a well-known American engraver, his most famous work being four prints of the battles of Lexington and Concord (1775). This engraving shows President Adams surrounded by the coats of arms of each state, with the eagle holding a banner reading "Millions for Defence, not a Cent for Tribute." Library of Congress.

Building the New Navy (1799). This print depicts the construction of the twenty-eight-gun frigate *Philadelphia*. When the ship ran aground in Tripoli Harbor in 1803, Lt. Stephen Decatur led a daring raid, boarding and burning it to prevent its being used by the Tripolitan pirates. Naval Historical Society.

*William Findley*
(1742–1821), by
Rembrandt Peale.
This pugnacious Irish
immigrant epitomized
the democratic middling
sorts who took control of
much of the culture of
the northern states in the
early nineteenth century.
When he retired from
the House of Represen-
tatives in 1817, he was
honored as the longest-
serving congressman.
Independence National
Historical Park.

*Thomas Jefferson*
(1743–1826), by
Rembrandt Peale. It is
surely the greatest irony
of American history that
this slave-holding aristocrat should be America's
supreme spokesman for
liberty, equality, and
democracy. Library
of Congress.

*Aaron Burr* (1756–1836), by John Vanderlyn. Burr is probably the most romanticized and vilified historical figure in American history—the subject of countless poems, songs, sermons, plays, and novels. Yale University Art Gallery. Bequest of Oliver Burr Jennings, B.A. 1917, in memory of Miss Annie Burr Jennings.

Washington, D.C., in 1801. The nation's capital remained for years primitive and desolate, with muddy streets, a swampy climate, and unfinished government buildings that stood like Greek temples in a deserted ancient city. Library of Congress.

*Apotheosis of George Washington* (c. 1800). This was one of the earliest depictions of
Washington ascending to heaven as a god. The most famous apotheosis of Washington
is that painted in 1865 by the Italian Constantino Brumidi in the Rotunda of the U.S.
Capitol. Courtesy of Winterthur Museum.

*Benjamin Rush* (1746–1813). Rush was the most well-known physician in the early Republic. Not only was he involved in every conceivable aspect of American culture, but he was responsible for bringing Adams and Jefferson together in their retirement, thus making possible the marvelous exchange of letters between the two ex-presidents. Library of Congress.

*Albert Gallatin* (1761–1849), by Rembrandt Peale. Gallatin, a French-Swiss immigrant, was Jefferson's and Madison's secretary of the treasury and the only official who came close to Hamilton in his understanding of public finance. After leaving the treasury, he had a long and productive career, including conducting research on the American Indians and founding the American Ethnological Society in 1842. Independence National Historical Park.

Meriwether Lewis
(1774–1809) and William
Clark (1770–1838). The
expedition across the
continent in 1803–1806
led by these two
captains was the greatest
adventure of exploration
in American history.
Independence National
Historical Park.

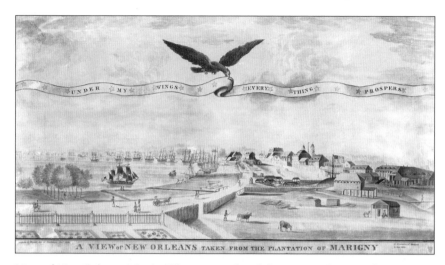

*View of New Orleans* (1803). "There is on the globe one single spot, the possessor of which is our natural and habitual enemy," said President Jefferson in 1802. "It is New Orleans, through which the produce of three-eighths of our territory must pass to market." The Mariners' Museum.

*James Wilkinson* (1757–1825), by Charles Willson Peale. Wilkinson is one of the most unscrupulous characters in American history. While commander of the U.S. Army, he remained secretly in the pay of the Spanish government. He was involved in numerous self-aggrandizing schemes, including the Burr conspiracy. Perhaps because Jefferson was one of Wilkinson's principal supporters, John Randolph called the general "the most finished scoundrel that ever lived." Independence National Historical Park.

FIAT JUSTITIA

John Marshall (1755–1835), by Rembrandt Peale. Marshall is the most famous chief justice of the Supreme Court in American history. During his long tenure on the Court from 1801 to his death, this Virginia Federalist participated in more than a thousand decisions, writing more than half himself. Collection of the Supreme Court of the United States.

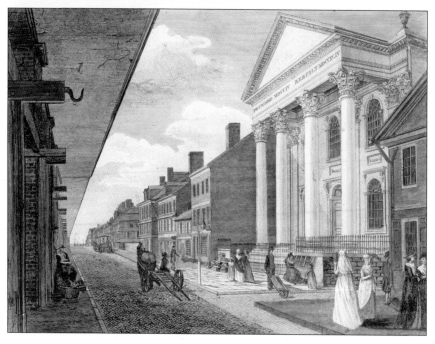

High Street, with the First Presbyterian Church (1800), by William Russell Birch. Birch was one of many British artists who migrated to the United States in the 1790s. He is most well known for his series of genre scenes of Philadelphia, designed, he said, to "show early improvements to the country" in order to encourage European immigration and investment. The Library Company of Philadelphia.

*The Artist in His Museum* (1822), by Charles Willson Peale. Peale was a painter, politician, scientist, tinker, and showman whose greatest masterpiece was his Museum. It was designed, he declared, to promote "the interests of religion and morality by the arrangement and display of the works of nature and art." The Pennsylvania Academy of Fine Arts.

*Exhuming the First American Mastodon* (1806–1808), by Charles Willson Peale. In 1806–1808 Peale painted this picture of his 1801 exhumation of the bones of a mammoth—perhaps the first organized scientific exhumation in American history. Peale displayed his mammoth in his celebrated museum and put the word "mammoth" on everyone's lips. The Peale Museum, Baltimore City Life Museums.

*Raphaelle and Titian Ramsay Peale,* by Charles Willson Peale. In a 1795 exhibition Peale displayed this famous *trompe-l'oeil* staircase portrait of two of his sons. The life-size portrait was set in a doorframe in Peale's Museum with a real wooden step built below the painted steps in order to add to the illusion; it is said that President Washington, visiting the Museum, was taken in by the illusion and courteously bowed as he passed the picture. Philadelphia Museum of Art.

Maison Carré and the Capitol at Richmond (1797). That Virginians would replicate as their new capitol in Richmond a Roman temple from the first century A.D. was a tribute to the prestige and persuasive powers of their former governor Thomas Jefferson. Shutterstock and courtesy of The Maryland Historical Society.

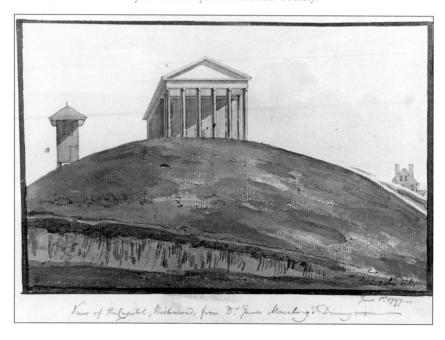

View of the Capitol, Richmond, from Dr James Maccleroy's Dining room.

President James Madison and Dolley Madison. That the slight and shy Madison, apparently a confirmed bachelor at age forty-three, married at all was surprising, but that his wife turned out to be the attractive and vivacious twenty-six-year-old widow Dolley Payne was truly remarkable. Library of Congress.

Pawtucket Bridge and Falls (1812). Thanks to the philanthropist Moses Brown (1738–1836) and the British immigrant Samuel Slater (1768–1835), Rhode Island became the center of cotton textile production in the early Republic. Courtesy of Rhode Island Historical Society.

*A Scene on the Frontier as Practiced by the Humane British and Their Worthy Allies* (1812), by William Charles (1776–1820). Charles was a Scottish-born engraver who emigrated to the United States, bringing with him the satirical techniques of the famous British caricaturists James Gillray and Thomas Rowlandson. Charles's most well-known political cartoons deal with the War of 1812. This one depicts the British encouraging the Indians to attack Americans on the Northwest frontier. Library of Congress.

*William Henry Harrison* (1773–1841), by Rembrandt Peale. Harrison came from one of the most distinguished Virginia families but made his mark in the Old Northwest both as an Indian fighter and territorial governor. He later became the ninth president of the United States. National Portrait Gallery, Smithsonian Institution/ Art Resource, NY.

Tecumseh (c. 1768–1813). Tecumseh, a Shawnee chief, was perhaps the most extraordinary Indian leader in American history. Together with his brother the Prophet he sought to unite and reform the Indians of the Northwest. He was killed fighting with the British during the War of 1812. Ohio Historical Society.

*The Capitol before 1814.* This ink and watercolor drawing attributed to Benjamin H. Latrobe was designed to display the picturesque character of the Capitol before it was burned by the British. Since it was drawn after the destruction, perhaps it was a way of emphasizing British brutality. Library of Congress.

Capture of the City of Washington. In August 1814 the British army set fire to many public buildings in the nation's capital, including the Capitol and the White House. Although burning non-military facilities was considered a violation of the laws of war, the British were probably retaliating for the Americans' burning of the Parliament and other buildings in the Canadian capital, York (Toronto), the previous year. Library of Congress.

*An Overseer Doing His Duty* (1798), by Benjamin H. Latrobe. This watercolor and ink wash, presumably depicting slavery on a farm near Fredericksburg, Virginia, seems satirical in intent. Courtesy of The Maryland Historical Society.

The Hartford Convention or LEAP NO LEAP.

*The Hartford Convention or Leap or No Leap* (1814), by William Charles.
From the beginning with Benjamin Franklin's "Join or Die" divided snake cartoon of the mid-eighteenth century, America's political cartoons were designed to influence viewers' understanding of current political events. In this case the cartoonist Charles attacks the Federalists, in particular Timothy Pickering, for being enticed by King George III to betray the United States. Above Pickering, who is praying for the success of "this great leap," Massachusetts tries to drag Connecticut and Rhode Island over the edge into secession. Library of Congress.

*Liberty Displaying the Arts and Sciences* (1790), by Samuel Jennings. Commissioned by the Library Company of Philadelphia, this was the first American painting that dealt directly with the abolition of slavery. The Library Company of Philadelphia.

*"Worldly Folk" Questioning Chimneysweeps and Their Master before Christ Church, Philadelphia* (1811–c. 1813), by John Lewis Krimmel. The German-born Krimmel was one of several artists in the early Republic who made a success of painting scenes from ordinary life, something that most serious artists scorned. The Metropolitan Museum of Art, Rogers Fund, 1942 (42.95.15). Image © The Metropolitan Museum of Art.

Shakers. The name "Shakers" was originally pejorative, mocking the religious group's rituals of trembling, dancing, and shaking. Their commitment to celibacy kept a rigid separation of the sexes, even in dancing, as this illustration shows. Library of Congress.

Lemuel Haynes (1753–1833). Haynes was the first black minister of the Congregational Church in America. He fought in the Revolutionary War and after he was ordained in 1785 he became minister of the west parish of Rutland, Vermont, where he remained for thirty years. Museum of Art, Rhode Island School of Design. Bequest of Lucy Truman Aldrich.

*Black People's Prayer Meeting* (1811–c. 1813), by John Lewis Krimmel. This genre scene by Krimmel may have been a caricature. As described by the Russian diplomat Pavel, who collected Krimmel's illustrations for his travel memoir, the black worshippers "leapt and swayed in every direction and dashed themselves to the ground, pounding with hands and feet, gnashing their teeth, all to show that the evil spirit was departing from them." The Metropolitan Museum of Art, Rogers Fund, 1942 (42.95.19). Image © The Metropolitan Museum of Art.

*Marius amid the Ruins of Carthage* (1807), by John Vanderlyn (1775–1852). Although Vanderlyn's painting, when shown in Paris, was awarded a Napoleonic gold medal, his fellow Americans were not much interested in such neoclassical works. Library of Congress.

*The City of New York* (1803), by William Russell Birch. This genre painting captures little of the dynamism of the most commercially developed city in America. Museum of the City of New York.

*Pennington Mills, Jones' Falls, Looking Upstream* (c. 1800), by Francis Guy (c. 1760–1820). Guy was a British immigrant who, though untrained in art, made a good living turning out crude landscapes by the dozens. His success infuriated serious artists and critics. College of the Maryland State Archives.

The Burning of the Richmond Theater (1812). Since the theater was associated with promiscuity and luxury, many clergymen saw this disaster, which took place on December 26, 1811, as God's punishment for America's sins. Sixty-eight people died, about 10 percent of the audience. Library of Congress.

*The United States Defeats the Macedonian*, by Thomas Birch (1779–1851). Birch, the son of William Russell Birch, concentrated on marine paintings, especially on the famous naval battles of the War of 1812. This painting depicts the battle between USS *United States* under the command of Stephen Decatur and HMS *Macedonian*. Library of Congress.

*Fourth of July in Centre Square* (c. 1810–1812), by John Lewis Krimmel. Much to the chagrin of the Federalists, and especially John Adams, the Republicans in the 1790s turned the Fourth of July into a major holiday that celebrated Thomas Jefferson as the author of the Declaration of Independence. The Pennsylvania Academy of Fine Arts.

*Travel by Stagecoach near Trenton, New Jersey* (1811–c. 1813), by Pavel Svinin. Stagecoach was the major means of travel in the early Republic. Since the coaches averaged about two to three miles per hour, the trip from New York to Philadelphia could take at least three days. The Metropolitan Museum of Art, Rogers Fund, 1942 (42.95.11). Image © The Metropolitan Museum of Art.

*Simon Snyder* (1759–1819), by Charles Willson Peale. Snyder was representative of the new democratic politicians emerging in the North in the early nineteenth century. Unpretentious and deeply religious, he won office, including the governorship of Pennsylvania, by celebrating his lack of gentility. Independence National Historical Park.

Marshall himself, like all "honest men who have honorable feelings," was increasingly "disgusted with…the political world" he saw around him, and was "much more gloomy" about the democratic future.[74] Everywhere the growth of democracy demanded the insulating of legal issues from popular politics; "for," as Marshall put it, "nothing is more to be deprecated than the transfer of party politics to the seat of Justice."[75] But even Marshall did not foresee all the implications of what was happening. In 1805, on the eve of the impeachment trial of Justice Samuel Chase, Marshall continued to concede that a legislature possessed judicial capacities and could overturn judicial opinions that it deemed unsound. So the separation of legislation from jurisprudence, politics from law, came hard to those reared in the old-fashioned tradition that legislatures were at heart just courts.

Yet, as American society became more commercial, with increasing numbers caught up in buying and selling and creating new modern sorts of property—property as venture capital, as a product of a person's labor and entrepreneurial skills—the judiciary's role in protecting property from capricious and irresponsible popular legislatures at both the state and federal levels became increasingly attractive to more and more people.[76] Consequently, many members of Jefferson's own party, who always talked about equal rights, began to accept the Marshall Court's message that all issues involving property rights were legal questions cognizable only by the courts, in effect, isolating these issues from partisan debate and the clashes of interest-group politics. Even the strongly pro-Jefferson Virginia Court of Appeals in 1804 acknowledged that the state legislature could do many things, but it could not violate private and vested rights of property.[77]

But could the state itself create private property? State legislatures could grant charters of incorporation, but once vested in individuals did these charters become rights that could no longer be touched by the granting agency? These questions bedeviled the politics of the states and eventually produced one of the most important legal developments of the first decade and a half of the Marshall Court.

AMERICANS WERE FAMILIAR with the use of public corporate charters. In the past the English crown and the colonial governments had

---

74. Marshall to C. C. Pinckney, 21 Nov. 1802, *Papers of Marshall*, 6: 125.
75. Marshall to Timothy Pickering, 28 Feb. 1811, *Papers of Marshall*, 7: 270.
76. Horwitz, *Transformation of American Law*, 31–62. For Marshall's conception of property, see Richard A. Brisbin Jr., "John Marshall and the Nature of Law in the Early Republic," *Va. Mag. of Hist. and Biog.*, 98 (1990), 62–71; Edward S. Corwin, "The Basic Doctrine of American Constitutional Law," *Michigan Law Review*, 12 (1914), 247–76.
77. Haskins, "Law Versus Politics," 19–20.

often granted monopolistic charters of incorporation to private persons and associations to carry out a wide variety of endeavors presumably beneficial to the whole society, such as founding a colony, maintaining a college, or creating a bank. In 1606 the English crown had given just such a charter to the Virginia Company to settle parts of North America. These corporate privileges had not been frequently granted or widely available; they had been made at the initiative of the government, not private interests; and they had recognized no sharp distinction between public and private. Although the Virginia Company had been composed of private entrepreneurs, it was as much public as it was private. The same was true of the seventeenth-century corporate charters of Massachusetts Bay, Connecticut, and Rhode Island, as well as those of Harvard, Yale, Dartmouth, and all the other colonial colleges. Although in the nineteenth century most of the colleges, especially those with religious affiliations, eventually became private institutions, at the time of the Revolution they were still regarded as public institutions with communal responsibilities, and as such they received tax money and public support.

Since these corporate charters tended to be exclusive monopolies given to a favored few, most of the American Revolutionary leaders in 1776 had viewed them with suspicion. In a republic, they believed, no person should be allowed to exploit the public's authority for private gain. Consequently, several of the states had written into their Revolutionary constitutions prohibitions against any man or group of men receiving special privileges from the community. The Massachusetts constitution of 1780, for example, had stated that "no man, nor corporation, or association of men, have any other title to obtain advantages, or particular and exclusive privileges, distinct from the those of the community, than what arises from the consideration of services rendered to the public."

Although the new Revolutionary states had expected to involve themselves directly in economic life and education, they soon discovered that what they wanted to do was more than they could handle, both administratively and fiscally. Because the new democratically elected legislatures were often unwilling to raise taxes to pay for all that the governmental leaders desired to do, the states were forced to fall back on the traditional premodern practice of enlisting private wealth to carry out public ends. Instead of doing the tasks themselves, as many devout republicans had expected, the states ended up doing what the crown and all pre-modern governments had done—granting charters of incorporation to private associations and groups to carry out a wide variety of endeavors presumably beneficial to the public, in banking, transportation, insurance, education, and other enterprises. The states did not intend to abandon their republican responsibility to promote the public good; they simply lacked the money to do it directly.

And of course there were many private interests that were only too eager to acquire these presumably exclusive corporate privileges.

Yet because of a republican aversion to chartered monopolies, the creation of corporations in the years following the Revolution provoked strenuous opposition and heated debate. In these decades attempts by the states to grant such corporate privileges to select individuals and groups immediately raised storms of protest.[78] Critics charged that such grants, even when their public purpose seemed obvious, such as those for the College of Philadelphia or the Bank of North America or the city of Philadelphia, were repugnant to the spirit of American republicanism, "which does not admit of granting peculiar privileges to any body of men." Such franchises and privileged grants may have made sense in monarchies as devices serving "to circumscribe and limit absolute power." Certainly the colonists had seen their various crown and corporate charters in just this defensive way. But now that only the people ruled, these grants of corporate privileges seemed pernicious, for, as Justice John Hobart of New York declared, "all incorporations imply a privilege given to one order of citizens which others do not enjoy, and are so far destructive of the principle of equal liberty which should subsist in every community."[79]

As a consequence of this kind of opposition, these corporations were radically transformed. As American society, in the North at least, spawned a variety of interests and became more democratic, it became increasingly difficult for the state legislatures to resist appeals to bestow these corporate privileges ever more widely, especially since many of their members were themselves involved in the businesses they were incorporating. With a huge proportion of the representatives in the state legislatures turning over annually, each special interest in society began clamoring for its own cluster of legal privileges. Eventually the corporate charter became, as James Sullivan of Massachusetts complained in 1792, merely "an indulgence to a few men in the state, who happened to ask the legislature to grant it to them."[80] What one community or group of

---

78. When in the Philadelphia Convention James Madison proposed that the federal government be given the explicit power to grant charters of incorporation, the Framers decided to finesse the issue by saying nothing in the Constitution about incorporations out of fear of arousing popular opposition to "mercantile monopolies." Frank Bourgin, *The Great Challenge: The Myth of Laissez-Faire in the Early Republic* (New York, 1989), 44.

79. *Pennsylvania Packet*, 2, 10 Sept. 1783, 7, 23 Aug., 25 Sept. 1786; Hendrik Hartog, *Public Property and Private Power: The Corporation of the City of New York in American Law, 1730–1870* (Chapel Hill, 1983), 90.

80. [James Sullivan], *The Path to Riches: An Inquiry into the Origin and Use of Money; and into the Principles of Stocks and Banks* (Boston, 1792), 37–38, 10, 43.

entrepreneurs had, others wanted as well, and so the corporate charters multiplied in ever increasing numbers.

Only about a half-dozen business corporations had been chartered in the entire colonial period. Now such corporate grants for businesses virtually turned into popular entitlements. The legislatures incorporated not just banks but insurance companies and manufacturing concerns, and they licensed entrepreneurs to operate bridges, roads, and canals. The states issued 11 charters of incorporation between 1781 and 1785, 22 more between 1786 and 1790, and 114 between 1791 and 1795. Between 1800 and 1817 they granted nearly 1,800 corporate charters. Massachusetts alone had thirty times more business corporations than the half dozen or so that existed in all of Europe. New York, the fastest-growing state, issued 220 corporate charters between 1800 and 1810.

It seemed clear as early as 1805, as a committee of New York City justifying multiple ferry leases put it, that "the only effectual method of accommodating the public is by the creation of rival establishments." "Thus," as one American noted in 1806, "if two baking companies are thereby permitted, where there was but one, bread may be cheaper in consequence; or if there are two banks thus instituted, and neither of them taxed, more of the people will be favoured by loans, than where there is but one bank; and a further increase will reduce even *the rate of interest*." Competition among corporations, including literary and scientific bodies, now seemed the best way of promoting the welfare of the whole community. In other words, the thinking behind the Charles River Bridge decision of the Supreme Court in 1837—that competition among corporations was good for the public—was already present a generation earlier.[81]

Eventually the pressure to dispense these corporate charters among special interests became so great that some states sought to ease the entire process by establishing general incorporation laws. Instead of requiring special acts of the legislature for each charter specifying the persons, location, and capitalization involved, the legislatures opened up the legal privileges to all who desired them. Beginning first with religious associations in the 1780s, the states, led by New York in 1811, extended the privileges of corporation to manufacturers, and later to banks and other entrepreneurial activities. With this multiplication not only was the traditional exclusivity of the corporate charters destroyed, but the public power

81. Thomas Cochran, *Frontiers of Change: Early Industrialization in America* (New York, 1981), 21; Hartog, *Public Property and Private Power*, 153; [Samuel Blodget], *Economica: A Statistical Manual for the United States of America* (Washington, DC, 1806), 17; Johann A. Neem, *Creating a Nation of Joiners: Democracy and Civil Society in Early National Massachusetts* (Cambridge, MA, 2008), 62.

of the state governments was dispersed. As early as 1802, James Sullivan, the perennial Massachusetts attorney general, warned that "the creation of a great variety of corporate interests...must have a direct tendency to weaken the powers of government." But the numbers only increased to the point where the governor of Massachusetts expressed the fear that so many corporate grants were being created "unsparingly and with an unguarded hand" that there was a real danger of the state government's ending up with "only the very shadow of sovereignty."[82]

Since many states were bewildered by the nature of these multiply-ing corporations—Were they public, were they private? Could the charters be revoked after they were granted? Were they vested rights?—the Supreme Court sooner or later had to try to sort the matter out.

In 1804 the Marshall Court grappled with the nature of a corporation for the first time. In *Head v. Providence Insurance Company*, Marshall stressed the traditional view of a corporation, that it was a public entity that presumably could be changed by the legislature that originally char-tered it. By a corporation the Court meant all entities chartered for public purposes—towns, turnpikes, canals, insurance companies, and colleges.

This stress on the need for a "public purpose" behind the state's activity, however, eventually forced the Supreme Court in *Terrett v. Taylor* (1815) to separate corporations into two kinds, public and private, a distinction new to American law. Legislatures could modify charters of public corporations, declared Justice Joseph Story, who wrote the decision; but such public cor-porations included only counties, towns, and cities. The charters of all the other corporations, including businesses and colleges, were private prop-erty. In overturning a Virginia statute in *Terrett*, Story's decision concluded by saying that "we think ourselves standing upon the principles of natural justice, upon the fundamental laws of every free government, upon the spirit and letter of the constitution of the United States, and upon the deci-sions of most respectable judicial tribunals." Story, however, never specified what "letter" of the Constitution he was referring to.[83]

If corporations such as banks and other businesses were indeed private, and not public, then it could be intelligibly argued that their charters

82. Oscar and Mary Handlin, *Commonwealth: A Study of the Role of Government in the American Economy: Massachusetts, 1774–1861* (Cambridge, MA, 1947, 1969), 106–33; E. Merrick Dodd, *American Business Corporations until 1860, with Special Reference to Massachusetts* (Cambridge, MA, 1954); Ronald E. Seavoy, *The Origins of the American Business Corporation, 1784–1855: Broadening the Concept of Public Service During Industrialization* (Westport, CT, 1982); Pauline Maier, "The Revolutionary Origins of the American Corporation," *WMQ*, 50 (1993), 68–69.

83. Sylvia Snowiss, "Text and Principle in John Marshall's Constitutional Law: the Cases of *Marbury* and *McCullough*," *John Marshall Law Review*, 33 (2000), 990.

were actually kinds of private property protected from subsequent violation or regulation by state authority. No one doubted the capacity of the
legislature to take private property for public purposes with compensation, that is, using the power of eminent domain, but this power, it was
now argued, could not be extended so far as to abridge rights expressly
vested prior to the legislature's assertion of its power — at least not without
some sort of compensation for such abridgements.[84] "In granting charters," declared William Robinson in the Pennsylvania assembly in 1786 in
defense of the charter of the Bank of North America, "the legislature acts
in a ministerial capacity"; that is, it acted as the crown had acted in mobilizing private resources for public purposes. This bestowing of charters,
said Robinson, "is totally distinct from the power of making laws, and it is
a novel doctrine in Pennsylvania that they can abrogate those charters so
solemnly granted." There was a difference between laws and charters.
Laws were general rules for the whole community; charters, argued Robinson, "bestow particular privileges upon a certain number of people.... Charters are a species of property. When they are obtained, they
are of value. Their forfeiture belongs solely to the courts of justice."[85] It
was a strained, premature argument, and it did not immediately take
hold; but it pointed the way to the future.

By 1802 Hamilton was contending that legislatures could not violate charters once granted. "The proposition, that a power to do, includes virtually, a
power to undo, as applied to a legislative body," he wrote, "is generally but
not universally true. All *vested rights* form an exception to the rule."[86] When
state legislatures in North Carolina, Virginia, Massachusetts, and New
Hampshire tried to change the charters of colleges they had once granted,
the boards of trustees contended that their charters were vested rights that
could no longer be tampered with. Yet many believed that institutions chartered to fulfill a public purpose had to be responsible to the public. "It seems

---

84. In 1776 most of the Revolutionary state constitutions did not provide for just
    compensation for the public taking of private property; but, following the adoption of
    the Fifth Amendment to the federal Constitution in 1791, this provision was explicitly
    added in nearly all the constitutions of states subsequently admitted to the Union,
    and where it was absent from the constitutions of the original states, judicial
    interpretation often inserted it. J.A.C. Grant, "The 'Higher Law' Background of the
    Law of Eminent Domain," *Wisconsin Law Review*, 6 (1930–1931), 70.
85. Mathew Carey, ed., *Debates and Proceedings of the General Assembly of
    Pennsylvania*...(Philadelphia, 1786), 11–12.
86. AH, "The Examination," 23 Feb. 1802, *Papers of Hamilton*, 25: 533. Edward S. Corwin
    called the protection of vested rights "the basic doctrine of American constitutional
    law." Corwin, "The Basic Doctrine of American Constitutional Law," *Michigan Law
    Review*, 12 (1914), 247–76.

difficult to conceive of a corporation established for merely private purposes," declared a North Carolina judge in 1805. "In every institution of that kind the ground of the establishment is some public good or purpose to be promoted."[87] With so many contrary legal arguments flying about, the issue had to be resolved at the highest judicial level.

The stage was set for the famous case *Dartmouth College v. Woodward*, decided by the Supreme Court in 1819. Dartmouth College had been incorporated by a royal charter in 1769. In 1815 the trustees of the college, who were Congregationalists and Federalists, removed John Wheelock, who was a Presbyterian and Republican, from the presidency of the college. Wheelock appealed to the legislature of New Hampshire, which revoked the old charter of 1769 and created a new corporation, Dartmouth University, with a new set of trustees who reinstated Wheelock to the presidency. The old Federalist trustees sued, arguing that the state legislature had violated their vested rights. The state supreme court rejected their argument, declaring in traditional fashion that Dartmouth was a public corporation subject to state control and regulation in the public interest. This decision was appealed to the Supreme Court of the United States.

In his creative decision Marshall contended that Dartmouth was a private corporation as defined by Story in *Terrett v. Taylor*. He then went on to declare (he said "it can require no argument") that the college's original charter was a contract under Article I, Section 10 of the United States Constitution and was thus immune to any state violation.[88] Although Marshall's reference to the text of the Constitution had often been peculiar to him and not generally shared by his colleagues on the Court, the idea that a charter was a kind of contract had been part of Federalist thinking for several decades. In 1802 New York senator Gouverneur Morris had used the presumed similarity of a charter and a contract to oppose the Jeffersonian Republicans' elimination of the circuit court positions created by the Federalists in the Judiciary Act of 1801. When you give an individual the right to make a toll road or bridge, said Morris, "can you, by a subsequent law, take it away? No; when you make a compact, you are bound by it."[89]

87. Harry N. Scheiber, "Public Rights and the Rule of Law in American Legal History," *California Law Review*, 72 (1984), 217–51; Neem, *Creating a Nation of Joiners*, 58–64; John S. Whitehead, *The Separation of College and State: Columbia, Dartmouth, Harvard, and Yale, 1776–1876* (New Haven, 1973), 16–21.

88. R. Kent Newmyer, *Supreme Court Justice Joseph Story: Statesman of the Old Republic* (Chapel Hill, 1985), 127–37; Newmyer, *Marshall and the Heroic Age of the Supreme Court*, 246–50.

89. *Debates in the Senate of the United States on the Judiciary During the First Session of the Seventh Congress* (Philadelphia, 1802), 39; Snowiss, "Text and Principle in John Marshall's Constitutional Law," *John Marshall Law Review*, 33 (2000), 991–92.

Although Marshall and his Court could scarcely have grasped the momentous implications for American business of their Dartmouth College decision, the decision did result in placing all private corporations under the protection of the United States Constitution. All private corporations, not just the four dozen or so educational institutions existing in 1819, but the hundreds of business corporations that had been created since the Revolution, had become different from their monarchical predecessors: most were no longer exclusive monopolies, and most were no longer public. They became private property belonging to individuals, not the state.

When Jefferson learned as early as 1816 of the argument the Federalist attorneys, including Daniel Webster, were making—that corporations created vested rights immune to subsequent legislative changes—he was furious. He could not believe that such an idea had any standing whatsoever. The notion that charters once publicly granted were beyond legislative tampering "may be a salutary provision against the abuses of a monarch," he told Governor William Plumer of New Hampshire, "but is most absurd against the nation itself." Such a doctrine, inculcated by "our lawyers and priests," he said, supposed "that preceding generations held the earth more freely than we do; had a right to impose laws on us, unalterable by ourselves, and that we, in like manner, can make laws and impose burdens on future generations, which they will have no right to alter; in fine, that the earth belongs to the dead and not the living."[90]

THERE WAS A CURIOUS PARADOX in these legal developments. Just as the private rights of individuals expanded in these years of the early Republic, so too did the public power of the states and municipal governments. Despite the generous bestowal of corporate charters on private interests, the republican belief that the government should have a distinct and autonomous sphere of public activity remained strong, especially among the new states west of the Appalachian Mountains.[91] Even in the

---

90. TJ to William Plumer, 21 July 1816, in L and B, eds., *Writings of Jefferson*, 15: 46–47. By the early 1820s Jefferson had come to believe that the federal judiciary, far from being what Hamilton had called "the least dangerous" branch, had "become the most dangerous branch" of the U.S. government, "sapping, by little and little, the foundations of the constitution, and working its change by construction. " AH, *Federalist* No. 78; TJ to M. Coray, 31 Oct. 1823, in L and B, eds., *Writings of Jefferson*, 15: 486–87.

91. Sandra F. VanBurkleo, "'The Paws of Banks': The Origins and Significance of Kentucky's Decision to Tax Federal Bankers, 1818–1820," *JER*, 9 (1989), 480–87; Sandra F. VanBurkleo, "'That Our Pure Republican Principles Might Not Wither': Kentucky's Relief Crisis and the Pursuit of Moral Justice, 1818–1826" (Ph.D. diss., University of Minnesota, 1988), ch. 6.

older states many Americans retained a republican faith in the power of government to promote the public good. Those who sought to protect the rights of individuals and private corporations did not deny the public prerogatives of the states. In fact, the heightened concern for the private vested rights of persons was a direct consequence of the enhanced public power the republican Revolution had given to the states and municipalities. Although the power of the federal government certainly declined in the decades following Jefferson's election as president, the public authority, the police powers, and the regulatory rights of the states and their municipalities grew stronger.

Separating the political from the legal, the public from the private individual, actually allowed for more vigorous state action as long as that action remained within the public realm and served what was called a "public purpose." Individuals may have had rights, but the public had rights as well—rights that grew out of the sovereignty of the state and its legitimate power to police the society. The state of New York, for example, remained deeply involved in the social and economic spheres. Not only did the state government of New York distribute its largess to individual businessmen and groups in the form of bounties, subsidies, stock ownership, loans, corporate grants, and franchises, but it also assumed direct responsibility for some economic activities, including building the Erie Canal.[92]

Even when the states began dissipating their newly acquired public power by reverting to the pre-modern practice of enlisting private wealth to carry out public ends by issuing increasing numbers of corporate charters, they continued to use their ancient police power to regulate their economies. Between 1780 and 1814 the Massachusetts legislature, for example, enacted a multitude of laws regulating the marketing of a variety of products—everything from lumber, fish, tobacco, and shoes, to butter, bread, nails, and firearms. The states never lost their inherited responsibility for the safety, economy, morality, and health of their societies.[93] The idea of a public good that might override private rights remained alive.

Despite all this state police power legislation and regulation, however, it was usually left to the courts to sort out and mediate the conflicting claims of public authority and the private rights of individuals. The more the state legislatures enacted statutes to manage and regulate the economy,

92. L. Ray Gunn, *The Decline of Authority: Public Economic Policy and Political Development in New York, 1800–1860* (Ithaca, 1988).

93. William J. Novak, *The People's Welfare: Law and Regulation in Nineteenth-Century America* (Chapel Hill, 1996), 15, 88.

the more judges found it necessary to exert their authority in order to do justice between individuals and make sense of what was happening. Precisely because of the exuberantly democratic nature of American politics, the judiciary right from the nation's beginning acquired a special power that it has never lost. By protecting the rights of minorities of all sorts against popular majorities, it has become a major instrument for both curbing that democracy and maintaining it.

# 13

# Republican Reforms

Despite all the increased violence and rioting, despite all the anxiety over America's climate, despite all the hand-wringing over so much licentiousness spreading everywhere, by the early nineteenth century most Americans continued to remain extraordinarily confident and optimistic about the future. They could readily respond to the overweening enthusiasm of poet and diplomat Joel Barlow in his Fourth of July oration of 1809. Public speakers on such memorable occasions, said Barlow, were called upon "to give utterance to the feelings of their fellow citizens," and that he intended to do. America, he said, had passed its infancy and was now looking forward confidently to its adolescence and its manhood. Providence had assigned Americans a special destiny, a theme iterated over and over in these years. The country was not only new to its own people, "but new also to the world." America required thoughts and principles different from those of the Old World. "There has been no nation either ancient or modern that could have presented human nature in the same character as ours does and will present it; because there has existed no nation whose government has resembled ours ... a representative democracy on a large scale, with a fixed constitution." The United States, said Barlow, was "the greatest political phenomenon, and probably will be considered as the greatest advancement in the science of government that all modern ages have produced."

But, Barlow added, Americans could not rest on their future promise; they had to work to achieve it. "Nations are educated like individual infants. They are what they are taught to be." Monarchies could exist with a corrupt and ignorant people, but republics could not. In order to sustain their republic, Americans had realized from the outset of the Revolution that they would have to throw off their older monarchical habits and thoughts and make themselves over. But they had every reason to believe that they were equipped to do so.[1]

---

1. Joel Barlow, *Oration, Delivered at Washington, July Fourth, 1809; at the Request of the Democratic Citizens of the District of Columbia* (Washington, DC, 1809), 3–6, 9.

They knew—their modern assumption lying at the heart of the Enlightenment told them so—that culture was something constructed, something made by people; and thus they could solve any problem by remaking what they thought and believed. If they could remake something in the physical world as intractable as the climate, then reforming something as man-made as their culture seemed much less challenging. Since free and republican America was "in a plastic state," where "everything is new & yielding," the country, said Benjamin Rush, "seems destined by heaven to exhibit to the world the perfection which the mind of man is capable of receiving from the combined operation of liberty, learning, and the gospel upon it."[2]

At the heart of the Revolution lay the assumption that people were not born to be what they might become. By exploiting the epistemology of John Locke, Americans had concluded that a child's mind was a blank slate, or, as one Quaker schoolmaster in 1793 called it, "soft wax." And since "the mind of the child is like soft wax, which will take the least stamp you put on it, so let it be your care, who teach, to make the stamp good, that the wax be not hurt."[3] Since, as Locke had democratically concluded, all knowledge came from the senses, and since, unlike reason, everyone was equally capable of receiving impressions through his or her senses, all young people could be molded to be whatever the teacher wanted them to be.[4]

And so Americans in the years following their Revolution set about reforming and republicanizing their society and culture. They aimed to continue the enlightened developments of the eighteenth century—to push back ignorance and barbarism and increase politeness and civilization. Indeed, as citizens of a popular-based republic, they needed more enlightenment than ever before. All aspects of life had to be republicanized—not only the society but also the literature, arts, law, religion, medicine, and even the family. One American even proposed the creation of a republican system of mathematics.

Many Americans, of course, had their hopes for the future mingled with doubts over their ability to become truly republican. Many of their

2. Donald J. D'Elia, "Dr. Benjamin Rush and the American Medical Revolution," American Philosophical Society, Proc., 110 (1966), 70, 101.

3. Jacqueline S. Reinier, "Rearing the Republican Child: Attitudes and Practices in Post-Revolutionary Philadelphia," WMQ, 39 (1982), 155.

4. In a number of extraordinary novels written in the 1790s the writer Charles Brockden Brown explored what the unreliability of sense impressions could mean for the spread of "falsehood and dissimulation" in America. Colin Jeffery Morris, "To 'Shut Out the World': Political Alienation and the Privatized Self in the Early Life and Works of Charles Brockden Brown, 1776–1794," JER, 24 (2004), 624.

hopes went unfulfilled; many of their reforms were foiled or compromised. Still, what is most impressive is the confidence that so many Revolutionary leaders expressed in their capacity to make over their society. The result was an outburst of reform sentiment that has been rarely duplicated in American history.

AMERICANS KNEW "that the mode of government in any nation will always be moulded by the state of education. The throne of tyranny," they told themselves, "is founded on ignorance. Literature and liberty go hand in hand."[5] It was the want of education that kept the mass of mankind in darkness and prejudice, in idleness and poverty, in paganism and barbarism. As the Massachusetts constitution of 1780 had stated, "Wisdom and knowledge, as well as virtue diffused generally among the people...[are] necessary for the preservation of their rights and liberties." But more was needed. If Americans were to sustain their republican experiment and remain a free and independent people, they must be taught not just their rights but also their duties as citizens. They must be educated in their moral obligations to the community.

The consequence of these attitudes was an unprecedented post-Revolutionary spate of speeches and writings on the importance of education. On the eve of the Revolution none of the colonies except those in New England had publicly supported schools. Even in New England the support had not been uniform: many of the towns had failed to meet their obligations to erect common or petty schools, and many more had refused to maintain the Latin grammar schools that prepared young boys for college. Many towns, such as Worcester, Massachusetts, in 1767, had urged their representative in the legislature "to relieve the people of the Province from the great burden of supporting so many Latin grammar schools."[6] And, of course, no parents in Massachusetts were required to send their children to school: the compulsion, such as it was, applied only to the towns to maintain petty or grammar schools.

Elsewhere in the colonies education had been very spotty. In New York, Philadelphia, and other coastal towns religious charity schools were the common institutions of elementary learning. Although a minister or some other patron could sponsor the education of a bright child, in all the colonies outside of New England education still remained solely the responsibility of parents. Sometimes parents hired itinerant freelance teachers or,

5. Simeon Doggett, A Discourse on Education (1797), in Frederick Rudolph, ed., Essays on Education in the Early Republic (Cambridge, MA, 1965), 155–56.
6. James Axtell, The School upon a Hill: Education and Society in Colonial New England (New Haven, 1974), 184.

like many of the Southern planters, employed Northern college graduates or indentured servants to tutor their children. Few children received
any formal education beyond learning to read and write.

Nine colleges had existed on the eve of the Revolution, and some of
them struggled to survive. Few Americans, in fact, attended college; only
about half of the members of the First Congress in 1789 had gone to college. The nine colleges together awarded fewer than two hundred B.A.
degrees a year, which is why Benjamin Rush called them the "true nurs-
eries of power and influence." At Columbia College's commencement in
May 1789 only ten students received B.A. degrees.[7]

Following the Revolution Americans began adding more colleges to
the original nine, and by 1815 they had created twenty-four more.
Soon colleges—mostly religiously inspired and short-lived—began to
be created by the dozens.[8] Everybody now wanted colleges, including
the first six presidents who repeatedly urged the creation of a national
university.

But colleges were supposed to train only gentlemen—a tiny proportion
of the society. Many leaders believed that it was the general populace
above all that needed to be educated and at the state's expense. The
Northwest Ordinance of 1787, organizing the territory north of the Ohio
River, expressed the general Revolutionary commitment to education. It
decreed that "religion, morality, and knowledge being necessary to good
government and the happiness of mankind, schools and the means of
education shall forever be encouraged." Six of the sixteen state constitutions formed before 1800 called explicitly for public aid to education. In
1784 New York created a board of regents to oversee a single comprehensive system of schools, pledging support for Columbia College and such
other schools as the regents might create. Massachusetts made similar
plans for a comprehensive three-tiered system of education building on
its earlier colonial legislation.[9]

Of all the Founders, Jefferson worked out the most detailed plans for
reforming the government and society of his state. Through extensive
changes in inheritance, landowning, religion, administration, and law, he
hoped to involve the people of Virginia personally in the affairs of

7. William Smith, *The History of the Province of New York*, ed. Michael Kammen
   (Cambridge, MA, 1972), 194.
8. Donald Tewksbury, *The Founding of American Colleges and Universities Before the
   Civil War* (New York, 1932).
9. BR, "Education Agreeable to a Republican Form of Government" (1786), in Dagobert
   D. Runes, ed., *The Selected Writings of Benjamin Rush* (New York, 1947), 98–99, 92;
   Lawrence A. Cremin, *American Education: The National Experience, 1783–1876*
   (New York, 1980), 116–17.

government. But nothing was more important to him than his plans for a state-supported system of education.[10] In his 1779 Virginia Bill for the More General Diffusion of Knowledge he, like Rush, proposed a three-tiered pyramid of local education. At the base would be three years of free elementary schools for all white children, boys and girls. The next level offered twenty regional academies with free tuition for selected boys "raked from the rubbish annually." Finally, the state would support the best ten needy academic students at the university level, the aristocracy of talent that he described as "the most precious gift of nature."[11]

Everywhere intellectual leaders drew up liberal plans for educating the American people. Unlike in England, where conservative aristocrats opposed educating the masses out of fear of promoting dissatisfied employees and social instability, American elites generally endorsed education for all white males.[12] In a republic that depended on the intelligence and virtue of all citizens, the diffusion of knowledge had to be widespread. Indeed, said Noah Webster, education had to be "the most important business in civil society."[13]

Most of the educational reformers in these years were less interested in releasing the talents of individuals than, as Benjamin Rush put it, in rendering "the mass of the people more homogeneous" in order to "fit them more easily for uniform and peaceable government." Pupils should be taught that they did not belong to themselves but were "public property." It was even "possible," said Rush, "to convert men into republican machines."[14] Even Jefferson, despite his emphasis on guarding the freedom and happiness of individuals, was more interested in promoting social unity and the public good.

Yet in the decades immediately following the Revolution, few of these elaborate educational plans came to fruition. Virginia repeatedly tried to erect a comprehensive school system along Jeffersonian lines, but the expense of such a system and the dispersed population prevented legislative adoption. In 1796 the Virginia legislature at least approved the creation of a system of elementary schools but left it to each county court to implement, in Jefferson's opinion, effectively allowing the county courts to emasculate what the legislature had promised.

10. TJ said as much in a letter to George Wythe, 13 Aug. 1786, *Papers of Jefferson*, 10: 244.
11. Dumas Malone, *Jefferson the Virginian* (Boston, 1948), 282–83.
12. Carl F. Kaestle, *Pillars of the Republic: Common Schools and American Society, 1780–1860* (New York, 1983), 33–35.
13. Noah Webster, *On the Education of Youth in America* (1790), in Rudolph, ed., *Essays on Education*, 59.
14. BR, "Of the Mode of Education Proper in a Republic" (1798), in Runes, ed., *Selected Writings of Rush*, 90, 88.

Elsewhere religious jealousies and popular opposition to tax increases for schools that still seemed to benefit only elites undermined support for comprehensive school systems. Too many ordinary farmers and artisans did not want their children compelled to go to school all day; they needed their labor at home. When little happened as a result of the 1784 act in New York, the state legislature tried again in 1795 and in 1805 to encourage the establishment of a comprehensive school system. Although many gentry leaders urged the need for public education, the public remained skeptical. Consequently, schooling continued in nearly all the states to be largely a private matter. In place of the elaborate plans for publicly supported education, reformers had to make do with privately supported charity schools, Sunday schools, and infant schools.

Even in New England, with its long tradition of public education, privately supported academies sprang up in the post-Revolutionary years to replace the older town-supported grammar schools that had existed in the colonial period. These academies, designed separately for both young men and women, became very important vehicles of education. As a Federalist complained in 1806, even "the middling class of society" was finding it "fashionable" to send their sons and daughters to these academies, often because the ambitious young people themselves pressed their parents to allow them to attend the schools.[15] Because the modern distinction between public and private was not yet clear, legislatures continued to grant public money periodically to some of these essentially private charity schools and academies.

Despite the spread of private education, however, the republican ideal of single, comprehensive, publicly supported systems of schooling did not die. Even though they were never adequately implemented, a series of legislative acts in states like New York and Massachusetts kept alive the republican idea of a three-tiered public-supported system for all people. A successful publicly funded modern educational system would come only in the common school movement of the second quarter of the nineteenth century.[16]

FORMAL SCHOOLING, OF COURSE, was never all that the Revolutionaries meant by education. Although many thought the Revolution was over in 1783 with the British recognition of American independence, Dr. Benjamin Rush knew better. "We have changed our forms of government," he said in 1786, "but it remains yet to effect a revolution in

15. J. M. Opal, *Beyond the Farm: National Ambitions in Rural New England* (Philadelphia, 2008), 97, 104–9.
16. Daniel Walker Howe, "Church, State, and Education in the Young American Republic," *JER*, 22 (2002), 1–24.

our principles, opinions, and manners so as to accommodate them to the forms of government that we have adopted."[17]

Rush was born in Philadelphia in 1745, and, like so many of the other Revolutionaries, he had no distinguished lineage: his father was an ordinary farmer and gunsmith. When Rush was five his father died, so his mother began running a grocery store to support the family. At the age of eight Rush was sent to live with a clergyman-uncle who saw to it that he received an education. After graduating from the College of New Jersey (Princeton) in 1760, Rush apprenticed as a physician in Philadelphia before leaving for further medical training at the University of Edinburgh. After returning to America in 1769, he became professor of chemistry at the College of Philadelphia and a participant in the Revolution both as a political leader and as a physician.

Since Rush came to believe that "the science of medicine was related to everything," he considered everything within his intellectual domain and had something to say about everything. In the decades following the Revolution Rush carried on what one historian has called "a one-man crusade to remake America."[18] "Mr. Great Heart," Jeremy Belknap called him, after the character in John Bunyan's *Pilgrim's Progress* who attacked all the giants and hobgoblins that stood in the way of getting to the Celestial City. Believing that he "was acting for the benefit of the whole world, and of future ages," Rush campaigned for every conceivable reform—for a national university, churches for blacks, temperance, healthy diets, the emancipation of the slaves, prison reform, free postage for newspapers, enlightened treatment of the insane, the education of women, animal rights, and the abolition of hunting weapons, oaths, dueling, and corporal and capital punishment. He even hoped eventually to eliminate all courts of law and all diseases. He was not so utopian, he said in 1786, as to think that man could become immortal, but he did believe that "it is possible to produce such a change in his moral character, as shall raise him to a resemblance of angels—nay, more, to the likeness of God himself."[19]

As republicans, Americans shared at least some of Rush's enthusiasm for reform, and their leaders enlisted every kind of media to change people's opinions, prejudices, and habits. Of these media the spoken and written word was most important. Every occasion demanded a lengthy speech, and

17. BR to Richard Price, 25 May 1786, *Letters of Rush*, 1: 388–90.
18. Editorial Note, *Letters of Rush*, 1: lxvii.
19. George W. Corner, ed., *The Autobiography of Benjamin Rush* (1948; Westport, CT, 1970), 161; D'Elia, "Rush and the American Medical Revolution," 101–2; BR, "The Influence of Physical Causes upon the Moral Faculty" (1786), in Runes, ed., *Selected Writings of Rush*, 209.

republican oratory was now celebrated as a peculiarly American form of communication. Groups sponsored public lectures on all sorts of topics and laid the foundations for the later lyceum movement. But it was printed matter, with its republican capacity to reach the greatest numbers of people, which came to be valued most. Private conversation and the private exchange of literary manuscripts among a genteel few might be suitable for a monarchy, but a republic required that politeness and learning be made more public.[20]

As republican citizens, many Americans, especially among the middling sort, became ever more anxious about acquiring gentility. People wanted more advice and etiquette manuals for every occasion or subject—from how to write letters to friends to how to control and clean their bodies. People, even gentry, who during their entire lives had never been wet all over now engaged in occasional bathing. In the 1790s public bathhouses were erected in some American cities as people began responding to the appeals for more cleanliness contained in scores of conduct manuals.[21]

All the various efforts to become more polite that had characterized eighteenth-century colonial society took on greater urgency under the new Republic. During the entire eighteenth century Americans published 218 spelling books designed to improve the writing of the English language, two-thirds of them in the final seventeen years of the century, between 1783 and 1800.[22] By the early nineteenth century Noah Webster's comprehensive speller, first published in 1783, had sold three million copies.[23] Although writing and spelling were important, they were not as important as reading. The few private libraries that had existed in the large cities in the colonial period were now supplemented by publicly supported libraries, which in turn sponsored increasing numbers of reading clubs, lectures, and debating societies.[24]

Most Americans now believed that anything that helped the spread of learning was good for their republic, for an informed citizenry was the source of republican freedom and security.[25] Although Americans could

20. David S. Shields, *Civil Tongues and Polite Letters in British America* (Chapel Hill, 1997), 316–17.
21. Richard L. Bushman, "The Early History of Cleanliness in America," *JAH*, 74 (1988), 1215–17; Kathleen M. Brown, *Foul Bodies: Cleanliness in Early America* (New Haven, 2009).
22. Russell B. Nye, *The Cultural Life of the New Nation, 1776–1830* (New York, 1960), 134; Konstantin Dierks, "Letter Writing, Gender, and Class in America, 1750–1800" (Ph.D. diss., Brown University, 1999), ch. 7.
23. Andrew Burstein, *Sentimental Democracy: The Evolution of America's Romantic Self-Image* (New York, 1999), 169.
24. Shields, *Civil Tongues and Polite Letters*, 322–23.
25. Richard D. Brown, *The Strength of a People: The Idea of an Informed Citizenry in America, 1650–1870* (Chapel Hill, 1996), 85–118.

not agree on what the citizenry should be informed about, they created new organizations for the collecting and conveying of knowledge at remarkable rates. Beginning with the reorganization of the American Philosophical Society in 1780, Americans began establishing many new learned academies and scientific societies. John Adams helped to form the American Academy of Arts and Sciences in Massachusetts. In 1799 the Connecticut Academy was created, and soon other states were establishing similar institutions.

In 1791 Congregational clergyman and historian Jeremy Belknap, concerned about the lack of any repository for historical documents in the United States, founded the Massachusetts Historical Society. The society was designed to preserve the materials that would "mark the genius, delineate the manners, and trace the progress of society in the United States."[26] It became the model for the New-York Historical Society (1804), the American Antiquarian Society (1812), and dozens of other historical societies created in other states in the early nineteenth century.

Everywhere institutions and organizations were burdened with the responsibility of imparting virtue and knowledge to the citizenry. Freemasonry, for example, came to see itself principally as an educational instrument for promoting morality. "Every character, figure, and emblem, depicted in a Lodge," declared a Masonic handbook, "has a moral tendency to, and inculcates the practice of virtue." But Masonry was not content with educating only its members; it sought to reach out and affect the whole society. Masonic brothers were involved in a multitude of public ceremonies and dedications—anointing bridges, canals, universities, monuments, and buildings. In 1793 President Washington himself, wearing a Masonic apron and sash, laid the cornerstone of the new United States Capitol in the planned Federal City. Masons, many of whom were artisans, architects, and painters, placed the fraternity's emblems, signs, and symbols on a wide variety of objects, including ceramics, pitchers, handkerchiefs, liquor flasks, and wallpaper—with the didactic hope of teaching virtue through the simple and expressive visual language of Masonry.[27]

26. Louis L. Tucker, *Clio's Consort: Jeremy Belknap and the Founding of the Massachusetts Historical Society* (Boston, 1990), 95.

27. Len Travers, "'In the Greatest Solemn Dignity': The Capitol Cornerstone and Ceremony in the Early Republic," Steven C. Bullock, "'Sensible Signs': The Emblematic Education of the Post-Revolutionary Freemasonry," and James Steven Curl, "The Capitol in Washington, D.C., and Its Freemason Connections," all in Donald R. Kennon, ed., *A Republic for the Ages: The United States Capitol and the Political Culture of the Early Republic* (Charlottesville, 1999), 155–76, 177–213, 214–67.

Printed matter flooded the new Republic. Three-quarters of all the books and pamphlets published in America between 1637 and 1800 appeared in the last thirty-five years of the eighteenth century. Few periodicals had appeared during the colonial period, and these had been frail and unstable, blossoming for a moment and dying like exotic plants. As late as 1785 only one American magazine existed, and it struggled to survive.[28]

Suddenly, this all changed. Between 1786 and 1795 twenty-eight learned and gentlemanly magazines were established, six more in these few years than in the entire colonial period. These magazines contained a rich mixture of subjects, including poetry, descriptions of new fossils, and directions for expelling noxious vapors from wells; and for the first time some of the magazines were aimed at female readers.

Although the Confederation had not done much to accelerate the movement of information throughout the country, the newly invigorated federal government was eager to change things. In 1788 there had been only sixty-nine post offices and less than two thousand miles of post roads to service four million people over half a continent. Congress's establishment of a national post office in 1792 created new routes and led to a proliferation of post offices throughout the country. By 1800 the number of post offices had grown to 903; by 1815 there were over three thousand post offices. Every little American town or hamlet wanted one. Since a post office was "the soul of commerce," a group of South Carolinians in 1793 naturally had petitioned for one. Without "such a direct, regular, and immediate communication by posts," the petitioners said, we are "kept in ignorance" and "know not anything which concerns us, either as men or as planters." To some observers the postal system seemed to be the most useful and rapidly improving feature of American life. "The mail has become the channel of remittance for the commercial interests of the country," said Jefferson's postmaster general, Gideon Granger, "and in some measure for the government." The postal system was helping to annihilate time and distances everywhere.[29]

Americans would soon make their postal system larger than the postal systems of either Britain or France. By 1816 the postal system had over thirty-three hundred offices, employing nearly 70 percent of the entire federal civilian workforce. The amount of mail increased just as quickly. In the year 1790 the postal system had carried only three hundred

28. Frank Luther Mott, A *History of American Magazines 1741–1850* (New York, 1930), 28–38.
29. Richard R. John, *Spreading the News: The American Postal System from Franklin to Morse* (Cambridge, MA, 1995), 50, 8, 54, 17–18.

thousand letters, one for about every fifteen persons in the country. By 1815 it transmitted nearly seven and a half million letters during the year, which was about one for every person. The post office was, as Benjamin Rush urged in 1787, the "only means" of "conveying light and heat to every individual in the federal commonwealth." And, unlike the situation in Great Britain and other European nations, the mail was transmitted without government surveillance or control.[30]

All these developments helped to speed up the rate at which information was communicated from one place to another. In 1790 it had taken more than a month for news to travel from Pittsburgh to Philadelphia; by 1794 that had been cut to ten days. In 1790 it had taken forty days to receive a reply to a letter sent from Portland, Maine, to Savannah, Georgia; by 1810 that time had been reduced to twenty-seven days.[31]

The postal system had its greatest effect on the circulation of newspapers. Congress's Post Office Act of 1792 allowed all newspapers, and not just those close to the centers of power, to be sent by mail at very low rates; in effect, newspaper circulation was subsidized by letter-writers. This act allowed for the dispersal of newspapers to the most remote areas of the country and nationalized the spread of information. In 1800 the postal system transmitted 1.9 million newspapers a year; by 1820 it was transmitting 6 million a year.[32]

In 1790 the country contained only 92 newspapers, only eight of them dailies. By 1800 this number had more than doubled, to 235, twenty-four of which were dailies. By 1810 Americans were buying over twenty-two million copies of 376 newspapers annually—even though half the population was under the age of sixteen and one-fifth was enslaved and generally prevented from reading. This was the largest aggregate circulation of newspapers of any country in the world.[33]

ALL THIS CIRCULATION of information could not have been achieved without the building of new postal roads and turnpikes. The need was obvious, Samuel Henshaw of Northampton, Massachusetts,

30. John, Spreading the News, 3, 4, 25–63.
31. Allen R. Pred, Urban Growth and the Circulation of Information: The United States System of Cities, 1790–1840 (Cambridge, MA, 1975), 36–42; John, Spreading the News, 17–18; Brown, Strength of a People, 85–118.
32. John, Spreading the News, 36–42.
33. Alfred M. Lee, The Daily Newspaper in America (New York, 1937), 715–17; Frank Luther Mott, American Journalism: A History of American Newspapers in the United States Through 250 Years, 1690–1940 (New York, 1941), 159, 167; Merle Curti, The Growth of American Thought, 3rd ed. (New York, 1964), 209; Donald H. Stewart, The Opposition Press of the Federalist Period (Albany, 1969), 15, 624.

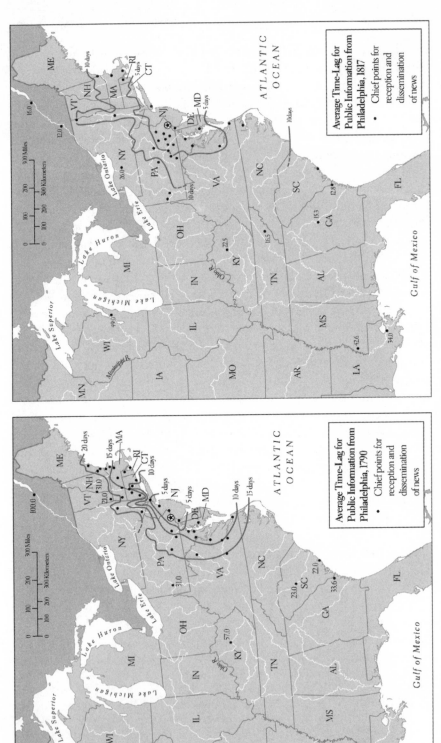

Source for both maps: Allan R. Pred, *Urban Growth and the Circulation of Information: The United States System of Cities, 1790–1840* (Cambridge, MA, 1973).

told his congressman, Theodore Sedgwick, in 1791. When the capital of the nation was in New York, said Henshaw, the people of the Connecticut Valley used to hear what was going on in the Congress. But once the capital moved to Philadelphia, "we scarce know you are in session." This, said Henshaw, "proves the necessity of post roads through all parts of the Union—people would then have early information & be influenced by it." Besides, he added, such post roads would be good for business.[34]

With these sorts of sentiments in the air, Americans began laying out roads at a frenetic pace. By 1810 they had created post roads that ran continuously from Brewer, Maine, not far from the northeastern border of the country, to St. Marys, Georgia, at the boundary with East Florida, a distance of 1,655 miles. Post roads in New York extended westward to Canandaigua in Iroquois country, which was nearly four hundred miles from New York City or Boston and had only recently been opened to white settlement. By 1810 New York had incorporated nearly a hundred turnpike companies, most of them since 1800. The busiest road in the country was the stage line between New York and Philadelphia, which in 1796 had four daily stage runs. In Pennsylvania roads ran from Philadelphia to Wheeling on the Ohio River, a distance of 389 miles, which usually took eight or nine days to travel. From Philadelphia continuous roads extended southwest into Tennessee as far as Knoxville. Other roads ran from Philadelphia to York, Pennsylvania, then south through the Shenandoah Valley and the towns of Hagerstown, Winchester, Staunton, and Abington. The South, however, had far fewer roads than the Middle States and the Northeast, and its population remained much more scattered and isolated.

The turnpikes were toll roads on which money was paid at gate entrances according to prescribed rates. They were often called "artificial roads" because, in contrast to the natural country roads, they contained artificial beds of gravel designed to support the weight of carriages and wagons. They were built with relatively level grades and were provided with sufficient convexity to allow for drainage. Often gates were established every ten miles or so, particularly at points where country roads "turned" into the turnpike. Considering that ordinary laborers made less than a dollar a day, the tolls were not cheap. In the state of Connecticut in 1808, four-wheeled carriages had to pay twenty-five cents for every two miles; a loaded wagon, twelve and one-half cents; a man and horse, four

34. Richard R. John and Christopher J. Young, "Rites of Passage: Postal Petitioning as a Tool of Governance in the Age of Federalism," in Kenneth R. Bowling and Donald R. Kennon, eds., *The House and Senate in the 1790s: Petitioning, Lobbying, and Institutional Development* (Athens, OH, 2002), 129.

cents; a mail stage, six and one-half cents; all other stages, twenty-five cents. These tolls supplied dividends to the investors who had bought shares in the corporation that built the road and maintained it.

The first major turnpike in the country was the Philadelphia to Lancaster road; it was completed in 1795 but much improved over the following decade. It was twenty-four feet wide and laid with eighteen-inch gravel in the middle decreasing to twelve inches on the sides for drainage. The road crossed three substantial bridges. At first the turnpike corporation returned only 2 percent per year on the investors' capital, but with the improvements on the road, usage increased, and the shares began returning 4 to 5 percent per year. With its success most of the rest of the Northern states began chartering turnpike companies. By 1810 twenty-six turnpike companies had been chartered in Vermont and more than twenty in New Hampshire. By 1811 New York had chartered 137 companies. As late as 1808, however, no state south of Virginia had established a turnpike company—another graphic reminder of the rapidly emerging distinction between the North and the South. Turnpikes that ran into new areas quickly led to a rush of new settlers eager to take advantage of the lower costs of transporting their produce. The Rome-Geneva turnpike in New York, for example, was completed in 1800 and soon reduced the cost of conveying a hundredweight of goods from $3.50 to 90 cents.

Getting a corporate charter and building the road, of course, did not guarantee success for the developers. Many of the turnpike companies failed because too many farmers evaded the tolls by using local detours. So common was the evasion that some began calling the roads "shunpikes."[35]

In 1802 Congress authorized the building of the National Road that would run from the East Coast to the Ohio River. But disputes over the route of the road delayed action. Finally, in 1806, Congress authorized a middle route beginning in the town of Cumberland in western Maryland; it later extended what came to be called the Cumberland Road (now U.S. 40) beyond Columbus to the Mississippi River at St. Louis by way of Vandalia. "In this way," President Jefferson told the Congress in February 1808, "we may accomplish a continued and advantageous line of communication from the seat of the General Government to St. Louis, passing through several very interesting points of the Western territory." Actual construction of the road did not begin until 1811.[36]

---

35. J. M. Opal, *Beyond the Farm: National Ambitions in Rural New England* (Philadelphia, 2008), 56–63.

36. TJ, Message to Congress, 19 Feb. 1808, in James D. Richardson, ed., *A Compilation of the Messages and Papers of the Presidents, 1789–1897* (Washington, DC, 1900), 1: 429.

At the same time Americans were building roads, they were improving their rivers and constructing canals. Because Americans, as Pennsylvania-born Robert Fulton pointed out, had such a strong prejudice in favor of wagons, it took a while for canal-building to take off. Fulton himself did not begin his career interested in canals. Indeed, he began as an artist and moved to England in 1787 to study painting with Benjamin West, an ex-Pennsylvanian who was known for his support of aspiring American artists. Although Fulton exhibited two canvases at the Royal Academy in 1791 and four in 1793, he soon came to realize that his genius lay in other directions. Influenced by some English aristocrats and scientists and the reformer and manufacturer Robert Owen, Fulton became involved in the operations of canals. In 1796 he published A *Treatise on the Improvement of Canal Navigation*, which he enhanced with superb drawings of aqueducts, bridges, inclined planes, and other canal devices. Fulton envisioned a series of canals designed for small boats being built everywhere to tie people and trade together. The Burr conspiracy, which threatened "to sever the western from the eastern states," convinced Fulton that canals could create a "sense of mutual interests arising from mutual intercourse and mingled commerce."[37]

Although Fulton eventually became preoccupied with various devices for conducting undersea warfare, he continued to stress the importance of canals to anyone who would listen. In 1811 he joined a commission, along with Mayor DeWitt Clinton of New York City, to explore the possibility of building a canal in the upper part of New York state.

Most of Fulton's many projects and proposals were ahead of their time. Only his development of the steamboat that traveled up the Hudson from New York to Albany in 1807 was well timed; this project, done in partnership with Robert R. Livingston, immortalized him.[38] Fulton was able to succeed with his steamboat where his predecessors John Fitch and James Rumsey had failed; not only was his boat technically superior, but most of his connections and patrons were better than those his rivals could muster. In 1811 Fulton sent his steamboat the *New Orleans* from Pittsburgh down the Ohio and Mississippi rivers to the port for which the boat was named, the first such craft on these Western waters. At the same time, New York City already had Fulton-built steam ferryboats carrying commuters across both the Hudson and East rivers. Fulton's first steam ferry on the East River, called *Nassau*, was a catamaran; it had a deck large enough to carry horses and wagons as well as foot passengers. People appreciated his time-saving inventions, and following his death in 1815

37. Wallace Hutcheon Jr., *Robert Fulton: Pioneer of Undersea Warfare* (Annapolis, 1981), 114–15.
38. Hutcheon, *Robert Fulton*, 4–15, 114–15.

both the Manhattan and Brooklyn streets leading to his ferry slips were renamed Fulton Street in his honor.[39]

As late as 1816 only a hundred miles of canals existed in the country. Yet these hundred miles were the products of at least twenty-five canal and lock companies. The two-and-one-half-mile-long canal at South Hadley Falls in western Massachusetts opened up in 1795 and took in over three thousand dollars in tolls the first year. In 1800 two more canals were built further north at Miller Falls and Bellows Falls, Vermont, making the Connecticut River navigable from the White River to the Atlantic. The most famous canal of the period was the Middlesex Canal that ran from Boston to the Merrimac River. It opened in 1804 and was twenty-seven miles long and thirty feet wide; it had twenty-one locks, seven aqueducts over rivers, and forty-eight bridges.

The canal companies were chartered and financed the same way as the toll roads. Although many of the canals failed to earn profits for their investors, many Americans were willing to try anything if there was a possibility of making a little money. Low-cost transportation to extensive markets, usually by rivers and other inland waterways, was a key to both commercial prosperity and a proliferation of labor-saving inventions. In this respect in the period up to 1812 the areas that benefited most from cheap water transportation and had the most inventive activity (as measured by the number of patents issued per capita) were New York and southern New England.[40]

Many saw the roads and canals not only as a means of making money for individual farmers but also, like Fulton, as devices for promoting union. In his 1806 message to Congress, President Jefferson foresaw the national debt soon being paid off, and thus he held out the prospect of using the federal surplus to support a system of internal improvements for the greatly enlarged nation. Since the federal funds, as Jefferson declared, came from duties on imports that were chiefly "foreign luxuries, purchased by those only who are rich enough to afford themselves the use of them," the taxes were justified in spite of their violation of republican principles. From the internal improvements, Jefferson promised, "new channels of communication will be opened between the States, the lines of separation will disappear, their interests will be identified, and their union cemented by new and indissoluble ties."[41]

President Jefferson, along with many other strict constructionist "Old Republicans," always believed that a constitutional amendment was

---

39. Hutcheon, *Robert Fulton*, 117.
40. Kenneth L. Sokoloff, "Inventive Activity in Early Industrial America: Evidence from Patent Records," *Journal of Economic History*, 48 (1988), 813–50.
41. TJ, Sixth Annual Message, 2 Dec. 1806, *Jefferson: Writings*, 529.

necessary to implement these plans, fearing that any implied enlargement of federal power over internal improvements would set a precedent
for further federal growth. Although Secretary of the Treasury Albert Gallatin was less scrupulous about the use of national power, he recognized
the political necessity of a constitutional amendment. Nevertheless, with
only the promise of a future amendment, he sought to get the process
going in April 1808 with his Report on Roads and Canals.

In his report Gallatin laid out his grandiose plans for the building of
roads and canals that would cement the parts of the country together, all
coordinated and paid for by the national government at a cost of $20 mil-
lion. Unfortunately for Gallatin, Congress, torn by Federalist opposition
and Republican rivalries, was no more interested in his report than it had
been earlier in Hamilton's Report on Manufactures. It did nothing to
implement Gallatin's plan until 1817, when it pledged the bonus due the
government from the new national bank for the improvement of the
nation's roads and canals. This Bonus Bill, however, much to the surprise
of nearly everyone, including its principal sponsor, John C. Calhoun, ran
into the strict constructionist scruples of President James Madison, who
vetoed it, on the grounds that the idea of implied powers threatened the
"definite partition" between the "General and State Governments" on
which the "permanent success of the Constitution" depended.[42]

PRECISELY BECAUSE REPUBLICS, as Benjamin Rush said, were
naturally "peaceful and benevolent forms of government," they inevitably
promoted humane reforms in accord with their "mild and benevolent
principles."[43] Jefferson thought that America was the most caring nation
in the world. "There is not a country on earth," he said, "where there is
greater tranquillity, where the laws are milder, or better obeyed..., where
strangers are better received, more hospitably treated, & with a more
sacred respect."[44] In the several decades following the Revolution Americans took very seriously the idea that they were more honest, more generous, and friendlier than other peoples.

Consequently, they were eager to create charitable and humanitarian
societies. Indeed, more humanitarian societies were formed in the decade
following the Revolution than were created in the entire colonial period.[45]

42. John Lauritz Larson, *Internal Improvement: National Public Works and the Promise of Popular Government in the Early United States* (Chapel Hill, 2001), 67–68.

43. Gordon S. Wood, *The Radicalism of the American Revolution* (New York, 1992), 192.

44. TJ to Maria Cosway, 12 Oct. 1786, *Papers of Jefferson*, 10: 447–48.

45. Merrill Jensen, *The New Nation: A History of the United States During the Confederation, 1781–1789* (New York, 1950), 141.

New England saw a virtual explosion of philanthropic organizations in the post-Revolutionary years. During the colonial period and prior to the formation of the Constitution in 1787, New Englanders had founded only seventy-eight charitable associations, most of these located in Boston. But with the new emphasis on people's moral sense and feelings of benevolence, things soon changed. In the decade following 1787, New Englanders formed 112 charitable societies; between 1798 and 1807, 158 more; and between 1808 and 1817, 1,101—creating in three decades nearly fourteen hundred benevolent organizations scattered in small towns all over the region.[46]

These associations were self-conscious replacements for traditional acts of individual and private charity, which were now described as impulsive and arbitrary. By organizing "upon a system; which inquires, deliberates, and feels a responsibility to the public," the charitable associations, declared the Reverend Edward Dorr Griffin of Massachusetts in 1811, were "the best repository of our gifts" and far more effective than the "little and widely scattered streams of individual munificence."[47]

Because the Federalist and Republican elites who created these institutions saw them as simply extensions of their public role as leaders of the society, they described them as public institutions designed to promote the public good. But as the state lost control of its creations and the idea of a unitary public good lost its coherence, these and other such organizations, like the chartered colleges, came to be regarded as private. These kinds of humanitarian and charitable associations represented the beginnings of what today is labeled "a civil society"—constituting the thousands of institutions and organizations that stand between the individual and the government. This emerging civil society in the early Republic was the major means by which Americans were able, to some extent at least, to tame and manage the near anarchic exuberance of their seething, boisterous society.

Voluntary associations in the early Republic sprang up to meet every human need—from the New York "Society for the Promotion of the Manumission of Slaves and Protecting such of them that have been or may be Liberated" to the Philadelphia "Society for the Relief of the Poor and Distressed Masters of Ships, their Widows and Children." There were mechanic societies, humane societies, societies for the prevention of pauperism, orphan asylums, missionary societies, marine societies, tract societies, Bible societies, temperance associations, Sabbatarian groups, peace societies,

46. Conrad E. Wright, *The Transformation of Charity in Post-Revolutionary New England* (Boston, 1992), 63.
47. Edward Dorr Griffin, *Sermon, Preached August 11, 1811, for the Benefit of the Portsmouth Female Asylum* (Boston, 1811), 16.

societies for the suppression of vice and immorality, societies for the relief of poor widows, societies for the promotion of industry, indeed, societies for just about anything and everything that was good and humanitarian.[48]

Some of these organizations, like the many immigrant aid societies that emerged in the cities, had social as well as humanitarian purposes. But most were charitable societies initially organized by paternalistic urban elites like John Jay, Noah Webster, and Benjamin Rush to deal with all the human miseries their newly aroused benevolent consciences told them they had an obligation to ease. These multiplying societies treated the sick, aided the industrious poor, housed orphans, fed imprisoned debtors, built huts for shipwrecked sailors, and, in the case of the Massachusetts Humane Society, even attempted to resuscitate those suffering from "suspended animation," that is, those such as drowning victims who appeared to be dead but actually were not. The fear of being buried alive was a serious concern at this time. Many, like Washington on his deathbed, asked that their bodies not be immediately interred in case they might be suffering from suspended animation.

In 1788 Dr. Rush had told the clergy that, whatever their doctrinal differences, "you are all united in inculcating the necessity of morals," and "from the success or failure of your exertions in the cause of virtue, we anticipate the freedom or slavery of our country." It was a message repeated over and over during the subsequent decades. Faced with such an awesome responsibility to inculcate morality, religious groups and others responded to the cause with an evangelical zeal and clamor that went beyond what Rush or anyone else in 1788 could have imagined. All the clergy came to realize that they could no longer rely on exposing the community's guilt through jeremiads; they could no longer count on reforming merely the "better part" of the society in the expectation that it would bring the rest along; and they could no longer just use government to create the right "moral effect." Ordinary people themselves had to be mobilized in the cause of virtue, through the creation of local moral societies, which in 1812 the great New England evangelical preacher Lyman Beecher labeled "disciplined moral militia."[49]

48. *American Museum*, 5 (1789), 555; Richard D. Brown, "The Emergence of Urban Society in Rural Massachusetts, 1760–1820," *JAH*, 61 (1974), 29–51; Richard D. Brown, "The Emergence of Voluntary Associations in Massachusetts, 1760–1830," *Journal of Voluntary Action Research*, 2 (1973), 64–73; Albrecht Koschnik, *"Let a Common Interest Bind Us Together"*: *Associations, Partisanship, and Culture in Philadelphia, 1775–1840* (Charlottesville, 2007).

49. BR, "To the Ministers of All Denominations," 21 June 1788, *Letters of Rush*, 1: 461–62; Lyman Beecher, *A Reformation of Morals Practicable and Indispensable: A Sermon Delivered at New Haven on the Evening of October 27, 1812* (Andover, MA, 1814), 18.

Middling members of these multiplying moral societies, which were at first often confined to rural villages, relied essentially on observation and the force of local public opinion. Members who were eager to support "the suppression of vice," such as the members of the Moral Society of the County of Columbia in New York in 1815, united to achieve that goal. They collected "the lovers of virtue of every name" and presented "a bold front to the growing licentiousness of the day"; and then, by erecting "a citadel, from which extended observations may be made," they exerted their "influence over the moral conduct of others," first by friendly persuasion, and then, if that did not work, by exposing the moral delinquents "to the penalties of law." The hopes were high: "character, that dearest earthly interest of man, will thus be protected, and thousands who are now settling down into incurable habits of licentiousness, will by these means be reclaimed."[50]

The growing and sprawling cities, however, needed more than moral societies to watch over and intimidate people. They needed new and substantial institutions, such as relief societies, hospitals, free schools, prisons, and savings banks, to improve the character of the weak and vicious of the society. The proliferation in the early nineteenth century of these new institutions eventually transformed and often eclipsed the humanitarian societies that enlightened gentry had formed in the immediate post-Revolutionary years in response to feelings of republican benevolence. All of these new institutions became parts of an expanding civic society.

By the second decade of the nineteenth century the goals and social complexion of these earlier urban philanthropic endeavors were changing. Ordinary middling sorts of people, usually pious newcomers from rural areas, were replacing the older paternalistic gentry as leaders of these charitable societies. In doing so, they transformed the emotional bonds tying them to the objects of their benevolence, substituting moral rectitude for gratitude.

The patrician gentry in the 1780s and 1790s had organized charitable societies for treating the sick, aiding widowed mothers, housing orphans, feeding imprisoned debtors, or resuscitating drowning victims out of a sense of Christian stewardship and paternalistic compassion befitting their genteel social position. They often seemed more interested in what their benevolence could do for their own feelings than for what it could do for the objects of their compassion. "How glorious, how God-like, to step forth to the relief of...distress," declared the twenty-four-year-old

---

50. "Formation and Constitution of the Columbia Moral Society," *Columbia Magazine*, 1 (1814–1815), 179–85.

DeWitt Clinton, a Columbia graduate, newly installed Freemason, and nephew of the governor of New York, in a 1793 oration. Enlightened caring gentry like Clinton wanted nothing more than "to arrest the tear of sorrow; to disarm affliction of its darts; to smooth the pillow of declining age; to rescue from the fangs of vice the helpless infant, and to diffuse the most lively joys over a whole family of rational, immortal creatures."[51] Paternalistic acts of charity by gentry like Clinton were disinterested deeds of sympathy for people whose character or behavior they did not expect to change fundamentally. All they expected was feelings of dependency and gratitude on the part of the recipients.

It was not gratitude, however, that the middle-class founders of the new reform institutions were interested in or expected. The new reformers wanted to imbue people not with deference and dependency but with "correct moral principles"; they aimed to change the actual behavior of people. These middling reformers had transformed themselves, often by strenuous efforts at self-improvement and hard work. Why couldn't others do the same? The compassionate charity of the paternalistic gentry, they believed, did not get at the heart of the problem of poverty. Indeed, in some cases they thought it aggravated the problem; many claimed, for example, that giving charity indiscriminately to the poor only perpetuated poverty. "Do not give to persons able to work for a living," declared a critic of the traditional paternalistic charity in 1807. "Do not support widows who refuse to put out their children. Do not let the means of support be made easier to one who does not work than to those who do."[52]

Instead of merely relieving the suffering of the unfortunate, as the earlier paternalistic gentry and benevolent associations had done, the new middle-class reformers sought to create institutions that would get at the sources of poverty, crime, and other social evils, mainly by suppressing the vices—gambling, drinking, Sabbath-breaking, profanity, horse racing, and other expressions of profligacy—that presumably were causing the evils. The middle-class moral reformers sought to remove the taverns and betting houses that tempted the weak and impressionable and to create institutions, such as schools and reformatory-type prisons, that would instill in people a proper respect for morality. Many of the middling reformers began attacking the sexual license and the spread of bastardy that had characterized the immediate post-Revolutionary decades. "The prostitution of women, which prevails to a high degree in all large cities," wrote publisher Mathew Carey in 1797, in one of the first writings

51. DeWitt Clinton, An Address, Delivered Before the Holland Lodge, December 24, 1793 (New York, 1794), 15.
52. Raymond A. Mohl, Poverty in New York, 1783–1825 (New York, 1971), 166.

on behalf of prostitution reform, "might be lessened by giving them encouragement to enter into various occupations which are available to them." But, said Carey, even more important than jobs in keeping women from prostitution was religion, especially "instruction of First-day or Sunday schools."[53]

AMERICANS DID NOT CONFINE their spirit of reform to just the United States and its own citizens. Throughout the period they created numerous missionary societies to bring the Bible and assorted tracts, schoolbooks, testaments, and other devotional literature to the heathen, first in the North American continent and then eventually in the farthest reaches of the globe. In 1787 the state of Massachusetts established the Society for Propagating the Gospel Among the Indians and Others in North America. Over the next thirty years a score of other major state and regional missionary societies were created, most of them supported by private bequests. The New York Missionary Society, formed in 1796, was the first voluntary interdenominational organization designed to propagate the gospel among the Indians. In 1801 the Connecticut assembly in association with the Presbyterian-inclined clergy of Connecticut adopted a Plan of Union that encouraged missionaries to the new settlements in the West and elsewhere to come together with the Congregationalists for their mutual benefit. Most of these missionary societies published journals and magazines to raise money and to keep the reforming spirit alive. In 1802 a group of Boston women formed the Cent Institution and agreed to deposit one cent a week in mite boxes for the purpose of "purchasing Bibles, Dr. Watts Psalms and Hymns, Primers, Catechisms, Divine Songs, Tokens for Children, etc.," which would be distributed by the Massachusetts Missionary Society that had been established in 1799.[54]

Soon, however, the goals of these missionary societies expanded beyond the North American continent, especially as the spread of French infidelity seemed to threaten the future of Christianity throughout the world. In 1804 the Massachusetts Missionary Society began to look outside of America for converts; the Cent Institution now saw itself "engaged in sending the gospel to lands unenlightened with its genial rays," wherever they might be. So popular did the idea of women's mite societies become

53. M. J. Heale, "Humanitarianism in the Early Republic: The Moral Reformers of New York, 1776–1825," *Journal of American Studies*, 2 (1968), 161–75; Clare A. Lyons, *Sex Among the Rabble: An Intimate History of Gender and Power in the Age of Revolution, Philadelphia, 1730–1830* (Chapel Hill, 2006), 321–22, 354–95.
54. Oliver Wendell Elsbree, *The Rise of the Missionary Spirit in America, 1790–1815* (Williamsport, PA, 1928), 63.

that English reformers picked it up. Indeed, throughout this period the American missionary societies, most of which were in New England, maintained strong ties and correspondence with their British counterparts; and thus most were appropriately Anglophile Federalists. Soon the women of Massachusetts were raising several thousand dollars annually for missions in lands as distant as Africa, the Middle East, East Asia, India, and the South Seas.[55]

In 1810 a group of enthusiasts formed the American Board of Commissioners for Foreign Missions that became for the next half century the largest organization devoted to sending benevolent workers abroad. The organizers justified their efforts by the oneness of humanity and need to bring the promise of Christian salvation to benighted souls everywhere. But the foreign missions were not just a religious responsibility; they were, the sponsors declared, a peculiar American responsibility. The United States above all other countries, they said, had the means and the message to bring republican civilization to the world.[56]

PROBABLY THE HUMANITARIAN REFORM that attracted the most worldwide attention was the Americans' effort to create new systems of criminal punishment. Since the colonial authorities had considered the lower orders incapable of restraining their passions by themselves, they had concluded that potential criminals could be controlled only through fear or force. Hence pillorying, whipping, and mutilating of the criminals' bodies had been standard punishments in the colonies, and carrying out these bodily punishments in public in front of local communities presumably had possessed the added benefit of overawing and deterring the spectators. Men and women in eighteenth-century Boston were taken from the huge cage that had brought them from the prison, tied bareback to a post on State Street, and lashed thirty or forty times "amid the screams of the culprits and the uproar of the mob."[57]

Everywhere in the eighteenth-century colonies criminals had their heads and hands pilloried and were exposed for hours on end to insults and pelting by onlookers. The stocks were even moved about, often to the particular neighborhoods of the criminals in order to make them feel mortification for their crimes and to teach lessons to the observers. In every punishment

55. Elsbree, *Rise of the Missionary Spirit*, 64.
56. William R. Hutchison, *Errand to the World: American Protestant Thought and Foreign Missions* (Chicago, 1987), 43–61.
57. *Recollections of Samuel Breck*, ed. H. E. Scudder (Philadelphia, 1877), 36–37; Linda Kealey, "Patterns of Punishment in Massachusetts in the Eighteenth Century," *American Journal of Legal History*, 30 (1986), 163–76.

the authorities were determined to expose the offender to public scorn, and with the lowliest of criminals, to do so permanently through mutilation. Persons with a brand on their foreheads or their ears cropped were forever condemned to the contempt of the intimate worlds in which they lived and object lessons to everyone of the consequences of crime.

Since few colonists had believed that the criminals were capable of being reformed or rehabilitated, capital punishment had been common not only for murder but for robbery, forgery, housebreaking, and counterfeiting as well. Prior to the Revolution, Pennsylvania had twenty capital crimes; Virginia had twenty-seven. Executions of the condemned criminals were conducted in public, and they drew thousands of spectators.

The republican Revolution challenged these traditional notions of punishment. Many of the Revolutionary state constitutions of 1776 evoked the enlightened thinking of the Italian reformer Cesare Beccaria and promised to end punishments that were "cruel and unusual" and to make them "less sanguinary, and in general more proportionate to the crimes."[58] Jefferson and other leaders drew up plans for liberalizing the harsh and bloody penal codes of the colonial period. In fact, Jefferson devoted more time to his Virginia bill for proportioning crimes and punishments than to any of the other reform bills he drafted during the Revolution.

A new republican order was emerging, and with it hopes of milder and more compassionate forms of punishment. Students at Yale and Princeton began debating the effectiveness of executing criminals. Did not such punishments do more harm than good? Maybe it was sensible for Britain to have nearly two hundred crimes punishable by death, for monarchies were based on fear and had to rely on harsh punishments. But, said many enlightened Americans, republics were different. They believed in equality and were capable of producing a kinder and gentler people. Americans must not forget, said Benjamin Rush, that even criminals "possess souls and bodies composed of the same materials as those of our friends and relatives."[59]

Everywhere enlightened Americans expressed doubts about the effectiveness of the old methods of criminal punishment. A sudden increase in crime in the 1780s suggested to many that bodily mutilations and executions did not deter crime after all. Sheriffs began refusing to cut off the limbs of criminals and to draw and quarter the bodies of those hanged, while others began rethinking the sources of criminal behavior. People, it seemed, were not born to be criminals; they were taught to be criminals by the world around them.

58. Louis Masur, *Rites of Execution: Capital Punishment and the Transformation of American Culture, 1776–1865* (New York, 1989), 72.
59. Lynn Hunt, *Inventing Human Rights: A History* (New York, 2007), 76.

If the characters of people were produced by their environments, as Lockean liberal thinking suggested, perhaps criminals were not entirely responsible for their actions. Maybe impious and cruel parents of the criminal were at fault, or maybe even the whole society was to blame. "We all must plead guilty before the bar of conscience as having had some share in corrupting the morals of the community, and levelling the highway to the gallows," declared a New Hampshire minister in 1796.[60] If criminal behavior was learned, then perhaps it could be unlearned. "Let every criminal, then, be considered as a person laboring under an infectious disorder," said one reformer in 1790. "Mental disease is the cause of all crimes."[61] If so, then it seemed that criminals could be salvaged, and not simply mutilated or destroyed. "A multitude of sanguinary laws is both impolitic and unjust," declared the 1784 New Hampshire Bill of Rights, "the true design of all punishments being to reform, not to exterminate mankind."[62]

These enlightened sentiments spread everywhere and eroded support for capital punishment in the new republican states. Not that the reformers had become soft on crime. Although Jefferson's code called for restricting the death penalty to treason and murder, he did propose the *lex talionis*, the law of retaliation, for the punishment of other crimes. So the state would poison the criminal who poisoned his victim and would castrate men guilty of rape, polygamy, or sodomy.[63] In Massachusetts in 1785 a counterfeiter was no longer executed. Instead, he was set in the pillory, taken to the gallows, where he stood with a rope around his neck for a time, whipped twenty stripes, had his left arm cut off, and finally was sentenced to three years' hard labor.

Although most states did something to change their code of punishment, Pennsylvania led the way in the 1780s and 1790s in the enlightened effort, as its legislation put it, "to reclaim rather than destroy," "to correct and reform the offenders" rather than simply to mutilate or execute them. Pennsylvania abolished all bodily punishments such as "burning in the hand" and "cutting off the ears" and ended the death penalty for all crimes except murder. Instead, the state proposed a scale of punishments based on fines and years of imprisonment.

With the reliance on imprisonment the Pennsylvanian reformers went beyond the Beccarian proposals for reform and challenged even the

60. Masur, *Rites of Execution*, 37.
61. Masur, *Rites of Execution*, 77; *American Museum*, 7 (March 1790), 137.
62. Masur, *Rites of Execution*, 72.
63. TJ, A Bill for Proportioning Crimes and Punishments in Cases Heretofore Capital (1776–1786), *Papers of Jefferson*, 2: 492–507.

punishing of criminals in public. Since people learned from what they saw, the cruel and barbaric punishments of monarchy carried out in public, said Thomas Paine, hardened the hearts of its subjects and made them bloodthirsty. "It is their sanguinary punishments which corrupt mankind." If people witness the miseries of the criminal being punished "without emotion or sympathy," said Rush, then "the principle of sympathy" itself "will cease to act altogether; and...will soon lose its place in the human heart."[64]

In the larger and less intimate worlds of the growing cities, communal punishments based on shaming the criminal and frightening the spectators seemed less meaningful, especially since the spectators, more often than not, reveled in witnessing the punishments. Instead of having their bodies publicly flogged or mutilated, the criminals, the reformers concluded, should be made to feel their personal guilt by being confined in prisons apart from the excited environment of the outside world, in solitude where the "calm contemplation of mind which brings on penitence" could take place. These new enlightened punishments, declared Edward Shippen in 1785, would bring "honor" to "our rising Empire, to set an Example of Lenity, moderation and Wisdom to the Older Countries of the World."[65]

Out of these efforts was created the penitentiary, which turned the prison into what Philadelphia officials called "a school of reformation." By 1805 New York, New Jersey, Connecticut, Virginia, and Massachusetts had followed Pennsylvania in constructing penitentiaries based on the principle of solitary confinement. Some criticized the practice on the grounds that it rendered the rehabilitated prisoners unfit for becoming useful members of society; these critics accepted the concept of penitentiaries but wanted the prisoners to participate in hard labor (and earn money) as well as having temporary periods of confinement in total solitude.

By the second decade of the nineteenth century, however, more and more Americans were having second thoughts about the penal reform

---

64. Masur, *Rites of Execution*, 65, 71, 80–82, 88, 87; Adam J. Hirsch, "From Pillory to Penitentiary: The Rise of Criminal Incarceration in Early Massachusetts," *Michigan Law Review*, 80 (1982), 1179–269; Linda Kealey, "Patterns of Punishment: Massachusetts in the Eighteenth Century," *American Journal of Legal History*, 30 (1986), 1631–76; Michael Meranze, "The Penitential Ideal in Late Eighteenth-Century Philadelphia," *Penn. Mag. of Hist. and Biog.*, 108 (1984), 419–50; Bradley Chapin, "Felony Law Reform in the Early Republic," *Penn. Mag. of Hist. and Biog.*, 113 (1989), 163–83; Thomas Paine, *Rights of Man* (1791), in Philip S. Foner, ed., *The Complete Writings of Thomas Paine* (New York, 1969), 1: 265–66; Hunt, *Inventing Human Rights*, 112.

65. Michael Meranze, *Laboratories of Virtue: Punishment, Revolution, and Authority in Philadelphia, 1760–1835* (Chapel Hill, 1996), 71; Masur, *Rites of Execution*, 82.

that a decade earlier had seemed so promising. In Massachusetts the state prison was soon overwhelmed by overcrowding, escapes, violence, and expenses far in excess of earnings. In 1813 the prisoners burned their workshops, and in 1816 they engaged in a full-scale revolt that resulted in one death. At the same time, the released inmates' high rate of recidivism began to cast doubt on the rehabilitative capacity of the penitentiary. By 1820 the penitentiary as a form of criminal punishment survived the criticism and doubts, but all sorts of proposals for restructuring and improving it were flying about.[66]

Yet at the outset liberals on both sides of the Atlantic enthusiastically celebrated what they took to be new humane forms of punishment. The penitentiary was of "pure American origin," noted a sympathetic British traveler in 1806, "and is happily adapted to the genius of the government of the country, mild, just, and merciful." The object was "to receive the vicious, and if possible, reclaim them to virtue; and is an admirable contrast to the sanguinary punishments of old governments, who, for even pecuniary offences, send them to the other world to be reclaimed there."[67] Nowhere else in the Western world, as enlightened philosophes recognized, were such penal reforms carried as far as they were in America.

SCHOOLS, BENEVOLENT ASSOCIATIONS, Masonic organizations, missionary societies, penitentiaries—all these were important for creating a civic society and making people more compassionate and republican. But none of them could compare in significance with that most basic social institution, the family. It was the family, John Adams had said in 1778, that was the "foundation of national morality."[68] Throughout the eighteenth century the family had been the primary place for teaching the young, carrying on work, disciplining the wayward, and caring for the poor and the insane. Yet the Revolution challenged all these familial relationships, not only unsettling connections between fathers and children and husbands and wives but also cutting some of the family's ties to the larger society and making it more private and insular. The family was becoming a much more republican institution.

Although the relationship between husbands and wives continued to be governed by the laws of coverture that gave husbands full control of their wives and their wives' property, wives were gaining a new sense of

---

66. Adam Jay Hirsch, *The Rise of the Penitentiary: Prisons and Punishment in Early America* (New Haven, 1992), 61–66.

67. John Melish, *Travels Through the United States of America in the Years 1806 and 1807, and 1809, 1810, and 1811* (London, 1813), 124.

68. Michael Grossberg, *Governing the Hearth: Law and the Family in Nineteenth-Century America* (Chapel Hill, 1985), 3; JA, *Diary and Autobiography*, 1: 123.

themselves as independent persons. Lucy Knox, the wife of General Henry Knox, told her husband in the midst of the Revolutionary War that everything was changing. When he returned from the war, he could no longer be the sole commander-in-chief of his household. Be prepared to accept, she warned, "that there is such a thing as equal command."[69]

With this remark Lucy Knox was not fundamentally challenging either her domestic situation or the role of women in her society any more than Abigail Adams was in her famous "Remember the Ladies" letter of 1776 in which she told her husband John that "all Men would be tyrants if they could" and predicted "a Rebellion" if the ladies' needs were not attended to. Both women were only playfully teasing their husbands. Yet teasing can often make a serious point, and in their bantering remarks both wives were undoubtedly expressing a self-conscious awareness of the legally dependent and inferior position of women that was capable of being changed.[70]

Such remarks certainly suggest that what earlier had been taken for granted was now beginning to be questioned, especially by a new generation of women. Catharine Sedgwick, who would go on to become a celebrated writer of domestic novels, recalled the marriage of her older sister in 1796 as "the first tragedy of my life." When she at age seven realized that her sister was now to be taken away and be governed by the will of her husband, she was crushed. In trying to console her, her sister's new husband told her that he "may" allow her sister to visit with her. Sedgwick never forgot that moment. "*May*! How my whole being revolted at the word—He had the power to bind or loose my sister."[71]

Although there was little change in the legal authority of men over their wives, people's consciousness was changing. Charles Willson Peale self-consciously painted his many family portraits with the husbands and wives on the same plane—an innovation that other artists adopted as well.[72] Women began to question the idea that marriage was their destiny and to defend the independence of spinsterhood (reinforced, at least in New England, by the fact that women considerably outnumbered men in the older communities). Some objected to the word "obey" in the marriage vows because it turned the woman into her husband's "slave."

69. Christopher Clark, *Social Change in America: From the Revolution Through the Civil War* (Chicago, 2006), 71.

70. Abigail Adams to JA, 31 March 1776, in Margaret A. Hogan and C. James Taylor, eds., *My Dearest Friend: Letters of Abigail and John Adams* (Cambridge, MA, 2007), 110.

71. Mary Kelley, *Private Women, Public Stage: Literary Domesticity in Nineteenth-Century America* (New York, 1984), 65.

72. David C. Ward, *Charles Willson Peale: Art and Selfhood in the Early Republic* (Berkeley, 2004), 136–39.

"Marriage," it was said, "ought never to be considered as a contract between a superior and an inferior, but a reciprocal union of interests, an implied partnership of interests."[73] The extraordinary proliferation of references in the 1790s to the marital bliss of Adam and Eve that Milton had portrayed in Book IV of *Paradise Lost* suggests that describing an ideal marriage was on many people's minds.[74] Indeed, popular writings everywhere set forth models of a perfect republican marriage—a companionate marriage. It was one based on love, not property. It was one based on reason and mutual respect. And it was one in which wives had a major role in inculcating virtue in their husbands and children.[75]

Under this kind of cultural pressure, even the laws began to change. The new republican states abolished the crime of petit treason, which had provided for harsher punishments for wives or servants who murdered their husbands or masters on the grounds that such murders were akin to subjects murdering their king. Women gained some greater autonomy and some legal recognition of their rights to divorce and to make contracts and do business in the absence of their husbands. Divorce, said Thomas Jefferson, would restore "to women their natural right of equality." In the colonial period only New Englanders had recognized the absolute right to divorce, but after the Revolution all the states except South Carolina developed new liberal laws on divorce, and in some states the rate of divorce increased sharply in the first decade of the nineteenth century. The new ideals of marriage made husbands more publicly responsible for their behavior, and the increase in the number of "runaway wife advertisements" in newspapers suggested that women were asserting themselves in new ways. Women were becoming more independently involved in the courts and legal affairs than they had been prior to the Revolution.[76]

73. Mary Beth Norton, *Liberty's Daughters: The Revolutionary Experience of American Women, 1750–1800* (Boston, 1980) 240–41, 235.
74. George Sensabaugh, *Milton in Early America* (Princeton, 1964), 195–217.
75. Linda K. Kerber, *Women of the Republic: Intellect and Ideology in Revolutionary America* (Chapel Hill, 1980); Jan Lewis, "The Republican Wife: Virtue and Seduction in the Early Republic," *WMQ*, 44 (1987), 689–712.
76. Frank L. Dewey, "Thomas Jefferson's Notes on Divorce," *WMQ*, 39 (1982), 212–23; Nancy F. Cott, "Divorce and the Changing Status of Women in Eighteenth-Century Massachusetts," *WMQ*, 33 (1976), 586–614; Sheldon S. Cohen, "The Broken Bond: Divorce in Providence County, 1749–1809," in Patrick T. Conley, ed., *Liberty and Justice: A History of Law and Lawyers in Rhode Island, 1636–1998* (East Providence, 1998), 224–37; Mary Beth Sievens, *Stray Wives: Marital Conflict in Early National New England* (New York, 2005); Sarah Leavitt, " 'She Hath Left My Bed and Board': Runaway Wives in Rhode Island, 1790–1810," *Rhode Island History*, 58 (2000), 91–104; Sara Tabak Damiano, "From the Shadows of the Bar: Law and Women's Legal Literacy in Eighteenth-Century Newport" (Honors thesis, Brown University, 2008), 122–54.

The Revolution challenged older English patterns of inheritance and the aristocratic legal devices that had sought to maintain the stem line of the estate (entail) and to sacrifice the interests of younger children to the eldest son (primogeniture). The Revolutionary state constitutions and laws struck out at the traditional power of family and hereditary privilege. No one hated the dead hand of the past more than Jefferson, and with Jefferson's Virginia taking the lead, all the states in the decades following the Revolution abolished both entail and primogeniture where they existed, either by statute or by writing the abolition into their constitutions. These legal devices, as the North Carolina statute of 1784 stated, had tended "only to raise the wealth and importance of particular families and individuals, giving them an unequal and undue influence in a republic, and prove in manifold instances the source of great contention and injustice." Their abolition would therefore "tend to promote that equality of property which is of the spirit and principle of a genuine republic."

Many of the states passed new inheritance laws that recognized greater equality among sons and daughters and gave greater autonomy to widows by granting them outright ownership of one-third of the estate rather than just the lifetime use that had been usual in the past. Such widows now had the right to alienate the land or to pass it on to their children of a second marriage. Most of the states also strengthened the ability of women to own and control property. In a variety of ways the new state laws not only abolished the remaining feudal forms of land tenure and enhanced the commercial nature of real estate, they also confirmed a new enlightened republican conception of the family.[77]

At the same time, various popular writings—such as the American novel *The Fatal Effects of Parental Tyranny* (1798)—added to the assault on patriarchy. Authors now imagined republican families in which children had much more equal relations with their parents than in the past. Indeed, most of the best-selling books throughout the Revolutionary era were didactic works that dealt with the proper relations between parents and children. They ranged from Oliver Goldsmith's *The Vicar of Wakefield* (Andrew Jackson's favorite novel) to John Gregory's *A Father's Legacy to His Daughters*.

*The Vicar of Wakefield* (first published in America in 1769) had at least nine different editions in various American cities before 1800, while Gregory's *Legacy* (first American edition in 1775) went through fifteen

---

77. Stanley N. Katz, "Republicanism and the Law of Inheritance in the American Revolutionary Era," *Michigan Law Review*, 76 (1977), 1–29; Holly Brewer, *By Birth or Consent: Children, Law, and the Anglo-American Revolution in Authority* (Chapel Hill, 2005).

editions and sold twenty thousand copies during this period of the early Republic.[78] In these works the republican family became bound together not by fear or force but by love and affection. Children were to be raised to be rational, independent, moral adults and were no longer to be compelled to follow parental dictates and marry for the sake of property and the perpetuation of the family estate. The individual desires of children now seemed to outweigh traditional concerns with family lineage.

So desirous were American readers for books celebrating the development of independent children that they turned Daniel Defoe's *Robinson Crusoe* into a longtime best seller. Between 1774 and 1825 Americans published 125 editions of Defoe's novel, all heavily abridged to meet American interests and sensibilities. Crusoe defied his parents and ran away from home. When cast alone on an island he turned to the Bible and discovered God and Christianity. Indeed, his solitary independence on the island became the source of his conversion experience. The novel told its readers that salvation was possible for the individual isolated from parents and society—a reassuring message for many young American men cut loose from their former social ties. Benjamin Franklin's *Autobiography* offered a similar message to young men who wanted to leave home and make it on their own. The first part of Franklin's memoirs began appearing shortly after his death in 1790. By 1828 twenty-two American editions of the *Autobiography* had been published, many of them abridged and adapted for younger readers. During the decades following the Revolution, resisting one's father and leaving home became an important motif in the many reminiscences written by that generation.[79]

The biblical commandment to honor one's father and mother no longer seemed as important as it once had been. Heavily abridged American editions of Samuel Richardson's *Clarissa* (an American best seller in 1786) turned the novel into an unequivocal attack on parental severity. Where Richardson had blamed both Clarissa's disobedience and her parents' arbitrariness for her downfall, the abridged American versions made the young daughter a simple victim of unjustifiable parental tyranny. In a variety of ways Americans were being told that patriarchy had lost some of its significance.[80]

78. Frank Luther Mott, *Golden Multitudes: The Story of Best Sellers in the United States* (New York, 1960), 40, 30; James D. Hart, *The Popular Book: A History of America's Literary Taste* (Berkeley, 1961), 61; Lewis, "Republican Wife," 696.

79. Joyce Appleby, *Inheriting the Revolution: The First Generation of Americans* (Cambridge, MA, 2000), 173.

80. Jay Fliegelman, *Prodigals and Pilgrims: The American Revolution Against Patriarchal Authority, 1750–1800* (Cambridge, MA, 1982), 86–87.

Not everyone, of course, accepted these changes with equanimity. A New Hampshire congressman was shocked by the familiarity he witnessed among New York families. "Fathers, mothers, sons & daughters, young & old, all mix together, & talk & joke alike so that you cannot discover any distinction made or any respect shewn to one more than to another." He was "not for keeping up a great distance between Parents & children, but there is a difference between sharing & stark mad."[81]

The Revolution had released egalitarian and anti-patriarchal impulses that could not be stopped. The republican family was becoming an autonomous private institution whose members had their own legal rights and identities.[82]

ALTHOUGH MOST AMERICANS understood "rights" in the post-Revolutionary years to mean simply the rights of men, some began asserting as well the rights of women. Judith Sargent Murray, daughter of a prominent Massachusetts political figure, writing under the pseudonym "Constantia," published an essay "On the Equality of the Sexes" in 1790, but it was not until the publication of A *Vindication of the Rights of Women* by the English feminist Mary Wollstonecraft in 1792 that discussion of the issue became widespread. In fact, copies of her work, which Aaron Burr called a "book of genius," could be found in more private American libraries of the early Republic than Paine's *Rights of Man*.[83] Although women did not need Wollstonecraft to tell them what to think, her book certainly released the pent-up thoughts of many women. As the Philadelphia Quaker Elizabeth Drinker put it, Wollstonecraft "*speaks my mind*."[84] Excerpts appeared at once, and by 1795 three American editions had been published.

Suddenly, talk of women's rights was everywhere. "The Rights of Women are no longer strange sounds to an American ear," declared the Federalist congressman Elias Boudinot of New Jersey in 1793. "They are now heard as familiar terms in every part of the United States."[85] In the 1790s Susanna Rowson, novelist, playwright, and actress, put on a series of plays dealing with the universal rights of men and women. Judith Sargent Murray, believing that "the stage is undoubtedly a very powerful

81. Norton, *Liberty's Daughters*, 236.
82. Grossberg, *Governing the Hearth*, 26–27.
83. Jon Kukla, *Mr. Jefferson's Women* (New York, 2007), 167–72; Nancy Isenberg, *Fallen Founder: The Life of Aaron Burr* (New York, 2007), 433.
84. Linda Kerber, *Toward an Intellectual History of Women: Essays* (Chapel Hill, 1997), 35.
85. Rosemarie Zagarri, "The Rights of Man and Woman in Post-Revolutionary America," *WMQ*, 55 (1998), 210; Rosemarie Zagarri, *Revolutionary Backlash: Women and Rights in the Early American Republic* (Philadelphia, 2007).

engine in forming the opinions and manners of a people," also tried her hand at playwriting in order to promote the cause of women's rights. Unfortunately, however, her effort, *The Medium*, produced in Boston in 1795, had only one performance.[86] Far more successful was the novel *The Coquette... Founded on Fact*, by Hannah Webster Foster and published in 1797. It spoke directly to women on the issues of women's education, employment, rights, and the double standard of sexual behavior; it remained immensely popular well into the nineteenth century.

Although in this early period no organized movement arose on behalf of women's rights, the way was prepared for the future. Murray, writing as "Constantia" in 1798, declared that she expected "to see our young women forming a new era in female history." In the decades following the Revolution women gained a new consciousness of their selfhood and their rights.[87]

It was a tricky problem for male reformers to claim rights for women while women remained legally dependent on men; any recognition of rights was bound to be picked up and used in unanticipated ways. When the Supreme Court of Errors in Connecticut in 1788 decided that a married woman had the right to devise her real property to whomever she wished, the decision was soon regarded as one "tending to loosen the bands of society."[88] Once the social bands were loosened, it was difficult to prevent slippage everywhere. Since rights were not really compatible with inferiority, it became harder and harder to maintain that inferiority. An 1801 poem began with a traditional recognition of women's subordination to men. "That men should rule, and women should obey,/ I grant their nature and their frailty such." Yet the poem ends on a very different note. "Let us not force them back, with brow severe,/ Within the pale of ignorance and fear,/ Confin'd entirely by domestic arts:/ Producing only children, pies and tarts."[89]

Many men, of course, were alarmed by what recognizing women's equal rights might mean. "If once a man raises his wife to an equality with himself," declared a Philadelphia writer in 1801, "it is all over, and he is doomed to become a subject for life to the most despotic of governments."[90] Timothy Dwight, president of Yale, earlier had been a leading

86. Larry E. Tise, *The American Counterrevolution: A Retreat from Liberty, 1783–1800* (Mechanicsburg, PA, 1998), 178–83.
87. Kerber, *Toward an Intellectual History of Women*, 23; Martha Tomhave Blauvelt, *The Work of the Heart: Young Women and Emotion, 1780–1830* (Charlottesville, 2007).
88. Marylynn Salmon, "Republican Sentiments, Economic Change, and the Property Rights of Women in American Law," in Ronald Hoffman and Peter J. Albert, eds., *Women in the Age of the American Revolution* (Charlottesville, 1989), 450–51.
89. Zagarri, "Rights of Man and Woman in Post-Revolutionary America," 225.
90. Zagarri, "Rights of Man and Woman in Post-Revolutionary America," 217.

advocate of offering women an education equal to that of men. But he was not prepared to accept the message Mary Wollstonecraft was preaching. If women shook loose from the family and became truly independent, he asked an imagined Wollstonecraft, "Who would make our puddings, Madam?" When she answered, "Make them yourself," he pressed her harder. "Who shall nurse us when we are sick?" and finally, "Who shall nurse our children?" With this last question concerning the role of mothers, Dwight has his imagined Wollstonecraft reduced to embarrassed silence.[91] Apparently, talk about women's equal rights was acceptable, as long as those rights did not actually affect women's traditional maternal role in the family.

Reconciling women's rights with their traditional family roles proved to be difficult. Some said that women's rights were actually duties—the responsibility of taking care of their husbands and children. Others said that the equality of the rights of men and women could be found only in a spiritual or social sense. Women in fact were now encouraged to mingle equally with men in nearly all social occasions—something that had not been common earlier. If both men and women had rights, then these rights had to be respected by both sexes. Although men were legally superior, they could not ride roughshod over the rights of women. In fact, in this enlightened age the treatment of women was supposed to be a measure of civilization. Did not "savages" regard their women as "beasts of burden"? If Americans wished to be considered refined and genteel, they certainly could not go back to those "barbarous days" when a woman was "considered and treated as the slave of an unfeeling master."[92] Still, despite the recognition of women's equal but different rights, almost everyone, including most women reformers, agreed that women had an essential female nature that should not be violated.

Indeed, many Americans came to believe that women, precisely because of their presumed female nature, had a special role to play in sustaining a republican society, especially one that was being torn apart by partisan fighting. Since virtue was increasingly identified with sociability and affability, with love and benevolence, rather than with the martial and masculine self-sacrifice of the ancients, it had become as much a female as a male quality. In fact, it was widely thought that women were even more capable than men of sociability and benevolence. "How often

91. Kerber, *Toward an Intellectual History of Women*, 36.
92. Antoine Louis Claude Destutt de Tracy, *Commentary and Review of Montesquieu's Spirit of the Laws* (Philadelphia, 1811), 72; Joseph Hopkinson, *Annual Discourse, Delivered Before the Pennsylvania Academy of the Fine Arts* (1810), in Gordon S. Wood, ed., *The Rising Glory of America*, rev. ed. (Boston, 1990), 337.

have I seen a company of men who were disposed to be riotous," declared a 1787 publication, "checked all at once into decency, by the accidental entrance of an amiable woman." Women seemed less burdened by artificial rules and more capable of demonstrating their natural feelings of affection than men. Indeed, "in the present state of society," said Joseph Hopkinson in 1810, women were "inseparably connected with every thing that civilizes, refines, and sublimates man."[93]

Because they had a particular talent for developing affective relationships and for stimulating sympathy and moral feelings, women, it was said, were better able than men to soften party conflict and bind the republican society together. Through their soothing influence on the often hot-headed passions of men, women could heal the dissentions that threatened to tear the country apart. The way to do this was to isolate and confine partisan politics to the exclusively male-dominated public sphere and to leave the private sphere—the world of drawing and dining rooms, of dances and tea parties, of places where the two sexes mingled—under the calming and socializing domination of women. Although some genteel women continued to try to use their social skills and various social institutions—salons, balls, and soirees—to influence politics, most tended to withdraw from the public world of divisive politics and to assume the disinterested responsibility of adjudicating conflict and promoting peace in the private world. The separation of government and society, public and private, that lay at the heart of the thinking of radicals like Paine and Jefferson in 1776 was now expanded and legitimized.[94]

If women had a special aptitude for refinement and sociability, then their first obligation was to civilize their children and prepare them for republican citizenship.[95] Since women's world was the home, the home became more significant than it had been earlier—a refuge from the nervous excitement and crass brutality that were increasingly coming to characterize the city and the commercial world in general. Women became responsible for the taste and respectability of the family and at the same time became the special purveyors of culture and the arts. Although women were excluded from participation in America's political institutions, William Loughton Smith of South Carolina told a female audience in 1796, nature had assigned women "valuable and salutary

---

93. Lewis, "Republican Wife," 689–721; James Fordyce, *Sermons to Young Women: A New Edition* (Philadelphia, 1787), 20; Hopkinson, *Annual Discourse*, in Wood, ed., *Rising Glory of America*, 337.

94. Catherine Allgor, *Parlor Politics: In Which the Ladies of Washington Help Build a City and a Government* (Charlottesville, 2000), 4–101; Zagarri, *Revolutionary Backlash*.

95. Lewis, "Republican Wife," 689–721.

rights" that were beyond men's control. "To delight, to civilize, and to ameliorate mankind...*these are the precious rights of woman*."[96]

Yet if wives and mothers had an important role in educating their husbands and sons in sociability and virtue, then they needed to be educated themselves. Too often, reformers said, women had been educated "not to their future benefit in life but to the amusement of the male sex."[97] They had been educated in frivolity and fashion; they had been taught to dress, to sew, to play the harpsichord, and to paint their faces, but not to use their minds in any meaningful manner. Republican women, it was hoped, would be different. They would scorn fashion, cosmetics, and vanity and would become socially useful and less susceptible to male flattery. Such republican women could become powerful forces in changing the culture. "Let the ladies of a country be educated properly," said Benjamin Rush, "and they will not only make and administer its laws, but form its manners and character."[98] Rush prescribed for women reading, writing, bookkeeping, geography, some natural philosophy, and especially the reading of history; this last was to be an antidote to novel-reading, which many reformers assumed was destroying women's minds. Because "the proper object of female education is to make women rational companions, good wives and good mothers," they need not be educated for the professions or for participation in the male world. Certainly, they should never be taught philosophy or metaphysics, which might destroy their feminine nature.[99]

Virtually every American reformer in this period, male and female, endorsed the education of women. In 1796 Massachusetts minister Simeon Doggett expressed astonishment that "one half of the human race have been so basely neglected." It was undoubtedly the consequence of barbarism that depressed "the delicate female...far below the dignity of her rank." In enlightened America, however, "this trait of barbarity" was rapidly disappearing and women were assuming "their proper rank."[100] American reformers went way beyond their English and European counterparts in urging that women be taught not just to sew, sing, dance, and play musical instruments but to think and reason and understand the world, if not like a man then at least more than they had in the past.[101]

96. Zagarri, *Revolutionary Backlash*, 177.
97. Kerber, *Toward an Intellectual History of Women*, 29.
98. BR, "Thoughts upon Female Education" (1787), in Rudolph, ed., *Essays on Education*, 36.
99. Zagarri, "Rights of Man and Woman in Post-Revolutionary America," 218.
100. Doggett, *Discourse on Education* (1797), in Rudolph, ed., *Essays on Education*, 159; Bullock, "'Sensible Signs,' in Kennon, ed., *A Republic for the Ages*, 196.
101. Norton, *Liberty's Daughters*, 271–72.

Consequently, during the two decades following the Revolution scores of academies were founded solely for the advanced instruction of females, a development unmatched in England. Although most of these academies were located in the Northern states, the young women, mostly from well-to-do families, came from all over the country. In addition to the usual ornamental subjects, they were taught grammar, arithmetic, history, and geography. For the first time in American history young women were able to acquire something resembling higher education in a formal and systematic way. Many of the women trained in these academies went on to achieve distinction in the nineteenth century.[102]

Once the rights of woman were discussed in public, their subversive implications could not always be contained. A writer in a Boston magazine of 1802 calling herself "Miss M. Warner" opened with a conventional listing of women's so-called rights: to cook for her husband, share in his troubles, and nurse him when he was sick. But then she paused and expressed what she assumed her readers must be feeling. These were not rights; "these are duties.... Agreed, they are/ But know ye not that Woman's proper sphere/ Is the domestic walk? To interfere/ With politics, divinity, or law,/ A much deserv'd ridicule would draw/ on Woman." Ridicule or not, many began pointing up the injustice involved in excluding "from any share in government one half of those who, considered as equals of the males, are obliged to be subject to laws they have no share in making!"[103]

Some Americans now even glimpsed the possibility of women becoming full-fledged citizens with the right to vote and hold political office. In 1764 James Otis had broached the issue of the right of women to political participation. But it was the Revolution itself that really raised women's consciousness. Women brought up in the post-Revolutionary decades had different expectations from their mothers. In her 1793 salutatory address at the Young Ladies Academy of Philadelphia, Priscilla Mason proclaimed the right and the responsibility of women to become orators. Not only were they equal to men in their ability to address political issues on public occasions, they were superior to men, as witnessed by the fact that many women had succeeded despite the best efforts of men to keep them down. "Our high and mighty Lords (thanks to their arbitrary constitutions)," declared Mason, "have denied us the means of knowledge, and then reproached us for the want of it." This bold young orator

102. Mary Kelley, *Learning to Stand and Speak: Women, Education, and Public Life in America's Republic* (Chapel Hill, 2006).
103. Zagarri, "Rights of Man and Woman in Post- Revolutionary America," 224, 226.

went on to call not just for equal education for women but for their equal participation in the learned professions and political office.[104]

Although some women in the 1790s began to assert themselves in public in this manner, public performances by women were generally frowned upon. Jefferson thought that if women were permitted to "mix promiscuously in the public meetings of men," the consequence would be a "depravation of morals." Even attending lectures with men present created some uneasiness.[105]

Given this experience and these attitudes, imagine the sensation created in Boston in 1802 by Deborah Sampson Gannett. This forty-two-year-old woman appeared onstage in female clothes to recount her experiences in the Revolutionary War as a disguised Continental Army soldier. Following her lecture, Gannett changed into a military uniform and demonstrated her ability to perform the soldier's manual exercise of arms.

After her spectacular appearance in Boston, Gannett went on a year's tour throughout New England and New York, playing mostly to packed houses—the first such lecture tour by an American woman. Yet her lectures, written by her mentor and memoirist Herman Mann, were ambivalent. Her mere presence, of course, awed many spectators, for she was attractive and not at all masculine. At the same time, however, Gannett needed to assure her audience that she was not the threat to the social order that she appeared to be. By 1802 a reaction against the egalitarian sentiments of Mary Wollstonecraft was taking place, and Gannett had to adapt to the new climate of opinion. Even Judith Sargent Murray had written that "we are not desirous to array THE SEX in martial habiliments."

Gannett admitted that what she had done twenty years earlier in joining the army in disguise was "a breach in decorum of my sex unquestionably," which "ought to expel me from the enjoyment of society, from the acknowledgement of my own sex." But then she went on to explain that she had been caught up in a frenzy of patriotism "that could brook no control" and had "burst the tyrant bands which *held my sex in awe*, and clandestinely, or by stealth, grasped an opportunity which custom and the world seemed to deny as natural privilege." In the end, however, she offset her assertion of freedom and independence for her sex by conceding that the proper role for women was to mold men and to be satisfied with the "dignified title and encomium of MISTRESS AND LADY, in our *kitchens* and in our *parlours*," and by acknowledging that "the *field* and the *cabinet* are the proper spheres assigned to our MASTERS and our LORDS." Still, the

104. Tise, *American Counterrevolution*, 161–63.

105. Alfred F. Young, *Masquerade: The Life and Times of Deborah Sampson, Continental Soldier* (New York, 2004), 202.

fact that she was traveling without male escort and lecturing to large audiences was an inspiring object lesson in female autonomy.[106]

Since the Revolution had made all Americans conscious of rights, feminists were bound to note that the Revolution had failed to fulfill its promises for women. Some, like the writer Charles Brockden Brown in his novel *Alcuin: A Dialogue* (1798) and the legal commentator St. George Tucker, saw an inconsistency between the Revolution's rhetoric and American practice. Tucker had to admit that women were taxed without their consent, like "aliens...children under the age of discretion, idiots, and lunatics."[107] For a brief period between 1790 and 1807 unmarried property-holding women took advantage of a clause in the New Jersey constitution that granted the franchise to all free inhabitants with property worth fifty pounds. Apparently some women voted for Federalist candidates too often, for critics began complaining that women were too timid and pliant and too dependent on male relatives for direction to exercise the ballot intelligently. In 1807 a Republican-sponsored law limited the franchise to white taxpaying male citizens. Few women in New Jersey seem to have lamented the loss of the vote.

Despite all the talk of women's rights, most women in this period were not yet eager to vote and participate in politics. The suggestions in the magazines of the day for female political equality were few and far between, and none of the major political leaders ever seriously considered the direct political participation of women in politics. "A woman in politics is like a monkey in a toy shop," declared the noted lawyer Jeremiah Mason, the Federalist U.S. senator from New Hampshire in 1814. "She can do no good, and may do harm." President Jefferson abruptly cut off any suggestion that women might be appointed to governmental office: it was "an innovation for which the public is not prepared, nor am I."[108] Although the gaining of political rights for women was never a realistic possibility in this period, there were isolated voices preparing the way for the future.

All this promotion of rights and reforms helped to strengthen the civil society that worked to hold the Republic together. But these particular rights and reforms did not begin to deal with the greatest evil afflicting American society—slavery.

106. Young, *Masquerade*, 220, 221, 223, 224.
107. Charles Brockden Brown, *Alcuin: A Dialogue* (New York, 1798), 57–59; Kerber, *Toward an Intellectual History of Women*, 37.
108. David Hackett Fischer, *The Revolution of American Conservatism: The Federalist Party in the Era of Jeffersonian Democracy* (New York, 1965), 184; TJ to Gallatin, 13 Jan. 1813, in Henry Adams, ed., *The Writings of Albert Gallatin* (Philadelphia, 1879), 1: 328.

# 14

## Between Slavery and Freedom

The greatest republican reform of the period was the anti-slavery movement. Of course, the Revolution freed only a fraction of the nearly half a
million slaves in the colonies in 1776—and many modern historians have
called the Revolution's inability to free all the slaves its greatest failure.
But the Revolution did accomplish a great deal: it created for the first
time in American history the cultural atmosphere that made African
American slavery abhorrent to many Americans.

By attacking slavery more fiercely than ever before, Revolutionary Americans freed tens of thousands of slaves. But the Revolution's libertarian and
egalitarian message had perverse consequences. It forced those Southerners
who chose to retain slavery to fall back on the alleged racial deficiencies of
blacks as a justification for an institution that hitherto they had taken for
granted and had never before needed to justify. The anti-slavery movement
that arose out of the Revolution inadvertently produced racism in America.

HEREDITARY CHATTEL SLAVERY—one person owning the life and
labor of another person and that person's progeny—is virtually incomprehensible to those living in the West today, even though as many as twenty-
seven million people in the world may be presently enslaved.[1] In fact,
slavery has existed in a variety of cultures for thousands of years, including
those of the ancient Greeks and Romans, the medieval Koreans, the
Pacific Northwest Indians, and the pre-Columbian Aztecs. The pre-Nor-
man English practiced slavery, as did the Vikings, the many ethnic groups
of Africa, and the early Islamic Arabs; indeed, beginning in the 600s Muslims may have transported over the next twelve centuries as many sub-
Saharan Africans to various parts of the Islamic world, from Spain to
India, as were taken to the Western Hemisphere.[2]

1. Lynn Hunt, *Inventing Human Rights: A History* (New York, 2007), 207.
2. As David Brion Davis has pointed out, a "French scholar, Raymond Mauny, estimates
   that between 600 and 1800 as many as fourteen million African slaves were exported to
   Muslim regions." Davis, *Challenging the Boundaries of Slavery* (Cambridge, MA,
   2003), 10.

Yet as ubiquitous as slavery was in the ancient and pre-modern worlds, including the early Islamic world, there was nothing anywhere quite like the African plantation slavery that developed in the Americas. Between 1500 and the mid-nineteenth century some eleven or twelve million slaves were brought from Africa to the Americas. The prosperity of the European colonies in the New World depended upon the labor of these millions of African slaves and their enslaved descendants. Slavery existed everywhere in the Americas, from the villages of French Canada to the sugar plantations of Portuguese Brazil.

Slavery in the New World was never a monolithic institution; it differed both in space and time, and slavery in British North America differed sharply from slavery in the rest of the New World. In the course of the seventeenth and eighteenth centuries the English mainland colonies imported about two hundred thousand African slaves, a small percentage of the millions who were brought to the Caribbean and South American colonies, where the mortality rates were horrendous. Far fewer slaves died prematurely on the North American mainland. In fact, by the late eighteenth century the slaves in most of the English mainland colonies were reproducing at the same rates as whites, already among the most fertile peoples in the Western world.[3]

By the eve of the Revolution white North American colonists possessed 460,000 African American slaves, about a fifth of the total population. Most were held in the South. In 1770 the largest colony, Virginia, had about 188,000 black slaves, slightly more than 40 percent of the colony's total population of 447,000. In 1770 South Carolina had the highest proportion of African American slaves to whites, 60 percent, or 75,000, of the total population of 124,000. In these Southern colonies slavery lay at the heart of the economy. The master-slave relationship supplied the standard for all other social relationships.

As it had been from the beginning in the seventeenth century, the South's economy was based on the production and sale of staple crops—exotic agricultural goods that commanded special significance in international markets. Each of the South's dominant slaveholding areas—the Chesapeake and the Lowcountry of South Carolina—had developed its own peculiar primary staple crop adapted to its climate and landscape, tobacco in the case of the Chesapeake and rice and indigo in the case of South Carolina.

Although both staples lent themselves to the development of plantation slave labor, they created different kinds of plantations and different

---

3. See "New Perspectives on the Transatlantic Slave Trade," to which the entire issue of January 2001 of the WMQ, 58 (2001), is devoted.

systems of slavery. Because of the nature of tobacco production, the plantations in the Chesapeake tended to be much smaller with many fewer slaves than those in South Carolina. On the eve of the Revolution less than 30 percent of the slaves in the Chesapeake area lived on plantations with twenty or more slaves. Indeed, over one-third of the slaves in the Chesapeake resided on small plantations with fewer than ten slaves. Because tobacco exhausted the soil rather rapidly, the small plantations and their labor forces in Virginia had to keep pushing westward in search of fresh lands, creating instability in the lives of both slaves and masters.

Tobacco, moreover, was not always associated with slave labor, and many non-slaveholding white families in the Chesapeake continued to grow it throughout the eighteenth century and beyond. Consequently, slaves in the Chesapeake lived in a world surrounded by whites. No Virginia county contained a majority of blacks. Even in those Virginia counties with the largest numbers of slaves, at least a quarter of the households owned no slaves at all.[4]

Slavery in the Lowcountry was different. Over 80 percent of the slaves in South Carolina lived on substantial plantations possessing twenty or more slaves. Only a tiny proportion — 7 percent — lived on small plantations with fewer than ten slaves. Unlike tobacco, rice cultivation required sizeable plantations; two-thirds of those in South Carolina exceeded five hundred acres. Rice was more laborious to produce than tobacco. One observer of the Lowcountry in 1775 noted that "the labour required for [rice] is only fit for slaves, and I think the hardest work I have seen them engaged in."[5] Unlike tobacco, rice did not exhaust the soil, and the need alternately to flood and drain the rice fields with tidewater meant that Lowcountry plantations necessarily remained close to estuaries. Consequently, the slaves and their descendants in South Carolina had a greater chance to remain on the same plantation for longer periods than was the case in Virginia. And they had fewer whites around them than in the Chesapeake. By 1790 eleven of the eighteen rural parishes of the Carolina Lowcountry were more than 80 percent black.

There were other differences. The Chesapeake plantations were much more diversified than those in Carolina, many of them growing wheat and other foodstuffs in addition to tobacco. In fact, in the decades leading

4. Philip Morgan, *Slave Counterpoint: Black Culture in the Eighteenth-Century Chesapeake and the Lowcountry* (Chapel Hill, 1998), 165.
5. Morgan, Slave Counterpoint, 148.

up to the Revolution more and more of the Virginia plantations, like Washington's Mount Vernon, began to replace tobacco with wheat. The spread of wheat production changed the nature of the skills the Chesapeake slaves needed. They had to learn to plow and take care of oxen and horses, which in turn required the growing of hay and other fodder and the manuring of land.

By the late eighteenth century the wheat-producing plantations in Virginia and Maryland had become highly organized operations with the slaves involved in a variety of specialized tasks. Growing wheat in place of tobacco, the planters began calling themselves "farmers," with their slaves becoming farm workers instead of plantation hands. Because the more diversified agriculture required less labor, many of the Chesapeake farmers began hiring out their slaves. This practice in turn suggested to some in the Upper South that slavery might eventually be replaced by wage labor.[6]

The Chesapeake slaves also engaged in many more diverse crafts than their counterparts in the Deep South. The British traveler Isaac Weld noted that the leading Chesapeake planters "have nearly everything they can want on their own estates. Amongst their slaves are found tailors, shoemakers, carpenters, smiths, turners, wheelwrights, weavers, tanners, etc."[7] While the Virginia slaves tended to supply many of the needs of their plantations, the situation was different in the Deep South. Rice was a more lucrative crop than tobacco; throughout the eighteenth century the profits from rice had accounted for one-half to two-thirds of the annual value of South Carolina's exports.[8] As a consequence, few South Carolina plantations were willing to sacrifice rice production in order to diversify and produce other goods, including provisions. In 1774 the manager of two Lowcountry plantations warned the owner against planting corn to supply food for the plantations. "If more corn is to be raised there than common, there must of consequence less Rice be planted, and the latter is the most profitable Grain." Instead, the manager urged that corn be purchased from the backcountry.[9]

6. Morgan, *Slave Counterpoint*, 170–75; Robert F. Dalzell Jr. and Lee Baldwin Dalzell, *George Washington's Mount Vernon: At Home in Revolutionary America* (New York, 1998), 132–33; Lorena S. Walsh, "Slave Life, Slave Society, and Tobacco Production in the Tidewater Chesapeake, 1620–1820," in Ira Berlin and Philip D. Morgan, eds., *Cultivation and Culture: Labor and the Shaping of Slave Life in the Americas* (Charlottesville, 1993), 170–99; Sarah S. Hughes, "Slaves for Hire: The Allocation of Black Labor in Elizabeth City County, Virginia, 1782 to 1810," *WMQ*, 35 (1978), 260–86.

7. Isaac Weld, *Travels Through the States of North America* (London, 1799), 1: 147.

8. Morgan, *Slave Counterpoint*, 148.

9. Morgan, *Slave Counterpoint*, 49–50.

Perhaps the most important distinction between the slave populations of the two regions was the different ways the two societies produced their slaves. On the eve of the Revolution over 90 percent of Virginia's slaves were American born and had assimilated much of Anglo-American culture, including the English language. To supply itself with slaves Virginia had come to rely on the fertility of the large number of its native-born female slaves, who had come to equal the males in number; by the time of the Revolution Virginia had stopped importing slaves and never again resumed importing them.

By contrast, only 65 percent of South Carolina's slaves were native born; over a third had been born in Africa. In the several decades following the Revolution South Carolina continued to import slaves, bringing in as many as seventy thousand, some from the West Indies, most of them from Africa. Indeed, South Carolina imported more slaves than any other colony on the North American mainland. Since most of the slaves brought into South Carolina from Africa were male adults, the natural growth of the slave population in the colony and state was retarded—the presence of a large number of native-born female slaves being the key to natural growth.

By the time the international slave trade was legally prohibited in 1808, South Carolina had imported about twice as many slaves as Virginia, even though its slave population of two hundred thousand was only half that of Virginia's. South Carolina's greater reliance on importation gave its slave society and culture an African tone and character that did not exist to the same degree in the Chesapeake. Most of the slaves in the Carolina Lowcountry carved out a distinctive culture for themselves, including not only their own African-English hybrid language, Gullah, but their own styles of personal display, including the wearing of beads and jewelry. Actually, everywhere in America the black slaves worked out their own syncretic forms for their African American culture—in their music, religion, funerals, humor, and entertainments. Whites had an especially hard time making sense of the dancing, singing, and rejoicing that took place at black funerals; they tended to dismiss these practices as "festive accompaniments" without realizing they were a ritual celebration of the deceased's journey back "home" to Africa.[10]

10. Morgan, *Slave Counterpoint*, 79, 594; Philip Morgan, "Black Society in the Lowcountry, 1760–1810," in Ira Berlin and Ronald Hoffman, eds., *Slavery and Freedom in the Age of the American Revolution* (Charlottesville, 1983), 89; John W. Blassingame, *The Slave Community: Plantation Life in the Ante-Bellum South* (New York, 1972), 17–40; Sylvia R. Frey, *Water from the Rock: Black Resistance in a Revolutionary Age* (Princeton, 1991), 41–42; Lawrence W. Levine, *Black Culture and Black Consciousness: Afro-American Folk Thought from Slavery to Freedom* (New York, 1977); Shane White and Graham White, *The Sounds of Slavery: Discovering African American History Through Songs, Sermons, and Speech* (Boston, 2005).

The nature of the staple also gave the Lowcountry Carolina slaves greater autonomy than their counterparts in the Chesapeake. Since producing rice did not require close supervision, the white planters came to rely on a task system of labor. Giving the slaves tasks to complete allowed the slaves who worked quickly opportunities for free time to grow their own crops or to produce goods for themselves or for sale. In 1796 the South Carolina legislature attempted to regulate this practice of the slaves selling and buying their own goods and thus implicitly legitimated it.[11]

Slaves in Virginia had no such free time and had much more difficulty earning extra money for themselves. Since tobacco needed considerable care and attention, producing it required a very different system of labor management. White planters in the Chesapeake relied on gang labor for the production of tobacco—using small units of closely supervised laborers who worked from sunup to sundown with no incentive to work quickly. Consequently, Chesapeake slaves developed all sorts of resourceful methods of malingering and shirking the work, frustrating their masters to no end.

Washington concluded that his slaves worked four times as fast when he was directly supervising them than when he was absent. Try as he might, he was never able to get his slaves to work efficiently, which was one of the initial reasons he came to oppose the institution. He realized that the slaves had no incentive to work hard and develop "a *good* name" for themselves. This he thought was slavery's greatest single flaw as a system of labor. He believed that people strove to do well in life in order to win the respect of others. But slaves had no opportunity to win respect or earn good reputations; hence their presumed lack of ambition. He often wondered what they might accomplish if they were free men.[12]

Although masters and slaves often developed close and sometimes even affectionate relationships, especially in the Chesapeake area, no one ever forgot that the entire system rested on violence and brute force. Masters in South Carolina sometimes branded their slaves and punished them with a ferocity that outsiders found appalling. Four hundred lashes washed down with salt and water was considered "but Slite punishment" compared to the ingenious cruelties some planters could think up to inflict on their disobedient slaves, including, as one observer noted, putting a slave "on the picket with his Left Hand tied to his left toe behind him and Right hand to the post and his Right foot on the pickets till it worked through his foot."[13]

11. John Campbell, "As 'A Kind of Freeman'? Slaves' Market Related Activities in the South Carolina Up Country, 1800–1860," in Berlin and Morgan, eds., *Cultivation and Culture*, 244.

12. Dalzell and Dalzell, *George Washington's Mount Vernon*, 129, 212–13.

13. Morgan, *Slave Counterpoint*, 393; Winthrop D. Jordan, *White over Black: American Attitudes Toward the Negro, 1550–1812* (Chapel Hill, 1968), 228–34.

Although master-slave relations were more brutal and more imper-sonal in the Lowcountry than in the Chesapeake, everywhere the slave system bred a pervasive sense of hierarchy. "Societies of men could not subsist unless there were a subordination of one to another," declared a Virginia lawyer in 1772. "That in this subordination the department of slaves must be filled by some, or there would be a defect in the scale of order."[14] More than anything else, that sense of hierarchy separated the Southern states from those of the North.

OF COURSE, THERE WERE ALWAYS MASTERS who took advantage of this subordination, especially with their female slaves. In the Lowcountry of South Carolina, the incidence of whites having slave concubines was often casually accepted and even treated with amusement. This was largely because whites and slaves tended to live farther apart from one another, and thus miscegenation was not as widespread as it was in the Chesapeake. In Virginia, where whites and slaves lived more closely together, such racial mixing became more common with increasing num-bers of mulattos.[15]

The Virginian Thomas Jefferson certainly lived among many mulattos. His father-in-law, John Wayles, had six children with a mulatto slave, Betty Hemings. When Jefferson married Wayles's daughter, Martha, these enslaved children, including the quadroon Sally Hemings, passed to Jef-ferson. Although the evidence is now overwhelming that Jefferson was sexually involved with Sally Hemings, that may be less important than the fact that miscegenation was part of his family and going on all around him at Monticello.[16] That alone may help explain Jefferson's deep fear of racial mixing.

Jefferson was in most respects a typical slaveholder. Although he always condemned slavery, he did own one of the largest slave populations in Virginia. Upon the division of his father-in-law's estate in 1774 he became, in fact, the second-largest slaveholder in Albemarle County. Thereafter the number of his slaves remained around two hundred—with increases through births offset by periodic sales to pay off debts. Jefferson was known to be a good master, reluctant to break up families or to sell slaves except for delinquency or at their own request. Nevertheless, between 1784 and 1794 he disposed of 161 people by sale or gift. It is true that

14. Morgan, *Slave Counterpoint*, 258.
15. Morgan, *Slave Counterpoint*, 405–7.
16. Annette Gordon-Reed, *The Hemingses of Monticello: An American Family* (New York, 2008), has mounted an enormous amount of persuasive evidence that Jefferson maintained Sally Hemings as his concubine.

Jefferson was averse to separating young children from their parents; but once slave boys or girls reached the age of ten or twelve and their working lives began, they were no longer children in Jefferson's mind.

Monticello was a working plantation, and Jefferson was eager to make it pay. His slaves may have been members of his "family," but they were units of production as well. Everywhere on his plantation he sought to eliminate pockets of idleness. If a slave was too old or too sick to work in the fields, he or she was put to tending the vegetable gardens or to cooking in the quarters. When one of his former head men named Nace became ill, Jefferson ordered that he be "entirely kept from labour until he recovers"; nevertheless, Nace was to spend his days indoors shelling corn or making shoes or baskets. Jefferson was willing to prescribe lighter work for women who were pregnant or raising infant children because they were actually breeding more property; thus, said Jefferson, "a child raised every 2 years is of more profit than the crop of the best laboring man." This was one of the times, he said, when "providence has made our interest and our duties coincide perfectly."[17]

"I love industry and abhor severity," declared Jefferson, and apparently he himself never physically punished a slave. Yet the coercion of the lash lay behind the workings of Monticello, as it did for all plantations. Jefferson certainly had no scruples in ordering disobedient slaves whipped; and those he could not correct he sold, often as a lesson to the other slaves. Jefferson ordered one particularly unmanageable slave to be sold so far away that it would seem to his companions "as if he were put out of the way by death." That Jefferson was considered to be a kind and gentle master suggests how pernicious the practice of slavery could be. As he himself pointed out, a master "nursed, educated, and daily exercised in tyranny, cannot but be stamped by it with odious peculiarities. The man must be a prodigy who can retain his manners and morals undepraved by such circumstances."[18]

ALTHOUGH NEARLY 90 PERCENT of all the slaves lived in the slave societies of the South, slavery was not inconsequential in the Northern parts of America. On the eve of the Revolution nearly fifty thousand slaves lived in the North. In the middle of the eighteenth century one out

17. Lucia C. Stanton, "'Those Who Labor for My Happiness': Thomas Jefferson and His Slaves," in Peter S. Onuf, ed., *Jeffersonian Legacies* (Charlottesville, 1993), 155, 150.

18. Stanton, "'Those Who Labor for My Happiness,'" in Onuf, ed., *Jeffersonian Legacies*, 158, 160; TJ, *Notes on the State of Virginia*, ed. William Peden (Chapel Hill, 1955), 162.

of every five families in Boston owned at least one slave. In 1767 nearly 9 percent of the population of Philadelphia was enslaved. In 1760 black slaves made up nearly 8 percent of the population of Rhode Island and nearly 7 percent of the population of New Jersey, most of them clustered around the port cities and towns.

By 1770 black slaves constituted 12 percent of the population of the colony of New York and a bit over 14 percent in the city of New York. Slaves were widely distributed in small units throughout the city; even as late as 1790 one out of every five households owned at least one slave. Indeed, the proportion of households in New York City and its surrounding counties owning slaves was greater than that of any Southern state — nearly 40 percent of the white households for the New York City area compared to 36.5 percent for Maryland and 34 percent for South Carolina. Of course, the number of slaves held by each household in New York City and its immediate hinterland was much smaller than those of the South, averaging fewer than four slaves per household.[19]

Most of the rural Northern slaves were farm laborers of one sort or another. Only in South County (then called King's County), Rhode Island, was there anything resembling the plantations of the South. These plantations, which produced dairy products and livestock, especially pacer horses, ranged from three-hundred-acre farms to large sprawling units that measured in square miles. The Narragansett Planters, as they were called, tried to live like Southern aristocrats, but the slave populations on their plantations tended to be much smaller, running about a dozen to a dozen and a half on each plantation. In South County the black proportion of the population ranged from 15 to 25 percent, making this area the most slave-ridden of any place in New England; indeed, the towns of South Kingstown and Charlestown in South County had proportions of black populations that rivaled those of Virginia, 30 to 40 percent. Some of the slaves may have been racially mixed, for many Narragansett Indians, devastated and scattered by King Philip's War in the previous century, had intermarried with blacks.[20]

In most parts of the Northern colonies slaves tended to live much closer to their white masters than the slaves of the South—usually jammed into the garrets, backrooms, and barns of their white owners rather than living in separate slave quarters. On the eve of the Revolution one-third

19. Gary B. Nash, "Slaves and Slaveowners in Colonial Philadelphia," WMQ, 30 (1973), 237; Shane White, *Somewhat More Independent: The End of Slavery in New York City, 1770–1810* (Athens, GA, 1991), 16.
20. Joanne Pope Melish, *Disowning Slavery: Gradual Emancipation and "Race" in New England, 1780–1860* (Ithaca, 1998).

or more of the Northern slaves lived in the several cities, where they performed a variety of tasks as domestics, teamsters, tradesmen, dock workers, and sailors. One out of four blacks in Rhode Island, for example, lived in the slave-trading entrepôt of Newport, where they constituted 20 percent of the city's population.[21] Despite this urban clustering of black slaves, however, the Northern colonies were not slave societies like those of the South, and slavery was just one form of labor among many and not the dominant model in the society.

PREVALENT AS IT WAS everywhere in colonial America, slavery in the first half of the eighteenth century was very much taken for granted. It was still a cruel and brutal age, as the system of criminal punishments revealed, and many believed that slavery was merely part of the natural order of things. An educated and enlightened slaveholder like William Byrd of Westover in Virginia never expressed any guilt or misgivings over the owning of dozens of slaves. Of course, by the end of the seventeenth century and the beginning of the eighteenth isolated conscience-stricken individuals spoke out against slavery, but they were few and far between, and mostly Quakers.

During the first half of the eighteenth century most Americans had simply accepted slavery as the lowest and most base status in a hierarchy of legal dependencies. The prevalence of hundreds of thousands of bonded white servants tended to blur the conspicuous nature of black slavery. With as much as half of colonial society at any moment legally unfree, the peculiar character of lifetime, hereditary black slavery was not always as obvious as it would become in the years following the Revolution when bonded white servitude virtually disappeared. Naturally, the leading Southern Revolutionaries—Washington, Jefferson, and Madison—all owned slaves; but so too did many of the Northern Revolutionaries—Boston's John Hancock, New York's Robert Livingston, and Philadelphia's John Dickinson. On the eve of the Revolution the mayor of Philadelphia possessed thirty-one slaves.[22]

The Revolution almost overnight made slavery a problem in ways that it had not been earlier. The contradiction between the appeal to liberty and the existence of slavery became obvious to all the Revolutionary leaders. They did not need to hear Dr. Johnson's famous quip "How is it we hear the loudest yelps for liberty among the drivers of negroes?" in order

21. William D. Pierson, *Black Yankees: The Development of an Afro-American Subculture in Eighteenth-Century New England* (Amherst, MA, 1988), 15.
22. Gary B. Nash, *The Unknown American Revolution: The Unruly Birth of Democracy and the Struggle to Create America* (New York, 2005), 32.

to realize the painful inconsistency between their talk of freedom for themselves and their owning of black slaves. If all men were created equal, as all enlightened persons were now saying, then what justification could there be for holding Africans in slavery? Since Americans "are by the law of nature free born, as indeed all men are, white or black...does it follow," asked James Otis of Massachusetts in 1764, "that 'tis right to enslave a man because he is black?...Can any logical inference in favor of slavery be drawn from a flat nose, a long or short face?"[23]

By the eve of the Revolution the contradiction had become excruciating for many, and Northerners, like Samuel Cooke in his Massachusetts election sermon of 1770, were anxious to confess that in tolerating black slavery "we, the patrons of liberty, have dishonored the Christian name, and degraded human nature nearly to a level with the beasts that perish."[24] Even some prominent slaveholding Southerners, like Thomas Jefferson, were willing to declare that "the rights of human nature [are] deeply wounded by this infamous practice [of importing slaves]," and that "the abolition of domestic slavery is the great object of desire in those colonies where it was unhappily introduced in their infant state."[25]

As early as 1774 both Rhode Island and Connecticut prohibited new slaves from being brought into their colonies. In the preamble to their law the Rhode Islanders declared that since "the inhabitants of America are generally engaged in the preservations of their own rights and liberties, among which that of personal freedom must be considered the greatest," it was obvious that "those who are desirous of enjoying all the advantages of liberty themselves should be willing to extend personal liberty to others." Other states—Delaware, Virginia, Maryland, and South Carolina—soon followed in abolishing the slave trade, South Carolina only for a term of years. Given the mounting sense of inconsistency between the Revolutionary ideals and the holding of people in bondage, it is not surprising that the first anti-slave convention in the world was held in Philadelphia in 1775.

Everywhere in the country most of the Revolutionary leaders assumed that slavery was on its last legs and was headed for eventual destruction. On the eve of the Revolution Benjamin Rush believed that the desire to abolish the institution "prevails in our counsels and among all ranks in

---

23. Samuel Johnson, *Taxation No Tyranny* (1775), in *Samuel Johnson: Political Writings*, ed. Donald J. Greene (New Haven, 1977), 454; James Otis, *The Rights of the British Colonists Asserted and Proved* (1764), in Bernard Bailyn, ed., *Pamphlets of the American Revolution, 1750–1776* (Cambridge, MA, 1965), 1: 439.

24. Bernard Bailyn, *The Ideological Origins of the American Revolution* (Cambridge, MA, 1967), 239.

25. TJ, *A Summary View of the Rights of British America* (1774), *Jefferson: Writings*, 115–16.

every province." With hostility toward slavery mounting everywhere among the enlightened in the Atlantic world, he predicted in 1774 that "there will be not a Negro slave in North America in 40 years."[26] Even some Virginians assumed slavery could not long endure. Jefferson told a French correspondent in 1786 that there were in the Virginia legislature "men of virtue enough to propose, and talents" to move toward, "the gradual emancipation of slaves." To be sure, "they saw that the moment of doing it was not yet arrived," but, said Jefferson, with "the spread of light and liberality" among the slaveholders that moment was coming.[27] Slavery simply could not stand against the relentless march of liberty and progress. That the Philadelphia Convention of 1787 was scrupulous in not mentioning "slaves," "slavery," or "Negroes" in the final draft of the Constitution seemed to point to a future without the shameful institution.

Predictions of slavery's demise could not have been more wrong. Far from being doomed, American slavery in fact was on the verge of its greatest expansion.

HOW COULD THE REVOLUTIONARY LEADERS have been so mistaken? How could they have deceived themselves so completely? The Founders' self-deception and mistaken optimism were understandable, for they wanted to believe the best, and initially there was evidence that slavery was in fact dying out. The Northern states, where slavery was not insignificant, were busy trying to eliminate the institution. Following the Americans' early efforts to abolish the slave trade, they began attacking the institution of slavery itself with increasing passion.[28]

In 1777 the future state of Vermont led the way in formally abolishing slavery. Its constitution of that year declared that no persons "born in this country, or brought from over sea, ought to be holden by law to serve any purpose, or servant, slave or apprentice" after they attained adulthood, unless "by their own consent," or by appropriate court-ordered legal proscription.[29] Then in 1780 the Revolutionary government of Pennsylvania,

26. Gary B. Nash, *Race and Revolution* (Madison, WI, 1990), 9; BR to Granville Sharp, 1 Nov. 1774, in John A. Woods, ed., "The Correspondence of Benjamin Rush and Granville Sharp, 1773–1809," *Journal of American Studies*, 1 (1967), 13.
27. Jefferson to Jean Nicolas Démeunier, 26 June 1786, *Papers of Jefferson*, 10: 63; Adam Rothman, *Slave Country: American Expansion and the Origins of the Deep South* (Cambridge, MA, 2005), 2.
28. For examples of these anti-slave expressions, see James G. Basker et al., eds., *Early American Abolitionists: A Collection of Anti-Slavery Writings, 1760–1820* (New York, 2005).
29. Patrick T. Conley and John P. Kaminski, eds., *The Bill of Rights and the States: The Colonial and Revolutionary Origins of American Liberties* (Madison, WI, 1992), 202.

admitting that slavery was "disgraceful to any people, and more especially to those who have been contending in the great cause of liberty themselves," provided for the gradual emancipation of the state's slaves.[30] In Boston free and enslaved blacks themselves took up the cause and used the Revolutionaries' language against the institution, declaring that "they have in common with all men a Natural and Unalienable right to that freedom which the Grat Parent of the Universe hath Bestowed equally on all menkind."[31] In 1783 the Massachusetts Superior Court held that slavery was incompatible with the state's constitution, particularly with its bill of rights, which declared that "all men are born free and equal." A New Hampshire court did the same. Rhode Island and Connecticut passed gradual abolition laws in 1784. In the Pennsylvania ratifying convention James Wilson predicted that emancipation of all the slaves in the United States was inevitable. The abolition of the slave trade, he said, would lay "the foundation for banishing slavery out of this country; and though the period is more distant than I could wish, yet it will produce the same kind [of] gradual change [for the whole nation] which was pursued in Pennsylvania."[32] New York in 1799 and New Jersey in 1804 provided for the gradual elimination of slavery, though as late as 1810 over 40 percent of white households in New York City still contained slaves.[33] Nevertheless, by the early nineteenth century every Northern state had provided for the eventual end of slavery. By 1790 the number of free blacks in the Northern states had increased from several hundred in the 1770s to over twenty-seven thousand; by 1810 free blacks in the North numbered well over one hundred thousand.

Even the South, especially Virginia, the largest state in the Union, gave signs of wanting to soften and eventually end the institution. The Virginia and Maryland masters certainly treated their slaves more paternalistically than their counterparts in South Carolina and Georgia. The Creole slaves of the Upper South benefited not only from better food, clothing, and housing but also from more intimate daily contact with their masters than those in the Deep South. On the eve of the Revolution many of Virginia's slaveholders had become more unwilling to break up families and had become more relaxed about slaves' visiting between plantations and about

30. Ira Berlin, *Many Thousands Gone: The First Two Centuries of Slavery in North America* (Cambridge, MA, 1998), 232.
31. Berlin, *Many Thousands Gone*, 232.
32. James Wilson, 3 Dec. 1787, *The Documentary History of the Ratification of the Constitution: Ratification by the States: Pennsylvania*, ed. Merrill Jensen et al., (Madison, WI, 1976), 2: 463.
33. White, *Somewhat More Independent*, 51.

slave truancy, even putting up with some slaves' running away for days or even weeks at a time as long as they eventually returned. (Since there were no free states as yet, there was no place to run to anyway.) Nevertheless, by the time of the Revolution literate young blacks, like Isaac Bee of Carter's Grove in Virginia, who, according to his master, "thinks he has a Right to his Freedom," were willing to run off and try "to pass" as free men.[34]

In the Upper South the black codes that had been passed at the beginning of the eighteenth century had fallen into neglect, and whites had become less concerned with racial separation than in the past. Fraternization between whites and black slaves had become more common, especially in drinking bouts, horse racing, cockfighting, and gambling. Slaves and lower-class whites often got together in drinking establishments. Blacks commonly supplied the music for white dances, which themselves became increasingly influenced by slave customs. Whites tended to treat the few free blacks in their midst much less severely than they would in the nineteenth century. Free blacks were allowed to acquire property, carry arms in militia groups, travel fairly freely, and even to vote in some areas.

The white evangelical Protestant groups of Baptists and later Methodists recruited blacks and mingled with them in their congregations. Some black evangelicals even preached to white congregations. Indeed, in the 1790s white residents of the Eastern Shore in Virginia pooled enough money to purchase the freedom of their black preacher. Not only were the Baptists and Methodists mixing whites and blacks, but these rapidly growing evangelical denominations were publicly voicing their opposition to slavery. When even Southerners like Jefferson, Patrick Henry, Henry Laurens, and St. George Tucker publicly deplored the injustice of slavery, from "that moment," declared the New York physician and abolitionist E. H. Smith in 1798, "the slow, but certain, death-wound was inflicted upon it."[35]

Other evidence from the Upper South seemed to reinforce the point. The increased hiring out of slaves convinced many in the Upper South that slavery would soon be replaced by wage labor. What could be a more conspicuous endorsement of the anti-slavery cause than having the College of William and Mary in 1791 confer an honorary degree on the celebrated British abolitionist Granville Sharp? That there were more anti-slave societies created in the South than in the North was bound to make people feel that the South was moving in the same direction of

34. Lorena S. Walsh, *From Calabar to Carter's Grove: The History of a Virginia Slave Community* (Charlottesville, 1997), 129.
35. Morgan, *Slave Counterpoint*, 415–18, 428–33, 652–54; Duncan J. MacLeod, *Slavery, Race and the American Revolution* (Cambridge, UK, 1974), 29.

gradual emancipation as the North, especially when these societies were publicly denouncing slavery as "not only an odious degradation, but an outrageous violation of one of the most essential rights of human nature."[36] In Virginia and Maryland some of these anti-slave societies brought "freedom suits" in the state courts that led to some piecemeal emancipation. If the slaves could demonstrate that they had a maternal white or Indian ancestor, they could be freed, and hearsay evidence was often enough to convince the courts. "Whole families," recalled one sympathetic observer, "were often liberated by a single verdict, the fate of one relative deciding the fate of many." By 1796 nearly thirty freedom suits were pending in Virginia courts.[37]

Other efforts in the Upper South to free slaves contributed to the sense that slavery was doomed everywhere in America. In 1782 Virginia allowed for the private manumission of slaves, and Delaware and Maryland soon followed with similar laws. Some slaves took advantage of these new liberal laws and worked to buy their own freedom. Of the slaves freed in Norfolk, Virginia, between 1791 and 1820, more than a third purchased themselves or were purchased by others, usually by their families. By 1790 the free black population in the Upper South had increased to over thirty thousand; by 1810 the free blacks in Virginia and Maryland numbered over ninety-four thousand. Many thought that the abolition of slavery itself was just a matter of time.

Some set forth what became the diffusionist position—that spreading slavery throughout the Western territories would make elimination of the institution easier. In 1798 Virginia congressman John Nicholas contended that opening up the Western Country to slavery would be a service to the entire Union. It would, he said, "spread the blacks over a large space, so that in time it might be safe to carry into effect the plan which certain philanthropists have so much at heart, and to which he had no objection, if it could be effected, viz., the emancipation of this class of men." Since the Constitution's restriction on acting against the slave trade until 1808 applied only to slaves brought into the states, Congress in 1798 prohibited the importation of slaves from abroad into the Mississippi Territory but purposefully allowed the introduction of slaves into the Western territories from elsewhere in the United States. A similar policy was followed in the newly organized Orleans Territory in 1804 when Congress forbade the importation of foreign slaves but allowed owners of slaves settling in the territory from other parts of the United States to bring their slaves with

36. Douglas R. Egerton, *Gabriel's Rebellion: The Virginia Slave Conspiracies of 1800 and 1802* (Chapel Hill, 1993), 13.
37. Berlin, *Many Thousands Gone*, 281; Egerton, *Gabriel's Rebellion*, 13.

them. The demand for slaves was so great in the Southwest that these restrictions were short-lived, and soon slaves were flowing into the Southwest not only from other parts of America but directly from Africa as well. But the diffusionist arguments voiced by slaveholders in the old states of the Upper South who had more slaves than they knew what to do with — self-serving as their arguments may have been—did suggest that many Southerners wanted to do away with slavery.[38]

Everywhere, even in South Carolina, slaveholders began to feel defensive about slavery and began to sense a public pressure against the institution that they had never felt before. Whites in Charleston expressed squeamishness about the evils of slavery, especially the public trading and punishment of slaves. Masters began toning down their fierce advertisements for runaway slaves and felt a need to justify their attempts to recover their slaves that they never had earlier. In the 1780s some of the Carolinian masters expressed a growing reluctance to break up families and even began manumitting their slaves, freeing more slaves in that decade than had been freed in the previous three decades.[39]

PERHAPS THE MAIN REASON many were persuaded that slavery was on its way to extinction was the widespread enthusiasm throughout America for ending the despicable slave trade. Everywhere in the New World slavery was dependent on the continued importations of slaves from Africa—*except* for much of the North American continent. But the fact that the Deep South and the rest of the New World needed slave importations to maintain the institution deluded many Americans into believing that slavery in the United States was also dependent on the slave trade and that ending the slave trade would eventually end slavery itself.

Those who held out that hope simply did not appreciate how demographically different North American slavery was from that in South America and the Caribbean. They were blind to the fact that in most areas the slaves were growing nearly as rapidly as whites, nearly doubling in number every twenty to twenty-five years. Living with illusions, white leaders concluded that if the slave trade could be cut off, slavery would wither and die.

38. Adam Rothman, *Slave Country: American Expansion and the Origins of the Deep South* (Cambridge, MA, 2005), 25–26, 31, 34.
39. Philip Morgan, "Black Society in the Lowcountry, 1760–1810," in Berlin and Hoffman, eds., *Slavery and Freedom in the Age of the American Revolution*, 114–15, 124–25. Still, compared to the Upper South the number of free blacks in South Carolina was negligible; as late as 1800 only about three thousand free blacks lived in the state. Morgan, *Slave Counterpoint*, 491.

All the initial eagerness to end the slave trade, especially among the planters of the Upper South, suggested to Northerners a deeper antagonism to slavery than was in fact the case. Perhaps some of the Virginia planters sincerely believed that ending the slave trade would doom the institution, but many others knew that they had a surplus of slaves. In 1799 Washington had 317 slaves, most of whom were either too young or too old and infirm to work efficiently. Even so, he had more slaves than he needed for farming wheat and foodstuffs, and he did not want to return to planting tobacco. Yet he had no desire to sell "the overplus...because I am principled against this kind of traffic in the human species." Nor did he want to hire them out, because he had "an aversion" to breaking up families. "What then is to be done?" he asked.[40]

Certainly Washington, like many other Virginia farmers, did not need more slaves and thus could welcome an end to the international slave trade. But not all Chesapeake planters were as scrupulous as Washington about not wanting to sell slaves and break up families, and they made the domestic slave trade in the Chesapeake flourish as never before. By 1810 one in five Chesapeake slaves was being sent westward to Kentucky and Tennessee.

Northerners scarcely understood what was happening. They had little or no appreciation that slavery in the South was a healthy, vigorous, and expansive institution. As far as they were concerned, the Virginia and Maryland planters were enthusiastically supporting an end to the international slave trade as the first major step in eliminating the institution. This assault on the overseas slave trade appeared to align the Chesapeake planters with the anti-slave forces in the North and confused many Northerners about the real intentions of the Upper South.

The Constitution drafted in 1787 gave South Carolina and Georgia twenty years to import more slaves from abroad, but everyone clearly expected that in 1808 Congress would act to end the trade, which in turn would lead to the eradication of slavery itself. Actually all the states, including South Carolina, stopped importing slaves on their own during the 1790s—actions that reinforced the conviction that slavery's days were numbered.

YET THE EXPLOSIVE PRO-SLAVERY RESPONSE by representatives from the Deep South to two petitions from the Pennsylvania Abolition Society to Congress in 1790 to end the slave trade and slavery itself should have indicated that the eradication of slavery was not going to be as predictable as many had thought. "Let me remind men who expect a

---

40. GW to Robert Lewis, 17 Aug. 1799, *Papers of Washington: Retirement Ser.*, 4: 256.

general emancipation by law," warned one outraged South Carolinian congressman, "that this would never be submitted to by the Southern States without civil war!" Despite such angry outbursts, however, confidence in the future remained strong, and James Madison and other congressmen from the Upper South were able to bury the petitions in 1790. Their desire to smother even talk about the problem of slavery rested on their deeply mistaken assumption that the Revolutionary ideals of "Humanity & freedom" were, as Madison put it, "secretly undermining the institution."[41] Raising noise about slavery, said Madison, could only slow down the inevitable march of progress. Besides, as President Washington pointed out, the petitions against slavery in 1790 were ill timed; they threatened to break apart the Union just as it was getting on its feet.

As early as 1786 Washington not only had vowed privately to purchase no more slaves but had expressed his deepest wish that the Virginia legislature might adopt some plan by which slavery could be "abolished by slow, sure, & imperceptible degrees." In the early 1790s, like others, he seemed to rest his hopes on the ending of the slave trade in 1808, and in early 1794 he actually introduced into the Senate a petition from the New England Quakers urging an end to American participation in the international slave trade. Although the Constitution forbade Congress from preventing the importation of slaves until 1808, Congress decided in 1794 that it had the authority to prohibit American citizens from selling captured Africans to foreign traders and to prevent foreign ships involved in the slave trade from being outfitted in American ports.[42]

Madison and Washington were not the only leaders who had a naïve faith in the future. Vice-President John Adams thought that when the imports of slaves were cut off, white laborers would become sufficiently numerous that piecemeal private manumissions of the slaves could take place. Oliver Ellsworth, the third chief justice of the Supreme Court and a strict, hard-headed Connecticut Calvinist, agreed. He believed that "as population increases, poor labourers will be so plenty as to render slaves useless. Slavery in time will not be a speck in our country."[43]

41. Richard S. Newman, "Prelude to the Gag Rule: Southern Reaction to Antislavery Petitions in the First Federal Congress," *JER*, 16 (1996), 571–72; JM to BR, 20 Mar. 1790, *Papers of Madison*, 13: 109.

42. GW to John Francis Mercer, 9 Sept 1786, *Washington: Writings*, 607; Charles Rappleye, *Sons of Providence: The Brown Brothers, the Slave Trade, and the American Revolution* (New York, 2006), 297.

43. Richard S. Newman, *The Transformation of American Abolitionism: Fighting Slavery in the Early Republic* (Chapel Hill, 2002), 33; Ellsworth quoted in J. J. Spengler, "Malthusianism in Late Eighteenth-Century America," *American Economic Review*, 25 (1935), 705.

Besides the Deep South's impassioned response to the 1790 Quaker petitions to end slavery, other signals suggested that slavery was not dying away. In 1803 South Carolina reopened its slave trade, a minor shock that should have prepared Americans for the big quake—the Missouri crisis of 1819—that lay ahead. Between 1803 and 1807 South Carolina brought in nearly forty thousand slaves, over twice as many in that four-year period as in any similar period in its history.[44]

With slavery slowly disappearing in the North and yet persisting in the South, the nation was moving in two different directions. By the beginning of the nineteenth century Virginia was still the largest state in the Union, with 885,000 people, nearly equal to the population of North Carolina, South Carolina, and Georgia combined. But its white population was expanding slowly, and tens of thousands of Virginians were pushing out of the Tidewater into the Piedmont and then even farther west and south into Kentucky and Tennessee in search of new land. At the same time, the black population in the Chesapeake was growing faster than the white population and was steadily being moved westward along with over two hundred thousand migrating white farmers. Although nearly one hundred thousand slaves were removed from Maryland and Virginia in the two decades after 1790, the black slave population of the Chesapeake still totaled well over five hundred thousand in 1810.

Each of the Chesapeake states of Maryland and Virginia responded differently to the rapidly growing slave populations. Although both states began manumitting slaves in the aftermath of the Revolution, Maryland freed many more than Virginia. Having no western piedmont to expand into, many of the Maryland planters were faced with either selling or freeing their slaves, and many chose to free them. By 1810 20 percent of Maryland blacks had gained their freedom, accelerating a process that continued up to the eve of the Civil War, when half the black population of the state had become free.

By contrast, only 7 percent of Virginia's black population was free by 1810, and by the eve of the Civil War the percentage of free blacks never got beyond 10 percent. White planters either moved out of the state with their slaves or sold their excessive slaves to whites in other states or to their fellow Virginians. The result was that an ever larger proportion of white Virginians, especially in the Piedmont, became slaveholders in the decades between 1782 and 1810. Prior to the Revolution the majority of

---

44. Jay Coughtry, *The Notorious Triangle: Rhode Island and the Slave Trade, 1700–1807* (Philadelphia, 1981); Stanley Lemons, "Rhode Island and the Slave Trade," *Rhode Island History*, 60 (2002), 95–104; Steven Doyle, *Carry Me Back: The Domestic Slave Trade in American Life* (New York, 2005), 19.

white Virginians had not owned slaves; by 1810 that had dramatically changed: the majority of white Virginians were now personally involved in the institution of slavery and the patriarchal politics that slavery promoted. With the spread of slavery to deeper levels of its population, Virginia became less and less the revolutionary leader of liberalism that it had been in 1776.[45]

MOST OF THE SOUTH became Jeffersonian Republican. As early as the Fourth Congress in 1795–1797, over 80 percent of the Southern congressmen voted in opposition to the Federalist administration. In the presidential election of 1796 the Federalist John Adams received only two Southern electoral votes in comparison to Jefferson's forty-three.[46]

But not all the South was Republican, at least not at first. During the 1790s parts of South Carolina had been strongly Federalist, especially the Lowcountry and the city of Charleston.[47] By 1800 Charleston had emerged as the most European and the least entrepreneurial-minded city of the large port cities of the United States. In the eighteenth century it had been one of the five largest colonial cities in North America with a flourishing commerce controlled by South Carolinian merchant-planters. But by the early nineteenth century merchants from the North and from Europe had taken over the city's countinghouses, and the Carolinian nabobs who had once been merchants became increasingly disdainful of all those who were engaged in trade.[48]

The swampy land of the Carolina Lowcountry tended to breed mosquitoes and malaria, which encouraged white families to abandon the area in the summer months. Consequently, many of the Lowcountry planters became absentee owners of their plantations, with hired white overseers managing the many black slaves. The early nineteenth century was the golden age for these sea island Carolina planters, who by 1810 owned over two hundred plantations, each with a hundred slaves or more. Although the Lowcountry had only one-fifth of the state's population, it contained three-fourths of its wealth. Its slaveholding planting class built huge mansions, bought elegant furniture, drank and ate the best of everything, dressed in the latest London fashions, intermarried with one another, voted for Federalists, and made believe they were English aristocrats.

45. Richard S. Dunn, "Black Society in the Chesapeake, 1776–1810," in Berlin and Hoffman, eds., *Slavery and Freedom in the Age of the American Revolution*, 49–82.
46. James Broussard, *The Southern Federalists, 1800–1816* (Baton Rouge, 1978), 11.
47. Broussard, *Southern Federalists*, 89–90, 235–40, 364–68, 371–73, 377–81, 390–91.
48. George C. Rogers Jr., *Charleston in the Age of the Pinckneys* (Columbia, SC, 1969).

In the coastal areas of the Lowcountry, where water was readily available, rice remained the principal staple, but planters in the lowlands also began turning to cotton, the long staple sort that was ideal for lace or fine linens. Although the long-staple cotton was lucrative, it was hard to grow and flourished only in the coastal areas. Many Carolinians would have liked to grow the short-staple cotton, which was appropriate for coarse fabrics and potentially very profitable, but they did not yet know how to process it easily. Separating the seeds from the cotton fibers by hand was so time-consuming and labor-intensive that results were measured in ounces rather than pounds.

Although sooner or later someone would have found a way to mechanize the process, it was left to a Massachusetts-born Yale graduate with an acute mechanical aptitude, Eli Whitney, to acquire the financial backing of Catherine Littlefield Greene, widow of General Nathanael Greene of Rhode Island, and come up with his invention of a cotton gin in 1793. His machine solved the perennial problem of removing seeds from the short-staple cotton; it, said Whitney, "required the labor of one man to turn it and with which one man will clean ten times as much cotton as he can in any other way before now, and also cleanse it much better than in the usual mode." Planters pirated Whitney's design and built large gins (short for engine) to process huge amounts of cotton. By 1805, in a little over a decade, cotton production in the South had multiplied thirty-fold, from two million pounds to sixty million pounds a year.[49]

The cotton gin turned the Carolina Upcountry into the greatest cotton producing area in the country. Prior to the 1790s the region had been dominated by yeoman farmers with few slaves raising tobacco for a little cash. By 1815 the interior of the state was full of small slaveholding cotton-producing planters, all eager to become aristocratic gentry like those of the Lowcountry. Cotton-production needed slaves, and the numbers multiplied dramatically. In 1790 five-sixths of all of the state's slaves had belonged to Lowcountry plantations; by 1820 most of the state's slaves were working in the Upcountry.[50]

From Carolina and Georgia, cotton and slavery soon moved to the new territories of the Southwest. Planters in the Natchez region quickly abandoned indigo and tobacco for the much more lucrative cotton. As early as 1800 a traveling minister in Mississippi noted that cotton was "now the staple commodity in the territory." Merchants

49. David S. Heidler and Jeanne T. Heidler, *Daily Life in the Early Republic, 1790–1820: Creating a New Nation* (Westport, CT, 2004), 68.
50. William W. Freehling, *The Road to Disunion: Secessionists at Bay, 1776–1854* (New York, 1990), 220.

from New Orleans began furiously competing with one another to line up contracts with cotton-producing planters. Since everyone presumed that only slaves could work the cotton fields, any effort to limit slavery in the Southwest was met with fierce opposition. The planters declared that without slaves, "the farms in this District would be but little more value by 1810 to the present occupiers than an equal quantity of waste land." In 1799 a Mississippi planter told his relatives back in Virginia to sell his property in Richmond and buy slaves. "I would take two Negros for it," he said. "They would here sell for 1,000 or 1200 Dollars." Everywhere in the Upper South increasing numbers of slaveholders either pulled up stakes and moved with their slaves to Mississippi or sold slaves at great profit to friends and relatives who were settling in the new territory. Between 1800 and 1810 the slave population of the Mississippi Territory increased from about thirty-five hundred to nearly seventeen thousand, with most of them producing cotton.[51]

In Orleans Territory sugar became the principal crop, especially following the slave rebellion and the collapse of the economy in Saint-Domingue. By 1802 seventy-five sugar plantations bordering the Mississippi River in lower Louisiana and staffed by slaves produced more than five million pounds of sugar annually; by 1810 sugar production had doubled. With rising sugar profits, the population of the area increased rapidly, with the number of slaves growing faster than the white population. In 1806 the *Louisiana Gazette* reminded slave-owners in the "middle and southern states" (identifying, as Washington had, the Upper South with the middle states) that the Orleans Territory offered "an outlet for the superabundance of their black population, and an extravagant price for what will shortly be to them, an incumbrance instead of an advantage." Slaves were flooded into Louisiana, turning New Orleans into one of the major slave markets in America. By 1810 New Orleans had become the largest city south of Baltimore and the fifth largest in the nation. By 1812 Louisiana had become a state.[52]

IN THE SOUTH AND SOUTHWEST there was democracy of a sort: some legislative elections, usually full white manhood suffrage, much talk of equal rights, and many rhetorical denunciations of "aristocrats." Beneath these democratic and egalitarian trappings, however, the politics

51. Rothman, *Slave Country*, 47–51.
52. Rothman, *Slave Country*, 77–78, 83, 94; Carlyle Sitterson, *Sugar Country: The Cane Sugar Industry in the South* (Lexington, KY, 1953); John G. Clark, *New Orleans, 1718–1812: An Economic History* (Baton Rouge, 1970), 219, 275.

of these Southern and Southwestern areas continued to be remarkably traditional and hierarchical.

Virginia's popular government, for example, bore little resemblance to the popular governments of New England. Not only was voting still confined to fifty-acre freeholders and done orally, but the wealthy Tidewater planters retained a disproportionate representation in the legislature. "The haughty and purse-proud landlords," noted a Massachusetts visitor, "form an aristocracy over the dependent democracy."[53] While this was no doubt an exaggeration that only a frosty Yankee could make, it contained more than a grain of truth. Unlike in the Northern states, the only elected officials in Virginia were federal congressmen and state legislators; all the rest were either selected by the legislature or appointed by the governor or the county courts, which were self-perpetuating oligarchies that dominated local government. Thus popular democratic politics in Virginia and elsewhere in the South was severely limited, especially in contrast to the states of the North, where nearly all state and local offices had become elective and the turbulence of politics and the turnover of offices were much greater.

Like Virginia, the other Southern states and territories—Kentucky, Tennessee, North Carolina, South Carolina, Georgia, Louisiana, Alabama, and Mississippi—continued to rely on mostly appointed local officials with the legislatures very much in control of government. Although the big slaveholding planters did not dominate all the political offices in these states, they set the tone for their societies; unlike in the North, where lawyers tended to dominate officeholding, many of the officeholders in these Southern and Southwestern states were themselves slaveholding farmers, with a vested interest in the institution of slavery.

That institution tended to create a different economy, society, politics, and culture than the North. While the North was coming to value labor as fit for all social ranks, much of the white population of the South was becoming more and more contemptuous of work and desirous of acquiring the leisure that slavery seemed to offer. Indeed, so great was the white cult of indolence that some Southerners began to worry about the discrepancy between an industrious North and a lethargic South. "Where there is Negro slavery," one concerned Virginian told Madison, "there will be laziness, carelessness, and wastefulness," not as much among the slaves as among the white masters. This Virginian even claimed that "our

53. James K. Paulding, "Slaves and Rivermen: Western Virginia, 1816," in Warren S. Tyron, ed., *A Mirror for Americans: Life and Manners in the United States, 1790–1870, as Recorded by American Travelers* (Chicago, 1952), 259.

intelligent Negroes are far superior in mind, morals and manners than those who are placed in authority over them."[54]

Slavery and the Southern economy tended to breed deference. Not only did the wealthy slaveholding planters' management of the overseas marketing of the staple crop, whether cotton or tobacco, help to reinforce a social hierarchy of patrons and clients, but ultimately, and more important, their patriarchal system of slavery sustained that hierarchy. The commercial institutions that were springing up in the North had no counterparts in the Southern states. The South contained fewer turn-pikes, fewer canals, fewer banks, fewer corporations, and fewer issuers of paper money than the North. Slavery even perversely affected the tax system and other public policies in the South. The Southern legislatures taxed their citizens much less heavily and spent much less on education and social services than did the legislatures of the North. "Slavery," as one historian has said, "had profoundly antidemocratic effects on American politics." The Southern planters could not afford to allow non-slavehold-ing majorities in their states to burden their peculiar "species of property," and they used their disproportionate representation in their state legisla-tures to protect themselves. For example, even though slaves made up only 16 percent of Kentucky's population, the minority of slaveholders in the state were able to write into Kentucky's 1792 constitution the nation's first explicit protection of slavery, declaring that "the legislature shall have no power to pass laws for the emancipation of slaves without the consent of their owners."[55]

In the early Republic North and South may have been both American and republican, both professing a similar rhetoric of liberty and popular government, but below the surface they were fast becoming different places—one coming to value common labor as the supreme human activity, the other continuing to think of labor in traditional terms as mean and despicable and fit only for slaves.

As THE SECTIONS gradually grew apart, each began expressing increasing frustration with the other, aggravating an antagonism that had been present from the beginning of the Revolution. Northerners, espe-cially New England Federalists, began to complain about what they saw

---

54. Drew R. McCoy, The Last of the Fathers: James Madison and the Republican Legacy (Cambridge, UK, 1989), 222–23.

55. Robin L. Einhorn, American Taxation, American Slavery (Chicago, 2006), 220, 232, 249, 236; Stanley Elkins and Eric McKitrick, "A New Meaning for Turner's Frontier: Part II: The Southwest Frontier and New England," Political Science Quarterly, 69 (1954), 572–76.

as unjustified Southern dominance of the federal government. They focused on the three-fifths clause of the Constitution that counted slaves as three-fifths of a person for the levying of direct taxes and for assessing representation in the House of Representatives and the Electoral College. Since the federal government had seldom directly taxed its citizens and was unlikely to do so very often, representation became the main issue people cared about.

In the Constitutional Convention of 1787 the aristocratic Gouverneur Morris had attacked the three-fifths clause as an unjust support for slavery, one that gave the slave states an incentive to import more slaves. But the Convention had overwhelmingly rejected Morris's proposal that the slaves not be counted at all, with only New Jersey voting for it. Once that proposal was defeated, the most plausible alternative to the three-fifths clause was to count the slaves as five-fifths, that is, as full persons, which would have given the slaveholding South even more political strength. But that alternative, suggested by both James Madison and John Rutledge, went nowhere. Caught between not counting the slaves at all and counting them fully, the Convention wrote the three-fifths compromise into the Constitution.

In 1787–1788 most Northern Federalists like Rufus King accepted the three-fifths compromise as the necessary price to be paid to keep the South in the Union. But with the rise of the Republican opposition in the 1790s climaxing with the election of Jefferson and a Republican Congress in 1800, the Federalists began to change their minds. They realized only too well that the Jeffersonian Republican party was Southern based and was solidly dependent on Southern slaveholding leadership. The fact that Jefferson won the election of 1800 with 82 percent of the electoral vote of the slave states and only 27 percent of the Northern states reinforced the Federalists' fear that the South was taking over the nation; indeed, the Federalists came to believe that their displacement from the national government was due almost entirely to the overrepresentation of the South in Congress and the Electoral College. Federalists like Timothy Pickering, the former secretary of state, began referring to Jefferson as the "Negro President" and began urging that the Constitution be amended to end this Southern dominance.[56]

Thus was born the idea of the "slave power" that was unfairly usurping control of the national government from the free states.[57] The fact that

---

56. Garry Wills, 'Negro President': Jefferson and the Slave Power (Boston, 2003).
57. Leonard L. Richards, The Slave Power: The Free North and Southern Domination, 1780–1860 (Baton Rouge, 2000); Don E. Fehrenbacher, The Slaveholding Republic: An Account of the United States Government's Relations to Slavery (New York, 2001).

Pickering and other Federalists tended to lump the free middle states, especially Pennsylvania, in with the Southern states as part of the Negro-based Republican takeover of the government reduces somewhat the cogency of their argument. But that may be less important than the politics of the matter. The Federalists needed an issue to combat the victorious Republicans, and their principled stand against slavery was the most effective means of mobilizing opposition to the Republicans in the North—at least until Jefferson in 1807 tried his disastrous experiment with the embargo that cut off all overseas trade.

DURING THE COURSE OF THE 1790s the earlier enthusiasm of those in the Upper South to liberalize their society and to create a looser slave regime began to dissipate. Probably nothing did more to diminish the initial optimism of many whites in Virginia about the end of slavery than the black rebellion in the French colony of Saint-Domingue on the island of Hispaniola. The rebellion began in 1790 with an uprising of free coloreds, a diverse group who numbered about thirty thousand and included French-educated planters, tradesmen, artisans, and small landowners. The insurgents had been infected with French revolutionary principles and now demanded equality with whites. The whites numbered about forty thousand, but they were bitterly divided between the grands blancs and the disorderly and marginalized petits blancs. Beneath the whites and the free coloreds were five hundred thousand African slaves.

Neither the free coloreds nor the whites realized the extent to which their clash over equality and the principles of the French Revolution was affecting the slaves. In August 1791 the slaves on the northern plains rose up, soon becoming a force of twelve thousand that began killing whites and destroying plantations. Brutal retaliation by the whites did not stop growing numbers of slaves from deserting the plantations. Confronted with this rebellion from below, officials in France belatedly sought to forge an alliance between the whites and the free coloreds and sent six thousand troops to put down the slave rebellion. But the whites and free coloreds were so divided by factions that the fighting became worse and eventually spilled over into the Spanish portion of Hispaniola (the present-day Dominican Republic). With the end of the French monarchy and the outbreak of war between France and England in 1793, English forces invaded the island and soon became entangled in the brutal racial wars. Although the great ex-slave leader of the revolt François-Dominique Toussaint L'Ouverture tried to preserve a multi-racial society, he could not contain the chaos that spiraled into what became the rebellion's eventual goal of eliminating from the island both slavery and whites.

Most Americans, including slaves, knew what was taking place in Saint-Domingue. Between 1791 and 1804 the American press carried regular reports of atrocities on the island. Moreover, thousands of refugees, both white and black, fled from the chaos, many of them to the United States, especially to the cities of Charleston, Norfolk, and Philadelphia. By 1795 as many as twelve thousand Dominguan slaves had entered the United States, bringing with them knowledge that slaves in the New World were capable of overthrowing white rule. Governor Charles Pinckney of South Carolina was not alone in realizing "that the day will arrive when [the Southern states] may be exposed to the same insurrection."[58]

Frightened of the contagion of this West Indian slave rebellion, most Southern states, but not Virginia, barred Dominguan slaves from entry. Consequently, many of them ended up in Virginia and throughout the decade of the 1790s stimulated wild fears of slave insurrections in the state. In June 1793 John Randolph reported overhearing two slaves planning "to kill the white people." When one of the slaves expressed skepticism about the plan, the other reminded him "how the blacks *has* kill'd the whites in the French Island…a little while ago." News of the rebellion in Saint-Domingue was everywhere, and the island could not help becoming a symbol of black liberation. Throughout the 1790s major slave conspiracies were uncovered in the Spanish colonies of Cuba and Louisiana, and slave rebellions actually broke out in Puerto Rico, Venezuela, Curaçao, and Grenada. As Federalist Rufus King pointed out, "*the example upon our slaves in the Southern states*" was obvious.[59]

During the 1790s talk of slave insurrections in the United States became increasingly prevalent—eroding whatever liberal feelings the Upper South hitherto had toward the ending of slavery. By the end of the decade, as one Virginia slaveholder put it, "the emancipation fume has long evaporated and not a word is now said about it."[60]

IN 1800 WHAT THE VIRGINIAN SLAVEHOLDERS had long dreaded finally arrived—a widespread conspiracy among their slaves to rise up and abolish slavery. In the area around Richmond a group of artisan-slaves enjoyed a much greater degree of liberty and mobility than they

58. Donald R. Wright, *African Americans in the Early Republic, 1789–1831* (Arlington Heights, IL, 1993), 89; David P. Geggus, ed., *The Impact of the Haitian Revolution in the Atlantic World* (Columbia, SC, 2001).

59. James Sidbury, *Ploughshares into Swords: Race, Rebellion, and Identity in Gabriel's Virginia, 1730–1810* (Cambridge, UK, 1997), 39–48; Donald Robinson, *Slavery in the Structure of American Politics* (New York, 1979), 364.

60. Egerton, *Gabriel's Rebellion*, 15.

had in the past. Slaves with skills were often able to hire themselves out where needed, pay their masters a share of their wages, and thus earn some money for themselves. These slave-artisans often mingled with both free-black and white artisans in a shadowy interracial underworld that floated between freedom and slavery. The twenty-four-year-old blacksmith Gabriel, owned by planter Thomas Prosser of Henrico County, in which Richmond was located, participated in this borderland world in which heady talk of liberty and natural rights was increasingly common. Already convicted and branded for fighting with a white man, Gabriel was on fire to destroy the system of slavery. He was not alone: as one of the black rebels, Jack Ditcher, declared, "We have as much right to fight for our liberty as any men."[61]

The timing of the conspirators was influenced by the explosive atmosphere of 1799–1800 when the Federalists and Republicans seemed to many to be on the verge of civil war. The Federalists in Virginia, who were mostly merchants and bankers confined to the thriving commercial cities of Richmond, Norfolk, and Fredericksburg, predicted that a Jefferson victory in the election of 1800 would lead to a liberation of the slaves, or worse, a slave insurrection. At the same time, the artisans in the towns, like their brethren in the North, were advocating a more equitable distribution of wealth and were attacking the Federalists for being rich drones who lived off of other men's labor. Amidst these kinds of charges and counter-charges with predictions of violence and armies clashing, Gabriel and other slave artisans thought that their slave insurrection would become part of a larger upheaval in Virginia and, perhaps, even in the nation.

Gabriel and his conspirators envisioned not simply a slave revolt but a republican revolution against rich merchants that would transform Virginia society. They believed that "the poor white people" and the "most redoubtable democrats" in Richmond would rise with them in rebellion against the existing order. But if the whites would not join the insurrection, then they would all be killed, with the exception of "Quakers, Methodists, and French people," since they were "friendly to liberty."[62]

Although Gabriel may not have originated the conspiracy, he quickly became its leader. Beginning around April 1800, he and other slave artisans began recruiting rebels in the taverns and religious meetings of Richmond and other towns. Five or six hundred men at least orally agreed to participate in the insurrection. Hoping eventually to have a thousand-strong army, the leaders tried recruiting from the rural

61. Egerton, *Gabriel's Rebellion*, 40.
62. Egerton, *Gabriel's Rebellion*, 49, 51; Sidbury, *Ploughshares into Swords*, 97.

plantations with less success than they had among the artisans. The rebels planned everything with military precision. They stole guns, made swords from scythes, and organized their army into three groups that would march on Richmond, the capital, under the banner of "Death or Liberty." Two of the groups planned to set diversionary fires in the warehouse district, while the main group led by Gabriel would seize the state's treasury, the magazine where military supplies were stored, and Governor James Monroe. The attack was set for August 30, 1800.

On the appointed day two slaves informed their master of the uprising, and at the same time a torrential rain flooded roads and bridges, making it impossible for the rebels to meet and coordinate their plans. The rebellion was doomed from the start.

At first some whites scoffed at the idea of a massive conspiracy, but as the white militia over the next several weeks hunted down dozens of rebels, white Virginians became more and more terrified as they learned of the scope of the miscarried insurrection. Eventually twenty-seven men, including Gabriel, were tried and hanged for their participation in the conspiracy; others were sold and transported out of the state. Some of the rebels knew only too well how to make the white Virginians squirm. One of them, speaking at his trial, declared, "I have nothing more to offer than what General Washington would have had to offer, had he been taken by the British and put to trial. I have adventured my life in endeavouring to obtain the liberty of my countrymen, and am a willing sacrifice in their cause."[63]

Governor Monroe thought it "strange" that the slaves should have embarked on "this novel and unexampled enterprise of their own accord." After all, he said, "their treatment has been more favorable since the revolution," and because of the end of the slave importations into the state, there were proportionally fewer of them. Unable to understand why the rebellion should have come from those slaves who suffered the fewest restrictions and experienced the greatest taste of liberty, Monroe could only conclude that some outsiders put them up to it.[64]

Virginia Federalists, eager to make political capital out of the conspiracy, were quick to blame the Republicans for their constant sermonizing on the doctrine of "liberty and equality." "It has been most imprudently propagated for several years at our tables while our servants were standing behind our chairs. It has been preached from the pulpits, Methodists and Baptists alike without reserve. Democrats have talked it, what else then

63. Egerton, *Gabriel's Rebellion*, 102.
64. Monroe to the Speaker of the General Assembly, 5 Dec. 1800, in Stanislaus M. Hamilton, ed., *Writings of James Monroe* (New York, 1900), 3: 208–9.

could we expect except what has happened?" We have learned a lesson, said the Virginia Federalists. "There can be no compromise between liberty and slavery." We must either abolish slavery or continue it. "If we continue it, it must be restricted, all the vigorous laws must be reenacted which experience has proved necessary to keep it within bounds.... If we will keep a ferocious monster within our country, we must keep him in chains." The two decades of liberalization had to come to an end. Otherwise these Virginians believed they would end up with "the horrors of St. Domingo."[65]

The New England Federalists picked up the refrain and taunted the Southern Republicans for having brought their misery upon themselves. "If any thing will correct & bring to repentance old hardened sinners in Jacobinism," said the *Boston Gazette*, "it must be *an insurrection of their slaves*." Hamilton's friend Robert Troup joked to Rufus King about how the Virginia Republicans "are beginning to feel the happy effects of liberty and equality."[66] Of course, the New England Federalists had little to fear from slave rebellions and were even willing to support the slave insurrection in Saint-Domingue as long as it hurt the Jacobinical French. The Adams administration supplied arms to Toussaint and at one point in 1798 actually intervened with naval support on Toussaint's behalf; it even encouraged the black leader to declare independence from France.

With the end of the Quasi-War with France in 1800 and Jefferson's election as president, American policy inevitably changed. After Napoleon failed to recover the colony for France in 1803, Haiti, as the black rebels called their new republic, finally became the second independent state of the New World; unlike the United States, Haiti succeeded in ending slavery and proclaiming racial equality at the moment of its independence. Although the United States was usually eager to encourage revolutions and during the nineteenth century was often the first state in the world to extend diplomatic recognition to new republics, in the case of the Haitian republic the nation behaved differently. Not until the Civil War did the United States recognize the Haitian republic.

GABRIEL'S CONSPIRACY was the final straw. The earlier liberal climate was already dissipating; now it definitely had to be eliminated. The planned slave insurrection convinced many Virginians that they had been terribly mistaken in loosening the bonds of slavery in the aftermath of the Revolution. They now sensed that slavery could not easily exist in a

---

65. Fredericksburg *Virginia Herald*, 22 Sept. 1800, in Gordon S. Wood, ed., *The Rising Glory of America*, rev. ed. (Boston, 1990), 361.
66. Egerton, *Gabriel's Rebellion*, 114.

society that extolled freedom. They agreed with Federalist critics that too much preaching of liberty and equality undermined the institution of slavery. The South would have to become a very different place from what many of them had envisioned in the 1780s. The earlier leniency in judging "freedom suits" in Virginia ended, and manumissions in the state rapidly declined. Southerners began reversing their earlier examples of racial mingling. The evangelical Protestant churches ended their practice of mixed congregations. The Southern states began enacting new sets of black codes that resembled later Jim Crow laws, tightening up the institution of slavery and restricting the behavior of free blacks. With the possibility of slaves running away to the free states of the North, despite the fugitive slave clause (Article IV, Section 2) of the Constitution, the planters of the Upper South could no longer regard truancy with the casualness they had earlier. Free blacks now had to carry papers or wear arm patches affirming their status; of course, this was partly for their own security, but the practices only reemphasized the identity between blackness and slavery.

Indeed, the very presence of free blacks now seemed to threaten the institution of slavery. "If blacks see all of their color [as] slaves," declared a Virginia lawmaker, "it will seem to them a disposition of Providence and they will be content. But if they see others like themselves free, and enjoying rights they are deprived of, they will repine."[67] This logic led the South to seek to expel all its free blacks and to abandon its earlier expectation that slavery would eventually come to an end.

In 1806 the Virginia legislature declared that any freed slave had to leave the state. In reaction Maryland, Kentucky, and Delaware prohibited those free blacks from seeking permanent residence within their borders. The Methodists and Baptists in the South revoked their previous stand against slavery, and the Southern societies promoting antislavery found themselves rapidly losing members. Virginia, which had been a symbol of hope at the time of the Revolution, increasingly turned inward and acted frightened and besieged. It developed an increasing contempt for the getting and spending—the capitalism—rapidly developing in the North and began to extol and exaggerate all those cavalier characteristics that Jefferson had outlined in the 1780s: its liberality, its candor, and its aversion to the narrow, money-grasping greed of the hustling Yankees.

Above all, the South now needed to justify slavery. If the institution was not going to disappear after all but was to continue, then it had to be

67. Duncan J. MacLeod, *Slavery, Race, and the American Revolution* (Cambridge, UK, 1974), 155–58; Ira Berlin, *Slaves Without Masters: The Free Negro in the Antebellum South* (New York, 1975), 36–41; Jordan, *White over Black*, 580.

defended. At the outset of the Revolution, many Southern leaders like Patrick Henry had proclaimed that slavery was an evil but had thrown up their hands about what to do about it. "I will not, I cannot justify it," Henry had said. But if slavery could not be eradicated, at least, he said, "let us treat the unhappy Victims with lenity, it is the furthest advance we can make towards Justice" and "a debt we owe to the purity of our Religion."[68] Here were the seeds of the idea of Christian and patriarchal stewardship that eventually became a major justification of the institution.

Other Southerners now began suggesting a more insidious apology for slavery—based on the presumed racial inferiority of the blacks. Somehow, it was insinuated, if the Africans were not and could never be equal to whites, then their subjugation made sense; slavery became a means of civilizing them. Of course, the eighteenth century scarcely had a modern notion of race, that is, a biologically based distinction that separated one people from another. Belief in Genesis and God's creation of a single species of human beings made any suggestion of fundamental natural differences among humans difficult to sustain. Although eighteenth-century thinkers obviously recognized that people differed from one another, most of them explained these differences by the workings of the environment or climate.

Now, however, some began to suggest that the characteristics of the African slaves might be innate and that in some basic sense they were designed for slavery. Although Jefferson was a committed environmentalist, in his Notes on the State of Virginia he had, nevertheless, intimated that the various characteristics of the blacks that he outlined—their tolerance of heat, their need for less sleep, their sexual ardor, their lack of imagination and artistic ability, and their musical talent—were inherent and not learned. He believed that the blacks' deficiencies were innate, because when they mixed their blood with whites', they improved "in body and mind," which "proves that their inferiority is not the effect merely of their condition of life." Still, Jefferson knew he was treading on precarious ground, where his "conclusion would degrade a whole race of men from the rank in the scale of beings which their Creator may perhaps have given them." Hence he advanced his conclusion "as a suspicion only, that the blacks, whether originally a distinct race, or made distinct by time and circumstances, are inferior to the whites in endowments both of body and mind."[69]

68. David Brion Davis, The Problem of Slavery in the Age of Revolution, 1770–1823 (Ithaca, 1975), 196.
69. TJ, Notes on the State of Virginia, ed. Peden, 138–43.

Unfortunately, said Jefferson, these natural differences were "a power-ful obstacle to the emancipation of these people." The only solution he could conceive of was to remove the freed blacks "beyond the reach of mixture." Although Jefferson had no apprehensions about mingling white blood with that of the Indian, he never ceased expressing his "great aver-sion" to racial mixing between blacks and whites. He could never really imagine freed blacks living in a white man's America, and thus he wanted all blacks sent to the West Indies, or Africa, or anywhere as long as it was out of the country. Whites and blacks had to remain "as distinct as nature has made them." Someday, he told Governor James Monroe of Virginia in 1801, the United States will "cover the whole northern, if not the south-ern continent, with a people speaking the same language, governed in similar forms, & by similar laws; nor can we contemplate with satisfaction either blot or mixture on the surface." By 1814 he was still repeating the same theme: the blacks' "amalgamation with the other color," he said, "produces a degradation to which no lover of his country, no lover of excellence in the human character can innocently consent."[70]

By the early nineteenth century others picked up Jefferson's suspicions of racial differences and expanded them. Scientists such as Charles Caldwell and Samuel Latham Mitchill raised doubts about climatic and environmental explanations for the differences between blacks and whites without explicitly repudiating the unitary creation of Genesis. Other sci-entists began laying the groundwork for the emergence of anthropologi-cal studies that would form the foundation for the pro-slavery arguments of the antebellum period. The slaves had no inherent capacity for free-dom, it was said, and thus the slaveholders had a Christian and patriar-chal responsibility to hold them in bondage and look after them. As one historian has concluded, blacks "had never before been so clearly defined as different and inferior, nor had their place in society ever before been so coherently and systematically deduced from those differences." And it was not just the black slaves who were victimized by this racist thinking; it was free blacks as well.[71]

The Revolution had unleashed anti-slavery sentiments throughout much of the country, but its emphasis on equal citizenship and equal rights presented increasing difficulties for the anti-slavery movement. Anyone who talked about emancipating the black slaves was confronted

---

70. TJ, *Notes on the State of Virginia*, ed. Peden, 138–43; TJ to James Monroe, 24 Nov. 1801, to Edward Coles, 25 Aug. 1814, *Jefferson: Writings*, 270, 1097, 1345.

71. Duncan J. MacLeod, "Toward Caste," in Berlin and Hoffman, eds., *Slavery and Freedom*, 235.

with the problem of what to do with the freedmen. Jefferson had warned that the two peoples could not live side by side as equal citizens. "Deep rooted prejudices entertained by the whites; ten thousand recollections, by the blacks, of the injuries they have sustained"—all this plus the inherent differences, he said, "will produce convulsions which will probably never end but in the extermination of the one or the other race."[72]

Even the most devoted abolitionists were anxious about what to do with the freedmen. With the increasing emphasis on black inferiority, expatriation of the blacks to some place outside of the United States became the only viable alternative to slavery. Even someone as sophisticated as Madison clung to the idea of colonizing blacks to some place outside of the country, although with decreasing confidence. He had promoted the idea ever since 1789, when he first suggested that an asylum "might prove a great encouragement to manumission in the southern parts of the U.S. and even afford the best hope yet presented of an end to slavery."[73] Although removal of blacks became increasingly unlikely after 1806, talk of it continued and led eventually to the formation of the American Colonization Society in 1816–1817. This idea that hundreds of thousands of African Americans might be resettled elsewhere was another one of the many illusions that this Founding generation of Americans entertained.

SUDDENLY, THE COUNTRY became obsessed with racial distinctions and the problem of freed blacks. Even in the North the liberal atmosphere of the immediate post-Revolutionary years evaporated, and whites began to react against the increasing numbers of freed blacks. Even an otherwise Northern liberal clergyman refused to marry mixed-race couples, fearing that such "mixtures" would eventually create "a particoloured race" in the city of Philadelphia. In 1804 and 1807 Ohio required blacks entering the state to post a five-hundred-dollar bond guaranteeing their good behavior and to produce court certificates proving they were free. Officials from Pennsylvania, the earlier heart of abolitionism, worried about the implications of all the freed Southern slaves migrating to their state. "When they arrive," declared a Philadelphian in 1805, "they almost generally abandon themselves to all manners of debauchery and dissipation, to the great annoyance of our citizens." In that same year, 1805, a crowd of whites chased a group of assembled blacks from the Fourth of July celebration in Philadelphia, thus ending what had always been a

---

72. TJ, *Notes on the State of Virginia*, ed. Peden, 138.
73. JM, Memorandum on an African Colony for Freed Slaves, ca. 20 Oct. 1789, *Papers of Madison*, 12: 438.

biracial commemoration in the City of Brotherly Love. Although Massachusetts had been quick to free its slaves, the state now passed laws prohibiting interracial marriages and expelling all blacks who were not citizens of one state or another.[74]

In New York in the second decade of the nineteenth century the Republican-dominated legislature took away the franchise of free blacks who had long possessed it, partly because they were black and partly because they had tended to vote for Federalists. The New York Federalists naturally had favored property qualifications for voting and did not oppose voting by blacks who could meet the property qualification. By contrast, the Republicans favored equal rights and universal manhood suffrage, but precisely for that reason could not tolerate blacks voting as equals with whites. At the same time as the New York Jeffersonian Republicans were denying the franchise to longtime black voters, they promoted illegal voting by Irish immigrants who were not yet citizens, knowing that such recent immigrants would vote for the Democratic-Republicans. Such were the strange and perverse consequences of republican equality and democracy.[75]

Whites in the North began copying the South in separating the races in ways they had not done earlier. Free blacks were confined to distinct neighborhoods and to separate sections of theaters, circuses, churches, and other places. Most Americans, both Northerners and Southerners, were coming to think of the United States as "a white man's country."

Yet could the states of the young Republic hang together suspended between slavery and freedom? That was the worrying question that tainted all the exuberance and optimism of early nineteenth-century Americans.

74. Clare A. Lyons, *Sex Among the Rabble: An Intimate History of Gender and Power in the Age of Revolution, Philadelphia, 1730–1830* (Chapel Hill, 2006), 224, 355; MacLeod, *Slavery, Race, and the American Revolution,* 163; Leon F. Litwack, *North of Slavery: The Negro in the Free States, 1790–1860* (Chicago, 1961), 81.

75. Harvey Strum, "Property Qualifications and Voting Behavior in New York, 1807–1816," *JER*, 1 (1981), 360–61; Leslie M. Harris, *In the Shadow of Slavery: African Americans in New York City, 1626–1863* (Chicago, 2003), 58–60.

# 15

# The Rising Glory of America

Despite Jefferson's valiant efforts to justify American genius, by the second decade of the nineteenth century many thought that the Europeans' jibes about America being a cultural wasteland might have been only too accurate after all. Where were the great writers, the great painters, the great playwrights? Despite the high hopes of the 1790s and the promise of being the most enlightened nation in the world, America seemed incapable of artistically creating anything that captured the attention of Europe. "Who reads an American book? or goes to an American play? or looks at an American picture or statue?" sneered the British critic Sydney Smith in 1820. Looking back, Ralph Waldo Emerson agreed that the country had failed to fulfill its earlier artistic promise. He thought his father's generation had contributed little or nothing to American culture, certainly not in Massachusetts. "From 1790 to 1820," he said, "there was not a book, a speech, a conversation, or a thought in the State."[1]

Subsequent generations of Americans have tried to explain what had happened. The new nation, they said, was too provincial and too dependent on European and English forms and styles to create a distinctive American culture. Americans in the early Republic, they contended, were too unwilling to exploit their indigenous materials, and too timid to create a genuine native culture; instead, in the words of Oliver Wendell Holmes, they had to wait for Emerson's "American Scholar" address to declare their cultural independence from the Old World.

Yet this conventional view that Americans in the first generation of the early Republic were too provincial and imitative of Europe, echoed by many modern generations of scholars, misunderstands the cultural aims of the American Revolutionaries. The Revolutionary leaders never intended to create an original and peculiar indigenous culture. Despite

---

1. Russell B. Nye, *The Cultural Life of the New Nation, 1776–1830* (New York, 1960), 257; *Journals of Ralph Waldo Emerson*, ed. Edward Waldo Emerson and Waldo Emerson Forbes (Boston, 1909–14), 8: 339.

all their talk of American exceptionalism and American virtue in contrast with European corruption, they were seeking not to cut themselves off from Europe's cultural heritage but to embrace it and in fact to fulfill it. It is a mistake to view America's post-Revolutionary emulation of Europe as a legacy of helpless dependence passed on from colonial days. Americans imitated European styles and forms not because in their naïveté they could do nothing else but because they wanted to. Their participation in European or English culture in the early years of the new Republic was intentional, undertaken with confidence and without apology. Their revolution was very much an international affair, an attempt to fulfill the cosmopolitan dreams of the Enlightenment.

Indeed, the Revolutionary generation was as cosmopolitan as any in American history. The Revolutionaries were patriots, to be sure, but they were not obsessed, as were some later generations, with separating America from the broad course of Western civilization. The Revolutionary leaders saw themselves as part of an international intellectual community, "the republic of letters." "Why may not a Republic of Letters be realized in America as well as a Republican Government?" demanded Jeremy Belknap in 1780. "Why may there not be a Congress of Philosophers as well as of Statesmen?" America ought to "shine as Mistress of the Sciences, as well as the Asylum of Liberty."[2]

Not only was the republic of letters based solely on merit, it transcended national boundaries as well. The American Revolution may have divided the British Empire, said Benjamin Rush, but it "made no breach in the republic of letters." Despite the war, Americans were eager to install British scientists in the American Philosophical Society. "Science and literature are of no party nor nation," said John Adams. When Benjamin Franklin was minister to France during the Revolutionary War, he issued a document to the English explorer Captain James Cook protecting him from American depredations at sea during his voyage of 1779. Franklin told all American ship commanders that they must regard all English scientists not as enemies but "as common friends of Mankind." When an American captain seized a British ship with some thirty volumes of medical lecture notes, Washington sent them back to England, saying that the United States did not make war on science. Jefferson justified sending some seeds to a French agricultural society in violation of his own embargo on the grounds that "these societies are always at peace, however the nations may be at war. Like the republic of letters, they form

2. Linda Kerber, *Federalists in Dissent: Imagery and Ideology in Jeffersonian America* (Ithaca, 1970), 3 n; Catherine O'Donnell Kaplan, *Men of Letters in the Early Republic: Cultivating Forums of Citizenship* (Chapel Hill, 2008).

a great fraternity spreading over all the earth, and their correspondence is not interrupted by any civilization."[3]

Being members of this trans-Atlantic intellectual fraternity enabled some Americans like the artist Robert Fulton and the poet Joel Barlow to spend most of their mature lives abroad without any sense of expatriation. And it allowed many Americans, much to the surprise of later generations, to embrace the cultural fellowship of the painters John Singleton Copley and Benjamin West and the scientist Count Rumford despite their loyalty to Great Britain.[4]

The American Revolutionaries intended, however, to be more than participants in this "republic of letters"; they aimed to be its leaders. Many of them came to believe that the torch of civilization was being passed across the Atlantic to the New World where it was destined to burn even more brightly. And why not? America had everything going for it, declared Joel Barlow in 1787; "the enterprising genius of the people promises a most rapid improvement in all the arts that embellish human nature."[5]

In light of their former colonial status and their earlier widespread expressions of cultural inferiority, their presumption of becoming the cultural leaders of the Western world is jarring, to say the least. Yet the evidence is overwhelming that the Revolutionary leaders and artists saw America eventually becoming the place where the best of all the arts and sciences would flourish.

Newspapers, sermons, orations, even private correspondence were filled with excited visions of future American accomplishments in all areas of learning. When the Revolutionaries talked of "treading upon the Republican ground of Greece and Rome" they meant not only that they would erect republican governments but also that they would in time have their own Homers and Virgils, in the words of historian David Ramsay, their own "poets, orators, criticks, and historians, equal to the most celebrated of the ancient commonwealths of Greece and Italy."[6]

Such dreams, bombastic as they seem in retrospect, were grounded in the best scientific thought of the day. This grounding undercut the

3. TJ to John Hollis, 19 Feb. 1809, in L and B, eds., *Writings of Jefferson*, 12: 252–54; Dumas Malone, *Jefferson the President: Second Term, 1805–1809* (Boston, 1974), 661.
4. On the cosmopolitanism of the Revolutionaries, see Arthur L. Ford, *Joel Barlow* (New York, 1971), 27, 31, 59, 61; and Allan Guttman, "Copley, Peale, Trumbull: A Note on Loyalty," *American Quarterly*, 11 (1959), 178–83.
5. Andrew Burstein, *Sentimental Democracy: The Evolution of America's Romantic Self-Image* (New York, 1999), 165–66.
6. Gordon S. Wood, *The Creation of the American Republic, 1776–1787* (Chapel Hill, 1969), 50; David Ramsay, *An Oration on the Advantages of American Independence* (1778), in Robert L. Brunehouse, ed., "David Ramsay, 1740–1815: Selections from His Writings," *American Philosophical Society, Trans.*, 55 (1965), 185.

Buffon-bred view that the New World was an undesirable human habitat and helped to give Americans the confidence to undertake their revolution. They knew, as philosopher David Hume had pointed out, that free states encouraged learning among the populace, and a learned populace was the best source of genius and artistic talent. But more important in convincing Americans that they might become the future artistic leaders of the world was the idea of the *translatio studii*, the ancient notion that the arts and science were inevitably moving westward.

From the beginning of the eighteenth century some Americans had dreamed that the arts were on their way to their wilderness. Even the founding of Yale College early in the century proved to Jeremiah Dummer that "religion & polite learning have bin traveling westward ever since their first appearance in the World." He hoped that the arts "won't rest 'till they have fixt their chief Residence in our part of the World."[7] With the publication in 1752 of Bishop Berkeley's "Verses on the Prospect of Planting Arts and Learning in America" (originally written in 1726), more and more Americans began to believe that the future belonged to them. Everyone knew that civilization and the arts had moved steadily westward—from the Middle East to Greece, from Greece to Rome, from Rome to Western Europe, and now, wrote Berkeley,

> Westward the course of Empire takes its way,
>    The first four acts already past,
> A fifth shall close the drama with the day;
>    Time's noblest offspring is the last.[8]

With Berkeley's poem reprinted in virtually every American newspaper and many magazines over the succeeding decades, more and more Americans became convinced that the arts were about to move from Western Europe to America, there to thrive as never before.[9] As early as 1759 the unsympathetic British traveler Andrew Burnaby noted that the colonists were "looking forward with eager and impatient expectation to that destined moment when America is to give the law to the rest of the world."[10]

---

7. Kenneth Silverman, *A Cultural History of the American Revolution* (New York, 1976), 10.
8. Berkeley quoted in Lewis P. Simpson, ed., *The Federalist Literary Mind: Selections from the Monthly Anthology and Boston Review, 1803–1811* (Baton Rouge, 1962), 34.
9. Silverman, *Cultural History of the American Revolution*, 10–11; Joseph J. Ellis, *After the Revolution: Profiles of Early American Culture* (New York, 1979), 7.
10. Andrew Burnaby, *Travels Through the Middle Settlements in North America: In the Years 1759 and 1760* (1775; Ithaca, 1960). Early in the nineteenth century John Adams recalled that ever since he was a young lawyer in Massachusetts it had been a common observation that the "arts, sciences, and empire had traveled westward" and that "the next leap would be over the Atlantic into America." JA to BR, 21 May 1807, in Adams, ed., *Works*, 9: 600.

So common became this theme of the *translatio studii* to eighteenth-century Americans that it led to the emergence of a new literary genre, the Rising Glory of America poem, which, it seems, every gentleman with literary aspirations tried his hand at. The most famous work with that title, "The Rising Glory of America," was Philip Freneau's and Hugh Henry Brackenridge's 1771 Princeton commencement poem. In it they predicted that Americans would in time have not only their own states, "not less in fame than Greece and Rome of old," but their own Homers and Miltons too. The poet John Trumbull echoed the same theme in predicting that painters, architects, musicians, and writers must inevitably find their place in this free and uncorrupted country:

> This Land her Steele and Addison shall view,
> The former glories equal'd by the new;
> Some future Shakespeare charm'd the rising age,
> And hold in magic chains the listening stage.[11]

Of course, not every American intellectual was sure of the New World's ability as yet to receive the inherited torch of Western culture, and some doubted whether America's primitive tastes could ever sustain the fine arts. Yet nearly all who became committed to the Revolution found themselves embracing a vision of America's becoming not only a libertarian refuge from the world's tyranny but also a worthy place where, in the words of Ezra Stiles, the enlightened president of Yale, "all the arts may be transported from Europe and Asia and flourish with...an augmented lustre."[12]

THE REVOLUTIONARIES, OF COURSE, never saw these dreams realized. Indeed, the gap between what they hoped for and what actually happened in the arts was so great that many historians have never been able to take their dreams seriously. Yet it would be a mistake to dismiss their hopes of America's becoming the eventual repository of Western learning as empty bluster. Not only did the Americans mean what they said, but their earnest attempts to implement that meaning had profound effects on American culture. By conceiving themselves as receiving and fulfilling the westward movement of the arts, the Revolutionaries inevitably became involved in powerful currents of cultural change sweeping through Europe in the eighteenth century.

11. Silverman, *Cultural History of the American Revolution*, 230.
12. Ezra Stiles, "Election Sermon" (1783), in John Wingate Thornton, ed., *The Pulpit of the American Revolution; or, the Political Sermons of the Period* (Boston, 1876), 460.

A century later these European currents would be labeled neoclassicism and disparaged as cold, formal, and sterile.[13] Yet to those who participated in this eighteenth-century artistic transformation, including Americans, neoclassicism represented not just another stylistic phase in the development of Western art but the ultimate realization of artistic truth, a promise of a new kind of enlightened art for an enlightened world. From the early eighteenth century, in France and England especially, amateur theorists had worked to distinguish several of the arts—usually painting, architecture, music, and poetry—from other arts and crafts and had designated them as possessing special capacities for civilizing humans. Numerous treatises systematically combined these "fine arts" together because of the presumed similarity of effect they had on audiences, spectators, and readers. Out of such efforts not only was the modern conception of aesthetics created, but the idea of measuring and judging nations and peoples by their artistic tastes and contributions was also born. These eighteenth-century developments radically transformed the aesthetic and social meaning of art. Paintings and literature were being taken out of the hands of the aristocratic courts and narrow elites and were being made into public commodities distributed to all literate members of the society eager to acquire reputations for polish and refinement.[14]

There were two interrelated aspects of this neoclassical transformation of the arts. One involved the purposes of art; the other involved a broadening of its public. For too long too many of the arts, such as the rococo paintings of François Boucher and Jean-Honoré Fragonard, seemed to have been the exclusive preserve of courtiers and a leisured aristocracy. Devotees of the rococo style, it was thought, looked upon the arts as a means of private pleasure, amusement, and display, as diversions from ennui or instruments of court intrigue. Such frivolous arts could scarcely be paid any special public veneration; indeed, with the courtly emphasis on amorous dalliance, lasciviousness, and luxury the arts could only be

13. On neoclassicism, see Hugh Honour, *Neo-Classicism* (Harmondsworth, UK, 1968), and the exhibition catalogue of the Royal Academy and the Victoria & Albert Museum, *The Age of Neo-Classicism* (London, 1972).

14. For these cultural changes, see R. G. Saisselin, "The Transformation of Art into Culture: From Pascal to Diderot," in Theodore Besterman, ed., *Studies on Voltaire and the Eighteenth Century*, 70 (Geneva, 1970), 3–25; R. G. Saisselin, "Tivoli Revisited or the Triumph of Culture," in Paul Fritz and David Williams, eds., *The Triumph of Culture: Eighteenth-Century Perspectives* (Toronto, 1972), 3–25; J. H. Plumb, "The Public, Literature and the Arts in the Eighteenth Century," ibid., 27–48; and Robert Rosenblum, *Transformations in Late Eighteenth-Century Art* (Princeton, 1970).

considered sources of personal corruption, effeminacy, and decadence, and hence dangerous to the social order.

Americans knew only too well that the fine arts, like painting or sculpture, in Benjamin Rush's words, "flourish chiefly in wealthy and luxurious countries" and therefore were symptoms of social decadence. Throughout his life, John Adams always had an extraordinarily sensuous attraction to beauty and the world of art. When he joined the Continental Congress in Philadelphia in 1774, he entered his first Roman Catholic church and, accustomed as he was to the stark simplicity of the Puritan churches of Massachusetts, was overwhelmed by the pomp of the service and the richness of the ornamentation. "Here is every Thing," he told his wife Abigail, "which can lay hold of the Eye, Ear, and Imagination." When he went to France in 1778 he was even more enchanted and overwhelmed by the beauty of Paris and Versailles, where "the Richness, the Magnificence, and Splendor is beyond all Description." Yet he knew that such art and beauty were the products of a hierarchical church and an authoritarian monarchy. As a good republican he knew "that the more elegance, the less virtue, in all times and countries." Buildings, paintings, sculpture, music, gardens, and furniture—however rich, magnificent, and splendid—were simply "bagatelles introduced by time and luxury in change for the great qualities and hardy, manly virtues of the human heart." The arts, he said, could "inform the Understanding, or refine the Taste," yet at the same time they could also "seduce, betray, deceive, deprave, corrupt, and debauch."[15]

Since the arts were associated with the politeness and gentility that many eighteenth-century people, including many Americans, were eager to acquire, they became a serious problem for enlightened reformers. How could the arts be promoted without promoting their evil consequences?

The solution was to change the character and purpose of art. Since those who feared being corrupted assumed that the arts, particularly the visual arts, had powerful effects on their beholder, it took only a slight shift of emphasis to transform art from a corrupting instrument of pleasure

15. JA to Abigail Adams, 9 Oct. 1774, 25 April 1778, April–May 1780, in Lyman Butterfield et al., eds., The *Book of Abigail and John: Selected Letters of the Adams Family, 1762–1784* (Cambridge, MA, 1975), 79, 210, 256; Neil Harris, *The Artist in American Society: The Formative Years, 1790–1860* (New York, 1966), 33–34; Wendell D. Garrett, "John Adams and the Limited Role of the Fine Arts," *Winterthur Portfolio*, 1 (1964), 243–55.

into a beneficial instrument of instruction. By the middle of the eighteenth-century European and English philosophers were already redi-
recting the content and form of art away from frivolous and voluptuous
private pleasure toward moral education and civic ennoblement. Infused
with dignity and morality and made subservient to some ideological force
outside themselves, the arts could become something more than charming ornaments of an idle aristocracy; they could become public agents of
reformation and refinement for the whole society.

At the same time as the social purpose of art was transformed, the
patronage of art expanded from the court and a few great noblemen to
embrace the entire educated public. Indeed, the two developments reinforced one another. Cultivation in the arts became a central means by
which eighteenth-century gentlemen sought to distinguish themselves.
Wealth and blood were no longer sufficient; taste and an awareness of the
arts were now necessary. Indeed, the English philosopher Lord Shaftesbury declared that morality and good taste were allied: "the science of
virtuosi and that of virtue itself become, in a manner, one and the same."[16]
Politeness and refinement were connected with public morality and
social order. The spread of good taste throughout the society would make
for a better and more benevolent nation.

Through the multiplication of newspapers, magazines, circulating
libraries, and book clubs, through the public exhibitions of paintings and
the engraving and distribution of prints, and through the formation of
salons, subscription assemblies, and concert halls—through all these
means Englishmen and other Europeans sought to exploit the arts in
order to reform their societies. In the process they turned the arts into
culture, into commodities, and created a central characteristic of modern
life. The polite essays of Joseph Addison and Richard Steele, the novels of
Samuel Richardson and Henry Fielding, the satiric prints of William
Hogarth, the history paintings of Benjamin West, even the vases of Josiah
Wedgwood, all in their different ways expressed this new moral and social
conception of culture. All were efforts to meet the new desire of a public
eager to learn how to behave, what to value, and why to be refined. To
possess this culture—to have correct taste and an amateur knowledge of
the arts and sciences—was to be a truly enlightened gentleman.

The effects of these developments on the arts and society were enormous. The arts became objects of special knowledge and examination, to

16. Stanley Grean, *Shaftesbury's Philosophy of Religion and Ethics: A Study in Enthusiasm*
(Athens, OH, 1967), 250; Lawrence Klein, "The Third Earl of Shaftesbury and the
Progress of Politeness," *Eighteenth-Century Studies*, 18 (1984–85), 186–214.

be placed in museums and studied in academies. Enlightened writers and painters sought to embody new ethical qualities in their work—truth, purity, nobility, honesty—to counteract the licentiousness and frivolity of their predecessors. The artist was no longer a craftsman catering to a few aristocratic patrons; he was to become a public philosopher academically educated and speaking to the society-at-large. Just as enlightened scientists and statesmen were seeking to discover the universal verities that underlay the workings of the universe and political states, so too were artists urged to return to long-accepted standards of excellence and virtue for the sake of the moral improvement of humanity.

For most eighteenth-century philosophes the return to the first principles of truth and beauty meant a recovery of antiquity. The only way for the moderns to become great, declared the influential German theorist Johann Joachim Winckelmann in his *On the Imitation of the Painting and Sculpture of the Greeks* (1755, Eng. trans. 1765), was "by imitating the ancients." For Winckelmann and other neoclassicists, originality meant little more than a return to origins.[17] Although Westerners, including the North American colonists, had long been involved with antiquity, the new enlightened interest in politeness and civic morality coupled with the archaeological discoveries of Herculaneum and Pompeii in the middle of the eighteenth century gave the classical past a new relevance, especially for those eager to emphasize republican values. The American Revolutionaries, in their images and writings, began playing down the martial qualities of antiquity and stressing instead its contributions to civility and sociability.[18]

Yet this new neoclassical use of antiquity was only the means toward a higher end—the discovery and imitation of Nature or those permanent and universal principles that transcended time, locality, and particularity. For Jefferson "natural" meant ideal, which is why he favored a "natural" aristocracy over an "artificial" one that was based on blood and family. Neoclassical art thus became a hostage against decline, a way of freezing time and maintaining an ideal permanence amidst the inevitability of social decay.

17. Winckelmann quoted in Eric Slauter, "Neoclassical Culture in a Society with Slaves: Race and Rights in the Age of Wheatley," *Early American Studies* (Spring 2004), 101.

18. Caroline Winterer, "From Royal to Republican: The Classical Image in Early America," *JAH*, 91 (2005), 1264–90; Caroline Winterer, *The Culture of Classicism: Ancient Greece and Rome in American Intellectual Life, 1780–1910* (Baltimore, 2002); Meyer Reinhold, ed., *The Classick Pages: Classical Readings of Eighteenth-Century Americans* (University Park, PA, 1975); Carl J. Richard, *The Founders and the Classics: Greece, Rome, and the American Enlightenment* (Cambridge, MA, 1994).

Comte de Volney's *Ruins; or, Meditations on the Revolution of Empires* was immensely popular in the United States—selling more than forty thousand copies within a few years of its publication in an English translation in 1795. Jefferson was so entranced by it that he began a new American translation, which he passed on to Joel Barlow to complete and publish in Paris in 1802. In addition to its anti-religious message and its indictment of monarchical tyranny and its celebration of liberty and equality, the book brought home to enlightened Americans the mortality of all states and reinforced their desire to build in stone and marble and to create depositories in order to leave to the future durable monuments of America's cultivation and refinement. But the book also seemed to suggest that an uncorrupted republican government might evade the decline and decay that had beset all other governments.[19]

EVEN PRIOR TO THE REVOLUTION some colonial painters had aspired to making their art significant. One of the early patrons of Benjamin West in Pennsylvania had told him to forget portraits and devote himself to "illustrating the moral effect of the art of painting."[20] West went to Europe and never returned, becoming in time president of Britain's Royal Academy and painter to George III. In a like manner John S. Copley of colonial Boston had yearned to make painting "one of the most noble arts in the world." But he could not convince his fellow colonial Americans to have anything other than their portraits painted. In fact, they regarded him as a mere artisan and what he did as just another "trade, as they sometimes term it, like that of a carpenter, tailor, or shewmaker." In frustration Copley left for England in 1774—alas! a moment too soon, for the Revolution changed everything.[21]

In 1789 young John Trumbull (second cousin to the poet of the same name and a son and brother to governors of Connecticut), realizing what the American Revolution meant for the arts, turned down a request to become Jefferson's personal secretary in order to pursue a career as a painter. He knew that in the past Americans had thought of painting as "frivolous, little useful to Society, and unworthy the attention of a Man

19. Constantin François Volney, *A New Translation of Volney's Ruins; or, Meditations on the Revolution of Empire* (Paris, 1802); *American Museum*, 8 (1790), 174–76; J. Meredith Neil, *Toward a National Taste: America's Quest for Aesthetic Independence* (Honolulu, 1975), 143.
20. Helmut von Erffa and Allen Staley, *The Paintings of Benjamin West* (New Haven, 1986), 9.
21. "Letters and Papers of John Singleton Copley and Henry Pelham, 1739–1776," Massachusetts Historical Society, *Coll.*, 71 (1914), 661–66.

who possesses talents for more serious occupations." Yet he believed that the Revolution offered an opportunity to alter the role of the arts and artists in society. By "commemorating the great Events of our Country's Revolution" in paintings and engravings, Trumbull hoped, he told Jefferson in 1789, "to diffuse the knowledge and preserve the Memory of the noblest series of Actions which have ever dignified the History of Man: — to give to the present and the future Sons of Oppression and Misfortune such glorious Lessons of their rights and of the Spirit with which they should assert and support them: — and even to transmit to their descendents the personal resemblance of those who have been the great actors in those illustrious scenes." Trumbull went on to become the principal painter of the American Revolution, depicting some of its great events, such as *The Death of General Warren at Bunker's Hill* and *The Signing of the Declaration of Independence*, and painting hundreds of portraits of its participants.[22]

Still, there was the problem of sumptuousness and decadence traditionally associated with art. If Americans were to exceed Europe in dignity, grandeur, and taste, they would need a new kind of art, something appropriate to their new independent status as a nation. Somehow they would have to create a strictly republican art that avoided the vices of monarchical over-refinement and luxury that were destroying the Old World. The solution lay in the taut rationality of republican classicism. It emphasized, as the commissioners who were charged with supervising the construction of public buildings in Washington, D.C., put it in 1793, "a grandeur of conception, a Republican simplicity, and that true elegance of proportion, which correspond to a tempered freedom excluding Frivolity, the food of little minds."[23]

Although such neoclassical thinking was cosmopolitan, it also possessed a nationalistic imperative. In this new enlightened age, Americans argued, nations had to distinguish themselves not by force of arms but, as the *Massachusetts Magazine* declared in 1792, "by art, science, and refinement."[24] It was therefore not paradoxical for American writers and artists to speak of emulating the best of European culture and in the same breath to recommend the need for native originality. Urging the exploitation of native themes and indigenous materials or the investigation of American antiquities and curiosities did not violate the neoclassical search for the eternally valid truths that underlay the particularities and

---

22. Trumbull to TJ, 11 June 1789, *Papers of Jefferson*, 15: 176–79; Irma B. Jaffe, *John Trumbull: Patriot Artist of the American Revolution* (Boston, 1975).
23. Harris, *Artist in American Society*, 42.
24. *Massachusetts Magazine*, 4 (1792), 434.

diversities of the visible world. Americans told themselves that they could "recur to first principles, with ease, because our customs, tastes and refinements, are less artificial than those of other countries."[25]

The principal criterion of art in this neoclassical era lay not in the genius of the artist or in the novelty of the work but rather in the effect of the art on the audience or spectator. Consequently, someone like Joel Barlow could believe that his epic of America, *Vision of Columbus* (later the *Columbiad*), precisely because of its high moral and republican message, could exceed in grandeur even Homer's *Iliad*.

George Washington certainly was impressed with Barlow, who labored over his six-thousand-line epic of future American greatness for twenty years. "Perhaps we shall be found, at this moment," Washington told Lafayette in May 1788, "not inferior to the rest of the world in the performances of our poets and painters." And he offered Barlow as an example of "a genius of the first magnitude;...and one of those Bards who hold the keys of the gate by which Patriots, Sages, and heroes are admitted to immortality."[26]

The Revolution gave Americans the opportunity to put all these neoclassical ideas about art into effect. It created a sudden effusion of artistic and iconographic works, the extent of which has never been fully appreciated. Neoclassical themes, especially embodied in the classical goddesses Liberty and Minerva, appeared everywhere—in paintings, newspapers, coins, seals, almanacs, flags, weathervanes, wallpaper, and furniture.

All these icons and images were designed to bear moral and political messages. The Revolutionaries continually interrupted their constitution-making and military campaigning to sit for long hours having their portraits painted or to design all sorts of emblems, Latin mottoes, and commemorative medals. One of the most famous icons they created was the Great Seal of the United States (seen most commonly on the one-dollar bill).

Franklin, Jefferson, and John Adams all took a stab at designing it—a measure of the importance they gave to the icons of the Revolution. Franklin proposed a biblical scene, that of Moses "lifting up his Wand, and dividing the Red Sea, and Pharaoh, in his Chariot overwhelmed with the Waters." Jefferson suggested a similar biblical scene, "the Children of Israel in the Wilderness." Adams proposed Hercules surveying the choice between Virtue and Sloth, the most popular of emblems in the eighteenth century. Since these designs proved "too complicated," as Adams

25. Neil, *Toward A National Taste*, 145.
26. GW to Lafayette, 28 May 1788, *Washington: Writings*, 680–81.

admitted, Congress turned the job over to the secretary of the Continental Congress, Charles Thomson, who finally worked out the present seal. The emblazoned eagle on one side was a symbol of empire. The pyramid on the other side, perhaps drawn from Masonic symbolism, represented the strength of the new nation. The all-seeing eye on the reverse stood for providence. And the Latin mottoes, *Novus Ordo Seclorum* — "a new order of the ages" — and *Annuit Coeptis* — "He has looked after us" — were taken from Virgil.[27]

ALTHOUGH MANY AMERICAN LEADERS sought to use art to further the Revolution, no one could match Charles Willson Peale in creating icons. He became a one-man dynamo on behalf of the patriot cause, completing sixty-five paintings in the year 1776 alone.[28] He was an extraordinary character — at one time or another artist, politician, scientist, tinker, and showman, yet remaining throughout his life, in his optimism and enthusiasm, as Benjamin Latrobe said, "a *boy* in many respects."[29]

Peale began life as an apprenticed saddle-maker, tried his hand as an upholsterer, silversmith, and clock and watch repairer, but eventually turned to painting portraits for money. Unlike Copley and Trumbull, Peale never lost the sense that his painting was a kind of craft or "business," not all that different from what he called "his other Trades."[30] Some gentry patrons, impressed with his artistic talent, sent him to London in 1767 to study with Benjamin West. When he returned to America in 1769, he threw himself into the Revolutionary movement. His radicalism cost him portrait commissions from wealthy Philadelphians, and at the end of the war he formally renounced politics and devoted all his energy to painting (sixty portraits of Washington alone), science, and raising his huge artistically inclined family, including such accomplished and prophetically named sons as Titian, Rembrandt, and Raphael. By the 1780s he was deeply involved in a variety of projects, ranging from an effigy of Benedict Arnold to a forty-foot-high Triumphal Arch spanning Market Street in Philadelphia and lit by a thousand lamps. Unfortunately,

27. Frank H. Sommer, "Emblem and Device: The Origin of the Great Seal of the United States," Art Quarterly, 24 (1961), 57–77; Burstein, Sentimental Democracy, 132–34; Steven C. Bullock, "'Sensible Signs': The Emblematic Education of Post-Revolutionary Freemasonry," in Donald R. Kennon, ed., A Republic for the Ages: The United States Capitol and the Political Culture of the Early Republic (Charlottesville, 1999), 203, 210.

28. Ellis, After the Revolution, 51.

29. David C. Ward, Charles Willson Peale: Art and Selfhood in the Early Republic (Berkeley, 2004), 146.

30. Neil, Toward a National Taste, 57–58; Ward, Peale, 16–17.

the arch caught fire and was destroyed, and its creator was nearly killed. But such disasters did not dampen Peale's enthusiasm. In one way or another he became involved in nearly all of Philadelphia's civic ceremonies during the 1780s and 1790s.

Peale's most famous creation was his museum, which was designed, he declared, to promote "the interests of religion and morality by the arrangement and display of the works of nature and art."[31] When he opened it in 1786 in concert with his brother James, he knew that educating the public in enlightened republicanism had to be its main justification. Peale added to his Philadelphia gallery of paintings, especially of the Revolutionary leaders, some fossils and a collection of stuffed birds and wild animals. When interest in this menagerie picked up, Peale included a miniature theater with transparent moving pictures.

In 1802 the museum was moved to the Pennsylvania State House (now Independence Hall), where it became a profitable institution attended by thousands of visitors. Unlike the European museums, which tended to open their exhibitions only to select or privileged groups befitting Europe's hierarchal societies, Peale's museum was designed as a republican institution open to anyone who could pay the twenty-five-cent admission fee. Peale wanted an admission fee, but only a small one, "for if a Museum was free to all to view it without cost," he said, "it would be over-run & abused—on the other hand, if too difficult of access, it would lose its utility; that of giving information generally." By 1815 Peale's museum was attracting nearly forty thousand visitors a year.[32]

In addition to the mammoth that he exhumed in 1802, Peale kept adding more and more creatures and curiosities to his museum, which he wanted to call the "Temple of Wisdom," but declined to do so for fear of offending religious sensibilities. His museum became the repository for specimens and artifacts collected by official explorations into the West, including the Lewis and Clark expedition. He hoped that his museum would "bring into one view a world in miniature" and teach visitors the overall design and rationality of the universe. Contemplating "the beautiful uniformity in an infinite variety of beings," he said in a notable address of 1800, would "raise us above ourselves." His view of the universe was thoroughly taxonomic. He even placed his portraits above the natural history cabinets in order to stress the natural order of a world dominated by man. He hoped that young children might learn from the harmony of nature to refrain from "cruelly, or wantonly tormenting" insects and other

31. Lillian B. Miller, *Patrons and Patriotism: The Encouragement of the Fine Arts in the United States, 1790–1860* (Chicago, 1966), 90.
32. Ward, *Peale*, 103–4.

natural creatures. Such knowledge, Peale said, would thus have the effect of "instilling and extending, as they advance in years, a sweet benevolence of temper toward their brethren."[33]

ALWAYS THE GOAL of every cultural effort during these post-Revolutionary years was to instill the right feelings in the spectators. "Emulation," seeing virtuous exemplars and becoming desirous of exceeding them, said Jefferson, was the best means of inculcating virtue in the society.[34] Anything that might inspire patriotic and republican sentiments, such as viewing Washington's statue or one of his many portraits, was encouraged, and anything that smacked of European dissipation and luxury, even something as seemingly innocuous as a semi-monthly tea assembly in Boston in the 1780s, was criticized. In 1783 Jeremy Belknap urged Congress to display all the trophies taken from the British during the war, since the sight of them would "fan the flame of liberty and independence."[35] In 1787 the New England founders of Marietta, Ohio, aimed to inspire the new settlers with the right spirit by calling the public squares in the town Capitolium and Quadranou in emulation of the Roman republic. With similar hopes of instilling the proper republican attitudes, Jefferson in the 1780s proposed some extraordinary classical names, including Assenisipia, Pelisipia, and Cherronesus, for the new states of the West.

When compared to the extravagant French effort in the succeeding years under the direction of Jacques-Louis David to put the arts into the service of revolution and republicanism, the American attempts to exploit the fine arts for the sake of their Revolution and their new Republic may seem pale and feeble.[36] Yet in the context of America's undeveloped

33. Charles Willson Peale, *Discourse Introductory to a Course of Lectures on the Science of Nature* (1800), in Gordon S. Wood, ed., *The Rising Glory of America, 1760–1820*, rev. ed. (Boston, 1990), 224, 225; David R. Brigham, *Public Culture in the Early Republic: Peale's Museum and Its Audience* (Washington, DC, 1995), 36; Charles Coleman Sellers, *Mr. Peale's Museum: Charles Willson Peale and the First Popular Museum of Natural Science and Art* (New York, 1980), 26–27; Sidney Hart, "'To Encrease the Comforts of Life': Charles Willson Peale and the Mechanical Arts," *Penn. Mag. of Hist. and Biog.* 110 (1986), 323–57; Ward, *Peale*, 105–7.

34. John Saillant, "The American Enlightenment," *Eighteenth-Century Studies*, 31 (1998), 264.

35. Kenneth R. Bowling, *The Creation of Washington, D.C.: The Ideas and Location of the American Capital* (Fairfax, VA, 1991), 5.

36. On the French revolutionary efforts, see James A. Leith, *The Idea of Art as Propaganda in France, 1750–1799* (Toronto, 1965); David Lloyd Dowd, *Pageant Master of the Republic: Jacques-Louis David and the French Revolution* (Lincoln, NE, 1948).

provincial situation in the eighteenth century and its relative lack of experience in the arts, the American Revolutionaries' aims and achievements are truly astonishing.

On the face of it, the creation of a monumental city like Washington, D.C., in the midst of the wilderness is incredible. But it becomes comprehensible in light of America's neoclassical aspirations, expressed, for example, in poet David Humphreys's vision of the United States as a rebirth of the ancient Roman republic. "What Rome, once virtuous, saw, this gives us now—/ Heroes and statesmen, awful from the plough."[37] Even little Goose Creek off the Potomac was renamed the Tiber.[38]

Probably no other American had more effect on America's public architecture than Jefferson, and no one emphasized the moral and public purposes of the arts more than he. He was "an enthusiast on the subject of the arts," he said, and of all the arts, architecture was his special "delight." He believed that nothing showed as much as "this beautiful art," and he spent his life "putting up and pulling down" buildings. (Indeed, Americans in this period were almost totally interested in architectural exteriors and spent very little time on interior design.)[39]

From France in the 1780s Jefferson badgered his Virginia colleagues into erecting as the new capitol of the state in Richmond a magnificent copy of the Maison Carrée, a Roman temple at Nîmes from the first century A.D. This classical building, he explained, "has pleased, universally, for nearly two thousand years," and it would be a perfect model for republican America. Indeed, the purpose of erecting such a Roman temple amidst the muddy streets of a backwoods town in Virginia, said Jefferson, was "to improve the taste of my countrymen, to increase their reputation, and to reconcile to them the respect of the world, and procure them its praise."[40] No matter that the Virginians had to interrupt their original plans and tear down some of what they had begun building to make room for Jefferson's model. No matter too that a Roman temple was hard to heat and was acoustically impossible. Other considerations mattered more. With the erection of this Virginia capitol Jefferson single-handedly influenced the classical style of public buildings in America. And he

37. David Humphreys, "Poem on the Industry of the United States of America" (1804), in Vernon Louis Parrington, ed., The Connecticut Wits (New York, 1954, new ed. 1969), 401.

38. John W. Reps, Monumental Washington: The Planning and Development of the Capital Center (Princeton, 1967), ch. 1.

39. Neil, Toward a National Taste, 150–51.

40. TJ to William Buchanan and James Hay, 26 Jan. 1786, to JM, 20 Sept. 1785, Papers of Jefferson, 9: 220–22, 8: 534–35.

helped to place a moral and civic burden on the arts that would prove difficult to sustain in subsequent years.

THE CULTURAL RELICS of these neoclassical dreams are with Americans still: not only in the endless proliferation of Greek and Roman temples but in the names of towns like Athens, Rome, Syracuse, and Troy; in the designation of political institutions like capitols and senates; in political symbols like the goddess Liberty and numerous Latin mottoes; and in poetry and songs like "Hail Columbia." But the spirit that once inspired these things, the meaning they had for the Revolutionaries, has been lost and was waning even as they were being created. Indeed, much of the culture inherited from the Revolutionary period remains only as an awkward reminder of the brevity of America's classical age.

With such high hopes and grandiose expectations the disillusionment among American artists and intellectuals in the years following the Revolution was profound. Culturally, the United States still seemed to be a provincial outpost of the British Empire. Most of the plays that Americans watched in the period were not American but British in origin and were performed by traveling British actors. Of the 160 plays professionally put on in Philadelphia between May 1792 and July 1794 only 2 were written by Americans. Even when native authors attempted something of their own, the English influence was inescapable. The play *Independence*, written in 1805 by the young South Carolina playwright William Ioor, was a perfect example. Despite its patriotic title, the play was based on an English novel, was set in England, and had only English characters. Seventy percent of the books Americans read were pirated English editions. About three-fourths of every issue of one of America's leading magazines, the *Columbian*, was borrowed from British sources. Most of the songs Americans sang were British songs. The homes and gardens of Americans were copies of English styles, and often in *retardataire* taste. In 1808 the artist William Birch issued his collection of engravings of *The Country Seats of the United States of America*, modeled on British publications dealing with the country estates of the English landed gentry and nobility, and found many eager buyers.[41]

41. Lawrence J. Friedman, *Inventors of the Promised Land* (New York, 1975), 9; Jeffrey H. Richards, *Drama, Theater, and Identity in the American New Republic* (Cambridge, UK, 2005), 2, 4; Heather Nathans, *Early American Theater from the Revolution to Thomas Jefferson: Into the Hands of the People* (Cambridge, UK, 2003), 86; Edward J. Nygren and Bruce Robertson, eds., *Views and Visions: American Landscape Before 1830* (Washington, DC, 1986), 25, 137–43.

So imitative were the arts that some Americans were ready to concede that they were European luxuries after all and thus dangerous to American republicanism. But others, such as Benjamin Henry Latrobe, were desperate to prove that the "arts have not an injurious, but a beneficent effect upon the morals, and even on the liberties of our country." While Europeans could take the arts for granted, Americans could not. Since, as Latrobe pointed out, "our national prejudices are unfavorable to the fine arts," the arts had to be repeatedly defended and justified. The peculiarly egalitarian and unstable character of American society, right from the beginning of the Revolutionary movement, had put the arts on the defensive.[42]

While eighteenth-century Europe had its own intellectual opponents of the arts (Rousseau being the most famous), there the debate over the place of the arts in society had been carried on for a century or more and had never endangered the legitimacy of art. But America's inexperience with the fine arts and the greater rapidity and intensity of its republican social revolution in comparison with Europe's forced it to telescope and compress its neoclassical transformation, leading to both the excited over-estimations and the exaggerated apologies, the "hothouse atmosphere of forced growth," as historian Neil Harris has described it.[43] Desiring to make the arts safe for republicanism, Americans placed a heavy moral and social burden upon them—heavier certainly than they bore in Europe—and left both the arts and artists little room for autonomy and originality. "While many other nations are wasting the brilliant efforts of genius in monuments of ingenious folly, to perpetuate their pride, the Americans, according to the true spirit of republicanism," wrote Jedidiah Morse in his 1791 geographic reader, "are employed almost entirely in works of public and private utility."[44]

It was evident that the arts in America had to be morally instructive and socially useful. But most Revolutionaries had assumed that the morality to be inculcated would be elitist and classical, emphasizing sobriety, rationality, and a noble stoicism. In the years following the Revolution, however, the morality of civic humanism became evangelicized and democratized, transformed into a shrill popular didacticism that some-times ended up resembling little more than prudery. Since art was judged by the moral lessons it taught, ministers like Timothy Dwight drew no

42. Latrobe, "Anniversary Oration," *Port Folio*, 3rd Ser., 5 (1811), 4.

43. Harris, *Artist in American Society*, 22.

44. Ruth M. Elson, *Guardians of Tradition: American Schoolbooks of the Nineteenth Century* (Lincoln, NE, 1964), 223; Michael T. Gilmore, "The Literature of the Revolutionary and Early National Periods," *The Cambridge History of American Literature*, ed. Sacvan Bercovitch (Cambridge, UK, 1994), 548.

sharp distinction between the sermons they delivered and the poetry they composed—everything had to be edifying.[45]

The theater especially had a reputation for licentiousness and corruption and consequently had been banned in every colony except Virginia and Maryland. One of the rules of Harvard College during the early 1770s declared that any undergraduate presuming "to be an Actor in, a Spectator at, or any Ways concerned in any Stage Plays, interludes or Theatrical Entertainments" would for the first offense be degraded and "for any repeated offence shall be rusticated or expelled." In New York City the Sons of Liberty had burned down a theater that had defied the law against theaters. In 1774 the Continental Congress had urged Americans to discourage "every species of extravagance and dissipation," including "exhibitions of shews, plays, other expensive diversions and entertainments."[46] Throughout the war the Congress had continued to recommend the suppression of play-going; in 1778 it declared that anyone holding an office under the United States would be dismissed if he encouraged or attended the theater. (This at the very moment the commander-in-chief was putting on Addison's *Cato* for the troops.) No one in 1789 could talk the old patriot Samuel Adams out of his belief that the theater subverted all those "Characteristics of a Republic which we ought carefully to maintain."[47]

Everywhere during the 1780s and 1790s—in New York, Philadelphia, Albany, Charleston, Portsmouth, Providence, Boston, and elsewhere—disputes broke out over the establishing of theaters. Of course, in most communities there were well-to-do elites that enjoyed the theater and had no problem with such expressions of luxury as tea parties and theatrical productions. But they had to contend with growing numbers, especially among the middling sorts like William Findley, who feared the influence of the theater and resented those wealthy merchants and luxury-loving professionals who favored it. These middling opponents argued that the theater stimulated debauchery, seduced young men, subverted religion, and spawned brothels. Some argued that it was the theater that had done the most to corrupt England, and thus it helped account for Britain's tyrannical behavior that brought about the Revolution. Others suggested that the theater contributed to the spread of the deception and dissimulation

45. Gilmore, "The Literature of the Revolutionary and Early National Periods," 548–49.
46. Nathans, *Early American Theater*, 13–36; G. Thomas Tanselle, *Royall Tyler* (Cambridge, MA, 1967), 5; William J. Meserve, *An Emerging Entertainment: The Drama of the American People to 1828* (Bloomington, IN, 1977), 61.
47. Kenneth R. Bowling, "A Capital Before a Capitol: Republican Visions," in Kennon, ed., *A Republic for the Ages*, 51.

that were serious problems in America's fluid society. "What was the talent of an actor?" asked the Presbyterian minister Samuel Miller, but the "art of counterfeiting himself, of putting on another character than his own, of appearing different than he is."[48] For many it seemed that the future of the new Republic itself had come to rest on preventing the performances of stage plays; "they only flourished when states were on the decline," declared critics in Pennsylvania in 1785.[49]

Only with great difficulty were those gentlemanly elites who favored the theater able to have most of the laws against the stage repealed in the decades following the Revolution; and they did so largely by stressing the theater's moral and civic purposes, sometimes sincerely but perhaps more often because these were the only justifications that could persuade an emerging middling popular culture obsessed with respectability. Washington loved the theater, but he had to defend it solely on the grounds that it would "advance the interest of private and public virtue" and "polish the manners and habits of society."[50]

Elbridge Gerry tried to change Samuel Adams's opinion of the theater by stressing that it was nothing more than a "school for morality."[51] In fact, plays had to be advertised as "moral lectures" or run the risk of being closed down. Shakespeare's *Othello* was billed as "a Series of Moral Dialogues in Five Parts, depicting the evils of jealousy, and other bad passions." So too was *Richard III* advertised as "The Fate of Tyranny," *Hamlet* as "Filial Piety," and Oliver Goldsmith's *She Stoops to Conquer* as "Improper Education." American theater managers cut and edited the imported British plays to the point where, as one critic complained, "the English comedy is reduced to the insipidity of a Presbyterian sermon."[52]

Everywhere apologists for the much feared theater were compelled to argue, as William Haliburton of Boston did in 1792, that the theater was the best "engine" for reforming the morals of the society and for suppressing vulgar vices like gambling, drinking, and cockfighting.[53] With clergymen

48. Ellis, *After the Revolution*, 133.
49. Nathans, *Early American Theater*, 37–70; Silverman, *Cultural History of the American Revolution*, 546–556; Ellis, *After the Revolution*, 129; *American Museum*, 5 (1789), 185–90.
50. Merle Curti, *The Growth of American Thought*, 3rd ed. (New York, 1964), 133.
51. Bowling, "Capital Before a Capitol," Kennon, ed., *A Republic for the Ages*, 51.
52. Playbill, in Wood, ed., *Rising Glory of America*, 281; Nye, *Cultural Life of the New Nation*, 264; Ellis, *After the Revolution*, 133–34; Richards, *Drama, Theater, and Identity in the American New Republic*, 69, 2; Nathans, *Early American Theater*, 86–88.
53. William Haliburton, *The Effects of the Stage...on the Manners of a People* (Boston, 1792), 11, 15, 21.

exploiting theatrical disasters, especially the devastating 1812 fire in Richmond that killed seventy-one persons, as evidence of God's just punishment for the evils of play-going, defenders were always hard-pressed to justify the presence of the stage in their communities. A Charleston, South Carolina, supporter told the people not to worry about the theater: the "morals and manners of this country are too chaste to leave reason to apprehend that any improper plays will be written here for perhaps centuries to come." When a person left the theater, it was said, he should "have no doubt about what was right and what was wrong,...and should testify...that he came away a better man than he went." With such rhetoric flying about, ambitious playwrights could scarcely think of themselves as anything but secular parsons.[54]

The new Republic seemed to have no place for idle pleasure. In comedies, the playwrights' moral messages continually got in the way of humor. If there were to be amusement, it had to be what was commonly called "rational amusement." The theater, wrote the sometime playwright and feminist Judith Sargent Murray, had to become "chaste and discreetly regulated." Then "young persons will acquire a refinement of manners; they will learn to think, speak and act with propriety; a thirst for knowledge will be originated; and from attentions, at first, perhaps, constituting only the amusement of the hour, they will gradually proceed to more important inquiries."[55]

Even the moral purpose of the arts was not always enough to justify them. Rather than simply describing the arts as benefactions to mankind, Americans felt compelled to measure them by their contributions to the country's material prosperity, celebrating them, for example, as stimulants to the marble, granite, clay, glass, and cotton industries.[56] In Benjamin Latrobe's oration before the Society of Artists in 1811, which, he said, was "an attempt to remove the prejudices which oppose the establishment of the fine arts among us," he hesitantly mentioned that, if necessary, "I could call up the spirit of commerce to aid me," which he then proceeded to do, listing Josiah Wedgwood's dishes, John Boydell's prints, and other "demons of cupidity, and of avarice" on behalf of the arts.[57]

UNDER THESE KINDS of utilitarian pressures the distinction between the fine and useful arts so painstakingly worked out over the previous century was now blurred. Since no one had any doubt of the

54. Silverman, *Cultural History of the American Revolution*, 554; Ellis, *After the Revolution*, 134; David Grimsted, *Melodrama Unveiled: American Theater and Culture, 1800–1850* (Chicago, 1968), 8; Meserve, *Emerging Entertainment*, 104–5.
55. Meserve, *Emerging Entertainment*, 154.
56. Elson, *Guardians of Tradition*, 233.
57. Latrobe, "Anniversary Oration," *Port Folio*, 3rd Ser., 5 (1811), 30.

value of the useful arts in contrast to the fine arts, Joseph Hopkinson went to great lengths to show how helpful the fine arts would be to "the carpenter, the mason, nay, the mechanic of every description."[58] But it was difficult to justify the fine arts to a large public, and American writers and artists like Alexander Wilson, Robert Fulton, and Samuel F. B. Morse eventually found it easy and more profitable to move into the more defensibly useful endeavors involving science and technology.

Young Morse, like other American painters, had been eager to pursue "the intellectual branch of the art," by which he meant history-painting, and in 1811 he went off to Europe to learn the art. Although his mother tried to set him straight—"you must not expect to paint anything in this country for which you will receive any money to support you, but portraits"—he returned from Europe with the "ambition to be among those who shall revive the splendor of the fifteenth century; to rival the genius of a Raphael, a Michael Angelo, or a Titian." Above all, he said, he did not want to end up "lowering my noble art to a trade,...degrading myself and the soul-enlarging art which I possess to the narrow idea of merely making money." The temptation was there, but he rejected it. "No, never will I degrade myself by making a trade of a profession. If I cannot live a gentleman, I will starve a gentleman."[59]

But no one would give a commission for a history painting, and Morse was eventually reduced to traveling about New England painting heads for fifteen dollars apiece. His idealized picture of the *Old House of Representatives*, from which he hoped to earn a fortune on tour, was not moralistically theatrical enough for viewers, and the tour was a failure; Congress refused to buy the painting, and it ended up cracked and dusty in a New York warehouse. Ultimately, Morse was able to find monetary reward only by inventing the telegraph and the code to which he gave his name.[60]

The neoclassical and republican desire to bring the arts to a wider public, to involve the whole citizenry in enlightenment and cultivation, created a popular cultural monster that could not be controlled. Instead of refining the taste of the people, the arts themselves, in their attempts to comprehend the ever enlarging public, became vulgarized. The self-taught artist John Durand may have advertised that his paintings were in

58. Joseph Hopkinson, "Annual Discourse, Delivered Before the Pennsylvania Academy of the Fine Arts" (1810), in Wood, ed., *Rising Glory of America*, 334.

59. James Thomas Flexner, *The Light of Distant Skies: American Painting, 1760–1835* (New York, 1954), 152.

60. Hopkinson, "Annual Discourse," in Wood, ed., *Rising Glory of America*, 330; Oliver W. Larkin, *Samuel F. B. Morse and the American Democratic Art* (Boston, 1954), 31–32.

accord with the "best taste and judgment in all polite nations in every age." But he knew that if he were to survive, he would also have to be willing, "either for cash, short credit, or country produce," to "paint, gild, and varnish wheel carriages; and put coats of arms, or ciphers, upon them, in a neater and more lasting manner than ever was done in this country."[61] No one wanted any sort of painting but portraits or landscapes, and those artists who sought to commemorate great historical events on canvas had to turn their paintings into panoramas, oversized spectacles designed for carnival-like exhibition. John Vanderlyn's effort to paint classical history, his *Marius Musing amid the Ruins of Carthage*, went unsold, and with well-to-do spectators, mostly Federalists, not all that eager to view anything French, even his huge panorama of Versailles lost money.[62]

The maudlin moralizing efforts of Parson Mason Weems to humanize George Washington for ordinary people were a vulgar perversion of the ennobling art of history-writing. Yet his brief popularized life of Washington, which included mythical stories such as young Washington cutting down the cherry tree, influenced American attitudes in ways that John Marshall's five-volume biography could not.

Marshall, who published his life and times of Washington between 1804 and 1807, was interested only in the public life of the great man, and in his first volume not even that: it covered the entire colonial period and scarcely mentioned the subject of the biography. Unlike Weems's biography, which concentrated on Washington's boyhood and early manhood, Marshall's second volume dismissed Washington's youth in a single page.

Although John Adams assured Marshall in 1806 that his biography of Washington would create "a more glorious and durable Memorial of your Hero, than a Mausoleum would have been, of dimensions Superiour to the proudest pyramid of Egypt," seven years later Adams told Jefferson that Marshall's work had indeed become "a Mausolaeum," resembling a pyramid that was "100 feet square at the base and 200 feet high," and all part of what he called "the impious Idolatry to Washington." Although Bushrod Washington, Marshall's collaborator, blamed the poor subscription sales of Marshall's *Life of George Washington* on the use of postal agents, who, he said, were mostly "democrats" who did not "feel a disposition to advance the work," the volumes were in

61. Flexner, *Light of Distant Skies*, 84; David Meschutt, "John Durand," in John A. Garraty and Mark Carnes, eds., *American National Biography* (New York, 1999), 7: 139–40.
62. Charles Coleman Sellers, *Charles Willson Peale*, vol. 2, *Later Life* (Philadelphia, 1947), 329.

fact too long, too formal, and too slowly published to attract many buyers.[63]

By contrast, Weems's fast-paced and fanciful biography sold thousands of copies and went through twenty-nine editions in two decades and a half following its publication in 1800. The public wanted Weems's human interest stories, even if they were fabricated. Weems's new sort of popular biography naturally disgusted some traditional reviewers, who said that the author "often transports us from a strain of religious moralizing...to the low cant and balderdash of the ranks and drinking table." But it awed others, who feared that this outrageous peddler-preacher and his popular biographies were endowed with "the power of doing considerable good, and considerable mischief, among the lower orders of readers in this country."[64]

Literature was supposed to be morally instructive, and most of the American novels published in the early Republic were intended to control sexual license and teach self-discipline, especially among young women. In fact, many of the novels, such as William Hill Brown's *The Power of Sympathy* (1789) and Hannah Foster's *The Coquette* (1797), were designed to replace the advice manuals, which were increasingly regarded, as one writer said, as "too generally tedious, and often uninteresting in the lively idea of youth." Better to insinuate morality "through the medium of history or even of fiction," which could "answer the same end, in a manner unquestionably more agreeable."[65]

Since these seduction novels were supposed to be true, their descriptions of the illicit love affairs became more and more obtrusively exciting and the overlaid moral lessons more and more transparent and gratuitous. Although themes of seduction tended to dominate the stories published in the periodicals of the period, most people ended up reading these sensual tales not to be reformed but to be titillated. Many of the seduction novels seemed to make the socially unacceptable but passionate suitor more attractive than the male character that society and the young woman's parents regarded as the appropriate mate. The writers railed against seduction, but at the same time they aroused sexual desire with erotically charged descriptions of the seductions. In Foster's *The Coquette*, for example, the libertine male character spends the night in the room of

63. JA to Marshall, 4 Feb. 1806, *Papers of Marshall*, 6: 425; to TJ, 13 July 1813, in Lester J. Cappon, ed., *The Adams-Jefferson Letters: The Complete Correspondence Between Thomas Jefferson and Abigail and John Adams* (Chapel Hill, 1959), 2: 349; Editorial Note, *The Life of George Washington*, *Papers of Marshall*, 6: 221.

64. Emily E. F. Skeel, ed., *Mason Locke Weems: His Works and Ways* (New York, 1929), 1: 55, 132.

65. Karen A. Weyler, *Intricate Relations: Sexual and Economic Desire in American Fiction, 1789–1814* (Iowa City, 2004), 29–74.

heroine Eliza Wharton and is seen sneaking away in the early morning hours by one of Eliza's female friends, who no doubt voiced the feelings of many readers in remarking: "My blood thrilled with horror at this sacrifice of virtue."[66]

INSTITUTIONS THAT WERE PRIMARILY DESIGNED to benefit artists had a hard time getting established. Artists in America initially tried to organize, as artists in England did, in order to create a school of the fine arts that would, as an advertisement promised, "supersede the necessity and save the expense of a foreign education." In 1794 Charles Willson Peale brought together thirty artists to form a society in emulation of the Royal Academy or the Society of Artists in England, to which he had belonged when he was in London. Peale's academy was designed for art instruction and exhibitions of the artists' works. The members of the society, which grew to over sixty in several weeks, called their organization "the Columbianum, or American Academy of the Fine Arts," a takeoff of "Athenaeum," which Americans in other cities were calling their institutions of cultural promotion. At the outset many of the members were foreign immigrants, especially English immigrants of middle age and often mediocre talent, including John James Barralet, Robert Field, and George Isham Parkyns, seeking to advance their careers in this new land of opportunity. These English immigrants, as Field told a colleague back home, saw a chance of "making a figure in an Academy of Arts and Sciences now establishing here, the plans of which is the most enlarged, liberal and grand of any in the world." To top it off, he said, President George Washington would become its honorary patron just as King George III was the patron of the Royal Academy.

This proposal of the president as patron was too much for Peale and the Jefferson Republicans, who saw themselves as simply a group of workmen coming together for mutual advantage; and they attacked the Englishmen as men "who fancy themselves a better order of beings," and "who started up from the hot-beds of monarchy, and think themselves lords of the human kind." Giuseppe Ceracchi, the hot-tempered Italian neoclassical sculptor who had come to America in the 1790s with the aim of erecting a hundred-foot marble memorial to American liberty and its heroes, was especially incensed by the monarchical suggestion of the Englishmen, and a spirited debate in the press followed.

This debate and the expression of support for radical republicanism angered many of the English immigrants and other conservative mem-

66. Rodney Hessinger, *Seduced, Abandoned, and Reborn: Visions of Youth in Middle-Class America, 1780–1850* (Philadelphia, 2005), 23–43.

bers, and early in 1795 eight of them withdrew to form another organization. The two organizations fought for weeks in the press over their names, until, first, the English separatist organization collapsed, and then several months later Peale's academy finally died as well.[67]

By the early nineteenth century supporters of the arts had come to realize that the English model of a learned academy of artists did not fit American conditions. If artistic institutions were to exist in America, they would have to be formed by prominent and well-to-do laymen and benefit not the struggling artists but a society very much in need of sophistication. The Society of Fine Arts in New York, formed in 1802 and later called the American Academy of the Fine Arts, set the pattern. Although its lay subscribers, such as Robert R. Livingston and the wealthy merchant John R. Murray, realized that such an academy might eventually help to "bring the Genius of this Country to perfection," they knew that there was a far more pressing need for the society to improve the artistic taste of the public, including not just middling artisans but even their fellow wealthy merchants, lawyers, and landowners. Since "the great Mass of our Gentry…want a little of the Leaven of Taste," lamented Murray, raising the gentry's taste had to be the first priority. Livingston and the other laymen wanted to display pieces sent from Europe, copies of the paintings of old masters and casts, as Livingston put it, of "the most admired works of the ancient Greek and Roman sculptors." Unfortunately, the American artists, who naturally wanted to display their own works, did not agree, and the academy divided and stagnated.[68]

A similar disparity of interests plagued the Pennsylvania Academy of Fine Arts, formed in 1805. The first exhibition, held in 1807, once again organized by Peale, was dominated by casts of European sculptures and several paintings by contemporary English artists and some old masters, which, since they came without labels, gave Peale a great deal of difficulty. He could not decide, for example, whether a picture entitled *Cain and Abel* was painted by Titian or Poussin.[69]

Having the wealthy lay patrons of the city encourage a love of art among the general public by these sorts of exhibitions was not what

---

67. Sellers, *Charles Willson Peale*, 2: 62–72; James Thomas Flexner, "The Scope of Painting in the 1790s," *Penn. Mag. of History and Biography*, 74 (1950), 74–89 (I owe this reference to John E. Crowley); Flexner, *The Light of Distant Skies*, 103, 109–10; Nygren and Robertson, eds., *Views and Visions*, 25, 137–43.
68. Miller, *Patrons and Patriotism*, 92; Flexner, *The Light of Distant Skies*, 159.
69. Flexner, *The Light of Distant Skies*, 161.

American artists wanted. They continued to desire an institution that would help them improve their craft and earn them some money. In 1810 a large group of Pennsylvania painters, architects, sculptors, and engravers—numbering a hundred within six months—tried once again to organize as the Society of Artists of the United States. At first the society tried to merge with the academy, but the different aims and interests were too great, and the effort failed. An attempt in 1809 to establish an academy of art in Boston came to nothing, largely because Gilbert Stuart, the great portrait painter and Boston's leading artist in residence, objected on the grounds that "too often the founders of such institutions were endowed with more wealth than knowledge of art."[70]

As long as artists were told that their primary task was to spread a knowledge of art throughout the society—in the words of William Tudor writing in Boston's *North American Review*, to "feel something of a *missionary spirit*" in improving "the taste of the publick"—they could scarcely develop much sense of artistic autonomy. Indeed, as historian Neil Harris points out, "the intellectual and moral autonomy of American artists did not disappear under civic attack; it never existed."[71]

These educational efforts to raise the people's artistic taste often became so frantic that they created their own distortions. Precisely because Susannah Rowson's racy story of seduction, *Charlotte Temple* (1794), went through forty-two editions in two dozen years, guardians of taste felt pressed to exaggerate the likes of British novelist Maria Edgeworth, whose heavily didactic novels ranked her, or so the *North American Review* claimed, among "the greatest reformers who have given a new direction to the faculties and opinions of mankind." Andrews Norton, an important Boston Federalist intellectual and later professor of sacred literature at Harvard, even thought that Edgeworth's works, all of which were intended to inculcate morality, integrity, and good sense, even at the expense of plot and character development, "entitle her to a reputation as enviable, perhaps, as that of any writer in English literature."[72]

By the early nineteenth century these developments were reshaping American culture. In the pre-democratic world of the eighteenth century cultivation or learning was considered to be unitary and homogeneous, involving all aspects of the arts and sciences, and regarded primarily as a personal qualification for participation in polite society. Indeed, to be learned was the equivalent of being a gentleman. Cultivated persons had

70. Harris, *The Artist in American Society*, 93–95; Miller, *Patrons and Patriotism*, 265.
71. *North American Review*, 2 (1815–1816), 161; Harris, *The Artist in American Society*, 97.
72. Daniel Walker Howe, *The Unitarian Conscience: Harvard Moral Philosophy, 1805–1861* (Cambridge, MA, 1970), 191.

no doubt of the existence of vulgar bucolic habits like bear-baiting or eating with one's hands, but they scarcely had seen these crude plebeian customs as some sort of popular culture set in competitive opposition to the enlightened republic of letters.

The Revolution and the relating of art to the public were not supposed to destroy the cultivated elite and threaten its standards but only broaden its sources of recruitment and elevate the taste of society as a whole. Yet the explosive expansion of literate middling sorts was having the opposite effect. The republic of letters was rapidly degenerating, "sliding," as Federalist Theodore Dehon complained in 1807, "inadvertently into a democracy."[73]

Many of the novels of the period were designed for untutored readers. They were small and easily carried and could be held in one hand. Their plots were straightforward, their vocabulary undemanding, and their syntax unsophisticated. Since they were often designed to instruct while they amused, they became an important means by which many marginally educated persons acquired an acquaintance with the larger world. The novels offered their readers who lacked a classical education Greek and Latin quotations conveniently translated. They also provided readers with devices—by contextually defining unusual words, for example—by which they could enlarge their vocabulary or improve their writing skills. Epistolary novels supplied models for readers to write their own letters. For women especially, novel-reading was a way of acquiring an education otherwise denied to them. In fact, all of these early American novels, observes their modern historian, "played a vital role in the early education of readers previously largely excluded from the elite literature and culture."[74]

The playwright and critic William Dunlap had been convinced that the theater was the most powerful engine for promoting morality in the society. But by the early nineteenth century he had come to realize that a significant distinction had arisen between "the wise and good," who learned "lessons [of] patriotism, virtue, morality, religion" from attending plays, and "the uneducated, the idle, and profligate," whose tastes were so bad as to lead "mercenary managers" to put on "such ribaldry or folly, or worse, as is attractive to such patrons, and productive of profit to themselves." Dunlap was torn between his desire to save the unenlightened and boorish populace from their degeneracy and his fear that they were corrupting the theater and turning it into "a breeding ground for ignorance

---

73. Theodore Dehon, "With Literature as with Government" (1807), in Lewis P. Simpson, ed., *The Federalist Literary Mind* (Baton Rouge, 1962), 186.
74. Davidson, *Revolution and the Word*, 73–79.

and depravity." He had tried to bring enlightenment to the populace, but people wanted only to be entertained. To keep his theater going he hired jugglers and acrobatic performers, including a man who whirled around on his head, with firecrackers attached to his heels. Even melodramas did not satisfy his audiences, and his theater went bankrupt in 1805. Dunlap had learned his lesson: he recalled that he was "one who had on trial found circumstances too strong for his desires of reform, and who, after a struggle of years (with ruined health and fortunes) gave up the contest without giving up the wish or the hope." If the legitimate drama were to continue in middle-class America, it had to meet popular taste and share the stage with bizarre novelty acts.[75]

Painting was likewise popularized. Many of the trained artists who emigrated from England, such as George Beck, William Winstanley, and William Groombridge, some of whom had seceded from Peale's Columbianum, were unable to make a living painting in America. Beck and Groombridge had to turn to schoolteaching, while Winstanley ended up copying Gilbert Stuart's portraits of Washington before returning to England. But Francis Guy, another expatriate from England, prospered brilliantly where others had failed. Guy was trained as a tailor and dyer in England and in the 1790s fled to America to escape his debts. Unable to make it as a dyer, he, in the words of Rembrandt Peale, "boldly undertook to be an artist, although he did not know how to draw." Nevertheless, without repudiating his occupational title as a dyer, he learned how to reproduce landscapes in a new and strange manner—by stretching over the window of a tent some thin black gauze upon which he traced an actual scene before transferring it to canvas. According to Peale, who concluded that Guy's "rough transcripts from Nature...were really good," this amateur artist *"manufactured"* these topographical pictures by the dozens and sold them for twenty-five dollars apiece.

That this self-taught artist was succeeding in Baltimore, while trained artists failed, enraged a female editor, Eliza Anderson, daughter of a distinguished Irish physician and fiancée of the French architect Maximilian Godefroy, who was exiled to the United States by Napoleon in 1805. Anderson could not get over the American tendency to believe that mere artisans—tailors and carpenters—could pretend to a taste in painting. Americans, she wrote in the Baltimore *Federal Gazette* in 1807, seemed unable to distinguish between the useful arts of artisans and the fine arts

---

75. Ellis, *After the Revolution*, 155; William Dunlap, *A History of the American Theater* (New York, 1832), 1: 130, 125; Jean V. Matthews, *Toward a New Society: American Thought and Culture, 1800–1830* (Boston, 1990), 132; Grimsted, *Melodrama Unveiled*, 20.

of real artists. "Apollo is somewhat aristocratic," she claimed, "and does not permit of perfect equality in his court.... The Muses are rather saucy, and do not admit of *workmen* to their levees." She advised Guy to return to his "soul-inspiring avocation of making pantaloons." As for Baltimore, Anderson concluded, it was "the Siberia of the arts."

Guy went on to become, along with the German immigrant John Lewis Krimmel, the English immigrant William Russell Birch, and the visiting Russian diplomat Pavel Svinin, one of the first genre painters in American history. These painters depicted people, buildings, and landscapes topographically, more or less as they were, not as the artistic conventions of the day dictated. Sophisticated critics like Eliza Anderson may not have liked their work, but many Americans did.[76]

Serious artists thought that genre scenes were too mean and lowly for their talent, and painters such as John Vanderlyn and Samuel Morse scorned the depicting of ordinary folk—except, said Vanderlyn, Italian peasants. With their lack of "fashion and frivolity," Italian peasants, Vanderlyn declared, were close enough to nature to possess a neoclassical universality that was worth depicting. But most major artists would have nothing to do with such common and humble subjects. William Dunlap mocked the former sign painter Jeremiah Paul for his crude efforts at genre painting. Paul, he said, was "one of those unfortunate individuals who, showing what is called genius in early life, by scratching the lame figures of all God's creatures, or every thing that will receive chalk or ink, are induced to devote themselves to the fine arts, without the means of improvement or the education necessary, to fit them for a liberal profession.... He was a man of vulgar appearances and awkward manners."[77]

Too many men, middling men, men of vulgar appearances and awkward manners, it seemed, were participating in all the arts, and serious artists and many of the elite despaired over what they saw as the increasing vulgarization of taste. As the social distinction between gentlemen and ordinary people blurred, cultivation itself seemed to have descended, as Dunlap grumbled, to "a certain point of mediocrity." The arts had become popularized, creating, complained disgruntled Federalists, a new kind of commodity culture, "widely and thinly spread," whose contributors

76. Flexner, "The Scope of Painting in the 1790s," *Penn. Mag. of History and Biography*, 74 (1950), 84–87; Martin P. Snyder, "William Birch: His Philadelphia Views," ibid., 73 (1949), 271–315; Snyder, "Birch's Philadelphia Views: New Discoveries," ibid., 88 (1964), 164–73.

77. Flexner, *The Light of Distant Skies*, 191–92, 112; William Dunlap, *A History of the Rise and Progress of the Arts of Design in the United States* (1834; New York, 1969), 1: 417, 418.

had become cultural "methodists," "feebly grasping at everything...fly-ing from novelty to novelty and regaling upon the flowering of litera-ture."[78] Members of the literati who clung to traditional humanist standards of the republic of letters found themselves beset by an avari-cious popular culture they could scarcely control, yet to which they bore a peculiar republican responsibility. "We know, that in this land, where the spirit of democracy is everywhere," wrote young biblical scholar Andrews Norton in 1807, "we are exposed, as it were, to a poisonous atmo-sphere, which blasts every thing beautiful in nature and corrodes every thing elegant in art." Nevertheless, these learned gentry like Norton believed that they had a special civic obligation to purify this poisonous atmosphere, "to correct blunders, to check the contagion of false taste, to rescue the publick from the impositions of dullness, and to assert the maj-esty of learning and of truth."[79]

In the minds of many, the future of the new Republic had come to rest on the cultivation of its public. Because the cultural atmosphere was drenched with civic and moral concerns, artists and critics alike found it impossible to justify any sort of independent and imaginative existence in defiance of the public. Two nude paintings—*Danae* by the Danish immi-grant Adolph Wertmüller and *Jupiter and Io* (renamed *Dream of Love*) by Rembrandt Peale—were exhibited in Philadelphia in 1814 to multitudes of paying viewers, but also to some intense criticism. Americans were naturally suspicious of the fine arts, wrote one critic in the *Port Folio*, but they have tolerated the arts "by representing them as able auxiliaries in the cause of patriotism and morals." But the exhibition of the two nude paintings did nothing for patriotism or morality. Instead, their exhibition offered, daily, scenes of "seducing voluptuousness to the young and thoughtless part of the city" of Philadelphia, which was such "a quiet, decent, moral city." True, admitted the critic, artists must be allowed "great latitude" for their imagination, and the critic "should be among the last to abridge the limits of their fancy." But these two nudes went too far; they violated "every consideration of morals and decorum, and even ordinary decency." He knew of "no apology for such licentiousness."[80]

78. Dunlap, A *History of the Rise and Progress of the Arts of Design*, 1; 417; Joseph Stevens Buckminster, "The Dangers and Duties of Men of Letters" (1809), and Robert H. Gardiner, "The Multiplicity of Our Literary Institutions" (1807), in Simpson, ed., *Federalist Literary Mind*, 100, 71, 55, 101.

79. Lewis P. Simpson, "Federalism and the Crisis of Literary Order," *American Literature*, 32 (1960), 260; Joseph Stevens Buckminster, "The Polity of Letters" (1806), in Simpson, ed., *Federalist Literary Mind*, 260, 184.

80. *Port Folio*, 4th Ser., 3 (1814), 35–38.

This sort of moralistic criticism led to the immediate withdrawal of the paintings and to a contrite public apology from the Society of Artists, which condemned the exhibition as "indecorous and altogether inconsistent with the purity of republican morals." The society, which represented dozens of various Philadelphia artists, went on to express its "deep regret" over the way these exhibitions were "evidently tending not only to corrupt public morals, but also to bring into disrepute those exhibitions which experience has proved to be important in cultivating a chaste taste for the fine arts in our country."[81]

Even the first copyright law in the country, adopted by Connecticut following the Revolution, put the needs of the society over the artist's right to earn what the market would bear. An artist's originality and individual inspiration could not count against such civic demands. When Wordsworth was criticized for writing too solitary and too unsocial a kind of poetry, what freedom from social obligations could an American poet expect?[82] Wordsworth's *Lyrical Ballads* was published only once in America before 1824. By contrast, Robert Bloomfield's *Farmer Boy* and its cult of sympathy had five American editions between 1801 and 1814. Indeed, all the great English Romantic poets—Coleridge, Byron, Keats, Shelley— were condemned or ignored in early nineteenth-century America, and Pope remained the most popular English poet until at least the 1820s.

The experience of painter Washington Allston reveals the tragedy of a romantic sensibility in a didactic neoclassical world. Born in 1779 in South Carolina, Allston was educated at Harvard where he became determined "to be the first painter, at least, from America." In 1801 he sold his inherited Carolina property and took off for England, where he befriended Samuel Taylor Coleridge. He returned to America in 1808 in order to fulfill his destiny but ended up painting portraits, which were all that Americans seemed to want. Frustrated, he returned once more to England in 1811, where his romantic artistic impulses found some success. Three years after the death of his wife in 1815, he returned once more to America. He brought with him *Belshazzar's Feast*, an unfinished canvas, which was supposed to become his masterpiece, but which over the next twenty-five years he never completed. When he declared in his *Lectures on Art*, published after his death, that "all effort at originality must end either in the quaint or the monstrous," he may have been reflecting on his own inability to express himself fully in a society that did not value originality.[83]

81. Harris, *The Artist in American Society*, 97; *Port Folio*, 4th Ser., 3 (1814), 154.
82. *North American Review*, 16 (1823), 102–3.
83. Virgil Barker, *American Painting: History and Interpretation* (New York, 1960), 339–51.

Some artists, like Allston's closest friend, Edmund Trowbridge Dana, rebelled against this suffocating neoclassicism. In 1805 Dana protested the great deference paid to the ancients. "One is hagridden...with nothing but the classicks, the classicks, the classicks!" he complained. He yearned for a literature of feeling. "In our day of refinement," he said, "very little is directed to the fancy or heart; for, from some cogency or other, it is unfashionable to be moved.... Establishment has crowded out sentiment," and readers were stuck with Alexander Pope and sitting "primly with Addison and propriety" instead of devouring Shakespeare. Dana wanted writers to appreciate that "the untutored gestures of children are more exquisite than the accomplished ceremony of courts."[84]

But Dana's was an isolated voice. Everywhere most American critics and artists urged the suppression of individual feeling and, instead, earnestly insisted on the moral and social responsibilities of the artist, an insistence that flowed not simply from the Americans' legacy of Puritanism or from their reading the Scottish moralists but from their Revolutionary aspirations for the arts. So deeply involved was the neoclassical commitment to society that most American writers and artists became incapable of revealing personal truths at the expense of their public selves, unwilling to regard beauty, as George Bancroft declared as late as 1827, as "something independent of moral effect." Indeed, the young Bancroft, who studied in Germany, found Goethe "too dirty, too bestial in his conceptions, and thus unfit for American consumption."[85] These were the sorts of sentiments that gave birth to the genteel society of the nineteenth century.

84. Edmund Trowbridge Dana, "The Works of Criticism" (1805), Simpson, ed., *Federalist Literary Mind*, 209–12.
85. Catherine O'Donnell Kaplan, *Men of Letters in the Early Republic: Cultivating Forums of Citizenship* (Chapel Hill, 2008), 201–2; Nye, *Cultural Life of the New Nation, 1776–1830*, 236; Russell B. Nye, *George Bancroft* (New York, 1964), 40.

# 16

# Republican Religion

Cultivated gentlemen like Thomas Jefferson may have relied on the arts and sciences to help them interpret and reform the world, but that was not the case with most average Americans. Nearly all common and middling people in the early Republic still made sense of the world through religion. Devastating fires, destructive earthquakes, and bad harvests were acts of God and often considered punishments for a sinful people. As they had in the mid-eighteenth century, people still fell on their knees when struck by the grace of God. People prayed openly and often. They took religion seriously, talked about it, and habitually resorted to it in order to examine the state of their souls. Despite growing doubts of revelation and the spread of rationalism in the early Republic, most Americans remained deeply religious.

As American society became more democratic in the early nineteenth century, middling people rose to dominance and brought their religiosity with them. The Second Great Awakening, as the movement was later called, was a massive outpouring of evangelical religious enthusiasm, perhaps a more massive expression of Protestant Christianity than at any time since the seventeenth century or even the Reformation. By the early decades of the nineteenth century American society appeared to be much more religious than it had been in the final decades of the eighteenth century.

The American Revolution broke many of the intimate ties that had traditionally linked religion and government, especially with the Anglican Church, and turned religion into a voluntary affair, a matter of individual free choice. But contrary to the experience of eighteenth-century Europeans, whose rationalism tended to erode their allegiance to religion, religion in America did not decline with the spread of enlightenment and liberty. Indeed, as Tocqueville was soon to observe, religion in America gained in authority precisely because of its separation from governmental power.

AT THE TIME OF THE REVOLUTION few could have predicted such an outcome. Occurring as it did in an enlightened and liberal age, the Revolution seemed to have little place for religion. Although some of the

Founders, such as Samuel Adams, John Jay, Patrick Henry, Elias Boudinot, and Roger Sherman, were fairly devout Christians, most leading Founders were not deeply or passionately religious, and few of them led much of a spiritual life. As enlightened gentlemen addressing each other in learned societies, many of the leading gentry abhorred "that gloomy superstition disseminated by ignorant illiberal preachers" and looked forward to the day when "the phantom of darkness will be dispelled by the rays of science, and the bright charms of rising civilization."[1] Most of them, at best, only passively believed in organized Christianity and, at worst, privately scorned and mocked it. Although few of them were outright deists, that is, believers in a clockmaker God who had nothing to do with revelation and simply allowed the world to run in accord with natural forces, most, like South Carolina historian David Ramsay, did tend to describe the Christian church as "the best temple of reason." Like the principal sources of their Whig liberalism—whether the philosopher John Locke or the Commonwealth publicists John Trenchard and Thomas Gordon writing as "Cato"—the Founders viewed religious enthusiasm as a kind of madness, the conceit "of a warmed or overweening brain." In all of his writings Washington rarely mentioned Christ, and, in fact, he scrupulously avoided testifying to a belief in the Christian gospel. Many of the Revolutionary leaders were proto-Unitarians, denying miracles and the divinity of Jesus. Even puritanical John Adams thought that the argument for Christ's divinity was an "awful blasphemy" in this new enlightened age.[2]

Jefferson's hatred for the clergy and organized religion knew no bounds. He believed that members of the "priestcraft" were always in alliance with despots against liberty. "To this effect," he said—privately, of course, not publicly—"they have perverted the purest religion ever preached to man, into mystery and jargon unintelligible to all mankind and therefore the safer engine for their purposes." The Trinity was nothing but "Abracadabra" and "hocus-pocus…so incomprehensible to the human mind that no candid man can say he has any idea of it." Ridicule, he said, was the only weapon to be used against it.[3]

1. Nicholas Collin, "An Essay on those inquiries in Natural Philosophy which at present are most beneficial to the United States of America," American Philosophical Society, Trans., 2 (1793), vii.

2. Henry May, The Enlightenment in America (New York, 1976), 72–73; [John Trenchard and Thomas Gordon], Cato's Letters…(London, 1748,) IV, No. 123; John Locke, An Essay Concerning Human Understanding (London, 1695), bk. IV, ch. 19; Jon Butler, Awash in a Sea of Faith: Christianizing the American People (Cambridge, MA, 1990), 195–96, 214–15.

3. TJ to Horatio Spafford, 17 March 1814, to James Smith, 8 Dec. 1822, in James H. Hutson, ed., The Founders on Religion: A Book of Quotations (Princeton, 2005), 68, 218.

Most of the principal Founders seemed to be mainly interested in curbing religious passion and promoting liberty. They attached to their Revolutionary state constitutions of 1776 ringing declarations of religious freedom, like that of Virginia's, stating that "all men are equally entitled to the free exercise of religion, according to the dictates of conscience." And they used this enlightened faith in liberty of conscience to justify disestablishing the Anglican Church everywhere.

The most lengthy and bitter fight for disestablishment took place in Virginia. Although the 1776 Virginia constitution guaranteed the "free exercise of religion" and the state legislature suspended the collection of religious taxes, the Anglican Church was not actually disestablished in 1776. Many Virginia leaders like Patrick Henry were willing to settle for some sort of multiple establishment, but others led by Jefferson and Madison wanted an end to all forms of state support for religion. They wanted to move beyond John Locke's plea for religious toleration; they wanted religious liberty, a different thing altogether. Consequently, the state legislature remained deadlocked for nearly a decade. The impasse was eventually broken in 1786 with the passage of Jefferson's famous Statute for Religious Freedom that abolished the Anglican establishment in Virginia.

With many of the Founders holding liberal and enlightened convictions, politics in the Revolutionary era tended to overwhelm religious matters. During the Revolution political writings, not religious tracts, came to dominate the press, and the clergy lost some of their elevated status to lawyers. The Revolution destroyed churches, interrupted ministerial training, and politicized people's thinking. The older established churches were unequipped to handle a rapidly growing and mobile population. The proportion of college graduates entering the ministry fell off, and the number of church members declined drastically. It has been estimated that scarcely one in twenty Americans was a formal member of a church.[4] All this has led more than one historian to conclude that "at its heart, the Revolution was a profoundly secular event."[5]

Many of the religious leaders themselves wholeheartedly endorsed this presumably secular revolution and its liberal impulses. Most Protestant

---

4. Russell B. Nye, *The Cultural Life of the New Nation, 1776–1830* (New York, 1960), 230; Franklin Hamlin Littell, *From State Church to Pluralism: A Protestant Interpretation of Religion in American History* (New York, 1962), 32.

5. Butler, *Awash in a Sea of Faith*, 195; John W. Chandler, "The Communitarian Quest for Perfection," in Stuart C. Henry, ed., *A Miscellany of American Christianity* (Durham, NC, 1963), 58; William Warren Sweet, *The Story of Religions in America* (New York, 1930), 322; Douglas H. Sweet, "Church Vitality and the American Revolution: Historiographical Consensus and Thoughts Towards a New Perspective," *Church History*, 45 (1976), 342, 344.

groups could think of no greater threat to religion than the Church of England, and consequently enlightened rationalists had little trouble in mobilizing Protestant dissenters against the established Anglican Church. Few clergymen sensed any danger to religion in the many declarations of religious freedom and in the disestablishment of the Church of England, which took place in most states south of New England. Even in Massachusetts and Connecticut, where religious establishments existed but were Puritan, not Anglican, Congregational and Presbyterian clergy invoked enlightened religious liberty against the dark twin forces of British civic and ecclesiastical tyranny without fear of subverting their own peculiar alliances between church and state. From all this enlightened and liberal thinking, the framers of the Constitution in 1787 naturally forbade religious tests for any office or public trust under the United States.

At the same time, the influence of enlightened liberalism ate away the premises of Calvinism, indeed, of all orthodox Christian beliefs. The Enlightenment told people they were not sinful but naturally good, possessed of an innate moral sense, and that evil lay in the corrupted institutions of both church and state. The rational deism of the Enlightenment could not be confined to the drawing rooms of the sophisticated gentry but spilled out into the streets. The anti-religious writings of Ethan Allen, Thomas Paine, the comte de Volney, and Elihu Palmer reached out to new popular audiences and gave many ordinary people the sense that reason and nature were as important (and mysterious) as revelation and the supernatural. For a moment at least the Enlightenment seemed to have suppressed the religious passions of the American people.[6]

All this emphasis on popular infidelity and religious indifference in Revolutionary America, however, is misleading. It captures only the surface of American life. The mass of Americans did not suddenly lose their religiousness in 1776, only to recover it several decades later. Certainly, the low proportion of church membership is no indication of popular religious apathy, not in America, where church membership had long been a matter of an individual's conversion experience and not, as in the Old World, a matter of birth.[7] In traditional European societies affiliation

6. On deism, see Kerry S. Walters, *The American Deists: Voices of Reason and Dissent in the Early Republic* (Lawrence, KS, 1992).
7. Jon Butler stresses the low proportion of church members or communicants among the eighteenth-century colonists, while Patricia U. Bonomi and Peter R. Eisenstadt emphasize the high proportion of church attendance. Jon Butler, "Coercion, Miracle, Reason," in Ronald Hoffman and Peter J. Albert, eds., *Religion in a Revolutionary Age* (Charlottesville, 1994), 19; Patricia U. Bonomi and Peter R. Eisenstadt, "Church Adherence in the Eighteenth-Century British American Colonies," WMQ, 39 (1982), 245–86.

with a dominant religion was automatic; people were born into their religion, and that religion could continue to order their lives, in the rituals of birth, marriage, and death, even if they remained religiously indifferent. In such societies the significant religious decision for a person was to break with the religious association into which he or she had been born. Consequently, religious indifference could exist alongside extensive, though merely formal, church membership. But in America the opposite became true: religious indifference meant having no religious affiliation at all; the important decision meant joining a religious association. People who wanted religion had to work actively and fervently to promote it. Consequently, huge surges of religious enthusiasm could exist alongside low church membership, membership, of course, being very different from churchgoing; in the older traditional churches only members could participate in Holy Communion and vote in church affairs.[8]

Thus the relatively small numbers of actual church members in the population did not suggest that Americans had become overly secularized or unduly antagonistic toward religion. There were, of course, fierce expressions of popular hostility to the genteel clergy with their D.D.'s and other aristocratic pretensions during the Revolutionary years. Yet this egalitarian anti-clericalism scarcely represented any widespread rejection of Christianity by most ordinary people.

Indeed, the total number of church congregations doubled between 1770 and 1790 and even outpaced the extraordinary growth of population in these years; and the people's religious feeling became stronger than ever, though now devoted to very different kinds of religious groups. Religion was not displaced by the politics of the Revolution; instead, like much of American life, it was radically transformed.

As the old society of the eighteenth century disintegrated, Americans struggled to find new ways of tying themselves together. Powerful demographic and economic forces, reinforced by the egalitarian ideology of the Revolution, undermined what remained of the eighteenth-century political and social hierarchies. As educated gentry formed new cosmopolitan connections in their learned societies and benevolent associations, so too did increasing numbers of common and middling people come together and find solace in the creation of new egalitarian and emotionally satisfying organizations and communities. Most important for ordinary folk was the creation of unprecedented numbers of religious communities.

The older state churches with Old World connections—Anglican, Congregational, and Presbyterian—were supplanted by new and in some

8. Bernard Bailyn et al., *The Great Republic: A History of the American People*, 4th ed. (Lexington, MA, 1992), 174.

cases unheard-of religious denominations and sects. As late as 1760 the Church of England in the South and the Puritan churches in New England had accounted for more than 40 percent of all congregations in America. By 1790, however, that proportion of religious orthodoxy had already dropped below 25 percent, and it continued to shrink in the succeeding decades. More and more people discovered that the traditional religions had little to offer them spiritually, and they began looking elsewhere for solace and meaning.

While nearly all of the major colonial churches either weakened or failed to gain relative to other groups during the Revolution, Methodist and Baptist congregations exploded in numbers. The Baptists expanded from 94 congregations in 1760 to 858 in 1790 to become the single largest religious denomination in America. The Methodists had no adherents at all in 1760, but by 1790 they had created over seven hundred congregations—despite the fact that the great founder of English Methodism, John Wesley, had publicly opposed the American Revolution. The Methodists benefited from having uneducated itinerant preachers who were willing to preach anywhere, on town greens, before county courthouses, on racing fields and potter's fields, on ferries, and even in the churches of other denominations.[9]

By 1805 the liberal Congregational minister of Salem, Massachusetts, William Bentley, was astonished to learn how rapidly the Methodists had grown. They claimed one hundred twenty thousand "in fellowship" and one million "attending their ministry," which, he exclaimed, was "a seventh of the population." They had four hundred traveling preachers and two thousand local preachers and had been very effective in gathering communicants by holding two to three hundred of what Bentley called "extraordinary meetings." And all this was accomplished, he declared with a certain amount of awe, in thirty-five years.[10] Organized nationally into circuits and locally into classes, the Methodists soon overtook the Baptists to become the largest denomination in America. By 1820 they had well over a quarter of a million formal members and at least four times that many followers.[11]

By the early nineteenth century enthusiastic groups of revivalist Baptists, New Light Presbyterians, and Methodists had moved from the

9. Stephen A. Marini, "The Revolutionary Revival in America" (unpublished paper); Mark A. Noll, *America's God: From Jonathan Edwards to Abraham Lincoln* (New York, 2002), 166.

10. William Bentley, *The Diary of William Bentley, D.D: Pastor of East Church, Salem, Massachusetts* (Gloucester, MA, 1962), 3: 192–93.

11. Dee E. Andrews, *The Methodists and Revolutionary America, 1760–1800: The Shaping of an Evangelical Culture* (Princeton, 2000), 76.

margins to the center of American society. But even more remarkable than the growth of these religions with roots in the Old World was the sudden emergence of new sects and utopian religious groups that no one had ever heard of before—Universal Friends, Universalists, Shakers, and a variety of other splinter groups and millennial sects.

This Second Great Awakening was a radical expansion and extension of the earlier eighteenth-century revivals. It was not just a continuation of the first awakening of the mid-eighteenth century. It was more evangelical, more ecstatic, more personal, and more optimistic. It did not simply intensify the religious feelings of existing church members. More important, it mobilized unprecedented numbers of people who previously had been unchurched and made them members of religious groups. By popularizing religion as never before and by extending religion into the remotest areas of America, the Second Great Awakening marked the beginning of the republicanizing and nationalizing of American religion. It transformed the entire religious culture of America and laid the foundations for the development of an evangelical religious world of competing denominations unique to Christendom.

Most of these religious associations called themselves denominations, not sects, for they had abandoned once and for all the traditional belief that any one of them could be the true and exclusive church for the society. Each religious association, called or "denominated" by a particular name, came to see itself simply as one limited and imperfect representative of the larger Christian community, each equal to and in competition with all the others, with the state remaining neutral in this competition.

Although none of these denominations claimed a monopoly of orthodoxy, out of their competition emerged Christian truth and morality that worked to unify the public culture in ways that defied nearly two thousand years of thinking about the relation of religious orthodoxy and the state. "Among us," wrote Samuel Stanhope Smith, the Presbyterian president of Princeton, "truth is left to propagate itself by its native evidence and beauty." It could no longer rely on the "meretricious charms" and "splendor of an establishment." In America, the clergy, "resting on the affections, and supported by the zeal of a free people," had to earn their way by vying with each other in being useful, and this competition turned out to be good for the society. "A fair and generous competition among the different denominations of Christians," said Smith, "while it does not extinguish their mutual charity, promotes an emulation that will have a beneficial influence on the public morals." Competition, emulation—these were the processes that justified much of what was going on in early nineteenth-century

American society, including arriving at the truth and rightness of a religious opinion that no one controlled.[12]

AT FIRST MOST OF THE FOUNDERS and other enlightened gentry
showed little awareness of what was happening. Although they assumed
that organized religion would become more rational and enlightened,
they hoped in the meantime to enlist it on behalf of their republican
Revolution, especially since most of them viewed religion as the best
means for fostering the virtue and public morality on which republicanism was based. The enlightened declarations on behalf of the rights of
conscience in the Revolutionary state constitutions did not initially signify a separation of church and state. Since the First Amendment at that
time applied only to the federal government, prohibiting only Congress,
and not the states, from interfering with "the free exercise" of religion,
the states felt free both to maintain establishments and to legislate in
religious matters. Not only did Connecticut and Massachusetts continue
their tax-supported Congregational establishments, but the Revolutionary constitutions of Maryland, South Carolina, and Georgia authorized
their state legislatures to create in place of the Anglican Church a kind
of multiple establishment of a variety of religious groups, using tax
money to support "the Christian religion." Many of the states outlawed
blasphemy, which they defined as attempts to defame Christianity, and
they sought to retain some general religious qualifications for public
office. Five states—New Hampshire, Connecticut, New Jersey, North
Carolina, and Georgia—required officeholders to be Protestant. Maryland and Delaware said Christians. Pennsylvania and South Carolina
officials had to believe in one God and in heaven and hell; Delaware
required a belief in the Trinity.[13]

Although the federal Constitution was very much a secular document,
not mentioning religion at all except for the reference in Article VII to
"the Year of our Lord," 1787, other important documents of the period,
including the Northwest Ordinance, did recognize the importance of
religion to good government. The peace treaty with Great Britain in 1783
opened with language familiar to British statesmen and to the devout
Anglican ear of John Jay, one of the negotiators of the treaty, "In the name
of the holy and indivisible Trinity." In 1789 some New England ministers
expressed to President Washington their dismay over the fact that "some

12. James H. Smylie, "Protestant Clergy, the First Amendment and Beginnings of a
    Constitutional Debate, 1781–91," in Elwyn A. Smith, *The Religion of the Republic*
    (Philadelphia, 1971), 149–50.
13. Smylie, "Protestant Clergy" in Smith, ed., *Religion of the Republic*, 117.

explicit acknowledgment of THE TRUE ONLY GOD, AND JESUS CHRIST whom he has sent," had not been "inserted somewhere in the Magna Charta of our country." Washington told the clergymen that "the path of true piety is so plain as to require but little political direction."[14]

Washington was about as ecumenical as any American of the time. Following his inauguration as president, he exchanged salutations with twenty-two major religious groups and continued the practice he had begun earlier of attending the services of various denominations, including Congregational, Lutheran, Dutch Reformed, and Roman Catholic. He expressed toleration for all religions, including the religions of Muslims and Jews. Except for an unknown number of African slaves who may have been followers of Islam, there were not many Muslims in America at the time of Washington's inauguration—perhaps only a small community of Moroccans in Charleston, South Carolina. But in 1790 several thousand Jews lived in the country, most of them in the cities of Newport, New York, Savannah, and Charleston.

Washington went out of his way to make Jews feel they were full-fledged Americans. In his famous letter of August 18, 1790, he thanked the members of the Touro Synagogue of Newport for their warm welcome during his tour of New England. He assured them that "happily the Government of the United States, which gives to bigotry no sanction, to persecution no assistance, requires only that they who live under its protection should demean themselves as good citizens." America, he said, was as much their home as anyone's. "May the Children of the Stock of Abraham, who dwell in this land," he wrote, "continue to merit and enjoy the good will of the other Inhabitants; while every one shall sit in safety under his own vine and figtree, and there shall be none to make him afraid."[15]

Washington's ecumenical spirit, however, did not flow from any indifference to the importance of religion to America's civic culture. Indeed, his first inaugural address conveyed more religious feeling than any of the subsequent presidential inaugural addresses in American history, except for Lincoln's second.[16] In November 1789 Washington quickly acceded to Congress's recommendation that he proclaim a National Day of Prayer and Thanksgiving to acknowledge on behalf of the American people "the

14. Forrest Church, So Help Me God: The Founding Fathers and the First Great Battle over Church and State (New York, 2007), 36.

15. GW to the Hebrew Congregation in Newport, Rhode Island, 18 Aug. 1790, Washington: Writings, 767; Patrick T. Conley and John P. Kaminski, eds., The Bill of Rights and the States: The Colonial and Revolutionary Origins of American Liberties (Madison, WI, 1992), 131–32.

16. Church, So Help Me God, 41.

many signal favors of Almighty God, especially by affording them an opportunity peaceably to establish a Constitution of government for their safety and happiness."[17] For all their talk of reason and enlightenment, Washington and the other leading Founders were more religious than they sometimes seem. Most of them had no quarrel with religion as long as it was reasonable and orderly. Washington was a member of his Anglican, later Episcopal, church vestry, and he remained a frequent churchgoer—though unlike his wife, Martha, he never became a member of his church, meaning that he did not partake of the Eucharist on communion Sundays. Washington, the perfect Freemason, considered himself enlightened in religious matters ("being no bigot myself to any mode of worship"), and he almost never knelt in prayer and seems never to have purchased a bible. Yet Washington, unlike Jefferson, had no deep dislike of organized religion or of the clergy as long as they contributed to civic life; indeed, as commander-in-chief in the Revolutionary War he had required all troops to attend religious services and had prescribed a public whipping for anyone disturbing those services.[18]

In his Farewell Address Washington stressed the importance of religion and morality for republican government and emphasized especially the religious obligation that lay behind the swearing of oaths. For all of his deistic-like talk of God as "the *Grand Architect* of the Universe," Washington was sure that the Architect intervened directly in human affairs; indeed, he thought that during the Revolution Providence had looked after not only the prosperity of the United States but also his personal well-being. He and Franklin, and, in fact, most of the Founders, believed in the efficacy of prayer as well as in some sort of afterlife.[19]

Jefferson took the possibility of an afterlife seriously. Despite his intense dislike of orthodox Christianity, he remained outwardly an Anglican and then an Episcopalian throughout his life. He was a regular churchgoer, was baptized and married in his parish, served on his local vestry, and sometimes attended church services in government buildings in Virginia. Jefferson was known for hypocrisy, but in this case his outward display of religious observance seems to have come from his deep aversion to personal controversy.

He learned his lesson about what not to say publicly about religion from his early indiscretions. In *Notes on the State of Virginia*, he had written that

17. *Annals of Congress*, 1st Congress, 1st session (Sept. 1789), 948, 949; Church, *So Help Me God*, 61, 64.

18. Gordon S. Wood, *Revolutionary Characters: What Made the Founders Different* (New York, 2006), 35; Church, *So Help Me God*, 46–47, 57.

19. GW to Watson and Cassoul, 10 Aug. 1782, in Hutson, ed., *Founders on Religion*, 18.

"it does me no injury for my neighbour to say there are twenty gods, or no god. It neither picks my pocket nor breaks my leg." Then in the preamble to his 1786 bill for religious freedom in Virginia, Jefferson had stated, to the astonishment of many, "that our civil rights have no dependence on our religious opinions, any more than our opinions in physics or geometry."[20] Since these public comments were drastically out of line with the opinions of ordinary people as well as most elite gentry, they raised a storm of criticism. Thereafter, Jefferson confined his derisive criticisms of Christianity to private letters and to those he believed would not object to his views.

In the election of 1800 these earlier awkward public comments led to his being called "a French infidel" and an "atheist"—certainly the most damaging charge his opponents ever made against him. "Should Jefferson prove victorious, there is scarcely a possibility that we should escape a *Civil War*," warned lawyer Theodore Dwight, in a typical Federalist outburst that appeared in the *Connecticut Courant* in 1800. "Murder, robbery, rape, adultery, and incest will be openly taught and practiced, the air will be rent with the cries of distress, the soil will be soaked with blood, the nation black with crimes."[21]

Although Jefferson, like all the Founders, had no doubt of the existence of God, he publicly suffered these charges of atheism, infidelity, and immorality in silence, privately dismissing them as the characteristic carping of bigoted Federalist clerics. He expected nothing but "the extreme of their wrath" from New England's clergymen. "I wish nothing," he said, "but their eternal hatred."[22]

Yet Jefferson very much wanted to win over to his Republican cause all those ordinary religious people who had voted for his opponent. To do so he knew he had to offset the Federalist accusations that he was an enemy of Christianity. Consequently, to the surprise of many Federalists, he had good things to say about religion in his first inaugural address. He also knew very well what effect he as president would have when in January 1802 he attended a church service held in the chamber of the House of Representatives. His attendance attracted wide public notice and astonished the Federalists. Even though other churches were available, Jefferson continued to attend church services in the House chamber and made available executive buildings for church functions. Sometimes the U.S. Marine Corps Band supplied music for the religious services. As

20. TJ, *Notes on the State of Virginia*, ed. William Peden (Chapel Hill, 1955), 159; TJ, Virginia Bill for Religious Freedom (1786), *Jefferson: Writings*, 346–48.
21. Jon Meacham, *American Gospel: God, the Founding Fathers, and the Making of a Nation* (New York, 2006), 278; Church, *So Help Me God*, 188.
22. Church, *So Help Me God*, 227.

president, however, Jefferson held to his vow never to call for any days of fasting and prayer as his two predecessors had done.

In 1803 upon receiving a copy of Joseph Priestley's *Socrates and Jesus Compared*, Jefferson was encouraged to set down his own similar thoughts in what he called his "Syllabus of an Estimate on the Merit of the Doctrines of Jesus, compared with Those of Others." He sent copies of this thousand-word essay to Priestley, to Benjamin Rush (who had asked him about his religious views), to a friend, John Page, and to members of his cabinet and family. He followed up this essay with an edited version of the New Testament in which he cut out all references to supernatural miracles and Christ's divinity and kept all the passages in which Jesus preached love and the Golden Rule. He called this collection "The Philosophy of Jesus." He told a friend that these works, which came to be called the Jefferson Bible, were "proof that I *am a real Christian*, that is to say, a disciple of the doctrines of Jesus, very different from the Platonists, who call *me* infidel."[23] Although he never published these works, word did get out that Jefferson had changed his religious views, a rumor that Jefferson was at great pains to deny.

In 1802 he sent a letter to the Baptists of Danbury, Connecticut, declaring that the First Amendment of the federal Constitution erected a "wall of separation between church and state."[24] It is unlikely that Jefferson had in mind the kind of high and often impenetrable wall between church and state that modern jurists have maintained. It is more likely that he had an exclusively political object. (In fact, he attended church services in the House of Representatives two days after writing this letter.)[25] For Jefferson the wall of separation may not have been the crucial point of his message anyway. For him, the wall was simply a means toward a larger end. It would give time for reason and free inquiry to work its way to the ultimate enlightenment he favored. In other words, the wall might protect the Baptists from the Standing Order of Connecticut Puritans in the short run, but Jefferson thought that in the long run both the Baptists and the Standing Order, like all religions based on faith and not reason, were slated for extinction. Indeed, as late as 1822 Jefferson continued to believe that "there is not a *young man* now living in the United States who will not die an Unitarian."[26]

23. Merrill D. Peterson, *Thomas Jefferson and the New Nation: A Biography* (New York, 1970), 960.

24. TJ to Messrs. Nehemiah Dodge and Others, 1 Jan. 1802, *Jefferson: Writings*, 510.

25. James H. Hutson, "Thomas Jefferson's Letter to the Danbury Baptists: A Controversy Rejoined," and Responses, *WMQ*, 56 (1999), 775–824.

26. Johann N. Neem, "Beyond the Wall: Reinterpreting Jefferson's Danbury Address," *JER*, 27 (2007), 139–54; TJ to Benjamin Waterhouse, 26 June 1822, in Hutson, ed., *Founders on Religion*, 221.

Of course, he could not have been more wrong. Jefferson did not understand the political forces behind his and Madison's success in getting his bill for religious freedom through the Virginia legislature. He may have thought that most Virginians accepted the enlightened thinking in his preamble, but the bill would never have passed without the overwhelming support of growing numbers of dissenting evangelical Presbyterians and Baptists in the state who hated the Anglican establishment so much that they did not care what the preamble said. It was not enlightened rationalism that drove these evangelicals but their growing realization that it was better to neutralize the state in matters of religion than run the risk of one of their religious opponents gaining control of the government.

Ultimately, an enlightened thinker like Jefferson could not speak for the popular Christian world of the early Republic. But someone like the New Light Separate Baptist Isaac Backus could. The separation of church and state that emerged in the early nineteenth century owed much to evangelical Christians like Backus. Born in Connecticut in 1724, and receiving only seven years of elementary education, Backus served his Middleborough, Massachusetts, parish for over sixty years, all the while defying the state's Congregational establishment. Throughout his career he preached, wrote, and traveled (a thousand miles a year) on behalf of the Baptist cause.[27]

To Backus true religion was vitally important to society, but it nonetheless had to rest ultimately on "a voluntary obedience to God's revealed will" and not on the coercive power of the government. Liberty of conscience for Backus was not, as it was for Jefferson, a consequence of the rationalistic and pagan Enlightenment. Backus and the Baptists came to their belief in the separation of church and state out of the exigencies of being a minority sect within tax-supported established church systems and out of the pietistic desire to create gathered voluntaristic churches of individual believers.

Although Backus and most other Baptists became good Jeffersonian Republicans, their support for the disestablishment of the Puritan churches did not signify the end of what Backus called the "sweet harmony" between church and state; it meant only that Christ's kingdom should be free to evangelize the society through persuasion aided by sympathetic but nonsectarian governments. Although Backus wanted no governmental interference with religion, he did expect government to

27. William G. McLoughlin, *Isaac Backus and the American Pietistic Tradition* (Boston, 1967); William G. McLoughlin, *New England Dissent, 1630–1833: The Baptists and the Separation of Church and State* (Cambridge, MA, 1971).

help religion create a climate in which Christian truth might prevail. Hence he and other Protestant evangelicals could support laws compelling church attendance and respect for the Sabbath and religious tests for governmental office even while advocating the separation of church and state.[28]

ALTHOUGH JEFFERSON MAY HAVE REMAINED oblivious to the increasingly religious character of the country, many other members of the elite soon realized what was happening; indeed, some of them developed a belated interest in religion themselves. Even when they privately scorned Christianity, they accommodated their outward behavior to the religiosity of the general populace. Franklin was only being wise in advising a friend in 1786 not to publish anything attacking traditional Christianity. "He that spits against the wind," he said, "spits in his own face." Thomas Paine destroyed his reputation in America with his scathing comments about Christianity in his *Age of Reason* (1794).[29]

It was one thing to denigrate Christianity in the privacy of one's home, but Paine spoke openly to common people in the streets. Upon his return to America from Europe in 1802, he was attacked everywhere in the press as a "lying, drunken, brutal infidel." Even former friends and sympathizers like the aged Samuel Adams grieved over what they took to be Paine's efforts to "unchristianize the mass of our citizens."[30] The great spokesman for the common sense of the common people had seriously misjudged the religiosity of that people.

During the Revolutionary era Hamilton had shed his youthful religious inclinations and had become a conventional liberal with deistic inclinations who was an irregular churchgoer at best. People even told stories about his joking references to religion. During the Philadelphia Convention of 1787 Franklin proposed to call in a minister each day to lead the delegates in prayers *"to the Creator of the universe"* in order to calm the rancor of the debates. Hamilton is supposed to have replied that the Convention did not need any "foreign aid." When Hamilton was later asked why the members of the Convention had not recognized God in the Constitution, he allegedly replied, "We forgot."

A decade or so later it was not so easy to forget God, and during the 1790s Hamilton began recovering his earlier interest in religion, partially in reac-

28. William G. McLoughlin, ed., *Isaac Backus on Church, State, and Calvinism: Pamphlets, 1754–1789* (Cambridge, MA, 1968), 61.
29. Thomas Paine, *The Age of Reason* (1794), in Eric Foner, ed., *Thomas Paine: Collected Writings* (Library of America, 1995), 825.
30. John Keane, *Tom Paine: A Political Life* (Boston, 1995), 457, 475–76.

tion to what he perceived to be the atheism of the French revolutionaries and their supporters in America. By 1801 in the aftermath of his fall from power he became increasingly devout. In 1802 he proposed the establishment of a Christian Constitutional Society—a network of interstate political clubs that would promote good works and the Federalist party. By the time of his death in 1804 he had become a true believer, desperate on his deathbed to receive Holy Communion from an Episcopalian minister.[31]

Many leaders came to realize that they had to make concessions to the growing evangelical religious atmosphere. In 1801 when the heir of several generations of Presbyterian divines Aaron Burr had become vice-president, he was criticized for not having been "in any place of public worship for ten years." Concerned about Burr's future career in politics, a close political associate reminded him of the Presbyterian vote and warned: "Had you not better go to church?"[32]

Other leaders also began thinking about going to church. In 1806 jurist St. George Tucker of Virginia, although a lifelong deist, became frightened enough by the social chaos that infidelity presumably was causing that he was willing to support state subsidies for Christian teachers regardless of their denomination. So too did Noah Webster, William Wirt, and John Randolph set aside their youthful deism in favor of the evangelical religion of the early nineteenth century. By 1806 William Cooper, who earlier had been contemptuous of churches, had come to believe "that our political Welfare depends much on adhering to the rules of religion," and he began encouraging and subsidizing the new churches of Otsego County, or at least those churches that were orthodox and conservative. Even enlightened Freemasonry became much more of a religious institution in the early decades of the nineteenth century.[33]

31. Douglass Adair, "Was Alexander Hamilton a Christian Statesman?" in Trevor Colbourn, ed., *Fame and the Founding Fathers: Essays by Douglass Adair* (Chapel Hill, 1974), 147–48 n; Max Farrand, ed., *The Records of the Federal Convention of 1787* (New Haven, 1911, 1937), 3: 471–72; Ron Chernow, *Alexander Hamilton* (New York, 2004), 708.

32. M[arinus] Willet to Aaron Burr, 8 Mar. 1801, in Mary-Jo Kline et al., eds., *Political Correspondence and Public Papers of Aaron Burr* (Princeton, 1983), 1: 522; Adair, "Was Alexander Hamilton a Christian Statesman?" in Colbourn, ed., *Fame and the Founding Fathers*, 149–59; May, *Enlightenment in America*, 326–34.

33. May, *Enlightenment in America*, 331; Jean V. Matthews, *Toward a New Society: American Thought and Culture, 1800–1830* (Boston, 1990), 30–31; Alan Taylor, *William Cooper's Town: Power and Persuasion on the Frontier of the Early American Republic* (New York, 1995), 348–49; Steven C. Bullock, *Revolutionary Brotherhood: Freemasonry and the Transformation of the American Social Order, 1730–1840* (Chapel Hill, 1996), 163–83.

In 1811 the distinguished jurist James Kent, the chief justice of the New York supreme court, actually acknowledged in a notable blasphemy case, *The People of New York v. Ruggles*, the legal connection between his state and religion. Although Kent recognized that New York had no formally established church, that its constitution guaranteed freedom of religious opinion, and that the state had no statute prohibiting blasphemy, he nevertheless declared that to revile with contempt the Christian religion professed by almost the whole community, as Ruggles had done, was "to strike at the roots of moral obligation and weaken the security of the social ties." That Kent was willing to declare Christianity to be part of the common law of the state of New York when he despised religious enthusiasm and in private called Christianity a barbaric superstition is a measure of just how intimidating the popular evangelical climate of the Second Great Awakening could be.[34]

Still, the proliferation of competing evangelical religious groups coupled with the enlightened thinking of the gentry soon eroded what was left of the idea of a European-like coercive state church. In the decades following the Revolution the remains of traditional church-state connections and establishments were finally destroyed: South Carolina in 1790, Maryland in 1810, Connecticut in 1818, New Hampshire in 1819, and Massachusetts in 1833.

ROMAN CATHOLICS on the European continent were certainly accustomed to church-state establishments, but in America any semblance of a Catholic establishment was impossible. Numbering about thirty-five thousand in 1790, they were still a tiny minority in all the states. Even in Maryland, which had the largest proportion of Catholics, they numbered only about fifteen thousand out of a Maryland population of nearly three hundred and twenty thousand at the time of the first census. All the colonies had politically discriminated against Catholics, but the Revolution created an atmosphere of greater tolerance. In 1783 Rhode Island repealed its 1719 statute preventing Catholics from voting and holding office. (The state eliminated similar restrictions on Jews in 1798.)

By the time John Carroll of Maryland became the first Catholic bishop in 1790, the Catholic Church of America had begun adapting to the

---

34. John T. Horton, *James Kent: A Study in Conservatism, 1763–1847* (New York, 1939), 190. By 1833 the distinguished jurist Joseph Story in his influential *Commentaries* declared that Christianity was part of the common law. Franklin Hamlin Littell, *From State Church to Pluralism: A Protestant Interpretation of Religion in American History* (New York, 1962), 48.

republican climate of America. In the 1780s Carroll had worked to make the Catholic Church an "independent national church" rather than simply a Catholic mission dependent on the Vatican. He argued that the American Revolution had given Catholics "equal rights and privileges with that of other Christians" and that Catholicism deserved to be independent of "all foreign jurisdiction." Carroll established a Catholic college in Georgetown, created a Sulpician seminary in Baltimore, promoted the use of English in the liturgy, and urged the publication of an English translation of the Catholic version of the Bible, which the Irish-born immigrant and devout Catholic publisher Mathew Carey undertook in 1790.

At the same time, Catholic laity began to participate actively in the organizing and the running of their churches, replicating the process that many of the Protestant groups had experienced in the colonial period. The practice of laymen forming trusteeships elected by people in the parish began in the cities but soon spread to the frontier areas. Without benefit of clergy Catholics banded together and formed religious societies, elected their leaders, purchased land for a church, and assumed responsibility for governing their church.[35]

Already Catholics were coming to accept the idea of separation of church and state and to think of themselves as just another Christian denomination—a position that the Roman Catholic Church as a whole did not formally endorse until the Second Vatican Council of 1962. In Maryland in the 1780s Catholics had opposed the proposal of a multiple establishment with tax money going to all Christian denominations out of fear that such a measure would be the first step toward reestablishing the Protestant Episcopal Church in the state. Carroll believed that the religious experiment of religious liberty, "by giving a free circulation to fair argument, is the most effectual method to bring all denominations of Christians to an unity of faith."[36]

Although fear of the anti-religious message of the French Revolution compelled Carroll and the American Catholic Church in the 1790s to revert to the use of Latin liturgy and the hierarchical appointment of priests, the process of local church government and lay control of the congregational parishes survived, largely because of the shortage of priests and bishops. And because Catholics remained everywhere a small minority in a sea of Protestants, they enthusiastically supported the idea of separation of church and state. In spite of continual pressures to

35. Jay P. Dolan, *The American Catholic Experience: A History from Colonial Times to the Present* (New York, 1985), 102; Thomas T. McAvoy, *A History of the Catholic Church in the United States* (Notre Dame, 1969), 61–91.

36. Dolan, *The American Catholic Experience*, 109.

become more like the Catholic churches of Europe in organization and character, the American Catholic Church essentially developed as just another Christian denomination among many.

The number of Catholics grew rapidly. In 1808 Bishop Carroll secured the creation of four new dioceses—in Boston, New York, Philadelphia, and Bardstown, Kentucky. This western outpost of Bardstown, the bishop of the diocese claimed, contained by 1815 nineteen Catholic churches and at least ten thousand communicants. With the acquisition of Louisiana and the addition of the diocese of New Orleans, Spanish and French Catholics became part of the United States. In 1819 two more dioceses were established in Richmond and Charleston, and by 1820 the number of Catholics in the country totaled nearly two hundred thousand.

Despite this rapid growth, the country remained overwhelmingly Protestant. Although most of the competing Protestant denominations were formally separated from the state, they tended to identify themselves with the nation. Most of the Protestant clergy were determined to prove that America's separation of church and state would not result in the infidelity and religious neglect that Europeans had expected. The evangelicals continually emphasized that America, although lacking a state-supported church, was nonetheless a nation of God, a Christian God, and a Protestant Christian God at that.

The nineteenth-century evangelical denominations knew Americans lived in a free country and could choose their religion at will; but this freedom and the lack of a traditional establishment did not mean that government had no responsibility for religion. The evangelicals repeatedly urged the United States government to recognize America's basis in Christianity by providing chaplains in Congress, proclaiming days of fasting and prayer, and ending mail delivery on the Sabbath. The clergy had no intention of creating a new church establishment or of denying the rights of conscience, declared Nathaniel William Taylor of Connecticut, the most important theologian of the Second Great Awakening. "We only ask for those provisions in law...in behalf of a common Christianity, which are its due as a nation's strength and a nation's glory."[37] Even the nineteenth-century public school system became suffused with what were essentially Protestant religious values. Americans thus created what one historian has called the paradox of a "voluntary establishment" of religion.[38]

37. Elwyn A. Smith, "The Voluntary Establishment of Religion," in Smith, ed., *Religion of the Republic*, 177.
38. Timothy L. Smith, "Protestant Schooling and American Nationality, 1800–1850," *JAH*, 53 (1967), 694; Smith, "Voluntary Establishment of Religion," in Smith, ed., *Religion of the Republic*, 154–82.

DESPITE JEFFERSON'S PREDICTION, there was as little chance of ordinary Americans becoming rational Unitarians as there was of their becoming Federalists. Evangelical Christianity and the democracy of these years, the very democracy with which Jefferson rode to power and destroyed Federalism, emerged together. As the Republic became democratized, it became evangelized.

Once common middling people—the likes of William Findley, Matthew Lyon, Jedediah Peck, and William Manning—found that they could challenge deistic indifference and the older staid religions as completely as they were challenging the aristocratic Federalists, they set about asserting their own more popular versions of Christianity with a vengeance. Indeed, in Massachusetts and Connecticut the Baptists and other dissenters became Jeffersonian Republicans because they could see no difference between the Federalists and the Standing Order of Congregational and Presbyterian establishments. In 1801 a "Baptist" writing in Connecticut in the *The Patriot, or Scourge of Aristocracy* complained that hitherto he had been "duped to believe that we must follow the old beaten track laid down by our rulers and priests, without examining whether it was right or wrong." But with the rise of the Jeffersonian Republican party those days were passing. This "Baptist" had now come "to suspect that every class of people have a right to shew their opinions on points which immediately concern them."[39]

With such democratic views came a new revitalized religion. In Otsego County, New York, the Republican evangelical Jedediah Peck pushed for daily Bible reading in the schools and berated the Congregational and Episcopalian Federalists as closet deists who denied biblical revelation and as aristocrats who were contemptuous of the plain style and folk Christianity of the common people of the county.[40] Middling people everywhere had a new heightened confidence to express their religious feelings publicly and politically. William Findley had been inducted as a ruling elder into the Reformed Presbyterian Church in 1770, and he remained a devout Presbyterian throughout his life. As a congressman from Pennsylvania, he promoted the interest of the Presbyterians and evangelical religion in every way he could. In 1807 he sponsored the incorporation of a Presbyterian church in the District of Columbia and throughout his many terms in office worked tirelessly to end mail delivery on Sunday.[41]

---

39. Nathan O. Hatch, *The Democratization of American Christianity* (New Haven, 1989), 25.
40. Taylor, *William Cooper's Town*, 285, 268.
41. John Caldwell, *William Findley from West of the Mountains: Congressman, 1791–1821* (Gig Harbor, WA, 2002), 280, 331, 333–34, 336, 379.

Although evangelical Christianity spread throughout America, it was most successful wherever authority and the social structure were weakest, wherever people were more mobile and separated from one another, and wherever the great demographic and commercial changes created the most anxieties and rootlessness. Out of the disintegration of authority and the resultant social turmoil and confusion, which could range from the severing of traditional social relationships to the more subtle sense that things simply seemed out of joint, many ordinary people became seekers looking for signs and prophets and for new explanations for the bewildering experiences of their lives. They came together without gentry leadership anywhere they could—in fields, barns, taverns, or homes—to lay hands on one another, to bathe each other's feet, to offer each other kisses of charity, to form new bonds of fellowship, to let loose their feelings both physically and vocally, and to Christianize a variety of folk rites.[42]

From the "love feasts" of the Methodists to the dancing ceremonies of the Shakers, isolated individuals found in a variety of rites and evangelical "bodily exercises" ungenteel and sometimes bizarre but emotionally satisfying ways of relating to God and to each other. The various emotional expressions of the revivalists—fainting, trances, involuntary cries, shouting, and speaking in tongues—were new and perhaps were even intentionally designed to distinguish the evangelicals from the staid and stuffy religions of the elites.

Examples of this sort of ecstatic behavior were sometimes frightening to witnesses. At a Methodist revival in Baltimore in 1789 many of the participants, recalled one observer, "went out at the windows, hastening to their homes," while others "lost use of their limbs, and lay helpless on the floor, or in the arms of their friends."[43] Sometimes the emotions got out of control. In an Ohio town in the early nineteenth century a middle-aged woman, who had been a Presbyterian, "got powerfully convicted" by the Methodism of her husband and children and, convinced by the devil that she was a reprobate, fell into a "black despair," from which she emerged believing "that she was Jesus Christ, and took it upon her, in this assumed character, to bless and curse any and all that came to see her." To the horror of her family and neighbors, she refused all food and drink, and two weeks later she "died without ever returning to her right mind." Convinced that the Methodists had brought about her death, some members of the community, recalled the great Methodist evangelist Peter Cartwright, "tried to make a great fuss about this affair, but they were afraid to go far with it, for fear the Lord would send the same affliction on them."[44]

---

42. Donald G. Mathews, *Religion in the Old South* (Chicago, 1977).
43. Andrews, *Methodists and Revolutionary America*, 80.
44. Peter Cartwright, *Autobiography*, ed. Charles L. Wallis (New York, 1956), 68–69.

When there were no trained clergy to minister to the yearnings of these often lost and bewildered men and women, they recruited leaders and preachers from among themselves, including women. The Baptists and Methodists were especially effective in challenging the traditional practice of having a settled and learned ministry, which was often Federalist. Indeed, the Baptists and Methodists scorned an educated clergy with their "senseless jargon of election and reprobation" and dismissed the traditional religious seminaries as "Religious Manufactories" that were merely "established for explaining that which is plain, and for the purpose of making things hard." Cartwright, who assailed whiskey, slavery, and extravagant dress along with his constant berating of the orthodox churches, readily admitted that he and his fellow evangelical preachers "could not, many of us, conjugate a verb or parse a sentence and murdered the king's English almost every lick, but there was a Divine unction that attended the word preached."[45] By 1812 Cartwright had become presiding elder of a district that extended into the territory of Indiana. While continuing to preach and hold quarterly conferences, he also supervised about twenty circuit preachers.

The most famous gathering of religious seekers took place in the summer of 1801 at Cane Ridge, Kentucky. There, huge numbers of people, together with dozens of ministers of several different denominations, came together in what some thought was the greatest outpouring of the Holy Spirit since the beginning of Christianity. Crowds estimated at fifteen to twenty thousand participated in a week of frenzied conversions. The heat, the noise, and the confusion were overwhelming. Ministers, sometimes a half dozen preaching at the same time in different areas of the camp, shouted sermons from wagons and tree stumps; hundreds if not thousands of people fell to the ground moaning and wailing in remorse; and they sang, laughed, barked, rolled, and jerked in excitement.

People "allowed each one to worship God agreeably to their own feelings," declared Richard McNemar, who was one of the Presbyterian preachers present at Cane Ridge. (He later broke from Presbyterianism, created a universal church of Christianity, and ended up as a Shaker.) "All distinction of names was laid aside," recalled McNemar of the camp meeting, "and it was no matter what any one had been called before, if now he stood in the present light, and felt his heart glow with love to the souls of men; he was welcome to sing, pray, or call sinners to repentance. Neither was there any distinction as to age, sex, color or any thing of a

---

45. Hatch, *Democratization of American Christianity*, 173, 174; Church, *So Help Me God*, 292.

temporary nature: old and young, male and female, black and white, had equal privilege to minister the light which they received, in whatever way the spirit directed."[46]

America had known religious revivals before, but nothing like this explosion of emotion. Of course, the outpouring of the Holy Spirit was accompanied by the pouring out of lots of intoxicating spirits, and critics of the excesses of Cane Ridge claimed that the frenzied excitement resulted in more souls being conceived than converted. But the extraordinary number of conversions that actually did take place during that heady week convinced many evangelists that there were multitudes of souls throughout the country waiting to be saved. This gigantic camp meeting at Cane Ridge immediately became the symbol of the promises and the extravagance of the new kind of evangelical Protestantism spreading throughout the West.

Following this great Kentucky revival of 1801 evangelical activity went wild. Peter Cartwright described camp meetings at which "ten, twenty, and sometimes thirty ministers, of different denominations, would come together and preach night and day, four or five days together," with the meetings sometimes lasting "three or four weeks." He saw "more than a hundred sinners fall like dead men under one powerful sermon," and witnessed "more than five hundred Christians all shouting aloud the high praises of God at once." He was certain that "many happy thousands were awakened and converted to God at these camp meetings."[47]

In the first twelve years of the nineteenth century the Methodists in Tennessee, Kentucky, and Ohio grew from fewer than three thousand to well over thirty thousand. According to the reports of circuit riders, Methodists in some parts of the Southwest grew even faster, from forty-six thousand in 1801 to eighty thousand by 1807. The Baptists made similar explosive gains. In the short period between 1802 and 1804 the Baptists in Kentucky increased from 4,700 to 13,500.[48] In the fast-growing new areas of the West the need for some kind of community, however loose and voluntary, and the need for building barriers against barbarism and sinfulness were most keenly felt.

Wherever the traditional structures of authority were disintegrating, new religious opportunities were opened up for those whose voices had not been heard before—the illiterate, the lowly, and the dependent. Both the Baptists and the Methodists encouraged public exhortation by

46. Richard McNemar, *The Kentucky Revival* (1808), in Gordon S. Wood, ed., *The Rising Glory of America, 1760–1820*, rev. ed. (Boston, 1990), 88.
47. Cartwright, *Autobiography*, ed. Wallis, 43.
48. Mathews, *Religion in the Old South*, 50.

women, and powerful female preachers, such as Nancy Grove Cram of frontier New York and the black preacher Dorothy Ripley of Georgia, awakened numerous men and women to Christ. Cram, who died prematurely in 1815, spent nearly four years preaching and during that time recruited at least seven active ministers to the loose organization that called itself the Christian Church. Even the conservative Protestant churches began emphasizing a new and special role for women in the process of redemption.[49]

Religion was in fact the one public arena in which women could play a substantial part. By the time of the Revolution nearly 70 percent of members of the New England churches were women, and in the decades following the Revolution this feminization of American Christianity only increased.[50] Some of the most radical sects, like Mother Ann Lee's Shakers and Rhode Island native Jemima Wilkinson's Universal Friends, even allowed for female leadership. Wilkinson's disciples claimed that she was Jesus Christ. This so scandalized people that Wilkinson was forced to leave southern New England, going first to Philadelphia and then to western New York, where she gathered wealth from her followers. Her death in 1819 led to the rapid dissolution of the sect. The Shakers, who believed in celibacy and had to recruit all of their members, became the first American religious group to recognize formally the equality of the sexes at all levels of authority.[51]

The democratic revolution of these years made it possible for not only middling sorts but also the most common and humble of people to assert themselves and champion their emotions and values in new ways. Because genteel learning, formal catechism, even literacy no longer mattered as much as they had in the past, the new religious groups were able to recruit converts from among hitherto untouched elements of the population. Under the influence of the new popular revivalist sects, thousands of African American slaves became Christianized, and blacks, even black slaves, were able to become preachers and exhorters.

49. Ruth Bloch, *Visionary Republic: Millennial Themes in American Thought, 1756–1800* (Cambridge, UK, 1985), 225; Hatch, *Democratization of Christianity*, 78–80.

50. Ann Douglas, *The Feminization of American Culture* (New York, 1977); Elaine Forman Crane, "Religion and Rebellion: Women of Faith in the American War for Independence," in Hoffman and Albert, eds., *Religion in a Revolutionary Age*, 80.

51. Stephen A. Marini, "The Revolutionary Revival in America" (unpublished paper), 28; Herbert A. Wisbey Jr., *Pioneer Prophetess: Jemima Wilkinson, the Publick Universal Friend* (Ithaca, 1964); David Hudson, *History of Jemima Wilkinson, a Preacheress of the Eighteenth Century; Containing an Authentic Narrative of Her Life and Character, and the Rise, Progress and Conclusion of Her Ministry* (Geneva, NY, 1821); Stephen J. Stein, *The Shaker Experience in America: A History of the United Society of Believers* (New Haven, 1992), 43, 48–49.

During the Revolutionary War serious money problems forced Stokely Sturgis, a Delaware owner of the black Allen family, to sell the parents and three young Allen children; Sturgis kept Richard Allen, a teenager, along with Richard's older brother and sister. At almost the same time he broke up the Allen family, Sturgis converted to Methodism, and Richard Allen and his older brother and sister soon did the same. "I was awakened and brought to see myself," Richard Allen recalled, "poor wretched and undone, and without the mercy of God, [I] must be undone." After suffering for a long period, said Richard, crying "to the Lord both night and day," and sure that "hell would be my portion, . . . all of a sudden my dungeon shook, my chains flew off, and, glory to God, I cried. My soul was filled. I cried, enough, for me the Saviour died."

Although Allen never attributed his and his siblings' conversion to the division of their family, the coincidence is compelling. His master, Sturgis, may also have suffered from having to sell some of the Allen family, for his conversion to Methodism led to his conviction that slavery was wrong. He allowed Allen and his two siblings to buy their freedom, which Richard did in 1780. Richard Allen caught the attention of Bishop Francis Asbury, the founder of American Methodism, and he became a Methodist preacher. Eventually he founded the African Methodist Episcopal Church and became a dedicated opponent of slavery and the Fugitive Slave Act of 1793.[52]

In the 1780s and 1790s another black preacher, Andrew Bryan, organized several Baptist churches in Georgia, including the first Baptist church for whites or blacks in Savannah. Bryan was born a slave but in 1795 purchased his own freedom. In the early nineteenth century a free black named Henry Evans founded the first Methodist church for blacks in Fayetteville, North Carolina. At first Evans's church was opposed by whites, but when his preaching led to a decline in the profanity and lewd behavior of the slaves, the whites began supporting it. By 1807 whites in increasing numbers were joining his church; by 1810 his congregation numbered 110 whites and 87 blacks.[53]

Initially the Baptists and the Methodists tended to condemn slavery and welcome blacks to full membership in their communion. In Wilmington, North Carolina, for example, the first Methodist congregation formed in 1784 was all black. By 1800 nearly one out of three American Methodists was

52. Andrews, *Methodists and Revolutionary America*, 88–89; Richard Newman, *Freedom's Prophet: Bishop Richard Allen, the AME Church, and the Black Founding Fathers* (New York, 2008).

53. Monte Hampton, "Henry Evans," *American National Biography*, ed. John A. Garraty and Mark Carnes (New York, 1999), 7: 607.

an African American. Mainly because whites eventually objected to integrated churches, African Americans like Richard Allen began organizing dozens of independent black congregations throughout much of America. During the first third of the nineteenth century, blacks in the city of Philadelphia alone built fourteen churches of their own, twelve of them Methodist or Baptist. Although historians know very little about the actual religious practices in the black churches, white observers emphasized praying, preaching, and especially singing as the central elements of black worship. The black churches in the North and the slave communities in the South stressed the expression of feelings, mixed African traditions with Christian forms, hymns, and symbols, and created religions that fit their needs.[54]

It was not just African Americans who brought more emotion to religion. Everywhere in America, among ordinary white folk, the open expression of religious feelings, along with singing, praying, and preaching, became more common than in the colonial period. The Revolution released torrents of popular religiosity and passion into American life. Visions, dreams, prophesying, and new emotion-soaked religious seeking acquired a new popular significance, and common people were freer than ever before to express publicly their hitherto repressed vulgar and superstitious notions. Divining rods, fortune-telling, astrology, treasure-seeking, and folk medicine thrived publicly. Between 1799 and 1802 a sect of New Israelites in Rutland, Vermont, claimed, according to a contemporary account, to be descended from ancient Jewish tribes with the "inspired power, with which to cure all sort of diseases"; the sect also had "intuitive knowledge of lost or stolen goods, and the ability to discover the hidden treasures of the earth, as well as the more convenient talent transmuting ordinary substances into the precious metals." Long-existing subterranean folk beliefs and fetishes emerged into the open and blended with traditional Christian practices to create a new popular religious syncretism that laid the basis for the later emergence of peculiarly American religions such as Mormonism.[55]

54. Hatch, *Democratization of Christianity*, 102–13; Albert J. Raboteau, *Slave Religion: The "Invisible Institution" in the Antebellum South* (New York, 1978); Mechal Sobel, *Travelin' On: The Slave Journey to an Afro-Baptist Faith* (Princeton, 1988); Sylvia R. Frey, "'The Year of Jubilee Is Come': Black Christianity in the Plantation South in Post-Revolutionary America," in Hoffman and Albert, eds., *Religion in a Revolutionary Age*, 87–124, esp. 97, 99, 103, 112; Charles Joyner, *Down by the Riverside: A South Carolina Slave Community* (Urbana, 1984); Margaret Washington Creel, "*A Peculiar People": Slave Religion and Community Culture Among the Gullahs* (New York, 1988); Paul E. Johnson, ed., *African-American Christianity: Essays in History* (Berkeley, 1994).

55. John L. Brooke, *The Refiner's Fire: The Making of Mormon Cosmology, 1644–1844* (Cambridge, UK, 1994), 31–32.

New half-educated enterprising preachers emerged to mingle exhibitions of book-learning with plain talk and with appeals to every kind of emotionalism. Common people wanted a religion they could personally feel and freely express, and the evangelical denominations offered them that, usually with much enthusiastic folk music and hymn singing. The lyrics of the Methodists' hymns were very sensuous, offering the congregations vivid images of Jesus' bloody sacrifice in order to better encourage repentance and a turn toward Christ. In many of the hymns Jesus appeared as the embodiment of overpowering love, ready and willing to receive the heart of the suppliant sinner. Not only did the period 1775–1815 become the golden age of hymn writing and singing in America, but it was also the period in which most religious folk music, gospels, and black spirituals first appeared. The radical Baptist Elias Smith alone produced at least fifteen different editions of colloquial religious music between 1804 and 1817.[56]

Obviously this religious enthusiasm tapped long-existing veins of folk culture, and many evangelical leaders had to struggle to keep the suddenly released popular passions under control. Bishop Francis Asbury repeatedly warned his itinerant Methodist preachers to ensure that visions were "brought to the standard of the Holy Scriptures" and not to succumb to the "power of sound."[57] In the new free environment of republican America some enthusiasts saw the opportunity to establish long-desired utopian worlds in which all social distinctions would be abolished, diet would be restricted, and goods and sometimes women would be shared.

Many, like those who joined the celibate Shakers, founded by the English immigrant Ann Lee, feared that the entire social order had collapsed, and thus they had to reconstitute sexual and family life from scratch. The Shaker communities that sprang up initially in New England and the eastern Hudson Valley had men and women living together in "families" of thirty to one hundred and fifty under the same roof, but with all their activities strictly separated. They knew what they were fleeing from. "The devil is a real being," said Mother Lee, whose followers considered her a "second Christ." Satan was "as real as a bear. I know, because I have seen and fought with him." Perhaps nothing is more revealing of the crisis of the social order in the early Republic than the growth of this remarkable religious group whose celibacy became an object of wonder to almost every foreign visitor. By 1809 the Shakers had established more

56. Stephen A. Marini, *Radical Sects of Revolutionary New England* (Cambridge, MA, 1982), 158; Hatch, *Democratization of Christianity*, 129, 146–61; Andrews, *Methodists and Revolutionary America*, 77.

57. Andrews, *Methodists and Revolutionary America*, 83.

than a dozen communities throughout the Northeast and the Midwest, with their several thousand members all seriously waiting for the Second Coming of Christ, which they believed was near at hand.[58]

THIS SECOND GREAT AWAKENING, like the democratic impulses of the Revolution, was very much a movement from below, fed by the passions of ordinary people.[59] To be sure, some Congregational clergy in New England saw in evangelical Christianity a means by which Federalists might better control the social disorder resulting from the Revolution. The Reverend Timothy Dwight even sponsored a revival at Yale to which a third of the student body responded. But these Federalist clergy, like Dwight and Jedidiah Morse, scarcely comprehended, let alone were able to manage, the popular religious upheaval that was spreading everywhere. Still, they did what they could to use evangelical religion to combat what they described as democratic infidelity and French-inspired madness.

On the eve of Jefferson's inauguration as president, Dwight and Morse founded the *New England Palladium* with the aim of strengthening "the government, morals, religion, and state of society in New England," and at the same time chastising "Jacobinism in every form, both of principle and practice." The orthodox clergy believed that they had every right to meddle with public morals and politics. Like most Federalist political leaders, the clerics assumed that since they were honest and pious, "opinions formed by such men are apt to be right." That was not the case with their Jacobinical enemies, wrote Dwight in one of his many articles for the *Palladium*. The Republicans were "men of loose morals, principles and lives. Are they not infidels...? Men who frequent public places, taverns and corners of the streets?" Such remarks reveal just how difficult it was for the Federalist leaders to accept the political, social, and religious changes taking place all around them. The issue facing them, as they saw it, was fundamental and beyond compromise: it was between "Religion and Infidelity, Morality and Debauchery, legal Government and total Disorganization."[60]

58. Lawrence Foster, *Religion and Sexuality: Three Communal Experiments in the Nineteenth Century* (New York, 1981), 31, 32.

59. Dixon Ryan Fox, "The Protestant Counter-Reformation in America," *New York History*, 16 (1935), 19–35; Clifford S. Griffin, "Religious Benevolence as Social Control, 1815–1860," *Mississippi Valley Historical Review*, 44 (1957), 423–44; Charles I. Foster, *An Errand of Mercy: The Evangelical United Front, 1790–1837* (Chapel Hill, 1960).

60. Church, *So Help Me God*, 268; Robert Edson Lee, "Timothy Dwight and the Boston Palladium," *New England Quarterly*, 35 (1962), 234; Dumas Malone, *Jefferson the President: Second Term, 1805–1809* (Boston, 1974), 373.

Despite their fear of Jeffersonian Republican infidelity, Morse and other mainstream New England Congregationalists soon came to realize that the most insidious enemy of their brand of Calvinism lay within their own Congregational ranks, within the Standing Order itself. Liberal Congregational ministers, who Morse thought were really infidels in disguise, had been growing in strength over the previous half century or more, especially in Boston and eastern urban centers of Massachusetts. Not only had the liberal clerics softened the confessions and rigors of Calvinism in the name of reason, but they had come to doubt and even deny the divinity of Christ. The appointment in 1805 of liberal clergyman Henry Ware as Hollis Professor of Divinity at Harvard College brought this long-existing proto-Unitarian threat to mainstream Calvinism to a head. For the orthodox Calvinists this appointment of a professor who denied the divinity of Jesus to the only college in the state that trained ministers meant "a revolution in sentiment in favor of what is called *rational* in opposition to *evangelical* religion."[61]

Morse and the "moderate Calvinists," as they were called, were outraged by this liberal takeover of the principal institution for educating Congregational clergymen. In response, in 1805 they formed a new journal, the *Panoplist*, with an evangelical, Yale-educated board, that launched attack after attack against the "unprincipled and designing men" in control of Boston's latitudinarian churches. Of course, the well-to-do liberal elites had their own journal, the *Monthly Anthology*, a sophisticated intellectual and literary publication that the evangelicals dubbed the "offspring of worldly ease and affluence." Although created about the same time, the learned *Monthly Anthology* had little in common with the polemically evangelical *Panoplist*, except that both were products of Federalist Congregational ministers and both were published in Boston.[62]

So alarming was this liberal threat that the mainstream Calvinists were even willing to come together with the New Divinity Calvinists in 1808 to form an alternative to Harvard, the Andover Theological Seminary, the first graduate school of theology in the United States. The New Divinity theology had been created by Samuel Hopkins, Congregational minister in Newport, Rhode Island, and was often called "Hopkinsianism." Drawing upon the ideas of Jonathan Edwards, the famous eighteenth-century Calvinist theologian, Hopkinsianism held to an uncompromisingly rigid

61. Peter S. Field, *The Crisis of the Standing Order: Clerical Intellectuals and Cultural Authority in Massachusetts, 1780–1833* (Amherst, MA, 1998), 114.
62. Field, *Crisis of the Standing Order*, 153; Catherine O'Donnell Kaplan, *Men of Letters in the Early Republic: Cultivating Forums of Citizenship* (Chapel Hill, 2008), 184–215.

brand of Calvinism in which sinners could do absolutely nothing to bring about their salvation. Although the New Divinity ministers had strange and logic-spinning techniques of preaching, they nevertheless had grown rapidly in the quarter century following the Revolution. By 1800 they had captured control of half the Congregational pulpits of New England, most of which were located in rural out-of-the-way areas in western Massachusetts and northern Connecticut.

In 1810 this alliance of moderate and extreme Calvinists founded a new Calvinist church in Boston, the Park Street Church, which the liberal Congregational clergy boycotted and dismissed for its "bigotry, illiberality, [and] exclusiveness." At the same time, Morse and the moderates joined the *Panoplist* with the Hopkinsian *Massachusetts Missionary Magazine* in order to bring Calvinist orthodoxy to the rest of America and to the world.[63]

WHILE THE NEW ENGLAND CONGREGATIONALISTS were coming apart—the formal division into Congregational and Unitarian churches would not take place for another decade or so—swelling numbers of dissenting Methodists and Baptists were threatening to engulf the Standing Order. Despite the scrambling efforts of the Congregational and Presbyterian clergy to meet the surging emotional needs of people, their position in New England steadily weakened. Although the legally established clergy in Massachusetts and Connecticut rarely held camp meetings, they were eventually compelled to adopt some of the new revivalist methods.

Wherever there was social disorder and anxiety, revivals flourished, even in Connecticut, the traditional "land of steady habits." Methodist preachers began entering the state in the late 1780s and increased their numbers over the next decade. Since the Methodists were Arminians, that is, believers in the possibility of striving to bring about one's own salvation, they had considerable advantages in recruiting converts over the established Presbyterians and Congregationalists, who generally clung, with varying degrees of rigidity, to the Calvinist belief in predestination—that God alone determined one's salvation. The Calvinists responded to the Methodist invasion of Connecticut with rocks and dogs, but eventually with revival efforts of their own.

63. Joseph A. Conforti, *Samuel Hopkins and the New Divinity Movement: Calvinism, the Congregational Ministry, and Reform in New England Between the Great Awakenings* (Grand Rapids, MI, 1981); Field, *Crisis of the Standing Order,* 174; J. M. Opal, *Beyond the Farm: National Ambitions in Rural New England* (Philadelphia, 2008), 76.

In 1798–1799 in Goshen, Connecticut, Asahel Hooker, a New Divinity clergyman, with his strict Calvinist belief in the doctrines of total depravity and predestination, launched a series of revivals that over the following decade swept through the town. The converts came from no particular age group, gender, or social rank. What they did share was growing anxieties over the fact that many in the community were leaving for Connecticut's Western Reserve in Ohio. Consequently, communicants in the congregation were asking themselves not only "What must I do to be saved?" but also "Shall I move to Ohio?" Even those who remained had reason to worry about broken family ties and the future of the community and to seek some assurance in religion.[64]

Yet in the end the efforts of the old Puritan churches to compete with the dynamic folk-like processes of the evangelicals were as ineffectual as the comparable efforts of the New England Federalists to outpopularize the Democratic-Republicans. Their static institutions based on eighteenth-century standards of deference and elite monopolies of orthodoxy were no match for the egalitarian-minded evangelicals.

In the slaveholding Old South social circumstances were different—more stable and more hierarchical; and there the spread of revivalism was complicated. At first the evangelical religions were not very successful in recruiting communicants. By 1790 only about 14 percent of Southern whites and fewer than 4 percent of blacks belonged to Baptist, Methodist, or Presbyterian churches, and much of this growth had come from the Scots-Irish migrations before the war and the collapse of Anglicanism following independence. The evangelicals did not gain much strength among the South's large unchurched population, white or black. And the situation did not change much over the next quarter century. By 1815 the combined membership of Baptists, Methodists, and Presbyterians grew slowly to just 17 percent of the white population and 8 percent of the black.

Part of the explanation of slow growth in the Old South came from the social disorder created by the Revolutionary War and the subsequent migrations of settlers westward. But more important in limiting growth were the radical egalitarian and anti-patriarchal impulses of the eighteenth-century evangelical religions in a slave-ridden society structured to resist such impulses. In 1784 the newly constituted Methodist Episcopal Church climaxed more than a decade of fierce anti-slavery preaching in America by enacting a rigorous set of rules designed to rid its membership of slaveholders. But such egalitarian and anti-slave

---

64. Richard D. Shiels, "The Origins of the Second Great Awakening in New England: Goshen, Connecticut, 1798–1799," *Mid-America: An Historical Review*, 78 (1996), 279–301.

sentiments could not be sustained: they did too much violence to the traditions and beliefs of both the slaveholding planters and ordinary Southern whites. It was only a matter of months, in fact, before stiff opposition from the Southern laity forced the Methodist leaders to repeal most of the new restrictions on slaveholding.

Even when the evangelical denominations made accommodations to slavery, their growth among common people in the Old South remained for decades slow and gradual. Ordinary Southern farmers resisted the appeal of evangelical preachers, frightened by the ways in which Baptists and Methodists challenged all those hierarchies that had lent stability to their daily lives. These Southerners wanted to maintain the deference of youth to the aged, the submission of children to parents and women to men, and the exclusive loyalties of individuals to family and kin. And they resisted the release of emotions that threatened these relationships. Because the Baptists and Methodists tended to undermine the ways in which ordinary people in the South structured their neighborhoods, their households, and their very being, these churches remained suspect in the minds of Southerners for decades. Many evangelical leaders eventually concluded, as a historian of Southern religion has put it, that "the ultimate success of evangelicalism in the South lay in appealing to those who confined the devil to hell, esteemed maturity over youth, put family before religious fellowship, upheld the superiority of white over black and of men over women, and prized their honor above all else." Southern evangelicalism had to make numerous concessions to the region's social and cultural realities, especially slavery.[65]

If social disorder was what lay behind the growth of evangelical religion, it was not something the system of slavery could long tolerate. Slavery, which necessarily shaped all dependency relationships in most Southern households, required a patriarchal social world that had little place for the disruptive effects of the wild and uncontrollable revivals of evangelical religion. Even Southern backcountry yeomen came to recognize the need for order. Consequently, wherever high proportions of black slaves were present in the Deep South evangelical religion tended to develop slowly.

65. Christine Leigh Heyrman, *Southern Cross: The Beginnings of the Bible Belt* (New York, 1997), 23–27, 255–56. On the conservatism of Southern white laymen in the face of the radical evangelical appeal, see Rachel N. Klein, *Unification of a Slave State: The Rise of the Planter Class in the South Carolina Backcountry, 1760–1808* (Chapel Hill, 1990); and Stephanie McCurry, *Masters of Small Worlds: Yeoman Households, Gender Relations, and the Political Culture of the Antebellum South Carolina Low Country* (New York, 1995). Of course, in time evangelical religion would flourish in the South.

But elsewhere, in places where the number of slaves was more limited or nonexistent, the situation was different. In the most disordered, dynamic, and fluid areas of the North and West the newly released religious yearnings of ordinary people often tended to overwhelm hierarchies of all sorts, including traditional religious institutions. Between 1803 and 1809, for example, more than half the Presbyterian clergy and church members of Kentucky, where slavery was less well established than it was in the Old South, were swept away by the torrents of popular revivalism.[66]

Of course, there were extensive efforts everywhere to reverse the extreme fragmentation, and in time these efforts at establishing some evangelical order would develop into middle-class discipline, self-improvement, and respectability.[67] But because the accounts of most early denominational historians tended to telescope this growth of refinement and organizational coherence in their particular churches, it has not always been fully appreciated just how disorderly the denominations' origins were.[68] Evangelical authoritarianism and respectability were slow to develop out of the social confusion of the immediate post-Revolutionary decades. It was at least a generation, for example, before the Methodists were able to tame the evangelical camp meeting.[69]

As THE OLDER ARISTOCRATIC WORLD of hierarchal churches fell apart (the growth of Roman Catholicism being the exception), the new revivalist Protestant clergy urged the common people to put their religious world back together on new democratic terms. The Scottish immigrant and renegade Presbyterian Thomas Campbell told the people in 1809 that it was "high time for us not only to think, but also to act, for ourselves; to see with our own eyes, and to take all our measures directly from the Divine standard."[70] Just as the people were taking over their

66. Ralph E. Morrow, "The Great Revival, the West, and the Crisis of the Church," in John Francis McDermott, ed., The Frontier Re-Examined (Urbana, IL, 1967), 78.
67. Daniel Walker Howe, "The Evangelical Movement and Political Culture in the North During the Second Party System," JAH, 77 (1991), 1216–39; Richard L. Bushman, The Refinement of America: Persons, Houses, Cities (New York, 1992).
68. Hatch, Democratization of Christianity, 97, 272 n. For some of the evangelical sects' initial efforts at establishing order, see Marini, Radical Sects, 116–35; and Hatch, Democratization of Christianity, 201–6.
69. Hatch, Democratization of Christianity, 52.
70. Mark A. Noll, America's God: From Jonathan Edwards to Abraham Lincoln (New York, 2002), 380; Donald G. Mathews, "The Second Great Awakening as an Organizing Process, 1780–1830: A Hypothesis," American Quarterly, 21 (1969), 23–43.

governments, so, it was said, they should take over their churches. Christianity had to be republicanized and made more popular. The people were their own theologians and had no need to rely on others to tell them what to believe. We must be "wholly free to examine for ourselves what is truth," declared the renegade Baptist Elias Smith in 1809, "without being bound to a catechism, creed, confession of faith, discipline or any rule excepting the scriptures."[71] From northern New England to southern Kentucky, Christian fundamentalists called for an end to priests, presbyters, associations, doctrines, confessions—anything and everything that stood between the people and Christ. The people were told that they were quite capable of running their own churches, and even clerical leaders of the conservative denominations like Presbyterian Samuel Miller were forced to concede greater and greater lay control.[72]

The people were everywhere "awakened from the sleep of ages," said the maverick Presbyterian Barton Stone—who was a product not of the frontier but of the American Revolution; and the people saw "for the first time that they were responsible beings" who might even be capable of bringing about their own salvation.[73] Although the strict Calvinists still tried to stress predestination, limited atonement, the sovereignty of God, and the inability of people to save themselves, conversion seemed to be within the grasp of all who desired it—a mere matter of letting go and trusting in Jesus. By emphasizing free will and earned grace, the Methodists especially gathered in great numbers of souls and set the entire evangelical movement in a decidedly Arminian direction, with people, in effect, able to will their own salvation. After hearing a Methodist preacher in Lynn, Massachusetts, in the early 1790s attack the Calvinist notion that only a few elect went to heaven, one middling artisan listener exclaimed, "Why, then, I can be saved! I have been taught that only part of the race could be saved, but if this man's singing be true, all may be saved."[74]

The Universalists did promise salvation for everyone and consequently thrived. Between 1795 and 1815 the Universalists organized twenty-three churches in the Connecticut River Valley of rural Vermont, especially under the leadership of Hosea Ballou, who denied the divinity of Christ and became Universalism's most important theologian. Although the

71. Smith, *The Loving Kindness of God Displayed in the Triumph of Republicanism in America* (n.p., 1809), 27.

72. Belden C. Lane, "Presbyterian Republicanism: Miller and the Eldership as an Answer to Lay-Clerical Tensions," *Journal of Presbyterian History*, 56 (1978), 311–14.

73. John Rogers, *The Biography of Elder Barton Warren Stone...* (Cincinnati, 1847), 45; Hatch, *Democratization of Christianity*, 70.

74. Paul G. Faler, *Mechanics and Manufacturers in the Early Industrial Revolution: Lynn, Massachusetts, 1780–1860* (Albany, 1981), 46.

Universalists were widely condemned, in their acceptance of universal salvation they were only drawing out the logic implied by many other denominations. One of the ministers who opposed them was Lemuel Haynes, apparently the first black minister ordained by a major denomination. Ordained as a Congregational minister in Connecticut in 1785, Haynes moved to a conservative church in Rutland, Vermont, which he served for thirty years. As a devout Calvinist, he assailed the Universalists sprouting up everywhere around him in Vermont. In his 1805 sermon Haynes satirized Universalism and compared Ballou to the serpent in the Garden of Eden, which had also promised "Universal Salvation." The sermon was widely republished and went through dozens of editions.[75]

Devout evangelicals still believed in Satan the harasser, but, unlike the Puritans of the seventeenth century, most no longer thought that the devil could possess the body of a person; only Christ and the Holy Spirit could possess, which made all the fainting, shouting, and bodily shaking of the suppliants acceptable. Sin was no longer conceived as something inherent in the depravity of human beings but as a kind of failure of a person's will and thus fully capable of being eliminated by individual exertion. Even some of the Calvinist Presbyterians and Separate Baptists felt compelled to soften their opposition to Arminianism in the face of the relentless challenges by free will believers; and many of them came to believe that the external moral behavior of people—their "character"—was more central to religious life than the introspective conversion of their souls.[76]

With ordinary people being told, as one preacher told them in 1806, that each individual was "considered as possessing in himself or herself an original right to believe and speak as their own conscience, between themselves and God, may determine," religion in America became much more personal and voluntary than it had ever been. People were freer to join and change their religious affiliation whenever they wished.[77] They

75. Randolph A. Roth, The Democratic Dilemma: Religion, Reform, and the Social Order in the Connecticut River Valley of Vermont, 1791–1850 (Cambridge, UK, 1987), 62; John Saillant, Black Puritan, Black Republican: The Life and Thought of Lemuel Haynes, 1753–1833 (New York, 2003); Richard Newman, "Lemuel Haynes," American National Biography, 10: 417–18. For the appeal of Universalism among workingmen in Philadelphia, see Ronald Schultz, "God and Workingmen: Popular Religion and the Formation of Philadelphia's Working Class, 1790–1830," in Hoffman and Albert, eds., Religion in a Revolutionary Age, 138.

76. Andrews, Methodists of Revolutionary America, 82; Marini, Radical Sects, 88; Marini, "Revolutionary Revival," 53–54; Richard Rabinowitz, The Spiritual Self in Everyday Life: The Transformation of Personal Religious Experience in Nineteenth-Century New England (Boston, 1989), 3–151.

77. Abel M. Sargent, The Destruction of the Beast in the Downfall of Sectarianism (n.p., [1806]), 15.

thus moved from one religious group to another in a continual search for signs, prophets, or millennial promises that would make sense of their disrupted lives. With no church sure of holding its communicants, competition among the sects became fierce. Each claimed to be right; they called each other names, argued endlessly over points of doctrine, mobbed and stoned each other, and destroyed each other's meetinghouses.

"All Christendom has been decomposed, broken in pieces" in this "fiery furnace of democracy," said the bewildered Federalist Harrison Gray Otis.[78] Not only were the traditional Old World churches fragmented but the fragments themselves shattered in what seemed at times to be perpetual fission. There were not just Presbyterians but Old and New School Presbyterians, Cumberland Presbyterians, Springfield Presbyterians, Reformed Presbyterians, and Associated Presbyterians; not just Baptists but General Baptists, Regular Baptists, Free Will Baptists, Separate Baptists, Dutch River Baptists, Permanent Baptists, and Two-Seed-in-the-Spirit Baptists. Some individuals cut their ties completely with the Old World churches and gathered around a dynamic leader like Barton Stone or Thomas Campbell who promised the restoration of the original Christian church—which is why they came to be called Restorationists. Other seekers ended up forming churches out of single congregations, and still others simply listened in the fields to wandering preachers like the eccentric Methodist Lorenzo Dow, who in the single year of 1805 traveled some ten thousand miles.[79]

Dow was a force of nature. He preached to more people, traveled to more places, and attracted larger audiences at camp meetings than any other preacher of his day. In 1804, for example, he spoke at between five hundred and eight hundred camp meetings. He also wrote books, publishing between 1800 and his death in 1834 over seventy editions of his works. With long hair and flowing beard and disheveled clothes, Dow cultivated the image of John the Baptist. Yet he was no otherworldly mystic; he was in fact a radical Jeffersonian who railed at aristocrats and supported equality everywhere he went. He condemned the "gentlemen or nobility" who sought to "possess the country and feel and act more than

78. Josiah Quincy, *The History of Harvard University* (Cambridge, MA, 1840), 2: 663.
79. On Dow, see Charles C. Sellers, *Lorenzo Dow: The Bearer of the Word* (New York, 1928); and Hatch, *Democratization of Christianity*, 36–40. On these religious developments, see in general Whitney R. Cross, *The Burned-Over District: The Social and Intellectual History of Enthusiastic Religion in Western New York, 1800–1850* (New York, 1965); John R. Boles, *The Great Revival, 1787–1805* (Lexington, KY, 1972); Donald G. Mathews, *Religion in the Old South* (Chicago, 1977); and Anne C. Loveland, *Southern Evangelicals and the Social Order, 1800–1860* (Baton Rouge, 1980).

their importance." Such elites thought of ordinary people as "peasants" whom they "put on a level with the animals, and treated as an inferior race of beings, who must pay these lords a kind of divine honor, and bow, and cringe and scrape."[80]

THE DIVISIVE EFFECTS of all this fragmentation were offset by a curious blurring of theological distinctions among the competing denominations. "In that awful day when the universe, assembled must appear before the judge of the quick and the dead, the question brethren," declared James McGready, one of the leaders in Kentucky's great revival, "will not be, Were you a Presbyterian—a Seceder—a Covenanter—a Baptist—or a Methodist; but, Did you experience the new birth? Did you accept of Christ and his salvation as set forth in the gospel?"[81] Some extreme evangelicals urged the creation of a simple Christian religion based on only the fundamentals of the gospel. They denounced all the paraphernalia of organized Christianity, including even the existence of a ministry.

Some radical evangelicals even thought they could end what the young Joseph Smith, the founder of Mormonism, called "this war of words and tumult of opinions" among the sects by appealing to the Bible, and especially the New Testament, as the lowest common denominator of Christian belief.[82] The Scriptures were to be to democratic religion what the Constitution was to democratic politics—the fundamental document that would bind all the competitive American Christian sects together in one national communion. The biblical literalism of these years became popular religion's ultimate concession to the Enlightenment—the recognition that religious truth now needed documentary proof. In that democratic age where all traditional authority was suspect, some concluded that individuals possessed only their own reason and the Scriptures—the "two witnesses," said Joseph Smith's grandfather, "that stand by the God of the whole earth."[83] Sects like the Shakers and later the Mormons came to believe that they needed some sort of literary evidence or written testimony to convince a skeptical world that their beliefs were, as the Shakers were anxious to show, not "cunningly devised fables" but rather manifestations of "the spirit of Eternal Truth."[84]

80. Hatch, *Democratization of Christianity*, 36–37.
81. Boles, *Great Revival*, 128–29.
82. Joseph Smith, *The Pearl of Great Price* (Salt Lake City, 1974), 47.
83. Asael Smith (1799), in William Mulder and A. Russell Mortensen, eds., *Among the Mormons: Historic Accounts by Contemporary Observers* (New York, 1958), 24.
84. Stein, *Shaker Experience*, 80–86.

All this emphasis on written evidence and fundamentalism gave the Bible special significance. As print was exploding in these years of the early Republic, it was inevitable that more and more ordinary people bought and read the Bible. No American editions of the entire Bible existed before 1782, yet by 1810 Americans were publishing over twenty editions of the Bible every year. Although by the early nineteenth century the Bible might have become merely a book among books, it was still the text most imported from abroad, most printed in America, and most widely read in all of America. Common people might have owned very few books, but those they did own usually included the Bible, which was read and known, often by heart.[85]

As early as 1798 the enterprising bookseller and future Washington biographer Parson Mason Weems pleaded with Philadelphia publisher Mathew Carey to publish a Protestant version of the Bible. If he did not, other printers would beat him to it. "You hear of nothing here now but printing the Bible," said Weems. "Everything that can raise a type is going to work upon the Bible." By 1801 Carey had a Protestant Bible out, and over the next decade and a half he produced a variety of Bibles to meet a diverse market—some printed on different kinds of paper, others bound in different kinds of leather, others set in different sizes of type, and still others provided with various maps and engravings—all at different prices. "Good engravings are a luxury," said Weems, "a feast for the soul.... The fame of them goes abroad and the Bible sells with Rapidity." Indeed, Carey's Bibles sold so well that he often had trouble keeping up with demand. Between 1801 and 1824 he brought out sixty editions of his Bibles and made substantial sums of money doing so.

As early as 1807 Carey had come to dominate Bible production in America. In addition to supplying booksellers everywhere, he furnished Bibles to common schools, Sunday schools, and in 1808 the Philadelphia Bible Society, the first of many such Bible societies to be founded in the United States. These societies soon began publishing their own Bibles in great numbers—hundreds of thousands of copies each year at vastly reduced prices.[86]

Reliance on the literalism of the Bible or on other literary evidence hardly stopped the confusion and fragmentation. Church publications and collections of testimonies proliferated, but there was no final authority, no supreme court of Christianity, to settle the interminable disputes among the sects over the Bible or any other testimony. And so the splintering went on, with many of the evangelist clergy desperately trying to bring the pieces together under some sort of common Christian rubric.

85. Paul C. Gutjahr, *An American Bible: A History of the Good Book in the United States, 1777–1880* (Stanford, 1999), 1.
86. Gutjahr, *American Bible*, 23–29; Peter J. Wosh, *Spreading the Word: The Bible Business in Nineteenth-Century America* (Ithaca, 1994).

In some areas churches as such scarcely existed, and the traditional identification between religion and society, never very strong in America to begin with, now finally dissolved. Churches no longer made any effort to embody their communities, and the church for many came to mean little more than the building in which religious services were conducted. The competing denominations essentially abandoned their traditional institutional and churchly responsibilities to organize the world here-and-now along godly lines; instead, they concentrated on the saving of individual souls. Church membership was no longer based on people's position in the social hierarchy but rather on their evangelical fellowship. Consequently, the new evangelical denominations were less capable than the traditional eighteenth-century churches had been in replicating the whole community and in encompassing a variety of social ranks within their membership. Instead, particular denominations became identified with particular social classes. While the Episcopalians (as the former Anglicans were now known) and the Unitarians (liberals who broke away from the more conservative Calvinist Congregationalists) became largely the preserve of social elites, the rapidly growing Baptists and Methodists swept up the middling and lower sorts of the population.[87]

Despite religion's separation from society, some Americans thought that religion was the only cohesive force capable of holding the nation together—"the central attraction," said Lyman Beecher in 1815, "which must supply the deficiency of political affinity and interest."[88] The traditional message of Christian love and charity came together with the Enlightenment's stress on modern civility and commonsense sociability to make the decades following the Revolution a great era of benevolence and communitarianism. Figures as diverse as Samuel Hopkins, Thomas Campbell, and Thomas Jefferson told people that all they had to do in the world was to believe in one God and to love one another.[89]

Not only did the new religious sects and movements Christianize American popular culture and bring many people together and prepare them for nineteenth-century middle-class respectability, but they also helped to legitimize the freedom and individualism of people and to make morally possible their commercial participation in an impersonal marketplace. Of

---

87. Donald M. Scott, *From Office to Profession: The New England Ministry, 1750–1850* (Philadelphia, 1978), 34, 47–48.
88. Lyman Beecher, *On the Importance of Assisting Young Men of Piety and Talents in Obtaining an Education for the Gospel Ministry* (New York, 1815), 16.
89. On the similarity of the messages of Hopkins, Campbell, and Jefferson, see H. Sheldon Smith, Robert T. Handy, and Lefferts A. Loetscher, *American Christianity: An Historical Interpretation with Representative Documents* (New York, 1960), 1: 516, 543–44, 579–86.

course, not every evangelical Christian was a capitalist or even an active participant in the marketplace. But in some basic sense evangelical religion and American commercialism were more than compatible; they needed one another. As Tocqueville later pointed out, "The Americans combine the notions of Christianity and of liberty so intimately in their minds that it is impossible to make them conceive of the one without the other."[90]

Conversion experiences did not leave most ordinary people incapacitated and unworldly; indeed, their "new births" seemed to fit them better for the tasks of this world. Religion increased their energy as it restrained their liberty, got them on with their work as it disciplined their acquisitive urges; it gave the middling sorts confidence that even self-interested individuals subscribed to absolute standards of right and wrong and thus could be trusted in market exchanges and contractual relationships.

Despite its strong repudiation of selfishness, even the New Divinity movement within New England Calvinism, in which many middling sorts like William Manning were involved, conceded that self-interest was no threat to a moral economic order; the movement even gave self-interest some moral legitimacy. Because the concept of universal disinterested benevolence made famous by the founder of New Divinity Calvinism, Samuel Hopkins, was grounded on the enlightened self-interest of people, it was able to set credible moral limits to their individualism and acquisitive behavior. Although Hopkinsianism declared that individuals could do nothing to bring about their own salvation and must work benevolently without hope of heavenly reward, nevertheless their benevolent character gave them some assurance that they were in fact saved and a higher sense of their own worth. The result was a moral benefit for the community without these self-assured individuals' having to repudiate their self-interest.[91]

Many middling people—those who were most mobile, most involved in commercial activity, from market farmers to craftsmen to petty businessmen—discovered in evangelicalism a kind of counter-culture that

90. Paul E. Johnson, "Democracy, Patriarchy, and American Revivals, 1780–1830," *Journal of Social History*, 24 (1990–91), 843–49; Alexis de Tocqueville, *Democracy in America*, ed. Phillips Bradley (1835; New York, 1956), 1: 306; Hugh Heclo, *Christianity and American Democracy* (Cambridge, MA, 2007). Naturally, some religious people could be very critical of the emerging market world. See Jama Lazerow, *Religion and the Working Class in Antebellum America* (Washington, DC, 1995), which contends that religion decisively affected the nature of antebellum labor protest.

91. William Breitenbach, "Unregenerate Doings: Selflessness and Selfishness in New Divinity Theology," *American Quarterly*, 34 (1982), 479–502; James D. German, "The Social Utility of Wicked Self-Love: Calvinism, Capitalism, and Public Policy in Revolutionary New England," *JAH*, 82 (1995), 965–98; Heclo, *Christianity and American Democracy*, 15–16.

offered them alternative measures of self-worth and social respectability and at the same time gave them moral justifications for their unusual behavior. "Liberty is a great cant word with them," complained a New Hampshire Federalist minister in 1811 of the local sectarians who were challenging the conservative Congregationalists. They tell their hearers, he grumbled—with more accuracy than sympathy—to cast aside "all their old prejudices and traditions which they have received from their fathers and ministers; who they say, are hirelings, keeping your souls in bondage, and under oppression. Hence to use their own language, they say, 'Break all these yokes and trammels from off you, and come out of prison; and dare to think, and speak, and act for yourselves.' "[92] It is not surprising that most of these radical evangelicals in New England and elsewhere became Jeffersonian Republicans: evangelicals and Republicans in the North were preaching the same message and drawing from the same social sources.

Being called by polite society "the scum of the earth, the filth of creation," the evangelicals made their fellowship, their conversion experiences, and their peculiar folk rites their badges of respectability.[93] They began to make strenuous efforts to bring their own passions and their own anarchic impulses under control and to create some order out of all the social disorder. To the horror of their unlearned itinerant preachers, some of them began proposing the establishment of seminaries to train their ministers. In the several decades following the founding of Andover Seminary in 1807, members of thirteen different Protestant denominations created fifty seminaries in seventeen states.[94] They began to cease their mocking of learning and tried to acquire some of the gentility they were repeatedly told they lacked. They staffed the moral societies that were springing up everywhere and denounced the dissolute behavior they saw about them—the profanity, drinking, prostitution, gambling, dancing, horse racing, and other amusements shared by both the luxurious aristocracy at the top of the society and the unproductive rabble at the bottom. By condemning the vices of those above and below them, the evangelicals struck out at both social directions at once and thereby began to acquire a "middle class" distinctiveness.

92. Nathan O. Hatch, "In Pursuit of Religious Freedom: Church, State, and People in the New Republic," in Jack P. Greene, ed., *The American Revolution: Its Character and Limits* (New York, 1987), 393–94.
93. William Gribbin, *The Churches Militant: The War of 1812 and American Religion* (New Haven, 1973), 102.
94. Natalie A. Naylor, "The Theological Seminary in the Configuration of American Higher Education: The Antebellum Years," *History of Education Quarterly*, 17 (1977), 20–23.

OTHERS WERE EXPERIENCING such radical disruption and bewilderment in their lives that they could only conclude that the world was on the verge of some great transformation—nothing less than the Second Coming of Christ and the Day of Judgment predicted in the Bible. Perhaps never before in the history of Christianity had the millennium seemed so imminent, and perhaps never before did so many people believe that the Final Days were upon them.

The turbulent decades following the Revolution saw a flourishing of millennial beliefs of various kinds, both scholarly and popular. Literally, millennialism referred to the doctrine held by some Christians on the authority of Revelation 20: 4–6. The traditional belief in the millennium usually had assumed that Christ's coming would precede the establishment of a new kingdom of God. The literal advent of Christ would be forewarned by signs and troubles, culminating in a horrible conflagration in which everything would be destroyed. Christ would then rule over the faithful in a New Jerusalem for a thousand years until the final Day of Judgment. Those who held such pre-millennial beliefs generally saw the world as so corrupt and so evil that only the sudden and catastrophic intervention of Christ could create it anew.

Flowing out of the heart of seventeenth-century Puritanism, this pessimistic eschatological tradition was significantly altered in America by the great eighteenth-century theologian Jonathan Edwards. Edwards conceived of the millennium occurring within history; that is, the Coming of Christ would follow, not precede, the thousand years that would constitute the final age of man on earth. These thousand years would be a time of joy and well-being in preparation for Christ's Final Coming. In the years following the Revolution, a number of important American ministers, including Edwards's grandson Timothy Dwight, president of Yale, and Joseph Bellamy and Samuel Hopkins, evangelized Edwards's millennial views, which helped to justify and explain the great social changes of the period. In fact, Hopkins's *Treatise on the Millennium*, published in 1793, became a handbook for a generation of American theologians.[95]

95. On millennialism, see J. F. Maclear, "The Republic and the Millennium," in Smith, ed., *Religion of the Republic*, 183–216; David E. Smith, "Millenarian Scholarship in America," *American Quarterly*, 17 (1965), 535–49; Ernest Lee Tuveson, *Redeemer Nation: The Idea of America's Millennial Role* (Chicago, 1968); James West Davidson, *The Logic of Millennial Thought: Eighteenth-Century New England* (New Haven, 1977); Sacvan Bercovitch, *The American Jeremiad* (Madison, WI, 1978); J.F.C. Harrison, *The Second Coming: Popular Millenarianism, 1780–1850* (New Brunswick, NJ, 1979); Melvin B. Endy Jr., "Just War, Holy War, and Millennialism in Revolutionary America," *WMQ*, 42 (1985), 3–25; and Ruth Bloch, *Visionary Republic: Millennial Themes in American Thought, 1756–1800* (Cambridge, UK, 1985).

Although some fundamentalist sects rejected this new Edwardsian interpretation of the millennium and continued to cling to the older apocalyptic view, most of the leading American churches pictured the cataclysmic Second Coming of Christ following rather than preceding the thousand years of glory and bliss.[96] Such an optimistic Adventist belief seemed much more appropriate for an improving progressive society that was undergoing a historic transformation.

By 1810, events of the previous fifty years, and especially those since 1789, had convinced the evangelical minister Jedidiah Morse that "God in his providence had been, and is preparing the world for some grand revolution, some wonderful display of his sovereign and almighty power." Taking as his text the prophecy of Daniel (12:4), "Many shall run to and fro and knowledge shall be increased"—a text used by other ministers as well—Morse went on to outline in typical fashion the signs of the coming millennium. Missionaries were spreading knowledge and Christianity to every corner of the world, even to the interior of Africa, and the collapse of both the papacy and the doctrine of Mahomet seemed to be "near at hand, even at the door." People, said Morse, will know when the beginning of the thousand years is upon them by the disappearance of the multiple languages and the conversion and return of the dispersed Jews to the Holy Land. Realizing that the gospel was at present being diffused everywhere and would eventually reach "every creature under heaven," Morse could only conclude that the prophecy of the coming millennium was "now fulfilling before our eyes."[97]

But the Federalist Morse was hardly unusual in his prophesying; indeed, there was scarcely a clergyman in these years, especially in New England, who did not read the signs of the times and predict that something momentous was happening. Baptist and Republican Elias Smith thought that the struggle for liberty and individual rights throughout the world set the present age apart from all previous ages in history. The rule of kings and priests was passing, led by the example of the republican government of the United States. In a sermon preached in the immediate aftermath of Jefferson's second inauguration as president in 1805, Smith suggested that Jefferson's re-election foretold the coming of the millennium. He believed that *"Thomas Jefferson is the angel who poured out his vial upon the river Euphrates, that the way of the kings of the east might be prepared."* The people of the world would know when Christ's favorite government was upon

96. Bloch, *Visionary Republic*, 217; Davidson, *Logic of Millennial Thought*, 275–76.
97. Jedidiah Morse, *Signs of the Times: A Sermon Preached Before the Society for Propagating the Gospel*...(Charlestown, MA, 1810), 22, 28.

them. It would be America's: it would consist of *"liberty, equality, unity and peace."*[98]

Other clergy also thought that the approaching age of perfection was beginning in America. The wandering Methodist Lorenzo Dow was convinced that just as "The Dawn of Liberty" was taking place in America, so too would the millennium begin in the United States. "America lay undiscovered for several thousand years," said Dow, "as if reserved for the era, when common sense began to awake her long slumber." It was "as if the Creator's wisdom and goodness" were waiting for "a 'NEW WORLD,'...for a new theatre for the exhibition of new things."[99]

Since the United States was itself leading humanity toward the earth's final thousand years of bliss, millennial hopes inevitably came to focus on contemporary events occurring in America as signs of the approaching age of perfection—a perfection that would be brought about, some said, "not by miracles but by means," indeed, "BY HUMAN EXERTIONS."[100] Although Samuel Hopkins's consistent Calvinism discouraged the sinner's hope of promoting his or her own salvation, nonetheless his *Treatise on the Millennium* offered a rosy view of the future. After emphasizing the usual spiritual resurrection that would occur at the onset of the millennium, Hopkins soon got to the part of his book that must have been especially appealing to many readers—his description of the concrete earthly benefits people could look forward to during the millennium. The thousand years preceding the apocalypse, he wrote, "will be a time of great enjoyment and universal joy." Family members will love one another, lawsuits will disappear, intemperance and extravagance will decline, and good health will be had by all. Men will learn how to farm more efficiently and smoothly. Artisans will improve their mastery of the "mechanic arts," with the result that "the necessary and convenient articles of life, such as all utensils, clothing, buildings, etc., will be formed and made, in better manner, and with much less labour than they now are." Men, Hopkins claimed, will learn how to cut rocks, pave roads, and build houses in new labor-saving ways. They will invent machines to level mountains and raise valleys. The millennium, he concluded, will bring about "a fullness and plenty of all the necessaries and conveniences

---

98. Elias Smith, *The Whole World Governed by a Jew; or, the Government of the Second Adam, as King and Priest...Delivered March 4, 1805, the Evening After the Election of the President and Vice-President* (Exeter, NH, 1805), 72–78; Hatch, *Democratization of American Christianity*, 184.

99. Hatch, *Democratization of American Christianity*, 185.

100. Timothy Dwight (1813) and Elephalet Nott (1806) in Davidson, *Logic of Millennial Thought*, 275, 276.

of life, to render all much more easy and comfortable in their worldly circumstances and enjoyments, than ever before." Hopkins admitted that it was tricky making all these predictions, but he hoped he had not made too many mistakes. Besides, he said, he was probably erring on the side of caution. By stressing that things were likely to be even better than his predictions, Hopkins guaranteed that his millennial message would be popular.[101]

This new post-millennial thinking represented both a rationalizing of revelation and a Christianizing of the enlightened belief in secular progress. Hopkins's predictions of a new world of "universal peace, love and general and cordial friendship" were not much different from those hopes for the future held by Jefferson and other secular radicals. This post-millennial thinking was optimistic and even at times materialistic; it promised not the sudden divine destruction of a corrupt world but a step-by-step human-directed progression toward perfection in this world. Every move westward across the continent and every advance in material progress—even new inventions and canal-building—was interpreted in millennial terms. Such millennial beliefs identified the history of redemption with the history of the new Republic. They reconciled Christianity with American democracy, and they explained and justified the anxious lives and the awakened aspirations of countless numbers of ordinary Americans for whom the world had hitherto never offered much promise of improvement.

101. Samuel Hopkins, A Treatise on the Millennium (Boston, 1793), in Wood, ed., Rising Glory of America (Boston, 1990), 43–53.

# 17

# Republican Diplomacy

The United States was born amidst a world at war. From 1792 to 1815, except for some brief armistices, Europe was torn apart by a ferocious struggle for dominance between revolutionary and later Napoleonic France and her many European enemies, especially Great Britain. It became the longest sustained global war in modern history. Before it was over, it had killed or maimed more than two million persons, overthrown numerous governments, and transformed boundaries throughout Europe. Fighting took place in nearly every part of Europe and in various regions of the world, including the Middle East, South Africa, the Indian Ocean, the West Indies, and Latin America. Almost every European country was involved at one time or another, either in alliance or at war with Britain or France.

For the new French republic the war was total. The French revolutionary leaders enlisted their entire society on behalf of the republican cause, which they said would be brought to all of Europe. With the execution of Louis XVI, exulted the radical Jacobin Georges Jacques Danton, France was flinging at the feet of monarchs "the head of a King." The French revolutionary leaders drafted their citizens and turned them into the world's first mass conscript army. By the end of 1794 the French army had grown to over a million men—not only the largest army the world had ever seen but one inspired by the most extraordinary revolutionary zeal. "No more maneuvers, no more military art, but fire, steel, and patriotism," declared Lazare Carnot, the organizer of the French revolutionary armies. "We must exterminate! Exterminate to the bitter end!"[1]

Against such revolutionary fervor, the British realized that this struggle would be different from the many previous clashes with their ancient enemy. The day in 1793 that Great Britain declared war on revolutionary France, the thirty-three-year-old prime minister, William Pitt, the brilliant son of the great minister who had won the Seven Years' War a generation

---

1. William Hague, *William Pitt the Younger* (New York, 2005), 279; Michael Howard, *War in European History* (Oxford, 1976), 80–81.

earlier, told Parliament that Britons were fighting not merely for a traditional balance of power in Europe but for their monarchy and their way of life, indeed, for "the happiness of the whole of the human race." The French, said Pitt, wish to bring their brand of liberty "to every nation, and if they will not accept of it voluntarily, they compel them. They take every opportunity to destroy every institution that is most sacred and most valuable in every nation where their armies have their appearance; and under the name of liberty, they have resolved to make every country in substance, if not in form, a province dependent on themselves." The cost in British blood and treasure of the nearly two and a half decades of war was astonishing—nearly three hundred thousand killed and over a billion pounds in money.[2]

Although the war took place in all parts of the world, it was not a single continuous war like the world wars of the twentieth century; instead, it was a series of wars, most of them very short and distinct. Every one of the great Continental powers—Austria, Prussia, and Russia—formed and dissolved coalitions against France in accordance with their particular interests. Being often more fearful of one another than of France, they were as willing to ally with Napoleon as to wage war against him. Only Britain, except for a year of peace in 1802–1803, remained continually at war with France throughout the period.

The Treaty of Amiens that Britain signed with France in 1802 left France in control of Belgium, Holland, the left bank of the Rhine, and Italy. This peace could not last, for it was no more acceptable to Britain than it was to Napoleon, who began to extend his sway over more and more parts of Europe. Britain declared war against France in 1803 and formed the Third Coalition with Austria and Russia against France. Napoleon crowned himself emperor in 1804 and made plans to invade England. In October 1805 the British navy under the command of Admiral Horatio Lord Nelson defeated the combined French and Spanish fleets off Cape Trafalgar. Nelson's victory destroyed Napoleon's plans for invading England and guaranteed Britain's control of the seas. Then at the end of 1805 Napoleon defeated the combined Austrian and Russian armies at Austerlitz (located in the present-day Czech Republic), which led to the collapse of the Third Coalition the British had mounted against the French.

President Jefferson saw at once the implications of Napoleon's victory at Austerlitz. "What an awful spectacle does the world exhibit at this

2. Arthur Herman, *To Rule the Waves: How the British Navy Shaped the Modern World* (New York, 2004), 332, 337; Hague, *Pitt the Younger*, 281, 282; Donald R. Hickey, *Don't Give Up the Ship: Myths of the War of 1812* (Urbana, IL, 2006), 7.

instant," he wrote in January 1806, "one man bestriding the continent of Europe like a Colossus, and another roaming unbridled on the ocean."[3] America was caught between these two leviathans, which, involved as they were in a life-or-death struggle for supremacy, could scarcely pay much attention to the concerns of the awkward young republic three thousand miles away. Napoleon thought that it would take at least two or three centuries before the United States could pose a military threat to Europe.

Americans, however, never fully appreciated this European disdain for their country's power. They had an extraordinary emotional need to exaggerate their importance in the world—a need that lay behind their efforts to turn their diplomacy into a major means of defining their national identity.

JEFFERSON AND THE REPUBLICANS, in control of the national government for the first time since the European war began, put forth a peculiar conception of the United States and its role in the world. Like the Federalists, they believed that the United States had to remain neutral amid Europe's quarrels. But more than the Federalists, they insisted, to the point of threatening war, on the right of the United States to trade with the European belligerents without restraint or restrictions. They held that free ships made free goods, which meant that neutrals had the right to carry non-contraband goods into the ports of a belligerent without their being seized by its opponent. They believed that the list of contraband articles—articles subject to seizure by the belligerents, including those owned by neutral nations—should be narrowly defined and not include, for example, provisions and naval stores. In addition, the Republicans believed that blockades of belligerent ports should be backed up by naval power and not simply declared on paper.

With the outbreak of war in the early 1790s and Britain in control of the seas, France and Spain found it much too risky to use their own ships to carry goods between their islands in the West Indies and Europe. Consequently, they had had thrown open their hitherto closed ports in the Caribbean to American commerce. American merchants as neutrals had begun developing a profitable carrying trade between the French and Spanish West Indies and the home countries in Europe, taking sugar, for example, from the French West Indies to France and returning with manufactured goods. By September 1794 Americans had completely absorbed all the foreign trade with the West Indies—British, French, and Dutch combined.[4]

3. Dumas Malone, *Jefferson the President: Second Term, 1805–1809* (Boston, 1974), 95.
4. Stanley Elkins and Eric McKitrick, *The Age of Federalism* (New York, 1993), 826 n8.

As the European wars continued, this re-export or carrying trade became even more profitable, increasing in value from $500,000 in 1790 to nearly $60 million by 1807. Between 1793 and 1807 the total value of all American re-exports was $493 million, an average of nearly $33 million a year.[5]

Not only did American merchants, especially New Englanders, dominate the re-export trade between the West Indies and Europe, but these shippers were also major re-exporters of goods from Asia. Sailing by way of Cape Horn, American merchants brought home products from Canton, China, and ports in the Indian Ocean, including teas, coffee, chinaware, spices, and silks, before shipping them on to Europe, especially to markets in the Netherlands as well as those in France, Italy, and Spain. In fact, between 1795 and 1805 American trade with India was greater than that of all the European nations combined.[6] At the same time, Americans imported the manufactured goods of Europe and Great Britain and re-exported most of them to the West Indies, South America, and elsewhere. During the crucial war years of 1798–1800 and 1805–1807 the value of goods in America's re-export trade exceeded the value of American-made goods sent abroad.

Many of the merchants involved in this re-export trade made fortunes, including William Gray, Elias Hasket Derby, and Joseph Peabody of Salem, Nicholas Brown II and Thomas P. Ives of Providence, John Jacob Astor and Archibald Gracie of New York, and Stephen Girard of Philadelphia. At the height of his business in 1807 Gray was worth over $3 million; he reputedly owned 115 vessels, annually employed three hundred seaman, and, as his obituary said in 1825, was "probably... engaged in a more extensive commercial enterprise than any man who has lived on this continent in any period of its history."[7]

All of this re-export trade turned the United States into the largest neutral carrier of goods in the world. In 1790 American ships had carried only about 40 percent of the value of all goods involved in America's foreign trade; by 1807 American ships were carrying 92 percent of a much larger volume—from combined imports and exports of $43 million in 1790 to $246 million in 1807. Between 1793 and 1807, the value of American imports and exports increased nearly sixfold, and American ship tonnage tripled. Even accounting for a price inflation of 26 percent between 1790 and 1807, these were impressive figures.[8]

5. Curtis P. Nettles, *The Emergence of a National Economy, 1775–1915* (New York, 1962), 396, 235.
6. Ted Widmer, *Ark of the Liberties: America and the World* (New York, 2008), 66.
7. Samuel Willard Crompton, "William Gray," *American National Biography*, ed. John A. Garraty and Mark C. Carnes (Oxford, 1999), 9: 453.
8. Hickey, *Don't Give Up the Ship*, 27.

With so much of its income and wealth involved in overseas trade, it was not surprising that the United States government vigorously supported freedom for neutral commerce on the high seas in wartime. Great Britain, as a strong naval power, however, never agreed with the liberal principles of wartime commerce that were so dear to the Americans. Since the British navy controlled the seas, the British government quite understandably thought that the American carrying trade between the French and Spanish West Indies and Europe was actually French and Spanish trade covered by the American flag. The British protested that this trade violated what they called the Rule of 1756, which stipulated that commerce prohibited in time of peace was also prohibited in time of war. This rule, which the British had first set forth during the Seven Years' War, thus enabled British prize courts (courts that judged the legitimacy of the seizure of enemy ships or enemy goods on neutral ships) to deny the right of neutral nations in wartime to trade with ports in belligerent countries that had been closed to them in peacetime—which had been the case for the Americans with the French and Spanish empires. Britain was especially eager to prevent the neutral United States from carrying goods between the Caribbean colonies of France and Spain and ports in Europe. The British denied that "free ships made free goods" and declared that they would take enemy property wherever they could find it, even from neutral ships on the high seas.

In order to comply with the British Rule of 1756 American shippers developed the legal fiction of the "broken voyage." By carrying goods from the French and Spanish colonies to ports in the United States, unloading and paying duties on them, and then reloading and receiving rebates on most of the duties before re-exporting them to France and Spain as presumably American and therefore neutral goods, American traders technically conformed to the British Rule of 1756. At first tacitly and then officially, as determined by a British admiralty court in 1800 in the case of the *Polly*, British authorities had accepted this practice of the "broken voyage," ruling that enemy goods became neutral property if imported into the United States before being re-exported. The American re-export trade thrived, and the Republicans became its great defenders.

The situation was bizarre. The Republicans in the Congress were those most determined to promote the neutral rights of Americans to carry belligerent goods throughout the world in wartime without fear of their vessels and crew being seized by the belligerents. Yet curiously nearly all the congressional Republicans came from areas in the South and West that supplied few if any of the ships and sailors that were being taken by the belligerents. By contrast, the section of the country, Federalist New England, that did supply the bulk of the ships and sailors for America's overseas commerce was the section most opposed to the Republicans' policy of defending America's neutral rights on the high seas. Republicans seemed obsessed with overseas trade even though most of them or their constituents were not directly engaged in it; they even carried their promotion of neutral rights to the point of wanting to prohibit America's participation in the very international trade that made a defense of neutral rights necessary. It seemed as if many Republicans really did not like overseas commerce yet were eager to defend the rights of Americans to engage in it.

In fact, many Republicans did dislike much of the overseas commerce they were defending, believing that there was something fraudulent about the commercial riches that the European wars were bringing to America. Merchants involved in the carrying trade, especially New England merchants, who were mostly Federalists, seemed to be prospering simply from America's neutrality. John Randolph objected strongly to having "this great agricultural nation" governed by urban merchants. He called the carrying trade—"this mushroom, this fungus of war"—utterly dishonest and wanted no part in defending it.[9]

Although Jefferson knew the re-export trade was lucrative, he too was not happy with a commerce that tended to get America involved in Europe's wars, especially with American ships' carrying the goods of belligerents. He believed that "a steady application to agriculture with just trade enough to take off its superfluities is our wisest course." By contrast, he said, the carrying trade fed on the evils of war and encouraged "a spirit of gambling" and the desire to make money without labor. Those merchants engaged in the wartime re-export trade produced nothing of their own and only profited from the work done by others. By becoming merely neutral carriers of goods, Americans, Jefferson concluded despairingly, were launched "into the ocean of speculation, led to over trade ourselves, tempted to become robbers under French colors, and to quit the pursuit of Agriculture the surest road to affluence and the best preservative of morals."[10] Not only did Jefferson, aristocratic Southern planter that he was, express disdain for what he thought were the low pecuniary motives of merchants, but he hated and thought "absurd" the fact that commerce was "converting this great agricultural country into a city of Amsterdam,—a mere headquarters for carrying on the commerce of all nations."[11]

9. Bradford Perkins, *Prologue to War: England and the United States, 1805–1812* (Berkeley, 1968), 111–12.
10. Burton Spivak, *Jefferson's English Crisis: Commerce, Embargo, and the Republican Revolution* (Charlottesville, 1979), 9; TJ to John Blair, 13 Aug. 1787, *Papers of Jefferson,* 12: 28.
11. Robert W. Tucker and David C. Hendrickson, *Empire of Liberty: The Statecraft of Thomas Jefferson* (New York, 1990), 213.

Despite this contempt for America's neutral carrying trade, which he thought benefited mostly his Federalist enemies, Jefferson as president devoted most of his diplomatic energies to defending it. As a result, he not only quarreled with Britain but nearly went to war with the former mother country, a war that above all he wanted to avoid. In trying to implement his policy, he ended up completely stopping the flow of all American overseas trade and at the same time repressing his fellow citizens to a degree rarely duplicated in the entire history of the United States. Jefferson's extraordinary efforts to defend the rights of neutrals to trade freely drove the country into a deep depression and severely damaged his presidency. He ended up violating much of what he and his party stood for.

NOT ONLY DID JEFFERSON and the Republicans have unusual ideas about America's political economy, but, more important, they possessed a radical appreciation of the role of commerce in international affairs and an inspired vision of what the world might be.

Jefferson's foreign policy grew out of his hopes for America's domestic economy. Unlike the Federalists, who anticipated the United States eventually—maybe in a half century or less—developing a diversified and balanced manufacturing economy like that of Great Britain, Jefferson and the other Republican leaders, but not many of their Northern followers, wanted the United States to remain predominantly rural and agricultural. Jefferson and Madison certainly did not want or expect America to become more like commercially developed Europe, at least not in the foreseeable future. Madison in the Constitutional Convention had warned of a time in the distant future when "a great majority of the people will not only be without landed, but any other sort of property," and reminded his colleagues that "we see in the populous Countries in Europe now what we shall be hereafter."[12] But he and many other Republicans hoped that that depressing future might be put off—for at least a century or two—by the prevalence of free land in America and by the fact that most Americans remained independent farmers. Believing in the same four-stage theory of social development as the Federalists, the Republican leaders had a vested interest in freezing time and holding America back from becoming sophisticated and luxury-loving like the nations of the Old World. And from the evidence of the seemingly unchanging rural and farming character of American society in the early nineteenth century, they were increasingly confident that the nation was pretty firmly fixed in the agricultural stage of development.

12. Max Farrand, ed., *The Records of the Federal Convention of 1787* (New Haven, 1911, 1937), 2: 203–4, 124.

While most Federalists were disappointed that the society was not becoming more urban, more complicated, and more hierarchical, the Republican leaders welcomed America's social stasis. They celebrated the dominance of farming and the absence of the large-scale urban manufacturing that was characteristic of the poverty and decadence that afflicted the Old World. Jefferson in his *Notes on the State of Virginia* had argued that no people in their right minds would ever voluntarily turn to manufacturing. The British and French had begun industrializing only because they had run out of land and their farmers had been forced to migrate to the cities and become dependent laborers working in houses of industry turning out gewgaws and other superfluities that no one actually needed. But Americans, said Jefferson, were not in that situation. "We have an immensity of land courting the industry of the husbandman." The more farmers the healthier the society, said Jefferson. "While we have land to labour then, let us never wish to see our citizens occupied at a work-bench, or twirling a distaff.... Let our work-shops remain in Europe."[13]

Although the Southern Republican leaders were opposed to European-style urban manufacturing, they were not opposed to commerce. Quite the contrary: overseas commerce was essential to preventing the development of large-scale manufacturing. Although Jefferson in the 1780s had talked wistfully of having America "stand with respect to Europe precisely on the footing of China," practicing "neither commerce nor navigation," so that "we should thus avoid wars, and all our citizens would be husbandmen," he realized this was "theory only, and a theory which the servants of America are not at liberty to follow." The American people had "a decided taste for navigation and commerce," and the country's political leaders had to take this taste into account. The best way to promote international trade was "by throwing open all the doors of commerce and knocking off its shackles."[14]

Opening up trade abroad became crucial for the Republican leaders. Desiring as they did the United States to remain predominantly rural and agricultural, they were confronted with the problem of ensuring sufficient markets for the agricultural surpluses of America's many hardworking and productive farmers. Since the Southern Republicans did not want America to develop huge urban centers, they could not assume the existence of a large domestic market for the surpluses of farm goods. If the farmers were unable to sell their produce somewhere, they would stagnate, slip into mere subsistence farming, and become idle and lazy and

13. TJ, *Notes on the State of Virginia*, ed. William Peden (Chapel Hill, 1955), 164–65.
14. TJ to G. K. van Hogendorp, 13 Oct. 1785, *Papers of Jefferson*, 8: 633.

eventually morally unfit for republican government. Hence developing markets abroad for America's agricultural produce became essential for sustaining America's experiment in republicanism. The Federalists, declared Jefferson, could not have been more wrong in thinking him "an enemy of commerce. They admit me a friend of agriculture, and suppose me an enemy to the only means of disposing of its produce."[15]

But since the European states would not open up their markets voluntarily, Jefferson and other Republican leaders thought that the only recourse America had was to "adopt a system which may shackle them in our ports as they do us in theirs." The English especially were pig-headed in resisting the liberalization of their commerce. Jefferson had concluded as early as the 1780s that "nothing will bring them to reason but physical obstruction, applied to their bodily senses." "We must shew them," he said, "that we are capable of foregoing commerce with them, before they will be capable of consenting to an equal commerce."[16] America had to create its own navigation system and use commercial retaliation against the European states, especially Great Britain, in order to compel them to free up their international trade.

The Republicans were confident of America's ability to bring economic pressure on Great Britain because they believed that it was more commercially dependent on the United States than the other way round. Although Britain was the chief purchaser of American exports, which the Republicans regarded as "necessaries," it was also selling America more goods than any other country. Because Britain supplied nearly 80 percent of America's imports, it seemed to the Republicans to be particularly dependent on American markets for its industries. And because the former mother country sent to America mostly manufactured "luxuries" or "superfluities," Britain seemed particularly vulnerable to American commercial coercion.[17]

Although Americans always overestimated the effectiveness of the nonimportation agreements of the 1760s and 1770s, many continued to see them as America's special weapon against Great Britain. "It is universally agreed," wrote the well-known merchant William Bingham in 1784, "that no country is more dependent on foreign demand, for the superfluous

15. TJ to William Jackson, 18 Feb. 1801, *Papers of Jefferson*, 33: 14; Spivak, *Jefferson's English Crisis*, 8; Drew R. McCoy, *The Elusive Republic: Political Economy in Jeffersonian America* (Chapel Hill, 1980), ch. 3.
16. TJ to G. K. van Hogendorp, 13 Oct. 1785, to JM, 18 March 1785, *Papers of Jefferson*, 8: 633, 40.
17. J.C.A. Stagg, *Mr. Madison's War: Politics, Diplomacy, and Warfare in the Early American Republic, 1783–1830* (Princeton, 1983), 14; Nettles, *Emergence of a National Economy*, 232–36.

produce of art and industry [than England];—and that the luxury and extravagance of her inhabitants, have already advanced to the ultimate point of abuse, and cannot be so increased, as to augment the home consumption, in proportion to the decrease that will take place on a diminution of foreign trade."[18]

In other words, if the Americans restricted their purchases of English luxury goods, there being no market elsewhere for them, the manufacturing poor in England would be thrown out of work, leading to hunger and rioting, which would force the government to change its policies. The possibility of taking advantage of England's susceptibility to this kind of economic coercion had been undermined by Jay's Treaty of 1795, which is why the Republicans hated it so much.

IN 1801 THE REPUBLICANS were at long last in control of the national government and in a position to bring pressure to bear on the British to break up their navigation system as soon as Jay's Treaty lapsed in 1803. Yet as important as this need for markets for America's agricultural produce was to the Republicans, it would be a mistake to see the foreign policy of the administrations of Jefferson and Madison as simply designed to compel Great Britain to open up more of its markets to American goods. The quarrel the Republicans had with Britain was much more political than economic. They did not want merely to change Britain's navigation policies; they wanted to change its monarchical regime.

The Republicans had never been happy with the foreign policy of the Federalist administrations, which they thought were decidedly biased toward the British. They especially resented British dominance over American commerce. By restricting the commerce of the former mother country, they believed, they could thrust a dagger into the heart of Britain's power.

Despite America's best efforts to establish trade with other nations in the aftermath of the Revolution, the country had not been able to throw off the hammerlock Britain had over American commerce. Never mind that much of America's prosperity rested on this commerce. They wanted to restrict it in order to enlarge it, or so they said publicly; actually they wanted much more.

The Republican leaders had multiple motives for their actions. They were actually less concerned with the country's commercial prosperity than they were with America's status in the world. They resented Europe's and especially Britain's view of the United States as a lesser nation. Not only did the Republicans dream of creating a new kind of world politics that would preclude the traditional resort to war, but, more important, as

18. McCoy, *The Elusive Republic*, 125.

citizens of a fledgling republic they wanted international acknowledgment of their nation's independence and identity, particularly from the former mother country. Since a nation's ability to exchange goods with other states in the world, along with its capacity to wage war, was a principal measure of its equal status as a sovereign state, the Republicans believed that resorting to economic coercion against Great Britain would be a fitting reminder that the United States had actually won the War of Independence.[19]

The Republicans came to power in 1801 very much committed to the liberal principles of international commerce that Americans had first sought to implement in the model treaty of 1776. Their ultimate aim, confused and confusing as it often was, was truly grandiose.

Although these liberal principles involved establishing free trade throughout the world, their purpose was not merely to promote commercial prosperity everywhere but to promote peace everywhere. If all nations treated foreign ships and goods as they treated their own ships and goods, commerce among nations would flow freely and dissolve the artificial mercantilist barriers the monarchies of Europe had erected. This free flow of commerce, many Republicans hoped, would tie nations together peacefully and change the way international politics had traditionally been conducted. The exchanges of commerce would substitute for the political rivalries of military-minded monarchical governments and create the possibilities for a universal peace. The secret was to get rid of monarchy and establish republics everywhere, which was why many Republicans clung so desperately to the idea of the French Republic, even when the reality of the Napoleonic dictatorship made that faith increasingly untenable.

The Republicans believed that republics were naturally peace-loving, while monarchies thrived on war-making. "Of all the enemies to public liberty," Madison had written in 1795, "war is, perhaps, the most to be dreaded, because it comprises and develops the germ of every other [enemy]." As "the parent of armies," not only did war promote "debts and taxes," but, he said, it also meant that "the discretionary power of the Executive is extended; its influence in dealing out offices, honors, and emoluments is multiplied; and all the means of seducing the minds, are added to those of subduing the force, of the people."[20] In 1806 the old radical Thomas Paine was still echoing these liberal sentiments. Precisely because Great Britain was a monarchy, Paine thought it would never make peace. The British government was "committed in a war system,"

19. David Armitage, *The Declaration of Independence: A Global History* (Cambridge, MA, 2007), 61.
20. JM, "Political Observations," 20 April 1795, *Papers of Madison*, 15: 518.

he told a visitor to his lodgings in New York, "and would prosecute it as long as it had the means."[21] In contrast to the Federalists, who believed that the only way to prepare for war was to build up the government and armed forces in a European manner, Republicans thought that the United States as a republic neither needed nor could safely afford a traditional army and navy and a bloated war-making government. "Our constitution is a peace establishment—it is not calculated for war," declared President Jefferson. "War would endanger its existence."[22]

It was just this sort of thinking that lay behind the Democratic-Republicans' excitement over the undersea warfare inventions of Robert Fulton. Fulton, who spent two decades abroad between 1787 and 1806 mingling with radicals like Thomas Paine and Joel Barlow, became convinced that submarines and torpedoes could revolutionize naval warfare. By being able to destroy warships "by means so new, so secret, and so incalculable," submarines, said Fulton, would render conventional naval warfare impossible. Not knowing where the underwater attacks would come from, sailors would be demoralized and fleets would be "rendered worthless." Without navies, nations, in particular Great Britain, would be compelled to liberalize their trade and practice the freedom of the seas that Americans had long advocated. This in turn would lead to the universal and perpetual peace that every enlightened person, but especially Americans, yearned for. Fulton built a prototype of a submarine and called it *Nautilus*. Although he knew his submarine was but an infant, he saw in it "an Infant hercules which at one grasp will Strangle the Serpents which poison and convulse the American Constitution."[23]

Fulton returned to the United States eager to demonstrate his new invention. In 1807 he used one of his torpedoes, which were actually mines, to blow up a brig in New York Harbor, an experiment that Washington Irving's *Salmagundi* mocked as the destruction of the British fleet in effigy. Nevertheless, the Republicans were excited. In a Fourth of July address in 1809 his friend and patron Joel Barlow declared that Fulton's submarine project "carries in itself the eventual destruction of naval tyranny" and the possibility of freeing "mankind from the scourge of naval wars."[24]

21. Lance Banning, *The Jeffersonian Persuasion: Evolution of a Party Ideology* (Ithaca, 1978), 253; John Melish, *Travels Through the United States of America, in the Years 1806 and 1807, and 1809, 1810, and 1811* (London, 1815), 61–62, 103.

22. Malone, *Jefferson the President: Second Term*, 76; Everett Summerville Brown, ed., *William Plumer's Memorandum of Proceedings in the United States Senate, 1803–1807* (New York, 1923), 470.

23. Wallace Hutcheon Jr., *Robert Fulton: Pioneer of Undersea Warfare* (Annapolis, 1981), 37.

24. Joel Barlow, *Oration, Delivered at Washington, July Fourth, 1809; at the Request of the Democratic Citizens of the District of Columbia* (Washington, DC, 1809), 8.

With this kind of support from a leading Republican intellectual and with the publication of his *Torpedo War and Submarine Explosions* in 1810, Fulton was invited to address the Congress and to conduct further tests of his underwater devices. The Republican Congress, despite its reputation for penny-pinching, even appropriated five thousand dollars to fund his experiments. Although Fulton had many doubters, especially in the navy and among the Federalists, Jefferson had nothing but praise for his devices. In April 1810 the former president told Fulton that he hoped that "the torpedo may go the whole length you expect of putting down navies." Indeed, he wished the scheme to succeed "too much not to become an easy convert & to give it all my prayers & interest.... That the Tories should be against you is in character, because it will curtail the power of their idol, England." Although most of Fulton's torpedo experiments were unsuccessful, the Jeffersonian Republican dream of creating the conditions for a universal peace did not die.[25]

When some Republicans urged that all diplomatic missions be replaced with consuls, which were all that was required to handle international trade, foreign observers were stunned. "They are singular, these people," declared the new Russian chargé in Washington. "They want commercial ties without political ties. It seems to me however that the one necessarily depends on the other." This may have been true for the old monarchical world, but not, in the eyes of the Jeffersonians, for the new republican world.[26]

Although Hamilton had thought Jefferson and Madison utopian dreamers, the Republican leaders were not completely naïve about the world. They feared, as Madison had written in 1792, that "a universal and perpetual peace...will never exist but in the imaginations of visionary philosophers, or in the breasts of benevolent enthusiasts." Nevertheless, because war was so foolish as well as wicked, the Republican leaders still hoped that the progress of reason might eventually end war; "and if anything is to be hoped," Madison had said, "every thing ought to be tried."[27] This deep desire to avoid a conventional war if at all possible became the driving force of Republican policy over the entire period.

The Republicans did concede that even republics might occasionally have to go to war. But if wars were declared solely by the authority of the people, and, more important, if the costs of these wars were borne directly and solely by the generation that declared them, then, Madison had

25. Hutcheon, *Robert Fulton*, 109; Robert J. Allison, *Stephen Decatur: American Naval Hero, 1779–1820* (Amherst, MA, 2005), 104–5.
26. Irving Brant, *James Madison: The President, 1809–1812* (Indianapolis, 1956), 69.
27. JM, "Universal Peace" (1792), *Madison: Writings*, 505.

written in 1795, "ample reward would accrue to the state." All "wars of folly" would be avoided, and only brief "wars of necessity and defence" would remain, and even these might disappear. "If all nations were to follow [this] example," said Madison, "the reward would be doubled to each, and the temple of Janus might be shut, never to be opened again."[28] This was an aspect of the liberal dream of a universal peace shared by the enlightened everywhere.

In a world of monarchies, however, the Republicans concluded that the best hope for the United States to avoid war was to create some sort of peaceful republican alternative to it. "War is not the best engine for us to resort to," said Jefferson; "nature has given us one *in our commerce*, which, if properly managed, will be a better instrument for obliging the interested nations of Europe to treat us with justice."[29] Peaceful coercions, using commercial discrimination against foreign enemies and backed ultimately by the withholding of American commerce, were, said Madison, "the most likely means of obtaining our objects without war."[30] In other words, most Republican leaders, especially Jefferson and Madison, believed in the use of economic sanctions—something that even today is often invoked as an alternative to the direct use of military force.

BEFORE JEFFERSON COULD ATTEMPT to use this powerful weapon against the former mother country, however, he needed to deal with the long-standing problem with the Barbary pirates.[31] In Jefferson's mind this was linked to the main problem with England itself, and that linkage made him much more eager to resort to military force in dealing with the Barbary States than he otherwise might have been.

Actually, when it came to promoting American interests, Jefferson was quite willing to put aside his most deep-rooted prejudices. In the summer of 1805 he even toyed with the possibility of forming an alliance with Britain in order to show both France and Spain (the latter had declared war on Britain in December 1804) that the United States could not be pushed around, especially on the issue of America's expansive boundaries of

28. Janus, the ancient Roman god, was noted not only for two-facedness. To commemorate him the Romans always left the temple of Janus open in time of war so that the god could come to their aid. The door was only closed when Rome was at peace.

29. TJ to JM, 28 Aug. 1789, *Republic of Letters*, 629; Gerald Stourzh, *Alexander Hamilton and the Idea of Republican Government* (Stanford, 1970), 266; Spivak, *Jefferson's English Crisis*, 6, 7.

30. JM, "Political Observations" (1795), *Papers of Madison*, 15, 518–19.

31. Frank Lambert, *The Barbary Wars: American Independence in the Atlantic World* (New York, 2005), 7.

Louisiana. It was unlikely that he ever would have gone that far. But dealing with the Barbary States was another matter. Since neither he nor Madison wanted the European states to take advantage of "the presumed aversion of this Country to war," the Republican leaders were certainly not going to let the "petty" tyrants of North Africa get away with anything.[32]

By the end of the eighteenth century the Barbary States of North Africa—Morocco, Algiers, Tunis, and Tripoli—had lost much of their former power in the Mediterranean world. They were no longer a threat to the great powers of Britain and France, which simply bought them off with annual tributes and used them to rid the Mediterranean of smaller rival trading peoples, such as the Danes or the Italian city-states. These smaller nations, without powerful navies or the resources to buy off the North African pirates, were vulnerable to having their ships and sailors seized and thus tended to leave the bulk of the Mediterranean trade to the great powers. The newly independent United States found itself in this vulnerable position.

As long as the American merchantmen had remained colonists of Great Britain, they had been protected by the British flag. But with independence, America's merchant ships became easy prey for these Barbary pirates, or privateers, which is the legal status most Europeans gave to the Muslim raiders. (Privateers had commissions from their governments and presumably only attacked ships belonging to states against which their governments had declared war.) The British government was delighted that commercial competition from the United States would be thwarted. "It is not probable the American states will have a very free trade in the Mediterranean," declared Lord Sheffield in 1784 on behalf of the British ministry; "it will not be in the interest of any of the great maritime powers to protect them there from the Barbary States."[33]

In 1784 Morocco captured an American ship but did not enslave its sailors; instead, in 1786 it signed a peace treaty with the United States, which still exists, making it the longest-standing treaty in American diplomatic history.[34] In 1785 Algiers, encouraged by Great Britain, captured two American ships and did enslave their crews. Lacking any resources, financial or otherwise, to retaliate, the Confederation Congress remained helpless, angered by the belief, as one American newspaper reported, that "those Barbarians are countenanced in their Depredations upon our

32. JM to TJ, 20 Aug. 1805, *Republic of Letters*, 1379–80; Lambert, *Barbary Wars*, 123.
33. Lambert, *Barbary Wars*, 47.
34. Robert J. Allison, ed., *Narratives of Barbary Captivity: Recollections of James Leander Cathcart, Jonathan Cowdry, and William Ray* (Chicago, 2007), xxxi.

Commerce by the British Court." Americans were convinced that the British government had the ultimate aim of making British ships the "Carriers of all the Property imported and exported between Britain and America."[35] Not only did this humiliation at the hands of these Muslim pirates contribute to the Americans' willingness to create a much stronger national government in 1787, but it intensified the rage many Americans felt toward the former mother country.

Throughout the 1780s Jefferson took a hard line against the Barbary States. He believed that they were so caught up in Islamic fatalism and Ottoman tyranny that their backward and indolent societies were beyond reform. He concluded that military force might be the only way to deal with these Muslim pirates. Offer them commercial treaties on the basis of equality and reciprocity, he said, and if they refuse and demand tribute, then "go to war with them."[36] John Adams disagreed. He thought it would be cheaper to pay tribute to these North African states than to go to war with them. "For an Annual Interest of 30,000 pounds sterling then and perhaps for 15,000 or 10,000 we can have Peace, when a War would sink us annually ten times as much." Jefferson countered with his own costs and calculations, including the creation of a "fleet of 150 guns, the one half of which shall be in constant cruise," all pointing to the advantages of fighting instead of paying tribute.[37] As these two ministers, one in Paris, the other in London, engaged in their debate over how best to deal with the Barbary States during the 1780s, they came to realize that the Confederation government was in no position either to go to war or to pay tributes.

Although the United States had ratified the liberal commercial treaty with Morocco in 1787, the Republic, even under the new federal Constitution, could not so easily deal with Algiers. In 1793, before the Washington administration could straighten out its policy toward the North African states and negotiate treaties with them, Algiers captured eleven more American ships and 105 sailors, who were enslaved along with the earlier captured sailors. These seizures finally goaded Congress into action. In 1794 it voted one million dollars to purchase a peace and ransom the American prisoners and another million to build a naval force of six frigates, marking the beginning of the U.S. Navy under the Constitution.

The growing split between Federalists and Republicans in Congress complicated matters. Being no longer part of the administration, Jefferson

35. Lambert, *Barbary Wars*, 48.
36. TJ to James Monroe, 11 Nov. 1784, *Papers of Jefferson*, 7: 511.
37. JA to TJ, 6 June 1786, to JA, 11 July 1786, in Lester J. Cappon, ed., *The Adams-Jefferson Letters: The Complete Correspondence Between Thomas Jefferson and Abigail and John Adams* (Chapel Hill, 1959), 1: 133–34, 141–43.

took a somewhat different view of the use of force. In fact, Jefferson's advocacy of military might in any circumstances was always limited. Force was sometimes justified, but never if it resulted in an expansion of executive power and the sacrifice of republican values. He and other Republicans saw the Federalist military buildup against Algiers as a ploy to enhance presidential power at the expense of liberty. Congressman William Branch Giles of Virginia joined a number of other Republicans in declaring that navies were "very foolish things" that could only lead to heavy taxes and a bloated office-laden European-type government. Better than building frigates at a horrendous expense, the United States should forget about the Mediterranean and protect America's coastline with some relatively inexpensive gunboats.[38]

The Federalists controlled Congress, however, and pushed on with negotiations and the building of the six frigates, some of which ended up being used against the French in the Quasi-War. In 1795 the United States agreed to a humiliating treaty with Algiers that cost a million dollars in tributes and ransoms—an amount equal to 16 percent of federal revenue for the year. The government realized that the frigates would not be ready for several years and that the country stood to gain more from trade in the Mediterranean than the peace treaty cost. As soon as the treaty was ratified in 1796, Congress, confident that there would be no more seizures of American ships, cut back the number of warships to three. The government opened negotiations with Tunis and Tripoli, which had begun seizing American merchantmen. By the end of the decade the United States had treaties with all the Barbary States, but the cost was exorbitant, $1.25 million, over 20 percent of the federal government's annual budget.[39]

Unfortunately, the Barbary States regarded treaties simply as a means of extracting more tributes and presents, and the threats and demands for more money, and the humiliations, continued. Tripoli felt it was not being treated equally with Algiers, and early in March 1801 it declared war on the United States and began seizing American merchant ships.

President Jefferson came to office several weeks later apparently determined to change American policy. "Nothing will stop the eternal increase of demand from these pirates," he told Secretary of State Madison in 1801, "but the presence of an armed force, and it will be more economical and more honorable to use the same means at once for suppressing their insolencies."[40] Yet Jefferson's strict construction of the Constitution made

---

38. Robert J. Allison, *The Crescent Obscured: The United States and the Muslim World, 1776–1815* (New York, 1995), 21.
39. Lambert, *Barbary Wars*, 93.
40. TJ to JM, 28 Aug. 1801, *Republic of Letters*, 1194.

him reluctant to engage the pirates offensively without a formal congressional declaration of war.

The Federalists, led by Hamilton in the press, pounced on this reluctance and forced the Republican Congress in 1802 to grant the president authority to use all means necessary to defeat the Tripolitan pirates. But the American blockade of Tripoli proved ineffective, mainly because the frigates could not maneuver in the shallow waters of Tripoli's harbor. At the same time, Secretary of the Treasury Gallatin and the Republicans in the Congress were concerned with the rising cost of maintaining a naval force in the Mediterranean. They feared the possibility of "increasing taxes, encroaching government, temptations to offensive wars, &c," more than the Barbary pirates.[41]

Still, the administration was determined to act, even if only with a minimum expenditure of funds and what President Jefferson referred to as "the smallest force competent" to the mission.[42] In 1803 it appointed a new experienced commander for the Mediterranean squadron, Commodore Edward Preble, and sent several small gunboats to the Mediterranean. Before Preble could deploy his new force, the frigate USS *Philadelphia* and its three-hundred man crew, commanded by twenty-nine-year-old William Bainbridge, was accidentally beached in Tripoli's harbor and had to surrender to an array of Tripolitan gunboats. The Pasha Yussef Karamanli of Tripoli set his initial demand for ransoming the newly captured American slaves at $1,690,000, more than the entire military budget of the United States.[43]

United States naval officers were determined to do something. On February 16, 1804, twenty-five-year-old Lieutenant Stephen Decatur and his seventy-man crew entered Tripoli's harbor under cover of darkness in a disguised vessel with the intention of burning the *Philadelphia*, thus preventing its being used as a Tripolitan raider. Since the American ship was deep in Tripoli's harbor, surrounded by a dozen other armed vessels and under the castle's heavy batteries, it was a dangerous, even foolhardy, mission; but it succeeded admirably, without the single loss of an American. This action, which Lord Nelson called "the most bold and daring act of the age," turned Decatur into an instant celebrity and inspired extraordinary outbursts of American patriotism. At age twenty-five Decatur became the youngest man commissioned a captain in U.S. naval history.[44]

41. Allison, *Crescent Obscured*, 29.

42. TJ, Second Annual Message, 15 Dec. 1802, in James C. Richardson, ed., *A Compilation of the Messages and Papers of the Presidents, 1789–1897* (Washington, DC, 1900), 1: 331.

43. Richard Zacks, *The Pirate Coast: Thomas Jefferson, the First Marines, and the Secret Mission of 1805* (New York, 2005), 30.

44. Lambert, *Barbary Wars*, 144; Allison, *Crescent Obscured*, 190; Fletcher Pratt, *Preble's Boys: Commodore Preble and the Birth of American Sea Power* (New York, 1950), 94–95; Allison, *Stephen Decatur*, 45–54; Allison, ed., *Narratives of Barbary Captivity*, lxi.

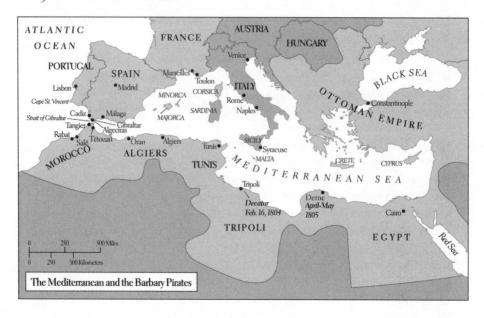

The Mediterranean and the Barbary Pirates

Emboldened by this success, Jefferson sent an even larger squadron to the Mediterranean under the command of Preble's senior, Samuel Barron, with the aim of punishing Tripoli. The expedition was to be paid for by a special tax on merchants trading in the Mediterranean, which the Federalists charged was an underhanded scheme to get the New England merchants to pay for the purchase of Louisiana. Following the advice of William Eaton, an ex-army captain and former consul to Tunis, the United States government authorized a loose alliance with the pasha of Tripoli's elder brother, Hamet Karamanli, who hoped to regain the throne his younger brother Yussef had taken from him. According to one historian, this was the U.S. government's "first overseas covert operation."[45]

In 1805 while the naval squadron besieged Tripoli, Eaton, who had an ambiguous status as an agent of the navy, and the pasha's brother Hamet marched west from Egypt five hundred miles across the Libyan Desert with a motley force of five hundred Greek, Albanian, and Arab mercenaries and a handful of marines. Their goal was to join up with Captain Isaac Hull and three American cruisers at Derne, the strategic Tripolitan port east of Tripoli. After a successful bombardment, Eaton's and Hull's marines took the fort at Derne. (This action later inspired the refrain of

45. Zacks, *Pirate Coast*, 377. The Arabic names and words have been transliterated in the form eighteenth-century English-speakers understood them, not in the more accurate modern transliteration.

the U.S. Marine Corps hymn, "to the shores of Tripoli.") Before Eaton could move his force against Tripoli, however, he learned that in June 1805 Tobias Lear, consul-general at Algiers, had signed a peace and commercial treaty with Tripoli ending the undeclared war.

Eaton felt betrayed by the U.S. government, and the war and what Eaton believed was its premature ending became caught up in partisan politics. The Federalists took every opportunity to chastise the Jefferson administration for its hesitancy in going to war against the Barbary States without a congressional declaration of war and for its ill-timed peace. Hamet did not get his throne back, but his family held in hostage was restored to him. The United States refused to pay any tribute to Tripoli, but it did pay a small ransom of sixty thousand dollars in order to get its imprisoned sailors released. Although the cynical European powers played down America's victory in this Tripolitan war, believing quite correctly that the pirates would ignore any treaty and would soon be back in business, many Americans celebrated it as a vindication of their policy of spreading free trade around the world and as a great victory for liberty over tyranny.

At the same time, however, many Americans could not ignore the contradiction between the Barbary States' enslaving seven hundred white sailors and their own country's enslaving hundreds of thousands of black Africans. As early as 1790 Benjamin Franklin had satirized this hypocrisy, and poets and playwrights juxtaposed the two forms of servitude in their works. Connecticut-born and Dartmouth-educated William Eaton had at once seen the contradiction upon his arrival in Tunis in 1799 as American consul. "Barbary is hell—," he wrote in his journal. "So, alas, is all America south of Pennsylvania; for oppression, and slavery, and misery, are there."[46]

BUT THIS CONTEST with the Barbary States was just a sideshow; the main act always involved America's relationship with Great Britain. Getting the British, however, to sign a liberal free trade treaty similar to that with Tripoli was highly unlikely. Not only would such a treaty be difficult to achieve, but it was not something that Jefferson really wanted, as events in 1805–1806 revealed.

Jefferson knew that America's prosperous trans-Atlantic carrying trade of French and Spanish colonial goods would require governmental

46. [Anon.], *The American in Algiers; or, The Patriot of Seventy-Six in Captivity* (New York, 1797), in James G. Basker et al., eds., *Early American Abolitionists: A Collection of Anti-Slavery Writings, 1760–1820* (New York, 2005), 242–61; Allison, *Crescent Obscured*, 92.

protection once war between Britain and France resumed, as it did in 1803. At first Britain seemed more or less willing to continue accepting the legal fiction of the "broken voyage," and America's carrying trade continued to flourish even though occasional seizures of American ships took place.

Suddenly in the summer of 1805 the Royal Navy began seizing scores of American merchant ships that assumed they were complying with the principle of the "broken voyage." Although Britain did not warn the United States of any change in policy, it had been contemplating tightening its treatment of the neutral carrying trade for some time. In the *Essex* decision in the spring of 1805 a British admiralty appeals court endorsed a change of policy and re-invoked the Rule of 1756 that had forbidden neutrals in time of war from trading within a mercantile empire closed to them in time of peace. By the new doctrine of the "continuous voyage," American merchants would now have to prove that they actually intended their voyages from the belligerent ports to terminate in the United States; otherwise the enemy goods they carried were liable to seizure.

This single decision undercut the lucrative trade that had gone on for years with only minor interruptions. By September 1805 Secretary of State Madison reported that America's merchants were "much alarmed" by the apparent change in British policy, for they had "several millions of property...afloat, subject to capture under the doctrine now enforced." Insurance rates quadrupled, and American merchants faced heavy losses. During the latter half of 1805 merchants in Philadelphia complained of over a hundred seizures, valued at $500,000.[47]

Many of the belligerents' vice-admiralty courts, which passed on the legality of the seizures, were remarkably impartial, but not all. Some of the British prize courts in the West Indies were corrupt and incompetent, and many of their decisions that went against American ship owners were later reversed by the High Court of Appeals in England. Because of these reversals, the actual number of condemnations was perhaps no more than 10 or 20 percent of the number of seizures. James Monroe, America's minister in London, told Secretary of State Madison in September 1805 that Britain "seeks to tranquillize us by dismissing our vessels in every case that she possibly can." But the appeals took time, usually four or five years, all the while the seized American ships were tied up in British ports.[48]

---

47. JM to TJ, 30 Sept. 1805, *Republic of Letters*, 1389; Donald Hickey, "The Monroe-Pinkney Treaty of 1806: A Reappraisal," WMQ, 44 (1987), 71.
48. Monroe to JM, 25 Sept. 1805, in Hickey, "Monroe-Pinkney Treaty of 1806," 72.

It was not the actual number of seizures that most irritated Americans; rather it was the British presumption that His Majesty's government had the right to decide just what American trade should be permitted or not permitted. It seemed to reduce America once again to the status of a colonial dependent. This was the fundamental issue that underlay America's turbulent relationship with Britain through the entire period of the European wars. *Aurora* editor William Duane went to the heart of the matter when in March 1807 he asked his readers, "Will you abandon your rights? Will you abandon your independence? Are you willing to become colonies of Great Britain?"[49]

From the 1790s through 1815 it was the Republicans alone who celebrated the Declaration of Independence and toasted as its author their leader, whom Joel Barlow called "the immortal Jefferson." The Republicans honored the Declaration, however, not for its promotion of individual rights and equality, as would be the case for all political parties after 1815, but for its denunciation of the British monarchy and its assertion that the new nation had assumed a "separate and equal Station...among the Powers of the Earth" — something the Republicans thought the Anglophilic Federalists were reluctant to acknowledge. Indeed, as late as 1823 Jefferson was still fulminating over the way the Federalists treated the Declaration, seeing it, he said, "as being a libel on the government of England...[that] should now be buried in utter oblivion to spare the feelings of our English friends and Angloman fellow citizens."[50]

The most humiliating grievance for Americans, the one that made them seem still under the thumb of the former mother country, was the British impressment of American seamen, a practice that John Quincy Adams labeled an "authorized system of kidnapping upon the ocean."[51] British captains of warships often stopped and inspected American commercial vessels even in American waters to see if there were any British subjects among the sailors. Such actions, said Jefferson, threatened American sovereignty. "We cannot be respected by France as a neutral nation, nor by the world ourselves as an independent one," he told Madison in 1804, "if we do not take effectual measures to support, at every risk, our authority in our own harbors."[52] The actual numbers of sailors that Britain impressed from American ships over this war period are unknown, the

---

49. Perkins, *Prologue to War*, 137.
50. Pauline Maier, *American Scripture: Making the Declaration of Independence* (New York, 1997), 170–75; Armitage, *Declaration of Independence*, 92, 165; TJ to JM, 30 Aug. 1823, *Republic of Letters*, 1876.
51. Malone, *Jefferson the President: Second Term*, 401.
52. TJ to JM, 15 Aug. 1804, *Republic of Letters*, 1335–36.

British admitting to more than three thousand, the Americans claiming at least double that figure.

The issue was serious and seemingly beyond compromise as long as Britain was in its life-or-death struggle with France. Since the Royal Navy needed to recruit at least ten thousand to twelve thousand new seamen every year, it relied heavily on impressing not only British subjects in their own seaports but also those who had deserted to the American merchant marine—a not insignificant number. According to estimates made by Secretary of the Treasury Gallatin, nine thousand of the twenty-four thousand sailors on American ships were actually British subjects—a figure, admitted Gallatin, that "was larger than we had figured."[53] With the Royal Navy seeming to be the sole obstacle to Napoleon's invasion of the British Isles, the British government naturally sought to get these sailors back and to discourage future deserters. It thus authorized its naval officers to board American merchant ships and impress into the British navy seamen who they believed were His Majesty's subjects and who lacked documents proving they were American citizens.

The British never claimed the right to impress American citizens, but since British and American sailors looked and sounded so much alike, aggressive British naval officers often made mistakes that might take years to correct. Although the United States did not employ press gangs to supply seamen for its navy, it never denied the right of the Royal Navy to impress British sailors on American ships in British ports. It did, however, deny Britain's authority to board American ships to impress men on the high seas. For their part, the British never admitted the right of the United States to do to them what they did to the United States; they never conceded the right of American naval officers to board British ships to impress American deserters—not that there were many of them. This discrepancy is what made impressment seem to the Americans to be an act of British neocolonialism.

The problem grew out of the British denial of the right of British subjects to expatriate and become citizens of another country. But, of course, despite the feelings of some Republicans that "man is born free" and "may remove out of the limits of these United States" at will, some Americans, especially in the judiciary, were not all that clear about the right of American citizens to expatriate either.[54] But the United States did offer immigrants a relatively easy route to naturalized citizenship—inconsistent

53. Hickey, "Monroe-Pinkney Treaty of 1806," 86.
54. Eugene Perry Link, *Democratic-Republican Societies, 1790–1800* (New York, 1942), 137; James H. Kettner, *The Development of American Citizenship, 1608–1870* (Chapel Hill, 1978), 271–73.

as that may have been with some judges' denial of the right of expatriation. Consequently, both nations often claimed the same persons as their own legitimate subjects or citizens.[55]

Neither Britain nor the United States could give way on the issue. It is easy to explain the British need to maintain impressment, which had become vital to Britain's security in its titanic struggle with Napoleon. But the Americans' fixation on impressment is not as easily explained. However brutal, the practice did not endanger the Americans' national security nor did the loss of even several thousand sailors threaten the existence of their navy or their merchant fleet. Since Americans did not deny the right of the British to search American ships for contraband goods, why, it was argued, could they not allow a search for British deserters — especially since, as Gallatin pointed out, over a third of American sailors were in fact British subjects?

Yet for most Americans, though not for most Federalists, none of this mattered. Impressment remained for most Republicans the rawest and most contentious issue dividing the United States and Britain. It was always first on the list of American complaints against British practices, and its abolition was always the sine qua non in negotiations with Britain. Although after 1808 the Republican leaders tended to place impressment behind neutral rights as a source of grievance, in the end they made it the most important of the reasons Americans went to war in 1812 against the former mother country.

Since most Americans, so British in heritage, language, and looks, could never be sure of their own national identity, they were acutely sensitive to any effort to blur the distinction between themselves and the British — something the Federalists were increasingly doing. The Federalist *Monthly Anthology* denied that there was any such thing as Americanness. Benjamin Rush in 1805 thought that most of the Federalists in Pennsylvania, "a majority of the old and wealthy *native* citizens," were "still Englishmen in their hearts." Indeed, Rush went so far as to say that Americans had "no national character, and however much we may boast of it, there are very few true Americans in the United States."[56]

Since a suffocating trans-Atlantic Englishness existed everywhere in the Americans' culture, it is not surprising that the Republicans came to see the British impressment of American sailors as a glaring example of America's lack of independence as a nation. The practice aroused so

---

55. Perkins, *Prologue to War*, 84–95.
56. Catherine O'Donnell Kaplan, *Men of Letters in the Early Republic: Cultivating Forums of Citizenship* (Chapel Hill, 2008), 201; BR to JA, 29 June, 14 Aug. 1805, *Spur of Fame*, 28, 31.

much anger precisely because it threw into the faces of the Americans the ambiguous and fluid nature of their national identity.

With both impressments of sailors and seizures of American ships increasing during the summer of 1805, Jefferson stopped talking of an alliance with Britain, and the American rapprochement with the former mother country that had begun with Jay's Treaty a decade earlier now came to an end. In his warlike message to Congress in December 1805 Jefferson called for the fortification of seaport towns, a substantial increase in the number of gunboats, the construction of six seventy-four-gun ships of the line, the creation of a naval militia reserve, and reorganization of the militia. Although he considered Britain's violation of neutral rights a greater "enormity" than Spanish intransigence over the Louisiana borders, he lumped them together as "injuries" that were "of a nature to be met by force only." If there were to be a war, he wanted it somehow to result in the acquisition of the Floridas.[57]

In response to the British injuries Congress considered cutting off all trade with the former mother country. Finally, however, in the spring of 1806 it passed a much milder Non-Importation Act, while rejecting the proposal to build the six ships of the line. Although the Non-Importation Act ignored the most important imports from Britain and prohibited only those British imports that Americans themselves could produce, the Republicans in Congress, fearful not only of spending money but of creating a military despotism, much preferred some sort of non-importation to building expensive ships. Furthermore, this bland measure was to be suspended until November 1806, provoking John Randolph's sneering (and prophetic) comment that it was "a milk and water bill, a dose of chicken broth to be taken nine months hence... too contemptible to be the object of consideration or to excite the feelings of the pettiest state in Europe."[58]

This Non-Importation Act and its suspension for nine months were designed to put pressure on the British and to give time for a special commission to Britain, composed of America's minister in London, James Monroe, and a Baltimore lawyer and former Federalist, William Pinkney, to seek a redress of America's grievances concerning impressment and neutral rights. Because the British violations of neutral rights and seizures of American ships resembled the situation that existed prior to the negotiation of the Jay Treaty, many thought that Monroe's and Pinkney's main mission was to negotiate a replacement for that treaty, which had expired in 1803.

57. Malone, *Jefferson the President: Second Term*, 69.
58. Malone, *Jefferson the President: Second Term*, 110.

Although American trade had flourished under the Jay Treaty, Jefferson and the Republicans had never liked the treaty, which had barred the United States from passing retaliatory commercial legislation. Jefferson called it "a millstone around our necks," and he had rejected British proposals to renew its commercial clauses when they had expired. If he had had his way, Monroe and Pinkney would have been authorized to deal with issues of neutral rights only, and not with issues of commerce. Jefferson, like many other Republicans, did not want to surrender the country's right to impose commercial sanctions against Great Britain, which it had yielded under the Jay Treaty. But pressure from Congress forced Jefferson to allow the Monroe-Pinkney mission to negotiate a whole host of issues between the two nations, including those concerning Anglo-American trade.[59]

Given Jefferson's feelings about the use of economic sanctions, the outlook for the treaty that Monroe and Pinkney sent back to the United States early in 1807 was not good. Since the treaty itself mentioned nothing about impressment on the high seas, Jefferson found it unacceptable and refused to send it to the Senate. "To tell you the truth," he supposedly said to a friend, "I do not wish any treaty with Great Britain." But since the British went out of their way to conciliate the Americans on the issue of impressment, informally promising to observe "the greatest caution" in impressing their sailors on American ships and to offer "immediate and prompt redress" to any American mistakenly impressed, Jefferson felt pressured to find other objections to the treaty.[60] What he particularly wanted to preserve was the right of the United States to retaliate commercially against Great Britain, the very thing the treaty was designed to avoid. "We will never tie our hands by treaty," he declared, "from the right of passing a non-importation or non-intercourse act, to make it in her interest to become just."[61] Although the commercial clauses gave Americans more advantages than they had had under the Jay Treaty, the unwillingness of Jefferson and many other Republicans to give up the weapon of commercial warfare probably doomed any treaty from the start.

With Napoleon's hopes of invading England shattered by Nelson's victory at Trafalgar in October 1805, the recently crowned French emperor turned to the weapon many Americans had been resorting to on and off for decades—economic sanctions against Great Britain.

59. Donald R. Hickey, *The War of 1812: A Forgotten Conflict* (Champaign: University of Illinois Press, 1990), 73.
60. Hickey, *War of 1812*, 14.
61. Merrill D. Peterson, *Thomas Jefferson and the New Nation: A Biography* (New York, 1970), 863–64.

Napoleon thus launched what came to be called the Continental System. In a series of decrees, beginning with the Berlin Decree in November 1806, issued five weeks after he had defeated the Prussians at Jena and Auerstädt and gained control of the ports on the North and Baltic seas, Napoleon believed he was in a position to stifle the British economy. He forbade all trade with the British Isles, ordered the confiscation of all goods coming from England or its colonies even when owned by neutrals, and made liable to seizure not only every British ship but any ship that had landed in England or its colonies. The British responded with a series of orders-in-council that proclaimed a blockade of all ports from which British goods were excluded and required neutral ships that wished to trade with these ports to stop in England and pay transit duties first. In December 1807 Napoleon answered with his Milan Decree, declaring that any neutral ship submitting to British trade regulations or even allowing a British search party to board was liable to seizure.

The net effect of all these regulations by the warring parties was to render all neutral commerce illegal and liable to seizure by one power or the other. Although by 1807 the French were seizing American ships in European ports, Britain's greater ability to capture Americans vessels (in 1805 and 1806 it was plundering about one of every eight American ships that put to sea) and its humiliating practice of impressment made Britain appear the greater culprit in American eyes. Indeed, it was difficult for many Republicans to think of France as the same kind of enemy as Great Britain.[62]

Fortunately for American trade, the economic sanctions imposed by both empires were never intended to starve their opponents into submission. Instead, they were exaggerated applications of traditional mercantilist principles designed to wreck each belligerent's commerce and to drain each other's specie. The British, for example, were happy to carry on trade with Napoleon as long as it was British goods in British ships. As the British prime minister declared, "The object of the Orders was not to destroy the trade of the Continent, but to force the Continent to trade with us."[63] Consequently, there were violations and loopholes everywhere, and trade continued to flourish. Still, the British and French trade restrictions did have some cost. Between 1803 and 1812 Britain and France and their allies seized nearly fifteen hundred American ships, with Britain taking 917 to France's 558.[64]

62. Perkins, *Prologue to War*, 74.
63. Hickey, *War of 1812*, 18.
64. Hickey, *War of 1812*, 19; Perkins, *Prologue to War*, 2.

THESE SEIZURES BY THE BELLIGERENTS, however, did not do as much damage to American commerce in this period as the United States eventually did to itself. In a desperate attempt to break the stranglehold that Britain and France had on American trade, the United States launched what Jefferson called a "candid and liberal experiment" in "peaceful coercion"—an embargo that forbade all Americans from sending any of their ships and goods abroad.[65] Perhaps never in history has a trading nation of America's size engaged in such an act of self-immolation with so little reward. Not only did this experiment fail to stop the belligerents' abuses of America's neutral rights, but the embargo ended up seriously injuring the American economy and all but destroying the Jeffersonian principle of limited government and states' rights.

Although the origins of this experiment in economic sanctions went back to the use of economic sanctions against the British in the 1760s and 1770s, the immediate precipitant of the embargo was the *Leopard-Chesapeake* affair.

On June 22, 1807, the American frigate USS *Chesapeake* sailed from Norfolk en route to the Mediterranean as part of a squadron sent to deal with the Barbary pirates. Not far out from Chesapeake Bay the fifty-gun HMS *Leopard* ordered the *Chesapeake* to allow a boarding party to search for British deserters. When the *Chesapeake* refused, the *Leopard* fired on the American warship, killing three American seamen, wounding sixteen others, and forcing it to lower its colors. The British boarded the American frigate and impressed four seamen as British deserters, only one of whom was actually a British subject.

Most Americans were outraged by this attack on an American warship. "This country," President Jefferson observed, "has never been in such a state of excitement since the battle of Lexington."[66] The president looked for some honorable way of redressing the attack peacefully but made some preparations for war in case it came. He issued a proclamation barring all British warships from American ports unless the ships were on diplomatic missions or in distress. He recalled all of America's ships from abroad, beefed up the country's harbor defenses, recommended building more gunboats, secretly made plans for the invasion of Canada, requested the state governors to mobilize one hundred thousand militiamen, and convened a special session of Congress for October 1807. He declared the British ships to be *"enemies,"* who should be treated as such. By contrast, the French ships were *"friends,"* who should be extended every courtesy.[67]

---

65. TJ, Eighth Annual Message to Congress, 8 Nov. 1808, *Jefferson: Writings*, 544.
66. Peterson, *Jefferson and the New Nation*, 876.
67. TJ to JM, 26 Aug. 1807, *Republic of Letters*, 1492.

Still, the president was anxious to avoid war with Britain and worried, with good reason, that his proclamation would not satisfy the patriotic ardor of his fellow citizens. He knew only too well that the United States was not ready for a war with Britain in 1807, but if a war had to come, he preferred it to be directed against England's newly found and incongruous ally, Spain. In August 1807 he told Madison "our southern defensive force can take the Floridas, volunteers for a Mexican army will flock to our standard, and rich pabulum will be offered to our privateers in the plunder of their commerce and coasts. Perhaps Cuba would add itself to our confederation."[68]

The British government did not want war either. Since the British government had never clearly claimed the right to impress from neutral warships, they disavowed the attack on the *Chesapeake* and recalled the naval commander who ordered it—though he was given another command. The British government offered to pay reparations and to return three of the four deserters, who were Americans; the fourth, who was a British subject, was summarily hanged, thus allowing the British government, Madison complained, to avoid "the humiliation of restoring a British subject" to America along with the other three seamen.[69]

Yet Jefferson wanted the British to disavow both the attack on the *Chesapeake* and the policy of impressment in general, and he thus considered the British response to be "unfriendly, proud, and harsh" and full of quibbles.[70] Because he remained deeply suspicious of British intentions, he could not help but welcome Napoleon's smashing victories over the armies of the British-led coalition that left the French emperor in complete control of the Continent. The President said in August 1807 that he had never expected to be "wishing success to Buonaparte," whose assumption of an imperial crown had ended once and for all the fiction that France was still a republic. But the English were as "tyrannical at sea as he is on land, and that tyranny bearing on us in every point of either honor or interest, I say, 'down with England.'" The warnings by the British-loving Federalists of what Napoleon might do to Americans were about "a future hypothetical" evil; we were now, he said, experiencing at the hands of the English "a certain present evil."[71]

That evil was revealed in a number of new British actions. These included instigating Indian threats in the Northwest, the brutal seizure

68. TJ to JM, 16 Aug. 1807, *Republic of Letters*, 1486.
69. JM to TJ, 20 Sept. 1807, *Republic of Letters*, 1499.
70. Malone, *Jefferson the President: Second Term*, 464.
71. TJ to Thomas Leiper, 21 Aug. 1807, in Ford, *Writings of Jefferson*, 9: 130. See Joseph I. Shulim, "Thomas Jefferson Views Napoleon," *Va. Mag. of Hist. and Biog.*, 60 (1960), 288–304.

of the neutral Danish fleet in Copenhagen (which seemed to make every neutral navy vulnerable to British confiscation), and the tightening up of the policy of impressment by allowing for impressments on neutral warships and by denying the validity of naturalization papers. The British duties now required on American goods bound for Europe seemed especially humiliating; they could only remind Americans of the former colonial regulations that they thought they had thrown off with the Declaration of Independence. William Cobbett, the irascible ex-Federalist journalist who had returned to England to become a vitriolic critic of the United States, summed up the hard-line position the British government was now taking: "Our power upon the waves enable us to dictate the terms, upon which ships of all nations shall navigate.... Not a sail should be hoisted, except by stealth, without paying a tribute."[72]

With the international situation worsening, few Republicans wanted outright war, but at the same time they wanted to do something to deal with the hostility of the monarchical Old World toward the neutral American Republic. The Republicans were increasingly anxious that not only was America's national independence at stake but their republican desire for a universal peace and their aversion to war's horrors and expenses were creating a false impression among the European powers—an impression, as Jefferson put it, that "our government is entirely in Quaker principles, and will turn the left cheek when the right has been smitten." This impression, he said in 1806, "must be corrected when just occasion arises, or we shall become the plunder of all nations."[73]

With the Non-Importation Act of 1806 in effect after a long delay, the president on December 18, 1807, announced a new policy, which eventually became an expanded version of economic retaliation—perhaps, with the exception of Prohibition, the greatest example in American history of ideology brought to bear on a matter of public policy.

In his brief message to Congress Jefferson recommended an embargo to protect the "essential resources" of "our merchandise, our vessels and our seamen," which were threatened by "great and increasing danger...on the high seas and elsewhere from the belligerent powers of Europe."[74] Although Jefferson had not fully explained to the Congress why the embargo was necessary, Congress acted immediately and in four days at the end of December 1807 passed the Embargo Act, which prohibited the departure of all American ships in international trade.

---

72. Perkins, *Prologue to War*, 187.
73. Roger H. Brown, *The Republic in Peril: 1812* (New York, 1964), 13.
74. TJ, Message to Congress, 18 Dec. 1807, in Richardson, ed., *Messages and Papers of the Presidents, 1789–1897*, 1: 433.

Although the act did not prohibit foreign ships, including British ships, from bringing imports to America, it forbade these foreign ships from taking on American exports, thus forcing them to sail away in ballast.

It was a very strange act, as self-contradictory as the Republican party itself. Although American thinking about the British vulnerability to economic sanctions had always emphasized the British need to sell their manufactured luxuries abroad, the embargo actually deprived the British of America's exports, which was much less harmful to the British economy than the loss of markets for their manufactured goods would have been. Of course, the embargo was accompanied by the implementation of the long-suspended Non-Importation Act, but this act only restricted some British imports, not all; exempt from prohibition were such items as Jamaican rum, coarse woolens, salt, and Birmingham hardware.[75] Throughout the life of the embargo Americans continued to import many British goods, which totaled at least half the volume of those they had imported in 1807 before the Republicans had invoked the Non-Importation Act. Although the Republicans never fully explained America's continued importation of British goods (carried on British ships, no less), Gallatin and others apparently felt that the federal government was so dependent on customs duties on its imports that cutting off all imports would have bankrupted it.

Barring American ships and goods from all overseas trade was a drastic act, but curiously neither Jefferson nor Republicans in the Congress made much of an effort to justify it to the country. This extraordinary measure went through Congress rapidly and with little debate. As Jefferson said, the choices were limited: it was either "war, Embargo, or nothing," and war and nothing were not really acceptable alternatives.[76] Certainly, the Republican supporters of the bill, knowing they had the votes, made little effort to defend the embargo; instead they kept calling for the question. The final vote in the House was eighty-two to forty-four. Jefferson said that half the opposition consisted of Federalists, the other half a mixture of the followers of the eccentric John Randolph, who thought the embargo was dictated by Napoleon and aimed at only Britain, and of "republicans happening to take up mistaken views of the subject."[77]

Secretary of the Treasury Gallatin in the cabinet may not have had a mistaken view of the embargo, but he certainly had doubts about it. Because he sensed the possible consequences of the embargo—"privations, sufferings, revenue, effect on the enemy, politics at home,

75. Forrest McDonald, *The Presidency of Thomas Jefferson* (Lawrence, KS, 1976), 107.
76. Malone, *Jefferson the President: Second Term*, 469.
77. Malone, *Jefferson the President: Second Term*, 486–87.

&c."—he wanted it to be temporary and designed only to recall America's ships and get them safely into port; indeed, if the embargo were to be permanent, he preferred going to war. Perhaps because of his sophisticated understanding of how economies worked, an understanding not shared by Jefferson or Madison, he realized that momentous actions by governments often had unanticipated consequences. He warned Jefferson that "governmental prohibitions do always more mischief than had been calculated; and it is not without much hesitation that a statesman should hazard to regulate the concerns of individuals as if he could do it better than themselves."[78] This was good Republican advice, but Jefferson ignored it.

It is not clear that Jefferson and Madison, who were the architects of the embargo, had thought through its implications. Although Madison was the more enthusiastic supporter of the measure, Jefferson certainly shared the Republican faith that almost anything was preferable to war, especially if that war had to be fought against a vigorous and powerful enemy and not a feeble Spain or a petty Barbary rogue-state. "As we cannot meet the British with an equality of physical force," as Jefferson later put it, "we must supply it by other devices"—whether those devices were Robert Fulton's submarine torpedoes or the withholding of America's exports.[79] With the belligerents' orders and decrees putting America's neutral commerce in an impossible situation, he thought that the embargo might buy time for something to be worked out diplomatically.

Instead of the president himself explaining to the country and the Congress the rationale for such an extreme act, Secretary of State Madison took on the task in three anonymous articles published in the Washington *National Intelligencer*, a pro-administration paper, several days after the enactment of the embargo. The embargo, Madison wrote, was "a measure of peace and precaution," without "a shadow of a pretext to make it a cause of war." It was a kind of test of America's republican character amidst a world of hostile monarchies. "Let the example teach the world that our firmness equals our moderation; that having resorted to a measure just in itself, and adequate to its object, we will flinch from no sacrifices which the honor and good of our nation demand from virtuous and faithful citizens." Relying on his Republican understanding of the contrasting political economies of America and Britain, Madison argued that while an embargo would deny Americans some British-made

78. Gallatin to TJ, 18 Dec. 1807, in Henry Adams, ed., *The Writings of Albert Gallatin* (Philadelphia, 1879), 1: 368.
79. TJ to Robert Fulton, 21 July 1813, in Malone, *Jefferson the President: Second Term*, 506.

"superfluities," the British "will feel the want of necessaries." America was blessed. It did not have to choose, as other injured nations did, "between graceful submission or war." With the embargo, a benign providence had given to America "a happy recourse for avoiding both." This experiment might even bring about a commercial world that Americans had dreamed about ever since the model treaty of 1776. The "embargo," said Madison, "whilst it guards our essential resources, will have the collateral effect of making it to the interest of all nations to change the system which has driven our commerce from the ocean." Madison, in other words, seems to have envisioned the embargo as an opportunity to initiate the enlightened dream of transforming the character of international relations.[80]

Although Jefferson eventually came to share Madison's grand vision, he initially saw the embargo as little more than a defensive device to prevent the capture of American ships, cargoes, and seamen. "The great objects of the embargo," he told the governor of Virginia in March 1808, "are keeping our ships and seamen out of harm's way."[81] He thought that an embargo for a certain length of time was "a less evil than war. But after a time it will not be so."[82] In the meantime, however, he believed that the withholding of American trade might bring pressure on the two belligerents, Britain and France, to negotiate "a retraction of the obnoxious decrees." The United States would prepare for war with the one that refused to withdraw its restrictions on American trade—though Jefferson and Madison knew only too well that the embargo hurt Britain more than France and that it would be Britain they would fight if the United States went to war.[83] To get ready for this possibility of war, Congress appropriated $4 million for eight new regiments for the U.S. Army, bringing it to about ten thousand men, new weapons for the militia, 188 additional gunboats, and harbor fortifications for the ports.

This military buildup created painful problems for Republican congressmen who had vowed never to vote for raising an army in time of peace. John Randolph urged delay and mocked his colleagues for their inconsistencies and contradictions. "We had just navy enough to bait the war-trap," he jeered, "to bring us into difficulties, not to carry us through them." The government was building gunboats to protect the harbors, and erecting

80. Irving Brant, *James Madison: Secretary of State, 1800–1809* (Indianapolis, 1953), 402–3; Malone, *Jefferson the President: Second Term*, 488–90.

81. TJ to William Cabell, 13 March 1808, in Spivak, *Jefferson's English Crisis*, 105.

82. TJ to Maj. Joseph Eggleston, 7 March 1808, in Malone, *Jefferson the President: Second Term*, 483.

83. TJ to JM, 11 March 1808, *Republic of Letters*, 1515; Tucker and Hendrickson, *Empire of Liberty*, 211.

forts in the harbors to protect the gunboats. The eight new regiments seemed to have no purpose—except as "a cause for laying taxes, which ruined those in public opinion who imposed them." If war were expected, then, said Randolph, the embargo made no sense at all. It was supposedly designed for peace, "at least such were the arguments adduced in its favor— that it would save all the expense of armies; that the annual millions other- wise to be thrown away upon armies would be saved; that we should keep close house and there would be no danger." The embargo, which Ran- dolph derided as the great American tortoise drawing in its head, a system of "withdrawing from every contest, quitting the arena, flying the pit," was, he said, totally incompatible with the raising of troops and the building of fleets. "If war be expected, you must raise the embargo, arm your mer- chantmen, and scuffle for commerce and revenue as well as you can."[84]

In the end the Republicans' long-standing fears of standing armies and a militarized government led them to label their measure, "an act to raise for a time an additional military force."[85] The act was in fact more than many Republicans had wanted or expected. Of course, passing an act was one thing, implementing it was quite another, and the army never attained its authorized strength during Jefferson's presidency. As a consequence, the British government could scarcely develop much respect for whatever military force the Americans were mustering.

At the same time, Congress enacted legislation closing loopholes in the embargo, including requiring bonds from vessels in the coastwise trade and forbidding the export of goods out of the country by land as well as by sea—which suggested that the policy was becoming much more than a defensive device to protect the capture of ships and seamen. The system leaked everywhere, but particularly in the Maine and the Lake Champlain borders with Canada. Ultimately Gallatin's Treasury Depart- ment, which administered the embargo, was authorized to use armed ships to search and detain vessels suspected of violating the embargo, especially those vessels engaged in the coastwise trade. Earlier exemp- tions were eliminated, new licenses and bonds were required, and licensed vessels had to be loaded under the supervision of revenue offi- cers. In its heyday the British navigation system regulating the trade of the eighteenth-century colonies had never been so burdensome.

Jefferson finally had to proclaim the Canadian–New York border area in a state of insurrection, and he ordered all civil and military officers to put

---

84. *Annals of Congress*, 10th Congress, 1st session (April 1808), 2: 1960–64; Malone, *Jefferson the President: Second Term*, 517.

85. Malone, *Jefferson the President: Second Term*, 517; *Annals of Congress*, 10th Congress, 1st session (April 1808), 2: 2849–52.

down the rebels. "I think it so important in example to crush these audacious proceedings, and to make the offenders feel the consequences of
individuals daring to oppose a law by force," he told the governor of New
York, "that no effort should be spared to compass the object."[86] Hamilton
could not have put it better. In using armed force to enforce the embargo,
including dispatching some army regulars, Jefferson was violating all of his
beliefs in minimal government. That he did so was a measure of how crucially important the embargo had become to him in what he called this
"age of affliction, to which the history of nations presents no parallel."[87]

In April 1808 Congress authorized the president to withdraw the embargo
against one or both of the belligerents if, in the judgment of the president,
one or both suspended hostilities during the congressional recess.

During the summer and fall of 1808 Jefferson, confused and sometimes
desperate, began emphasizing the experimental character of the
embargo—that it was a trial in peaceful coercion. Perhaps under the influence of Madison, the embargo now became less a defensive and protective
device and more an offensive and coercive measure to compel the
belligerents to remove their trade restrictions. Indeed, Jefferson now saw it
as a means of "starving our enemies," by which he meant the British.[88]

Jefferson seems to have had an exaggerated idea of America's international clout. He continued to think, for example, that he could use the
European war to acquire the Floridas. When he learned of Napoleon's
troubles with Spain in the summer of 1808, he told his secretary of the
navy, Robert Smith of Maryland, that this might be the moment for the
United States to take possession of "our territory held by Spain, and so
much more as may make a proper reprisal for her spoliations." A few
months later he thought that if Napoleon succeeded in Spain, the French
emperor would be so gratified to have America's neutral carrying trade
with the Spanish colonies that he would repeal most of his restrictive
decrees, "with perhaps the Floridas thrown into the bargain."[89]

Given Jefferson's evolving belief that a grand experiment in peaceful
coercion was being tried, the stakes could not have been higher, and
inevitably he became obsessed with its enforcement. He would tolerate
no violations, and, as he said, "I set down the exercise of commerce,

86. TJ to Tomkins, 15 Aug. 1808, in L and B, eds., *Writings of Jefferson*, 12: 131–33.
87. TJ to Captain McGregor, 26 Aug. 1808, in H. A. Washington, ed., *The Writings of Thomas Jefferson* (Washington, DC, 1853), 5: 356.
88. TJ to Rodney, 24 Apr. 1808, in L and B, eds., *Writings of Jefferson*, 12: 36; Malone, *Jefferson the President: Second Term*, 585.
89. Joseph I. Shulim, "Thomas Jefferson Views Napoleon," *Va. Mag. of Hist. and Biog.*, 60 (1952), 295; TJ to Monroe, 28 Jan. 1809, in L and B, eds., *Writings of Jefferson*, 12: 241–42.

merely for profit, as nothing when it carries with it the danger of defeating the objects of the embargo."[90] He thought the real needs of the American citizens must not become "a cover for the crimes against their country, which unprincipled adventurers are in the habit of committing."[91]

The New England Federalists were furious. With their region bearing the brunt of the enforcement, they urged resistance and civil disobedience. The Republican clergyman William Bentley of Salem, Massachusetts, was astonished to see several Boston papers taking "a decided part against our own Country in favour of the British."[92] During the summer and fall of 1808 a number of New England towns flooded the president with petitions calling for the suspension of the embargo, so much so that Jefferson later recalled that he had "felt the foundations of the government shaken under my feet by the New England townships."[93] The towns complained that their ships were lying idle in the harbors and that thousands of sailors, dock workers, and others employed in mercantile activities were out of work. The inhabitants of the little border town of St. Albans, Vermont, told the president that they could not understand how stopping their trade with Canada could possibly help the United States if it hurt the people of St. Albans. "Exchanging their surplus production for many of the conveniences, and even necessaries, of life," they said, was what the townsmen did; it was the source of their daily existence.[94]

The commercial losses were substantial. During the first year of the embargo the Massachusetts fleet, which comprised nearly 40 percent of the nation's total tonnage, lost over $15 million in freight revenues alone, a sum equal to the entire income of the federal government in 1806. During 1808 American exports declined nearly 80 percent (from $103,343,000 to $22,431,000) and imports declined nearly 60 percent (from $144,740,000 to $58,101,000).[95] Most of the decline in exports took place in the last three-quarters of 1808, as stricter enforcement of the embargo steadily took effect.

As a measure of the extent to which ideology trumped commercial interests, the Republican legislatures of the Mississippi and Orleans

90. Spivak, *Jefferson's English Crisis*, 117.

91. Malone, *Jefferson the President: Second Term*, 590, 591.

92. William Bentley, *The Diary of William Bentley, D.D: Pastor of East Church, Salem, Massachusetts* (Gloucester, MA, 1962), 3: 313.

93. Malone, *Jefferson the President: Second Term*, 613.

94. James Duncan Phillips, "Jefferson's 'Wicked Tyrannical Embargo,'" *New England Quarterly*, 18 (1945), 466–78; *American Register*, 3 (1808), 450–52.

95. Samuel E. Morison, *Maritime History of Massachusetts, 1783–1860* (Boston, 1921), 189; Douglas North, "The United States Balance of Payments, 1790–1860," *Trends in the American Economy in the Nineteenth Century*, National Bureau of Economic Research, Studies in Income and Wealth, 24 (Princeton, 1960), 590–92.

territories supported the embargo even as the Southwestern cotton planters suffered severe losses. The value of exports from New Orleans and Mobile fell precipitously and would not return to pre-embargo levels until 1815. The house of representatives of the Mississippi Territory told Congress that "our produce lies unsold and unsaleable in our Barns." Still, as good Republicans most of the cotton planters blamed Britain and Europe, and not the Jefferson administration, for their plight.[96]

Although administration officials may have exaggerated the extent of smuggling, they became determined to tighten up the system even more. Congress called for the closing of all ports to the armed vessels of both France and Great Britain and for the prohibition of all imports from both belligerents. During the summer of 1808 Gallatin told the president that "Congress must either vest the Executive with the most arbitrary powers and sufficient force to carry the embargo into effect, or give it up altogether."[97] Faced with these choices, the administration opted to enforce the embargo even more harshly, and early in January 1809 Congress passed and Jefferson signed an extremely draconian enforcement act.

This act closed all additional loopholes and granted the president extraordinary powers to capture and punish any violators, including powers that were clearly contrary to the search-and-seizure provisions of the Fourth Amendment. Almost nothing could be loaded onto vessels or moved in oceanic commerce without a permit or license, usually backed by a large bond; and the federal authorities were granted enormous discretion in deciding who was to be permitted to trade. "This was regulatory authority of astonishing breadth and administrative discretion of breathtaking scope," concludes a modern historian of administrative law.[98] The United States government was virtually at war with its own people, especially those in Massachusetts, whose opposition to the embargo, said Jefferson, "amounted almost to rebellion and treason."[99] For their part, "the people of Massachusetts," declared the state's senate, "will not willingly become the victims of a fruitless experiment."[100]

The embargo revived the fortunes of the Federalist party in New England, New York, and Maryland, but not as much as the Federalists

96. Adam Rothman, *Slave Country: American Expansion and the Origins of the Deep South* (Cambridge, MA, 2005), 54.
97. Gallatin to TJ, 29 July 1808, in Adams, ed., *Writings of Gallatin*, 1: 399.
98. Jerry L. Mashaw, "Reluctant Nationalists: Federal Administration and Administrative Law in the Republican Era, 1801–1829," *Yale Law Journal*, 116 (2007), 1655.
99. Malone, *Jefferson the President: Second Term*, 639; TJ to Lehre, 8 Nov. 1808, in L and B, eds., *Writings of Jefferson*, 12: 191.
100. Malone, *Jefferson the President: Second Term*, 652.

had expected. By 1808, for example, the fourteen Federalist congressmen that the South had sent to Washington in 1800 had diminished to seven.[101] Nevertheless, the Federalists taunted the Republicans with hypocrisy and inconsistency and mocked the Jeffersonians' pretensions to limited government and their earlier fears of executive power. As the parties reversed their traditional positions, everything was turned upside-down. The Massachusetts legislature condemned the enforcement measures as "unjust, oppressive, and unconstitutional and not legally binding on the citizens of this state." In language reminiscent of the Virginia and Kentucky resolutions of 1798, the Connecticut governor declared that the state legislatures had the right and duty "to *interpose* their protecting shield between the right and liberty of the people, and the assumed power of the general government."[102] The Republicans responded with a Hamilton-like defense of their actions. They were not trying to establish a military despotism, declared Senator William Branch Giles of Virginia; instead, they were merely seeking the means "necessary and proper for carrying into effect a great national and Con-stitutional object...and thus to make a last effort to preserve the peace of the nation."[103]

The pressure to repeal the embargo mounted, especially among Repub-lican congressmen from the Northeast. With the unity of the Republican party that had sustained the embargo for over a year finally disintegrating, Congress voted to end this liberal experiment in peaceful coercion.

Both Republican leaders, Jefferson and Madison, were opposed to the repeal of the embargo; they thought that a few more months of enforce-ment might have succeeded in compelling Britain to relax its commercial restrictions.[104] Both Republican leaders believed that a great opportunity to teach the world a new way of dealing with international conflicts had been lost. "There never has been a situation of the world before in which such endeavors as we had made would not have secured our peace," Jefferson lamented. "It is probable there never will be such another." He was filled with regret that this grand and enlightened experiment

---

101. James H. Broussard, *The Southern Federalists, 1800–1816* (Baton Rouge, 1978), 107.
102. Malone, *Jefferson the President: Second Term*, 653, 654.
103. Malone, *Jefferson the President: Second Term*, 639; *Annals of Congress*, 10th Congress, 2nd session (Dec. 1808), 19: 276.
104. At least one modern econometrician agrees that the British experienced more economic suffering than the Americans did and that the embargo failed because of the lack of sufficient political will in America. Jeffrey A. Frankel, "The 1807–1809 Embargo Against Great Britain," *Journal of Economic History*, 42 (1982), 291–308. See also Perkins, *Prologue to War*, 205.

had failed; it had been "made on motives which all mankind must approve."[105]

The embargo was ended on March 4, 1809, on the day the new president, James Madison, took office. In its place Congress substituted nonintercourse with both Britain and France; that is, it retained the embargo with these two nations but now permitted trade with all other nations. At the same time, it authorized the incoming president to reopen trade with whichever nation ended its violations of America's neutral rights. Three years later President Madison called for a declaration of war against Great Britain; yet because the Republicans were still in charge of the Congress and the presidency, it was to be a war like no other.

105. Malone, *Jefferson the President: Second Term*, 644, 657; TJ to Monroe, 28 Jan. 1808, in Ford, ed., *Writings of Jefferson*, 9: 243; to Judge St. George Tucker, 25 Dec. 1808, in Malone, *Jefferson the President: Second Term*, 657.

# 18

## The War of 1812

The War of 1812 is the strangest war in American history. It was a war in its own right but also a war within a war, a part of the larger war between Britain and France that had been going on since France's National Convention declared war on Britain in February 1793. Although the total American casualties in the war were relatively light—6,765—far fewer in the entire two and a half years of war than those killed and wounded in a single one of Napoleon's many battles, it was nonetheless one of the most important wars in American history. It was, said Virginia's John Taylor, the philosopher of agrarian Republicanism, a "metaphysical war, a war not for conquest, not for defense, not for sport," but rather "a war for honour, like that of the Greeks against Troy," a war, however, that "may terminate in the destruction of the last experiment in...free government."[1]

The United States told the world in 1812 that it declared war against Great Britain solely because of the British impressment of American sailors and the British violations of America's maritime rights. Yet on the face of it, these grievances scarcely seemed to be sufficient justifications for a war, especially a war for which the United States was singularly unprepared. In 1812 the U.S. Army consisted of fewer than seven thousand regular troops. The navy comprised only sixteen vessels, not counting the dozens of gunboats. With this meager force the United States confronted an enemy that possessed a regular army of nearly a quarter of a million men and the most powerful navy in the world, with a thousand warships on the rolls and over six hundred of them in active service.

Yet President James Madison was supremely confident of success. Indeed, right after Congress declared war Madison personally visited all the departments of government, something never done before, said the controller of the treasury, Richard Rush, the young son of Benjamin Rush. The president, who presumably abhorred war, gave a pep talk to

1. Norman K. Risjord, *The Old Republicans: Southern Conservatism in the Age of Jefferson* (New York, 1965), 145.

everyone "in a manner," said Rush, "worthy of a little commander-in-chief, with his little round hat and huge cockade."[2]

From beginning to end the war seemed as ludicrous as its diminutive commander-in-chief with his oversized cockade, the symbol of martial spirit. The British against whom the United States declared war in June 1812 did not expect war and did not want it. In fact, just as America was declaring war in June 1812, the British government repealed the orders-in-council authorizing the seizure of American ships and the impressment of American sailors that presumably had been a major cause of the war—too late, however, for the Americans to learn of the British action and reverse their decisions already taken. It turns out that many Americans did not want to go to war either; indeed, the leaders of the governing Republican party were devoted to the idea of creating a universal peace and had spent the previous decade desperately trying to avoid war. Nevertheless, it was the Republican party, which most loathed war and all that war entailed in taxes, debt, and executive power, that took the country into the war, and some Republicans did it with enthusiasm.

The vote for war in the Congress (in the House of Representatives seventy-nine to forty-nine and in the Senate nineteen to thirteen, the closest vote for a declaration of war in American history) was especially puzzling. The congressmen who voted for the war were overwhelmingly from the sections of the country, the South and West, that were farthest removed from ocean traffic and least involved in shipping and thus least affected by the violations of maritime rights and the impressments that were the professed reasons for declaring war. At the same time, the congressmen most opposed to the war were from the section of the country, New England, that was most hurt by the British impressment of American sailors and British violations of America's maritime rights.

Perhaps the infusion of new members helps explain Congress's decision to go to war.[3] In 1810 sixty-three new congressmen were elected to a

2. J.C.A. Stagg, *Mr. Madison's War: Politics, Diplomacy, and Warfare in the Early American Republic, 1783–1830* (Princeton, 1983), 3; Henry Adams, *History of the United States of America During the Administration of James Madison* (1889–1891; New York, 1986), 452.

3. On the differing views of historians over the causes of the war, see Louis M. Hacker, "Western Land Hunger and the War of 1812," *Mississippi Valley Historical Review*, 10 (1924), 366–95; Julius W. Pratt, *Expansionists of 1812* (New York, 1925); George R. Taylor, "Agrarian Discontent in the Mississippi Valley Preceding the War of 1812," *Journal of Political Economy*, 39 (1931), 471–505; Warren H. Goodman, "The Origins of the War of 1812: A Survey of Changing Interpretations," *Mississippi Valley Historical Review*, 28 (1941–1942), 171–86; Reginald Horsman, *The Causes of the War of 1812* (Philadelphia, 1962); and Bradford Perkins, ed., *The Causes of the War of 1812: National Honor or National Interest?* (New York, 1962).

142-seat House of Representatives. The Twelfth Congress contained a number of young "War Hawks," such as Henry Clay of Kentucky, Felix Grundy of Tennessee, and John C. Calhoun of South Carolina, who were eager to take strong measures against Great Britain. Since many of the War Hawks were from the West, however, it is not at all clear why they should have been so concerned for the nation's maritime rights. Representatives from Ohio, Kentucky, and Tennessee cast more votes for the war (nine) than did those from the New England states of New Hampshire, Vermont, Rhode Island, and Connecticut. In fact, New England congressmen voted twenty to twelve against the war, and most of the twelve votes in New England for the war came from congressmen representing the frontier areas of New Hampshire and Vermont.

This paradox of Western support for a war that was ostensibly about maritime rights led historians at the beginning of the twentieth century to dig beneath the professed war aims in search of some hidden Western interests. They argued that the West supported the war because it was land hungry and had its eyes on the annexation of Canada. Others refined this interpretation by contending that the West was less interested in land than it was in removing the British influence over the Indians in the Northwest. Still others argued that low grain prices aroused Western resentment against British blockades of America's Continental markets.

But since the West had only ten votes in the House of Representatives, it could not by itself have led the country into war. It was the South Atlantic states from Maryland to Georgia that supplied nearly half (thirty-nine) of the seventy-nine votes for war. This Southern support for war led other historians to posit an unspoken alliance between Westerners who wanted Canada and Southerners who had their eyes on Florida. Yet Pennsylvania, which presumably had little interest in the West or Florida, provided sixteen votes for the war, the most of any state.[4]

Although the vote for the war may remain something of a puzzle to some historians, one thing is clear: the war was very much a party issue,

---

4. On the votes for the war, see David S. Heidler and Jeanne T. Heidler, eds., *Encyclopedia of the War of 1812* (Annapolis, 2004), 571–74; this *Encyclopedia* also has an extensive bibliography on the war. For some of the many articles dealing with the votes for the war, see Leland R. Johnson, "The Suspense Was Hell: The Senate Vote for War in 1812," *Indiana Magazine of History*, 65 (1969), 247–67; Ronald I. Hatzenbuehler, "Party Unity and the Decision for War in the House of Representatives," *WMQ*, 29 (1972), 367–90; Ronald I. Hatzenbuehler, "The War Hawks and the Question of Congressional Leadership in 1812," *Pacific Historical Review*, 45 (1976), 1–22; Rudolph M. Bell, "Mr. Madison's War and Long-Term Congressional Voting Behavior," *WMQ*, 36 (1979), 373–95. On Pennsylvania, see Victor Sapio, *Pennsylvania and the War of 1812* (Lexington, KY, 1970).

with most Republicans being for the war and all the Federalists against it. In fact, the war became the logical consequence of the Republicans' diplomacy since 1805. As early as February 1809 President-elect Madison said as much to the American minister in London, William Pinkney. If America repealed the embargo and the British orders-in-council remained in effect, said Madison, "war is inevitable."[5] He believed war was inevitable because impressment and neutral rights had come to symbolize what he and other Republicans wanted most from Britain— unequivocal recognition of the nation's sovereignty and independence.

THE FIFTY-EIGHT-YEAR-OLD MADISON was presumably as well prepared for the presidency as anyone in the country. He had been involved in public service in one way or another during his entire adult life. He had been a principal force behind the calling of the Philadelphia Convention in 1787 and had composed the Virginia Plan that formed the working model for the Constitution. He was the co-author of the *Federalist*, surely the most important work of political theory in American history. He had been the leader and the most important member of the House of Representatives at the beginning of the new government in 1789. More than any other single person he was responsible for the congressional passage of the Bill of Rights. He was the co-founder of the Republican party and had been secretary of state for the entire eight years of Jefferson's presidency.

Despite all of Madison's experience, however, he seemed awed by the prospect of becoming president. When in his timidly delivered inaugural address he referred in a conventional manner to his "inadequacies" for the high office, he appeared to mean it. He was by far the most uncharismatic president the country had yet experienced. His three predecessors had fit the king-like office much better than he. They either had been virtual royalty, as in the case of Washington, or had tried to be royalty, as in the case of Adams, or had achieved dominance by being the anti-royal people's president, as in the case of Jefferson. Madison was none of these; he was not made for command. He lacked both the presence and the stature of his illustrious predecessors; indeed, as one observer noted, during social gatherings in the White House, "being so low in stature, he was in danger of being confounded with the plebeian crowds and was pushed and jostled about like a common citizen."[6]

Madison could be congenial in small groups of men, where he liked to tell smutty stories, but in large mixed groups he was shy, stiff, and

---

5. Irving Brant, *James Madison: The President, 1809–1812* (Indianapolis, 1956), 37.
6. Catherine Allgor, *A Perfect Union: Dolley Madison and the Creation of the American Nation* (New York, 2006), 250.

awkward—"the most unsociable creature in existence," concluded one female observer. Consequently, his gregarious wife, Dolley—who was described by an ungallant English diplomat as having "an uncultivated mind and fond of gossiping"—tended to dominate their social gatherings.[7] When Madison held official dinners as president, Dolley, a large woman who dwarfed her husband, seated herself at the head of the table with Madison's private secretary seated at the foot. Madison himself sat in the middle and was thus relieved of having to look after his guests and control the flow of conversation. But so alarmed did Dolley become over what she felt was the lack of regard paid Madison that she arranged for "Hail to the Chief" to be played at state receptions to rouse people to proper respect when her husband entered the room. As a brilliant Washington hostess, Dolley Madison, the "presidentess," as she was called, created a public persona that rivaled that of her husband, who was seventeen years her senior. Her social skills and energy encouraged dozens of congressmen to bring their wives with them to the capital—something they had not done during Jefferson's presidency.

With his retiring personality and his constrained conception of the presidency, Madison was never able to control the Republican party to the extent Jefferson had. He fully accepted the Republican principle of executive deference to the people's representatives in Congress but made none of the necessary efforts to manage the legislature as Jefferson had. He was unable, as one Pennsylvania Republican noted, to "hook men to his heart as his predecessor could."[8]

Because by 1808 the congressional Republican caucus clearly controlled the nomination of the party's candidate for the presidency, it concluded that the president was in some measure its creature. As Congress gathered up the power draining away from the executive, it sought to organize itself into committees in order to initiate and supervise policy. But the rise of the committee system only further fragmented the government into contending interest groups. Madison thus faced a raucous Congress and a bitterly divided Republican party, various factions of which were opposed to his presidency. In trying to promote unity among the Republicans, the president allowed his critics to deny him the selection of his trusted ally, Albert Gallatin, as secretary of state. Instead, he felt compelled to appoint to that important post Robert Smith, the undistinguished secretary of the navy in Jefferson's cabinet and a person totally unfit to be secretary of state.

7. Andrew S. Trees, *The Founding Fathers and the Politics of Character* (Princeton, 2004), 111; Ralph Ketcham, *James Madison: A Biography* (New York, 1970), 428.
8. Stagg, *Mr. Madison's War*, 507.

Madison ended up with a cabinet considerably weaker than that of any of his presidential predecessors. Madison's cabinet, as John Randolph observed with his usual poisonous perceptivity, "presents a novel spectacle in the world, divided against itself, and the most deadly animosity raging between its principal members—what can come of it but confusion, mischief, and ruin?"[9]

THE NEW PRESIDENT was immediately confronted with the ending of the embargo, which he wanted to continue. In its place Congress put the Non-Intercourse Act of 1809, which opened trade with the rest of the world but prohibited it with both Britain and France; it also authorized the president to reopen trade with whichever belligerent repealed its trade restrictions and recognized American neutral rights. With trade to the rest of the world reopened, the opportunities for evading the prohibition on trading with the belligerents were great, and many American ships took off ostensibly for neutral ports only to end up in Great Britain. Since British control of the seas prevented many American merchants from sailing to France, the Non-Intercourse Act actually favored Britain over France, a circumstance that left Madison at a total loss: how could he coerce Britain with an act that actually benefited the former mother country? Britain reacted to the Non-Intercourse Act by issuing new orders-in-council in April 1809 that went some way toward meeting the Americans' complaints, though the British government was always reluctant to admit that it was making any concessions whatsoever.

Unfortunately, the British minister in Washington, David M. Erskine, had already reached an agreement with the Madison government that was not in line with the thinking of the British ministry in London. Erskine ignored several key instructions from his government, which disavowed his agreement when it learned of it, including one instruction stating that, while opening up American trade with Britain, the United States should allow the British navy to enforce the continued American prohibition on trade with France—a humiliating neocolonial stipulation that Madison rejected outright. The two nations could not be farther apart. While America wanted free neutral trade with both belligerents, Britain wanted a neutral United States that would help it defeat Napoleon.[10]

Misled by Erskine into believing that Britain would repeal its trade restrictions, President Madison in April 1809 proclaimed that trade with

9. Ketcham, *Madison*, 485.
10. Bradford Perkins, *Prologue to War, 1805–1812: England and the United States* (Berkeley, 1968), 218.

the former mother country was now open. When in the summer of 1809 the United States learned that the British government had recalled Erskine and repudiated his agreement, the country had no choice but to reimpose non-intercourse with Britain. When Secretary of the Treasury Gallatin complained that the Non-Intercourse Act was hurting the duties from trade and creating a federal deficit, Congress was forced to turn its policy inside out and once again reopen trade with the belligerents.

Republican policy was always caught in a dilemma. If the government restricted trade with Britain, which Madison and other Republicans wished to do, it lost considerable revenue from the duties on imports. With such a loss of revenue the government would be compelled to raise taxes or borrow money, which no good Republican wanted to do. As a way out of this dilemma, Madison at first sought an old-fashioned navigation act, Macon's Bill No. 1 (named for Congressman Nathaniel Macon of North Carolina), which allowed British and French goods to enter American ports as long as they were carried in American ships. When an unlikely combination of Republican dissidents who wanted war and Federalists who feared it defeated this bill, a still much divided Congress passed Macon's Bill No. 2 in May 1810. This bill once again opened trade with both Britain and France, with the provision that if either belligerent revoked its restrictions on neutral commerce, the United States in ninety days would restore non-intercourse against the other. Madison, who yearned to restore the embargo, was disgusted with the bill; though named for him, even Macon voted against it. As trade with Britain flourished, many Republicans, as one congressman complained, thought the new policy was simply offering "up the honor and character of this nation to the highest bidder."[11]

Madison's only hope for this awkward policy was that its bias in favor of Britain might inspire Napoleon to remove his restrictions on American trade, which by 1810 were actually resulting in more French than British seizures of American ships and goods. Thus the president was primed to receive favorably an ambiguous note from France's foreign minister, the duc de Cadore, issued in the summer of 1810 declaring that Napoleon would revoke his decrees after November 1, 1810, but only on the condition that the United States first re-establish its prohibitions on British commerce. Since this conditional declaration did not actually fulfill the provisions of Macon's Bill No. 2, the Cadore letter, as it was called, generated much controversy, with the Federalists denouncing it as trickery and the most rabid Republicans hailing it as France's penance for its violations of American rights.

11. *Annals of Congress*, 11th Congress, 2nd session (April 1810), 21: 1772; Perkins, *Prologue to War*, 241; Risjord, *Old Republicans*, 107.

Ambiguous as the Cadore letter was, it was enough for Madison, who was eager to escape from his awkward situation. On November 2, 1810, he publicly proclaimed that France had met the requirements of the Macon Bill and that if Britain failed to revoke its orders-in-council over the next ninety days, non-intercourse would be reimposed on Britain on February 2, 1811. Chief Justice Marshall could scarcely believe what was happening and declared that the president's claim that France had revoked its decrees was "one of the most astonishing instances of national credulity... that is to be found in political history."[12] Although Madison well understood the equivocal nature of the Cadore letter, he felt he had to grasp at the opportunity to pressure the British into some sort of relaxation of their commercial restrictions. At any rate, he was only too eager to resume the policy of commercial sanctions against Great Britain that he had dreamed of implementing since the Revolution.

Madison, however, confronted a Republican party in the Congress that was breaking apart, and the resultant factions always threatened to coalesce in opposition to the administration. There were the Old Republicans of '98, or Quids, led by John Randolph; the supporters of New Yorkers George Clinton and his nephew DeWitt Clinton, who was challenging Madison for the presidency; and the Invisibles in the Senate, led by William Branch Giles of Virginia and Samuel Smith of Maryland, the brother of the secretary of state, Robert Smith. Robert Smith's mounting indiscretions at last gave Madison the opportunity to dismiss him from the cabinet and install his old opponent and fellow Virginian James Monroe as secretary of state. But the Smith family of Maryland in opposition only added to the disarray of the Republicans. Jefferson became so fearful of the disorder that he pleaded for unity. "If we schismatize on men and measures, if we do not act in phalanx," he told the Republican journalist William Duane in the spring of 1811, "I will not say our *party*, the term is false and degrading, but our *nation* will be undone. For the Republicans are the nation."[13]

Whether the Americans, never mind the Republicans, were really a nation was the issue. Was the United States an independent nation like other nations with an explicit and peculiar tribal character? Could Americans establish their separate identity only by fighting and killing Britons to whom they were cultural kin and whom they so much resembled?

In July 1811 Madison called Congress to meet in an early session in November in order to prepare the country for war, which seemed to be

12. James H. Broussard, *The Southern Federalists, 1800–1816* (Baton Rouge, 1978), 136.

13. Stagg, *Mr. Madison's War*, 61.

the only alternative if commercial sanctions failed. Despite the Cadore letter, Napoleon continued to enforce his various decrees making all neutral ships that brought goods from Britain to the Continent liable to confiscation. But the French emperor seized only some American ships but not all, thereby hoping to create sufficient confusion to prevent the British from repealing their own commercial restrictions, which they had always justified as acts of retaliation that would last only as long as Napoleon's Continental System.

In February 1811 Congress had passed a new Non-Importation Act that turned away British ships and goods coming to America but allowed American ships and produce to go to England. At the same time, the act required American courts to accept the president's proclamation as conclusive evidence that France had indeed repealed its decrees—a strange stipulation that suggested the widespread doubts that Napoleon was behaving honestly. In fact, declared John Quincy Adams from his post in St. Petersburg, Napoleon's conduct was so blatantly deceptive as "to give sight to the blind."[14] When the British government declared that it was unconvinced that France had abandoned its Continental System and that it would therefore not relax in any way its own commercial restrictions, Madison's policy collapsed in failure. Other than throwing up the country's hands in surrender, the United States had no choice now but war.

Although some suggested that the United States might have to fight both belligerents simultaneously in what was called a "triangular war," it was virtually inconceivable that the Republicans would go to war against France. Although Madison was well aware of "the atrocity of the French Government" in enforcing its "predatory Edicts," he, like Jefferson, always believed "that the original sin against Neutrals lies with G.B."[15]

It seemed to the Republicans as if the Revolution of 1776 was still going on. The United States was trying to establish itself as an independent sovereign republic in the world, and Britain, much more than France, seemed to be denying that sovereign independence. As one congressman put it in 1810, "The people will not submit to be colonized and give up their independence."[16] Even British concessions were now viewed suspiciously. When the British government in May 1812 offered to give the Americans an equal share of the ten thousand licenses it issued to merchants trading with the continent, Madison rejected the offer outright as degrading to American sovereignty. Most alarming to the Republicans was the quisling-like

14. Stagg, *Mr. Madison's War*, 56.
15. JM to TJ, 15 June 1810, 22 June 1810, *Republic of Letters*, 1636–37.
16. *Annals of Congress*, 11th Congress, 2nd session (April 1810), 21: 1868.

behavior of the New England Federalists, who endlessly harassed the Republicans for their timidity and inconsistencies all the while supporting continued ties and trade with Great Britain. Just as the Federalists in 1797–1798 had accused the Republicans of being more loyal to France than to America, so now the Republicans accused the Federalists of aiding and abetting the former mother country. Just as the Federalists in 1797–1798 had thought that the Republicans were trying to bring the Jacobinical French Revolution to America, so now the Republicans thought the Federalists were seeking to reverse the results of not just the Jeffersonian revolution of 1800 but the original Revolution of 1776. In the eyes of many Republicans this threat of the Federalists' undoing the Revolution and breaking up the Union seemed real, perhaps more real than the threat of invasion by the French had been to the Federalists in 1797–1798.

The New England Federalists continually worried about their declining political fortunes even as the administration's unpopular policies of commercial coercion gave them false hopes of regaining power. By 1809 many citizens of Massachusetts were looking to their state to protect them from the machinations of the Republicans in Washington. Some even began talking of New England seceding from the Union. Fear and dislike of the Republicans and what they represented in the spread of democratic politics made many Federalists rethink the significance of America's break from Great Britain. Compared to Catholic France or that country's atheistic revolutionaries, Britain seemed more and more to be, in the words of Timothy Pickering, "the country of our forefathers, and the country to which we are indebted for all the institutions held dear to freemen."[17]

Because most Americans were anxiously trying to establish their distinct national identity, such Anglophilic sentiments were bound to be misinterpreted and used against the Federalists. The leader of the Federalists in the House of Representatives, Josiah Quincy, realized only too keenly the mistakes many of his colleagues were making in professing an emotional attachment to Great Britain. Not only did such professions do "little credit to their patriotism," but they did "infinitely less to their judgment. The truth is," he said in 1812, "the British look upon us as a *foreign nation*, and we must look upon them in the same light."[18]

Confronted by a Napoleonic tyranny and the democratic rumblings at their feet, the New England Federalists could scarcely restrain their affection for England, which seemed to them to be a rock of stability in a revolutionary world gone mad. This was why their Republican opponents,

17. Henry Adams, ed., *Documents Relating to New England Federalism, 1800–1815* (Boston, 1877), 389.
18. Perkins, *Prologue to War,* 61.

like Joseph Varnum, Republican congressman from Massachusetts and Speaker of the House of Representatives in 1810, believed that they could not trust the Federalists, even in Varnum's case those from his own state. Varnum had "for a long time been convinced," he told a colleague in March 1810, "that there was a party in our Country, fully determined to do everything in their power, to Subvert the principles of our happy government, and to establish a Monarchy on its ruins; and with a view of obtaining the aid of G.B in the accomplishment of their nefarious object, they have Inlisted into her service, and will go all lengths to Justify and support every measure which she may take against the Nation." Establishing America's separate identity as a nation was difficult enough, the Republicans believed, without having a large segment of the society yearning to reconnect with "a foreign nation, whose deadly hate has pursued us from the day when America said she would be free."[19]

With many Republican leaders holding these sorts of opinions, the war in their minds became both a second war for independence and a defense of republicanism itself. In this sense the Federalists helped contribute to the Republicans' move toward war; they made many Republicans feel that not only was the Union in danger but further vacillation—talking of war and doing nothing—had become impossible. A few Federalists, like Alexander L. Hanson of Maryland, even welcomed the possibility of war, confident that the Republicans would so mismanage it as to discredit their party and bring the Federalists back into power.[20]

The Republicans offered a variety of reasons why they felt they had to move toward war, most having to do with saving both republicanism and the nation's honor; but ultimately they were compelled to go to war because their foreign policy left them no alternative. America had been engaged in a kind of warfare—commercial warfare—with both Britain and France since 1806. The actual fighting of 1812 was only the inevitable consequence of the failure of "peaceful coercion." Wilson Cary Nicholas of Virginia put his finger on the problem early in 1810. The failure of "every mode of coercion short of war," he told Jefferson, now left little room for choice. "We have exhausted every means in our power to preserve peace. We have tried negotiations until it is disgraceful to think of renewing it, and commercial restrictions have operated to our own injury. War or submission alone remain." In deciding between these alternatives, Nicholas, along with many other Republicans, could not "hesitate a

19. Roger H. Brown, *The Republic in Peril: 1812* (New York, 1964), 15; Felix Grundy, *Annals of Congress*, 12th Congress, 1st session (May 1812), 24: 1407–8.
20. Richard Buel Jr., *America on the Brink: How the Political Struggle over the War of 1812 Almost Destroyed the Young Republic* (New York, 2005), 92–97, 133–35, 151–53, 242.

minute." By June 1812 the need to go to war with Great Britain, declared Secretary of State James Monroe, had become inescapable. "We have been so long dealing in the small way of embargoes, non-intercourse, and non-importation, with menaces of war, &c., that the British government has not believed us. We must actually get to war before the intention to make it will be credited either here or abroad."[21]

Perhaps some good would come out of a war. Some predicted it would destroy the parties and bring the country together. "The distinction of Federalists and Republicans will cease," declared Felix Grundy in May 1812; "the united energies of the people will be brought into action; the inquiry will be, are you for your country or against it?"[22] Some Republicans even came to see the war as a necessary regenerative act—as a means of purging Americans of their pecuniary greed and their seemingly insatiable love of commerce and money-making. They hoped that the war with England might refresh the national character, lessen the overweening selfishness of people, and revitalize republicanism.[23] "War," said the enterprising Baltimore journalist Hezekiah Niles in 1811, "will purify the political atmosphere....All the public virtues will be refined and hallowed; and we shall again behold at the head of affairs citizens who may rival the immortal men of 1776." When told that a war might be expensive, a Maryland congressman responded with indignation. "What is money?" he said. "What is all our property, compared with our honor and our liberty?" Americans must put aside their partisan divisions and concern for profits, urged the editors of the Richmond Enquirer. "Forget self," they said, "and think of America."[24]

SINCE THE REPUBLICANS BELIEVED that war was a threat to republican principles, whatever kind of war they fought would have to be different from the wars the Old World had known. As Secretary of the Treasury Albert Gallatin pointed out at the outset, the Republicans needed to conduct a war without promoting "the evils inseparable from it...debt, perpetual taxation, military establishments, and other corrupting or anti-republican habits or institutions."[25]

21. Wilson Cary Nicholas to TJ, 4 Feb. 1810, Papers of Jefferson: Retirement Ser., 2: 195; James Monroe to John Taylor, 13 June 1812, in Stanislaus Murray Hamilton, ed., The Writings of James Monroe (New York, 1901), 5: 206.
22. Annals of Congress, 12th Congress, 1st session (May 1812), 24: 1410.
23. Steven Watts, The Republic Reborn: War and the Making of Liberal America, 1790–1820 (Baltimore, 1987), 63–107.
24. Niles' Weekly Register, 1 (1811–1812), 252; Annals of Congress, 12th Congress, 1st session (Jan. 1812), 658; Watts, The Republic Reborn, 101.
25. Albert Gallatin to TJ, 10 March 1812, in Henry Adams, The Life of Henry Gallatin (New York, 1879), 455–56.

Although the Republicans in the Congress knew that the country's armed forces were not ready for any kind of combat, they nonetheless seemed much more concerned about the threat the American military might pose to the United States than to Great Britain. Armies and navies, said John Taylor of Caroline, "only serve to excite wars, squander money, and extend corruption."[26] Thus the Republicans prepared for the war in the most curious and desultory manner. They had strengthened the army and navy in 1807, but in 1810 wondered whether they really needed these military increases after all, even though the possibility of war was still in the air.[27] Since armies and navies cost money, strengthening them meant new taxes, and that was not what good Republicans voted for.

In the spring of 1810 the Republican Congress, confronted with the dilemma of increasing taxes, decided instead to debate the possibility of reducing all the expensive armed forces. John Taylor of South Carolina (not to be confused with Virginia's John Taylor of Caroline) wanted the army substantially cut back and the whole navy put in mothballs, except for those vessels used to carry dispatches. Since the country was not actually at war, said Congressman Richard M. Johnson of Kentucky, there was no need for the military. "Unless you use them, the Army and Navy, in times of peace, are engines of oppression." Yet in the next breath Johnson, befitting his hawkish reputation, was ready to go to war against both Britain and France at the same time. His colleague from Kentucky, Samuel McKee, declared that "even if war itself was certain, it would be perfectly unnecessary to keep on foot this establishment." "For defence from a foreign foe," he preferred the militia—the citizen-soldiers, "the hardy sons of the country"—to the corrupt dregs of the regular army. "Would any gentleman be willing to submit the defence of everything he holds dear, to men who have loitered out their days in camps and in the most luxurious ease and vice?" As for the navy, what purpose could it have? Since it could never be large enough to take on the British navy, better that the United States have none at all. Since the existence of military establishments only bred war, which in turn magnified executive power, McKee would reduce the American military as drastically as he could. Never mind simply reducing the army, declared Congressman Macon; it ought to be abolished outright. But the Congress did not want to go that far, and by a two-to-one margin it voted merely to reduce the army and navy, not to eliminate them entirely.[28]

26. Risjord, *Old Republicans*, 109.
27. Risjord, *Old Republicans*, 102.
28. *Annals of Congress*, 11th Congress, 2nd session (April 1810) 21: 1864–1876, 1885.

Following the election of more War Hawks to the Twelfth Congress in 1810, however, talk of war became more and more prevalent. Still, the Republicans in Congress remained reluctant to face up to the implications of going to war, and so they dawdled and debated.

Finally Congress in January 1812 added twenty-five thousand regular troops to the ten thousand previously authorized. In addition, it provided for the raising of fifty thousand one-year volunteers, with the states rather than the national government, however, having the authority to appoint the volunteer officers; and in April 1812 it authorized the president to call out one hundred thousand militiamen who would serve for six months. But efforts to classify by age and arm the militia were stymied by state jealousies. Some congressmen even objected to the phrase "the militia of the United States"; it was, they said, the "militia of the several States," until called into the service of the United States.[29] Since the militia (and some included the volunteers as well) could not legally serve abroad, there were doubts raised over the government's plans to invade Canada as a means of bringing pressure to bear on Great Britain.

At least Congress voted for an army; the navy was another matter. A bill to build twelve ships of the line and twenty frigates ran into stiff opposition. Congressman Adam Seybert of Pennsylvania predicted that such an increase in the navy would have the most awful consequences. Unlike the army, the navy would not be disbanded at the end of the war and thus, as "a *permanent* Naval Establishment," might "become a powerful engine in the hands of an ambitious Executive." Not only was a navy expensive, it would lead to impressment and naval conscription. "If the United States shall determine to augment their navy, so as to rival those of Europe, the public debt will become permanent; direct taxes will be increased; the paupers of the country will be increased; the nation will be bankrupt; and, I fear," concluded Seybert, "the tragedy will end in a revolution."[30]

With such dire results predicted, it was not surprising that the Republican Congress at the end of January 1812 finally decided that the United States did not actually need a navy to fight the impending war. The House by a vote of sixty-two to fifty-nine defeated the proposal to build twelve ships of the line and twenty-four frigates. Nathaniel Macon of North Carolina was only one of many Republicans who in the early months of 1812 voted against all attempts to arm and prepare the navy, who opposed all efforts to beef up the War Department, who rejected all tax increases, and yet who in June 1812 voted for the war.[31]

29. *Annals of Congress*, 12th Congress, 1st session, (Feb. 1812), 23: 1027.
30. *Annals of Congress*, 12th Congress, 1st session, (Jan. 1812), 23: 824–833.
31. Risjord, *Old Republicans*, 127.

After much hand-wringing over the problem of paying for the war, the Congress finally agreed to some tax increases, but only on the condition they were to go into effect when war was actually declared. The president was relieved that at last the Republicans in Congress had "got down the dose of taxes. It is the strongest proof," he told Jefferson in March 1812, "they could give that they do not mean to flinch from the contest to which the mad conduct of G.B. drives them."[32] Taxes would only cover a portion of the cost of the war; the rest would have to be borrowed. Of course, in 1811, even as war seemed increasingly likely, the Republicans had killed the Bank of the United States, which some knew was the best instrument for borrowing money and financing a war. This failure to re-charter the BUS proved to be disastrous for the war effort.

In other respects too the government was ill prepared for war, partly because many people did not believe that it was actually going to have to fight. Many congressmen wanted to go home for a spring recess in 1812. When the recess was denied, many of them left anyway, making it difficult to gather a congressional quorum even as the country was presumably moving toward war. As late as May 1812, the British minister in Washington was totally confused about what the Republicans were up to, the signals were so mixed. Could a country go to war when its War Department, with only the secretary and a dozen inexperienced clerks, was so chaotically disorganized? With no general staff, the secretary of war communicated directly with individual generals and acted as the army's quartermaster general. The United States, complained the secretary of war, William Eustis, presented the "rare phenomenon" of a country going to war with an army lacking staff support.[33] In April 1812 many Republicans opposed a bill providing for two assistant secretaries of war, even though it had been suggested by the president. Some Republicans thought that such additional offices were the opening wedge to executive tyranny. But with Federalist help the bill squeaked through.

Finally, on June 1, 1812, President Madison delivered his war message to Congress. He dwelt exclusively on Britain's impressment of sailors from American ships and its abuses of American neutral rights—the two issues for Republicans that most flagrantly violated the sovereign independence of the United States. Indeed, said Madison, evoking the ominous phrase of the British Declaratory Act of 1766, the recent British aggressions against American shipping had rested on nothing but their "claim to regulate our external commerce in all cases whatsoever." In effect, the president said, Great Britain was already in "a state of war

32. JM to TJ, 6 March 1812, *Republic of Letters*, 1688.
33. Stagg, *Mr. Madison's War*, 160.

against the United States."[34] On June 18, Madison signed the congressional declaration of war, which was enthusiastically supported by many Republicans who for the previous six months had voted against all attempts to prepare for the war.

Although Congress had created an army on paper, the actual army on the eve of the war consisted of 6,744 men, scattered across the nation at twenty-three different forts and posts. New York, for example, had less than a third of the men needed to defend its harbor.[35] The generals responsible for leading the army were not very impressive. Although sixty-one-year-old Henry Dearborn was a distinguished Revolutionary War veteran and former secretary of war in Jefferson's cabinet, he was more interested in politics than in war-making and reluctant to assume a command. Nevertheless, "Granny," as he came to be called by his troops, was appointed the senior major general responsible both for commanding the Northern Department and for drawing up the initial plans for invading Canada. Fifty-nine-year-old William Hull had been in the Revolutionary War, but he had suffered a stroke and his best days were behind him. Since he was the governor of Michigan Territory and the only candidate for a command in the territory, he was appointed brigadier general in charge of the North Western Department, a command that was separate from Dearborn's. The junior officers were not in better shape. There were only twenty-nine field-grade officers (colonels and majors), many of them either incompetent or too old for active service. Winfield Scott, a twenty-six-year-old newly appointed lieutenant colonel, was an energetic and brilliant exception. He thought most of his fellow officers were "swaggerers, dependents, decayed gentlemen... *utterly unfit for any military purpose whatever.*"[36]

After much jousting between the Congress and the president over the appointment of more officers, Madison by the end of the year had issued commissions to over eleven hundred individuals, 15 percent of whom immediately declined them, followed by an additional 8 percent who resigned after several months of service. By November 1812, ten months after Congress had authorized increasing the regular army by twenty-five thousand, only 9,823 men had been recruited—hardly surprising since the recruiting officers often could not even offer the recruits a decent uniform and a pair of shoes. By the end of 1812 a real army scarcely existed. Very few of its companies were at full strength, and very few of the recruits had any training whatsoever for combat.

34. JM, War Message to Congress, 1 June 1812, *Madison: Writings*, 691.
35. Leonard D. White, *The Jeffersonians: A Study in Administrative History* (New York, 1951), 216.
36. Jon Latimer, *1812: War with America* (Cambridge, MA, 2007), 56.

MANY AMERICANS INITIALLY SAW the war as a way of dealing with the problem of the Indians in the Northwest. Ever since the Treaty of Greenville in 1795, the Indians of the Northwest Territory had been pushed back by relentless hordes of white settlers. Finally in 1805 the Shawnee chief Tecumseh and his half brother Tenskwatawa (better known as the Prophet) attempted to halt this steady encroachment by forming some sort of confederation. The Prophet led an Indian revival movement that denounced white ways and white goods and preached a return to the virtues of traditional Indian culture. At the same time, Tecumseh—an impressive, commanding man and perhaps the most extraordinary Indian leader in American history—attacked the practice of making land cessions to the Americans, dozens of which had been made under Jefferson's presidency. He proposed that the Northwestern tribes adopt a policy of common landowning in order to resist white expansion. From Prophet's Town at the junction of the Wabash and Tippecanoe rivers in Indiana Territory, the Shawnee brothers spread their message throughout the region, resulting in 1810 in an alarming increase in Indian raids on white settlers.[37]

Although the ideas of Tecumseh and the boastful Prophet alienated as many Indians as they inspired, Americans in the Northwest believed they faced a well-organized Indian conspiracy. William Henry Harrison, governor of the Indiana Territory, was eager to establish Indiana's statehood and pleaded for troops to crush the conspiracy. "If some decisive measures are not speedily adopted," he told the secretary of war in the summer of 1811, "we shall have a general combination of all the tribes against us."[38] Since the administration was preoccupied with its negotiations and possible war with Great Britain and did not want an Indian war, it was reluctant to give Harrison any regular troops. But under pressure from the other territorial governors in the region, the federal government finally gave way and committed a regiment of regulars to Harrison's command. By the fall of 1811 Harrison had assembled an army of two hundred and fifty regulars, one hundred Kentucky volunteer riflemen, and six hundred Indiana militiamen.

Taking advantage of Tecumseh's absence in the South, where the Indian leader was recruiting more tribes to his cause, Harrison marched upon Prophet's Town. He camped outside of the town on November 6, 1811, apparently intending to enter the Indian settlement the next day to order the tribes to disperse. Urged on by the Prophet, six or seven hundred Indians surprised Harrison's troops during the pre-dawn hours of

37. John Sugden, *Tecumseh: A Life* (New York, 1997).
38. Donald R. Hickey, *The War of 1812: A Forgotten Conflict* (Urbana, IL, 1989), 25.

November 7 and inflicted about two hundred casualties before being driven off. Although Harrison's force suffered twice as many casualties as the Indians, it was able the next day to burn the abandoned Prophet's Town, thus enabling Harrison to call the Battle of Tippecanoe a victory.

Although the Madison government claimed that this ambiguous victory had brought peace to the Northwest frontier, Westerners in the region knew differently and stressed their continued vulnerability to Indian attacks, especially if the Indians were supported by the British in Canada. It was not surprising therefore that an invasion of Canada became central to America's war plans in 1812. Not only would such an invasion help to pressure the British to make peace, but it would end their influence with the Northwestern Indians once and for all and bring about Britain's full compliance with the peace treaty of 1783. Although Madison's government always denied that it intended to annex Canada, it had no doubt, as Secretary of State Monroe told the British government in June 1812, that once the United States forces occupied the British provinces, it would be "difficult to relinquish territory which had been conquered."[39]

Besides the possibility of removing the Indian threat, the Republicans had other reasons for wanting to take Canada from Great Britain: they thought it was already filled with Americans. Many Loyalists who had fled the Revolution lived in Canada, and since the 1790s perhaps fifty thousand American citizens, many frustrated with the archaic system of landholding in New York, had left the United States in search of cheap land and had moved into the southwest corner of Lower Canada (present-day Quebec) and into Upper Canada (present-day Ontario, and southwest of Lower Canada). With so many Americans willing to leave the United States for cheap land, it is no wonder the Republicans were worried about the strength of their countrymen's attachment to the nation. Canada was becoming less a sterile snow-clad wilderness and more a collection of substantial British colonies that the United States could no longer ignore. Smuggling over the northern border had undermined the embargo and weakened other Republican efforts to restrict trade with Britain. Moreover, evidence mounted that Canada was becoming a major source of supply for both the British West Indies and the mother country itself, especially for timber. With the development of Canada freeing the British Empire from its vulnerability to American economic restrictions, President Madison was bound to be concerned about Canada.

ALTHOUGH GROWING, Canada seemed especially vulnerable to an American invasion. It had only about five hundred thousand people com-

pared to the nearly eight million in the United States, and it was still economically rather undeveloped. Since two-thirds of the people of Lower
Canada were of French descent, their loyalty to the British crown was
doubtful. Upper Canada, that is, the Niagara area, which was the most
likely site of an invasion, had a white population of only seventy-seven
thousand, of whom one third or more were American in origin and perhaps sympathy.[40] In mid-July 1812 Governor Daniel Tompkins of New York
was sure that half the militias of both Lower and Upper Canada "would
join our standard."[41] Since the Canadian frontier from Quebec to Mackinac Island at the junction of Lake Huron and Lake Michigan stretched
well over a thousand miles, it seemed difficult to defend. Jefferson expressed
the confidence of many Republicans in 1812 when he predicted the invasion of Canada would be "a mere matter of marching."[42]

The plan for invasion involved a three-pronged attack on the areas of
Detroit, Niagara, and Montreal. Although Montreal was supposedly the
main objective, the unwillingness of Massachusetts and Connecticut to
supply militia for the assault on Montreal made the western attack on the
Detroit frontier seem more feasible. William Hull and his two thousand
troops were to march from Ohio to take the British Fort Malden south of
Detroit. Hull's officers, who jealously quarreled over precedence with
one another, had little confidence in their commander, dismissing him as
old and indecisive even before the force set out. When Hull's troops
reached the Canadian border in July 1812, two hundred members of the
Ohio militia refused to cross over into Canada, claiming that they were a
defensive force only and could not fight outside of the United States.

Hull hoped for little or no resistance. He urged the people of Canada
to remain in their homes or join the American cause; perhaps as many as
five hundred did in fact desert the Canadian militia. Although Fort
Malden was only lightly defended, Hull was worried about his supply
lines and kept delaying his attack. When he learned that Fort Mackinac,
at the junction of Lake Huron and Lake Michigan, had surrendered to
British forces on July 17, he became more apprehensive, fearing that Indians from the north would now descend on him. Without Fort Mackinac
in American hands, Hull believed that Fort Dearborn at the present site
of Chicago could not be held, and he ordered its evacuation, which eventually took place on August 15. On August 6, 1812, Hull finally ordered an
attack on Fort Malden, only to cancel it the next day when he heard that
British regulars were on their way to the threatened fort. When Hull next

40.  Latimer, 1812, 42.
41.  Walter R. Borneman, 1812: The War That Forged a Nation (New York, 2004), 57.
42.  Hickey, War of 1812, 73.

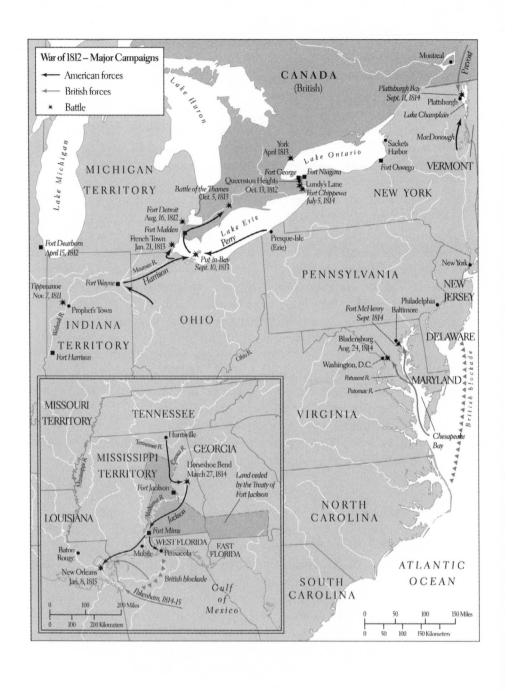

War of 1812 – Major Campaigns

← American forces
← British forces
✱ Battle

decided to retreat to Detroit, many of the militia officers wanted to remove him from command, but the regular officers stopped the mutiny.

The British commander, Major General Isaac Brock, the governor of Upper Canada, took advantage of Hull's timidity and mobilized his troops to march on Detroit. His force included a mixture of two hundred fifty regulars, four hundred militia, and about six hundred Indians under Tecumseh's leadership. Capitalizing on Hull's dread of Indian atrocities, Brock arranged to have a bogus document fall into American hands in order to feign having more Indian troops than he actually had. Hull, paralyzed with fear that he was cut off from his supplies and faced an overwhelming force, including Indians that might massacre the women and children in the Detroit fort, surrendered on August 16, 1812, without firing a shot. After taking Detroit, Brock annexed the whole territory of Michigan and made it part of the dominion of His Majesty George III.

Hull's surrender of Detroit shocked everyone, and rather unfairly he alone was held responsible for the disaster. Hull was eventually courtmartialed for cowardice and neglect of duty and was sentenced to death, with a recommendation of mercy because of his Revolutionary War service and advanced age. Madison accepted this recommendation and commuted Hull's punishment to dismissal from the army. With the loss of the forts at Detroit, Mackinac, and Dearborn, the whole Northwest lay open to British invasion and Indian raids.

Although the administration wanted someone else to command the Western forces, it was compelled by local pressure, especially from Kentucky, to appoint William Henry Harrison, the alleged hero of Tippecanoe, as the commanding general to replace Hull. In the winter of 1812–1813 Harrison sent a detachment of eight hundred fifty troops to protect settlers at Frenchtown eighteen miles southwest of Malden (now Monroe, Michigan). Attacked on January 21, 1813, at the River Raisin by a force of about twelve hundred British and Indians, the outnumbered Americans surrendered. When the British troops had left with the American prisoners who could walk, the Indians allied to the British became drunk and massacred dozens of the wounded prisoners who had been left behind. "Remember the Raisin" became an American rallying cry throughout the Northwest.

The invasions of the eastern portions of Canada were no more successful. Although Major General Henry Dearborn was presumably responsible for the area from Niagara eastward to New England, he scarcely seems to have comprehended what was expected of him. As customs collector for Boston, he was reluctant to leave New England. Although he had helped design the invasion plan and had received explicit instructions, he nevertheless wondered to the secretary of war about "who was to have command of the operations in Upper Canada; I take it for granted," he said, "that my command does not extend to that distant quarter." Instead of launching an attack on Montreal from Albany and thus relieving some of the pressure on Hull in the West, Dearborn spent months in New England trying to recruit men and build coastal defenses.[43]

When Dearborn seemed confused about his responsibilities for the Niagara campaign, Governor Daniel Tompkins of New York took matters into his own hands and appointed Stephen Van Rensselaer commander-in-chief of the New York militia. Although Van Rensselaer had no military experience, he was a Federalist, and Tomkins thought this appointment might ease some of the Federalist opposition to the war. In October 1812 Van Rensselaer with four thousand troops successfully attacked Queenston Heights on the British side of the Niagara River, and in the process killed the heroic General Brock, who had returned from Detroit to take command of the British defense. When Van Rensselaer sought to send the New York militia to reinforce the troops in Queenston Heights, they, like the militia in the West, developed constitutional scruples and refused to leave the country. Consequently, the American force, numbering about a thousand men, was soon overwhelmed by British reinforcements and on October 13, 1812, was forced to surrender. The Battle of Queenston Heights became a rich site of memory for the victorious Canadians and an important stimulus for their own emerging nationalism. Brock's death turned him into a cult figure in Upper Canada, and numerous streets, towns, and a university were named after him.[44]

In the East, General Dearborn had not yet begun to move against Canada. Only in November 1812, after prodding by the exasperated secretary of war, did Dearborn's army, numbering between six and eight thousand men, set out from Albany northward toward Canada. Again the state militia refused to cross the border, and Dearborn abandoned his feeble attempt at an invasion. His entire venture, recalled a contemporary, was a "miscarriage without even the heroism of disaster."[45]

The three-pronged American campaign against Canada in 1812 had been a complete failure. What was worse, the failure was due less to the superiority of the Canadian resistance and more to the inability of the United States to recruit and manage its armies.

THE WAR AT SEA IN 1812 helped to take some of the sting out of that failure. Although the Republicans in Congress had decided in January 1812 not to build any new ships, seventeen ships, including seven

43. Latimer, 1812, 71.
44. Latimer, 1812, 82–83.
45. Stagg, Mr. Madison's War, 268.

frigates, still survived from the naval buildup during the Quasi-War with France in the late 1790s. The U.S. Navy had no large ships of the line that carried seventy-four guns, but three of the frigates, the USS *Constitution*, the USS *President*, and the USS *United States*, had forty-four guns and were bigger and sturdier than most other foreign frigates. Although Britain had hundreds of vessels, they were spread about the world. In 1812 Britain had only one ship of the line and nine frigates operating out of its North American stations at Halifax and Newfoundland.

The *Constitution*, captained by Isaac Hull, thirty-nine-year-old nephew of General William Hull, was the first American warship to acquire fame in the war. After escaping from a British squadron in July 1812 in one of the longest and most exciting chases in naval history, the *Constitution* on August 19 defeated HMS *Guerrière*, a thirty-eight-gun frigate under the command of Captain Richard Dacres, who earlier had contemptuously challenged the American naval commanders to frigate-to-frigate duels at sea. When during the engagement, which took place 750 miles east of Boston, a British broadside bounced harmlessly off the *Constitution*'s hull, one of the crew supposedly exclaimed that "her sides are made of iron," and the legend of "Old Ironsides" was born. The London *Times* was stunned by the American victory. Since "never before in the history of the world did an English frigate strike to an American," the paper predicted that the victory was likely to make the Americans "insolent and confident."[46]

As a consequence of the *Constitution*'s victory, Madison's government gave up its original idea of keeping the navy bottled up in the harbors as floating batteries. Instead, America's ships were divided into three squadrons and ordered to fan out over the central Atlantic trade routes and to take advantage of every opportunity to meet and destroy the enemy. In October 1812 the *United States* under the command of thirty-three-year-old Stephen Decatur, the hero of Tripoli in 1804, showed brilliant seamanship in defeating and capturing HMS *Macedonian* six hundred miles west of the Canary Islands. A prize crew sailed the *Macedonian*, which was only two years old, across the ocean—a very risky venture—and into the harbor of Newport, Rhode Island. Since the *Macedonian* was the first and only British frigate ever brought into an American port as a prize of war, its capture made Decatur a hero all over again. The officers and crew of the *United States* received $300,000 in prize money, the largest award made for the capture of a single ship during the war.[47]

---

46. Borneman, *1812*, 84; Harry L. Coles, *The War of 1812* (Chicago, 1965), 81.

47. In 1820 the forty-one-year-old Decatur was killed in a duel by James Barron, the disgraced captain of the *Chesapeake*, who had surrendered to a British warship in 1807. Hickey, *War of 1812*, 96; Robert J. Allison, *Stephen Decatur: American Naval Hero, 1779–1820* (Amherst, MA, 2005), 115–19, 123–28, 200–211.

A series of successful single-ship engagements followed, including the victory of the *Constitution*, now captained by William Bainbridge, over HMS *Java* off the coast of Brazil in December 1812. During the war there were eight sloop and brig engagements, and in all but one the American ships were victorious. Losing these single-ship engagements was a new experience for British seamen. In twenty years of naval warfare and numerous single engagements between British and French frigates, only once, in 1807, had the British ever been beaten. "It is a cruel mortification," said one British minister, "to be beat by these second-hand Englishmen upon our own element." In all, the American navy in 1812 defeated or captured seven British warships, including three frigates, and fifty merchantmen and lost only three small warships, each with eighteen guns or less.[48]

But the real American threat to Britain on the high seas came from the country's privateers, the naval equivalent of the militia and what one Republican called "our cheapest and best navy."[49] Most of the five hundred registered privateers were small vessels that made only a single cruise; only about two hundred of the five hundred were large enough to carry fifty men or more. Although there may have been only fifty privateers at sea at any one time, they were generally very profitable. Operating off the coast of Canada and in the West Indies, the American privateers captured 450 prizes in the first six months of the war. (Throughout the remainder of the war they would capture 850 more British merchant vessels.) The most successful privateers were James D'Wolf's *Yankee*, sailing out of Bristol, Rhode Island, which captured eight British vessels valued at $300,000, and the *Rossie*, operating out of Baltimore, which seized eighteen ships worth nearly $1,500,000. American privateers did enough damage to British trade in the West Indies to temporarily force insurance rates up to 30 percent of the value of the cargo.[50] Although America's successes at sea in 1812 were of little strategic significance in determining the outcome of the war—the British navy soon recovered its dominance of the oceans—they did boost American morale and help to compensate for the disgraceful defeats on land.

IN 1812 AMERICA'S NAVAL SUCCESSES may even have helped Madison win a second term as president. Although two-thirds of the

---

48. Hickey, *War of 1812*, 98.
49. Latimer, *1812*, 88.
50. Hickey, *War of 1812*, 96–97; Coles, *War of 1812*, 95–99; Latimer, *1812*, 90; George C. Daughan, *If by Sea: The Forging of the American Navy—From the Revolution to the War of 1812* (New York, 2008), 430.

Republican congressmen supported Madison as the nominee of the party (with Elbridge Gerry of Massachusetts as the vice-presidential nominee), many of the Northern Republican congressmen, disillusioned with Madison's leadership and the dominance of the Virginia Dynasty, wanted someone more sympathetic to Northern commerce. Consequently, Republican members of the New York state legislature selected DeWitt Clinton, the handsome and popular mayor of New York City, as their Republican nominee for the presidency. The Federalists decided to nominate no one but instead to support Clinton without formally endorsing him, for fear of undermining his Republican backing outside of New York.

In the November 1812 election Clinton carried all the seaboard states from New Hampshire through Delaware and part of Maryland. Madison won all the rest, including Pennsylvania, which further established its role as the keystone state in the Republican party. The revelation that the Federalists were supporting Clinton helped carry Pennsylvania for the president. Madison received 128 electoral votes to Clinton's 89, a smaller margin of victory than the president had received in 1808. The Republicans lost seats in Congress, especially in New York, Massachusetts, and New Hampshire. The Federalists captured control of most of the states of New England as well as the states of New Jersey, Maryland, and Delaware. By taking advantage of the mismanagement of the war and the frightening news of the savage Baltimore riots in the summer of 1812, the Federalists made their most striking electoral gains since the 1790s. The Federalists mistakenly thought the fortunes of the Republicans were dying and theirs were on the rise.

THE GOVERNMENT STRUGGLED to recover from the failures of 1812. As long as Britain was holding American territory and winning the war, it was impossible to make the former mother country come to terms. Canada had to be successfully invaded, and that meant the United States' military forces would have to be beefed up and reformed. In the winter of 1812–1813 Madison replaced Secretary of War William Eustis with John Armstrong, a New Yorker and the leader of the abortive Newburgh mutiny in 1783 (the attempt by some Continental Army officers to pressure the Congress), and Secretary of the Navy Paul Hamilton with William Jones, a Philadelphia merchant and former congressman. Congress finally agreed that the country needed a navy and in January 1813 voted to construct six additional frigates and four ships of the line. Prodded by Madison, Congress also provided for an additional twenty-two thousand regular troops and raised the pay of the soldiers in order to spur enlistments. It added staff officers and improved the ordering and distribution of supplies to the army. Under these wartime pressures Republican congressmen were being compelled to swallow many of their principles.

What they were not willing to give up, at least not easily, was their traditional opposition to any kind of internal taxation. But there were problems. If the Republicans were to avoid imposing internal taxes, they needed the revenue from customs duties on imports, most of which were British goods. Yet the Non-Intercourse Act, which was part of the war effort, presumably prohibited the importation of British goods. Non-importation made no sense, declared Congressman Langdon Cheves, a War Hawk from South Carolina. "It puts out one eye of your enemy, it is true," he said in December 1812, "but it puts out both your own. It exhausts the purse, it exhausts the spirit, and paralyses the sword of the nation."[51]

Although most Republicans disagreed with Cheves and refused to abandon the weapon of commercial discrimination, they were still reluctant to resort to the imposition of any internal taxes. Secretary of the Treasury Gallatin had urged internal taxes from the beginning, which had helped provoke the most radical Republicans into labeling him "the Rat—in the Treasury."[52] Now at the outset of 1813 Gallatin faced having to pay for the war by borrowing and by issuing treasury notes. But borrowing proved difficult, especially with the New England Federalists working to stymie all lending of money to the government. In March 1813 Gallatin informed the president that the government had scarcely enough funds to carry on for a month. But an offer of Russian mediation of the conflict, which the United States readily accepted, improved the prospects for peace, and Gallatin was able to extract enough money from creditors to see the government through the year 1813. Finally, in June 1813 the Republicans closed their severely divided ranks enough to pass a comprehensive tax bill, which included a direct tax on land, a duty on imported salt, and excise taxes on stills, retailers, auction sales, sugar, carriages, and negotiable paper. All these taxes, however, were not to go into effect until the beginning of 1814—revealing once again, as one Virginia congressman put it, that "everyone is for taxing every body, except himself and his Constituents."[53]

THE GOVERNMENT'S PLAN for the campaign of 1813 was to attack Kingston, Britain's major naval base on Lake Ontario, York (present-day Toronto), the capital of Upper Canada, and then Fort George and Fort Erie, which controlled the Niagara River. Since America's failures in 1812 had been due in large part to Britain's control of the Great Lakes,

51. *Annals of Congress*, 12th Congress, 2nd session (Dec. 1812), 25: 249.
52. Philadelphia *Aurora*, 30 Jan. 1812, in Hickey, *War of 1812*, 120.
53. Hickey, *War of 1812*, 122.

especially Ontario and Erie, the U.S. government was determined to reverse that situation. Believing that Kingston was too strongly garrisoned, General Dearborn and his naval opposite Commodore Isaac Chauncey decided to attack York instead and destroy the shipping there. In late April 1813 a detachment of sixteen hundred men under the command of Brigadier General Zebulon M. Pike, the explorer who had discovered Pike's Peak in 1806, sailed out of Sackets Harbor, on the eastern edge of Lake Ontario, and attacked York on the northwest corner of the lake. The Americans overwhelmed the defenders of York, which had only six hundred inhabitants, but suffered heavy casualties, including General Pike. They then proceeded to loot and burn the town, including its public buildings, aided by disgruntled British subjects who came from the countryside. When the Americans evacuated the town, they took with them provisions and military stores and £2,500 from the public treasury; they even took some books from the subscription library, most of which were soon returned. (But the Canadians did not get the government's mace back until 1934.) Commodore Chauncey made another destructive raid on York in July, taking what little public property that was left. The British remembered the burning of their Canadian capital when in the following year they burned Washington.[54]

The Americans had less success in the Niagara region. After taking Fort George in May 1813, the American forces failed to follow up their initial victory, and the British soon recovered. Fierce fighting went on through the rest of the year with the British eventually ousting the Americans from both Fort George and Fort Niagara. By December 1813 not only had the Americans lost control of the Niagara frontier, but General Dearborn had been relieved of his command, to be replaced by the notorious General James Wilkinson.[55]

Although the Americans were not able to gain control of Lake Ontario in 1813, their experience on Lake Erie was different. In the spring of 1813 Oliver Hazard Perry, a twenty-seven-year-old naval officer from Rhode Island, began assembling a fleet of nine vessels at Presque Isle (present-day Erie, Pennsylvania); and in the late summer he sailed for Put-in-Bay, off South Bass Island toward the western end of the lake. On September 10, 1813, Perry's squadron traded broadsides with a smaller British squadron for over two terrible and bloody hours. When Perry's flagship, the USS *Lawrence* (twenty guns), was reduced to a battered hulk, he transferred to the USS *Niagara* (twenty guns) and carried on the fight for another hour, finally forcing the British ships to surrender. On the

54. Latimer, *1812*, 133.
55. Latimer, *1812*, 195.

back of an old letter Perry scribbled his famous message to General Harrison: "We have met the enemy and they are ours."[56] His victory could scarcely have been more significant, for it enabled the Americans to reverse all the defeats they had suffered in 1812.

With the loss of the British fleet on Lake Erie, Sir Henry Proctor, the British commander in charge of the newly acquired Michigan Territory, knew his situation had become untenable. He thus decided to withdraw from Malden and Detroit and, with his Indian allies led by Tecumseh, retreat northward to the Thames River. Following close on Proctor's tail was General Harrison with three thousand men, mostly Kentucky volunteers commanded by Congressman Richard M. Johnson, on leave from his legislative duties. Harrison crossed into Canada and on October 5, 1813, caught up with Proctor at Moraviantown. With only 430 soldiers and about six hundred Indian warriors, Proctor's bedraggled and demoralized force was quickly overrun. In this Battle of the Thames (known to Canadians as the Battle of Moraviantown) Johnson, or one of his troops, killed Tecumseh, shattering his Indian confederacy. When the Indians learned of Tecumseh's death, recalled a member of the Kentucky militia, they "gave the loudest yells I ever heard from human beings and that ended the fight." Johnson used his claim that he had killed the famous Indian chief to gain the vice-presidency in 1836.[57]

Earlier Tecumseh had helped inspire some Creek Indians, known as Red Sticks, into resisting the American encroachments on the Southern frontier. In 1810 the United States had annexed most of West Florida. Then in 1813, following the outbreak of the war, American troops occupied the last remaining piece of West Florida, the district of Mobile that reached to the Perdido River. (This turned out to be the only piece of conquered territory retained by the United States as a result of the war.) At the same time, clashes among the Creeks themselves, who occupied most of present-day Alabama, escalated into a larger war with the United States. In August 1813 a party of Creeks overran Fort Mims, a stockade located forty miles north of Mobile in southeastern Mississippi Territory, and massacred hundreds of Americans. Despite being warned, the commander of the fort had doubted the possibility of any Indian attack and had left the gates of the stockade open. The result was horrific. "Indians, Negroes, white men, women and children lay in one promiscuous ruin," declared a member of an American burial party. "All were scalped, and the females of every age were butchered in a manner which neither decency nor language will permit me to describe." Although the attacking

56. Coles, *War of 1812*, 129.
57. Latimer, *1812*, 189.

Creeks lost a hundred or so of their men, they killed nearly 250 whites and perhaps another 150 blacks and friendly Indians. This massacre sent shock waves throughout the Southwest.[58]

Andrew Jackson, a major general in the Tennessee militia, took charge and moved south with several thousand Tennessee volunteers, including a twenty-seven-year-old Davy Crockett and a twenty-year-old Sam Houston. Jackson fought a series of inconclusive engagements through the fall and winter of 1813–1814. Jackson was having problems holding his army together, but, believing that no army could exist "where order & Subordination are wholly disregarded," and being a disciplinarian like none other, he knew what to do. Twice he raised his own gun to stop militiamen from leaving, and finally he had a young soldier who had refused to obey an order court-martialed and shot, the first such execution since the Revolution. The lesson took, and, as Jackson pointed out, "a strict obedience afterwards characterized the army." With his militiamen now more frightened of him than the Indians, Jackson led his army against a band of a thousand or more Red Sticks and on March 27, 1814, at Horseshoe Bend on the Tallapoosa River, wiped it out. With over eight hundred of the Creek warriors killed in the battle against a loss of only forty-five Americans, even tough-minded "Old Hickory" had to admit that the "carnage was dreadful." "My people are no more!" cried a surviving chief, Red Eagle. "Their bones are bleaching on the plains of the Tallushatchee, Talladega, [and] Emuckfaw."[59]

On August 9, 1814, all the Creeks were forced to sign the harsh Treaty of Fort Jackson. Despite instructions from Washington to the contrary, Jackson sought to punish even those Indians who were allies of the United States. They had, he said, "forfeited all right to the Territory we have conquered."[60] The treaty gave to the whites over twenty-two million acres of land—more than half of the territory belonging to the Creeks. Although his superiors in Washington were furious, Westerners were elated. Jackson had broken the Creek nation and, as he himself boasted, had seized the "cream of the Creek country, opening up a communication from Georgia to Mobile." Although victory in this Creek war did not strategically affect the war with Great Britain, it "could fairly be described," concludes one historian, "as the most decisive and most significant victory won by the United States in the entire War of 1812."[61]

58. Latimer, 1812, 220.
59. Borneman, 1812, 151; Latimer, 1812, 221.
60. Latimer, 1812, 369.
61. Stagg, Mr. Madison's War, 362.

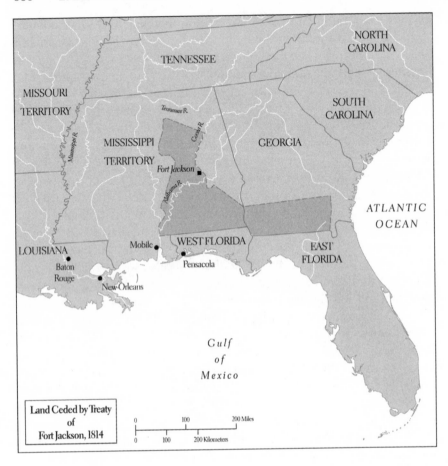

DESPITE AMERICAN VICTORIES in the Northwest and Southwest, however, the strategic center of the northern frontier along the Niagara and St. Lawrence rivers remained deadlocked. After two years of campaigning, the Americans had not been able to capture and hold any Canadian territory. Equally frustrating was the war at sea. By 1813 Britain's great naval superiority was finally making itself felt. Needing American foodstuffs in the West Indies and the Iberian Peninsula, where the British army was busy fighting the French, Britain at first had left American trade essentially untouched. And always there were Americans eager to earn money supplying the British. But beginning in December 1812 Britain began blockading Delaware and the Chesapeake; and by mid-1813 it extended its naval blockade from Long Island to the Mississippi. New England was left open until 1814 to allow the New Englanders to continue to supply Halifax and the Royal Navy offshore and to encourage that section's separatist peace movement.

By the end of 1813 nearly all of America's warships were either destroyed or bottled up in their ports. With most of America's merchant ships driven from the high seas, the country's commerce was effectively stymied. Exports fell from a peak of $108 million in 1807 to $27 million in 1813 and $7 million in 1814. Imports plummeted from a high of $138 million in 1807 to less than $13 million by 1814. The government's revenue fell as well, from over $13 million in 1811 to $6 million by 1814. Still, a great deal of illegal trade went on with Canada in the Northeast and with the Southeast through Amelia Island in Florida, just south of the Georgia border, and it was not easy to stop. As one enterprising American smuggler recalled, "Men will always run great risks—when great personal profits are expected to be realized." In 1813 an American lieutenant and his soldiers attempted to arrest thirteen suspected smugglers operating out of a little New York town on the border with Canada. But they quickly discovered that the community was not at all supportive of their efforts. The smugglers were soon released from jail, and instead the lieutenant was arrested; his commander, General Pike, had to bail him out.[62]

Because of this excessive leakage, Madison at the end of 1813 made one final effort at an embargo. In December Congress passed the most restrictive measure it had ever enacted. The act forbade all American ships from leaving port, prohibited all exports, outlawed the coasting trade, and gave government officials broad powers of enforcement. The act was so draconian that Congress had to spend the next several months softening some of its effects. Finally, at the end of March 1814—less than four months after he had recommended the new commercial restrictions— Madison, under immense pressure to resume trade both for revenue and diplomatic reasons, called for the repeal of the embargo and the Non-Importation Act.

Although there was severe fighting at Chippewa and Lundy's Lane in the Niagara region in July 1814, it was inconclusive, and the British decided to take the war to the United States. They intended to invade New York at Lake Champlain and, taking advantage of New England's sympathy for the British cause, possibly break up the Union. As a diversion to help the Champlain invasion, they planned on bombarding and raiding the Atlantic and Chesapeake coasts. Finally, they aimed to launch an attack on New Orleans at the mouth of the Mississippi. With Napoleon's abdication in April of 1814—a disaster in Republican eyes—more British soldiers and resources could now be directed at America. Up to now the American war had been an absurd sideshow for the British; indeed, the editor of the

---

62. Latimer, 1812, 263, 130–31.

*Edinburgh Review* thought that half the people of Britain did not even realize that their country was at war with America.

The British invaded New York in the late summer of 1814 along the route General John Burgoyne had followed in 1777, with an imposing force of fifteen thousand men, many of them veterans of the Napoleonic War, perhaps, as one historian has said, "the finest army ever to campaign on American soil."[63] Yet the army's success depended on British control of Lake Champlain, and that was not to be. On September 11, 1814, a thirty-year-old American naval commander, Thomas Macdonough, and his fleet of four ships and ten gunboats decisively defeated a British squadron of more or less equal size in Plattsburgh Bay. Macdonough had set multiple anchors with springs on their cables that allowed them to wind about, that is, rotate 180 degrees and bring fresh batteries to bear on the enemy. He showed brilliant seamanship that in the opinion of one historian entitles him to be remembered as "the best American naval officer" in the war.[64] The British defeat, one of the most crucial in the struggle, compelled its invading army to withdraw to Canada.

The British were much more successful in their invasion of the Chesapeake. During the previous year the British navy had plundered the coastal towns of Chesapeake Bay. But now the British planned a more serious assault focusing on Baltimore and Washington, the American capital. American officials were slow to perceive the danger, believing that since Washington had no strategic significance the British were not likely to attack it. By mid-August 1814 the British admiral, Sir Alexander Cochrane, and General Robert Ross had arrived in the Chesapeake with two dozen warships and over four thousand British regulars. On August 24 the British soldiers easily overran a motley collection of American militia at Bladensburg, Maryland, just northeast of the District of Columbia. This rout allowed the British to invade Washington that night and burn the White House, the Capitol (which contained the Library of Congress), and other public buildings. When Rear Admiral George Cockburn, the British commander of the Royal Marines and the officer most insistent on attacking Washington, came upon the office of the *National Intelligencer* that night, he was determined to get revenge. The *Intelligencer* had been especially critical of Cockburn, portraying him as something of a barbarian. The British commander ordered the destruction of the

---

63. Coles, *War of 1812*, 167.

64. Donald R. Hickey, *Don't Give Up the Ship: Myths of the War of 1812* (Urbana, IL, 2006), 154.

newspaper's offices and its printer's type. "Be sure that all the c's are destroyed," he told his men, "so the rascals can't abuse my name anymore."[65]

The British justified the burning of Washington as retaliation for the Americans' burning of York in Canada the previous year. While President Madison was with the army outside the capital, his wife, Dolley, gathered up state papers and some White House treasures, including a Stuart portrait of George Washington, and escaped in the nick of time. The British forces led by Ross and Cockburn discovered a table set in the White House with forty covers. The officers dined on the food and wine, with Cockburn drinking a toast to "Jemmy" before he ordered the presidential mansion burned. The flames of the burning buildings in the capital could be seen nearly thirty miles away.[66]

After plundering Alexandria, the British moved on Baltimore. Admiral Cockburn and General Ross landed their forty-five hundred marines and soldiers on September 12, 1814, and defeated a force of thirty-two hundred American militiamen, but at the cost of Ross's life. Meanwhile, Admiral Cochrane bombarded Fort McHenry, firing over fifteen hundred rounds in a twenty-five-hour period on September 13 and 14. A Georgetown Federalist lawyer, Francis Scott Key, witnessed the heavy British bombardment; when he saw the American flag still flying the next morning over the fort, he was inspired to write the poem that became "The Star-Spangled Banner." When set to the music of an English drinking song, Key's creation, according to the recollection of Julia Anne Hieronymus Tevis, a young woman going to school in Washington, D.C., in 1814, became a stirring success. She thought "'The Star-Spangled Banner' should be a consecrated song to every American heart," not because of "any particular merit in the composition," but because of "the recollection of something noble in the character of a young and heroic nation."[67] By mid-century the song was widely considered to be the country's unofficial national anthem, a status the Congress made official in 1931.

DESPITE THE AMERICANS' ABILITY to hold Fort McHenry, which compelled the British to withdraw from the Chesapeake, they now faced a series of crises. Blamed for the burning of the capital, John Armstrong resigned as secretary of war and was replaced by James Monroe, who

---

65. Latimer, 1812, 320.
66. Latimer, 1812, 319.
67. Julia Anne Hieronymus Tevis, in Joyce Appleby, ed., *Recollections of the Early Republic: Selected Autobiographies* (Boston, 1997), 77.

continued as secretary of state as well. The government was having diffi-culty raising troops and keeping those it had recruited. Over 12 percent of American troops deserted during the war, almost half of them in 1814. Paying for the war was becoming almost impossible. The government's attempts to borrow money failed miserably as potential lenders refused to buy American bonds, especially as the Federalists continued to discour-age lending to the government. In the summer of 1814 many of the prolif-erating state banks were forced to suspend specie payments for the extraordinary amount of paper notes they had put in circulation since the demise of the Bank of the United States in 1811. Without a national bank the government was unable to transfer funds across the country or to pay its mounting bills. In the fall of 1814 Treasury Secretary George W. Camp-bell said the government needed $50 million, but he had no idea how to raise it. In October he resigned as secretary of the treasury, and in Novem-ber the government defaulted on the national debt. For all intents and purposes the public credit was defunct, and the United States govern-ment was bankrupt.

Campbell was replaced by Alexander Dallas, a moderate Pennsylvania Republican. Dallas stunned his fellow Republicans with his recommen-dations for new internal taxes and a national bank that was an enlarged version of the bank the Republicans had only recently done away with. Although Congress reluctantly agreed to the new taxes, including a whis-key excise tax that was heavier than the one that had precipitated the Whiskey Rebellion in 1794, it rejected Dallas's proposed bank, at least for the time being. President Madison, reversing his earlier strict construc-tionist view of 1791 that a national bank was unconstitutional, now favored such a bank modeled on the Bank of England.

AN EVEN MORE SERIOUS PROBLEM for the Republicans was the opposition of the Federalists to the war—an opposition so intense that it perhaps made the war the most unpopular in American history. Federalists everywhere, but especially in New England where they were strongest, incessantly and passionately spoke out against the conflict, so clogging "the wheels of war," said Madison, that its objective was undermined and the enemy was encouraged "to withhold any pacific advances otherwise likely to be made."[68] The Federalists believed that it was exclusively a partisan struggle that could only promote France and the Virginia Dynasty, and they were joined in opposition by the Standing Order of the Congregational and Presbyterian clergy, who secretly and sometimes

---

68. JM to TJ, 17 Aug. 1812, to Richard Cutts, 8 Aug. 1812, *Papers of Madison: Presidential Ser.*, 5: 165, 127.

openly prayed for England's victory over France and America.[69] Most important, many of the Federalists did more than express orally and in writing their opposition to the war; indeed, they committed what today would probably be regarded as seditious if not treasonous acts. The zealous "Blue Light" Federalists, so called because they were thought to have alerted British warships of American sailings by flashing blue lights, discouraged enlistments in the army, thwarted subscriptions to the war loans, urged the withholding of federal taxes, and plotted secession from the Union. They bought British government bonds at a discount and sent specie to Canada to pay for smuggled goods. The Federalist governors in New England even refused to honor the War Department's requisition of their state militias. The governor of Massachusetts actually entered into secret negotiations with the British, offering part of Maine in return for an end to the war.[70] Although the president condemned this Federalist defiance as threatening the basis of the Union, he wisely did not press the issue. He had great confidence, as he politely and calmly told a rather frantic Mathew Carey, who was predicting "a bloody civil war" that would "crush republicanism for centuries," that "the wicked project of destroying the Union of the states is defeating itself." That deep and calm confidence in most people's support for the Union and in the ultimate success of the United States in the war was the secret of Madison's presidential leadership.[71]

Although some New England extremists called for making a separate peace with England and for secession from the Union, most Federalist leaders, as Madison correctly surmised, were more cautious. Federalists such as Harrison Gray Otis of Massachusetts came to realize that the calling of a convention of New England states to express their grievances against the national government and the Virginia Dynasty might be the best way of moderating the extremism in the region.[72] By the time the convention of twenty-six delegates from the New England states met in Hartford in mid-December 1814 the embargo had been repealed, Bonaparte had fallen, and the earlier sense of crisis had passed.

69. On the clergy's role during the war, not only in support of the Federalists but in support of the Republicans as well, see William Gribbon, *The Churches Militant: The War of 1812 and American Religion* (New Haven, 1973).

70. For a severe indictment of the Federalists, see Buel, *America on the Brink*, 54–55, 117–18, 156–64, 169, 172, 192, 200, 209, 215, 220, 242.

71. Mathew Carey to JM, 1 Aug. 1812, 12 Aug. 1812, 21 Jan. 1813, 25 Jan. 1813; JM to Mathew Carey, 19 Sept. 1812, *Papers of Madison: Presidential Ser.*, 5: 109–10, 148–49, 601–3, 614–18, 335, quotations at 601–2 and 335.

72. James M. Banner Jr., *To the Hartford Convention: The Federalists and the Origins of Party Politics in Massachusetts, 1789–1815* (New York, 1970).

In its report issued on January 5, 1815, the convention condemned the Republicans for their "visionary and superficial theory in regard to commerce" and their "ruinous perseverance in efforts to render it an instrument of coercion and war." The report emphasized the paradoxes of the Republicans' policy by pointing out the "fatal errors of a system which seeks revenge for commercial injuries in the sacrifices of commerce, and aggravates by needless wars, to an immeasurable extent, the injuries it professes to redress." Revealing their anger and anxiety over what was happening socially all around them, the Federalists also condemned the Republicans both for "excluding from office men of unexceptionable merit" and for distributing offices "among men the least entitled to such distinction." The report went on to lament the involvement of "this remote country, once so happy and so envied,... in a ruinous war, and excluded from intercourse with the rest of the world." But the convention rejected secession and a separate peace with Britain. Sounding more Republican than the Republicans, the report reminded readers that the Madison administration had not been able to avoid "the embarrassments of old and rotten institutions." It had lusted for power, abused executive patronage, taxed exorbitantly, and spent wastefully. Most important, said the convention, the Republicans seemed to have forgotten that "unjust and ruinous wars" were "the natural offspring of bad administrations, in all ages and countries."[73]

The Federalist convention, held in secret, contented itself with proposing a series of amendments to the Constitution that summed up New England's grievances over the previous decade and a half. These amendments called for eliminating the three-fifths representation of slaves in Congress; preventing the admission of new states, future embargoes, and declarations of war without a two-thirds majority of Congress; and ending Virginia's dominance of the executive by prohibiting the president from serving more than one term and by preventing the same state from providing two presidents in succession. The New England Federalists hoped that these proposals would lessen the influence of the South and West in the country and restore sectional balance.

Unfortunately for the Federalists, their report arrived in Washington just as news came that a peace treaty between the United States and Great Britain had been signed. Since the declaration of war in 1812 had been in part a bluff to force Britain to take American demands seriously, Madison had begun pursuing peace almost from the beginning; but he

73. Theodore Dwight, *History of the Harford Convention: With a Review of the Policy of the United States, Which Led to the War of 1812* (New York, 1833), 354, 355, 367, 368, 369–70. The convention's "Report" is on pp. 352–379.

wanted it on American terms, namely, an end both to Britain's commercial restrictions and, more important, to its policy of impressment.

When the Russian government made its offer of mediation in March 1813, Madison assigned two commissioners to join John Quincy Adams in St. Petersburg—Albert Gallatin, who was tired of running the treasury, and James A. Bayard, a moderate Delaware Federalist. The British declined the Russian mediation but offered to open direct negotiations with the United States, which eventually took place in Ghent, Belgium, between August and December 1814. Madison added to the peace commission the War Hawk Henry Clay of Kentucky and Jonathan Russell of Rhode Island, who was minister to Sweden. It was a strong commission, composed of the best America had available; by contrast, Britain's delegation was made up of second-raters, its top people being tied up with European affairs.

The American delegation was an odd mixture of personalities, with the flamboyant Clay coming home from a night of gambling just as the crusty Adams was rising to say his prayers. But they got along, thanks to Gallatin. The British began with very tough terms—a permanent Indian reservation in the Old Northwest, American but not British demilitarization on the Great Lakes, cession of northern Maine, and access to the Mississippi River. The Americans rejected these terms outright and, to the surprise of the British, seemed unfazed by the news of the burning of Washington. For their part the British kept delaying in hopes of an even more impressive British victory. But when they learned of their failures at Baltimore and Plattsburgh, the British gave way and agreed to a peace that simply restored the *status quo ante bellum*, without mentioning any of the issues of neutral rights and impressment that had caused the war. The opinion of the duke of Wellington, the future victor at Waterloo, that America could not be easily conquered and certainly not without naval superiority on the Great Lakes clinched the willingness of the British to settle without gaining any of their original terms. The treaty was signed on Christmas Eve 1814.

News of the peace treaty did not reach Washington until February 13, 1815. In the meantime, on January 8 at New Orleans, Andrew Jackson and a force of about 4,700 achieved a smashing victory over five thousand British regulars, commanded by General Sir Edward Pakenham, the brother-in-law of the duke of Wellington. Jackson's troops included regulars, militia, and volunteers, mostly from Tennessee and Kentucky; he also had the help of the notorious Jean Lafitte and his hundreds of fellow smugglers and pirates who maintained a base at Barataria, forty miles south of New Orleans. The British columns surrounded by mist marched into withering American fire that went on for hours. Eventually the British called for a truce to withdraw their wounded and then retreated to the fleet. Although the British persisted for several more weeks in trying to force a passage up the Mississippi and in attempting to take Mobile, they finally gave up when news of the peace treaty arrived.

The American victory at New Orleans was so overwhelming—the British suffered two thousand casualties, including the death of General Pakenham, to Jackson's seventy—that the Americans came to believe that the United States had really won the war and dictated the peace terms, even though the peace treaty had already been signed. But Jackson's victory did in fact clinch the treaty, and news of it thoroughly discredited the report of the Hartford Convention, which many thought was a treasonous act. The Federalists were scorned and ridiculed, and they never recovered politically.

The war had not weakened the Americans' sense of responsibility for the enlightenment of the world; in fact, it strengthened it. In August 1815 David Low Dodge, a wealthy Connecticut merchant living in New York, organized the New York Peace Society. Dodge claimed that his society was "probably the first one that was ever formed in the world for that specific object." In the meantime the Reverend Noah Worcester of Brighton, Massachusetts, had written the *Solemn Review of the Custom of War*, a searing indictment of war that called for the establishment of peace societies. The book was published in December 1814 and in the next fifteen months went through five editions, with many more in subsequent years. Worcester took his own advice and in December 1815, with the aid of William Ellery Channing, formed the Massachusetts Peace Society, which sought to turn "the attention of the community to the nature, spirit, causes, and effects of war." In 1819 the London Peace Society gave credit to the Americans for creating the model for peace societies, which were made for "promoting the general amelioration of humanity."[74]

ALTHOUGH THE WAR WITH BRITAIN was over, there was still fighting to be done, and, as a consequence of the war, Americans now had the ships to do the fighting. During the war, the Barbary States had taken advantage of America's inability to retaliate, and once again they had captured American merchant ships and imprisoned their crews. With the ratification of the Peace Treaty of Ghent between the United States and Great Britain, however, the Americans were finally free to take action, and on March 3, 1815, Congress declared war on Algiers. The United States sent two squadrons, totaling seventeen warships, into the Mediter-

---

74. Merle Eugene Curti, *The American Peace Crusade, 1815–1860* (1929; New York, 1965), 8–20.

ranean, the largest naval fleet the country had ever assembled. After losing several vessels to the American forces, the Algerines capitulated and
signed a treaty with the United States.

Threatened by the powerful American naval squadrons, Tunis and
Tripoli soon followed the Algerian example. The Americans demanded
the release of not only their own prisoners but the prisoners of other
nations as well. "To see the stars and stripes holding forth the hand of
retributive justice to the barbarians, and rescuing the unfortunate,
even of distant but friendly European nations, from slavery" filled an
American observer on the spot and Americans back home as well with
pride. By ending the Barbary practices of tributes and ransoms, the
Americans accomplished what no European nation had been willing
or able to accomplish. John Quincy Adams, from his new post in London as minister to Great Britain, thought that America's "naval campaign in the Mediterranean has been perhaps as splendid as anything
that has occurred in our annals since our existence as a nation."[75]

It is not surprising, therefore, that Americans came to believe that the
Treaty of Ghent with Great Britain had been written on their terms.
Although the treaty seemed to have settled none of the issues that had
caused the War of 1812, it actually had settled everything. It was true that
the treaty never mentioned the issues of impressment and neutral rights
that were the ostensible causes of the war, but that did not matter. It was
not merely the fact that the end of the European war rendered the
issues of neutral rights moot; more important was the fact that the
results of the war vindicated what those issues had come to symbolize—
the nation's independence and sovereignty. As President Madison
declared during the war, not to have waged it would have announced to
the world that "the Americans were not an independent people, but
colonists and vassals."[76] Most important, the war ended without seriously jeopardizing the grand revolutionary experiment in limited republican government.

President Madison had appreciated this from the beginning and had
behaved accordingly. Just before the war began, noted Richard Rush,
Madison had suggested that "the difference between our government and
others was happily this: that here the government had an anxious and difficult task at hand, the people stood at ease—not pressed upon, not
driven, ... whereas elsewhere *government* had an easy time, and *the people*
[had] to bear and do everything, as mere *ambition*, will, or any immediate

75. Lambert, *Barbary Wars*, 194, 195.
76. Walter A. McDougall, *Promised Land, Crusader State: The American Encounter with
    the World Since 1776* (Boston, 1997), 35.

impulse dictated." Madison was not like other men, said Rush; his mind was "fertile and profound in these sorts of reflections."[77]

To the consternation of both friends and enemies Madison remained remarkably sanguine during the disastrous events of the war. Better to allow the country to be invaded and the capital burned than to build up state power in a European monarchical manner. It was a Republican war that Madison sought to wage in a republican fashion. Even during the war the president continued to call for embargoes as the best means for fighting it. As his secretary of the navy William Jones came to appreciate, Madison's republican principles were the source of his apparently weak executive leadership. "The President," Jones observed in 1814, "is virtuous, able and patriotic, but...he finds difficulty in accommodating to the crisis some of those political axioms which he has so long indulged, because they have their foundation in virtue, but which from the vicious nature of the times and the absolute necessity of the case require some relaxation."[78]

Madison resisted that relaxation of republican political axioms. He knew that a republican leader should not become a Napoleon or even a Hamilton. Although he had tried to lead the Congress, he had not badgered it, and he had not used executive patronage to win influence. With no wartime precedents to guide him, he knowingly accepted the administrative confusion and inefficiencies, the military failures, and the opposition of both the Federalists and even some members of his own party, calm in the conviction that in a republic strong executive leadership could only endanger the principles for which the war was fought.[79]

As the City of Washington declared in a formal tribute to the president, the sword of war had usually been wielded at the expense of "civil or political liberty." But this was not the case with President Madison in the war against Britain. Not only had the president restrained the sword "within its proper limits," but he also had directed "an armed force of fifty thousand men aided by an annual disbursement of many millions, without infringing a political, civil, or religious right." As one admirer noted, Madison had withstood both a powerful foreign enemy and widespread domestic opposition "without one trial for treason, or even one prosecution for libel."[80]

77. Ketcham, *Madison*, 586.
78. Irving Brant, *James Madison: Commander in Chief*, 1812–1836 (Indianapolis, 1961), 329.
79. Ketcham, *Madison*, 586, 604.
80. Brant, *Madison: Commander in Chief*, 419, 407.

Although historians have had difficulty appreciating Madison's achievement, many contemporaries certainly realized what he had done. It is not surprising, therefore, that fifty-seven towns and counties throughout the United States are named for Madison, more than for any other president.[81] "Notwithstand[ing] a thousand Faults and blunders," John Adams told Jefferson in 1817, Madison's administration had "acquired more glory, and established more Union than all his three Predecessors, Washington, Adams, Jefferson, put together."[82] Although Adams with this statement may have been tweaking the pride of the man who had defeated him for the presidency in 1800, he was essentially correct. The War of 1812 did finally establish for Americans the independence and nationhood of the United States that so many had previously doubted. And everyone but the Federalists sensed it. The war, declared the "republican citizens of Baltimore" in April 1815 in what became a common refrain through much of the country,

> has revived, with added luster the renown which brightened the morning of our independence: it has called forth and organized the dormant resources of the empire: it has tried and vindicated our republican institutions: it has given us that moral strength, which consists in the well earned respect of the world, and in a just respect for ourselves. It has raised up and consolidated a national character, dear to the hearts of the people, as an object of honest pride and a pledge of future union, tranquility, and greatness.[83]

With the spread of sentiments like these it was not surprising that Americans came to think of the War of 1812 as "the second war for independence." The war, they claimed, had at last given them a "national character," something that George Washington and others had only yearned for three decades earlier. As a result of the war, said Albert Gallatin, the people "are more American; they feel and act more as a nation."[84] The internal struggle that had gone on from 1789 over the direction of the

---

81. Forrest Church, So Help Me God: The Founding Fathers and the First Great Battle Over Church and State (New York, 2007), 350.

82. JA to TJ, 2 Feb. 1817, in Lester J. Cappon, ed., The Adams-Jefferson Letters: The Complete Correspondence Between Thomas Jefferson and Abigail and John Adams (Chapel Hill, 1959), 2: 508; Robert A. Rutland, The Presidency of James Madison (Lawrence, KS, 1990).

83. Watts, The Republic Reborn, 317.

84. Len Travers, Celebrating the Fourth: Independence Day and the Rites of Nationalism in the Early Republic (Amherst, MA, 1997), 205; Gallatin to Matthew Lyon, 7 May 1816, in Henry Adams, ed., The Writings of Albert Gallatin (Philadelphia, 1879), 1: 700.

United States finally seemed to be over. People now called for an end to party bickering and for uniting as one great family. The grand republican experiment had survived. "Our government is now so firmly put on its republican tack," Jefferson assured Lafayette in France, "that it will not be easily monarchised by forms."[85]

85. TJ to Lafayette, 23 Nov. 1818, in Gilbert Chinard, ed., *The Letters of Lafayette and Jefferson* (Baltimore, 1929), 396.

# 19

# A World Within Themselves

By the end of the War of 1812 the United States was becoming, in the minds of its citizens, a nation to be reckoned with. Its population, approaching that of England, had grown rapidly, numbering now nearly eight and a half million people, including one and a half million African Americans. The population had more than doubled in the twenty-five years since the first census in 1790—and continued to grow faster than nearly every other nation in the Western world.

In 1815 the United States comprised eighteen states and five territories. To the original thirteen states had been added Vermont (1791), Kentucky (1792), Tennessee (1796), Ohio (1803), and Louisiana (1812). The territories were Indiana (1809), Illinois (1809), Michigan (1805), Mississippi (1798), and Missouri (1812). Not only had the United States doubled in size, but its older eighteenth-century society, especially in the North, had been dramatically transformed. Americans, or at least the Northerners among them, were more egalitarian, more enterprising, and more self-confident than they had been in 1789.

With the fall of Napoleon and the restoration of the Bourbons in France, Europe was experiencing a conservative reaction to decades of revolutionary upheaval, leaving America the only beacon of republicanism remaining in a thoroughly monarchical world. The Americans' emotional connection with Britain was at last broken, and they had acquired a new sense of their own national character. Their perspective was no longer eastward across the Atlantic but westward across their own expansive continent. Anyone aged forty or older born in America had once been a monarchical subject of His Majesty George III; anyone younger than forty—and they comprised over 85 percent of the population—had been born a republican citizen of the youthful United States. The generation that had framed the Constitution and launched the new federal government was passing, and a new generation of Americans was emerging.

Of the forty-one members who attended the last meeting of the Constitutional Convention in 1787, only eleven still lived, and of these only two were still actively influential in national politics: President Madison, the last president to wear his hair in a queue, and Rufus King, senator from New York. Charles Pinckney, another Framer, had retired from the South Carolina legislature in 1814, but his political career was not over: he would successfully run for Congress in 1818. When Madison left the presidency in 1817, he and Secretary of State Monroe were the only members of his administration who had been in public life at the beginning of the new national government. The turnover in the Congress was even more dramatic. Nearly all the major congressional leaders in 1815 were under age forty, including Henry Clay, Langdon Cheves, John C. Calhoun, William Lowndes, and Felix Grundy.[1]

By 1815 CHANGE WAS EVERYWHERE, but especially in the North. The War of 1812 cleared the air of much traditional thinking about commerce and made it much easier for Americans to come to a more honest appreciation of their society's preoccupation with economic development and money-making, at least in the Northern states. By 1815 a new generation of leaders was much less apt to wring its hands over the obsessively acquisitive character of American society and was much more aware of the importance of domestic manufacturing and internal trade to the growing wealth of the nation.

With the embargo and the non-intercourse acts, far fewer manufactured imports from Britain were available, and this meant rising prices for such manufactured items. This in turn led both to a sudden increase in the number of patents and also to an inducement for more and more investors to shift their capital out of overseas shipping into domestic manufacturing. Before 1808 only fifteen cotton mills existed in the United States; by the end of 1809 eighty-seven mills had been added. Everywhere in the North, but especially in New England, small factories were springing up. "Our people have 'cotton mill fever' as it is called," declared Moses Brown of Rhode Island in 1810. "Every place almost occupied with cotton mills. . . . Spinning yarn and making cloth is become our greatest business."[2]

By inviting the English immigrant Samuel Slater to Rhode Island in 1790, Brown himself had contributed to this explosion of mills. He helped

1. Gaillard Hunt, As We Were: Life in America, 1814 (1914; new ed. Stockbridge, MA, 1993), 8–10.
2. Kenneth L. Sokoloff, "Inventive Activity in Early Industrial America: Evidence from Patent Records, 1790–1846," Journal of Economic History, 48 (1988), 813–50; Barbara M. Tucker, Samuel Slater and the Origins of the American Textile Industry, 1790–1860 (Ithaca, 1984), 89.

Slater use his knowledge of cotton textile machinery that he had smuggled out of England to set up a factory. By 1794 Slater had built a large part of the mill that survives today in Pawtucket, Rhode Island. By 1795 he built a second mill, and between 1803 and 1807 he and his associates started twelve more. Of all the mills in existence in the United States in 1808, nearly half belonged to Slater and his associates or to one of his former employees. Between 1808 and 1812 the embargo and the war prompted the creation of thirty-six cotton mills and forty-one woolen mills in Rhode Island and southern Massachusetts. "There is probably more business done here, than at any other factory in America," declared a young minister describing Slatersville, Rhode Island, in 1812. "On a spot where a few years ago there was but two or three houses, there is a village of 64 families and 500 people in some way employed about the factory."[3]

The growth of manufacturing was not confined to New England. By 1814 Tench Coxe estimated that 243 cotton mills operated within fifteen states. Pennsylvania alone had 64. By 1820 well over a quarter of the labor force in New England and the Mid-Atlantic States was working in small factories, making everything from shoes to textiles. But such statistics are misleading; not only was at least 30 percent of the manufacturing labor force in 1820 composed of women and children, but this factory work did not include the extraordinary amount of manufacturing taking place in rural family households.

Unlike Britain and Europe, this American rural manufacturing was not usually the result of mercantile capitalists subcontracting work to impoverished cottagers and landless laborers in so-called putting-out systems; it was more often the consequence of ongoing farm families becoming part-time manufacturers and entrepreneurs in order to better themselves by making some extra money. Even farmers who were not growing crops for export abroad were nonetheless scrambling to create goods to exchange in local markets—working with their wives and children spinning cloth or weaving hats, dressing deer skins and beaver pelts, making hoops and barrels, distilling whiskey or cider, and fabricating whatever they might sell to local stores. In 1809 an English-born leather dresser, Talmadge Edwards, who had migrated to America in 1770, hired country girls to come to his tannery in upstate New York to cut out gloves, which Edwards then sent to farmers' wives for sewing and finishing. By 1810 he discovered he had a market for his gloves among the households in the Albany area. From these modest beginnings grew the flourishing glove and mitten industry of the United States.

3. J. M. Opal, *Beyond the Farm: National Ambitions in Rural New England* (Philadelphia, 2008), 157.

In 1810 90 percent of the $42 million total textile production of the nation came from family households. As early as the 1790s Henry Wansey, a British visitor, had noted that in both Massachusetts and New Jersey housewives in every farming household kept their families busy carding and spinning woolen and linen cloth "in the evenings and when they are not in the fields." Even earlier the French visitor Brissot de Warville had found "almost all" the households of Worcester, Massachusetts, "inhabited by men who are both cultivators and artisans; one is a tanner, another a shoemaker, another sells goods; but all are farmers." Manufactures, it was said, were "rising in all their varied form in every direction, and pursued *with an eye to profit* in almost every farm house in the United States." By 1809 households in the little town of Franklin, Massachusetts, were producing six thousand straw hats a year for sale in Boston and Providence.[4]

In many Northern agricultural towns people seemed to be doing everything but farming. By 1815 even the tiny town of Mount Pleasant, Ohio, with a population of only five hundred persons, had several dozen artisans and manufacturing shops, including three saddlers, three hatters, four blacksmiths, four weavers, six boot and shoe makers, three cabinet makers, one baker, one apothecary, two wagon makers, two tanneries, one wool-carding-machine maker, two wool-carding machinists, one wool-spinning machinist, one flax spinner, and one nail factory. Within a six-mile radius of this little Ohio town were nine merchant mills, two gristmills, twelve sawmills, one paper mill, one woolen factory, and two fulling mills.[5]

With so much manufacturing and so many internal exchanges going on, the Republican leaders had to adjust their ideas of political economy. As early as 1799 Congressman Albert Gallatin had recognized that America had become commercially and socially different from the former mother country. In Britain, he told the Congress, the different trades and occupations were "so well distinguished that a merchant and a farmer are rarely combined in the same person; a merchant is a merchant, and nothing but a merchant; a manufacturer is only a manufacturer; a farmer is

---

4. Claudia Goldin and Kenneth Sokoloff, "Women, Children, and Industrialization in the Early Republic: Evidence from the Manufacturing Censuses," *Journal of Economic History*, 42 (1982), 745–46; Thomas C. Cochran, *Frontiers of Change: Early Industrialism in America* (New York, 1981), 57; Henry Wansey, *Journal of an Excursion* (1796; New York, 1969), 47, 101; James A. Henretta, "The War for Independence and American Economic Development," in Ronald Hoffman et al., eds., *The Economy of Early America: The Revolutionary Period, 1763–1790* (Charlottesville, 1988), 81, 80.

5. George Rogers Taylor, *The Transportation Revolution, 1815–1860* (New York, 1962), 206–7.

merely a farmer; but this is not the case in this country." In America, by contrast, "the different professions and traders are blended together in the same person; the same man being frequently a farmer and a merchant and perhaps a manufacturer."

The consequence, said Gallatin, was that the United States was no longer the exclusively agricultural nation that Jefferson idealized. Nearly everyone was a farmer, and something else besides. "Go into the interior of the country," he said, "and you will scarcely find a farmer who is not, in some degree, a trader. In a grazing part of the country, you will find them buying and selling cattle; in other parts you will find them distillers, tanners, or brick-makers. So that, from one end of the United States to the other, the people are generally traders."[6]

By the end of the War of 1812 even Jefferson realized that circumstances had radically changed since he had expressed his hostility toward manufacturing in his *Notes on the State of Virginia*. Who in 1785, he asked in January 1816, could have foreseen the "rapid depravity" into which Europe would sink in the subsequent decades? Who could have imagined that two such distinguished nations as Britain and France would defy "those moral laws established by the Author of nature between nation and nation" and "would cover the earth and sea with robberies and piracies"? Americans, he said, had experienced what in 1785 they had not believed possible, "that there exists both profligacy and power enough to exclude us from the field of interchange with other nations: that to be independent for the comforts of life we must fabricate them for ourselves. We must now place the manufacturer by the side of the agriculturist." Anyone opposed to domestic manufacturing, Jefferson now concluded, must be willing either to be reduced to a dependency on Great Britain or "to be clothed in skins, and to live like wild beasts in dens and caverns."

Since Jefferson wanted neither alternative, he had to concede "that manufactures are now as necessary to our independence as to our comfort." He vowed he would in the future purchase homemade goods and thereby "wrest that weapon of distress from the hand which has wielded it." Still, he hoped that Americans would manufacture only enough goods to meet their domestic demand and would not end up, like England, creating urban factories into which their surplus labor would be drawn.[7]

Indeed, so averse were Americans to English-style urban factories that much of the textile production remained scattered among farm families. Slater's mills not only employed whole families, including young children, but confined the work to the spinning of yarn; the yarn was then

6. *Annals of Congress*, 5th Congress, 3rd session (Jan. 1799), 9: 2650.
7. TJ to Benjamin Austin, 9 Jan. 1816, *Jefferson: Writings*, 1369–72.

"put out" to be woven by hand-weavers in the homes of families throughout the area. Nineteen out of twenty Americans continued to live in rural places, that is, places smaller than twenty-five hundred persons. In the two decades between 1800 and 1820 the percentage of the labor force employed in agriculture actually increased from 89.5 percent to 91.7 percent.[8]

By 1820 sixty-one urban places dotted the map, but only five were cities with populations over twenty-five thousand—New York, Philadelphia, Baltimore, Boston, and New Orleans. Altogether, these urban places held less than 7 percent of the total American population. By contrast, England in 1821 had well over a third of its population in cities, and more than 20 percent lived in cities larger than twenty thousand. America contained nothing resembling London with its million and a quarter people and had no burgeoning industrial cities like Leeds or Manchester.

By 1815 the United States thus remained a predominantly rural, agricultural society, on the surface not all that different from the society of the eighteenth century. Yet beneath that surface much had changed. The early Republic may have been still overwhelmingly rural, still overwhelmingly agricultural, but it was also now overwhelmingly commercial, perhaps, in the North at least, the most thoroughly commercialized society in the world. The Americans' desire to trade was "a passion as unconquerable as any with which nature has endowed us," Henry Clay told the House of Representatives in 1812. "You may attempt to regulate—you cannot destroy it."[9]

America's intense involvement in overseas commerce and the carrying trade between 1792 and 1805—because of the European wars—tended to mask what was happening commercially within the United States itself. While Americans were trading with places all over the world, they were also trading with one another and creating a continental marketplace. Suddenly, the vision some had had in the aftermath of Independence that Americans constituted "a world within ourselves, sufficient to produce whatever can contribute to the necessities and even the superfluities of life," was being realized.[10]

The rapid development of domestic trade created the heightened demand almost everywhere for internal improvements—new roads, new canals, new ferries, new bridges—anything that would help increase the speed and lower the cost of the movement of goods within the country,

8. James L. Huston, *Securing the Fruits of Labor: The American Concepts of Wealth Distribution, 1765–1900* (Baton Rouge, 1998), 89.

9. Clay, 22 Jan. 1812, *Annals of Congress*, 12th Congress, 1st session, 23: 918.

10. Cathy Matson and Peter Onuf, "Toward a Republican Empire," *American Quarterly*, 37 (1985), 496–531.

and, as John C. Calhoun said in 1817, in a common opinion, help "bind the republic together." All this worked to convince Americans, as the governor of Pennsylvania declared in 1811, that "foreign commerce is a good but of a secondary nature, and that happiness and prosperity must be sought for within the limits of our own country." This growing belief that domestic commerce of the United States was "incalculably more valuable" than its foreign commerce and that "the home market for productions of the earth and manufactures is of more importance than all foreign ones" represented a momentous reversal of traditional thinking.[11]

Americans had always carried on an extraordinary amount of internal trade with one another, but rarely had they appreciated its worth to their society. They had tended to believe that such domestic trade—say, between Lancaster, Pennsylvania, and Philadelphia—had no real value unless goods were further shipped outside of the country. Inland trade by itself, they thought, could never increase a community's aggregate wealth; it could only move it about. The "meer handling of Goods one to another, no more increases any wealth in the Province, than Persons at a Fire, increase the Water in a Pail, by passing it thro' twenty or Forty hands." Such passing of wealth around the community from hand to hand, William Smith of New York had declared in 1750, "tho' it may enrich an Individual," meant that "others must be poorer, in an exact proportion to his Gains; but the Collective Body of the People not at all."[12]

Because of this kind of traditional thinking, Americans had tended to attach a special importance to overseas commerce. They had believed that a society could increase its aggregate wealth only by selling more beyond its borders than it bought, that is, by having a favorable balance of foreign trade. As one American put it in 1786, "Only exports make a country rich."[13] With such zero-sum mercantilist assumptions, Americans had not extended much respectability to internal traders and retail shopkeepers. They certainly had not granted such traders and shopkeepers the highly regarded status, or the right to claim the title, of "merchant,"

11. Calhoun quoted in Oscar and Lillian Handlin, *Liberty in Expansion, 1760–1850* (New York, 1989), 197; *Niles' Weekly Register*, 1 (1811–1812), 282, 3; Mathew Carey (1822), quoted in Nathan Miller, *The Enterprise of a Free People: Aspects of Economic Development in New York State During the Canal Period, 1792–1838* (Ithaca, 1962), 42.

12. John Crowley, *This Sheba, Self: The Conceptualization of Economic Life in Eighteenth-Century America* (Baltimore, 1974), 88, 97–99, 38–39; [William Smith], *The Independent Reflector*, ed. Milton M. Klein (Cambridge, MA, 1963), 106.

13. [Anon.], *The Commercial Conduct of the United States of America Considered, and the True Interest Thereof, Attempted to Be Shewn By a Citizen of the New York* (New York, 1786), 4.

which belonged exclusively to those who exported goods abroad and thus presumably earned real wealth for the society.

By the early nineteenth century, however, anyone who was involved in trade of any sort, even retail shopkeepers, was claiming the title of "merchant." Instead of defining "commerce" as Montesquieu had—"the exportation and importation of merchandise with a view to the advantage of the state"—many Americans, at least in the North, now equated "commerce" with all the exchanges taking place within the country itself, exchanges in which not only both parties always gained but the society did as well. "There is no word in the English language that more deceives a people than the word *commerce*," wrote Hezekiah Niles in his *Weekly Register* in 1814. People everywhere "associate with it an idea of great ships, passing to all countries—whereas the rich commerce of every community is its *internal*; a communication of one part with other parts of the same.... In the United States, (were we at peace) our *foreign* trade would hardly exceed a *fortieth* or *fiftieth* part of the whole *commerce* of the people."[14]

Niles, whose *Register* was America's first national news magazine, was one of the leaders in turning Americans inward. During the War of 1812 he called for an end to all foreign influence and the development of domestic manufacturing and trade. The war, he said, was beneficial to America because it will "bring about a blessed union of the people, in directing them to look AT HOME for all they desire."[15]

Of course, not everyone accepted the new thinking. "Perhaps the most controversial subject of political economy," declared DeWitt Clinton in 1814, "is whether the home or foreign commerce is most productive of national wealth." The Southern planters with their need to market their staples abroad could never acknowledge the superiority of internal trade.[16]

BY THE SECOND DECADE of the nineteenth century the Republicans had won such an overwhelming victory that the Federalist "aristocrats" no longer seemed to matter either politically or socially. The result was that the middling people in the North, who were participating in all the buying and selling and made up the bulk of the Northern Jeffersonian Republicans, never developed the same acute self-consciousness of being "middling" as their counterparts in England. There the aristocracy was much more firmly

---

14. Montesquieu, *Spirit of the Laws*, ed. Franz Neumann (New York, 1949), I, bk. xx, ch. 13, p. 323; *Niles' Weekly Register*, 6 (1814), 395.
15. *Niles' Weekly Register*, 3 (1812), 328.
16. DeWitt Clinton, *An Introductory Discourse delivered before the Literary and Philosophical Society of New York, on the Fourth of May, 1814* (New York, 1815), 37.

established and less open to easy entry. Wealthy tradesmen and business-men and other aspiring middling sorts usually had to wait a generation or more and then acquire land before they could move up into the ranks of the gentry. Consequently, in England the term "middle class" took on a much more literal meaning than it did in America: it came to describe that stratum of people who lay between the dominant aristocracy and the working class and were self-consciously distinguished from each of the extremes.

But by the second decade of the nineteenth century in America, in the North at least, the ambitious, go-getting middling sorts were collapsing into themselves all levels of income and all social ranks and had come to domi-nate American culture to a degree that the middle class in England never achieved. It was as Franklin in the 1780s had predicted: "the almost general mediocrity of fortune that prevails in America" had obliged "its people to follow some business for subsistence," turning America into "the land of labour."[17] The growing numbers of commercial farmers, mechanics, clerks, teachers, businessmen, and industrious, self-trained would-be professionals could scarcely think of themselves as the "middle" of anything; they consid-ered themselves to be the whole nation and as a consequence gained a powerful moral hegemony over the society, especially in the North.

When Noah Webster later came to define "gentleman" in his *Diction-ary*, he saw it simply as a courtesy title, of general address, applied most appropriately to "men of education and good breeding, of every occupa-tion." "Of every occupation"—that was the key to the changes taking place. By the early decades of the nineteenth century many lawyers could no longer think of themselves merely as gentlemen who sometimes prac-ticed some law. Law, at least for those who did not use it merely as a stepping-stone to politics, was becoming a technical and specialized pro-fession that wholly occupied the person engaged in it, making it no differ-ent really from the occupations of artisans and tradesmen. Much to the chagrin of aristocratic Federalists, not just law but all the professions had become income-producing occupations. "Our Lawyers are mere lawyers, our physicians are mere physicians, our divines are mere divines," com-plained John Sylvester John Gardiner, perhaps Boston's most distin-guished man of letters in the first decade of the nineteenth century. "Everything smells of the shop, and you will, in a few minutes conversa-tion, infallibly detect a man's profession."[18]

17. BF, "Information to Those Who Would Remove to America" (1784), *Franklin: Writings*, 975–83.
18. John Sylvester John Gardiner, "The Scholar and Gentleman United" (1806), in Lewis P. Simpson, ed., *The Federalist Literary Mind: Selections from the Monthly Anthology and Boston Review, 1803–1811* (Baton Rouge, 1962), 81.

The distinction between gentlemen and commoners did not entirely disappear, but it was buffeted and further blurred. When working with one's head became no different from working with one's hands, then the distinction between gentlemen and commoners became less and less meaningful. As early as 1802 the buyer of a church pew in a New England meetinghouse called himself a "gentleman," but the seller labeled him a "blacksmith." Visiting foreigners were amazed to find so many adult white males, including draymen, butchers' boys, and canal workers, being addressed as gentlemen. Outraged Federalists tried to make fun of the vulgar for claiming to be equal to gentlemen and men of education. But such satire rang hollow when no one felt embarrassed over such claims.

Since the 1790s American leaders had yearned to make their society more homogeneous, but they had hoped that that homogeneity would come from raising ordinary people to their level of gentility and enlightenment. Instead, ordinary folk were collapsing traditional social differences and were bringing the aristocracy down to their level. The many academies and colleges that were sprouting up everywhere, especially in the North, were not enlightening the society as expected; instead, they were annually producing "multitudes of half-educated candidates for public confidence and honor," which accounted for so many trying "to *crowd themselves* into the learned professions."[19] Many foreigners were surprised to discover that the social and cultural distinctions common to the nations of Europe seemed in America, as Tocqueville later put it, "to have melted into a middle class."[20] Although the upper ranks of Americans may have lacked the elegant manners and refined courtesy of the European aristocracy, ordinary Americans were far less vulgar and uncultivated than their European counterparts.

Crossing the Allegheny Mountains westward in 1815, the English immigrant Morris Birkbeck was struck by "the urbanity and civilization that prevail in situations remote from large cities." Americans, said Birkbeck, "are strangers to rural simplicity: the embarrassed air of an awkward rustic, so frequent in England, is rarely seen in the United States." Birkbeck attributed the social homogeneity of the Americans to "the effects of

19. Lawrence A. Cremin, *American Education: The National Experience, 1783–1876* (New York, 1980), 2: 249–334; Donald G. Tewksbury, *The Founding of American Colleges and Universities Before the Civil War, with Particular Reference to the Religious Influences Bearing upon the College Movement* (New York, 1932), 55–132; Natalie A. Naylor, "The Ante-Bellum College Movement: A Reappraisal of Tewksbury's Founding of American Colleges and Universities," *History of Education Quarterly*, 13 (1973), 261–74; Opal, *Beyond the Farm*, 128, 127.

20. George Wilson Pierson, *Tocqueville in America*, abridged by Dudley C. Lunt (New York, 1959), 44.

political equality, the consciousness of which accompanies all their intercourse, and may be supposed to operate most powerfully on the manners
of the lowest class." It was as if the sharp distinction between politeness
and vulgarity that characterized European society had in America somehow become mingled and made into one—creating, said an unhappy
James Fenimore Cooper, the "fussy pretensions" of the "genteel vulgar"
who got their manners "second hand, as the traditions of fashion, or perhaps the pages of a novel."[21]

American society, or at least the Northern part of American society,
was coming more and more to resemble what Franklin and Crèvecoeur
had imagined in the 1780s, a society that seemed to lack both an aristocracy and a lower class. "Patrician and plebeian orders are unknown...,"
wrote the Federalist-turned-Republican Charles Ingersoll in 1810, drawing out the logic of what had been conventional American wisdom
since the mid-eighteenth century. "Luxury has not yet corrupted the
rich, nor is there any of that want, which classifies the poor. There is no
populace. All are people. What in other countries is called the populace, a compost heap, whence germinate mobs, beggars, and tyrants, is
not to be found in the towns; and there is no peasantry in the country.
Were it not for the slaves of the south," wrote Ingersoll, "there would be
one rank."[22]

The exception is jarring, to say the least, but no more jarring than
Ingersoll's larger generalization. By modern standards his judgment that
America had become classless and composed of one rank seems absurd.
From today's perspective, the distinctions of early nineteenth-century
society are vivid, not only those between free and enslaved, white and
black, male and female, but also those between rich and poor, educated
and barely literate. Despite the celebration of commerce, the many participants in business may have failed as often as they succeeded. People
talked about being "busted" or of "going to smash": one out of five house-
holders could expect to become insolvent at least once.[23] Yet understanding the wonder and the astonishment of observers like Ingersoll requires
taking seriously the ways in which the Northern society of the early

21. Morris Birkbeck, *Notes on a Journey in America, from the Coast of Virginia to the
Territory of Illinois* (London, 1819), 37, 108, 98; Cooper quoted in Edwin H. Cady, *The
Gentleman in America: A Literary Study in American Culture* (Syracuse, 1949), 121.
22. Charles Jared Ingersoll, *Inchiquin, the Jesuit's Letters* (1810), in Gordon S. Wood, ed.,
*The Rising Glory of America, 1760–1820* (New York, 1971), 387.
23. Opal, *Beyond the Farm*, 175; Peter J. Coleman, *Debtors and Creditors in America:
Insolvency, Imprisonment for Debt and Bankruptcy, 1607–1900* (Madison, WI, 1974),
287–88; Scott A. Sandage, *Born Losers: A History of Failure in America* (Cambridge,
MA, 2005), 7; Bruce H. Mann, *Republic of Debtors: Bankruptcy in the Age of American
Independence* (Cambridge, MA, 2002), 36.

Republic concocted the myth of a new middle-class society that celebrated its homogeneous egalitarian character.

To be sure, there were great discrepancies of wealth in the early Republic. The South had its great slaveholding planters while most farmers had few or no slaves. Even in the North wealth was far more unequally distributed in the decades following the Revolution than it had been before.[24] Yet not only did Republican political leaders continue to hold out the vision of an egalitarian society of small producers, but many Northerners felt they were in fact living in a more egalitarian society; and in a strange way they were correct. After all, wealth, compared to birth, breeding, ethnicity, family heritage, gentility, even education, is the least humiliating means by which one person can claim superiority over another; and it is the one most easily matched or overcome by exertion.

From this point of view the popular myth of equality in the early Republic was based on a substantial reality—but a psychological more than an economic reality. British traveler John Melish thought that most Northern states in 1806 resembled Connecticut, where, he said, "there is no feudal system, and no law of primogeniture; hence there are no overgrown estates on one hand, and few of those employed in agriculture are depressed by poverty on the other." Despite this celebration of Connecticut's equality, however, Melish went on to say that the farms in the state were very unequal in size, ranging "generally from 50 to 5000 acres."

Still, Melish emphasized, Americans felt remarkably equal to one another. They "have a spirit of independence, and will brook no superiority. Every man is conscious of his own political importance, and will suffer none to treat him with disrespect. Nor is this disposition confined to one rank; it pervades the whole and is probably the best guarantee for the continuance of the liberty and independence of the country."[25]

IN ORDER TO JUSTIFY and legitimate their claim to be all the people, these egalitarian-minded middling sorts needed, above all, to link themselves to the greatest event in their young history, the Revolution. Since most of the political elite who had led the Revolution were gentlemen-aristocrats, and slaveholding aristocrats at that, they had little to offer

24. See James T. Lemon and Gary Nash, "The Distribution of Wealth in Eighteenth-Century America: A Century of Change in Chester County, Pennsylvania, 1693–1802," *Journal of Social History*, 2 (1968), 1–24; Allan Kulikoff, "The Progress of Inequality in Revolutionary Boston," *WMQ*, 28 (1971), 375–412; Lee Soltow, "Economic Inequality in the United States in the Period from 1790 to 1860," *Journal of Economic History*, 31 (1971), 822–839; Jackson Turner Main, "Trends in Wealth Concentration Before 1860," ibid., 445–57.

25. John Melish, *Travels Through the United States of America, in the years 1806 and 1807, and 1809, 1810, and 1811* (London, 1815), 100, 48–49.

the burgeoning groups of enterprising artisans and businessmen as models for emulation or justification. If the middling artisans and entrepreneurs who were coming to dominate Northern American culture in the early nineteenth century were to find among the Revolutionary Founders a hero they could relate to, only Benjamin Franklin, the former printer who had risen from the most obscure origins to worldly success, could fulfill their needs. Only Franklin could justify the release of their ambition.

Franklin died in 1790, and his *Autobiography* was not published until 1794. Between that year and 1828 twenty-two editions were published. After 1798 editors began adding the Poor Richard essays, and especially *The Way to Wealth*, to editions of the *Autobiography*. Franklin's life became an inspiration to countless young men eager to make it in the world of business. Reading Franklin's life and writings at age eighteen, Silas Felton of Marlborough, Massachusetts, was encouraged to change his life. Since, as he said in his memoir written in 1802 at age twenty-six, "Nature never formed me to follow an Agricultural Life," he did not pursue his father's farming career but instead turned to teaching and then to storekeeping, at which he was successful. He was interested in politics and was an insatiable reader, devouring not only newspapers and "many volumes...that contained true genuine Republicanism" but also Franklin's writings and indeed everything he could lay his hands on that would improve his mind and refine his manners—all of which he dutifully listed in his memoir. Like Franklin founding his Junto for ambitious artisans in early Philadelphia, Felton in 1802 helped to organize the Society of Social Enquirers in Marlborough, a group of twelve middling men who met monthly in order to improve themselves and their society. The group debated the amount of wealth people needed and the importance of credit in the economy; it devised a plan for reforming the town's schools, and some of the society served on the local school committee. Nothing was more important to these middling men than "a good education."

Felton was a good Jeffersonian Republican. He harbored a deep resentment toward the local "priests" and "other Aristocrats," that is, the Federalist Calvinist clergy and their lay supporters. These Federalists tried to keep people like him down and were always "discouraging Learning, among the lower Class of people." By "lower class" he meant that large deferential majority who had lived too long under patriarchal rule. The "bigoted" and "sour-hearted" priests preached pessimistic sermons about depravity and sin and sought to destroy the kind of youthful and middling ambition that he and countless others in the North were expressing.[26]

26. Rena L. Vassar, ed., "The Life or Biography of Silas Felton Written by Himself," *American Antiquarian Society, Proc.*, 69 (1959), 120, 127–28, 129–30; Opal, *Beyond the Farm*, 137, 132–37, 147–48, 135.

Although Felton never became very rich or famous, he did eventually become a substantial member of his modest community—a town clerk, a selectman, a justice of the peace, and a representative to the General Court for three terms. He epitomized, in other words, the kind of self-improving sort who hated the Federalists for "conspiring against reason and republicanism," and in reaction he celebrated the dynamic and middling Northern society composed of "probably the happiest people upon the earth."[27]

Other Franklin readers were even more successful. In 1810 sixteen-year-old James Harper left his father's farm on Long Island for New York City after reading Franklin's *Autobiography*. Eventually he founded one of the most successful publishing firms in the country and became mayor of New York. Chauncey Jerome was another success story. The son of a blacksmith, he became a prosperous clockmaker in New Haven, with three hundred men in his employ, and mayor of the city; indeed, he was one of those enterprising individuals who turned Connecticut into the clockmaking center of the world. In his memoir he marveled at how far he had risen and could not help describing his arrival in New Haven in 1812 as a nineteen-year-old just as Franklin had, wandering alone "about the streets early one morning with a bundle of clothes and some bread and cheese in my hands."[28]

Franklin emerged for businessmen everywhere as the perfect model of the "self-made man," struggling by himself to rise from humble origins in order to achieve wealth and respectability. Haughty Federalists could only shake their heads in disgust at all those vulgar sorts who had come to believe "that there was no other road to the temple of Riches, except that which runs through—Dr. Franklin's works."[29]

The "self-made man" became such a familiar symbol for Americans that its original novelty has been lost.[30] Of course, there had always been social mobility in Western society, at some times and in some places more than others. Eighteenth-century Americans had always experienced a good deal of it. But this social mobility in the past generally had been a mobility of a peculiar sort, an often sponsored mobility in which the

27. Opal, *Beyond the Farm*, 135, 136.
28. Chauncey Jerome, *History of the American Clock Business*, in Joyce Appleby, ed., *Recollections of the Early Republic: Selected Autobiographies* (Boston, 1997), 183.
29. Joseph Dennnie, *Port Folio*, 1 (14 Feb. 1801), in J. A. Leo Lemay and P. M. Zall, eds., *Benjamin Franklin's Autobiography* (New York, 1986), 250. In his famous work *The Protestant Ethic and the Spirit of Capitalism* (1905), the great German sociologist Max Weber found Franklin to be the perfect exemplar of the modern capitalistic spirit.
30. Irvin Wyllie, *The Self-Made Man in America: The Myth of Rags to Riches* (New Brunswick, NJ, 1954); John G. Cawelti, *Apostles of the Self-Made Man* (Chicago, 1965); Daniel Walker Howe, *Making the American Self: Jonathan Edwards to Abraham Lincoln* (Cambridge, MA, 1997).

patronized individual acquired the attributes of the social status to which he aspired while at the same time he tried to forget and disguise the lowly sources from whence he had come. As indicated by the pejorative terms— "upstarts," "arrivistes," "parvenus"—used to disparage those participants unable to hide their rise, social mobility traditionally had not been something to be proud of. Hamilton certainly did not brag about his obscure background; indeed, most of the Founders did not like to talk about their humble origins. But by the nineteenth century many of those new middling sorts who had risen were boasting of their lowly beginnings in imitation of Franklin. Washington Irving mocked the "outrageous extravagance" of the manners and clothes of the wife of a nouveau riche Boston tradesman. Yet Irving could not help admiring her lack of "foolish pride respecting her origins"; instead of being embarrassed by her background, she took "great pleasure in telling how they first entered Boston in Pedlars trim."[31]

Early nineteenth-century England was experiencing extensive social mobility, but it was nothing compared to the rate of upward mobility among contemporary Americans. Already, independent mobile men were bragging of their humble origins and their lack of both polish and a gentleman's education. They had made it, they said, on their own, without family influence, without patronage, and without going to Harvard or Princeton or indeed any college at all. For many Americans the ability to make and display money now became the only proper democratic means for distinguishing one man from another.

Of course, most Federalists were outraged by these attempts to make wealth the sole criterion of social distinction. The socially established families of Philadelphia looked down upon the nouveau riche businessman John Swanwick even though he was one of the wealthiest men of the city; they regarded him as "our Lilliputian, [who] with his dollars, gets access where without them he would not be suffered to appear."[32] Catharine Maria Sedgwick, author and daughter of an esteemed Federalist family, spoke for all of the old aristocracy when she said of the emerging nineteenth-century money-based hierarchy, "wealth, you know, is the grand leveling principle."[33]

Some of the ambitious middling sorts declared that they did not need formal educational institutions to learn about the world and get ahead. Like William Findley, they "prefer[red] common sense and common

31. William L. Hedges, "Washington Irving: Nonsense, the Fat of the Land and the Dream of Indolence," in Matthew J. Bruccoli, ed., *The Chief Glory of Every People* (Carbondale, IL, 1973), 156–57.

32. Roland M. Baumann, "John Swanwick: Spokesman for 'Merchant-Republicanism' in Philadelphia, 1790–1798," *Penn. Mag. of Hist. and Biog.*, 97 (1973), 141.

33. Stow Persons, *The Decline of American Gentility* (New York, 1973), 50.

usage" to pompous theories and pretentious words picked up in college classrooms. Through newspapers, almanacs, tracts, chapbooks, periodicals, lectures, novels, and other media, those who were eager to improve themselves sought to obtain smatterings of knowledge about things that previously had been the exclusive property of college-educated elites — learning to write legibly, for example. *Niles' Weekly Register* became a regular source of information for these striving middling people, and no one was a more devoted subscriber than William Findley. Near the end of Findley's life the personal property he had accumulated was very modest, appraised at less than five hundred dollars; but it contained a large number of books, including Samuel Johnson's *Dictionary* and Adam Smith's *Wealth of Nations*, with which he had educated himself.[34]

Others, however, like Jedediah Peck, who had begun their assaults on the aristocracy by ridiculing fancy book-learning and genteel manners, ultimately accepted the need for educational institutions. Peck, for example, eventually became the father of the common school system of New York. In the end many of the new middling sorts did not repudiate the politeness and learning of the Enlightenment; instead they popularized and vulgarized that politeness and learning and turned both into respectability. Reacting to the Federalists' many snubs and jeers, many of the middling people began seeking to acquire some of the refinement of the aristocracy, to obtain what the leading historian of this process has nicely called "vernacular gentility." Americans socially and culturally set about constructing what one observer astutely noted was "a most uncommon union of qualities not easily kept together—simplicity and refinement"—the very qualities that came to constitute the nineteenth-century middle class.[35]

In seeking to become genteel, many of these wealthy middling sorts came to resemble the "molatto gentleman" that Benjamin Franklin had mocked—a "new Gentleman, or rather a half Gentleman, or Mungrel, an unnatural Compound of earth and Brass like the Feet of Nebuchadnezzar's Image." These were the people who bought the increasing numbers of books and manuals to teach themselves manners and politeness, including various abridged editions of Lord Chesterfield's *Letters to His Son*. Daniel Drake, a famous physician in the West, recalled growing up in late eighteenth-century Kentucky, where books were scarce, reading

---

34. John Caldwell, *William Findley from West of the Mountains: Congressman, 1791–1821* (Gig Harbor, WA, 2002), 356, 377; Cathy N. Davidson, *Revolution and the Word: The Rise of the Novel in America* (New York, 1986), 68.
35. Richard L. Bushman, *The Refinement of America: Persons, Houses, Cities* (New York, 1992), xiii; *American Monthly Magazine*, 2 (1818), 469.

Chesterfield's *Letters*, which "fell in mightily close with my tastes, and not less with those of father and mother, who cherished as high and pure an idea of duty of good breeding as any people on earth."[36] But, as one young woman recognized, in the struggles of those seeking to become refined "an easy unassuming politeness...is not the acquirement of a day."[37] For some of these new middlebrow Americans, buying a tea service or placing a piano in their parlor came to be the mark of being cultivated and genteel. Out of these efforts was born the middle-class Victorianism of the nineteenth century.

Honor—that aristocratic sense of reputation—decreased in significance for the new middle-class society. Except for the South and the military, which retained many aristocratic values, the concept of honor was attacked as monarchical and anti-republican. As honor came under assault, so too did dueling, which was the special means by which gentlemen protected their honor. Although Aaron Burr's killing of Alexander Hamilton in 1804 in a duel led to much condemnation of the practice, it was the spread of egalitarian sentiments that most effectively undermined it. When even servants began challenging others to duels, many gentlemen realized that the code of honor had lost its cachet.

As Tocqueville later pointed out, Americans, in the North at least, came to replace aristocratic honor with middle-class morality. Virtue lost much of the rational and stoical quality befitting the antique heroes the Revolutionary leaders had emulated. Temperance—that self-control of the passions so valued by the ancients and one of Cicero's four cardinal virtues—became mainly identified with the elimination of popular drunkenness—"a good cause," declared the Franklin Society for the Suppression of Intemperance in 1814, in which "perseverance and assiduity seldom fail of securing the denied object." The hustling entrepreneur Parson Weems labeled a republic "the best government for morals," by which he mainly meant "the best remedy under heaven against national intemperance"; it "imparts a joy that loathes the thought of drunkenness."[38]

If indeed the Americans had become one homogeneous people and the people as a single estate were all there was, then many Americans now became much more willing than they had been in 1789 to label their

36. Daniel Drake, *Pioneer Life in Kentucky*, in Appleby, ed., *Recollections*, 60.

37. Martha Tomhave Blauvelt, *The Work of the Heart: Young Women and Emotion, 1780–1830* (Charlottesville, 2007), 192.

38. *Franklin Society for the Suppression of Temperance* (Broadside: Greenfield, MA, 23 Feb. 1814); Mason L. Weems, *The True Patriot; or, An Oration on the Beauties and Beatitudes of a Republic* (Philadelphia, 1802), 37.

government a "democracy." At the time of the Revolution, "democrat" had been a pejorative term that conservatives leveled at those who wanted to give too much power to the people; indeed, Federalists identified democracy with mobocracy, or, as Gouverneur Morris said, "no government at all." "Simple democracy," declared a Federalist editor in 1804, was even more abhorrent than "simple monarchy." Even Madison in *Federalist* No. 10 had said that pure democracies "have ever been spectacles of turbulence and contention; have ever been found incompatible with personal security, or the rights of property; and have in general been as short in their lives, as they have been violent in their deaths."[39]

But increasingly in the years following the Revolution the Republicans and other popular groups, especially in the North, began turning the once derogatory terms "democracy" and "democrat" into emblems of pride. Even in the early 1790s some contended that "the words Republican and Democratic are synonymous" and claimed that anyone who "is not a Democrat is an aristocrat or a monocrat."[40] The Democratic-Republican Societies disappeared, but their name lingered on; and soon many of the Northern Republicans began labeling their party the Democratic-Republican party. Early in the first decade of the nineteenth century even neutral observers were casually referring to the Republicans as the "Dems" or the "Democrats."[41]

With these Democrats regarding themselves as the nation, it was not long before people began to challenge the traditional culture's aversion to the term "democracy." "The government adopted here is a DEMOCRACY," boasted the populist Baptist Elias Smith in 1809. "It is well for us to understand this word, so much ridiculed by the international enemies of our beloved country. The word DEMOCRACY is formed of two Greek words, one signifies the people, and the other the government which is in the people.... My Friends, let us never be ashamed of DEMOCRACY!"[42]

In 1816 many members of Congress discovered just how powerful the people in this democracy could be. In March of that year Congress passed a Compensation Act, which raised the pay of congressmen from

---

39. David Hackett Fischer, *The Revolution of American Conservatism: The Federalist Party in the Era of Jeffersonian Democracy* (New York, 1965), 156; James H. Broussard, *The Southern Federalists, 1800–1816* (Baton Rouge, 1978), 309.

40. Sean Wilentz, *The Rise of American Democracy: Jefferson to Lincoln* (New York, 2005), 70.

41. See, in general, Everett Somerville Brown, ed., *William Plumer's Memorandum of Proceedings in the United States Senate, 1803–1807* (London, 1923).

42. Elias Smith, *The Loving Kindness of God Disposed in the Triumph of Republicanism in America* (n.p., 1809), 14–15.

six dollars per diem to a salary of fifteen hundred dollars a year. The vote in the House was eighty-one to sixty-seven, and in the Senate, twenty-one to eleven—with both Federalists and Democratic-Republicans on both sides of the vote. Congress had not received a raise since 1789 and had repeatedly complained that the per diem set at the beginning of the government was no longer adequate. Robert Wright, a Maryland congressman and former governor of the state, argued in the House that in the old days the representatives "lived like gentlemen, and enjoyed a glass of generous wine, which cannot be afforded at this time for the present compensation."[43]

Some analysts figured out that the new salary of fifteen hundred dollars a year came out to be about twelve dollars a day: Congress had thus doubled its pay. The press, both Federalist and Democratic-Republican, picked up on the issue and fanned the passions of people to heights rarely seen. Kentucky congressman Richard M. Johnson declared that "the poor compensation bill excited more discontent" than any other bill or event in the history of the young Republic—more "than the alien or sedition laws, the quasi war with France, the internal taxes of 1798, the embargo, the late war with Great Britain, the Treaty of Ghent, or any other one measure of the Government." Jefferson agreed. "There has never been an instance before of so unanimous an opinion of the people," he observed, "and that through every State in the Union."[44] If he had still been president, he said, he might have vetoed the bill. Earlier he had pointed out that the "drudgery" of office and the bare "subsistence" provided for officeholders in a republic were "a wise & necessary precaution against the degeneracy of the public servants." Such parsimonious views, which were actually aristocratic in nature, had inevitably increased Jefferson's popularity among Republican plebeians who resented paying taxes to pay for what seemed to be the high salaries of their public officials.[45]

Now the people had a chance to make their resentment felt. Throughout the country public meetings composed of both political parties denounced the law that had raised the salaries of congressmen. Several state legislatures along with Fourth of July orators bitterly condemned it. Glasses were raised in criticism; the compensation law, noted one New

43. C. Edward Skeen, "Vox Populi, Vox Dei: The Compensation Act of 1816 and the Rise of Popular Politics," JER, 6 (1986), 259–60.

44. Skeen, "Vox Populi, Vox Dei," JER, 6 (1986), 259–60.

45. TJ to De Meunier, 29 April 1795, in Paul Leicester Ford, ed., The Works of Thomas Jefferson: Federal Edition (New York, 1904), 8: 174.

York editor, was "toasted until it is black." In Georgia opponents even burned the members of Congress in effigy.[46]

Critics of the raise were especially incensed at Congressman Wright's indiscreet comment about not being able to enjoy a good glass of wine and cited it over and over to great effect. Popular outrage was unprecedented, and the reputation of Congress was severely tarnished. Even congressmen who had voted against the law had to promise humbly to work to repeal it and to return the salary they had already received. In the fall elections of 1816 nearly 70 percent of the Fourteenth Congress was not returned to the Fifteenth Congress. In January 1817 a chastened lame-duck Fourteenth Congress met to debate the issue of exactly what representation meant, and by and large it determined that the people had every right to instruct their congressmen. At this session, the last of his long career as a congressman, William Findley spoke passionately about the need to pay the people's representatives adequately. Ordinary middling people like him, who "have to support their families by their industry in any occupation," needed more than just enough money to cover their expenses. "Agreeable to all the principles of our government," said Findley, in summing up his view of representation that he had promoted from the beginning of his career, "all classes, and all interests ought to be represented in Congress.... The wages might be made so low that but one class, viz.: the wealthy who could afford the expense, and did not depend on their own personal industry would serve. But this," he said, in defense of the middling world he had helped create, "would change the nature of our government."[47] Despite Findley's plea for a decent salary, Congress at the end of the session repealed the Compensation Act but left it to the next Congress to set the members' pay, which it eventually did at eight dollars a day.

The issue marked an important point of transformation in American politics. It was "productive of good," declared the Republican *National Intelligencer*, "in so far as it has been the means of teaching the Representatives of the people a lesson of accountability, which will not be soon forgotten."[48] Congress was not to be a deliberative body set apart from the people; the representatives were not to stand above the people making impartial judgments as wise umpires in order to promote some abstract good. It was as the comte de Volney had said in his radical book, *Ruins*, which so enthralled Jefferson: Just as the enlightened wanted no mediators between themselves and God—no priests—so too did good republi-

---

46. Skeen, "Vox Populi, Vox Dei," *JER*, 6 (1986), 261.
47. Caldwell, *William Findley from West of the Mountains*, 370–72.
48. Skeen, "Vox Populi, Vox Dei," *JER*, 6 (1986), 272.

cans want no mediators between themselves and their rulers. Instead, congressmen and other officials were to be simply temporary agents of those who elected them, and they were bound to adhere as closely as possible to the will of their constituents.[49]

A new era in popular democratic politics had clearly emerged, and new modern politicians like Martin Van Buren realized that they could no longer rely on the elitist ideas of the Founders. For all of their greatness, those Founders, Van Buren said, had possessed many fears, fears of democracy that popular American experience since 1800 had laid to rest.

IN THIS DEMOCRATIC SOCIETY heroic individuals, like the Founders, no longer mattered as much as they had in the past. What counted was the mass of ordinary people, with the term "mass" being used positively for the first time in reference to "almost innumerable wills" acting to create a process that no one of them clearly intended. No country in history ever resembled the United States "in the points of greatness, complexity, and the number of its relations," declared the *North American Review* in 1816. It was a country so caught up in shifting currents, "rapid, powerful, accumulated in the mass, and uncertain in ... direction," that it was "scarcely possible for the mind to fix upon any ... ground of policy or just calculation" of what to do. America was in the hands of "Providence," and this traditional religious term now became identified with "progress" and with the natural principles of society created by the mass of busy people following their individual desires free from all sorts of artificial restraints, especially those imposed by government.[50]

As people became more confident that the social process was naturally progressive, earlier talk of the successive stages of social development tended to fall away, and people became less and less worried about entering the advanced commercial stage of the civilizing process. America was unique, declared Republican Nathaniel Cogswell in 1808. It "possesses all the excellencies of the ancient and modern Republics, without their faults," said Cogswell, whom the Federalists tried to mock as "one of Mr. Jefferson's idolators" and "proselytes to democracy." "It possesses, if I may so express myself, the seeds of eternal duration." America, said recent Harvard graduate Pliny Merrick in 1817, would never suffer the fate of

49. Constantin Francois Volney, *A New Translation of Volney's Ruins; or, Mediations on the Revolution of Empires* (Paris, 1802), 1: 152.

50. Gordon S. Wood, *The Radicalism of the American Revolution* (New York, 1992), 360; *North American Review*, 3 (1816), 345–47.

Greece and Rome. Its political institutions were "susceptible of infinite improvement," said Merrick, who went on to a distinguished legal career in Massachusetts; they "will endure unhurt by the ravages of time, and...future ages will be their witness, that 'decay's effacing fingers' are too feeble to crush their massive columns!"[51]

With new progressive conceptions of the social process, educated and reflective observers found it increasingly difficult to hold to the eighteenth-century conspiratorial notion that particular individuals were directly responsible for all that happened. The kind of conspiratorial thinking that lay behind the Bavarian Illuminati scare in the 1790s, for example, no longer had quite the same appeal for many educated ministers and Yale professors. Conspiratorial interpretations of events—attributing complicated concatenations of events to the motives of particular individuals—still thrived (witness the popularity of the "slave power conspiracy"), but with the spread of scientific thinking about society many of these sorts of conspiratorial interpretations began to seem increasingly primitive and quaint.[52]

Changing their conception of how things happened in society was only one of many transformations Americans experienced in the early nineteenth century. Although nature had been important to liberally educated eighteenth-century Americans, it was not America's wilderness or its landscape the Revolutionary gentlemen of the Enlightenment had sought to celebrate. Instead, they had honored the natural order of a Newtonian universe that transcended all national boundaries. In 1789 geographer Jedidiah Morse had seen nothing special, just "curious," in Niagara Falls; instead of the wilds of nature, Morse, like most enlightened eighteenth-century Americans, had admired well-laid-out villages and productive land. The British immigrant artist William Strickland likewise had known the difference between civilization and nature, and, speaking for the enlightened everywhere in the eighteenth century, he had wanted no part of raw nature. In 1794 Strickland had told people back in Britain that he went "about 50 miles beyond Albany, just sufficiently near the verge of barbarism to give me an idea of the

51. Nathaniel Cogswell, *An Oration, Delivered Before the Republican Citizens of Newburyport...on the Fourth of July 1808* (Newburyport, 1808), 18–19; *Monthly Anthology and Boston Review* (Boston, 1808), 450; Pliny Merrick, *An Oration, Delivered at Worcester, July 4, 1817* (Worcester, 1817), 9–10.
52. Gordon S. Wood, "Conspiracy and the Paranoid Style: Causality and Deceit in the Eighteenth Century," *WMQ*, 39 (1982), 439–41; David B. Davis, *The Slave Power Conspiracy and the Paranoid Style* (Baton Rouge, 1969); Thomas L. Haskell, *The Emergence of Professional Social Science: The American Social Science Association and the Nineteenth-Century Crisis of Authority* (Urbana, IL, 1977).

country in a state of nature which having once seen I feel not the least inclination to revisit."[53]

By the early nineteenth century, however, artists were changing their view of the untamed landscape. They were beginning to explore the wilds and forests of America and to paint what they now called the sublime grandeur of nature, including Niagara Falls. "Do not our vast rivers," declared Joseph Hopkinson to the Pennsylvania Academy of the Fine Arts in 1810, "vast beyond the conception of the European, rolling over immeasurable space, with the hills and mountains, the bleak wastes and luxuriant meadows through which they force their way, afford the most sublime and beautiful objects for the pencil of the Landscape?" The wilderness was no longer a source of fear and revulsion; it had become a source of admiration and pleasure. Indeed, some even began "lamenting the melancholy progress of improvement" and the "savage hand of cultivation."[54]

The Enlightenment was passing in other ways as well. All of the learned and scientific societies formed in the period, from the American Academy of Arts and Sciences in 1780 to the Literary and Philosophical Society of New York in 1814, rested on the eighteenth-century assumption that science or learning (the two were equated) was what distinguished cultivated gentlemen from savages and made them citizens of the world. For the enlightened members of these societies, science was cosmopolitan, taxonomic, and contemplative. The study of nature raised man "above vulgar prejudice" and enabled him "to form just conceptions of things." It expanded "his benevolence," extinguished "everything mean, base, and selfish in his nature," gave "a dignity to all his sentiments," and taught "him to aspire to the moral perfections of the great author of all things."[55]

This sort of enlightened contemplative science was not supposed to be connected too closely to the nitty-gritty of life. Although Jefferson had always emphasized that knowledge in the New World should be useful and applicable to "the common business of life," he was appalled by the idea that medical research might go on in hospitals. As far as he was concerned, hospitals were charitable institutions for the sick and the destitute, not places for science. Utility was important for eighteenth-century

53. Edward J. Nygren and Bruce Robertson, eds., *Views and Visions: American Landscape Before 1830* (Washington, DC, 1986), 226, 37–40, 58.

54. Joseph Hopkinson, *Annual Discourse* (1810), in Wood, ed., *Rising Glory of America*, 336; Washington Irving, *A History of New York* (1809), in James W. Tuttleton, ed., *Washington Irving: History, Tales and Sketches* (New York, 1983), 489.

55. *New York Magazine*, 5 (1794), 472, 474.

enlightened science but not all-encompassing. "The cultivation of knowledge, like the cultivation of virtue, is its own reward," declared DeWitt Clinton, in one of the last echoes of the Enlightenment's impulse. By 1814 not only had classical virtue become a behaviorist morality for the American masses, but enlightened knowledge was no longer its own reward: it had become an everyday instrument for the promotion of American prosperity.[56]

By the early nineteenth century, scientists, under pressure to explain their serene detachment from the world, were strenuously subverting the Enlightenment for the sake, in the words of Dr. Thomas Ewell, of "the dignity of independence and the glory of usefulness" and urging each other to turn their backs on the generalities of European science in the name of American particularities.[57] The contemplative and cosmopolitan sciences of the eighteenth century, physics and astronomy, now gave way to the more vital and patriotic sciences of biology and chemistry.

The eighteenth-century abstractions of the Enlightenment no longer seemed relevant. As the Jeffersonian chemist and émigré from England Thomas Cooper declared in 1817, "The days of metaphysical philosophy when the learned argued from generals to particulars...are gone by." Knowledge was acquired from the bottom up and could no longer deal "in abstract propositions" and be the exclusive business of the learned, elevated few; it belonged to everyone and had to enter "into our everyday comforts and conveniences." Cooper even justified the study of chemistry for its usefulness in the preparing and marinating of food.[58]

He was not alone in this desire to give chemistry a down-home usefulness, a peculiarly American desire that British critics enjoyed mocking. Jefferson urged Cooper to apply his chemistry "to domestic objects, to malting, for instance, brewing, making cider, to fermentation and distillation generally, to the making of bread, butter, cheese, soap, to the incubation of eggs, etc." John Adams agreed. He told John Gorham, professor of chemistry at Harvard, that chemists ought to forget about "deep discovery" and instead concentrate on giving "us the best possible bread, butter, cheese, wine, beer, and cider."[59]

56. TJ to John Banister Jr., 15 Oct. 1785, *Papers of Jefferson*, 8: 636; to Joseph C. Cabell, 28 Nov. 1820, in Ford, ed., *Writings of Jefferson*, 10: 166; Joseph Dorfman, *The Economic Mind in American Civilization, 1606–1865* (New York, 1946), 2: 503–4; DeWitt Clinton, *An Introductory Discourse, Delivered Before the Literary and Philosophical Society of New York, May 4th, 1814* (New York, 1815), 38.

57. John C. Greene, "Science in the Age of Jefferson," *Isis*, 49 (1958), 24.

58. Thomas Cooper, *Port Folio*, 5th Ser. (1817), 408–13.

59. Hugo A. Meier, "Technology and Democracy, 1800–1860," *Mississippi Valley Historical Review*, 43 (1957), 622; Edward Handler, "'Nature Itself Is All Arcanum': The Scientific Outlook of John Adams," American Philosophical Society, *Proc.*, 120 (1979), 223.

In its search for some sort of foundation in the popular mass, science kept sinking into curiosity-hunting and gimmickry. Charles Willson Peale, despite his devotion to the taxonomic and contemplative majesty of the natural world, nevertheless loved novelties and used all sorts of amusements to attract customers to his museum. He eventually resorted to hiring a popular musical performer who played five different instruments simultaneously, using all parts of his body. Following Peale's death the museum passed into the enterprising hands of P. T. Barnum, becoming part of his traveling circus—a romantic ending for an Enlightenment institution.

Others too had sought in a good Enlightenment manner to find a taxonomic principle under which a multitude of phenomena could be gathered. Dr. Samuel L. Mitchill thought he had discovered an element, which he called septon, that was the cause of decay and of most diseases, including cancer, leprosy, scurvy, and ringworm. But no physician went as far as Dr. Benjamin Rush in seeking the universal theory that would purge medicine of its complexities and mysteries.

Rush had inherited a system of medicine that numbered diseases in the hundreds. Dr. William Cullen, Rush's teacher in Edinburgh, for example, recorded 1,387 diseases and remedies. Rush came to equate this complicated array of diseases with the ancien régime of monarchy. He wanted to severely systemize his nosology and create an enlightened medicine that ordinary people would find as reasonable and comprehensible as they found republican government. "It is no more necessary that a patient should be ignorant of the medicine he takes, to be cured by it," he said, "than that the business of government should be conducted with secrecy, in order to insure obedience to the laws." If the Old World's medicine were sufficiently simplified and republicanized, he argued, medicine could be "taught with less trouble than is taken to teach boys to draw, upon paper or slate, the figures of Euclid." Even nurses and wives could be taught to administer remedies. Rush lectured his students in English, urged an end to the prescribing of medicines and writing of dissertations in the "dead language" of Latin, and even took to prescribing medicines and remedies by direct mail and through the newspapers.

But he let his enlightened reform of medicine get out of hand. Influenced by his classmate at Edinburgh John Brown, who had reduced the number of diseases to two, Rush carried the simplification to its ultimate conclusion and reduced all the hundreds of diseases to only one—fever, caused by convulsive tension in the blood vessels. As a good advocate for the Enlightenment, Rush believed that "truth is an unit. It is the same thing in war—philosophy—medicine—morals—religion—and government; and in proportion as we arrive at it in one science, we shall discover it in others." Just as there was but one God and one source of sovereignty in government, the people, so, Rush contended, there had to be only one source of disease, with the cure being purging and bleeding.

Rush had acquired much of his reputation as a physician by his heroic participation in the Philadelphia yellow fever epidemic of 1793. Despite his courageous devotion to his patients during the epidemic, however, Rush had lost many of them, largely because of his routine bleeding. Rush tended to bleed all his patients regardless of the nature of their illnesses. From consumption to cancer, he treated all diseases by reducing tension through purging and blood-letting. Unfortunately for his patients, he overestimated the amount of blood in the human body. He thought most people had twelve quarts of blood, double the six quarts in the average person. Since he often took from his patients as many as five quarts of blood in a day and a half, it is not surprising that so many of them died. The Federalist journalist William Cobbett termed Rush's method of bleeding "one of those great discoveries which are made from time to time for the depopulation of the earth." This became one of the statements that Rush used in his successful suit for libel against Cobbett.[60]

Rush even came to believe that mental illness was caused by excessive fever in the brain, with bleeding as the remedy. But Rush's eighteenth-century simplification turned out to be too extreme. Inevitably, many physicians and scientists became disillusioned with such Enlightenment a priori theories, and they reacted by swinging to the opposite extreme, leaving medicine and other sciences drowning in a sea of empiricism and Baconian fact-gathering.[61]

By the early nineteenth century old-fashioned enlightened scientists were criticized for their "careless flights of fancy" when all they needed was "an accumulation of well ascertained facts"—facts that could be gathered democratically by everyone and that would speak for themselves. Theories did not matter anymore; just gather the facts, and knowledge would automatically emerge. "In composing a work like the present," said physician James Mease of his Picture of Philadelphia (1811), "the author is of opinion that the chief object ought to be the multiplication of facts, and the reflections arising out of them ought to be left to the reader." Mease told his readers that 14,355 gallons of oil were used in

60. Richard Harrison Shryock, Medicine and Society in America, 1660–1860 (New York, 1960), 70; Carl Binger, Revolutionary Doctor: Benjamin Rush, 1746–1813 (New York, 1966), 229.
61. Whitfield J. Bell, Early American Science: Needs and Opportunities for Study (Williamsburg, 1955), 8–9; Donald J. D'Elia, "Dr. Benjamin Rush and the American Medical Revolution," American Philosophical Society, Proc., 110 (1966), 227–34.

city lamps per year and that 8,328 printed sheets were put out by the eight daily newspapers. In setting forth facts in this manner, Mease intended his readers to reach their own conclusions about the character of Philadelphia.[62]

If everything were being left to the reader in this way, then perhaps everyone, in good republican or democratic fashion, could become his own expert and make his own decisions about everything. Charles Nisbet, the president of Dickinson College in Pennsylvania, saw his worst nightmare being realized. With Americans relying so much on individual judgment, he fully expected, he said, to see soon such books as "Every Man his own Lawyer," "Every Man his own Physician," and "Every Man his own Clergyman and Confessor."[63] Dr. Daniel Drake in fact concluded that specialized medical knowledge was no longer the preserve of a few. "Hitherto," Drake told a group of Ohio medical students in the early nineteenth century, "the philosophers have formed a distinct caste from the people; and the like kinds have been supposed to possess a divine right of superiority. But this delusion should be dispelled, indeed is fast disappearing, and the distinction between scientific and the unscientific dissolved. . . . All men to a certain extent may become philosophers."[64]

With every ordinary person now being told that his ideas and tastes, on everything from medicine to art and government, were as good as if not better than those of "connoisseurs" and "speculative men" who were "college learnt," it is not surprising that truth and knowledge, which had seemed so palpable and attainable to the enlightened late eighteenth century, now became elusive and difficult to pin down.[65] As popular knowledge came to seem as accurate as the knowledge of experts, the borders the enlightened eighteenth century had painstakingly worked out between religion and magic, science and superstition, naturalism and supernaturalism, became blurred. Animal magnetism now seemed as legitimate as gravity. Popular speculations about the lost tribes of Israel seemed as plausible as scholarly studies of the origins of the Indian mounds of the Northwest. Dowsing for hidden metals appeared as rational as the workings of

62. Port Folio, 4th Ser., 6 (1815), 275; Patricia Cline Cohen, A Calculating People: The Spread of Numeracy in Early America (Chicago, 1982), 154.

63. James H. Smylie, "Charles Nisbet: Second Thoughts on a Revolutionary Generation," Penn. Mag. of Hist. and Biog., 98 (1974), 201.

64. Daniel Drake, "Introductory Lecture for the Second Session of the Medical College of Ohio," Henry D. Shapiro and Zane L. Miller, eds., Physician in the West: Selected Writings of Daniel Drake (Lexington, KY, 1970), 171.

65. Hopkinson, Annual Discourse, (1810), in Wood, ed., Rising Glory of America, 333; Nathan Hatch, The Democratization of American Christianity (New Haven, 1989), 45.

electricity. And crude folk remedies were even thought to be as scientific as the bleeding cures of enlightened medicine.

The result was an odd mixture of credulity and skepticism among many middling Americans. Where everything was believable, everything could be doubted. Since all claims to expert knowledge were suspect, people tended to mistrust anything outside of the immediate impact of their senses. They picked up the Lockean sensationalist epistemology and ran with it. They were a democratic people who judged by their senses only and who doubted everything that they had not seen, felt, heard, tasted, or smelled. Yet because people prided themselves on their shrewdness and believed that they were now capable of understanding so much from their senses, they could be easily impressed by what they sensed but could not comprehend. A few strange words spoken by a preacher, or hieroglyphics displayed on a document, or anything written in highfalutin language could carry great credibility. In such an atmosphere hoaxes of various kinds and charlatanism and quackery in all fields flourished.[66]

IN THE NEW DOWN-TO-EARTH populist world of the nineteenth century, the previous century's idea of the benefaction of science to mankind inevitably became identified with hardheaded utilitarianism. The rush of technological inventions in these years—steamboats, clocks, lamps, and numerous machines for doing everything from carding wool to cutting nails—was not unanticipated by Enlightenment philosophers like Jefferson, but the new business significance given to them was. While some of the devices of these years, like Jefferson's moldboard, were the result of the detached ingenuity of enlightened gentlemen-scientists, most inventions were the products of middling men of humble origins, such as Oliver Evans and Thomas Blanchard, seeking not fame but more efficient and more profitable ways of doing things.[67]

Oliver Evans, perhaps the most important inventor of his generation, was born in Delaware in 1755 and apprenticed to a wheelwright at age sixteen. With labor costs so high compared to those in England, clever young Americans like Evans immediately sought to devise machines that would cut down on the use of manual labor. Like other middling inventors in these years, Evans, once he got going inventing one thing, quickly

66. Neil Harris, *Humbug: The Art of P. T. Barnum* (Boston, 1973); Karen Halttunen, *Confidence Men and Painted Women: A Study of Middle-Class Culture in America, 1830–1870* (New Haven, 1982).

67. Kenneth L. Sokoloff and B. Zorina Khan, "The Democratization of Invention During Early Industrialization: Evidence from the United States, 1790–1846," *Journal of Economic History*, 50 (1990), 363–78.

thought of other machines for saving time and money. He first developed a carding machine for combing fibers for spinning and later a grain-grinding machine that led to a fully automated flour mill—setting the standards for flour-milling for the next several generations. After 1800 he concentrated on what became his most important invention, his high-pressure steam engine. In 1806 he opened his Mars Works in Philadelphia, and during the following decade he supervised the construction of dozens of steam engines and boilers, which became the driving force for most steamboats and factory machinery throughout the country.[68]

Thomas Blanchard was born in Sutton, Massachusetts, in 1788. He disliked both farming and the little schooling he had, but by concocting an apple-paring machine at age thirteen he demonstrated an early aptitude for inventiveness. Working in his older brother's tack-making shop, he created a tack-counting device and later a machine that cut and headed five hundred tacks per minute, which he was able to sell for five thousand dollars. Blanchard's experience, like that of other middling inventors of these years, demonstrates that most of the many inventions of the period were based not on any rare technical expertise or on extensive financial resources but rather on commonly available knowledge that an ordinary worker with some ingenuity and modest amounts of capital could apply to a specific problem. Among Blanchard's numerous inventions the most important was his unusual turning lathe that allowed for the production of irregular wooden shapes, including gun stocks. He took out over two dozen patents for his many inventions.[69]

With example after example of middling people like these becoming rich and successful, it was hard to think of scientific education as anything other than a means of releasing individual talents for the individual's profit, which was increasingly a pecuniary one. In Europe, said the *North American Review* in 1816, wealth was a prerequisite for new discoveries in science. In America, however, "we do all these as a means of acquiring wealth." Lacking the "large establishments and expansive endowments" of the Europeans, Americans, said Jacob Bigelow, in his 1816 inaugural lecture as Rumford Professor of the Application of Science to the Useful Arts at Harvard, had fundamentally altered the nature and sociology of scientific investigation. In Europe, the branches of the physical sciences were "pursued by learned men" interested in abstract theory. By contrast, the sciences in America have been pursued by ordinary

68. Neil L. York, "Oliver Evans," *American National Biography* (New York, 1999), 7: 617–18; Eugene S. Ferguson, *Oliver Evans: Inventive Genius of the American Industrial Revolution* (Greenville, DE, 1980).

69. Carolyn C. Cooper, "Thomas Blanchard," *American National Biography*, 2: 939–40.

"ingenious men" who, "unambitious of fame" and possessed with "a spirit or enterprise and perseverance" and "a talent of invention," have mainly "had utility for their object." Consequently, said Bigelow, who went on to develop what was labeled the science of technology, "we have had few learned men, but many useful ones," which "has entitled us to the character of a nation of inventors."[70]

This nation of inventors was creating new kinds of heroes. As early as 1796 an English author of children's stories popular in the United States argued in a tale entitled "True Heroism" that the great men of the present could no longer be the "kings, lords, generals, and prime ministers" who had shaped public life in the past. Instead, the true heroes now were becoming those who "invent useful arts, or discover important truths which may promote the comfort and happiness of unborn generations in the distant parts of the world." This was a message that Americans readily responded to, much to the disgust of the Federalists. Inventors and talented workmen were no doubt important, declared a writer in the *Port Folio* in 1810, "but if we crown with civic wreath every fortunate patentee of a steam engine or carding machine, every judicious speculator in merinos or Fezzan sheep, what honours have we left for wisdom and virtue?"[71]

By the early nineteenth century technology and prosperity were assuming for Americans the same sublime and moral significance that the Enlightenment had reserved for the classical state and the Newtonian universe. Eli Whitney, inventor of the cotton gin, and Robert Fulton, creator of the steamboat, became national heroes to the hundreds of thousands of artisans and others in the country who worked with their hands. Roads, bridges, and canals were justified by their fostering of "national grandeur and individual convenience," the two now being inextricably linked.[72] It was not virtue or sociability that held this restless and quarrelsome people together, said architect and economist Samuel Blodgett in 1806; it was commerce, "the most sublime gift of heaven, wherewith to harmonize and enlarge society." If America were ever to "eclipse the grandeur of European nations," it could not be in Hamilton's Old World terms of building a great and powerful nation; it had to be in America's new Jeffersonian terms: in its capacity to further the material welfare of its ordinary citizens.[73]

70. Jacob Bigelow, *Inaugural Address, Delivered in the Chapel of the University at Cambridge, December 11, 1816* (Boston, 1817), 12, 13, 15, 16–17.
71. Isaac Kramnick, "Republican Revisionism Revisited," *AHR*, 87 (1982), 662; *Port Folio*, 3rd Ser., 4 (1810), 571–72.
72. Charles G. Haines, *Considerations on the Great Western Canal* (Brooklyn, 1818), 11.
73. Samuel Blodgett, *Economica: A Statistical Manual for the United States of America* (Washington, DC, 1806), 102.

AT THE OUTSET many members of the Revolutionary elite, including Benjamin Rush, Noah Webster, and Francis Hopkinson, had inadvertently contributed to the popularization and vulgarization of the culture. Many of them had attacked the study of the "dead languages" of Greek and Latin as time-consuming, useless, and unrepublican without appreciating the unintended consequences of their attacks. Such study of Greek and Latin, Rush had said, was "improper in a peculiar manner in the United States" because it tended to confine education only to a few, when in fact republicanism required everyone to be educated.[74]

Yet when some of these enthusiastic republican gentlemen began to glimpse the populist and anti-intellectual results of these attacks on liberal learning, they began to have second thoughts about what they had said. Even Rush, though he retained his dislike of the heathenish classics on religious grounds, by 1810 came to realize that "a learned education" ought once again to "become a luxury in our country." If college tuitions were not immediately raised, he said, "the great increase in wealth among all classes of our citizens" would enable too many ordinary people, particularly plain farmers, to pay for a college education for their sons "with more ease than in former years when wealth was confined chiefly to cities and to the learned professions." It was one thing for a practical knowledge of "reading, writing, and arithmetic...to be as common and as cheap as air," said Rush; in a republic everyone should have these skills, and "they should be a kind of sixth or civic sense." But it was quite another thing with a college liberal arts education. "Should it become universal, it would be as destructive to civilization as universal barbarism."[75]

Rush had come to perceive that middlebrow adoption of liberal learning was insidiously draining its integrity away without anyone's being the wiser. In fact, the middling sorts were diluting everything they touched. The enlightened clergyman from Salem, Massachusetts, William Bentley, who commanded twenty languages, possessed a library of four thousand volumes, and knew something about everything, had very high hopes for the spread of knowledge through newspapers. For several decades, beginning in the early 1790s, this polymath made available his encyclopedic knowledge to his fellow citizens in regular essays in the local papers. Twice a week he presented digests of the most important

74. Meyer Reinhold, *Classica Americana: The Greek and Roman Heritage in the United States* (Detroit, 1984), 129, 124.
75. BR to James Hamilton, 27 June 1810, *Letters of Rush*, 2: 1053. Others too thought that the number of those attending colleges and academies in the United States ought to be limited, "since but few men can, or ever ought to live by their learning." David Barnes, *A Discourse on Education* (Boston, 1803), 11.

domestic and foreign news, including notices of new books and significant scientific discoveries. He often illustrated his columns with original
documents, which usually he himself had translated. In his news sum-
maries Bentley aimed to get beyond "the conversation of the day, or the
reports of passing moment," in order for his readers to understand "the
causes which produce interesting events." He hoped that his biweekly
columns and newspapers in general would become an important means
of elevating the knowledge of "all classes of readers."

By 1816 his enlightened dreams of newspapers becoming agents of education for the public had dissipated. The press, he now realized, had
become simply a source of "public entertainment," filled with inconsequential and parochial pieces of information. "The great number of newspapers," he ruefully recognized, "put in circulation every incident which
is raised in every local situation.... So not a fire, an accident, a fear or a
hope but it flies quickly throughout the union." How could judicious
analyses of foreign policy and careful discussions of domestic politics
compete with such trivial and ephemeral incidents of daily life? "The
public mind," Bentley complained, "is already unaccustomed to weigh
these things," and consequently was sinking into a sea of mediocrity.[76]

Most Federalists and many disillusioned Republicans like Rush and
Bentley thought that America would be better off with the Visigoths at
the gates than with this degradation and disintegration from within.

BUT IT WAS TOO LATE. Not only were the middling people popularizing America's culture, but they were as well creating the country's
sense of identity, even its sense of nationhood. Many Americans had
hoped that participation in the War of 1812 would in an aristocratic manner vindicate the honor of the new Republic and establish its reputation in
the world. But by the end of the war America's conception of its national
character was becoming much more indebted to the middling people's
go-getting involvement in commerce and enterprise. These ambitious,
risk-taking entrepreneurs, who were coming into their own by the second
decade of the nineteenth century, were the generation that imagined the
myth of the American dream. They went way beyond the eighteenth century's earlier celebration of America as "the best poor man's country" and
created, as Joyce Appleby, the foremost historian of this post-Revolutionary
generation, points out, "a new character ideal...: the man who developed

76. Richard D. Brown, *Knowledge Is Power: The Diffusion of Information in Early
America, 1700–1865* (New York, 1989), 212–15; William Bentley, *The Diary of William
Bentley, D.D: Pastor of East Church, Salem, Massachusetts* (Gloucester, MA, 1962),
4: 370.

inner resources, acted independently, lived virtuously, and bent his behavior to his personal goals." The middling sorts who created this ideal extolled hard work and ingenuity and wrote the hundreds of stories of "the self-made man," which, says Appleby, appeared "as a recognizable type for the first time in this era." In short, these middling men invented America's sense of itself as a land of enterprising, optimistic, innovative, and equality-loving Americans. Even today their sense that America is a land of opportunity and enterprise remains alive and influential.[77]

Although this peculiar identity was a Northern middle-class creation, it quickly came to be embraced by the nation as a whole. In fact, Northern characteristics of enterprise and hard work were now categorized as "national" while Southern qualities were viewed as sectional or regional, "a development," notes Appleby, "that the Virginians who initiated the move for a 'more perfect union' provided by the Constitution could never have predicted."[78]

Although most Southern farmers were not slaveholders and many of the plain folk of the South valued hard work as much as any ambitious Northern artisan, these ordinary Southern folk could never give the same kind of enterprising middling tone to Southern society that existed in the North. There were fewer middling institutions in the South—fewer towns, schools, newspapers, businesses, manufacturing firms, banks, and shops. And there were fewer middling people in the South—fewer teachers, physicians, clerks, publishers, editors, and engineers. The antebellum South never became a middling commercial-minded society like that of the North. Its patrician order of large slaveholders continued to dominate both the culture and the politics of the section.

Although the great Southern planters celebrated the advance of republicanism and the destruction of monarchy everywhere, their confidence in republicanism, unlike that of the Federalists of the North, was necessarily based on their ability to take the hierarchy and deference of their slave society for granted. Yet, as opposition to slavery grew in the North, the Southern planters began to create ever more elaborate apologies and defenses of their "peculiar institution." Many of the younger planters were even beginning to argue that the very existence of civilization depended on slavery. By 1815 the South seemed sharply separated from the North in ways that had not been true a generation earlier.

In 1789 the South and especially Virginia had been the impelling force in creating the nation. By 1815 the South and slaveholders still seemed to be in

77. Joyce Appleby, *Inheriting the Revolution: The First Generation of Americans* (Cambridge, MA, 2000), 11, 10.
78. Appleby, *Inheriting the Revolution*, 126.

control of the national government. President Madison was a slaveholder. So too were Speaker of the House Henry Clay, James Monroe, the secretary of state, and George W. Campbell, the secretary of the treasury. All the Republican leaders of the House were slaveholders. In 1815 the United States had four missions in Europe: two of them were held by slaveholders. The chief justice of the United States was a slaveholder, as were a majority of the other members of the Court. Since 1789 three of the four presidents, two of the five vice-presidents, fourteen of the twenty-six presidents pro tempore of the Senate, and five of the ten Speakers of the House had been slaveholders.[79]

Nevertheless, despite this political dominance, many slaveholding Southerners had a growing uneasiness that the South was being marginalized by the dynamic, enterprising, and egalitarian North, which was rapidly seizing control of the nation's identity. By 1815 Virginia was still the most populous state in the nation, with nearly nine hundred thousand people. But the growth of its white population had slowed dramatically, its land was depleted, and it no longer possessed its earlier confidence that it would always be in charge of the nation. Many of its vigorous and ambitious younger people were fleeing the state. In fact, as many as 230 men born in Virginia before 1810, including Henry Clay, were eventually elected to Congress from other states.[80]

While the North was busy building schools, roads, and canals, Virginia was in decline. As early as 1800, according to one Virginian, Albemarle County, Jefferson's home county, had become a "scene of desolation that baffles description." Farms were "worn out, washed and gullied, so that scarcely an acre could be found in a place fit for cultivation." Even as the Virginia planters were celebrating the yeoman farmer and the agricultural way of life, some of them sensed that their best days were behind them. In 1814 John Randolph spoke for many of them in reflecting on the decline and ruin he saw in Virginia's Tidewater.

> The old mansions, where they have been spared by fire (the consequence of the poverty and carelessness of their present tenants), are fast falling into decay; the families, with a few exceptions, dispersed from St. Mary's to St. Louis; such as remain here sunk into obscurity. They whose fathers rode in coaches and drank the choicest wines now ride on saddlebags, and drink grog, when they can get it. What enterprise or capital there was in the country retired westward.[81]

79. Hunt, *As We Were*, 42–43.
80. Susan Dunn, *Dominion of Memories: Jefferson, Madison and the Decline of Virginia* (New York, 2007), 42.
81. Avery O. Craven, *Soil Exhaustion as a Factor in the Agricultural History of Virginia and Maryland, 1606–1860* (1926; Gloucester, MA, 1965), 83; Edmund Quincy, *Life of Josiah Quincy of Massachusetts* (Boston, 1867), 354.

The Southern planters, bewildered and besieged by the fast-moving commercial developments in the North, reacted, as Jefferson did, by turning inward, blaming conniving, mercenary, hypocritical Yankees for their problems, and becoming increasingly anxious and defensive about slavery. Although in the first decade of the nineteenth century foreign travelers had observed how confident most Virginians were that slavery would eventually disappear, that confidence soon dissipated. In 1815 an English visitor was struck by how much Virginians talked about slavery. It was "an evil uppermost in every man's thoughts," an evil, he noted, "which all deplore, many were anxious to flee, but for which no man can devise a remedy." Soon, however, many Southerners became less and less willing to talk about slavery in front of strangers.[82]

BY THE END OF THE WAR OF 1812 the eighteenth-century Enlightenment in America was clearly over. The people of the United States no longer had the same interest in a cosmopolitan connection with Europe. France no longer influenced American thinking, and with the demise of the Federalists, the cultural authority of England lost much of its fearsomeness. Most Americans abandoned any lingering sense that they were "secondhand" Englishmen and concluded that they no longer needed to compete with Europe in a European manner. Instead, they turned in on themselves in admiration at their own peculiarities and spaciousness.

In 1816, much to the chagrin of Jefferson and other enlightened figures, Congress enacted a duty on imported foreign books. Jefferson protested, as did Harvard, Yale, and other elite institutions, including the American Philosophical Society and the American Academy of Arts and Sciences, but to no avail. "Our Government," declared the chairman of the Senate Finance Committee in defense of the tariff,

> is peculiar to ourselves and our books of instruction should be adapted to the nature of the Government and the genius of the people. In the best of foreign books we are liable to meet with criticism and comparisons not very flattering to the American people. In American editions of these the offensive and illiberal parts are expunged or explained, and the work is adapted to the exigencies and tastes of the American reader. But withdraw the protection, our channels of instruction will be foreign; our youth will imbibe sentiments, form attachments and acquire habits of thinking adverse to our prosperity, unfriendly to our Government, and dangerous to our liberties.[83]

82. Appleby, *Inheriting the Revolution*, 225.
83. Merle Curti, *The Growth of American Thought*, 3rd ed. (New York, 1964), 245.

Although Jefferson was appalled by this sort of parochial and unenlightened thinking—this repudiation of everything the cosmopolitan Enlightenment had been about—his own despairing reaction to the nineteenth-century world he saw emerging was not much different. He himself withdrew mentally from Europe. Nature had placed America in an "insulated state," he told Alexander von Humboldt in 1813. It "has a hemisphere to itself. It must have its separate system of interests, which must not be subordinated to those of Europe." He loathed the new democratic world that America had become—a world of speculation, banks, paper money, and evangelical Christianity; and he railed against this world that was full of "pseudo-citizens...infected with the mania of rambling and gambling," and indeed turned his back on it, withdrawing more and more to the sanctuary of his mountaintop home, Monticello. He had come to believe, as he said in 1813, that, in the face of this Northern obsession with money and commerce, the principles of free government that he had struggled so long to promote now must retreat "to the agricultural States of the south and west, as their last asylum and bulwark." All he could do to counteract the threat posed by the "pious young monks from Harvard and Yale" was to hunker down in Virginia and build a university that would perpetuate true republican principles. "It is in our seminary," he told Madison, "that that vestal flame is to be kept alive."[84]

Although the world of the early nineteenth century was spinning out of Jefferson's control or even his comprehension, no one had done more to bring it about. It was Jefferson's commitment to liberty and equality that justified and legitimated the many pursuits of happiness that were bringing unprecedented prosperity to so many average white Americans. His Republican followers in the North had created this new world, and they welcomed and thrived in it. They celebrated Jefferson and equal rights and indeed looked back in awe and wonder at all the Founders and saw in them heroic leaders the likes of which they knew they would never see again in America. Yet they also knew they now lived in a different world, a bustling democratic world that required new thoughts and new behavior.

Americans had begun their experiment in national republicanism seeking a classic and cosmopolitan destiny in a Western trans-Atlantic

84.  TJ to Alexander von Humboldt, 6 Dec. 1813, in L and B, eds., Writings of Jefferson, 14: 22–23; to William H. Crawford, 20 June 1816, in Ford, ed., Writings of Jefferson, 10: 34–35; to Henry Middleton, 8 Jan. 1813, in L and B, eds., Writings of Jefferson, 13: 203; Robert E. Shalhope, "Thomas Jefferson's Republicanism and Antebellum Southern Thought," Journal of Southern History, 42 (1976), 542; TJ to JM, 17 Feb. 1826, Jefferson: Writings, 1514.

world they felt very much a part of. Many of them sought to receive the best of Western culture, and some of them even wanted to emulate the powers of Europe by building a similar fiscal-military state. But by 1815 most Americans had come to perceive their destiny in America itself, by becoming an unprecedented kind of democratic republic.

Indeed, with Europe restored to monarchy after 1815 and the monarchies joined together in a Holy Alliance against liberalism and revolution, Americans were coming to believe that their democracy was all the more peculiar and significant. "Alliances, Holy or Hellish, may be formed, and retard the epoch of deliverance," declared Jefferson; they "may swell the rivers of blood which are yet to flow." But they will eventually fail. America would remain as a light to the world showing that mankind was capable of self-government.[85]

Yet beneath the Americans' excitement over their newfound Americanness lay what Jefferson bemoaned as "the miseries of slavery." The War of 1812 was no sooner concluded than the country became seriously divided over the admission of Missouri as a slave state. That crisis stripped away the illusions that both the North and the South had entertained about slavery. Suddenly, Northerners came to realize that slavery was not going to disappear naturally, and Southerners came to realize that the North really cared about ending slavery. From that moment few Americans had any illusions left about the awful reality of slavery in America.

To Jefferson the crisis was "a fire bell in the night," filling him and many other Americans with the terror that they had heard "the knell of the Union." Jefferson feared that all he and "the generation of 1776" had done "to acquire self-government and happiness to their country" was now to be sacrificed and thrown away by the "unwise and unworthy passions of their sons."[86]

The Missouri crisis, said Jefferson, was "not a moral question, but one merely of power."[87] He was wrong. It was a moral question, and the passions of the sons of the Founders were neither unwise nor unworthy; indeed, they had been his passions as well—the love of liberty and the desire for equality. No American had spoken more eloquently or more fully for the radical impulse of the Enlightenment than Jefferson. No one had expressed the radical meaning of the Revolution—the deposing of tyrannical kings and the raising up of common people to an unprecedented degree of equality—than Jefferson. Yet he always sensed that his

85. TJ to Lafayette, 4 Nov. 1823, in Ford, ed., *Writings of Jefferson*, 10: 280.
86. TJ to Charles Pinckney, 30 Sept. 1820, in L and B, eds., *Writings of Jefferson*, 15: 280; TJ to John Holmes, 22 April 1820, *Jefferson: Writings*, 1434.
87. TJ to Lafayette, 26 Dec. 1820, in Ford, ed., *Writings of Jefferson*, 10: 180.

"empire of liberty" had a cancer at its core that was eating away at the message of liberty and equality and threatening the very existence of the nation and its democratic self-government; but he had mistakenly come to believe that the cancer was Northern bigotry and money-making promoted by Federalist priests and merchants.

In light of Jefferson's belief that "the earth belongs in usufruct to the living" and that each generation must be free of burdens inherited from the past, there was something perversely ironic in his bequeathing slavery to his successors. But he put all his trust in the ability of the country to educate and enlighten the future generations of Americans. This confidence in education and the future, he confessed in 1817, "may be an Utopian dream, but being innocent, I have thought I might indulge in it till I go to the land of dreams, and sleep there with the dreamers of all past and future times." Although Jefferson in his final years tried to retain his sunny hopes for the future, he had twinges of an impending disaster whose sources he never fully understood. He and his colleagues had created a Union devoted to liberty that contained an inner flaw that would nearly prove to be its undoing. The Virginians who had done so much to bring about the United States knew in their souls, as Madison intimated in his advice to his country from beyond the grave, that there was a "Serpent creeping with his deadly wiles" in their Arcadian "Paradise." Like Madison, many of the older generation came to realize that "slavery and farming are incompatible."[88] The Civil War was the climax of a tragedy that was preordained from the time of the Revolution. Only with the elimination of slavery could this nation that Jefferson had called "the world's best hope" for democracy even begin to fulfill its great promise.[89]

88. TJ to J. Correa de Serra, 25 Nov. 1817, in L and B, eds. *Writings of Jefferson*, 15: 157; JM, "Advice to My Country" (1834), *Madison: Writings*, 866; Dunn, *Dominion of Memories*, 26.

89. TJ, First Inaugural Address, 4 March 1801, *Jefferson: Writings*, 493.

# Bibliographic Essay

Over the past three decades or so, the period of history covered by this book has experienced a renaissance in historical writing, involving the production of many more books than can be cited in this essay. Consequently, this bibliography is very selective.

Much of the proliferation of works on the early Republic came from the formation of the Society for Historians of the Early American Republic (SHEAR) in 1977 and the launching of the *Journal of the Early Republic* (JER) in 1981. This organization and its journal have turned the period into one of the most exciting and significant in American history.

Since there were so many great men in the period, biographies, many of them multivolume, have been written and continue to flourish. Douglas Southall Freeman, seven volumes on Washington (1948–1957); James Thomas Flexner, four volumes on Washington (1965–1972); Dumas Malone, six volumes on Jefferson (1948–1981); Irving Brant, six volumes on James Madison (1941–1961); and Page Smith, two volumes on Adams (1962). Early in the twentieth century Albert Beveridge wrote four laudatory volumes on John Marshall (1916–1919) that still stand up.

It seems that scarcely a year now passes that one or another of the Founders does not have his life portrayed in print. Probably the best single-volume study of Washington is Joseph J. Ellis, *His Excellency: George Washington* (2004). Good single-volume studies of other Founders are the following: Merrill D. Peterson, *Thomas Jefferson and the New Nation: A Biography* (1970); for a superb brief life, see R. B. Bernstein, *Thomas Jefferson* (2003); Ron Chernow, *Alexander Hamilton* (2004), but Gerald Stourzh, *Alexander Hamilton and the Idea of Republican Government* (1970) excels in placing this leading Federalist in an eighteenth-century context; John Ferling, *John Adams: A Life* (1992); Ralph Ketcham, *James Madison: A Biography* (1971), but for an excellent short biography, see Jack N. Rakove, *James Madison and the Creation of the American Republic* (1990); Jean Edward Smith, *John Marshall: Definer of a Nation* (1996), but for a good short study, see Charles F. Hobson, *The Great Chief Justice: John Marshall and the Rule of Law* (1996).

Each of these Founders also has his own mammoth papers project under way (or in the case of Hamilton, completed), each promising to publish virtually everything written by and to the great man. Nearly all the leading Founders have volumes of their selected writings available in the Library of America. Jefferson's exchange of letters with two of his fellow Founders is in two volumes edited by Lester J. Cappon, *The Adams-Jefferson Letters* (1959); and in three volumes edited by James Morton Smith, *The Republic of Letters: The Correspondence Between Thomas Jefferson and James Madison, 1776–1826* (1995).

Even Aaron Burr, forever disgraced but forever fascinating, has had two volumes of his correspondence edited by Mary-Jo Kline and published in 1984. The standard biography of him is Milton Lomask, *Aaron Burr*, 2 vols. (1979, 1982). The most recent life is a defense of Burr, Nancy Isenberg, *Forgotten Founder: The Life of Aaron Burr* (2007).

Many secondary figures in the period have excellent biographies. To name only several, see Talbot Hamlin, *Benjamin Henry Latrobe* (1955); Winifred E. Bernard, *Fisher Ames: Federalist and Statesman, 1758–1808* (1965); George C. Rogers Jr., *Evolution of a Federalist: William Loughton Smith of Charleston, 1758–1812* (1962); Robert Ernst, *Rufus King: American Federalist* (1968); Samuel Eliot Morison, *Harrison Gray Otis, 1765–1848: The Urbane Federalist* (1969); Harry Ammon, *James Monroe: The Quest for National Identity* (1971); George Athan Billias, *Elbridge Gerry: Founding Father and Republican Statesman* (1976); John Mack Faragher, *Daniel Boone: The Life and Legend of an American Pioneer* (1992); James J. Kirschke, *Gouverneur Morris: Author, Statesman, and Man of the World* (2005); and Walter Stahr, *John Jay: Founding Father* (2005). Two collective studies of the Founders are Joseph J. Ellis, *Founding Brothers: The Revolutionary Generation* (2000) and Gordon S. Wood, *Revolutionary Characters: What Made the Founders Different* (2006).

In the 1960s the origins of political parties commanded the attention of political scientists and political sociologists. Since these scholars were not historians, they were primarily concerned with forming generalizations about politics that were applicable to the experience of newly developing nations in the decade or so following World War II. Consequently, they were not always sensitive to the differentness of the past, and their books often presented a very ahistorical and anachronistic view of America's early political parties. See especially William Nesbit Chambers, *Political Parties in a New Nation: The American Experience, 1776–1809* (1963); Seymour Martin Lipset, *The First New Nation: The United States in Historical and Comparative Perspective* (1963); Rudolph M. Bell, *Party and Faction in American Politics: The House of Representatives, 1789–1801* (1973); and John F. Hoadley, *Origins of American Political Parties, 1789–1803* (1986).

In more recent years, historians more sensitive to time and place have challenged this political science conception of "the first party system." See Richard Buel Jr., *Securing the Revolution: Ideology in American Politics, 1789–1815* (Ithaca, 1972); Ronald P. Formisano, *The Transformation of Political Culture: Massachusetts Parties, 1790s–1840s* (New York, 1983); Ralph Ketcham, *Presidents Above Party: The First American Presidency, 1789–1829* (1984); James Roger Sharp, *American Politics in the Early Republic: The New Nation in Crisis* (1993); Stanley Elkins and Eric McKitrick, *The Age of Federalism: The Early American Republic, 1788–1800* (1993), which is a monumental study of the high politics of the 1790s sympathetic to the Federalists; and Joanne B. Freeman, *Affairs of Honor: National Politics in the New Republic* (New Haven, 2001), which nicely captures the peculiar political culture of the 1790s. The first section of Sean Wilentz's monumental study *The*

*Rise of American Democracy: Jefferson to Lincoln* (2005) is pertinent to the early Republic; Wilentz's work is a throwback to a traditional approach to politics, focusing on elections, parties, and the maneuvering of elite white males in government.

Most historians nowadays seek to write political history that views politics through the lenses of race, gender, and popular culture. Consequently, they are interested primarily in the symbols and theatrics of politics—the varied ways common people, including women and blacks, expressed themselves and participated in politics, whether in parades, dress, or drinking toasts. For examples, see Doron Ben-Atar and Barbara B. Oberg, eds., *Federalists Reconsidered* (1998); and Jeffrey L. Pasley, Andrew W. Robertson, and David Waldstreicher, eds., *Beyond the Founders: New Approaches to the Political History of the Early Republic* (2004). On popular politics in the 1790s, see Simon P. Newman, *Parades and the Politics of the Street: Festive Culture in the Early American Republic* (1997); and David Waldstreicher, *In the Midst of Perpetual Fetes: The Making of American Nationalism, 1776–1820* (1997).

Over the past three decades many historians have also developed a new conception of the early Republic, bridging the professional chasm that earlier separated those who concentrated on the colonial and Revolutionary periods from those who focused on the early Republic. Historians now tend to conceive of the Revolution much more broadly than they did in the past and have extended its reach into the early decades of the nineteenth century. Historians now write books that run from 1750 or 1780 to 1820 or 1840. This new periodization makes the Revolution far more significant and consequential for the early nineteenth century than it had been earlier.

As a result, there is a stronger sense of the changes that took place over this extended Revolutionary period, not just politically but socially and culturally. On this subject, see Gordon S. Wood, *The Radicalism of the American Revolution* (1992). Over the past generation increasing numbers of historians have turned to social and cultural subjects rather than just focusing on prominent individuals. They now write about extended social developments that cut through the Revolutionary era and transcended the traditional political dates—the role of women and families, the emerging professions, the decline of apprenticeship, the rise of counting, the transformation of artisans, the changing of urban mobs, the development of the postal system, and so on. On these subjects, see Donald M. Scott, *From Office to Profession: The New England Ministry, 1750–1850* (1986); W. J. Rorabaugh, *The Craft Apprentice: From Franklin to the Machine Age* (1986); Patricia Cline Cohen, *A Calculating People: The Spread of Numeracy in Early America* (1982); W. J. Rorabaugh, *The Alcoholic Republic: An American Tradition* (1979); Paul G. Faler, *Mechanics and Manufactures in the Early Industrial Revolution: Lynn, Massachusetts, 1780–1860* (1981); Sean Wilentz, *Chants Democratic: New York City and the Rise of the American Working Class, 1788–1850* (1984); Paul A. Gilge, *The Road to Mobocracy: Popular Disorder in New York City, 1763–1834* (1987); and Richard R. John, *Spreading the News: the American Postal System from Franklin to Morse* (1995).

Even legal historians have become less interested in the decisions of Chief Justice Marshall and more interested in the relation between law and society. For examples, see William E. Nelson, *Americanization of the Common Law: The Impact of Legal Change on Massachusetts Society, 1760–1830* (1975); and Morton J. Horwitz, *The Transformation of*

*American Law, 1780–1860* (1977). Much of this new legal research was inspired by James Willard Hurst. See his "Old and New Dimensions of Research in United States Legal History," *American Journal of Legal History*, 23 (1979), 1–20.

One of the most important contributors to this new look at the relation of the Revolution to the first few decades of the early Republic is the extraordinarily ambitious and fruitful project *Perspectives on the American Revolution*, supported by the United States Capitol Historical Society and conceived and led by Ronald Hoffman and Peter J. Albert. For nearly twenty years, from the early 1980s to the end of the twentieth century, Hoffman and Albert, supplemented by occasional guest editors, brought out almost a dozen and a half volumes on various important issues connected with the American Revolution and its aftermath — everything from women, slavery, and Indians to religion, social developments, and patterns of consumption.

A host of issues has been enlivened by connecting the Revolution to the decades of the early Republic and emphasizing its cultural implications. The Enlightenment, for example, has been broadened to include politeness and civility and not just the growth of deism and reason. On this cultural conception of the Enlightenment, see Richard L. Bushman, *The Refinement of America: Persons, Houses, Cities* (1992); David S. Shields, *Civil Tongues and Polite Letters in British America* (1997); and Lawrence E. Klein, *Shaftesbury and the Culture of Politeness: Moral Discourse and Cultural Politics in Early Eighteenth-Century England* (1994). Henry F. May, *The Enlightenment in America* (1976), Robert A. Ferguson, *The American Enlightenment, 1750–1820* (1997), Gary L. McDowell and Jonathan O'Neill, eds., *America and Enlightenment Constitutionalism* (2006), and Andrew Burstein, *Sentimental Democracy: The Evolution of America's Romantic Self-Image* (1999) are important studies. On the influence of antiquity, see Carl J. Richard, *The Founders and the Classics: Greece, Rome, and the American Enlightenment* (1994); and Caroline Winterer, *The Culture of Classicism: Ancient Greece and Rome in American Intellectual Life, 1780–1910* (2002). On the origins of American exceptionalism, see Jack P. Greene, *The Intellectual Construction of America: Exceptionalism and Identity from 1492 to 1800* (1993). The authoritative history of early American Freemasonry is Steven C. Bullock, *Revolutionary Brotherhood: Freemasonry and the Transformation of the American Social Order, 1730–1840* (1996). The best historical study of citizenship is James H. Kettner, *The Development of American Citizenship, 1608–1870* (1978).

On the creation of the new national government, see the surveys by Stanley Elkins and Eric McKitrick, *The Age of Federalism: The Early American Republic, 1788–1800* (1993); and John C. Miller, *The Federalist Era, 1789–1801* (1960). On the creation of a federal bureaucracy, see the pathbreaking work by Leonard D. White, *The Federalists: A Study in Administrative History* (1948). For the English model of a "fiscal-military" state, see John Brewer, *The Sinews of Power: War, Money and the English State, 1688–1788* (1989). Particularly important for understanding the Hamiltonian vision of this "fiscal-military" state is Max M. Edling, *A Revolution in Favor of Government: Origins of the U.S. Constitution and the Making of the American State* (2003). For other accounts of state-building in the 1790s, see Carl Prince, *The Federalists and the Origins of the U.S. Civil Service* (1978); and especially Richard R. John, *Spreading the News: The American Postal System from Franklin to Morse* (1995). Richard H. Kohn, *Eagle and Sword: The Federalists and the Creation of the Military Establishment in America, 1783–1802* (1975) is important for understanding the Federalists' goals. Samuel Flagg Bemis's, *Jay's Treaty: A Study in Commerce and Diplomacy* (1923) and *Pinckney's Treaty: A Study of America's Advantage from Europe's Distress, 1783–1800* (1926) are classics on foreign policy in the 1790s. Jerald A. Combs, *The Jay Treaty: Political Battleground of the Founding Fathers* (1970) is broader than its title would suggest.

On the origins of the Bill of Rights, see Patrick T. Conley and John P. Kaminiski, eds., *The Bill of Rights and the States: The Colonial and Revolutionary Origins of American Liberties* (1991); Richard Labunski, *James Madison and the Struggle for the Bill of Rights* (2006); and Leonard W. Levy, *Origins of the Bill of Rights* (1999). For a modern analysis of the constitutional significance of the Bill of Rights, see Akhil Reed Amar, *The Bill of Rights: Creation and Reconstitution* (1998).

On financial matters in the 1790s, see E. James Ferguson, *The Power of the Purse: A History of Public Finance, 1776–1790* (1961); and Edwin J. Perkins, *American Public Finance and Financial Services, 1700–1815* (1994).

Leland D. Baldwin, *Whiskey Rebels: The Story of a Frontier Uprising* (1939) and William Hogeland, *The Whiskey Rebellion: George Washington, Alexander Hamilton, and the Frontier Rebels Who Challenged America's Newfound Sovereignty* (2006) are narratives of the insurrection, while Thomas P. Slaughter, *The Whiskey Rebellion: Frontier Epilogue to the American Revolution* (1986) is more analytical.

Richard Hofstadter, *The Idea of a Party System: The Rise of Legitimate Opposition in the United States, 1780–1840* (1969) is a lucid account that does not quite break from the anachronistic secondary sources on which it is based. For the emergence of the Republican party, see Noble E. Cunningham Jr., *The Jeffersonian Republicans: The Formation of Party Organization, 1789–1801* (1957). Lance Banning, *The Jeffersonian Persuasion: Evolution of a Party Ideology* (1978) is crucial for understanding the intellectual fears that held the Republican party together; but Joyce Appleby, *Capitalism and a New Social Order: The Republican Vision of the 1790s* (1984) better captures the optimistic market orientation of the Northern Republicans. For the classic account of the ideology that underlay the Revolution and the Republicans' fear of state power, see Bernard Bailyn, *The Ideological Origins of the American Revolution* (1967). On the extralegal associations that promoted the Republican party, see Eugene Perry Link, *Democratic-Republican Societies, 1790–1800* (1942); and Albrecht Koschnik, *"Let a Common Interest Bind Us Together": Associations, Partisanship, and Culture in Philadelphia, 1775–1840* (2007).

On the French Revolution in America, see Charles D. Hazen, *Contemporary American Opinion of the French Revolution* (1897). Jay Winik, *The Great Upheaval: America and the Birth of the Modern World, 1788–1800* (2007) has brief but stirring accounts of the French Revolution and Catherine the Great's Russia, along with a discussion of America in the 1790s. On French influence in American affairs, see Harry Ammon, *The Genet Mission* (1973).

On John Adams and the crisis of the late 1790s, see Alexander DeConde, *The Quasi-War: Politics and Diplomacy in the Undeclared War with France, 1797–1801* (1966); Stephen G. Kurtz, *The Presidency of John Adams: The Collapse of Federalism, 1795–1800* (1957); and John Patrick Diggins, *John Adams* (2003). Manning J. Dauer, *The Adams Federalists* (1953) captures some of the desperation of the High Federalists in 1798. On Adams's public life, in addition to John Ferling, *John Adams: A Life* (1992), see James

Grant, *John Adams: A Party of One* (2005). David McCullough, *John Adams* (2001) is more a sensitive account of Adams's marriage to Abigail than an analysis of his public career. Other perceptive studies of Adams's character include Joseph J. Ellis, *Passionate Sage: The Character and Legacy of John Adams* (1993); and Peter Shaw, *The Character of John Adams* (1976). For Adams's political theory, see John R. Howe Jr., *The Changing Political Thought of John Adams* (1964); and C. Bradley Thompson, *John Adams and the Spirit of Liberty* (1998).

On the press in the 1790s, see Jeffrey L. Pasley, *"The Tyranny of the Printers": Newspaper Politics in the Early American Republic* (2001); and Marcus Daniel, *Scandal and Civility: Journalism and the Origins of American Politics* (2009). On immigration in the 1790s, see Marilyn C. Baseler, *"Asylum for Mankind": America, 1607–1800* (1998); and Michael Durey, *Transatlantic Radicals and the Early American Republic* (1997). The Alien and Sedition Acts are best covered in James Morton Smith, *Freedom's Fetters: The Alien and Sedition Laws and American Civil Liberties* (1956). But for understanding the peculiar eighteenth-century context in which freedom of the press has to be viewed, see Leonard W. Levy, *Emergence of a Free Press* (rev. ed., 1985). For the Republicans' response to the Alien and Sedition Acts, see William J. Watkins, *Reclaiming the American Revolution: The Kentucky and Virginia Resolutions and Their Legacy* (2004).

The watershed election of 1800 has attracted much recent historical attention. See James Horn, Jan Ellen Lewis, and Peter S. Onuf, eds., *The Revolution of 1800: Democracy, Race, and the New Republic* (2002); Susan Dunn, *Jefferson's Second Revolution: The Electoral Crisis of 1800 and the Triumph of Republicanism* (2004); John Ferling, *Adams vs. Jefferson: The Tumultuous Election of 1800* (2004); Bruce Ackerman, *The Failure of the Founding Fathers: Jefferson, Marshall, and the Rise of Presidential Democracy* (2005); and Edward J. Larson, *A Magnificent Catastrophe: The Tumultuous Election of 1800, America's First Presidential Campaign* (2007). An earlier work, Daniel Sisson, *The American Revolution of 1800* (1974), tries to capture the radical meaning of Jefferson's election, but it does not succeed as well as James S. Young, *The Washington Community, 1800–1828* (1966), which, despite an unhistorical focus, rightly stresses the Republicans' fear of power.

For the Jeffersonians in power, see Marshall Smelser, *The Democratic Republic, 1801–1815* (1968); Nobel E. Cunningham Jr., *The Jeffersonian Republicans in Power: Party Operations, 1801–1809* (1963); and Forrest McDonald, *The Presidency of Thomas Jefferson* (1976).

On banking in Jeffersonian America, see Bray Hammond, *Banks and Politics from the Revolution to the Civil War* (1957); Howard Bodenhorn, *State Banking in Early America: A New Economic History* (2003); and J. Van Fenstermaker, *The Development of American Commercial Banking: 1782–1837* (1965). For Jefferson's problems with debt, both public and private, see the illuminating study by Herbert E. Sloan, *Principle and Interest: Thomas Jefferson and the Problem of Debt* (1995). On urban development, see David T. Gilchrist, ed., *The Growth of the Seaport Cities, 1790–1825* (1967).

On Gallatin, see Henry Adams, *The Life of Albert Gallatin* (1879); and Raymond Walters Jr., *Albert Gallatin: Jeffersonian Financier and Diplomat* (1957). Theodore J. Crackel, *Mr. Jefferson's Army: Political and Social Reform of the Military Establishment, 1801–1809* (1987) and Robert M. S. McDonald, *Thomas Jefferson's Military Academy: The Founding of West Point* (2004) explain the paradox of the war-hating, anti-military Jefferson founding West Point.

On Jefferson's dismantling of the Federalist bureaucracy, see Leonard D. White, *The Jeffersonians: A Study in Administrative History, 1801–1829* (1951). See also Noble E. Cunningham Jr., *The Process of Government Under Jefferson* (1979); and Robert M. Johnstone Jr., *Jefferson and the Presidency* (1979). Of course, as in all periods of Jefferson's life, the appropriate volumes of Dumas Malone's biography are helpful.

David Hackett Fischer, *The Revolution of American Conservatism: The Federalist Party in the Era of Jeffersonian Democracy* (1965), looks at party competition in the early nineteenth century with fresh eyes. Indispensable for understanding politics in the early Republic is Philip Lampi's monumental *Collection of American Election Data, 1787–1825.* The collection of data for presidential, congressional, gubernatorial, and state legislative elections is available online via the American Antiquarian Society's Web page: "A New Nation Votes: American Election Returns, 1787–1825." On the right to vote, see Chilton Williamson, *American Suffrage: From Property to Democracy, 1760–1860* (1960); and Alexander Keyssar, *The Right to Vote: The Contested History of Democracy in the United States* (2000).

On the Federalists' cultural reaction to the Jeffersonian victory, see Linda K. Kerber, *Federalists in Dissent* (1970); and William C. Dowling, *Literary Federalism in the Age of Jefferson: Joseph Dennie and the Port Folio, 1801–1811* (1999). See also James H. Broussard, *The Southern Federalists, 1800–1816* (1978). For John Randolph and the spirit of '98, see Norman K. Risjord, *The Old Republicans: Southern Conservatism in the Age of Jefferson* (1965). Fine studies of politics in two states are Donald J. Ratcliffe, *Party Spirit in a Frontier Republic: Democratic Politics in Ohio, 1793–1821* (1998) and Andrew Shankman, *Crucible of American Democracy: The Struggle to Fuse Egalitarianism and Capitalism in Jeffersonian Pennsylvania* (2004).

On the society of the early Republic, see Christopher Clark, *Social Change in America: From the Revolution Through the Civil War* (2006); Alice Felt Tyler, *Freedom's Ferment: Phrases of American Social History from the Colonial Period to the Outbreak of the Civil War* (1962); and especially Joyce Appleby, *Inheriting the Revolution: The First Generation of Americans* (2000). J. M. Opal, *Beyond the Farm: National Ambitions in Rural New England* (2008) is a sensitive and subtle study of ambition in the early Republic. On the excessive drinking in the early Republic, see W. J. Rorabaugh, *The Alcoholic Republic: An American Tradition* (1979). On rioting in the colleges, see Steven J. Novak, *The Rights of Youth: American Colleges and Student Revolt, 1798–1815* (1977). Paul A. Gilje, *Rioting in America* (1996), is the best survey of the general subject of rioting.

On the development of the West, see Malcolm J. Rohrbough, *Trans-Appalachian Frontier: People, Societies, and Institutions, 1775–1850* (3rd ed., 2008); and Reginald Horsman, *The Frontier in the Formative Years, 1783–1815* (1970). On the new cities of the West, see Richard C. Wade, *The Urban Frontier: Pioneer Life in Early Pittsburgh, Cincinnati, Lexington, and St. Louis* (1964). Andrew R. L. Cayton has become the premier modern historian of the early Midwest. See his *The Frontier Republic: Ideology and Politics in the Ohio Country, 1780–1825* (1986); *Frontier Indiana* (1996); and a series of jointly edited volumes: Cayton and Peter S. Onuf, eds., *The Mid-West and the Nation: Rethinking the History of an American Region* (1990); Cayton and Fredrika J. Teute, eds., *Contact Points: American Frontiers from the Mohawk Valley to the Mississippi, 1750–1830* (1998); Cayton and Susan E. Gray, eds., *The American Midwest: Essays on Regional History* (2001); and Cayton and Stuart D. Hobbs, eds., *The Center of a Great Empire: The Ohio Country in the Early American Republic* (2005).

Two especially important books that deal with the West and land speculation are Alan Taylor, *William Cooper's Town: Power and Persuasion on the Frontier of the Early American Republic* (1995); and Stephen Aron, *How the West Was Lost: The Transformation of Kentucky from Daniel Boone to Henry Clay* (1996). Land policy and land laws are covered in Malcolm J. Rohrbough, *The Land Office Business: The Settlement and Administration of American Public Lands, 1789–1837* (1968).

Writing on the Lewis and Clark expedition is immense. See Stephen Dow Beckham et al., *The Literature of the Lewis and Clark Expedition: A Bibliography and Essays* (2003). For a fast read, see Stephen E. Ambrose, *Undaunted Courage: Meriwether Lewis, Thomas Jefferson, and the Opening of the American West* (1996). For a more scholarly study, see James P. Ronda, *Finding the West: Explorations with Lewis and Clark* (2001). Arthur Furtwangler, *Acts of Discovery: Visions of America in the Lewis and Clark Journals* (1999) and Thomas P. Slaughter, *Exploring Lewis and Clark: Reflections on Men and Wilderness* (2003) treat the journals very imaginatively. There are many selectively edited versions of the explorers' journals. One example is Frank Bergon, ed., *The Journals of Lewis and Clark* (1995).

On the Louisiana Purchase, see the superb narrative by Jon Kukla, *A Wilderness So Immense: The Louisiana Purchase and the Destiny of America* (2003) and the relevant chapters in George Dangerfield, *Chancellor Robert R. Livingston of New York, 1746–1803* (1960). For more analytical and contextual studies of the Purchase, see Peter J. Kastor, *The Nation's Crucible: The Louisiana Purchase and the Creation of America* (2004); and Alexander DeConde, *This Affair of Louisiana* (1976). On the Burr conspiracy, see the books cited earlier on Burr, together with Thomas Abernethy, *The Burr Conspiracy* (1954); and Buckner F. Melton Jr., *Aaron Burr: Conspiracy to Treason* (2002).

On the theories of America having a deleterious effect on all living creatures, Antonello Gerbi, *The Dispute of the New World: The History of a Polemic, 1750–1900* (1973) is basic. On the native peoples in this period, see Gregory Evans Dowd, *A Spirited Resistance: The North American Indian Struggle for Unity, 1745–1815* (1992); Reginald Horsman, *Expansion and American Indian Policy, 1783–1812* (1967); Francis Paul Prucha, *American Indian Policy in the Formative Years: The Indian Trade and Intercourse Acts, 1790–1834* (1962); and Anthony F. C. Wallace, *Jefferson and the Tragic Fate of the First Americans* (1999). For a sensitive study of the irony in that tragic fate, see Bernard W. Sheehan, *Seeds of Extinction: Jeffersonian Philanthropy and the American Indian* (1973). For a pathbreaking work on Indian-white relations, see Richard White, *The Middle Ground: Indians, Empires, and Republics in the Great Lakes Region, 1650–1815* (1991). With the Iroquois in upstate New York and Canada, the ground was different, according to Alan Taylor, *The Divided Ground: Indians, Settlers, and the Northern Borderlands of the American Revolution* (2006). On the Cherokees, see two superb books by William G. McLoughlin, *Cherokees and Missionaries, 1789–1839* (1984) and *Cherokee Renascence in the New Republic* (1986).

On the politics of the judiciary in this period, see William R. Casto, *The Supreme Court in the Early Republic: The Chief Justiceships of John Jay and Oliver Ellsworth* (1995); Richard E. Ellis, *The Jeffersonian Crisis: Courts and Politics in the Young Republic* (1971); Andrew Shankman, *Crucible of American Democracy: The Struggle to Fuse Egalitarianism and Capitalism in Jeffersonian Pennsylvania* (2004); and Maeva Marcus, ed., *Origins of the Federal Judiciary: Essays on the Judiciary Act of 1789* (1992). Indispensable for understanding the Supreme Court in its earliest years is Maeva Marcus et al., eds., *The Documentary History of the Supreme Court of the United States, 1789–1800* (1985–). On the Court, see also the relevant volumes in the Oliver Wendell Holmes Devise History of the Supreme Court of the United States, the multi-volume history of the Court endowed by Justice Holmes on his death: Julius Goebel, *Antecedents and Beginnings to 1801: History of the Supreme Court of the United States* (1971); George Lee Haskins and Herbert A. Johnson, *Foundations of Power: John Marshall, 1801–1815* (1981).

In addition to the books on Marshall cited earlier, see R. Kent Newmyer, *John Marshall and the Heroic Age of the Supreme Court* (2001); see also Newmyer's superb biography of Story, *Supreme Court Justice Joseph Story: Statesman of the Old Republic* (1985).

The origins of judicial review are treated in Edward S. Corwin, *The "Higher Law" Background of American Constitutional Law* (1955); and Charles G. Haines, *The American Doctrine of Judicial Supremacy* (1932). For an important corrective to the idea that judicial review meant judicial supremacy, see Larry Kramer, *The People Themselves: Popular Constitutionalism and Judicial Review* (2004). Efforts to place *Marbury v. Madison* in historical context include Christopher Wolfe, *The Rise of Modern Judicial Review: From Constitutional Interpretation to Judge-Made Law* (1986); J. M. Sosin, *The Aristocracy of the Long Robe: The Origins of Judicial Review in America* (1989); Robert Lowry Clinton, *Marbury v. Madison and Judicial Review* (1989); and William E. Nelson, *Marbury v. Madison: The Origins and Legacy of Judicial Review* (2000). Especially important in understanding the development of judicial review is Sylvia Snowiss, *Judicial Review and the Law of the Constitution* (1990).

On the development of the corporation see Oscar and Mary Flug Handlin, *Commonwealth: A Study of the Role of Government in the American Economy: Massachusetts, 1774–1861* (1947, 1969); E. Merrick Dodd, *American Business Corporations Until 1860, with Special Reference to Massachusetts* (1954); Ronald E. Seavoy, *The Origins of the American Business Corporation, 1784–1855: Broadening the Concept of Public Service During Industrialization* (1982); Hendrik Hartog, *Public Property and Private Power: The Corporation of the City of New York in American Law, 1730–1870* (1983); and Johann N. Neem, *Creating a Nation of Joiners: Democracy and Civil Society in Early National Massachusetts* (2008).

Benjamin Rush has yet to find a biographer worthy of his importance. But see Nathan G. Goodman, *Benjamin Rush: Physician and Citizen, 1746–1813* (1934); Carl Binger, *Revolutionary Doctor: Benjamin Rush, 1746–1813* (1966); and David F. Hawke, *Benjamin Rush: Revolutionary Gadfly* (1971). On education in the early Republic, see Lawrence A. Cremin, *American Education: The National Experience, 1783–1876* (1980); and Carl F. Kaestle, *Pillars of the Republic: Common Schools and American Society, 1780–1860* (1983). Important for understanding newspapers and the spread of information in the period are Richard D. Brown, *Knowledge Is Power: The Diffusion of Information in Early*

*America, 1700–1865* (1989); Richard D. Brown, *The Strength of a People: The Idea of an Informed Citizenry in America, 1650–1870* (1996); and Frank Luther Mott, *American Journalism: A History of American Newspapers in the United States Through 250 Years, 1690–1940* (1941). On the emergence of humanitarian institutions, see Conrad E. Wright, *The Transformation of Charity in Post-Revolutionary New England* (1992).

On criminal punishment and penal reform, see Louis Masur, *Rites of Execution: Capital Punishment and the Transformation of American Culture, 1776–1865* (1989); Michael Meranze, *Laboratories of Virtue: Punishment, Revolution, and Authority in Philadelphia, 1760–1835* (1996); and Adam Jay Hirsch, *The Rise of the Penitentiary: Prisons and Punishment in Early America* (1992).

John Lauritz Larson, *Internal Improvement: National Public Works and the Promise of Popular Government in the Early United States* (2001) is the best study of the politics of internal improvements in the period.

On the development of various moral reform associations, see Charles I. Foster, *An Errand of Mercy: The Evangelical United Front, 1790–1837* (1960); and Clifford S. Griffin, *Their Brothers' Keepers: Moral Stewardship in the United States, 1800–1865* (1960). On missionaries, see Oliver Wendell Elsbree, *The Rise of the Missionary Spirit in America, 1790–1815* (1928); and William R. Hutchison, *Errand to the World: American Protestant Thought and Foreign Missions* (1987).

On women in the period, see Mary Beth Norton, *Liberty's Daughters: The Revolutionary Experience of American Women, 1750–1800* (1980); and Mary Kelley, *Learning to Stand and Speak: Women, Education, and Public Life in America's Republic* (2006). Linda K. Kerber has two important books on women in the early Republic: *Women of the Republic: Intellect and Ideology in Revolutionary America* (1980) and *Toward an Intellectual History of Women: Essays* (1997). Rosemarie Zagarri, *Revolutionary Backlash: Women and Politics in the Early American Republic* (2007) is a particularly significant study.

The literature on slavery has been growing rapidly in the past several decades. Basic for understanding the subject are David Brion Davis's *The Problem of Slavery in Western Culture* (1966) and his *The Problem of Slavery in the Age of Revolution, 1770–1823* (1975). For the best and most thorough account of slave life in the Chesapeake and in the Lowcountry of South Carolina and Georgia, see Philip D. Morgan, *Slave Counterpoint: Black Culture in the Eighteenth-Century Chesapeake and the Lowcountry* (1998). Also indispensable are two books by Ira Berlin, *Many Thousands Gone: The First Two Centuries of Slavery in North America* (1998) and *Generations of Captivity: A History of African American Slaves* (2003). Additional studies of slave culture are John W. Blassingame, *The Slave Community: Plantation Life in the Anti-Bellum South* (1972); Sylvia R. Frey, *Water from the Rock: Black Resistance in a Revolutionary Age* (1991); Lawrence W. Levine, *Black Culture and Black Consciousness: Afro-American Folk Thought from Slavery to Freedom* (1977); and Shane White and Graham White, *The Sounds of Slavery: Discovering African American History Through Songs, Sermons, and Speech* (2005). Adam Rothman, *Slave Country: American Expansion and the Origins of the Deep South* (2005) and Steven Doyle, *Carry Me Back: The Domestic Slave Trade in American Life* (2005) are important for the domestic slave trade. Winthrop Jordan, *White over Black: American Attitudes Toward the Negro, 1550–1812* (1968) remains a classic.

For studies of the plantations of two important Founders, see Robert F. Dalzell Jr. and Lee Baldwin Dalzell, *George Washington's Mount Vernon: At Home in Revolutionary America* (1998); Henry Wiencek, *An Imperfect God: George Washington, His Slaves, and the Creation of America* (2003); and Lucia C. Stanton, *Free Some Day: The African-American Families of Monticello* (2000). But for a detailed study of slavery at a less well known plantation, see Lorena S. Walsh, *From Calabar to Carter's Grove: The History of a Virginia Slave Community* (1997).

On Gabriel's Rebellion, see Douglas R. Egerton, *Gabriel's Rebellion: The Virginia Slave Conspiracies of 1800 and 1802* (1993); and James Sidbury, *Ploughshares into Swords: Race, Rebellion, and Identity in Gabriel's Virginia, 1730–1810* (1997).

On free blacks, see Ira Berlin, *Slaves Without Masters: The Free Negro in the Antebellum South* (1974); and Leon F. Litwack, *North of Slavery: The Negro in the Free States, 1790–1860* (1961). Gary B. Nash has several important books on blacks in the Revolution and in the following decades: *Forging Freedom: The Formation of Philadelphia's Black Community, 1720–1840* (1988); *Race and Revolution* (1990); and *The Forgotten Fifth: African Americans in the Age of Revolution* (2006). See also Douglas R. Egerton, *Death or Liberty: African Americans and Revolutionary America* (2009). For abolitionism, see Arthur Zilversmit, *The First Emancipation: The Abolition of Slavery in the North* (1967); and especially Richard S. Newman, *The Transformation of American Abolitionism: Fighting Slavery in the Early Republic* (2002). Duncan J. MacLeod, *Slavery, Race and the American Revolution* (1974) demonstrates how republican equality helped to create racism.

The standard surveys of culture in the period are Russell B. Nye, *The Cultural Life of the New Nation, 1776–1830* (1960) and Jean V. Matthews, *Toward a New Society: American Thought and Culture, 1800–1830* (Boston, 1990). Especially important are Kenneth Silverman, *A Cultural History of the American Revolution: Painting, Music, Literature, and the Theater in the Colonies and the United States from the Treaty of Paris to the Inauguration of George Washington* (1976); and Joseph J. Ellis, *After the Revolution: Profiles of Early American Culture* (1979).

On the theater, see Jeffrey H. Richards, *Drama, Theater, and Identity in the American New Republic* (2005); and Heather Nathans, *Early American Theater from the Revolution to Thomas Jefferson: Into the Hands of the People* (2003). On painting, see Neil Harris, *The Artist in American Society: The Formative Years, 1790–1860* (1966); and James Thomas Flexner, *The Light of Distant Skies: American Painting, 1760–1835* (1969). Harris's book is particularly rich and imaginative. On the novel, see Cathy N. Davidson, *Revolution and the Word: The Rise of the Novel in America* (1986).

On Charles Willson Peale, see David R. Brigham, *Public Culture in the Early Republic: Peale's Museum and its Audience* (1995); and Charles Coleman Sellers, *Charles Willson Peale* (1947) and *Mr. Peale's Museum: Charles Willson Peale and the First Popular Museum of Natural Science and Art* (1980).

The most important work on religion in the early Republic is Nathan Hatch, *The Democratization of American Christianity* (1989). On the separation of church and state, see Thomas J. Curry, *The First Freedoms: Church and State in America to the Passage of the First Amendment* (1986); and A. James Reichley, *Religion in American Public Life* (1985). Other important studies of religion in the early Republic are Edwin S. Gaustad,

*Neither King nor Prelate: Religion and the New Nation, 1776–1826* (1993); Mark Noll, *America's God: From Jonathan Edwards to Abraham Lincoln* (2002); Jon Butler, *Awash in a Sea of Faith: Christianizing the American People* (1990); Christine Leigh Heyrman, *Southern Cross: The Beginnings of the Bible Belt* (1997); and Dee E. Andrews, *The Methodists and Revolutionary America, 1760–1800: The Shaping of an Evangelical Culture* (2000). The essays collected in Elwyn A. Smith, ed., *The Religion of the Republic* (1971), are important in relating evangelical Protestantism to republicanism.

Peter S. Field, *The Crisis of the Standing Order: Clerical Intellectuals and Cultural Authority in Massachusetts, 1780–1833* (1998) is important for the Unitarian controversy in Massachusetts. For the background to the Unitarian movement, see Conrad Wright, *The Beginnings of Unitarianism in America* (1955). On the New Divinity movement, see Joseph A. Conforti, *Samuel Hopkins and the New Divinity Movement: Calvinism, the Congregational Ministry, and Reform in New England Between the Great Awakenings* (1981). John R. Boles, *The Great Revival, 1787–1805* (1972) and Donald G. Mathews, *Religion in the Old South* (1977) are important for evangelical revivalism. Jay P. Dolan, *The American Catholic Experience: A History from Colonial Times to the Present* (1985), is an excellent survey of American Catholicism.

The issue of the Founders and religion has generated an enormous amount of writing, especially in the past two decades. Among the most moderate and sensible accounts are James H. Hutson, *Religion and the Founding of the American Republic* (1998); Jon Meacham, *American Gospel: God, the Founding Fathers, and the Making of a Nation* (2006); Frank Lambert, *The Founding Fathers and the Place of Religion in America* (2003); and Forrest Church, *So Help Me God: The Founding Fathers and the First Great Battle over Church and State* (2007).

On millennialism, see James West Davidson, *The Logic of Millennial Thought: Eighteenth-Century New England* (1977); J.F.C. Harrison, *The Second Coming: Popular Millenarianism, 1780–1850* (1979); and Ruth Bloch, *Visionary Republic: Millennial Themes in American Thought, 1756–1800* (1985).

The underlying eighteenth-century liberal assumptions about international politics are explored in Felix Gilbert, *To the Farewell Address: Ideas of Early American Foreign Policy* (1961). Gilbert's book has not been taken as seriously as it ought to have been, largely because he relied heavily on French instead of English sources; but the English materials back up his thesis. On another important work that investigates the thinking behind the commercial and foreign policy of the Jeffersonians, see Drew R. McCoy, *The Elusive Republic: Political Economy in Jeffersonian America* (1980). On the foreign policy itself, see Bradford Perkins, *Prologue to War: England and the United States, 1805–1812* (1968); and Robert W. Tucker and David C. Hendrickson, *Empire of Liberty: The Statecraft of Thomas Jefferson* (1990). Lawrence S. Kaplan, *Jefferson and France: An Essay on Politics and Political Ideas* (1967) captures the idealism of Jefferson. On the embargo, see Burton Spivak, *Jefferson's English Crisis: Commerce, Embargo, and the Republican Revolution* (1979). On the Southern Spanish-American borderlands, see J.C.A. Stagg, *Borderlines in Borderlands: James Madison and the Spanish-American Frontier, 1776–1821* (2009).

On the Barbary pirates, see Robert J. Allison, *The Crescent Obscured: The United States and the Muslim World, 1776–1815* (1995); and Frank Lambert, *The Barbary Wars: American Independence in the Atlantic World* (2005).

J.C.A. Stagg, *Mr. Madison's War: Politics, Diplomacy, and Warfare in the Early American Republic, 1783–1830* (1983) is indispensable for understanding the War of 1812, as, of course, is Henry Adams, *History of the United States of America During the Administration of James Madison* (1889–1891). Roger H. Brown, *The Republic in Peril: 1812* (1964) and Steven Watts, *The Republic Reborn: War and the Making of Liberal America, 1790–1820* (1987) have imaginative accounts of America's willingness to go to war. See also Bradford Perkins, *Castlereagh and Adams: England and the United States, 1812–1823* (1964).

Of the many brief accounts of the war, the best is Donald R. Hickey, *The War of 1812: A Forgotten Conflict* (1989). See also his *Don't Give Up the Ship: Myths of the War of 1812* (2006). Jon Latimer, *1812: War with America* (2007) views the war from a British or Canadian point of view. Richard Buel Jr., *America on the Brink: How the Political Struggle over the War of 1812 Almost Destroyed the Young Republic* (2005) provocatively indicts the Federalists for their seditious behavior. James M. Banner Jr., *To the Hartford Convention: The Federalists and the Origins of Party Politics in Massachusetts, 1789–1815* (1970) superbly describes the Federalists' attitudes and stresses their moderate purposes in calling the Convention.

On the economy of the period, see Curtis P. Nettles, *The Emergence of a National Economy, 1775–1815* (1962); Stanley L. Engerman and Robert E. Gallman, eds., *The Cambridge Economic History of the United States*, vol. 2, *The Long Nineteenth Century* (2000); Douglas C. North, *The Economic Growth of the United States, 1790–1860* (1966); and James L. Huston, *Securing the Fruits of Labor: The American Concepts of Wealth Distribution, 1765–1900* (1998). Barbara M. Tucker, *Samuel Slater and the Origins of the American Textile Industry, 1790–1860* (1984) is the best study of that extraordinary entrepreneur.

The origins of liberal capitalism have generated a great deal of controversy among historians. Some historians have suggested that many farmers, especially in New England, were still pre-modern in their outlook, interested far more in patrimony and kin than in capitalistic aggrandizement. See James A. Henretta, *The Origins of American Capitalism: Selected Essays* (1991); Allan Kukikoff, *The Agrarian Origins of American Capitalism* (1992); and Christopher Clark, *The Roots of Rural Capitalism: Western Massachusetts, 1780–1860* (1990). Winifred Barr Rothenberg, *From Market-Places to a Market Economy: The Transformation of Rural Massachusetts, 1750–1850* (1992) sought to clear the "transition to capitalism" debate of a lot of theoretical cant by asking some basic questions about the rural New England economy that could be empirically verified.

Joyce Appleby, *Inheriting the Revolution: The First Generation of Americans* (2000) and Gordon S. Wood, *The Radicalism of the American Revolution* (1992), using other evidence, endorse Rothenberg's view that rural capitalism arose at the end of the eighteenth century. Appleby, in particular, nicely captures the early nineteenth-century culture out of which the myth of the self-made man arose. On capitalism, see also Paul A. Gilje, ed., *Wages of Independence: Capitalism in the Early American Republic* (1997). Of the many works on artisans, see Howard B. Rock, *Artisans of the New Republic: The Tradesmen of New York City in the Age of Jefferson* (1978); Bruce Laurie, *Working People of Philadelphia, 1800–1850* (1980); Ronald Schultz, *The Republic of Labor: Philadelphia Artisans and the Politics of Class, 1720–1830* (1993); Charles G. Steffen, *The Mechanics of Baltimore: Workers and Politics in the Age of Revolution, 1763–1812* (1984); and Rosalind Remer, *Printers and Men of Capital: Philadelphia Book Publishers in the New Republic*

(1996). Stuart M. Blumin, *The Emergence of the Middle Class: Social Experience in the American City, 1760–1900* (1989) is the best study of the development of the middle class out of an eighteenth-century society divided between a gentry elite and commoners.

On debt and bankruptcy, see Peter J. Coleman, *Debtors and Creditors in America: Insolvency, Imprisonment for Debt and Bankruptcy, 1607–1900* (1974); Scott A. Sandage, *Born Losers: A History of Failure in America* (2005); and Bruce H. Mann, *Republic of Debtors: Bankruptcy in the Age of the American Independence* (2002).

Susan Dunn, *Dominion of Memories: Jefferson, Madison and the Decline of Virginia* (2007) is the best book on the decay of the once most powerful state in the Union.

# Index